Forensic archaeology

Forensic archaeology

A global perspective

EDITED BY

W.J. Mike Groen

Netherlands Forensic Institute (NFI), The Hague, The Netherlands

Nicholas Márquez-Grant

Cranfield Forensic Institute, Cranfield University,
Defence Academy of the United Kingdom, Shrivenham, UK
and
Institute of Human Sciences, School of Anthropology
and Museum Ethnography, University of Oxford, Oxford, UK

Robert C. Janaway

School of Archaeological Sciences, University of Bradford,
Bradford, UK

Publication of this volume is kindly supported by:

Netherlands Forensic Institute
Ministry of Security and Justice

WILEY Blackwell

This edition first published 2015 © 2015 by John Wiley & Sons, Ltd.

Registered Office
John Wiley & Sons, Ltd., The Atrium, Southern Gate, Chichester, West Sussex, PO19 8SQ, UK

Editorial Offices
9600 Garsington Road, Oxford, OX4 2DQ, UK
The Atrium, Southern Gate, Chichester, West Sussex, PO19 8SQ, UK
111 River Street, Hoboken, NJ 07030-5774, USA

For details of our global editorial offices, for customer services and for information about how to apply for permission to reuse the copyright material in this book please see our website at www.wiley.com/wiley-blackwell.

Library of Congress Cataloging-in-Publication Data applied for.

ISBN: 9781118745984

A catalogue record for this book is available from the British Library.

Wiley also publishes its books in a variety of electronic formats. Some content that appears in print may not be available in electronic books.

Cover image:
Figure 1: Mock crime scene investigation of a clandestine burial. © NFI
Figure 2: A mass grave in the province of Cordoba, Argentina. Excavated by EAAF in 2013. © EAAF
Figure 3: GIS image combining digital photography, 3D scan of the grave pit and Total Station data. © NFI
Figure 4: JPAC-CIL recovery team members set up a grid at a Vietnam War-era aircraft crash site, Khammouan, Lao People's Democratic Republic, May 2011. © US Department of the Navy, Thiep Nguyen.
Figure 5: An air crash site in the Madang province, Independent State of Papua New Guinea, related to WWII. Excavated by the JPAC-CIL in 2010. © Air Force Staff Sgt Aaron Allmon II.

Set in 8.5/10.5pt Meridien by SPi Publisher Services, Pondicherry, India

1 2015

MIX
Paper from responsible sources
FSC
www.fsc.org
FSC® C013604

Contents

Biographies of editors

W.J. Mike Groen, MA, holds a Masters' degree in Archaeology from Leiden University, the Netherlands. His past academic and professional experience relates to archaeological theory and methodology, field archaeology and physical anthropology. As a field archaeologist, he was involved in archaeological excavations in several Dutch municipalities in the western part of the Netherlands between 1994 and 2006. As a physical anthropologist, he was attached to the Leiden Medical University Centre (LUMC) between 2002 and 2012, and was involved in both the recovery and analysis of human remains from late medieval and post-medieval contexts. Since 2006, he has been employed as a forensic archaeologist by the Netherlands Forensic Institute (NFI) in The Hague. He is a guest staff member at the Bioarchaeological Section of the Faculty of Archaeology, Leiden University, the Netherlands, and lectures in Human Taphonomy and Osteoarchaeology at several Dutch universities. He is also responsible for introducing forensic archaeology in the Netherlands in 2005 and for the creation of the Forensic Archaeology Project Group within the European Network of Forensic Science Institutes (ENFSI) in 2013. As a forensic archaeologist, he has been involved in more than 650 forensic cases in the Netherlands and abroad. At the time of writing, he is completing his PhD thesis in Physical Anthropology at the LUMC on the socio-cultural and taphonomic influence on the use and reliability of physical anthropological models in an archaeological context.

Nicholas Márquez-Grant, PhD, is a lecturer in forensic anthropology and Course Director in Forensic Archaeology and Anthropology at Cranfield Defence and Security, Cranfield University, UK. He is also a research associate of the Institute of Human Sciences, School of Anthropology and Museum Ethnography, Oxford University, UK. Having worked as a specialist in human skeletal remains from archaeological sites for over 15 years, he has considerable experience in the excavation and study of cremated and unburnt bone from prehistoric sites, to 20th century conflict sites, from a variety of geographical areas. Between 2008 and 2013, he worked full time as a forensic anthropologist and archaeologist for independent forensic science providers in the United Kingdom, working for over 20 police forces and attending numerous crime scenes and mortuaries, and dealing primarily with the search, location, recovery and identification of human remains. He has acted as an expert witness on several occasions in the United Kingdom and has trained Crime Scene Investigators from a number of national and international police forces. He regularly delivers lectures to students, other scientists and police officers, and he has taught physical anthropology since 2001 at Oxford University, UK. Dr Márquez-Grant has published a number of papers and edited volumes on the subject of forensic anthropology and archaeology and undertakes research in the fields of taphonomy, trauma and methods of identification in physical/forensic anthropology.

Robert C. Janaway, BSc, MIFA, is a lecturer in forensic and archaeological sciences at the University of Bradford, UK. He has been involved in archaeological excavation and the examination of degraded materials for over 30 years. After working on a range of excavations while still at school, he originally trained as an archaeological conservator at University College, Cardiff, UK. On graduation, he worked for Bath Museums Service and the University of Leeds, UK, before moving to the Department of Archaeological Sciences at Bradford in 1987. His research specialisation is the excavation and analysis of degraded textiles and other materials associated with decomposing cadavers, and he has published in both archaeological and forensic literature. He was amongst the first archaeologists in the United Kingdom to apply their techniques to the investigation of crime scenes and in particular clandestine graves, and was a co-editor of *Death Decay and Reconstruction* (1987), which explored the overlap between forensic and archaeological approaches. His police casework includes the excavation of crime scenes, with the recovery of both human remains and other evidential material. He has been asked to examine clothing, paper and other personal effects in a severely degraded condition recovered from bodies in a range of putrefied states. He was an assessor for forensic archaeology for the Council for the Registration of Forensic Practitioners (CRFP) and was subsequently involved in establishing the Forensic Archaeology Expert Panel of the Institute for Archaeologists (IfA), of which he is currently chair. He also wrote the Forensic Archaeology component standards for the Forensic Science Society.

Biographies of contributors

Alexey Abramov, PhD, works at the Department of Forensic Medical Criminology, Moscow Regional State Bureau of Forensic Medicine, Russia. In 2003, he graduated from the Russian State Medical University, majoring in Paediatrics. After his graduation, he specialised in the fields of Forensic Medicine and Criminalistics. Dr Abramov has participated, as a forensic anthropologist, in several mass disaster incidents in Russia and abroad.

Rafael de Abreu e Souza, MSc, is a doctoral student at the Public Archaeology Laboratory, University of Campinas, Brazil, with a special focus on historical archaeology and archaeology of the contemporary past. He is a member of the Archaeology of Repression and Resistance Research Group at the National Council for Scientific and Technological Development, Brazil. He has developed programmes in forensic archaeology and coordinated archaeological excavations on sites related to the Brazilian dictatorship, human rights violations and political disappearances. He is also a member of two Brazilian archaeological teams: the Araguaia Working Group (GTA) and the Forensic Archaeology and Anthropology Group (GAAF).

Anil Aggrawal, MD, PhD, is Director Professor of Forensic Medicine and Toxicology at the Maulana Azad Medical College, New Delhi, India. He holds a medical degree in forensic medicine from the All India Institute of Medical Sciences, New Delhi. In 1996, he was awarded a WHO fellowship, under which he taught at Shiga University of Medical Sciences, Japan, and the Armed Forces Institute of Pathology, Washington, DC, US. Professor Aggrawal is Founder and Editor-in-Chief of the *Anil Aggrawal's Internet Journal of Forensic Medicine and Toxicology* (available at: http://www.anilaggrawal.com/ij/indexpapers.html) and has published several books and numerous scientific articles on medical and forensic topics.

Amin Attia Alemam, BDS, is one of the first promoters for the use of dental sciences in the Libyan legal sector (forensic odontology). He submitted, starting in 2005, related proposals to the Libyan Ministry of Justice and the Libyan Ministry of Higher Education. During the Libyan revolution (2011), he cooperated with the Centre of Expert Witnesses to the Court of Laws and Research in Benghazi and was, as forensic odontologist, co-responsible for the identification of victims. He is attached, as an instructor in forensic odontology, to the Department of Forensic Sciences, University of Benghazi, Libya, and founded the Libyan Society of Forensic Odontology (LSFO). Currently, he is pursuing a Masters' degree in the United Kingdom.

Khudooma Saeed Al Naimi, MSc, holds a Masters' degree in forensic anthropology from the University of Central Lancashire, UK. Since 2001, he has been employed at the Forensic Biology Section of the General Directorate of Abu Dhabi Police, UAE. His duties include crime scene investigation, laboratory examination of evidence and training of new staff. His research interests include, among other things, forensic anthropology (e.g. the effect of firearms on human bone), forensic biology and forensic entomology. He is a member of the American Academy of Forensic Sciences (AAFS) and the International Association of Identification (IAI). In 2005, he participated, as a forensic anthropologist, in the identification of war victims in Bosnia and Herzegovina.

Susan Appleyard, MA, is an independent human rights researcher. She has worked for the UN Office of the High Commissioner for Human Rights, the UN Department of Political Affairs, the International Commission of Jurists, Human Rights Watch and Child Soldiers International in Nepal and throughout Asia-Pacific for over 10 years. She is currently completing a Masters' degree in forensic anthropology and archaeology at Cranfield University, UK.

Edward Ashby, MA, is an independent consulting archaeologist. He holds a Masters' degree in archaeology and a PgDip in forensic science from Auckland University, New Zealand. His research is focused around cultural resource management and forensic archaeology. Edward has worked with the Chief Coroner of New Zealand in developing protocols for the recovery of skeletal remains, and has published in the *Australian Journal of Forensic Sciences*.

José Pablo Baraybar, MA, MSc, has consulted and trained on the use of forensics in cases of human rights violations in the Americas, Africa and South East Asia. He is a founding member of the Peruvian Forensic Anthropology Team (EPAF) and has worked as a forensic anthropologist for the International Criminal Tribunal for Rwanda (ICTR) in 1996 and as chief forensic anthropologist/archaeologist for the International Criminal Tribunal for the former Yugoslavia (ICTY) from 1996 to 2002. In 2002, he created the Office of Missing Persons and Forensics (OMPF) in Kosovo and served as its Head until 2007. During his tenure as Head of OMPF, he was awarded the UN 21 Award. In 2011, he was awarded the Judith Lee Stronach Human Rights prize by the Centre for Justice and Accountability in San Francisco, US.

Radoslav Beňuš, PhD, is Associate Professor at the Department of Anthropology, Comenius University, Slovakia, and a court expert in forensic anthropology. His professional interests include physical and forensic anthropology. The main field of his research in physical anthropology lies in palaeopathology and the epidemiology of diseases of historical populations. In forensic anthropology, his main interests are the taphonomic changes in the human body, the distinction between peri-mortal and post-mortal skeletal alterations, the determination of biological profile and the identification of unknown persons. Dr Beňuš is a member of the Main Committee of the Slovak Anthropological Society, the European Anthropological Association (EAA) and the Palaeopathology Association (PPA).

Soren Blau, PhD, is the senior forensic anthropologist at the Victorian Institute of Forensic Medicine, Melbourne, Australia, where she has been employed since 2005. Additionally, she is an adjunct senior lecturer at the Department of Forensic Medicine, Monash University, Australia, and a founding fellow of the Royal College of Pathologists of Australasia (RCPA). In addition to numerous journal publications, she co-edited a book titled *Handbook of Forensic Anthropology and Archaeology* (2009). Dr Blau undertakes domestic and international forensic anthropology casework, as well as contributing to international training courses on aspects of DVI and the application of forensic anthropology and archaeology to the investigation of human rights violations.

Tomasz Borkowski, PhD, works at the Wrocław Museum of Archaeology, Poland, where he specialises in the late Middle Ages and post-medieval periods. Additionally, Dr Borkowski lectures in postgraduate studies in forensic archaeology at the University of Wrocław, Poland.

Matteo Borrini, PhD, holds a doctorate in evolutionary biology and ecology from the University of Rome 'Tor Vergata', Italy. He is a principal lecturer and programme manager of the BSc (Hons) forensic anthropology programme at Liverpool John Moores University, UK. Currently, he is the only expert witness in forensic archaeology and forensic anthropology for the Italian State Prosecutor Office (registered at the Criminal Court of La Spezia). He has led dozens of archaeological and bioarchaeological excavations and was a scientific consultant for the National Geographic Society (Vampire Forensic Project). He is involved in the search, recovery and identification of missing people and murder victims, and is also devoted to the study of forensic archaeology and anthropology in the context of WWII. For his contribution to the location and identification of missing army soldiers, Dr Borrini was designated as an honorary member of the Commonwealth-Italian Joint Committee of the Commonwealth War Graves Commission (CWGC).

Ilian Boyanov, PhD, is a senior lecturer at the Department of Archaeology, New Bulgarian University, where he has been employed since 2008. Additionally, he is an adjunct lecturer at the Faculty of Law, University of National and World Economy, Bulgaria, where he has lectured in forensic archaeology since 2009. In addition to numerous journal publications, he has edited a book titled *Forensic Archaeology: A Brief Training Course* (2010). Dr Boyanov undertakes domestic and international archaeology and forensic archaeology fieldwork and casework.

Eileen Buitrago Pérez, BA, has studied anthropology at the Externado de Colombia University. She has trained in forensic anthropology since joining the Colombian Interdisciplinary Team on Forensic Work and Psychosocial Assistance (EQUITAS) in 2010. She has worked with victims' families that have suffered serious human rights violations, in particular extra-legal executions. She is experienced in working in interdisciplinary teams and with minority groups.

Luis L. Cabo, MSc, is the Director of the Bioarchaeology and Forensic Laboratory at the Mercyhurst Archaeological Institute, Mercyhurst University, US. With a background in biology and anthropology, before joining Mercyhurst's forensic team in 2003, he took part in more than a dozen major archaeological and paleontological projects in Europe and the Americas, with chronologies from middle Palaeolithic to late Middle Ages. Mercyhurst's team processes an average of more than 100 cases per year, including outdoor recoveries, fatal fire scenes, burials and mass disasters.

Gonçalo Carnim, BSc, is a forensic anthropologist at the National Institute of Legal Medicine and Forensic Sciences in Portugal. He is responsible for the identification of skeletal remains and assists forensic pathologists in the determination of cause and manner of death when badly decomposed bodies are involved. He also lectures in forensic anthropology, in pre- and post-graduation courses.

Jan Cemper-Kiesslich, PhD, is Assistant Professor at the Interfaculty Department of Legal Medicine and the Department of Antiquities at the University of Salzburg, Austria, where he lectures in forensic genetics, bioarchaeology and molecular archaeology. Additionally, he is the quality management representative for the Forensic Laboratories (DNA and Toxicology) according to EN DIN ISO/IEC 17025. His research activities focus on DNA typing involving forensic applications, mainly working on human remains from archaeological excavations and historical finds from Austria, Southern Germany and beyond. As well as publishing numerous scientific articles in monographs, national and international journals, Dr Cemper-Kiesslich is Co-founder and Editor-in-Chief of the ArchaeoPlus series and the president of the Centre of Archaeometry and Applied Archaeology Salzburg (CAMAS).

Nak-Eun Chung, MD, PhD, has been the Director of the Disaster Victims Identification team of the Republic of Korea since 2005 and is the Chief Medical Examiner at the Division of Forensic Medicine, National Forensic Service, Seoul. He has published diverse scientific articles and books on the use of computer models in medicine and on DVI work. Dr Chung is Vice-President (Honourable) of the International Association of Law AND Forensic Science (IALFS), and, since 2012, the Chair of the Asia-Pacific Medico-Legal Association (APMLA).

Sónia Codinha, PhD, is a postdoctoral research fellow at CENCIFOR (South Branch of the National Institute of Legal Medicine) where she is developing research on craniofacial identification. She holds an MSc in forensic anthropology (University of Granada, Spain) and a PhD in biological anthropology (University of Coimbra, Portugal). Dr Codinha has been working in the laboratory on human skeletal remains from archaeological contexts and forensic cases, has excavated on several archaeological sites and has participated in forensic missions in Guinea-Bissau and Spain.

Derek Congram, PhD, holds a doctorate in archaeology from Simon Fraser University, Canada. Since 1999, he has worked in conventional and forensic archaeology in 13 countries for governments, non-governmental organisations and international organisations, including the UN and the International Criminal Court (ICC). Dr Congram's primary research interests include spatial analysis and GIS-modelling of body disposal sites in armed conflict contexts and the search for and identification of missing persons from the Spanish Civil War.

Cecily Cropper, BA (Hons), received a degree in archaeology from Cardiff University, UK. From 1999 to 2001, she worked within the UN forensic exhumation team in Bosnia, Kosovo and Croatia. This was followed by 2 years as senior forensic archaeologist with the International Commission on Missing Persons (ICMP). From 2009 to 2012, she worked as the forensic archaeologist with the Department of Forensic Science in Kosovo, as a member of the European Union's Rule of Law mission (EULEX). She acted as a consultant to the UK Foreign and Commonwealth Office in Iraq, worked for various police services within the United Kingdom and the Channel Islands, and participated as a forensic scientist with the UN mission in Cyprus. She has trained police and forensic professionals in the United Kingdom and South Africa, and has mentored and trained forensic teams in Cyprus and Kosovo.

Eugénia Cunha, PhD, has been Full Professor of Anthropology at Coimbra University, Portugal, since 2003. Professor Cunha is also a national consultant for forensic anthropology at the National Institute of Legal Medicine and Forensic Sciences (INMLCF, I.P.), Portugal, and the President of the Forensic Anthropology Society of Europe (FASE) since 2009.

Annamaria Diana, BSc, MA, MSc, is a PhD candidate in human osteoarchaeology at the University of Edinburgh, UK. She holds a Bachelor's degree in archaeological sciences and a Master in classical archaeology from the University of Siena, Italy, and an MSc in human osteoarchaeology from the University of Edinburgh, UK. She has been involved as tutor, occasional lecturer and demonstrator in undergraduate archaeology courses and in the human osteoarchaeology and forensic anthropology MSc courses at the same university from 2011 to 2014. She has worked as a field archaeologist and physical anthropologist in Italy, Morocco, Romania Georgia and the U.A.E. Her PhD research looks at the impact of climate change on medieval human skeletal populations from Romania.

Dennis C. Dirkmaat, PhD, D-ABFA, is the Chair of Applied Forensic Sciences Department at Mercyhurst University, in Erie, Pennsylvania, US, and is Director of the Anthropology Masters programme (Forensic and Biological Anthropology Concentration). He has conducted over 400 forensic anthropology and forensic archaeology cases for the coroner, medical examiner and police agencies throughout Pennsylvania, New York and Ohio, US. He has published numerous articles and book chapters on the role of archaeology and forensic anthropology in forensic investigations, fatal fire scenes and mass fatalities, including *A Companion to Forensic Anthropology* (2012). He participated as a forensic anthropologist in four plane crash incidents, including Shanksville, Pennsylvania, US, in 2001. He also directed the scene of recovery operations for a plane crash in Buffalo, New York, US, in 2009. Dr Dirkmaat is the chair of the Scene of Search and Recovery, and Co-Chair of the Anthropology Sub Committee of the US Scientific Working Group–DVI (SWG-DVI).

Marija Djurić, MD, PhD, is Full Professor of Anatomy at the School of Medicine, University of Belgrade, Serbia, and the Founder and Head of the PhD course 'Skeletal Biology' (conducted in English) at the same institution. She holds a doctorate in physical anthropology from the University of Novi Sad, Serbia. In 1995, she founded the Laboratory for Anthropology, which housed numerous research projects focusing on physical and forensic anthropology (particularly skeletal age markers, anthropological and pathological characteristics of skeletal remains), bone biomechanics and the structural basis of bone fragility. She has been an expert consultant in forensic anthropology since 1998. She has performed anthropological analyses in a number of excavated mass graves from World War II and recent conflicts in the former Yugoslavia. Professor Djuric has published numerous research articles in international scientific journals.

Miluše Dobisíková, RNDr, is a graduate of the Faculty of Science, Charles University, Prague, Czech Republic. She worked at the Department of Haematology and Forensic Anthropology of General University Hospital II, Prague. Since 1991, she has worked at the Department of Anthropology of the National Museum in Prague, where she was Head until 2003. She specialises in forensic anthropology and bioarchaeology and is a court expert in the field of forensic anthropology and serology.

Alexey Dolgov, MD, is a forensic medical doctor at the Department of Forensic Medical Criminology, Moscow Regional State Bureau of Forensic Medicine, Russia. From 2002 to 2009, he was the chief forensic medical expert of the Baikal Regional Bureau of Forensic Medicine in Chita, Russia. From 2009 to 2012, he was the deputy chief of the same laboratory.

Denise Donlon, PhD, holds a doctorate in physical anthropology, is Curator of the Shellshear Museum of Physical Anthropology and a senior lecturer in the Department of Anatomy and Histology, University of Sydney, Australia. She coordinates courses in comparative primate anatomy and forensic osteology and supervises postgraduate students. Her research interests include forensic anthropology of the Sydney region, dental and postcranial skeletal variation and Australian Aboriginal burial archaeology. She is a consultant to the NSW Department of Forensic Medicine, where she assists in the identification of skeletonised remains. Dr Donlon is also a member of the RAAF Specialist Reserves, where her role is in the recovery and identification of Australian war dead.

Florent Ducrettet, MD, leads the Department of Anthropology–Thanatology–Odontology of the Forensic Sciences Institute of the French National Gendarmerie (IRCGN). He is also a medical doctor in the Medical Service of the French Armed Forces and operates in France and around the world. He has co-authored scientific articles on forensic casework and methodology.

Constantine Eliopoulos, PhD, is a lecturer in forensic anthropology at Liverpool John Moores University, UK. As a practitioner for over a decade, he has worked on several projects involving mass graves in places such as Cyprus, Iraq, Sierra Leone and Grenada with the non-governmental organisation Physicians for Human Rights (PHR) and the UN. Dr Eliopoulos' research has focused on forensic taphonomy, human skeletal biology and palaeopathology, and he has published several papers in international peer-reviewed journals.

Asya V. Engovatova, PhD, is the Vice-Director of the Institute of Archaeology, Russian Academy of Sciences, Moscow, Russia, and Head of the Department of Rescue Archaeological Research in Moscow. Dr Engovatova has directed numerous archaeological excavation projects, focussing on the use of modern field methods.

Shari Eppel, MA, is a Zimbabwean, and the Director of the non-governmental organisation Solidarity Peace Trust. She has worked in the field of transitional justice for more than a decade and was the primary author of the Catholic Commission for Justice and Peace History, *Breaking the Silence, Building True Peace: A Report on the Disturbances in Matabeleland and the Midlands 1980–1987*, which remains the definitive history of the Gukurahundi era. A psychologist by training, she has worked with victims of torture for nearly 20 years. She began studying for a Masters' degree in forensic anthropology at Mercyhurst University, US, in August 2012. Once qualified as a forensic anthropologist, she intends to resume her earlier work from the 1990s, which combined both psychosocial and forensic anthropology skills, in order to 'heal the dead' in Matabeleland.

Kinga Éry, PhD, is a retired archaeologist and physical anthropologist. Her research area is osteoarchaeology of the Carpathian Basin population from the 3rd to the 16th century AD. Dr Éry worked in the Déri Museum in Debrecen, Hungary (1955–1956), the Hungarian Natural History Museum in Budapest (1957–1969), the King Stephen Museum in Székesfehérvár, Hungary (1970–1973), the Bakony Museum in Veszprém, Hungary (1973–1982), the Hungarian Natural History Museum in Budapest (1983–1991) and the Hungarian National Museum in Budapest (1992–1994).

Lilia Escorcia Hernández, PhD, is a forensic anthropologist with a doctorate in physical anthropology. She has experience in research, as coordinator and contributor for inter-institutional projects, as well as the development and elaboration of expert opinions and publications in the fields of physical anthropology and forensic archaeology. Dr Escorcia currently works in the Laboratory for Forensic Anthropology at the Institute of Anthropological Research (IIA) of the National Autonomous University of Mexico.

Francisco Etxeberria, MD, PhD, is Full Professor of Legal Medicine at the University of the Basque Country, Spain; Professor at the Basque Institute of Criminology; and the Director of the Sociedad de Ciencias Aranzadi – a scientific institution which has undertaken research in forensic anthropology and pathology. Since 2000, Professor Etxeberria has participated in over 200 exhumations and has generated publications and promoted the use of these scientific disciplines (anthropology, pathology) in the context of human rights investigations.

Martin Paul Evison, PhD, has been Full Professor and research group leader at the Northumbria University Centre for Forensic Science, UK, since 2010. From 2005 to 2010, he was the Director of the Forensic Science Program at the University of Toronto, Canada. Before moving to Canada, he was a member of the Department of Forensic Pathology at Sheffield University, UK, where he led a research group in forensic human identification and practised as the regional forensic anthropologist. He has given written and oral evidence in forensic anthropology and archaeology cases in the UK courts, and has participated in human rights investigations in Brazil, Kenya and Kosovo. Professor Evison has recently published on the utility of forensic anthropology in the investigation of suspicious death with collaborators in São Paulo, Brazil.

Roxana Ferllini, BSc, MA, MFSSoc, is an independent researcher and author. From 2002 to 2013, she was coordinator of the MSc programme in forensic archaeological sciences, University College London, UK. She has participated in human rights investigations in Rwanda, Kosovo, the Middle East and Spain, and was involved in forensic investigations in the United Kingdom. She was a consultant for the Organism of Judicial Investigation and an instructor at the Judicial School, Costa Rica, during the 1990s. From 1989 to 1998, she was an associate professor at the Departments of Anthropology and Legal Medicine, University of Costa Rica.

Maria Teresa Ferreira, PhD, holds a doctorate in forensic anthropology. She has coordinated several excavations of human remains in archaeological contexts in Portugal. She has also participated in fieldwork in Guinea-Bissau and Spain as a forensic anthropologist. In recent years, Dr Ferreira has focused on taphonomic research.

Andrea Fischer was Senior Inspector (*Kriminaloberkommissar*) at the German Federal Police Force (BKA) and a member of the Crime Scene Unit of the BKA from 2006 to 2013. In addition to her main duties, she also supported the BKA Forensic Archaeology team and the EU ISEC-project 'Fingerprints and DNA on Human Skin'. Since 2011, she has also been a member of the Disaster Victim Identification Team of the BKA. In November 2013, she was transferred to the management-level staff of the BKA (Executive Board of the CID Working Group).

Luis Fondebrider is an Argentine forensic anthropologist, co-founder and current president of the Argentine Forensic Anthropology Team (EAAF), a scientific non-governmental organisation created in Argentina in 1984 to investigate the whereabouts of people who disappeared in the country during the period 1976–1983. He has, as a member of the EAAF, participated in and/or conducted forensic investigations of cases of political/ethnic violence in Chile, Bolivia, Brazil, Paraguay, Peru, Colombia, Venezuela, El Salvador, Guatemala, Haiti, Croatia, Bosnia, Kosovo, Romania, Georgia/Abkhazia, Cyprus, Iraq, South Africa, Namibia, Zimbabwe, DRC, Ethiopia, Libya, Thailand, Vietnam, the Philippines, Indonesia, East Timor and the Solomon Islands, among others. Additionally, he also lectures in forensic anthropology at the Faculty of Medicine, University of Buenos Aires, Argentina.

Gillian Fowler, MSc, is a lecturer in forensic anthropology and archaeology in the School of Life Sciences at the University of Lincoln, UK. She is a forensic anthropologist and archaeologist with extensive experience working in post-conflict mass grave exhumations in Guatemala and more recently in Afghanistan, where she is a consulting forensic anthropologist for Physicians for Human Rights (PHR). In addition to international consultancy, Gillian undertakes casework for UK police forces and is a fellow of the Royal Anthropological Institute (RAI).

Raffaela Arrabaça Francisco, MSc, holds degrees in biomedicine from the Baron of Mauá University Centre, and is specialist in forensic sciences and holds a Masters degree in forensic anthropology from the Medico-Legal Centre (CEMEL), Department of Pathology and Legal Medicine, Ribeirão Preto Medical School, University of São Paulo, Brazil. As a forensic expert, she is a member of the Araguaia Working Group (GTA) and the vice-coordinator of the Forensic Archaeology and Anthropology Group (GAAF) of the Human Rights

Secretariat of the Presidency of the Republic. She is developing her PhD thesis in forensic anthropology at CEMEL, Ribeirão Preto Medical School.

Claudia Garrido Varas, PhD, holds a doctorate in physical anthropology. She is employed as a forensic odontologist at the Special Forensic Identification Unit (UEIF) in Chile. She is currently working on commingled human skeletal remains and examines patterns of asymmetry and sexual dimorphism in the appendicular skeletons of the modern Chilean population. Dr Garrido Varas' recent publications include *The 'Unidad Especial de Identificación Forense' and Human Rights in Chile* (Garrido and Intriago 2012) and *Managing Commingled Remains from Mass Graves: Considerations, Implications and Recommendations from a Human Rights Case in Chile* (Garrido and Intriago 2012).

Patrice Georges, MA, is an archaeologist and physical anthropologist at the National Institute of Preventive Archaeological Research (INRAP), France. He is also attached to the Laboratory of Anthropology of Past and Present Populations at the University of Bordeaux, France. After completing an additional degree in criminal science, he became a reserve officer of the Department of Anthropology–Thanatology–Odontology of the Forensic Sciences Institute of the French National Gendarmerie (IRCGN). He is appointed as a forensic expert at the Toulouse Court of Appeal, France. His expertise in medieval history, archaeology, physical anthropology and his excavation experience in France and abroad, including Egypt, have led to numerous archaeological publications. Since his appointment in the Reserve Force, he has co-authored scientific articles on forensic archaeology.

Ana Carolina Guatame García, MSc, is a forensic anthropologist and currently Director of the Colombian Interdisciplinary Team on Forensic Work and Psychosocial Assistance (EQUITAS). She was educated at the University of the Andes, Colombia, and the University of Central Lancashire, UK. She obtained a scholarship to carry out graduate studies in the United Kingdom and has conducted academic projects on river searches. In addition, she has extensive experience in the documentation of human rights abuses and on issues of psycho-social necessities of families of missing persons and social politics. She is a diplomat of the Latin American Forensic Anthropology Association (ALAF).

Marco Aurelio Guimarães, MD, PhD, is the chief forensic anthropologist of the Medico-Legal Centre (CEMEL), Department of Pathology and Legal Medicine, Ribeirão Preto Medical School, University of São Paulo, Brazil. He is the senior lecturer responsible for the disciplines of forensic medicine and bioethics. He undertakes local and national criminal forensic anthropology casework, mainly related to the investigation of human rights violations on political deaths and the disappeared from the dictatorship years in Brazil, including excavations undertaken in the search for human remains by the Araguaia Working Group (GTA). Dr Guimarães was recently designated by the Human Rights Secretariat of the Presidency of the Republic to coordinate the anthropology area in the Forensic Archaeology and Anthropology Group (GAAF).

Ian Hanson, MSc, MIfA, is the Deputy Director of Forensic Science for Archaeology and Anthropology at the International Commission on Missing Persons (ICMP), responsible for managing operations and the scientific process of search, location, recovery and examination. Previously, he was senior lecturer in forensic archaeology at Bournemouth University, UK. He has 26 years of excavation experience, with more than 16,000 hours spent working on field investigations. Since 1997, he has undertaken human rights and forensic investigations for the UNICTY, UNDPKO, FCO, ICMP and other agencies in the Balkans, Middle East, Central America and Africa. As an expert witness and report writer, he has advised non-governmental organisations on forensic science, operational and field management matters since 2000. He is an expert advisor for the Serious Organised Crime Agency, UK (SOCA) and a Fellow of the American Academy of Forensic Sciences (AAFS).

Lourdes Herrasti, MA, holds a degree in history and archaeology and specialises in osteoarchaeology. Since 1980, she has been a member of the Anthropology Department at the Sociedad de Ciencias Aranzadi, Spain. She has directed many archaeological excavations comprising human remains from prehistory to the mediaeval period. Since 2000, she has participated in more than 200 mass grave exhumations from the Spanish Civil War and reported on findings. She has also published on this topic.

Ute Hofmeister, MA, is Regional Forensic Coordinator for the Americas for the International Committee of the Red Cross (ICRC). She specialises in forensic archaeology and anthropology with particular focus on documentation and management of forensic data and on issues of psycho-social necessities of families of missing persons applied to human rights and humanitarian investigations. Since 1995 she has worked for various organisations (UN, ICTY, ICMP, EAAF, FAFG), mainly in the Balkans and Latin America, until joining the ICRC in 2005. Since then, she has advised and trained governments, forensic experts and civil society organisations in over 40 countries on issues concerning the search and identification of missing persons, particularly in humanitarian and human rights contexts, management of dead bodies in conflict and disasters and support to families of the missing.

Beatrice Hudson, BA (Hons), MSc, gained her qualifications from the University of Otago, New Zealand, and Durham University, UK, and a CoP in forensic science from Auckland University, New Zealand. She works as an independent archaeological and osteological consultant in New Zealand. Her research interests include Southeast Asian and Pacific palaeopathology and burial practices – in particular health and the mortuary process in pre- and post-contact Maori – and the application of archaeological methods to forensic casework.

John Hunter, OBE, BA, PhD, FSA, MIFA, FFSSoc, has been Full Professor of Archaeology and Ancient History at the University of Birmingham, UK, since 1996. Apart from performing research excavation and survey in Scotland, he began to develop forensic archaeology in 1988, and has co-authored his third book on the subject, *Forensic Approaches to Buried Remains* (Hunter et al. 2013). He is involved operationally throughout the United Kingdom, has worked in Bosnia, Iraq and the Falklands, and routinely lectures to police and forensic professionals. He helped found the Forensic Search Advisory Group, was a lead assessor for the Council for Registration of Forensic Practitioners (CRFP) and was primary in setting up the current validation system for Forensic Archaeology. Professor Hunter is a Royal Commissioner on the Ancient and Historical Monuments of Scotland, an appointee of the Cathedral Fabrics Commission for England at Worcester Cathedral and sits on the National History Museum Scientific Advisory Panel (human remains).

Marisol Intriago Leiva, MSc, is a Chilean forensic anthropologist and Head of the Special Forensic Identification Unit of the Forensic Medical Service (SML). From 2003 to 2010, she worked within a multidisciplinary SML team that analysed cases involving human rights abuses linked to the military dictatorship in Chile (1973–1990), as well as other complex cases. Since 2011, she has been in charge of the implementation of identification protocols at the SML, in addition to the coordination of forensic analysis in the laboratory and field, which aims to identify and determine injury in human rights abuses and criminal cases.

Carlos Jácome Hernández, PhD, is Full Professor at the Sociology and Anthropology Department, University of Concepcion, Chile. He holds Archaeological (National School of Anthropology and History) and Physical Anthropological (National Autonomous University of Mexico) degrees and a PhD from the University of Montreal, Canada. He has worked as an independent expert witness and forensic advisor in humanitarian cases and for different committees of relatives of the illegally detained/disappeared since 2000. Most of Professor Jácome's work has been in Mexico, but he has also worked in other regions of America and Europe.

Christian Jackowski, MD, PhD, is Full Professor and Director of the Institute of Forensic Medicine at the University of Bern, Switzerland. He studied Medicine and Business Administration in Magdeburg; Germany; and Bern, Switzerland. He has worked, as a forensic pathologist with special research interest in forensic imaging, at five different Institutes of Forensic Medicine in Germany, Sweden and Switzerland. Professor Jackowski has participated in over 60 scientific publications.

Pavel Jamnik, BA, holds a degree in Political Science (University of Ljubljana). He has worked at the Ministry of the Interior, in the criminal police directorate and is presently a member of the Government Commission on Concealed Mass Graves in Slovenia. Since 2001, he has led the criminal investigation of post-WWII mass graves in the Republic of Slovenia. He introduced archaeological methods to the police investigation of mass graves, which then became the standard for forensic police cases related to buried human remains. He also participates in cave excavations and Palaeolithic archaeology. He has published around 100 professional and scientific articles on Palaeolithic archaeology and post-WWII mass graves.

Rimantas Jankauskas, PhD, is Full Professor at the Department of Anatomy, Histology and Anthropology, Faculty of Medicine, Vilnius University, Lithuania, and a senior specialist at the State Forensic Medicine Service, Ministry of Justice. He serves on the editorial board of *Anthropologischer Anzeiger*, and is an active participant in the Palaeopathology Association. His close collaboration with various scholars and professionals in archaeology, medicine and forensics resulted in the successful completion of projects such as the identification of the remains of former Estonian president K. Päts (died in exile in Russia in 1957), the burials of the Radziwill family (16th–17th century), the Napoleonic mass grave in Vilnius (1812) and the identification of KGB victims (1944–1947). Professor Jankauskas has published widely in scientific journals on topics ranging from palaeopathology and human osteology to forensic anthropology and human biology.

Marie Louise Jørkov, PhD, holds a doctorate in physical anthropology from Copenhagen University, Denmark. As forensic anthropologist, she has been on missions to Iraq investigating mass graves and has worked cases for the Danish National Police, in Denmark and abroad, in connection with identification and trauma analysis. She is a member of the Danish DVI-team and affiliated with the International Humanitarian Rosters (IHB) under the Danish Ministry of Foreign Affairs. Her research interests include skeletal trauma and human identification, dietary studies based on stable isotope analysis, palaeopathology and demography. Dr Jørkov is currently holding a postdoctoral fellowship from the Danish Council for Independent Research/Humanities at the Institute of Forensic Medicine, Copenhagen University, where she investigates health and diet in Denmark during the industrial period.

Fabian Kanz, PhD, is Associated Professor at the Department of Forensic Medicine, the Medical University of Vienna, Austria, where he has lectured in forensic anthropology since 2010. He has also been sworn in as an expert on forensic anthropology by the Austrian Minister of Justice since 2011. In addition to journal publications on topics in forensic anthropology, he has published numerous scientific articles in monographs concerning bioarchaeological research on human remains from archaeological excavations. He participates in domestic and international forensic anthropological casework, as well as in national and international regular archaeological excavations. Dr Kanz is currently leading the development of a Masters' programme in forensic science, the first such program to be offered in Austria.

Yi-Suk Kim, MD, PhD, is Assistant Professor at the Ewha Womans University School of Medicine, Seoul, Republic of Korea, where he lectures in gross anatomy and forensic anthropology. Dr Kim's fields of interest are physical and forensic anthropology, clinical anatomy and human osteology.

Karsten Klenke is a senior inspector (*Kriminaloberkommissar*) with the German Federal Police Force (BKA) and has been a member of the Crime Scene Unit and the DVI-tem of the BKA since 1998. He is one of the initiators of the establishment of the Forensic Archaeology Working Group within the BKA Crime Scene Unit and is presently coordinating its actions.

Geoffrey C. Knupfer, MBE, BA (Hons), MSc, Dipl (Dunelm), PGCE, FCSFS, is a forensic scientist and investigator. His areas of interest include major crime investigation, review and management, crime scene investigation, forensic ballistics and forensic archaeology. He is a former Detective Chief Superintendent in the UK Police Service and, in that role, was an advisor to the (UK) Home Office on policing technologies. Since retirement, he has lectured and examined at universities and colleges in the United Kingdom. In 2005, he was appointed consultant forensic scientist to the Independent Commission for the Location of Victims Remains (ICLVR). In 2006, this role was combined with that of Head of the ICLVR Investigation Team. He is a fellow of the Chartered Society of Forensic Sciences, a member of the International Association for Identification (IAI), and a founding member of the Forensic Search Advisory Group (FSAG).

László Kovács, DSc, is a retired archaeologist and numismatist. He was the Deputy Director of the Institute of Archaeology in the Research Centre of Humanities of the Hungarian Academy of Sciences. His research field is 10th–11th century Hungarian archaeology. He was one of the critics regarding the misidentification of the skeletal remains of the Hungarian poet Sandor Petofi (1823–1849). Dr Kovács has participated in archaeological excavations related to human identification since 1992.

U-Young Lee, MD, PhD, is Assistant Professor at the Department of Anatomy, College of Medicine, The Catholic University of Korea, Republic of Korea, and Entrusting Medical Examiner (Forensic Autopsy and Forensic Anthropology) at the National Forensic Service, Seoul, Republic of Korea. Dr Lee's field of research is the use of 3D-human models (morphometric studies) within physical and forensic anthropology, clinical anatomy and human osteology.

Roosje de Leeuwe, MA, BEng, has worked as a forensic archaeologist at the Netherlands Forensic Institute (NFI) since 2011. After finishing a bachelor's degree in Maritime Engineering and working as an engineer for a few years, she changed careers and completed a 4-year Masters' degree in North-west European Prehistoric Archaeology at Leiden University, the Netherlands, specialising in late prehistory, maritime archaeology and African archaeology. She worked as a field archaeologist in contract archaeology for nearly a decade and taught a course in Maritime Archaeology at Leiden University before switching to forensics.

José M. López Mazz, PhD, is Full Professor at the Archaeology Department, University of the Republic, Uruguay. He is also attached, as anthropologist and archaeologist, to the University of the Republic, École Hautes Etudes Sciences Sociales, France. In addition, Professor López Mazz coordinates the Uruguayan Forensic Anthropology Investigation Team (GIAF).

Sandra Lösch, PhD, studied Physical Anthropology with Biology at the Ludwig-Maximilian-University of Munich (LMU), Germany. She has published numerous scientific articles concerning bioarchaeological investigations on human remains from archaeological excavations.

She works on regional and international forensic anthropological cases, as well as on national and international archaeological excavations. Since 2010, she has been head of the Department of Physical Anthropology at the Institute of Forensic Medicine at the University of Bern, Switzerland.

Anthony Lowe, MA, obtained his Masters' degree in London, UK. He started out working in Middle Eastern archaeology in the 1980s, but now works as an historical archaeologist in Sydney, Australia, with a focus on 19th century European settlement. Since 2006, he has been privileged to be able to contribute to Missing in Action (MIA) recoveries in Southeast Asia for the Australian Defence Forces (ADF), assisting in site investigation and documentation.

Alicia Lusiardo, MA, holds a Masters' degree in forensic anthropology from the University of Florida, US. She is a diplomat and a former president of the Latin American Forensic Anthropology Association (ALAF), and works as a forensic anthropologist for the Uruguayan Forensic Anthropology Investigation Team (GIAF). She developed and has taught the 'Forensic Anthropology 1' course of UF's Forensic Science Distance Learning Program since 2006 and, since 2010, the 'Forensic Anthropology' course of the Centre for Legal Studies (CEJ) in Madrid, Spain.

Niels Lynnerup, MD, PhD, DMSc, is Full Professor and Head of the Unit of Forensic Anthropology at the Department of Forensic Medicine, University of Copenhagen, Denmark. He became a medical doctor in 1988, received his doctorate from the University of Copenhagen in 1995, and his Doctor of Medical Science degree in 2013. His forensic anthropological research comprises both the living (photogrammetry, gait analyses) and the dead (radiocarbon techniques and the utilisation of CT-scanning and 3D-visualisation techniques). Professor Lynnerup is the author or co-author of 130 research papers and numerous book chapters.

Lynn Maalouf is a Beirut-based writer, activist and trainer whose work focuses on the issue of the missing and disappeared persons in Lebanon. She headed the Lebanese program of the International Centre for Transitional Justice (www.ictj.org) for 5 years, conducted a process that led to the drafting of a bill for the disappeared and missing in Lebanon and conceived and implemented an oral history project, 'Badna Naaraf' (We Want to Know), with high school and university students, about citizens' daily life during the Lebanese conflict. She also co-founded 'Act for the Disappeared', a local non-governmental organisation that focuses on raising awareness among the youth about the issue of the missing and disappeared in Lebanon and elsewhere. She scripted *Blue Line*, a 20-minute fiction film, which gained multiple awards at international film festivals; she is currently working on a feature-length script.

Rita Clovis Maalouf, MSc, MC, is a US-educated and trained forensic scientist who has worked in Lebanon since 2008 as an independent consultant in the criminal investigation of murder and violent crimes, taking on cases for various clients, including the Lebanese Supreme Court Criminal Branch, as the first forensic expert approved by the Lebanese Ministry of Justice. Prior to her work in Lebanon, she worked at the Forensic Science Medical Group in Washington, DC, US, where she assisted in the forensic psychiatric evaluations of individuals accused of US federal crimes. Academically, she is currently teaching forensic science at the American University of Science and Technology in Beirut, Lebanon, and is pursuing her PhD in forensic entomology at the Nicolaus Copernicus University in Toruń, Poland.

Brian Manns, BA, has an Associate Diploma in Museum Studies from the University of Sydney, Australia. He served for 25 years in the Australian Regular Army, in the infantry and saw overseas and active service in Malaysia, New Zealand and East Timor. In 2000, he left the Regular Army to become the Manager of the Australian Army's Museum Network. In 2006, he commenced his current work of searching for and recovering Australia's wartime missing and established a permanent unit in 2010. He has led recovery teams in Vietnam, Indonesia, Malaysia and Papua New Guinea.

Carina Marques, MSc, holds a Masters' degree in physical anthropology from the University of Coimbra, Portugal, and is presently completing a PhD thesis on the evolution and skeletal evidences of neoplastic diseases. She is a researcher at CIAS (Centro de Investigação em Antropologia e Saúde, University of Coimbra) and CENCIFOR (Centro de Ciências Forenses, INML). Her main interests are paleopathology and forensic anthropology, areas in which she has been conducting research, fieldwork and teaching activities.

Julie Martin, BA, is a freelance field archaeologist in the United Kingdom with over 20 years' experience in a variety of archaeological settings; she teaches field techniques for the Kent Archaeological Field School. In 2010, she became the archaeological consultant for the Vietnamese-American charity 'The Returning Casualty'. She is currently studying for an MSc degree in forensic archaeology and anthropology at Cranfield University, UK.

Soňa Masnicová, PhD, is a biological/forensic anthropologist. She is Associate Professor at the Department of Criminalistics and Forensic Sciences at the Academy of the Police Force in Bratislava, Slovakia. She holds a PhD in physical anthropology from Comenius University, Bratislava, and a habilitation in Security and Legal Protection of Persons and Property from the Academy of the Police Force, Bratislava. Her major research includes areas of skeletal biology, especially palaeopathology and forensic anthropology. Dr Masnicová is consultant for forensic anthropology at the Institute of Forensic Medical Expertise – Forensic.sk, a member of the Slovak Anthropological Society (member of the Main Committee), and a member of the European Anthropological Association (EAA).

Eliška Maxová, MA, MSc, is a graduate of the Faculty of Philosophy and Arts, University of West Bohemia, Czech Republic. She holds Masters' degrees in archaeology and anthropology of past populations. She specialises in bioarchaeology and burial archaeology, especially on relations between morphological variability and post-marital residence in the La Téne Period population of Bohemia.

Dallas Mazoori is currently completing her Juris Doctor at the University of New South Wales, Australia. She is a former member of the Transitional Justice Unit of the Afghanistan Independent Human Rights Commission (AIHRC) where she led efforts in the compilation of the country's conflict mapping report. She has also consulted for the UN and the International Centre for Transitional Justice. Most recently, she worked on Physicians for Human Rights' (PHR) 3-year Afghanistan Program, culminating in the *Securing Afghanistan's Past: Human Identification Needs Assessment and Gap Analysis* report.

Niamh A. McCullagh, MA, MSc, is a senior forensic archaeologist with the Independent Commission for the Location of Victims Remains (ICVLR) and has been working with them since 2007. She worked for 6 years as a professional archaeologist in the commercial and research-based sectors before specialising in forensic archaeology and crime scene investigation at the University of Bradford, UK, in 2006. As an independent forensic archaeologist specialising in search, Niamh has been involved in advising on domestic criminal cases, training police forces and a number of research projects specific to Ireland and the Irish burial environment.

Maria B. Mednikova, DSc, PhD, is a physical anthropologist and leading researcher at the Department of Theory and Methods of Archaeology, Institute of Archaeology of Russian Academy of Sciences in Moscow. She has participated in archaeological excavations and provided bioarchaeological and forensic expertise related to the excavated human remains. Dr Medinikova has also participated in the identification of burials of famous Russian historical persons.

Raquel Meléndez González is a police inspector who entered the Spanish National Police (CNP) in 1996. She has worked in different branches within the Police, including the divisions of intelligence and information gathering, civil protection, public security and scientific police. In the latter, she worked for over 10 years in the investigation of serious violence including homicides, sexual assaults and fire scenes. After her work with the scientific police, she moved as instructor to the Centre of Actualisations and Specialisation of the Training and Development Division of the CNP where she teaches police officers with the latest techniques and methods.

Mária Molnos is a research associate at the Hungarian Network of Forensic Science Institutes (ISZKI) where she works under the supervision of Professor Éva Susa on the identification of people who have died in uncertain circumstances between 1945 and 1962. She is responsible for the organisation of the research materials and database. She participated in the search for the unmarked graves at the Prisoner Cemetery of Vác, and the New Public Cemetery (parcels 301 and 298) in subsequent documentation and identification of the exhumed bodies.

Franco Mora, BA, studied archaeology at the Catholic University of Peru, trained as a bioarchaeologist early in his career and in forensic anthropology since joining the Peruvian Forensic Anthropology Team (EPAF) in 2007. He has worked on several cases as both Prosecutor's and Defence expert in Peru, as well as other countries such as Colombia, Guatemala, the Democratic Republic of Congo, Somaliland and Mexico.

Konstantinos Moraitis, PhD, is Assistant Professor in forensic anthropology and Head of the Forensic Anthropology Unit at the Department of Forensic Medicine and Toxicology, School of Medicine, University of Athens, Greece. In addition to assisting in forensic cases of human identification for the police and medico-legal agencies in Greece, he has been involved in humanitarian missions in Bosnia, Kosovo and Cyprus. His research interests include forensic anthropology, skeletal biology, taphonomy and trauma analysis.

Livia Margarita Muñoz Andrade, MSc, graduated from the Central University of Venezuela as a physical anthropologist. She also holds a Masters' degree in Police Management and Administration. Her additional specialisations include criminology, teaching and education management. She works as forensic anthropologist and chief criminal investigator at the Attorney General's Office, Caracas, Venezuela. She also participated in the exhumation of the remains of Simón Bolívar 'The Liberator' (15 July 2010) in Caracas and was responsible for the final report concerning the bioanthropological analysis of this notable citizen.

Ralf Neumann, BA, is a senior inspector (*Kriminaloberkommissar*) at the German Federal Police Force (BKA). After graduating from the Federal University of Applied Administrative Sciences, he worked in the field of economic crime focusing on investment fraud, real property fraud and violations of the German Stock Corporation Act/stock market and stock prices manipulation. Following a devastating tsunami in late 2004, he was repeatedly deployed to Thailand with the DVI-team of the BKA. In autumn 2005, he joined the BKA Crime Scene Unit where he has been a member of the 'Forensic Archaeology' Working Group from the very beginning. Besides working at numerous crime scenes and examining exhibits in the laboratory, he has gained extensive experience in the field of search and excavation. He has repeatedly given lectures on issues of crime scene work in Germany and abroad.

W. Coen Nienaber, BA, BSc, is a career archaeologist and has been with the University of Pretoria, South Africa, since 1995. He has collaborated with the South African Police Services and other law enforcement and judicial institutions in the recovery of human remains in forensic settings and human rights cases. He is an active researcher in the field of burial archaeology and has extensive experience in cultural resources management projects involving human remains and graves in the southern African region. He has published and presented on the subject in various forms and is a member of several national and international professional associations in the field.

Sergey Nikitin, MD, graduated from the Moscow Medical Institute, Russia, and specialises in the field of forensic medicine. He has been a forensic medical doctor at the Bureau of Forensic Medical Examination, Moscow, since 1973. Between 1984 and 2006, he worked at the Department of Archaeology, Moscow State University, Russia, where he developed new methods related to the superimposition of photographic images on skulls and the plotting of portraits on the skull using computer programs.

Franck Nolot, MSc, is a forensic anthropologist at the Department of Anthropology–Thanatology–Odontology of the Forensic Sciences Institute of the French National Gendarmerie (IRCGN). He holds a Masters' degree in Anthropology of Past and Present Populations from the University of Bordeaux, France. He provides training in forensic anthropology and archaeology for Crime Scene Technicians and leads a university internship. Additionally, he teaches a graduate course on forensic sciences at the Laboratory of Medical Ethics and Legal Medicine, René Descartes University, France. He has co-authored scientific articles on the above-mentioned topics.

Zuzana Obertová, PhD, is a biological/forensic anthropologist, currently residing in New Zealand. She holds a PhD in biological anthropology from Comenius University in Bratislava, Slovakia and Eberhard-Karls University in Tübingen, Germany. Due to her interest in researching disease patterns in past and present populations, she is currently undertaking doctoral studies in epidemiology/community health at the University of Auckland, New Zealand. Before coming to New Zealand, she was employed as a research fellow at the Institute of Forensic Medicine in Düsseldorf, Germany. She is currently a Board Member of the Forensic Anthropology Society of Europe (FASE).

José Vicente Pachar Lucio, MD, specialises in anatomical pathology. He also holds a Masters' degree in forensic pathology from the University of London, UK. He is employed as a forensic pathologist at the Institute of Legal Medicine and Forensic Sciences, Republic of Panama, and has 20 years of experience in medico-legal cases, including forensic anthropology (e.g. skeletonised, burned or dismembered remains and human remains in an advanced state of decomposition).

Thomas J. Parsons, PhD, has been the Director of Forensic Science at the International Commission on Missing Persons (ICMP) in Sarajevo, Bosnia and Herzegovina since 2006. He supervises a large team forensic science staff in a multidisciplinary approach to identification of missing individuals involving forensic archaeology, anthropology, pathology and high-throughput DNA analysis. These sciences have been applied to investigation and/or human identification of mass graves, missing persons' cases, and mass disasters worldwide, often on a very large scale. The ICMP has made DNA identification matches to over 18,000 individuals. ICMP training and capacity building are also large parts of ICMP forensic activity, currently with large programs in Libya and Iraq. He is on the editorial board of *Forensic Science International Genetics*, a Board Member of the US Scientific Working Group on DVI (SWG-DVI) and a Board Member of the American Association for the Advancement of Science (AAAS) Committee for Scientific Responsibility and Freedom. Prior to joining the ICMP, Dr Parsons was Chief Scientist at the US Armed Forces DNA Identification Laboratory.

Anja Petaros, MD, graduated from the Rijeka University School of Medicine, Croatia, in 2009. She is employed at the Department of Forensic Medicine and Criminalistics, Rijeka University School of Medicine, where she established the Anthropological Laboratory and is in charge of the forensic anthropological analysis of skeletal remains from WWII, post-WWII mass burials and recent forensic cases. She lectures in forensic anthropology and anthropometry at the Rijeka University School of Medicine and is currently preparing a PhD thesis on the application of virtual anthropology methods in the assessment of sexual dimorphism from the mastoid region. She is the online-publishing editor of *Acta Medico-Historica Adriatica*. From 2009 on, she has acted as the Croatian delegate in the International Society for the History of Medicine (ISHM); and in 2012, she was nominated as a Board Member of the Forensic Anthropology Society of Europe (FASE).

Andrew T. Pietruszka, PhD, is a forensic underwater archaeologist with the US Department of Defence Joint POW/MIA Accounting Command's Central Identification Laboratory (JPAC-CIL). He holds a Masters' degree in underwater archaeology from East Carolina University, US, and a doctorate in Anthropology from Syracuse University, US. His comprehensive experiences in archaeology include work on both terrestrial and maritime sites throughout the United States, the Caribbean, Southeast Asia, Europe and West Africa. Dr Pietruszka's research interests include marine remote sensing, method and theory in maritime archaeology, forensic archaeology and anthropology, human osteology, the preservation and management of cultural resources, and African-European contact in West Africa.

Joyce Stockins Ramírez, MSc, holds a BA in Archaeology from the College of Wooster, Ohio, US. During her studies, she spent 2 months at the National Museum of Ireland and her archaeological thesis won the Vivian L. Holliday Prize and an honourable mention at the Congress of the Central States Anthropological Society in 2004. In 2007, she earned a Masters' in forensic archaeology from University College London, University of London, UK. She participated in the recovery of human remains and other materials from the debris of the Twin Towers in New York, after the 9/11 attacks. Since 2010 she has been part of the Special Forensic Identification Unit of the Chilean Forensic Medical Service (SML), working as the Archaeology Coordinator within a multidisciplinary team that analyses cases involving human rights abuses linked to the military dictatorship in Chile (1973–1990), as well as other complex criminal cases.

Jean Richebé, MSc, is a forensic anthropologist at the Department of Anthropology–Thanatology–Odontology at the Forensic Sciences Institute of the French National Gendarmerie (IRCGN), with a career in the French National Gendarmerie Forces. He provides training in forensic anthropology and archaeology for Crime Scene Technicians and leads a university internship. He also lectures in a graduate course on forensic sciences at the Laboratory of Medical Ethics and Legal Medicine, René Descartes University, France. He has published scientific articles on the above-mentioned topics.

Adnan Rizviç, BSc, joined the International Commission on Missing Persons (ICMP) in January 2000 and was instrumental in the establishment of ICMP's Identification Coordination Division in Tuzla and was in charge for development of Forensic Database Management System. In January 2004, he became Deputy Director of ICMP's Forensic Sciences Department. He has previously worked for Physicians for Human Rights (PHR) as their Forensic Program Coordinator in Bosnia and Herzegovina. He has a degree in Engineering Science from Tuzla University, Bosnia and Herzegovina. Following the 9/11 disaster, he participated in sessions of KADAP Group (Kinship and Data Analyses Planning Panel) working on developing a consensus on the protocol needed to evaluate the genetic profiles that will be used to identify the victims of the World Trade Center using DNA technology. He has also worked on several major mass fatality incidents including the crash of Kenya Flight 507, the Thailand Tsunami Victim Identification, Typhoon Frank-Philippines and, most recently, he is involved in ICMP's forensic activities in Iraq.

Ann H. Ross, PhD, is a board certified diplomate of the American Board of Forensic Anthropology, and a Full Professor and the Co-Director of the Forensic Sciences Institute, North Carolina State University, US. Professor Ross consults for the Office of the Chief Medical Examiner and law enforcement agencies in North Carolina, US, and has participated in exhumations and identifications for the Panamanian Truth Commission, Bosnia and Chile.

Azrat Safarov, BSc, is a Masters' student at the SARE Centre, Russian State University for the Humanities, Moscow, Russia.

Vivian Scheinsohn, PhD, is an Argentine archaeologist and researcher at the National Scientific and Technical Research Council (CONICET) and the Anthropological and Latin-American Thought National Institute (INAPL). She lectures at the Anthropology Department of the Faculty of Arts, University of Buenos Aires, Argentina, in Argentine Archaeology and has specialised in Patagonian Archaeology.

Stefan Schmitt, MSc, is the Director of the Physicians for Human Rights (PHR) International Forensic Program. He holds a bachelor's degree in physical anthropology from the Universidad del Valle, Guatemala, and a Masters' degree in Criminology from Florida State University, US. Prior to joining PHR in 2006, he worked for 10 years at the Florida Department of Law Enforcement as a Crime Scene and Digital Video Enhancement Analyst. Before that he lived in Guatemala, where he founded the country's first Forensic Anthropology Team in 1992. Internationally, he has worked for the International Criminal Tribunals for Rwanda (ICTR) and the former Yugoslavia (ICTY) and as a forensic consultant to the UN in countries such as Iraq, Afghanistan and Liberia.

Eline M. J. Schotsmans, PhD, is a post-doctoral researcher in forensic archaeology and taphonomy at the Laboratory of Anthropology of Past and Present Populations (PACEA) at the University of Bordeaux, France, and an honorary fellow at the University of Bradford, UK. She obtained her doctorate at the University of Bradford, specialising in lime burials. Dr Schotsmans has worked on various forensic cases in collaboration with the Belgian DVI-team, the University of Bradford, the University of Leuven, various UK police forces and Kenyon International Emergency Services.

Yves Schuliar, MD, PhD, is the Director of Education and Research at the Forensic Sciences Institute of the French National Gendarmerie (IRCGN). He holds a medical degree in Forensic Medicine and a doctorate in Forensic Sciences from the University of Lausanne, Switzerland. In addition, he is a medical doctor (Brigadier General) within the Medical Service of the French Armed Forces and the Head of the Forensic Sciences education programme at the Laboratory of Medical Ethics and Legal Medicine, René Descartes University, Paris, France. He is also appointed by the French Supreme Court and the Paris Court of Appeal as a forensic expert. Dr Schuliar has published numerous scientific articles on forensic sciences, forensic medicine and criminal investigation.

Fernando Serrulla, MSc, PhD, has been a forensic pathologist within the Spanish Ministry of Justice from 1988, and holds a Masters' degree in forensic anthropology. He is an expert in legal and forensic medicine, criminology and assessment of personal injury. He became a member of the Asociacion Española de Paleopatología in 1989, after encountering Professor Francisco Etxeberría and his passion for bones. He is the Director of the *Journal for Forensic Pathologists of Galicia* (www.agmf.es), Director of the Forensic Anthropology Unit of the Spanish Institute of Legal Medicine of Galicia, a founding member of the Spanish Association of Anthropology and Forensic Odontology (AEAOF) and a member of the Anthropology Section of the Aranzadi Science Society. Dr Serrulla has participated in more than 20 studies related to the Spanish Civil War.

Mario Šlaus, PhD, is Full Professor at the Department of Forensic Medicine, University of Zagreb School of Medicine, Croatia, and Full Professor of Physical Anthropology at the Department of Archaeology, University of Zadar, Croatia. He has also worked at the Croatian Academy of Sciences and Arts (CASA) in Zagreb, first at the Department of Archaeology, and, from 2012, as the Director of the Anthropological Centre of the CASA. His main fields of research include physical anthropology, bioarchaeology and forensic anthropology. From 1993 to the present, he has participated in *pro bono* work related to the recovery, identification and analysis of the cause of death of 2143 victims from the Yugoslav War. He established and developed the osteological collection at the Croatian Academy of Sciences and Arts, which currently holds approximately 5500 skeletons from 34 archaeological sites in Croatia, dating from the Mesolithic to the Historic period.

Amanda Sozer, PhD, is the President of SNA International. She received her bachelor's degree from Rutgers University, US, and her doctorate from the University of Tennessee-Oak Ridge Graduate School of Biomedical Sciences at Oak Ridge National Laboratory, US. She has worked in human identification and forensics for 23 years directing forensic laboratories and programmes. Dr Sozer served as a technical contractor to the US National Institute of Justice (NIJ) and following 9/11 served on and facilitated the NIJ Kinship and Data Analysis Panel for the World Trade Centre victim identification effort and was instrumental in writing NIJ's *Lessons Learned from 9/11: DNA Identification in Mass Fatality Incidents* report (2006).

Andrej Starović, BSc, is a professional archaeologist, working since 2002 at the National Museum in Belgrade, Serbia, as curator of the Early Neolithic Collection. He was one of the founders and Head of the Department of Anthropology of the Petnica Science Centre, Serbia, an institute known worldwide for its extracurricular education of talented students in the field of different sciences. During his career, he has organised over 50 archaeological field projects and written four books, numerous scientific papers and created several exhibitions on prehistory. Since 2001, he has been included in the practice of forensic archaeology, working on mass grave cases in Serbia.

Jon Sterenberg, MSc, has been a professional archaeologist since 1983 and continues to work as a freelance consultant archaeologist in Australia. He has worked in the field of forensic archaeology since the late 1980s and worked in the Balkans for 11 years with the International Criminal Tribunal for the former Yugoslavia (ICTY) and the International Commission on Missing Persons (ICMP). He has employed his skills to locate and recover human remains from a diverse range of single, multiple and mass graves around the world including Australia, the Balkans, Africa, the United Kingdom, East Timor, the Solomon Islands and Iraq. He continues to follow and support the expanding role of forensic archaeology and anthropology within crime scene and humanitarian work.

Éva Susa, PhD, is the General Director of the Hungarian Network of Forensic Science Institutes (ISZKI). She is a forensic anthropologist and senior judicial counsellor. Her main area of research is forensic exhumation and identification of individuals who have died in ambiguous circumstances and who were buried in unmarked graves between 1945 and 1962 (e.g. parcel 301 in the New Public Cemetery, Prisoner Cemetery of Vác, Hungary). Dr Susa also writes forensic anthropological testimonies and expert reports at the requests of police, courts and so forth.

Mátyás Szőke is retired Director of the King Matthias Museum in Visegrád, Hungary, and specialises in the archaeology and history of Visegrád, especially the Medieval Period. He has also performed excavations at Mount Beuvray (a Gallic opidium) in France. Responding to the invitation of the Budapest Network of Forensic Science Institutes, he participated in diverse excavations associated with the graves of the victims of communism. One of his latest projects was the excavation of a mass grave of prisoners of a labour camp, buried near the Austrian border in 1945.

Morris V. Tidball-Binz, MD, is the forensic coordinator for the International Committee of the Red Cross (ICRC). He was the co-founder and first Director of the Argentine Forensic Anthropology Team (EAAF); advisor for the Grandmothers of Plaza de Mayo; researcher for Amnesty International (UK) and later Head of its Americas Department; he has also managed regional and international human rights programmes for other non-governmental organisations. He joined the ICRC in 2004. He has carried out forensic case work, dissemination and training applied to human rights and humanitarian investigations in over 70 countries in all regions. His publications include manuals, scientific articles and contributions in the fields of medical documentation of torture; monitoring prison conditions; forensic investigations into the missing; and the management of human remains in armed conflicts and catastrophes.

Maciej Trzciński, PhD, is Full Professor and Head of Postgraduate Studies in forensic archaeology at the Department of Forensic Sciences, the Faculty of Law, University of Wrocław, Poland. Professor Trzciński is also a member of the Scientific Association of Polish Archaeologists, the Archaeological Commission of the Polish Academy of Sciences, the Polish Forensic Society and the International Union for Prehistoric and Protohistoric Sciences.

Cláudia Umbelino, PhD, is Assistant Professor at the Department of Life Sciences, Faculty of Sciences and Technology, University of Coimbra, Portugal, and a researcher at the Research Centre for Anthropology and Health (CIAS). She holds a doctorate in biological anthropology and lectures in palaeoanthropology (Anthropology and Evaluation of the Biological Profile) and palaeodiets (Human Evolution and Biology Master).

Carolina Puerto Valdivieso, BA, is a physical anthropologist and a physical anthropology masters student educated at the National University of Colombia. She has specialised in forensic anthropology, criminal investigation and pedagogy. She works at the Colombian Interdisciplinary Team on Forensic Work and Psychosocial Assistance (EQUITAS) and has experience as a forensic expert in the analysis of human remains, university teaching and research projects on issues of violence such as missing persons and child abuse.

Birgit Van Denhouwe, MA, has been a police inspector and member of the Belgian DVI-team since 2007. She specialises in the search and recovery of clandestinely buried or hidden human bodies. She holds a Masters' degree in archaeology and a postgraduate certificate in forensic research. Additionally, she has participated in several international short courses, for example Forensic Archaeology and Anthropology (UK), Crime Scene Investigation (US) and Physical Anthropology (the Netherlands).

Miguel Ángel Vázquez Díaz has been an inspector in the Spanish National Police (CNP) since 1993. He has worked in different roles within the police including Immigration and Border Agency roles, Civil Protection, Judicial Police and Scientific Police. It was within the Scientific Police that he was responsible for the Local Brigade of one of the largest metropolitan areas of Madrid for 4 years. After this role, taking into account his experience as an investigator, he joined the Training and Career Development Centre for the Police as an instructor. Here, he teaches and trains active police officers with regard to new scientific techniques. He has also developed a number of collaborations with other police forces in the country as well as abroad, for example, the CNP Unit in Galicia, the Navarre Police, the French National Police and the Mexican Federal Police. He also collaborates with the Complutense University of Madrid, Spain, in the formation of specialist detectives.

Jana Velemínská, PhD, has been Assistant Professor at the Department of Anthropology and Human Genetics, Faculty of Science, Charles University, Prague, Czech Republic, since 1989. Her research areas are biomedical anthropology, forensic anthropology and bioarchaeology. Dr Velemínská has published, as author or co-author, nearly 60 scientific articles.

Petr Velemínský, PhD, has been a curator and researcher at the Department of Anthropology of the National Museum in Prague, Czech Republic, since 1989, and Head of this Department since 2004. His research covers the study of the relationship between biological variability, socio-economic conditions and health among past populations – particularly from the period of the last two millennia – and the estimation of basic demographic characteristics – sex and biological age – and the study of sexual dimorphism of the human skeleton. Dr Velemínský has published, as author or co-author, approximately 100 scientific articles.

Elizaveta Veselovskaya, PhD, is the Head of the Laboratory of Anthropological Reconstruction, Institute of Ethnology and Anthropology, Russian Academy of Sciences. She graduated from the Department of Anthropology, Moscow State University, Russia, and has been working at the famous Gerasimov Laboratory under the supervision of Dr Lebedinskaya and Dr Balueva since 1982. Dr Veselovskaya has performed more than 50 sculptural and nearly 200 digital portrait reconstructions of skulls belonging to Russian historical figures.

Roland Wessling, MSc, is employed by Cranfield University, UK, as a part-time research fellow in forensic archaeology and anthropology, is the Director of Operations for the Inforce Foundation and is a consultant forensic archaeologist. He holds a Masters' degree in forensic archaeology from Bournemouth University, UK. He worked as a forensic archaeologist in the Balkans for the International Criminal Tribunal for the former Yugoslavia (ICTY) and has been deployed on forensic operations in countries such as Cyprus and Iraq for the 'Inforce Foundation'. He was also involved in the excavation of 250 British and Australian soldiers from WWI in Fromelles, France. He regularly contributes to Inforce's training and exercise programmes and workshops for forensic scientists and police forces, mostly in the United Kingdom, but also in Colombia, and lectures regularly at California State University, US. He is one of the authors and an editor of *The Scientific Investigation of Mass Graves: Towards Protocols and Standard Operating Procedures* (Cox et al. 2008).

Christian Zingg, PhD, studied chemistry at the Swiss Federal Institute of Technology in Zürich (ETH Zürich), Switzerland, including 6 months at the University of Strathclyde in Glasgow, UK. He wrote his dissertation at the Institute of Forensic Science at the University of Lausanne, Switzerland. In 2005, after 5 years of experience at the Forensic Science Service of the City Police of Zürich (WD Zürich), Dr Zingg became the Head of the Forensic Crime Scene Unit of the Cantonal Police in Bern, Switzerland.

References

Cox, M., Flavel, A., Hanson, I., Laver, J. and Wessling, R. (eds.) 2008. *The Scientific Investigation of Mass Graves. Towards Protocols and Standard Operating Procedures*. Cambridge, Cambridge University Press.

Garrido Varas, C. E. and Intriago Leiva, M. 2012a. The "Unidad Especial de Identificación Forense" and Human Rights in Chile. *Cadernos de GEEvH* 1, 32–41.

Garrido Varas, C. E. and Intriago Leiva, M. 2012b. Managing commingled remains from mass graves: Considerations, implications and recommendations from a human rights case in Chile. *Forensic Science International* 219 (1–3), e19–e24.

Hunter, J., Simpson, B. and Sturdy Colls, C. 2013. *Forensic Approaches to Buried Remains*. Chichester, Wiley Blackwell.

Foreword by Clyde Collins Snow†

Forensic archaeology 1970–1984

In the early 1960s, I was employed as an anthropologist at the Federal Aviation Agency (FFA) Civil Aeromedical Institute (CAMI) in Oklahoma City, United States. My primary duty was to conduct research in human factors safety in commercial and general aviation – most of which involved the anthropometric characteristics of aviation populations such as pilots, flight attendants, air traffic controllers and passengers. I also participated in the investigation of major aircraft accidents, where I applied my skills as a physical anthropologist to help identify the often fragmented and badly burned bodies of the victims.

After a couple of years, local law enforcement officials in the state of Oklahoma, hearing of my experience in identification, began to ask if I could help them in the investigation of skeletal remains found in a forensic context. Although such activities were not within my official responsibilities, the CAMI director recognised them as a significant contribution to the local community and gave me permission to accept such case *pro bono*.

Up to this point, my Oklahoma cases typically began when a deputy sheriff from an outlying county walked into my laboratory, plopped a cardboard box full of dirt-encrusted bones on my desk and said something like 'Hey Doc, can ya'll tell me who these here bones is?' Invariably, upon examining the contents, I found that not only many bones and teeth were missing, but those recovered had been fragmented by the careless and unskilled excavators – law enforcement officers using picks and shovels. In most instances, I found that they had done more damage to the skeleton than the original perpetrator, who had merely fired a couple of bullets into the victim or had hit him with a tyre iron or a baseball bat!

One such case involved the remains of a six-year-old girl who had gone missing in Oklahoma City in 1967. Quail hunters had discovered a shallow grave in a rural area. It had been opened by animal scavengers, and bones and teeth had been scattered over a considerable area. A hasty and careless recovery effort conducted by police investigators working through the night in bad light and rainy weather resulted in the loss of, and damage to, the bones and associated evidence. The grave itself had been reduced to a mud-hole, destroying any stratigraphic evidence it might have offered. This loss was disturbing, and I wondered if a more rational approach might have yielded valuable evidence that might have pointed to the perpetrator.[1] Although I had chosen to specialise in physical anthropology for my doctoral degree, my undergraduate and graduate work at the University of Arizona (Tucson) included a few lecture courses in archaeology, and I had learned to appreciate the meticulous and painstaking care that professional archaeologists use in unearthing the remains of our prehistoric ancestors. Thus, I began to realise that a similar approach would be useful in recovering the bones of more recent murder victims.

The Raspberry Ranch case – 1970

The chance to put this idea to work came in the summer of 1970 when an agent of the Oklahoma State Bureau of Investigation (OSBI) informed me that he had found a place where he suspected that two murder victims might be located. It was on the Raspberry Ranch, a large cattle ranch about 35 miles (around 56.5 km) north of Tulsa, Oklahoma. When questioned, the ranch owner told the agent that one night in 1967, a long-vacant bunkhouse on the ranch had mysteriously burned to the ground. On a visit to the site, investigators found a rusty fuel can; analysis at the OSBI laboratory showed that it contained residue of an accelerant.

The law enforcement officers had been led to the site by a man convicted of a drug offence, who offered to

† *POSTSCRIPT FROM THE EDITORS.* During the preparation phase of this volume, the editors learnt that Dr Clyde Snow, aged 86 years, had sadly passed away on 16 May 2014. Although we did not have the privilege to meet him face to face, we were honoured that he had kindly agreed to write this preface, especially as we fully recognise the impact of his ideas and pioneering actions have had on the development of forensic archaeology worldwide. We are saddened that the world has lost one of the world's foremost forensic anthropologist and wish his relatives all the strength they need to go through this hard time.

[1] I published a paper on this case which appeared in the *Journal of Forensic Sciences* in early 1970 (Snow and Luke 1970). Although a few anthropologists in the United States and abroad had served as consultants to coroners to help in skeletal identification for many decades, this title marked the first time that the term 'Forensic Anthropology' appeared in the scientific literature.

give information on the victims in return for a lighter sentence. He identified them as Tulsa residents Mr Kenneth Ray Painter and Miss Betty Joan Smith, who were both in their mid-20s. They had not been seen alive since 1967 – some 3 years prior to the discovery of the bone fragments at Raspberry Ranch. At the time of their disappearance, they had been scheduled to testify as witnesses for the prosecution in a case against a drug dealer in Tulsa, Oklahoma, and were murdered to keep them from testifying. The informant said that three other men had been hired to kill them and dispose of their bodies. He said that the victims were first shot with a pistol, placed in the trunk of a car and driven to the isolated house on the ranch. Upon arrival, the car trunk was opened, and it was found that they were still alive, so both were finished off with close-range shotgun blasts to the head. Their bodies were then carried into the house and placed in the front room of the house with their heads close to the wall dividing it from the kitchen. They were then doused with several gallons of accelerant and set afire.

The OSBI agent asked me to come to the site and help him inspect it. I did so and found that all that was left were the stone foundation walls, part of an old chimney and a few fragments of burned timber. Surface vegetation from the surrounding grassland had grown over the area (Figure 1). Walking into the old living area, I found few fragments of burned bone that I suspected were human.

It was immediately apparent that, if any useful evidence was to be recovered, the site would have to be excavated with great care. I asked that it be secured until it could be excavated by archaeologists. At the University of Oklahoma (OU), I recruited three archaeology graduate students, Mr Towana Spivey, Miss Judy McNatt and Mr Mike Richards, to conduct the project over a long weekend in early October. Graduate students worked cheap in those days – it was agreed that each be paid 15 dollars a day, provided with food and drink (they requested bread, bologna sausage, eggs and bacon, doughnuts, coffee, some soft drinks and a case of beer) and that they bring their own camping equipment and tools to conduct the excavation. Meeting them at the site, I asked them to inspect it and develop their own plan of excavation. They went to work, first removing the surface vegetation, and then laid out a grid (Figure 2). I told them to inform me when they had completed their work and returned to my laboratory in Oklahoma City.

After 3 days, they called to let me know that they had finished the dig, and I returned to inspect their work. As diagrammed in Figure 3, it was very shallow: beneath the surface vegetation, there were a few centimetres of ash and charred debris under which was a thin, fire-hardened clay representing the original ground surface. Removing the layer of ashy debris, they had screened the contents of each grid and placed the recovered items in paper bags labelled with the

Figure 1 Raspberry Ranch site.

Figure 2 Raspberry Ranch grid layout.

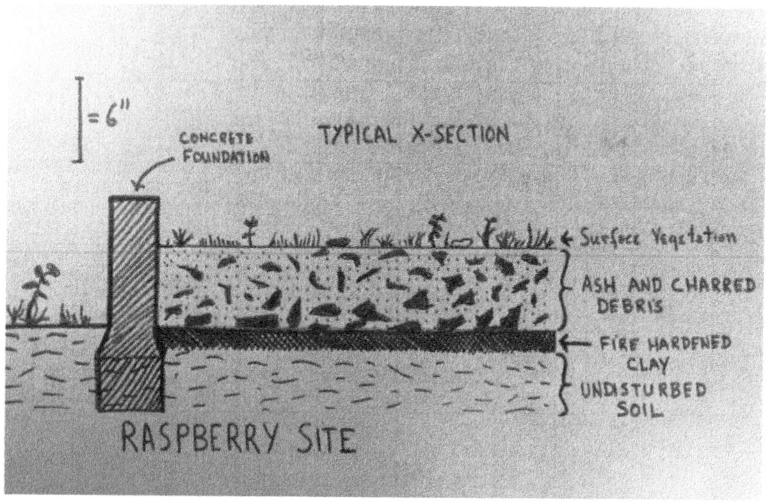

Figure 3 Raspberry Ranch stratigraphy.

grid coordinates. In all, they had collected several hundred small fragments of burned bone. Some metal artefacts including a cartridge case from a .38 calibre handgun, blue jean buttons, a woman's hair clip, a brassiere clasp and a small gold wedding ring had also been recovered.

When brought to my laboratory, the contents of the bags were found to contain 846 bones or bone fragments. Based on morphological details, many could be definitely classified as *human* or *non-human*. The latter group included a few beef bones that had been butchered for culinary purposes, but the majority were from rodents and other small mammals such as skunks and opossums which, over many years, had lived and died beneath the house. Already completely skeletonised, their surfaces were charred and darkly discoloured by direct exposure to fire. By contrast, the human fragments were calcined and nearly white, indicating that they had been exposed to much higher temperatures – probably due to direct exposure to an accelerant. These colour differences proved helpful in sorting many fragments that could not be definitely diagnosed based on anatomical detail. In all, we classified 508 items as human.

With the non-human fragments eliminated, we could then determine the number of human fragments found within each grid square. It was found that the heaviest concentrations were in a couple of squares located in the front room immediately adjacent to the wall that had separated it from the kitchen. Among the human materials, 73 fragments were from the skull, and these were also more frequent in the squares adjacent to the wall. Post-cranial fragments from vertebrae and limb bones tended to be more frequent in grid squares closer to the centre of the room.

Further study of the human fragments showed that they represented two individuals of markedly different body size lying side by side, with the smaller individual on the left. From the few fragments that displayed age indicators, I concluded that both were young adults in their late 20s or early 30s. The blue jean buttons and a man's belt buckle were found in the area where the bone fragments of the larger individual were concentrated. The woman's hair clip, brassiere attachment and wedding ring were closely associated with the smaller individual who was, therefore, probably female.

From the distribution of the fragments and artefacts, we were able to roughly diagram the original positions of the bodies (Figure 4). They lay side by side in the front room of the house with their heads close to the wall separating it from the kitchen, with the male on the right and the female on his left.

Most damning of all was some evidence that both victims had died violently. This was in the form of a number of cranial fragments that displayed lead pellets embedded in their inner (endocranial) surfaces, indicating that they had sustained close-range shotgun wounds to the head (Figure 5).

The victims were not married; but when questioned by police, Miss Betty Smith's relatives identified the wedding ring as one bought in Mexico where she and Mr Painter posed as husband and wife while buying drugs to smuggle into the United States.

Insofar as I have been able to determine, the Raspberry Ranch site was the first in which archaeologists were used in a forensic case. The case also illustrates two very important aspects of forensic archaeology. First, the

Figure 5 Cranial fragments with embedded shotgun pellets.

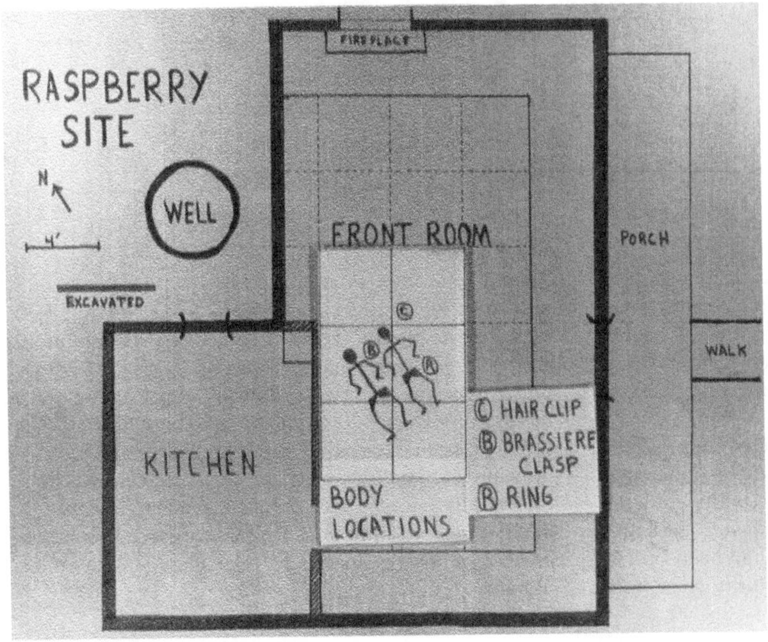

Figure 4 Raspberry victims locations inferred from the distribution of bone fragments.

scientific evidence independently corroborated the informant's story, which otherwise might have been regarded as a self-serving fabrication in an attempt to gain a lighter sentence in his own case. Second, the forensic evidence – small and very fragile fragments of burned bone – simply could not have been recovered without the painstaking and meticulous methodology employed by professional archaeologists. In the following years, whenever possible, I recruited their services to help me in the recovery of skeletal remains from clandestine graves in Oklahoma and other states.

Forensic archaeology and human rights – Argentina 1984

In 1984, I was asked to go to Argentina to help in the recovery of the thousands of men, women and children who had been 'disappeared' during the brutal military dictatorship that ruled the country between 1976 and 1983. Most of these *desaparecidos* had been buried in unmarked graves as *ningún nombre* (NN) in municipal cemeteries throughout the country.[2] By the time I arrived, several hundred skeletons had already been unearthed by using gravediggers and even bulldozers to open the graves in large areas of the cemeteries where not only the *desaparecidos* but also ordinary unidentified bodies were buried in unmarked graves. The results were a forensic disaster. Upon inspection, the skeletons recovered in these hasty exhumations, I found that not only many bones, teeth and artefacts had been lost but also that the skeletons of the *desaparecidos* had been hopelessly commingled with those of the ordinary unidentified dead.

We were able to prevail upon President Raúl Alfonsín of the new democratic government to call a halt to such hasty exhumations until a properly trained team of forensic anthropologists and archaeologists was available to conduct them. Fortunately, I was able to recruit a small group of anthropology and medical students who were willing to dedicate themselves to this project. This group, the *Equipo Argentino de Antropología Forense* (EAAF), founded in 1984, was the pioneer in the scientific investigation of human rights violations. We began by excavating the graves of the *desaparecidos* using the same time-honoured methods used by generations of professional archaeologists to exhume our prehistoric ancestors, ensuring that all of the bones, teeth and associated artefacts were recovered (Figure 6).

We also found that statistics could be a valuable tool in tracking down the disappeared (Snow and Bihurriet 1992). Before they left power, the bureaucrats within the military and police death squads had destroyed the

Figure 6 EAAF archaeologist excavating a *desaparecido* grave in 1984.

[2]This practice of arranging that the victims of the military and police 'death squads' be buried as *ningún nombre* (NNs) in municipal cemeteries was a convenient way of getting rid of the bodies since, in Argentina, a small annual 'grave tax' is imposed on the next-of-kin to pay for the maintenance of the grave. If the tax is not paid for several years, the grave is opened and the bones transferred to an *ossario* (bone yard), containing the bones of hundreds of other dispossessed dead whose families were too poor to pay the tax or had simply died out. Although the identities of the *desaparecidos* was known to the perpetrators, by having them buried as NNs, they could be certain that after 5 or 10 years, their bones, thrown into an *ossario*, would be inextricably commingled with hundreds of other skeletons. In effect, the murderers were saved the labour of digging clandestine graves for their victims.

records of their murderous activities, making it extremely difficult to trace the ultimate fate and burial places of the *desaparecidos*. However, they overlooked the fact that cemetery administrators were also bureaucrats and had kept excellent records, including the sex, approximate age, cause of death and grave location of all NNs buried in their graveyards. Analysis of these records enabled us to find which cemeteries showed a statistically significant rise in NN burials between 1976 and 1983 – the seven years when the *Junta* was in power. Once such a cemetery was identified, further analysis helped us distinguish which NN graves were more likely to be those of the *desaparecidos*. This was because there were strong differences in age, sex and causes of death between the disappeared and ordinary NNs. Within the latter group, over 96% were elderly males listed as having died of natural causes. By contrast, the average age of the disappeared was 25.9 years, and only 4.4% were aged over 50 years, 30% were females and the great majority had died of gunshot wounds to the head (Snow 1984). Thus, for example, when selecting NN graves for exhumation, we could be virtually certain that it was truly a disappeared person if the cemetery records showed it to be a young female with a gunshot wound to the head. More recently, we have used a similar statistical approach to determine the burial location of disappeared persons in Guatemala (Snow et al. 2008).

After recovery, they were removed to a morgue where they could be cleaned and examined in more detail to determine the cause of death (a gunshot wound to the back of the head in close to 90% of the cases) and, when possible, establish positive identification through dental records, ante-mortem X-rays or, in later years, by DNA. Finally, we prepared reports documenting our findings for submission to the investigating judges. One major project was the exhumation of a large mass-grave located in a remote corner (*Sector 134*) of the municipal cemetery of Avellaneda, a suburb of Buenos Aires; by 1990, the skeletons of nearly 400 *desaparecidos* were recovered from that site (Figure 7) (Doretti and Snow 2003).

In 1985, the Argentine Supreme Court recognised the significance of the work conducted by the EAAF by asking it to provide expert witness testimony for the prosecution in the trial of the generals and admirals who ruled the country during the dark years (1976–1983) of the *Junta* and which resulted in the conviction of several for terms of eight years to life imprisonment. Thus these young students, who themselves could easily have been targeted for disappearance a few years before (many of the *desaparecidos* were university students), were instrumental in bringing their country's oppressors to justice.

Beginning in 1988, the EAAF began to be called to other countries to help in the investigation of human rights violations. In several cases, they were instrumental in recruiting and training local anthropology and archaeology students in the formation of teams to continue such work in their own countries. The 'spin-off' groups included the *Equipo Peruano de Antropología Forense* (EPAF) and the *Fundación de Antropología Forense de Guatemala* (FAFG).[3] The FAFG is now the largest forensic

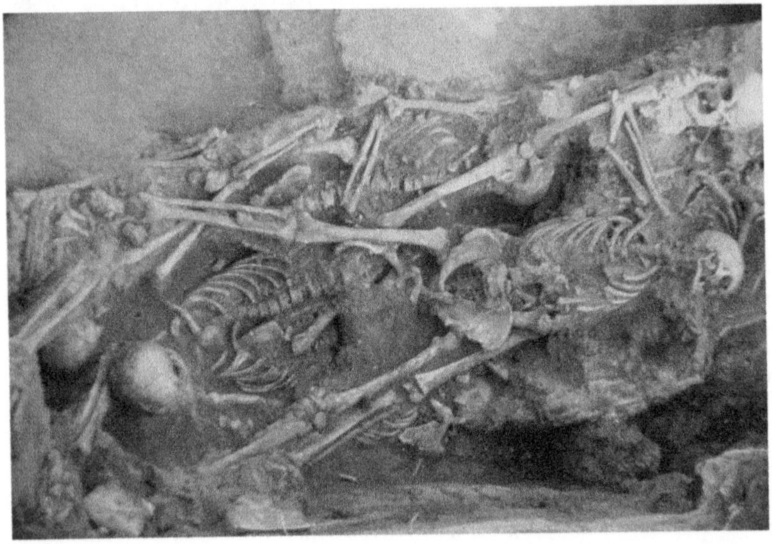

Figure 7 A *desaparecidos* mass grave.

[3] An outstanding alumnus of the Guatemalan group is one of its founders, Mr Stefan Schmitt, who is now Director of the International Forensic Program of Physicians for Human Rights (PHR).

anthropology operation in the world with a staff of over 100 archaeologists, physical anthropologists, DNA experts and other forensic specialists (Snow et al. 2008).

From these beginnings, the EAAF has continued its work not only in Argentina but has led or participated in investigations in close to 40 countries throughout the world (Doretti and Snow 2003).

Conclusion

This volume, *Forensic Archaeology: A Global Perspective*, brings together scholars from throughout the world to remind us that the ultimate goal of crime scene investigation is to reconstruct an event in time and that, above all, a clandestine grave is a crime scene. Forensic archaeologists bring unique and vital skills to such investigations. First, almost magically, they are able to transform evidence distributed in the three spatial dimensions into a fourth – *time*. In other words, they transform the evidence into a coherent story that tells us how the crime was committed. Second, only their painstaking and meticulous methodology ensures that *all* of the pertinent evidence is collected and preserved. Even the finest forensic anthropologists, pathologists, DNA experts and other medico-legal specialists working in the best-equipped morgues and laboratories are helpless to resolve the case without the evidence the forensic archaeologist brings to them.

References

Doretti, M. and Snow, C.C. 2003. Forensic anthropology and human rights: the Argentine experience. In D.W. Steadman (ed.), *Hard Evidence: Case Studies in Forensic Anthropology*, 290–310. Upper Saddle River, Prentice Hall.

Snow, C.C. 1984. Sex, age and other statistical characteristics of the desaparecidos. In E. Sabato (ed.), *NUNCA MÁS: Informe de la Comisión Nacional sobre la Desaparicion de Personas*, 293–299. Buenos Aires, Editorial Universitaria de Buenos Aires.

Snow, C.C. and Bihurriet, M.J. 1992. An epidemiology of homicide: ningun nombre burials in the province of Buenos Aires from 1970 to 1984. In T.B. Jabine and R.P. Claude (eds.), *Human Rights and Statistics: Getting the Record Straight*, 328–363. Philadelphia, University of Pennsylvania Press.

Snow, C.C. and Luke, J.L. 1970. The Oklahoma City child disappearances of 1967: forensic anthropology in the identification of skeletal remains. *Journal of Forensic Sciences* 15, 125–153.

Snow, C.C., Peccerelli, F.A., Susanávar, J.S., Robinson, A.G. and Najera Ochoa, J.M. 2008. Hidden in plain sight: X. X. burials and the Desaparecidos in the Department of Guatemala, 1997–1986. In J. Asher, D. Banks and F. J. Scheuren (eds.), *Statistical Methods for Human Rights*, 89–116, New York, Springer.

Foreword by Jeremy Sarkin

Department of Public, Constitutional and International Law, University of South Africa, Pretoria, South Africa
Former Chair-Rapporteur, United Nations Working Group on Enforced or Involuntary Disappearances

Over the past 100 years, at least 200 million people have been killed as a result of international crimes, including genocide and crimes against humanity (Sarkin 2008a). During this period, millions of individuals have gone missing, and most remain unaccounted for, as a result of a variety of events such as wars, natural disasters, human trafficking and a range of other crimes including enforced disappearances (Sarkin in press-b). In the 20th century, mass atrocities occurred in places such as Armenia, Bosnia and Herzegovina, Burundi, Cambodia, China, the Democratic Republic of Congo, Ethiopia, Guatemala, India, Indonesia, Iraq, Libya, Nigeria, Pakistan, Rwanda, the Soviet Union, Sri Lanka, Syria, Turkey and Uganda (Sarkin 2010). At the same time, almost every country suffers the consequences of catastrophic events, including disasters, as a result of which many people cannot be found or identified. As a result, every year, hundreds of thousands of people are killed or go missing from a variety of causes, in all regions of the world. Finding people affected by these happenings, and finding out what happened to them, is critically important not only for their families but also to hold those responsible accountable for their actions, where crimes have occurred.[1] Finding out what happens to such people should have a deterrent effect, as those who wish to carry out such deeds may come to realise that the bodies they want to hide are more likely to be detected in the future, and what happened to victims and who perpetrated the deeds could be determined by the use of a variety of scientific techniques leading to the discovery of the perpetrator.

The use of forensic science, DNA technology in particular, in human rights work has developed rapidly over the past 15 or so years (HRC 2009). Over this period, the procedures and processes used have advanced quickly. As a result, the science has become a vital aid in processes of ensuring justice. One of the areas of major growth has been the application of forensic anthropology and forensic archaeology to human rights. This has occurred not only for reasons of simply determining the truth about what occurred, but there has also been a vital need to provide evidence in international or hybrid courts where prosecutions have occurred that deal with such matters. Over the past 20 years, the international community has developed a large number of institutions and processes to bring perpetrators of mass crimes to book (Sarkin 2012).

For successful prosecutions to occur, evidence is needed that can be used in a courtroom, to prove that wrongdoing transpired. Forensic evidence can often prove the factual aspect of the crime, but also the *mensrea*, or criminal intent, needed to convict someone. Criminal intent must be proved by way of evidence showing that a perpetrator intended to commit the crime. Proving both deed and intent of a perpetrator is thus critical to a successful prosecution. Without proving criminal intent, a conviction will not result. Forensics, in its widest sense, has played, and will play, a more critical role in proving both the factual and intent aspects of crimes.

The use of forensic evidence has grown exponentially. Today, it is often the only available evidence proving the commission of a crime, especially in the area of enforced disappearances but in other crimes as well. Today, it is more likely, because of forensic evidence, that families will be able to get closure, at least to some degree, as the science of discovering and identifying mortal remains has become easier and cheaper. There will be a much greater degree of certainty as to what happened, and if the remains found belong to a specific person. This I have seen for myself in a range of places where I have worked, including Morocco, Timor-Leste and Bosnia and Herzegovina, which will be discussed in the following. These missions took place in the context of my being a member of the United Nations Working Group on Enforced or Involuntary Disappearances from 2008 to 2014, and Chair-Rapporteur of the Group from 2009 to 2012. I have worked, however, in many other countries on these, and similar issues.

In Morocco, the investigation that I did in 2009, as part of the Working Group on Enforced or Involuntary Disappearances, found that the process of identifying

[1]Interview with UN Working Group on Enforced or Involuntary Disappearances Chair-Rapporteur Jeremy Sarkin on the Secret Detention Study, *Essex Human Rights Review*, 2011, 57–67.

victims found in graves identified by state officials was at times controversial. Some families refused to accept that the graves they were shown contained the remains of their loved ones (HRC 2010a). Some families asked how they could rely on the word of government officials in the identification process. The families demanded DNA testing to ascertain whether the remains in a specific grave were those of their loved ones. As a result of the families being uncertain about the identity of remains, we recommended that the bodies found in various burial sites should be formally identified, so that the identifications could be fully accepted by the victims' families. The Working Group recommended that when doubt existed, DNA testing should be conducted (HRC 2010a). The families want and need certainty. Forensic science can assist in this regard. These events also raise issues concerning the independence of the process and reliability of the results that are significant issues.

In the Timor-Leste report (Sarkin 2008b) that I wrote which served at the Human Rights Council in 2012 (HRC 2012) that investigated disappearances that occurred in that country, mainly during the time of the occupation of the country by Indonesia between 1975 and 1999, we noted that there has been some success in determining the location of some of the people who disappeared. Various grave sites have been exhumed. Because local capacity was not available, the November 12, Committee, an association of people in Timor-Leste who survived the Santa Cruz massacre that occurred in 1991, in cooperation with forensic experts from the Victorian Institute of Forensic Medicine (VIFM) and the Argentine Forensic Anthropology Team (EAAF), examined 16 bodies of Santa Cruz massacre victims. As a result, 11 victims were identified by way of DNA testing. In 2010, the government contracted an international forensic team and a further nine bodies were found. There has been less success dealing with possibly 4000 children who were taken from Timor-Leste to Indonesia. Our report noted that international assistance should be provided both materially and for the development of a forensic unit with the requisite expertise and capacity and that assistance with DNA capabilities was needed. It was further noted that there were no clear rules of procedure related to the process of managing human remains and that there were no rules of procedure for mortal remains after their exhumation, including the conditions for storage. The report called for an appropriate legislative framework to deal with forensic examinations and the necessary procedures. The report noted that managing a forensic process is an important aspect of ensuring justice. The report further noted that the assistance of outside forensic institutions, as had been occurring, should be further actively sought, and that processes to ensure that DNA testing occurs more often should be enhanced and promoted (HRC 2012, section 32). These lessons are ones that emerge from this book as well. *Forensic Archaeology: A Global Perspective* makes it clear that international assistance can be provided from a variety of sources, and there is a need for forensic techniques to be used as widely as possible.

In the former Yugoslavia in the early 1990s, between 100,000 and 150,000 people were killed. In Bosnia and Herzegovina alone, about 32,000 people disappeared in events some of which have been classified as genocide (Sarkin and Fowler 2010), out of a total of 40,000 who disappeared altogether in the Western Balkans. Even though perpetrators attempted to hide the bodies of their victims, and moved the remains under cover of darkness, once they determined that the whereabouts of the graves had been found, using large earth-moving equipment intermingling the human remains and making identification much more difficult, about 25,000 people's remains have been individually identified in Bosnia and Herzegovina. Despite the perpetrators hiding and then disturbing the graves, scientists, including forensic archaeologists, were able to determine when the graves were excavated, when some of them were exhumed, when some of the graves were refilled, what was used to dig the graves, when the bodies were placed in the graves, and who were in the graves. A variety of techniques were used to identify the remains. Various items found in the graves, including clothing, papers and other objects, were used to assist the process of human identification, and the process to determine when the atrocities had occurred, how, by whom and a variety of other questions.

In my report to the Human Rights Council on the mission by the Working Group to Bosnia and Herzegovina that served before the Human Rights Council in 2011 (HRC 2011), the issue of the forensic work being done in that country was examined. It was determined that a massive number of exhumations and identifications have been done, despite limited resources and equipment. It was noted that the conditions under which those who perform the exhumations work are often very inadequate, and more resources ought to be assigned to this work.

Forensic science, including forensic archaeology, has played a key role in determining what happened to the 8000 men and boys who disappeared and were killed in Srebrenica, in Bosnia and Herzegovina.[2] Without the integrated multidisciplinary forensic processes, involving a range of professionals including forensic archaeologists, forensic anthropologists, pathologists,

[2]For more information, see the report to which contributed that is forthcoming: *Bosnia and Herzegovina: Accounting for Missing Persons from the Conflict: A Stocktaking*, International Commission on Missing Persons (ICMP).

DNA experts and information technologists, the denials of perpetrators, especially in various criminal trials, would have been difficult to overcome. This is critical as determining the truth about what occurred is an issue of vital significance in Bosnia and Herzegovina. As the United Nations Development Program (UNDP) noted in 2009 'there are different interpretations of truth in Bosnia and Herzegovina; the number of victims remains the subject of political manipulation, since there are no formal activities aimed at establishing circumstances and facts regarding the crimes committed; about 13,000 persons are still registered as missing; there is no comprehensive programme of reparation; the public remains unsatisfied with the reform of institutions, and many other issues' (UNDP 2009). As a result of the forensic work, there is now absolute certainty, in most quarters, about who the victims were, and when, where and by whom these victims were killed. The daughters, mothers, grandmothers, sisters and other family members now know what happened, and know that their loved ones are no longer alive. The certainty about what occurred is a result of the use of forensic science. Not only have the human remains been identified, but the science has been used in court cases in a variety of settings including at the International Criminal Tribunal for the former Yugoslavia (ICTY). Prosecutions have occurred as a result of these processes and even civil cases (Sarkin 2006), such as that against the Dutch government whose peacekeepers were alleged to have not stopped the atrocities while in a position to do so, have been brought. Forensic archaeology has played a critical role in the search, recovery and identification of these and other human remains, as well as other evidence that supports the detection of victim identity, the cause of death and other ancillary issues. The role of forensics has also played a role, to a lesser or greater extent in a range of conflict ridden or post-conflict societies. Processes of forensic examination can also have an effect on processes of reconciliation (Daly and Sarkin 2007; Sarkin and Daly 2004). It can also assist wider transitional justice processes at work in a country (Sarkin 2011; 2011–2012).

In this context, dealing with forensic issues, particularly in the field of disappeared or missing people, has become a burgeoning and critically important field of late, especially in the human rights arena. The forensics associated with the search, recovery and identification of human remains has progressed rapidly in the very recent past. Forensic archaeology that is applied to both human remains, as well as other evidence that is discovered, has grown in leaps and bounds and has become a critical part of the forensic science applied today, especially in the context of mass graves.

Forensic science can play a critical part in ensuring that various rights of people affected by these issues are supported. Some of the rights that affect those who have disappeared or gone missing, as well as other victims that can be assisted by forensic sciences, include the right to life, the right not to be tortured, the right to liberty, the right to dignity, the right to a fair trial, the right to an identity, the right of access to justice and the right to the truth. A variety of sources confirm the existence of the right to the truth including Article 32 of Additional Protocol I to the Geneva Conventions, of 12 August 1949. This recognises the right of families to know the fate of their relatives. Article 24(2) of the International Convention for the Protection of All Persons from Enforced Disappearance, adopted in 2006 by the United Nations, sets out the rights of victims to know the truth about the circumstances of the enforced disappearance. The Convention also provides that victims are entitled to know the progress and results of any investigation and the fate of disappeared persons.[3] The Convention also sets out State Party obligations to take appropriate measures. The right to the truth is both a collective and an individual right. Individual victims have the right to know the truth about violations that affected him or her. However, the truth also has to be told at the level of society for a variety of reasons including as a means to ensure that those responsible for such acts are held accountable and as a means to deter perpetrators from recommitting such offences in the future (Sarkin in press-a).

A variety of institutions have played a role in finding the truth. These include courts, tribunals and a range of other bodies, including Truth and Reconciliation Commissions (TRCs). The role that TRCs have played, as far as forensic investigations are concerned, has been dependent on the mandates given to such institutions, the length of time that they have had to undertake their work and the resources at their disposal. In South Africa, the TRC recognised different types of truth, including narrative, historical, forensic and social varieties.

The relevance and importance of forensics in truth discovery cannot be underestimated. It is through forensics that the right to the truth has become important and much more meaningful. Through forensics, the right to the truth has become much more of a reality for the families of those who have disappeared or people killed as a result of a variety of events. Resolution 61/155 of the General Assembly on disappeared persons, for this reason, emphasises the importance of forensics in the process of identifying disappeared persons. In its resolution on Forensic Genetics and Human Rights,[4] the Human Rights

[3]Keep on Investigating until there is Clarification: Interview with UN Chair-Rapporteur Jeremy Sarkin on Disappearances in Nepal, *Informal Journal Nepal*, 2011.

[4]Resolution 10/26 Forensic Genetics and Human Rights: A/HRC/RES/10/26.

Council noted that: 'forensic genetics, when applied in an independent manner and subject to international standards, may effectively contribute to the identification of the remains of victims, to the restitution of identity to those persons illegally taken away and to address the issue of impunity'.

In its General Comment on the Right to the Truth in Relation to Enforced Disappearances the Working Group on Enforced or Involuntary Disappearances found that:

> The right to know the truth about the fate and the whereabouts includes, when the disappeared person is found to be dead, the right of the family to have the remains of their loved one returned to them, and to dispose of those remains according to their own tradition, religion or culture. The remains of the person should be clearly and indisputably identified, including through DNA analysis. The State, or any other authority, should not undertake the process of identification of the remains, and should not dispose of those remains, without the full participation of the family and without fully informing the general public of such measures. States ought to take the necessary steps to use forensic expertise and scientific methods of identification to the maximum of its available resources, including through international assistance and cooperation. (HRC 2010b, section 6)

Thus, much can and should be done, particularly by states, to give meaning to the right to the truth. Bolstering the availability and skill associated with forensic sciences should be enhanced and made more widely available. As was urged in the resolution adopted by the Human Rights Council on Forensic Genetics and Human Rights, states ought to consider using forensic genetics in compliance with international standards that are accepted by the scientific community in relation to quality assurance and control, and to safeguard, where appropriate, due respect for the principles of protection and confidentiality of information and restricted access to such information.[5]

More resources ought to be devoted to its provision, and more dedicated personnel ought to be given to the agencies carrying out this essential service. The legislative framework also ought to be created, which clearly states that these techniques ought to be made available when needed.

While a number of publications have emerged recently dealing with forensic archaeology, none of these are as comprehensive, wide-ranging or relevant as *Forensic Archaeology: A Global Perspective*. This is a work of major significance. It pulls together most of the most highly regarded experts working in different countries to deal with the science as it is being applied in their countries. As a result, it is possible to observe the trends and processes that are being applied in a large number of settings. Gathering all the experiences that are occurring across the globe is of utmost significance, as while the field of forensic archaeology is well developed and well known in certain parts of the world, it is less developed in other parts. This publication, which gathers best practices, and a variety of techniques that are being used for various purposes, will not only be useful to forensic archaeologists but to a range of others interested in the field. The work of forensic archaeologists and the techniques they use is now an issue of cross-disciplinary importance. The work of detecting graves, exhuming them and determining whose remains are contained therein, is the work of many different experts working together. Thus, the book should appeal to humanitarian and human rights organisations, an array of academics and experts in fields such as law, odontology, forensic pathology, geophysics, forensic genetics, ballistics, radiology and computer science, among others. It will have definite appeal to law enforcement officers, archaeologists, anthropologists, criminologists and a range of other social scientists, to name but a few. The book should play a valuable role in training a new generation of scientists in the field, as well as state agencies and others to become more adept at providing this important service. The publication should also spur new research into the country settings discussed in the book, but also advance the research techniques used in the field. It should also be a catalyst in providing new and available techniques to places where the science is vitally needed. At the present time, there are many places that are dependent on a few skilled institutions to do this type of work. Hopefully, this work can become an integral part of the service that all law enforcement agencies provide. This service should be a routine part of all investigation agencies in all countries, and not only those where there have been mass atrocities or major disasters. All countries likely at some point have to deal with mass tragedy, never mind ordinary crime where these techniques will be of fundamental importance. The book will certainly be most useful to raise awareness in a variety of quarters about what is possible. Hopefully, states take due notice of the processes that can occur and give meaning to the human rights of victims and their families that can be assisted by using forensic science in identifying and returning the remains of those killed. The identity of victims and their cause of death should be established with certainty and due diligence (ICRC 2009). In this way, the right to dignity and a variety of other human rights that exist can be supported and give real meaning to victims and their families.

[5] Human Rights Council Resolution 10/26 Forensic Genetics and Human Rights: A/HRC/RES/10/26.

References

Daly, E. and Sarkin, J. 2007. *Reconciliation in Transitional Societies: Finding Common Ground*, Philadelphia, University of Pennsylvania Press.

HRC (Human Rights Council) 2009. *Forensic Genetics and Human Rights* A/HRC/RES/10/26.

HRC (Human Rights Council) 2010a. A/HRC/13/31/Add.1, § 106.

HRC (Human Rights Council) 2010b. A/HRC/16/48.

HRC (Human Rights Council) 2011. A/HRC/16/48/Add.1.

HRC (Human Rights Council) 2012. A/HRC/19/58/Add.1.

ICRC (International Committee of the Red Cross) 2009. *Guiding Principles/Model Law on the Missing*, Geneva, ICRC.

Sarkin, J. 2006. Reparation for gross human rights as an outcome of criminal versus civil court proceedings. In M. Bossuyt, K. De Feyter, P. Lemmens, S. Parmentier and F. Reyntjens (eds.), *Reparation for Victims of Gross and Systematic Human Rights Violations*, 151–188, Antwerp, Intersentia.

Sarkin, J. 2008a. Review: atrocity, punishment and international law. *Human Rights Quarterly* 30, 1028–1042.

Sarkin, J. 2008b. Achieving reconciliation in divided societies: comparing the approaches in Timor-Leste, South Africa and Rwanda. *Yale Journal of International Affairs* 3, 11–28.

Sarkin, J. 2010. Why the responsibility to protect (R2P) as a doctrine or (emerging) norm to prevent genocide and other massive human rights violations is on the decline: the role of principles, pragmatism and the shifting patterns of international relations. *Politorbis: The Swiss FDFA Journal* 47, 51–64.

Sarkin, J. 2011. The role of the International Criminal Court in reducing massive human rights violations such as enforced disappearances in Africa: towards developing transitional justice strategies. *Studies in Ethnicity and Nationalism* 11, 130–142.

Sarkin, J. 2011–2012. Enhancing the legitimacy, status and role of the International Criminal Court by using transitional justice or restorative justice strategies. *Interdisciplinary Journal of Human Rights Law* 6, 83–102.

Sarkin, J. 2012. Why the prohibition of enforced disappearance has attained jus cogens status in international law. *Nordic Journal of International Law* 81, 537–583.

Sarkin J. (in press-a) Putting in place processes and mechanisms to prevent and eradicate enforced disappearances around the world. *South African Yearbook of International Law.*

Sarkin J. (in press-b) Enforced disappearance as continuing crimes and continuing human rights violations. In B.M. Leyh, Y. Haeck, C. Burbano-Herrera, D. Contreras-Garduno (eds.), *The Realization of Human Rights: When Theory Meets Practice*. 389–414. Antwerp, Intersentia.

Sarkin, J. and Daly, E. 2004. Too many questions, too few answers: reconciliation in transitional societies. *Columbia Human Rights Law Review* 25, 101–168.

Sarkin, J. and Fowler, C. 2010. The responsibility to protect and the duty to prevent genocide: lessons to be learnt from the role of the international community and the media during the Rwandan genocide and the conflict in the former Yugoslavia. *Suffolk University Transnational Law Review* 33, 35–87.

UNDP (United Nations Development Programme) 2009. *Transitional Justices Guidebook for Bosnia and Herzegovina: Executive Summary*, 17–14.

Foreword by Colin Hope

National Search Adviser, National Crime Agency, UK

A number of years ago, I recall being quietly but very deliberately taken to one side by a gentleman I'd only recently met. During a brief and very private conversation, he actually said very little, but what he said has stayed with me to this day.

> Thank you, your explanations and the kind words helped. We appreciate what has been done.

To provide a little context, I was a relatively inexperienced Police Search Adviser at that time. The Police Search Adviser is a specialist officer trained to plan and manage complex search operations initiated by the Police Service in the United Kingdom. These search operations include those that relate to the search for evidence, for the victims of crime, or to the search for missing persons. In this case, I had been managing a search for an elderly man who had been missing from his family for several weeks, and our Police Search Team had just recovered his remains. I was speaking to the elderly man's son.

The search had been a challenging one, in difficult weather conditions. In truth, the search had not gone particularly well; our activities had been the subject of interest from the media and local community members, and a number of us struggled under a degree of pressure. The end result was expected but very sad. My brief conversation with his son helped refocus my perspectives. Regardless of the difficulties that my organisation and I had encountered, the work was important. It was of enormous significance to the family to know what had happened. In concluding the searches with the 'find' (of his remains), we were able to help with closure for the family and to provide some answers about what happened.

People become 'lost' in many ways, for example as a result of criminal activity, accident or other form of misadventure. It seems obvious, but the need to know what happened is the most basic requirement for the family and friends left behind when a loved one is 'lost'. Search helps to provide information and contributes answers relevant to this 'need to know'. Moving forward to today, as National Search Adviser with the National Crime Agency in the United Kingdom, I am reminded of the raw emotions involved in these cases on an all-too-regular basis.

It is commented in this book that in many ways the search for what is left behind (our defined 'locatable' items, in this case human remains) is in part a search for truth. In my view, this is absolutely the case within the context of law enforcement, where a search will routinely form part of an investigation.

Such investigations must be conducted in a professional, effective, often innovative and always transparent manner. The investigation will be open to scrutiny at every level and is routinely carried out in circumstances best described as adversarial. The investigation will be conducted within a framework defined by legislation, policy and experience of what is 'best practice'. Professional and motivated personnel are required, together with a clear understanding and awareness of applicable evidential and procedural requirements. Subject matter experts will be engaged by investigators to provide guidance and support not available within the police service. In all regards, the pressure on those leading the investigation can be immense.

In the United Kingdom, the Police Service is recognised as having a mature, developed and experienced approach to search. The methodologies, strategies and tactics employed are based on a foundation of excellent training, delivered by the Police National Search Centre and the College of Policing. Selected police officers are trained in the techniques of 'how' to search, how to plan and manage a search and how to engage with the most appropriate specialist support.

The service has developed a considerable range of specialist assets including search dogs and technical equipment. Especially, trained officers, for example those trained in the search of hazardous environments, are available. The use of 'external' search assets, for example Mountain and Lowland Rescue Teams and Search and Rescue Dogs, is a regular feature of search operations.

Systematic search procedures are employed and are supported with expertise and guidance available from agencies including Crime Operational Support at the National Crime Agency. Technical expertise and equipment is provided by the Centre for Applied Science and Technology at the Home Office. All of these assets are deployed when appropriate as part of what is described as a 'blended' approach to search and the operation is managed by the Police Search Adviser, described earlier.

Additional support is often required from experts in the academic and scientific communities. Forensic geologists, biologists and, of course, archaeologists are frequently engaged to provide their expertise, advice and support in all phases of a search operation. On a personal level, I have worked closely with Nicholas Márquez-Grant and Robert C. Janaway and have been grateful for the considerable benefits resulting from their involvement. I am also very aware of the consistent support that Mike Groen provides to colleagues within the 'Nationale Politie' (National Police) in the Netherlands. Forensic archaeology is an essential component of a search operation that seeks to locate and recover human remains, and the expertise that exists within this discipline is relied on to be effective, informed and delivered with integrity and a passion for doing the right thing. That this expertise is offered so readily is very welcome.

Despite the mature and developed approach that we have to search in the United Kingdom, nothing can or should stand still. Innovation and development needs to continue if we, as the search community, are to provide the best available service to families of 'lost' loved ones. Innovation and the need for expert support, advice and guidance are the primary reasons for my acknowledgement of the importance of this book.

In this volume, the experience and approach of forensic archaeologists from across the world are brought together. The challenges that each of the contributors have faced in their own unique search environment are identified and discussed. The solutions that they were able to implement and the effectiveness of new and in many cases innovative processes are explained. The detail included is impressive and gives us the opportunity to see what has worked in a range of varied and challenging search environments and conditions. Key practitioners are identified. In short, this work provides us with an opportunity to share the best practice that is constantly evolving. It identifies who we should speak to. In doing so, it places the collective search community into a position where, on the basis of this shared expertise, we can continue to develop and deliver the best service possible.

I'm reminded again of a more recent comment made by a family member of a 'lost' loved one.

> We're grateful to you for the hard work you're putting in; you don't have to do it. We will be eternally grateful for what you've done.

My view is clear. As a Police Officer and a Police Search Adviser, I believe that we do have to carry out this type of work. It is the right thing to do and families need to know what happened to their 'lost' loved ones. We also need to conduct the work in the most efficient and effective manner possible. I firmly believe that this book will help us to achieve this.

Preface

What is forensic archaeology? The answer to this question seems to correlate with the geographical residency and the professional background of the person asked. If asked of a forensic anthropologist educated in North America, the answer will probably be that forensic archaeology, or the recovery of human remains in police work, is a sub-discipline of forensic anthropology. An archaeologist educated in Central or Eastern Europe will probably answer that it is the application of archaeology in researching extrajudicial executions performed during World War II and the following Communist era. Most of the forensic specialists working for non-governmental or intergovernmental organisations will probably state that it is the application of archaeological theories and methodology to the excavation of mass graves. Forensic archaeologists educated in Northwest Europe will mostly define it as an archaeological discipline that can be of use during Crime Scene Investigation (CSI) and that sometimes can also be studied at a (post) graduate level. If asked of the general public, the answer will most likely associate forensic archaeology with artefact looting, excavation of historical cemeteries or mass grave sites, CSI-related television series or the study of historical individuals such as Tutankhamun or Ötzi the Iceman.

Since the perception and practice of forensic archaeology is not uniform across the globe, the idea arose to publish a volume about forensic archaeology as a discipline in its own right. The idea behind the intended volume was to show how forensic archaeology is defined and practised in different countries. To show the full developmental potential of forensic archaeology and to raise its theoretical and methodological framework to what it should be: an academic discipline with theories and methodology specially developed to reconstruct and interpret human behaviour from the retrieved material finds and features at a crime scene or a place of incident within the context of law. This idea was developed further during the first European Meeting on Forensic Archaeology (EMFA) that took place at The Hague, the Netherlands, in August 2012. This meeting, which was held at the Netherlands Forensic Institute (NFI), was organised jointly by the Dutch NFI and the Forensic Archaeology Expert Panel of the British Institute for Archaeologists (IfA) chaired by Robert C. Janaway. During the meeting, presentations were given about the perception and practice of forensic archaeology in several European Countries and organisations. The presentation given by Nicholas Márquez-Grant covered those European countries that were not represented at the meeting. After a short but fruitful discussion with Nicholas, Rob and myself, it was decided to try to combine the EMFA papers into a volume on European forensic archaeology. This idea was subsequently discussed with Wiley-Blackwell Publishers. After additional dialogue, it was decided to extend the number of contributions in the planned volume by contacting potential authors in countries and organisations outside Europe. The overall goal of the volume shifted accordingly from a European perspective to a global one. After extensive research and the sourcing of contributions from across the globe, the final manuscript was completed one and a half years later and sent for publication.

Forensic archaeology (as is the case in all archaeology) is about team work and sharing ideas. Its theories and methodology have been developed over several decades of field work and scholarship, and collaborative working is at the heart of this important discipline. This volume therefore owes thanks to many people who – at times unknowingly – have helped to foster it. Without all of you, this volume would not have been possible.

W.J. Mike Groen
April 2014

Acknowledgments

We would like to express our sincere gratitude to all of our contributors. They have provided excellent and detailed research and analysis without which this volume would not have been possible. We also appreciate their patience during the progression of this volume. Special appreciation goes to Dr Clyde Snow, Professor Jeremy Sarkin and Mr Colin Hope who gave their time and expertise to write prologues to this volume. Their forewords convey valuable perspectives from the fields of forensic archaeology/anthropology, international law and the police service respectively. We were sad to learn that Dr Snow passed away during the preparation of this volume. The editors are also indebted to the team at Wiley-Blackwell, in particular Rachael Ballard, Laura Bell and Fiona Seymour for their support to see this project through. Likewise we would like to thank Denny Collie and Lucy Douglas (ELES Editing, UK) and Sandeep Kumar (SPi Global), for diligently and effectively proofreading the entire manuscript and preparing the print proofs, respectively.

We are much obliged to our friends and colleagues Dr Emma Brown and Roosje de Leeuwe for their helpful comments on several chapters in this volume. Grateful thanks also go to all our family members, plus many other friends and colleagues, who have patiently helped us to achieve this work and to make this volume come to light for the benefit of forensic archaeology and forensic science in general.

We are also very grateful to the Netherlands Forensic Institute (NFI) for supporting and helping to fund this project.

W.J. Mike Groen, Nicholas Márquez-Grant
and Robert C. Janaway
June 2014

Glossary of abbreviations

AAAS	American Association for the Advancement of Science
AAD	Archaeology and Anthropology Division (ICMP)
AAFS	American Academy of Forensic Sciences
AAHU	Australian Army History Unit
ACT	Australian Capital Territory
ADF	Australian Defence Force
AEAOF	*Asociación Española de Antropología y Odontología Forense* (Spanish Association of Forensic Anthropology and Odontology)
AFP	Australian Federal Police
AFSO	Afghanistan Forensic Science Organisation
AIA	*Asociación de Investigaciones Antropológicas* (Association for Anthropological Research, Argentina)
ALAF	*Asociación Latinoamericana de Antropología Forense* (Latin American Forensic Anthropology Association)
BDA	*Bundesdenkmalamt* (Austrian Federal Monuments Office)
BiH	*Bosna i Hercegovina* (Bosnia and Herzegovina)
BKA	*Bundeskriminalamt* (German Federal Criminal Police Office)
CCJ	Criminal Court Judge, Lebanon
CEMEL	*Centro de Medicina Legal* (Medical Medicine Centre, Brazil)
CHA	Cultural Haritage Act (*Zakon o kulturni dediščini*)
CICPC	*Cuerpo de Investigaciones Científicas, Penales y Criminalísticas* (Scientific, Penal and Criminal Investigation Corps, Venezuela)
CIfA	Chartered Institute for Archaeologists, UK
CIL	Central Identification Laboratory, US
CING	Cyprus Institute of Neurology and Genetics
CMP	Committee on Missing Persons, Cyprus
CNP	*Cuerpo Nacional de Policía* (National Police Corps of Spain)
COINCET	*Consejo Nacional de Investigaciones Científicas y Técnicas* (National Scientific and Technical Research Council, Argentina)
CPA	Criminal Procedure Act, Slovenia (*Zakon o kazenskem postopku*)
CRFP	Council for the Registration of Forensic Practitioners, UK
CSI	crime scene investigation
CSIs	Crime Scene Investigators
CWGC	Commonwealth War Graves Commission
Dept ATO	Department of Anthropology–Thanatology–Odontology of the Forensic Science Institute of the National Gendarmerie
DVI	disaster victim identification
EAAF	*Equipo Argentino de Antropología Forense* (Argentine Forensic Anthropology Team)
EAFG	*Equipo de Antropología Forense de Guatemala* (Guatemalan Forensic Anthropology Team)
EMFA	European Meeting on Forensic Archaeology
ENFSI	European Network of Forensic Science Institutions
EPAF	*Equipo Peruano de Antropología Forense* (Peruvian Forensic Anthropology Team)
EQUITAS	*Equipo Colombiano Interdisciplinario de Trabajo Forense y Asistencia Psicosocial* (Colombian Interdisciplinary Team on Forensic Work and Psychological Assistance)
ESR	Environmental Science & Research, New Zealand
EU	European Union
EWG	Expert Working Group, ENFSI
FAFG	*Fundación de Antropología Forense de Guatemala* (Guatemalan Forensic Anthropology Foundation)
FARC	Forensic Anthropology Research Centre, University of Pretoria, South Africa
FCO	Foreign and Commonwealth Office, UK
FSS	Forensic Science Service, UK
GAF	*Grupo Antropología Forense* (Forensic Anthropology Group, Chile)
GIAF	*Grupo de Investigación en Arqueología Forense* (Forensic Archaeology Investigation Team, Uruguay)
GIS	Geographic Information System
GPR	ground-penetrating radar
GPS	Global Positioning System
GTA	*Grupo de Trabalho Araguaia* (The Araguaía Working Group, Brazil)
HRW	Human Rights Watch
ICC	International Criminal Court
ICLVR	Independent Commission for the Location of Victims' Remains
ICMP	International Commission on Missing Persons
ICRC	International Committee of the Red Cross
ICTJ	International Centre for Transitional Justice

ICTR International Criminal Tribunal for Rwanda
ICTY International Criminal Tribunal for the former Yugoslavia
IEC International Electrotechnical Commission
IFM Institute of Forensic Medicine, Slovenia (*Inštitut za sodno medicino*)
IICCMER *Institutul de Investigare a Crimelor Comunismului şi Memoria Exilului Românesc* (Institute for the Investigation of Communist Crimes and the Memory of the Romanian Exile)
IICCR *Institutul de Investigare a Crimelor Comunismului în România* (Institute for the Investigation of Communist Crimes in Romania)
IML *Instituto Médico-Legal* (Medico-Legal Institute, Brazil)/*Instituto de Medicina Legal* (Institute of Legal Medicine)
IMLCF *Instituto de Medicina Legal y Ciencias Forenses* (Institute of Legal Medicine and Forensic Sciences, Panama)
INAH *Instituto Nacional de Antropología e Historia* (National Institute for Anthropology and History, Mexico)
INLA Irish National Liberation Army
INML *Institutul Naţional de Medicina Legala* (National Institute of Legal Medicine of Romania)
INMLCF, I.P. *Instituto Nacional de Medicina Legal e Ciências Forenses, I.P.* (National Institute of Legal Medicine and Forensic Sciences, Portugal)
IO Investigation Officer, India
IRA Irish Republican Army
IRCGN *Institut de Recherche Criminelle de la Gendarmerie Nationale* (Forensic Science Institute of the French National Gendarmerie)
ISF Internal Security Forces, Lebanon
ISO International Organization for Standardisation
ISZKI *Igazságügyi Szakértői és Kutató Intézetek* (Hungarian Network of Forensic Science Institutes)
JPAC-CIL Joint POW/MIA Accounting Command's – Central Identification Laboratory, US
KGB *Комитет государственной безопасности* (Soviet Committee for State Security)
KNA *Kwaliteitsnorm Nederlandse Archeologie* (Dutch Archaeology Quality Standard)
LGGRTC *Lietuvos Gyventojų Genocido ir Rezistencijos Tyrimo Centras* (The Genocide and Resistance Research Centre of Lithuania)
MACR Missing Air Crew Report, US
MAFMM Ministry for the Affairs of Families of Martyrs and Missing, Libya
MCI Medical Council of India
MDC Movement for Democratic Change, Zimbabwe
ME medical examiner
MFI mass fatality incidents
MHR Ministry of Human Rights, Iraq
MIA Missing in action
MIM Mass Identification Manager
MLI Medical-Legal Institute, Iraq
MNI minimum number of individuals
MNIT *Muzeul Naţional de Istorie a Transilvaniei* (National Museum of History of Transylvania, Romania)
MPI Missing Persons Institute for Bosnia and Herzegovina
MPTT Missing Persons Task Team, South Africa
MR-Hypothesis middle-range hypothesis
MR-Theory middle-range theory
NAFOL National Forensic Science Laboratory, Nepal
NCA National Crime Agency, UK
NFFA National Forensic Framework Agreements, UK
NFI *Nederlands Forensisch Instituut* (Netherlands Forensic Institute)
NFS National Forensic Service, Republic of Korea
NGO Non-governmental Organisation
NHRC National Human Rights Commission, Nepal
NN *Nomen Nescio* (unknown person)
NSW New South Wales, Australia
NZHPT New Zealand Historic Places Trust
OAH Operation Aussies Home, Australia
OHCHR Office of the High Commissioner for Human Rights
OIJ *Organismo de Investigación Judicial* (Judicial Investigative Bureau, Costa Rica)
PG Project Group, ENFSI
PG Prosecutor General, Lebanon
PHR Physicians for Human Rights
PJT *Policía Técnica Judicial* (Judicial Technical Police, Venezuela)
PMI Post-mortem interval
POW prisoner of war
PPE Personal protective equipment
QAA Quality Assurance Agency, UK
RAAF Royal Australian Air Force
RAN Royal Australian Navy
RAS Russian Academy of Sciences
RNA Royal Nepal Army
RL/A Recovery Leader/Anthropologist, JPAC-CIL

SAB *Sociedade de Arqueologia Brasileira* (Society for Brazilian Archaeology)
SENAMEFC *Servicio Nacional de Medicina y Ciencias Forenses* (National Service of Medicine and Forensic Sciences, Venezuela)
SML *Servicio Médico Legal* (Medico-Legal Service, Chile)
SOCO Scenes of Crime Officer
SOP Standard Operating Procedure
SWGANTH Scientific Working Group for Forensic Anthropology, US
SWGDVI Scientific Working Group on Disaster Victim Identification, US
TRC Truth and Reconciliation Commission
TSD Time since Deposition
UAE United Arab Emirates
UBA *Universidad de Buenos Aires* (University of Buenos Aires, Argentina)
UCV *Universidad Central de Venezuela* (Central University of Venezuela)
UEIF *Unidad Especial de Identificación Forense* (Special Forensic Identification Unit)
UK United Kingdom
UN United Nations
UNED *Universidad Estatal a Disancia* (Distance State University)
UNHCR United Nations High Commission for Refugees
UNLP *Universidad de La Plata* (University of La Plata, Argentina)
UoAFAU Forensic Anthropology Unit of the Department of Forensic Medicine and Toxicology, Medical School, University of Athens, Greece
US United States
UWC-A Unrecovered War Casualties – Army, Australia
VIFM Victorian Institute of Forensic Medicine, Australia
VTMT *Valstybinė Teismo Medicinos Tarnyba* (Lithuanian State Forensic Medicine Service)
WGA War Grave Sites Act, Slovenia (*Zakon o vojnih grobiščih*)
WWI World War I
WWII World War II
ZANLA Zimbabwe National Liberation Army, armed wing of ZANU-PF
ZANU-PF Zimbabwe African National Union – Patriotic Front
ZAPU Zimbabwe African People's Union
ZIPRA Zimbabwe People's Revolutionary Army, armed wing of ZAPU

Introduction

W.J. Mike Groen[1], Nicholas Márquez-Grant[2,3] and Robert C. Janaway[4]

[1] *Netherlands Forensic Institute (NFI), The Hague, the Netherlands*

[2] *Cranfield Forensic Institute, Cranfield University, Defence Academy of the United Kingdom, Shrivenham, UK*

[3] *Institute of Human Sciences, School of Anthropology and Museum Ethnography, University of Oxford, Oxford, UK*

[4] *School of Archaeological Sciences, University of Bradford, Bradford, UK*

The purpose of this volume is to explore the origins, history, present and future of forensic archaeology, as understood and practised across the globe. This volume was produced by the generous participation of 127 contributors who provide a valuable insight into how forensic archaeological specialists, whose work has made significant contributions to the development of this discipline, use archaeological theory and methodology within their police forces, forensic institutes, private forensic providers, universities, museums, archaeological units, intergovernmental organisations or nongovernmental organisations (NGOs). Above all, they discuss their personal experience and practice within different legal traditions that not only required exceptional, logistical, legal and ethical challenges but also, at times, psychological stress and threats to personal safety.

Today, forensic archaeology is being practised in numerous criminal, medico-legal, humanitarian and civil law contexts. Despite this, there are only a few publications that discuss the forensic archaeological theory and methodology – and then also mostly related to the investigation of human rights violations (e.g. mass graves) – on a supranational level (e.g. Connor and Scott 2001a; Cordner and McKelvie 2002; Juhl 2005; Steadman and Haglund 2005; Juhl and Olsen 2006; Tuller and Đurić 2006; Cox et al. 2008; Hanson 2008; Steele 2008; Blau and Ubelaker 2009; Cheetham and Hanson 2009; Dirkmaat 2012a; Crossland 2013; Gupta 2013). It could be even said that most of the 'traditionally employed archaeologists have no notion of this particular application of archaeology' (Juhl and Olsen 2006, 412). The editors hope that this volume will aid and contribute to the exposure of forensic archaeology and that it will be helpful in defining the role of a forensic archaeological specialist, and consequently in the development of forensic archaeology practice on a global scale. Despite the achievements of forensic archaeology in specific jurisdictions across the globe, this discipline is still unknown in most countries. It is still more the exception rather than the rule that forensic archaeological specialists, be it archaeologists, forensic anthropologists, forensic pathologists or police officers, are routinely requested to assist in a case where they could potentially offer valuable information. This underuse of forensic archaeology is partly explained by the assumption that 'forensic archaeological techniques are not realistically applicable at many crime scenes due to time (and personnel) constraints' (Dirkmaat et al. 2008, 42), and the common belief that 'archaeological excavation techniques can be employed by anyone' (Márquez-Grant et al. 2012, 605).

The editors believe that this volume, with contributions on 40 country-specific medico-legal settings, two forensic archaeological expert groups and 15 (non) governmental organisations are a testimony to the prospects and significance regarding the use of archaeological theories and methodology in a legal setting, be it as part of criminal-, medico-legal- or civil law investigation, or with regard to humanitarian work associated with past human rights violations. We hope that these contributions – some written by researchers at the start of their careers, others by senior and well-established forensic archaeologists, forensic anthropologists, forensic scientists, forensic pathologists or police officers – will help archaeologists, criminal investigators, forensic scientists, prosecutors, lawyers, judges, human rights organisations and others to value the potential forensic archaeology has to offer in recording (outdoor) scenes; in establishing the link between the victim, the offender and the crime; and in reconstructing the human behaviour that took place at these scenes. This volume should also serve as a good starting point for supporting each other in a global network of forensic archaeological specialists, and to serve researchers and upcoming forensic experts. We also believe that the development of quality assurance, certifications and accreditation in forensic archaeology is essential, as is the advancement of the forensic archaeological theoretical framework, and the improvement of its field methodology. We do not have the luxury to stand still and not to improve ourselves.

Forensic archaeology: defining its context

In this volume, forensic archaeology is discussed *an sich*, and therefore independent of forensic anthropology, although forensic archaeology and forensic anthropology, especially in the Americas, are closely related. It is acknowledged that forensic archaeology owes greatly to many forensic anthropologists; several of them are the main contributors to some of the chapters in this volume. It is also acknowledged that different countries define forensic archaeology differently.

This introduction provides a working definition of forensic archaeology, as used within this volume, and focuses on the development of this discipline during the past and current century. The professional background of the forensic specialists, who use archaeological theories, methods and techniques regularly in their casework, is also discussed.

Forensic archaeology: a working definition

Forensic archaeology is defined in this volume as *a forensic discipline that uses archaeological theories, methods and techniques in a legal context*. This definition, although similar to the definitions and descriptions of forensic archaeology as used by forensic specialists, mostly forensic archaeologists and/or anthropologists (e.g. Morse et al. 1976, 1983, 1984; Skinner 1987; Hunter et al. 1994, 1996; Dirkmaat and Adovasio 1997; Scott and Connor 1997, 2001; Christ 2001; Connor and Scott 2001b; Haglund 2001; Skinner et al. 2003; Blau 2004; Blau and Skinner 2005; Hunter and Cox 2005; Menez 2005; Oakley 2005; Connor 2007; Dirkmaat et al. 2008; Hanson 2008; Blau and Ubelaker 2009; Cox 2009; Dirkmaat 2012a; Dirkmaat and Cabo 2012; Hochrein 2012; Hunter et al. 2013), is primarily intended as a broad-spectrum working definition. A more tailored definition will be provided in the final part of this volume, Concluding Remarks.

It is also important to define what is not included in the above definition. First, the use of forensic science in traditional archaeological research projects falls outside the definition, since this research does not take place *for the courts* within a criminal, medico-legal, humanitarian or civil law context. To quote Hunter and Cox (2005, 2): 'Here is the confusion between the words "science" and "forensics"'. Second, the physical anthropological/bioarchaeological analysis and identification of historical individuals, including facial reconstruction on historical/archaeological skeletons, also fall outside the definition. This kind of research does not take place within the context of law, and is primary historical in nature. Finally, this definition also excludes the archaeological excavation and analysis of historical mass graves, battlefields, execution sites, or extermination centres, if the primary goal of excavation falls outside the criminal, medico-legal, humanitarian or civil law setting.

Despite the above, we do recognise that some of the successful work undertaken on historical individuals and mass graves has helped to promote (i.e. public interest) the forensic archaeological and anthropological disciplines, leading in some countries to the further promotion of these for more recent cases.

A brief history of forensic archaeology 1943–2000

It could be argued that buried contextual evidence, as a tool to confirm war crimes in a medico-legal context, was first used in the Katyn Forest, near Smolensk, Russia, in spring/summer of 1943. In this forest, several mass graves were exhumed and researched by representatives of the Red Cross and the International Katyn Commission, consisting of forensic experts (mostly pathologists and anatomists) from different European countries, but under the supervision of the government of Nazi Germany. The investigation proved that the mass execution and burial of several thousand Polish nationals (mostly military officers and intelligentsia) in the Katyn Forest was not committed by Nazi Germany, but by the Soviet People's Commissariat for Internal Affairs (NKVD), in the spring of 1940 (e.g. Raszeja and Chróścielewski 1994; Cienciala et al. 2007).[1] A second International Commission, likewise under the supervision of the government of Nazi Germany, participated in the exhumation of 91 mass graves near the town of Vinnytsia, Ukraine, also in 1943. These mass graves were related to the mass execution of thousands of citizens (mostly ethnic Ukrainians) by the NKVD in 1937–1938 (e.g. Dragan 1986; Kamenetsky 1989). The details related to the above-mentioned exhumations were widely distributed by the government of Nazi Germany as part of an anti-Soviet propaganda campaign. The post-World War II (WWII) investigation of war crimes, crimes against humanity and genocide, committed by the European Axis Powers and the Japanese Empire, was done – to the editors' knowledge – without using the available archaeological knowledge and experience at that time.[2]

---

[1]For more information on the findings of the International Katyn Commission, see http://www.warsawuprising.com/doc/katyn_documents1.htm (last accessed 11 January 2014).

[2]In the immediate aftermath of WWII in Europe Dr Keith Mant, later Professor and Head of the Department of Forensic Medicine at Guy's Hospital Medical School in London, UK, made important observations in the field that would develop into forensic taphonomy. These observations were done during exhumations of both single and multiple WWII graves in north-western Europe, on behalf of the British Army (e.g. Mant 1950, 1987).

In the 1970s, the North American forensic anthropologists started to promote archaeology as a discipline that could be useful in providing contextual information about the *in situ* position of the excavated human remains, in order to aid the forensic anthropological identification of these remains (e.g. Imaizumi 1974; McLaughlin 1974; Morse et al. 1976, 1983, 1984; Bass and Birkby 1978; Kerley 1978; Boyd 1979; Snow 1982; Skinner and Lazenby 1983; Brooks and Brooks 1984; Sigler-Eisenberg 1985; Skinner 1987; Lovis 1992; Poirier and Bellantoni 1996; Dirkmaat and Adovasio 1997; Scott and Connor 1997; Dirkmaat and Cabo 2012; Foreword by Clyde Collins Snow, this volume). The need for development of controlled excavations by trained professionals became obvious as increasing number of cases involving human remains recovery – by unskilled law enforcement officials – resulted in poorly recovered human remains and loss of associated evidence (e.g. Morse et al. 1976, 1984; Skinner and Lazenby 1983; Sigler-Eisenberg 1985; Cabo and Dirkmaat, Chapter 31, this volume; Foreword by Clyde Collins Snow, this volume).

In 1984, the families of the disappeared in Argentina contacted the American Association for the Advancement of Science (AAAS) to send a delegation of forensic scientists to Argentina in order to assist in the search, recovery and identification of their disappeared family members (Fondebrider and Scheinsohn, Chapter 43, this volume; Foreword by Clyde Collins Snow, this volume). Argentina, like many countries in Latin America, had a tumultuous history of political and social unrest and internal armed conflict. More often than not, it was the State and its affiliated armed groups (e.g. Death Squads) that were responsible for the violation of human rights, such as kidnappings, extrajudicial killings and disappearance of the remains of the executed individuals (e.g. Snow et al. 1984; Americas Watch and PHR 1991; Joyce and Stover 1991; Stover and Manuel 1991; EAFG 1993; Crossland 2000; Stover and Ryan 2001; Fondebrider 2002, 2009, 2012; Doretti and Snow 2003; Juhl 2005; Juhl and Olsen 2006; Bernardi and Fondebrider 2007; Ferllini 2007; Egaña et al. 2008; Zarankin and Funari 2008). The arrival of US forensic anthropologists in Argentina led to the establishment of a NGO, the Argentine Forensic Anthropology Team (*Equipo Argentino de Antropología Forense* – EAAF) in 1984 (e.g. Snow et al. 1984; Joyce and Stover 1991; Crossland 2000; Stover and Ryan 2001; Doretti and Snow 2003; Steadman and Haglund 2005; Bernardi and Fondebrider 2007; Egaña et al. 2008; Flavel and Barker 2009; Fondebrider 2009, 2012; Fondebrider and Scheinsohn, Chapter 43, this volume; Foreword by Clyde Collins Snow, this volume). In the same year, another NGO, Physicians for Human Rights (PHR), was established in Boston, United States (Schmitt et al., Chapter 53, this volume). The PHR focused (and still does) on the use of medicine and science to stop mass atrocities, and on the investigation of severe human rights violations. In 1989, another Latin American NGO was established, the Chilean Forensic Anthropology Group (*Grupo Antropología Forense* – GAF; Intriago Leiva et al., Chapter 45, this volume); this was followed by the establishment of the Guatemalan Forensic Anthropology Team (*Equipo de Antropología Forense de Guatemala* – EAFG) in 1992 (e.g. Americas Watch and PHR 1991; Stover and Manuel 1991; EAFG 1993; Stover and Ryan 2001; Steadman and Haglund 2005; Flavel and Barker 2009; Fondebrider 2009; Peccerelli, personal communication 2013; Foreword by Clyde Collins Snow, this volume). The EAFG was redesigned to a foundation (*Fundación de Antropología Forense de Guatemala* – FAFG) in 1997.

All the above-mentioned NGOs were driven to assist the families of the victims of political violence in finding out what happened to their loved ones. To answer the question: Were they dead or alive? And if dead, where were their bodies? Consequently, these NGOs also developed a series of forensic excavation protocols and post-mortem analyses of the remains that fitted into the (national) humanitarian and judicial processes. The PHR and the Latin American NGOs were also responsible for answering these questions in almost all forensic archaeological/anthropological missions related to human rights violence prior to 1996. For example, in 1991 the PHR launched a reconnaissance mission to Iraqi Kurdistan, followed by a mass grave excavation campaign in 1992 (e.g. EAAF 1992; Middle East Watch and PHR 1992, 1993; Scott and Connor 1997). These campaigns also included archaeologists and physical/forensic anthropologists from the United States, the EAAF, the EAFG and the GAF.

Parallel with the above-mentioned developments in the Americas in the late 1980s, the archaeological theory and methodology was also introduced to the European criminal, medico-legal and humanitarian contexts. The fall of communism in the late 1980s in Central and Eastern Europe allowed, for example, the investigation of human rights violations committed by the previous communist regimes (e.g. Jankauskas et al. 2005; Kola 2005; Mark 2010; Neamţu and Ţînţariu 2010; Jankauskas, Chapter 13, this volume; Susa et al., Chapter 11, this volume; Trzciński and Borkowski, Chapter 15, this volume). The first medico-legal European investigation related to the use of archaeology in a regular police enquiry – to the editors' knowledge – took place in 1988, when the forensic archaeological theory and methodology was applied in the United Kingdom (e.g. Hunter et al. 1994, 1996, 2013; Hunter and Cox 2005; Cox 2009; Hunter and Cropper, Chapter 23, this volume). In 1990–1991, a team of Australian and Soviet archaeologists and anthropologists excavated three mass graves associated with WWII Nazi mass burials of Jewish victims at Serniki and Ustanovka, Ukraine, this in process of acquiring evidence for the

Australian War Crimes Prosecutions that were conducted between 1986 and 1992 (Wright 1995).

In 1993, an *ad hoc* international tribunal was established, the United Nations (UN) International Criminal for Former Yugoslavia (ICTY).[3] The ICTY had jurisdiction over crimes and human rights violations committed on the territory of the former Yugoslavia since 1991. The year 1996 saw two important developments; first the ICTY asked the PHR to conduct mass grave excavations in Bosnia and second an intergovernmental organisation, the International Commission on Missing Persons (ICMP) was established with headquarters in Sarajevo, Bosnia and Herzegovina (Hanson, Chapter 48, this volume; Hanson et al., Chapter 3, this volume). In 1997, the ICTY started to employ its own forensic archaeologists and anthropologist (e.g. Wright et al. 2005; Wright 2010), followed a few years later by the ICMP (Hanson, Chapter 48, this volume). All these developments resulted in the formation of many multidisciplinary excavation teams across the territory of the former Yugoslavia, with individuals from all over the globe (e.g. PHR 1993, 1994, 1996; Owsley et al. 1996; Stover and Peress 1998; EAAF 2000; Haglund et al. 2001; Cordner and McKelvie 2002; Skinner et al. 2002; Stover and Shigekane 2002; Jessee and Skinner 2005; Juhl 2005; Skinner and Sterenberg 2005; Juhl and Olsen 2006; Ferllini 2007; Hanson 2008; Fondebrider 2009; Sterenberg 2009; Wright 2010; Djurić and Starović, Chapter 18, this volume; Hanson, Chapter 48, this volume; Hanson et al., Chapter 3, this volume; Šlaus and Petaros, Chapter 5, this volume). In 1994, a second *ad hoc* tribunal was established, the UN International Criminal Tribunal for Rwanda (ICTR), to examine the genocide that took place in Rwanda in the same year.[4] The ICTR had jurisdiction over crimes and human rights violations committed in Rwanda, or by Rwandan citizens in nearby States, in 1994. In 1995–1996, the PHR gathered a team to excavate a mass grave site related to the genocide (e.g. Connor and Scott 2001b; Haglund et al. 2001; Stover and Ryan 2001; Cordner and McKelvie 2002). In 1997, a PHR team was sent to Afghanistan to investigate allegations of mass graves containing the remains of executed Taliban prisoners (Skinner 2007).

What about the professional background?

In the North American Boasian four-field anthropology approach (archaeology, cultural anthropology, linguistics and physical anthropology), forensic archaeology is primarily seen as the outdoor location and recovery of human remains within the context of forensic anthropology, and is therefore mainly practised by forensic anthropologists (e.g. Dirkmaat and Adovasio 1997; Connor and Scott 2001b; Haglund 2001; Owsley 2001; Scott and Connor 2001; Gould 2007; Dirkmaat et al. 2008; Ubelaker 2009; Kranioti and Paine 2011; Dirkmaat and Cabo 2012; Cabo and Dirkmaat, Chapter 31, this volume; Congram, Chapter 27, this volume). However, there are also North American forensic anthropologists/archaeologists who see an important role for the archaeologist during the process of recovery (e.g. Krogman 1943a, 1943b; Morse et al. 1976, 1984; Bass and Birkby 1978; Boyd 1979; Duncan 1983; Morse 1983; Stoutamire 1983; Sigler-Eisenberg 1985; Mant 1987; Skinner 1987; Lovis 1992; Poirier and Bellantoni 1996; Christ 2001; Owsley 2001; Scott and Connor 2001; Gould 2002; Skinner et al. 2003; Gould 2004, 2007; Bellantoni 2005; Connor 2007; Holland and Connell 2009; Skinner and Bowie 2009; Larson et al. 2011; Snow 2011; Emanovsky and Belcher 2012; Tuller 2012).[5]

In the United Kingdom and most of Northern Europe, archaeology and physical anthropology are seen as separate disciplines that have originated from distinctly different educational departments: archaeology and anatomy, forensic medicine or biology, respectively. Subsequently, forensic archaeology in these countries is recognised as an independent discipline – grounded in archaeological science – and is therefore practised by archaeologists (e.g. Hunter et al. 1994, 1996, 2013; Connor and Scott 2001b; Hunter 2002, 2009; Hunter and Cox 2005; Menez 2005; Cox 2009; de Leeuwe and Groen, Chapter 14, this volume; Hunter and Cropper, Chapter 23, this volume; Janaway, Chapter 24, this volume; Schuliar et al., Chapter 8, this volume). To complicate the matter of definition even further, many of the forensic anthropologists working in the United Kingdom have an educational background in archaeology (Cox 2009, 31–32). In fact, physical anthropology/bioarchaeology is also commonly taught in archaeological departments in the United Kingdom and the Netherlands. Moreover, in some European countries, forensic anthropology is seen as a medical discipline and is practised accordingly by forensic pathologists, or medically trained anatomists (e.g. Blau and Ubelaker 2009; Kranioti and Paine 2011; Márquez-Grant et al. 2012).

In Latin America (e.g. Steadman and Haglund 2005; Fondebrider 2009) and some European countries (e.g. İşcan 1981; Kranioti and Paine 2011; Márquez-Grant et al. 2012), the term *forensic anthropology* is 'used in its widest sense, comprising the activities of both archaeologists and anthropologists who are concerned with the

[3]For more information, see http://www.icty.org/sections/AbouttheICTY (last accessed 11 January 2014).

[4]For more information, see http://www.unictr.org/ (last accessed 11 January 2014).

[5]See also Dirkmaat et al. (2005) on mass graves.

investigation of cases of criminal and political violence' (Fondebrider 2009, 73).

Finally, forensic archaeology is sometimes also seen as a supplementary forensic discipline that is practised by – sometimes archaeologically educated – police officers, especially by the specialised crime scene investigators (e.g. Neumann et al., Chapter 9, this volume; Van Denhouwe and Schotsmans, Chapter 2, this volume).

To summarise, the professional title of a forensic specialist who uses archaeological theories, methods and techniques within the legal context depends on the country where this specialist is working, and therefore also on his or her professional background. The overlap between forensic archaeology and forensic anthropology is real and sometimes inevitable 'and difficult for forensic investigators outside the disciplines to recognise. In fact, it is sometimes difficult for those within the disciplines to recognise' (Scott and Connor 2001, 103–104). Skinner et al. (2003, 81) even propose the use of a new working title; the 'forensic bio-archaeologist', this 'to unite the roles of physical anthropologist and archaeologist because it usefully implies a broader skill base including the biological sciences such as botany, entomology and zoology as well as some familiarity with surveying and excavation techniques including site formation processes and material culture.'

The above-mentioned differences in perceptions of the forensic archaeological specialists are not surprising: not only are there country-specific discrepancies in the educational background, training, and organisation of the specialists – be it archaeologists, forensic anthropologists, forensic pathologists, or police officers, there are also important differences in the country-specific police and judicial settings in which these specialists are working. For example, archaeological education and training at some Dutch and British Archaeological departments maintains a strong focus on pedology, ecology and physical anthropology. Subsequently, the theories, methods and techniques taught at these departments can be easily used, with some modification, within the criminal, medico-legal, humanitarian or civil law settings. The above-mentioned differences in perception can also be, to a certain extent, explained by country-specific dissimilarities in population number and density; crime rate and crime behaviour; elapse time for crimes, such as murder; historical developments, such as military conflicts or violations of human rights (e.g. the presence of mass graves); and geography and climatic conditions. For example, a largely forested country, with a stable democracy and a low crime rate will probably not have enough forensic cases to train and sustain specialised forensic archaeologists, and will, as a consequence, probably use its police officers or forensic pathologists to perform the excavation and recovery of human remains.

Despite the above, the editors believe that forensic archaeological casework should be – ideally – practised by an academically educated and trained specialist with a long history in traditional archaeological excavations. It is important not only to have knowledge of how to dig and what methods and techniques to use but also to have the experience that enables appropriate recording and interpretation of what is being dug, regarding the sequence of events surrounding the creation of the grave, the deposition of a body, or an object, and all the activities that occurred after the deposition of the body or object (e.g. backfilling, concealing, etc.). With this in mind, it is fair to indicate that most of the forensic anthropologists, forensic pathologists and police officers do not possess the theoretical background and methodological skills that come with a traditional archaeological education and, as importantly, an extensive post-training field experience. This observation is not unique. Several professional organisations improved their quality assurances, and/or pursuit of accreditation of members who perform outdoor field recovery. For example, the US-based Scientific Working Group for Forensic Anthropology (SWGANTH) published a document on Scene Detection and Processing[6]; the Latin American Forensic Anthropology Association (*Asociación Latinoamericana de Antropología Forense* – ALAF) is, at the time of writing, in the process of establishing standard professional requirements for forensic anthropologists/archaeologists (Fondebrider, personal communication 2013); the British Institute for Archaeologists (IfA) Forensic Archaeology Expert Panel just finished its standardisation and accreditation process (Janaway, Chapter 24, this volume); and the European Network of Forensic Science Institutions (ENFSI) recently created the Project Group Forensic Archaeology to examine the potential of forensic archaeology in Europe (Groen, Chapter 25, this volume).

The archaeology in forensic archaeology

Although archaeological theories and methodology have already been transferred from the archaeological into the forensic context, this has often been done 'independently of the paradigms behind them' (Connor and Scott 2001b, 1). This introductory chapter will therefore discuss the application of archaeological theory in the first instance, followed by a discussion on archaeological

[6]For more information, see http://swganth.startlogic.com/Scene%20Detection%20and%20Processing%20Rev%200.pdf (last accessed 11 January 2014).

methodology. By discussing the archaeological theory first, it is intended to convey a point, the precedence of archaeological theory over methodology. The above will be followed by a discussion of the constraints and challenges archaeology has to face when operating within the context of law. Finally, the nine potential areas of engagement, in which archaeological knowledge and expertise could be used within the context of the law, will be specified.

Archaeological theory

Archaeology, like all academic disciplines, has its own scientific paradigm, theoretical framework, methodology and principles. One part of its theoretical framework is derived from the social sciences (e.g. history, sociology and cultural anthropology); the other part from the natural sciences (e.g. biology and earth sciences). Archaeology is therefore both a Science and a Humanity. The primary goal of archaeology is the study and reconstruction of human activity in the past, primarily through the systematic recovery and analysis of the so called *archaeological record*, or the physical evidence of the past. The archaeological record consists of the physical remains of the once living humans and other organisms, the material culture,[7] and the archaeological features (i.e. non-portable manmade objects) left behind by human and animal activity, and the environmental data.

All archaeologists use a theoretical framework to interpret the archaeological record, and there are different theoretical viewpoints within archaeology.[8] Archaeologists do not always agree on which explanatory framework should be used for interpretation. This is not surprising since archaeology attracts scholars from an endless range of backgrounds, and its research topics diverge from an interpretative study of Viking symbolism to the determination of mineral and chemical components in late medieval pottery. It could be said that most of today's theoretical viewpoints lie somewhere between the extreme hyper-positivistic processualism of the 1960s–1970s and the extreme hyper-relativist post-processualism of the 1980s–1990s. Extreme hyper-positivistic processualism states that archaeology, as a science, should only apply scientific methods in its research, and that it should only focus on finding general laws to explain human adaptations and change.[9] Extreme hyper-relativist post-processualism stresses that archaeology can never be objective, that cross-cultural laws do not exist, and that the social and cultural dynamics and their meanings should be the main focus of archaeological research.[10] Despite the above-mentioned disagreements, the practice of archaeology is fairly coherent, since it aims at answering questions through the recovery and analysis of the archaeological record. Archaeologists furthermore agree that this record should not only be interpreted within its context (i.e. its place in time and space) and association but also within an explanatory theoretical perspective that integrates the excavated record with the ecological data and assumptions about human behaviour. Most of today's archaeologists will also agree that human behaviour is patterned, that this pattern is reflected in the archaeological record that is the result of human behaviour and that the contextual recording and analysis of the archaeological record can be used to understand the patterns in human behaviour that led to the deposition/construction of the archaeological record in the first place. Finally, most of today's archaeologists will also agree that all archaeological interpretations and reconstructions are affected by their social and historical context.

Archaeological methodology

Archaeological methodology describes 'the procedures and approaches used to carry out a piece of archaeological research whether it is an excavation, survey, artefact study, or any other kind of analysis' (Darvill 2002, 259). Archaeological field methodology is always research question driven, since field research is almost always

[7] Material culture can be subdivided into artefacts (any movable object that has been manufactured, used or modified by humans), architecture and eco-facts (plant and animal remains found on an archaeological site).

[8] For more information on archaeological theory, see for example Bentley et al. (2009) or Johnson (2010).

[9] Processualism, also known as New Archaeology, is strongly associated with a positivist view of the past, an ecosystemic approach, and a hypothetico-deductive research philosophy. It holds that archaeologists are able to develop accurate, objective information about the past human behaviour by applying the scientific method and the ethno-historical approach to their investigations. Archaeologist should further develop hypotheses and test these hypotheses quantitatively with the obtained archaeological record (e.g. Binford 1962, 1968, 1977, 1981; Binford and Binford 1968; Watson et al. 1971; Schiffer 1972; Clarke 1973).

[10] Post-processualism, also known as interpretative archaeology, developed in the early 1980s in response to the processual framework that, accordingly to the post-processual archaeologists, treated the cultural change independently of human social relations and the human beings as passive objects totally modified by external dynamics. Post-processualism refers to different theoretical frameworks (e.g. Neo-Marxism, Structuralism, Contextual Archaeology), all with their own theoretical thoughts. Generally speaking, post-processualism states that the interpretation of the archaeological record is infected by our own subjective interpretation and social factors (multiple interpretations of the past are therefore possible), sees the archaeological record as a communicative medium and considers the role of individuals (i.e. agents) as the driving force for all archaeological patterning (e.g. Hodder 1982a, 1982b, 1983, 1985, 1991; Miller and Tilley 1984; Shanks and Tilley 1987a, 1987b; Trigger 1989).

destructive. An excavation will destroy the context of the archaeological record. This context, defined as the position of an item or feature in time and space, should therefore be 'established by measuring and assessing the associations, matrix, and provenance' (Darvill 2002, 98) of all within the archaeological record present finds and features. Archaeologists are experienced in recognising site specific contexts, their research value and how these contexts came to be created. Context and association are of paramount importance in archaeology, even more important than the archaeological record *an sich*. Archaeological finds are always recorded *in situ* (i.e. in their original position and context) and may only then be removed from the site. Archaeological features are, generally speaking, unmovable and are normally destroyed during their investigation. They must therefore be recorded and studied *in situ*.

Archaeology is all about the development and refinement of systematic and reliable field methodology for management, control and three-dimensional documentation of complex sites. Archaeological field methods and techniques are developed to systematically search for, and reliably document the context of, and association within, the archaeological record, and to limit the bias during the sampling and recovery of archaeological finds and features (i.e. the empirical evidence). Today's field methods and techniques are the result of more than 100 years of refinement and testing on numerous archaeological sites from different contexts (depositional environments) all over the world. Archaeological field methods and techniques are fully integrated with Geographic Information Systems (GIS)[11] to help understand the stratigraphic[12] sequence and associations on an archaeological site, and to help understand and record the human and natural site formation processes and site specific degradation (taphonomic transformations) of the archaeological record (i.e. the pre-depositional, depositional and post-depositional activities).[13] Understanding taphonomic transformations (taphonomy[14] and degradation of materials), or the condition of the archaeological material at the time of excavation, is essential since these transformations may distort, mask or even delete a part of the (excavated) archaeological record, and can therefore cause misinterpretations during the process of reconstruction (e.g. Clarke 1973; Schiffer 1976, 1983, 1987). Taphonomic transformations also influence the concept of taphonomic time, defined as 'the archaeological concept of relative time' (Sorg and Haglund 2002, 7).

To summarise: archaeological field methodology is 'more than just digging a neat square hole' (Sigler-Eisenberg 1985, 651). There is also no 'universal methodology' to process an archaeological site, and this is also likely to vary in forensic work, on a case-by-case basis (e.g. different contexts and dissimilar research aims and objectives). The simplistic view of archaeological field methodology not only ignores the explanatory theories needed to comprehend the excavated archaeological record but also the diversity and complexity of the archaeological field methods and techniques. Non-archaeologists often lack the knowledge of context specific limitations and effectiveness of these methods and techniques, and of the justification for their application in a particular context. The key concept is the ability to be able to select an appreciated field method or technique. It is also important to have the flexibility to modify a method or technique, if necessary. If used well, archaeological field methodology is able to provide access to spatial behaviour and taphonomic time, and therefore to the reconstruction of past human behaviour (the pre-depositional and depositional activities). Taphonomic time can be accessed through the analysis of the transformed archaeological record *in situ*, the recognition and interpretation of site stratigraphy and the understanding of taphonomic history (the post-depositional activities) of the site. Spatial behaviour can be accessed through the use of proper archaeological documenting and mapping techniques, understanding

[11] GIS is a software application that enables collection, storage, retrieval, manipulation, analysis, management and visualisation of spatial data (i.e. spatial database) and images with a geographical reference (e.g. soil maps, air photographs, and cadastres). GIS is widely used within archaeology, since it helps archaeologists to interpret the archaeological record, and hence the human behaviour, within a geographic setting (e.g. Chapman 2006; Conolly and Lake 2006).

[12] Archaeological stratigraphy is related to natural processes and human activities that resulted in (soil) deposits and, in time, have accumulated to form geological and archaeological layers and features. Stratigraphic relations and associations are therefore necessary to understand processes and behaviours that created the archaeological site (e.g. Harris 1989). Modern archaeological excavations methodology follows the site-specific stratigraphic principles.

[13] Pre-depositional activities comprise all past human behaviours that took place at an archaeological site. Depositional activities are associated with all cultural and natural activities that were expressed through the means of archaeological record, and that resulted in the insertion of this record in the archaeological context, for example by loss, abandonment or intentional burial. Post-depositional processes comprise all cultural and natural activities that have altered or destroyed the archaeological record after its inclusion in the archaeological context, and before the archaeological excavation (e.g. Clarke 1973).

[14] Taphonomy can be defined as the 'context related study of organic decomposition'. In traditional archaeology, taphonomic studies address all stages of research: 'from site formation process through diagenesis and sampling procedures to analytical techniques and interpretative perspectives' (Stallibrass 2000, vii).

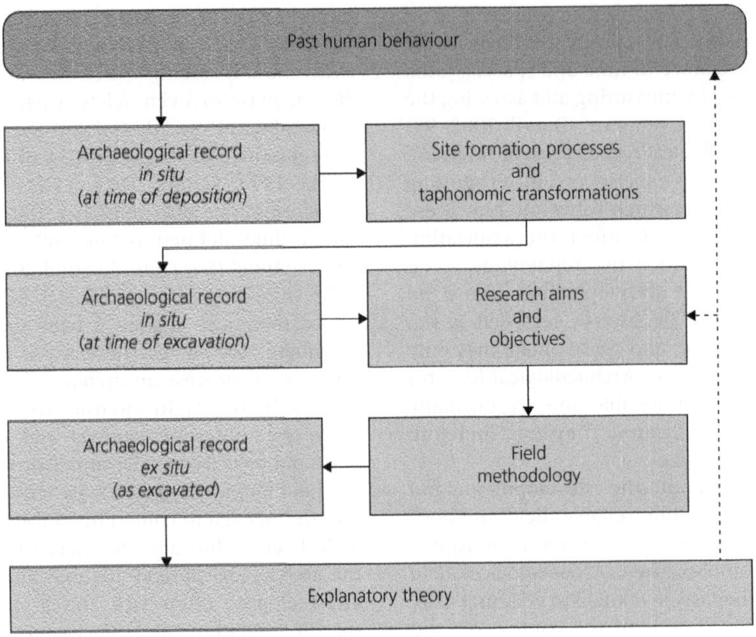

Figure I.1 The structure of an archaeological interpretation.

of the site formation process, and the spatial arrangement of the archaeological record *in situ* (Figure I.1).

Additionally, the use of GIS geodatabases will not only allow a reliable and systematic spatial analysis of the excavated site and the excavated archaeological record, but also a comparison with the spatial analyses related to other archaeological sites. In this way information obtained from distinct archaeological sites can be combined to research human behaviour on a supra-site level. The use of GIS also allows predictive modelling, for example the extrapolation of today's archaeological knowledge to predict the location of previously unknown archaeological sites.

Legal context and ethics

Forensic archaeology is not simply 'a straightforward transference of methodology, but rather the application of archaeological theory to forensic circumstances' (Hunter 2002, xxvi). Forensic archaeological time frame, research questions, evidentiary procedures (e.g. chain of custody and evidential value of finds and features), judicial constrains and reporting (i.e. court testimony) differ strongly from the ones used within the traditional archaeology. Additionally, knowledge of law enforcement and law procedures, unnecessary in traditional archaeology, is an integral part of forensic archaeology. As is the possibility that one's work could be re-examined by the Defence or Prosecution in the court of law (e.g. Sigler-Eisenberg 1985; Hunter and Knupfer, 1996; Hunter et al. 1996, 2013; Cox 1998; Christ 2001; Haglund 2001; Hunter 2002; Dilley 2005; Juhl and Olsen 2006; Cerone 2007; Rainio et al. 2007; Cheetham and Hanson 2009; Henneberg 2009; Crossland 2013). General knowledge of criminology and forensic sciences (criminalistics) is also required. Forensic archaeology should further be flexible enough in its approach to adapt its archaeological theories and methodology to the criminal, medico-legal, humanitarian or civil laws settings. On the other hand, there should also be national standards (where appropriate aligned to international practice, especially when concerning mass grave excavation) that will allow for inter-site comparison, recognition of possible patterns and relationships and for the justification of the methods and techniques used during the forensic investigation (e.g. Skinner 1987; Haglund et al. 2001; Cordner and McKelvie 2002; Schmitt 2002; Skinner et al. 2003; Jessee and Skinner 2005; Cox et al. 2008; Cheetham and Hanson 2009). Additionally, innovations from the field of affiliated forensic sciences[15] and practices[16] must also be incorporated into forensic archaeological field

[15] For example forensic botany (e.g. Coyle 2005; Hall and Byrd 2012), forensic entomology (e.g. Gennard 2007; Byrd and Castner 2009), forensic anthropology (e.g. Cox and Mays 2000; Komar and Buikstra 2008), forensic geology (e.g. Pye 2007; Tibbett and Carter 2008), and geoforensics (e.g. Ruffell and McKinley 2008; Pirrie et al. 2013).

[16] For example cadaver dogs (e.g. Rebmann et al. 2000).

methodology to strengthen its effectiveness. Finally, the results provided by forensic archaeology will have an impact on the psychological and legal ramifications for the victim's relatives and their community (e.g. Crossland 2000, 2011, 2013; Connor and Scott 2001b; Cordner and McKelvie 2002; Fondebrider 2002, 2009; Stover and Shigekane 2002; Skinner et al. 2003; Williams and Crews 2003; Hunter and Cox 2005; Bernardi and Fondebrider 2007; Skinner 2007; Egaña et al. 2008; Gassiot Ballbé and Steadman 2008; Pollock 2008; Steele 2008; Congram and Sterenberg 2009; Flavel and Barker 2009; Blau and Fondebrider 2010; Mark 2010; Gupta 2013; Powers and Sibun 2013).[17]

Archaeology and law: the areas of engagement

The use of (modified) archaeological theories and methodology within the context of law could cover different types of casework. The nine most important, and somewhat simplified, areas of engagement or requests are the following:

- Domestic police service cases, in particular during field surveys or searches for missing persons (presumably dead and buried) or objects; excavation of clandestine burials; controlled exhumations at regular cemeteries; (sub)surface field recovery of scattered and/or heavily burned (calcified) human remains; and dating of skeletonised human remains and buried objects (e.g. Imaizumi 1974; McLaughlin 1974; Morse et al. 1976; Bass and Birkby 1978; Boyd 1979; Sigler-Eisenberg 1985; McDonald and Ross 1990; Spennemann and Franke 1995; Ubelaker et al. 1995; Hunter et al. 1996, 2001, 2013; Dirkmaat and Adovasio 1997; Nawrocki et al. 1998; Dirkmaat 2002; Sauer et al. 2003; Blau 2004; Hunter and Cox 2005; Congram 2008; Reinecke and Hochrein 2008; Steadman et al. 2008, 2009; Ubelaker and Rife 2008; Hunter 2009; Hochrein 2012; Rainwater et al. 2012; Dirkmaat et al., 2013; Foreword by Colin Hope, this volume). The legal context in this type of casework is covered by the national judiciaries. The commissioning authority is the Public Prosecution Office, the Police and/or the Judiciary.
- Mass fatality events resulting from natural disasters, building fires, transportation accidents or terrorist attacks (Disaster Victim Identification – DVI, or Mass Fatality Incident – MFI) (e.g. Sledzik 1996, 2009; Dirkmaat and Adovasio 1997; Dirkmaat and Hefner 2001; Gould 2002, 2004; Dirkmaat and Miller 2003; Sledzik et al. 2003, 2009; Blau 2005; Gould 2007; Reinecke and Hochrein 2008; Waterhouse 2009; Dirkmaat et al. 2010, 2013; Blau and Briggs 2011; Dirkmaat 2012b; Mundorff 2012; Rainwater et al. 2012). The legal context in this type of casework is covered by the national judiciaries, often in the form of a request, to assist in the area of mass fatality event. The documentation and evidence gathered from these sites could also be used for prosecution if the event was caused by a terrorist attack.
- Investigations of human rights violations (i.e. extrajudicial killings, war crimes, crimes against humanity and genocide) in medico-legal context for reason of prosecution, the location and recovery of victims, the determination of the legal personal identity of these victims and the exposure of the committed atrocities (e.g. Skinner 1987; PHR 1994, 1996; Wright 1995, 2010; Owsley et al. 1996; Stover and Peress 1998; Connor and Scott 2001b; Haglund et al. 2001; Hunter et al. 2001; Scott 2001; Stover and Ryan 2001; Haglund 2002; Schmitt 2002; Skinner et al. 2002, 2003; Stover and Shigekane 2002; Doretti and Snow 2003; Blau and Skinner 2005; Dirkmaat et al. 2005; Jessee and Skinner 2005; Juhl 2005; Steadman and Haglund 2005; Wright et al. 2005; Juhl and Olsen 2006; Tuller and Durić 2006; Cox et al. 2008; Hanson 2008; Steele 2008; Cattaneo 2009; Crossland 2013). The legal context in this type of casework is generally covered by the national judiciaries and/or the UN Convention on Prevention and Punishment of the Crime of Genocide (1948), the UN Declaration of Human Rights (1948), the Geneva Conventions (1949) and the Rome Statute (1998–2002) that led to the physical establishment of the permanent International Criminal Court (ICC) in The Hague, the Netherlands, in 2002 (e.g. Schmitt 2002; Dirkmaat et al. 2005; Juhl and Olsen 2006; Foreword by Jeremy Sarkin, this volume).
- Investigations of human rights violations in a humanitarian setting, mostly related to the past century's oppressive governments and/or paramilitary organisations. This type of casework is related to the location and recovery of victims whose disappearance is a direct result of political violence, the determination of legal personal identity of these victims and the exposure of the committed atrocities (e.g. Joyce and Stover 1991; PHR, 1996; Crossland 2000, 2011; Fondebrider 2002, 2009, 2012; Doretti and Snow 2003; Blau and Skinner 2005; Juhl 2005; Steadman and Haglund 2005; Juhl and Olsen 2006; Bernardi and Fondebrider 2007; Klonowski 2007; Egaña et al. 2008; Gassiot Ballbé and Steadman 2008; Steele 2008; Congram and Sterenberg

[17]In compliance to the above, the editors expressed their wish to limit the publication of photographs with sensitive material (i.e. photographs of recognisable persons or decomposing human bodies) in this volume to a minimum. All contributors to this volume responded positively to this request and submitted sensitive photographs only if they thought that these photographs had a significant contribution to their chapter, and only after acquiring the appropriate permission.

2009; Blau and Fondebrider 2010; Wright 2010; Gupta 2013). Additionally, the documentation and evidence gathered from these investigations will produce a more accurate image of the historical past and can be used in (future) prosecution of human rights violations or civil law actions. These investigations, mostly performed by NGOs that work closely with the families of victims, differ to some extent from the above-mentioned medico-legal investigations. For example, due to passed amnesty laws or expired period of limitation. Additionally, these NGOs are generally not only responsible for the recovery and identification of the victims but also for the conduction of a preliminary investigation that could lead to locating the graves of the victims, and for the training of local professionals to continue this work at local level. The legal context in this type of casework is generally covered by national judiciaries, the above-mentioned international laws, and special commissions of enquiry (e.g. Truth and Reconciliation Commissions – TRCs).

- Humanitarian investigation that could lead to the recovery, repatriation and determination of the legal personal identity of the remains of missing military service personnel related to past century's military conflicts (e.g. World Wars I and II, the Korean War and the Vietnam War) (e.g. Wood and Stanley 1989; Holland and Mann 1996; Hoshower 1998; Webster 1998; Holland et al. 2002; Mann et al. 2003; Gojanović and Sutlović 2007; Palo et al. 2007; Emanovsky and Belcher 2012). The legal context in this type of casework is generally covered by national judiciaries or international treaties between the country that performs the investigation and the country on which territory this investigation takes places.
- Controlled exhumations of conventional burials at regular cemeteries for DNA sampling purposes outside the criminal, medico-legal or humanitarian setting, for example for identification purposes of the unknown individuals (NNs or *nomen nescio*). The legal context is this type of casework is covered by the national judiciaries.
- Archaeological investigations in the context of civil law. For example, during boundary disputes, or search for a missing grave at a regular cemetery. The legal context in this type of casework is covered by national judiciaries.
- On-site investigation related to the destruction of archaeological sites and monuments, illicit digs and artefact looting, especially in assessing the financial and archaeological damage caused by the destruction and looting, and examining of possibilities to link the looted sites to the looters (e.g. Bellantoni and Cooke 1996; Poirier and Bellantoni 1996; Prentice 2006). The legal context in this type of casework is generally covered by the National Archaeological Resources and/or the Cultural Heritage Protection Acts, and regulations concerning the illegal metal detector search, digging or picking up artefacts or relics from protected archaeological contexts or former battlefield sites.
- Investigations related to illegal selling of archaeological or historical artefacts, especially in determining the authenticity and the financial value of these artefacts. The legal context in this type of casework is generally covered by the above mentioned Archaeological Resources and/or Cultural Heritage Protection Acts and additional regulations.

Organisation of the volume

The chapters in the volume are ordered loosely according to a set of questions sent to the contributors to this volume to help them structure their chapters in a similar way. The following set of questions was asked:

- Please provide a description of the medico-legal framework in your country, in particular concerning the investigation of a crime scene or mass grave.
- How is forensic archaeology defined in your country or organisation?
- If forensic archaeology does exist, please provide a brief background and history on the use of this discipline.
- Do forensic archaeologists exist in your country or organisation? And if yes, in what capacity and where are they based?
- If forensic archaeologists do not exist, are archaeological theories and methodology employed by other forensic scientists or police officers?
- If forensic archaeology does exist, is there a system of accreditation? Are there any training opportunities?
- If forensic archaeology does exist, please provide a description of the type of cases in which archaeological theories and methodology are being employed.
- Please provide a description of future trends regarding forensic archaeology in your country or organisation.

The volume itself is divided into five parts. Part 1 explores forensic archaeology as practised in Europe; Part 2 concentrates on the Americas; and Part 3 on Africa, Asia and Oceania. Part 4 accounts for the (non) governmental organisations that regularly use forensic archaeological theories and methodology during their casework. Parts 1–4, discussed more extensively later, are structured alphabetically, in accordance with the first letter of the country or (non)governmental organisation. Part 5, Concluding Remarks, provides answers to the above-mentioned set of questions, an overall discussion, and a proposal for a new forensic archaeological theoretical framework.

Part 1 Europe

This section of the book contains 23 European country-specific chapters; one chapter on the quality assurances in British forensic archaeology (Chapter 24); and one chapter on the forensic archaeological collaboration within the European Network of Forensic Science Institutes (Chapter 25). The country-specific chapters can be generally subdivided into chapters that tend to focus on the use of forensic archaeology during crime scene investigations (Chapters 2, 8, 9, 14 and 23); chapters that integrate forensic archaeology into their forensic anthropological research (Chapters 1, 7, 10, 12, 16, 17, 21 and 22); and chapters that focus primarily on WWII and the human rights violations performed by past governments and/or paramilitary groups (Chapters 3, 4, 5, 6, 11, 13, 15, 18, 19 and 20).

Individuals in additional 11 European countries (Albania, Armenia, Azerbaijan, Estonia, Finland, Georgia, Ireland, Latvia, Sweden, Turkey and Ukraine) were approached, but could not commit to this volume due to different reasons.

Part 2 The Americas

Part 2 contains seven American chapters; three chapters from North America (Chapters 27, 29 and 31); two chapters from Central America (Chapters 28 and 30); and two chapters from South America (Chapters 26 and 32). All these chapters focus, among other things, on the interaction between forensic archaeology and forensic anthropology.

The number of countries in the Americas section is somewhat distorted, due to the inclusion of six Latin American (non) governmental organisations in Part 4 of the volume.

Part 3 Africa, Asia and Oceania

Part 3 contains 10 chapters; three chapters from Africa (Chapters 36, 39 and 42); five chapters from Asia (Chapters 34, 35, 37, 40 and 41); and two chapters from Oceania (Chapters 33 and 38). One chapter in Part 3 (Chapter 40) discusses an anthropological module and its potential for forensic archaeology.

Africa and Asia are also represented in contributions in Part 4 of this volume. Individuals in four additional Asian countries (Israel, Japan, Sri Lanka and Thailand) were approached, but due to a variety of reasons they could not commit to this volume.

Part 4 (Non) Governmental Organisations

Part 4 contains chapters from 15 (non) governmental organisations. Four of these organisations are NGOs that were primarily founded to investigate human rights violations in Latin America: the Argentinian Forensic Anthropology Team (EAAF) (Chapter 43), the Colombian Interdisciplinary Team on Forensic Work and Psychological Assistance (EQUITAS) (Chapter 46), the Peruvian Forensic Anthropology Team (EPAF) (Chapter 52) and the Uruguayan Forensic Archaeology Investigation Group (GIAF) (Chapter 56). One chapter discusses a Chilean governmental organisation, the Medico-Legal Service (SML) (Chapter 45). Two chapters discuss intergovernmental organisations that were primarily founded to examine human rights violations in Europe: the Independent Commission for the Location of Victims Remains (ICLVR) (Chapter 47), and the International Commission on Missing Persons (ICMP) (Chapter 48). Three chapters discuss NGOs that were primarily formed to examine human rights violations in an international context: the International Committee of the Red Cross (ICRC) (Chapter 49), the Inforce foundation (Chapter 50) and the Physicians for Human Rights (PHR) (Chapter 53). One chapter focuses on the human rights violations during the Spanish Civil War (Chapter 55), and one chapter on the human rights violations during and after the Vietnam War (Chapter 57). Three chapters focus on locating, recovery and repatriation of missing military service personnel from past military conflicts. One chapter focuses on Australian military personnel (Chapter 44), one on Portuguese military personnel (Chapter 54) and one on US military personnel (Chapter 51). The last-mentioned chapter discusses the work of a US governmental organisation (JPAC-CIL), with special focus on the use of forensic underwater archaeology.

Individuals in three additional NGOs were approached, but could not be included in this volume due to other commitments or the political situation in their countries.

References

Americas Watch and PHR (Physicians for Human Rights) 1991. *Guatemala: Getting Away With Murder*. New York, Human Rights Publications.

Bass, W.M. and Birkby, W.H. 1978. Exhumation: the method could make the difference. *FBI Law Enforcement Bulletin* 47(7), 6–11.

Bellantoni, N.F. 2005. The bone sleuth. The state archaeologist role in forensic investigation. *News from the Connecticut State Museum of Natural History*, 1–2. Connecticut Archaeology Center, University of Connecticut.

Bellantoni, N.F. and Cooke, D.G. 1996. Criminal investigations: a forensic archaeology case study from Connecticut. *Forensic Archaeology: a Humanistic Science* 19(10), 13–14. US Department of the Interior, CRM Archive Issue.

Bentley, R.A., Maschner, H.D.G. and Chippindale, C. (eds.) 2009. *Handbook of Archaeological Theories*. Plymouth, AltaMira Press.

Bernardi, P. and Fondebrider, L. 2007. Forensic archaeology and the scientific documentation of human rights violations: an Argentinian example from the early 1980s. In R. Ferllini (ed.), *Forensic Archaeology and Human Rights Violations*, 205–232. Springfield, Charles C. Thomas.

Binford, L.R. 1962. Archaeology as anthropology. *American Antiquity* 28, 217–225.

Binford, L.R. 1968. Some comments on historical versus processual archaeology. *Southwestern Journal of Anthropology* 24, 267–275.

Binford, L.R. (ed.) 1977. General introduction. In *For Theory Building in Archaeology: Essays on Faunal Remains, Aquatic Resources, Spatial Analysis, and Systematic Modelling*, 1–10. London, Academic Press.

Binford, L.R. 1981. *Bones: Ancient Man and Modern Myths*. New York, Academic Press.

Binford, S.R. and Binford, L.R. (eds.) 1968. *New Perspectives in Archaeology*. Chicago, Aldine Press.

Blau, S. 2004. Forensic archaeology in Australia: current situations, future possibilities. *Australian Archaeology* 58, 11–58.

Blau, S. 2005. One chance only: advocating the use of archaeology in search, location and recovery at disaster scenes. *The Australian Journal of Emergency Management* 20, 19–24.

Blau, S. and Briggs, C.A. 2011. The role of forensic anthropology in Disaster Victim Identification (DVI). *Forensic Science International* 205, 29–35.

Blau, S. and Fondebrider, F. 2010. Dying for independence: proactive investigations into the 12 November 1991 Santa Cruz massacre, Timor Leste. *The International Journal of Human Rights* 15, 1249–1274.

Blau, S. and Skinner, M. 2005. The use of forensic archaeology in the investigation of human rights abuse: unearthing the past in East Timor. *The International Journal of Human Rights* 9, 449–463.

Blau, S. and Ubelaker, D.H. (eds.) 2009. *Handbook of Forensic Anthropology and Archaeology*. Walnut Creek, Left Coast Press.

Boyd, R.M. 1979. Buried body cases. *FBI Law Enforcement Bulletin* 48(2), 1–7.

Brooks, S.T. and Brooks, R.H. 1984. Problems of burial exhumation, historical and forensic aspects. In T.A. Rathburn and J.E. Buikstra (eds.), *Human Identification: Case Studies in Forensic Anthropology*, 64–86. Springfield, Charles C. Thomas.

Byrd, J.H. and Castner, J.L. (eds.) 2009. *Forensic Entomology: the Utility of Arthropods in Legal Investigation*. 2nd edition. Boca Raton, CRC Press.

Cattaneo, C. 2009. Forensic anthropology and archaeology: perspectives from Italy. In S. Blau and D.H. Ubelaker (eds.), *Handbook of Forensic Anthropology and Archaeology*, 42–48. Walnut Creek, Left Coast Press.

Cerone, J. 2007. The nature of International Criminal Law and implications for investigations. In R. Ferllini (ed.), *Forensic Archaeology and Human Rights Violations*, 24–54. Springfield, Charles C. Thomas.

Chapman, H. 2006. *Landscape Archaeology and GIS*. Stroud, Tempus.

Cheetham, P.N. and Hanson, I. 2009. Excavation and recovery in forensic archaeological investigation. In S. Blau and D.H. Ubelaker (eds.), *Handbook of Forensic Anthropology and Archaeology*, 141–149. Walnut Creek, Left Coast Press.

Christ, T.A.J. 2001. Bad to the bone? Historical archaeologists in the practice of forensic science. *Journal of Historical Archaeology* 35, 39–56.

Cienciala, A.M., Lebedeva, N.S. and Materski, W. 2007. *Katyn: a Crime without Punishment*. New Haven, Yale University Press.

Clarke, D. 1973. Archaeology: the loss of innocence. *Antiquity* 47, 6–18.

Congram, D.R. 2008. A clandestine burial in Costa Rica: prospection and excavation. *Journal of Forensic Sciences* 53, 793–796.

Congram, D. and Sterenberg, J. 2009. Grave challenges in Iraq. In S. Blau and D.H. Ubelaker (eds.), *Handbook of Forensic Anthropology and Archaeology*, 441–453. Walnut Creek, Left Coast Press.

Connor, M.A. 2007. *Forensic Methods: Excavation for the Archaeologist and Investigator*. Lanham, Altamira Press.

Connor, M.A. and Scott, D.D. 2001a. Archaeologists as forensic investigators: defining the role. *Historical Archaeology* 35.

Connor, M.A. and Scott, D.D. 2001b. Paradigms and perpetrators. *Journal of Historical Archaeology* 35, 1–6.

Conolly, J. and Lake, M. 2006. *Geographical Information Systems in Archaeology*. Cambridge, Cambridge University Press.

Cordner, S. and McKelvie, H. 2002. Developing standards in international work to identify missing persons. *International Review of the Red Cross* 848, 867–884.

Cox, M. 1998. Criminal concerns: a plethora of forensic archaeologists. *The Archaeologist* 33, 21–22.

Cox, M. 2009. Forensic anthropology and archaeology: past and present – a United Kingdom perspective. In S. Blau and D.H. Ubelaker (eds.), *Handbook of Forensic Anthropology and Archaeology*, 29–41. Walnut Creek, Left Coast Press.

Cox, M. and Mays, S. 2000. *Human Osteology in Archaeology and Forensic Science*. London, GMM.

Cox, M., Flavel, A., Hanson, I., Laver, J. and Wessling, R. (eds.) 2008. *The Scientific Investigation of Mass Graves. Towards Protocols and Standard Operating Procedures*. Cambridge, Cambridge University Press.

Coyle, H.M. (ed.) 2005. *Forensic Botany. Principles and Applications to Criminal Casework*. Boca Raton, CRC Press.

Crossland, Z. 2000. Buried lives: forensic archaeology and the disappeared in Argentina. *Archaeological Dialogues* 7, 146–159.

Crossland, Z. 2011. The archaeology of contemporary conflict. In T. Insoll (ed.), *The Oxford Handbook of the Archaeology of Ritual and Religion*, 285–306. Oxford, Oxford University Press.

Crossland, Z. 2013. Evidential regimes in forensic archaeology. *Annual Review of Anthropology* 42, 121–137.

Darvill, T. 2002. *The Concise Oxford Dictionary of Archaeology*. Oxford, Oxford University Press.

Dilley, R. 2005. Legal matters. In J.R. Hunter and M. Cox (eds.), *Forensic Archaeology: Advances in Theory and Practice*, 177–203. London, Routledge.

Dirkmaat, D.C. 2002. Recovery and interpretation of the fatal fire victim: the role of forensic anthropology. In W.D. Haglund and M.H. Sorg (eds.), *Advances in Forensic Taphonomy: Methods, Theory, and Archaeological Perspectives*, 451–472. Boca Raton, CRC Press.

Dirkmaat, D.C. 2012a. Documenting context at the outdoor crime scene: why bother? In D.C. Dirkmaat (ed.), *A Companion to Forensic Anthropology*, 48–65. Chichester, Wiley-Blackwell.

Dirkmaat, D.C. 2012b. Forensic anthropology at the mass fatality incident (commercial airliner) crash scene. In D.C. Dirkmaat (ed.), *A Companion to Forensic Anthropology*, 136–156. Chichester, Wiley-Blackwell.

Dirkmaat, D.C. and Adovasio, J.M. 1997. The role of archaeology in the recovery and interpretation of human remains from an outdoor forensic setting. In W.D. Haglund and M.H. Sorg (eds.), *Forensic Taphonomy: The Post-Mortem Fate of Human Remains*, 39–64. Boca Raton, CRC Press.

Dirkmaat, D.C. and Cabo, L.L. 2012. Forensic anthropology: embracing the new paradigm. In D.C. Dirkmaat (ed.), *A Companion to Forensic Anthropology*, 3–40. Chichester, Wiley-Blackwell.

Dirkmaat, D.C. and Hefner, J.T. 2001. Forensic processing of the terrestrial mass fatality scene: testing new search, documentation and recovery methodologies. *Proceedings of the American Academy of Forensic Sciences* 7, 241–242.

Dirkmaat, D.C. and Miller, W. 2003. Scene recovery efforts in Shanksville, Pennsylvania: the role of the Coroner's Office in the processing of the crash site United Airlines Flight 93. *Proceedings of the American Academy of Forensic Sciences* 9, 279.

Dirkmaat, D.C., Cabo, L.L., Adovasio, J.M. and Rozas, V. 2005. *Commingled Remains and the Mass Grave: Considering the Benefits of Forensic Archaeology*. Paper presented at the 57th Annual Meeting of the American Academy of Forensic Sciences, New Orleans, February 21–26.

Dirkmaat, D.C., Cabo, L.L., Ousley, S.D. and Symes, S.A. 2008. New perspectives in forensic anthropology. *Yearbook of Physical Anthropology* 51, 33–52.

Dirkmaat, D.C., Symes, S.A. and Cabo-Perez, L.L. 2010. Forensic archaeological recovery of the victims of the Continental Connection Flight 3407 crash in Clarence Center, NY. *Proceedings of American Academy of Forensic Sciences* 16, 387.

Dirkmaat, D.C., Olson, G.O., Klales, A.R. and Getz, S. 2012. The role of forensic anthropology in the recovery and interpretation of the fatal-fire victim. In D.C. Dirkmaat (ed.), *A Companion to Forensic Anthropology*, 113–135. Chichester, Wiley-Blackwell.

Doretti, M. and Snow, C.C. 2003. Forensic archaeology and human rights: the Argentine experience. In D.W. Steadman (ed.), *Hard Evidence: Case Studies in Forensic Anthropology*, 290–310. New Jersey, Upper Saddle River.

Dragan, A. 1986. *Vinnytsia: a Forgotten Holocaust*. Jersey City, Svoboda Press.

Duncan, J. 1983. Search techniques. In D. Morse, J. Duncan and J. Stoutamire (eds.), *Handbook of Forensic Archaeology and Anthropology*, 4–19. Tallahassee, Rose Printing Company.

EAAF (Equipo Argentino de Antropología Forense) 1992. *EAAF 1992 Annual Report*. Buenos Aires. Available at: http://eaaf.typepad.com/ar_1992/AnnualReport1992.pdf (last accessed 15 February 2014).

EAAF (Equipo Argentino de Antropología Forense) 2000. *EAAF 2000 Annual Report: Kosovo*. Buenos Aires. Available at: http://eaaf.typepad.com/pdf/2000/08Kosovo2000.pdf (last accessed 15 February 2014).

EAFG (Equipo de Antropología Forense de Guatemala) 1993. *Informe de Investigaciones Antropológico Forenses. Aldea Chichupac, Rabinal, Baja Verapax*. Guatemala City, EAFG.

Egaña, S., Turner, S., Doretti, M., Bernardi, P. and Ginarte, A. 2008. Commingled remains and human rights investigations. In B.J. Adams and J.E. Byrd (eds.), *Recovery, Analysis and Identification of Commingled Human Remains*, 57–79. Totowa, Humana Press.

Emanovsky, P.D. and Belcher, W.R. 2012. The many hats of a recovery leader: perspectives on planning and executing worldwide forensic investigations and recoveries at the JPAC Central Identification Laboratory. In D.C. Dirkmaat (ed.), *A Companion to Forensic Anthropology*, 567–592. Chichester, Wiley-Blackwell.

Ferllini, R. 2007. Human rights violations, past and present: consequences and interventions. In R. Ferllini (ed.), *Forensic Archaeology and Human Rights Violations*, 3–23. Springfield, Charles C. Thomas.

Flavel, A. and Barker, C. 2009. Forensic anthropology and archaeology in Guatemala. In S. Blau and D.H. Ubelaker (eds.), *Handbook of Forensic Anthropology and Archaeology*, 426–440. Walnut Creek, Left Coast Press.

Fondebrider, L. 2002. Reflections on the scientific documentation of human rights violations. *International Review of the Red Cross* 84/848, 885–891.

Fondebrider, L. 2009. The applications of forensic anthropology to the investigation of cases of political violence: perspectives from South America. In S. Blau and D.H. Ubelaker (eds.), *Handbook of Forensic Anthropology and Archaeology*, 67–75. Walnut Creek, Left Coast Press.

Fondebrider, L. 2012. The application of forensic anthropology to the investigation of cases of political violence. In D.C. Dirkmaat (ed.), *A Companion to Forensic Anthropology*, 639–648. Chichester, Wiley-Blackwell.

Gassiot Ballbé, E. and Steadman, D.W. 2008. The political, social and scientific contexts of archaeological investigations of mass graves in Spain. *Archaeologies: Journal of the World Archaeological Congress* 4, 429–444.

Gennard, D.E. 2007. *Forensic Entomology: an Introduction*. Chichester, Wiley-Blackwell.

Gojanović, M.D. and Sutlović, D. 2007. Skeletal remains from World War II mass grave: from discovery to identification. *Croatian Medical Journal* 48, 520–527.

Gould, R.A. 2002. WTC archaeology: what we saw, what we learned, and what we did about it. *The SAA Archaeological Record*, November issue, 11–17.

Gould, R.A. 2004. Disaster archaeology at the West Warwick, RI, nightclub fire scene. *The SAA Archaeological Record* 4, 1–7.

Gould, R.A. 2007. *Disaster Archaeology*. Salt Lake City, University of Utah Press.

Gupta, N. 2013. Local communities, national governments and forensic and archaeological investigations of human right violations. *Archaeologies: Journal of the World Archaeological Congress* 9(1), 106–131.

Haglund, W.D. 2001. Archaeology and forensic death investigations. *Journal of Historical Archaeology* 35, 26–34.

Haglund, W.D. 2002. Recent mass graves: an introduction. In W.D. Haglund and M.H. Sorg (eds.), *Advances in Forensic Taphonomy: Methods, Theory, and Archaeological Perspectives*, 243–261. Boca Raton, CRC Press.

Haglund, W.D., Connor, M. and Scott, D.D. 2001. The archaeology of contemporary mass graves. *Journal of Historical Archaeology* 35, 57–69.

Hall, D.W. and Byrd, J.H. 2012. *Forensic Botany: a Practical Guide*. Chichester, Wiley-Blackwell.

Hanson, I. 2008. Forensic Archaeology: approaches to international investigations. In M. Oxenham (ed.), *Forensic Approaches to Death, Disaster and Abuse*, 17–28. Bowen Hills, Australian Academic Press.

Harris, E.C. 1989. *Principles of Archaeological Stratigraphy*. 2nd edition. London, Academic Press.

Henneberg, M. 2009. The expert witness and the court of law. In S. Blau and D.H. Ubelaker (eds.), *Handbook of Forensic Anthropology and Archaeology*, 490–494. Walnut Creek, Left Coast Press.

Hochrein, M. 2012. Crime scene perspective: collecting evidence in the context of the criminal incident. In D.C. Dirkmaat (ed.), *A Companion to Forensic Anthropology*, 101–112. Chichester, Wiley-Blackwell.

Hodder, I. 1982a. *Symbols in Action. Ethnoarchaeological Studies in Material Culture*. Cambridge, Cambridge University Press.

Hodder, I. (ed.) 1982b. *Symbolic and Structural Archaeology*. Cambridge, Cambridge University Press.

Hodder, I. 1983. *The Present Past: an Introduction to Anthropology for Archaeologists*. New York, Pica Press.

Hodder, I. 1985. Postprocessual archaeology. In M.B. Schiffer (ed.), *Advances in Archaeological Method and Theory: Volume 8*, 1–26. New York, Academic Press.

Hodder, I. 1991. *Reading the Past: Current Approaches to Interpretation in Archaeology*. 2nd edition. Cambridge, Cambridge University Press.

Holland, T.D. and Connell, S.V. 2009. The search for and detection of human remains. In S. Blau and D.H. Ubelaker (eds.), *Handbook of Forensic Anthropology and Archaeology*, 129–140. Walnut Creek, Left Coast Press.

Holland, T.D. and Mann, R.W. 1996. Forensic aviation archaeology: finding and recovering America's MIA remains. *Cultural Resource Management* 19, 29–31.

Holland, T.D., Anderson, B.E. and Mann, R.W. 2002. Human variables in the postmortem alteration of human bone: examples from U.S. war casualties. In W.D. Haglund and M.H. Sorg (eds.), *Advances in Forensic Taphonomy: Method, Theory, and Archaeological Perspectives*, 262–273. Boca Raton, CRC Press.

Hoshower, L.M. 1998. Forensic archaeology and the need for flexible excavation strategies: a case study. *Journal of Forensic Sciences* 43, 53–56.

Hunter, J.R. 2002. Foreword: a pilgrim in forensic archaeology – a personal view. In W.D. Haglund and M.H. Sorg (eds.), *Advances in Forensic Taphonomy: Methods, Theory, and Archaeological Perspectives*, xxv–xxxii. Boca Raton, CRC Press.

Hunter, J.R. 2009. Domestic homicide investigations in the United Kingdom. In S. Blau and D.H. Ubelaker (eds.), *Handbook of Forensic Anthropology and Archaeology*, 363–373. Walnut Creek, Left Coast Press.

Hunter, J.R. and Cox, M. (eds.) 2005. *Forensic Archaeology: Advances in Theory and Practice*. London, Routledge.

Hunter, J.R. and Knupfer, G.C. 1996. The police and judicial structure in Britain. In J.R. Hunter, C. Roberts and A. Martin (eds.), *Studies in Crime: an Introduction to Forensic Archaeology*, 24–39. London, B.T. Batsford.

Hunter, J.R., Heron, C., Janaway, R.C., Martin, A.L., Pollard, A.M. and Roberts, C.A. 1994. Forensic archaeology in Britain. *Antiquity* 68, 758–769.

Hunter, J.R., Roberts, C. and Martin, A. (eds.) 1996. *Studies in Crime: an Introduction to Forensic Archaeology*. London, B.T. Batsford.

Hunter, J.R., Brickley, M.B., Bourgeois, J., Bouts, W., Bourguignon, L., Hubrecht, F., De Winne, J., van Haaster, H., Hakbijl, T., de Jong, H., Smits, L., van Wijngaarden, L.H. and Lüschen, M. 2001. Forensic archaeology, forensic anthropology and human rights in Europe. *Science & Justice* 41, 173–178.

Hunter, J.R., Simpson, B. and Sturdy Colls, C. 2013. *Forensic Approaches to Buried Remains*. Chichester, Wiley Blackwell.

Imaizumi, M. 1974. Locating buried bodies. *FBI Law Enforcement Bulletin* 43(8), 2–5.

İşcan, M.Y. 1981. Concepts in teaching forensic anthropology. *Medical Anthropology Newsletter* 13, 10–12.

Jankauskas, R., Barkus, A., Urbanavičius, V. and Garmus, A. 2005. Forensic archaeology in Lithuania: the Tuskulėnai mass grave. *Acta Medica Lituanica* 12, 70–74.

Jessee, E. and Skinner, M. 2005. A typology of mass grave and mass grave-related sites. *Forensic Science International* 152, 55–59.

Johnson, M. 2010. *Archaeological Theory: an Introduction*. 2nd edition. Oxford, Wiley-Blackwell.

Joyce, C. and Stover, E. 1991. *Witnesses from the Grave*. Boston, Little Brown.

Juhl, K. 2005. *The Contribution of (forensic) Archaeologists to Human Rights Investigation of Mass Graves*. AmS-NETT 5, Museum of Archaeology, Stavanger. Available at: http://am.uis.no/getfile.php/Arkeologisk%20museum/publikasjoner/ams-nett/Mass_Graves2.pdf (last accessed 15 February 2014).

Juhl, K. and Olsen, O.E. 2006. Social safety, archaeology and the investigation of contemporary mass graves. *Journal of Genocide Research* 8, 411–435.

Kamenetsky, I. (ed.) 1989. *The Tragedy of Vinnytsia: Materials on Stalin's Policy of Extermination in Ukraine 1936–1938*. New York, Ukrainian Historical Association.

Kerley, E.R. 1978. Recent developments in forensic anthropology. *Yearbook of Physical Anthropology* 21, 160–173.

Klonowski, E. 2007. Forensic anthropology in Bosnia and Herzegovina: theory and practice amidst politics and egos. In R. Ferllini (ed.), *Forensic Archaeology and Human Rights Violations*, 148–169. Springfield, Charles C. Thomas.

Kola, A. 2005. *Archeologia Zbrodni. Oficerowie Polscy Na Cmentarzu Ofiar NKWD W Charkowie*. Toruń, Wydawnictwo Uniwersytetu Mikołaja Kopernika w Toruniu.

Komar, D.A. and Buikstra, J.E. 2008. *Forensic Anthropology. Contemporary Theory and Practice*. New York, Oxford University Press.

Kranioti, E.F. and Paine, R.R. 2011. Forensic anthropology in Europe: an assessment of current status and application. *Journal of Anthropological Sciences* 89, 71–92.

Krogman, W.M. 1943a. Role of a physical anthropologist in the identification of human skeletal remains, I. *FBI Law Enforcement Bulletin* 12(4), 17–40.

Krogman, W.M. 1943b. Role of a physical anthropologist in the identification of human skeletal remains, II. *FBI Law Enforcement Bulletin* 12(5), 12–28.

Larson, D.O., Vass, A.A. and Wise, M. 2011. Advanced scientific methods and procedures in the forensic investigation of clandestine graves. *Journal of Contemporary Criminal Justice* 27, 149–182.

Lovis, W.A. 1992. Forensic anthropology as mortuary anthropology. *Social Science & Medicine* 34, 113–117.

Mann, R.W., Anderson, B.E., Holland, T.D., Rankin, D.R. and Webb, J.E. 2003. Unusual 'crime' scenes: the role of forensic anthropology in recovering and identifying American MIAs. In D.W. Steadman (ed.), *Hard Evidence: Case Studies in Forensic Anthropology*, 108–116. New Jersey, Upper Saddle River.

Mant, A.K. 1950. A study in exhumation-data. MD Thesis, University of London.

Mant, A.K. 1987. Knowledge acquired from post-war exhumations. In A. Boddington, A.N. Garland and R.C. Janaway (eds.), *Death, Decay and Reconstruction: Approaches to Archaeology and Forensic Science*, 65–78. Manchester, Manchester University Press.

Mark, J. 2010. What remains? Anti-communism, forensic archaeology, and the retelling of the national past in Lithuania and Romania. *Past and Present* 206(Supplement 5), 276–300.

Márquez-Grant, N., Litherland, S. and Roberts, J. 2012. European perspectives on the role of the forensic archaeologist in the UK. In D.C. Dirkmaat (ed.), *A Companion to Forensic Anthropology*, 598–625. Chichester, Wiley-Blackwell.

McDonald, J.J. and Ross, A.C. 1990. Helping the police with their enquiries: archaeology and politics at Angophora reserve rock shelter, N.S.W. *Archaeology and Oceania* 25, 114–121.

McLaughlin, J.E. 1974. *The Detection of Buried Remains*. Yuba City, Study of Andermac.

Menez, L.L. 2005. The place of a forensic archaeologist at a crime scene involving a buried body. *Forensic Science International* 152, 311–315.

Middle East Watch and PHR (Physicians for Human Rights) 1992. *Unquiet Graves. The Search for the Disappeared in Iraqi Kurdistan*. New York, Human Rights Publications.

Middle East Watch and PHR (Physicians for Human Rights) 1993. *The Anfal Campaign in Iraqi Kurdistan*. New York, Human Rights Publications.

Miller, D. and Tilley, C. (eds.) 1984. *Ideology, Power, and Prehistory*. Cambridge, Cambridge University Press.

Morse, D. 1983. Introduction. In D. Morse, J. Duncan and J. Stoutamire (eds.), *Handbook of Forensic Archaeology and Anthropology*, 1–3. Tallahassee, Rose Printing Company.

Morse, D., Crusoe, D. and Smith, H.G. 1976. Forensic archaeology. *Journal of Forensic Sciences* 21, 323–332.

Morse, D., Duncan, J. and Stoutamire, J. (eds.) 1983. *Handbook of Forensic Archaeology and Anthropology*. Tallahassee, Rose Printing Company.

Morse, D., Dailey, R.C., Stoutamire, J. and Duncan, J. 1984. Forensic archaeology. In T.A. Rathburn and J.E. Buikstra (eds.), *Human Identification: Case Studies in Forensic Anthropology*, 53–64. Springfield, Charles C. Thomas.

Mundorff, A.Z. 2012. Integrating forensic anthropology into Disaster Victim Identification. *Forensic Science, Medicine, and Pathology* 8, 131–139.

Nawrocki, S.P., Schmidt, C.W., Williamson, M. and Reinhardt, G. 1998. Excavation and analysis of human remains from the Fox Hollow serial homicide site, Hamilton County, Indiana. *Proceedings of American Academy of Forensic Sciences* 4, 205–206.

Neamţu, M. and Ţînţariu, A.-L. 2010. *5 Years of Activity. The Institute for the Investigation of Communist Crimes and for the Memory of the Romanian Exile*. Bucharest, IICCMER. Available at: http://www.iiccr.ro/index.html/about_iiccr/5_years_of_activity/?lang=en&section=about_iiccr/5_years_of_activity (last accessed 20 February 2014).

Oakley, K. 2005. Forensic archaeology and anthropology: an Australian perspective. *Forensic Science, Medicine, and Pathology* 1, 169–172.

Owsley, D.W. 2001. Why forensic anthropologist needs the archaeologist. *Journal of Historical Archaeology* 35, 35–38.

Owsley, D.W., Strinović, D., Šlaus, M., Kollmann, D.D. and Richardson, M.L. 1996. Recovery and identification of civilian victims of war in Croatia. *Forensic Archaeology: a Humanistic Science* 19(10), 33–36. US Department of the Interior, CRM Archive.

Palo, J.U., Hedman, M., Söderholm, N. and Sajantila, A. 2007. Repatriation and identification of Finish World War II soldiers. *Croatian Medical Journal* 48, 528–535.

PHR (Physicians for Human Rights) 1993. *Report of a Preliminary Site Exploration of a Mass Grave near Vukovar, Former Yugoslavia*. Boston, PHR.

PHR (Physicians for Human Rights) 1994. *Report of a Preliminary Medicolegal Investigation of a Series of Clandestine Graves near Pakracka Poljana, Former Yugoslavia*. Boston, PHR.

PHR (Physicians for Human Rights) 1996. *Report of a Preliminary Site Exploration of a Mass Grave near Vukovar, Former Yugoslavia*. Boston, PHR.

Pirrie, D. Rufferl, A. and Dawson, L.A. (eds.) 2013. *Environmental and Criminal Geoforensics*. Bath, Geological Society Special Publication 384.

Poirier, D.A. and Bellantoni, N.F. 1996. Forensic archaeology: a humanistic science. *Forensic Archaeology: a Humanistic Science* 19(10), 3–4. US Department of the Interior, CRM Archive.

Pollock, S. 2008. Archaeology as a means for pace or a source of violence? An introduction. *Archaeologies: Journal of the World Archaeological Congress* 4(3), 356–367.

Powers, N. and Sibun, L. 2013. Forensic archaeology. In P. Graves-Brown, R. Harrison and A. Piccini (eds.), *The Oxford Handbook of the Archaeology of the Contemporary World*, 40–53. Oxford, Oxford University Press.

Prentice, G. 2006. The archaeological damage assessment report. In S. Hutt, M.P. Forsyth and D. Tarler (eds.), *Presenting Archaeology in Court. Legal Strategies for Protecting Cultural Resources*, 85–106. Oxford, Altamira Press.

Pye, K. 2007. *Geological and Soil Evidence. Forensic Applications*. Boca Raton, CRC Press.

Rainio, J., Lalu, K. and Sajantila, A. 2007. International forensic investigations: legal framework, organisation, and performance. In R. Ferllini (ed.), *Forensic Archaeology and Human Rights Violations*, 55–75. Springfield, Charles C. Thomas.

Rainwater, C.W., Crowder, C., Hartnett, K.M., Fridie, J.S., Figura, B.J., Godbold, J., Warnasch, S.C. and Adams, B.J. 2012. Forensic anthropology at the New York City Office of Chief Medical Examiner. In D.C. Dirkmaat (ed.), *A Companion to Forensic Anthropology*, 549–566. Chichester, Wiley-Blackwell.

Raszeja, S. and Chróścielewski, E. 1994. Medicolegal reconstruction of the Katyn Forest massacre. *Forensic Science International* 68, 1–6.

Rebmann, A., David, E. and Sorg, M.H. 2000. *Cadaver Dog Handbook. Forensic Training and Tactics for the Recovery of Human Remains*. Boca Raton, CRC Press.

Reinecke, G.W. and Hochrein, M.J. 2008. Pieces of the puzzle: FBI evidence response team approaches to scenes with commingled evidence. In B.J. Adams and J.E. Byrd (eds.), *Recovery, Analysis and Identification of Commingled Human Remains*, 31–55. Totowa, Humana Press.

Ruffell, A. and McKinley, J. 2008. *Geoforensics*. Chichester, Wiley-Blackwell.

Sauer, N.J., Lovis, W., Blumer, M.E. and Fillion, J. 2003. The contributions of archaeology and physical anthropology to the John McRae case. In D.W. Steadman (ed.), *Hard Evidence: Case Studies in Forensic Anthropology*, 117–126. New Jersey, Upper Saddle River.

Schiffer, M.B. 1972. Archaeological context and systemic context. *American Antiquity* 37, 156–165.

Schiffer, M.B. 1976. *Behavioural Archaeology*. New York, Academic Press.

Schiffer, M.B. 1983. Toward the identification of formation process. *American Antiquity* 48, 675–706.

Schiffer, M.B. 1987. *Formation Process of the Archaeological Record.* Albuquerque, University of New Mexico Press.

Schmitt, S. 2002. Mass graves and the collection of forensic evidence: genocide, war crimes, and crimes against humanity. In W.D. Haglund and M.H. Sorg (eds.), *Advances in Forensic Taphonomy: Methods, Theory, and Archaeological Perspectives,* 277–292. Boca Raton, CRC Press.

Scott, D.D. 2001. Firearms identification in support of identifying a mass execution at El Mozote, El Salvador. *Journal of Historical Archaeology* 35, 79–86.

Scott, D.D. and Connor, M. 1997. Context delicti: archaeological context in forensic work. In W.D. Haglund and M.H. Sorg (eds.), *Forensic Taphonomy: the Postmortem Fate of Human Remains,* 27–38. Boca Raton, CRC Press.

Scott, D.D. and Connor, M. 2001. The role and future of archaeology in forensic science. *Journal of Historical Archaeology* 35, 101–104.

Shanks, M. and Tilley, C. 1987a. *Re-Constructing Archaeology.* Cambridge, Cambridge University Press.

Shanks, M. and Tilley, C. 1987b. *Social Theory and Archaeology.* Cambridge, Polity Press.

Sigler-Eisenberg, B. 1985. Forensic research: explaining the concept of applied archaeology. *American Antiquity* 50, 650–655.

Skinner, M. 1987. Planning the archaeological recovery of evidence from mass graves. *Forensic Science International* 34, 267–287.

Skinner, M. 2007. Hapless in Afghanistan: forensic archaeology in political maelstrom. In R. Ferllini (ed.), *Forensic Archaeology and Human Rights Violations,* 233–265. Springfield, Charles C. Thomas.

Skinner, M. and Bowie, K. 2009. Forensic anthropology: Canadian content and contributions. In S. Blau and D.H. Ubelaker (eds.), *Handbook of Forensic Anthropology and Archaeology,* 87–103. Walnut Creek, Left Coast Press.

Skinner, M. and Lazenby, R.A. 1983. *Found! Human Remains: A Field Manual for the Recovery of the Recent Human Skeleton.* Burnaby, Archaeology Press.

Skinner, M. and Sterenberg, J. 2005. Turf wars: authority and responsibility for the investigation of mass graves. *Forensic Science International* 151, 221–232.

Skinner, M., York, H.P. and Connor, M.A. 2002. Postburial disturbance of graves in Bosnia-Herzegovina. In W.D. Haglund and M.H. Sorg (eds.), *Advances in Forensic Taphonomy: Methods, Theory, and Archaeological Perspectives,* 293–308. Boca Raton, CRC Press.

Skinner, M., Alempijevic, D. and Djuric-Serejic, M. 2003. Guidelines for international forensic bio-archaeology monitors of mass grave exhumations. *Forensic Science International* 134, 81–92.

Sledzik, P.S. 1996. Federal resources in mass disaster response. *Cultural Resources Management* 19, 19–20.

Sledzik, P.S. 2009. Forensic anthropology in disaster response. In S. Blau and D.H. Ubelaker (eds.), *Handbook of Forensic Anthropology and Archaeology,* 374–387. Walnut Creek, Left Coast Press.

Sledzik, P.S., Miller, W., Dirkmaat, D.C., de Jong, D.L., Kauffman, P.J., Boyer, D.A. and Hellman, F.P. 2003. Victim identification following the crash of United Airlines Flight 93. *Proceedings of the American Academy of Forensic Sciences* 9, 195–196.

Sledzik, P.S., Dirkmaat, D., Mann, R., Holland, T., Mundorff, A.Z., Adams, B., Crowder, C. and De Paolo, F. 2009. Disaster victim recovery and identification: forensic anthropology in the aftermath of September 11. In D.W. Steadman (ed.), *Hard Evidence: Case Studies in Forensic Anthropology.* 2nd edition, 289–302. Upper Saddle River, Prentice Hall.

Snow, C.C. 1982. Forensic anthropology. *Annual Review of Anthropology* 11, 97–131.

Snow, C.C. 2011. *Letter to Dr D.C. Dirkmaat Regarding the Proposal to Change the Name of the AAFS Forensic Anthropology Section, 29 July 2011.* Available at: http://panthsectionnamechange.wordpress.com/a-letter-by-clyde-snow/ (last accessed 15 February 2014).

Snow, C.C., Levine, L., Lukash, L.G., Tedeschi, C., Orrego, C. and Stover, E. 1984. The investigation of the human remains of the 'disappeared' in Argentina. *American Journal of Forensic Medicine and Pathology* 5, 297–299.

Sorg, M.H. and Haglund, W.D. 2002. Advancing forensic taphonomy: purpose, theory, and process. In W.D. Haglund and M.H. Sorg (eds.), *Advances in Forensic Taphonomy: Methods, Theory, and Archaeological Perspectives,* 3–29. Boca Raton, CRC Press.

Spennemann, D.H.R. and Franke, B. 1995. Archaeological techniques for exhumations: a unique data source for Crime Scene Investigation. *Forensic Science International* 74, 5–15.

Stallibrass, S. 2000. AEA 1993 Conference at Durham: editorial. In J.P. Huntley and S. Stallibrass (eds.), *Taphonomy and Interpretation: Symphosia of the Association for Environmental Archaeology No. 14,* v–vii. Oxford, Oxbow Books.

Steadman, D.W. and Haglund, W.D. 2005. The scope of anthropological contribution to human right investigations. *Journal of Forensic Sciences* 50, 23–30.

Steadman, D.W., Sperry, K., Snow, F., Fulginiti, L. and Craig, E. 2008. Anthropological investigations of the Tri-State Crematorium incident. In B.J. Adams and J.E. Byrd (eds.), *Recovery, Analysis and Identification of Commingled Human Remains,* 81–96. Totowa, Humana Press.

Steadman, D.W., Basler, W., Hochrein, M.J., Klein, D.F. and Goodin, J.C. 2009. Domestic homicide investigations: an example from the United States. In S. Blau and D.H. Ubelaker (eds.), *Handbook of Forensic Anthropology and Archaeology,* 351–362. Walnut Creek, Left Coast Press.

Steele, C. 2008. Archaeology and the forensic investigation of recent mass graves: ethical issues for a new practice of archaeology. *Archaeologies: Journal of the World Archaeological Congress* 4, 414–428.

Sterenberg, J. 2009. Dealing with the remains of conflict: an international response to crimes against humanity, forensic recovery, identification, and repatriation in the former Yugoslavia. In S. Blau and D.H. Ubelaker (eds.), *Handbook of Forensic Anthropology and Archaeology,* 416–425. Walnut Creek, Left Coast Press.

Stoutamire, J. 1983. Excavation and recovery. In D. Morse, J. Duncan and J. Stoutamire (eds.), *Handbook of Forensic Archaeology and Anthropology,* 20–47. Tallahassee, Rose Printing Company.

Stover, E. and Manuel, A. 1991. *Guatemala: Getting Away With Murder.* New York, Americas Watch and PHR.

Stover, E. and Peress, G. 1998. *The Graves: Srebrenica and Vukovar.* New York, Scalo.

Stover, E. and Ryan, M. 2001. Breaking bread with the dead. *Journal of Historical Archaeology* 35, 7–25.

Stover, E. and Shigekane, R. 2002. The Missing in the aftermath: when do the needs of victims' families and international war crimes tribunal clash? *International Review of the Red Cross* 848, 845–866.

Tibbett, M. and Carter, D.O. (eds.) 2008. *Soil Analysis in Forensic Taphonomy: Chemical and Biological Effects of Buried Human Remains*. Boca Raton, CRC Press.

Trigger, B. 1989. *A History of Archaeological Thought*. Cambridge, Cambridge University Press.

Tuller, H.H. 2012. Mass graves and human rights: latest developments, methods, and lessons learned. In D.C. Dirkmaat (ed.), *A Companion to Forensic Anthropology*, 157–174. Chichester, Wiley-Blackwell.

Tuller, H.H. and Durić, M. 2006. Keeping the pieces together: comparison of mass grave excavation methodology. *Forensic Science International* 156, 192–200.

Ubelaker, D.H. 2009. Historical development of forensic anthropology: perspectives from the United States. In S. Blau and D.H. Ubelaker (eds.), *Handbook of Forensic Anthropology and Archaeology*, 76–86. Walnut Creek, Left Coast Press.

Ubelaker, D.H. and Rife, J. 2008. Approaches to commingling issues in archaeological samples: a case study from Roman era tombs in Greece. In B.J. Adams and J.E. Byrd (eds.), *Recovery, Analysis, and Identification of Commingled Human Remains*, 97–122. Totowa, Humana Press.

Ubelaker, D.H., Owsley, D.W., Houck, M.M., Craig, E., Grant, W., Woltanski, T., Fram, R., Sandness, K. and Peerwani, N. 1995. The role of forensic anthropology in the recovery and analysis of Branch Davidian compound victims. *Journal of Forensic Sciences* 40, 335–340.

Waterhouse, K. 2009. *The Use of Archaeological and Anthropological Methods in Fatal Fire Scene Investigations*. Defence Research and Development Canada Centre for Security Science, Canadian Police Research Centre, Document no: DRDC CSS TN 2009-04.

Watson, P.J., LeBlanc, S.A. and Redman, C.R. 1971. *Explanations in Archaeology: an Explicitly Scientific Approach*. New York, Columbia University Press.

Webster, A.D. 1998. Excavations of a Vietnam-era aircraft crash site: use of cross-cultural understanding and dual forensic recovery methods. *Journal of Forensic Sciences* 43, 277–283.

Williams, E.D. and Crews, J.D. 2003. From dust to dust: ethical and practical issues involved in the location, exhumation, and identification of bodies from mass graves. *Croatian Medical Journal* 44, 251–258.

Wood, W.R. and Stanley, L.A. 1989. Recovery and identification of World War II dead: American grave registration activities in Europe. *Journal of Forensic Sciences* 34, 1365–1373.

Wright, R., 1995. Investigating war crimes: the archaeological evidence. *The Sidney Papers* 7, 39–44.

Wright, R. 2010. Where are the bodies? In the ground. *The Public Historian* 32, 96–107.

Wright, R., Hanson, I. and Sterenberg, J. 2005. The archaeology of mass graves. In J.R. Hunter and M. Cox (eds.), *Forensic Archaeology: Advances in Theory and Practice*, 137–158. London, Routledge.

Zarankin, A. and Funari, P.P.A. 2008. 'Eternal sunshine of the spotless mind': archaeology and construction of memory of military repression in South America (1960–1980). *Archaeologies: Journal of the World Archaeological Congress* 4(2), 310–327.

PART 1
Europe

CHAPTER 1

Forensic archaeology and anthropology in Austria

Fabian Kanz[1] and Jan Cemper-Kiesslich[2]

[1] *Department of Forensic Medicine, Medical University of Vienna, Austria*

[2] *Interfaculty Department of Legal Medicine, University of Salzburg, Austria*

Introduction

In general, archaeological disciplines are closely linked to the local historical, climatic and geographical conditions within the area of research. This is especially true for forensic archaeology, including aspects of the legal system and crime statistics such as the number of missing persons or murder cases. This chapter gives an overview of Austria's geographical and legal characteristics with regard to forensic archaeological and closely related anthropological works, the educational institutions involved and future perspectives.

Overview of Austria

Austria is a federal Republic with an area of 83,879 km^2. It is divided into nine administrative states called *Bundesländer*. The country is landlocked and is geographically situated in Central Europe with borders to the Czech Republic, Germany, Hungary, Italy, Lichtenstein, Slovakia, Slovenia and Switzerland. The country is mountainous, with the Alps occupying about 60% of the territory, and about 43% of Austria is forested. Two-thirds of Austria (68%) is located higher than 500 m above sea level. The climate is characterised by distinct seasons, with an overall temperature between 8 and 10 °C in the most populated areas. Austria has a population of approximately 8.5 million, an average of around 100 people per square kilometer, with more than a quarter of the whole population concentrated around the capital Vienna, which hosts all the federal authorities. Additional agglomerations are found around the cities of Linz and Graz, the Inn valley and the Rhine valley to the west of the country.[1]

The legal framework affecting forensic archaeology and anthropology

The intersection of five federal bodies forms the framework of forensic archaeology and anthropology: the police, attached to the Federal Ministry of the Interior (*Bundesministerium für Inneres*), the prosecution and sworn-in experts from the Federal Ministry of Justice (*Bundesministerium für Justiz*), the Federal Monuments Office (*Bundesdenkmalamt*) of the Federal Ministry of Education, the Arts and Culture Ministry (*Bundesministerium für Unterricht, Kunst und Kultur*) and the Federal Ministry of Science and Research (*Bundesministerium für Wissenschaft und Forschung*). The regulations of federal laws and state laws in the nine federal states of Austria affect work in this new field.

Federal laws include the criminal code, which regulates criminal procedures and autopsy regulations for the coroner's inquest. Additional federal laws affecting the work of forensic archaeologists and anthropologists in Austria are the Austrian state or independence treaty (*Staatsvertrag betreffend die Wiederherstellung eines unabhängigen und demokratischen Österreich; Vienna, May 15 1955*), which regulates the procedures on war graves, and also the Monument Protections Act (*Denkmalschutzgesetz*), which defines archaeological sites. These federal laws are supplemented by the civil code, which respects the landowner's rights.[2,3]

Because of the federal system with the division into states there are additionally nine state laws dealing with different corpse and burial regulations.

In Austrian law there is a particular system of sworn-in experts, the so-called *Allgemein beeideter und gerichtlich zertifizierter Sachverständiger*,[4] who can be called in by the

[1]For more information, see: http://www.statistik.at/ (last accessed October 2013).

[2]For more information, see: http://www.justiz.gv.at (last accessed October 2013).

[3]For more information, see: http://www.ris.bka.gv.at (last accessed October 2013).

[4]For more information, see: http://www.sachverstaendige.at/ (last accessed October 2013).

Forensic Archaeology: A Global Perspective, First Edition. Edited by W.J. Mike Groen, Nicholas Márquez-Grant and Robert C. Janaway.

prosecutor if police forces do not have the expertise to complete the investigation by themselves. These sworn-in experts have to fulfil several requirements, including 10 years of experience in the field, trustworthiness, equipment and expertise verified by a court examination executed by two experts and a judge. If they fulfil these requirements, they will be sworn in by the court and their names will be published in a public list of experts by the Ministry of Justice.[5] At the moment there are four sworn-in archaeological experts on this list, but none for forensic archaeology and just one sworn-in expert for forensic anthropology (the first author).

Forensic archaeology and anthropology in Austria

Forensic archaeology

To our knowledge there is only one group in Austria dealing with forensic archaeology, the Study Group Forensic Archaeology (*Arbeitskreis Forensische Archäologie*).[6] This group is associated with the Institute of Prehistory and Historic Archaeology (*Institut für Urgeschichte und Historische Archäologie*) at the University of Vienna. This institute also has a unit working on modern archaeology. The study group was founded in 2005 by Mr Peter Pesseg and Mr Thomas Pototschnig, and focuses predominantly on the search and recovery of World War II (WWII) mass graves, namely in Rechnitz in the state of Burgenland.

Forensic anthropology

In Austria forensic anthropology as a discipline was introduced for the first time in 2010 in the Department of Forensic Medicine (*Department für Gerichtsmedizin*) at the Medical University of Vienna; however, a unit for physical anthropology was established in the department as early as 1958.

Forensic archaeology and anthropology within the police

Austrian police can be subdivided into Municipal Police Forces (*Gemeindesicherheitswache*) and the Federal Police Force (*Bundespolizei*), which is subdivided into nine administrative state commands. There are no official forensic archaeologists or anthropologists employed in these police forces. In the curricula of the Police Academies as well there are no archaeologists or anthropologists involved in teaching or training. The same is true for the curricula of Austrian forensic pathologists (*Facharzt für Gerichtsmedizin*). Austrian Federal Police students get an introduction and a guideline as to how to work forensically at a crime scene. They are taught photography, photogrammetry and how to measure and draw crime scenes to create an evidence report. There is a standardised evidence report form used by Austrian police forces so that every policeman would be able to document non-complex crime scenes. For more complex crime scenes the Austrian Federal Police force has its own specialised Scene of Crime units (*Tatortgruppen*). These small groups, which generally perform the searches for clandestine burials and subsequent exhumations, consist, very often, of highly motivated policemen who are interested in extending their knowledge of archaeology and anthropology. They try to do so with self-study or external educational programmes. There are varying levels of knowledge of archaeological skills within these groups, since they are not taught at the police schools. Therefore groups in Vienna seek to compensate the lack of professional archaeological teaching programmes with a few former archaeologists who are currently finishing their regular police-training programme.

Institutions connected to (forensic) archaeological and anthropology research

Five Austrian institutions are involved with (forensic) archaeological and anthropological research:

- The Federal Monuments Office (*Bundesdenkmalamt* (BDA)),[7] which has dependencies in most Austrian states and monitors the National Monument Protection Act. The BDA decides about excavation permits for archaeological sites and runs an archaeological site cadastre including the former graveyards and cemeteries in Austria. The BDA recently developed guidelines for excavations[8] where human remains have been found or are expected. These guidelines demand that an anthropologist or an anthropologically trained archaeologist accompany such excavations.
- The Austrian Black Cross (*Österreichisches Schwarzes Kreuz* (ÖSK))[9] was founded in 1919 and represents the Austrian War Graves Commission (*Kriegsgräberfürsorge*), which takes care of the graves and memorials of WWI and WWII soldiers of all nations who died within the borders of Austria.
- The Vienna Institute for Archaeological Science (VIAS)[10] is an interdisciplinary research platform for Archaeological Science at the University of

[5]For more information, see: http://www.sdgliste.justiz.gv.at (last accessed October 2013).
[6]For more information, see: http://www.akforensik.at (last accessed October 2013).
[7]For more information, see: http://www.bda.at/ (last accessed October 2013).
[8]For more information, see: http://www.bda.at/downloads/1990/Richtlinien (last accessed October 2013).
[9]For more information, see: http://www.osk.at/ (last accessed October 2013).
[10]For more information, see: http://vias.univie.ac.at/ (last accessed October 2013).

Vienna which consists of several laboratories. The unit for Geophysical Prospection, Geodesy and Photogrammetry is an institution recognised as outstanding in the development of new large-scale prospection possibilities.

- The Centre of Archaeometry and Applied Molecular Archaeology Salzburg (CAMAS)[11] was established in order to offer a joint regulated and directed procedure whenever osseous human remains are discovered during an archaeological or historical excavation, with a special focus on the synoptic evaluation of physical anthropology, ancient DNA data and radiological images in conjunction with the conventional archaeological record.
- The Vienna Environmental Research Accelerator (VERA)[12] is an institution at the University of Vienna which hosts an accelerator mass spectrometry (AMS) facility (particle accelerator) for ^{14}C radiocarbon dating. VERA was strongly involved in the development of the 'bomb peak' dating technique for the estimation of post-mortem interval for post-WWII skeletonised human remains (Wild et al. 2000).

The demand for forensic anthropology and archaeology investigations

About 75,000 Austrians die each year, and in 1,300 cases the prosecutors request a legal autopsy to clarify whether third-party negligence can be excluded.[13] In the majority of cases the autopsies take place in one of the four Austrian Institutions for Forensic Medicine, in Innsbruck, Graz, Salzburg or Vienna. The authors can exclude about two-thirds (800–900 per year) of these investigations because they are conducted at their Institutes in Salzburg-Linz and Vienna.

Every year about 100–150 attempted murders are reported to the police, approximately 50 of them involving a murdered person. There are about 10 unidentified bodies each year, in addition to about 15 cases represented by skeletonised remains. Additionally, in 2012, 34 people were reported missing in Austria from the previous 5 to 10 years and another 33 individuals had been missing for more than 10 years.[14] The authors assume that the Central Federal Registration System and health and social insurance IDs are responsible for this comparatively low number of missing and unidentified persons. Usually the police forces are successful in identifying the areas to be searched for a missing person and, in the case of a fatality, ascertaining the identity of unknown remains found. Furthermore, due to the individual social insurance ID, which is recorded at each contact with the Austrian health care system (visit and treatment), it is simple to use medical recordings, such as computed tomography (CT) scans or dental panoramic radiographs, for identification. To our best knowledge we can estimate the demand for classic forensic archaeological investigations (excavations) to be about five to ten cases per year in which human remains have been buried subsurface.

The applied investigation flow for buried and surface skeletonised remains

We can only report on the protocols used at the Departments for Forensic Medicine in Vienna and Salzburg. If the police are called to a reported crime scene with the potential of discovering human remains, they frequently ask the federal BDA for assistance during ground preparation for building construction. The BDA sends an archaeologist who is familiar with the archaeological situation at the site and who may be able to comment on the date of the remains. If the finding place is not registered in the archaeological site cadastre of the BDA, the archaeologist will decide if the remains are archaeological or recent by the inspection of possible accompanying artefacts. If the remains are classified as archaeological, the BDA employee will take over and instigate the procedures of the Monument Protection Act, which will lead, in most cases, to an excavation that has to be financed by the landowner. If the remains are classified as recent, the BDA archaeologist will leave the site and the police will proceed with their investigations. This means that they start procedures with the state prosecutor, who will lead all future stages. The prosecutor has to decide whether the police on site, a specialised crime scene investigation group or external experts should do the crime scene documentation. In most cases where external experts are involved, this will be a forensic pathologist (*Facharzt für Gerichtsmedizin*) from the nearest forensic medical institution, because of the 24-hour on-call duty complementing the specialised crime scene investigation group. If this forensic pathologist is from the Department of Forensic Medicine in Vienna and the remains found are skeletonised, they call in the Forensic Anthropology Unit (*Fachbereich Forensische Anthropologie*) for assistance. The Unit will take over the excavation process and all further

[11]For more information, see: http://archaeoplus.sbg.ac.at/camas.html (last accessed October 2013).
[12]For more information, see: http://isotopenforschung.univie.ac.at/en/vera/ (last accessed October 2013).
[13]For more information, see: http://www.statistik.at/(last accessed October 2013).
[14]For more information, see: http://www.statistik.at/ (last accessed October 2013).

investigation. In other regions the forensic pathologist on duty/in charge will feel competent to supervise the excavation on site. However, there is no special training in archaeological methodology for Austria's forensic pathologists.

Services offered by the forensic anthropology units in Austria

Within our institutes we have standardised procedures for the finding of skeletonised remains. Normally the prosecutor will order this process or the forensic pathologist will call for assistance from the Forensic Anthropological Unit. In practice, in most cases the police forces will bring the skeletonised remains to the nearest Department of Forensic Medicine for investigation. Basically we offer the following services:

- The recovery of remains on site; if this is rejected by the prosecutor, we provide Standard Operating Procedures (SOPs) for the recovery of surface and subsurface findings. These SOPs define in which order activities at the scene (e.g. photography, evidence marking, documentation of climatic conditions, proper securing of inorganic and organic remains) have to be undertaken, and they are accompanied by a checklist to ensure that our requirements for further analysis are fulfilled.
- Once the remains arrive in the lab the first step is to discover if the remains are of human or non-human origin.
- This is followed by a Minimum Number of Individuals (MNI) analysis to estimate the number of persons represented by the remains.
- For each identified individual a time-since-death or post-mortem interval (PMI) estimation is conducted by traditional methods such as UV detection of remaining collagen (Hunger 1978), or more sophisticated methods such as citrate content in bone (Kanz et al. 2014; Schwarcz et al. 2010) and bomb peak dating by ^{14}C radiocarbon analysis (Danner 2006; Lynnerup et al. 2005; Ubelaker et al. 2006). Estimation of the PMI is essential for the prosecutor to decide whether the remains are of forensic/medico-legal interest or can be treated as archaeological findings. In Austria homicide does not prescribe it but normally the prosecutor decides for an archaeological case if the PMI is greater than 50 years.
- Assigning a biological profile consisting of sex, age, ancestry, body height and left- or right-handedness where possible.
- Examining ante-mortem conditions, especially trauma and pathological conditions, which are likely to leave traces on the hard tissues and may serve as unique identifying features.
- A unit for craniofacial reconstruction is currently being built up based on the experiences of the Centre for Anatomy and Human Identification at the University of Dundee (Wilkinson and Rynn 2012), and this might support the identification process in the future.
- If there are any macroscopic or microscopic traces on the hard tissues, the cause of death due to blunt or sharp force trauma or gunshot may be reconstructed.
- The identification of post-mortem modifications (taphonomy) to reconstruct the circumstances of the burial or body deposition.
- An expert witness report on the investigation and analysis which can be used in court.

Training and education opportunities in forensic archaeology and anthropology

At the moment there are no studies, either in forensic archaeology or in forensic anthropology, offered by Austrian Universities. There are periodic workshops on forensic archaeology and anthropology organised by ARCHEOskills,[15] an association of student representatives from all German-speaking countries. Most of the lecturers in these 1- or 2-day workshops are associated with the earlier-mentioned Study Group Forensic Archaeology based in Vienna. There is a wide range of BA, MA and PhD studies in archaeology offered by the Universities in Innsbruck, Salzburg, Graz and Vienna. Physical anthropology can only be studied through the BA, MA and PhD programmes at the University of Vienna. A curriculum for an MS in Forensic Sciences, with a significant focus on forensic archaeology and anthropology, is currently under way at the Medical University of Vienna. The start of this course is planned for late 2014.

Conclusion and future developments

Beyond any doubt, there is a need for general improvement of forensic archaeology and anthropology in Austria. Education is required to train future experts in these fields of expertise. Regulations for the service of forensic archaeology and anthropology, as well as an increased awareness of these disciplines by the prosecutors, are also required. This enhanced awareness might be administered by expert talks at postgraduate seminars. Furthermore, regulations and procedures have to be developed to ensure that these specialists are routinely employed during excavations or when special forensic finds are made in the field.

[15]For more information, see: http://www.archaeoskills-dasv.org/ (last accessed October 2013).

Although most expertise is available in Austria, due to the changes in universities becoming semi-privatised rather than state-run, it is increasingly difficult for prosecutors and the police to rely on civil servant specialists employed at the universities to conduct such special investigations. Therefore the budget to assign external experts has to be increased, or people with the necessary expertise have to be employed by the police force itself. This demands a necessary development for the (re)organisation of federal institutions as mentioned earlier, as well as the development of additional educational programmes. We hope to contribute to this necessary development by offering a Master's programme in Forensic Science, which will also serve as a platform for exchange and discussion on best practice for invited international scholars. Additionally, national guidelines for forensic archaeological and anthropological work should improve the situation, followed by the accreditation of such experts and institutions realised by the well-established Austrian system of sworn-in experts.

Acknowledgment

We would like to acknowledge the following people for their valuable input, especially on the legal framework in Austria: Professor Edith Tutsch-Bauer (Head of Department of Forensic Medicine, University of Salzburg), Professor Daniele Risser (Head of the Department of Forensic Medicine, Medical University of Vienna), Mr Christoph Blesl and Dr Bernhard Hebert (Federal Monuments Office) and Professor Claudia Theune-Vogt (Head of the Department of Prehistoric and Historic Archaeology, University of Vienna). Last but not the least, we thank the members of the specialised crime scene investigator groups from the State Police Upper Austria, the State Police Lower Austria and the State Police of Vienna. We would also like to thank Mr Nik Green for the improvement of the English manuscript.

References

Danner, B. 2006. Kernwaffen-Induziertes Radiocarbon (14C) und die Liegzeitbestimmung von Menschlichen Skelettresten. Thesis, University of Ulm.

Hunger, H. 1978. Liegezeitbestimmung an Skelettfunden im Erdboden. In H. Hunger and D. Leopold (eds.), *Identifikation*, 50–99. Leipzig, Barth.

Kanz, F., Reiter, C. and Risser, D. U. 2014. Citrate content of bone for time since death estimation: results from burials with different physical characteristics and known PMI. *Journal of Forensic Sciences* 59, 613–620.

Lynnerup, N., Bentzer, N. K. and Heinemeier, J. 2005. Radiocarbon dating of human remains in a forensic medical context. *Scandinavian Journal of Forensic Science* 11, 11–14.

Schwarcz, H. P., Agur, K. and Jantz, L. M. 2010. A new method for determination of post-mortem interval: citrate content of bone. *Journal of Forensic Sciences* 55, 1516–1522.

Ubelaker, D., Buchholz, B. and Stewart, J. 2006. Analysis of artificial radiocarbon in different skeletal and dental tissue types to evaluate date of death. *Journal of Forensic Sciences* 51, 484–488.

Wild, E. M., Arlamovsky, K. A. and Golser, R., et al. 2000. C-14 dating with the bomb peak: an application to forensic medicine. *Nuclear Instruments & Methods in Physics Research Section B-Beam Interactions with Materials and Atoms* 172, 944–950.

Wilkinson, C. and Rynn, C. (eds.) 2012. *Craniofacial Identification*. Cambridge, Cambridge University Press.

CHAPTER 2

DVI Belgium: victim identification and necrosearch

Birgit Van Denhouwe[1] and Eline M.J. Schotsmans[2,3]

[1] *Federal Police, DVI, Brussels, Belgium*

[2] *PACEA UMR 5199, Université de Bordeaux, Bordeaux, France*

[3] *Department of Forensic and Archaeological Sciences, University of Bradford, Bradford, UK*

Introduction

In Belgium, forensic archaeology is a part of *necrosearch* (see definition later), carried out by the Belgian Disaster Victim Identification (DVI) team. For the past 16 years the Belgian DVI has developed methods and techniques for forensic archaeology and necrosearch: the search, detection and recovery of hidden and buried human remains with the aim of safeguarding as much evidence as possible.

Belgium and the Belgian police

Belgium is a small country in Western Europe that is located at the North Sea Channel across from the United Kingdom, adjoining the Netherlands, Luxembourg and France. Since its independence in 1830, Belgium has reconciled regional and cultural identities in a single federal structure. The federal state is made up of communities and regions. There are three communities in Belgium, based on language and cultural diversities: the Flemish community with Dutch as its official language, the French community with French as its main language and the German community, which speaks German. Furthermore, Belgium has three regions based on historical economic interests: the Flemish region, the Capital region with Brussels and the Walloon region. The country is further divided into 10 provinces and 589 municipal councils.[1]

Belgium's jurisdiction is complex. Regions have authority in fields that are associated with their territory. The Federal State's authority includes justice, defence, federal police, social security finance, foreign affairs and domestic affairs.

The Belgian police force is divided into (i) the federal police, responsible for federal and more specialised tasks, and (ii) the local police, consisting of 195 smaller police units, responsible for either one municipal council[2] or several municipal councils.[3] DVI Belgium is a support unit within the federal police which is part of the Special Units of the Belgian Federal Police (*Commissariaat-Generaal Special Units/Commisariat-Général Special Units* (CGSU)).[4] The team works closely with the Missing Persons Unit (*Cel Vermiste Personen/Cellule Personnes Disparues*), another support unit.

In Belgium a support unit never starts its own investigation. Support units assist and support other units with their investigation. After the support has been given, a support unit withdraws itself and will no longer be involved in the investigation.

In general, when a person is missing or when an unidentified body is found, the local or federal investigators ask the Missing Persons Unit for tactical support and the DVI team for technical support.

Medico-legal framework

In Belgium, there are many shortcomings regarding the medico-legal framework. As of 2013 there was still no legislation on medico-legal investigations, no uniformity of the study of forensic pathology and no accreditation of experts.

There are 27 forensic pathologists in Belgium who are connected to academic forensic medicine centres. Furthermore, there are an unknown number of

[1]For more information, see: www.belgium.be (last accessed June 2013).

[2]There are 50 single municipal police zones (*éėngemeentezone/zones monocomunales*).

[3]There are 145 multiple municipal police zones (*meergemeentezone/zones pluricommunales*).

[4]This used to be the structure at the time of writing of this chapter (2013). In 2014 DVI Belgium was moved to the Technical and Scientific Police Unit DJT (Directie van Technische en Wetenschappelijke Politie/La Direction de la Police Technique et Scientifique).

Forensic Archaeology: A Global Perspective, First Edition. Edited by W.J. Mike Groen, Nicholas Márquez-Grant and Robert C. Janaway.

independent forensic doctors who act as forensic experts, but do not have a specialised degree in forensic medicine. Since 2002 forensic medicine is officially recognised as a specialisation of medicine. This means that a forensic pathologist has to study medicine for a duration of 7 years, followed by training in forensic medicine, which takes 5 years. Unfortunately, the specialisation in forensic medicine is not compulsory. A general practitioner can work as a forensic doctor without training in forensic medicine.

The Belgian law on establishing death has remained unchanged since the Napoleonic Code (1804), leading to an outdated legislation. Any doctor can ascertain the death of anyone (with the exception of a brain-dead potential organ donor). Most doctors do not have the necessary forensic knowledge and skills to assess or investigate a death in unknown or unnatural circumstances. This leads to misinterpretations of legal terms, overlooked non-natural deaths and sometimes to late intervention by the police and the law. Furthermore, the juridical authorities are free to decide whether or not a medico-legal investigation will take place. Despite internationally established criteria for medico-legal autopsies and recommendations by the Council of Europe (2000), Belgium has no guidelines or legislation regarding medico-legal investigations into cases of suspicious death. This has bearings on the medico-legal quality and contributes to a very low number of autopsies and, therefore, many overlooked crimes (autopsies are only carried out in 1–2% of all deaths). The Royal Belgian Association of Forensic Medicine (*Koninklijk Belgisch Genootschap voor Gerechtelijke Geneeskunde/Société Royale de Médecine Légale de Belgique*) pleads for a uniform, continued, inter-university training of forensic pathologists, the accreditation of experts and a legislation regarding medico-legal investigations.

Forensic archaeology in Belgium

There are limited professional opportunities for forensic archaeologists in Belgium. Most forensic excavations are performed by the Belgian DVI. There is no education or course that offers training in forensic archaeology or the application of archaeological techniques in a legal context. Furthermore, there is no commercial development of forensic archaeology and no existing system of consultancy. Some forensic archaeologists are linked to universities and perform research in the broader subject of taphonomy or physical anthropology, but most have to remain in close contact with other international organisations and universities to practice their profession.

When skeletal remains are found outside the context of an official excavation, the police are notified and the DVI team will, in most cases, be called for an assessment. If the remains appear to be archaeological, the archaeological heritage of the specific region will be contacted (detailed in Quintelier et al. 2011). If the context indicates that the remains are from a World War I or II soldier, the DVI team will contact the Office of War Graves of the Institute for Veterans – National Institute of War Invalids, War Veterans and Victims of War,[5] which takes care of the recovery, analysis, identification, registration and repatriation of the remains.[6] When the discovery is unique or when it concerns more than one military victim, support will be given by archaeologists of the Flemish Heritage Institute (*Agentschap Onroerend Erfgoed*) or Archeo 7 (an archaeological service in western Flanders).[7] Guidelines for municipalities and police, in case remains of war victims are detected, are published by Breyne (2004).

Education and training

There is no Belgian university which offers specific academic education (at Bachelor's or Master's level) in forensic archaeology. One could argue that there is a need for proper postgraduate education in forensic archaeology. But the limited professional opportunities make a postgraduate course in forensic archaeology less appropriate. It would be good, however, to establish course modules in forensic archaeology linked to other forensic subjects.

In Belgium there are several modules/courses in the broader sense of the word 'forensic'. Forensic medicine can be studied at the Universities of Antwerp, Leuven, Brussels, Ghent and Liège. An overview of education in physical/forensic anthropology in Belgium is summarised by Quintelier et al. (2011). The Erasmus University College Brussels has a Bachelor's degree course in Biomedical Laboratory Technology which focuses on forensic investigations. Hasselt University pays attention to forensic archaeology and anthropology in their Master's degree course in Forensic Science. From September 2014 onwards a minor in forensic science will be established within the MSc in Biomedical Sciences at the University of Leuven.

---

[5]*Dienst Oorlogsgraven van het Instituut voor Veteranen – Nationaal Instituut voor Oorlogsinvaliden, Oudstrijders en Oorlogsslachtoffers* (IV-NIOOO)/*Service Sépultures Militaires de l'Institut des Vétérans – Institut National des Invalides de Guerre, Anciens Combattants et Victimes de Guerre* (IV-INIG).

[6]For more information, see: www.warveterans.be (last accessed June 2013).

[7]Intergemeentelijke Archeologische Dienst van de zuidelijke Westhoek (Heuvelland, Ieper, Langemark-Poelkapelle, Mesen, Poperinge, Vleteren en Zonnebeke).

An additional course which leads to a certificate in forensic investigation is organised by the Erasmus University College Brussels (*Postgraduaat Forensisch Onderzoek*).

DVI Belgium

Belgium started its DVI team in 1987 and has its office in Etterbeek (Brussels).[8] The first major disaster faced by the Belgian DVI was the accident with the Herald of Free Enterprise, also known as the Zeebrugge ferry disaster. As a result of this incident, in which 193 people of different nationalities lost their lives, and through its involvement in several mass disasters and major incidents in Belgium and abroad, the Belgian DVI has become more professional over the years.

To date, its main task is to recover and identify the victims of disasters, incidents and individual forensic cases. Over the years the DVI team has taken part in many individual identifications and a variety of disasters such as a major hotel fire in Antwerp (1994, Belgium), an aircraft accident in Bucharest (1995, Romania), the Tsunami (2004, Thailand), a train accident in Buizingen (2010, Belgium) and the identification and repatriation of 28 victims who died in a bus accident (2012, Switzerland). While victim identification is the main mission of the DVI team, another important task is necrosearch, defined later.

Over the past years the DVI team, which originally consisted of only police officers with no archaeological background, learned the skill of forensic archaeology through practice. Since 2007 a police inspector with a qualification in conventional archaeology has been added to the team. The inspector took several additional international courses in physical anthropology, forensic archaeology and forensic techniques. In 2012 another police inspector who has a Master's degree in Criminology and an additional MSc in Forensic Archaeology, acquired in the UK, joined the team.

In 2013, the DVI core team consisted of eight members who are employed full-time (including the two aforementioned police inspectors with archaeological background). Additionally, DVI volunteers, called DVI Pool Members, are part of other federal police units. They are policemen or civilians who work across Belgium and can be deployed in case of major incidents or to reinforce the team when several operations take place at the same time.

The Dutroux case: the birth of necrosearch

In 1996, Belgium was faced with the serial killer Marc Dutroux. Dutroux kidnapped and sexually abused six girls between 8 and 19 years of age and murdered four of them. The Belgian police asked the British police Chief John Bennett for advice regarding the search and detection of human remains. John Bennett, a Detective Superintendent of Gloucestershire Constabulary, led the investigation into the crimes of Fred and Rosemary West in the early 1990s in the United Kingdom. Bennett gave the Belgian police technical and tactical advice in their search for the bodies of the murdered girls and instigated the use of a ground-penetrating radar (GPR). With the help of architect-engineers and forensic investigators all properties of Marc Dutroux were searched for hiding places. Additional support, mainly for the outside searches, was received from the Dutch military Recovery and Identification Unit (*Berging-en Identificatiedienst*). Captain Harry Jongen, also known as 'the Nose', had 30 years of experience in forensic archaeology and botany. In the absence of a forensic archaeologist, Jongen taught the Belgian investigators the basics of forensic searches and helped locate the graves of two of the murdered girls. With the Dutroux case the Belgian version of forensic archaeology, named necrosearch, was born.

After the Dutroux case, DVI Belgium built up more experience in necrosearch with major homicide cases such as the serial killers Michel Fourniret in 2004 and Ronald Jansen in 2010.

Necrosearch

Definition

As determined in an internal police protocol (3 September 2009), necrosearch is 'the search, detection and recovery of hidden and illegally buried human remains and objects in different environments which requires a specialised technical knowledge and whereby the located remains are recovered in accordance with the standard forensic techniques'.[9] In other words, necrosearch implies the use of archaeological techniques for forensic investigations with the aim to safeguard as much evidence as possible. Necrosearch is also used for the recovery of scattered human remains on the surface.

The first policemen (local or federal) attending the scene can call upon any police support unit for specific

[8]For more information, see: www.polfed-fedpol.be/org/org_cg_dsu_dvi_en.php (last accessed June 2013).

[9]'Het opsporen, lokaliseren en bergen van verborgen en begraven lichamen en voorwerpen in diverse milieus waarvoor een gespecialiseerde technische kennis nodig is en waarbij de gevonden resten worden geborgen conform de heersende normen van forensische technieken'.'La recherche, la localisation et la récupération de corps et objets cachés et enfouis dans des environnements divers pour lesquels une connaissance technique spécialisée est nécessaire et où les restes retrouvés sont récupérés conformément aux normes des techniques légales en vigueur'.

help (including the DVI team). Usually, the investigation of a forensic case (suspicious death or missing person) is managed by a federal or local investigation team in consideration with a magistrate who can also contact any police support unit.

When the investigator has evidence or suspects that a victim is hidden or buried, the support of the DVI team is requested. This implies the start of a necrosearch operation. Every necrosearch operation is organised by the DVI team and carried out according to the same methodology, consisting of four stages: (1) information gathering, (2) site preparation, (3) search and location, and (4) excavation and recovery.

Stage 1: gathering of information

All searches require a starting point derived from key data of the investigation. Usually, one or more DVI members attend a strategy meeting with the forensic investigators, the tactical investigators, other (police) services, experts, the Public Prosecutor and/or the investigating judge. During this meeting, the DVI members try to obtain as much information as possible regarding the ongoing investigation (offender profile, missing person's background, witnesses, type of crime, etc.) and regarding the site (surface vegetation, soil maps, groundwater level, security, building layout and architectural plans, accessibility, limitations and satellite images (Google Earth etc.). With the permission of the investigators and/or the public prosecutor (permission is not granted in case of embargo) and, if necessary, the permission of the owner of the site, the DVI then visits the location. A survey is carried out to obtain a better image of the site and to verify the limits and boundaries of the scene. All this information is key to good coordination and to assembling the right search teams, workforce and equipment.

Stage 2: site preparation

Securing the site

During a necrosearch operation three perimeters are established to secure the site. Their size varies according to whether or not the grave or human remains are localised.

The *isolation perimeter* is the outer boundary. Only people with a reason to be near the search or recovery should be allowed within this perimeter. This perimeter is useful to exclude the media and the public. A record or log should be kept of all the people who enter and exit and the times at which they do so.

The second perimeter is the *search perimeter*, established around the actual search area. Anyone who participates in the search for the grave or remains is allowed within this boundary. The search perimeter also has an entrance and exit which is monitored. This entrance is also the start of a common approach path in case human remains are detected.

The third perimeter, the *exclusion perimeter*, is the inner boundary, which is only established when a grave is localised or when human remains are detected. The only people authorised to access this perimeter are the people who are participating in the actual excavation and/or recovery of the remains and in the sieving of the soil. In practice this encompasses members of the DVI, the Civil Protection, the Laboratory for Technical and Scientific Police, the forensic pathologist and, if necessary, other experts (partners in necrosearch explained later).

Documentation of the site

Before proceeding to search and/or recovery, it is necessary to document the site as it exists. Photographs are taken and sketches are made from different angles. Sometimes video recordings are made. Furthermore, the site is mapped and metric measurements are taken. The Belgian DVI has a total station (an optical surveying instrument) that can be used for this purpose.

Safety measures

When carrying out a necrosearch operation, various safety measures are taken. Personnel should wear personal protective equipment (PPE) for their own protection and safety (e.g. safety shoes) and protective crime scene clothing to prevent cross contamination of evidence (e.g. crime scene suits, shoe covers, gloves and hair covers). In case of bad weather a shelter is provided for all personnel and to protect evidence. Furthermore, the grave and/or the human remains is/are shielded from spectators and the media.

Organisation outside the search area

It is important to have all workforces, materials and facilities necessary for the operation close to the search area. Usually space is provided within the isolation perimeter for vehicles, containers, temporary storage units, supplies and sanitary facilities.

Stage 3: search and location

Searching for the remains of a missing person can be a difficult task. Clear organisation with pre-arranged search strategies and good communication with all parties involved are critical to the success of a search.

Search techniques can be either non-invasive or invasive. Non-invasive search uses non-destructive methods in which searches are performed by visually looking for evidence of a burial or surface scatter. They include line walking, the use of cadaver dogs and almost all of the geophysical methods such as metal detection, GPR, thermal imaging and resistivity meters. Invasive methods are used when non-invasive methods are not successful or as a follow-up to visual searches. Invasive methods include probing, digging test trenches or using heavy equipment.

Stage 4: excavation and recovery

Every crime scene involving human remains is different. As such the archaeological techniques used to excavate a site must be adapted. However, the general methodology of an excavation and the removal of remains are similar. The use of systematic and controlled approaches is important, no matter the condition or the context of the recovery scene.

Buried human remains

Burials have specific characteristics. In most situations the burial fill and burial cut can be recognised from the original soil. When a burial is discovered, the DVI team will plan a recovery strategy on the basis of the known stratigraphy, the soil profile and taphonomic information. There are several methods to excavate a single inhumation. In Belgium most bodies are recovered by digging an access trench to the side of the body, by excavating the grave cut (Figure 2.1) or by the pedestal method in which all soil around the body is removed, leaving the body in place on a pedestal of soil (Figure 2.2). Half-sectioning the grave or the stratigraphic method are less often applied by the Belgian DVI because of time pressure and because not all DVI members have a background in archaeology. The chosen method is case-dependent and decided upon consultation with the appointed forensic pathologist.

In brief, the grave area will be cleared and the soil or sediment layers that overlie the grave will be excavated and sieved for any material evidence, as well as sampled for botanical or entomological evidence. Every stage of the recovery is recorded, and each context is numbered so that all materials, exhibits and samples seized are documented in terms of precise contextual location. The fill above and to the sides of the body will be removed until the remains are exposed using the appropriate equipment such as trowels, plasterers' leaves and brushes. The position of the body is recorded carefully through photographs, video and other documentation. If necessary, the forensic pathologist will perform a first external examination *in situ*, and more samples will be taken. The next step is lifting of the body or body parts. Methods of lifting depend on the environment and the condition of the remains. Sometimes it is necessary to bag the hands and feet to avoid losing body parts such as fingers, toes or nails (Figure 2.2). If the remains are skeletonised they are lifted individually, numbered and bagged. After the removal of the body any remaining fill is removed and sieved. The process of sieving can also be part of the search process (stage 3), while looking for small bones in the soil or mud. Once the grave has been completely cleared, it is photographed, documented and measured against fixed reference points, often using the total station.

Surface human remains

While a buried body is usually related to a crime, (scattered) surface remains could be related to a homicide, suicide or natural mortality. Surface remains can be found on the surface or in a ditch, they can be uncovered or covered by debris, and they can be undisturbed or disturbed. However, surface remains are likely to be disturbed since they are easily accessible by animals and subject to all weather conditions. First, the body or body parts are numbered, documented and photographed. Next, they are removed from the scene and packaged accordingly. When scattering is extensive, every effort is made to recover as many body parts as possible.

The members of the Laboratory for Technical and Scientific Police (see later) are, together with the

Figure 2.1 A dummy is recovered by DVI members during an exercise as part of the Ibis group training program. They remove the grave fill following the grave cut.

Figure 2.2 The excavation of a homicide victim recovered by the pedestal method. Hands and feet are bagged to avoid losing fingers, toes, nails and possible trace evidence such as hair, fibres or DNA.

appointed forensic doctor/pathologist, in charge of the crime scene and the technical crime scene investigation. When the DVI is called in, they share this responsibility and are in charge of all activities which require forensic archaeological techniques and methods.

Partners in necrosearch

Forensic archaeologists and/or the DVI team will never work at a forensic scene by themselves. Good collaboration with different partners forms the basis of a successful necrosearch operation. The main partners of the DVI team are described later.

Services and units inside the Belgian police force

Laboratory for Technical and Scientific Police

Every judicial department in Belgium (19 in total) has its own Laboratory for Technical and Scientific Police (*Laboratorium van Technische en Wetenschappelijke Politie (LTWP)/Laboratoire de Police Technique et Scientifique (LPTS)*). Similar to Scene of Crime Officers (SOCOs) or Crime Scene Investigators (CSIs) in the United Kingdom, the task of the LTWP is to process the crime scene, that is to take photographs, secure and examine the crime scene, and locate, identify, preserve, record and collect traces and evidence. When a burial or human remains are discovered, the site automatically turns into a crime scene and the assistance of the LTWP is indispensable.

Cadaver dog unit

The Belgian cadaver dog unit *(Dienst Hondensteun – Speurhonden Menselijke Resten/Service d'Appui Canin – Chiens de Recherche de Restes Humains)* consists of four dog handlers and four dogs. The cadaver dogs are used to locate human remains by detecting the scent of human decomposition. They also search for blood traces. There is a close collaboration between the DVI team and the cadaver dog unit and they are involved in most of the necrosearch operations.

National Technical Support Unit

The National Technical Support Unit (NTSU) was established in 1996 within the Special Units of the Federal Police. Their main task is to support the Special Units technologically, usually in relation to sensitive cases. Examples of their technological support are the interception of data or different forms of imaging.

During a necrosearch operation, the NTSU supports the DVI by providing trained personnel and search equipment such as GPR, thermal imaging and X-ray instruments.

Metal detectors are provided by the Technical Support Team (*Technisch Steunteam/Equipe d'Appui Technique*) from the Waterway Police, another unit within the Belgian Federal Police.

Services and experts outside the Belgian police force

Civil protection/Ibis group

The Civil Protection (*Civiele Bescherming/Protection Civile*) provides logistical support during a necrosearch operation (manpower, materials and means). Therefore it is one of the most important partners of the DVI. In Belgium, the Civil Protection is divided into five units. Volunteers within the Civil Protection are specifically trained in necrosearch by the DVI, because necrosearch operations require specific methods and skills such as handling of a mechanical digger or sieving, and

Table 2.1 The crime rates in Belgium from 2005 to 2012.

	2005	2006	2007	2008	2009	2010	2011	2012
Murder/manslaughter	962	917	913	884	932	947	1,062	1,005
Other crimes	998,434	1,021,896	1,033,517	1,042,744	1,066,363	1,071,064	1,109,910	1,072,768
Total	999,396	1,022,813	1,034,430	1,043,628	1,067,295	1,072,011	1,110,972	1,073,773

sometimes assisting with the excavation (Figure 2.1). This group with trained members of the Civil Protection is called the Ibis group. Members of the Ibis group will get priority to work with the DVI during a necrosearch operation.

Belgian national institute for criminalistics and criminology

The Belgian National Institute for Criminalistics and Criminology (*Nationaal Instituut voor Criminalistiek en Criminologie* (NICC)/*Institut National de Criminalistique et de Criminologie* (INCC)) is a government institute which provides forensic science services to the Belgian police forces.[10] It is located in Brussels and is part of the Ministry of Justice. The institute is accredited by the international ISO/IEC 17025 norm and is a member of the European Network of Forensic Science Institutes (ENFSI) since 1992. The NICC contributes to a necrosearch operation by providing expertise in, for example, microtraces, entomology, biology, fibres and textiles.

Experts and universities

The Ministry of Justice can refer the analysis of human remains and other evidence to consultants or independent experts such as forensic pathologists, forensic anthropologists, forensic odontologists and forensic entomologists. Most experts are linked to Belgian or foreign universities.

There are nine DNA laboratories in Belgium, among which one is the NICC/INCC; the others are attached to a university or are private accredited laboratories.

The universities and the government can also ask for the technical support of the DVI team. In 2012 the DVI carried out a survey and provided the technical support for a Burundian mission led by the Belgian government and the University of Leuven, after an official request by the Burundian government to help with the search, recovery and identification of the remains of the last Burundian King, Charles Ntare V.

Foreign partners

Good collaboration with foreign partners is necessary, and more so in a small country such as Belgium. The Belgian Federal Police and the DVI have a good relationship with police forces in all neighbouring countries. More specifically, there is close collaboration with the Netherlands Forensic Institute (NFI). Other foreign partners include the Interpol and international experts (pathologists, anthropologists, universities).

Statistics

Belgium has relatively low crime rates.[11] The average ratio of murder/manslaughter to the total number of crimes is 0.09% (Table 2.1).

Since the Dutroux case and the start of necrosearch operations in Belgium, the number of operations carried out by the DVI has increased while the number of necrosearch operations has remained fairly stable (Figure 2.3). Other DVI operations include ante-mortem (missing person) and post-mortem (unidentified body) data collection; recovery of victims (other than buried, hidden or skeletonised) as a result of a mass fatality, accident, natural cause of death or other; forensic diving (locating, registering, recovering and preserving of traces under water); technical and coordinating support in extensive house searches and giving advice when animal or archaeological remains are encountered.

About one-fifth of the necrosearch operations in Belgium are successful, resulting in the discovery of a body (Figure 2.4). The rate of success depends on the chosen methods.

Research and development

The Belgian DVI team is keen to improve their techniques and methods. Therefore it has a close collaboration with several universities. Furthermore, it organises courses in necrosearch for the Ibis group (see earlier) and other support services with the aim of optimising collaboration and the quality of the work.

The Belgian DVI has three different field sites at their disposal which can be used for research and development. The three sites are part of the Belgian Military and located in Lombardsijde, Meerdaal and Bertrix. At those field sites several experiments have been conducted over the years in collaboration with other police units and the universities of Leuven

[10] For more information, see: www.incc.fgov.be (last accessed June 2013).

[11] Criminality statistics are available at: www.polfed-fedpol.be/crim/crim_stat_nl.php (last accessed June 2013).

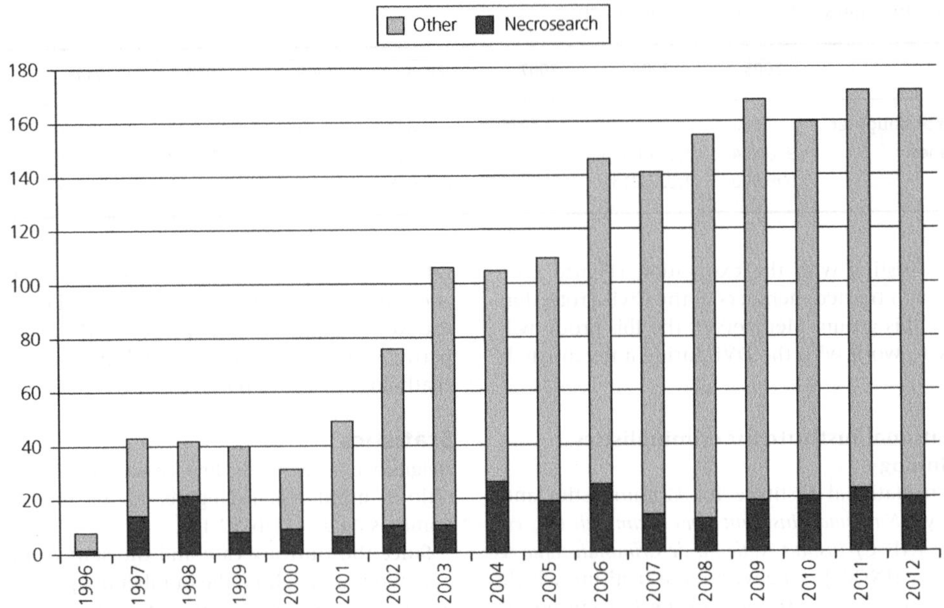

Figure 2.3 Number of necrosearch operations amongst a total annual number of operations by the DVI.

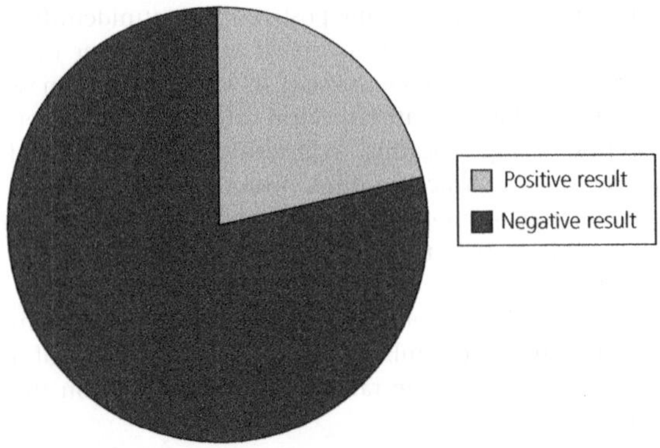

Figure 2.4 Over one-fifth (22%) of all necrosearch operations carried out in Belgium since the start of necrosearch results in the discovery of human remains (positive result).

(Belgium), Liège (Belgium), Amsterdam (the Netherlands) and Bradford (the United Kingdom). Pigs have been buried there or left on the surface to investigate entomofaunal colonisation, to sample volatile organic compounds (VOCs) released by the corpses, to analyse temperature differences by thermal imagery with both airborne and ground-based cameras, to study GPR responses to burials which differ in size and depth, to assess surface indicators, soil disturbance and environmental changes caused by the burials, and to investigate normal and atypical burials such as the inclusion of lime. This research led to several publications in the forensic field (Brasseur et al. 2012; Dekeirsschieter et al. 2009; Schotsmans et al. 2012; Stefanuto et al. 2012).

The field sites are also used for training purposes for the Ibis group (see earlier). Pigs and dogs have been buried or left on the surface to teach and refine necrosearch and excavation skills. The participants have to carry out a search and apply archaeological techniques during the forensic excavation. The Belgian DVI team also delivers international training. For instance, in 2012 members of the DVI team trained six Burundian police officers (East Africa) in necrosearch and victim identification (Figure 2.5). This was part of a police reformation project between Burundi and Belgium aiming to change corruption, abuse and the unnecessary use of weapons within the Burundian police.

The Belgian DVI is motivated to collaborate with its national and international partners and keen to learn up-to-date methods and techniques in conventional archaeology, forensic archaeology, forensic anthropology and other forensic sciences.

Conclusion

Clearly, there is a demonstrated value of archaeological expertise within criminal investigations. In Belgium, most forensic excavations are performed by the Belgian DVI as part of necrosearch operations. There are limited professional opportunities for forensic archaeologists in Belgium since there is no commercial development of forensic archaeology, no existing system of consultancy and no specific education.

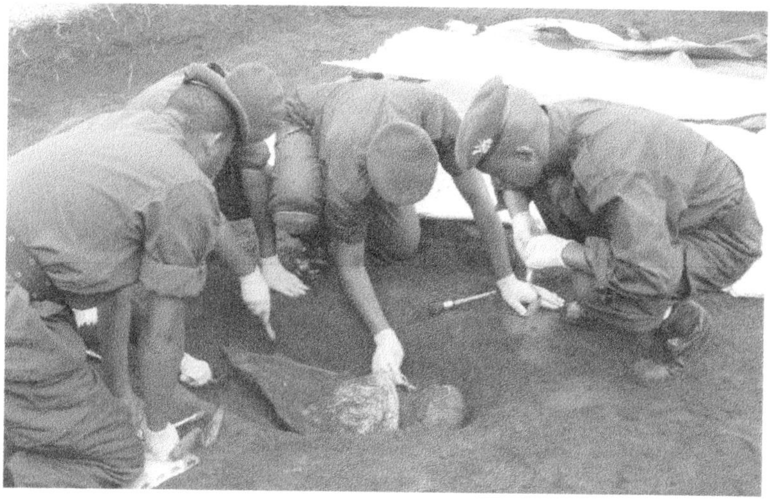

Figure 2.5 In 2012, the Belgian DVI team trained six Burundian police officers in necrosearch and forensic archaeology.

Acknowledgements

Thanks to all current and past DVI core team members, DVI pool members and Ibis members for their engagement and effort on DVI cases since 1987. The authors would also like to thank former DVI commander Joan De Winne for his support, encouragement and advice.

References

Brasseur, C., Dekeirsschieter, J. and Schotsmans, E. M. J. et al. 2012. Comprehensive two dimensional gas chromatography-time-of-flight mass spectrometry for the forensic study of cadaveric volatile organic compounds released in soil by buried decaying pig carcasses. *Journal of Chromatography A* 1255, 163–170.

Breyne, P. 2004. *Omgaan met Bodemvondsten. Opgravingen WOI.* Brugge, Vademecum.

Council of Europe, 2000. Recommendation no. R (99) 3 on the harmonisation of medico-legal autopsy rules and its explanatory memorandum. *Forensic Science International* 111, 5–29.

Dekeirsschieter, J., Verheggen, F. J. and Gohy, M. et al. 2009. Cadaveric volatile organic compounds released by decaying pig carcasses in different biotopes. *Forensic Science International* 189, 46–53.

Quintelier, K., Malevez, A., Orban, R., Toussaint, M., Vandenbruaene M. and Yernaux, G. 2011. Belgium. In N. Márquez-Grant and L. Fibiger (eds.), *The Routledge Handbook of Archaeological Human Remains and Legislation*, 47–60. London, Routledge.

Schotsmans, E. M. J., Denton, J. and Dekeirsschieter, J. et al. 2012. Effects of hydrated lime and quicklime on the decay of buried human remains using pig cadavers as human body analogues. *Forensic Science International* 217, 50–59.

Stefanuto, P.-H., Schotsmans, E. M. J., Wilson, A. S. and Focant, J. F. 2012. Grave soil analysis by TD-GCxGC-ToFMS. *6th European Academy of Forensic Science Conference (EAFS)*, The Hague.

Further Reading

Beauthier, J.-P. 2011. *Traité de Médecine Légale*. Brussels, Groupe De Boeck, 567–572.

Beauthier, J.-P., De Valck, E., Lefevre, P. and De Winne, J. 2009. Mass disaster victim identification: the Tsunami experience. *The Open Forensic Science Journal* 2, 54–62.

Bockstaele, M., Bruggeman, W. and Bryssinckx, J. et al. 2009. *De Zoeking Onderzocht*. Antwerpen-Apeldoorn, Maklu.

De Coninck, D. 2004. *Marc Dutroux, het Stilste Jongetje van de Klas*. Antwerpen, Houtekiet.

De Poot, D. and De Winne, J. 2007. *Als Doden een Gezicht Krijgen*. Leuven, Uitgeverij Van Halewyck.

Schotsmans, E. M. J., Van de Voorde, W., De Winne, J. and Wilson, A. S. 2011. The impact of shallow burial on differential decomposition to the body: a temperate case study. *Forensic Science International* 206, e43–e48.

Van de Voorde, W. 2010. *Handboek Forensische Geneeskunde*. Brugge, Die Keure.

Websites

www.belgium.be
www.co7.be/nl/archeo7.html
www.incc.fgov.be
www.onroerenderfgoed.be
www.polfed-fedpol.be
www.polfed-fedpol.be/crim/crim_stat_nl.php
www.polfed-fedpol.be/org/org_cg_dsu_dvi_en.php
www.polfed-fedpol.be/pub/inforevue/inforevue3_08/IR032008-4-nl.pdf
www.warveterans.be

CHAPTER 3

Bosnia and Herzegovina: forensic archaeology in support of national and international organisations undertaking criminal investigations and identifying the missing from 1996 to 2013

Ian Hanson, Adnan Rizviç and Thomas J. Parsons

Internet Control Message Protocol ICMP, Sarajevo, Bosnia and Herzegovina

Historical background

This chapter deals with the success of forensic archaeology as one of several forensic sciences in a multidisciplinary system assisting in criminal and missing persons investigations in Bosnia and Herzegovina (*Bosna i Hercegovina* (BiH)). The work undertaken between 1996 and 2013 remains the largest continuous forensic operation ever undertaken in which forensic archaeology and anthropology have supported death investigations and identifications. Over 200 sites have been assessed and excavated per year, and over 22,000 people have been identified. The potential for archaeological sciences to contribute to investigations became clear as soon as Yugoslavia began to break up. Events at Vukovar in 1991, where many people were documented by the United Nations (UN) to have been killed and buried, demonstrated that search and excavation techniques would be useful to locate and recover the dead (United Nations 1994). The conflict in former Yugoslavia lasted between 1991 and 2001, and spread to Bosnia in 1992, ending there in 1995.

The war in BiH resulted in an estimated 100,000 deaths, out of a population of 3.9 million (Institut National d'Études Démographiques 2013). Between the end of the war in 1995 and November 2004, the International Committee of the Red Cross (ICRC) (Tidball-Binz and Hofmeister, Chapter 49) received in total over 21,700 requests to trace missing persons (ICRC 2004). By 2006 the International Commission on Missing Persons (ICMP) (Hanson, Chapters 3 and 48) had determined that 22,129 were missing, based on numbers represented by records collected when blood samples were provided by missing relatives, rising to 23,354 in 2013. As of 2012, The Missing Persons Institute (MPI) for BiH reported records of 34,965 missing persons which are currently being verified. Since the signing of the Dayton Peace Agreement in 1995, extensive measures have been undertaken to account for the missing and to determine the circumstances of their disappearance (ICMP 2014).

The criminal investigations were spear-headed by the International Criminal Tribunal for the former Yugoslavia (ICTY), which had undertaken criminal investigations since 1993, prosecuting crimes against humanity, war crimes and other offences committed on the territory of the former Yugoslavia since 1991, and which has charged 161 persons. Its indictments address crimes committed from 1991 to 2001 against members of various ethnic groups in Croatia, BiH, Serbia, Kosovo and the former Yugoslav Republic of Macedonia. More than 60 individuals have been convicted and currently more than 30 people are in different stages of proceedings before the Tribunal in 2013. All ICTY indictees for offences in BiH have been charged. War crime trials continue at state level. Excavations of mass graves have been the key to providing physical evidence of events for numerous prosecutions, with the Tribunal undertaking excavations between 1996 and 2001. Since 2002 state and canton prosecutors in BiH have issued court orders for site evaluations and excavations.

Support for recovery and identification has been led by the ICMP, which was established in 1996 to develop cooperation of the parties with the Dayton Peace Agreement (December 1995) in locating the missing from the 4-year conflict and to assist them in doing so. The ICMP became operational, supporting excavations

Forensic Archaeology: A Global Perspective, First Edition. Edited by W.J. Mike Groen, Nicholas Márquez-Grant and Robert C. Janaway.

and using modern forensic methods to conduct identifications, with the aim of improving identification success rates, supporting families and the rule of law. From 2000 ICMP lab analysis and then excavation monitoring support began. Today, missing persons investigations have identified 70% of the *c.* 30,000 missing. The primary source of this success has been the use of a scientific process supporting large-scale excavations and examinations, and utilising DNA-assisted identification techniques, which, through the use of cutting-edge throughput technology, has ensured a high level of accuracy. Some 25,000 bodies have been recovered from grave sites all over the country (represented by many more cases). Some 8,000 of these individuals were identified by presumptive methods (most prior to 2001), and over 14,000 identifications have been resolved with DNA as the primary contributor to identification. An estimated 9000 recovered cases (bodies and body parts) which have not been identified or claimed are currently in BiH's 12 mortuaries. Some 9000 people reported missing remain unaccounted for (ICMP 2013).

This scientific process to locate and find the missing and process that information to achieve identification has relied on the political will of the authorities in BiH to engage in this practice and to build a governmental, institutional and legal framework that allows families of the missing to assert their rights and for thousands of mortal remains to be located, excavated and identified. During and after the conflict, United Nations (UN) agencies and the ICRC recorded and documented events and produced a list of the missing. Working groups established dialogues between parties. Coordinating the work being done by the three sides in BiH was essential in order to achieve progress in the region. In 1997 a proposal was made to create the MPI for BiH. Additionally a proposal built upon an initiative launched by the Office of the High Representative (OHR)[1] in 1997 called the Joint Exhumation Process (JEP) permitted the three former warring parties to conduct exhumations relevant to their own missing persons. Exhumations and analysis were undertaken by entity commissions until the MPI became operational in 2008. Work in the early years of the process was supported by Finnish experts in 1996 and Physicians for Human Rights (PHR) between 1996 and 1999 (Schmitt et al., Chapter 53). Coordination of the JEP was eventually handed over to the ICMP, and in the summer of 2000, the ICMP founded the MPI for BiH. Political developments and consultation with the ICMP, government officials, families of the missing and others led to the agreement for the MPI to function as a state-level entity in August 2005, with directors and members of the management bodies in place by the summer of 2007. The implementation of the MPI marks a milestone in the history of BiH and the ICMP and provides a model for transitional justice that can be applied in many other situations and areas of the world. The MPI provides BiH with a national mechanism to address the issue of persons missing as a result of the conflict in BiH, regardless of their ethnic, religious or national origin. It also ensures that mass grave sites are protected, catalogued and properly excavated, and will ensure that relatives of the missing are able to participate in the work of searching for missing persons.[2] The MPI have undertaken excavations since 2009, coordinated with the prosecutor's office, cantonal police forces, the ICMP and state-registered pathologists.

The application of archaeology to support investigations in Bosnia between 1996 and 2013 can be discussed within these two main foci: international criminal investigations, and national criminal and missing people's investigations supported by international agencies.

International investigations

Organisation

The ICTY began field operations in 1996, conducting the search for and excavations of mass graves for the purpose of collecting evidence for its ongoing war crimes prosecutions in The Hague. Several investigation teams worked across BiH, with a forensic field team that supported scene examinations in Brcko, Bosanski Samac, Bihac, Prijedor and the area around Srebrenica. In 1996 the field team was supplied by PHR, who undertook exhumations of mass graves related to Srebrenica events at Cerska, Nova Kasaba, Lazete and Branjevo Farm. Some 650 bodies and body parts were recovered (PHR 1997). PHR were also contracted to the ICMP between 1997 and 1999 to provide forensic assistance. From 1997 to 2001 ICTY excavations were conducted by their own teams, drawn internationally from both existing national teams undertaking humanitarian work and professional field archaeologists.

Process

The field teams undertook search, location and excavation, and separate mortuary teams undertook autopsy and sampling of cases. Cause and manner of death was

[1]The Office of the High Representative (OHR) is an *ad hoc* international institution responsible for overseeing implementation of civilian aspects of the Peace Agreement ending the war in Bosnia and Herzegovina. For more information, see: http://www.ohr.int/ohr-info/gen-info/default.asp?content_id=38519 (last accessed October 2013).

[2]For more information, see: http://www.ic-mp.org/icmp-worldwide/southeast-europe/bosnia-and-herzegovina/ (last accessed October 2013).

determined by pathologist-led mortuary teams, but identification of the dead was not systematic, only taking place in a few cases pertinent to prosecutions. Bosnian pathologists for the most part undertook the signing of death certificates after the bodies were transferred to local authorities, and where identity – mostly by presumptive methods (e.g. identification documents, clothing and personal effects) – could be determined (ICMP 2014). In many cases it was several years before cases were transferred and re-examined. The chief scientists or medical staff of the field and mortuary teams produced reports concerning excavation and examination work, and presented testimony at the Tribunal concerning this.

Sites had to be checked and cleared of ordnance before search and excavation could take place. There were explosive ordnance disposal (EOD) officers contracted to the teams who were in full-time attendance. Security concerns surrounded the conduct of investigations and excavations. Security was provided by members of the NATO-led IFOR (Implementation Force) (later SFOR, Stabilisation Force) mission to the country. They were deployed to provide very necessary security for the field teams and the crime scenes. The work was often undertaken in areas where known perpetrators were at large, where there was hostility towards the work being undertaken and where SFOR teams were conducting operations to seize suspected war criminals. These and other issues relating to the management and logistics of these mass grave excavations are discussed by Wright and Hanson (2009).

Standard operating procedures evolved for the fieldwork so that all relevant evidence was identified, documented and catalogued. This moved away from a trend that searched for graves by probing for bodies to conduct archaeological analysis, which was key to determining the site formation history, dating and stratigraphic sequence of graves, and the connections between them. Field and mortuary procedures collected anthropological data that might assist with identifications, and detailed analysis was undertaken to determine cause of death. A combination of evidential recording and collection from the scene of crime and exhibiting archaeological artefacts developed. Procedures were developed to ensure that information recorded could be used for both criminal prosecution and identification purposes.

ICTY investigation teams undertook work to pinpoint grave locations through witness information and other sources. This was partially successful, but highlighted problems later encountered by MPI in gaining accurate information from witnesses years after traumatic events, and then successfully interpreting it. The breakthrough in locating many grave sites came with the provision to the ICTY of aerial imagery taken during the conflict by the North Atlantic Treaty Organization (NATO) reconnaissance aircraft. Although only used to locate sites around Srebrenica, this archived imagery when combined with other information sources and analysis was vital in locating many sites. The field team operating during 1997–2000 under archaeologist/anthropologist Professor Richard Wright (Emeritus Professor of Anthropology, University of Sydney, Australia; e.g. Blau and Sterenberg, Chapter 33) realised the importance of using a multidisciplinary approach to site search and excavation, with imagery, witness information and analysis on the ground pinpointing locations from a macro to a micro scale. Experts were drawn in to provide sampling and analysis in the field (e.g. Brown 2006), and the Tribunal widely sought assistance for evidence analysis of soils, ballistics and watches, and for physical matching from international agencies and experts such as the US Bureau for Alcohol, Tobacco and Firearms (ATF) and Netherlands Forensic Institute (NFI) (Manning 2001). Furthermore, the excavation process of both primary and secondary grave sites provided intelligence to feedback into investigations to pinpoint related graves, execution sites, holding locations and group identities of the cases recovered. The result was that some 82% of the substantial mass graves found relating to the missing after the Srebrenica events in 1995 were pinpointed and tested between 1996 and 2000 by the ICTY field teams. These contained an estimated 72% of cases recovered related to these events. Aerial imagery did not unfortunately pinpoint grave sites further across BiH during this time.

The excavation and examination procedures established in the field and mortuary by the ICTY forensic teams set an example, which continues to be followed. Protocols, standards and documentation developed by various organisations including the Coalition Provisional Authority (CPA) in Iraq, by Bournemouth University, Inforce Foundation in the United Kingdom (Wessling, Chapter 50) and the ICMP were founded on the procedures developed during this mass grave investigation work (e.g. Bureau of Democracy, Human Rights and Labor and Bureau of Public Affairs 2003; Cox et al. 2008; Tuller et al. 2009).

Archaeological approaches

Search and location

Search methods between 1996 and 2001 relied on both witness information and imagery. For a sample of 49 potential sites indicated by imagery and then searched for by the ICTY field team, 44 were found to be graves (a 90% success rate). For many of these sites there was no corresponding witness information at the time. For a sample of 13 sites where only witness information was available, the success rate in finding the locations dropped to 54%. This mirrors rates found in later years for some sites investigated with ICMP support.

Once potential locations were determined, assessment from the ground initially focused upon use of imagery or witness description to guide teams to areas within 50 m of graves. Assessment of topographic and vegetative features then focused the search. In many cases, at primary graves, remains and the evidence of executions and robbing of graves could be pinpointed. Plants favouring disturbed soil grew in blocks over graves, or there were observable exposed subsoils, mounding and depressions. Other sites were covered with imported soil and debris used to conceal locations. For all sites, the area of disturbance visible in imagery and on the ground was always larger than the footprint of the grave; identifying this signature was key to locating the buried landscape.

Trenching to locate land surface and grave structure was the most rapid (and very successful) technique used to test and probe sites. Many graves were in potentially mined areas, which precluded techniques such as field walking and geophysical survey from use. It was not efficient or necessary to de-mine large areas to undertake wider search when imagery was so accurate. For example, a sequence of 12 secondary graves along the Cancari Road was pinpointed using aerial imagery. Their presence was confirmed by de-mining a narrow approach to the target area and then excavating a discreet peripheral test trench to confirm grave structure and the presence of multiple human remains, at a rate of three sites a day (Wright 1998). An additional grave in the sequence was not revealed on imagery and was pinpointed later by a witness. These graves yielded several thousand cases representing an estimated 2076 identified bodies (Janc 2010). Two were excavated by the ICTY in 1998 as a sample. The remainder were excavated between 2001 and 2009.

Excavation

The approaches to these excavations utilised techniques commonly used in research excavations, and rescue excavations in the United Kingdom. The priority was to ensure an understanding of the stratigraphic sequence of each site, identifying the site history and determining the properties of each grave. These approaches are discussed in some detail by Wright et al. (2005).

A stratigraphic understanding of each grave was key for many primary sites to demonstrate that graves had been disturbed or robbed or contained sequences of deposits – information that was easily lost if the stratigraphic relationships were not identified and recorded. The buried piles of bodies were often found to have reduced decay rate (a topic discussed by Haglund 2001; Haglund et al. 2001; Hanson 2004) and remained as a solid deposit that sealed evidence on the grave's surfaces (the walls and floors). The spread of 'spoil' or excess soil (from the creation of the grave) left after backfilling sealed the land surface around graves upon which perpetrators and vehicles operated. These layers often thinned out to a 'feather edge' (as described by Harris 1979, 32), which could be identified. A known edge could then be followed and surfaces, cuts and deposits identified and excavated. Exposure of these land surfaces was vital to identify and record the grave extent and structure, tool marks, trace and physical evidence such as shell cases and cranial bone fragments resulting from mass executions. This gave assured context to dating evidence and allowed comparison.

A technique often used was to remove the undifferentiated backfilled or capping soils (which were over and around the graves) in thin spits using excavators with toothless ditching buckets, which acted as giant trowels, leaving a clean surface upon which soil differences could be discerned. This was undertaken until the buried land surface or grave edge was identified. Excavation then moved from this arbitrary technique to one of stratigraphic recognition and excavation, exposing the extent of the grave and the related activity in the plan (Figure 3.1). All archaeological deposits were then revealed, noted and excavated. In this way the relationship between deposits, the context of evidence and deposits pre-dating events could be determined, allowing reconstruction. Issues regarding using various excavation techniques from experiences in BiH are discussed by Hanson (2004).

Exposure of the grave in the plan and recording of the surfaces allowed a 3D reconstruction of the grave's shape and details to be considered. In this way, if walls of graves needed to be removed for access or logistical reasons, stratigraphic relationships were recorded and understood beforehand. There is often space within graves to excavate without requiring removal of walls (Figure 3.2). The issues around the excavation approaches and engineering required around mass graves are discussed by Wright et al. (2005) and Cheetham et al. (2008).

Dating sites and determining the time of death of those in mass graves was key to demonstrating when specific events occurred, allowing them to be linked in the investigation. Aerial imagery provided specific dates of events, or a date range for occurrence of ground disturbance from 'before' and 'after' images. Botanical evidence around and beneath bodies could indicate if graves were open in high summer or autumn. Within the excavated graves, many self-winding watches were recovered, with a day/date window. They typically stop within 36–48 h of their last movement, and thus each presented a potential estimated time of death (Wright et al. 2005). Ballistic evidence also narrowed time ranges for when events occurred. If shell cases found within graves beneath undisturbed bodies had head stamps showing they were manufactured in 1994, they provide a *terminus post quem*; the grave cannot have been constructed earlier than 1994.

Figure 3.1 Lazete 2 primary grave during excavation in 2000, looking east, with the field stripped of topsoil. Multiple archaeological contexts revealed in plan, representing six phases of activity (Image courtesy: ICTY).

Figure 3.2 Lazete 2 primary grave, during excavation, looking east. Archaeologists and anthropologists clean and recover evidence, after removal of grave fill. The grave is 4 m wide and 38 m long (Image courtesy: ICTY).

Evidence recovered through careful archaeological excavation demonstrated the *modus operandi* of perpetrators. Vehicle tracks and machine bucket tool marks impressed in the grave floors demonstrated that a series of graves were excavated by the same machine. Blindfolds found at locations where prisoners were held, and also in multiple graves, thus associated with multiple cases, were determined to be made from common material (ICMP 2006; Manning 2001).

Issues

The difficulties of recognising stratigraphic relationships through the examination of test trenches were identified. Narrow trenches limited the ability to determine the sequence of archaeological contexts, potentially impacts the ability to interpret and thus accurately determine events related to investigations in question. This led to a need at times to reassess trenches and expand them, and use surface stripping to expose land surfaces and subsoils to fully identify the stratigraphic sequence. It was also necessary to re-excavate graves, to answer investigative questions not previously resolved, by undertaking additional assessment and stratigraphic analysis (e.g. Hanson 2012; Peccerelli 2000).

Bringing together specialists from across the world with varying experience, skills, inherited scientific approaches, terminologies, languages, expectations and understanding the work made for complex management organisation. For example, having integrated crime scene management and chain of custody standards as the norm on excavations was not the experience of some team members coming from human rights and field archaeology backgrounds.

The Tribunal focused on larger mass graves related to several specific criminal investigations, with a strategy to gather evidence for specific prosecutions between 1996 and 2001. They did not therefore systematically identify the missing and recover remains from smaller sites across BiH. The prime objective was not identification, or national coordination. Other excavations during this time were undertaken by local groups, PHR and national commissions to find as many missing as possible (e.g. Skinner et al. 2002). The lack of an overall nationally coordinated effort to undertake the search and excavation process impacted on the standards of exhumation and examination work undertaken, with delays in identifications and repatriations. These are issues that continue even today.

National investigations

Organisation

The Tribunal did not continue undertaking excavations after 2001. Work continued with national commissions and prosecutors supported by the ICMP. Some continuing monitoring by the ICTY took place from 2001. Commission staff, pathologists or ICMP staff continued to provide reports and testimony in The Hague in the Netherlands concerning investigative matters, such as new excavation findings, identifications and cause and manner of death of victims.

The national commissions, supported with technical assistance by PHR and the ICMP, were concerned with locating all of the missing, as well as providing evidence for prosecutions. This meant organising search and recovery from a wider range of site types than the ICTY dealt with, which posed many significant challenges. Work in the years immediately after the conflict was to some degree haphazard and lacked coordination. International efforts were made to assist with this.

PHR monitored and assisted a total of 508 exhumation sites in which the bodies of at least 1427 individuals were recovered in Bosnia. It left behind a comprehensive and transparent record of all of its work, which was focused on the eventual identification of the missing. In support of that goal, PHR collected ante-mortem data and created a database available to pathologists who would eventually close cases. It became clear in the years immediately following the conflict that the increasing number of cases excavated from graves and other sites were accumulating with little success in identifying them (ICMP 2014). The PHR initiative to identify Srebrenica missing had resulted in only 70 identifications by 1999 (Vollen 2001). Few dental records survived. There were very few ante-mortem hospital records or X-rays. There was clear difficulty in gaining positive identifications with many secondary graves and caves containing so many commingled body parts. Only 5–8% of cases related to the fall of Srebrenica in July 1995 had enough ante-mortem and post-mortem information to make an accurate assessment of identification (Sterenberg 2009). Recognition of cases through families examining images of clothing and personal effects was equally problematical. Families recognised clothing only 40% of the time; however, when their indications were checked against DNA matching of the family to the related remains, only 6.9% of clothing recognitions proved to be correct (Huffine et al. 2001).

Given these issues, the ICMP initiated and set up a DNA laboratory system, now operating under a well-established quality management system and accredited to ISO/IEC 17025 standards by an internationally recognised accreditation body. Comparisons of DNA profiles from unidentified skeletal remains were made to large-scale, regional databases of DNA profiles from families of the missing to establish a 'DNA-led' process of identification. Genetic kinship matching conducted computationally provided reliable and highly accurate bases for identifications. In a vast majority of instances, DNA matching provided the first evidence of identification, which was later combined with other types of ante-mortem and post-mortem comparisons to provide positive identifications and the issuance of death certificates. Over 14 000 identifications have been made in this way in BiH.[3] The DNA matching has also provided an excellent tool for re-associations of commingled or dispersed body parts, and acts as an evidence-matching tool between crime scenes such as primary and secondary grave sites, where re-associated body parts provide a physical link between locations. Furthermore, the positive identifications through DNA matches provide dating evidence for graves, as the individuals in them often have a known time of disappearance. If victims were seen alive on 26 May 1992, they cannot have been buried in a grave before that date. The identified cases therefore provide a *terminus post quem* for burial in that grave.

The commissions and MPI have undertaken investigative work from their regional offices across all of BiH, locating thousands of sites. Many of them are small in size or surface sites, with 66% of all sites excavated in BiH having contained only one or two bodies. It was vital that these small excavations were undertaken. Location of these sites has relied to a great extent on witnesses. The distribution of a sample of sites can be seen in Figure 3.3. These tend to mirror the areas of ethnic cleansing, conflict and confrontation lines.

[3] For more information, see: http://www.ic-mp.org/activities/technical-assistance/dna/ (last accessed October 2013).

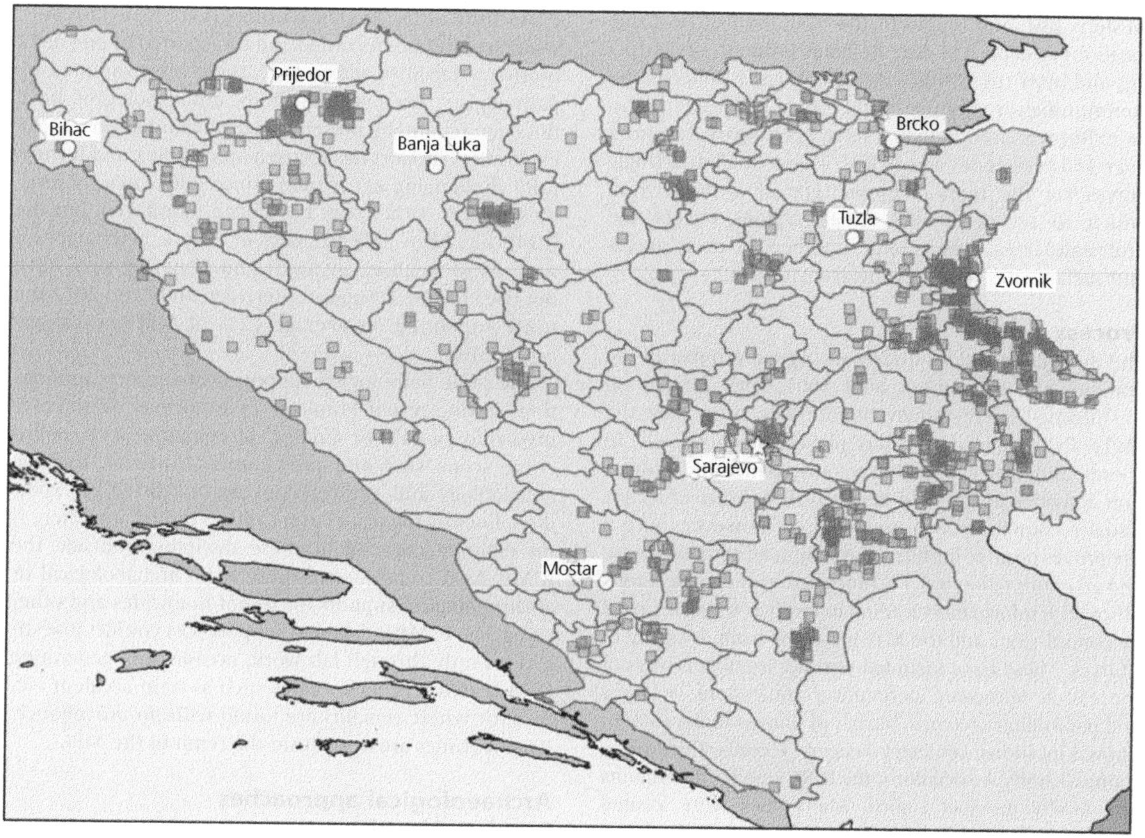

Figure 3.3 Trend in the distribution of field sites in BiH from which remains were recovered during 1996–2012. The sample of 1277 sites includes graves, cemeteries, buildings, burnt buildings, caves, lakes, rivers and surface locations. Data from ICMP fDMS database (Image courtesy: M. Venemeyer, ICMP).

The majority (67%) of cases assessed in the ICMP fDMS database[4] have come from mass graves. The number of large graves found and excavated has dropped since 2009. The work of PHR, commissions and the MPI (including the ICTY's work) has, however, maintained a momentum of site investigations over the years, with an average of at least 200 sites being assessed and excavated a year. This is likely to be an underestimation, as not all commission data are available.

There is regional variation in distribution of the sites from which bodies have been recovered. Epicentres of violence are starkly indicated; the Srebrenica region, Gornje Podrinje (comprising the towns of Visegrad, Foca and Gorasde) and the Krajina region together account for 65% of sites investigated by the ICTY and supported by PHR and the ICMP. This reflects both an intensity of search and location efforts and the numbers of missing in these areas.

Looking at the estimated numbers of cases recovered nationally, we see the impact of the recovery efforts concerning Srebrenica grave sites, which account for a majority (57%). When Krajina is included, these two areas account for three-quarters (74%) of all recovered cases recorded in the ICMP fDMS database.

The overall regional site distribution shows variation in types of site. The majority of cave sites found are in

[4]ICMP has designed an integrated Forensic Database Management System (fDMS). This searchable database links all information related to the identification process from field excavation, missing persons data, family reference data, examinations, DNA processes, profiles and matching to match report generation. Components of the fDMS are provided to governments and other authorities to help create a state-level central record of missing persons. The ICMP maintains a database of 150 000 genetic profiles obtained from relatives of the missing and government authorities worldwide. In BiH, over 71 361 blood reference samples and 32 730 post-mortem samples have been submitted to the ICMP, which has issued 16 166 match reports.

western BiH, and represent the utilisation of available locations to deposit bodies. Remains found in caves during and after the conflict were frequently collected by communities or volunteers and buried in cemeteries, to be exhumed later. Remains have been recovered from over 100 cemeteries across BiH. These small and single graves are the most common type of location from which to recover bodies in all regions except the Srebrenica area, where large numbers of mass graves and surface sites reflect events from 1995.

Process

The three commissions undertook a great number of site searches and excavations after 2001, with a focus on the missing from their own communities. Since 2008, the MPI's Exhumation Unit has played the lead role in coordinating and conducting reconnaissance and excavation activities in the field across BiH. A court order for initial reconnaissance is not required; however, once a site proves positive for human remains, all activities cease and an exhumation order is processed by the prosecutor's office. The information leading to location of graves used by commissions and the MPI has come from a variety of sources. These have included testimonies of survivors of the event, witnesses, perpetrator confessions, military and paramilitary records, burials of known individuals in known locations, cemetery keepers' records, third-party claims (Family Associations, the ICRC), police documents and family member claims. Many sites were located shortly after the war as they were known to survivors, the media and communities, and were well documented. It has been common practice that field investigators will visit and probe sites based solely on witness information. Often, reconnaissance work is primarily conducted in the spring, especially for surface remains, when vegetation growth does not impede search. Depending on the complexity of the site and the number of expected victims, the MPI will arrange for technical assistance from auxiliary, heavy machinery, de-miners, and specialists such as divers. This support includes the ICMP field teams. Although the MPI investigators have many years of experience working in the field, remarkably few staff hold actual technical competencies or certifications in relevant disciplines (ICMP 2014).

Once a site provides positive results, usually through test trenching and surface search, the MPI informs the court system, currently the BiH State Prosecutor's Office, which in turn will issue an exhumation order. They appoint an investigating prosecutor, a pathologist (responsible for the recovery, forensic examination and identification of the deceased) as well as crime scene staff, who are responsible for establishing and maintaining the forensic integrity of all evidence of forensic interest (crime inspectors and/or technicians are from local police units). This complies with the BiH Criminal Procedure Code (Bosnia and Herzegovina Office of the Prosecutor 2003). Evidence numbers are issued to cases, which are logged, recorded and transported to one of 12 mortuary facilities across BiH. These are examined by pathologists. For many facilities, anthropologists have not been habitually present during examinations. ICMP excavation support has focused on complex and technically challenging excavations since 2001, mainly large mass graves. Other sites have been monitored, but the ICMP has been able to assist in only a percentage of sites. Most small excavations and cemetery sites have not used technical support. Between 2009 and 2012 the ICMP supported on average 12% of MPI excavations across BiH.

The same pathologists support death scene examinations during recent homicide or suspicious death cases involving burials or finding of remains, with police crime scene staff and prosecutors. However, forensic archaeology and anthropology are not listed as expert disciplines by the prosecutor's offices in BiH, and there is no national capacity in these disciplines outside the ICMP. As a consequence there is no archaeological or anthropological support for recent homicides and other cases. The ICMP is asked to support post conflict investigations only through lab work, occasionally generating DNA match reports for cases such as train accident victims, or where remains are found with no provenance. Recent crimes are not within the remit of the MPI.

Archaeological approaches

Search and location

Witnesses have been the key to providing information for many graves. However, the accuracy of information is often lacking, and such information provides a general location only. The ability to locate graves through physical testing, for example digging test trenches, is dependent on multiple intelligence sources pinpointing a location to search. Physical trenching of locations has often ended in no grave being found. Witness information may be second or third hand, witnesses may have observed events under stress, their recollections may be limited and they may be understandably reluctant to return to locations. For the years 1996–2012 no remains were recovered from some 43% of sites attended by the ICMP, the ICTY and PHR. They yielded either no remains or non-conflict-related cases. The early post-war years were more successful, with more witnesses and fresher memories. Unsuccessful search is also exacerbated by court orders, which may specify only an exact geographical location that can be investigated, and because of the limits of current search techniques employed. Sites attended that yield no cases are a continuing issue today, with implications for resource and cost-effectiveness. Each year a number of graves excavated by MPI that did yield remains are found to pre-date the conflict, and so are not of interest in terms of identifying the missing from 1992 to 1995. Assessment of remains recovered but not identified from two regions of Bosnia show that at least 14% are not related to the conflict, and included remains of German soldiers from World War II (WWII), and Austro-Hungarian soldiers from World War I (WWI). Most pre-conflict remains recovered, however, relate to those exhumed from cemeteries which were buried in the last 50 years but were mistaken for or recovered as conflict-era cases. Prosecutors are responsible for the disposal of these cases and work with embassies and war dead commissions to repatriate cases determined to be foreign nationals. Some 200 cases assessed as soldiers from the German army of WWII are currently held in BiH mortuaries. The issue of witness accuracy is not a situation unique to Bosnia, and has been noted in other investigations, for example in Guatemala or Iraq.

Limits to the accuracy of site location information for suspected grave sites are further suggested by a comparison of the estimated number of bodies expected at a sample of grave sites (based upon data taken from the standardised support requests from MPI to the ICMP) against actual cases found. There was an overestimate of 36% between the suspected number compared to those excavated. Estimates often change as more intelligence is forthcoming once site work begins.

The physical search techniques relied upon by commissions and the MPI have been based primarily on search on foot to detect changes detectable on the ground, and to trench suspected locations. Ground search has limitations in a heavily mined country such as BiH, and vegetation covers the ground over time. Trenching provides a limited view of what is underground and the nature of soils that might indicate graves. It is a basic approach; however, it is fast and relatively simple to undertake. It has been relied upon by MPI and the prosecutor's office to pinpoint graves.

Other search techniques have been tested for suitability to locate graves. Dogs trained to locate remains have been tried to a limited extent without success. The application suffered from deploying dogs that had not been trained specifically to find skeletal remains, and applied limited scientific methods to guide search strategy. Geophysical techniques have been tested by the ICMP (Sterenberg 2009) and can successfully pinpoint ground disturbance (Cheetham 2005). However, the fact that geophysical techniques are slower than trenching, do not find graves but anomalies that might be graves (that need to be tested anyway), cannot be utilised until areas are de-mined and require costly specialist equipment and operators means the equipment has not been applied in BiH operations.

As stated, the most effective sensing technique to have assisted in finding graves has been aerial imagery. It has pinpointed the location of 90% of secondary graves related to the 1995 Srebrenica events. Imagery provides both a precise location and datable evidence of when events occurred. Unfortunately aerial imagery has been used in very few areas of the country. It has been perceived by the MPI and other agencies as unavailable and an expensive investment, and, until recently, analysis had not been undertaken to determine the success rates of its application.

Analysis undertaken by the ICMP in 2012 has shown there is potential for imagery that was regularly taken during 1992–1995 from aircraft and satellites to be further utilised. Imagery from commercial scientific sources such as the geographical SPOT satellite is archived. In 2013 the ICMP, together with the UN Operational Satellite Applications Programme (UNOSAT), purchased SPOT images. Although the resolution (10 m) is relatively poor, image analysis has both shown known mass grave sites and indicated new suspected locations. Of far more potential is the archived military imagery taken by the US Air Force (USAF) Lockheed U2 aircraft and other surveillance platforms during the war years. Thousands of very high-resolution images from across BiH exist that have not yet been assessed. The images were mostly taken for military purposes, but graves appear in them as a by-product. Review of this imagery by analysts for grave sites has been neither automatic nor systematic (Netherlands Institute for War Documentation 2002). In 2013 the ICMP supported the BiH office of the prosecutor in reaching an agreement with the US government to assist in coordinating analysis of further archived imagery. The ICMP has worked with the MPI and the prosecutor to produce lists of suspected site locations as a new focus of analysis for imagery analysts. The first images have been provided. It is likely that such aerial imagery will prove to be key in finding new grave sites of the remaining missing.

Imagery is not useful for locating all grave sites and remains. One difficulty for the MPI has been searching the diversity of locations in BiH, which vary regionally. Many caves in Herzegovina were utilised to dispose of remains. These sites often also contain munitions and rubbish. Specialist climbing, safety and support requirements are needed for excavation (e.g. Klonowski 2007; Simmons 2002). Cases recovered are commingled, and the key to assisting effective examinations is to undertake detailed survey of remains before lifting and determining discrete body parts. Wells were also utilised to dispose of bodies. In BiH many are waterlogged. As with caves, specific approaches and equipment are needed, but space can be confined and with water logging and decomposition comes the risk of pockets of gas. In many instances the specialist rescue teams undertake the recovery of remains. The limitations of workspace make careful excavation problematical.

Recovering remains from large bodies of water like rivers and lakes also requires complex organisation and qualified divers and equipment. There has been no systematic search of water in BiH, despite the known preference for disposal in water during the conflict, and elsewhere as a result of homicide. Opportunities have arisen when water levels have been lowered in dam lakes to recover remains. Some 450 cases were located when Perucac Lake levels were reduced in 2010, and extensive line searches and some excavations took place. These cases represented a minimum number of individuals (MNI) of 97 (Alicehajic et al. 2012) and still had viable DNA for identifications.

Rubbish and refuse dumps have been frequently used for disposal. There are obvious issues with health and safety of work teams and contamination. Stability of rubbish deposits when excavating at depth requires battering and stepping engineering works to prevent section collapse. These sites seem problematical as there can initially appear to be limited stratigraphy in the mixed rubbish deposits. However, layers and sequences of disturbance can be discerned and provide sequencing and dating evidence. Collections of artefacts from deposits around remains can provide insight into the date of deposition when analysed. In 2013 the excavation of the Sarajevo city garbage dump began, with an estimated 200,000 m^3 of rubbish and soil excavated in steps to search for human remains reported dumped and hidden in the conflict under 20–30 m of deposits.

All of these site types pose difficulties in recovery, need time for detailed survey and excavation, and tend to recover remains as complex commingled cases. Operations are costly when and if resources and the necessary equipment are available to undertake the work. In many cases, such as for rivers or lakes, there is a lack of suitable equipment, so only limited successful search has been undertaken. In some instances the expertise to tackle a site such as a cave or rubbish dump is not available to canton-level investigators and prosecutors, with the result that work has not yet been completed or attempted because it was not deemed practical.

A large number of cases are recovered from surface sites. These may be in forested locations or in abandoned or burnt buildings. Recovery tends to be by visual search, with a bias towards the recovery of large and obvious bones. Limited use has been made of gridding or systematic line search or other methods. Repeat visits to locations typically yield more remains.

To succeed in finding graves a combined use of techniques is needed, narrowing down search from a wider area to pinpointing a suspected micro location. Systematic search of suspected areas is required, not only to find graves but also to eliminate areas from investigation. As the search for further graves re-examines areas already searched, and patterns of grave location are analysed, accurate recording of site coordinates is needed.

Excavation

With a reliance on witness information, there has been limited use of archaeological recording and analysis to undertake crime scene reconstructions. Teams of workmen from canton mortuaries and machine operators are used for excavation. Many of them have been working for two decades on missing persons' excavations. The excavation techniques used by commissions and the MPI (at sites without ICMP involvement) have centred on locating remains and expanding excavations around cases until they are exposed. Years of experience have brought skill in identifying remains and grave structures and straightforward differences in soils, but core archaeological skills in stratigraphic recognition, recording and analysis are lacking.

Machines remove soil from around and over bodies. Shovels, picks and hand tools are then used to clean around cases, which are then numbered. These are generally examined *in situ* by the pathologist and photographed and noted. Survey is usually limited to one or two points on a case from a datum or baseline. There is no archaeological recording.

Excavations have seen a trend shifting from recovery of cases from large mass graves to smaller sites and cemetery exhumations since 2009. This reflects the completion of the 'store' of mass graves identified by the ICTY between 1996 and 2000, but which were excavated later. Those (mostly secondary grave) sites represented a significant percentage of the total cases recovered in BiH for the years between 1996 and 2008, with some 5700 identified individuals in all. There is a dearth of witness information for additional larger mass grave locations nationally, though many are suspected. The MPI has drawn up lists of suspected sites that it has not yet pinpointed. These are estimated to contain around 3500 of those still missing.

Excavation remains hazardous. The number of sites which required the assistance of specialists from the Mine Action Centre and civil protection teams for the years between 2009 and 2012 was at least 27, with 47 incidents involving unexploded ordnance or other risks to MPI site personnel. A percentage of sites turn up ordnance that was not expected. In July 2013, two blocks of downtown Sarajevo were closed to traffic as a live 155 mm artillery shell was removed safely from an excavation. Some sites have been impossible to excavate to date due to mine issues.

There continues to be a high rate of site investigation, and planning for excavations and reconnaissance. On average at least 200 excavations a year since 1996 have been undertaken. The return for these endeavours has greatly diminished since 2008, with a significant decrease in the number of cases recovered per site. An estimated 1500 cases were recovered each year between 1996 and 2008. This dropped to less than 400 a year between 2009 and 2012, with the backlog of 'stored' graves completed, as mentioned earlier. This is a slowed rate of return on the considerable effort that the MPI continues to invest in its field operations, and again reflects the lack of large grave sites found in recent years.

ICMP technical support

ICMP technical support in BiH has focused on assisting with the detection of sites, the identification and recording of archaeological records, the efficient recovery and recording of skeletal remains, and the survey and coordinate location of graves sites and bodies. Teams are tasked with record-keeping of all activities undertaken in the field. When the ICMP attends excavations it generally undertakes the analysis and recording. It has been relied upon to do so; there have been limited funds to employ archaeological staff to replicate the ICMP's work. All permanent national forensic archaeological and anthropological staff in BiH are employed by the ICMP. There has been a different work environment for these forensic archaeologists in recent years compared to the work of secured crime scenes under the ICTY. Family members expect to visit excavations to observe and bear witness; the ICMP strongly supports family groups and communities in identifying the missing (Figure 3.4).

ICMP staff attendance has focused support on large mass grave sites. Although these sites (holding 10 or more individuals) account for only 13% of sites excavated since 2001, they contain the majority of cases (67%). They have taken up much ICMP technical support time in the field due to their scale, the need for machine excavation and the extent to which commingled remains require archaeological and anthropological expertise for effective excavation.

ICMP standards require careful excavation that identifies each individual body or body part and separately records and surveys them. This simplifies the rest of the scientific process. The more accurate and controlled the excavation, the faster and more cost-effective are the examination, sampling and DNA analysis. If a body can be identified and collected intact, then the examination is straightforward and the sampling for DNA limited to one or two samples. If a body is collected as several body parts, or is mixed up with other bodies, then a longer time is required to examine the remains, and more samples need to be taken. This is in part determined by the properties of the grave; an undisturbed primary grave with 50 complete bodies is straightforward. A secondary grave of commingled remains may have 50 bodies, but they might be recovered as 150 body parts, which have to be re-associated, and sampled. This relationship between simple and complex sites and therefore simple and complex cases is a core issue which explains variation in recovery standards, examinations and ability to identify the missing.

For primary and secondary mass graves, the digital surveying of the distribution of archaeological contexts, remains and evidence has fundamental importance in being able to record and identify deposits that provide information on the distribution of body parts belonging to the same individual. In coordination with osteological and DNA-matching data, information on how bodies were placed in graves and the position and identification of each body part and deposit is proving crucial in assessing links between primary and secondary graves, determining if all remains have been recovered from certain events and if more graves are yet to be found. This assessment cannot be done if no accurate surveying data have been collected.

ICMP archaeologists provide technical assistance in assessing whether graves are related to the conflict in BiH. An excavation in 2012 held remains associated with artefacts of WWII German soldiers in deposits which could be shown in the stratigraphic sequence to pre-date the conflict of 1992–1995. Stratigraphic analysis of a simple

Figure 3.4 Excavation in 2006 of Hodzici 1 (Snagavo 4), a secondary grave related to Lazete 2. Family members visiting to view the work pray and look at personal effects (Image courtesy: ICMP).

cleaned, drawn and photographed section provided this information, demonstrating cases that were not relevant to missing persons from the conflict, and which precluded the need to take expensive DNA or radiocarbon dating samples. Archaeologists also provide assistance in dating graves, with artefacts found with remains, on rubbish such as wrappers and cans, or manufacturing dates on shell cases from archaeological contexts providing dating, and providing evidence. Dating evidence also helps to support or refute witness or other information.

Field teams record all data from sites they attend into the ICMP fDMS database. This has accumulated historical field data from various organisations and databases. Data have been merged for intended transfer to the MPI's Exhumation Unit to use as a national asset, allowing analysis and management of operational field-related information. To date, the ICMP has over 3700 sites in BiH recorded (ICMP 2014). Standard reports are generated for all sites attended to augment investigation records or be used as evidence.

Issues

The ICMP has encountered several issues in BiH related to the problems already described. These are common in post-conflict countries that need to rebuild everyday criminal investigative and rule of law systems, as well as provide the additional requirements of a missing persons program.

It is clear from the analysis of re-exhumed cases that the recovery of remains during and immediately after the war years led to misidentifications. This has been due in part to variable exhumation standards, and a lack of a standardised national examination and management process, with simple cases becoming complex. It is also due to a reliance on presumptive methods of identification in the immediate post-war years.

Crime scenes have not been systematically mapped and recorded. Sites investigated by commissions and by the MPI are not collated on a complete database, and records are disparate. To this end it has proved difficult to make some overall assessments and data comparisons, and to model and predict search for further graves, because all figures are not available.

The cantonal teams employed to undertake site location and excavation lacked formal training in archaeological excavation and recording. A lack of institutional positions for staff in the required disciplines has left a national deficit of qualified personnel. No scientific standards for the excavation and examinations have been implemented nationally.

Conclusion

National efforts and international support for investigations in BiH have been extensive and sustained. The figures for the number of excavations, recoveries, identifications and prosecutions speak for themselves. Forensic archaeology has played a key role in assisting in this work, while developing and seeing innovative processes used. More forensic archaeological excavations and excavation hours have been undertaken in BiH than anywhere else in the world. While many practical issues have been encountered, these are to be expected with the scale and complexity of work, and solutions to problems continue to be found. The integration of archaeological approaches into multidisciplinary criminal and identifications systems has been a great success.

Acknowledgements

A great number of individuals and a number of organisations have been involved in the remarkable story of forensic archaeology in BiH. While a complete list is too long to specify, we would like to acknowledge the very broad and formative contributions from many in the field including William Haglund and Richard Wright. Individuals at the ICMP, past and present, who have played a key role in establishing the environment in which forensic archaeology has been so successfully employed include Jon Sterenberg, Mark Skinner, Sharna Daley, Renee Kosalka, Matthew Vennemeyer, Cheryl Katzmarzyk, Rifat Kesetoviç, Jeffrey Buenger, Goran Peka, Klaudia Kuljuh, Samira Krehiç, Matthew Holiday, and current directors Andreas Kleiser, Adam Boys and Kathryne Bomberger. Parts of this chapter benefited greatly from information summarised from the ICMP 'Stocktaking' report for BiH that is in preparation at the time of this writing, and we acknowledge the contributions by Renee Kosalka and others whom we have listed to that work.

References

Alicehajic, E., Jugo, A. and Huel, R. et al. 2012. Perurac Lake, Bosnia: a multidisciplinary operation to locate, recover and examine DNA samples, and identify the missing from Balkans conflicts. *Proceedings of the American Academy of Forensic Sciences*. February 2012. Volume XVIII.

Bosnia and Herzegovina Office of the Prosecutor. 2003. *Criminal Procedure Code of Bosnia Herzegovina*. Official Gazette of Bosnia and Herzegovina, 3/03. Sarajevo, OHR.

Brown, A. G. 2006. The use of forensic botany and geology in war crimes investigations in NE Bosnia. *Forensic Science International* 163, 204–210.

Bureau of Democracy, Human Rights and Labor and Bureau of Public Affairs 2003. *Mass Graves of Iraq: Uncovering Atrocities*. DRL Fact Sheet. Washington, DC. Available at: http://2001-2009.state.gov/g/drl/rls/27000.htm (last accessed 16 August 2013).

Cheetham, P. 2005. Forensic geophysical survey. In J. Hunter and M. Cox (eds.), *Forensic Archaeology: Advances in Methods and Theory*, 62–95. London, Routledge.

Cheetham, P., Cox, M., Flavel, A., Hanson, I., Haynie, T., Oxlee, D. and Wessling, R., 2008. Search, location, excavation and recovery. In M. Cox, A. Flavel, I. Hanson, J. Laver and R. Wessling (eds.), *The Scientific Investigation of Mass Graves*, 183–267. Cambridge, Cambridge University Press.

Cox, M., Flavel, A., Hanson, I., Laver, J. and Wessling, R. (eds.) 2008. *The Scientific Investigation of Mass Graves*. Cambridge, Cambridge University Press.

Haglund, W. D. 2001. Recent mass graves, an introduction. In W. D. Haglund and M. H. Sorg (eds.), *Advances in Forensic Taphonomy: Method, Theory, and Archaeological Perspectives*, 243–261. Boca Raton, CRC Press.

Haglund, W. D., Connor, M. and Scott, D. D. 2001. The archaeology of contemporary mass graves. *Journal of Historical Archaeology* 35(1), 57–69.

Hanson, I. D. 2004. The importance of stratigraphy in forensic investigation. In K. Pye and D. Croft (eds.), *Forensic Geoscience: Principles, Techniques and Applications*, 39–47. Bath, Geological Society Special Publication 232.

Hanson, I. D. 2012. *Evaluation of Branjevo farm Mass Grave Report and Images*. ICMP Report (ICMP.FSD.AA.568.2.doc).

Harris, E. 1979. *Principles of Archaeological Stratigraphy*. London, Academic Press.

Huffine, E., Crews, J., Kennedy, B., Bomberger, K. and Zinbo, A. 2001. Mass identification of persons missing from the break-up of the former Yugoslavia: structure, function, and role of the International Commission on Missing Persons. *Croatian Medical Journal* 42(3), 271–275.

ICMP 2006. *Summary Report, Hodzici Road 01 Grave*, BiH. ICMP Report (ICMP.FSD.EXEX.217.1 doc).

ICMP 2014. *Bosnia and Herzegovina. Missing Persons from the Armed Conflicts of the 1990s: A Stocktaking*. ICMP Sarajevo.

ICRC 2004. *Bosnia-Herzegovina: Almost 17 000 Still Missing a Decade After War Ends*. News Release 04/140. Available at: http://www.icrc.org/eng/resources/documents/misc/673myj.htm (last accessed 16 August 2013).

Institut National d'Etudes Démographiques – Base de Données des Pays Développés. Available at: http://www.ined.fr/fichier/s_rubrique/302/publi_pdf2_04_pope1101_avdeev.2.en.pdf (last accessed 10 December 2014).

Janc, D. 2010. *Update to the Summary of Forensic Evidence-Exhumation of the Graves and Surface Remains Recoveries Related to Srebrenica and Žepa – April 2010*. ICTY Report. The Hague, Office of the Prosecutor ICTY.

Klonowski, E. 2007. Exhumations in Bosnia and Herzegovina: caves as mass graves, from recovery to identification. In M. Brickley and R. Ferllini (eds.), *Forensic Anthropology: Case Studies from Europe*, 183–202. Springfield, Charles C. Thomas.

Manning, D. 2001. *Srebrenica Investigation: Summary of Forensic Evidence-Mass Graves Exhumed in 2000*. ICTY Report. The Hague, Office of the Prosecutor ICTY.

Netherlands Institute for War Documentation 2002. Appendix II intelligence and the war in Bosnia 1992-1995: the role of the intelligence and security services: Chapter 7, 'imagery intelligence in Bosnia'. In *Srebrenica: A 'Safe' Area*, 277–312. Amsterdam, NOID.

Peccerelli, F. 2000. *Lazete 2 (LZ02C) Bosnia and Herzegovina Excavation and Exhumation Report*. ICTY Report. The Hague, Office of the Prosecutor ICTY.

Physicians for Human Rights 1997. PHR completes largest forensic study in its ten year history, unearths critical evidence in Bosnia and Croatia. *Newsletter of Physicians for Human Rights* Volume X, no. 1. Boston, PHR.

Physicians for Human Rights 1997. *Bosnia Projects Annual Report*, January–December 1997. Boston, PHR

Simmons, T. 2002. Taphonomy of a karstic cave execution site at Hrgar, Bosnia-Herzegovina. In W. D. Haglund and M. H. Sorg (eds.), *Advances in Forensic Taphonomy: Method, Theory, and Archaeological Perspectives*, 263–275. Boca Raton, CRC Press.

Skinner, M., York, H. P. and Connor, M. A. 2002. Post burial disturbance of graves in Bosnia-Herzegovina. In W. D. Haglund and M. H. Sorg (eds.), *Advances in Forensic Taphonomy: Method, Theory, and Archaeological Perspectives*, 293–308. Boca Raton, CRC Press.

Sterenberg, J. 2009. Dealing with the remains of conflict: an international response to crimes against humanity, forensic recovery, identification, and repatriation in the Former Yugoslavia. In S. Blau and D. H. Ubelaker (eds.), *World Archaeological Congress Handbook of Forensic Archaeology and Anthropology*, 416–425. Walnut Creek, Left Coast Press.

Tuller, H., Hofmeister, U. and Daley, S. 2009. Spatial analysis of mass grave mapping data to assist in the reassociation of disarticulated and commingled human remains. In B. J. Adams and J. E. Byrd. (eds.), *Recovery, Analysis and Identification of Commingled Human Remains*, 7–29. Totawa, Humana Press.

United Nations 1994. *Final Report of the United Nations Commission of Experts Established Pursuant to Security Council Resolution* 780, 1992.

Wright, R. 1998. *Report on Excavations in Eastern Bosnia for ICTY 1998*. ICTY Report. The Hague, Office of the Prosecutor ICTY.

Wright, R. and Hanson, I. 2009. Working for the UN as a forensic archaeologist. In S. Blau and D. H. Ubelaker (eds.), *World Archaeological Congress Handbook of Forensic Anthropology and Archaeology*, 468–478. London, Routledge.

Wright, R., Hanson, I. and Sterenberg, J. 2005. The archaeology of mass graves. In J. Hunter and M. Cox (eds.), *Forensic Archaeology: Advances in Theory and Practice*, 137–158. London, Routledge.

Vollen, L. 2001. All that remains: identifying the victims of the Srebrenica massacre. *Cambridge Quarterly of Healthcare Ethics* 10, 336–340.

CHAPTER 4

Forensic archaeology in Bulgaria – problems and perspectives

Ilian Boyanov

Department of Archaeology, New Bulgarian University, Sofia, Bulgaria

Historical background

The development of forensic archaeology in Bulgaria corresponds to the country's social and economic development, and consequently lags behind in comparison with most Western European countries and the United States. To a large extent, it developed in the shadow of forensic medicine and criminalistics, slowly forging forward as an independent field of study. The beginning of Bulgarian forensic medicine is associated with the establishment of the Chair of Forensic Medicine at the Medical Faculty in Sofia after the end of World War I (WWI) (Radanov 2009, 23). The organisation of forensic medical expert investigation in Bulgaria was established later, in accordance with the needs of judicial practice.

Criminalistics in Bulgaria developed in a similar fashion. For the period up to the end of World War II (WWII), criminological know-how spread mainly by means of forensic medicine and the achievements of other European countries in the field, particularly Austria. The next period in the development of criminalistics was quite different from the first. A typical feature of this development after WWII was its unconditional link to Soviet criminalistics and the detrimental split from Western European criminalistics, motivated by the unfounded denial of the principles on which it was based. One fact that can be quoted as having an essentially detrimental influence was that Bulgaria left the Interpol in 1951, and was accepted as a member of that organisation again only after the fall of the totalitarian regime in 1989. Then again, the introduction of criminalistics as a mandatory subject at the Faculty of Law, and later at the academy of the Ministry of Interior, had a favourable effect on its development (Cekov 1998, 46). A Central Laboratory for Court Expertise (*Централна лаборатория за съдебни експертизи*) was also established with the Ministry of Justice in 1961.

Archaeologists and forensic experts teamed up for the first time in connection with the controversy around the identification of the grave of the national hero Vassil Levski at the St. Petka of the Saddlers church in the 1980s (Ovcharov and Valev 2013). Unlike some of the Western European countries and the United States, however, in this case it was the archaeologists from NAIM – BAS who turned to their colleagues in forensics at the Central Laboratory for Court Expertise for assistance. After this first 'encounter', forensic archaeology remained more or less disregarded by investigation services for nearly 30 years. It became an independent field of study only in 2008, when it was introduced as a subject in the Department of Archaeology of New Bulgarian University, and then in the Faculty of Law at the University of National and World Economy in 2009.

Definition

Today, the term *forensic archaeology* in Bulgaria means two things: the application of forensic methods in studying and interpreting archaeological finds, and resorting to archaeological methods, mostly excavation and exhumation, in investigating contemporary crimes. Archaeologists are sometimes also being included during inquiries associated with looted archaeological sites. The time limit by prescription for contemporary crimes is accepted as a maximum of 75 years, beyond which the probability of the perpetrator of a given crime being alive – and hence subject to criminal prosecution – becomes minimal. According to contemporary Bulgarian law, criminal prosecution was excluded by prescription for an even shorter period of time, which was just 20 years. It was only in 1990 that the National Assembly passed an amendment to the Criminal Code (Наказателен кодекс), whereby the criminal prosecution in respect of the murder of two or more persons was excluded by prescription when it was not instigated in the course of

Forensic Archaeology: A Global Perspective, First Edition. Edited by W.J. Mike Groen, Nicholas Márquez-Grant and Robert C. Janaway.

35 (not 20) years (Item 1 of Article 80 (1) of the Criminal Code). The objective of this amendment was solely aimed at instigating criminal prosecution of the persons guilty of the mass murders in the labour camps in Bulgaria under the communist regime (Boyanov 2010, 7–8, 2012, 13). Interest in forensic archaeology has increased in recent years in connection with the criminological characteristics of the murders and the number of convictions adjudged.

Medico-legal framework

Crime trends in Bulgaria

Criminological statistics indicate that offences against the person ranked fourth in the structure of crimes in the 1980s, with 13.3% in the structure of reported crimes. During this period, murders with subsequent convictions had an almost identical relative share of 0.8–0.9%. This leads to the concerning conclusion that there was a stability of such crimes in the last years of the totalitarian regime.

Subsequently the high rate of murder in the beginning of the 1990s, which exceeded the number of five murders per 100,000 people, was followed by a sharp decline in the homicide rate of up to 3 per 100,000. This, however, is still twice as large as the European Union (EU) average, which was 1.6 per 100,000 in the period between 1999 and 2001. A steady downward trend began after 2000. The number of homicide cases continued to decline in absolute values in 2010, but because of the dynamic situation with population numbers caused by the intensive migration processes, it is difficult to pinpoint precise figures per 100,000. In 2009 and 2010 there was a stable trend of return to pre-1990 levels of less than or approximately two murders per 100,000. This trend of decline in the homicide rate in Bulgaria followed the general European trend. Nevertheless, Bulgaria still registered higher values in comparison with most EU member states (Bezlov et al. 2011, 62–63).

The considerably smaller number of perpetrators sentenced for premeditated murder after 1990 cannot be explained with a decline in the number of murders, as the actual situation was quite different. There are two main reasons for the existing anomaly: the incomparably lower degree of solved crimes compared to the preceding period, and the crisis in the judicial system. The omissions existing in Bulgarian legislation in respect to grave crimes also contributed to the smaller number of persons sentenced for murder. Another factor behind the low degree of solved crimes is the omissions in investigation and the collection of evidence, particularly in the case of buried human remains, because of the absence of forensic archaeologists.

The killing of another person with malice aforethought is the gravest crime against the person. In addition to the main *corpus delicti* (Article 115 of the Criminal Code), the law also lists specific cases of premeditated murder (Article 116 of the Criminal Code). The high degree of public risk of this type of crime obligates investigation authorities to take timely measures for the rapid resolution of the cases supported with evidence (Mihaylov 2002, 270–271). According to the provisions of procedure provided in Bulgaria, forensic expert assessment is the only mandatory one, which is explained by the fact that its subject – man – is the most valuable subject protected by law. It is precisely in relation to this expert assessment that forensic archaeology forged its way in Bulgaria, because when it mandatorily accompanies the investigation of a cadaver the expert assessment is directly related to the collection of new evidence (Manev 2010, 228).

Expert assessment according to Bulgarian legislation

Expert assessment is appointed by the court in the cases in which specialist knowledge is necessary in the field of science, art or technology, for the purpose of elucidating some circumstances of the case (Article 144 (1) of the Criminal Procedure Code). It is a means of collecting and checking evidence in criminal procedure. Expert assessment is carried out by appointment of the investigation authorities and involves examination by experts in a certain field of science, art or technology. The expert witnesses study the existing evidence, or that collected in the process of their investigation, on the basis of and within the range of the specialist knowledge they have. It is important to note that knowledge in the field of legal science is not included in the scope of specialist knowledge and therefore expert witnesses do not have the right to draw conclusions on legal matters (Mihaylov 2002, 258). Evidence is assessed by a procedure established by the Criminal Procedure Code, which guarantees the necessary completeness, comprehensiveness and objectivity of the expert assessment. The objective of the latter is to establish facts related to the relevant crime which investigation authorities cannot find by themselves and provide for the case, because they do not have the necessary specialist knowledge. These facts, established by an expert, are evidence in the criminal procedure sense of the word. This means that, in its procedural nature, expert assessment is an act of investigation, a means of procedure for collecting case evidence where specialist knowledge is required, as provided by Article 144 (1) of the Criminal Procedure Code. This is also confirmed by the provision of Article 136 (1) of the Criminal Procedure Code which lists expert assessment among the means of collecting and verifying evidence. The results of expert assessment are submitted by the relevant expert in a conclusion, in the form established by the law. An expert conclusion constitutes a means of providing evidence reproducing the facts established by means of expert assessment and constituting evidence on the case.

Expert assessments are classified on different grounds in Bulgarian legislation, being mandatory or not, as the case may be. Those assessments which can clarify the circumstances on the case listed in Article 144 (2) of the Criminal Procedure Code are mandatory. All these circumstances, however, are the subject of forensic expert assessment. All other expert assessments not listed in this legal text are not mandatory and are appointed at the discretion of the investigation authorities. The principle of *iuranovit curia* is valid in respect to the state procedure authorities who conduct the case and appoint an expert assessment. However, it is impossible to require these officials to have profound specialised knowledge in all spheres of natural and public life which may arise in any criminal case (Manev 2010, 229). They themselves decide when specialist knowledge for elucidating certain circumstances in the case is required.

The essence of an expert witness's activity in the procedure finds expression in his/her procedural rights and obligations. Above all, we should note that an expert has a number of rights in the procedure without which it would be impossible to fulfil this function and which a regular witness does not and cannot have. Expert witnesses have the right to familiarise themselves with the written and material evidence in the case which refers to the issues of expert assessment. They can also require additional materials and take part in conducting individual investigative actions, if necessary, in order to fulfil the task assigned (Article 150 (1) of the Criminal Procedure Code). This makes an expert an authority who, in a certain sense, contributes actively to revealing the objective truth in a case, unlike witnesses who only have to outline what they have perceived directly in a statement (Pavlov 1996, 276).

Expert assessment is also particularly and essentially important as a specialised study within and for the needs of a pending criminal trial. Suffice it to mention that, in order to prepare a conclusion, an expert witness applies knowledge and skills in which the state procedural authority cannot have specialist knowledge, or of which it only has a general idea. This means, at least, that the respective authority who commissions an expert assessment will be unable to gauge the depths of the specialised study, the methodology and means used, and so on. Nor can it understand fully the specialised means of getting the results from the expert assessment and the forming of expert conclusions.

The state procedural authority may or may not adopt (entirely or in part) the opinion of an expert. In compliance with the basic principle of decision-making by inner conviction (Article (1) of the Criminal Procedure Code) and the independence of the court and pre-trial proceeding authorities (Article 10 of the Criminal Procedure Code), the law has provided Article 154 (1) of the Criminal Procedure Code, according to which the conclusion of an expert is not binding upon the court and pre-trial proceeding authorities. However, the next paragraph of the same Article states that where an authority disagrees with the conclusion of an expert it shall be obligated to provide reasons thereof. This general clause opens various opportunities for interaction between a state procedural body and an expert witness. On the one hand, on the basis of considerable practical experience over the years, the court of the pre-trial authority finds shortcomings in the expert examination, mainly from the point of view of formal requirements and indicators in the work of the expert. However, it is difficult for the former to provide reasons in essence as this authority does not have specialised knowledge and skills. In this case, the decision-making authority questions the conclusion of the expert witness with a view to further development and specification and, more rarely, commissions a new expert assessment because the conclusion is not well justified and raises doubts about its correctness. Because of the destructive character of archaeological studies in particular, a repetition of assessment is well-nigh impossible. On the other hand, the procedural authority may accept the results of the expert assessment without reservations, inasmuch as the formal requirements for the appointment and execution of an expert assessment have been kept, and there are no visible indicators that the expert has not fulfilled his/her obligations involving the expert assessment in good faith, thus making the conclusion clearly unacceptable. In the case of miscarriage of justice, the responsibility is transferred to the expert witness. On the basis of these conditions, there is no doubt that the expert assessment and the expert witness are of crucial importance in procedures involving criminal cases.

Problems

In spite of the development of forensic archaeology as an independent subject in recent years, the discussion about the concrete role of archaeologists in criminal investigation was still topical in the near past (Haglund 2001, 27). Some authors do not fully accept the role of archaeology in the investigation of contemporary crimes. For example, Knight (1987, 60) thinks that archaeologists can be of assistance at a crime scene only in cases where there are doubts about when the individual has died. But since archaeological principles are based on relative rather than absolute criteria, the evidence collected during the excavation of a victim on the day following the murder can be just as much as that found at the excavation of a 10-, 100- or 1000-year-old grave. In Bulgaria, too, the medical examiner is the only available scientist from the point of view of criminal investigators. This leads to the opinion that it is sufficient to resort to his/her services during the exhumation of human remains and that, therefore, the participation of an archaeologist is not necessary, as one can also see from the provisions of the already repealed Article 131 (3) of the Criminal Procedure Code.

The application of archaeological expertise at a crime scene usually takes the form of borrowing methods and techniques, rather than using the archaeologists themselves. Medical examiners were the first to expand their participation in criminal investigations from laboratory tests to identify human bone remains as being present at the discovery of such remains, for example buried victims of crime. Their training, however, remains mainly in the sphere of laboratory tests, which makes it necessary to look for other specialists in the process of field work. It was precisely these needs that forged the way for forensic archaeology. In the not-so-distant past – and even today – in Bulgaria the absence of forensic archaeologists at the discovery of human remains frequently leads to the destruction of the context of the crime scene by untrained criminal investigators. This causes problems for medical examiners, who find themselves hampered because of lost or faulty recorded information at the discovery of these remains. Thus the number of unsolved crimes, particularly murders, because of incorrect inspection of the remains and the materials associated with them becomes unacceptably high and logically necessitates the inclusion of various specialists in the work on the crime scene, including forensic archaeologists.

It can be seen from what has been said so far that according to current Bulgarian legislation forensic archaeologists can be invited to work on a crime scene in the role of a forensic expert, mostly during the excavation of human remains. According to the provisions of Article 131 (3) of the Criminal Procedure Code valid until recently, however, the exhumation of a body at a regular cemetery was allowed by the court or the prosecutor only when the first examination of the body (autopsy) was incomplete and gave rise to suspicions that the conclusions were not objective. The presence of a forensic expert and certifying witnesses is mandatory and, if possible, that of persons providing additional technical assistance. The record drawn up during an exhumation at a regular cemetery requires recording the main stages of the exhumation of the body, as well as the condition of the grave before and after the exhumation, and after the reinterment of the body and refilling of the grave. Bone and tissue samples for laboratory examination are also taken during the exhumation (Cekov 1998, 342–343). One of the main problems is that the law does not provide a special procedure during the excavation of clandestinely buried human remains after a crime. Thus the participation of a medical examiner or a forensic archaeologist at work on a crime scene is not obligatory in practice, which provides the defence counsel with the opportunity to question the methods of excavation and collection of evidence (Judgment No. 99 on the dockets for the year 2010; II Criminal College of the Supreme Court of Cassation). What is more, the current Criminal Procedure Code does not have a special provision in respect to exhumation. According to Article 157 (3) of the Criminal Procedure Code, exhumation of a body is only allowed with the authorisation of the court or the prosecutor in the presence of an expert witness, that witness being a forensic medical examiner.

Court is the ultimate test of the forensic archaeologist's credibility. Impartiality in investigation and interpretation of evidence is imperative if justice is to be done. Credibility in court relies very much on experience and qualifications, as well as upon having the essential professional and interpersonal skills to ensure that evidence can be given with confidence and credibility (Hunter and Cox 2005, 21). In addition, it is not enough to be proficient as an archaeologist. An understanding of basic criminal law is essential (Kittichaisaree 2001). Failure to control confidential information at work in a judicial context may not only put at risk the case itself or the rights of the suspect, but can also place potential victims at risk. The grave responsibility that the opinion expressed by the experts may reflect on the life of other people also exists in the context of the court.

Role and future

The works of the archaeologist and the criminal investigator share a common basis: both try to understand the nature, the sequence and the reasons for certain events in the past. In the last few decades it has become clear that there are two emerging roles of forensic archaeology (Skinner et al. 2003; Spennemann and Franke 1995). The first includes the necessary skills and techniques to understand and interpret the history of the crime scene. The results of these are the first things taken into account by investigators, and the interpretation of taphonomic changes is usually essential in the process of excavation of the remains. The second, no less important, role is the reconstruction and interpretation of the events which occurred when the body was being buried. What a criminal investigator and an archaeologist share in their work on a crime scene and an archaeological site has been noted repeatedly (Dupras et al. 2006, 7–9). In short, both strive to preserve the physical and spatial integrity of potential evidence or remains, to make conclusions based on the context that can be supported with arguments and can be defensible in court.

Without doubt, field work, where the individual experience of every single specialist is essential, is the main aspect of forensic archaeology (Owsley 2001, 38). The key to the successful adaptation of archaeology in a forensic context lies in the application of all techniques and methods established over the years, but after they have been modified, or in the inclusion of new ones according to the requirements of the investigation. Archaeology raises questions and seeks facts, but as a destructive science its invasive methods are applied only in cases when concrete problems have to be solved. There are essential differences in the questions whose answers archaeology and forensic archaeology seek. The most important difference is that identification of the perpetrator of the crime is of prime importance to the latter (Hunter 1999). In forensic archaeology, evidence is not used to understand various aspects of human conduct but to reconstruct the specific features of a concrete event (Connor and Scott 2001, 3). These problems are not always clear in a forensic context. On the contrary, in many cases it is precisely the method of investigation and collection of evidence that is questioned in court (Erzinclioglu 2000, 39 *et seq.*). This is a major problem in Bulgaria, since forensic archaeologists may be summoned as expert witnesses by either the prosecution or the defence. Thus, instead of supporting the charges, the evidence they give in court can compromise the methods used by the crime investigators in favour of the accused, or even contribute to their acquittal.

Perspectives

Although forensic archaeology is developing quickly in Western Europe and the United States, in Bulgaria it is just taking its first steps. Luckily, this delay is due above all to the small number of grave crimes involving buried human remains – or at least that is what official statistics say. But does it really reflect what has been happening in Bulgaria in the last couple of decades? The answer to this question remains elusive, whether unconsciously or intentionally. Should one look at Bulgaria's recent past, one will see that, besides the thousands of victims of the People's Court after 9 September 1944, the murders committed by the then ruling party did not cease in the following decades.

Soon after the communist regime came to power in Bulgaria, one of the main tasks the Bulgarian Communist Party (*Българска комунистическа партия*) set before State Security was to organise and carry out the confinement of persons dangerous for the people's power in the so-called labour corrective colonies – in other words concentration camps – which were organised after the Stalinist model and which functioned until 1962. After the fall of the totalitarian regime on 10 November 1989, the prosecution established that life in those camps was exceedingly difficult. Of the 1501 inmates who passed through the camp near Lovech alone, 155 fell victim to the terror within, and the death certificates of 147 of these have been found. To this day, the graves of the victims have not been located or investigated, which does not allow the court to judge whether the reasons stated in the death certificates are valid.

Investigation of criminal liability for the murders began only after 10 November 1989, and covered only the operation of the last camps near Lovech and Skravena because detailed documentation for the rest was not discovered. Investigation proceedings were launched in March 1990 and the case dragged on to 2002, when it was closed by a judgment of the Supreme Court, whose main argument in support of this decision was the expiry of the prescription period, in spite of the voted amendment to the Criminal Code (Hristov 1999). The Bulgarian parliament did not resort to the experience of other countries, such as Germany for example, where the legislative body voted that there cannot be a period of prescription for the crimes perpetrated on the territory of the former German Democratic Republic during the totalitarian regime. Thus the only penalty for the defendants in this case was their 3-year remand into custody.

Conclusions

In Bulgaria so far, no National Assembly has suggested that the period of prescription for the gravest crime, murder, should be made redundant – a remnant of the Soviet penal doctrine introduced in Bulgarian laws after the establishment of the totalitarian regime. Redundancy of prescription would provide the opportunity for a new field of operation of forensic archaeology in Bulgaria, more precisely the localisation and investigation of the supposed mass graves in the communist labour camps. Better cooperation between criminal investigators and archaeologists also requires amendments to the Criminal Procedure Code pertaining to expert assessment and investigative action, and exhumation in particular. In this sense, it would be better for the procedure provided in Article 157 (3) of the Criminal Procedure Code to be obligatory not only during an exhumation authorised by the court or the prosecution, but also during overall crime scene examination associated with buried human remains. The application of archaeological techniques and methods in such cases would contribute to a higher degree of solved grave crimes, and the participation of a forensic archaeologist in collecting and recording evidence would make the work of medical examiners and the prosecution much easier. In some investigations the presence of archaeologists might be unnecessary (although it is never redundant), but in other cases they provide valuable and sometimes much-needed assistance. In any case, if not obligatory, the participation of a forensic archaeologist in such investigations is desirable and necessary, and could only help police and law-enforcement authorities.

References

Bezlov, T., Gunev, F. and Gerganov, A. 2011. *Тенденции на престъпността в България 2000-2010 г.* София.

Boyanov, I. 2010. *Съдебна археология.* София, Авалон.

Boyanov, I. 2012. Съдебна археология – често задавани въпроси. *Годишник на Департамент Археология* VII, 13–21.

Cekov, C. 1998. *Криминалистика.* София.

Connor, M. and Scott, D. 2001. Paradigms and perpetrators. *Journal of Historical Archaeology* 35(1), 1–6.

Dupras, T., Schultz, J., Wheeler, S. and Williams, L. 2006. *Forensic Recovery of Human Remains: Archaeological Approaches.* Boca Raton, CRC Press.

Erzinclioglu, Z. 2000. *Maggots, Murder and Men.* Colchester, Harley Books.

Haglund, W. D. 2001. Archaeology and forensic death investigation. *Journal of Historical Archaeology* 35(1), 26–34.

Hristov, H. 1999. *Секретното дело за лагерите.* София.

Hunter, J. 1999. The excavation of modern murder. In J. Downes and T. Pollard (eds.), *The Loved Body's Corruption*, 209–223. Glasgow, Cruithne Press.

Hunter, J. and Cox, M. 2005. *Forensic Archaeology: Advances in Theory and Practice.* London, Routledge.

Kittichaisaree, K. 2001. *International Criminal Law.* Oxford, Oxford University Press.

Knight, B. 1987. Murder in the laboratory. *New Scientist* December–January Issue, 59–63.

Manev, N. 2010. *Наказателно-процесуално право.* София.

Mihaylov, G. 2002. *Криминалистика.* София.

Owsley, D. W. 2001. Why the forensic anthropologist needs the archaeologist? *Journal of Historical Archaeology* 35(1), 35–38.

Ovcharov, D. and Valev, P. 2013. *Науката срещу агресивното невежество: Погребан ли е Апостола на свободата в църквата "Св. Петка Самарджийска"?* София.

Pavlov, S. 1996. *Наказателен процес на Република България.* София.

Radanov, S. 2009. *Съдебна медицина.* София, Ciela.

Skinner, M. F., Alempijevic, D. and Djuric-Srejic, M. 2003. Guidelines for international forensic bio-archaeology monitors of mass grave exhumations. *Forensic Science International* 134, 81–92.

Spennemann, D. H. R. and Franke, B. 1995. Archaeological techniques for exhumation: a unique data source for crime scene investigations. *Forensic Science International* 74, 5–15.

CHAPTER 5

Croatia (Hrvatska): from WWII and the 1991 war to contemporary forensic cases

Mario Šlaus[1] and Anja Petaros[2]

[1] *Anthropological Center of the Croatian Academy of Arts and Sciences, Zagreb, Croatia*

[2] *Department of Forensic Medicine and Criminalistics, Rijeka University School of Medicine, Rijeka, Croatia*

Introduction

Croatia belongs to a select group of countries that has probably benefited the most through the implementation of archaeological techniques in criminal investigations during its recent history, although the concept of forensic archaeology is still not recognised. Throughout and immediately after the 1991 War in Croatia that followed the dissolution of the former Yugoslavia more than 11,000 individuals had been reported missing (Anđelinović et al. 2005). A well-organised and professional search for the victims/missing or displaced individuals was imperative, and resulted in the formation of a government-sponsored interdisciplinary exhumation and identification team – a body whose very existence highlights the importance of archaeology in human rights investigations and contemporary forensic contexts (Šlaus et al. 2011).

Unfortunately, despite having recognised the contribution that archaeological techniques can make to these types of investigations and in their application, the recovery of human remains in Croatia is still under the authority of different types of law enforcement, military, legal medicine or at best anthropology agencies or government bodies, resulting in a situation where forensic archaeology is, at best, marginalised, while the figure of the forensic archaeologist is virtually non-existent. For this reason, in this chapter we will discuss the application of both archaeological and anthropological practices in Croatian legal settings.

Forensic archaeology history in Croatia

Since forensic archaeology is regarded as a relatively young discipline that developed during the last couple of decades (Haglund et al. 2001), the period during and immediately after the 1991 war in Croatia can be considered as the starting point for the development and implementation of archaeological practice and techniques in the legal setting and mass graves investigation in modern Croatia.

The 1991 war between Croatia and Serbia that followed the dissolution of the former Yugoslavia caused extensive material destruction and loss of life. The conflict was characterised by executions and mass burials of both civilians and the army and intentional destruction of private and government property. All together, from 1991 to 1995, there were more than 14,000 war-related deaths in Croatia (Šlaus et al. 2007a), 11,000 individuals had been reported missing and, of those, more than 4,000 were presumed dead (Brkić et al. 2004). To deal with this humanitarian crisis, the Croatian government established the Committee for Imprisoned and Missing Individuals (*Komisija za Zatočene i Nestale*), which gathered forensic experts from different disciplines and involved them in the process of recovering and identifying war-related victims (Kranioti and Paine 2011; Šlaus et al. 2011). The recovery process carried out under the auspices of the Committee started in 1995 when large parts of previously occupied Croatian territories were liberated in the military operation 'Storm'. However, as early as 1991 forensic medicine specialists and local forensic practitioners began to be involved in the recovery of victims and were thus, in a sense, obliged to develop their own basic recovery and anthropology techniques, as no forensic archaeologists or anthropologists were as yet involved in this process. With the formation of the Committee, a multidisciplinary team was formed and other forensic specialists (pathologists, odontologists, anthropologists with a background in archaeology, radiologists and molecular biologists) began to be called upon to participate in one of the biggest human identification processes in history (Huffine et al. 2001). This led to the development of a recognised *Croatian Model for the Search for Imprisoned and Missing Persons* that among its main points includes the recovery process of individuals buried in mass graves (Ministry of Veterans' Affairs 2013a). Apart from governmental and

Forensic Archaeology: A Global Perspective, First Edition. Edited by W.J. Mike Groen, Nicholas Márquez-Grant and Robert C. Janaway.

local assistance, the recovery and identification process was supported by international cooperation through the creation of humanitarian organisations. As early as 1992, teams of international experts started performing site surveys in order to identify potential mass graves in various parts of Croatia (Juhl 2005). In May 1993, in response to events that took place on the territory of the former Yugoslavia, the United Nations (UN) established the International Criminal Tribunal for the former Yugoslavia (ICTY) (ICTY 2013a). Formal excavations under the auspices of the ICTY started in July 1996 (ICTY 2013b). Foreign forensic archaeologists and anthropologists participated in the excavations by providing seasonal consulting, monitoring and advising on burial-scene location, forensic analysis and excavation. However, as the ICTY teams were involved only in solving burials relevant for war crime trials, the majority of recoveries and identifications carried out in Croatia were undertaken by the national Committee for Imprisoned and Missing Individuals. Since 2004, the same tasks have been undertaken by the Division for Imprisoned and Missing Individuals (*Uprava za Zatočene i Nestale*) on behalf of the Commission for Imprisoned and Missing Persons (*Povjerenstvo za Zatočene i Nestale*). Apart from UN involvement in the post-war recovery/identification process practice and the formation of the International Commission on Missing Persons (ICMP) (Hanson, Chapters 3 and 48, this volume; Huffine et al. 2001), a simultaneous international project was started. In 1995 the US–Croatia forensic anthropology project, in which specialists from the Smithsonian Institution (Washington DC, US) and the University of Knoxville, Tennessee (US), along with those from the Croatian Academy of Sciences and Arts and the University of Zagreb (Croatia), commenced the formation of a forensic data bank which gathered skeletal biological data from the recovered remains (Šlaus et al. 2011), thus helped the identification process through such measures as developing discriminant functions for sexing various skeletal components, and establishing large, computerised databases that facilitated the identification process (Šlaus et al. 2003, 2007a,b).

Thanks to the joint effort of the aforementioned organisations and the dedication of individual forensic specialists, to date 144 mass graves and 1700 individual burials have been excavated and 4684 victims have been recovered. Of these, 3796 have, so far, been positively identified (Pavelić 2013). Today, out of a total of 2,509 persons that are reported as missing in Croatia (in a population of 4,284,889), 1,703 (68% of the total number of missing individuals) are individuals who disappeared during the 1991 war in Croatia (Ministry of Interior 2013).

Following the creation of the Independent Republic of Croatia in 1991, excavations and exhumations of mass graves related to atrocities during, and in the immediate aftermath of, World War II (WWII) were also carried out (Borić et al. 2011) (the first being excavated as early as 1992 near Donji Macelj).

The recovery of forensically significant skeletal remains and the medico-legal framework in Croatia

To date, in Croatia there is no specific regulation on how the recovery of human skeletal remains should be conducted and, somewhat similarly, there are no clear guidelines as to when these can be considered to be of forensic significance. Generally, skeletal remains that are dated to the twentieth century are regarded as modern and often forensically significant finds (Šlaus et al. 2011). Based on this definition, three main categories of modern and 'forensically significant' human skeletal remains can be found in Croatia: (1) casualties of the 1991 war (1991–1995), (2) remains related to the period of WWII and its immediate aftermath (victims of armed conflicts, those killed by Croatia's pro-Nazi regime and those killed and who disappeared during the communist regime), and (3) recent forensic cases (homicide cases, unidentified bodies, mass disaster victims).

Skeletal remains and mass graves can be located in two different ways: by an elaborate system of collection of relevant data and testimonies encouraged mainly by governmental bodies or civic associations (analysis of archives, historical documents and collection of testimonies followed by on-site investigations and site surveys), or by accident. In the latter case, the police are called to the scene and usually the opinion of an archaeologist (most often from the local museum) is requested regarding the age of the remains (whether they represent a forensic case or archaeological finding).

1991 war remains

If the remains are believed to have belonged to victims of the 1991 war (based on the recovered personal artefacts and grave characteristics), they are treated as a forensic finding and immediately passed on to and handled by the Division for Imprisoned and Missing Individuals (of the Ministry of Veterans' Affairs, hereinafter 'the Ministry') (Šlaus et al. 2007a). The excavation process runs into several stages, which start with the coordination of all participants involved, screening for any unexploded explosive devices and determination of the micro location (ground-penetrating radar (GPR), trial excavations, probing, etc.) and ends with crime scene investigation and recovery of the bodies following the basic archaeological principles including photographing and mapping of the site and body positions (Ministry of Veterans' Affairs 2013b). The excavation process requires the presence of the State Attorney, the relevant county court, the relevant law enforcement police administration (Ministry of Interior), the Division for Exhumations

(Ministry of Defence) and the relevant medico-legal institutions (Ministry of Health) (Ministry of Veterans' Affairs, 2013a). The operational expert Division for Exhumations of the Croatian Ministry of Defence (*Odjel za Ekshumacije Ministarstva Obrane*) is the main body involved in the recovery and transportation of the remains, while the Department of Forensic Medicine carries out the anthropological and forensic analysis of the recovered remains. The whole process is undertaken following protocols in line with Croatian law needs (e.g. chain of custody) and, once finished, the complete documentation of the excavation is brought to the Directorate of the Division for Imprisoned and Missing Individuals (Ministry of Veterans' Affairs 2013a). In general, archaeologists are not involved in the excavations. Although in the beginning on many occasions forensic anthropologists with archaeological background helped to locate and recover the remains, the recovery of bodies has been more commonly left to military units and professional gravediggers (assisted by speleologists, well diggers, etc.). Specialists in legal medicine, some of them skilled in archaeological techniques, acted on site as external associates whose expertise was sought mainly for identification purposes but also to monitor and guide the process of excavation and extraction of the remains (Strinović et al. 2001).

WWII and post-war remains

As remains pertaining to the 20th century can be considered forensically important, human remains from WWII and the subsequent historical period also represent forensic cases. However, these were recovered and analysed in a different manner. For a number of years, an initiative to establish a government body that would deal with the recovery, identification and burial of the remains related to WWII has remained unrealised (Šlaus et al. 2011). Finally, in December 2012 the Croatian Parliament passed a law on the research, planning and maintenance of military and WWII cemeteries and post-war victims (*Zakon o istraživanju, uređenju i održavanju vojnih groblja, groblja žrtava Drugog svjetskog rata i poslijeratnog razdoblja* – NN 143/12), which came into force on January 2013. This law regulates the treatment and burial of remains from WWII and the post-war period. Since there was no specific act regulating actions required in the finding, recovery and analysis of historical war casualties, the articles that relate to forensic investigations in general were applied to these cases (these articles will be discussed in the section dedicated to recent forensic skeletal finds). At that time, the decision as to whether to carry out the investigation and exhumation of remains allegedly pertaining to WWII and the post-war period, and whether to consult medico-legal or other experts, depended on the existence of a reasonable suspicion that a criminal offense had been committed and, at the time, exclusively on the decision of the investigating judge.

This, obviously, did not satisfy the need for a thorough and professional treatment of all remains and/or graves pertaining to WWII and post-war victims. The approach to the site and processing, if any, depended on the preparation, training and knowledge of the authorities and experts present at the scene (e.g. trained medico-legal specialists with adequate knowledge of archaeological field methods and even archaeologists were sometimes present to perform the recovery while at other times this, unfortunately, was not the case). Cases where no investigation authority warrant had been issued after the finding of the remains have been reported. However, even in these cases the remains were packed and transported to the competent Department of Legal Medicine for an opinion and/or final storage since the former legal framework has not solved the issue of saving and storage of unidentified skeletal remains. Other cases where the necessary anthropological and legal analysis of the remains was hampered refer to situations in which medico-legal or other specialists were not called to participate in or monitor the excavation of the remains. The remains have been brought to the Department commingled in transport boxes/sacks with no additional photographic material or data on the spatial distribution of the remains on the site (e.g. remains recovered during construction and infrastructure projects).

The new law should help overcome such limitations and avoid repeating unnecessary mistakes. The new Law on the Research, Planning and Maintenance of Military Cemeteries, Cemeteries of WWII and the Post-War Period Victims (Table 5.1) empowers the Ministry to take pertinent actions for the documentation, transfer and caring of the remains of WWII and post-war victims, if it is in the public interest or if the remains are found during infrastructure, urban, archaeological, caving and other works (Article 5). Thus, with the new law, the question of the remains of WWII and post-war victims passed into the hands of the Division for Imprisoned and Missing Individuals, which now has two sections: one for victims of the 1991 war, and another for WWII and post-war victims (Ministry of Veterans' Affairs 2013a). The Ministry acts in cooperation with other authorities and with professional organisations to determine the number of victims in each discovered grave or mass grave (Article 7). That is, in case of founded suspicion about the existence of post-war burials and/or graves, the Ministry has to notify the competent State Attorney's Office and the Ministry of Interior and, in coordination with these organs, having received a proper warrant, proceeds with the investigation of the site (Article 10). Articles 18, 19 and 22 of this law are those that most strictly refer to the actions that should be undertaken in case of an accidental unearthing of skeletal remains that are thought to have belonged to WWII and post-war victims.

Table 5.1 Articles from the law on the research, planning and maintenance of military cemeteries, cemeteries of WWII and the post-war period victims referring to the actions that need to be undertaken after accidental discovery of human skeletal remains from the WWII and post-war period.

Article 18

(1) If during infrastructure, urban, construction, archaeological and other work [...], remains that can be reasonably assumed to have belonged to WWII–post-war victims are found, the investor or contractor shall, without delay, immediately stop the work and notify the Ministry and the Police Department of the Ministry of Interior [...].

(3) Upon receipt of the notification [...], the competent Police Directorate of the Ministry of Interior shall [...] within 3 days, notify the State Attorney's Office and the Ministry.

(5) The extent of the intervention – the exhumation, identification and treatment of human remains [...] shall be determined by the competent investigating judge.

Article 19

In accordance with the warrant issued by the judge responsible for the investigation, the Ministry will organise the exhumation, processing and identification of the remains [...].

Article 22

The Ministry may conduct both the exhumations and permanent disposal of the remains if it is required in the public interest, and when it has been regarded by the judicial authorities as being out of their jurisdiction and competence.

Table 5.2 Articles from the 'Criminal Procedure Code' that refer to the involvement of other professionals and experts in crime scene investigation.

Article 304

(2) Based on the warrant issued by the State Attorney, the crime scene investigation [...] can be performed by an investigator [...] or the police [...].

Article 306

(1) The authority conducting the investigation, the reconstruction or the experiment may seek professional assistance from an expert in criminalistics, traffic science or other disciplines who shall, if necessary, undertake measures to discover, secure and describe traces and other evidence, execute the necessary measurements as well as recordings, photography, sketching and collection of other data.

(2) An expert witness may also be summoned to be present during the crime scene investigation, reconstruction or experiment, if his/her presence would be useful for an expert's findings and opinion.

The new law does not specify which specialists should be involved in the recovery process. These are named and coordinated by the Ministry, specifically by the Division for Imprisoned and Missing Individuals. Accordingly, the excavation is handled mostly by the Division for Exhumations of the Croatian Ministry of Defence. Whether to carry out the excavation of remains allegedly belonging to WWII and post-war victims is now decided on the basis of the forensic (State Attorney) or civic (the Ministry) significance of the find (although it is not clear what makes a find and its recovery of public interest).

Recent forensic cases

Recent forensic skeletal finds are treated by law as any other forensic case. The State Attorney decides whether a crime scene investigation is needed, based on reasonable suspicion of criminal activity. Further actions are conducted pursuant to the Criminal Procedure Code (*Zakon o Kaznenom Postupku* – NN 152/08, 76/09, 80/11, 143/12). In Table 5.2, Articles 304 and 306 dedicated to the crime scene investigation that may refer also to recovery of accidentally unearthed remains or bodies are reported.

Based on the articles of the Criminal Procedure Code, experts of different disciplines are allowed to be present and/or assist in the crime scene investigation. However, the decision as to who should be engaged in the crime scene investigation process is left to the State Attorney and the competent authority conducting the investigation, who can fail to recognise the importance of having a medico-legal specialist or a forensic anthropologist or archaeologist at the scene. In cases where skeletal remains are unearthed and law enforcement agencies decide to seek the participation of an expert, they usually consult a medico-legal specialist, while the expertise/assistance of forensic anthropologists and archaeologists is almost never sought. Even then, the participation of the medico-legal specialist at the crime scene is often requested when the remains have been already unearthed by law enforcement personnel. It must be taken into consideration that recovery techniques and archaeological theory of medico-legal specialists and the police greatly vary between individuals, and that many of them acquire their first archaeological training at the crime scene (Dupras et al. 2006). During crime scene investigation law enforcement personnel follow standardised working methods and specific protocols described in specialised literature (e.g. *The Guide for Forensic Technicians*, published by the Ministry of Interior), which, however, fails to describe the specific actions for the investigation of crime scenes involving human skeletal remains or burials. Therefore, law enforcement personnel act on the exhumation scene following the general rules and protocols used in other crime scene investigations, relying on their skills and resources. On these occasions, more attention during the investigation is given to recovery of body remains, physical artefacts and personal items than to specific site features. Many of the tasks that are attributed to forensic archaeologists in specialised literature (Skinner et al. 2003) are performed in Croatia by police officers (ground search methods, survey techniques, mapping, excavation, artefact collection) or medico-legal specialists (basic recognition of remains, recognising the relationship, position of the bodies), while others are simply omitted (field sample collection, disclosure of site formation, recognition of soil layers and delineation of walls, dendrochronology, differentiating primary from secondary burials, dating and interpretation of the burial site, etc.). In addition, in cases when a relatively small amount of osteological material is recovered (for instance just a couple of bones) these remains are directly transported to the Departments of Forensic Medicine or Pathology in the nearest local hospitals without any attempt to recover relevant forensic archaeological data. Obviously, in both scenarios the possibility of losing evidentiary spatial and temporal burial data is very real. Although it is known that criminal scenes involving human skeletal remains are among the most complex (Dupras et al. 2006), the fact that such cases are very rare in a country like Croatia (with a rather small population of 4.3 million people) does not facilitate improvements in the working mode. Despite this, the identification procedure performed at the Department of Legal Medicine is of a high level, even though the involvement of physicians skilled in forensic anthropology techniques or forensic anthropologists themselves varies between cases (e.g. only the practitioners most familiar with state-of-the-art forensic anthropology rely on the US Scientific Working Group for Forensic Anthropology (SWGANTH) protocols during the processing and analysis of the remains). However, the current practice and experience in the medico-legal framework as well as the opinions and future intentions of the authorities performing crime scene investigations indicate progress in understanding the importance of a multidisciplinary approach in the investigation of remains.

Current status of forensic archaeology and forensic anthropology practice in Croatia

There is no doubt that a large number of mass graves resulting from conflicts that have marked the 20th century still remain undiscovered and concealed in Croatia. So far 144 mass graves related to the 1991 war have been excavated and the existence of hundreds of graves related to WWII and the post-war period has been postulated (based on different types of official and unofficial data). The importance of discovering, recovering, when possible identifying and guaranteeing a proper burial to all victims is upheld by Croatian laws, instituted as they are on the values and principles of international humanitarian law (Ferllini 2003). While Croatia has developed well-equipped, experienced and thoroughly professional recovery teams that have proven to be highly effective in the recovery and identification of victims of war crimes, the role of the forensic archaeologist remains marginalised and overshadowed by other disciplines. The current state of affairs, in which archaeologists are called on to simply date the recovered remains (separating ancient from modern remains), results in a situation where advances in archaeological theory and practice are not being taken advantage of in excavation practices. It can, therefore, be argued that in Croatia forensic archaeology in general, and more particularly the role of the forensic archaeologist, still remains unrecognised and thus ignored, with no professionals being truly involved in forensic archaeology (even though some archaeologists can be involved as expert witnesses in legal matters about forgery and robbery of archaeological items). This is similar, yet different, to the perception of forensic anthropology that has proven its importance during the identification and analyses of victims of the 1991 war in Croatia. While the contribution that this field has made to the location, recovery and identification of human remains is fully appreciated, professionals practising exclusively forensic anthropology are non-existent. While physical anthropology and bioarchaeology in Croatia are practiced by people with archaeological, anthropological or medical backgrounds, forensic anthropology is almost always left to medical doctors working in pathology departments, or more often in departments of forensic medicine. A total of four university departments of forensic medicine (in the cities of Osijek, Rijeka, Split and Zagreb) and a couple of hospital divisions for pathology and forensic medicine perform identification of skeletal remains in Croatia. In addition, in Zagreb physical anthropologists/bioarchaeologists from the Anthropological Centre of the Croatian Academy of Arts and Sciences participate in identification performed at the Department of Forensic Medicine, University of Zagreb.

Since there are still problems in formalising the role of archaeologists and anthropologists during forensic cases, there is no forensic anthropology or forensic archaeology society in Croatia and therefore no national guidelines or policies for these disciplines. Archaeologists, anthropologists and medical doctors working on skeletal remains (archaeological and recent) act independently as members of different professional organisations – The Croatian Anthropological Society (*Hrvatsko Antropološko Društvo*), the Croatian Archaeological Society (*Hrvatsko Arheološko Društvo*), the Croatian Society of Medico-legal Specialists and Toxicologists (*Hrvatsko Društvo Sudskih Medicinara i Toksikologa*) and the Croatian Society of Pathology and Forensic Medicine (*Hrvatsko Društvo za Patologiju i Sudsku Medicinu*) (the latter two are sections of the Croatian Medical Association (*Hrvatski Liječnički Zbor*)). There is no society that gathers different forensic professional profiles, possibly because of the small number of such specialists in Croatia. Some attempts to gather different forensic specialists have been made through the establishment of the Croatian Association Forensic Scientists (*Hrvatska Udruga Forenzičara*) (which did not include either an archaeological or an anthropological subsection) and that of the newly founded Croatian Forensic Association (*Hrvatsko Društvo Forenzičara*). The education of these specialists takes place in different faculties (Faculty of Philosophy – Ethnology and Cultural Anthropology and Archaeology study programs, Faculty of Science, Faculty of Medicine). At present no university programs or courses dedicated exclusively to forensic archaeology exists in Croatia. Forensic anthropology courses exist in the form of required courses at the Faculty of Philosophy of the Universities of Zagreb and Zadar (Anthropology and Archaeology study programs) and at the University Department of Forensic Sciences, University of Split (MA programs in forensics), and as an elective course at the Faculty of Science, University of Zagreb (MA program in biology) and at the Faculty of Medicine, University of Rijeka (the courses are open exclusively to the faculty's full-time students). No master's degrees, PhD programs or national training programmes/courses exist specifically for forensic archaeology/anthropology (although some talks on the topics have been organised for the police). At best, PhD researches that focus on forensic anthropology topics are conducted as part of other biomedical/social doctoral programs. In Croatia no accreditation program for these disciplines exists.

However, in the last couple of years the need for both a more multidisciplinary approach and broader knowledge in forensics has been recognised, although the question of whether it will lead to the formalisation of the roles that forensic archaeologists and anthropologists have in forensic analyses or to mandatory anthropological and archaeological training for professionals already involved in crime scene investigation and identification unfortunately still remains open. That is not to say that there has been no progress in this matter in Croatia. There has been, but it has been frustratingly slow. Today, both law enforcement personnel and forensic medicine practitioners, when asked, recognise the importance of including another allied professional (archaeologist or anthropologist) during the investigation process who will provide them with his/her expertise. Moreover, in 2011 a new specialisation programme for medico-legal doctors has been established (NN 100/11) which, for the first time in Croatia, also includes mandatory training in forensic anthropology and forensic odontology at the Anthropological Centre of the Croatian Academy of Arts and Sciences, and the Zagreb Faculty of Dentistry. The growing number of scientific papers published in the combined areas of forensic anthropology, archaeology and legal medicine confirm the recognition of the disciplines among practitioners (Borić et al. 2011; Kuharić et al. 2011; Leksan et al. 2005; Petaros et al. 2013; Petrovečki et al. 2007, 2008; Šlaus et al. 2003, 2007a,b, 2013).

Conclusion

In conclusion, the development of forensic anthropology and archaeology in Croatia today rests on the interest, experience and persistence of a few individuals who practice these disciplines and who, by themselves or through their departments, pursue additional training and accreditation outside Croatia. The factors hindering the implementation of specific measures that would improve the development of these fields are primarily a lack of communication between different forensic professionals (sometimes law enforcement agencies are not aware that they can seek anthropological or archaeological support or when they are they do not know whom to contact) and, of course, financial, legislative and organisational limitations. It is, however, vitally important to develop in the future a full recognition of the benefits that anthropological and archaeological expertise can bring to some forensic contexts if Croatia is truly determined to locate, recover, identify and analyse the remaining individuals missing from the 1991 war, as well as those individuals who have perished in previous armed conflicts. This of course depends both on the authorities performing crime scene investigation and on anthropologists and archaeologists who wish to pursue this type of career in forensics.

Acknowledgements

The authors would like to thank Professor Alan Bosnar, Professor Dražen Cuculić and Assistant Professor Valter Stemberga from the Department of Forensic Medicine and Criminalistics, Rijeka University School of Medicine, Rijeka, and especially Professor Mladen Marcikić from the Clinical Unit for Forensic Medicine, University Hospital Osijek, Osijek, for their invaluable testimonies, experience and suggestions. The authors have really appreciated also the affability, understanding, advice and the will for further cooperation between our disciplines expressed by the Head of the General Crime Division of Primorje – Gorski kotar County (Ministry of Interior), Robert Tomac. The time that all these colleagues have dedicated to us and their rich experience helped us to further strengthen and improve this chapter, allowing us to be included with the state-of-the-art work of other institutions and forensic professionals.

References

Anđelinović, Š., Sutlović, D., Erceg, I., et al. 2005. Twelve-year experience in identification of skeletal remains from mass graves. *Croatian Medical Journal* 46, 530–539.

Borić, I., Ljubković J. and Sutlović, D. 2011. Discovering the 60 years old secret: identification of the World War II mass graves victims from the island of Daksa near Dubrovnik, Croatia. *Croatian Medical Journal* 52, 327–335.

Brkić, H., Šlaus, M., Jerolimov, V. and Petrovečki, M. 2004. Dental evidence of exhumed human remains from the 1991 War in Croatia. *Collegium Antropologicum* 2, 259–266.

Dupras, T. L., Schultz, J. J., Wheeler, S. M. and Williams, L. J. 2006. *Forensic Recovery of Human Remains: Archaeological Approaches*. Boca Raton, CRC Press.

Ferllini, R. 2003. The development of human rights investigation since 1945. *Science & Justice* 43, 219–224.

Haglund, W. D., Connor, M. and Scott, D. D. 2001. The archaeology of contemporary mass graves. *Historical Archaeology* 35, 57–69.

Huffine, E., Crews, J., Kennedy, B., Bomberger, K. and Zinbo, A. 2001. Mass identification of persons missing from the break-up of former Yugoslavia: structure, function and role of the International Commission on Missing Persons. *Croatian Medical Journal* 42, 271–275.

ICTY (International Criminal Tribunal of the Former Yugoslavia). 2013a. *About the ICTY*. Available at: http://www.icty.org/sections/AbouttheICTY (last accessed 30 June 2013).

ICTY (International Criminal Tribunal of the Former Yugoslavia). 2013b. *First exhumation by ICTY to begin in Srebrenica area*. Available at: http://www.icty.org/sid/7329 (last accessed 1 June 2013).

Juhl, K. 2005. *The Contribution by (Forensic Archaeologists) to Human Rights Investigation of Mass Graves*. Stavanger, Arkeologisk Museum.

Kranioti, E. F. and Paine, R. R. 2011. Forensic anthropology in Europe: an assessment of current status and application. *Journal of Anthropological Sciences* 89, 71–92.

Kuharić, J., Kovačić, N., Marušić, P., Marušić, A. and Petrovečki, V. 2011. Positive identification by a skull with multiple epigenetic traits and abnormal structure of the neurocranium, viscerocranium, and the skeleton. *Journal of Forensic Sciences* 56, 788–793.

Leksan, I., Marcikić, M., Nikolić, V., Radić, R. and Selthofer, R. 2005. Morphological classification and sexual dimorphism of hyoid bone: new approach. *Collegium Antropologicum* 29, 237–242.

Ministry of Veterans' Affairs. 2013a. *The missing* [*Nestali*]. Available at: http://www.branitelji.hr/nestali (last accessed 30 June 2013).

Ministry of Veterans' Affairs. 2013b. *Croatian model* [*Hrvatski model*]. Available at: http://www.branitelji.hr/hr-model (last accessed 30 June 2013).

Ministry of Interior. 2013. *National record of missing persons* [*Nacionalna Evidencija Nestalih Osoba*]. Available at: http://www.nestali.hr/ (last accessed 30 June 2013).

Pavelić, B. 2013. Croatia and Serbia identify wartime dead together. *Balkan Transitional Justice*, 5 February 2013. Available at: http://www.balkaninsight.com/en/article/croatia-and-serbia-jointly-search-for-missing (last accessed 25 May 2013).

Petaros, A., Šlaus, M., Čoklo, M., Šoša, I., Čengija, M. and Bosnar, A. 2013. Retrospective analysis of free-fall fractures with regard to height and cause of fall. *Forensic Science International* 226, 290–295.

Petrovečki, V., Mayer, D., Šlaus, M., Strinović, D. and Škavić, J. 2007. Prediction of stature based on radiographic measurements of cadaver long bones: a study of the Croatian population. *Journal of Forensic Sciences* 52, 547–552.

Petrovečki, V., Salopek, D., Topić, I. and Marušić, A. 2008. Chronic unreduced anterior shoulder dislocation: application of anatomy to forensic identification. *American Journal of Forensic Medicine and Pathology* 29, 89–91.

Skinner, M., Alempijević, D. and Djurić-Srejić, M. 2003. Guidelines for international forensic bioarchaeology monitors of mass grave exhumation. *Forensic Science International* 134, 81–92.

Strinović, D., Škavić, J., Zečević, D., et al. 2001. Experience based on the model of identification in mass casualties [Iskustva Bazirana na Modelu Identifikacije u Masovnim Stradavanjima]. In J. Škavić (ed.), *10th International Meeting on Forensic Medicine Alpe-Adria-Pannonia*, 55–62. Zagreb, Croatian Medical Association.

Šlaus, M., Strinović, D., Škavić, J. and Petrovečki, V. 2003. Discriminant function sexing of fragmentary and complete femora: standards for contemporary Croatia. *Journal of Forensic Sciences* 48, 509–512.

Šlaus, M., Strinović, D., Pećina-Šlaus, N., et al. 2007a. Identification and analysis of human remains recovered from wells from the 1991 War in Croatia. *Forensic Science International* 171, 37–43.

Šlaus, M., Strinović, D., Petrovečki, V. and Vyroubal, V. 2007b. Contribution of forensic anthropology to identification process in Croatia: examples of victims recovered in wells. *Croatian Medical Journal* 48, 503–512.

Šlaus, M., Novak, M. and Vodanović, M. 2011. Croatia/Hrvatska. In N. Márquez-Grant and L. Fibiger (eds.), *The Routledge Handbook of Archaeological Human Remains and Legislation*, 83–96. London, Routledge.

Šlaus, M., Bedić, Ž., Strinović, D. and Petrovečki, V. 2013. Sex determination by discriminant function analysis of the tibia for contemporary Croats. *Forensic Science International* 10, e1–e4.

CHAPTER 6

Forensic archaeology in the Czech Republic

Petr Velemínský[1], Miluše Dobisíková[1], Eliška Maxová[1] and Jana Velemínská[2]

[1] *Department of Anthropology, National Museum, Prague, Czech Republic*

[2] *Department of Anthropology and Human Genetics, Faculty of Science, Charles University, Prague, Czech Republic*

Introduction

Research areas of forensic archaeology in the Czech Republic

Although each artefact documenting people's lives in the past is considered an archaeological find, even if it is only a few years old, in the Czech Republic archaeology is seen particularly as a discipline studying finds of more than 100 years of age, and archaeological research seldom considers any more recent finds. The situation has started changing only in recent years as more and more researchers/archaeologists realise the necessity of studying the events of our great-grandparents' era, that is where witnesses are still alive. Interest in recent times was also encouraged by the fall of communism in the late 1980s, which allowed unlimited opportunities to study the modern period in Middle European territory without an ideological undertone. Moreover, the existence of a range of recent monuments is threatened by modern construction activities. For example, unless they are architecturally interesting, industrial buildings from the 20th century are not often perceived as being valuable, documenting the technical level of the given period. If they are situated on a locally attractive plot of land, they are at risk of being torn down to make room for buildings that are more lucrative for the given municipality or city (commercial administrative centres etc.). First, such research focuses on identifying and clarifying events during the war conflicts which afflicted Czechoslovakia and from 1993 onwards the Czech Republic, in the 20th century. Consistent exploration of mass graves allowed national and/or personal identification (Funk et al. 2011; Konečná et al. 2012, Nenutil et al. 2011). An example is an endeavour to find and identify pilots killed above our territory during World War II (WWII) (Rak 2012; Trojan 2013).

The second area includes the exploration of graves/tombs with the aim of identifying the remains of historic persons. Research of the remains of historic persons has a long tradition in Bohemia, as the first such research dates to the turn of the 19th and 20th centuries (Matiegka 1912). This was not long after the French police officer Alphons Bertillon introduced the use of anthropometric methods to identify offenders. This group also includes the earlier-mentioned researches of particular WWII victims (e.g. Trojan 2013).

Last but not least, the study of modern execution sites can be included in this category as well. An example is the study of human remains found in execution sites in Vodňany or Bečov over Tepla (Likovský and Veleminský 2006; Mašková and Michálek 2006). Based on an archaeological context, attempts were made to reconstruct events preceding the death of individuals and the manner and cause of death (Sokol 2003).

Forensic archaeology in the Czech Republic

The present position of forensic archaeology in the Czech Republic

All the mentioned types of investigations are linked by the current application of archaeological principles, techniques and methodologies, methods of forensic anthropology and criminal science; hence, they represent the forensic archaeology specialisation.

The work of forensic anthropologists is based on the methods of biological or skeletal anthropology, which they further develop within the frame of their professional activities and the research tasks set out by their institutions. These institutions most often comprise institutes of forensic medicine, universities or national institutes of public health. Forensic anthropologists must at least hold an MSc degree in anthropology from a faculty of natural sciences. They must have passed a specialist state board examination of the Ministry of Health or completed a postgraduate program focusing on biological (skeletal) anthropology. These specialists may then work as judicial experts who identify unknown human remains, such as dead bodies or their parts, skeletal remains or other biological evidence. However, identification as a legal act *per se* falls under the jurisdiction of the court, with judicial experts merely

Forensic Archaeology: A Global Perspective, First Edition. Edited by W.J. Mike Groen, Nicholas Márquez-Grant and Robert C. Janaway.

preparing the source documents for such identification. In specific cases, judicial experts are summoned by a 'ruling' issued by the authorities involved in criminal proceedings (the police) or the court, on the basis of which they draw up an expert opinion stamped with a seal of office. A judicial expert may be nominated by any state organ, scientific institution or university and is appointed as an expert in a specific field by the presiding county judge or the Minister of Justice, who also swears the expert in. Once appointed, the expert is recorded in the register of judicial experts of the given court, though the expert's scope of activity may involve the whole country. Experts are appointed in accordance with Act No. 36/1967 Coll. on judiciary experts and interpreters as amended later by Act No. 444/2011 Coll. Such an appointment requires that the candidate has Czech citizenship, be knowledgeable and experienced in the given field and possess personal characteristics that guarantee that the required activities will be duly carried out. Moreover, the candidate must provide his/her consent to the appointment. In urgent cases when a judiciary expert in a given field is not on hand for some reason, an available expert may be summoned *ad hoc*. In exceptional and especially complex cases that require special scientific assessment, the investigating officer, public prosecutor or president of the court (presiding judge) may decide to summon a state institution to either submit an expert opinion or to review the report submitted by the judiciary expert. Skeletal findings at locations with the aspect of a funereal component of a certain community's settlement (archaeological localities) are excavated and removed by archaeologists. Others, especially isolated findings, fall within the jurisdiction of the police and are uncovered and removed by its technicians and handed over to a specialised institution, either the corresponding institute or department of forensic medicine or the Criminalistics Institute in Prague (*Kriminalistický ústav Praha*). Archaeologists are not usually summoned to such locations. Police investigations are strictly confidential and involve the participation of police experts or judiciary experts from the field of forensic medicine or anthropology, who are also bound by a pledge of secrecy. The examination of potentially present, or on the contrary absent, artefacts is within the jurisdiction of the police, who if necessary consult the relevant judiciary or other experts. Findings relating to WWII, which remains a rather sensitive social issue, are to date examined predominantly by the police.

Institutes or departments of forensic medicine form part of either medical faculties or county hospitals. The bodies of persons who have suffered a sudden or violent death are autopsied at these institutions and any findings of human remains in a given territory are examined there. The qualification required for working in the field of forensic medicine involves passing the state board examination before a committee from the Ministry of Health, while further professional development is ensured by the Institute for Postgraduate Training in Healthcare (*Institut Postgraduálního Vzdělávánive Zdravotnictví* – IPVZ).

The institution responsible for dealing with and resolving technical and laboratory problems as part of police investigations in the Czech Republic is the Criminalistics Institute in Prague. Apart from dealing with technical issues of the police investigation, it is responsible for the methodological management of the departments of criminalistics technology and expertise (*Odbor Kriminalistické Technikya Expertíz* – OKTE) attached to the county police directorates. It is also the only institution within the police force in the country authorised to investigate skeletal remains. In accordance with Police President Binding Directive No. 135/2010, only those findings of human remains where a period of 20 years has not yet elapsed from the date the given investigation was launched are considered to be relevant in criminal proceedings. Once this period has elapsed, such remains may not be used to demonstrate a crime, given the binding statute of limitations. According to their relevance, such remains are either destroyed or handed over to a museum with an anthropological collection. Employees of the Criminalistics Institute must pass a state board examination, which involves both their given speciality and legal issues related to their activities. The Institute's laboratories have accredited standard procedures.

The framework of forensic archaeology in the Czech Republic

Researches in the field of forensic archaeology are based on the same legislative framework as other archaeological researches. By law, archaeological research in the Czech Republic can be performed by the Institute of Archaeology of the Czech Academy of Sciences (*Archeologický ústav Akademie věd České Republiky*), which also gives its opinion on the protection of archaeological heritage. In justified cases, the Ministry of Culture of the Czech Republic (*Ministerstvo kultury České Republiky*), upon agreement with the Academy of Sciences of the Czech Republic (*Akademie věd České Republiky*) and upon request, can grant permission to universities, colleges, museums and other institutions and/or a physical entity who have the necessary professional qualifications to conduct archaeological research ('the authorised organisations'). The required professional qualification is a minimum of a master's degree in archaeology and 2 years of professional practice. The authorised institutions must provide premises for the temporary storage of archaeological finds and a laboratory for the processing of artefacts. They are obliged to notify the

Institute of Archaeology when research has begun, and to report the results to them (§ 21 of the Act No. 20/1987 of Coll., on State Monument Care, as amended). At present, more than a 100 state and private institutions authorised to perform archaeological research are active in the Czech Republic. In the Czech Republic, only archaeology graduates are eligible to conduct archaeological research whereas anthropology graduates are not. The archaeologist decides on the course of the research and which professionals from other fields should be included, that is whether an anthropologist should be invited to a find of human skeletal remains.

According to an amendment to the Act on State Monument Care (*Zákon o státní památkové péči*) of 2005, movable archaeological finds (including human skeletons) are the property of the region in the territory of which they were found. This is not applicable if they were found within the frame of a research performed by an organisation promoted by a municipality. In such a case they are the property of the municipality. If they are found within the frame of research performed by a state organisation they become the property of the Czech Republic. Movable archaeological finds that are regional property are deposited in a museum promoted by the region; if they are municipality property they are deposited in a museum promoted by the municipality or the region. Finally, finds discovered by state organisations are usually deposited in museums promoted by the Czech Ministry of Culture.

All the earlier-mentioned rules are part of the Act on State Monument Care, which became effective in 1987. Some parts of it have been revised in recent years. By legislation, archaeological research is sometimes conditioned by the Act on Town and Country Planning and Building Code (*Zákon o územním plánování a stavebním řádu*) (i.e. 'the Building Act'), the Act on Nature and Landscape Protection (*Zákon o ochraně přírody a krajiny*) or the European Convention on the Protection of the Archaeological Heritage (*Úmluva o ochraně architektonického dědictví Evropy*) of 2002.

In the case of an isolated find of human skeletal remains with no indication of date, the primary question is whether it is an 'archaeological' or 'forensic' find. If human skeletal remains are more than 20 years old they are not considered important under Criminal Law, since the statute of limitation in the case of murder is 20 years, and any criminal act cannot be proven.

Special legislation regarding the approach to the remains of victims of war conflicts that occurred in the Czech Republic territory does not exist. In this case we particularly think of victims of WWI and WWII whose relatives are likely to be found. Similarly, there is no special legislation in the case of the finding of skeletal remains within ecclesiastical properties. The Church gives their opinion in this case. If victims of criminal offences are buried by the perpetrators, only members of the Police of the Czech Republic can excavate such findings. Archaeologists are not invited to such cases – to 'clandestine graves'. In 2012, a little girl was murdered in Prague on returning from school. The perpetrator buried her body in a nearby forest. This was found by the police on the basis of olfactory and biological traces. Incidentally, in the Czech Republic there are about 2 murders per 100,000 inhabitants annually.

Professional institutes specialising in forensic archaeology

In the Czech Republic there is no organisation or institute dedicated to forensic archaeology. Research falling within this branch is performed by archaeologists in cooperation with forensic or biological anthropologists, historians and/or criminalists.

Subsequent cooperation with physicians and scientists of various specialisations (radiologists, anatomists, geneticists, entomologists, botanists, geologists) is also fundamental. Thus people from a range of professional fields take part in the research. In the Czech Republic there are no specialised forensic archaeologists yet, or, strictly speaking, people specialising solely in this topic. A periodically published journal devoted to forensic archaeology is not issued. An association of forensic archaeologists does not exist either.

The situation of 'forensic archaeology' in the Czech Republic is well illustrated by a case from 2007, when the discovery of skeletal remains in the territory of Brteč village near Vysoké Mýto was reported to the local police department. The police were authorised to secure evidence, remove, excavate the skeletal remains and transfer them to the Institute of Forensic Medicine of the Medical Faculty of Charles University and the Hradec Králové Teaching Hospital for forensic medical examination. Once the results of these expert examinations were available and the discovered artefacts had been dated, it was concluded that the mass grave most probably dated back to WWII and the criminalistics investigation was stopped as the statute of limitations had passed. Thus, the skeletal findings became irrelevant for forensic science and it was possible to submit the remains to a subsequent anthropological examination for scientific purposes.

Until then, police officers had had no prior experience with the excavation of multiple burials and thus the bones of individual persons were mixed up. Given this unqualified manipulation, only basic demographic data and the cause of death could be determined and it was not possible to fully identify the individual skeletons (Konečná et al. 2012).

The teaching of forensic archaeology

Forensic archaeology has not yet been clearly defined in the Czech Republic or, more precisely, this specialisation of archaeology has not yet been accredited in any university. The only opportunity for interested persons is to attend lectures concurrently at various faculties; archaeology and history is studied at the Faculty of Philosophy and Arts, biological anthropology at the Faculty of Science, medicine at the Faculty of Medicine, and criminal science at the Czech Police Academy. As for textbooks, the situation is optimal since students can use available foreign literature (e.g. Black and Ferguson 2011; Cox and Mays 2000; Cox et al. 2007; Ferrlini 2007). There is also appropriate literature available in the Czech language. Some information on forensic archaeology methods – excavation, documentation, sampling and exhuming of human remains, geophysical prospection – is partly summarised in the book written by L. Prokeš (2007). However, this book was written primarily for bioarchaeology students, and is mainly based on cases from past populations of the area. Of course, Czech students have an opportunity to study the specialisation abroad.

In the Czech Republic, the designation 'forensic' (e.g. anthropology, medicine and chemistry) is etymologically associated with forensic investigations and evidence gathering, mainly as part of criminal proceedings. The methods used in forensic sciences are usually identical to those used to investigate 'non-criminal or non-judicial' cases. The development of these methods is mainly based on the study and examination of general biological rules and these methods become 'forensic' once they are applied to specific cases under investigation. During the investigation of findings that are not older than 20 years (i.e. those considered important by criminal law), even when archaeological methods are applied, the term 'forensic archaeology' is practically never used. If an archaeological location, for example, is disturbed in the form of theft of certain artefacts or skeletal remains, then these acts are assessed and judged in accordance with the penal code.

There have been recent discussions on establishing a new field of study called 'archaeology of modernity' at the University of West Bohemia in Pilsen. This would deal with artefacts and events of the recent past, including war conflicts of the 20th century, and would also include forensic archaeology issues.

Methods and techniques used in the field of forensic archaeology studies

The methods of exploration, processing and evaluation of localities and finds in the case of forensic archaeology are not basically different from usual archaeological practices. The procedures are identical in the research of any prehistoric or historic era. Similarly to common archaeological research, both destructive and non-destructive methods are used here. Similarly, bioanthropological processing of skeletal remains is based on the same anthropological methods which are currently used by forensic anthropology and anthropology of past populations (e.g. Buikstra and Ubelaker 1994; Cox and Mays 2000, Stloukal et al. 1999).

Case studies in forensic archaeology

Of the war conflict events in the last century, the findings of WWI graves and mass graves at the end of WWII received by far the most publicity; these were graves at extermination camps, during death marches or graves dating to the expulsion of German inhabitants from the territory of former Czechoslovakia. If they were found after accidental exposure they were uncovered unprofessionally, which considerably limited the results of the subsequent research, whether it was bone materials, accessories or other artefacts (Konečná et al. 2012; Nenutil and Rak 2011; Rak 2012). Therefore, targeted locating of graves according to contemporaries' information or using aerial photography was approached recently.

Identification of historical individuals

As mentioned earlier, research of skeletons of historic persons has a big tradition in the Czech area. As early as 1900, Jindřich Matiegka studied the remains of the writer Pavel Josef Šafárik (Matiegka 1912). Subsequently, this biological anthropologist verified the authenticity of the remains of a number of historical Czech persons. Matiegka's research was followed by the recent research of the remains of the Danish astronomer Tycho Brahe, which ruled out his assumed poisoning (Rasmussen et al. 2013). Emanuel Vlček continued this research in the second half of the 20th century and processed the remains of about 60 members of the Přemyslid, Luxembourg, Jagiellonian and Habsburg dynasties, clerical persons and saints, and also important cultural, political and scientific persons (e.g. Bohuslav Martinů, Jan Masaryk). His research in many cases verified the authenticity of the remains and frequently corrected previous opinions of the health of those persons (Vlček 1997, 2000a,b). Vlček (1989) also studied the skulls of parachutists who attempted to take Reinhard Heidrich's life. He based the identification on a comparison of dental finds and the status of the dead parachutists' teeth. These were taken from photographs made by the German criminal service.

The methods of 'forensic archaeology' were partly applied at a survey of the skeletal remains of the nobleman General Johann Sporck. The general participated in a number of battles and suffered several injuries. The X-ray photographs of the skull of General Johann Sporck showed many small, irregularly placed deep shadows detectable on the affected places, mainly on the facial and chin regions. By means of an electron raster microscope it appeared that they represented lead splinters. As it is known that at that time cavalry pistols were charged with cut lead splinters there is a tangible relation between the described facial defects and the shotgun wounds which Sporck incurred at Mellerstadt (Dobisíková et al. 1999). The field of forensic archaeology can also include the search for the remains of the politician Milada Horakova, who was executed by the communist regime in the 1950s on the basis of trumped-up charges of conspiracy and treason. Her remains were allegedly cremated, but the urn was never found. According to witnesses and historians, there is evidence that the body was not cremated after her execution and autopsy, and was transported or rather 'snatched' by friends and placed in one of the tombs of her husband's family. In 2010, the search for the remains of Milada Horakova was initiated, the indicated tombs were opened and the individuals buried there were exhumed. However, on the basis of anthropological, osteological and genetic analysis (only the DNA of Horakova's daughter was available), the presence of the politician's skeleton was excluded from these tombs.[1]

WWI prisoner graves

The history of WWI raises interest as well. Although a number of publications have been devoted to it, war conflicts did not take place in our territory and an archaeological workplace specialising in the history of WWI has not been established yet in our country. War memorials are represented by prisoner-of-war camps and nearby cemeteries.

Soon after the Czechoslovak Republic (CSR) was constituted, in 1925, an inventory of military prisoner cemeteries in CSR was made in cooperation with orthodox priests, focused on Serbian WWI prisoners. In Bohemia 172 cemeteries were found, in Moravia 38 and in Slovakia 139, that is 349 cemeteries in total. The largest cemeteries were in Velké Meder-Čalovo, Broumov and Jindřichovice.

The best known cemetery is in Jindřichovice (the Sokolov region), the land being offered by the earl Nostic, who most probably initiated the establishment of the cemetery. At present, the cemetery is commemorated only by the Jindřichovice Museum, where 8000 small coffins with the exhumed remains of prisoners, mostly coming from the former Yugoslavia territory, are deposited, and there is also a detailed model constructed according to the original plans by a local citizen. Exhumation of skeletal remains was conducted in the period from 1926 to 1932, and 7100 Serbian and 189 Russian WWI prisoners of the Jindřichovice, Písek, Cheb, Chomutov and Chodová Planá cemeteries were exhumed (Beranová and Bruženák 2012; Brandl 1937).

WWII mass graves

In 2007, a mass grave with well-preserved skeleton remains of at least five individuals was discovered near Vysoké Mýto (Ústí nad Orlicí region). Undertaking DNA analysis was not cost-effective or possible due to the commingling of bones, indicating that most bones would have had to be sampled. Genetic analysis has not been carried out due to financial restrictions on research. Basic demographic data and the cause of death (a gunshot wound to the head) were determined in all individuals (Konečná et al. 2012). The direction and location of the gunshot wounds was typical of execution. All individuals could be deemed to be of Caucasoid origin, which was supported by making a 2D reconstruction of the physical appearance of the skull. Such 2D reconstruction, along with contemporary information, was also used in an attempt at individual identification; however, it was not successful. Remains of textiles and leather were evaluated and concluded to be part of German uniforms; the ammunition found belonged most probably to the Russian automatic gun Tokarev, type TT6-33 (Konečná et al. 2012).

In August 2010 the human remains of 16 individuals were found near Dobronín which raised considerable emotion. By oral tradition, the remains should have belonged to persons of German nationality shot or killed with shovels and pickaxes just after the end of WWII. The graves were uncovered by policemen along with archaeologists. The police did not invite any biological anthropologist to the uncovering of the human remains. The bones were sampled and the samples used for DNA examination for comparison with living relatives. However, the bioanthropological investigation did not find any evidence of the alleged cause of death. Moreover, after comparison with other information given by contemporaries it is evident that a thorough investigation of the events leading to the death of the buried persons is needed.[2] The findings from Dobronín confirmed the fact that discovery and excavation of skeletal remains should always be undertaken with a biological anthropologist. Only this can ensure finding information which may disappear when skeletons are uncovered, and at the same time ensure that the bones are positioned in such a way as to avoid damaging them.

In 2013, the remains, according to historians, of the greatest tank ace of WWII, Kurt Knispel, were found. His body was identified in an unmarked mass grave

[1]For more information, see: http://www.ceskatelevize.cz/porady/10268447803-tela-nevydavat/20956226945/ (last accessed 17 November 2014).

[2]For more information see: http://www.policie.cz/clanek/dobronin-profily-dna-obeti-stanoveny.aspx and http://www.rozhlas.cz/zpravy/regiony/_zprava/policiste-uzavreli-vysetrovani-zabitych-nemcu-z-dobronina--1154144 (last accessed 17 November 2014).

containing 15 German soldiers. Identification of Kurt Knispel was made easier thanks to a preserved military tag on his neck, which highlights the need for careful excavation and recording of objects associated with an individual. Bioanthropological investigation of the remains was later performed (Trojan 2013).[3] A survey of 'mass graves' with remains from disturbed interments also took place in the cemetery in Stribro in western Bohemia. Among other things, efforts were made to find the remains of specific Soviet citizens who died in Stribro at the end of WWII. The research revealed some major differences between the actual situation in the ground and the written evidence, and confirmed the suitability of field surveys on 20th century sites (Funk et al. 2011).

In the case of the aforementioned surveys of mass graves from WWII, criminal investigation proceedings were no longer involved.

WWII airplane crashes

The case of a crashed plane in Bělotín (Přerov region) was also appropriate for forensic investigation. Archaeologists, historians and the police of the Czech Republic participated in the research, which was conducted under the auspices of the Museum of Suchdol over Oder (District Nový Jíčín). Based on a find of a board gun shell and evidence given by a contemporary, remains of a Soviet plane that crashed at Bělotín in 1945 were sought. A survey probe was used which revealed the wreckage of aircraft Il 2 'Shturmovik'. The place was located precisely using a ground-penetrating radar (GPR), and when topsoil was removed and excavation conducted, board guns, a lot of cannon and machine-gun ammunition, an engine with a preserved nameplate, armour plating and other aircraft fragments were revealed. Under a 13 mm thick armour partition wall, burned bone fragments were found, belonging to one of the missing aviators, and later a Soviet military medal was found – 'Order of the Red Star' (*Orden Krasnoi Zvezdy*) – with a preserved number, which was used for precise identification of the pilot (Rak 2012).[4] On the other hand, in the case of a crashed aircraft found near Nynice (Pilsen region), explored by amateurs and without documentation, the identity of neither the plane nor the pilot has as yet been clarified (Rak 2012).

Surveys that helped clarify and identify the events of WWI and WWII were often primarily initiated by specialised societies, clubs or associations. Most of these organisations were established in the Czech Republic after the political changes in the early 1990s. They were usually founded by historians, both professionals and amateurs. They often bring together people who are interested in searching and repairing military equipment (e.g. The Military History Club Náchod (*Klub vojenské historie Náchod*), Military Car Club Plzen (*Klub vojenských automobilů Plzeň*), or they are associations of local patriots (e.g. the Czudek brothers from Náves at Jablunkov). Often these are aeronautical-historical societies, which in addition to looking for and excavating aircrafts are interested in aircraft modelling and history (e.g. SLET Pilsen (*SLET Plzeň*), East Czech Aviation Archive (*Východočeský letecký archív*), Prague Aviation Archive (*Pražský letecký archív*), Aviation history group Kovářská (*Leteckohistorická skupina Kovářská*), Klimkovice – pyrotechnic surveys (*Klimkovice – pyrotechnický průzkum*), the Friends of Suchdol over Odra River – Military History Section (*Klub přátel Suchdolu nad řekou Odrou – Sekce vojenské Historie*) (Rak 2012).

Conclusion

The aforementioned studies focusing on WWI and WWII events, especially surveys of mass graves, basically constituted the first collaboration between the police and archaeologists. Although this collaboration to date has not always worked effectively or ideally, and has not benefited any of the parties, it is likely that in the future it will deepen and intensify, not only with regard to the identification of war victims, but also potentially in cases of criminal proceedings, where the remains of victims are buried (clandestine graves). It cannot be ruled out that the ranks of the police will include persons with archaeological training who will be capable of conducting archaeological research. On the basis of the increased interest in military archaeology, combat archaeology or generally archaeology of conflicts of the 20th century, interest in forensic archaeology in the Czech Republic can be expected to increase in the following years. It is expected that the field of forensic archaeology will be accredited in the next few years at a university in the Czech Republic, with the resulting emergence of a specialised workplace/department, as well as the establishment of a professional journal devoted to this specialisation of archaeology.

[3]For more information, see: http://www.lidovky.cz/historici-na-znojemsku-nasli-ostatky-nemeckeho-tankoveho-esa-p6p-/lide.aspx?c=A130409_155827_lide_ape and http://www.novinky.cz/domaci/298538-historici-nasli-na-znojemsku-ostatky-streleckeho-esa-wehrmachtu.html (last accessed 17 November 2014).

[4]For more information, see: http://www.leteckemuzeum.eu/news/nalezeni-a-vyzvednuti-trosek-sovetskeho-bitevniku-il-2-belotin-17-10-2009/ (last accessed 17 November 2014).

References

Beranová, R. and Bruženák, V. 2012. Ozvěny Velké Války. Zajatecký Tábor Jindřichovice 1915–1918. Muzeum v Sokolově.

Black, S. and Ferguson, E. 2011. *Forensic Anthropology: 2000 to 2010*. Boca Raton, CRC Press.

Brandl, H. 1937. *Festshriftzur 400 Jahrfeier der Stadt Heinrichsgrün*. Obec Jindřichovice v Krušných Horách.

Buikstra, J. E. and Ubelaker, H. D. (eds.) 1994. Standards for data collection from human skeletal remains. Proceedings of a seminar at the field museum of Natural History. *Arkansas Archaeological Survey Research Series* 44, 206.

Cox, M. and Mays, S. 2000. *Human Osteology in Archaeology and Forensic Science*. Cambridge, Cambridge University Press.

Cox, M., Flavel, A., Hanson, I., Laver, J. and Wessling, R. (eds.) 2007. *The Scientific Investigation of Mass Graves: Towards Protocols and Standard Operating Procedures*. Cambridge, Cambridge University Press.

Dobisíková, M., Vyhnánek, L., Velemínský, P., Kuželka, V. and Čejková, I. 1999. Palaeopathology and historical personality of general Johann Sporck (1595–1679). *International Journal of Osteoarchaeology* 9, 297–301.

Ferrlini, R. 2007. *Forensic Archaeology and Human Rights Violations*. Springfield, Charles C. Thomas.

Funk, L., Hložek, J., Marková, S. et al. 2011. Historický a archeologický výzkum městského hřbitova ve Stříbře (Historical and archaeological survey of the main cemetery in the town of Stříbro). Kuděj - Časopis pro kulturní dějiny. *Západočeská Univerzita* 12, 31–51.

Konečná, L., Drozdová, E. and Šafr, M., 2012. Identifikace jedinců z hromadného hrobu. *Česká Antropologie* 61(1), 23–28.

Likovský, J. and Velemínský, P. 2006. Lidské kostrové pozůstatky z popraviště ve Vodňanech. *Archeologické Rozhledy* 58(4), 810–812.

Mašková, P. and Michálek, J. 2006. Archeologický výzkum v poloze 'Na šibenici' ve Vodňanech (okres Strakonice). Příspěvek k archeologii popravišť v Čechách. *Archeologické Rozhledy* 58(4), 790–809.

Matiegka, J. 1912. *Pozůstatky Slavných Mužů a Žen a jich Identifikace*. Praha, Vlastním nákladem vydal Jan Otto.

Nenutil, J. and Rak, M. 2011. *Exhumace obětí II. světové války: předpoklady, východiska, výzkum*. Plzni, Vydavatelství Západočeské Univerzity.

Nenutil, J., Rak, M., Friedl, L. et al. 2011. Archeologický výzkum na městském hřbitově ve Stříbře. In J. Nenutil and M. Rak a kol (eds.), *Exhumace obětí II. světové války: předpoklady, východiska, výzkum*, 79–82. Plzni, Vydavatelství Západočeské Univerzity.

Prokeš, L. 2007. *Posmrtné změny a jejich význam při interpretaci pohřebního ritu (ke vztahu mezi archeologií a forenzními vědami)*. Archaeologia Mediaevalis Moravica et Silesiana Suppl. 1. Brno, UAM Filosofická fakulta Masarykovy univerzity.

Rak, M. 2012. *Možnosti Archeologie 20. Století. Archeologie Konfliktů*. Disertační práce. Plzeň, Filosofická fakulta Západočeské Univerzity.

Rasmussen, K, Kučera, J., Skytte, L. et al. 2013. Was he murdered or was he not? – Part I: analyses of mercury in the remains of Tycho Brahe. *Archaeometry* 55(6), 1187–1195.

Sokol, P. 2003. Šibenice v Bečově nad teplou a archeologie popravišť. *Archeologické rozhledy* 55(4), 736–766.

Stloukal, M., Dobisíková, M., Kuželka, V. et al. 1999. *Antropologie. Příručka pro studium kostry*. Praha, Národní Muzeum.

Trojan, J. 2013. Historici našli na Znojemsku ostatky střeleckého esa Wehrmachtu. *Noviny Právo* 9 (dubna 2013).

Vlček, E. 1989. Identifikace lebek parašutistů z Resslovy ulice v Praze. *Časopis/lékařů českých* 128(8), 247–253.

Vlček, E. 1997. Nejstarší přemyslovci. Atlas kosterních pozůstatků prvních sedmi historicky známých generací Přemyslovců s podrobným komentářem a historickými poznámkami. *Fyzické osobnosti českých panovníků* I. díl. Praha, Vesmír.

Vlček, E. 2000a. *Čeští králové I. Atlas kosterních pozůstatků Českých králů Přemyslovské a Lucemburské dynastie s podrobným komentářem a historickými poznámkami. Fyzické osobnosti českých panovníků* II. díl. Praha, Vesmír.

Vlček, E. 2000b. *Čeští králové II. Atlas kosterních pozůstatků Českých králů Ladislava Pohrobka, Jiřího z Poděbrad a Habsburků pohřbených v Praze s podrobným komentářem a historickými poznámkami. Fyzické osobnosti českých panovníků* III. díl. Praha, Vesmír.

Websites

Czech television program 'Body not to be issued' [*Těla Nevydávat*]. Availableat: http://www.ceskatelevize.cz/porady/10268447803-tela-nevydavat/20956226945 or http://www.csfd.cz/film/297984-tela-nevydavat/filmoteka/

http://www.policie.cz/clanek/dobronin-profily-dna-obeti-stanoveny.aspx

http://www.rozhlas.cz/zpravy/regiony/_zprava/policiste-uzavreli-vysetrovani-zabitych-nemcu-z-dobronina--1154144

http://www.lidovky.cz/historici-na-znojemsku-nasli-ostatky-nemeckeho-tankoveho-esa-p6p-/lide.aspx?c=A130409_155827_lide_ape;

http://www.novinky.cz/domaci/298538-historici-nasli-na-znojemsku-ostatky-streleckeho-esa-wehrmachtu.html

http://www.leteckemuzeum.eu/news/nalezeni-a-vyzvednuti-trosek-sovetskeho-bitevniku-il-2-belotin-17-10-2009/

Websites related to archaeological legislation

List of organisations for execution of archaeological excavations (see. § 21 par.2, Act No.20/1987 Col.). Available at: http://www.arup.cas.cz/?p=8169. Accessed 17 November 2014.

Act No. 20/1987 Coll. on national protection and conservation of monuments (or State Monument Care) (Zákon č. 20/1987 Sb. o státní památkové péči). Available at: http://www.arup.cas.cz/wp-content/uploads/2010/11/zakon_pamatkovapece_aktualni2008.pdf. Accessed 17 November 2014. (in Czech language)

Act No. 183/2006 Coll., on zoning and building regulations (Zákon č. 183/2006 Sb., o územním plánování a stavebním řádu (changes: č. 68/2007 Sb., 191/2008 Sb., 223/2009 Sb., 227/2009 Sb., 345/2009 Sb., 379/2009 Sb.). Available at: http://www.tzb-info.cz/pravni-predpisy/zakon-c-183-2006-sb-o-uzemnim-planovani-a-stavebnim-radu-stavebni-zakon. Accessed 17 November 2014. (in Czech language)

Charter for the protection and management of European archaeological heritage (Úmluva o ochraně architektonického dědictví Evropy). Available at: http://www.kr-kralovehradecky.cz/cz/krajsky-urad/kultura/obecne-predpisy/umluva-o-ochrane-architektonickeho-dedictvi-evropy-3660/. Accessed 17 November 2014. (in Czech language)

CHAPTER 7

Forensic archaeology in Denmark

Marie Louise Jørkov and Niels Lynnerup

Unit of Forensic Anthropology, Institute of Forensic Medicine, Copenhagen, Denmark

Introduction

The Forensic Anthropology Unit of the Department of Forensic Pathology is part of the Institute of Forensic Medicine at the University of Copenhagen. The Institute houses all aspects of forensic medicine, including forensic toxicology, genetics, anthropology, pathology and odontology. The Forensic Anthropology Unit has worked with Danish archaeologists for 50 years, and regularly participates in conventional archaeological excavations and physical anthropological analysis of excavated human remains (e.g. Lynnerup 2009; Lynnerup et al. 2013).

The use of forensic archaeology, that is the use of archaeological methods in a medico-legal context, is a relatively new field of expertise in Denmark. During the last decade forensic archaeological cases have been few and far between. This is not least because there simply are few cases of buried bodies in Denmark. Indeed, buried bones found during excavations (building, garden work, home improvement) which are reported to the police often turn out to be of animal origin. In cases of buried human remains, where it is evident that it concerns a recently deceased and interred individual, the police, more often than not, do not find it necessary to use archaeological expertise. The few instances where archaeologists have been employed by the police have usually been in connection with surveying and locating presumed burial sites, including locating evidence material, such as cartridge casings, in connection to homicides.

Description of Danish medico-legal framework

The Danish medico-legal framework is non-adversarial, and it is for the judge, and the judge alone, to decide whether expert evidence, or indeed any kind of evidence, is admissible. In other words, there are no specific rules or statements indicating, or setting, a certain prescribed standard for expert evidence or who can be an expert witness (which would include forensic medical or archaeological evidence), as is known from, for example, the United States with the Fry and the Daubert rulings (Tancredi and Giannini 1994).

Thus, forensic evidence, including forensic archaeological evidence, is called for by the prosecution, and the judge can decide admissibility, if contested. There are no codified ways for presenting or writing up reports, or for giving expert opinion in court, although a certain *modus operandi* has been developed especially by the forensic medical community and the forensic (police) technical community (Saukko 2013). If called for, forensic archaeological reports would be written up following the general standards and ways developed by the forensic pathological and anthropological institutes and units. Archaeological reports concerning surveying and excavation will be written up according to the regular Danish archaeological qualifications and standards.

The few instances where archaeologists have been used in forensic work, surveying, locating and exhuming dead bodies, are mainly due to the scarcity of crimes. The Danish murder rate is around 1 per 100,000 (population of *c.* 5 million) and has been at this level for decades (Rogde 2013; Tangmose Larsen and Lynnerup 2011).

Short description of Danish forensic institutes

Denmark has three forensic institutes at Copenhagen, Århus and Odense. These institutes are part of the universities of Copenhagen, Århus and southern Denmark (Odense), respectively. Forensic genetics is only performed at the institute in Copenhagen, as is forensic anthropological anthropometry, facial recognition and gait analysis (study of human motion). Forensic toxicology is practiced at both the institutes in Copenhagen and in Århus, while forensic pathology and forensic anthropological skeletal analysis is practiced at all three institutes. There is no specific forensic archaeological unit in Denmark. However, the Danish National Police (*Rigspolitiet*) have initiated an *ad hoc* collaboration with archaeologists from the Moesgaard museum in Århus and from a local museum,

Forensic Archaeology: A Global Perspective, First Edition. Edited by W.J. Mike Groen, Nicholas Márquez-Grant and Robert C. Janaway.

Museum Lolland-Falster, in southern Denmark. Both the forensic institutes at Copenhagen and Odense have an extensive collaboration with archaeologists and maintain archaeological osteological collections (Lynnerup 2009; Lynnerup et al. 2013). Thus, all archaeologically excavated human remains end up at these two institutions for analysis and curation. Currently the two institutions house some 50,000 skeletons, predominantly from the medieval period. The archaeologists or physical/forensic anthropologists have never been allowed to conduct full excavation of buried human remains associated with modern crime scenes. This has either been done by the scene of crime officers alone or together with a forensic pathologist. Unfortunately none of these are excavators or have any training in excavation techniques.

Search for scattered human remains is also done by the police and their dogs, which specialise in the decomposition odour of (human) bones. Unfortunately, this may result in missing elements, painstaking collection of animal bones and possibly loss of evidence.

All these services are exclusively requested by the police, that is private persons or organisations cannot request these services.

Forensic archaeology at present in Denmark

Since there is no academic degree in forensic, biological or physical anthropology or forensic archaeology in Denmark, the extant practitioners in the field (four) reflect different paths taken to the subject area, which may be a biological, medical or archaeological academic degree or a degree from a non-Danish university. There is no formalised training, but given the close cooperation with archaeologists, informal training actually reflects substantial analyses of archaeological skeletal cases.

Being part of a university means that a certain degree of scientific work is required, which is generally reflected in publications in peer-reviewed journals.

Representative examples of Danish casework

Archaeological techniques were applied in the course of forensic work in 2003. A person had gone missing 30 years earlier, was assumed murdered, and was buried in a sand dune landscape. The police needed help to narrow down the search field and called for archaeological assistance from the local museum (Museum Lolland-Falster). The archaeologist surveyed the area and once a possible site was identified, the surface was scraped in thin centimetre spits using a mechanical excavator overseen by the archaeologist.

However, the archaeologist could quite quickly conclude that no disturbance of soil had taken place within the last 600 years. The actual burial was never found.

In another case a witness had pointed out a location in a small wood where a body was presumed to be buried. Archaeologists from the Moesgaard museum were called for by the police and assisted by guiding the police in the cleaning of leaf surfaces and other residue in order to identify a possible outline of a grave. It became clear that there were several disturbances of the ground. But as it turned out, these disturbances had all been made by the police dogs in previous attempts to locate the grave (L. Krants Larsen, personal communication, 2013).

One of the more recent and probably biggest assignments yet where the archaeologists have assisted the police was in a case of locating a child's grave. The Scene of Crime officer contacted the archaeologists from the Moesgaard museum. The ground was searched by the archaeologists using a ground penetrating radar (GPR); however, the results did not prove to be helpful in this type of soil. Instead the suspected area was dug up by a mechanical excavator in thin spit layers supervised by the archaeologists. There were several disturbances. However, the area turned out to be a small pet cemetery. Not one of the graves contained a human child (L. Krants Larsen, personal communication, 2013).

Archaeologists have also been employed to sieve soil in order to collect evidence such as cartridge casings, fired bullets or other material that could help in identification. One case was in connection to a double homicide in the outskirts of a wood. The Scene of Crime officers contacted the archaeologists from the Moesgaard museum as they needed help to recover any evidence material from the crime scene. The archaeologists used metal detectors to locate ejected cartridge casings on the surface, followed by sieving of top layers of soil. Their method resulted in the finding of another eight fired bullets (L. Krants Larsen, personal communication, 2013). A second case where sieving was conducted was after a body had been found dumped in a slurry tank. Nothing on the body could help the police identify the person. Again, assistance from the archaeologists at the Moesgaard museum was called for by the Scene of Crime officer. In this case they were asked to water-sieve the slurry tank to recover any items that could be useful. Besides remnants of duct tape, nothing was found (L. Krants Larsen, personal communication, 2013). Further inquiries and investigation of the local area identified the person as an illegal immigrant possibly dumped there b fellow illegal immigrants after his death (Detective Chief Inspector P. Nielsen, personal communication, 2013).

Yet by far the most finds of human bones are made when such material is encountered accidentally, for example among deceased medical doctors' materials or trophy skulls (e.g. Lynnerup and Iversen 2006). The police are then alerted, and the human remains brought to the institutes of forensic medicine. The forensic anthropologist then examines the remains, and writes up a report, not least focusing on the presumed dating of the remains, for example historical or recent. In approximately five cases per year a radiocarbon dating is performed to determine more definitely whether the material is indeed historical (or, at least, given the so-called bomb pulse, from before 1954). Skeletal material found in such circumstances and probably older than 50–60 years will not be investigated further by the police.

Conclusion and future prospects for forensic archaeology in Denmark

Forensic archaeology has until now been sparingly used in Denmark. This is mostly a reflection of there being few cases where a forensic archaeological approach would be crucial, but also of a lack of knowledge among the police (who would need to request these services) and the forensic pathologists (who may end up assisting in exhumations). One may hope that the recent upgrading of forensic anthropology in Denmark may result in a change. Forensic anthropologists in Denmark work closely with both archaeologists and forensic pathologists, and would thus seem to be in a good position to introduce forensic archaeological methods to the forensic community. Yet it is difficult to see a more substantial use of forensic archaeology in Danish casework, and probably not in terms of archaeologists specialising in forensics.

References

Lynnerup, N. 2009. Retsantropologi. Ugeskrift for Læger 171, 2643–2645.

Lynnerup, N. and Iversen, L. 2006. Trophy skulls in Denmark. *Scandinavian Journal of Forensic Medicine* 12(2), 64–66.

Lynnerup, N., Jørkov, M. L. and Kastmand Larsen, P. 2013. Retsantropologi. In J. L. Thomsen (ed.), *Nordisk lærebog i Retsmedicin*, 336–346. Copenhagen, FADL's Forlag.

Rogde, S. 2013. Drab. In J. L. Thomsen (ed.), *Nordisk lærebog i Retsmedicin*, 136–142. Copenhagen, FADL's Forlag.

Saukko, P. 2013. Retsmedicineren og myndighederne. In J. L. Thomsen (ed.), *Nordisk Lærebog i Retsmedicin*, 22–36. Copenhagen, FADL's Forlag.

Tancredi, L. R. and Giannini, A. J. 1994. The admissibility of scientific evidence in psychiatric malpractice: junk science and the Daubert case. *Journal of Clinical and Forensic Medicine* 1(3), 145–148.

Tangmose Larsen, S. and Lynnerup, N. 2011. Medico-legal autopsies in Denmark. *Danish Medical Bulletin* 58(3), A4247.

CHAPTER 8

Forensic archaeology in the French context: the role of the Forensic Sciences Institute of the French National Gendarmerie

Yves Schuliar[1], Patrice Georges[1,2], Florent Ducrettet[1], Franck Nolot[1] and Jean Richebé[1]

[1] *Department of Anthropology–Thanatology–Ondotology, Forensic Sciences Institute of the French National Gendarmerie, Rosny-sous-Bois cedex, Paris, France*

[2] *National Institute of Preventive Archaeological Research – UMR 5608, Centre de recherches archéologiques de Midi-Pyrénées nord ZAC Albasud – Impasse de Lisbonne, Montauband, France*

Introduction

Many authors praise the qualities of archaeologists who recover human bones or rely on their methods of investigation that follow the same rigorous techniques as the forensic approach (Baccino 2011; Dupras et al. 2006; Ubelaker 1984). In particular, archaeologists can distinguish human bones from animal bones; they have knowledge of excavation techniques related to human skeletons and, if also trained in anthropology, are able to perform palaeobiological analyses (Morse et al. 1983). However, the presence of (forensic) archaeologists at crime scenes in France is quite rare. The following reasons explain this low demand:

- The vast size of the French territory and the forensic chain of command in the Gendarmerie, with difficulties of using external specialists.
- Most forensic cases do not concern buried or burned human remains and therefore the need for an archaeologist is not widely recognised or requested in France.
- The lack of information and awareness within the police and medico-legal staff about this particular skill.

Since its creation, the Forensic Science Institute of the National Gendarmerie (*Institut de Recherche Criminelle de la Gendarmerie Nationale* – IRCGN)[1] has continued to improve its methods and means of intervention for better gathering of evidence. It is organised to address cases of buried human bodies in terms of human and material resources, in harmony with other organisations in the forensic chain, regardless of institutional affiliation. For 20 years, the Department of Anthropology–Thanatology–Odontology (Dept ATO) of the IRCGN has been the most important French laboratory for forensic anthropology, and the only one with a steady and continuous activity in this field. Over the past 3 years, an average of more than 110 cases per year have required anthropological expertise, besides providing advice or intervention to the investigator (advice or interventions), or teaching and research projects. Especially forensic anthropologists, but also other specialists of this department (forensic odontologists), are involved in crime scene investigation.

The Dept ATO has developed its field methodologies on crime scenes based particularly on the Anglo-Saxon experience. It is also engaged in important programs of training and research. Indeed, the National Gendarmerie is the only institution in France to have formalised forensic archaeology in the last 3 years, allowing protocols for the treatment of cases from the scene of the crime (excavation of clandestine graves) to the laboratory. The Dept ATO is indeed a unique structure in France. Despite the number of records processed every year, forensic archaeology within the framework of the forensic services today remains largely unknown in the French forensic community. This contribution is thus the occasion to detail all the activities of forensic archaeology in this department, to point out the strong links that exist with (medically based) forensic anthropology and to present some basic methodological principles. The originality and quality of French expertise need to be highlighted.

[1]The creation of the IRCGN dates back to 1992. Previously, it was the Technical Department of Criminal Investigation.

Forensic Archaeology: A Global Perspective, First Edition. Edited by W.J. Mike Groen, Nicholas Márquez-Grant and Robert C. Janaway.

Forensic chain of command within the Gendarmerie

Apart from occasional initiatives coming from forensic medicine laboratories or police forces drawing from the vast pool of archaeologically educated physical anthropologists (non-physicians) – France is one of the countries in the world where preventive archaeology is well developed – the use of forensic archaeology appears to be specific, from an institutional point of view, to the National Gendarmerie.

The National Gendarmerie comprises military staff and is subject, as is the French National Police (*Police Nationale*), to the Ministry of the Interior; it constitutes one of the national police forces in France (the National Police is responsible for the big cities in France and the Gendarmerie for the remainder of the country). Forensic sciences in the Gendarmerie system are organised on three different major levels and, far from being hermetically sealed, allow the involvement of practitioners and methods of forensic archaeology at local, departmental and national levels.

In the entire Gendarmerie system, the local level is the level at which Proximity Crime Scene Technicians (*Technicien en Identification Criminelle de Proximité* – TICP) become involved. Their main task is the technical treatment of all acts of criminality, especially petty ones. They are responsible for carrying out simple procedures for the Technical and Scientific Police (*Police Technique et Scientifique* – PST). Many cases show that they can be the first responder where a human body is accidentally discovered. In this context, they ask to be reinforced by the Criminal Investigation Unit (*Cellule d'Investigation Criminelle* – CIC), a special unit with Crime Scene Technicians (*Technicien en Identification Criminelle* – TIC) who are able to respond to cases that are beyond the skills and/or resources of the TICP.

In each department, the headquarters of the Gendarmerie therefore has at its disposal a CIC and a technical platform for taking into account a serious crime scene and performing technical and scientific acts. Crime scene technicians are in a position to request tests beyond their areas of expertise from the IRCGN or any other forensic laboratory. A new member of staff at the departmental level called Coordinator of Criminalistic Operations (*Cordinateur des Opérations de Criminalistique* – COCrim) is a real crime scene engineer. He plans, develops a hypothesis and directs sampling on complex crime scenes. He is the technical correspondent of the forensic laboratories and experts. Thus he contributes to the success of the investigation by providing technical and scientific responses to the officer in charge.

Local and departmental levels are able to generate cases requesting the expertise of forensic archaeology. They can be managed initially *in situ* at these levels before potentially asking for a national team. However, as with the IRCGN, the Dept ATO (a team of 15 individuals composed of archaeologists, anthropologists, odontologists and forensic pathologists from the Gendarmerie and the active and reserve armies) does not generally intervene without the official request of the investigator in charge. A significant number of cases are under the jurisdiction of the national police or more directly the investigative magistrates (*Juge d'Instruction*) and public prosecutor (*Procureur*). This is primarily for investigators, where on-site and/or laboratory investigations (post-mortem evaluation) of fortuitously discovered (mostly human) bones indicate that archaeological expertise is generally required.

The training of crime scene technicians (TICs) provided at the National Training Centre of the Judicial Police (*Centre National de Formation de Police Judiciaire* – CNFPJ) in Fontainebleau (Seine-et-Marne) includes theoretical and practical courses in archaeology excavation. Student TICs are regularly faced with the search for buried skeletons (Figure 8.1). This exercise aims to identify a crime scene, to hold and protect it ('to freeze the scene'), and to engage the human and material resources necessary for the exhumation of a skeletonised body without departing from the basic principles of forensic sciences. This requires, in particular, for forensic archaeology as for other disciplines of crime scene techniques, the documentation of everything on site, through the stages of the removal process to the

Figure 8.1 Training of crime scene technicians (TIC): burying a skeleton (© P. Georges/French National Gendarmerie).

sampling (see later) (Figure 8.2). This introduction to forensic archaeology is essential for the Gendarmerie missions, in France and abroad.

This training is conducted jointly with the Department of Forensic Entomology of the IRCGN. One of the main assets of the IRCGN is indeed to be able to provide, right from the field phase, all stakeholders potentially useful in the understanding and treatment of such a crime scene. What is true for the exercises is of course valuable for a real event. The full spectrum of all forensic disciplines is in fact available. The principle of a multidisciplinary team is particularly persuasive through the combined action of the Dept ATO and the entomology department, which are trained to work together. The skills of the entomology department are not limited to entomological work, as their arrival at crime scenes allows them to use an approach the Dept ATO considers today because of the particularly interesting feedback on forensic archaeology given by their work (Gaudry 2010).

More obviously, the national level is the one which is the most relevant for forensic archaeology, always linked to, but not replacing, the lower levels. Indeed, it is at this national level that complex cases are handled by the IRCGN. A forensic adviser ensures the coherence of the operational chain of the National Gendarmerie and sees to the implementation of the doctrine, the application of protocols, the quality assurance and the adequacy of forensic sciences. The IRCGN can be considered as an experts' unit, which is able to act immediately and is available 24 h/day. Among the four divisions of the IRCGN, the 'forensic human identification' division, including the Dept ATO and the Entomology Department, is the one which most frequently uses archaeological methods. But, depending on the nature of the crime scene (for instance a case of cremation) or the findings made in a grave or excavation and/or bones upon release, other departments of the IRCGN are also required. The unique location of the laboratory in this case turns out to be a considerable asset.

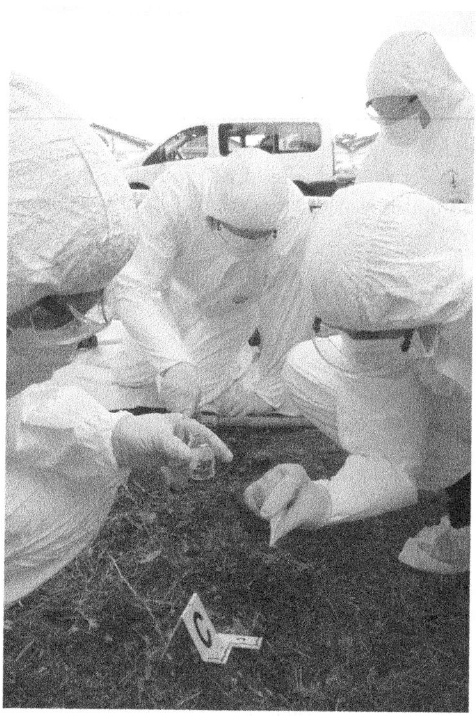

Figure 8.2 Training of crime scene technicians (TIC): sampling of entomological remains (© P. Georges/French National Gendarmerie).

More or less recent judicial developments amply demonstrate the interest in such an organisation. This is especially true since the IRCGN is reinforced by a mobile laboratory (unique in France) and two deployable units created by the laboratory according to events: the DVI team (*Unité Gendarmerie d'Identification de Victimes de Catastrophes* – UGIVC) (Schuliar and Jam 2007) and the National Criminal Investigation Unit (*Unité Nationale d'Investigation Criminelle* – UNIC). When deployed, the latter unit is part of the investigation and supports, thanks to its experience and technical means, the local units.

Assets are adapted according to the difficulty of a case, combining local and departmental units with highly specialised national units, which can be rapidly deployed on the frontline. Three levels may thus be distinguished:

- 1st level (stations): to secure the crime scene and perform basic investigations and description
- 2nd level (crime scene investigation units): crime scene investigations, sampling and crime scene management
- 3rd level (IRCGN, STRJD): expertise and support (complex crime scenes, disasters), training and research and development (R&D), forensic intelligence

Forensic archaeology in France

In France, the existence of archaeology in forensic criminal investigation is not yet formalised (Duday and Guillon 2006). Moreover, the term 'forensic' is not recognised by the Academy in French language. Forensic archaeology remains an alien subject for academic or traditional archaeology even if one agrees that forensic teams investigating crimes against humanity must now integrate trained archaeologists and physical anthropologists (Haglund 2008), whose roles are sometimes also mixed.

It is important to point out the low number of cases of human remains buried in a criminal context and considered as interesting from a forensic archaeological point of view. However, no database offers reliable statistics.

The only way to be satisfied in this context is to consider studies conducted by the Department of Entomology of the IRCGN, in the knowledge that this department deals with all archaeological cases. It appears that *c.* 4% of the treated cases involve completely or partially buried bodies, mainly in rural areas. Regarding the conditions of burial, only 2% of real burial cases (partially recovered bodies are excluded) require archaeological input. Moreover, between 1987 and 2008, of 33 discoveries of buried corpses registered in the laboratory database, 28 were concerned with archaeological contribution (Gaudry 2010).

Nevertheless, in the early years, one part of the archaeo-anthropological activity of the Dept ATO was deliberately oriented towards archaeological techniques. Due to their teaching and research remits, several other high-level French university laboratories could easily claim similar dynamics. In 2002, a French academic team pointed out the importance of people trained in the search for human skeletons in the field (Adalian et al. 2002). But the Dept ATO, thanks to its policy of specialist recruitment and training, and other Gendarmerie members, such as at the departmental level (training provided: see later) always maintained close relationships with archaeology and archaeo-anthropological methods. Recently, those links were strengthened by scientific cooperation, particularly internships and academic essays. Exchanges are also fruitful with professional archaeology, the integration of specialists of preventive archaeology being one among many aspects. Thus the Dept ATO is at the forefront of controlling all the phases of forensic archaeology and forensic anthropology (field preparation phase, laboratory analysis and research programs) in France. It is important to note, at the same time, that this department, led since its creation by a forensic pathologist, always chose to work in a multidisciplinary way, systematically combining forensic pathologists, forensic anthropologists, forensic dentists, criminalists and, for the last 3 years, forensic archaeologists for important cases.

Experience of the French National Gendarmerie

Although it is impossible to review every case, here are some methodological issues that cannot be considered as recommendations but, however, may serve as a basis for discussion for past and future cases. These remarks reflect the experience gained during the past 20 years by the Gendarmerie.

From search and location ...

Many discoveries of human skeletons or scattered bones are accidental, and the Dept ATO is requested to conduct systematic research. It should be noted that for this phase, the Dept ATO does not generally act alone. With its Signal–Image-Speech department, the IRCGN can deploy a team using ground-penetrating radar (GPR) (non-destructive investigation) (Figure 8.3). It is impossible to detail here the advantages and limits, but with specialised dog teams dedicated to search for human remains (Canine National Investigation Group; *Centre National d'Instruction Cynophile de la Gendarmerie* – CNICG) (Figure 8.4), this could be considered as a complementary method. These teams can be engaged jointly or independently, depending on the nature of the research, the type of field, area, etc.

Whatever method is used, recovered remains cannot be distinguished with any certainty in any sedimentary

Figure 8.3 Real case in France: research with ground-penetrating radar (© F. Nolot/French National Gendarmerie).

environment. There is no way of being 100% certain of finding the bones buried. All the methods have a particular scope and defined limits. These may be inherent to the method itself or due to the particularities of the field. That is why the use of a dedicated mechanical shovel equipped for the occasion is essential (Georges et al. 2012) (Figure 8.5).

Unlike some methodological books on Forensic Archaeology (e.g. Dupras et al. 2006; Morse et al. 1983), and contrary to what is done when searching for mass graves, we strongly recommend the use of an auger, as for most discovered graves currently excavated. The field chosen from the information given by the documentary investigation is then probed according to a more or less regular grid. Forensic pathologists and forensic anthropologists base their research on the discovery of bones and objects belonging to the deceased. Each positive finding (recovery of a bone fragment, clothing, etc.) helps to define the search area, which

Figure 8.4 Real case in France: specialised dog searches for human remains (© F. Nolot/French National Gendarmerie).

does not take into account the limits of excavation. This approach may have very serious consequences for the integrity and, consequently, the recognition of the individuals concerned. Mr Hugh Tuller (JPAC-CIL) and Dr Marija Djuric (Laboratory of Anthropology of the University of Belgrade) recently published a very interesting article on the subject (Tuller and Djuric 2006). Such a methodology is in fact indicative of the absence of consideration regarding the stratigraphic information, particularly the search for the limits of the burial site, and consequently shows that the scene is not treated as a whole or, worse, is partially destroyed. The auger which reveals the presence of buried remains is not in fact a tool used in French archaeology. It does not allow a proper assessment. The mechanical excavator has proved to be the best tool to locate forensic buried remains, and not only to probe or clear an area (Figure 8.6). Stripping with a shovel (mechanical digger), running retroactively, under the trained eye of an archaeologist, is the best way to discover features in which there may be buried human remains. It is simple to use and, unlike the GPR on wheels, can be used in difficult field conditions. This is a particularly efficient tool. Its use in a large area, however, requires a digging management plan, including the rehabilitation of the field. In addition, using a mechanical shovel may constitute an interface between research and excavation, but can only be used for one or the other of these operations. Above all, this does not prevent other localisation approaches. The use of a mechanical shovel reduces the requirement for human resources, thus allowing people to work on more precise tasks. It can be a very effective tool, even for tricky things; it also addresses issues of profitability, which are important in a forensic context.

The importance of this operation requires a thorough preparation phase, which ensures the quality of research and gives credibility to the results. Only the application

Figure 8.5 Real case in France: Using a shovel equipped for the occasion (© F. Nolot/French National Gendarmerie).

Figure 8.6 Presentation to the Gendarmerie National Tactical Training Centre: exhumation of a buried skeleton (© P. Georges/French National Gendarmerie).

of a well-thought-out and recognised methodology makes it possible to ensure that the absence of a result is a lack of real information. Whatever the method(s) chosen, it is necessary to carry out, beforehand, a review of the literature. In some cases, this directs research to certain areas and/or explains the location of the remains. To achieve this, the Dept ATO has used aerial photographs since its inception (Schuliar et al. 1998) with different partners, both public and private, to search for buried bodies. Tests with infrared (IR) radiation have been conducted, but the results were inconclusive. If aerial means are available in the Gendarmerie, such an approach is now used prior to any exploration (by observation or ground introspection) through satellite coverage of the territory (digital resources). This information is a great help in planning the operation (access conditions, area calculation, etc.). It offers an environmental approach to identifying abnormalities, microreliefs (sciographical index) and vegetation cover (phytographic index). The latter requires IRCGN resources the Dept ATO does not have. In several recent cases of accidental discoveries of human bones, a brief literature review was conducted to try to gather archaeological information explaining in particular the presence of bones at that point. Consultation of local archaeological surveys may be of great interest.

... To excavation

The search for a clandestinely buried human body is undoubtedly the most difficult part of a forensic investigation, following the discovery and the clearing of the pit in which the body lies. It is fundamental for any interpretation and explanation to the judge and depends largely on the quality and reliability of observations and data collected in the field. This is why the Dept ATO recommends graphic surveys rather than a set of listed measures, for it is true that the 3D laser scan belonging to the IRCGN allows opportunities for research in the field of forensic archaeology including the creation of a so-called fixing site state unit. The search activity involves some basic principles that incorporate four stages of forensic management of the crime scene: (i) evaluation, protection and safety, (ii) observation, (iii) deduction and confrontation, and (iv) documentation and removal. However, unlike other crime scenes, the archaeological scene is, in the case of a burial, already fixed. This does not preclude the process of 'freezing the site' for obvious reasons of preservation of evidence and the safety of the team involved. But from a technical point of view, the search will 'unfreeze the site', at successive stages, preserving time for (photo) graphic registration. Even if it is a question of skeletons, we can keep talking as the forensic pathologist examines the body at the scene. The archaeological and anthropological operation, which is essential, however, could *de facto* be compared to this type of activity. Like the process of removing the body from the scene by the forensic pathologist, archaeological methods allow the recording of data concerning *in situ* human bodies (badly decomposed or skeletonised).

French preventive archaeology is particularly advanced in this area, a situation the Dept ATO took advantage of. Indeed, until the 1970s, archaeo-anthropologists were almost exclusively interested in the history and evolution of population – research topics most often considered in an isolated way. What proved to be important in this archaeo-anthropological approach was the number and dating of skeletons. Their presence on site at the time of the search was not necessary and therefore uncommon. The contribution of osteoarchaeological studies to the knowledge of sepulchral sets in France, under the leadership of Dr Henry Duday and following the pioneering work of Dr André Leroi-Gourhan, led to the establishment of funeral archaeo-thanatology (e.g. called 'field anthropology'), which is implemented as soon as the field phase is complete (Duday 2005, 2006; Tuller and Djuric 2006). The latter took off with the proliferation of preventive archaeology searches, osteoarchaeological observation allowing the demonstration of the possible involvement of natural or anthropogenic factors involving potential graves. Concomitantly, specialists of the Dept ATO also undertook their first missions according to the cases received.

Each anthropic or natural action always leaves marks in the ground. By extension, the stratigraphic approach consists of identifying the limits of the excavation. Decomposition of the body and organic elements, and even the action of the insect fauna, explains why pits become more or less visible depending on the substrate. It is important to recognise the walls of an excavation and their shape. This seems obvious but is still only very rarely done in France, the use of a grid again being the main archaeological approach. Finding the edges of a pit excludes all the artefacts buried and found outside the pit, *stricto sensu*, which the condition of excluding the action of burying animals. A grid will also tend to collect clues that are not indicative. So, the excavation inside the pit allows the time required for digging to be estimated. The Anglo-Saxons emphasize the possibility of identifying tool marks or paint chips made by tools used to dig deeper graves (Godwin 2000). This often saves time and efficiency (only human bones are oriented towards anthropological laboratories) in terms of laboratory tests. Again, joint training with entomologists and forensic pathologists of the IRCGN ensures quality processing at the crime scene. Checking the principles of search is at least facilitating or orientating the work of the laboratory.

These precepts are also valuable in the context of the study of cremations and scattered bones. It would be a mistake to believe that the structures of cremation vary, even if the use of a grid can possibly be justified, notably on the basis of time constraints. But it is important not to forget that the set-up of a grid, which overcomes some points of intervention in the field, can significantly increase the tasks of the laboratory and is only really needed when the context requires it. Thus, in the context of a cremation, it will facilitate the micro-geolocalised recovery of bone fragments, but the problem of recognition still remains.

Research and development process

Apart from training the crime scene technician (see earlier), the IRCGN has also been involved for several years in two academic courses in partnership with Paris-Descartes University: a postgraduate diploma in Criminalistics and a postgraduate diploma in Coordination of Criminalistic Operation (see earlier). The Dept ATO presents its experience and part of its activity, including forensic archaeology, as a whole discipline and an introduction to questions on anthropology. In 2009, an essay specifically dedicated to forensic archaeology was also presented (Georges 2009). At the end of the same year, an oral presentation on forensic archaeology was made to the main representatives of the Gendarmerie and French Police forensic specialists during a conference organised by the IRCGN. The Dept ATO regularly responds to various challenges, such as in 2010 when the methods of excavation of buried bodies and management of criminal mass graves were presented (Figure 8.6). A presentation at the National Training Centre for Police Forces (*Centre National d'Entrainement des Forces de Gendarmerie* – CNEFG), at Saint-Astier (Dordogne), was designed *in situ* for gendarmes coming from different European countries (Spain, Portugal, Romania, etc.) and for anti-riot police forces who might possibly face such situations during overseas missions. In June 2013, in Saint-Astier, the Dept ATO was hired on the same issue in the context of the European Police Services Training (EUPST). The mission was to find and excavate a pit with several bodies (mass grave) using a mechanical shovel.

In the same spirit, the publishing policy aims to reveal to all the participants at the scene of crime the goals, methods and benefits of the intervention of forensic archaeologists. Our publications to the French forensic specialists, based on the broad French experience in preventive archaeology, concern the following issues:

- Current research: application of technology for any buried archaeological object
- Detection of clandestine graves, especially the use of a mechanical shovel
- Experimental project (using pigs) to write guidelines

Conclusion

Twenty years ago the Gendarmerie founded forensic archaeology in France, based in particular on the Anglo-Saxon experience. The originality and quality of French expertise must also be underlined in particular, however, because of the Dept ATO's experience of preventive archaeology. This department also benefits from the central multiplicity of expertise at the IRCGN, composed of highly qualified and experienced experts in the vast majority of forensic science disciplines. It is therefore necessary to follow cases throughout the forensic chain from excavation to laboratory work. The number of cases processed annually is also the largest in France among the laboratories of forensic anthropology.

The experience of the Dept ATO relating to forensic archaeology reveals how the field phases, namely the treatment of the crime scene with archaeology (research, excavation and removal processes), are crucial for a case. For the search of serial facts, each case must be treated systematically. However, to date, this procedure is still largely neglected in France, although thought is currently being given to the subject. If some specific interventions may be mentioned – they have the merit of being based on the recognised expertise of people in the field – the Gendarmerie is so far the only institution to have formalised this approach, relying on its nationwide network of units and a high level of competence in this area. Academic education of the anthropologists who built the Dept ATO, linked with the professional world of archaeology and 20 years of experience of working closely with forensic pathology in a context of multidisciplinary approach, contributes to the explanation.

References

Adalian, P., Signoli, M. Lalys, L. et al. 2002. Intérêt de la présence d'une équipe spécialisée pour la levée de corps en anthropologie médico-légale. *Journal de Médecine légale droit Médical* 45, 375–377.

Baccino, E. 2011. L'Anthropologie forensique (AF), ou anthropologie médicolégale, est-elle un nouveau métier? *La Revue de Médecine Légale* 2(1), 1–3.

Duday, H. 2005. *Lezioni di Archeotanatologia. Archeologia Funeraria e Antropologia du Campo.* Rome, Soprintendenza archeologica di Roma et École Française de Rome.

Duday, H. 2006. Archaeothanatology or the archaeology of death, translated by C. J. Knüssel. In R. Growland and C. Knüssel (eds.), *Social Archaeology of Funerary Remains*, 30–56. Oxford, Oxbow Books.

Duday, H. and Guillon, M. 2006. Understanding the circumstances of decomposition when the body is skeletonized. In A. Schmitt, E. Cunha and J. Pinheiro (eds.), *Forensic Anthropology and Medicine*, 117–157. Totowa, Humana Press.

Dupras, T. L., Schultz, J. J., Wheeler S. M. and Williams L. J. 2006. *Forensic Recovery of Human Remain: Archaeological Approaches.* Boca Raton, CRC Press.

Gaudry, E. 2010. The insects' colonisation of buried remains. In J. Amendt, C. P. Campobsso, M. Lee Goff and M. Grassberger (eds.), *Current Concepts in Forensic Entomology*, 273–311. Heidelberg, Springer.

Georges, P. 2009. *L'Archéologue a-t-il sa Place sur la Scène de Crime? Localiser, Fouiller, Prélever les Vestiges Criminalistiques Enfouis. De l'Expérience Anglo-Saxonne au Savoir-faire Français.* Unpublished, University of Paris 5-René Descartes.

Georges, P., Ducrettet F., Nolot F., Richebé J. and Schuliar Y. 2012. Problématiques et règles d'emploi criminalistiques des engins de chantier pour la recherche de cadavres enfouis. L'expérience de l'Institut de recherche criminelle de la Gendarmerie nationale (France). *Revue Internationale de Criminologie et de Police Technique et Scientifique* 3(1), 363–374.

Godwin, G. M. (ed.) 2000. *Criminal Psychology and Forensic Technology. A Collaborative Approach to Effective Profiling.* Fayetteville, CRC Press.

Haglund, W. D. 2008. L'archéologie et l'anthropologie médico-légales dans le contexte international. In J.-P. Demoule and B. Stiegler (eds.), *L'avenir du Passé. Modernité de l'Archéologie*, 114–131. Paris, La Découverte.

Morse, D., Duncan, J. and Stoutamire, J. (eds.) 1983. *Handbook of Forensic Archaeology and Anthropology.* Tallahassee, Bills Bookstore.

Schuliar, Y. and Jam, D. 2007. Organisation de l'Unité gendarmerie d'identification des victimes de catastrophes (UGIVC): exemples de mise en œuvre. *Revue Francophone des Laboratoires* 37(392), 59–68.

Schuliar, Y., Richebe, J., Crispino, F. and Delemme, E. 1998. Méthodes de recherches de cadavres. *Journal de Médecine Légale Droit Médical* 41(3–4), 253–260.

Tuller, H. and Đurić, M. 2006. Keeping the pieces together. Comparison of mass grave excavation methodology. *Forensic Science International* 156, 192–200.

Ubelaker, D. H. 1984. *Human Skeletal Remains. Excavation, Analysis, Interpretation, Manuals on Archaeology 2*, 2nd edition. Washington DC, Taraxacum Press.

CHAPTER 9

The Working Group 'Forensic Archaeology' at the German Bundeskriminalamt

Ralf Neumann, Karsten Klenke and Andrea Fischer
Bundeskriminalamt, ZD31-General Crime Scene Work, Wiesbaden, Germany

Introduction

This chapter describes the proceedings of the German Working Group 'Forensic Archaeology' (*Arbeitsgruppe Forensische Archäologie*) of the Crime Scene Unit (*Tatortgruppe*) at the Federal Criminal Police Office (*Bundeskriminalamt* – BKA) and offers an overview of forensic archaeology in Germany.

It should be noted, however, that our statements make no claim to completeness or definitiveness. The information developed for this chapter should be regarded as an assessment only since – despite intense efforts and research of various authorities, universities and institutes – we have found no other institution in Germany which specifically uses archaeological methods to support law enforcement work. In 2008, Mr Dirk Krause and Mrs Carla Nübold of the German Association of State Archaeologists (*Verband der Landesarchäologen*), Stuttgart Government Headquarters, published a study on the professional situation of archaeologists in Germany as part of a project entitled Discovering the Archaeologists of Europe.[1] The authors aptly describe how difficult it is to collect reliable data for Germany.

In Germany, archaeology is predominantly perceived as a classic academic science in the context of the protection and preservation of cultural heritage. Unfortunately, it is largely overlooked as an important element of an interdisciplinary approach to a crime scene.

So, has everything been said now for Germany? The answer has to be: No, it is not that simple! Germany has experts for every subject area in forensic science, but one must know where to find them.

Key data on the Federal Republic of Germany as a starting point for forensic archaeology

It can be guessed from the following facts what a crime investigator who is enthusiastic about excavating may expect in Germany: Germany consists of 16 federal states, with Bavaria (70,550 km^2) being the largest state and the city state of Bremen being the smallest covering 419 km^2. As regards the population, however, the federal state of North-Rhine Westphalia has the largest number of inhabitants (17.845 million). In this respect, too, Bremen with its 661,000 inhabitants is the federal state with the smallest population. The capital Berlin is also an individual federal state and, at the same time, Germany's largest city with a population of 3.461 million. In late 2012, a total of 81.8 million[2] people lived in the Federal Republic of Germany, which covers an area of 357,000 km^2. Half of the population lives in urban areas (Statistisches Jahrbuch 2012).

Germany is situated in a temperate climate zone. Frequent changes in the weather and moist Atlantic influences throughout the year provide for mild winters and summers that are not too hot. Extreme weather conditions are very rare.

Even though Germany is an industrial country and, statistically speaking, 229 persons live here per km^2, it is still one of the most densely wooded countries in Europe. In 2011, a good 30% of its territory consisted of wooded areas. A total of 13.4% of the land is used for housing and transport (Statistisches Bundesamt 2012). To the north lies the North German Lowland with its coastal areas bordering the North Sea and the Baltic Sea. The south is a predominantly mountainous region, even

[1] For more information, see: http://www.discovering-archaeologists.eu (last accessed July 2013).

[2] On 31 May 2013, the Federal Statistical Office published the results of the 2011 census according to which recent German population estimates would need rectification; the correct number of people living in Germany should, hence, amount to about 80.2 million. In particular, the estimated number of inhabitants in some cities, such as Berlin, was reportedly too high.

Forensic Archaeology: A Global Perspective, First Edition. Edited by W.J. Mike Groen, Nicholas Márquez-Grant and Robert C. Janaway.

alpine at the borders with Austria and Switzerland. In contrast to the densely populated Ruhr region in the west, Germany's east is scarcely populated in some areas and has numerous lakes.

Those facts about Germany suggest that a perpetrator has every opportunity in practice to dispose of a dead body. It would be possible at any time to bury or leave a human body in the wilderness or to dispose of it in urban settlements.

The Police Crime Statistics for 2011 recorded a total of 614 accomplished homicides (murder and voluntary manslaughter) in Germany.[3] In relation to the total population, this is a low rate compared to other countries. However, the number of undiscovered homicide offences has been under discussion for many years (e.g. Rückert 2000). The forensic autopsy rate in Germany continues to be low and it is likely that numerous violent crimes against life are overlooked for this reason.

To forensic archaeology, however, it is irrelevant how many homicides are committed or remain undiscovered because forensic autopsies have been omitted. In such cases, there is a dead body which does not have to be searched for and recovered. Instead, the number of missing persons may provide a lead – but only if those persons remain missing for a long time.

Between 50,000 and 60,000 persons are reported missing throughout Germany every year. In simple terms, *c.* 500 persons are reported missing every day but just as many are found and/or are heard of again. About 1% remains missing. The number of missing persons is not recorded in the crime statistics. This is presumably due to the great daily fluctuations in the databases, and only few cases have a criminal background. The aforementioned data were collected by the Missing Persons Unit of the BKA.[4]

Overview of the relevant organisations

Germany is a federal republic comprising 16 states. Each federal state has its own police force and police law. In addition to the task of warding off danger, criminal prosecution falls within the jurisdiction of the federal states, regardless of the seriousness of the offence. In the first instance, the decisive factor is the location of the offence alone.

In addition to the local police offices and higher-ranking authorities for regions or cities (usually the police headquarters), each federal state has a State Criminal Police Office (*Landeskriminalamt*). In simplified terms, a State Criminal Police Office is the central agency of a federal state which supports or takes over complex investigations from the local police.

Further police organisations have been established at the federal level. The Federal Border Police (formerly known as *Bundesgrenzschutz* – BGS) was founded to protect the borders as well as the railways and air traffic. Entrusted with quite a number of additional tasks, the Federal Border Police was developed into today's Federal Police (*Bundespolizei* – BPol) whose responsibilities are determined by the Act on the Federal Police.

Besides the predominantly uniformed Federal Police, the BKA was established as a criminal police authority acting across state borders from 1952. Originally conceived as a mere central agency for exchanging information, the BKA was – over the decades – given its own responsibilities and its own law, the BKA Act. In brief, the BKA's law enforcement tasks are the fight against terrorism and internationally organised crime. Moreover, it is a service office functioning as a central agency, *inter alia*, for all disciplines of forensic science (Division KT). The Division Central CID Services (*Zentrale Kriminalpolizeiliche Dienste* – ZD) includes, for example, operational services. The BKA's Crime Scene Unit with its Working Group Forensic Archaeology (*Arbeitsgruppe Forensische Archäologie*), hereafter Working Group, is such an operational service. Thus, the Working Group is an element of the services offered and can be approached for support by all German law enforcement authorities.

Despite all the legal regulations in force, it goes without saying that only a general sense of cooperation and mutual assistance between the federation and the states paves the way for successful police work. For this reason, investigations are often carried out jointly. In prominent criminal cases, federal and state officers sometimes work together in joint teams.

When it comes to recovering a body, the aforementioned regulations mean that the location of the excavation initially determines which police authority is responsible. If in need of assistance, the local authority contacts the respective State Criminal Police Office. Only after the State Criminal Police Office has agreed or has at least been informed, the BKA may be asked for support. Experience gained over the years with regard to forensic archaeology has shown that a lack of technical means was not the main reason for requesting the BKA's help. Rather, general advice and coordination were required for locating and excavating a body. Reinforcement of the evidence recovery and excavation staff also played a role on some occasions.

Besides the aforementioned police authorities at federal and state level, there are further organisations which can enforce the law, for example the customs authorities.

[3]Federal Criminal Police Office, Publications, Police Crime Statistics, PCS 2011, page 18, recorded cases, attempts excluded. Available at: http://www.bka.de (last accessed December 2013).

[4]BKA Unit SO11-3.

They are, however, not concerned with forensic archaeology and therefore need not be addressed here.

Forensic archaeology at the police offices in the federal states

The Working Group sent a questionnaire to all 16 State Criminal Police Offices on 12 November 2012. This questionnaire was designed to gain an overview of forensic archaeology within the police all over Germany. It included the following six questions:

1 Are any members of the police force dealing with forensic archaeology?
2 Have any advanced training courses been attended?
3 How many operations with an archaeological background have been carried out during the past 10 years, and have any bodies been discovered in this context?
4 How strong is the need for assistance?
5 Is there any interest in workshops/information events on this topic?
6 Do you maintain any contacts with experts specialising in searching for and excavating bodies?

All 16 State Criminal Police Offices replied by 22 February 2013. It has come to light that, both in theory and practice, little experience has so far been gained throughout Germany. Most of the police offices are interested in the subject. A majority also expressed the wish to be able to ask for help in individual cases.

In detail, the answers can be summarised as follows:

- In response to the question on whether *points of contact were available*, 11 federal states answered 'no'. In five federal states, some colleagues are already dealing with the issue.
- In 11 federal states, no *advanced training courses* have been held on forensic archaeology. Five federal states reported events, lectures, etc. on the topic.
- The question pertaining to *previous operations* with an archaeological background showed that 12 federal states had not collected any information or had no knowledge of such operations. In four federal states, bodies were discovered in connection with forensic archaeology.
- The need for *general operational assistance*, for example from the BKA, was expressed by 11 federal states. Two federal states did not answer this question, and three federal states were not interested in such an offer.
- According to the survey, 12 federal states are interested in workshops/information events. Four states are not interested.
- Eight federal states confirmed and specified *contacts* with experts.

The answers show that the individual federal states approach the issue very differently. In some states, on the one hand, there have been numerous excavations and a great open-mindedness towards the subject; on the other hand, a complete lack of interest has been observed.

The lack of figures provided on operations, however, indicates that many search and excavation measures were presumably carried out by local police services without involving the respective State Criminal Police Office. This assumption is supported by the fact that the Working Group already assisted police authorities whose State Criminal Police Offices answered the question about operations with 'none' or 'not known'.

To obtain a reliable overview, a nationwide survey would have to be repeated and addressed to every single local criminal police service.

The role of the Public Prosecutor's Office

The decision on whether to carry out search and excavation measures lies with the Public Prosecutor's Office (*Staatsanwaltschaft*). They obtain a search warrant from a judge which must, depending on the case, be issued for searches regarding a suspect or a witness. The costs incurred are borne by the Public Prosecutor's Office.

Most public prosecutors are not familiar with search methods and excavation processes. Before action is taken, advice is therefore required with regard to the search strategy, technical means, recovery of physical evidence, prospects of success and especially any damage and costs to be expected. Fortunately, costs have not played a predominant role in the past. Experience has shown that – given the lack of alternatives – the Public Prosecutor's Office was willing to support some very costly search and excavation measures.

The role of medico-forensic institutes in the context of forensic excavations

There are 32 medico-forensic institutes all over Germany (*Deutsche Gesellschaft für Rechtsmedizin*).[5] The vast majority are affiliated with a university. Depending on the region, the nearest medico-forensic institute can be very far away from a requesting police service. Cooperation between the police and the medico-forensic institutes is very good and uncomplicated.

Upon request, the medico-forensic institutes send their staff to the crime scene – but this is not the rule. Medico-forensic specialists usually see a body only after it has been taken to their institute.[6]

[5]For more information, see: http://www.dgrm.de (last accessed July 2013).

[6]If there is no initial suspicion of a crime, a post-mortem examination on the spot is often carried out by a medical doctor on call or the respective general practitioner who has not necessarily undergone additional forensic training. This shortcoming has often been criticised but the situation has not improved. From the police's point of view, this is definitely a disadvantage and one of the reasons why comparatively few autopsies are carried out in Germany.

At the request of the police, medico-forensic institutes make their personnel available for forensic excavations and almost all of them have probably accompanied excavations in the past. The institutes have confirmed – upon inquiry – that the relevant expertise is available in this respect. However, to the best of our knowledge there is only one medico-forensic institute which permanently employs an archaeologist. Moreover, very few institutions employ physical anthropologists on a permanent basis.

So, the medico-forensic institutes are not specifically geared up for forensic archaeology. Their expertise is, of course, still required and the presence of their specialists is always helpful when bodies have been discovered.

The offices for cultural heritage preservation and the Association of State Archaeologists

The German legal provisions concerning archaeological excavations fall within the jurisdiction of the individual federal states. For this reason there is no uniform national law, but one of the 16 state laws is applicable depending on the location.

The offices for cultural heritage preservation have a supervisory function in the field of protecting and preserving cultural heritage in their respective federal states. These offices thus decide where and by whom an archaeological excavation may be carried out. Usually, however, they are not involved in the actual forensic excavation process. The Working Group highly values their expertise. In the context of inter-authority assistance, police offices usually find a competent contact person there who can give advice and, if the need arises, even assist in excavations.

The Association of State Archaeologists (*Verband der Landesarchäologen*) predominantly consists of staff of the state offices for cultural heritage preservation. This association is not an authority but promotes the exchange of experience and comments on questions and problems linked with the protection and preservation of cultural heritage. It also advises the legislator with regard to proposed legislation.

The Association of State Archaeologists can give the police valuable advice on forensic excavations or the enhancement of relevant knowledge/skills.

The departments of archaeology at universities

Numerous German universities offer good conditions for studying the different subjects of archaeology. It is, however, not possible to study forensic archaeology in Germany. No university offers such a course of studies. Consequently, the professional title 'forensic archaeologist' is not used in this country.

Numerous graduates of archaeology leave university every year but they rarely find permanent employment at state institutions, not to mention a job with a law enforcement authority. The Working Group does not know of any archaeologist in Germany who was specifically recruited for developing relevant expertise within the police force.

As experience shows, the archaeological departments at German universities are very helpful when it comes to providing advice to police authorities. Cooperation between the police and universities in the field of basic and advanced training may be a potential approach towards improving forensic archaeology in Germany in the future.

The *Hochschule für Technik und Wirtschaft* (University of Applied Sciences) in Berlin offers bachelor's and master's degree courses in excavation techniques. Elsewhere, institutions offer vocational training for excavation technicians (*Grabungstechniker*) without a university degree. In the opinion of the Working Group, the studies or vocational training in excavation techniques seem to be best adapted to the police's needs. There are good opportunities for future cooperation in this context too.

The War Graves Commission (*Kriegsgräberfürsorge*)

The German War Graves Commission is an association financed by donations and public subsidies. Among other things, the association has taken on the task of transferring German victims of the two world wars to war grave sites. In March 2013, the Working Group received a brief report from the association with regard to the status of their work and their course of action.

While in western Europe and North Africa this work was completed around the end of the 1970s, in eastern Europe the task could only be tackled as a result of the political changes following 1990. Since that time, about 800,000 other German soldiers killed in action have been reburied. The work has not yet been completed (Head of the War Grave Care Division, personal communication, 2013).

For the purpose of finding mortal remains, the association uses records drawn up by the German Armed Forces (*Wehrmacht*) of the Third Reich. Exposed bones are identified on the basis of personal belongings and ID badges of the soldiers killed in action. If ascertained in this context, the cause of death is recorded. In many cases, it is already revealed by the written records of the *Wehrmacht*.

Meticulous archaeological methods or documentation techniques are not applied, though. It was only in individual cases that geophysical techniques were applied for detecting graves (Head of the War Grave Care Division, personal communication, 2013).

The Working Group Forensic Archaeology at the Bundeskriminalamt

The formation of the Working Group

In 2001, Mönchengladbach criminal police asked the BKA's Crime Scene Unit for assistance in the search for the body of an adolescent boy. The father of this boy's girlfriend had killed the teenager and had subsequently buried him in his own allotment garden. The man did so because he feared that his daughter would tell her boyfriend that her father had sexually abused her in the past. The cruelty of the offence was reinforced by the fact that the murderer forced his daughter to act as his accomplice. She had to lure the unsuspecting boy into a trap and subsequently help her father remove the body. Many years passed before she admitted the truth and led the police to the place where the boy had been buried.

The murderer had hastily buried his victim after the crime, dug him up again, poured petrol over him, set fire to him and finally buried the charred remains once again. Thanks to the witness's statements, the mortal remains were discovered very quickly. The BKA's Crime Scene Unit had to recognise, however, that there was a great degree of uncertainty on how to excavate human remains professionally. Subsequently, the Working Group Forensic Archaeology was established for the purpose of carrying out excavations correctly.

Soon afterwards, in 2002, another case engendered an extension of the task we had set ourselves. Wuppertal police asked for cooperation and advice concerning the search for a body. There were no witnesses in this case and the police only had a vague idea of where to look for the body. Since the area concerned was much too large, however, it was impossible to carry out excavations. Since then, the Working Group has been dealing with all possibilities of locating human remains or other objects reported to be buried or concealed – in addition to the subject of excavation techniques.

The Working Group's role as a central service unit

The Working Group regards itself as a service unit for all police authorities in Germany. It currently consists of 10 criminal police officers who, in addition to their original occupations as crime scene and forensic officers, give particular attention to this topic with all related disciplines.

Their objective is to give advice to investigators, to assist in preparatory works and subsequently support searches and excavations. The central idea is to ensure that police authorities/forensic teams need not make themselves familiar with the subject every time anew and in a time-consuming way. Instead, the knowledge and practical experience gained from previous cases is to be preserved and enhanced.

To meet this requirement, networking with experts from the subject areas concerned (e.g. archaeologists, geologists, physical anthropologists) is indispensable. Their practical experience gained in similar cases is of special interest. Their professional training alone does not automatically enable archaeologists to provide guidance for measures of that kind.

Sources for obtaining technical equipment and operational logistics are continuously ascertained and listed. The Working Group itself holds the necessary excavation tools but heavy clearing machinery is requested from other organisations, such as the Federal Agency for Technical Relief (*Bundesanstalt Technisches Hilfswerk* – THW) or the stand-by police. Body-tracker dogs are usually made available by the police of the federal state concerned.

As regards geophysical measuring instruments (ground penetrating radar (GPR), geomagnetics, etc.), contacts are maintained with various institutes, authorities, companies or freelance geophysicists.

Despite largely positive experiences in this respect, we unfortunately have to point out that, in individual cases, providers of geophysical methods made their equipment available at high cost although there was little prospect of success and there might have been cheaper alternatives. It is quite likely that financial interests played a decisive role in this context and that the service providers described the prospects of success or their efficiency too optimistically.

For this and other reasons, the Working Group considers each case individually and always develops a search strategy adapted to the individual circumstances. The excavation technique also differs from case to case.

To our knowledge, no other German police authority has a comparable Working Group dealing with forensic archaeology. The enquiries made with the State Criminal Police Offices (see earlier) have, however, shown that there are at least some police authorities which address or have addressed the issue. Some offices have already gathered in-depth practical experience in relevant cases. At present, there is no regular exchange of information and no fixed network in Germany; however, this would be desirable in the future.

Representative case examples

Case example 1 (military training ground)

A 21-year-old woman had been missing since June 2000. She had disappeared 4 days after her wedding, being 3 months pregnant. Only after having been urged by friends, her husband reported his wife missing several days later. During forensic examinations in the couple's flat, a tracker dog responded to a carpet. The murder squad in charge suspected the husband of having killed his wife.

For a long time it was impossible to collect sufficient evidence for a conviction. The investigation dragged on for years. Four years later, another attempt was made to solve the case. When the investigation was taken up again, special attention was paid to a detail which had been impossible to clarify until then. In the post-commission phase, the victim's husband had stayed on a military training ground for about 30 min. He had parked his car on an emergency runway. The investigators asked themselves why the husband was interested in that piece of land and whether his wife's body might be found there.

In 2004, the murder squad asked the Working Group for assistance. It was requested to help in determining a search area and an appropriate search strategy and, if required, to carry out excavations to locate the body.

The military training ground was too large for a search territory. The area therefore had to be narrowed down. Based on the location of the car, a displacement/time calculation was made taking into account the nature of the terrain and the weight of the body carried (about 50 kg). The emergency runway was lined with open fields bounded by woods. To the south-east, however, there were several earth walls which obstructed the view from the runway to the open fields (Figure 9.1). Although the British military used to patrol the premises every day, the perpetrator would not have been visible behind the earth walls. He could have dug a grave unnoticed, especially since a small group of trees also offered protection against discovery. The other parts of the emergency runway were clearly visible. For this reason, the searches were focussed on the area behind the earth walls.

The following search strategy was determined in this case:

- Walking all over the territory to detect irregularities
- Aerial photographs taken by a police helicopter from a low flight altitude
- Inspection of the territory by a highly experienced and specialised archaeologist from the Office for Cultural Heritage Preservation of Mainz (Rhineland-Palatinate)
- Searches assisted by body-tracker dogs
- Searches by means of metal detectors (large loop)
- Examination of the area by use of a test bar
- Removal of the upper soil layer

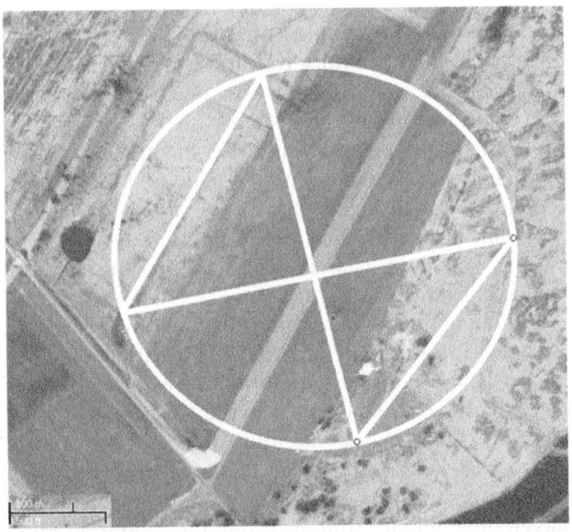

Figure 9.1 Military training ground with position of the car and indication of the relevant area, based on the displacement/time calculation.

The area inspection and the analysis of the aerial photographs revealed some conspicuous spots in the search territory. Moreover, the aerial photographs showed suspicious areas outside the defined territory. The body-tracker dogs showed special interest in the sector near the aforementioned group of trees. Machine excavators, under the direction of the archaeologist, carefully removed the upper soil layer from all areas concerned (*c.* 3000 m^2). Underneath the upper soil layer, suspicious soil elements were further exposed manually by members of the Working Group. However, in the end the body was not found.

The abortive attempt to find the body as well as new information suggested that the terrace of the house formerly inhabited by the couple might be a potential site for an excavation (Figure 9.2). In the period following the offence, the suspect had built a terrace outside the house which he had sealed with a concrete slab. A non-destructive search of the terrace by means of GPR revealed an irregularity in the ground (Figure 9.3). This area was opened by use of a concrete saw. The subsequent excavation was made manually and with fine tools. Unfortunately, the body was not found here either. The anomaly discovered in the radar image had been caused by building rubble (measuring 160 cm in length, 50 cm in width and 20 cm in depth) in the otherwise homogeneous sandy soil.

This case has been chosen to demonstrate that there is no guarantee for successful searches. Depending on the terrain, an individual search strategy has to be

Figure 9.2 House and terrace.

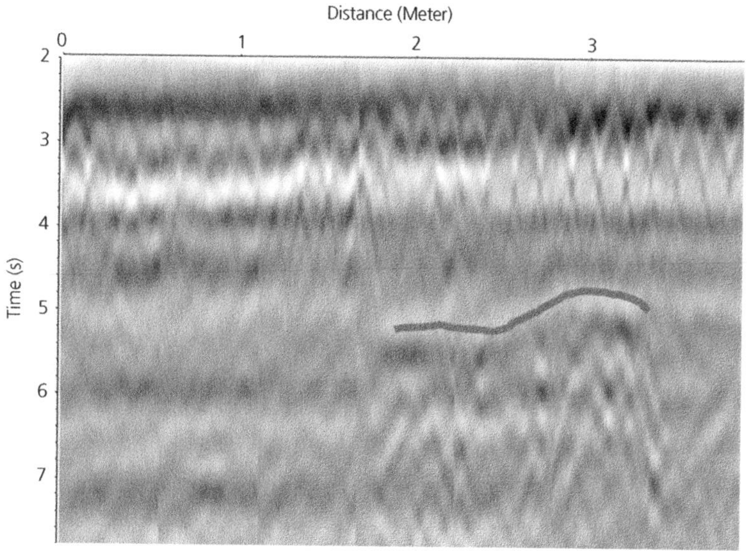

Figure 9.3 GPR image showing irregularities in the ground.

developed. Knowledge of the case-specific details and simple considerations (e.g. displacement/time calculation), site inspections and aerial photographs can help narrow down a search area to a considerable extent.

It remains to be said that the aforementioned wife has not been found to date. However, an important witness for the defence later confessed in a hearing that he had provided the husband with a false alibi. The husband had told him that he was responsible for the offence. The husband was subsequently convicted for manslaughter although his wife's body had not been found.

Case example 2 (additional crime scene work carried out after discovery of a body)

A businessman had been missing since March 2003. The State Criminal Police Office in charge conducted an investigation on suspicion of homicide. Many years later, in May 2008, forestry workers doing marking work in a wood near a motorway discovered parts of a human skeleton in a hole in the ground.

Subsequent searches of the forest with body-tracker dogs, an on-site inspection by a search team of the stand-by police and the excavation of the hole resulted in the discovery of further human bones. The dental chart and further examinations clearly identified the human remains as those of the missing businessman.

The medico-forensic specialists and investigating officers ascertained, however, that various bones, clothes, the watch and jewellery were missing. The Working Group was therefore tasked with finding and seizing the missing body parts and objects.

According to the crime scene report provided, the forensic scientists were not sure whether the perpetrator had buried the body in a hole or whether he had put it on the forest ground and covered it with soil, sand and leaves. After the skeleton parts had been excavated, the place of discovery was again filled up with the forest soil previously removed (Figure 9.4).

In the light of these circumstances, the members of the Working Group decided to proceed as follows:

- Removing the upper soil layer
- Taking soil samples
- Opening the site of discovery once again
- Sieving the soil
- Searching the environment by use of metal detectors

The soil piled up was explored by means of poking bars and marked. Subsequently, the exact boundaries of the pit were determined and the level was prepared, in which the upper soil layer was removed from the outside to the inside until a transition from solid and old needle/root layers to loose sandy soil could be identified (Figure 9.5).

The first excavation seemed to indicate that the hole was 80–100 cm long, 40–50 cm wide and *c.* 45 cm deep, but further work revealed real dimensions of 210 × 130 cm and a depth of 75 cm (Figure 9.6). The excavated soil (fill of the grave) was sieved and additionally screened by a metal detector. Further tarsal and carpal bones as well as teeth, some skin fragments and scalp hairs were discovered in this context. Based on the individual sites of discovery and the features of the hole in the ground, it was ascertained that the body had been in a lateral position with the head pointing to the south-east.

At the edge of the grave, the offender had cut off roots between 1 and 2 cm thick. Sand found at the head and tail ends of the pit indicated that animals had partly dug out the body. This explained why the skeletal parts were scattered within a radius of about 15 m. The surrounding

Figure 9.4 Excavation site covered with tree trunks and branches.

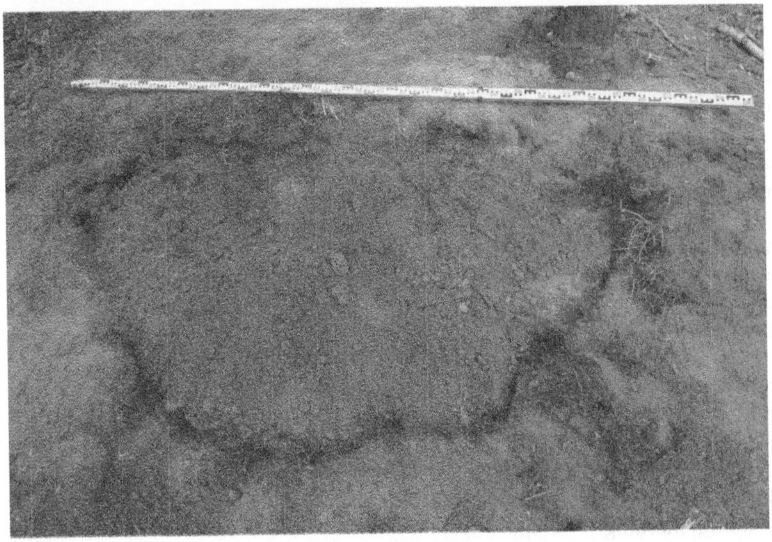

Figure 9.5 Boundaries of the excavation site.

forest soil was raked off, sieved and searched by means of a metal detector. Thus further bones were discovered.

All in all, the second search measure resulted in the discovery of another 23 human bones, 2 human teeth and various skin particles and hairs. The true dimensions of the hole and the position of the body were reconstructed. The missing watch and jewellery were not found, but it can be assumed that those objects were not actually left behind on the scene since the body was buried unclothed.

This description shows that only an archaeological approach could provide certainty as to whether the perpetrator had laid the victim onto the forest ground or buried him in a hole. During the first searches, the forensic scientists had not dug deep enough so that various skeletal parts as well as skin and hair particles had been left in the grave. Its dimensions had been misinterpreted.

Summary, conclusion and outlook

The number of forensic excavations in Germany cannot be verified with certainty. It is difficult to collect such information because some cases are not reported by the local police services. They are not actually obliged to do so. The total number of forensic excavations is probably rather low, particularly when the figures are considered broken down into the individual federal states. Under these circumstances, it is doubtful that archaeologists will be employed by the police.

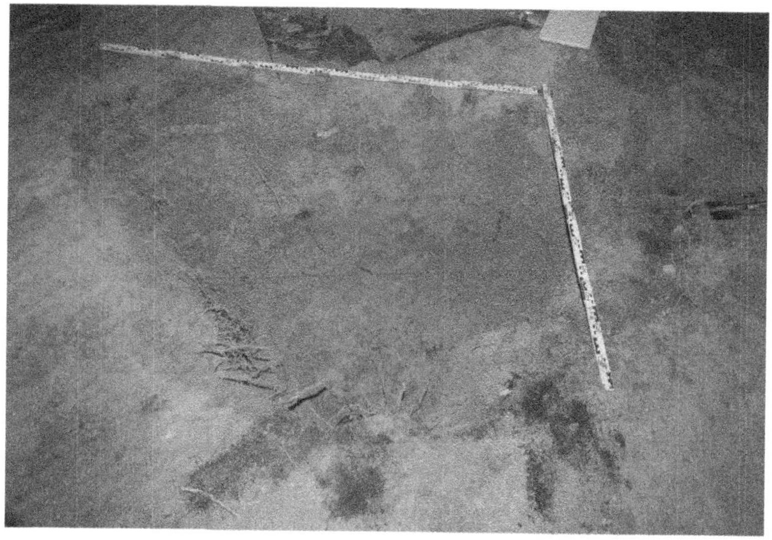

Figure 9.6 Exposed grave, about 210 × 130 cm.

Nevertheless, a certain awareness of the forensic-archaeological approach to an excavation site is developing. Corresponding opportunities for basic and advanced training should pay due regard to this development in the future. In the opinion of the Working Group, it would be useful for the police to build up 'centralised' expertise.

Outside the police, excellent expertise is available, for example, at universities/institutes and offices for the preservation and protection of cultural heritage. The law enforcement authorities can benefit from increased networking and cooperation with these institutions.

As far as technical localisation methods are concerned, the results achieved so far are not satisfactory. Progress may be expected from further practical experience with technically refined devices and continuous market monitoring.

While still evolving in Germany, forensic archaeology is often well established abroad. An active exchange of experience with other countries could bring about benefits for all those involved.

References

Krausse, D. and Nübold, C. 2008. *Discovering the Archaeologists of Europe: Germany.* Verband der Landesarchäologen in der Bundesrepublik Deutschland. Available at: http://www.discovering-archaeologists.eu/germany.html (last accessed 9 July 2013).

PSC (Police Crime Statistics). 2011. *Federal Criminal Police Office.* Available at: www.bka.de (last accessed July 2013).

Rückert, S. 2000. *Tote Haben Keine Lobby. Die Dunkelziffer der Vertuschten Morde.* Hamburg, Hoffmann und Campe.

Statistisches Jahrbuch. 2012. *Statistisches Bundesamt, Wiesbaden.* Available at: https://www.destatis.de/DE/Publikationen/StatistischesJahrbuch/StatistischesJahrbuch2012.pdf?__blob=publicationFile (last accessed 8 December 2014).

CHAPTER 10

Forensic archaeology in Greece

Konstantinos Moraitis[1] and Constantine Eliopoulos[2]

[1] *Department of Forensic Medicine and Toxicology, School of Medicine, University of Athens, Athens, Greece*

[2] *Research Centre in Evolutionary Anthropology and Palaeoecology, School of Natural Sciences and Psychology, Liverpool John Moores University, Liverpool, UK*

Introduction

Greece is a country with a rich history where archaeological investigations have been taking place for centuries. Local archaeological authorities (Ephorates of Antiquities) and foreign archaeological missions or schools established in Greece have conducted excavations throughout the country (Biers 1996; Eliopoulos et al. 2011a). The same cannot be said about forensic archaeology, as this discipline is virtually non-existent. When a body of forensic interest is discovered, it is law-enforcement personnel who recover the remains. In these cases, crime scene procedures are followed, but there is no reference to forensic archaeology. The purpose of the present work is to provide a description of the medico-legal framework in Greece concerning the investigation of an outdoor crime scene, and also the type of forensic cases in which archaeological theories, principles and methods are employed.

The medico-legal framework in Greece

In Greece, the medico-legal death investigation is organised in such a way that two systems run in parallel, a State and a University System. There are 13 State Medico-Legal Services (*Iatrodikastikes Ipiresies*) operated by the Ministry of Justice, Transparency and Human Rights. The majority of these services operate in hospitals, while others operate in dedicated facilities. These local services cover the entire country and are responsible for the forensic investigation of deaths occurring within their jurisdiction. The University System includes the Departments of Forensic Medicine in Athens, Thessaloniki, Crete, Ioannina and Alexandroupolis, which are staffed with personnel trained mainly in forensic pathology and toxicology (Mavroforou and Michalodimitrakis 2002). Being a university, this system also includes teaching and research. Forensic DNA analysis is offered by both State and University laboratories, while other forensic services such as fingerprint, trace evidence, firearm and tool-mark analyses are provided exclusively by the Forensic Science Division of the Hellenic Police.

The Department of Forensic Medicine and Toxicology at the University of Athens Medical School is the only institution in Greece that offers forensic anthropological services (Eliopoulos et al. 2011a). Since 1999, the department's forensic anthropologist (first author) has actively participated in cases where skeletal remains are involved by providing anthropological examinations at the request of the Court, Prosecution Office or police. However, the academic recognition of forensic anthropology in Greece as a discipline dates to 2008 with the establishment of the Forensic Anthropology Unit (*Monada Dikastikis Anthropologias* – UoAFAU) at the department. In addition to the usual forensic cases involving the establishment of a biological profile, personal identification, evaluation of skeletal trauma and estimation of the post-mortem interval, the Unit also undertakes examinations aimed at estimating the age of living individuals with no identification documents who are arrested and declared to be underage. Since 1999, when the Department first started to offer anthropological services, an average of 12 cases is investigated every year, with a steadily increasing number in recent years.

Forensic archaeology casework

Greece

In Greece, human remains that are discovered from sites undergoing development or from locations that are not part of an archaeological excavation are reported to the police (Eliopoulos et al. 2011a). In such cases, police officers, crime scene investigators and a forensic pathologist, who is charged with the legal responsibility for investigating and certifying the cause of death, will

Forensic Archaeology: A Global Perspective, First Edition. Edited by W.J. Mike Groen, Nicholas Márquez-Grant and Robert C. Janaway.

attend the scene and recover the reported remains. According to the Greek Penal Code, the time frame for prosecution for life felonies or capital offences is 20 years (Eliopoulos et al. 2011a). The medico-legal system does not involve archaeologists in outdoor crime scene investigation of human remains. However, in recent years there have been some changes with the establishment of the UoAFAU (Eliopoulos et al. 2011a). The forensic anthropologists of the Unit have visited a number of scenes in order to confirm that the remains are human and to determine whether they are recent or archaeological. This decision is made by the forensic anthropologist or pathologist, since most Greek archaeologists have very little experience with human remains. In the vast majority of these cases, their role was to conduct a scene search in order to recover additional skeletal elements following a recovery of human remains by the police. These scenes contained surface remains in the majority of cases. Even though the Unit's personnel do not include any archaeologists, its members have received training in archaeological methods. Therefore, archaeological search and excavation techniques are employed at all scenes where decomposing or skeletonised human remains are recovered. In recent years there has been an increase in the need for specialised retrieval and recovery of human remains because of the growing rate of crime and illegal immigration, especially in southern Europe (Cattaneo and Baccino 2002).

Most of the surface remains were disarticulated, scattered across the surface and altered by mammalian carnivores. Although scavengers may modify a scene significantly, a study discussing the implications that scavenging has on human remains recovered from outdoor locations in Greece showed that body retrieval was usually incomplete when the recovery was carried out solely by police investigators (Moraitis and Spiliopoulou 2010). This is due to the fact that police officers in Greece, like in most countries are not trained in human osteology and archaeological recovery techniques. Potentially, this can cause problems, especially in cases of commingled remains, but a systematic recovery can eliminate such complications. Experience has shown that having an anthropologist with archaeological training as a member of the recovery team ensures that all skeletal elements and maximum contextual information are collected.

A category of routine casework is the result of the funerary customs of Greece. The unusual practice of exhuming the dead 3–5 years after burial, placing the bones in boxes and keeping them in ossuaries can lead to a large number of human remains above ground at any given time. As a consequence, human bones can find their way to places not normally expected to be found (Eliopoulos 2006). These cemetery remains can sometimes be misinterpreted as the result of a crime, but a careful examination of the context and other attributes of the bones can help rule out foul play (Eliopoulos et al. 2011b). Some of these attributes can include bleaching of the remains, as this procedure usually takes place for medical specimens. This bleaching is achieved by chemical methods and must be differentiated from bleaching occurring as a result of sun exposure. Another modification is that resulting from the forensic autopsy, where various skeletal elements are sectioned. These sections are very specific in their form and location and should not be confused with dismemberment or post-mortem damage. In countries where embalming is a common procedure, the artefacts of this process can help identify remains of a cemetery origin. However, in Greece embalming is required by law only to make the body suitable for transportation (Government Gazette 210/A63/1975); therefore, embalming artefacts are very rare. In addition, the location of the discovery is an important element: remains found near a cemetery or a medical school may very well be the result of an improper disposal of skeletons (Eliopoulos et al. 2011b).

The application of archaeology in mass grave investigation: the Cyprus Project

Another application of forensic archaeology has been the involvement of the authors of the present work in the Cyprus Project. This is a project run by the non-governmental organisation Physicians for Human Rights (PHR) (Schmitt et al., Chapter 53, this volume) for the government of the Republic of Cyprus. The project aims at the recovery, identification and repatriation of the remains of citizens of Cyprus and Greece who were killed during the 1974 invasion of Cyprus by Turkey (Borowiec 2000; Drousiotis 2000). One important part of this project was to recover the remains that had been exhumed and returned to families of Greek soldiers by the Greek army in the period between 1979 and 1981. The exhumations conducted by PHR in 1999 revealed that these repatriations by the Greek army, even though they had been conducted with good intention, were not scientifically sound and most families were given the wrong remains. The main reason was that the exhumations were performed by individuals who did not have the necessary knowledge or training. As members of the PHR Cyprus Project team, the authors travelled to several locations within Greece in order to recover these remains employing archaeological methodology, and return them to Cyprus where a DNA analysis was performed at the DNA Identification Laboratory of the Cyprus Institute of Neurology and Genetics (CING) (Drousiotis 2008). Due to the funerary customs of Greece, some of these remains were found in boxes kept in ossuaries, while others had been buried in family graves along with the remains of other individuals. A detailed history of the inhumations that had taken place in each grave was taken from the families prior to any exhumation efforts. Having knowledge of the biological profile, skeletal pathologies and cause of death of the individuals within the grave greatly enhanced our ability to arrange the commingled remains and recover only the skeletal elements of interest to the investigation.

The following section presents some characteristic cases that highlight the anthropological/archaeological involvement in the recovery of human remains and outdoor crime scene investigation in Greece.

Case reports

Case 1

A partially skeletonised body was found in a rural area of the Euboea Island by a passer-by (Figure 10.1). A forensic pathologist and a forensic anthropologist visited the site of discovery at the request of the police and proceeded to examine the scene. The remains were recorded and photographed *in situ* as part of the investigation.

The body was found in a prone position, and a systematic search using taphonomic knowledge and principles was used. This resulted in an almost complete recovery of all the available skeletal elements, including bones such as the hyoid. The hyoid bone is of particular forensic importance since fracture to one or both of the greater horns can be a characteristic sign of manual strangulation (Shepherd 2002). In addition, several items were identified as being part of the scene and were collected. These included an insulin pen used to inject insulin for the treatment of diabetes that was found in proximity to the body. In the course of the investigation it was concluded that the victim had probably committed suicide by use of insulin. The victim was diabetic and was an insulin user, but the large number of insulin cartridges found at the scene indicated that the dosage would have been fatal for the individual if administered in a short period of time. Other items found at the scene, such as a deteriorating piece of newspaper, helped to establish the post-mortem interval. This newspaper fragment was photographed at the scene, but was not preserved intact during transportation to the morgue, as it was attached to the body. Another taphonomic finding was the presence of insect pupal casings (puparia) where the body was found, indicating that decomposition had taken place at the site of discovery. Finally, large parts of the body had been mummified as they were exposed to the open air, with the exception of the right hand, which was underneath the body. This had created a moist environment and led to the saponification of the hand.

All these observations that took place during the recovery process helped the post-mortem examination significantly. The interpretation of the changes observed on the body was made possible by an extensive photographic recording and a careful and systematic recovery at the scene.

Case 2

In another case, human remains were discovered in a coastal area just north of Athens, when a dog was seen carrying a human limb. Investigators from the Hellenic Coast Guard conducted a search of the area and found a decomposing body nearby. A forensic anthropologist was called at the request of the Coast Guard to the scene in order to perform an examination of the body *in situ*

Figure 10.1 The body within dense vegetation with personal effects that can be seen in the foreground.

and direct the recovery efforts. The body was in a prone position and large concrete slabs had been placed over it in order to conceal it from view (Figure 10.2).

Evidence of fire damage was also found on the body, which was most likely an attempt to prevent identification. However, only a few areas of the body showed some evidence of charring, indicating that the burning was incomplete. No signs of fire were found in the vegetation surrounding the body, but when the area was searched by crime scene investigators some evidence of fire was discovered nearby. At a distance of about 100 m there was an area of recently burned vegetation. It was apparent that the perpetrators had attempted to burn the body at a different location and when they did not succeed, they moved it to the location where it was found. Further evidence for transportation was provided by a piece of thick wire around the victim's waist, which was probably used to drag the body.

The examination of the victim at the scene revealed that he had sustained sharp force injuries, including some to the posterior part of the head. Post-mortem modifications of the body included signs of scavenging of the limbs. The right lower leg had been removed by scavengers, most probably dogs, and despite the extensive search of the surrounding area, it was never recovered. Puncture and scoring marks were also found on the lower limbs, hands and upper torso.

Once the initial assessment of the scene was completed, the body, which was partially buried, had to be fully exposed. The concrete slabs were removed carefully by a backhoe in order to enable the excavation of the remains. Standard archaeological tools such as trowels, brushes and wooden picks were used to remove the vegetation, debris and soil surrounding the body. When the remains were fully exposed, photographs and notes were taken. The findings indicated that the body was set on fire, then placed in an area with vegetation and, finally, covered by slabs. This case illustrates how the application of taphonomic principles and archaeological methods can aid in the reconstruction of the events surrounding death.

Future trends regarding forensic archaeology in Greece

The application of principles of forensic taphonomy and forensic archaeology is important as they can provide some vital information about the scene, the victim, the perpetrators and the events that took place there. Following the guidelines and procedures described by practitioners of the discipline is the only way to ensure that an outdoor scene investigation is thorough (Connor 2007; Dupras et al. 2006; Litherland et al. 2012). Unfortunately, in most parts of the world police investigators are not given training in archaeology and as a result much important information is unnoticed and undocumented (Menez 2005).

Equally important is the knowledge of taphonomic principles. By assessing a scene where surface remains have been found, the investigator can determine the exact location of original deposition and decomposition. Finds such as soil discolouration, pupal casings and some skeletal elements can indicate where a body has decomposed. This in turn can help with the search for the rest of the skeleton, as the spatial distribution of bones follows somewhat predictable patterns when all the taphonomic variables are considered (Haglund and Sorg 1997, 2002). In addition, it can provide a smaller area for a detailed search where items essential to the

Figure 10.2 The body in prone position with concrete slabs on top of it.

investigation, such as bullets or a murder weapon, can be found. As illustrated in the case studies presented earlier, scene examinations by UoAFAU staff have resulted in the discovery of additional skeletal elements, or the finding of information such as the location of body decomposition. Even though many parts of the world today do not have forensic anthropologists as part of the medico-legal system (İşcan and Quatrehomme 1999), Greece is fortunate to have anthropologists with an archaeological training who can conduct scene examinations.

In Greece, although forensic archaeology as a discipline does not exist and it is not likely to be established in the near future, principles of forensic archaeology are employed by individuals who have been trained accordingly. This includes the members of the UoAFAU who are called to several crime scenes every year. It is hoped that the practice of employing staff with specialised knowledge will continue in the field of forensic investigation in Greece.

References

Biers, W. R. 1996. *The Archaeology of Greece: An Introduction*. 2nd edition. New York, Cornell University Press.

Borowiec, A. 2000. *Cyprus, a Troubled Island*. Westport, Praeger Publishers.

Cattaneo, C. and Baccino, E. 2002. A call for forensic anthropology in Europe. *International Journal of Legal Medicine* 116, N1–N2.

Connor, M. A. 2007. *Forensic Methods. Excavation for the Archaeologist and Investigator*. Lanham, Altamira Press.

Drousiotis, M. 2000. *1619 Guilts*. Nicosia, Diafaneia Publishing.

Drousiotis, M. 2008. The tragic end of a suicide mission. *Eleftherotypia*, 23 May 2008.

Dupras, T. L., Schultz, J. J., Wheeler, S. M. and Williams, L. J. 2006. *Forensic Recovery of Human Remains: Archaeological Approaches*. Boca Raton, CRC Press.

Eliopoulos, C. 2006. The creation of a documented human skeletal collection and the application of current aging and sexing standards on a Greek skeletal population. Unpublished PhD thesis, University of Sheffield.

Eliopoulos, C., Moraitis, K., Vanna, V. and Manolis, S. K. Greece. 2011a. In N. Márquez-Grant and L. Fibiger (eds.), *The Routledge Handbook of Archaeological Human Remains and Legislation*, 173–183. Abingdon, Routledge.

Eliopoulos, C., Moraitis, K., Reyes, F., Spiliopoulou, C. and Manolis, S. K. 2011b. Guidelines for the recognition of cemetery remains in Greece. *American Journal of Forensic Medicine and Pathology* 32, 153–156.

Government Gazette of the Hellenic Republic. 210/A63/1975.

Haglund, W. D. and Sorg, M. H. (eds.) 1997. *Forensic Taphonomy: The Postmortem Fate of Human Remains*. Boca Raton, CRC Press.

Haglund, W. D. and Sorg, M. H. (eds.) 2002. *Advances in Forensic Taphonomy: Method, Theory and Archaeological Perspectives*. Boca Raton, CRC Press.

Işcan, M. Y. and Quatrehomme, G. 1999. Medicolegal anthropology in France. *Forensic Science International* 100, 17–35.

Litherland, S., Márquez-Grant, N. and Roberts, J. 2012. Forensic archaeology: from crime scene to court. In N. Márquez-Grant and L. Fibiger (eds.), *Forensic Ecology Handbook: From Crime Scene to Court*, 23–48. Oxford, Wiley-Blackwell.

Mavroforou, A. and Michalodimitrakis, E. 2002. Forensic pathology on the threshold of the 21st century and the need for harmonization of current practice and training: the Greek concept. *American Journal of Forensic Medicine and Pathology* 23, 19–25.

Menez, L. L. 2005. The place of a forensic archaeologist at a crime scene involving a buried body. *Forensic Science International* 152, 311–315.

Moraitis, K. and Spiliopoulou, C. 2010. Forensic implications of carnivore scavenging on human remains recovered from outdoor locations in Greece. *Journal of Forensic and Legal Medicine* 17, 298–303.

Shepherd, R. 2002. *Simpson's Forensic Medicine*. 12th edition. London, Arnold.

CHAPTER 11

Forensic archaeology and anthropology in Hungary: current trends and future perspectives

Éva Susa[1], Kinga Éry[2], László Kovács[2], Mátyás Szőke[2] and Mária Molnos[1]

[1]*Igazságügyi Szakértői és Kutató Intézetek (ISZKI), Budapest, Hungary*

[2]*Retired Scientist*

This chapter is in memory of Alán Kralovánszky (1929–1993), archaeologist, and a prominent representative of the exhumations for humanitarian reasons in Hungary.

Introduction

The term *forensic archaeology* is not applicable in Hungary. The police do not use archaeological methods and archaeologists are not included in police investigations. Investigations are coordinated by the police according to administrative or criminal law regulations, with the assistance of either a forensic medical or a forensic anthropological expert. In cases of accidentally finding skeletal remains, the procedure is the same as in cases of exceptional death, and the case has to be clarified in cooperation with a forensic expert.

Training facilities and institutional frameworks

Currently there is no educational training for forensic archaeology in Hungary, and there is none planned. Universities of Arts and Sciences offer archaeology courses. Archaeologists take part in forensic excavations if required, but their role is limited to professional procedure in connection with excavation. Thus, there are no dedicated forensic archaeologists in Hungary. In forensic excavation cases archaeologists apply theoretical and practical archaeological methods. Universities of Natural Sciences offer anthropology courses. The examination of skeletal remains has previously been and is currently mostly done by biological anthropologist experts, who are biologists at MSc level. They are qualified to determinate sex, age, metric and morphological features of the skeleton and to perform biological reconstructions (all general features and personal identifications). Historically, forensic medicine has existed in Hungary for 200 years. Forensic pathologists assist in the identification of bygone persons more and more frequently today, even though they have not studied biological anthropology.

Forensic exhumations in Hungary

Indirect forensic investigations have taken place in Hungary since the end of the archaeological period (from 1711 onwards). The post-1711 civilian or military dead were buried in individual or mass graves, churchyards, civil cemeteries or outside cemeteries. Many may have been buried in a prison cemetery in an unmarked grave or with a pseudonym. The dead persons of this period could be citizens, famous historical persons, sovereigns, lords and their family members, national martyrs, soldiers, victims of historical events, or persons who have died or have been executed in prison (e.g. victims of the revolution in 1848, one of the two World Wars (WWI and WWII), the revolution in 1956, or victims of the holocaust or communist terror) (Éry 1990; Susa 1995, 2000).

During the last centuries human identification has attracted greater interest and value in connection with wars and different political events. The largest number of requests is connected to changes in the political system (the end of the Communist era in 1989). Family members, civil organisations and churches were now looking for persons buried in unmarked graves or who had died in Hungary after 1711. The authors of this chapter were involved in numerous exhumations and human identifications related to such cases (e.g. Éry and Susa 1994, 1996; Susa 1998, 2000; Susa and Éry 1995; Susa and Molnos in press).

Exhumations relating to the identification of deceased persons were performed previously, for example in the 1950s. For instance internal affairs personnel were looking for László Rajk (Interior Minister of Hungary between 1946 and 1948), who was executed by the

Forensic Archaeology: A Global Perspective, First Edition. Edited by W.J. Mike Groen, Nicholas Márquez-Grant and Robert C. Janaway.

regime, and his comrades (Susa and Molnos 2002, 2004). Those of the authors qualified as forensic anthropologists knew about the exhumations which took place in the 1960s, when social democrat leaders who had been executed or died in prisons were sought. However, the excavations were not completed in rows; instead graves were excavated which were distinguished by certain marks, thus excavating many graves in several cemeteries. As described in later studies by the authors some remains were uncovered and were later reburied elsewhere (Susa and Molnos 2002, 2004).

The concept of the humanitarian exhumation and ISZKI

As recognised since the time of Antigone (Sophocles), relatives have the right to mourn and bury their dead. After a successful humanitarian archaeological exhumation and reburial this concept remains constant.

In Hungary the concept of the humanitarian archaeological excavation is widely known. The terminology was established by the archaeologist Dr Alán Kralovánszky, who designated the forensic archaeological investigations thus in response to the political changes in 1989. These excavations are conducted in the presence of the relatives or those who requested the exhumation from the experts who are working to reconstruct past events. Relatives can provide valuable information about burial conditions and circumstances, for instance the time, place and biological characteristics of the deceased person (Susa and Molnos 2002, 2004, 2013).

The permission of the National Humanitarian Committee (*Nemzeti Kegyeleti és Emlékhely Bizottság* – NKEB) must be officially requested before humanitarian exhumations can take place. In the absence of relatives the state or NKEB can exercise humanitarian rights. Unfortunately so-called 'volunteer actions' might take place when other organisations undertake an arbitrary request; these actions are based on an incorrect interpretation of legal regulations. Forensic exhumations in Hungary are conducted by institutes under the supervision of the Ministry of Justice, especially by the Network of Forensic Science Institutes (*Igazságügyi Szakértői és Kutató Intézetek* – ISZKI). The purpose of a grave's exhumation – besides cemetery exhumations – is mostly human identification, followed by the reburial of the body in its final, more appropriate place (Éry 1990).

The research group of ISZKI was created in 1989 by the Ministry of Justice in order to identify deceased persons. The first request of the new regime was the exhumation of Imre Nagy (the martyred Prime Minister of Hungary, who died in 1958) and his comrades after Nagy's rehabilitation in 1989, in which Dr Alán Kralovánszky (archaeologist), Dr László Harsányi and Dr Árpád Szabó (forensic pathologists), and Dr János Nemeskéri (forensic anthropologist) participated. The membership of this team changed after 1990, the group being consolidated under the leadership of the first author (ÉS). The authors of this chapter still actively work in the ISZKI team (Susa and Molnos in press).

Prior to archaeological excavation research begins with data collection by forensic anthropologists and their assistants. The ISZKI database (January 2013) contains 2790 names of the disappeared, with additional data. It includes information about persons executed as criminals or who died in prison for other reasons between 1945 and 1962 (Susa and Molnos 2002, 2004). Generally the data collected for one or more persons include the burial time, manner and place of burial, and biological and other characteristics of the dead person. The group will mark the excavation site, although if there is no positive indication of a burial site, excavation cannot be undertaken.

The ISZKI team conducted several forensic exhumations and cemetery excavations from 1989 on request (*c.* 250 cases). The results taken from exhumation scenes concurred with burial characteristics for the given time periods based on written information included in our database. The data were published previously in several reports (Susa and Molnos in press).

The exhumations took place between 28 and 57 years after the deaths of the individuals. In many cases there are differences between the periods before and after 1956 in the depths of the graves, the position and burial of corpses, the aluminium tag around the ankle, burial accessories and the quality of the coffin or wooden box. People who died after 1956 were not buried as deep, many of them lying prone in poor-quality wooden boxes, rather than in coffins (Éry et al. 1994; Susa 2007; Susa and Molnos 2004, 2013).

Besides increasing professional knowledge, this work requires moderation and responsibility since the positive and negative results can deeply affect the feelings of families involved or may even affect a whole nation (Éry 1990).

Excavation of individual graves

The history of the Budapest New Public Cemetery, Plots 298, 300 and 301

The Budapest New Public Cemetery is one of the biggest cemeteries in Europe. It was opened in 1886, and nowadays covers *c.* 207 hectares. It is currently the final resting place of *c.* 3 million people. Persons executed for political reasons and the victims of political trials were buried in the farthest plots from the entrance gate. These are plots 298 and 301. In these plots excavations can be performed based on the exact location of the grave (whether it is totally separate, between other tombs, the number of the plot is known, etc.). The data collected refer to a grave in a specified row; the exact location can be specified only by searching. Graves or their markings may have disappeared, due to artificial markings being used for humanitarian or political reasons. Therefore official data on graves may well be incorrect.

Investigation is hampered if (political) persons buried on the same day were incorrectly buried, either through lack of concern or on purpose. Consequently the research team seeking a specific deceased person may have to exhume several graves buried on the same day.

There are 28 rows in plot 301, each containing 40 graves (a total of 1120 graves). Most of the graves are 'free of charge', containing the unidentified dead from hospitals, remains of bodies from dissection chambers and the corpses of animals used in experiments. The burials took place between January 1952 and 1977. The present condition of the plot is mostly poor due to excavations in 1960 and landscaping in1989.

Plot 298 adjoins plot 301, but is smaller. It consists of 23 rows, each containing 45 graves (a total of 1035 graves). This plot contains victims from an earlier obscure period. From 1945 the graves were dug from either side and then met in the middle. The plot was completely full by December 1951. This plot also contains *gratis* graves. The graves are not currently in good condition due to previous excavations and landscaping. Plot 300 is close to plots 298 and 301, and contains a monument to the Hungarian revolution of 1956.

Archaeological excavations are performed by the third (LK) and fourth (MS) author of this chapter, with the assistance of cemetery labourers. The second author (KÉ) also participates in the practical archaeological excavations, together with the first author (ÉS), who has also experience in different types of forensic excavation.

In cemetery conditions the first task is to label the identified grave approximately, using either measurements or steps. It is necessary to open a section large enough not just for the grave but to allow archaeologists to work outside the grave. Excavations are always conducted using archaeological hand tools, contrary to the 'industrial' method using spade, shovel and hoe, which uncover the bones randomly. The research team should keep the humanitarian character of the excavation in mind, since family members, relatives or others (e.g. parishioners, members from a civil organisation, journalists) may be present.

The purpose of the work is the excavation of whole remains (a skeleton in a coffin if it exists) in the position in which they were buried, to gather information about the burial method (e.g. lying face up or down, the position of the limbs, binding) and to discover additional items (Figure 11.1). These items can have great value, for example, buttons, remnants of clothing, small personal objects or the aluminium (less often iron) numbered tags around the ankle of the prisoners, which allow the remains to be dated (Figure 11.2). These numbers, when compared to prison registration, can help to exclude or verify the identification of a person. Our research team's work proved that these numbers correspond to the numbers in the registration book in a given period.

The difference between a forensic and an archaeological excavation is that in forensics one cannot consider the whole documentation of the excavation and transporting of all the remains. Instead the expert has to decide on the scene if the remains belong to the person in question or not. The final decision as to correct identification is based on laboratory tests – fortunately, nowadays it is possible to compare DNA profiles with the relatives of the deceased. All valuable morphological data (height, physique, cranial characteristics, bone fractures, injuries and illnesses, amputation) in the documentation or given by the relatives, documented dental status, prostheses, glass eyes, etc. have to be considered, and then if the probability is high the corpse

Figure 11.1 Skeleton (in prone position) from grave Nr. 301/15/19 in the Budapest New Public Cemetery.

can be transferred to the anthropological laboratory of NFSI for further investigation. This is also the usual protocol in doubtful cases.

On the other hand, if the remains prove to be negative regarding positive identification or where the remains are older (archaeological) than the victim one is searching for, the remains have to be reburied after photographic documentation so the data can be used later in doubtful cases.

Determination of the sex of a skeleton in 95% of the cases can be predicted on the basis of the measurable and describable phenomena, but biological age can only be estimated within 10–15 years. According to these facts we can only give a general description of the remains. The time interval since burial can also only be estimated within 50–100 years. Moreover, the success of the identification may depend on the condition of the skeleton (intact, decomposed, incomplete or complete) and the context and number of individuals in that mass grave which may provide clues as to who is buried at that particular location (Éry 1990; Éry and Susa 2001; Éry et al. 1994; Susa and Molnos 2002).

If reliable data are available about the location, method of burial and the circumstances of death, the probability of successful identification significantly improves. Without the aforementioned data it is not really possible to identify a person.

Figure 11.2 Grave Nr. 15/19, Plot 301 of the Budapest New Public Cemetery. Feet in socks, the so-called aluminium tags around the ankles.

The partial excavation of the Vác Prison Cemetery, personal identification of Dr Bálint Hóman

Excavation can be performed if the burial site of the person being sought is not exactly known. An example of this is the partial excavation of the Vác prison cemetery in 2000, where a prison cemetery was incorporated into a citizens' cemetery.

Vác is a small town located in the northern part of Hungary at a bend in the Danube, where a prison and a penitentiary were established in 1855; prior to that a hospital prison operated in the building. In the 1950s many state prisoners were kept here. The dead were buried in the so-called prison cemetery outside town.

First we had to establish what the system of burial was in this neglected cemetery, overgrown with vegetation and with very few gravestones, and to differentiate between the civil and prison areas of the cemetery. A complex archaeological excavation was conducted. With the use of machines the whole area was cleared of trees, bushes and other vegetation, and the ground was excavated to a depth of 1 m. This surface was shovelled to clear the area, so that the graves with mixed soil were separated from the undisturbed subsoil (Figure 11.3).

Figure 11.3 The excavation of the prison cemetery in Vác in 2000, with cleared burial locations.

After the prison cemetery was identified, we attempted to identify the chronological order of the burials and thus find the grave of the person searched for.

The local government in Vác and the Ministry of Justice gave financial assistance for the partial humanitarian excavation of the Vác prison cemetery in 2000. Prior to excavation, data had been collected for years (archives, data concerning interior affairs and prisons, records of evidence, exhumation reports from 1960 onwards, registry data, etc.). According to our research (focusing on the period 1945–1962) 115 burials were definitely connected to the Vác prison, where people died in the prison or the prison hospital. Moreover, persons who died elsewhere (e.g. in a labour camp) but were moved to Vác for burial could also be identified.

After removing the surface of the excavated area (*c.* 950 m^3) it was estimated that there could be 285 graves (yellowish, yellow-blackish and blackish) in the cemetery, randomly arranged. The colours of the soil indicated a relatively chronological order. The deepest layer, corresponding to the oldest burials, was yellowish, the black layer nearest to the surface corresponded to burials in the 1950s. Data from the archives showed that the excavated area contained a civil cemetery in the 19th century; these were the yellow grave patches. 156 civilian graves were counted, and 41 graves were completely excavated. We also uncovered skeletons from the black-coloured graves, these remains having been buried in the 20th century. Altogether 129 graves were identified and 68 graves were completely excavated.

Unfortunately complete excavation and reconstruction was impossible at the time, since the remains could not be identified. The year of burial, and the completely random, sometimes multilayered, grave patches from different periods did not give a clear picture of the area. Based on the map of grave patches and the available written information it was difficult to identify the persons buried here, because the relatives who requested the excavation (the living family members requested forensic exhumations and identifications in 30 cases) did not have enough biological information about their dead either.

Biological-anthropological examination of 109 remains was performed. Despite the partial excavations and difficulties in identification, due to missing personal information, identification in three cases was positive.

An outstanding success from these cases was the identification of Dr Bálint Hóman (1885–1951). He was a famous historical personality, politician, historian and numismatist. According to our team's research he died in the Vác prison and was buried in the Vác prison cemetery in 1951. We were able to identify his most likely burial place with the help of the personal information collected. Positive identification of the late Dr Bálint Hóman was proven using dental records, photographic superimposition (Figure 11.4) and comparative DNA tests with his son (Susa et al. 2001).

Excavation of mass graves

Kőszeg, Lovagló Ridge, identification of a mass grave of Jewish holocaust victims

Kőszeg is a small town located on the western border of Hungary near Austria. It played a key role in WWII as a station on the way to the concentration camps. The following case proves how the report of a private person (or civil organisation) can be important for the identification of a mass grave. In 2008 a verifying excavation was conducted in the forest of Kőszeg (Lovagló Ridge) at the boundary of the town. A civilian who remembered this event from his childhood uncovered human skeletal remains such as crania.

It was widely known that at the end of 1944 and the beginning of 1945 many people were forced to labour in the brickyard and brewery of Kőszeg. Many of them died

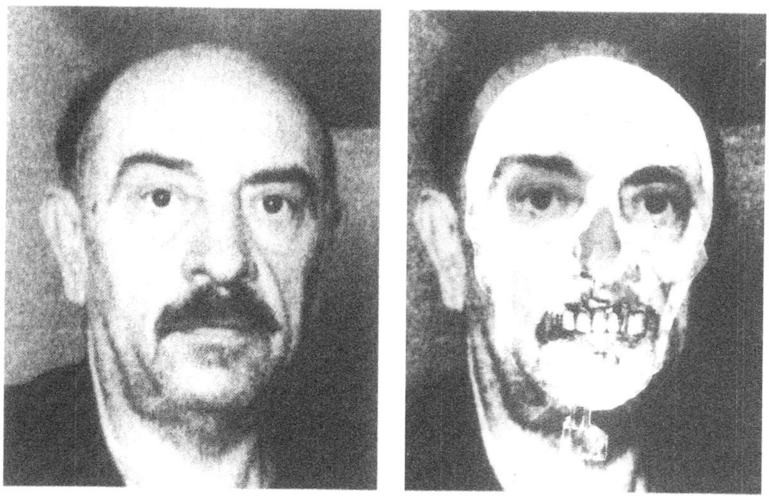

Figure 11.4 Photos of the late Bálint Hóman, exhumed in the Prison Cemetery of Vác, from his lifetime and photographic superimposition.

from cold weather, starvation, disease or infection. It was known that the dead persons were buried in a mass grave in Lovagló Ridge. The amateur researcher noticed five approximately parallel hollows lying east to west *c.* 13×22m in size. Skeletal remains and clothes were found buried in one of the hollows. The forensic anthropological examination assumed that the remains had risen near to the surface after more than 60 years after burial.

The research group of ISZKI started to collect all written and oral data that could be found, and it was verified that in the autumn of 1944 and spring of 1945 German and Arrow Cross soldiers forced people to labour, typically trench and rampart digging. Many women and men died from weakness, typhoid, enteritis, starvation, frostbite and also violence. According to earlier administrative documents there was a partial exhumation by official organisations in that area in 1947, and around 2500 corpses were transported to Budapest, where the remains were reburied in the Jewish Cemetery district.

At the request of the city of Kőszeg, and with financial assistance from the local government and the Ministry of Education and Culture, the research group conducted a partial humanitarian excavation in 2008.

It was assumed at the scene that the area could be the burial place of the citizens who were forced to labour and who died in 1944. After the area was cleared, a 13×22m wide section was excavated until the bones were uncovered, along with clothing remnants (Figure 11.5). The excavation proved that the corpses were deposited from one end of the grave. The bodies were not piled up as is usually seen in mass graves, but were lying close to each other. However, without any personal data, identification was impossible, and after documentation the section was reburied.

It was concluded that the site discovered by the civilians contains a mass grave of civilian victims. Outer clothing and large amounts of cut hair were found in the almost 2×2.20m wide and 11m long grave at a depth of 100–110cm. Under the *c.* 10cm thick layer of clothes the corpses were found at a depth of 130–140cm covered with a layer of thick yellow loam *c.* 20cm deep. The corpses were placed transverse and opposite to each other in the grave and the bodies were outstretched. They partly covered each other, but occasionally some corpses were placed longitudinally at the edge of the grave. The corpses were found lying at least one on top of another, so according to the size of the opened section with 40–50 dead, this means that there were at least 100 dead bodies in the ground.

Most of the dead (predominantly men) were buried in only a thin shirt and trousers. The fact that the dead and their outer clothing were buried in different layers indicated that disabled or infected persons were stripped when still alive and after death they were buried separately.

Clothing with historical value, such as woollen overcoats, shorts and trousers, ties, long Jaeger underpants and a knitted cuff were also examined. The textile remnants were of good quality. Other findings from the grave included a leather belt, leather boots, buttons, a pocket knife and an item which looked like a shawl (Figure 11.6).

Clear evidence indicating the time of burial was not found, but based on our knowledge, the 20th century clothes of the dead indicate that these people were forced to labour, and died sometime between 1944 and 1945.

The research group suggested that the area should be protected as a humanitarian place of memorial. In this case our work was successful, because the local

Figure 11.5 Kőszeg, Lovagló Ridge, excavation of a mass grave, archaeological exhumation of skeletal remains.

Figure 11.6 Kőszeg, Lovagló Ridge, excavation of a mass grave, the remains lying opposite each other, feet in shoes.

government of Kőszeg has established a memorial to the holocaust victims.

The examination of the skeletal remains from the mass grave of Soroksári Road, Budapest

A type of forensic examination is the investigation of a mass grave after civilians (e.g. cemetery labourers) have excavated and exhumed the area. In this case the forensic expert examines only the skeletal remains. This forthcoming work has previously been published in detail.

In September 1993 a mass grave was discovered in an excavated area, when an east–west canal was being dug in Budapest, 50–60 m north of the embankment of the South Railway Bridge, between the Danube Bank and Soroksári Road. This building site was originally planned to be a plaza. A machine damaged the southern wall of the grave, causing serious damage to the skeletal remains. There was a *c.* 5 cm thick limestone layer above and below the bodies. According to the construction workers the grave could be 5×5 m of limestone covered by soil. The exhumation was conducted by cemetery labourers and not by experts. According to their description the corpses were piled up randomly. The bone layer was 100–150 cm thick in the middle and 30–40 cm thick at the sides. The workers did not find any textile, leather, metal or other objects in the grave, so there was no evidence as to the time of burial or identification of the dead. The case received media attention; people wanted to know who the dead might be, and when and why they died.

The first possibility was that the dead were Jews executed during WWII; a second was that they were soldiers who died in the hospital. The second possibility was supported by the fact that they were buried without clothes. The location of the grave was difficult as it was situated at an earlier railway freight yard near the Danube Bank. This train station was established in 1879 and used until 1992, but by the autumn of 1993 it had totally disappeared. On earlier maps railroad warehouses were located around the mass grave, and after landscaping in 1993 a remnant of the north–south brick wall was uncovered 1.5 m from the edge of the grave. This was probably part of one of the warehouse walls. Based on some descriptions it seems likely that during WWII trains coming from hospitals were often stationed there, and the area near the Danube Bank was used to impound labourers.

We have presented the complex anthropological investigation of the salvaged skeletal remains in many publications. In this chapter we propose that the dead were buried in a 20th century mass grave, they were all men aged between 16 and 60, they were not part of a regular army, they were not urban residents who had been shot, they did not belong to the Hungarian ethnic group and they came from a less-developed region, since they appeared to suffer from malnutrition (Éry and Susa 1994; Susa 2007).

Recsk, searching for an expected mass grave

The next study is an example of another case type, as it had a negative result. From 1950 until 1953 there was a forced labour camp in Recsk operated by State Security Authorities (*ÁllamVédelmi Hatóság*). Some members of the alliance of ex-prisoners who were still alive requested an excavation of the grave. Recsk is a tiny settlement in north-east Hungary. It played a role in recent history as a location of the Hungarian Gulag.

The National Memorial Foundation for Recsk requested the excavation, together with family members whose relatives died due to intolerable conditions in

Recsk between 1950 and 1953. The result of the excavation was negative. It is estimated that 16 persons were buried in the area near the cemetery of Recsk. Based on the description of the cemetery by labourers and eye witnesses a mass grave was assumed. According to them a depression could be seen on the ground above the graves, which was now overgrown with bushes. The dead were buried in tool boxes made by the prisoners.

In 2000 the research group of ISZKI opened an archaeological section at the edge of the Recsk civil cemetery in the area indicated by those requesting the excavation. The ground was excavated until undisturbed subsoil was reached. In spite of earlier descriptions the group found no proof of burials in the indicated area. It was therefore declared that there were no graves in that site. Our team assumed that the inhabitants protected the upper western side of the cemetery with trenches, which allowed rainwater to drain down the overgrown hill. The water was then directed to Zsebe. These depressions were thought to be graves.

Later investigation by the research team proved that the burial of only one person could be connected to Recsk. The rest of the burials took place elsewhere (Susa and Molnos in press).

Conclusion

A better understanding of these historical events can be gained from more than historical research. On the one hand, it is beneficial to view a historical event with hindsight; on the other hand, information and documents may be lost as the event regresses. Moreover, people who might remember the facts may die without having told their story.

In the past 22 years the ISZKI group of forensic archaeologists and anthropologists have identified several persons who have died recently in uncertain circumstances and who are buried in unmarked graves; this has helped us to clarify facts about recent historical events in Hungary.

References

Éry, K. 1990. Personal Identification on the Deeds of Recent and Past Times in Hungary. Personal communication.

Éry, K. and Susa, É. 1994. The anthropological examination of the 20th century mass-grave Soroksar Round, Budapest. *Anthropologiai Közlemények* 36, 3–19.

Éry, K. and Susa, É. 1996. Skeletal ageing based on the cranial sutures in the identification process. In B. É. Bodzsár and C. Susanne (eds.), *Studies in Human Biology*, 95–102. Budapest, Eötvös University Press.

Éry, K. and Susa, É. 2001. XIX. és XX. századi férfi csontvázak Magyarországról. *Antropológiai Közlemények* 42, 53–58.

Éry, K., Susa, É. and Varga, T. 1994. Data on the estimation on the rib and personal identification. *Proceedings of the IV. International Meeting on Forensic Medicine, Alpen-Adria-Pannonia*, Italy, Grado, 12–14 May, 55–58.

Susa, É. 1995. Forensic anthropology in Hungary at the end of the 20th century. *Anthropologiai Közlemények* 37, 113–123.

Susa, É. 1998. Forensic anthropological data of recent history, SAXA LOQUUNTUR II. Workshop and Shrine – on a High Level – in Lágymányos 1912–1997 Memorials [*Műhely és Szentély - nem Középiskolás Fokon - Lágymányoson*], 199–204.

Susa, É. 2000. Identification of Hungarian historical persons. *Acta Biologica Szegediensis* 44, 175–178. Available at: http://www2.sci.u-szeged.hu/ABS/ (accessed 8 December 2014).

Susa, É. 2007. Forensic Anthropology in Hungary. In M. Brickley, and R. Ferllini (eds.), *Forensic Anthropology: Case Studies from Europe*, 203–215. Springfield, Charles C. Thomas.

Susa, É. and Éry, K. 1995. *Forensic Experts' Opinion About the Remains of Captain Steimetz*. OSZ: 6151/1995. Forensic expert report for the Court.

Susa, É., Éry, K., Kovács, L. and Szőke, M. 2001. A Váci Rabtemető kegyeleti-régészeti feltárásának szakértői problémái. *Fiatal Igazságügyi Orvosszakértők* VII, Fóruma. Kaposvár. CD edition.

Susa, É. and Molnos, M. 2002. Az 1945 – 1962 között büntetés-végrehajtási intézetben elhaltak és jeltelen sirokban eltemetettek temetési helyeinek kutatása. *Anthropologiai Közlemények* 43, 55–62.

Susa, É. and Molnos, M. 2004. Jeltelen eltemetések (1945–1962) kutatása. *Trezor 3. Az átmenet évkönyve, Állambiztonsági Szolgálatok Történeti Levéltára*, 245–253.

Susa, É. and Molnos, M. (in press). *Kegyelet és Végtisztesség. A Kommunista Diktatúra Áldozatainak Exhumálása és Azonositása.* Under publication.

CHAPTER 12

Forensic archaeology in Italy: the difficult birth of a discipline

Matteo Borrini
Research Centre in Evolutionary Anthropology and Palaeoecology, School of Natural Sciences and Psychology, Liverpool John Moores University, Liverpool, UK

The discipline and its perception in Italy

To better understand the perception of forensic archaeology in Italy, a starting point could be the general definition of the forensic archaeologist as 'an expert of the recovery of everything, corpse and crime evidence, that nature or human have concealed in the subsoil' (Borrini 2007, 20).[1] A more exhaustive Italian definition describes the discipline as

> the importing of archaeological methodologies on the *scena crimins*, especially when it is buried, as in the case of concealed human bodies. Of the techniques used, those of fundamental support are field walking (survey) for scene identification and the recovery of associated items (evidence); the analysis of stratigraphic seriation for context dating, for time since death estimation (*Post-Mortem Interval – PMI*), and/or for reconstruction of the corpse's deposition; the techniques for remains recovery and taphonomic reconstruction (Borrini 2008, 396). [Authors' translation]

To appreciate the reach of the contribution offered by the application of forensic archaeology in crime scene investigation, it is important to specify that nowadays in Italy archaeological excavation is perceived as an analysis based on the stratigraphic principles developed by Harris (1979) and Carandini (1996), with the distinction of different layers through physical and functional characteristics (*Unità Stratigrafiche* – stratigraphic units). This means that when it is claimed that forensic archaeology is the application of archaeological techniques at the crime scene, it is first of all the use of expertise in identifying different soil layers in terms of physical characteristics (shape, colour, composition, consistency) and manner of formation (e.g. a trench as the result of human digging action or natural erosion).

Archaeology is also perceived, however, as the *science of documentation* (Borrini and Lusa 2012, 38), and so applying archaeological techniques means applying specific methods to map sites, layers, sections and remains, as well as data collection during the excavation and the post-excavation reconstruction of the events that gave rise to seriation.

In addition to all these aspects, which represent the archaeologist's role in the excavation of the site/crime scene, it is useful to remember that archaeological techniques include systematic field walking and survey strategies for the search of buried/concealed remains (also with the help of geophysical instruments such as ground-penetrating radar – GPR), as well as depositional taphonomy and the analysis of the areal dispersion of the remains to reconstruct their original position (Borrini et al. 2011).

An example of the contribution of forensic archaeology in Italy, where the author has been involved as a consultant, is a case concerning the assessment of a possible combat fatality.

According to the statements, the remains appeared to have been unearthed in an area of the Gothic Line[2] during amateur research with metal detectors. The only evidence that seemed to date the remains to World War II (WWII) was a single metallic identity tag. Before allowing the removal of the remains and their inhumation in a military cemetery, the prosecutor wanted to ascertain the effective correlation of the identity tag with the corpse, excluding the possibility that it had been bought in the antiquities market and used to mask the recent concealment of a murder victim (staging).

[1]Translated from Italian by the author.

[2]The Gothic Line or Green Line (*Grüne Linie*) was the last defence line used in Italy by the German Nazi army during the final stage of WWII, between the summer of 1944 and the spring of 1945; it ideally ran between mountains from the west coast (Massa Carrara) to the east coast (Pesaro).

Forensic Archaeology: A Global Perspective, First Edition. Edited by W.J. Mike Groen, Nicholas Márquez-Grant and Robert C. Janaway.

As the remains and the dog tag had already been partially manipulated and moved, only the complete stratigraphic excavation of the neighbouring area made it possible to identify other related bones, which resulted in primary deposition along with other artefacts clearly attributable to WWII. Also, the stratigraphic approach documented how the soldier, killed by a grenade, was lying inside an individual trench (fox hole), clarifying the doubts of the judicial authority and facilitating the reconstruction of historical events.

Despite what is illustrated, it is quite difficult to delineate the typical scenarios in which forensic archaeologists are involved in Italy. A forensic archaeologist is defined here as an expert in field-walking strategies to search for concealed materials and somebody who is experienced in stratigraphic excavation of buried evidence, collection and documentation.

Forensic archaeology is still quite uncommon in Italy, due on the one hand to the complexity of the legal system and the forensic pathologists' control of death investigations, and on the other hand to the lack of knowledge of the discipline and its undoubted potential (Márquez-Grant et al. 2012, 602). Consequently scientific publications of case reports are also quite rare.

To facilitate the understanding and the conscious use of these disciplines a distinction between forensic archaeology and forensic anthropology has been proposed (Borrini 2008, 395–396): while the search and recovery of concealed remains is the prerogative of forensic archaeology, the identification of unnamed bodies is the responsibility of forensic anthropology. Although both are therefore considered separate disciplines, with the common goal of bringing a name and justice to unidentified victims, excavation techniques have been applied mostly by physical/forensic anthropologists (Cattaneo et al. 2006) or – even more often – by medical examiners during crime scene assessment activities.

Accuracy in (buried) evidence collection and documentation ensured by stratigraphic methodologies (systematic excavation with recognition of different soil layers, their interpretation as a result of human/natural action and their graphic rendering) has been successfully adopted. There are examples of murder investigations related to charred bodies in vehicles (Porta et al. 2013), during the recovery of pieces of evidence related to WWII carnage (Borrini 2008, 398–399) and during the investigation of skeletonised remains scattered at an outdoor scene (Borrini 2011a, 118). More uncommon is the application of archaeological techniques during the search for and/or recovery of clandestine graves connected to homicides (Cattaneo 2009, 42–48; Cattaneo et al. 2009).

Crime scene framework: the Italian law's perspective

In Italy it is possible to identify two different *domini* of investigations into suspected deaths: the prosecutor (*Pubblico Ministero* – PM) for the legal aspects (ex art. 113 and 244 c.p.p.[3]) and the medical examiner (*Medico Legale*) appointed by the PM for the scientific side.

The judicial authority, represented by the PM, is usually involved when the Judicial Police (*Polizia Giudiziaria* – PG) informs him by a formal act, *notitia criminis*, as indicated ex art. 108 bis and 347 c.p.p.

It is not uncommon that the forensic pathologist who will perform the autopsy is not the same medical examiner on duty who ascertained the death at the crime scene; but in complex cases (e.g. a clandestine grave) or after an extended intelligence activity usually the PM immediately designates a pathologist for the *scena criminis* inspection, recovery of the body and post-mortem examination.

From this brief view it seems clear that the crime scene investigation in Italy is mainly the prerogative of the First Officer Attending (first responder police officer), of the PG forensic team and of the medical examiner appointed by the prosecutor. Unfortunately the cooperation between the different agencies involved in the investigation and with other scientific consultants is often difficult, due to the scarce synergy related to different points of professional view and lack of comprehension of overall prerogative (Magni et al. 2008, 160).

In Italian law, the judicial inspection of the crime scene is done to 'preserve the state of the places, the search and recovery of elements and pieces of evidence related to the crime and of all useful elements for the identification of perpetrators and victim, and for the complete reconstruction of the dynamic of the crime' (Carrella Prada and Tancredi 2006).[4]

It is relevant to emphasise that the Penal Procedure Code (*Codice di Procedura Penale*, art. 348 and 354 c.p.p.) gives the police the authority to proceed with the inspection even without the presence of the prosecutor 'if there is a danger that things, pieces of evidence and places could change'; this precarious situation is certainly represented by the occasional discovery of a corpse hidden in a clandestine grave (i.e. brought to light by building operations) or of a body/skeletonised remains at an outdoor scene. As a matter of fact the Italian Code (art. 359 c.p.p.) provides for recourse to further, more specifically technical analysis, which can then be delegated to specialists during the preliminary investigation; this means that the possible appeal to practitioners such as forensic

[3]*c.p.p.* is the abbreviation of the *Codice di Procedura Penale* – Penal Procedure Code of the Italian Republic.
[4]Translated from Italian by the author.

archaeologists (as well as forensic anthropologists) is deferred until after the first inspection.

What has been described shows a fundamental aspect of on-the-spot investigation: as a *means of gathering evidence* it is free from any technical judgment. From the Italian regulatory point of view, in fact, an inspection must secure all possible sources of evidence protecting the *status quo* of the scene. From this perspective, archaeological excavation cannot be performed during the crime scene inspection, because it is not a simple soil removal, but a scientific excavation using an approach that involves the distinction between different layers based on their physical characteristics (shape, colour consistency, composition) and stratigraphic tangible connections (e.g. which layer covers the others), and consequently the removal of the strata from the most recent to the oldest (Borrini 2007). Fortunately, Italian practice and legislation include photography, fingerprinting and collection of evidence and biological traces within inspection activities, permitting – at least theoretically – access to the scene by the forensic archaeologist even during initial activities.

Another possible obstacle to the intervention of the forensic archaeologist at the crime scene may be represented by art. 116 att. c.p.p., which is interpreted as a rule that attributes the right to give clearance for the removal of the body from the scene only to a magistrate. The activity of the forensic archaeologist, indeed, is essentially the recovery of the body from the clandestine grave or the scattered remains from an outdoor scene. Properly interpreted, the second paragraph of that article, however, would allow the archaeologist to be present as the PM's consultant during the disinterment of a corpse, if evidence of a serious crime has been detected. This condition is clearly identifiable whenever the crime scene is characterised by a clandestine grave.

Luckily it is possible to find some legal mechanisms that allow the archaeologist to attend the crime scene (Borrini and Lusa 2012, 96): Articles 348 (IV paragraph), 327-*bis* and 391-*sexies*, which regulate the evidence, the defence investigation and the access to the crime scene, and also Articles 359, 225 and 117, which are related to the appointment of the consultant.

Possible gaps in the Italian situation

Unfortunately, the wide range of potential offered by forensic archaeology in Italy (Borrini and Lusa 2012, 35), as also indicated by the international scenario, has not yet been applied to the fields of search for buried corpses and/or evidence, and recovery after a mass fatality (DVI work).

For example, perhaps due to the strict rules as well as to the personnel authorised for the intervention (military, civil protection or pathologists), no archaeologist – and no anthropologist – was involved in the investigation of the Viareggio train disaster of 30 June 2009, when the explosion of an LPG transporter destroyed several buildings, killing and burying the victims (Borrini 2011a, 123).

This is a case which offered clear parallels with other international experiences (Dirkmaat 2009; Dirkmaat et al. 2010, 387; Milligan et al. 2012, 395–396), where the methodologies for documented removal of debris had also been adopted for the proper recovery/identification of the victims. Unfortunately, nothing similar to the Weldon Spring Protocol (Dirkmaat et al. 1995, 2001) has actually been adopted in Italy.

It is, however, important to mention that examples of guidelines for the applications of basic archaeological methods to the *scena criminis*, such as recovery and mapping of remains (buried or from an outdoor scene), photographic documentation and personal protective equipment (PPE) use, have recently been proposed (Borrini 2011b, 237–268) and developed (Borrini and Lusa 2012, 109–115) for use in Italy.

The position of forensic archaeology in Italy

Usually the opportunity for Italian investigators to make use of forensic archaeology is provided either by the open-mindedness of the prosecutor in charge or by the presence in the university of a research collaboration between archaeologists and forensic scientists. The university, in addition to the list of expert witnesses from which the prosecutor or the judge can appoint their consultant (ex art. 225, 233, 255 c.p.p.), is in fact the only suitable place where forensic archaeologists can be found.

The placement of a professional archaeologist *strictu senso* – not necessarily a forensic one – is difficult in Italy, where the profession may be exercised either in a freelance capacity or as a state official (Galasso 2009, 35–53). In the first case the archaeologist works individually or in cooperatives and companies, while in the second case they work for the Ministry for Cultural Heritage (*Uffici di Soprintendenza*) as a functionary or inspector.

Due to the type of assignment carried out by government officials, it is rather difficult to identify the forensic archaeologist, while it is easier for a freelance consultant to undertake the appropriate training to enable them to assist the judicial authority.

It does not seem necessary to use the list of archaeologists (ex Legislative Decree 12 April 2006, Art. 95, paragraph 2) – individual or grouped in institutions, companies and cooperatives – who are qualified for verification activities in the field of preventive archaeology (law 109/205). In fact, there are specific qualifications for the assessment of the historical value of an archaeological site that is subject to construction activity; it would seem more appropriate instead to use the registers of expert witnesses present in the State Prosecutor Offices and Civil Courts, which include personnel with proven experience in the investigative field. The register is held by the President of the Court, who also directs a committee composed of the Public Prosecutor (*Procuratore della Repubblica*), the President of the Forensic Board (*Presidente del Consiglio dell'Ordine Forense*) and the President of the Board or experts from the applicant's discipline. The committee makes decisions on admission criteria, examines the admission requests and ensures the revision of the register every 2 years, removing the experts who no longer meet all the legal requirements (art. 69 norme att. c.p.p.).

In addition, universities with specific research projects and/or academic courses in forensic archaeology can provide expert staff for investigations, which may be more appropriate than those from the *Uffici di Soprintendenza*.

Lately a limited increase in the involvement of forensic anthropologists at the crime scene would appear to promote the use of stratigraphic techniques for the *in situ* recovery and documentation of remains, with an appropriate recognition of the layers and the enhancement of their value as useful indicators of human/natural actions for the reconstruction of the crime dynamics. The close connection between archaeology and physical anthropology in the Italian context should not be surprising considering the possibility of interdisciplinary education and training for those who want to pursue a career in these disciplines, both in the recovery and analysis of skeletal remains. It is important to note that archaeological academic programmes in Italian universities can include osteological/anthropological theory and practical laboratory sessions, while lectures and modules on stratigraphic excavation and documentation methodologies are almost absent in the courses for students of scientific/biological disciplines. Thus it is possible, within an archaeological academic programme, to be trained in survey, excavation and documentation techniques as well as in osteological analysis for the anthropological study of skeletonised remains. This kind of practitioner is sometimes called a bioarchaeologist, a figure that requires additional forensic training before entering into the investigative field.

Possible future developments

General considerations

If we look at recent surveys (Márquez-Grant et al. 2012, 602), the situation in Italy is far from settled. 'At present, there is only one criminal expert witness in forensic archaeology registered at the State Prosecutor Office and Civil Court in Italy. He has applied archaeological methods to the recovery of bodies from actual crime scenes as well as to the recovery of remains of World War II soldiers buried in mass graves', but '[a] publication by Borrini (2007), the only one of its kind in Italy, is solely on forensic archaeology and should help to promote the discipline'.

One of the major obstacles to the proper start of forensic archaeology in Italy is represented by the word *archaeology* (Borrini and Lusa 2012, 15–18).

First of all, the term introduced by the 17th century French antiquarian Jacques Spon (Manacorda 2002), which refers to the study (λόγος – *logos*) of old remains (ἀρχαῖος – *archaios*), suggests that this specialist deals exclusively with ancient enigmas – or ideally, cold cases from the forensic point of view.

In the second place, archaeology in Italy has always been taught in Faculties of Arts and Letters, which have facilitated its assimilation with History of Art or Philosophy: not statistic-based or scientific disciplines that are not be useful in crime scene investigation. Fortunately the discipline is more recently being taught in more appropriately named departments, such as Sciences of Cultural Heritage or Archaeological Sciences. Nevertheless, it is still very difficult to make it clear to prosecutors and investigators that archaeology

> is a science as well as the archaeologist is a scientist. Through the identification, recovery and subsequent analysis of material traces left 'on' and 'in' the land (overground and underground) from past populations, the archaeologist is able to reconstruct real events (battles, town foundations, simple concrete gestures such as the lighting of a fire), but also to infer social, cultural and populationist dynamics. Archaeology becomes a science when systematic protocols for collection and documentation of elements are applied from which, with a deductive logic based on physical, biological and behavioural laws, it infers the existence of human and natural actions occurring in a context precisely placeable in space and time (Borrini and Lusa 2012, 16). [Authors' translation]

If the validity and reliability of archaeology as a science is applied by archaeologists to their ordinary work and publications, freedom from ambiguity – and so the success of forensic archaeology – is dependent on the validity of paperwork regarding the application of forensic techniques to ancient remains.

It is certainly useful to apply new investigative methods to better reconstruct past events with more accurate data (Borrini 2012, 484; Borrini and Mariani in press). It is convenient to test new archaeological methods before they are applied to the crime scene, but it is important to underline that this is *archaeology with forensic techniques* and it is not forensic archaeology (Borrini and Lusa 2012, 22). This misuse of terminology, which is not beneficial for the discipline, is not rare in Italy, and is sometimes even used to make courses and conferences more attractive to new generations of students. If this misunderstanding can be avoided and

Table 12.1 Schematic representation of the contribution of forensic archaeology in the Italian legal scenario, with bibliographic examples of case reports, when they are present.

Investigative scenario	Legal references	Forensic archaeology contribution	References
Investigations of *crimes that offend religious sentiment*	Concealment of a corpse (art. 412 c.p.p.) often associated with murder; aggravating circumstance for art. 61, 434, 449, 450, 451 c.p.p.	Survey Stratigraphic excavation Evidence collection Mapping and documentation	Porta et al. (2013)
	Removal of corpse (art. 411 c.p.p.)	Survey Stratigraphic excavation Evidence collection Mapping and documentation	Cattaneo (2009) Cattaneo et al. (2009)
Investigations related to *concealment of elements from other crimes*	(art. 374, 379 c.p.p.) Aggravating circumstances for art. 61, 434, 449, 450, 451 c.p.p.	Survey Stratigraphic excavation Evidence collection Mapping and documentation	Proposed by Borrini and Lusa (2012) Still not applied
Investigation of *crimes against public safety*	Arson (art. 423 c.p.p.)	Debris removal with stratigraphic criteria Evidence collection Reconstruction of the status quo ante fire destruction Mapping of samples collected by other experts	Proposed by Borrini and Lusa (2012) Still not applied
	Collapse (art. 434 c.p.p.)	Debris removal with stratigraphic criteria Evidence collection Reconstruction of the status quo ante collapse Mapping of samples collected by other experts	Proposed by Borrini and Lusa (2012) Still not applied
	Intentional disaster (art. 449, 450, 451 c.p.p.)	Debris removal with stratigraphic criteria Evidence collection Reconstruction of the status quo ante the event Mapping of samples collected by other expert	Proposed by Borrini and Lusa (2012) Still not applied
	Massacre (art. 285, 422 c.p.p.) also possibly related to WWI	Survey Stratigraphic excavation Evidence collection Mapping and documentation Reconstruction of the status quo ante the event	Borrini (2008)
Honour the fallen in war	law n. 204, 9 January 1951 law n. 87, 12 June 1931	Survey Stratigraphic excavation Evidence collection Mapping and documentation Reconstruction of battle events	Borrini (2011a) Turchetto et al. (2008)

solved, it will be possible to create more distinct postgraduate courses for both those who will dedicate their profession to historical research and for those who will work at the crime scene.

It is relevant that there are no degrees totally focused on forensic archaeology and only a few postgraduate courses or classes are offered in universities, such as in Florence, Milan or Rome (Papal Theological University 'San Bonaventura').

Future goals

Forensic archaeology in Italy could be further developed by the application of recovery techniques not only in classic murder investigations (in which the corpse is seldom concealed) but also in the investigation of Mafia murders, where clandestine graves are more frequent.

It is also important not to forget how many soldiers lost their life in Italy during WWII: around 90,000 Allied soldiers (Blaxland 1979) and 215,000 German/Italian troops (Jackson 2009). Although most of them were recovered in the immediacy of the conflict, under the soil of the peninsula there are still huge numbers of unknown missing soldiers that need to be recovered and identified. For this reason, and through cooperation with organisations such as the Commonwealth War Grave Commission, it is important to focus attention on the recovery and identification of soldiers' remains which are occasionally discovered or brought to light by treasure hunters looking for military relics.

If WWI recoveries are more historical (Piccinini et al. 2010, 329–333), the recovery and identification of WWII casualties could still have forensic interest for the Military Tribunal (i.e. war crime investigation); it also certainly has a strong emotional impact on the family members of victims/soldiers who are still alive.

Search for missing people

Regarding the dramatic situation of missing people, it is important to emphasise that the last survey of the Ministry of the Interior (Extraordinary Commissioner of the Government for Missing Persons 2012) states that more than 27,000 people are missing in Italy, 62% of these are missing for unknown reason (but not for voluntary leaving), and therefore are potentially dead (killed by accident). If it is assumed that the majority of these corpses were concealed by the perpetrator or by natural events (i.e. death at an outdoor scene, especially for the elderly or those suffering from Alzheimers), it appears quite clear that archaeological survey techniques could be useful for the identification of the clandestine grave/deposition site.

Recent cases that are still open in Italy (often involving the disappearance of girls or young women) have stressed the importance of field walking, GPR and cadaver dog surveys, and have also revealed that the police, civil protection and volunteer teams lack the necessary expertise to conduct a systematic survey of large areas. To meet these needs, the non-profit association National and European Multidisciplinary Equipe for Special Investigation (NEMESI)[5] has been established, with the aim of creating a multidisciplinary team for the application of archaeological/anthropological techniques for a comprehensive survey of the area in conjunction with inspection by cadaver dogs. Thanks to the contribution of academic and professional staff qualified in dog training, forensic investigation, archaeology and anthropology this association is devoted to the training of canine units, both to assist in cases of missing live persons (mantrailing dog) and in corpse searches (cadaver dog). NEMESI's innovative approach not only utilises dog/handler units, but also trains canine units and on-foot volunteers in basic field-walking techniques and the correct approach to the *scena criminis* (i.e. preserving potential evidence, use of PPE), and prepares operative units to support the judicial authority in the search for the missing (living and dead).

Forensic archaeology can indeed provide the necessary background to understand the geology of the territory, prioritising the search in the most likely areas to support the investigators' intelligence activity. It can propose a traditional field-walking survey and assist with geophysical tools when necessary; it can provide a scientific and immediate check of each anomaly found by stratigraphic excavation, thus ensuring timely intervention of the most appropriate practitioners for the recovery of buried evidence at the scene.

The development of these aspects of forensic archaeology in response to families searching for a missing relative, as well diffusing the discipline to a wider use and exploiting its potential, is currently the aim of the Italian Academy of Forensic Sciences (*Accademia Italiana di Scienze Forensi*).[6] The Academy aims to bridge the cultural, professional and operational gap in the development of forensic disciplines in Italy, assisting investigative agencies (*Polizia di Stato* and *Arma dei Carabinieri*) and university institutes, so far the only ones involved in the field. The mission of this non-profit institution is therefore to organise (mainly through professional training courses, conferences and publications) a scientific-technical and operational support for all the subjects involved in the investigation: judicial authority, investigative agencies, lawyers, expert witnesses.

Acknowledgement

The author is especially grateful to the lawyer Vincenzo Lusa for the legal contribution offered in the promotion and development of forensic archaeology in Italy.

References

Blaxland, G. 1979. *Alexander's Generals: The Italian Campaign 1944–1945*. London, William Kimber.

Borrini, M. 2007. *Archeologia Forense*. Bologna, Lo Scarabeo.

Borrini, M. 2008. Archeologia forense e antropologia identificativa: due discipline, un fine comune. Casi studio. *Atti del XVII Congresso dell'Associazione Antropologica Italiana*, 395–402.

[5]For more information see: www.nemesi.co (last accessed 4 December 2014).

[6]For more information see: www.acisf.org (last accessed 20 March 2014).

Borrini, M. 2011a. Forensic anthropology: a typical Italian case report to understand possible future developments. *Archivio per l'Antropologia e la Etnologia* CXLI, 117–126.

Borrini, M. 2011b. Antropologia Forense: Protocollo e Linee Guida per il Recupero e lo Studio Dei Resti Umani. Unpublished PhD thesis, University of Rome 'Tor Vergata'.

Borrini, M. 2012. More than a cold case: the frozen murder of Iceman – a heinous or a merciful crime scene? *Proceedings of the American Academy of Forensic Sciences – 64rd Annual Scientific Meeting* 18, 484.

Borrini, M. and Lusa, V. 2012. *La prova Occulta. L'Indagine Forense sub Suolo alla Luce Della Procedura Penale Italiana.* Milano, Lo Scarabeo.

Borrini, M. and Mariani, P. P. (in press). La sepoltura di Teodosia, l'archeologia e l'antropologia forense come strumenti d'identificazione nel caso di una sepoltura a camera del sito di Sheik-Abada (Antinuopolis). In R. Pintaudi (ed.), *Antinoupolis*. Ist. Florence, Papirologico G. Vitelli.

Borrini, M., Mariani, P. P., Murgia, C., Rodriguez, C. and Tumbarello, M. V. 2011. Contextual taphonomy: superficial bone alterations as contextual indicators. *Journal of Biological Research* 84, 217–219.

Carandini, A. 1996. *Storie Dalla Terra*. Torino, Einaudi.

Carrella Prada, O. and Tancredi, D. M. 2006. *Il Sopralluogo Giudiziario Medico-Legale. Norme, Metodologia ed Elementi Medico-Forensi per l'Attività Investigativa*. Roma, Società Editrice Universo.

Catteneo, C. 2009. Forensic anthropology and archaeology: perspectives from Italy. In S. Blau and D. H. Ubelaker (eds.), *Handbook of Forensic Anthropology and Archaeology*, 42–48. Walnut Creek, Left Coast Press.

Cattaneo, C., Mazzucchi, A., Poppa, P. and Salsarola D. 2006. Il ruolo dell'antropologo forense dal recupero alla diagnosi di causa di morte: un case report. Il Processo di Umanizzazione. *Atti del XVI Congresso degli Antropologi Italiani (Genova, October 29–31 2005)*. Milano, Edicolors Publishing.

Cattaneo, C., Salsarola, D., Porta, D., Poppa, P., Gibelli, D. and Grandi, M. 2009. Evolution of forensic archaeology in Italy: a 10 year experience. *Oral communication 21st Congress of the International Academy of Legal Medicine*, Lisboa.

Dirkmaat, D. C. 2009. Forensic archaeological documentation and recovery of the victims of the Continental Connection Flight 3407 crash in Clarence, NY. *The 43rd Annual Meeting of the National Association of Medical Examiner, San Francisco, CA.*

Dirkmaat, D. C., Quinn, A. and Adovasio, J. M. 1995. New methodologies for search and recovery. *Disaster Management News*, 1–2 December 1995.

Dirkmaat, D. C., Hefner, J. and Hochrein, M. 2001. Forensic processing of the terrestrial mass fatality scene: testing new search documentation and recovery methodologies. *Proceedings 53rd Annual Meeting of American Academy of Forensic Sciences* 7, 241–242.

Dirkmaat, D. C., Symes, S. A. and Cabo, L. L. 2010. Forensic archaeological recovery of the victims of the Continental Connection Flight 3407 in Clarence Centre, NY. *Proceedings 62nd Annual Meeting of American Academy of Forensic Sciences* 16, 387.

Extraordinary Commissioner of the Government for Missing Persons. 2012. Il *Commissario Straordinario del Governo per le Persone Scomparse Nona Relazione Semestrale Giugno 2012*. Ministero dell'Interno Roma. Available at: http://www.interno.gov.it/ (last accessed 20 March 2014).

Galasso, G. 2009. *L'Archeologo dalla Formazione alla Professione*. 3rd edition. Albanella, Edizioni Agenzia magna Grecia.

Harris, E. C. 1979. *Principles of Archaeological Stratigraphy*. London, Academic Press.

Jackson, W. 2009. *The Mediterranean and Middle East*. Uckfield, Naval & Military Press.

Magni, P., Massimelli, M., Messina, R., Mazzucco, P. and Di Luise, E. 2008. *Entomologia Forense. Gli Insetti Nelle Indagini Giudiziarie e Medico-Legali*. Torino, Edizioni Minerva Medica.

Manacorda, D. 2002. *Lo Scavo Archeologico. Cenni Atorici e Principi Metodologici*. AA.VV. Il mondo dell'archeologia. Roma, Ist. Treccani.

Márquez-Grant, N., Litherland, S. and Roberts, J. 2012. European perspectives and the role of the forensic archaeologist in the UK. In D. C. Dirkmaat (ed.), *A Companion to Forensic Anthropology*, 598–625. Chichester, Wiley-Blackwell.

Milligan, C. F., Bartelink, E. J. and Murad, T. A. 2012. San Bruno gas pipeline explosion: responding to a neighbourhood-wide disaster. *Proceedings 64th Annual Meeting of American Academy of Forensic Sciences* 18, 395–396.

Piccinini, A., Coco, S., Parson, W. et al. 2010. World War One Italian and Austrian soldier identification project: DNA results of the first case. *Forensic Science International: Genetics* 4, 329–333.

Porta, D., Poppa, P., Regazzola, V. et al. 2013. The importance of an anthropological scene of crime investigation in the case of burnt remains in vehicles: 3 case studies. *American Journal Forensic Medical Pathology* 34(3), 195–200.

Turchetto, M., Lafisca, A., Borrini, M. and Vanin, S. 2008. A study of the entomofauna on some WWII skeletons from a 'Foiba' in NW-Italy. *Atti del Convegno EAFE European Association of Forensic Entomology 2008.*

CHAPTER 13

Forensic archaeology in Lithuania

Rimantas Jankauskas

Department of Anatomy, Histology and Anthropology, Faculty of Medicine, Vilnius University, Vilnius, Lithuania

Introduction: historical background

Various wars and social disasters have left numerous mass or unidentified graves in Lithuania, which nowadays have become an object of bioarchaeology that requires close collaboration between natural sciences and humanities. In some cases elements of forensic archaeology, defined as the application of knowledge and skills of archaeology in legal processes, were applied. The beginning of forensic archaeology in Lithuania has a tradition starting from the early 1960s (Garmus et al. 1999), with experience gained from earlier excavations of the mass graves of the Holocaust (Markulis 1966; Nainys 1972), exhumation and identification of historical persons (Doveika and Korsakas 1981; Nainys 1972) and numerous forensic-osteological/anthropological (determination of age, sex, stature and individual traits on 'fresh' materials with the ultimate purpose of identification of an individual) and bioarchaeological (all the range of analyses of skeletal materials from archaeological contexts) works. A set of original population-specific forensic anthropological methods have been developed and validated (Garmus 1974, 1992; Nainys 1972; Nainys and Anusevičienė 1984) among those most widely used. However, complete archaeological and legal procedures were applied during the last couple of decades in the cases of victims of Nazi occupation and of the Communist regime only. 'Forensic archaeology' is a new concept in Lithuania, understood primarily as a practical application of combined knowledge of archaeology, forensic and physical anthropology and bioarchaeology.

Medico-legal framework

Being at the crossroads of medicine (practice and research) and legal arenas, the formal position of forensic medicine in Lithuania is changing. For a long time it was considered to be primarily a branch of medicine, thus medico-legal structures (under different names) until the 1990s were under the auspices of the Ministry of Health. For several years forensic services were affiliated to one of the universities (thus becoming subject to the Ministry of Science and Education), and during the last years all structure was given to the Ministry of Justice. Such subordination is considered to guarantee a more independent status of the service. Now, the State Forensic Medicine Service (*Valstybinė Teismo Medicinos Tarnyba* – VTMT), under the Ministry of Justice of the Republic of Lithuania (*Lietuvos Respublikos Teisingumo Ministerija*), has central administration and specialised laboratories (serology and DNA, toxicology, histology, medical criminalistics) localised in Vilnius, and regional divisions that are located in five major cities and nine Lithuanian county towns. Regional divisions perform routine examinations (autopsies, investigations of living persons) and submit materials to specialised laboratories in case more specialised investigations are required.

Crime rates in Lithuania reflect profound changes in the political and economic situation, the mode of life and the moral climate during the last couple of decades. The total number of criminal offences reached its peak in the mid 1990s. The number of murders in 1993 was 480, 523 in 1994 and 502 in 1995; since then there has been a steady decrease (212 in 2012). However, the homicide rate per 100,000 inhabitants (8.0–7.5) remains one of the highest in the European Union (Crime Statistics 2013; Tavares et al. 2012). This decrease resulted from the improvement of the economic situation and the control of organised crime: nowadays, the majority of homicides occur due to alcohol abuse and daily-life conflicts, victims of which are seldom hidden in clandestine graves. Thus the need for true forensic exhumations (regrettably, no analysis of such cases was performed) is diminishing. The role of medico-legal experts is usually limited to conventional autopsies and providing their conclusions to legal institutions; collection of all circumstantial evidence is entirely the responsibility of the police. There are no institutionalised forensic archaeologists in Lithuania. Few cases of 'pure forensic' exhumation cases are performed by police and supervised by forensic pathologists, without the application of archaeological techniques.

Forensic Archaeology: A Global Perspective, First Edition. Edited by W.J. Mike Groen, Nicholas Márquez-Grant and Robert C. Janaway.

It is only recently that the sites of mass graves from the 19th century and World War I and II (WWI and WWII) graves are being given the status of archaeological objects, that is becoming formally protected by the Department of Cultural Heritage (legislation is still in preparation). This way the 'grey area' between traditional archaeology and 'pure' forensics is being covered. Such sites are especially suffering from illegal excavations now; regrettably the police are informed *post factum* and remains that have already been disturbed are transported to VTMT for examination. Cooperation with heritage institutions and archaeologists is almost entirely absent.

One of the few points of collaboration between archaeologists and legal institutions is the looting of archaeological sites and the illegal trade (local and especially international smuggling) of artefacts. Archaeologists are invited as experts to evaluate the damage and estimate the value of the artefacts.

Cases of application of forensic archaeology

Only during recent years has the potential of archaeologically gained evidence from the past (location, excavation and recovery of human remains and associated artefacts, reconstruction of events related to burial), especially in combination with bioarchaeology, palaeopathology and forensic archaeology, begun to be acknowledged, as archaeologists – some of them with basic training in osteology – are involved in some exhumation cases. Archaeology students are only given a short review of the potential application of archaeology in legal issues, as well as discussions of specific cases. No elements of archaeology are included in police training programmes. This chapter is a summary of the results of 'good practice' of such collaboration. Cases are discussed in chronological order (i.e. dates of analysis), thus demonstrating the evolution of the field. At the same time, specific problems of these interdisciplinary works are outlined.

Exhumations of the victims of Nazi occupation

The occupation of Lithuania by Nazi Germany (1941–1944) caused great loss of population; the special 'target' of the Nazis and their local collaborators was the Jewish population of several hundred thousand people. Consequently, the formerly flourishing local Jewish community became virtually extinct, almost 95% being annihilated. This is probably the highest percentage of Holocaust victims in Europe (Bubnys 2005).

Exhumations after WWII

Series of exhumations by legal authorities were performed during 1951–1963. These investigations were performed in selected sites only, data were submitted to legal institutions and no detailed scientific analysis was made (Figure 13.1). Only group identification (number of individuals, sex and age) in the field was made, paying specific attention to signs of violence and other material evidence (Markulis 1966; Nainys 1972). The aim of these investigations was limited to the legal requirements of that time – to provide evidence for courts performing formal prosecution of military criminals. No questions about the identity of the victims were raised (eventually, even the ethnicity of

Figure 13.1 General view of human remains exhumed in 1962 in Katkiškės village, Lazdijai district, Lithuania.

the victims was hidden under the euphemism of 'Soviet citizens'). After this series of trials, this tragic period was almost forgotten. It is only during the last decade that memories have been revived, locations of execution being marked and protected by the state. Delayed justice is now being sought for these innocent victims (Jankauskas 2009).

Excavation in 2008

In 2008, the State Genocide and Resistance Research Centre of Lithuania (*Lietuvos Gyventojų Genocido ir Rezistencijos Tyrimo Centras* – LGGRTC) obtained information about a possible site of mass graves on the western outskirts of Vilnius. The site was in a forest, on the slope of a steep hill. At the request of the State prosecutor and the LGGRTC, a trial 2 × 2 m trench was excavated by archaeologists from the Department of Archaeology, Vilnius University. Skeletal remains were sent for forensic anthropological analysis. It was established that the trench contained the commingled remains of at least 32 individuals with numerous traces of peri-mortem gunshot wounds (17 on skulls and 10 on other bones, with entrance diameters of *c.* 9.2–9.7 mm) entering the bodies from various directions. Associated artefacts (personal belongings and coins) clearly indicated the time of death as the summer of 1941. Parallel questioning of evidence and documentary sources supported these findings – in July 1941, about 200 hostages (inhabitants of Vilnius, mostly Jews, but also some university students) were transported by Nazis to this site and executed with machine guns at previously dug trenches. In the mid 1960s, the site was disturbed by marauders, which evidently caused the disarrangement and commingling of remains. At the request of the local Jewish community, no further excavations were conducted, and the remains were officially reburied at the same site; a small memorial sign was erected. This case stressed the importance of the coordination of archaeology and forensic anthropology, although neither complete excavation nor even an attempt for individual identification was performed, in case of ethically sensitive events and reducing political tensions.

Identification of historical personalities

Identification of the remains of Kristijonas Donelaitis

Kristijonas Donelaitis (1714–1780), a Lutheran priest, lived and worked in the territory of east Prussia, and wrote the first classic Lithuanian language poem that has become one of the principal works of Lithuanian poetry. He was buried in the parish church of Tolminkiemis (*Tollmingkehmen*). After WWII this territory was annexed by the Soviet Union and today is known as Kaliningrad district. The church was abandoned, and the grave of K. Donelaitis was forgotten. In 1967, an archaeological expedition from the Institute of the History of Lithuania uncovered 25 graves beneath the ruins of the church; the two most recent became the subject of further forensic analysis. This revealed that both remains belonged to elderly males, individual No.1 (the older one) being subsequently identified as K. Donelaitis. As there was no portrait of him, the reconstruction of the face was performed by V. Urbanavičius, student of M. Gerasimov (Doveika and Korsakas 1981; Nainys 1972). This case evoked great interest in society and contributed to raising the profile of forensic anthropology.

Identification of the Radvilos (Radziwill) family remains

The Radvilos (*Radziwill*) family were highly prominent historical figures from the 16th century in the Grand Duchy of Lithuania and in the Polish–Lithuanian Commonwealth, producing many notable personalities in Lithuanian, Byelorussian, Polish and general European history and culture. It appears that the family, who had reached the peak of their influence in the 16th and 17th centuries, considered Dubingiai (today a small village) to be their patrimony, as they themselves chose it to be their burial pantheon. During the upheaval of war during 1655–1665, the church and palace of Dubingiai were plundered and destroyed and the Radvila family bodies removed from their basement grave and scattered throughout the church. They were later hidden again, to avoid a recurrence, but their grave was then forgotten. It was only during archaeological excavations conducted by archaeologists from Vilnius University in 2004 that a secondary burial containing the remains of eight adult individuals was found. During the complex research of the team of forensic anthropologists, historians, art critics and archaeologists from 2004 to 2008, the remains were identified employing various techniques including specific taphonomy, analysis of pathologies, analysis of available portraits and skull-portrait superimpositions, statistical testing of probability and DNA identification. It was considered to be one of the most significant historical and archaeological discoveries in Lithuania in past decades, and the remains were given a state reburial (Kuncevičius et al. 2009). This case was of special importance for the development of archaeology, anthropology and forensics, as it demonstrated the potential of such collaboration for society.

Investigation of mass graves

The excavation and subsequent analysis of several historic mass graves is briefly discussed in this chapter; although not strictly forensic, this was a good opportunity to apply both archaeological and bioarchaeological methods, thus contributing to the development of skills that might be used in more recent cases.

Napoleonic mass grave from the 1812 Russian campaign

A mass grave was discovered during construction works on the site of the former barracks of the Soviet Army, in the northern suburbs of Vilnius, in the late autumn of 2001. At first, several alternative hypotheses were considered, connecting this mass grave to the successive military and oppression activities of the area (i.e. the Tsarist, Nazi and Stalinist periods) (Jankauskas 2009). Representatives from the Lithuanian Prosecutor General's office therefore attended the site and started collecting evidence. Human bones were submitted to the VTMT. However, some preliminary observations made on uniform remains (especially buttons showing the Imperial Eagle and numbers of regiments) led to the conclusion that this mass grave was one of the Great Army's, returning from the disastrous campaign in Russia in 1812 (Signoli et al. 2004). In 2002, excavation took place covering a total area of *c.* 600 m². The complete mass grave was located in an L-shaped trench about 40 m long and up to 10 m wide, starting 2 m below current ground level, which corresponded to former suggestions that this was an L- or V-shaped trench for French artillery battery. Two teams were employed. French anthropologists applied a qualitative approach, using the methodology of funeral or forensic anthropology, previously applied to plague mass graves and forensic cases (Adalian et al. 2002); and local archaeologists from Vilnius University and bioanthropologists used a regular quantitative approach. Due to methodological differences between the two teams, the preliminary results were slightly different. The time constraint made the two techniques complementary. The accumulation of bodies on two sides of the pit showed that the trench was filled from its edges; it is highly probable that corpses were thrown from the side of the trench by the people in charge of the burial. The anatomical position of numerous skeletons strongly suggests that the bodies were handled very little; moreover, some positions are very different from that of rigor mortis, suggesting that the intense cold had frozen victims in the position of their death, this being preserved by the rapid burial of corpses. Other data such as the simultaneous burial of horses and men also demonstrated the context of crisis; burial of corpses wearing clothes was clearly revealed by the location of different uniform remains in corresponding positions. Analysis of buttons and other uniform fragments allowed the identification of the remains of soldiers and officers from *c.* 40 various regiments. The minimum number of individuals was 3269, males being predominant, although at least 29 females were definitely present. The density was about seven bodies per square metre, apparently identical along the entire trench. Detected unhealed traumas cannot be associated with combat wounds. Most often, peri-mortal spiral and comminuted fractures of long bones were found, probably occurring during the crude handling of bodies around the time of their disposal. In summary, archaeological and bioanthropological data coincide with historical records describing the burial of about 37,000 dead French soldiers in eight locations by the troops of Kutuzov and local officials in defensive trenches made by the French garrison in Vilnius. One such location was examined.

This case, although historical, was of major significance for promoting the discipline due to the development of professional relations between specialists of different institutions, including foreign ones, gaining practical skills in mass grave investigations (including techniques, logistics, etc.) and, finally, awareness of general public and legal institutions.

Excavation of a German military WWI cemetery

Experience gained during the excavation of a Napoleonic mass grave was extensively used in this excavation. In July 1915 the German army had occupied Panevėžys, at the centre of north-east Lithuania. A gymnasium building was transformed into a military hospital. Soldiers deceased in the hospital were buried in a cemetery arranged in the former school's garden. Historical data indicate that 580 German soldiers were buried there. At least at the beginning, Russian soldiers were buried there as well. German troops had evacuated by the end of 1918, but the cemetery remained. Regrettably, during the Soviet occupation in 1947 the cemetery was demolished, tombstones were crushed and removed, and the area was used as a school stadium. It was only in 2005 that the decision was taken by the local municipality to exhume the remains for subsequent reburial in the German military cemetery in Klaipėda. In 2005, a total area of 4070 m² was investigated, and 191 burial places containing the remains of 830 individuals were found, plus seven more remains in 2010. Inhumations were found in orderly group burials, containing from 1 to 17 individuals oriented east–west and parallel to each other. Archaeological finds include ID tags, personal items, some ammunition, residues of uniforms and medical devices. Routine anthropological analysis was performed on the site. However, personal identification was only possible for 26 individuals (18 identification tags, and 8 wedding rings with engraved initials). Most of the remains belong to males up to 30 years of age. There were, however, the remains of five females. Data on the health status of military personnel was obtained. The highest number of pathologies observed was various traumas, some of them with signs of treatment and healing. Evidence on the causes of those lesions is scarce: several deformed bullets (11 cases, 1 of them still in the cranial cavity) and comminuted fractures of limb bones prove the use of shotguns; in a few cases, blast injuries could be the cause (comminuted fractures of several bones from the same area); furthermore, the presence of cut/stab wounds suggests the use of bayonets and swords. However, a significant number of skeletons (115) were covered with lime, suggesting death from other causes, possibly infectious disease; the presence of chronic disease treatment is suggested by a certain number (32) of osteoperiosteal lesions. The presence of dissected bodies (13 cases) indicates systemic analysis of mortality causes. All this indicates the functioning of a large hospital with qualified staff and at least several specialised departments. Such a large sample was a unique opportunity to perform anthropological analysis of remains coming from a well-known context (Jankauskas et al. 2011). Experience gained during such excavations strengthened the skills of archaeologists in mass burial excavations, enabled bioarchaeologists to develop protocols for examination of numerous remains, increased their skills in analyses of modern-era traumas and signs of relatively modern medical interventions on remains. Moreover, it also indicated the possibility of individual identification by artefacts in the context of war.

Excavations of the victims of the Communist regime

At the end of WWII, Lithuania, as all of eastern Europe, came under the dominance of another oppressive system. In Lithuania, strong resistance against the Soviet Communist regime had already begun in the summer of 1944, and armed resistance continued until 1953 (Kuodytė and Tracevskis 2004). The regime implemented its system with massive deportations of 'unreliable' persons and their families, military operations causing numerous casualties, imprisonment and executions of participants and even potential supporters of resistance. The result was another series of numerous clandestine burials.

The Tuskulėnai site

One such site was the area of Tuskulėnai, close to downtown Vilnius. According to data found in the former Soviet Committee for State Security (*Комитет государственной безопасности* – KGB) headquarters, from 28 September 1944 until 16 April 1947, a total of 767 people were executed (seven more died before their execution) in the Soviet People's Commissariat for State Security (*Народный комиссариат государственной безопасности* – NKGB)/Soviet Ministry of State Security (*Министерство государственной безопасности* –MGB) prison. The majority (613 people) were charged with treason, and sentenced under Article 58 of the RSFSR Criminal Code. The executions were carried out by special groups of NKGB/MGB staff. After the executions, the corpses were buried secretly in a mass grave on the former estate on Tuskulėnai. The details of executions and the locations of burial sites were secret under the Soviet regime. In 1994, evidence about these facts became available to the officials of the Republic of Lithuania. The Decree of the President of the Republic No 216 (25 January 1994) was issued and accordingly a working group consisting of archaeologists, anthropologists and forensic medicine experts was formed. The initial goal was to exhume and identify two prominent persons of the Roman Catholic Church and anti-Soviet resistance. In June 1994, exhumation and identification work began. During the field seasons of 1994 and 1995, 706 remains were exhumed. During the construction of memorial works to the victims in the summer of 2003, 18 more skeletons were found. Very few archaeological artefacts were found (some details of personal belongings, clothes, eyeglasses, medallions, pencils, etc.).

Excavation, subsequent analysis and identification of individuals buried in this particular mass grave were challenges and a serious examination of former experience and available skills and resources was required. Each skeleton was excavated individually by archaeologists and bioanthropologists, given a registration number and after initial examination and field form completion was transported to the forensic anthropology laboratory. In the laboratory, each skeleton was analysed according to routine protocols collecting post-mortem evidence – sex, age, stature as well as individual traits (such as healed traumas, traces of diseases and treatment, dental status, peri-mortal lesions). Simultaneously, the collection of ante-mortem evidence took place – research in the former KGB archives, analysis of letters and requests from relatives and other documentary data. Later two data sets (ante-mortem and post-mortem evidence) were compared, as the initial data survey suggested that individuals executed on the same date (as a rule during the night in a special chamber in the KGB prison) may have been taken for burial simultaneously. During the fieldwork, 44 pits containing 1–154 skeletons were found. Thirty-two pits were found under a disturbed stone pavement, later identified as a former garage (Figure 13.2). Eight pits were outside the garage and formed a separate row. Five more small pits were found later at the northern end of the garage, approximately at the sites of former doors, where trees had subsequently been planted. In total, the remains of 720 males and four females were found. Their age ranged from 19 to 66 years. The position of the bodies in the pits clearly indicates careless disposal of the bodies. The overwhelming majority of the skulls of the deceased (97%) had peri-mortal lesions. In 492 cases, lesions were caused by one bullet in 110 cases; by two bullets in 31 cases; by three bullets in 13 cases; by four bullets in 5 cases; and by six bullets in 1 case. The calibre of the bullets varied from 5.6 to 9.0 mm, corresponding with indications of evidence that different handguns were used for executions. In the majority of cases, bullets had entered the occipital area (more often to the left side), the exit site of the bullet being in

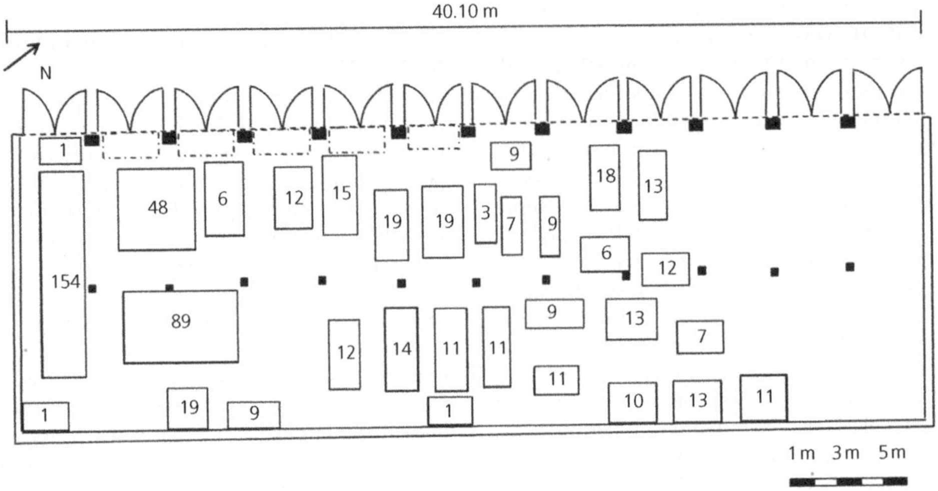

Figure 13.2 Tuskulėnai case: schematic drawing of the former garage found in 1994 indicating pit numbers.

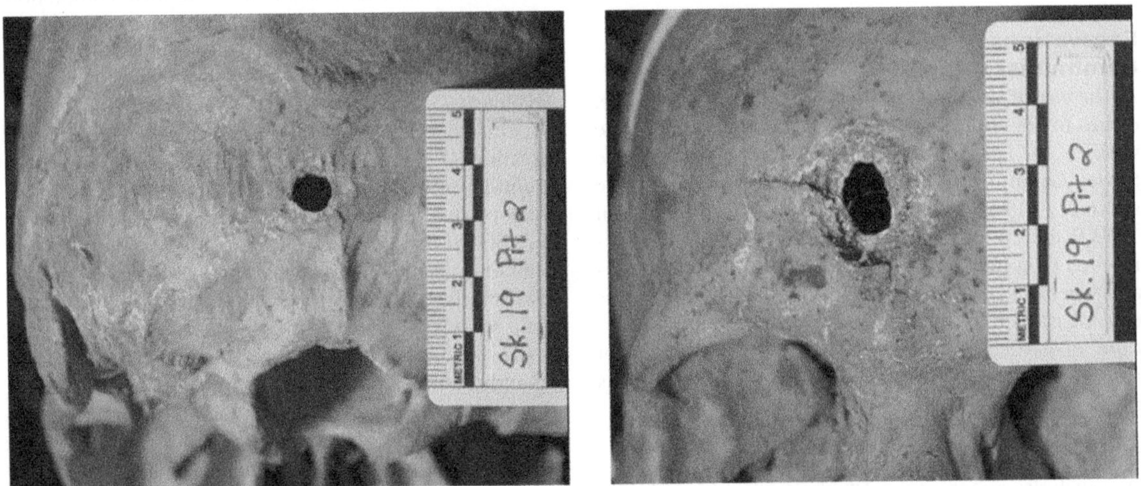

(a) (b)

Figure 13.3 Typical case of execution: (a) general view of skull with visible bullet exit on forehead; (b) bullet entrance in occipital area.

the frontal area or face, thus proving that the victims were shot from behind (Figure 13.3). Multiple shots and bullets impacted in the skull vault (Figure 13.4) also proving the application of control shots when the body was lying on the concrete floor of the execution room. Different kinds of skull lesions were also documented: 118 were made with a blunt instrument, 106 were stab wounds, and 4 were cuts or indicated striking. The majority of stab wounds were performed with four-edged instruments (possibly a pick or ice axe) (Figure 13.5). In six cases, quadrangular 3 × 3 cm entrance and 0.5 × 0.5 cm exit holes in the skulls were found, proving that a bayonet had been used on the prone victim. Archival data indicate that executions were performed subsequently by two execution squads (Vasilij Dolgirev operated from 1944 to 1946, and Boris Prikazchikov from 1946 to 1947), and peri-mortem trauma varied over time and between security personnel in the Tuskulėnai case; for example there is a higher frequency of stab wounds in the victims of the Prikazchikov squad (Bird 2013).

KGB files of executed persons contained information about age, sex and approximate stature. Often descriptions of faces were given in files, but this information was inaccurate and not very informative for further identification. The most important information from the files was the photographs of victims, the dates of executions and the number of executed persons. Some additional photos and descriptions were received from relatives of victims.

Initial comparison of execution details (periodic executions of several persons, sometimes up to two dozen each night, with intervals between executions from several days to 2–3 weeks) and numbers of individuals per pit was the basis of the working hypothesis for subsequent systematic identification. It was suggested that the bodies from one execution were transported for burial simultaneously and people executed on one night could be in one pit. During the cross-matching of data from reports of executions (number of executed persons, their group and individual identification traits) and numbers of bodies with their traits that could be significant for identification in particular pits, important details of the deposition of bodies were elucidated. It became evident that individuals executed in the late autumn/winter/early spring of 1944/1945, 1945/1946 and 1946/1947 were buried in the garage (later demolished), as the ground there was less frozen and easier to dig in the cold period of the year. Among the KGB files a letter was found complaining about burial difficulties in winter. The construction of the burial pits proves that the executions were planned; some were up to 4 m deep, with wooden supports, and the bodies were stacked neatly in several layers separated by tar paper. According to this system, individuals executed in the summer of 1945 were buried outside: in the summer of 1995 a separate row of eight pits was discovered. It should be that the bodies in these pits were covered with corrosive disinfecting chemicals.

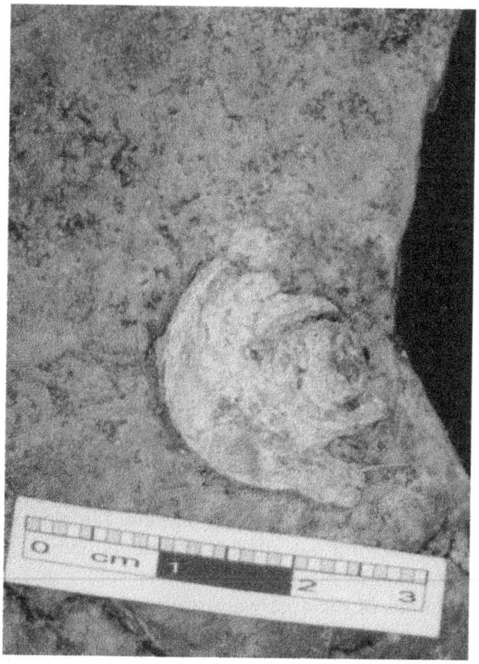

Figure 13.4 Impacted bullet in skull vault.

The next step in the process of identification was the selection of potential individuals for further identification. The main method was video skull/portrait superimposition. During the cross-matching of individual data from KGB files and video superimposition results, over 50 individuals were identified, and the identification process continues.

Finally, the remains were transported to the specially built memorial columbarium and placed in separate numbered caskets. This columbarium was officially opened in November 2004. Further identifications are being performed on official request, and the potential

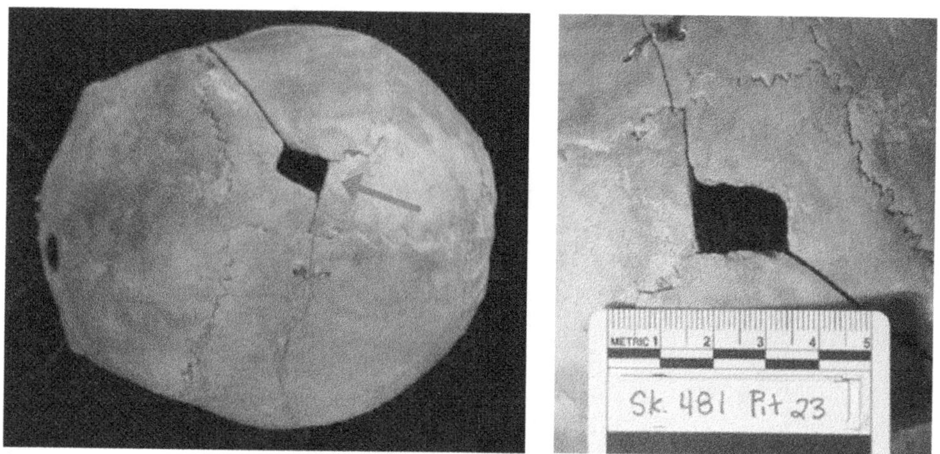

(a) (b)

Figure 13.5 Quadrangular opening (sign of bayonet?) in skull vault: (a) general view (arrow indicates the opening); (b) close-up.

number of identifiable individuals is likely to increase. Successful identification is now being enabled by the progress of technology, especially the implementation of DNA analysis. In 2007 one victim was identified by DNA examination – it was established that the individual encoded as case 203 was the father of two persons (brother and sister), with a probability of 99.97% and 99.91%. A control sample provided a definite negative result (Jankauskas et al. 2005; Jankauskas 2009).

Excavations of remains post-WWII anti-Soviet resistance

In September 2010, during regular archaeological excavations, a mass grave was found in Rietavas (a small town in western Lithuania). Disorderly position of the bodies and associated artefacts indicated that this could be a clandestine anti-Soviet guerrilla grave: it was routine practice for the KGB authorities to dispose of bodies in such a manner (often dumping them in refuse pits etc.) (Figure 13.6). Further excavation was performed under the supervision of local police, and the remains were transported to the VTMT. Forensic analysis revealed that the remains are of one female and four males, their ages ranging from 20 to 45 years, all of them containing bullet wounds. Two showed traces of bullets entering under the chin and leaving the skulls in skull vaults, evidently suicide shots. Such data were reported to the LGGRTC, and archival research suggested that this grave might be the result of a special operation performed on 26 January 1952, when five guerrillas were annihilated: group identification traits closely corresponded with individual data indicated in the report of Soviet Peoples Commissariat for Internal Affairs (*Народный комиссариат внутренних дел* – NKVD/MGB). Photographs of three individuals were obtained from relatives, and skull-portrait superimpositions resulted in a complete match, thus confirming the identity of all three persons. A decision about the identity of the remaining two was made on the basis of age differences (one of them was 21, another 40 years old at the time of death). Regretfully, attempts at identification using DNA analysis failed due to degradation of the DNA (apparently due to burial in very humid ground). The aforementioned identifications helped to perform a complete reconstruction of the events that took place that day. In total, 400 Soviet soldiers and militiamen were involved; after surrounding the hiding place in the woods, combat took place for several hours, and apparently the last two remaining guerrillas chose suicide instead of surrender. This served as a good example of formal and informal collaboration between various institutions (Žygelis 2012). The remains were returned for official burial.

A further example of successful collaboration is the search for remains in another site. At this time, LGGRTC initiated the work in the woods of south-east Lithuania, close to the village of Zervynos. According to documents in their disposition, on 20 May 1952, a secret group of special agents and MGB soldiers reached the bunker hideout where four guerrillas were hiding. Hand grenades were thrown into the underground bunker, and fire broke out; however, there was retaliatory shooting from the hideout. After brief fighting the bunker was completely burned, and the bodies were buried on the site. In the summer of 2012, a planned archaeological investigation took place; the site of the bunker was excavated completely, but no human remains were found except for a few charred fragments (later identified as fragments of distal end of tibia, talus, etc.). The surroundings of the area were searched, and a shallow pit was noted. In this pit, highly disturbed fragmentary human remains were found (the disturbance being

Figure 13.6 Position of bodies found in Rietavas case.

apparently caused by wild animals). The remains were submitted by local police to the VTMT for routine examination. Analysis revealed fragments of four males, aged 20–30 years, with multiple lesions, some of which could be peri-mortem: one bullet wound on the skull vault, one penetrating bullet wound on the upper thoracic vertebrae, one blunt blow into the left angle of the left mandible. However, the majority of cracks and fractures could be post-mortem, caused by repeated freezing and unfreezing, when the remains were deposited close to the surface. Thus, the data from the forensic anthropological analysis concurred with archival data as to the circumstances of the event. Attempts at individual identification were made. Due to extreme fragmentation of the skulls no skull-portrait superimpositions were made (portraits of two individuals were available). However, DNA identification was partially successful. Four skeletal samples (two from skull fragments and two from femurs) were taken for DNA extraction using standard procedures, and mouth mucosa samples were obtained from two sisters of individuals that supposedly died in this episode. A DNA sample from one femur revealed a 65.8% match of alleles analysed with the sample of one of the females, and it was concluded that indeed one of the individuals might be the brother of one of the DNA donors. Regrettably, DNA profiles from remaining bone fragments were either not extracted or were insufficient for identification. In summary, on the basis of all evidence and laboratory tests it was finally concluded that the skeletal fragments of four males found in the Zervynos forest are indeed the remains of four guerrillas who died on 20 May 1952, and their remains were returned for official burial.

Another case is the example of rejection of hypotheses about post-war inhumations. LGGRTC received requests based on oral evidence that guerrillas and their supporters were secretly inhumed in the vicinity of the former local Soviet militia headquarters in Dusetos (eastern Lithuania). Archaeological excavation on the site began in the autumn of 2012. The remains of four individuals in unconventional burial positions, some of them disturbed during former earthworks, were found with no associated artefacts. However, artefacts found above the remains were suggestive of deposits from the 17th to 18th centuries. The remains were submitted to the VTMT for further investigation. Analysis revealed that the skeletons are of two males and two females, ranging in age from 20 to 50 years; the skeletons were heavily eroded post-mortem due to acidic soil, but no peri-mortal lesions were detected. Moreover, heavy dental attrition of all individuals appeared to be characteristic of the Late Mediaeval–Early Modern populations of Lithuania (Miliauskienė and Jankauskas 2009), and not the mid 20th century. Based on this evidence the conclusion was drawn that the burials are at least 100, possibly 200 and more years old, and the case was closed.

All these cases demonstrated the validity of the application of archaeological methods, as they supplied valuable information that was used for identification. As the literature indicates, details of execution and disposal of bodies are solid evidence of the attempts of those performing this systematic killing to dehumanise victims, to destroy evidence purposely and to deny responsibility (Komar 2008), to bury the social memory of violence and in this way strengthen the terror-based regimes (Ferrándiz 2006). The resolution of these cases served to reconcile and to provide historic justice.

Conclusions

It is evident that the close collaboration of professionals from various fields (legal institutions, forensic medicine and archaeology, professional archaeologists from museums and universities – three of them have participated so far) in all stages of investigation is essential in the identification process of historical and legal cases. All these cases attracted great interest from the mass media and general public, although the value of archaeology was not emphasised. However, our experience revealed practical implementation problems for forensic archaeology that will be valid for other countries as well. In general, it is not an easy task due to the interdisciplinary character of the field as such different authorities (medical, legal, universities) with sometimes different expectations are involved. Very often such work is performed on the basis of informal ('horizontal') contacts and initiative. Missing feedback especially from legal institutions can be an obstacle in the improvement of methodologies. Insufficient workload plus limited resources, especially valid for small countries, can lead to loss of skills and difficulties in obtaining new technologies, consequently leading to unreliable results, which in turn can cause neglect by authorities. One can hope that such examples will raise local police awareness of the potential of archaeology in the investigation of modern crimes; in any case, if the VTMT were to be involved from the beginning of the investigation, the inclusion of archaeologists would be one of the first steps.

References

Adalian, P., Signoli, M., Lalys, L. et al. 2002. Intérêts de la présence d'une équipe spécialisée pour la levée de corps en anthropologie médico-légale. *Journal de Médecine Légale, Droit Médical, Victimologie, Dommage Corporel* 45, 375–377.

Bird, C.E. 2013. State-Sponsored Violence in the Soviet Union: Skeletal Trauma & Burial Organization in a Post-World War II Lithuanian Sample. Unpublished PhD thesis, Michigan State University.

Bubnys, A. 2005. *The Holocaust in Lithuania Between 1941 and 1944.* Vilnius, Genocide and Resistance Research Centre of Lithuania.

Crime statistics in Lithuania, Latvia, Estonia for the period of January–December 2012. Available at: http://www.ird.lt/viewpage.php?page_id=55 (last accessed 2 December 2013).

Doveika, K. and Korsakas, K. (eds.) 1981. *Kristijono Donelaičio Palaikų Tyrinėjimo Medžiaga.* Vilnius, Mokslas.

Ferrándiz, F. 2006. The return of Civil War ghosts. *Anthropology Today* 22(3), 7–12.

Garmus, A. 1974. Opredelenije pola po metričeskim priznakam kostej goleni. *Sudebno-Medicinskaja Ekspertiza* 26(2), 8–10.

Garmus, A. 1992. Problems of the person's identification from pelvic bones. *Medicina Legalis Baltica* 1–2, 22–29.

Garmus, A., Jankauskas, R. and Urbanavičius, V. 1999. Prospects of Lithuanian forensic anthropology. *Acta Medica Lituanica* 6(3), 238–241.

Jankauskas, R. 2009. Forensic anthropology and mortuary archaeology in Lithuania. *Anthropologischer Anzeiger* 67(4), 391–405.

Jankauskas, R., Barkus, A., Urbanavičius, V. and Garmus, A. 2005. Forensic archaeology in Lithuania: the Tuskulėnai mass grave. *Acta Medica Lituanica* 12(1), 70–74.

Jankauskas, R., Miliauskienė, Ž., Stankevičiūtė, D. and Kuncevičius, A. 2011. Im Osten etwas Neues: anthropological analysis of remains of German soldiers from 1915–1918. *Anthropologischer Anzeiger* 68(4), 393–414.

Komar, D. 2008. Patterns of mortuary practice associated with Genocide. *Current Anthropology* 49(1), 123–133.

Kuncevičius, A., Jankauskas, R., Laužikas, R., Stankevičiūtė, D. and Rutkauskaitė, I. 2009. *Radvilų Tėvonija Dubingiuose.* Vilnius, Vilniaus Dailės Akademijos Leidykla.

Kuodytė, D. and Tracevskis, R. 2004. *The Unknown War. Armed anti-Soviet Resistance in Lithuania in 1944–1953.* Vilnius, Genocide and Resistance Research Centre of Lithuania.

Markulis, J. 1966. Teismo Medicinos Tarnybos Raida Lietuvoje (1795–1965). Unpublished PhD thesis, Vilnius University.

Miliauskienė, Ž. and Jankauskas, R. 2009. Dental wear patterns in Lithuanian and Latvian palaeoanthropological samples. *Archaeologia Baltica* 12, 88–94.

Nainys, J.V. 1972. *Identifikacija Ličnosti po Proksimalnym Kostiam Konečnostei.* Vilnius, Mokslas.

Nainys, J.V. and Anusevičienė, O.V. 1984. Nekotoryje anatomo-antropologičeskije osobennosti kostej predplečja. *Archiv Anatomii, Gistologii i Embriologii* 86(3), 60–68.

Signoli, M., Ardagna, Y., Adalian, P. et al. 2004. Discovery of a mass grave of Napoleonic period in Lithuania (1812, Vilnius). *Comptes Rendus Palevol* 3, 219–227.

Tavares, C., Thomas, G. and Bulut, F. 2012. Crime and criminal justice, 2006-2009. *Eurostat: Statistics in Focus* 6.

Žygelis, D. 2012. Sugrįžę iš nebūties: partizanų palaikų identifikavimas. *Genocidas ir Rezistencija* 31, 5–14.

CHAPTER 14

Forensic archaeology in the Netherlands: uncovering buried and scattered evidence

Roosje de Leeuwe and W.J. Mike Groen
Netherlands Forensic Institute (NFI), The Hague, the Netherlands

Introduction

The Netherlands is a relatively small country and reasonably densely populated (Demographic Yearbook 2009–2010). Despite this, it can be considered quite safe with a low murder rate (*c.* 150 murders per year[1] per 16.8 million people; 1.1 murders per 100,000 people). About 2% of these murdered people end up buried in a clandestine grave.

Forensic archaeology exists in the Netherlands and is defined as an archaeological discipline that combines archaeological theory and methodology with theory, methods and techniques from forensic science (criminalistics), within the context of (criminal) law. Dutch forensic archaeology furthermore combines the abovementioned with criminological, pedological and ecological knowledge at a (crime) site to document and interpret the encountered finds and features (e.g. Groen 2007). Central to Dutch forensic archaeological research is the location, identification and documentation in a verifiable manner, *in situ* and in context, of any finds and features needed for further forensic analysis.

Forensic archaeology in the Netherlands is based at the Netherlands Forensic Institute (*Nederlands Forensisch Instituut* – NFI) in The Hague along with over 30 other areas of forensic expertise. The NFI is an agency of the Dutch Ministry of Security and Justice and provides services to clients within the criminal justice chain.[2] At present there are two full-time forensic archaeologists (the authors) active for the whole of the Netherlands[3] and the Dutch Caribbean overseas territories. Most forensic archaeological reports are written in accordance with the Bayes' theorem to express the most likely outcome.[4] In addition, Dutch forensic archaeology is concerned with the development and refinement of archaeological field methods and techniques that may be relevant in forensic archaeological case studies and the applied research of human (below ground) decomposition processes (taphonomy). The various types of forensic case analysis in which forensic archaeologists assist are described in more detail further on in this chapter.

Medico-legal framework and the role of a forensic archaeologist

According to Hirsch Ballin (2012, 41) the Dutch criminal process can be divided into three main stages: the pre-trial stage (*Voorbereidendonderzoek*) in which the criminal investigation (*Opsporingsonderzoek*) is carried out, the trial stage (*Eindonderzoek*) and the execution stage. The judge, public prosecutor (*Officier van Justitie* – OvJ) and defence attorney debate during the trial stage. This debate is focused on the discussion and verification of the technical evidence and the written testimonials of witnesses – heard by the police or examining magistrate (*Rechter Commissaris* – RC) – and court-appointed expert witnesses. Since most of the aforementioned testimonies and reports have been established during the criminal investigation (pre-trial phase), this investigation is crucial for the final judgment by the judge.

---

[1]Based on statistics from 2008 to 2011 by the Central Bureau of Statistics in the Netherlands (CBS).

[2]For more information, see: http://www.forensicinstitute.nl (last accessed 31 July 2013).

[3]The maximum travel time from the NFI to anywhere in the Netherlands is about three hours.

[4]Bayes' theorem is a way to work out the probability (likelihood) of the presence of a characteristic given a particular piece of evidence. It compares the probability (likelihood) of finding particular evidence in view of the hypothesis A (e.g. the tool mark was made with the spade X) versus the probability (likelihood) of finding particular evidence in view of the hypothesis B (e.g. the tool mark was not made with the spade X). Using this theorem it is also possible, in light of new information, to update the probability that a proposition is true (e.g. Stoel and Sjerps 2012).

Forensic Archaeology: A Global Perspective, First Edition. Edited by W.J. Mike Groen, Nicholas Márquez-Grant and Robert C. Janaway.

Dutch criminal investigation is inquisitorial, with the suspect merely as the subject of investigation, especially during the pre-arrest stage (Hirsh Ballin 2012). The Dutch Public Prosecution Service (*Openbaar Ministerie* – OM) is responsible for this investigation and – together with the police – collects evidence that could constitute the basis for a trial. The public prosecutor's (and police's) role in this investigation is impartial: he is obliged to investigate not only the incriminating but also the exculpatory evidence. The defence can also play a role in the investigation by requesting that the examining magistrate investigate certain aspects of the case (Hirsh Ballin 2012). These additional investigations can also be performed by the NFI forensic scientists, if requested by the defence and granted by the examining magistrate. The examining magistrate plays a central role in the pre-trial investigation as he guarantees the impartiality and independence of this investigation.

The Dutch National Police Corps (*Korps Nationale Politie*)[5] is responsible for the actual criminal investigation, under the supervision of the public prosecutor (sect. 13 Police Act). The Crime Scene Investigation (CSI) departments (*Forensische Opsporing* – FO) of the Regional Constabularies (*Regiokorpsen*) are responsible for the identification, processing and collection of all types of physical evidence at a crime scene. The regional Scene of Crime Officers (SOCOs) can be assisted during the investigation by members of the Central Operational Cooperation Division (*Dienst Landelijke Operationele Samenwerking* – DLOS), a nationwide operating unit of police specialists. The NFI forensic scientists can also assist the SOCOs during CSI at the request of the examining magistrate, the public prosecutor or the regional CSI department. The SOCOs will examine some of the collected evidence at their police laboratories; other evidence will be sent to the NFI or other forensic laboratories for (additional) analysis.

The NFI is funded by the Dutch government to support the National Police Corps, the Public Prosecution Service and the judicial system in case-related investigation and analysis (a service-level agreement). Besides case-related investigation and analysis, the NFI researches and develops new forensic methods and techniques, functions as a centre of knowledge and expertise, and houses the Dutch DNA databank. The NFI has no legally defined duties or powers; nor does it hold a state monopoly. The NFI forensic scientists are independent from the Public Prosecution Service and the police and can only be ordered to perform an investigation by the examining magistrate or the trial judge. All NFI forensic scientists have to comply with specific requirements. The NFI generally employs experienced professionals[6] and then trains them in forensics to meet their standards. Every scientist has to do an internal oral exam before a committee, which includes an external forensic scientist who specialises in the relevant field of expertise, after completing courses and assisting in casework for about 2 years before becoming a reporting scientist. The compulsory forensic courses include criminalistics, reporting, penal law, court room training and Bayesian reasoning, as well as additional training in the expert's own field of expertise.[7]

Dutch forensic archaeologists are NFI forensic scientists and are officially recognised as specialists in their field of expertise. As a result, they have an assigned role in the criminal process. Generally the SOCOs will call, on behalf of the public prosecutor, the NFI forensic archaeologist to assist them at a (potential) crime scene. However, it is important to note that the Public Prosecution Service and the SOCOs are not obliged to do this.

The forensic archaeologist will report his/her findings to the examining magistrate or the public prosecutor, depending on the stage of the criminal investigation. It is also possible that he/she will be required to testify before the examining magistrate, or during the actual trial in Court.

History of forensic archaeology in the Netherlands

The history of forensic archaeology in the Netherlands is quite brief. It did not exist until 2005. Before that time the SOCOs exhumed clandestine burials, sometimes with the aid of a forensic pathologist or a medically trained forensic anthropologist. As they had no, or very limited, archaeological experience, no spatial recording of the crime scene took place. In April 2005 Mrs Doris Eerhart (forensic adviser, NFI) and Professor George Maat (professor in anatomy and physical anthropology at the Leiden University Medical Centre (LUMC), then also a forensic anthropologist at the NFI) advised the NFI to contact an archaeologist (the second author) in relation to an already exhumed clandestine burial. Thereafter, the profession of forensic archaeology

[5]On 1 January 2013, all Dutch regional police forces and the Dutch Police Service Agency (*Korps Landelijke Politiediensten* – KLPD) merged into the National Police Corps of the Netherlands (*Korps Nationale Politie*) with 10 Regional Constabularies (*regiokorpsen*).

[6]The minimum requirements for a trainee forensic archaeologist at the NFI are a master's degree in archaeology and a minimum of six years' experience in (regular) archaeological fieldwork in north-western Europe.

[7]For example in the field of forensic archaeology additional training in physical anthropology, pedology, botany and human taphonomy is required.

developed rapidly and the importance of a forensic archaeologist at a (potential) crime scene associated with buried bodies was recognised by the Public Prosecution Service and the police.

From October 2006 onwards a forensic archaeologist was employed full time by the NFI. As the workload steadily grew, a second forensic archaeologist was employed full time at the NFI in 2009. At first (forensic) archaeological methods were only applied to cases associated with clandestine burials (survey and excavation) and exhumations at regular cemeteries. For example, the application of a forensic archaeologist at a crime scene provided information about the grave pit, the time since burial and the possibility of using stratigraphically assorted soil samples. Soon it became apparent that archaeological theory and methodology could also be applied to other types of forensic investigations (e.g. dating of human remains and recovery of scattered or burned human remains) and at an earlier phase in the criminal investigative process.

Although it is obligatory for an NFI forensic archaeologist to possess working knowledge in physical anthropology, in the Netherlands forensic archaeology and forensic anthropology are regarded as two separate fields of expertise. The NFI forensic archaeology is grounded in academic archaeology and focuses almost entirely on the (potential) CSI and analysis (field work). The NFI forensic anthropology is grounded in medicine and focuses on analysis of human skeletal material (laboratory work). The NFI policy furthermore states that a medical degree is needed to be able to practice forensic anthropology fully at the NFI.

Casework

Forensic archaeological casework mostly takes place at a crime scene. Exceptions are in cases where a forensic archaeologist is consulted during a meeting, on the telephone or by email. The case load varies and usually peaks in spring and autumn. Some casework, for example a search for a missing and presumed buried person or an exhumation on a cemetery, can be planned in advance. Other cases will present themselves *ad hoc*. For this purpose the NFI forensic archaeologists have their own four-wheel-drive vehicle readily equipped with materials needed to perform crime scene investigation. Usually they will be accompanied by the logistical technical support unit (*Logistiek-Technische Ondersteuning*) of the NFI. This unit is, for example, able to provide tents, generators, lights, an electrical sieve and even a complimentary coffee machine during the forensic archaeological field work.

Dutch forensic archaeological casework, which entails different types of investigation, is discussed in more detail in the following sections.

Spatial analysis

Spatial documentation and the use of a Geographical Information System (GIS)[8] application for processing data and information are an integral part of archaeology and forensic archaeology in the Netherlands. One goal of forensic archaeological research is to contribute to a reconstruction of the human and natural activities that took place on and around a (possible) crime scene. As archaeologists are experienced in spatial documentation, assistance can be through a GIS analysis including, for example, documented crime scene information, (aerial) photos, topographic maps, soil and vegetation maps and historical information derived from the National Archaeological Database of the Netherlands (ARCHIS2). The ARCHIS2 database is only accessible to archaeologists and contains all regular archaeological sites, fieldwork, finds, reports, etc. The crime scene information is documented with the aid of a Total Station[9] and a Differential Global Positioning System (DGPS).[10]

In summary, the GIS analysis is used to document, store, process, analyse and visualise different sources of data and information for (geo)spatial analysis.

Forensic survey for buried human remains or objects

When a person goes missing, it generally takes time before it becomes apparent that he/she might be murdered and buried somewhere. After that it may take some additional time for the police to narrow down the potential area with the clandestine grave. As a result a forensic survey (or search) may take place anywhere between a week and several decades after the disappearance of a person. Experience teaches us that it

[8]GIS is a software application that enables collection, storage, retrieval, manipulation, analysis, management and visualisation of spatial data (i.e. geodatabase) and images with a geographical reference (e.g. soil maps, air photographs and cadastres). GIS is widely used within archaeology, since it helps archaeologists to interpret the archaeological record, and hence the human behaviour, within a geographic setting (e.g. Chapman 2006; Conolly and Lake 2006).

[9]Total Station is an optical electronic device that combines the possibilities of a theodolite (to measure angles) with a distance meter. The spatial position of the feature can be documented in a horizontal grid (X and Y) and in height (Z). With these data a digital map can be drawn in GIS.

[10]The DGPS is a GPS system that uses a ground station next to the available satellites. The ground station provides differential corrections to improve the accuracy of the GPS signal, from several metres to a few centimetres.

becomes more difficult to find a clandestine burial with the passage of time.

A Dutch forensic survey is related to the question of whether there is (or was) a buried (remainder of a) body or object within the designated area. The purpose of the survey is therefore to exclude the presence of a buried object or body, to locate a buried object or body or to provide presumptive evidence that an object or body has been buried within the surveyed area in the past. The forensic survey consists of two phases.

1 During the phase of the preliminary desk research the available information regarding the survey area is processed, analysed and visualised in a GIS application. The GIS analysis not only provides information on the geographical, pedological and ecological values in the survey area, but also on the state of expected decomposition (taphonomic expectation) of the presumably buried object or body, in relation to the duration of burial (the missing period). This is important since the taphonomic state of decomposition, together with the pedological and ecological conditions within the survey area, will directly influence the viability of survey methods that can be used successfully.
2 During the fieldwork phase the designated area will be first visually inspected for suspicious features (e.g. soil and vegetation markers) and then further investigated by a range of archaeological (e.g. probing, auguring (Figure 14.1), test pits, trenching and scraping), geophysical (e.g. GPR, metal detector, magnetometer) and canine survey methods (e.g. Connor 2007; Hunter and Cox 2005; Larson et al. 2011; Pringle et al. 2012). The geophysical and canine methods are not deployed by the NFI, but by the nationwide operating DLOS police unit.

The evidential value of observations obtained from a forensic survey depends heavily on the local conditions, the presumptive duration of the burial and the chosen search strategy and methodology. Thus, the probative value of a forensic survey depends – among other things – on the local vegetation, soil type and structure, the time since the disappearance, the taphonomic expectation, the size and depth of the (grave) pit, the applied survey methods and the available time.

Figure 14.1 Examining a soil feature with the aid of an auger.

Dutch NFI forensic archaeological survey reports therefore almost always use two hypotheses and evaluate the outcome of the survey using the Bayesian approach. For example, the survey results are more (or less) likely given hypothesis A (there is no buried body within the survey area) than given hypothesis B (there is a buried body within the survey area). The Bayesian approach is not used in cases where it can be 100% excluded that a buried body or object is present within the search area.

Forensic recovery of fragmented human remains above ground

Forensic recovery focuses on the detection, identification, documentation and securing of fragmented human remains found on the (sub)surface or in a structure, for example a burned car. The remains are secured within their context. That is to say, the spatial relationship of these remains to each other and to other forensically important features (such as structures and personal items) is documented. During documentation several archaeological research and mapping methods and techniques are used, individually or in combination.

In the Netherlands forensic archaeological recovery mostly concerns severely burned – and therefore fragmented – human bodies. Complete skeletonisation of human remains above ground is a rarity in the Netherlands. As mentioned, the Netherlands is a densely populated country and many people undertake outdoor activities. Walking (the dog) or cycling are popular ways to spend spare time in the open air and is allowed in the Netherlands almost everywhere. As a result, human remains on (sub)surface are usually found by the general public long before they are able to fully skeletonise.

An exception to these findings was the discovery of the scattered skeletonised remains of a man found in the woods in 2011. This recovery was performed by the forensic archaeologists, together with the SOCOs and the NFI forensic pathology department. Pieces of clothing and human skeletal remains were discovered in 45 locations, spread out over an area of *c.* 500 m^2. The primary spot of decomposition was detected due to the presence of a Cadaver Decomposition Island (e.g. Carter et al. 2007), an area with disturbed plant growth and several human ribs and vertebrae. All items were catalogued, photographed with a north arrow, a unique documentation letter and a measuring rod. The spatial position of all items was documented within the Dutch

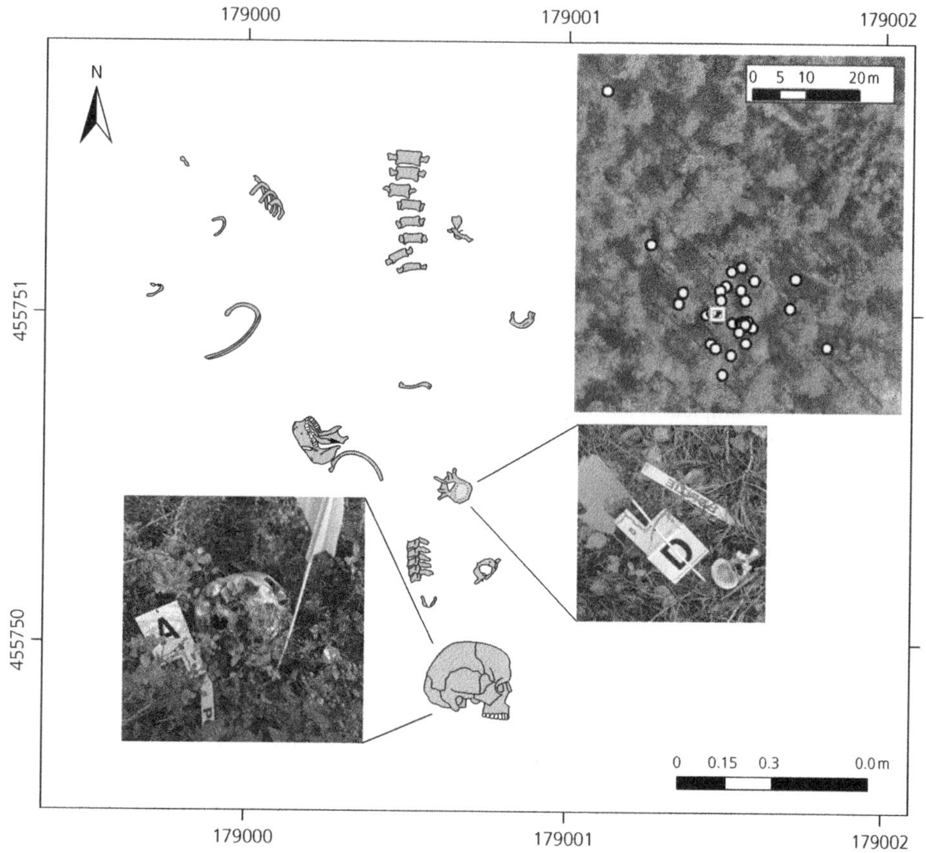

Figure 14.2 Example of the recovery and GIS analysis of skeletonised human remains in a forest. The *X*-axis and *Y*-axis show the Dutch National Grid coordinates (fictional for the purpose of this article). The inset on the top right is an overview of the crime scene with the spatial distribution of the localised skeletonised human remains. The photos in the lower left and lower right are crime scene photos of two skeletal parts *in situ*.

National Grid (*Rijksdriehoekstelsel*) with the aid of a Total Station and a differential GPS. After fieldwork, all field data were analysed in a GIS application (Figure 14.2).

The incorporation of the Dutch ecological database (*Soortenbank*) in the forensic archaeological GIS analysis made it clear that wild boar (*Sus scrofa*) and fox (*Vulpes vulpes*) were quite common in the area where the scattered human remains were found. The first were probably responsible for the miniscule splintering of the bones and the latter for the displacement of several of the body parts before skeletonisation. The GIS analysis therefore clarified the position and displacement of the recovered skeletal remains, some of which, like the entire lower left arm, were scattered up to 20 m away from the Cadaver Decomposition Island.

The time since deposition (TSD), defined as the time interval elapsed between the time of body deposition at the location where the body was found and the time of the discovery, could be estimated on the basis of observed plant growth and collected moss samples that overgrew some skeletal elements. The plants within the Cadaver Decomposition Island, mostly dwarf shrubs, were starting to recover. This recovery could take up to four years (e.g. Marchenko 2001). The moss attached to several skeletal elements was still reasonably small and must have started to grow on the skeletal tissues attached after skeletonisation. All collected plants were analysed by the NFI's Non-Human Biological Traces (*Niet-Humane Biologische Sporen* – NHBS) group. Considering all data, the TSD was estimated to be two–three years.

Dating analysis

A major task in forensic science is to determine the time between the death of an individual and the discovery of the remains (post-mortem interval – PMI). TSD of buried items can also be dated. This could be done archaeologically by dating the context in which the item is found *in situ* and in context, by using stratigraphy, knowledge of the local soil types and the ARCHIS2 database. The ARCHIS2 database is especially useful since it enables the forensic archaeologist to check the vicinity and history of a (potential) crime scene.

An example of TSD dating in relation to a buried object was a half-buried box of *c.* $2 \times 1\,m^2$ and *c.* 1 m high. The SOCOs found this box in a wooded area, near a place where a sexual crime was suspected. The box was buried by the suspect and it was suspected that the interior of this box could be associated with the sexual offence. The question facing the forensic archaeologist was 'how long ago was the box buried at the site?' The forensic archaeologist excavated a cross section over the sides and top of the box to examine the stratigraphy of the soil and vegetation (living plants and litter) that covered the box. While doing this several plants that were growing in the soil were sampled. A small maple tree (*Acer pseudoplatanus*) that was half covered by soil was also collected. The examination of the cross section revealed that the soil was deposited on the box no longer than one year earlier. The collected plants were examined at the NFI by the Non-Human Biological Traces group. The NFI biologists concluded that some of the collected plants were probably covered by soil in the autumn, thereby determining the year and season in which the box was buried on the location.

A long occupational history ensures a rich archaeological record underground. The Netherlands is no exception and skeletal elements from former inhabitants surface on a regular basis. Usually these are recognised as human when brought to the police station, but the question of whether they are old (i.e. historical) or of forensic relevance still remains. Three methods are generally used by NFI forensic archaeologists to date skeletal material: (1) contextual dating, (2) visual dating and (3) radiocarbon dating.

Contextual dating usually involves whole skeletons or individual human bones (Figure 14.3) and is the fastest dating method available. Even when the skeleton or bone has already been extracted, given that the condition of the location before the excavation is known, it is usually still possible to (TSD) date it. Knowledge of the context in which the skeletal remains were found is furthermore almost always essential for determining the date. The forensic archaeologist may therefore be required to investigate the site for the presence of soil features, guide artefacts and ecological evidence (as already described earlier). In addition, since site conditions can sometimes also affect the reliability of certain dating methods,[11] it is strongly advisable to let a forensic archaeologist inspect the site.

Unfortunately, the context of skeletal body parts that are sent to the NFI by the CSI departments for additional analysis is often unknown. In those cases visual and radiocarbon dating can help. In visual dating the wear patterns found on teeth (occlusal attrition) and the observable conservation status of the skeletal material is inspected. Through this method, a low probability statement can be made regarding the PMI and/or TSD of the skeletal parts. Visual dating has severe limitations and is only used as an additional dating method, in combination with either a carbon or a contextual date.

Figure 14.3 Dating bones on the basis of their context and stratigraphy.

Through radiocarbon dating the age of organic materials to *c.* 45,000 years ago can be determined (e.g. Hajdas et al. 2009). This method provides certainty and probability statements regarding one or more time intervals within which the person whose skeletal remains were dated must have died. Carbon dating can also be used within the forensic context (e.g. Alkass et al. 2011; Hua 2009) and is to date the method most applied to human skeletal elements without context at the NFI. However, this method also has some limitations. For example, before present (BP) results younger than *c.* 275 BP will – due to the ^{14}C fluctuations in the atmosphere (wiggles) – correspond with several calibrated calAD ranges, varying from *c.* AD 1500 to *c.* AD 1950. If the skeletal age of the deceased person, or the turnover speed of the human bone tissue (e.g. Hedges et al. 2007) is added to these calAD results, the outcome could be forensically significant. In the Netherlands, *c.* 48% of carbon-dated human remains brought in by

[11]For example, the reliability of radiocarbon dating can be strongly influenced by the presence of humic acids in the soil from which the human skeletal remains to be dated were recovered.

the CSI departments between 2008 and mid 2014 as a possible forensic case ($N=64$) resulted in such a doubt. About 44% dated older, ranging from before WWII to as far back as 7500 BC. These remains were transferred from the police to a regular archaeological service. In the end, only *c.* 8% of the carbon-dated human bones were certainly younger than *c.* 1950 and thus of possible forensic relevance, emphasising the importance of using contextual or other (non-radiocarbon) dating methods.

Forensic excavation (of a clandestine burial)

A forensic excavation consists of a systematic archaeological excavation in a verifiable manner, and the documentation and securing of a clandestine burial. The use of archaeological field techniques and methods, for example, ensures that the stratigraphy of the (grave) pit is accurately mapped, that a maximum potential of finds and features is identified and documented *in situ* and in context, and that relevant evidence (e.g. soil and vegetation samples) is sampled and secured. The securing of evidence during a forensic excavation is a collaborative effort between the regional operating SOCOs and the NFI forensic archaeologist, sometimes in collaboration with other NFI forensic experts.

The choice of excavation method depends on the specific objective, the taphonomic expectation and the environment of the clandestine burial. A multitude of techniques is available, for example trial trenches, horizontal layers, cross sections, platforms or a combination of these (e.g. Cheetham and Hanson 2009; Connor 2007; Hunter and Cox 2005). This choice is crucial, since it not only determines the finds and soil features that can be identified and later analysed, but also the likelihood that the buried human remains or objects are uncovered intact during the excavation.

In general, the following excavation sequence is used in the Netherlands. First, a 3D scan of the situation encountered is performed by the Expert Team Visualisation and Reconstruction (ETV&R) of the nationwide operating DLOS. Then the situation is evaluated and soil found in the vicinity of the grave (residue from when the pit was dug) is examined and sieved. Next, the outline of the grave pit on the surface is uncovered by scraping off a thin layer of soil with the aid of a sharp shovel. Following this the filling in the grave pit is removed by hand, using either a new or sterile trowel or a wooden spatula. The latter is used in proximity of the remains, as care is taken not to touch these remains with any sharp objects. The most applied method of excavation is a careful removal of the filling of the grave pit, without touching the grave pit walls.

The filling is removed in horizontal layers, revealing any anomalies or trace evidence *in situ*. Soil features, samples and all collected evidence are documented *in situ* and in context with a Total Station within the earlier defined 3D grid. All soil excavated from the grave pit is sieved through a mesh (4 mm width). When the excavated body or object – after the removal of the soil – is clearly visible, another 3D scan is performed. It is important to be able to adapt the excavation method during the investigation process, for example when new questions arise or unexpected evidence is encountered. It may, for example, be required to excavate a part of the grave filling first, in order to make a vertical section and review the stratigraphy within the grave. Or, in cases with deep grave pits (the deepest hand-dug clandestine grave so far encountered in the Netherlands was 1.7 m), it may be necessary to create a working platform in an adjacent pit, parallel to the grave pit, in order to be able to excavate and reach the buried remains.

After the human remains are secured from the grave pit, the walls and bottom of the pit will be further examined for the presence of tool marks, shoe prints and other evidence (e.g. Hochrein 1997; 2002). For example, it is possible to derive the approximate shape and size of a digging tool from a tool mark, and large plant roots, if damaged during the original digging, can sometimes possess microscopic metal fragments of digging tools. Additionally, plant roots that were damaged during the original digging of the grave pit and partly recovered afterwards can be used to determine the time interval in which the grave pit was originally dug. The empty grave pit (and the encountered tool marks) will be 3D-scanned (Figure 14.4). Finally, all stratigraphical soil layers in the pit will be sampled for additional pedological and pollen analysis.

In the winter of 2010 an NFI forensic archaeologist was called to a crime scene in the woods. A woman buried in a shallow grave had been found by a passer-by with a dog. While excavating the grave, the forensic archaeologist found soil features and sods turned over by a certain type of digging tool. Also, as part of a standard procedure, the archaeologist took soil samples from several locations in and around the grave. After careful removal of the grave's fill, the measurements of the empty grave – as it had been dug originally – were taken. The information about the width and shape of the digging tool was passed on to the SOCOs and three digging tools were found in the suspect's garage. One tool met the criteria as described by the forensic archaeologist.

The soil samples, along with the digging tool, were brought to the NFI for further investigation by the Non-Human Biological Traces group. A match was found between the pollen spectrum present in the soil sampled from the bottom of the grave pit and the pollen spectrum found on the digging tool. This pollen spectrum could moreover not be matched to the spectrum found in the suspect's backyard or those found at other places where the suspect declared that he had used his digging tools. The trial judge determined that the pollen match

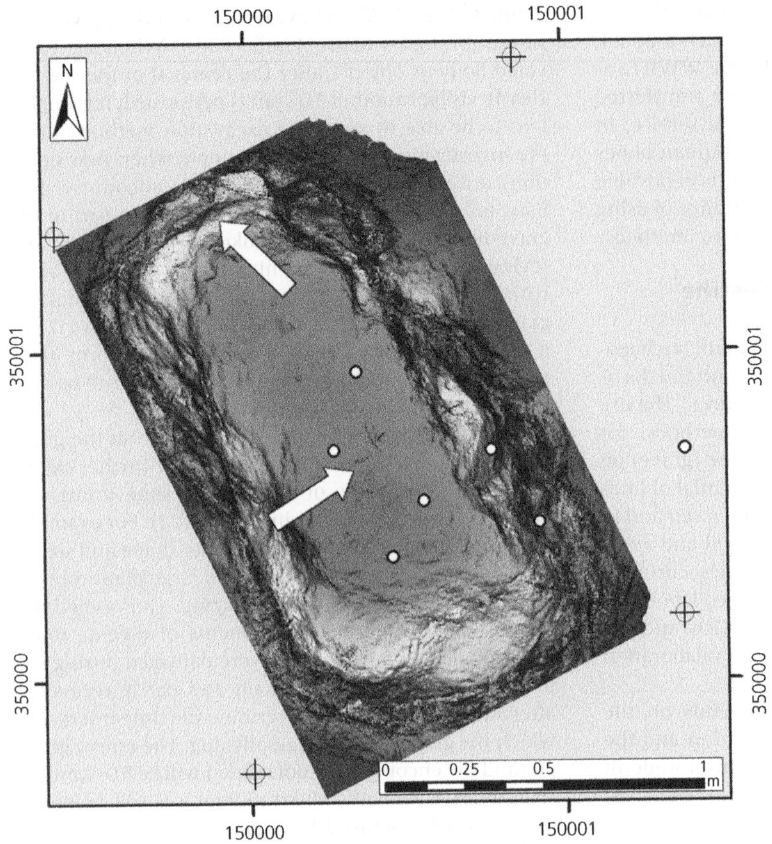

Figure 14.4 Example of a 3D scan of an empty grave pit. The *X*-axis and *Y*-axis show the Dutch National Grid coordinates (fictional for the purpose of this article). The lower arrow points to a shoe print at the bottom of the pit, found after the removal of the body. The top arrow points to a mark in the pit wall left by a digging tool, possibly a shovel. The white dots are locations of soil samples (source 3D scan: Expert Team Visualisation and Reconstruction (ETV&R) of the DLOS).

was strong evidence. The recorded depth of the grave was also used by the judge as evidence. The suspect apparently had bragged to a friend that he 'buried his girlfriend two spades deep', which, according to the trial judge, corresponded with the recorded depth of the grave pit. On the basis of this and other evidence the suspect was convicted.

Forensic exhumation (at a regular cemetery)

In the Netherlands the term *exhumation* refers to the disinterring of a body buried in a regular cemetery following a conventional legal burial. Two types of exhumations are executed by forensic archaeologists. One is the disinterring, documentation and recovery of a corpse in a regular cemetery for forensic follow-up investigation in a criminal case. The physical remains are secured according to the *chain of custody* (i.e. the collection, custody, control, transfer, analysis and disposition of the evidence from the crime scene to the court room). If necessary, the stratigraphy of the grave can be documented and soil samples can be taken for additional toxicological analysis. It is important, specifically with fragile remains such as those of infants, that this type of exhumation is performed by the trained hand of a forensic archaeologist, instead of a digging machine (Figure 14.5).

The second type of exhumation is only done for identification purposes. The remains of unknown individuals (*Nomina Nesciis* – NNs) are now exhumed and sampled for DNA. In the Netherlands the DNA of the NNs is recorded in the Missing Persons Databank (*Databank Vermiste Personen*) as standard procedure since 2010. In 2012 the National Missing Persons Bureau (*Landelijk Bureau Vermiste Personen* – LVBP) of the National Police made an inventory of all buried NNs at Dutch cemeteries from 1920 onwards.[12] The inventory came up with several hundred NNs whose DNA was not in the Missing Persons Databank. Since most of the NNs were buried in communal graves, and these graves

[12]With the exception of WWII victims and soldiers, who are usually investigated by a special Recovery and Identification Unit of the Royal Dutch Army (*Bergings en Identificatiedienst van de Koninklijke Landmacht* – BIDKL).

Figure 14.5 Exhumation of a grave in a cemetery by a forensic archaeologist.

could be theoretically evacuated in the Netherlands after 10 years, a plan was drawn up to exhume all NNs (or at least most of them) buried at Dutch cemeteries and to sample their remains for identification purposes.

The question as to why you would need a forensic archaeologist to assist in the second type of exhumation is often asked and best answered by the following example. In the spring of 2013 eight NN graves in the province of Groningen were exhumed and their remains sampled. The cemetery had been in use since the 19th century and the exhumed graves dated from 1935 to 1997. Most of the NNs had drowned and either been washed ashore or were found at sea. One of the exhumed NNs was a man buried in 1941 in a grave numbered 'No 2'. The exact date of the burial was unknown and no other description of the man was given. The skull appeared to be missing from the skeletal remains encountered in grave No 2. This is not uncommon for a body retrieved from water, but is inconvenient for DNA sampling (the Dutch DNA procedure aims for a femoral bone sample and a tooth). It became complicated when a second set of skeletal remains, with a skull, turned up in grave No 2. The potential problem was solved when the forensic archaeologist concluded that the second set of remains predated the first set: the soil feature in which the second set was found was disturbed by the coffin in which the first set was encountered. The second set was therefore an older burial, probably from the 19th century. Besides this, the encountered skull within the second set of remains also had distinctive feminine features. Without the forensic archaeologist the encountered skull might have been sampled for DNA and a 'wrong' DNA profile could have been entered in the Missing Persons Databank.

This example is not an exception. Many cemeteries, in particular the older ones where the handwritten card catalogue administration was first transferred to a 1980s floppy disk and later on to a digital catalogue system, seem to experience (previously unknown) errors in their grave administration. An additional problem is that people who managed the handwritten catalogue and floppy disks have already retired or are even deceased.

Accreditation of forensic archaeological casework

In the Netherlands all archaeologists have to conduct fieldwork under the Dutch Archaeology Quality Standard (*Kwaliteitsnorm Nederlandse Archeologie* – KNA).[13] The Netherlands signed the European Convention on the Protection of the Archaeological Heritage (Revised), also known as the Malta Convention, in 1992, but the treaty was not officially implemented until 2007. Dutch archaeology, however, started to transform its quality system from the 1990s onwards, from work done by universities and municipal archaeological departments towards a fully fledged commercial market. Under the new law archaeological investigation could only be performed by parties (the archaeological contractor) who have demonstrated that they were capable of doing this correctly (e.g. Willems and Brandt 2004). Furthermore, this investigation had to be funded by the disturbing party (the developer). In addition, the archaeological investigation had to be done according to the 'accepted standards', as accepted and maintained by the Dutch archaeological community. To assure that the quality of the archaeological investigation did not suffer under the demands of the developer, a quality norm was needed. In 1999 a national preparatory committee was therefore established, in which all archaeological sectors: universities, municipalities, private enterprises, all levels of government, the Dutch Association of Archaeologists (*Nederlandse Vereniging van Archeologen* – NVvA) and even the developers were represented. Since archaeological work is difficult to standardise, and there was a consensus that most of this work is in fact a scientific process which should not be made inflexible by too many prescriptions, the committee took the

[13]For more information, see: http://www.sikb.nl/pagina.asp?id=183 (last accessed 31 July 2013).

approach that the focus of the quality assurance should not be on a detailed specification of products, but on the process of the archaeological fieldwork. For example, all steps in an excavation had to be described and all participants defined. So instead of defining in detail what needs to be done, the KNA standard describes who is allowed to do it. For example, to draw up an excavation work plan or to identify contexts, features and structures on an archaeological site, an archaeologist is required to have a minimum of three years of fieldwork experience in north-western European archaeology after finishing a degree in archaeology. The KNA is meant for all archaeological phases: from desk-based assessment to filing finds in a depot and reports in a national e-depot (DANS) within two years after the completion of the fieldwork.

Unfortunately Dutch forensic archaeology could not be accredited under the KNA, as the Dutch Archaeology Quality Standard also describes how archaeological field data should be published and finds should be deposited. These are requirements that forensic archaeologists, due to the forensic nature of their work, would not be able to fulfil. Forensic reports cannot be published as they are not public and the 'finds' are considered forensic evidence and cannot therefore be stored in a regular archaeological depot. Besides, most forensic archaeological 'finds' would not even qualify as 'archaeological', as they are too recent (<50 years of age). Furthermore, there is already a quality norm that is appropriate for CSI work: the ISO/IEC 17020, a norm for quality management. At the time of writing, the Dutch Quality Manual for Forensic Archaeology (*Kwaliteitshandboek Forensische Archeologie*) is under development, based on the KNA and the ISO/IEC 17020 norm. The latter is in compliance with the implementation of the ISO/IEC 17020 norm in the field of CSI in Europe in the future (e.g. Groen, Chapter 25, this volume).[14] The NFI forensic archaeological accreditation process will hopefully be finished in 2015.

Training, education and European cooperation

One of the strengths of the NFI is that it invests in the training and education of the police officers, public prosecutors, examining magistrates and trial judges in technical matters. Training the SOCOs and informing other police officers, the examining magistrates and the public prosecutors about the possibilities of forensic archaeology is furthermore essential to promote this discipline across the Netherlands. For example, the Dutch Police Academy (*Politieacademie*) offers the SOCOs a 2-day training course biannually in forensic archaeology. In this training course the students receive a basic knowledge of dating methods and forensic archaeological field methods, such as excavating a clandestine burial (Figure 14.6).

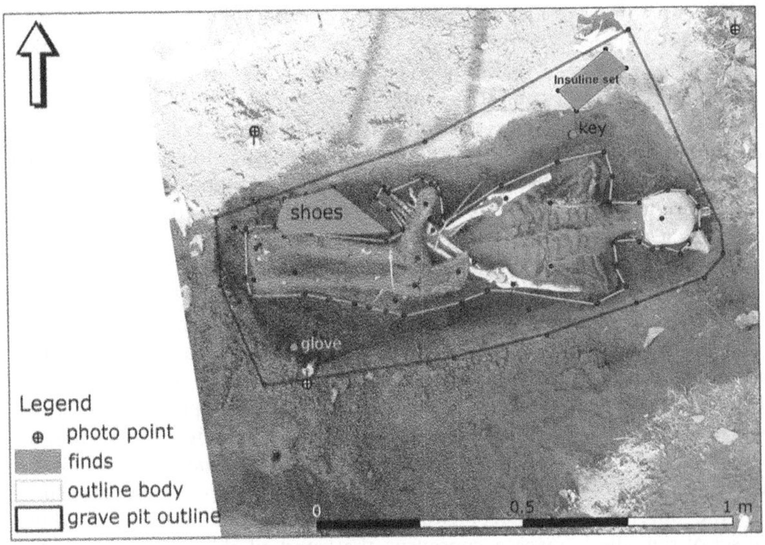

Figure 14.6 A practice grave at the Police Academy visualised in a GIS application.

[14]This is a joint project with participation from the European Network of Forensic Science Institutes (ENFSI) and the European cooperation for accreditation (EA). For more information, see: http://www.european-accreditation.org/publication/ea-5-03-ta (last accessed 31 July 2013).

For this purpose plastic skeletons, including clothing and personal items, are buried in grave pits months before training. As excavating is far too complex to teach in a 2-day training course, the aim of the training is to let the SOCOs understand the concepts of forensic archaeology and its research possibilities, methods and limitations. In addition, experience shows that when a SOCO has participated in forensic excavation training, he/she will find it easier to estimate the necessities of an excavation plan at a real crime scene. Other forensic archaeological courses involve, for example, teaching the Dutch Royal Navy (*Koninklijke Marine*) divers, who assist the police at underwater crime scenes, the possibilities, methods and necessity of documenting a crime scene underwater and recording their observations. Lectures in human taphonomy and forensic archaeology are also taught at several universities by the NFI forensic archaeologists throughout the Netherlands. Although forensic archaeology, as an archaeological degree, is not taught at Dutch universities, it is regarded as a subdiscipline of archaeology.

To understand how forensic archaeology is being practiced in Europe, to meet foreign colleagues and to create an environment for the exchange of experiences in forensic archaeology, the NFI and the British Institute for Archaeologists (IfA) Expert Panel Forensic Archaeology (Janaway, Chapter 24, this volume) felt it was time to establish an annual European Meeting on Forensic Archaeology (EMFA). The first two meetings were held at the NFI; the first on 30 August 2012, and the second on 30–31 August 2013. The second meeting was also used to inaugurate the Forensic Archaeology Project Group of the European Network of Forensic Science Institutes (ENFSI) (Groen, Chapter 25, this volume).

Research and development

The NFI forensic archaeology has four focus points regarding research and development: human taphonomy, improvement of dating methods, the use of GIS within a forensic context and the improvement of survey and recovery methods. The R&D relating to dating methods focuses, for example, on the refinement of (often forgotten) non-radioactive dating methods, for example, the use of ultraviolet (UV) light in relation to the auto-fluorescence of bone collagen and the use of luminol in relation to the chemiluminescence of bone tissue (e.g. Ramsthaler et al. 2011).

An example of an NFI GIS project is the criminological analysis of clandestine burials. From 2005 onwards the NFI forensic archaeologists have been present at all crime scenes in the Netherlands concerning a clandestine burial of an adult person (on average about three a year). The relevant data on all these burials, such as the geographic location and soil type, the grave dimensions, the presence of tool marks, the time since disappearance, the taphonomic stage and the method of discovery, are recorded in a forensic archaeological GIS database. Even with the limited number of cases (at the time of writing $N=23$), patterns emerge within the database. For example over 78% of the excavated graves were located in sandy soils, despite the fact that sandy soils cover just over 40% of the Netherlands. These percentages could mean that most clandestine grave pits in the Netherlands were dug in sandy soils, or – more plausibly – that grave pits dug in sandy soils are easier to find with the survey methods at hand, as opposed to clandestine grave pits dug in clay soils.

As the limited number of cases in the forensic archaeological GIS database made a statistical analysis unreliable and the criminological analysis of crime-related data falls outside the skills of the NFI forensic archaeologists, the GIS database project was extended to a specialist from the National Police Corps and the Criminology Department of Leiden University. At the time of writing the number of cases has increased to over 130, mostly dating before 2005, and the preliminary results look promising. Hopefully the GIS analysis of the data associated with clandestine burials from the past will reveal the (statistically) most likely places to search for a missing and presumed buried person in the future.

Conclusion

The aim of this chapter was to give insight into how forensic archaeology is organised in the Netherlands. As a relatively young archaeological specialisation its applications are still expanding in the field of crime scene work. Dutch forensic archaeology has been accepted by the examining magistrates, public persecutors and CSI departments. The forensic archaeological field methods are applied at a variety of (potential) crime scenes, while the underlying archaeological theory and methodology is being used to modify the way crime scenes are recorded and (pedological and ecological) evidence is looked at.

This does not mean that forensic archaeology in the Netherlands is without challenges; there are still SOCOs who believe that forensic archaeology is just a technical skill that can be acquired through attending a two-day training course. In our view, to be a forensic archaeologist requires field experience acquired through extensive fieldwork on regular archaeological projects and subsequently within a forensic archaeological setting, and a strong theoretical and methodological background obtained during regular archaeological academic education.

References

Alkass, K., Buchholz, B. A., Druid, H. and Spalding, K. L. 2011. Analysis of ^{14}C and ^{13}C in teeth provides precise birth dating and clues to geographical origin. *Forensic Science International* 209, 34–41.

Carter, D. O., Yellowlees, D. and Tibbett, M. 2007. *Cadaver Decomposition in Terrestrial Ecosystems*. Faculty Publications, Department of Entomology. Paper 251. Lincoln, University of Nebraska.

Chapman, H. 2006. *Landscape Archaeology and GIS*. Stroud, Tempus.

Cheetham, P. N. and Hanson, I. 2009. Excavating and recovery in forensic archaeological investigations. In S. Blau and D. H. Ubelaker (eds.), *Handbook of Forensic Anthropology and Archaeology*, 141–149. Walnut Creek, Left Coast Press.

Connor, M. A. 2007. *Forensic Methods. Excavation for the Archaeologist and Investigator*. Plymouth, AltaMira Press.

Conolly, J. and Lake, M. 2006. *Geographical Informations Systems in Archaeology*. Cambridge, Cambridge University Press.

Demographic Yearbook 2009–2010. Department of Economics and Social Affairs, United Nations Publication ST/ESA/STAT/SER.R/40.

Groen, W. J. 2007. De forensische archeologie: een vak apart. *Archeobrief* 3, 18–21.

Hajdas, I., Michczyński, A., Bonani, G., Wacker, L. and Furrer, H. 2009. Dating bones near the limit of the radiocarbon dating method: study case mammoth from Niederweningen, ZH Switzerland. *Radiocarbon* 51, 675–680.

Hedges, R. E., Clement J. G., Thomas C. D. and O'Connell, T. C. 2007. Collagen turnover in the adult femoral mid-shaft. *American Journal of Physical Anthropology* 133, 808–816.

Hirsch Ballin, M. G. H. 2012. *Anticipative Criminal Investigation: Theory and Counterterrorism Practice in the Netherlands and the United States*. The Hague, T.M.C. Asser Press.

Hochrein, M. 1997. The dirty dozen: the recognition and collection of tool marks in the forensic geotaphonomic record. *Journal of Forensic Identification* 47, 171–198.

Hochrein, M. J. 2002. An autopsy of the grave: recognising, collecting, and preserving forensic geotaphonomic evidence. In W. D. Haglund and M. H. Sorg (eds.), *Advances in Forensic Taphonomy. Method, Theory, and Archaeological Perspectives*, 45–70. Boca Raton, CRC Press.

Hua, Q. 2009. Radiocarbon: a chronological tool for the recent past. *Quaternary Geochronology* 4, 378–390.

Hunter, J. R. and Cox, M. (eds.) 2005. *Forensic Archaeology: Advances in Theory and Practice*. London, Routledge.

Larson, D. O., Vass, A. A. and Wise, M. 2011. Advanced scientific methods and procedures in the forensic investigation of clandestine graves. *Journal of Contemporary Criminal Justice* 27, 149–182.

Marchenko, M. I. 2001. Medico-legal relevance of cadaver entomofauna for the determination of the time of death. *Forensic Science International* 120, 98–109.

Pringle, J. K., Ruffell, A., Jervis, J. R., Donnelly, L., McKinley, J., Hansen, J. and Morgan, R. 2012. The use of geoscience methods for terrestrial forensic searches. *Earth-Science Reviews* 114, 108–123.

Ramsthaler, F., Ebach, S. C., Birngruber, C. G. and Verhoff, M. A. 2011. Post-mortem interval of skeletal remains through the detection of intraosseal hemin traces: a comparison of UV-fluorescence, luminol, Hexagon-OBTI®, and Combur® tests. *Forensic Science International* 209, 59–63.

Stoel, R. D. and Sjerps, M. 2012. Interpretation of forensic evidence. In S. Roeser, R. Hillerbrand, P. Sandin and M. Peterson (eds.), *Handbook of Risk Theory: Epistemology, Decision Theory, Ethics, and Social Implications of Risk*, 136–158. Dordrecht, Springer.

Willems, W. J. H. and Brandt, R. W. 2004. *KNA 2.1* [*Dutch Archaeology Quality Standard*] – English version, The Hague.

Websites

Dutch Archaeology Quality Standard (KNA) (in Dutch). Available at: http://www.sikb.nl/pagina.asp?id=183 (accessed 16 August 2014).

National Research Agenda Archaeology (in Dutch). Available at: www.noaa.nl (accessed 16 August 2014).

Netherlands Forensic Institute. Available at: http://www.forensicinstitute.nl/ (accessed 16 August 2014).

CHAPTER 15

Forensic archaeology in Poland: theory and practice

Maciej Trzciński[1] and Tomasz Borkowski[2]

[1] *Department of Forensic Sciences, Faculty of Law, Administration and Economics, University of Wrocław, Wroclaw, Poland*

[2] *Museum of Archaeology Wrocław, Wroclaw, Poland*

Introduction

The term *forensic archaeology*, which is in widespread use in English-speaking countries (e.g. Byeres 2011; Hunter and Cox 2005), is still insufficiently recognised in central and eastern Europe. Forensic archaeology in Poland is often confused with the archaeology of law, which, in fact, focuses mainly on studies of the material remains of past criminal penalties, for example excavations in places where once gallows, pillories and other corporal punishment devices stood. Problems with the correct perception of forensic archaeology result from the small number of Polish publications available (e.g. Głosek 2004; Kola 2005; Trzciński 2013) and the lack of tradition in this matter. Nevertheless, Polish archaeologists have actually carried out forensic excavations (Sojka 1974), but they were not referred to as such. Instead, they were called the implementation of forensic methods in archaeology or vice versa. Cooperation between both disciplines, however scarce, was known of in Poland from as early as the 1960s and has always been very fruitful (Gruza et al. 2008; Kwiatkowska-Wójcikiewicz 2011).

Legal framework

The legal framework underpinning the practical work of the forensic archaeologist is based mainly on penal proceedings. The primary legislation in this case is the Penal Code (the Act from 6 June 1997 – the Penal Code – *Journal of Laws* No. 89, position 555 with subsequent amendments). It regulates, among others, the fundamental issue of conducting a crime scene examination. It also introduces a distinction between the examination of a place, a person and a thing (Article 207 § 1). It regulates separately on the issue of conducting an autopsy (Article 209) and the possibility of carrying out an exhumation (Article 210).

The legal basis that allows for judicial authorities (state police, prosecutor, court) to request help from an archaeologist during an investigation also makes provision for the possibility of appointing an expert witness, consultant or specialist. It should be clearly emphasised, however, that in each of these situations, an archaeologist will perform only actions that are ordered by the authority. A forensic archaeologist working for a judicial authority can play the role of an expert witness, who can conduct a specialised examination (which may be in the form of archaeological excavations) as well as that of a so-called *ad hoc* consultant, who in the course of an investigation may be asked some specific questions by a prosecutor or the police. An archaeologist can also take part in proceedings as a so-called specialist (Article 205 of the Penal Code), if the examination requires the use of technical equipment, recording measurements, taking photographs, making calculations or securing evidence.

The judicial authorities who currently undertake research involving the implementation of forensic archaeology in Poland are mostly prosecutors who work at the Institute of National Remembrance[1] (*Instytut Pamięci Narodowej* – IPN), a state institution established in 1999 that is focused on researching crimes against the Polish Nation, studying cases of war crimes and so-called communist crimes. At this point Article 105 of the Polish Penal Code should be mentioned as it excludes a statute of limitation in cases of the following crimes: against peace, against humanity and war crimes.

It should also be noted that increasingly forensic excavations result from routine rescue archaeology that accompanies construction works. This occurs when, during archaeological monitoring, human remains are unearthed. The practice shows that cases of this type are usually not contemporary crimes, but rather the accidentally discovered graves of World War II (WWII) soldiers. At the occurrence of such cases, when, apart from archaeologists, a prosecutor and the police appear on

[1] http://ipn.gov.pl/en/about-the-institute

Forensic Archaeology: A Global Perspective, First Edition. Edited by W.J. Mike Groen, Nicholas Márquez-Grant and Robert C. Janaway.

site, it is evident that there is an urgent need for cooperation between these two very different spheres as they use different professional terminology. Up to the present it seems that prosecutors or police officers do not know the full possibilities of archaeology, which they may only associate with Indiana Jones or the pyramids of Giza. Therefore, they are unaware of the kind of questions they should ask and what type of support they could gain. Archaeologists, on the other hand, do not always realise that they are not being asked to take part in normal archaeological excavations, but in a crime scene investigation, headed not by an archaeologist but by a prosecutor. In addition, items discovered during forensic archaeology excavations are not only 'artefacts', but are primarily exhibits.

The most common forms of forensic archaeology in Poland

In Poland there are four main forms of forensic archaeology:

1 Excavations on sites of war crimes or genocide
2 Excavations on battlefields
3 Historical research (both prehistoric and contemporary)
4 Excavations and recording on plane crash sites

Occasionally, there are instances that involve the use of forensic archaeology to locate deposits of war plunder or for solving civil cases, for example to determine old field boundaries or to locate foundations of buildings that are no longer extant. The implementation of forensic archaeology in the daily work of police and prosecutors, however, is not common practice. Archaeologists, pathologists and physical anthropologists are not employed permanently by the police. They may be appointed as an expert witness and their professional skills are verified by the court.

Excavations on sites of war crimes or genocide

In this context, a very important event in the recent history of Poland and Russia might be recalled – namely, the case of the Katyn massacre (about 20,000 Polish prisoners of war (POW) and civilians were executed by the People's Commissariat for Internal Affairs (NKVD) in 1940). The excavations, started in the early 1990s by Polish teams (e.g. Głosek 2004; Kola 2005), are still continuing (most recently in Kharkiv and Bykivnia). In the 1990s, a number of archaeological excavations also commenced in the locations of former concentration camps, for example Bełżec and Sobibór.

The first step in this process of genocide or war crimes' investigations is locating mass graves. In most cases, the perpetrators have attempted to conceal the graves, for example by planting trees or covering the area with rubble. Determining the locations of mass graves is usually accomplished by taking a series of aerial or satellite photographs, which may point to some landscape anomalies or a specific pattern of vegetation growth that could indicate ground disturbance. The chemical testing of soil might also be very helpful. A high concentration of phosphorus would indicate intense decomposition processes on a site. Increasingly in this type of research, geophysical methods are involved, mainly ground-penetrating radar (GPR) and electrical resistivity surveys (Koźmiński et al. 2009, 22–32). Finally, there are the most time-consuming and, unfortunately, invasive methods of geological coring that have been applied, for example in Kharkiv and Katyn (e.g. Cox et al. 2008).

Further work during the excavation of these mass graves is undertaken in close collaboration with pathologists and physical anthropologists. Examinations carried out in situ often reveal the perpetrators' modus operandi. In the cases of war crimes, the perpetrators often use firearms. Hence, during this work, forensic examinations of firearms and ammunition (ballistics) are frequently undertaken. Sometimes, alongside the bodies, various personal items such as documents that were deliberately hidden within uniforms or boots are recovered. In this case, the forensic examination of documents is very useful. Physicochemical analyses may enable their reconstruction and as a result, even from a poorly preserved document, the identity of the bearer can be recovered.

An interesting example in this respect is the examination of records from the POW camp in Żagań/Sagan (Stalag VIII C). In 1972, within the ruins of one of the destroyed buildings, burnt camp documentation was found. Work carried out in forensic laboratories have made it possible not only to separate the charred sheets of paper, but also to decipher the writing under infrared analysis. It was discovered that among the documents were permits for the German camp crew, which bore signatures. This allowed for the identification of the camp commander and his deputy and became the evidence for the prosecution of this Nazi crime (Sojka 1974).

Studies of war crimes and genocide have always had many aspects. Obviously, personal items found on a site become evidence for the prosecution, but we ought to bear in mind another important aspect of this research – the purely human one – the restoration of the identity and dignity of the victim.

Currently in Poland, very frequent exhumations of war crime victims' remains are conducted or of soldiers who fell on battlefields (mainly German and Soviet soldiers).

There are also numerous ongoing exhumations of the communist regime victims' remains from the 1940s and 1950s and these are mainly conducted by the Institute of National Remembrance. An example of such an undertaking is the exhumations carried out in 2011 in one of Wrocław's cemeteries.

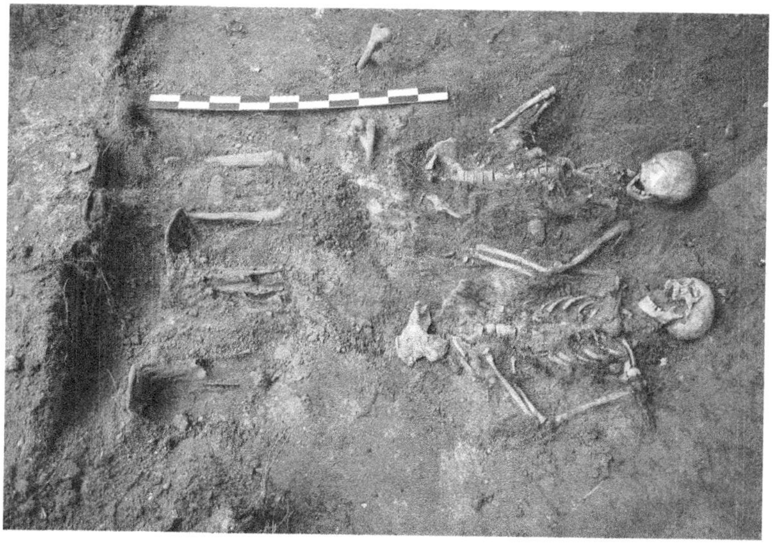

Figure 15.1 Wrocław, Old Town Park. Burial of a German soldier and a civilian (Photo: R. Jarysz, Museum of Archaeology, Wrocław).

In the last few years several thefts from the Nazi extermination camp of Auschwitz-Birkenau have occurred. In 2009, the notorious theft of the sign over the gate with the inscription *Arbeit Macht Frei* took place. Such actions force archaeologists to undertake rescue excavations just to secure sites from such destruction. The main purpose is to protect human remains and personal belongings. Victims' identification remains a secondary issue since in this case it is rather impossible.

Excavations on battlefields

More and more frequently, battlefields are becoming the subjects of specialised research. The primary goal is to verify by excavation the written sources that were not always objective for various reasons or were simply untrue. Research on a battlefield, even after several hundred years, provides a unique opportunity to collect material that would allow for the reconstruction of the course of a given battle, and sometimes to find weapons and victims. Battlefield excavations have been successfully carried out on both prehistoric sites as well as WWII ones (Lynch and Cooksey 2007; Meller 2009).

In 2010 employees of the Museum of Archaeology in Wrocław monitored earthworks in the Old Town Park in Wrocław. The area is located between two lines of medieval and post-medieval fortifications in Wrocław. The archaeologists expected to uncover architectural remains and layers linked with moats and ramparts. Instead, in one of the trenches, at a depth of about 0.8 m, a human skull was uncovered. The excavation revealed a double burial (Figure 15.1). Even a cursory examination enabled the excavators to establish that the burial dated from WWII. Injuries noticed on both skulls suggested the violent death of both interred individuals. The skeletons were accompanied by many small objects: buttons, braces, belt buckles and boots. Amongst them were also personal items: a small leather wallet, corroded razor fragments, a pocket mirror and a small fragment of a gold signet ring with the initials BB (Figure 15.2). A dog tag was found next to one of the skeletons. Unfortunately, it was made of aluminium that reacted with the mortar lime from the surrounding walls and made identification impossible. This unexpected discovery during a routine archaeological monitoring job caused quite a stir. The archaeologists informed the police, the prosecutor's office and the office of the Voivodship Monuments' Conservator. The prosecutor decided to transfer the remains to the Department of Forensic Medicine in Wrocław and to

Figure 15.2 Wrocław, Old Town Park. Heinrich Biskupek's father's signet-ring (BB Bernard Biskupek) (Photo: T. Gąsior, Museum of Archaeology, Wrocław).

undertake an examination aimed at determining the cause of death.

After completing the necessary documentation, the archaeologists began to explore the burials. Consultants, specialising in the identification of uniforms of WWII soldiers, confirmed that the buttons and buckles found next to one of the skeletons were from a German uniform. This provided the reason for contacting the *Pamięć* (Remembrance) Foundation, which protects memorials, cemeteries and war graves. It cooperates with, amongst others, the German War Graves Commission (*Volksbund Deutsche Kriegsgräberfürsorge*), so it has access to German archives from WWII. The Foundation staff, based on information provided by the archaeologists concerning the manner and location of the burial, were able to determine that one of the victims was probably a young stretcher-bearer, Heinrich Biskupek, born 3 June 1923 in Godulla-Hütte (now Ruda Śląska in Upper Silesia, Poland). The identification was facilitated by the aforementioned fragment of a signet ring with the initials BB, which probably belonged to Heinrich's father, Bernard. Heinrich Biskupek served in the 174th Infantry Regiment, which belonged to the 81st Infantry Division. The reason for Biskupek's stay in Wrocław is not exactly known. At that time his regiment was stationed in Courland. German archives provided information that Heinrich Biskupek committed suicide on 5 May 1945, one day before the Festung Breslau agreement of surrender was signed. His skull bears traces of bullet wounds (both entry and exit ones – Figure 15.3). The ballistics analysis proved that it was a short-range shot to the right temple. One can hardly imagine the atmosphere in the besieged city a short time before the surrender (Wrocław (Breslau in German) in 1944 was declared *Festung Breslau* – a closed fortress; the Siege of Breslau lasted 82 days until 6 May 1945).

If Heinrich Biskupek had been captured and held as a POW by Soviets, his situation would have been worsened by his Polish surname. The identification of the second individual is not entirely certain. Due to the date of death (he had to die very close in time to Biskupek because they were interred in the same grave), he was probably a civilian called Georg Otto, born on 4 December 1895, who was probably a refugee from the east or the west of Germany. Many people in 1945 fled to the west to evade the Red Army. Wrocław (Breslau) was also out of the range of the Allies' carpet-bombings, and thus appeared to be a safe haven. This is why there were also many refugees from western Germany. The discovery of the burial and the identification of the individuals made it possible to attempt to make contact with the victims' living relatives (Gross 2010).

Figure 15.3 Wrocław, Old Town Park. Heinrich Biskupek's skull (Photo: R. Jarysz, Museum of Archaeology, Wrocław).

Historical research

Cooperation between archaeologists and historians on various projects has often resulted in the use of forensic examinations in these cases. This concerns, for example, anthropometric studies conducted during the exhumations of Polish royals and nobles (Widacki 1992), or one recently carried out by the Central Forensic Laboratory which was the reconstruction of the appearance of Nicolaus Copernicus, whose remains were discovered by archaeologists in 2005.

Excavations and recording on plane crash sites

The cooperation of archaeologists and forensic specialists on the sites of plane crashes has proved to be very fruitful. This concerns both disasters that took place decades ago as well as recent ones. Polish archaeologists worked on the crash site in Smolensk, Russia, in October 2010 (the Polish President and many other officials were killed in this disaster).

Archaeological methods include detailed ground examination and meticulous planning, which may be helpful in determining the exact location of the plane crash. Geophysical methods enable researchers to find and record even the smallest of items and these can be parts of a destroyed plane or personal belongings of victims. Traces and items found and secured by archaeologists are subjected to specialist forensic analyses. The methods most often applied in these cases are audio forensic analysis, which examines the contents of flight recorders ('black boxes'), toolmarks' examination and finally DNA analysis, which is helpful in identifying victims of disasters and is commonly used (Włodarczyk 2010).

Forensic archaeology may also deal with WWII military aircraft crashes. In autumn 2008, archaeologists from the Museum of Archaeology in Wrocław discovered a wreck of a German medium bomber, a Heinkel He 111 near Wrocław. The site had been located using metal detectors (Figure 15.4). Test trench No. 1 was opened in an area with a high concentration of signals, which indicated the presence underground of a large number of metal artefacts. Topsoil was removed both by hand and mechanically.

Figure 15.4 Kamień, Wrocław district. Aerial view of Heinkel He 111 crash site (Photo: T. Gąsior, Museum of Archaeology, Wrocław).

The greatest area of unnatural discolouration was found within test trench No. 9, where an aluminium oxide concentration was noticed. Some of these irregularities, especially those of a more considerable depth and containing artefacts, were defined as features. The largest of them was feature No. 4 in test trench No. 14. It was kidney-shaped in plan and had dimensions of 3.0 × 1.5 m (Figure 15.5). Its depth was 0.8 m. There were two fills distinguished: the upper one was a dark brown soil mixed with aluminium oxide and the lower one was a light brown soil with yellow sand lenses. Beneath the bottom of the pit, in the central part, there was a smear of a bluish substance, probably an oil product (Figure 15.6). Within the fills of feature No. 4, numerous artefacts were found. Among many metal fragments, small parts of an aircraft's engine were also identified (which may explain the origin of the aforementioned bluish smear). The other features were smaller. It should be assumed that all of them were created at the same time as a result of the aircraft crash. These features' fills also contained tiny aircraft parts mixed with soil and layers of charcoal or scorched soil.

Other non-invasive methods apart from metal detecting were used on the site. First, the site was tested by GPR. The test area was 28 × 100 m. The data-processing results indicated a large cluster of anomalies. Test trench No. 1, whose position, based only on metal detector scanning, was located in the centre of this cluster. An electrical resistivity survey covered an area of 25 × 20 m. The electrodes were spaced at a distance of 1.5 × 1.5 m, and the maximum depth range was 2.0 m. One of the clearer anomalies was feature No. 4 within test trench No. 14. A large number of artefacts were recovered from the topsoil. The aluminium fragments of the aircraft fuselage, cartridges of 7.92 and 13 mm calibre, parts of a Plexiglas cockpit, navigation instruments and many other items were found. There were also small human bones among the fragments of the crashed plane. They belonged to three males aged 19–24 years. In addition, three distinctive buckles used to fasten parachute harness straps were found. Portions of the machine enabled it to be identified as a Heinkel He 111, a medium bomber. According to historical sources, many examples of this type of aircraft were shot down while supplying Festung Breslau in spring 1945. They belonged mostly to the fourth Bomber Regiment Kampfgeschwäder 4 (KG 4) 'General Wever' and to the so-called Herzog Group. The excavations not only established the time when the aircraft was shot down (March–April 1945), but also enabled the reconstruction of the unsuccessful attempt at an emergency landing – it resulted in the crash and the death of all the crew members (Gross 2009, 228–234).

Figure 15.5 Kamień, Wrocław district. Scene of the crash of a shot down Heinkel He 111 during excavations (Photo: M. Gross, Museum of Archaeology, Wrocław).

Figure 15.6 Kamień, Wrocław district. Scene of the crash of a shot down Heinkel He 111 during excavations (Photo: M. Gross, Museum of Archaeology, Wrocław).

Conclusions

It seems that the advantages of the practical application of forensic archaeology have to date been underestimated or overlooked in Poland. There is no doubt that specialised forensic archaeology training can be very useful in the work of police and prosecutors in the case of recently committed crimes. Unfortunately, when it comes to training or an accreditation system for future forensic archaeologists there is a lack of programmes. Currently the only institution in Poland offering such a course is the University of Wrocław, where in 2010 a course entitled Postgraduate Studies in Forensic Archaeology was launched. The course is addressed not only to graduate archaeologists. Among students are also prosecutors, historians and, occasionally, policemen. In addition, in 2013 a manual of forensic archaeology was published (Trzciński 2013). Police training schools have not introduced even the most basic principles of forensic archaeology into their training programme. At present, the police do not see a need for regular cooperation with archaeologists. Therefore, there are no counterparts of the disaster victim identification (DVI) units which work successfully in western Europe. Forensic archaeology is still a new discipline in Poland. Its research capabilities and social usefulness have not been perceived to date or have only been implemented solely in cases connected with war crimes. The opportunities for forensic archaeology in criminal cases, for example in searching and identifying missing persons, are still ignored.

References

Byeres, S.N. 2011. *Introduction to Forensic Anthropology*. Boston, Pearson.

Cox, M., Flavel, A., Hanson, I., Laver, J. and Wessling, R. 2008. *The Scientific Investigation of Mass Graves: Towards Protocols and Standard Operating Procedures*. Cambridge, Cambridge University Press.

Głosek, M. (ed.) 2004. *Katyń w Świetle Badań Terenowych 1994–1995*. Toruń, Duet.

Gross, M. 2009. Badania archeologiczne na stanowisku z II wojny światowej w miejscowości Kamień, Gm. Długołęka. pow. wrocławski. *Silesia Antiqua* 45, 228–234.

Gross, M. 2010. Festung Breslau w wykopie. *Archeologia Żywa* 6(52), 60–62.

Gruza, E., Goc, M. and Moszczyński, J. 2008. *Kryminalistyka – Czyli Rzecz o Metodach Śledczych*. Warszawa, Wydawnictwa Akademickie i Profesjonalne.

Hunter, J. and Cox, M. 2005. *Forensic Archaeology: Advances in Theory and Practice*. London, Routledge.

Kola, A. 2005. *Archeologia Zbrodni. Oficerowie Polscy na Cmentarzu ofiar NKWD w Charkowie*. Toruń, Wydawnictwo Uniwersytetu Mikołaja Kopernika w Toruniu.

Koźmiński, L., Brzozowska, M., Kościuk, J. and Kubisz, W. 2009. Wykorzystanie możliwości nowoczesnego skanowania 3D w oględzinach miejsca zdarzenia i ich dokumentowania. *Kwartalnik Prawno-Kryminalistyczny* 2(2), 22–32.

Kwiatkowska-Wójcikiewicz, V. 2011. *Oględziny Miejsca. Teoria i Praktyka*. Toruń, Dom Organizatora.

Lynch, T. and Cooksey, J. 2007. *Battlefield Archaeology*. Chalford, Tempus.

Meller, H. (ed.) 2009. *Schlachtfeldarchäologie*. Halle, Tagungen des Landesmuseums für Vorgeschichte Halle.

Sojka, T. 1974. Kryminalistyczna Problematyka Zbrodni Wehrmachtu na Jeńcach Wojennych. (Na Przykładzie Obozów Jenieckich w Żaganiu). Unpublished PhD thesis, Department of Forensic Sciences, University of Wrocław, Poznań.

Trzciński, M. (ed.) 2013. *Archeologia Sądowa w Teorii i Praktyce*. Warszawa, Wolters Kluver.

Widacki, J. 1992. *Detektywi na Tropach Zagadek Historii*. Kraków, Wydawnictwo Wawelskie.

Włodarczyk, R. 2010. *Działania Kryminalistyczne Medyczne i Organizacyjne w Sytuacjach Zdarzeń Masowych ze Szczególnym Uwzględnieniem Identyfikacji Genetycznej Zwłok i Szczątków Ludzkich z Pogorzeliska*. Szczytno, Wydawnictwo Wyższej Szkoły Policji w Szczytnie.

CHAPTER 16

Forensic archaeology in Romania: present and future of a new discipline

Annamaria Diana
Edinburgh University, School of History, Classics and Archaeology, William Robertson Wing, Old Medical School, Edinburgh, UK

Introduction

This chapter will attempt a reconstruction of the current attitude of Romanian academic institutions, archaeologists and the general public towards the role of forensic archaeology (and forensic anthropology) in the legal-forensic framework, and in archaeological fieldwork. It will also discuss whether this science has actually reached Romania, and, if not, will analyse the reasons by suggesting future actions to be taken.

Forensic sciences, archaeology and anthropology

First, a clarification of the meaning of the expression *forensic archaeology* is needed. This fairly new discipline defines the application of archaeological excavation methods and procedures to the crime scene (Hunter and Cox 2005), especially for unearthing war crimes and humanitarian recovery (Dupras et al. 2006, 5). There is a substantial difference between exhumation and recovery by excavation, the latter being a scientific process aiming at exposing and recovering not only the remains but also the related evidence by following specific protocols (Cox et al. 2008, 216).

The concept of forensic archaeology has not yet been 'officially' introduced in Romania. However, results that are achieved elsewhere through this specialisation are obtained in this country with the contribution of a range of disciplines which apply forensic anthropological methods to criminal cases.

Medico-legal sciences and all the specialisations resulting from courses related to them (medicine, law and forensic anthropology) are generally considered the most reliable disciplines, located at the top of this hierarchical structure. Legal medicine is defined by the Romanian National Legal Medicine Board as 'a medical specialisation which applies the principles and methodologies of medical sciences to the legal field'.[1] This discipline aims to pursue justice by using medical evidence in forensic cases in order to solicit legal institutions and parties involved, and to protect the interest of the victim.[2]

Furthermore, it is important to stress that in Romania archaeology and physical anthropology (and related disciplines such as forensic anthropology) are two separate and independent fields. For example, in the academic world, people still find it hard to accept the existence of researchers specialising in *human osteoarchaeology*, that is holding a title combining the knowledge of physical/forensic anthropological and archaeological studies. It is therefore clear that the road towards the consideration and use of forensic sciences applied to archaeology or vice versa is still long, unless new courses are created following an increasing interest in this discipline.

Historical background and legal framework

Mention of forensic medicine in the Romanian countries appears as early as the 17th century, under the reigns of Princes (*Voivods*) Matei Basarab (1588–1654) and Vasile Lupu (1595–1661), in Romanian documents such as *The Romanian Book of Rules from Royal Laws* (*Cartea Românească de Invăţătură de la Pravilele Împărăteşti*) (1646) and *The Mending of Law* (*Îndreptarea Legii*) (1652), where clear references are made to the use of expert witnesses in criminal cases (Buda 2012).

In 1865 the first penal code established the role of medical doctors in trials. However, the person who reformed the whole medico-legal system was Professor Mina Minovici (1858–1933), who converted the city morgue in 1892 into the first Medico-Legal Institute

[1] For more information, see: http://www.legmed.ro/?doc=1237833997 (last accessed October 2013).
[2] For more information, see: http://www.legmed.ro/?doc=1237833997 (last accessed October 2013).

Forensic Archaeology: A Global Perspective, First Edition. Edited by W.J. Mike Groen, Nicholas Márquez-Grant and Robert C. Janaway.

(*Institutul de Medicină Legală*) ever known, acknowledging the fact that forensic medicine had to be a separate discipline training forensic specialists (Dumitrascu et al. 1995). His brother, Nicolae Minovici, Professor Mina Minovici's closest collaborator and the creator of the first forensic medicine chair at the University of Cluj-Napoca, was director of the Institute between 1932 and 1938.[3]

After a flourishing period, the Institute created by Minovici risked being demolished by the Romanian Communist Party (*Partidul Comunist Român* – PCR), whose members did not understand the necessity 'of doctors for dead people'. However, the intervention and the efforts of Professor Moise Terbancea, director of the Institute from 1973 to 1989, allowed the institute and its medico-legal network to survive (Dumitrascu et al. 1995).

Forensic institutions and associations

There are several public and private institutions dealing with crime and forensic cases in Romania today. Those establishing guidelines and coordinating the system are mainly based in Bucharest, which represents the core and 'benchmark' for police and tribunals from all over the country.

The National Institute of Legal Medicine (*Institutul Naţional de Medicină Legală* – INML) is the entity establishing legal, organisational and theoretical guidelines for forensic institutes, public and private associations and forensic specialists in Romania. The medico-legal system is in fact based on a pyramidal structure, including 53 institutes and offices coordinated by the INML, which is subordinate to the Superior Counsel of Legal Medicine (*Consiliul Superior de Medicină Legală*). Those institutions all collaborate with the Ministry of Justice, the Ministry of Public Administration and the Ministry of Internal Affairs.[4]

The Forensic Institute (*Institutul de Criminalistică*), a departmental branch of the National Police (*Poliţia Română*), has been recognised by the European Network of Forensic Science Institutes (ENFSI) (Groen, Chapter 25, this volume) since 2005 and, in addition to chemistry and physics laboratories, also has a forensic anthropology and facial reconstruction laboratory.

There are also two official private associations recognised by the government (H.G. nr 1240/2005): the Association of Forensic Scientists of Romania (*Asociaţia Criminaliştilor din România*) and the Romanian Society of Criminology and Forensic Sciences (*Societatea Româna de Criminologie şi Criminalistică*). Both aim to promote research and improve legal and scientific methods within the forensic framework.

Whilst these institutions mainly deal with contemporary criminal cases and carry out research in medical subjects, most humanitarian excavations have been promoted and organised by the Institute for the Investigation of Communist Crimes and the Memory of the Romanian Exile (*Institutul de Investigare a Crimelor Comunismului şi Memoria Exilului Românesc* – IICCMER). This organisation was created in 2009, when the Institute for the Investigation of Communist Crimes (*Institutul de Investigare a Crimelor Comunismului în România* – IICCR) was merged with the National Institute for the Memory of Romanian Exile (*Institutul Naţional pentru Memoria Exilului Românesc* – INMER) with the aim of investigating forgotten crimes and possibly bringing their perpetrators to court (Mark 2010, 284). Among the Institute's main objectives are 'to administer and analyse, in a rigorous and scientific manner, the memory of the Communist Regime in Romania (1947–1989), as well as its consequences' and 'to make public the acts of violence, the abuses and the crimes carried out from the direct order of the Communist Party' (Neamţu and Ţânţariu 2010, 6).

The Institute is directed by a Scientific Council, composed of 14 Romanian and international non-profit members specialising in historical[5] and political science studies, and an Executive Board, again represented by political and historical experts. It is responsible for the coordination of four research departments (Department for Ideology and Culture; Department for the Analysis of Society, Economy and Institutions; Department for Public Policies and Partnerships; and Department for Exile and Minorities) (Neamţu and Ţânţariu 2010, 10–17).

Among the publications edited by academic and private institutions involved in the medico-legal framework, the *Romanian Journal of Legal Medicine*, founded in 1936 by Professor Nicolae Minovici, is the best known Romanian publishing platform for researchers of all branches of forensic science from Romania and other countries. It is interesting to note that its editors clearly declare the journal to be open to contributions from disciplines other than strictly medico-legal sciences, which may present papers and works where forensic and legal aspects have been touched upon, for example human osteoarchaeological papers describing the analysis of modern human skeletal remains (Panaitescu et al. 2008).

[3]For more information, see: http://www.legmed.ro/?doc=1237833847 (last accessed November 2013).

[4]*Raport Asupra Activitatii Retelei de Medicină Legală în Anul 2011*. Romanian Society of Legal Medicine. For more information, see: http://www.legmed.ro/doc/dds2011.pdf (last accessed October 2013).

[5]In Romania those holding a history degree might have an archaeological background and training, or actually be professional archaeologists, as these disciplines are included under the main history department.

Medico-legal 'experts' and expert witnesses

Coroners and medically trained forensic anthropologists can collaborate with the police, or other private or public institutions. As a general trend, it looks as if those who have a medical degree are considered more suitable for duties related to the identification and analysis of human remains in a criminal context.

When cases are taken to court, the system can be flexible, and several specialists can play the role of expert witness (with the right requirements established by the Law, art. 201 of the Penal Code), but archaeologists and archaeologically trained physical anthropologists/ human osteoarchaeologists are not yet considered possible candidates for such a role. However, medico-legal experts are usually called as expert witnesses when the police deal with crime scenes that need the intervention of experts in human remains. Their role is liminal as it involves the application and the knowledge of both medical and legal principles.

In order to play the role of expert witness, a medico-legal medical doctor needs to meet some minimum requirements, which include a title in legal medicine, at least 5 years of activity as a specialist and being a member of the Romanian Society of Legal Medicine. They should also be clean from any legal infraction that could affect the practice of this profession and be able to profess the medical activity in Romania in conformity with the country's legislation. Those who wish to act as expert witnesses need to take an exam organised by the INML which, if they pass, allows them to be included in a list of recommended expert witnesses, and this will be communicated to the court and might be used in forensic cases.[6]

Crime trends and the role of coroners

In 2012 the dependents of medico-legal institutions in Romania conducted almost 20,000 autopsies, more than half of them represented by victims of violent death. These statistics include the analysis of 102 skeletonised remains and age estimations for 487 cases.[7] Table 16.1 shows a summary of the number of victims per type of accident/violent crime from 1996, 1997, 2007 and 2012, showing a decrease in crime trends.

Last year's INML final report in particular laments the government's lack of interest in coroners' working conditions around the country. It is in fact stated that they are often forced to carry out autopsies in 'more or less improvised conditions' and under a very high risk of biological contamination, demonstrated by the increasing number of staff affected by TBC and hepatitis: a situation apparently completely ignored by the authorities (*Raport RNML* 2012).[8] It is a complicated issue in a country facing financial, political and cultural crisis – like many other European countries today.

Forensic archaeology as a means of restoring the memory of silent victims

World War II (WWII), the Holocaust and the rise of the Romanian Communist Party caused the persecution and the violent death of thousands of opponents and minorities. The 1989 Revolution, which was a strikingly violent one in Romania, also caused hundreds of deaths and scenes of violence from both sides that are still impressed on people's minds today.

Table 16.1 Mortal crimes/accidents as listed in the official reports of the Romanian Legal Medicine Institutes.

Type of crime/accident	Year			
	1996	**1997**	**2007**	**2012**
Homicide and mortal lesions	1034	1047	565	489
Road accidents	3699	3344	3152	2163
Work accidents	479	432	372	219
Voluntary and involuntary intoxication		1246		
Post-partum and post-abortum deaths	63	56		
Suicides	2933	3474	2705	2753

Source: Adapted from the Reţeaua Naţională de Medicină Legală website.

[6]For more information, see: http://www.legmed.ro/?doc=1237739799& (last accessed October 2013).
[7]For more information, see: http://www.legmed.ro/?doc=1237824528 (last accessed October 2013).
[8]For more information, see: http://www.legmed.ro/?doc=1237824528 (last accessed October 2013).

The promotion of investigations aimed at finding these victims' remains and reburying them in a respectful and dignified manner was – and still is – of vital importance to their families and the public. The last couple of decades have been astonishingly important for activists and associations involved in the identification of both perpetrators and victims of crimes against humanity. Historical surveys, interviews of witnesses, fieldwork, conferences and workshops (Neamţu and Ţânţariu 2010, 66–96) have been conducted by volunteers and specialists, who have shown a strong commitment and resolution in not letting the memories of those actions fade away and be left unpunished, as will be seen in the following paragraphs.

The IICCMER special investigations

The IICCR since 2005 and the IICCMER since 2009 have organised inquiries often resulting in archaeological fieldwork aiming at locating and possibly excavating and recovering the mortal remains of people arbitrarily killed in particular in the years between 1945 and 1989 (Neamţu and Ţânţariu 2010, 26). The Institute's experts and collaborators have conducted special investigations to identify various kinds of burial sites, including execution victims' individual or double burials, penitentiary cemeteries and mass graves. However, for sites in the proximity of or within cemeteries, in some cases the continuity of use of the cemetery after the 1950s and the depth of the prisoners' graves made it impossible to conduct archaeological excavations which would have taken an unaffordable amount of time and money in order to be conducted fully.

Between the 1940s and the late 1960s penitentiaries around the country were dedicated to the retention and the re-education of individuals considered to be criminals and a menace to the state – mostly intellectuals and political opponents. These were perceived as politically dangerous individuals and were therefore 'legally' secluded in penitentiaries. In some of those institutes of detention torture, physical and psychological punishment, humiliation and starvation were everyday practices as part of this re-educational programme.[9]

The best-known penitentiaries with the harshest conditions, and where the most 'dangerous' prisoners were held, were those in Aiud, Sighet, Gherla and Râmnicu Sărat. An unofficial estimate based on eye witnesses and local obituary documents claims that between 1945 and 1964 *c.* 700 convicts (half of them convicted for political reasons) died in Aiud.[10]

The Sighetu Marmaţiei excavations

In 2006 the IICCR promoted the excavation of human remains from the Cemetery of the Poor (*Cimitirul Săracilor*) in Sighetu Marmaţiei (Maramureş, north-western Romania), a multicultural and multi-ethnic area, with Hungarian and Jewish communities among the largest in the country during the 1930s–1940s (Rotariu 2002). Within a couple of decades, this village experienced a double tragedy: first the creation of two ghettos under the Hungarian administration for the reclusion and isolation of 12,000 Jews, who were eventually deported to extermination camps, and then, at the beginning of the 1950s, the use of the prison for political convicts (Petrov and Budeancă 2006).

The IICCR intended to carry out a forensic archaeological excavation at the Sighet penitentiary in order to recover and identify the remains of political convicts whose bodies had been apparently scattered among those of the orphans and other individuals in the Cemetery of the Poor. The excavation was conducted by two archaeologists, Dr Gheorghe Petrov (National Museum of History of Transylvania, *Muzeul Naţional de Istorie a Transilvaniei* – MNIT) and Mr Horaţiu Groza (History Museum, Turda – *Muzeul de Istorie, Turda*), helped by expert members of the IICCR, the police and forensic specialists. Two trenches were opened in the south-east area of the cemetery, yielding respectively 6 and 12 graves which contained adult and juvenile individuals. Some of the adult burials showed anomalous characteristics, such as orientation and position of the body against the Christian tradition (Petrov and Budeancă 2006). Meanwhile, Dr Cosmin Budeancă, an IICCMER specialist in social history, and the local police conducted interviews of former guardians and employees, and gained access to the memoirs of one of the convicts at the time when the crimes were committed (Petrov and Budeancă 2006, 3).

Although the excavation did not allow the identification of those whose names were included in the list of political prisoners, it provided information about the disrespectful and approximate burial of some of the dead. The bones recovered at this site did not have a name, and they will probably never be identified. As a result, the efforts of the IICCMER and its supporters allowed the creation of the Sighet Memorial to the Victims of Communism and the Resistance (*Memorialul Victimelor Comunismului şi al Rezistenţei*), which is the first and best-known example in Romania of the attempt to create a 'sanctuary' for the mortal remains of victims of

[9]Source: IICCMER. For more information, see: http://www.iiccr.ro/pdf/ro/arhiva_documente/deplasare_salcia.pdf (last accessed 24 December 2013).

[10]Source: IICCMER. For more information, see: http://www.iiccr.ro/ro/presa/comunicate/comunicate_de_presa_2012/iiccmer_demareaza_o_campanie_de_investigatii_arheologice/ (last accessed October 2013).

violent repression, and which reminds us that the absence of evidence should never allow the loss of the memory of crimes against humanity.

The Ostrov labour colony

In 2007 another special investigation was launched for the identification of the burial site of prisoners from the labour camp of Ostrov (Brăila, south-east Romania), where in 1959 alone 5000 political convicts were detained and used for various forced labour duties.

It had been reported to the IICCR that crimes against humanity at the camp intensified between 1952 and 1953, when unmotivated violence, punishments, abuses and the profanation of the convicts' dead bodies are just some of the abominations described by witnesses. It was acknowledged that 63 convicts died following torture and punishment, and many others were left scarred for life.[11]

However, no information has been provided so far on the final results of this investigation.

The hospital penitentiary of Târgu Ocna

Between 2011 and 2013 the IICCMER and the MNIT promoted a series of campaigns aimed at locating and excavating graves containing the mortal remains of former political prisoners in the areas surrounding the cemetery of Târgu Ocna's (Bacău county) hospital prison.[12] Specialists involved included archaeologists Dr Gheorghe Petrov, Mr Paul Scrobota (History Museum Aiud – *Museul de Istorie Aiud*) and Mr Horaţiu Groza, and historian Dr Marius Oprea (Director of the IICCMER Special Investigations bureau).

Sources showed that between 1950 and 1954 at least 54 people considered 'politically dangerous' died in this correction institute, and many more up to the mid 1960s. The building was used to detain prisoners affected by TBC until 1977, when it changed its function to an institute for mental illnesses; a function it retained until 1997. The identification of their burial place was quite difficult given the high concentration of graves and the cemetery's continuous use since then. Moreover, the political convicts' bodies were buried without coffins or a cross indicating the grave location. However, the burials were eventually identified in 2011 and resulted in a still ongoing series of excavation campaigns, the results of which are still due to be published.[13]

The Periprava labour colony

In September 2013 the IICCMER organised the excavation of the north-west corner of the Periprava cemetery in order to locate the burials of individuals detained in the labour colony of Periprava village (Tulcea, Dobrogea region). The multidisciplinary team included Dr Dan Ţălnaru (IICCMER general manager until 2013), lawyer Dr Oana Axinia, historians Mr Andrei Lascu, Mr Dumitru Lăcătuşu and Mr Constantin Vasilescu, and archaeologists Dr Constantin Băjenaru and Mr Dan Vasilescu.[14]

A double burial and three individual burials containing the skeletons of prisoners who died between 1958 and 1963 were identified and excavated (Băjenaru and Vasilescu 2013).

The double burial, coded M1, immediately showed several anomalies: the two bodies uncovered, bones in anatomical position, were in fact oriented east–west (contrary to the Christian tradition) (Figure 16.1). The second skeleton's skull in particular showed dislocation of the cervical vertebrae, evidencing that the body was forced into the coffin. Moreover, metallic wires were found at the lower limb level, where the legs were crossed, suggesting that they might have been tied up during disposal of the body (Băjenaru and Vasilescu 2013, 2).

On the contrary, the other three individual burials were oriented west–east, according to the Christian practice, although it was obvious that the bodies had been placed in the grave with very little care or in an unusual way, such as the individual from context M3. This individual's head was resting on the right side, chin facing the south, the left arm parallel to the body, while the right arm was bent and the hand resting dorsally under the chin (Figure 16.2). The right foot was missing, but no further interpretation has been provided by the investigators at the time of writing (Băjenaru and Vasilescu 2013, 3).

Eventually, all skeletons showed evidence of a negligent burial, although M1 displayed more obvious anomalies (Băjenaru and Vasilescu 2013, 4). A detailed physical anthropological analysis of the bones and DNA tests are to follow, and will provide more information about the identity of those individuals, which so far are considered by the investigators to be probable convicts.

This case is a brilliant example of how a forensic archaeological investigation can be successfully conducted with

[11]Source: IICCMER. For more information, see: www.iiccr.ro/pdf/ro/arhiva.../deplasare_salcia.pdf (last accessed November 2013).

[12]Source: IICCMER For more information, see: http://www.iiccr.ro/en/press/press_releases/iiccmer_starts_a_new_archaeological_investigation_in_search_for_the_political_prisoners_dead_at_targu_ocna/ (last accessed October 2013).

[13]Source: IICCMER For more information, see: http://www.iiccr.ro/en/press/press_releases/iiccmer_starts_a_new_archaeological_investigation_in_search_for_the_political_prisoners_dead_at_targu_ocna/ (last accessed October 2013).

[14]Source: IICCMER For more information, see: http://www.iiccr.ro/en/press/press_releases/iiccmer_starts_a_new_archaeological_investigation_in_search_for_the_political_prisoners_dead_at_targu_ocna/ (last accessed November 2013).

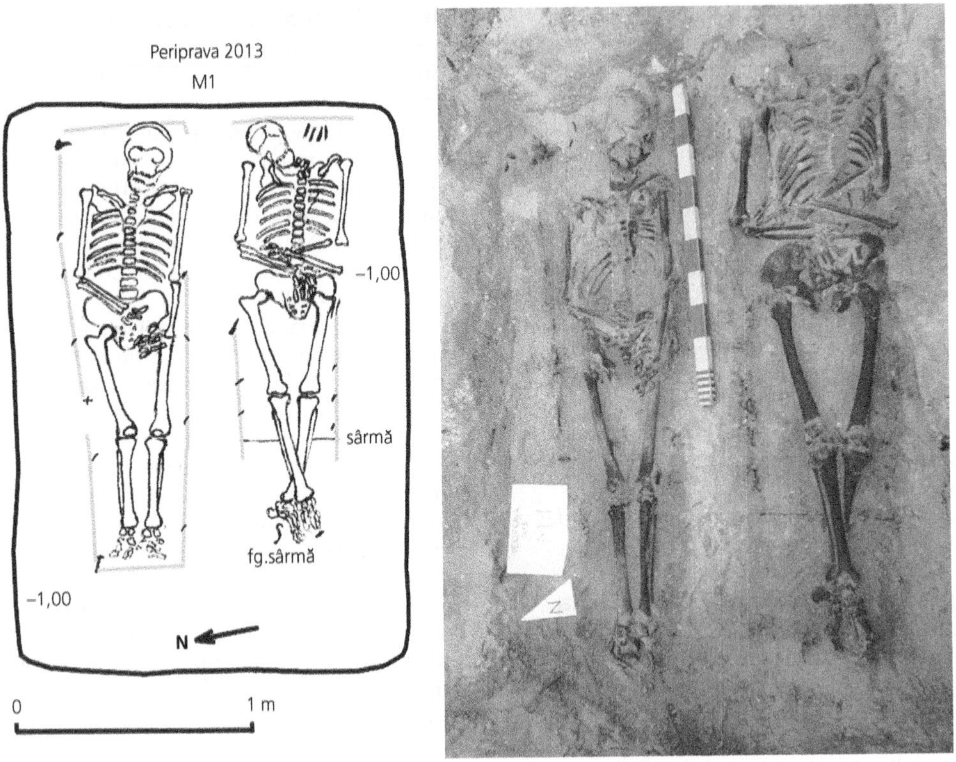

Figure 16.1 Plan and photograph of context M1 (Image courtesy: Băjenaru and Vasilescu 2013, 8/9).

Figure 16.2 Photo showing context M3: note missing right foot and the right arm's unusual position (Image courtesy: Băjenaru and Vasilescu 2013, 14).

the contribution of archaeologists, historians and medico-legal experts. The General Prosecutor will now be responsible for the prosecution and punishment of Periprava's former commander, who is at the time of writing 85 years old and still free despite his crimes committed at the labour camp: he is in fact accused of causing the deaths of more than 100 people.

Identification and recovery of remains of victims of summary executions

Since 2005 more than 20 victims from individual or double graves, all males of different ages, executed alone or in small groups, have been identified. A few cases will be herein reported, mostly from 2007, the year when many successful exhumation and identification campaigns were finalised.

Between 2 and 4 July 2007 in the village of Glodghileşti (Burjuc, Hunedoara, western Romania) a search for a supposed victim of the Securitate soldiers was launched by members of the IICCR (Dr Andrei Muraru, Dr Cosmin Budeancă and Dr Mihail Bumbeş), IICCR collaborators (archaeologists Dr Gheorghe Petrov, Mr Paul Scrobota and Mr Horaţiu Groza), and legal and forensic specialists from Timişoara and Deva. The information provided by eye witnesses and living relatives allowed the reconstruction of the events that resulted in the fatal shooting of miller Iosif Orşa by two Securitate officers dressed in civilian clothes (Muraru et al. 2007). A bullet was found in the abdominal area – as one of the eye witnesses had stated – and showed that the injury was not fatal. According to the victim's relatives and eye witnesses, in fact, the family was not allowed to take care of the man's injuries. He was eventually left to die, and then buried in a location not far from his own home. He was and still is remembered as the 'unknown hero' by people in the village (Muraru et al. 2007).

Again in 2007, between April 24 and 25, another important investigation was opened in the Bistriţa-Năsăud county by a team composed of military prosecuting authorities, the police, forensic experts from Bucharest, coroners from Bistriţa, archaeologists (Dr Alexandru Matei, deceased, former director of the Zalău History Museum, Andrei Lascu and Mihai Bumbes) and IICCR members (Dr Cosmin Budeancă and Dr Marius Oprea, Director of the IICCR at the time). They planned and organised the systematic forensic excavation of two burial sites, located in two nearby villages and respectively containing the remains of four young individuals aged 16–20 and of two older individuals, all males, summarily executed on the same day, 9 March 1950 by the Securitate soldiers (Petrov and Budeancă 2007, 1). The excavation was supervised by Dr Gheorghe Petrov and Mr Horaţiu Groza and allowed the identification of the victims, who were all shot in the head and buried at the same location where the executions had taken place.

In October 2007, in Odoreu (Satu Mare), archaeologists Dr Alexandru Matei, Mr Paul Scrobota and Mr Horaţiu Groza performed an excavation aimed at recovering the remains of the civilian Tira Gheza, who was executed with three other locals for refusing to be sent to work in the Soviet Union by the local party members on 14 August 1949 (Matei 2007). Coroner Petru Varodi identified a blunt force trauma to the back of the skull, and a gunshot hole to the right scapula, confirming that the man's death was the result of a violent action (Matei 2007).

In a recent case, the body of war veteran and anti-Communist partisan Ioan Ienea was exhumed before his relatives, 60 years after his unjustified execution in his own home, in Caraş-Severin, south-western Romania, by the Security troops. The IICCMER appointed Dr Gheorghe Petrov (MNIT), Mr Paul Scrobota and Mr Horaţiu Groza for the excavation of the burial site. The recovered human remains showed evidence of Ioan Ienea's arbitrary murder by the Securitate troops in 1950.[15]

These cases are not the only ones, and more families and public and private institutions are now interested over the last decade in the reopening of cold cases or the exhumation of burials in the attempt to shed light on the dynamics and motivations (if there were any) that led to the execution of those individuals.

Discovery and excavation of Holocaust mass graves

The search for Holocaust victims in Romania is a very 'hot', recent task, and a more sensitive subject than in other countries where this kind of investigation has been carried out more intensively and almost immediately after WWII. Some publications have analysed and discussed the Romanian Holocaust and the deportation of minorities in general (Ioanid 1993; Ioanid et al. 2009), but there is still no certainty of the number of individuals imprisoned and killed as a consequence of the application of racial laws in Romania.

The 'Elie Wiesel' National Institute for the Study of the Romanian Holocaust (*Institutul Naţional pentru Studierea Holocaustului din România 'Elie Wiesel'*) is today the official

[15]For more information, see: http://www.iiccr.ro/ro/presa/comunicate/comunicate_de_presa_2013/osemintele_unei_alte_victime_a_securitatii_deshumate_in_cadrul_unei_actiuni_a_iiccmer_ioan_ienea/ (last accessed October 2013).

body dealing with research activities, and trying to shed light on this dark chapter in the history of the country. It is believed that between 280,000 and 380,000 Romanian and Ukrainian Jews died during the Holocaust period in the Romanian territory (Friling et al. 2004). This is one of the highest – maybe the highest – number of victims of Jewish origin in Europe. The aforementioned Institute promoted in 2011 the archaeological excavation of a mass grave in a forest near the city of Popricani (Iaşi County) (Ungureanu 2011, 11), directed by Dr Adrian Cioflâncă, researcher at the History Institute 'A.D. Xenopol' of Iaşi and member of the 'Elie Wiesel' Institute, and Dr Neculai Bolohan (University of History 'Alexandru Ioan Cuza', Iaşi), who coordinated the archaeological team.[16] This resulted in the exhumation of the bones of 36 individuals of Jewish origin: 15 males, 9 females and 12 children/adolescents (Florian 2013, 168). The osteological analysis revealed several blunt force, blade and gunshot injuries to their bones, and that their murder was caused by a violent attack carried out with several kinds of weapons including blades and guns.

Investigations also showed that they were all fairly wealthy individuals, and that they were killed at the same spot where the bodies were disposed of (Florian 2013). The case was brought to the Bucharest Military Appeal Court in 2012 in order to legally and officially recognise the Ion Antonescu (1882–1946) government's genocide charges against Jewish communities in Romania for the first time since 1941. This was an important historical step: in fact, thousands of people are believed to have been massacred by Romanian and German soldiers in this area in June 1941, and consequently much fieldwork can – and hopefully will – still be carried out.

The application of forensic methods in archaeology

The recovery of human skeletal remains by a team of archaeologists (University of Alba Iulia, Archaeology Department) from the Lumea Noua site (Middle Basin of the Mureş River) and their analysis, conducted by the forensic anthropological laboratory at the 'Mina Minovici' National Institute of Legal Medicine (INML) (Panaitescu et al. 2008), is a good example of the Institute's journal editor's willingness to promote the collaboration between specialists from different backgrounds, but aiming to obtain the same results. In this case study, the joint work of archaeologists and medically trained forensic anthropologists allowed the interpretation of a very peculiar context and the identification of taphonomic and peri-mortem damage to the bones.

Between 2003 and 2005 a large quantity of human bones was recovered and radiocarbon-dated 5570±40 BP – 5650±40 BP (*c.* 4548–*c.* 4341 BC, 95% confidence interval). These bones included cranial fragments showing evidence of cranial traumatic injuries and were recovered together with a small stone axe.

The excavation was carefully and systematically conducted in order to allow the recording of spatial and quantitative information. The laboratory conducted the osteological analysis with the awareness of the excavation's results, which had showed a complicated context including several individuals whose bones were commingled. It was eventually concluded that the depressed fractures and abrasions on the cranial vault of some individuals were the result of interpersonal violence or ritual ceremonies (Panaitescu et al. 2008, 267–268).

This case study is an example of how violence in the past can be reconstructed thanks to the confluence of archaeology and forensic sciences, and more will hopefully be seen in the near future in this country.

Future perspectives

Historical and demographic information could be recovered in larger amounts if forensic techniques were applied in archaeological contexts. As an example, the numerous late medieval cemeteries being excavated across Romania have often yielded family tombs or mass graves where human remains were simply exposed, photographed and recovered without following a specific protocol. Spatial recording, numbering of the bones based on operational guidelines, and the meticulous recording and measuring of the bones *in situ* are only a few of the actions that are usually not taken.

The main reason for this is that most excavations involving urban cemeteries are rescue interventions, which have to be conducted in a very limited amount of time, and usually without the participation of physical anthropologists, who are generally referred to when the skeletal remains have already been exposed, lifted and taken to the processing laboratory.

Romanian researchers have shown quite an early interest and originality in the forensic field. It is therefore hoped that a future improvement in the critical financial situation will allow the allocation of more funds for academic research and the introduction of new courses of study and training for specialists in 'new' disciplines such as forensic archaeology.

As shown in this paper, there is still a strong distinction between archaeologists, physical anthropologists and medico-legal specialists in Romania. This, however,

[16]For more information, see: http://www.ziaruldeiasi.ro/local/zeci-de-evrei-masacrati-si-ingropati-in-padurea-popricani~ni724p (last accessed November 2013).

has not impeded public and private institutions and specialists from collaborating and obtaining excellent results in both archaeological and forensic investigations, helping to shed light not only on the most recent, but also on the ancient history of this country.

The creation of new courses and professional figures able to apply both forensic and archaeological methods will definitely help the development of these new disciplines and allow Romanian specialists to become more involved in the European forensic research network.

References

Băjenaru, C. and Vasilescu, D. 2013. *Raport Privind Diagnosticul Archeologic Efectuat în Cimitirul de la Periprava, Com. C.A. Rosetti, Jud. Tulcea.* Rapoarte IICCMER. Available at: http://www.iiccr.ro/pdf/ro/Raport%20Periprava%20sep2013.pdf (last accessed 9 October 2013).

Buda, O. 2012. Vasile Lupu and Matei Basarab rulings: Cultural identity and forensic provisions, 1646, 1652. *Romanian Journal of Forensic Science* 82(4), 1073–1076.

Cox, M., Hanson, I., Flavel, A., Laver, J. and Wessling, R. 2008. *The Scientific Investigation of Mass Graves: Towards Protocols and Standard Operating Procedure.* Cambridge, Cambridge University Press.

Dumitrascu, D. L., Shampo, M. A. and Kyle R. A. 1995. The Institute of Forensic Medicine established by Dr Mina Minovici. *Mayo Clinic Proceedings*, 70(8), 776.

Dupras, T., Schultz, J., Wheeler, S. and Williams, L. 2006. *Forensic Recovery of Human Remains. Archaeological Approaches.* Boca Raton, Taylor and Francis Group.

Florian, A. 2013. Archive: The Holocaust of Romanian Jews. A new legal document. *Sfera Politicii* XXI 173(1), 168–177.

Friling, T., Ioanid, R. and Ionescu, M. E. (eds.) 2004. *Comisia Internaţională Pentru Studierea Holocaustului în România.* Raport final. Iaşi, Polirom.

Hunter, J. and Cox, M. 2005. *Forensic Archaeology: Advances in Theory and Practice.* London, Routledge.

Ioanid, R. 1993. *The Holocaust in Romania: The Iaşi Pogrom of June 1941.* Cambridge, Cambridge University Press.

Ioanid, R., Kelso, M. and Cioaba, M. L. (eds.) 2009. *The Tragedy of the Deported Roma Population (1942-1945).* Iaşi, Polirom.

Mark, J. 2010. What remains? Anti-communism, forensic archaeology, and the retelling of the national past in Lithuania and Romania. *Relics and Remains, Past and Present* Supplements 5, 276–300.

Matei, A. 2007. *Raport Privind Exhumarea lui Tira Gheza din Odoreu, Satu Mare, Executat de Securitate în 16 August 1949.* Rapoarte IICCMER. Available at: http://www.iiccr.ro/ro/proiecte/investigatii_speciale/raport_tira_gheza/ (last accessed 28 November 2013).

Muraru, A., Budeancă, C. and Bumbeş, M. 2007. *Misterul Unei Execuţii Sumare a Securităţii din 1950, Dezlegat de Institutul de Investigare a Crimelor Comunismului în România. 'Eroul Necunoscut', aşa cum era Ştiut Iosif Orşa în Zonă, a Fost Exhumat de IICCR. Proba Incontestabilă a Execuţiei: un Glonţ de Calibrul 7,62 mm Găsit între Rămăşiţele Pământeşti.* Available at: http://www.iiccr.ro/pdf/ro/investigatii_speciale/iosif_orsa.pdf (last accessed October 2013).

Neamţu, M. and Ţânţariu, A. -L. 2010. *5 Years of Activity. The Institute for the Investigation of Communist Crimes and for the Memory of the Romanian Exile.* Rapoarte IICCMER. Available at: http://www.iiccr.ro/index.html/about_iiccr/5_years_of_activity/?lang=en&section=about_iiccr/5_years_of_activity (last accessed 28 November 2013).

Panaitescu, V., Roşu, M., Gligor, M., Matei, L. and Sîrbu, A. 2008. Cranial fractures identified in a late Neolithic population, exhumed from the Middle Basin of the Mureş river—'Lumea Nouă' (Romania). *Romanian Journal of Legal Medicine* 4, 261–268.

Petrov, G. and Budeancă, C. 2006. *Raport Privind Cercetările Arheologice Desfasurate în Cimitirul Saracilor din Sighetu Marmaţiei (Jud. Maramureş) în Perioada 2-4 Noiembrie 2006.* Rapoarte IICCMER. Available at: http://www.iiccr.ro/pdf/ro/investigatii_speciale/raport_sighet.pdf (last accessed 10 December 2014).

Petrov, G. and Budeancă, C. 2007. *Raport Privind Sondajele Arheologice Efectuate în Satul Halmasau, Com. Spermezeu şi pe Dealul Sasa-Poieni (Jud. Bistriţa-Nasaud) 24 - 25.04.2007.* Rapoarte IICCMER. Available at: http://www.iiccr.ro/ro/proiecte/investigatii_speciale/raport_halmasau/ (last accessed 28 November 2013).

Raport RNML 2012—Raport Asupra Activităţii Retelei de Medicină Legală în Anul 2011. Reţeaua Naţională de Medicină Legală. Available at: http://www.legmed.ro/doc/dds2011.pdf (last accessed October 2013).

Rotariu, T. (ed.) 2002. *Recensmântul Din 1941.* Transilvania, Editura Presa Universitară Clujeană.

Ungureanu, E. 2011. *Raport de Activitate Pentru 2011.* Ministerul Culturii şi Patrimoniului Naţional, Institutul Naţional pentru Studierea Holocaustului din România 'Elie Wiesel'.

CHAPTER 17

Forensic archaeology in the Russian Federation

Alexey Abramov[1], Elizaveta Veselovskaya[2], Alexey Dolgov[3], Asya V. Engovatova[4], Maria B. Mednikova[5], Sergey Nikitin[3] and Azrat Safarov[6]

[1] *Department of Biomedical Research of Main Department of Criminalistics, Investigation Committee of Russia, Moscow, Russia*

[2] *Laboratory of Anthropological Reconstruction, Institute of Ethnology and Anthropology, Russian Academy of Sciences, Moscow, Russia*

[3] *Department of Forensic Medical Criminology, Moscow Regional State Bureau of Forensic Medical Expertise, Moscow, Russia*

[4] *Institute of Archaeology, Russian Academy of Sciences, Moscow, Russia*

[5] *Department of Theory and Methods of Archaeology, Institute of Archaeology of Russian Academy of Sciences, Moscow, Russia*

[6] *SARE Centre, Russian State University for the Humanities, Moscow, Russia*

Introduction

Today forensic archaeology, defined as the involvement of physical anthropological and archaeological experts in fieldwork, does not exist in Russia as a separate science. We are currently seeing only the initial stages of its development, and there are several problems it is facing. In this chapter the authors try to explain the methods which they believe should prompt faster development of this discipline in Russia. They also highlight the problems hindering the development of this science.

The authors feel obliged to discuss some people and several interesting studies which have been conducted within the last decades in Russia and to share their thoughts on the prospects of development of this sphere. These cases demonstrate both the positive and negative sides of forensic expert collaboration in Russia today, as well as the lack of field specialists in archaeology for medico-legal cases.

The medico-legal system in Russia and its role in forensic archaeology

At the time of writing, forensic archaeology, as a medico-legal discipline, is not practiced in Russia; neither the national police, nor the forensic institutions, nor the Investigative Committee of the Russian Federation (*Следственный Комитет Российской Федерации*) has forensic archaeological departments, and this discipline has no legal or judicial status. Forensic archaeology exists only within academic forensic and research institutions. All of its elements exist independently, and their interaction is more often observed at the level of the personal initiative of certain experts, rather than through legal means (there are no legal algorithms of interaction).

In Russia there is Archaeology and Forensic Medicine, with a division dealing with forensic anthropology, consisting only of medical doctors and social and physical anthropologists, providing theoretical support. The police also have a forensic department, as does the Investigative Committee of the Russian Federation (investigating significant crimes including murders). However, none of these bodies are united, and their interaction is strictly regulated.

Let's consider the legal system in the area of criminal law as applied to the most common scenario: the discovery of a burial which could potentially be a criminal case. In this case the actions and procedures of law enforcement, investigative, judicial and expert bodies are strictly regulated.

- *Step one* – The local unit of the regional police, having received such information, sets off for the place of discovery to verify the accuracy of the information.
- *Step two* – The investigative team arrives at the place of discovery, led by an investigator of the Investigative Committee. The group consists of a police criminalist from the forensic centre of the Ministry of the Interior of the Russian Federation (*эксперт-криминалист экспертно-криминалистического центра – МВД* (MVD)), and at this stage of the examination, working as a Scene of Crime Officer, a forensic pathologist from the forensic medical service. The forensic medical service is a separate structure independent of the police and clinical pathology; it is a separate division of medical ministry, based in local and regional bureaus.

Forensic Archaeology: A Global Perspective, First Edition. Edited by W.J. Mike Groen, Nicholas Márquez-Grant and Robert C. Janaway.

The group also includes a police officer from the operative investigation department (a police officer of the regional criminal investigation service (*следователь оперативно-следственного отдела*)). According to protocol:

- The investigator from the Investigative Committee draws up a report of the inspection of the scene.
- The Scene of Crime Officer (Police Criminalist) takes photographs, fixes the traces and secures the exhibits.
- The forensic medical expert inspects and describes everything related to the corpse or human remains; he passes this information to the investigator, who registers it in the protocol.
- The police officer from the operative investigation department (the criminal investigation service of the Russian criminal police (*оперативно-розыскная часть уголовного розыска криминальной полиции*)) interviews witnesses and draws up a layout of the scene or the place of discovery of the corpse. Usually the corpse is discovered by a witness, who reports this to the police. After that the police initiate an exhumation. In most cases the body is exhumed by an ordinary (archaeologically untrained) worker. When examining the scene of crime, the Scene of Crime Officer produces a sketch (not to scale), which may include the dimensions of the scene. These dimensions are fixed in the protocol of examination. The sketch of the scene reflects the surrounding buildings and place in body position or apartment scheme. There are no specific operating procedures or accreditation standards used by the police or medical examiners at this stage.

- *Step three* – The human remains are sent to a regional morgue, where they are examined by the forensic medical expert (forensic pathologist). The report is submitted either to the police or to the regional investigation department.
- *Step four* – The forensic medical expert may send part of the skeleton (if the corpse is skeletonised) for research to the medical forensic (or other) department, to establish a biological profile and the prescription of the burial. He or she may also send partial remains to the investigator. The procedure is defined by the investigator in this case. The remaining bones of the skeleton may be buried.
- *Step five* – If it is established that the burial is criminal or its prescription, subject to the examination report provided by the forensic pathologist (forensic anthropologist), does not exceed 15 years, a criminal case is opened (if there are signs of criminal death or the person is unidentified) or an investigation check is initiated. If the burial is older than 15 years, an investigation is not usually conducted and the remains are reburied in a local cemetery as the remains of an unknown person. Such cases occur in Russia rather frequently, and clandestine graves may be found, for instance, on construction sites, or in gardens or parks which used to be cemeteries years ago. Usually it is the forensic experts and police criminal investigators who attend the scene.

In compliance with the scheme of interactions, experts in the field of forensic anthropology (forensic medical criminologists) or other physical anthropologists and archaeologists are not involved in the study, search and excavation of a clandestine grave or a deposition site.

As can be seen, experts in forensic anthropology or archaeology are not usually attracted to the study of burial sites. They only attend and examine the scene when the burial is either a mass grave or a disaster. Subject to the examination protocol, forensic anthropologists participate in cases of disasters or mass grave exhumation. If they are engaged in the research, it is only in the final stages, which seems wrong to the authors.

Case studies

In this section the authors describe several real cases that demonstrate possible scenarios of the sequence of events and schemes of interaction of experts of different types. It also shows the value of such disciplines and interaction and how these can be applied to future cases of criminal investigation. These cases have been helpful in promoting the disciplines through the media.

Case study 1: Examination of the remains of the Romanovs (the Russian Imperial family)

This is probably a unique case for Russia where examination procedures are performed by a team of experts from different fields of expertise working together on a legal basis.

The place of burial was determined by historical documents detailing the shooting and burial, and also by the contribution of Alexander Avdonin and Geliy Ryabov – volunteers, who in 1979 initiated a secret excavation. Their excavation revealed human remains, after which they concealed the excavation and kept the information secret until the early 1990s (Ryabov 1998).

The forensic examination was ordered by Dr V. Volkov, Chief Assistant Prosecutor of the Sverdlovsk Region, on 23 August 1991. The order was issued to the Chief Forensic Bureau of the Russian Ministry of Public Health and Sverdlovsk Regional Bureau of Forensics. The case was initiated due to political reasons, the Soviet Union ending in 1991.

In August 1993, criminal proceedings in the case of the discovery of unidentified skeletal remains were initiated and taken over by the Office of the Prosecutor General of the Russian Federation.

However, in spite of the participation of an expert in archaeology, Dr L. Koryakova, the first steps in the investigation were taken hastily and without due care. The remains were first removed from the burial site (Ganina Yama, a 9 foot (c. 2.75 m) deep pit in the Four Brothers mine near the village of Koptyaki, 15 km north of Yekaterinburg) by forensic experts, including forensic anthropologists. Unfortunately, certain measures to protect the bones were not taken (Figure 17.1).

To deal with the challenge of identifying the remains, the Chief Forensic Expert of the Russian Ministry of Public Health, Dr Vitaliy Tomilin, was allowed to invite leading experts, both Russian and from abroad, to assist in the research. About 50 volunteer specialists from Moscow, St. Petersburg, Voronezh, Kiev, Saratov, Krasnoyarsk and other regions of Russia officially participated in forensic studies of the case.

Forensic anthropological analysis

A separate study and inventory of all skeletal items was carried out, with the aim of obtaining information regarding the sex, age and height, as well as the number of persons buried, and their anthropological and individual features (Figures 17.2 and 17.3).

The experts used a range of approved forensic methodologies (macroscopic and microscopic) accepted in Russia. These methodologies differ from the procedures applied in other countries. There are no published protocols for physical/forensic anthropological examination in Russia. The experts choose therefore methodologies and techniques that seem appropriate for each case. However, all used methodologies and

Figure 17.1 Non-archaeological exhumation of the remains of the Romanovs.

Figure 17.2 Preliminary examination, registration and restoration of the skeletal remains, delivered to the experts from the place of burial.

Figure 17.3 These works were performed in August–October 1991. All bones (totalling over 700 objects) were marked into 10 indexed groups.

Table 17.1 Biological profile of the individuals buried as revealed by information obtained from their skeletons.

Skeleton number	Sex	Age (years)	Stature (cm)	Ancestry
1	Female	40–50	164–168	Caucasoid (European)
2	Male	51–60 or more	171–177	Caucasoid (European)
3	Female	20–25	161–165	Caucasoid (European)
4	Male	About 50	165–169	Caucasoid (European)
5	Female	About 20	166–169	Caucasoid (European)
6	Female	20–24	162–166	Caucasoid (European)
7	Female	40–50	163–168	Caucasoid (European)
8	Probably male	40–50	163–167	Not established
9	Male	Over 60	173–180	Caucasoid (European)

techniques are based on commonly accepted attributes of sexual dimorphism and evidence of bone growth and degeneration (e.g. Pashkova 1963; Tomilin 2000).

This stage of the examination started in October 1991 and was completed in June 1992. From the biological profiles the experts concluded that the skeletal remains submitted for examination belonged to nine persons (Table 17.1).

However, at that stage of the examination it was impossible to match the bones to their corresponding skeletons. This omission could have been made during the removal of the remains from the burial site. At first only large bones were removed, after which the grave was refilled. At the second exhumation, which took place in October 1991, a forensic expert from Krasnoyarsk, Mr Vyacheslav Lysiy, examined 16 m^2 of soil and found over 250 more objects. The remains were washed and screened (screen mesh 4–5 mm), and a large quantity of teeth, bones, fragments of bones, clothes and bullets were found (Abramov 1994). There were also ceramic chips, which was in accordance with published information from the state archives that the Romanovs' murderers used an acid kept in ceramic containers, in order to conceal the evidence (the bodies). Chips from these containers were found in the mass grave discovered in the Ganina Yama pit. This discovery gave the crime scene investigation (CSI) experts proof that that was the mass grave for which they were searching.

Comparison of biological attributes revealed similarities between examined and presumptive objects but failed to positively identify the skeletons (Table 17.2). Comparisons of ante-mortem information and the biological profiles of the skeletons failed to identify Tsarevich Alexei Nikolaevich of Russia and one of his sisters.

Reconstruction of the fragmented skulls was carried out alongside other studies. Bones and their fragments found during both explorations of the grave were used to reconstruct skull specimens (Figure 17.4). The results of the reconstruction proved the applicability of the anatomical characteristics of the skulls to the comparative research for identification, partial definition of the

Table 17.2 Results of comparative analysis of the data relating to the skeletons and presumptive persons.

Presumptive persons	Skeleton number								
	1	2	3	4	5	6	7	8	9
1. Tsar Nikolas II				+				+	
2. Alexandra Romanova	+						+		
3. Olga Romanova			+		+	+			
4. Tatiana Romanova			+		+	+			
5. Maria Romanova			+		+	+			
6. Anastasia Romanova			+		+	+			
7. Dr Eugene Botkin		+							+
8. Anna Demidova	+						+		
9. Alexei Trupp		+							+
10. Ivan Kharitonov				+				+	

described attributes (i.e. biological profile and discovered essential diagnostic features) and the comparative study using the superimposition methodology (superimposition of photographic images of the skull and an intra-vitam image of the head).

The work was performed in the Forensic Centre of the Ministry of the Interior. Dr Sergey Abramov developed a unique computer methodology for the photographic superimposition of intra-vitam or ante-mortem images and skulls (Abramov 1997; Abramov et al. 2001). Using this method, by September 1992 experts had performed 77 comparative studies of the 9 examined skulls using 40 ante-mortem photographs of the 6 members of the Romanov family, and single images of Dr E. Botkin and A. Demidova.

In February 1994, in Yekaterinburg, 16 further studies were performed using additional photographic images of the servant and the cook, and also of N. Romanov and A. Demidova. Photographic images of the Romanovs, E. Botkin, A. Demidova, A. Trupp and I. Kharitonov, and other related documents stored in the Russian State Archives were used as identification material. Verbal descriptions of physical attributes were

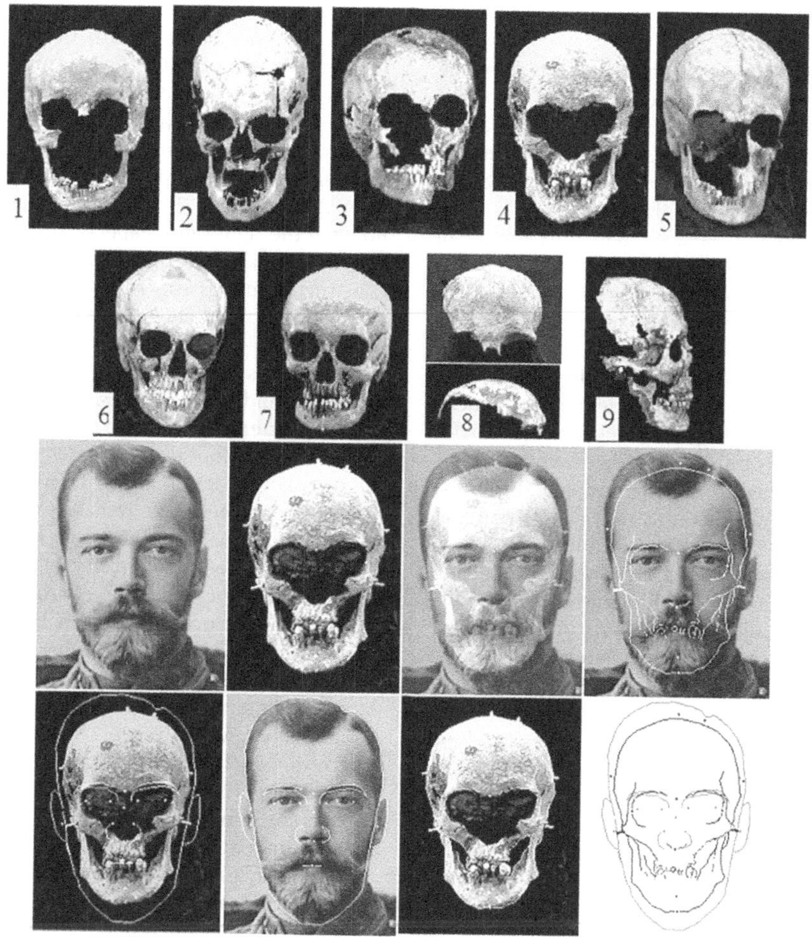

Figure 17.4 The photographic superposition with photos of Tsar Nicholas II.

compared to those of the presumed persons. Wax reconstructions of the skulls made by Sergey Nikitin showed a high degree of similarity to the ante-mortem photographic images of the aforementioned persons.

The studies proved to a high degree of accuracy (over 80%) that five skeletons, subject to epigenetic traits and other features commonly found in these skeletons, belonged to individuals of this family group:

1 Skeleton no. 4 – Romanov Nikolai Aleksandrovich
2 Skeleton no. 7 – Romanova Alexandra Feodorovna
3 Skeleton no. 3 – Romanova Olga Nikolaevna
4 Skeleton no. 5 – Romanova Tatiana Nikolaevna
5 Skeleton no. 6 – Romanova Anastasia Nikolaevna

Concerning the other four skeletons, based on elimination and biological profile regarding age and sex, it was determined that the remains belonged to the following:

1 Skeleton no. 1 – Demidova Anna Stepanovna
2 Skeleton no. 2 – Botkin Evgeny Sergeevich
3 Skeleton no. 8 – Kharitonov Ivan Mikhailovich
4 Skeleton no. 9 – Trupp Alexei Egorovich

The studies were performed using a unique method of computer craniofacial superimposition (TADD), specially developed by Dr Sergey Abramov for this case.

The rate of false identification is 1.389e – 15, that is, it is possible to find a group of nine persons with a similar set of appearance attributes (ante-mortem versus post-mortem) twice in 100 trillion cases, or less frequently. This rate was constituted by the sum of statistical probability, including certain factors (place and conditions of burial, quantity of skeletons, biological profiles, and similarity to the missing persons, results of craniofacial superimposition, etc.). The remains of Romanova Maria Nikolaevna and Romanov Alexei Nikolaevich were not found among the studied bones.

DNA analysis

Due to the lack of technical facilities required for the examination in Russia, the work was performed in the Forensic Science Service laboratories of the UK Home Office in the town of Aldermaston, United

Kingdom, within the scope of the Russian–British agreement.

The leader of the Russian group was Dr P. Ivanov, the head of the laboratory for genetic analysis of the Chief Forensic Examination Bureau of Russia; Dr P. D. Gill, the head of molecular-genetic research department at the Forensic Science Service (FSS) branch in Aldermaston, was the leader of the UK team.

As a result the experts managed to identify the sex of all the examined remains to a high degree of accuracy. The identified remains belonged to four male and five female individuals. A family group of five persons was revealed among the nine analysed skeletons. The identified individuals included the father, the mother and three daughters. DNA analysis revealed lack of genetic relationship of the remaining four skeletons either with the members of the examined family or *inter se*.

mtDNA was obtained from bone and dental samples of all nine studied individuals, as well as those of two reference samples: from Prince Philip, Duke of Edinburgh, who's mother was a nephew of the Russian empress Alexandra Feodorovna Romanova (genetic distance of four generations) and from two descendants of the Romanovs – Duchess Xeniya Sheremetieva-Sphiri and a member of the Fife ducal family (who preferred to stay incognito), separated by four and five generations respectively from the Emperor Nikolas II. The resulting identification was successful (Tomilin 1998). Thus, the case proves that such examinations require the participation of experts in different fields, starting from the initial stage of exploration of the burial site. In the authors' opinion forensic archaeology is highly appropriate to such cases in order to maximise the evidence obtained from careful recovery of the remains etc.

Case study 2: Archaeological input into the search and identification of burials of historical figures

On 10–11 December 2012, the Institute of Archaeology of the Russian Academy of Sciences in Moscow carried out work to determine the state of burials of the family of General Alexei P. Yermolov (Алексей Петрович Ермолов) (1777–1861) and to identify the remains. The Yermolovs' family burial vault consists of six crypts separated by brick walls, located on the ground floor of the right side-chapel of Trinity Church. The following members of the Yermolov family were buried in four crypts: Alexei P. Yermolov (d. 1861), Alexei's father Peter A. Yermolov (d. 1832), Alexei's son Claudius (Omar) A. Yermolov (d. 1894) and Alexei's daughter-in-law Barbara Yermolova (d. 1897).

Alexei P. Yermolov (24 May (N.S. 4 June) 1777, Moscow – 11 April (N.S. 23 April) 1861, Moscow) was a military leader and statesman who participated in many major wars of the Russian Empire from the 1790s to the 1820s: the Polish Uprising of 1794, the Russian–Persian War (1796), the War of the Third Coalition (1803–1806), the War of the Fourth Coalition (1806–1807), the Patriotic War of 1812, the War of the Sixth Coalition (1812–1814), the Caucasian War (1816–1864) and the Russian–Persian War (1826–1828). He was General of Infantry (1818), General of Artillery (1837) and Commander in Chief during the Caucasian War.

On 25 September 2012, during the renovation of the floors in the right side-chapel of Trinity Church (Свято-Троицкая церковь) in the Oryol a significant amount of construction debris was revealed in the space between the floor and the arches of the crypts, where fragments of the general's epaulettes, frameworks of icons, coins and fragments of stove tiles were found. In addition, the builders found human bones, as well as a military uniform and artefacts related to funeral rites. The regional administration appealed to the Ministry of Culture of the Russian Federation for help in conducting the research to protect the remains, due to the lack of appropriately qualified specialists in the Oryol region. At the request of the Ministry of Culture a group of experts from the Institute of Archaeology, Russian Academy of Sciences (RAS), left for the Oryol city to conduct the excavation and analysis of the finds.

In accordance with the programme agreed by the parties, their aims were as follows:

1. The study and analysis of the literature and archive recordings related to the construction of the church, crypts and circumstances of the burials of the Yermolov family
2. Ascertaining the state of the crypts and the time and circumstances of destruction of the graves
3. Conducting an anthropological and archaeological identification of the remains found in the crypts

In the field and laboratory work, in addition to the head of the excavation, Deputy Director Institute of Archaeology, RAS, Dr A. Engovatova, the following experts participated in the excavation: Dr M. Mednikova (physical anthropologist), Dr T. Shvedchikova (physical anthropologist), O. Radyush (archaeologist) and N. Shvedchenko (specialist in photogrammetry). Restoration, conservation and research of details of the uniform were conducted by Y. Voronin, O. Orfinskaya and O. B. Lantratova.

Fixing the archaeological objects in the research process was carried out in accordance with the methodological guidelines and requirements of the Regulations on the Procedure of the Archaeological Fieldwork (archaeological excavations and prospecting), and Compelling a Scientific Report Documentation.

Historical/archival research was conducted to clarify the circumstances of construction of Trinity Church and the burial vault, and the circumstances of the burial and reburial of the Yermolov family.

During this examination the whole complex of necessary works on monitoring and fixing was carried out. Initially, experts photographed the crypts, then a video was filmed and fixed using photogrammetry techniques, after which natural observations and measurements of the crypt were made and plans on a scale of 1:1000 were drawn. Preliminary anthropological definition of the remains and scanning of the skull using a 3D scanner was made. All detected materials were entered into a field inventory.

After a visual inspection and primary photofixation without descending to the crypt it was decided to hold the remote photo and video filming of the crypt internally to fix the situation, creating an accurate 3D model and definition of further action. As a result N. Shvedchenko created a 3D model of the crypt at the time of its initial examination by experts of the Institute of Archaeology, RAS (Figure 17.5). A plan of the crypts was drawn up later, on the basis of the reconstruction and field measurements.

The crypt of Alexei P. Yermolov (no. 2) and Peter A. Yermolov (no. 1) had dimensions of 240–200 × 180–170 cm and a height of up to 170 cm. The metal coffin of Alexei P. Yermolov, which was partly recessed into a wall niche, measured 230 × 85 × 70 cm. Remote robotics photography confirmed that the metal coffin had been opened roughly in the middle (the centre of the lid had a hole); there were only small fragments of the coffin, bones and small objects inside it. At the site of his father's burial, Peter A. Yermolov, there were the remains of a man; the skull and the wall of a wooden coffin could be clearly seen. Close to the longitudinal wall and near the hole in the metal coffin lay a fragment of a black marble memorial plaque with the letters CL – obviously related to the burial of Claudius A. Yermolov.

Figure 17.5 3D model of the Yermolov crypt.

Following the photography the Institute of Archaeology, RAS, experts examined the remains of a man lying on the spot where the remains of Peter A. Yermolov should have been located. The skull was damaged in the occipital area, which was almost absent. The arms were folded across the body, with the palms of the hands uppermost. Below there were the remains of the clavicle, ribs, several cervical and thoracic vertebrae and pelvic bones. One femur was lying between the wall of the tomb and the wall of the crypt, and the second was missing. The tibiae were *in situ*, but anatomical position of the bones was violated (space entanglement). The remains were located directly on the boards of the base of the coffin. After excavating lower down, the brick floor of the crypt was traced. Some preserved clothing was found on the deceased, including parts of his uniform near the hand and chest, and probable remnants of underwear on the pelvic bones. A. Tikhomirov, researcher of local history at the Oryol museum, confirmed that the details refer to the bureaucratic uniform of the Oryol province in the 1820s, which confirms the identification of the remains as Peter A. Yermolov.

However, fragments of military uniform (the upper part of the collar embroidered with gold thread with a button, parts of the sleeves with military buttons) were lying on the remains. A. Tikhomirov established that the buttons belonged to the uniform of Alexei P. Yermolov himself, the crossed cannons and the number 2 being depicted on them. The uniform in which he was probably buried was that of the General of Artillery, the chief of the second Horse Artillery Battery. In the area of the legs details of boots were found. Judging by the shape, some parts referred to a second pair of footwear, which were shoes. Thus, the footwear could be both from Peter A. Yermolov and from Alexei P. Yermolov. In the area of the legs were also found fragments of foil with cutouts, probably from the shell of the coffin. The metal coffin was hexagonally shaped. The coffin had significant damage at the base and had been displaced a little along the longitudinal axis. The space between the coffin and the wall of the crypt was filled with fragments of bricks and wood from the boards of the grave. On top of the debris a femur was lying. Its outer surface was gray. The physical anthropologists defined this as belonging to another individual, unlike the femur lying in the burial site of Peter A. Yermolov.

After conducting a physical anthropological examination at the church the human remains were returned to the crypt, where they were laid out in anatomical alignment on the burial place of Peter A. Yermolov. Some bones apparently belonging to Alexei P. Yermolov were placed inside a metal coffin.

Three 2D skull images (full-face, half-face and three-quarter) were printed on the basis of the 3D image. Three graphic reconstructions were performed using current craniofacial reconstruction software, which applies certain standards of thickness of facial soft coverings as well as a regression equation of separate facial elements, based on the skull size. Craniofacial concordance software was applied to create a verbal description of the deceased (i.e. a description of intra-vitam or ante-mortem appearance), and also to design the basic facial proportions. Historians could also refer to the ante-mortem portraits of General Alexei P. Yermolov and his father. Thereafter graphic reconstructions and portraits, facial proportions and verbally described characteristics were correlated. Consequently, experts confirmed a significant concordance of facial reconstructions and the portrait of the father of General Alexei P. Yermolov. Identification was based on the analysis of the schedules of proportion evaluation and the correlation of verbally described characteristics. Case identification was carried out by anthropologists and an expert in forensics, which provided the most professional selection of methods for identification using bones.

Search for Japanese WWII prisoners of war graves

In 1945, there were about 639,000 Japanese prisoners after World War II (WWII). Within the next 5 years the prisoners of war lived in special camps and were engaged in the construction of dams, buildings and industrial objects. Thousands of Japanese soldiers died in the years of captivity. Over 77,000 Japanese prisoners of war (c. 12% of the total number of the prisoners from Japan) were captive in the territory of the Chita Region, in the Zabaikalye Territory (Galickiy 1991, 66). Places of burial of the prisoners are still found in the territory of the region. However, published official information concerning the quantity and location of such mass graves is very scarce.

In 1991 the governments of the USSR and Japan signed the agreement for the prisoners of war. Subject to this document the Russians accepted the obligation to provide all possible assistance to the Japanese in the search and return of the remains of Japanese prisoners of war deceased in USSR territory. A special group, including mostly experts from the Japanese Ministry of Public Health and former prisoners of war and their relatives, as well as Russian forensic experts and KGB officers, was formed for the remains search. No archaeologists were included in this group.

The Russians, in the scope of the intergovernmental agreement, provided the Japanese with archive recordings giving evidence of the location of the prisoners of war on Russian territory after WWII and their burial locations. The mass graves were located in the territories of prisoner camps. Russian local authorities facilitated the search on site: they recruited personnel (experts and workers) to handle the exhumation, arranged accommodation and catering for the search group, provided site protection and security for the group members and assisted in preparation activities for the cremation and shipment of the discovered remains.

Archive recordings specifying the location and the number of the buried prisoners of war became primarily important in the search for burial sites. In practice, there were many discrepancies in the quantity of the discovered remains. The number of skeletal remains found turned out to be in conflict with official information concerning the number of the buried prisoners. Having studied the archive recordings, the Japanese would delegate a search group, consisting of four/five representatives from the Japanese Ministry of Public Health. Trial excavations were carried out at the estimated place of burial (a cemetery with individual graves) with the purpose of evaluating the final scope of work. The remains discovered at this stage were left on the site. The next year (after reconnaissance) the principal search team, consisting of the same experts as previously, worked on site. The work time of the team was limited and varied from 7 to 30 days. The search works were performed in the first half of summer or in the first half of autumn.

On arrival at the Russian destination the representatives of the Japanese party would refer to the regional ministry of public health with an application for a Russian forensic expert as a specialist in anthropological issues. The authors should mention that it has only been since 2005 that forensic experts (medical criminology) started to participate in excavation works as specialists in the field. All skeletal remains removed from the burial were regarded as the remains of Japanese prisoners of war as they all had certain anthropological attributes (Asians). Certain archive data were also taken into consideration (e.g. documents on the location of the burials).

A Russian forensic expert (medical criminologist of the local state bureau of forensic examination) was present on the site during excavation works and performed an examination of all the discovered remains in order to estimate sex, age-at-death and ancestry of the person (or persons) buried. Later on the forensic expert issued a report on the results of the examination of skeletal remains. The third author (AD) examined c. 450 remains between 2005 and 2011. The depth of burial of the remains varied from 40 to 200 cm. In some burial sites experts also found elements of clothing such as metal belt-buckles and uniform metal buttons. Due to taphonomic processes the bones of the feet, hands, clavicles, sternum and vertebrae were rarely found in burials. Ribs and their fragments were discovered in 20% of cases. Skeletal remains were mostly represented by long bones, hip bones and cranial bones. The excavation works were carried out by manual digging (without the participation of any archaeologists); excavating machinery was used only for mass graves 1.5–2 m deep. The significant duration of the excavation works

Figure 17.6 Excavation of the Japanese WWII prisoners of war.

(Figure 17.6) could have been caused by such reasons as inconsistencies in documents containing information about the places of burials, lack of efficient methodologies of discovering remains in the ground (including lack of ground-penetrating radar (GPR)) or short terms of work of the search team.

The discovered skeletal remains were studied with the purpose of defining the sex and the ancestry of the buried persons as there was no need to identify these individuals, for example, by means of DNA analysis. The sex was defined using the methodology of Dr V. Zvyagin, that is subject to the anatomical skull characteristics of the skull. The methods of Dr M. Gerasimov (1949) and Dr A. Zubov (1970) were successfully applied when defining ancestry. The measurements were carried out using a sliding calliper. Thereupon the remains were cremated and buried with dignity in Japan.

Prospects for development of forensic archaeology and its role in Russia

Forensic archaeology as a science cannot be regarded as a separate discipline. It is closely related to such areas as archaeology, taphonomy, forensic medicine (including forensic anthropology) and criminalistics.

In our opinion forensic archaeology should be divided into two fields, depending on its role. These are archaeological/historical on the one hand and criminalistic on the other hand. This distinction is partly due to the lack of experts in the field of forensic archaeology in Russia, which leads to the need for cooperation between specialists from different areas.

Considering the character of the Russian law enforcement system, as well as the leading role of investigative and police forces as initiators in any case, the authors suppose that forensic anthropologists and archaeologists can only be an auxiliary institution participating in investigations. This is established by Russian legislation and procedures of prosecution of the inquiry. Therefore the participation of archaeologists and other experts in Russia is limited to excavation and exhumation works on graves and examination of the remains.

At present forensic anthropology and archaeology is a daydream for Russian experts, lacking the support and understanding of the majority. However the authors hope that such an institution will be established in the Investigative Committee of the Russian Federation. The existence of such an institution and experts in independent structures unconnected with the police and Investigative Committee is impossible due to legal peculiarities of Russian legislation.

Current Russian legislation provides for engaging experts in any field to participate in investigation procedures, but, as a rule, archaeologists and anthropologists are invited *post factum* (on discovery and exhumation of the remains). The authors believe that forensic archaeology can play a substantial role in the investigation of war crimes, genocide or clandestine graves.

The authors further believe that the leading role in forensic anthropology and archaeology should be given to investigative and police forces as initiators of the investigation. It is dictated by the necessity to follow the statutory procedures leading to the investigation and solution of the crime. Thus, in Russia the role of archaeologists and historians in the excavation of clandestine graves is an auxiliary one. Their main task is to provide investigators and expert services with the necessary consulting and methodological assistance, and in some cases, to take an active part in the investigation (at the stage of excavation and exhumation). However at present there is no institution of forensic archaeology in Russia.

The existing legislation in Russia envisages the involvement of any specialists as experts by the investigating bodies, and its situation benefits the possibility of development of the criminalistic direction of forensic anthropology. In the authors' opinion the criminalistic direction of forensic archaeology can play a significant role in cases of investigation of war crimes, genocide and discovery of criminal burials.

The development of historical direction, by contrast, appears to be somewhat difficult. This is due to the fact that the current Russian legislation provides for the work of forensic experts only on request by the police, investigative bodies or the court. Other organisations or individuals do not have the opportunity to apply to the state expert institutions at an official level. In the authors' opinion this circumstance prevents the official development of the historical direction of forensic archaeology.

Conclusion

In conclusion, the authors would like to state that the cases described and the ideas proposed in this chapter, however categorical they might sound, reflect the opinion only of a small group who are interested in the proposed theme; there is potential for further development of the discipline in more recent criminal cases. The authors' work in this area has just begun and they hope for mutual cooperation with the international scientific community.

References

Abramov, S. 1994. A mystery of Imperial Remains. Proceedings of the conference 'The latest chapter in the history of the royal family: the results of the study of the Yekaterinburg tragedy'. Yekaterinburg, Association of the Urals, Middle Ural Book Publishing House, 75.

Abramov, S. 1997. Computerization of Comparative Studies in Craniofacial Identification (Methodology and Practice). Unpublished PhD thesis, Moscow.

Abramov, S., Avetisyan, A., Afanaseva, O. et al. 2001. New technologies in craniofacial identification. *Scientific and Practical Journal Forensic Medical Examination* 3, 25.

Galickiy, V. 1991. Japanese prisoners of war in the Soviet Union: the truth and speculation. *Military Historical Journal RATOBOREC* 4, 66.

Pashkova, V. 1963. *Essays on Forensic Osteology*. MEDGIZ – State Publishing House of Medical Literature, Moscow.

Ryabov, G. 1998. *As it Was. The Romanovs: The Concealment of Bodies, Search, Effects*. POLITBURO, Moscow.

Tomilin, V. 1998. *Repentance/Materials of the Government Commission*. VIBOR, Moscow.

Tomilin, V. (ed.) 2000. *Medical and Forensic Identification*. NORMA-INFRA, Moscow.

CHAPTER 18

Forensic archaeology in Serbia: from exhumation to excavation

Marija Djurić[1] and Andrej Starović[2]

[1] *Laboratory for Anthropology, Institute of Anatomy, Faculty of Medicine, Belgrade, Serbia*

[2] *National Museum in Belgrade, Serbia*

Introduction

Challenges and limits in the development and practice of forensic archaeology in Serbia

In Serbia, forensic archaeological methods were used for the first time in 2001 at the mass grave of Batajnica (see case study 1), for tasks related to the excavation of mass graves. Although the first experience with archaeologists in a forensic context was positive, leading to the complete retrieval of evidence for the final identification of human remains, as well as to an accurate interpretation of the events that surrounded burial, the involvement of forensic archaeologists remains isolated in forensic practice. Up to now, there have been only few occasions, primarily associated with mass grave excavation, when archaeologists were requested to join a forensic team. Thus far, archaeologists in Serbia are not yet recognised as professionals who are valuable in forensic cases, and they are not asked to attend court as expert witnesses.

The absence of forensic archaeologists in our judicial system could be related to several facts. Apart from one PhD course in biological anthropology at the School of Medicine in Belgrade, which contains several topics related to forensic context, forensic archaeology still has no place in the educational system in our country. Despite a number of attempts from Serbian medically trained forensic anthropologists to generate interest in forensic archaeology among prospective professionals and institutions (police, court, etc.), there are no courses or at least official guidelines sufficiently competent to explain to judges and police officers all the benefits that skilled archaeologists can provide in crime scene investigation. Furthermore, the budgets of police units and courts are often limited, which causes a tendency to avoid all personnel perceived as unnecessary. In addition, promising forensic archaeologists are arriving from academic archaeological backgrounds. They usually do not recognise or describe themselves as forensic experts, although it is legally possible to apply to our Ministry of Justice (*Ministarstvo Pravde*) for the list of experts that can be employed in particular forensic cases.

A brief report on cases where forensic archaeology has been employed

Case study 1: Batajnica

In the late spring of 2001 archaeologists were appointed for the first time to the excavation of graves in a forensic context. Initially, Serbian police anti-organised crime unit (*Uprava za borbu protiv organizovanog kriminala Ministarstva unutrašnjih poslova Republike Srbije*) collected information about the potential mass graves in a suburb of Belgrade (Batajnica) that might contain the mortal remains of suspected victims of the Kosovo conflict of 1999, killed during the North Atlantic Treaty Organization (NATO) bombings of Serbia. The procedure and the collection setting of assumed graves were carried out in accordance with the rules outlined by the District Court of Belgrade. The Institute of Forensic Medicine (*Institut za Sudsku Medicinu*) at the University of Belgrade, Faculty of Medicine was appointed by the court in order to organise the exhumation process. This is standard procedure in Serbia. However, the general lack of any previous experience in the investigation of mass graves suddenly created a situation with high humanitarian and political pressure. Therefore, the requirement for a large-scale excavation forced the Institute's forensic experts to create a careful methodology, recognising the need for archaeological methods and principles, in order to cope with the hard task of recovering composite mass graves with complex burial stratigraphy and commingled human remains. That is why the first task was to gather a multiskilled expert team, including experts from the Laboratory for Anthropology (*Laboratorija za Antropologiju*), University of Belgrade, Faculty of Medicine, led by the first author

Forensic Archaeology: A Global Perspective, First Edition. Edited by W.J. Mike Groen, Nicholas Márquez-Grant and Robert C. Janaway.

(MD), and a small team of skilled archaeologists from the National Museum in Belgrade (*Narodni Muzej u Beogradu*), led by the second author (AS). By special request of the Serbian government (based on an agreement between the Ministry of Foreign Affairs and the International Commission on Missing Persons – ICMP; Hanson, Chapter 48, this volume), the court also allowed forensic archaeologists and anthropologists from the ICMP to observe the recovery process (monitoring process in 2001), and to assist in the excavations (during the field seasons in 2002).

In two subsequent years (2001–2002) during the three fieldwork campaigns, a series of five mass graves were discovered and explored within the area of the Special Anti-terrorist Unit (*Specijalna Antiteroristička Jedinica* – SAJ) facilities complex, located in Batajnica, c. 17 km north-west of Belgrade. The Unit, as well as its facilities at Batajnica, has existed since the early 1990s. Technically, a total of eight pits were recorded there (BA01–BA08), but BA04, BA06 and BA08 had been dug next to regular grave pits, and presented temporary deposition sites (e.g. Jessee and Skinner 2005, 57), with the remains of clothes, shoes, plastic sheeting pieces and some remains of body parts. Only the pits numbered BA01, BA02, BA03, BA05 and BA07 were real mass graves, containing complete remains of victims and body parts.

Spatial distribution of the Batajnica grave pits led to the following conclusions: in five mass graves, 705 human bodies were recorded and recovered, a total of the minimum number of individuals (MNI) in each pit: BA01 – 36 individuals, BA02 – 269 individuals, BA03 – 39 individuals, BA05 – 287 individuals and BA07 – 74 individuals.

Batajnica 1

Archaeological excavations started at the beginning of June 2001, in sensitive methodological and political circumstances. In fact, this took place only 2 years after the war in former Yugoslavia and the bombardment of Serbia, and some of the police officers involved in actual fieldwork may also have been connected to previous activities at the burial site. Archaeologists in the team were initially required to establish the original size, shape and position of the suspected burial pit. Later, we were employed to excavate the pit carefully to find and expose suspected human remains and to record the forensic context (dynamic of the creation of the grave, human activities surrounding burial process as well as later taphonomic changes). The initial problem was the early use of heavy machinery (a huge digger) by the police to locate the pit. For this reason we arrived at a very disturbed site, with no regular surface to survey as the starting point. The site was located outside the SAJ's firing ranges, in the 'no man's land' on the right bank of the river Danube.

Large tents were erected over the site itself and over the temporary mortuary facility where the remains were examined. After that, we started with hand trowelling of the surface, in order to locate the borders of the pit more precisely. A grid (1 × 1 m) was laid out, covering a wide area of the site. The border lines soon became visible, and the excavation began. The grave pit itself was not large – c. 5 × 3 m, with a total depth of c. 2 m. The first remains of bodies and body parts appeared *in situ* around 0.5 m in depth from the actual surface (Figure 18.1). Just next to the north-west edge of the pit, burnt tire tracks belonging to a heavy machine were recorded. Through contextual analysis of the stratigraphy, it was concluded that the grave pit had been created using a huge mechanical digger, with a pretty steep accessing ramp (Figure 18.2).

During the excavations, the remains of 36 individuals were recovered, comprising 13 males, 14 females and 9 children. In addition, there was an 8-month foetus. It was observed that the majority of bodies were commingled and concentrated at the centre of the pit, where a burning area had been created. Under the bodies a plastic sheeting had been spread, on which lay a series of five wooden railway cross ties. These were attached to the pit walls (just above the bottom of the pit) and set parallelly. The entire construction, together with the physical residue of petrol, implies that there was a clear intention to burn the bodies.

Many forensically important artefacts have been collected during the excavation, such as personal documents, papers, jewellery, money and so on. Everything was carefully recorded (using plotting, videography and photography). All of these artefacts could help in the final identification of the human remains.

Batajnica 2–8

After finishing our fieldwork at the end of June 2001 at site BA01, we were informed of a series of additional mass graves located inside the firing range of SAJ. Exhumation of the bodies in the next mass grave pit (labelled as BA02) took place during the late summer of the same year without the presence of archaeologists. The Institute of Forensic Medicine in Belgrade, responsible for this part of the excavation, concluded that archaeological work significantly extends the time for recovery and that archaeologists are not necessary! A mixed team of national forensic experts, mostly medical doctors, conducted very complex fieldwork stratigraphically, excavating the southernmost grave pit, recovering almost 300 bodies. The recovery operation was complicated by a number of factors. First, some remains were incomplete; second, the remains were badly contorted and commingled, making the tracing of arms and legs very difficult; third, a large number of vehicle tires with their constituent wire reinforcing had been burned in a vain attempt to destroy the remains; and fourth, this was a large site containing more than 250 sets of remains. According to the words of Dr M. Skinner, the

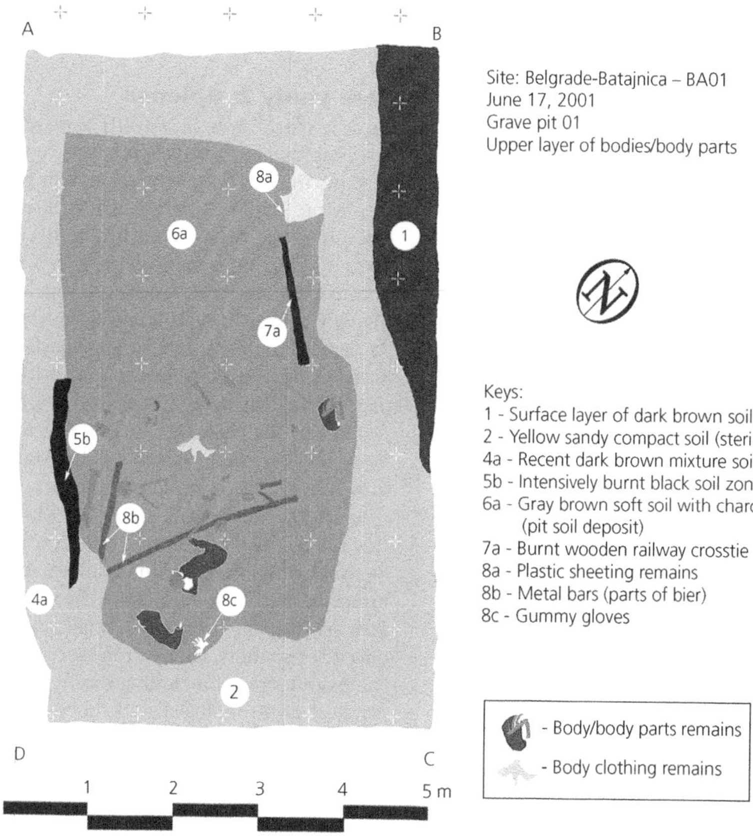

Figure 18.1 Technical plan of the archaeological situation in the grave pit at the BA01 site, upper layer (Drawing: A. Starović).

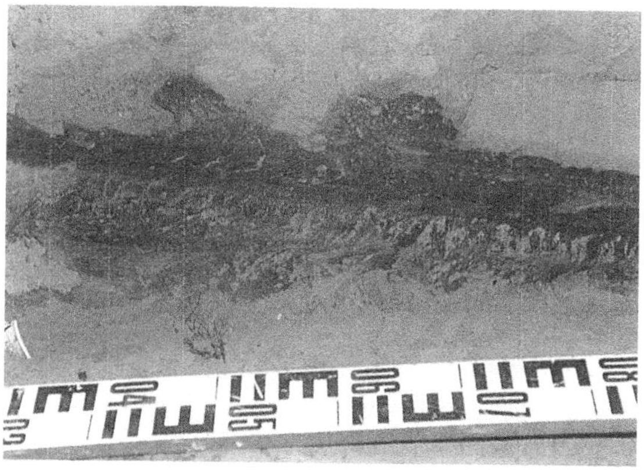

Figure 18.2 Detail of the heavy machine burnt tyre track on the access ramp to the grave pit at the BA01 site (Photo: Institute of Forensic Medicine, Faculty of Medicine, Belgrade).

ICMP senior anthropologist and official monitor during the excavations of BA02, 'this mass grave was among the most difficult sites to exhume ever monitored by staff from ICMP' (ICMP 2002, 6).

For the excavation of the pits labelled BA03, BA05 and BA07, the same team of archaeologists was employed again. Generally, two methodological approaches were used during the whole excavation process at Batajnica: the *pedestal method* (pit labelled BA02 and, partially, BA01) as used by the forensic experts (mostly medical doctors) and the *stratigraphic method* (pits labelled BA03, BA05 and BA07) as used by the archaeologist.

As graves were created using the same techniques, subjected to the same disposal method and exposed to the same taphonomic conditions, we used this opportunity to compare the two methodologies in order to evaluate the efficiency of the excavation, focusing on an analysis of recovered unassociated bones (Tuller and Djuric 2006). The first grave (BA02) excavated using the pedestal method had been perceived to have a disproportionately larger amount of unassociated bones than did the second (BA05), which used the stratigraphic method. The results of the experience suggest that the archaeologically based stratigraphic method is more appropriate for such complex sites, because it assists in maintaining body parts articulated to each other, and because it is more helpful in understanding the grave formation process and context.

BA03, BA05 and BA07, although very complicated from the viewpoint of their internal stratigraphy, presented the majority of complete bodies for final study and identification, as well as the most carefully recorded, retrieved and collected artefacts of interest for forensic purposes. More than 400 individuals, their personal effects (clothes, shoes, IDs, jewellery, wallets, watches and so on), as well as bullets and shell cases, labels with numbers attached to the clothing of some victims and even one complete empty coffin were instructive elements for later analysis and archaeo-forensic interpretation of the dynamics and internal chronology of the events that had created the mass graves.

Thanks to the great professional assistance of the ICMP experts Mr J. Sterenberg, Dr M. Skinner and Mr H. Tuller, as well as the ICMP's technical and financial support, we were able to plan and conduct our fieldwork prudently. Spatial 3D recording (x, y and z) of each finding was made using the Total Station, which helped to speed up plotting, and, later on, to produce more accurate spatial and stratigraphic analysis. Pit BA03, with a size of c. 17 × 3 m and a depth of 2.5 m (ICMP 2004, 7), revealed a single deposit of bodies, similar to BA01. However, BA03, contrary to BA01, is not a *primary grave* (ICMP 2004, 7). Further, BA07 (c. 14 × 3 m in size and up to 2.7 m deep) had 5 separate body deposits, while the largest one, BA05 (25 × 3 m and up to 2 m deep) contained 13 separate body deposits! It is likely that 13 different trucks emptied the bodies into the mass grave.

Evidence of intense fire activity within all four grave features was observed by the archaeological team on initial surface cleaning, and during the excavation itself. Vehicle tires were placed in the bottom and more or less throughout the grave to assist in the cremation of the remains. A number of bodies were damaged by this fire, some of them severely. In addition, huge parts of large vehicles (trucks, refrigerator trucks, dumpers), as well as burnt tires, have been found in the context of the burial sites.

In addition to the basic archaeological research tasks (locating the gravesite, exposing, cleaning, recording and plotting bodies and other forensic evidences), we also concentrated on (i) the transfer of any recovered human remains and artefacts of forensic interest to an on-site team from the Institute of Forensic Medicine in Belgrade for further analysis; and (ii) ensuring that if possible the entire site excavation would be under the control of an experienced archaeologist, in order to recover as much evidence as possible relating to site formation, body deposition and consequent backfilling or robbing activity within the grave.

In summary, we have approached our fieldwork just 'like any other archaeology' (J. Sterenberg, personal communication). Nevertheless, several methodological papers based on our new forensic experience from Batajnica have been published (cf. Skinner et al. 2003; Tuller and Djuric 2006).

Case study 2: Oplenac

During World War II (WWII) the German army killed 40–50 soldiers – the loyalists of the Yugoslav government in exile, in the area of Oplenac, near the town of Topola in central Serbia. Oplenac historically houses the mausoleum of the Serbian Royal Family Karadjordjević. In 2012 and 2013 the mausoleum received much attention because Prince Paul's remains, together with those of his wife and son, were eventually returned there after 71 years. Prince Paul was the Yugoslav regent who was accused by the communist authorities of signing the pact with Germans in 1941, and therefore he spent the rest of his life in exile. Finally, the remains of the last Yugoslav King Petar II and Queen Maria have also been transferred and reburied at Oplenac.

In 2007, the District Court in Kragujevac requested that the Institute of Forensic Medicine in Belgrade should organise a field survey in order to collect any practical information that could help in the quest for the potential area of suspected burial. A small team of three experienced researchers, led by Professor D. Dunjić as the medical examiner and including the first author (MD) as the physical anthropologist and the second author (AS) as the archaeologist, conducted a full day of field research there. From an interview with the director of the local museum, we found out that during WWII, the Oplenac memorial complex had been used as a command centre by the regional German army. This is the place where the very first local Serbian rebels were captured, and then killed by shooting. Although the entire zone of Oplenac used to be a 'forbidden city' for civilians during the war and occupation, oral history had preserved its memory as a burial place. It was said that 'they were killed and buried in young oak wood, and after a while, some brave local farmer, employed for the short term by German military authorities, has carved on an oak tree bark a Christian cross filled with wax – forming a *zapis*' (M. Gavrilovic, personal communication). In Serbian, the word *zapis* signifies an old Slavic ritual of the sacrifice of a specific oak tree, making the sign of the Holy Cross on it. (This might be a mixture of Christian and ancient pagan tradition, related to the cult of the deceased.) In addition, a small quarry of high-quality marble rock had been mentioned as the surrounding area of the suspected execution site.

That was merely information that we have obtained. A practical problem was the fact that virtually the entire slope of the Oplenac hill today is covered with dense oak forest, and our major concern was related to the possibility of recognising the named rock quarry at the foothill of Oplenac. As a final point, we have found a good 'candidate' on the southernmost steep slope of the hill. Fortuitously, we have even found the mark on the oak tree (Figure 18.3), and previous stories turned

Figure 18.3 Carved cross (*'zapis'*) on the oak tree bark at the Oplenac site, near Topola (Photo: M. Djurić, Laboratory for Physical Anthropology, Faculty of Medicine, Belgrade).

out to be true. We later focused on a visualisation study around the oak tree, and a pretty regular rectangular shape (roughly 10 × 2 m in size) between two rows of oak trees has been detected.

As a trial test, surface scraping was conducted in the zone, and after only a half an hour we found a series of artefacts in the backfill of the grave, directly related to the case: several small buttons from clothing, as well as two Serbian wartime coins dated 1942. That is how it came to be the so-called *terminus ante quem*, that is the earliest possible time of suspected events.

Unfortunately, a group of amateurs led by the director of the local Oplenac complex museum decided to exhume the skeletal remains from the mass grave at Oplenac by themselves, with no supervision by forensic professionals. For this reason, all the important information about the formation process, dynamics, stratigraphy, and so on are missing today. All the bones were put together, so no further contextual analysis was possible.

Anthropological analysis of the Oplenac mass grave skeletal remains was conducted by the Military Medical Academy (*Vojno-Medicinska Akademija*) and Laboratory for Anthropology (*Laboratorija za Antropologiju*) from the Faculty of Medicine, University of Belgrade, and it was concluded that a minimum of 28 young males were buried at this location. Some of the skeletons had visible traumata, probably caused by projectiles.

Case study 3: Kragujevac – Fiat

In 2011 the High Court in Kragujevac, after it had heard about the fieldworks at Batajnica and Oplenac, again invited our forensic team, headed by the first author, to investigate a new site in the area of the contemporary Fiat car factory. The team comprised a senior archaeologist (the second author), and three young archaeologists and physical anthropologists, the field crew members. A chance discovery of human bones had been made just a week earlier, reported by local ground workers during the mechanical excavation of draining channels. In fact, the well-known Italian car company Fiat, after buying the complex of the Serbian Zastava car factory, had initially decided to reconstruct old buildings, including the entire surface area between the structures (roads, parking places etc.) The easternmost flat zone, next to a small hill, was designated to become a huge parking place for heavy trucks, and that is why radical excavations were conducted there.

Historical sources that we have found indicated the possibility that the discovery of human remains may be associated with tragic events at the end of WWII. Namely, numerous series of executions took place during the winter of 1944 in Kragujevac, when the new communist government prosecuted and killed several hundred people from central Serbia convicted of collaboration with the German occupiers. The victims, according to local oral history, were buried in a collective grave (or graves?) without any marking.

The starting point for the forensic field research was pretty unclear, because the original land surface was unrecognisable. The entire plateau (measuring c. 800 × 200 m) was radically reshaped for the purpose of a large parking place during the 1970s, and the original surface was completely removed mechanically years ago. In order to identify the physical boundaries of the suspected burial pit (or pits?) we began with fine scraping of the wide zone around the discovered human bones. Soon after, we recovered many remains of human bones, scattered on the surface. Initially, our basic research dilemma was whether the site features consisted of one single long grave pit or of a series of parallel pits, dug next to each other. Further detailed spatial analysis of the grave units and context finally indicated (most likely) the occurrence of one single very large shallow pit, not deeper than 0.5–0.7 m. Its shape used to be pretty much irregular, with clear borders to the south, east and west, which were archaeologically observed. It was obvious that the burial pit extends significantly to the north, under the concrete sidewalk and the neighbourhood building.

After the removal of the first excavation layer (0.2 m deep), the skeletal remains of 11 individuals concentrated in three groups became visible. Careful cleaning (Figure 18.4) demonstrated that the skeletons were quite well preserved in an undisturbed position, and some artefacts (parts of footwear, coats, leather belts, mirrors, combs, decorative buttons, rings and wallets) were found associated with some individuals. The position of the bodies and discovery of numerous bullet shell cases (from guns, machine guns, rifles, pistols) indicated that executions were carried out in the pit (Figure 18.5). This is why we were able to conclude

Figure 18.4 Ongoing work at the Kragujevac – Fiat site (Photo: M. Dakić, Laboratory for Physical Anthropology, Faculty of Medicine, Belgrade).

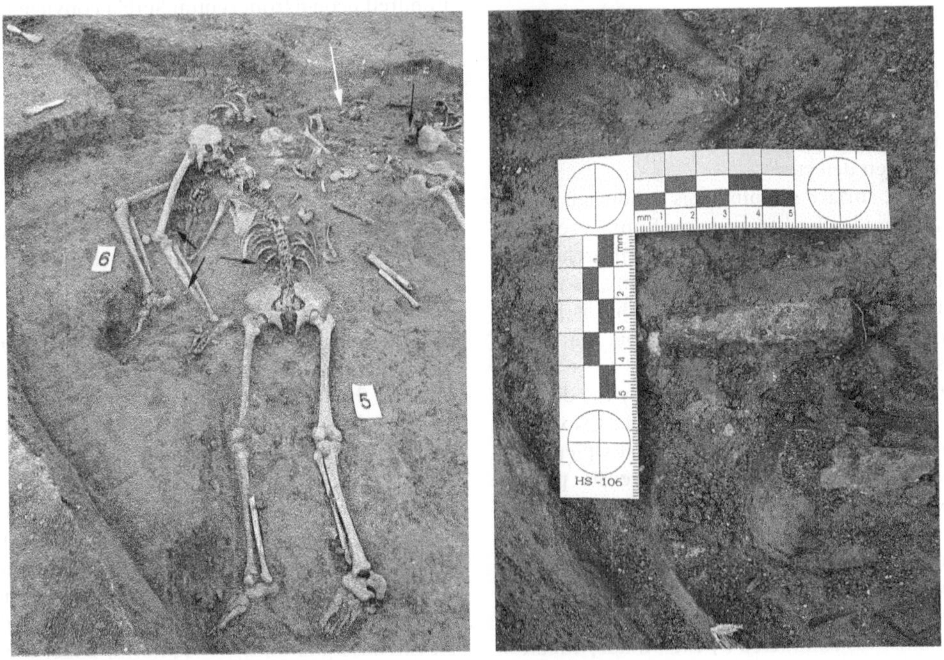

Figure 18.5 On the left: grouped skeletons *in situ*, with marked personal clothes (arrows), and shell cases, Kragujevac – Fiat, grave pit. On the right: detail of a shell case found *in situ* between human bones (Photos: M. Dakić, Laboratory for Physical Anthropology, Faculty of Medicine, Belgrade).

that the site belongs to the so-called grave execution site (GES), and to primary inhumation site (PIS) as well, according to adopted mass grave typology (Jessee and Skinner 2005, 75).

Quite a peculiar finding – a fully preserved group of c. 10 wax candles – was discovered next to the northern profile of our trench. Some witnesses have claimed that local people (probably the victims' relatives), after the shooting, used to come here and light the candles, 'in the name of the souls of the deceased'.

According to the results of our excavations and further physical anthropological analysis, we concluded that the MNI buried at this location was 27. Sex was estimated for a total of 16 individuals: 11 males and 5 females. Studying the entire skeletal material (disarticulated bones and individual skeletons) we concluded that all the individuals were adults, except one whose age at the time of death was c. 17 years.

After finishing the fieldwork and laboratory research, our forensic team finally transferred all material to the judge in Kragujevac in order to continue the ongoing judicial process. It was specifically emphasised in our report that the mass grave pit in the Kragujevac Fiat site was not entirely forensically explored. We highly recommended continuing the field excavations, after removing the old internal power station building, in order to find and research the northern extension of the grave pit.

Case study 4: Belgrade – Ada Ciganlija

In 2010 the Serbian government began the rehabilitation process of General Dragoljub (Draža) Mihailović, under the authority of the High Court in Belgrade. Draža Mihailović was a famous Serb pro-monarchist leader who had organised rebel guerrillas (known as the Chetniks) during WWII, after the German occupation. Historical records of the Chetniks are controversial, because at least some of their military units also collaborated with the Axis, fighting against Tito's partisans and committing many crimes against local civilians. In 1946 the communist Yugoslav authorities caught Draža Mihailović and detained him in Ada Ciganlija prison, located in an island area of the River Sava, in Belgrade.

On 15 July 1946 the Military Council of the Supreme Court of the Federal People's Republic of Yugoslavia (*Vojni savet Vrhovnog suda Federativne Narodne Republike Jugoslavije*) sentenced and convicted (among others) Draža Mihailović for collaborating with the German occupiers between 1941 and 1945, and for suppressing the uprising of the people of Yugoslavia and the liberation war led by communists. Draža Mihailović was convicted for active political and military cooperation with the occupier, for leading the country into civil war under the pretext of fighting against communism, for inciting discord among the peoples of Yugoslavia and for crimes against the people, and the undermining of a new constitutional democratic system (Kesar and Lukić 1990). The place of execution and his unmarked grave have so far remained secret. That is why the High Court (*Viši Sud*) in Belgrade in June 2011 requested that the Institute of Forensic Medicine in Belgrade conduct exhumations and forensic investigation at the site, which included the external area of the former Ada Ciganlija prison's northern wall, because several indirect witnesses identified that very location as the possible place of Draža Mihailović's burial. The Institute has formed a team consisting of a forensic anthropologist and a senior archaeologist (the authors of this chapter) and several other technicians, students and workers.

Two months before the employment of our forensic team, the State Commission for Investigation of Secret Mass Graves (*Državna Komisija za Ispitivanje Tajnih Masovnih Grobnica*)[1] also found on this location some burnt skeletal material and artefacts (glass and metal), suggesting that these findings could be related to a suspected grave. However, the analyses of the skeletal material in the Laboratory of Anthropology in Belgrade determined that the bones actually belonged to animals, and that no finding could be related to the context of the tomb of General Draža Mihailović.

The forensic team finally started work in August 2011 and experienced many difficulties in locating the site. First, a long time had elapsed since the burial, and the entire location and its surface had been extensively reshaped, in order to create what is today Belgrade's swimming beach (Ada Ciganlija island was linked to the city by a huge manmade causeway, forming an artificial river lake). Second, the investigators had to consider the possibility of the manipulation of Draža Mihailović's body after death, including reburial and/or devastation. Finally, according to some historical data, more than one executed and buried person could also have existed, so the suspected grave pit itself could be even larger.

The first survey of the area confirmed the complexity of the case, since the given data about the position of the prison's north wall was very inaccurate. We therefore had to find the remains of the prison building (visualisation of the grass field, measuring the distances, etc.). Once we had determined the position of the north and west walls, we were able to find the corner where

[1] In 2008 the Serbian government established the State Commission for Investigation of Secret Mass Graves after September 12, 1944 (*Državna Komisija za Tajne Masovne Grobnice nakon 12. Septembra 1944)*, located at the Institute of Contemporary History *(Institut za Savremenu Istoriju)* in Belgrade. The basic mission of the Commission is to research and collect all data about crimes against civilians from the autumn of 1944, when the new communist government took power in Serbia.

the two walls met. According to the previously collected statements of several witnesses, that corner might be a significant point of reference for determination of the exact position of the hole where the bodies were reportedly dropped after being shot. (Essentially, no regular grave pit had been dug, but an already existing hole for producing lime plaster was dug when the prison was active, and it was widened and reused to put the body/bodies in.) Excavations were conducted in a block of c. 100 m², in the 'quest' for the grave pit, and human remains that could be linked to the case. After almost an entire month of field research, the final results were rather disappointing. In fact, excavations did reveal the remains of the western and northern walls of the prison enclosure, and a well-preserved brick pavement was discovered on the external side of the wall. Just next to the original pavement, we found many artefacts that could have been connected to the suspected execution: shell cases, bullets, small underwear buttons, the sole of a jackboot, even a 'ladle' for the filtration of liquid lime (Figure 18.6). During our careful excavations, we also found many bones, all belonging, however, to animals. A total of six deep pits were detected, but the contents were always suspected, consisting of fairly modern artefacts (glass bottles, plastic and contemporary garbage). Only Pit 4 actually contained at its bottom the remains of lime plaster (Figure 18.6) and shell cases. However, no human remains, bones or any other artefacts were detected.

At the end of our field research, by courtesy of the Monting Company of Belgrade, we used a high-quality professional ground-penetrating radar (GPR) to explore the entire area, in order to find any disorder or anomaly in soil layers at depths greater than 1.5 m, along the northern wall of the prison. Afterwards, we organised probing of this area, for example test-excavating with a mini-digger, to check every single disturbance noticed by the GPR. Those probes have confirmed that deep soil irregularities were caused by later digging for the city water supply. Finally, in the court report we concluded that our research did not reveal any evidence suggesting that the remains of an unidentified person were buried at the specified location.

Conclusion

Displayed case studies illustrate the use of archaeology in a number of investigations of mass graves. When archaeologists were used for the first time in 2001, we believed that this was due to exceptional circumstances and the importance of the case. The intention of the competent court in an (at the time) very turbulent political situation, with high media attention focused on questions related to genocide and war in ex-Yugoslavia, was to conduct excavations in the best way, which included the gathering of a large team of skilled experts of all required profiles. Later, the engagement of archaeologists depended on the importance of the case, the financial resources available to the court and the courts' assessment as to whether the presence of archaeologists was necessary. Generally, archaeology is not used as standard in the excavation of individual forensic cases. Certainly, the official education of forensic archaeologists and development of protocols for the excavation of individual and mass graves (accepted by the court and

Figure 18.6 Vertical cross section of Pit 4, Belgrade – Ada Ciganlija, showing the remains of the lime plaster (white stains) (Photo: M. Dakić, Laboratory for Physical Anthropology, Faculty of Medicine, Belgrade).

the police) would be helpful for the promotion of the discipline in Serbia.

References

ICMP 2002. *Exhumation in Serbia, 2001 (Summary)*. Available at: www.ic-mp.org/wp-content/uploads/2008/02/batajnica-2001-eng.pdf (last accessed 30 March 2013).

ICMP 2004. *Batajnica Summary Report. Forensic Monitoring Activities*. Available at: www.ic-mp.org/wp-content/uploads/2008/02/icmp-fsd-16-04-2-doc.pdf (last accessed 30 March 2013).

Jessee, E. and Skinner, M. 2005. A typology of mass grave and mass grave-related sites. *Forensic Science International* 152(1), 55–59.

Kesar, J. and Lukić, D. 1990. *Ne Osećam se Krivim: Draža Mihailović pred Sudom: Stenografske Beleške sa Suđenja Vođi Četničkog Pokreta*. Beograd: Akvarijus.

Skinner, M., Alempijevic, D. and Djuric-Srejic, M. 2003. Guidelines for international forensic bio-archaeology monitors of mass grave exhumations. *Forensic Science International* 134(2–3), 81–92.

Tuller, H. and Djuric, M. 2006. Keeping the pieces together: Comparison of mass grave excavation methodology. *Forensic Science International* 156(2), 192–200.

CHAPTER 19

Forensic archaeology in the Slovak Republic

Soňa Masnicová[1], Radoslav Beňuš[2] and Zuzana Obertová[2,3]

[1] *Department of Criminalistics and Forensic Science, Academy of Police Force in Bratislava, Bratislava, Slovak Republic*

[2] *Department of Anthropology, Comenius University, Bratislava, Slovak Republic*

[3] *Waikato Clinical School, University of Auckland, Hamilton, New Zealand*

The state of forensic archaeology in Slovakia

The field of forensic archaeology, defined as the application of archaeological theory, methods and techniques in a legal context, is not yet sufficiently established in Slovak judicial and forensic practice. The institutions involved in archaeological research in Slovakia, such as departments of archaeology at several universities, the Archaeological Institute of the Slovak Academy of Sciences (*Archeologický Ústav Slovenskej Akadémie Vied*) and several private archaeological organisations offer neither training in forensic archaeology nor professional archaeological services for forensic purposes. The current situation stems probably from the fact that the Slovak police only require the services of archaeologists in cases involving damage or devaluation of archaeological heritage or counterfeiting of archaeological finds.

In the following sections we will first describe the legislation and procedures undertaken by the state authorities in cases involving the looting of archaeological sites. Next, we will discuss the legal background in relation to war graves from World War I and II (WWI and WWII). Furthermore, we will provide information on forensic practices and methods used in Slovakia in surveys for corpses and clandestine graves. We will also summarise the procedures associated with the recovery of human remains from clandestine graves and the type of expertise required in such cases.

Legislation and procedures undertaken by state authorities in cases of looting of archaeological sites

In the past 20 years archaeological sites in Slovakia have suffered from 'invasions' by modern treasure hunters, so-called 'detector-men'. These men left traces of their activity at each of the better-known archaeological sites in Slovakia. Our country seems to be a paradise for people with metal detectors, who leave behind empty holes in the ground for the archaeologists to find. Rare objects of our cultural heritage are often sold at auctions and trade markets and so end up in private collections.

According to the police c. 1000 detector-men operate currently in Slovakia. In 2012, six cases of illegal archaeological activity were reported, out of which two minor cases were resolved by a fine and two further detector-men were accused and are awaiting trial. The perpetrators in such cases can be sentenced to up to 5 years in prison, and in severe offences even up to 10 years.

Until recently, the state legislation was ineffective in dealing with these serious crimes. However, our legislation is improving (Revised § 249 of the Act No. 300/2005 Coll. of the Criminal Code) and the law changes are facilitated by the newly formed Section of Cultural Heritage Protection at the Presidium of the Police Force (*Úsek Ochrany Kultúrneho Dedičstva na Prezídiu Policajného Zboru*), which regulates the activities of the respective police force authorities. In addition, the police have started to cooperate more closely with the experts, mainly archaeologists from the Monuments Board of the Slovak Republic (*Pamiatkový Úrad Slovenskej Republiky*).

If citizens suspect looting of archaeological sites they can notify the Regional Monuments Board, the Monuments Board of the Slovak Republic, the Ministry of Culture of the Slovak Republic or the local municipality. When unauthorised archaeological research or archaeological sites damaged or devaluated by excavations have been detected and there is a suspicion that an offence has been committed under § 249 of the Criminal Code (Act No. 300/2005 Coll.), an employee of the Regional Monuments Board will proceed in accordance with § 43 (2) of the Monuments Act (Act No. 49/2002 Coll.) and will refer the matter to law enforcement agencies. Before the matter is referred, the unauthorised activity needs to be well documented. The Regional Monuments Board will submit this documentation as part of a criminal complaint to the local Criminal Police

Forensic Archaeology: A Global Perspective, First Edition. Edited by W.J. Mike Groen, Nicholas Márquez-Grant and Robert C. Janaway.

at the District Headquarters of the Police Force or to the District Prosecutor's Office.

The relevant regulations of the Monuments Board and the Regional Monuments Boards for the protection of archaeological finds and archaeological sites (Glaser-Opitzová and Feníková 2012) state that when a person directly observes that an archaeological site or other natural place has been surveyed with a metal detector by an unknown person, the witness is required to notify the police at the emergency phone line 158 or directly contact the Department of Cultural Heritage Protection at the Presidium of the Police Force. At the site it is necessary to document and photograph the disturbed archaeological site, damaged archaeological finds and archaeological context. It may also be useful to photograph any objects associated with the unauthorised activity, such as a car or tools.

In the event of any unauthorised activities, such as surveying, excavation, collection, transfer or possession of movable archaeological finds, criminal proceedings led by the Department of Cultural Heritage Protection at the Presidium of the Police Force will commence. During these proceedings experts, mostly archaeologists from the Regional Monuments Board and the Monuments Board of the Slovak Republic, may be requested to assess the value of the damaged archaeological site and potentially also the value of the illegally removed archaeological finds. These experts are also authorised to determine the value of archaeological finds seized by the Police Force for the purpose of calculating the financial damage for the criminal proceedings. In addition, they may also participate in the search of the suspect's property at the request of the Police Force.

War graves from WWI and WWII

In the Slovak Republic the care for war graves is regulated by Act No. 130/2005 Coll. on War Graves, including amendments which define a War Grave. Following this Act, war graves are under the care of municipalities. The state administration of the war graves is undertaken by the Ministry of Interior of the Slovak Republic and by the district offices at the county level. The Ministry also manages the Central Register of War Graves (*Ústredná Evidencia Vojnových Hrobov*) and makes decisions about exhumations of potential war victims. Therefore, when a war grave is located, the Public Administration Section of the Ministry of Interior needs to be contacted. The data in the Central Register are continuously verified and updated. In order to make the information from the Central Register available to the public, a website[1] has been established.

Currently, there is hardly any systematic archaeological or anthropological research which targets the identification of victims of WWI and WWII. War graves are mostly identified through incidental discoveries. When human remains are detected, forensic pathologists are called to participate at the exhumation and they subsequently examine the remains. In some cases, personal identification of the remains is attempted in collaboration with historians. There were cases when, in cooperation with relevant German authorities, remains of several German soldiers were identified on our territory (Štuller et al. 2008, 2011).

Search for clandestine graves

Perpetrators sometimes try to dispose of human bodies so that their victims will never be found and consequently crucial evidence of the crime will be destroyed. In Slovakia, this type of criminal activity is being increasingly undertaken in recent years by locally organised underworld gangs, which are sometimes also supported by international organised crime groups. The situation started to deteriorate rapidly in the second half of the 1990s when the number of murders began to rise due to the expansion of organised crime groups into every region in Slovakia. For example, one of these groups killed more than 10 people and buried the victims in very deep places, such as foundations of dams during construction. Another group forced their victims to dig their own graves before murdering them. In most of these cases, the criminals chose remote rural areas to hide the bodies. However, there are also some Slovak cases in which the bodies or body parts were concealed in other places, such as buried under the floorboards within a house or stored in a refrigerator. In the first case, the body was discovered following information from a witness, while in the second case the body parts were discovered in the fridge when it was bought with other contents of a garage. One of the most peculiar cases in recent years was when, following information from a witness, the police searched an apartment in which they found the mummified body of a child, and then got to know that the family lived in that apartment with the dead child for 2 years.

For these reasons, a survey of clandestine graves and corpses became one of the most pressing issues that the Police Force of the Slovak Republic had to deal with. Police officers from Criminal Police Unit specialising in this work organise and undertake surveys for missing persons who might be deceased. The officers who undertake these surveys are called 'police searchers' and they work in an investigation unit that focuses on one

[1]For more information, see: http://www.vs.sk/uevh (last accessed 30 March 2014).

of the essential tasks performed by a police force in accordance with § 2 (1e) of the Act No. 171/93 Coll. on the Police Force. The survey procedure for locating persons and objects is governed by the Regulation of the Minister of Interior of the Slovak Republic No. 53/2007. In this phase of the investigation the survey is carried out by police investigators, who use police information and police procedures and methods without involving other professionals and experts. The involvement of civilian experts will only be requested when human remains or other traces suggesting the presence of a human body (e.g. personal items, clothing) are found.

After a person is reported missing, primary information about the disappearance of the person is verified and in case there is a suspicion the person might have died a violent death a search for the missing person will be declared. The investigation is traditionally comprised of the verification of last sightings, his/her place of residence and investigation of last known movements. Gradually, the search will focus on the place where the missing person was last seen or where he/she could be regularly encountered. At this stage in the investigation, a suspicion prevails that these places may also be the places where a body or body parts can be uncovered. Therefore, a search will be undertaken with the help of specially trained cadaver dogs; special equipment, such as instruments for detecting soil disturbance; special techniques, such as thermal vision, ground-penetrating radar and multispectral photography; and chemical probing for the detection of decomposition products.

If a large area needs to be examined in order to find a buried body, a larger number of police officers will be deployed to search the landscape. In case the area is very large, a skirmish line will be used for prospection. The searching party concentrates on spotting changes of the ground surface. An effective approach, which is used frequently in Slovak practice, is deploying specially trained cadaver dogs.

The Department of Cynology (*Odbor Kynológie*) is an independent functional unit within the Presidium of the Police Force constituted in 1991 by the Regulation of the Minister of Interior of the Slovak Republic No. 4/1991. One of the sections of the Cynology department specialises in training dogs to search for cadavers. In connection with this activity the Police Force in Slovakia recently started to train dogs to search for bodies or body parts in water. Their current positive results have justified the establishment of this new subsection (Berek 2000; Krajník 2009).

According to the investigators, in forensic practice clandestine graves, bodies, body parts or skeletal remains are most commonly found either following information given by a witness or the perpetrator, who will lead the police to the place where the body has been hidden, or they are found accidentally during excavation work, or in farming activities or in not easily accessible terrain and landfills. Police cynologists with cadaver dogs are the most commonly used means in police surveys for clandestine graves in Slovak practice. The second most common method used is the survey of large areas by a skirmish line of police officers who search for visual indicators suggesting the location of clandestine graves.

Other approaches, such as using specialised technology, are less developed. Some representatives of the police express the opinion that using helicopters with thermal vision is not useful in the search for corpses. However, they acknowledge that this method can be applied when locating cadavers in the early stages of decomposition, which lie on the surface, in a meadow or other open spaces. Another survey instrument that is rarely used in practice is ground-penetrating radar (GPR). One reason for avoiding this method is that the police lack the experts and the equipment necessary and they are not used to cooperating with civilians who may have both the expertise and the technical equipment, such as forensic archaeologists.

Recently, the Slovak media gave a lot of attention to a case of a young woman who went missing in 2003 and during the search the police actually used GPR, which was borrowed from abroad after a request from the Minister of the Interior. Based on the GPR technology 11 sites were identified in a location indicated by a suspect who confessed murdering the young woman and burying her body in this place. However, the body has not been found. Later, the suspect stopped cooperating with the police and he withdrew his confession. Due to the high profile of this case several other survey methods were used, including a survey using visual indicators in a skirmish line, aerial photography and cadaver dogs. Despite repeated efforts from the police to find the body following information gained throughout the investigation and also information from the public, the body of the young woman has still not been found.

On-site procedures for the recovery of bodies or skeletal remains

After the discovery of a clandestine grave potentially containing human remains, police investigators undertake the excavation and secure the human remains by using their own methods and procedures. Procedures that need to be followed on the site of a body recovery are briefly described in the Criminal Procedure Code (Act No. 301/2005 Coll.) but are mainly governed by the Regulation of the Minister of Interior of the Slovak Republic No. 53/2007 on the procedure for searching for persons and objects.

After a police station receives a report that human remains have been found, the local police officers will examine the site where the body was found and will interview the person who discovered the body and ensure his/her participation on all required actions. The local police officers will also secure the site in order to ensure that the area and the body are preserved in their original state. They will cordon the area off and demarcate a single access path. Before the arrival of the investigators, police officers present at the site will secure any forensic evidence, particularly in cases where the evidence may be easily damaged or lost.

The group of investigators usually includes a senior investigator, a crime scene technician and a police officer from the investigation unit of the Judicial and Criminal Police (*Úrad Justičnej a Kriminálnej Polície*), but more investigators and other specialists may be involved depending on the complexity of the case. At the scene the investigators will undertake a thorough inspection of the body and the surrounding area. They will traditionally document the scene in a written protocol and with photographs, but occasionally other means of documentation, such as drawings and videos may be used. In some cases, specialist members of the Police Force, such as dog handlers and other crime scene technicians, as well as specialists from other fields of expertise will be called to attend the scene. In most cases, a forensic pathologist is called in order to give an opinion on the circumstances of the person's death. In some cases, the corpse can be initially examined by a physician, as is routine in cases of non-suspicious deaths, if a physician has an authorisation for this kind of examination from the Health Care Surveillance Authority under § 42 of Act No. 576/2004 Coll. on Health Care and Health Care Services.

The Regulation of the Minister of Interior of the Slovak Republic No. 53/2007 on the procedure for searching for persons and objects also governs the specific procedure required for the recovery of human remains. However, this particular section is quite brief. Soil and other substances and objects that covered the skeletal remains should be removed and the individual stages of the recovery process should be documented photographically. A forensic anthropologist or a forensic pathologist should be invited to the scene in order to provide his/her expertise on, amongst others things, the post-mortem interval of the find, that is whether the remains are recent or historical with respect to time since death. In the majority of cases in our country, only forensic pathologists, not forensic anthropologists, are called to the scene. When the remains are considered to be historical, that is older than 50 years, the police will hand the case over to the archaeologists. When the pathologist concludes that the find may be recent, the recovery process will continue and the layer of soil beneath the remains will be examined to the depth of c. 3 cm. In justified cases, the use a metal detector is recommended. In addition, from the area immediately beneath and around the body samples of soil, insects, larvae and pupae should be secured.

All bones need to be secured for the forensic anthropological analysis. Skeletal remains must be handled with care and special attention should be paid to the skull, teeth, vertebrae and small bones. Bones should be sent to the specialist individually wrapped in paper. Loose teeth should be packed individually.

Specific procedures and methods applied at the site of recovery of human remains are described in forensic textbooks and police officers are educated about them during courses held at the Academy of Police Force in Bratislava (*Akadémia Policajného Zboru v Bratislave*) (e.g. Krajník 2005). As mentioned earlier, the entire excavation, documentation and securing of the human remains in Slovakia is exclusively undertaken by the police under the leadership of a senior investigator by applying their own methods and procedures, which oftentimes grossly differ from methods recommended by forensic archaeologists.

The experts that police will engage at the site of recovery of human remains are either forensic pathologists or forensic anthropologists in case skeletonised remains are uncovered. Forensic pathologists usually work for Institutes of Forensic Medicine at universities, such as the Institute of Forensic Medicine at the Medical Faculty of the Comenius University in Bratislava, Institute of Forensic Medicine and Medical Expertise at the Jesenius Medical Faculty in Martin, and Institute of Forensic Medicine at the Medical Faculty of the Pavol Jozef Safarik University in Kosice. Alternatively, forensic pathologists can also work for private expert organisations, such as Forensic.sk (Institute of Forensic Medical Expertise). Experts from the field of forensic anthropology are university graduates in anthropology (more specifically in biology with a specialisation in biological anthropology), who also need to undergo a special training and subsequently pass a test on the Experts Code (Act No. 382/2004 Coll.), Criminal Procedure Code (Act No. 301/2005 Coll.), Criminal Code (Act No. 300/2005 Coll.) and other relevant legislation relating to the activities of expert witnesses.

After the documentation and securing of all evidence, the body will be examined and an autopsy will be performed at a medico-legal institute which is regulated by § 156 of the Criminal Procedure Code (Act No. 301/2005 Coll.). The aim of the examination and the autopsy is to ascertain the identity of the deceased person and the circumstances and cause of death. A medico-legal assessment is also mandatory in the case of skeletal findings, while an anthropological assessment is only undertaken if law enforcement authorities (usually the investigator) issue such a request. In Slovak forensic practice a forensic anthropologist is only requested when the identification of skeletal remains has not been successful for a long period of time and hinders the investigation of the related offence. The conditions under which an expert (with any type of expertise) can be engaged are summarised in § 143 of the Criminal Procedure Code (Act No. 301/2005 Coll.).

Conclusion

In conclusion, the Slovak police work closely with archaeologists only in cases of damage or devaluation of archaeological heritage sites or counterfeiting of archaeological finds. There is currently no systematic research of war graves from WWI and WWII and associated identification of victims of wars undertaken in Slovakia.

In this chapter we have summarised the Slovak legislation and forensic practice with respect to searches for the remains of missing persons in cases of suspected violent deaths as well as the police procedures followed on the scene when bodies, body parts or skeletal remains are discovered. We showed that in the mentioned situations Slovak law enforcement uses its own methodology and procedures, which are oftentimes very different to methods recommended by forensic archaeologists. The methodological discrepancies may be partly the reason why the remains of many missing persons remain undiscovered and the corresponding offences unsolved.

Nevertheless, we hope that this book and our chapter may facilitate a change in the current practice in Slovakia towards better communication and cooperation between the law enforcement authorities and experts in forensic archaeology.

References

Act No. 49/2002 Coll. On Protection of Monuments and Historic Sites ('Cultural Heritage Monuments Act'). *The Slovak Republic Law Digest 23*, published on 2 February 2002.

Act No. 130/2005 Coll. The War Grave Act. *The Slovak Republic Law Digest 58*, published on 16 March 2005.

Act No. 171/93 Coll. On the Police Force. *The Slovak Republic Law Digest 46*, published on 6 July 1993.

Act No. 300/2005 Coll. The Criminal Code. *The Slovak Republic Law Digest 129*, published on 2 July 2005.

Act No. 301/2005 Coll. The Code of Criminal Procedure. *The Slovak Republic Law Digest 130*, published on 2 July 2005.

Act No. 382/2004 Coll. On Experts, Interpreters and Translators. *The Slovak Republic Law Digest 162*, published on 26 May 2004.

Act No. 576/2004 Coll. On Health Care and Health Care Services. *The Slovak Republic Law Digest 243*, published on 1 November 2004.

Berek, A. 2000. Špeciálne cvičený pes na vyhľadávanie mŕtvol v policajnej praxi. In P. Masárová (ed.), *Efektívne Využívanie Služobných Psov v Policajnej Praxi s Dôrazom na Detekciu Drog a Záchranársku Činnosť*, 35–38. Bratislava, Prezídium Policajného Zboru - Odbor kynológie.

Glaser-Opitzová, R. and Feníková, A. 2012. *Metodická Inštrukcia k Výkonu Špecializovanej Štátnej Správy Pamiatkového Úradu SR a Krajských Pamiatkových Úradov na Ochranu Archeologických Nálezov a Archeologických Nálezísk*. Bratislava, Pamiatkový Úrad Slovenskej Republiky.

Krajník, V. (ed.) 2005. *Kriminalistika*. Bratislava, Akadémia Policajného Zboru.

Krajník, V. (ed.) 2009. *Policajná Kynológia*. Bratislava, Akadémia Policajného Zboru.

Regulation of the Minister of Interior of the Slovak Republic No. 4/1991 (internal regulation).

Regulation of the Minister of Interior of the Slovak Republic No. 53/2007 (internal regulation).

Štuller, F., Novomeský, F., Krajčovič, J., Macko, V. and Straka, Ľ. 2008. The late results of WWII – the human remains: how to handle them? *Book of Abstracts and Lectures. 1st Slovak – Czech Scientific Congress of Forensic Medicine with International Participation*, 18–21 June 2008, Gabčíkovo, Slovakia, 10. Bratislava, Comenius University.

Štuller, F., Novomeský, F., Krajčovič, J. and Straka, Ľ. 2011. Skelettreste aus dem Zeitraum des Zweiten Weltkriegs. *Rechtsmedizin* 21(2), 136–140.

Website

The Central Register of War Graves. Available at: http://www.vs.sk/uevh/ (accessed 20 August 2014).

CHAPTER 20

Inclusion of archaeology in criminal investigations – Slovenia

Pavel Jamnik

Ministry of the Interior, Criminal Police Directorate, Ljubljana, Slovenia

Introduction

Slovenia is a country with just two million inhabitants. There are relatively few serious criminal offences against life and limb; from 2007 to 2012 there were 9.4 murders and 8.2 manslaughters per year per 100,000 inhabitants (Ministry of the Interior, annual statistics). In the majority of such cases, the perpetrator is identified immediately or very shortly after the event. There are rare cases of people going missing as a result of a criminal offence. Fewer still are cases when a buried body or remains are found after a long period. In such cases cooperation between the police and archaeologists in reading the stratigraphy of the burial would be useful; however, the manner of cooperation is not yet regulated. Another field of cooperation between archaeology and police would potential be for smuggling and illicit trade in movable cultural heritage.

Apart from the general police work from recent homicides, a specific phenomenon in Slovenia, as a former Yugoslav republic, is the presence of mass graves as a result of mass killings of military and political opponents immediately after the end of World War II (WWII). In May 1945, thousands of soldiers and civilians from all over Yugoslavia were on the run through Slovenia, the westernmost part of Yugoslavia. Over 600 gravesites have been discovered in Slovenia (Ferenc 2012, 5). Some of them contain the remains of thousands of people, others only a few. It was only after the democratic changes in 1991 that the attitude to these mass graves changed in Slovenia. A shift from mass graves protected and covered-up by secret services and police to the so-called awareness of the crime occurred (Jamnik 2009), which meant that gravesites were recognised as scenes of crime, and buried human remains as unidentified victims of criminal offences. As a consequence, legal changes concerning the marking and treating of these gravesites took place as well as their examination. On the one hand there were police investigations and legally defined criteria for carrying out exhumation[1] and, on the other, exhumation to satisfy the wishes of victims' relatives for proper burial. Both processes have intertwined and complemented each other, with the aim of acquiring as much information as possible from the graves containing unidentified and not easily identifiable victims. We realised very early on that such work requires the presence of archaeological experts, or at the very least some archaeological knowledge on the part of the excavators.

Prior to exploring the investigation of mass graves, a brief outline is provided of the medico-legal framework in Slovenia, in particular with reference to cases where archaeology is or may be utilised.

Medico-legal framework with regard to mass graves

In the framework of the Commission of the Government of the Republic of Slovenia on Concealed Mass Graves in Slovenia (*Komisija Vlade Republike Slovenije za Reševanje Vprašanj Prekritih Grobišč*), which was founded by the Slovenian Government as early as 1990, special work methodology for probing and exhumation was drawn up. The Commission members tried to harmonise this with police requirements as to the necessary activities affecting the gravesites on the one hand, and a reduction of costs and speedy exhumation on the other.

We provide here a more detailed presentation of legal bases and practice regarding the introduction of archaeology into the forensic examination of mass grave exhumation. This is a rather lengthy process but nevertheless it can serve as an interesting example and experience for other countries. There are a number of acts that were set in place.

[1]Exhumation in Slovenia is a legal term for the excavation of human remains for the purposes of criminal investigation – a so-called urgent investigative act, which is ordered by the investigating judge on the prosecutor's office initiative.

Forensic Archaeology: A Global Perspective, First Edition. Edited by W.J. Mike Groen, Nicholas Márquez-Grant and Robert C. Janaway.

The Criminal Procedure Act (CPA) (*Zakon o Kazenskem Postopku Republike Slovenije*) (Official Gazette of RS, No 63/1994, 70/1994) (*Uradni List Republike Slovenije*) tasks a court-appointed medical expert with the physical act of exhumation of human remains pursuant to an investigating judge's order. In practice, these are court-appointed experts of the Institute of Forensic Medicine at the Faculty of Medicine in Ljubljana (*Inštitut za Sodno Medicino Medicinske Fakultete v Ljubljani*), who perform the necessary expert procedures for the police and court, such as autopsies, determining the cause and time of death, toxicology examinations, etc. The Cultural Heritage Act (CHA) (*Zakon o Kulturni Dediščini*) (Official Gazette of RS, No. 16-485/2008 and 123/2008) considers as archaeology everything older than 50 years, but in unclear cases of finding human remains, at least in the first stage, the police is always involved. That means that the post-war graves are the responsibility of archaeology and the police at the same time.

The War Gravesites Act (WGA) (*Zakon o Vojnih Grobiščih*) (Official Gazette of RS, No. 6572003) lays down in paragraph v 7 of Article 28 that 'for an already recorded alleged gravesite, where the existence of human remains has not been proved but can reasonably be suspected, the Ministry may issue a permit for the performance of procedures of determining the existence of a war gravesite. The Ministry shall inform the Police and State Prosecutor's Office thereof' [authors' translation]. With the adoption of this Act it became legally possible to verify the existence of a number of WWII grave or deposition sites, whose micro-location is known only approximately or even unknown, while the other collected data undoubtedly point at the existence of a concealed gravesite. In practice this is done by probing and excavating the ground. In Article 27, the WGA also enables a covered gravesite to be excavated, if so requested by relatives, natural and legal persons who have a legitimate interest to make such a request.

The test pits and excavation made possible under the WGA first needed to be regulated methodologically to avoid disrespectful handling of human remains or disrespectful or destructive probing and excavation. For this reason, in 2006, the Government Commission prepared the *Protokol Izkopov Prikritih Vojnih Grobišč* (Protocol of the Procedure of Excavating a War Gravesite), which defines the competences of individual entities involved in the investigation of post-war gravesites as well as legal ways of carrying out individual procedures. The Commission adopted the Protocol at its seventh regular session on 21 June 2006, and it defines the sequence of including individual investigative and custodian entities in the treatment of an individual gravesite.

When a yet unknown gravesite is discovered, the police begin to investigate whether the grave is a result of a criminal offence. If it appears to be a war grave, a state prosecutor may, on the basis of a crime report by the police, file an application with the competent court for an investigation to be initiated, and propose that the investigating judge carries out investigative acts to obtain evidence and find the perpetrator. One of these investigative measures is to order exhumation/excavation of human remains. If the remains are older and turn out to be archaeological, then the site and remains are passed to archaeological competence.

If the investigating judge does not order investigative acts, it means that the police and prosecutor's work is complete until any new or additional facts arise. From here on, activities at gravesites can be performed pursuant to the WGA. The Government Commission on Concealed Graves may adopt a proposal for a decision for exhumation and reburial of remains found in a war grave. On the basis of this proposal, the Government can decide if public interest exists, that the Ministry of Labour, Family, Social Affairs and Equal Opportunities (*Ministrstvo za Delo, Družino, Socialne Zadeve in Enake Možnosti*) should finance and lead the procedure of excavation, or it may decide on co-financing with other entities that have a legitimate interest.

Such an approach can confirm or rule out allegations on the existence of a grave which were not confirmed or ruled out in a police investigation, while excavation may provide new or additional facts on the basis of which a pre-trial or criminal procedure, which had to be terminated previously because the possibilities provided by the Criminal Procedure Act were exhausted, could continue (Government Commission 2006b).

Even before the adoption of the Protocol the Commission prepared theoretical positions for the performance of works, such as the Methodology of Carrying out Excavation, which is a result of experience gained from both 'classically' performed court-ordered exhumations as well as exhumations based on a method suited to archaeological work (Government Commission 2006a). The most important points of the Methodology of Carrying out Excavation are as follows (after Jamnik 2008a, 89; 2011, 288):

> *Test pits* can be carried out: at suspected gravesites where the specific location of the interment is unknown, at burial sites where the area of the burial site needs to be marked off (e.g. trenches, bomb craters, caves) or at places where oral sources (e.g. witness interviews) indicate a burial site, and finally where the location by a visual inspection of the field is not obvious. It is also recommended that these test pits, performed by machine or by hand should be *c.* 1 × 1 m or 0.5 × 2 m, to the depth of any human remains. When first bone remains are found as a result of the test pits or evaluation trenches, all works immediately stop. During this evaluation phase, an anthropological or forensic expert has to be present on site to provide an opinion as to whether the bones found are human or not. [Authors' translation]

> *Excavation* is performed following forensic, archaeological and anthropological methods. This means that the same way of removing soil layers (or stratigraphic units) over skeletons is used as employed by archaeologists in their work, whilst human remains are protected and documented by using forensic principles (photo documentation, protecting traces of injuries, isolation and identification of associated items). Given the progress of the forensic science, it is recommended that DNA samples are taken from the human remains *in situ* to minimise contamination and store for subsequent analyses. With regard to any objects or items found in the grave, the protocols indicate that these are of much value regarding victim identification, dating and the events surrounding the deposition. For this reason they have to be protected in accordance with forensic principles and documented. As these objects have at the same time a historical significance and have to be protected and stored accordingly, they are handed over to a museum institution, which processes and uses them as museum exhibits. [Authors' translation]

In addition, the exhumation work is contracted out and a call for tenders advertised by the Ministry of Labour, Family, Social Affairs and Equal opportunities. The tender should have the following conditions for the excavation:

- The contracting institution or company should ensure that the excavation will not affect a larger area than necessary for the exhumation of skeletal remains.
- The excavation is done by separate removal of soil layers to achieve the exhumation of entire skeletal remains, thus ensuring that skeletal remains do not get mixed if possible.
- Skeletal remains are photographically documented during excavation, separately and together.
- The spot where objects are found with skeletal remains is recorded, photographed and these artefacts are stored as historical items for further restoration work. If an object is considered potential evidence in the opinion of the competent police representative, it is dealt with in accordance with forensic principles.
- The contracting authority or contractor shall make sure that skeletal remains are kept separated by individuals and stored in suitable and secure premises until reburial.

The Cultural Heritage Act (CHA) (*Zakon o Kulturni Dediščini*) (Official Gazette of RS, No. 16-485/2008 and 123/2008) was adopted in 2008, and it classified clandestine mass graves among immovable cultural heritage. The system of protection and work at mass burial sites thus became a subject under the Ministry of Culture. In Article 3 the CHA places covered gravesites among cultural heritage and thus any investigation and excavation must be carried out in accordance with the conditions for examination and removal of archaeological layers. Immediately after the adoption of the CHA, the Ministry of Culture did not get involved in works concerning post-war graves. However, in 2010 there were some cases when the extent of probing exceeded the authorised framework and the Ministry of Culture as the authority implementing the CHA reacted. On 14 March 2011 the Ministry of Culture informed the Ministry of Labour, Family, Social Affairs and Equal Opportunities, the Office of the State Prosecutor General, the General Police Directorate, the Supreme Court, the Institute of Forensic Medicine, the Institute for the Protection of Cultural Heritage of Slovenia, the Commission on Concealed Mass Graves and the concession operator for exhumation and reburial of foreign soldiers of the proper manner of carrying out works at gravesites under Articles 31 and 33 of the CHA.

In the document it says that the operator, in the course of works during which archaeological remains could become physically altered, must hire a professional archaeologist and physical anthropologist to lead the work. An exception as regards the acquisition of cultural heritage approvals is a court-ordered exhumation of bodies. However, in this case also the observance of archaeological standards is recommended, the only difference being that the documentation and protection of objects and skeletal remains discovered is done in accordance with the principles of forensic examination.

Control over performance of work in the field and decision making on the arrangement of the gravesite after the work is finished is under the competence of the conservation specialist of the regional unit of the Institute of the Protection of Cultural Heritage of Slovenia in the area of which the works are carried out (Ministry of Culture 2011).

With this notice of the Ministry of Culture, the rules of obtaining permission for work were at last defined in detail, and the methods of work and its documentation laid down in a legal basis after work had been carried out at concealed gravesites since 2006. Excavations and probing have slowed down somewhat in recent years; therefore it is not entirely clear in practice how the principles of precise archaeological work method will be married with lower methodological needs of work at concealed gravesites. It needs to be stated quite openly that some kind of struggle was going on to take over this area, as it is connected to, among other things, the contract for archaeological works and control over the performance of work. It will have to be borne in mind that a demand for equally high methodological standards as apply in archaeology would be an unnecessary exaggeration, which would make things considerably more expensive. It would also lead to an attempt to divert an investigation of post-war mass graves into a scientific sphere of archaeology, which – given that relatives of those killed are still alive and that in several gravesites there are human remains with preserved tissues – cannot be a legitimate and justified wish. Exaggerated precision of documentation and positioning of a discovery and skeleton could only be an end in itself, which would only slow down the work and make it more expensive. When archaeologists started to be included in excavations of mass graves the author tried to define the necessary and pertinent criteria of archaeological work at mass gravesites and to point out the important differences between investigating a 'classical' archaeological site and a 'recent' mass gravesite.

With concealed mass graves the situation is different than in the case of classic archaeological sites. Graves are physically obscured to a certain extent; however, in almost all cases there are oral sources testifying to the presence of graves in the vicinity. On their basis, even though oral sources cannot be deemed the only source, it is possible to reconstruct many details, including the date of the killings. A mass grave investigation therefore almost does not look for answers to the same questions as archaeology does, that is when, why and for how long. A mass grave investigation is interested in the questions who (are the victims and perpetrators), in what way (were they killed), with what (type of weapon) and how (was the grave constructed and covered/concealed). If we just compare the stratigraphy aspect, in archaeology the stratigraphic position of discoveries and their sites is of fundamental importance for interpretation. In archaeology, the interpretation of deposit sequence is the point of departure for further work. With mass gravesites, the question of stratigraphy is almost negligible. We are only interested in whether it was a concurrent burial and how the burial site was covered and concealed – simple questions that do not require such precise excavation techniques as with archaeological work. As a consequence, the documentation of a burial site excavation is also less demanding than the documentation of an archaeological grave excavation. The division of the excavation area into areas, sectors or strata, which serves accurate documentation of the excavation work and the recording of discoveries in archaeological excavation, is almost never needed. Precise sketches and positioning of excavated skeletal remains at a mass gravesite would lead work towards exclusively scientific treatment of mass gravesites and increase costs of the excavation. In our opinion, such documentation is not needed for WWII graves in Slovenia as it serves no further purpose. In documenting mass gravesites, a basic sketch supported by photographs of individual skeletons and accompanying objects suffices. The reason for applying the archaeological work method at concealed gravesites is that the result thus obtained is intended for judicial proceedings and the method must follow suit. Archaeological work methods are here used to assist legal and forensic science.

One of the important differences between an archaeological individual grave and a mass gravesite of post-war killings is that there are living relatives or supposed relatives of the victims. For this reason a greater consideration to any sensitivity or a greater degree of reverence and respect is called for, as there is emotional involvement of relatives who have obtained an authorised permit for excavation. The psychological aspect applies here, as it would appear that relatives find it hard to accept their dead being a subject of archaeological processing.

Another important difference between gravesites and classic archaeological locations that needs to be taken into account is the relatively short time from the emergence of a particular mass grave. In many cases this means that human remains have not yet been skeletonised and that remains of soft tissue or hair are present, or that human remains are even naturally mummified; likewise with materials such as textiles. In such cases, due to the decomposition processes, work needs to be done as fast as possible and excavators must devote more attention to personal protection as they would in excavating an archaeological gravesite. All these points also apply if an archaeologist participates in the exhumation of a victim of recent murder or manslaughter (Jamnik 2008b, 183).

Further mass gravesite investigations will show which direction the work will take, whether it will be in unnecessary insistence on the full methodology of excavation and documentation of mass gravesites as archaeological sites or a methodology adapted to the needs of specific research corpus of mass gravesites. Given the experience so far, some harmonisation will still be needed, as the archaeological profession has already pointed out that in their opinion the level of documentation of the excavation of mass gravesites done in 2006 and 2007 was insufficient.

> [T]he excavation method is indeed archaeological and an archaeologist and anthropologist are present, however, it does not in any way meet the minimal standards of archaeological methodology of excavation for several reasons – an acute lack of funds, strictly limited time of excavation, documentation reduced to photographing only, surveyance measurements are just local (Josipovič 2011, 473). [Authors' translation]

From 2006 to 2010 Josipovič directed a total of eight excavations, for which the author can say, from the point of view of a police investigator of mass gravesites, that they met all the necessary requirements for further work and that the documentation was entirely satisfactory. Any more extensive documenting would be, as already mentioned, unnecessary and an end in itself.

Historical developments of mass grave exhumation/excavation in the republic of Slovenia

This section presents the origins and development of the excavation of mass graves in Slovenia which took place alongside the legal definition of methods of work that was presented in the preceding chapter.

In 1996 and 1999 during construction works in Celje and Maribor (Tezno-Bohova) a large number of human bones were found in anti-tank trenches (Ferenc 2012, 36–63). The exhumations of human remains were undertaken by the Institute of Forensic Medicine upon an investigating judge's order. These were the first exhumations of mass gravesites of post-war killings in Slovenia. There was no practice or experience of such specific excavations and no qualified or experienced archaeologists were employed. The process followed was that human bones were taken from the grave as they were found, and skeletons were then reconstructed next to the grave. Along with skeletal reconstruction a basic forensic medical examination was performed. It turned out that reconstructing the correct skeletal was enough of a problem, let alone matching the objects found with the skeletons (Figure 20.1).

In 2001 the municipality of Slovenska Bistrica started excavating a mined bomb shelter above the town. The excavation was done by digging into the ruined bomb shelter from the front; the bones found were then examined in front of the bomb shelter, where the basic forensic medical examination was done. The work was performed in difficult and spatially limited conditions, and therefore the physical excavation of the bomb shelter needed to be finished as soon as possible. As the bodies were covered with loam and could only be accessed by digging from the front they could not be exhumed while maintaining the anatomical position. A total of 431 victims were exhumed, the majority of whom still had a considerable amount of tissue preserved (Ferenc 2012, 65–76).

In 2005 an excavation of a gravesite at Bodovlje near Škofja Loka was conducted. It has since become a textbook example of how not to do an excavation. Physical removal of soil from above the skeletons was done by machines with brute force literally down to the skeletons. When human remains were found, the ground beside the gravesite was dug down to below the level of the gravesite, from where a very imprecise frontal excavation was performed. The bones were collected from the gravesite as they were found. Only after the excavation attempts were made to put the skeletons together at the Institute of Forensic Medicine, which carried out the excavation (Ferenc 2012, 83–87).

Such excavations show that it is essential to change the work method. If we wish to get at least some data from the gravesite on the manner of the execution and on the victims, the excavation method needs to be changed and qualified and/or experienced archaeologists employed. The first exhumation based on the principles of forensic anthropology, and an archaeologically comparable method, during the investigation of post-war killings in Slovenia was carried out at the gravesite of Jelenca near Šmarjeta na Dolenjskem in 2003 (Jamnik 2008a, 84). The investigating judge appointed the Institute of Forensic Medicine (IFM) to oversee the exhumation. As during previous exhumations, due to objective circumstances in the excavation of gravesites, some data were lost. The author of this chapter, who led the police investigation of the gravesite, suggested that 'an archaeologically comparable excavation' should be carried out. During exhumations performed until then the bones had been literally plucked from the ground and no attempt was made to excavate whole skeletons. As a consequence, it was not possible to determine the position of objects found next to the bodies and by the end of the excavation, the bones were completely mixed

Figure 20.1 Tezno pri Mariboru, 1999, non-archaeological exhumation of human remains (photo: Pavel Jamnik).

Figure 20.2 Lovrenška grapa, 2006, archaeological method of gravesite excavation associated with exhumations, led by an archaeologist (photo: Pavel Jamnik).

up. The initiative was accepted by the IFM. After the exhumation representatives of the IFM and the police agreed that such work, even though it takes longer than the excavation methods used until then, yields important and complex data on victims and especially a much greater quantity of data (Ferenc 2012, 80–82).

In 2006 and 2007, in addition to police exhumations done previously, the first excavations based on the adopted 'methodology' were carried out on the Government Commission's proposal at gravesites Lovrenška grapa (Figure 20.2), Žovšče in the garden of the Loka castle and on Pohorje (Ferenc 2012, 106–109). Archaeologist Mr D. Josipovič was in charge of the excavation and documentation. It was the first time that he had overseen professional archaeological work. From 2006 to 2010 Mr Josipovič led eight excavations that from the author's viewpoint as investigator met all the requirements needed. Anything more extensive would, as already mentioned earlier, only be an end in itself. Even though the excavation at the Areh na Pohorju gravesite was conducted under time pressure as it was late autumn, the work done was important as 'profile' documenting (Figure 20.3) of a grave hollow with human remains proved how a methodologically correct approach to excavation can yield data that would be lost forever with a different kind of excavation. In the excavated gravesite there were 190 bodies (Leben-Seljak 2007, 1).

An important excavation was carried out when a motorway was being built near Lesce airport in November 2006. The excavation was done pursuant to the Criminal Procedure Act, which means it was done for the needs of criminal proceedings. The excavation was done in accordance with the Government Commission's methodology by the IFM. With archaeologically comparable work, skeletons of 35 people were excavated (Ferenc 2012, 103–105). This excavation was particularly important as the Government Commission's methodology became accepted also for excavations ordered by the judicial system in the case of a criminal investigation. The work done by an archaeologically comparable method yielded excellent results as to the manner of execution and burial, and individual injuries on skeletons could be reconstructed. Two separate burials of bodies at different times could be distinguished and objects matched to the skeletons (Figure 20.4).

Figure 20.3 Areh na Pohorju, 2007, a view of a cleared profile of a grave pit (photo: Pavel Jamnik).

The last major work on a covered gravesite was so specific that it was clear right from the start that the removal of bodies will represent a methodological *novum* both in Slovenia and worldwide. In 2009 the Government

Figure 20.4 Lesce, 2006, archaeological method of gravesite excavation associated with criminal investigation, led by a forensic medicine expert (photo: Pavel Jamnik).

Figure 20.5 Huda jama, 2009, mummified bodies in horizontal pit (photo: Pavel Jamnik).

Commission started excavating the pits of an abandoned coal mine, Huda jama, near Laško, where according to known data several thousand people were killed in May 1945 and thrown into mine shafts, which were then filled. Over several months miners removed *c.* 150 m of material from completely filled pits. They had to remove 11 partition walls, made of reinforced concrete and more than 1 m thick, which were installed after the killings to cover the gravesite. When the gravesite was discovered on 4 March 2009, investigators encountered an unimaginable sight of hundreds of human bodies that, for the most part, were mummified due to a specific climate in the mine (Ferenc et al. 2011). A team of forensic medicine experts from the IFM and criminal forensic experts spent several months removing bodies from the horizontal part of the mine's pit and a part of a vertical shaft. A total of 778 bodies were removed, and several thousand mummified victims are still in the mine shaft awaiting further decision on the way to remove and bury them. Bodies were stratigraphically removed since they were placed on top of each other in the horizontal pit and intertwined and squashed due to the pressure of other bodies in the horizontal shaft. Even though the work was excruciatingly exhausting, physically and psychologically, every effort was made to document the removal of human remains from the mine in a form that was at least to some extent suitable for archaeological documentation, although in this case the criminal forensic and anthropologically forensic medical processing had priority (Figures 20.5 and 20.6).

Figure 20.6 Huda jama, 2009, fully preserved mummified bodies (photo: Pavel Jamnik).

Perspectives

Through the years, Slovenia managed, with the cooperation of criminal forensics, forensic medicine, anthropology and archaeology and under the auspices of the Government Commission on Concealed Graves, to formulate and regulate how the work at post-war mass graves should be carried out. Even though the current regulation imposes an entirely archaeological approach to work at mass gravesites, in practice both in civil-sanitary and judicially ordered exhumations for reasons of criminal investigations, the work is done by using a somewhat curtailed archaeological method, but an archaeological method nonetheless.

Experience of working with archaeological experts during mass grave excavations has made the police consider whether archaeological expertise might be useful in investigating current criminal offences. As with criminal investigation work all possibilities and know-how have to be considered that might lead to identification of the perpetrators and clarification of the circumstances of a criminal offence. With better documentation and recognition of traces left at the scene, we have identified archaeological know-how as a positive possibility. Thus we have started acquainting investigators, as part of their regular training, with the possibility of engaging an archaeological expert in cases when a buried body is found and the stratigraphy of the burial could shed some light on how the offence was committed. So far we have not had a case where we could check the results of such cooperation.

The next segment of cooperation between the police and archaeology is the area of illicit trade in art and criminal offences connected to the destruction of cultural heritage. Here cooperation goes both ways. The police inform archaeological and museum institutions of cases and the institutions make sure the objects are stored appropriately and give the police as much information as possible on concrete objects or places they originate from. Such cooperation includes an exchange of know-how and has already taken place in some cases at police training courses, when an archaeologist presented the specifics of his profession, thus giving police officers some knowledge the police education system does not provide.

Forensic archaeology as a sub-branch of archaeology is not represented as part of the university study of archaeology. This means that archaeologists in Slovenia cannot institutionally acquire specific knowledge of forensic archaeology, which would make it possible to include a forensic archaeologist in an investigative team on account of his forensic skills obtained during his or her education. With its specific methodology, archaeology can be included in the investigation of criminal offences as a tool for securing traces of a criminal offence to the best possible degree. Cooperation in the investigation of mass graves is successful and regulated. Engaging an archaeologist as an external expert in cases that seem to need archaeological skills will show whether a step forward will need to be taken in the area of archaeologists' education and some additional expertise required.

There have been initiatives recently to introduce new work methods in forensic investigations, or, more specifically, geological ones, which in this case are quite close to the archaeological knowledge of recognition or reading the so-called stratigraphic column. A study was done by the Forensic Laboratory of the Ministry of the Interior, where mineral composition, density and colour of 15 soil samples from different locations were compared, which can be key evidence that connects a location and/or victim in an investigation, and comparisons made of traces found at a crime scene (Štibelj 2012).

The Slovenian criminal police and Forensic Laboratory of the Ministry of the Interior try to introduce and adopt as many multidisciplinary approaches as possible in searching for, securing and documenting traces of criminal offences.

References

Ferenc, M. 2012. *Prekopi Žrtev iz Prikritih Grobišč*. Ljubljana, Znanstvena založba FF.

Ferenc, M., Mehmedalija, A. and Jamnik, P. 2011. *Huda Jama*. Ljubljana, Družina.

Government Commission. 2006a. *Methodology of Carrying out Excavation*. Slovenian Government Commission on Concealed Mass Graves. Document No. 17400-22/2005-10, 26 January 2006.

Government Commission. 2006b. *Protocol of the Procedure of Excavating a War Gravesite*. Slovenian Government Commission on Concealed Mass Graves. Document No.17400-22/2005-30, 21 June 2006.

Jamnik, P. 2008a. Metodološki okviri izvedbe sodno odrejenih ekshumacij ter sondiranj in prekopov, izvedenih v okviru vladne komisije. In J. Dežman (ed.), *Poročilo Komisije Vlade Republike Slovenije za Reševanje Vprašanj Prikritih Grobišč 2005–2009*, 83–91. Ljubljana, Družina.

Jamnik, P. 2008b. Covered mass grave in Slovenia. The amount of archaeological work involved in unearthing grave sites and determining their existence? *Prispevki za Novejšo Zgodovino* 48, 173–186.

Jamnik, P. 2009. The awareness of crime. In M. Čoh (ed.), *Totalitarizmi – Vprašanja in Izzivi*, 95–112. Ljubljana, Študijski Center za Narodno Spravo.

Jamnik, P. 2011. Fizični posegi v grobišča. In J. Dežman (ed.), *Poročilo 3 Komisije Vlade Republike Slovenije za Reševanje Vprašanj Prikritih Grobišč 2005–2009*, 287–293. Ljubljana, Družina.

Josipovič, D. 2011. Prispevek arheologa pri izkopu prikritih grobišč v letih 2006–2009. In J. Dežman (ed.), *Poročilo 3 Komisije Vlade Republike Slovenije za Reševanje Vprašanj Prikritih Grobišč 2005–2009*, 473–502. Ljubljana, Družina.

Leben-Seljak, P. 2007. *Mnenje o Kosteh, Najdenih pri Ekshumaciji Povojnega Grobišča na Arehu – Lokacija A3. Antropološko Poročilo 9 November 2007*. Unpublished report. 1-12.Žiri.

Ministry of Culture. Document No. 62290-1/2010/6, 21 January 2011.

Štibelj, K. 2012. Use of different investigation methods of soil for forensic purpose. *Geologija* 55(1), 141–150.

CHAPTER 21

The use of archaeology in the criminal and medico-legal context in Spain

Nicholas Márquez-Grant[1,2], Miguel Ángel Vázquez Díaz[3] and Raquel Meléndez González[3]

[1] *Cranfield Forensic Institute, Cranfield University, Defence Academy of the United Kingdom, Shrivenham, UK*

[2] *Institute of Human Sciences, School of Anthropology and Museum Ethnography, University of Oxford, Oxford, UK*

[3] *Centro de Actualización y Especialización, División de Formación y Perfeccionamiento, Policía Nacional, Madrid, Spain*

Introduction

Archaeology is increasingly seen in Spain as a discipline which can provide much support in the search, location and recovery of buried and surface human remains in criminal and medico-legal contexts. The increasing awareness in recent years regarding the benefits and the maximisation of evidence during the recovery of a buried, partially buried or surface-deposited body if archaeological methods, theory and principles are followed is significant. Likewise, promoting this value to archaeology and the use of archaeologists in police work is the number of publications in recent years related to forensic archaeology.

The concept of *forensic archaeology* is becoming established as an increasing number of cases involving buried remains from clandestine graves, as well as the recent exhumations in cemeteries to obtain DNA samples, are being investigated. These are very visible nowadays in the media, especially with regard to the search for missing persons (presumably dead). The latter has perhaps raised public pressure to ensure that the right techniques and the right scientific methodology are used. The collaboration between the armed forces and institutes of legal medicine with archaeologists based outside the armed forces and mainly at universities is a synergy which seems to provide very positive outcomes. Moreover, the concept of forensic archaeology has also been present in the humanitarian context in the *praxis* regarding the search, location, excavation and recovery of human remains from the Spanish Civil War. Over 300 mass graves have been excavated in the last decade or so where there is a strong archaeological presence in the scientific teams carrying out the task, and it could be said that this has also enhanced the profile of forensic archaeology in Spain (Etxeberria et al., Chapter 55, this volume).

In this chapter we provide a bibliographical review of the use of archaeology and its application to criminal investigation in Spain. This is followed by a brief overview of the judicial and medico-legal framework in Spain with special reference to the armed forces and in particular the National Police Corps of Spain (*Cuerpo Nacional de Policía* – CNP).[1] This chapter also highlights some of the involvements of archaeologists in forensic cases, and a number of case studies from the CNP are presented. Finally, a summary of the situation in Spain shows an optimistic future for forensic archaeology in this country.

Literature review: the rise of archaeology in the forensic context in Spain

The use of (forensic) archaeology in Spain, taking into account its principles, theory and practice, is reflected in a number of publications which emphasise its value in criminal or medico-legal investigation. In the year 2000, a chapter was dedicated to search and excavation by F. J. Puchalt Fortea in a book on police and forensic anthropological identification (Villalaín Blanco and Puchalt Fortea 2000). Although the author, who is a forensic pathologist and specialist in forensic anthropology, summarises in his article the protocols already published by the United Nations (UN) in 1991, he does state clearly that if a methodical recovery of a buried or semi-buried body is not undertaken, much information can be lost which *a posteriori* would have consequences for a correct examination of the human remains and any interpretation of the evidence. Moreover, this author provides the reader (e.g. forensic pathologist, forensic anthropologist) with the information that it is possible to learn archaeology, for example by working in 'traditional' archaeological digs under the supervision and guidance of archaeologists. It has to be said, however, that to undertake the most correct archaeological

[1] For more information, see: www.cnp.es (last accessed October 2013) or Otero (2011).

Forensic Archaeology: A Global Perspective, First Edition. Edited by W.J. Mike Groen, Nicholas Márquez-Grant and Robert C. Janaway.

excavation and interpret the different contexts it can take many years of experience of working on many different sites.

José Manuel Reverte Coma in his book on forensic anthropology (1999) dedicates only one page to what he determines as the discovery of the remains, focusing only on the importance of recovering as much of the skeleton or human remains as possible. Nevertheless, in some of Reverte Coma's media appearances and interviews between 1995 and 1997 (N. Márquez-Grant, personal observation), he indicated that the excavation of clandestine graves should be conducted as archaeologists do, and that these archaeological practices should be followed. In addition, in his 1999 book he does provide a section at the end on the search of clandestine graves through an assessment of the landscape (e.g. botany) and using instruments such as ground-penetrating radar (GPR). He also mentions how in his involvement with an excavation by a UN team in El Salvador, the forensic team was comprised of archaeologists.

A decade later, in 2010, archaeological techniques were again incorporated in a book on criminalistics and forensic sciences, for a readership of both professionals and students. However, these still appeared under the umbrella or heading of a larger chapter on forensic anthropology (Robledo Acinas and Sánchez Sánchez 2010). The inclusion of archaeology under the umbrella of forensic anthropology seems to be well established in a number of countries worldwide (see other chapters, this volume), although in others, forensic archaeology and forensic anthropology are two quite separate – although at times overlapping – disciplines (e.g. Márquez-Grant et al. 2012). In fact, the excavation section in the chapter of Robledo Acinas and Sánchez Sánchez (2010) has no mention of the word 'archaeology' or 'archaeologist', and the text tends to follow established protocols from other publications in North America or Britain.

Sometimes there appears to be the impression that anyone can hold a tool and dig without the need of an archaeologist, which is a serious misperception and irresponsibility. In any case, we need to remind some professionals that it is not about how to dig, but *how to dig well*, document and interpret what has been dug. With this in view, the value of archaeological methods and the experience of an archaeologist have also been highlighted in journal articles. For example, Manuel Polo Cerdá published a letter (2002) with the title Archaeology and Forensic Medicine (*Arqueología y Medicina Forense*) in a medical journal. Here, the author used the term *forensic archaeology* and emphasised the importance of using archaeological techniques and professionals with this experience. Márquez-Grant et al. (2011) published an article with the title *El Papel de la Arqueología en la Investigación Criminal* (The Role of Archaeology in Criminal Investigation) in a journal with a readership mainly in the area of forensic medicine. This article did mention the important role that archaeology can have in the justice system, mainly for the search, location and excavation of clandestine graves. In addition, the paper outlined some of the skills required of a forensic archaeologist and the different types of cases in which the involvement of an archaeologist is advisable in order to maximise the gathering of evidence.

The use of archaeology as a useful tool does not only result in awareness in published work (mainly within forensic anthropology or forensic medicine), but also within police circles too. For example, the first author (NMG) has been invited to deliver talks on forensic archaeology to students including officers from *Ertzaintza*, *Guardia Civil* and CNP in the master's programme in Forensic Anthropology at the *Universidad Complutense de Madrid*. The different types of cases involving or requiring a forensic archaeologist, the protocols followed and the type of documentation are the main focus of these lectures, and the questions asked by the officers who are students on the course confirm the interest in this topic. More important is the knowledge that some police officers have entered the force with a degree in history (with a specialisation in archaeology). This is another major promoter of the value of archaeology in criminal investigation. With this in view, the role of the second author of this chapter (MAVD), a Police Inspector at CNP and an instructor to the scientific police, is very significant. His publication, *La Arqueología como Instrumento Forense* (Archaeology as a Forensic Tool, Vázquez Díaz 2011), is original in that it has been written by a police officer with an archaeological background and, more importantly, it has been published in a police (CNP) journal (*Ciencia Policial*). To summarise, the value and methods of archaeology have been emphasised in recent years and help to promote the use of forensic archaeology in particular with regard to some cases in Spain involving buried or partially buried human remains.

Recently, a number of commercial companies have begun to offer services or courses in forensic archaeology; however, the term 'forensic' has been used primarily within the context of the Civil War Mass Graves. In Valencia, courses have also been organised since the year 2000 by Dr Delfín Villalaín and Dr Manuel Polo on Forensic Anthropology and Archaeology.[2]

Of significance are the recommendations published both in Spanish and in English by the Spanish Association

[2]For more information, see: http://grupopaleolab.blogspot.co.uk/ (last accessed October 2013).

of Forensic Anthropology and Odontology (*Asociación Española de Antropología y Odontología Forense* – AEAOF).[3] These protocols (Serrulla 2013b), published in June 2013, are very positive with regard to promoting forensic archaeology. In the first chapter, on the topic of recovery of human remains from both surface deposits and burials, the authors indicate (Crespo and Polo 2013, 18) that for buried remains it will be necessary to involve an archaeologist or professionals who have enough archaeological experience.[4] This mention of an archaeologist or archaeological techniques once again demonstrates the awareness of professionals in Spain, especially amongst those practising forensic anthropology and criminalistics, regarding the importance of involving an archaeologist. This is particularly true in cases of buried remains which fall mainly under the direction of the forensic pathologist (*médico forense*). In addition, a publication by the Ministry of Justice (*Ministerio de Justicia*) with regard to the 'stolen kids' or *niños robados* (Cubero 2012) has been written jointly by the directors of a number of different medico-legal institutes, the National Institute of Toxicology and Forensic Sciences (*Instituto Nacional de Toxicología y Ciencias Forenses* – INTCF), and includes amongst the authors two forensic anthropologists (Fernando Serrulla and Santiago Crespo). In this document, which includes recommendations for good practice, it states (Cubero 2012, 17–18) that it is advisable to use the expertise of a forensic archaeologist with regard to exhumations.[5]

Lastly, the term *forensic archaeology* (*arqueología forense*) can be found well established and applied in Spain to the recovery of Historical Memory (*Memoria Histórica*), which, regarding human remains, aims to search and locate the victims of the Civil War (1936–1939) and the Francoist dictatorship that followed (1939–1975). Therefore, *forensic archaeology* appears as a book title (e.g. Polo Cerdá 2008) as well as in keywords to published papers (e.g. Herrasti Erlogorri and Jiménez Sánchez 2012). In this latter article by Herrasti and Jiménez (2012) it is clearly indicated that the archaeological excavation of mass graves from the Civil War and in the context of Human Rights' investigations since the year 2000 (see Etxeberria et al., Chapter 55, this volume) makes archaeology an invaluable discipline within forensic sciences. A number of student dissertations have also been produced relating to forensic archaeology (e.g. Ortega Ruiz 2011; Sánchez Marcos 2009) although within the Spanish context mostly with a focus on clandestine burials form the Spanish Civil War.

As can be seen, awareness and promotion of forensic archaeology in Spain has risen in recent years and continues to rise. Much of this development at present is triggered by those forensic doctors or pathologists, as well as police officers, who have specialised or have a background in forensic anthropology. In the following sections of this chapter, we introduce the medico-legal framework in Spain and a number of scenarios or cases are presented where archaeological methodology or archaeologists have proved valuable, with special reference to those investigated by the CNP.

A brief overview of the police and medico-legal framework in Spain

In Spain, as in many other countries, there are a number of police forces working simultaneously which, apart from their own legislation, fall under one particular law (*Ley Orgánica 2/86*). The administrative organisation of the country results in the coexistence of three police structures: state, regional and local. Thus, there are two forces which operate nationally: the National Police Corps (CNP) and the Civil Guard (*Guardia Civil*). There are also three forces which operate at a regional (Autonomous Communities) level: the Basque Police (*Ertzaintza*), the police in Catalonia (*Mossos d'Esquadra*) and the police in Navarre (*Policía Foral de Navarra*). In addition, there are specific CNP sections (CNP4) for the regions of Andalusia, Galicia, Madrid and Valencia. Finally, there are numerous local police forces for every municipality or local government.

In the latest statistics, 390 intentional homicides took place in Spain in 2011 (a rate of 0.8% for every 100,000 inhabitants).[6] Since the majority of the most serious crimes occur in urban centres, on many occasions it is the CNP which deals with them (Figure 21.1). The CNP organises its work according to a number of areas: Security (*Comisarías Generales de Seguridad Ciudadana*), Counterterrorism (*Información*), Criminal Investigation (*Policía Judicial*), Immigration (*Extranjería y Fronteras*)

[3]For more information, see: www.aeaof.com (last accessed October 2014).

[4]*En el caso de que los restos se encuentren inhumados será necesaria la participación o bien de un* ***arqueólogo*** *o bien de personas cualificadas o con conocimientos suficientes en* ***arqueología*** *por cuanto la exhumación se realizará siguiendo los métodos y las técnicas de esta disciplina.* [Our emphasis]

[5]*Si se considerase una exhumación con alto grado de dificultad, aún en el caso de tratarse de inhumaciones en el interior de cementerios se recomienda la presencia de un* ***Experto en Arqueología Forense*** *para la búsqueda, localización y excavación de una inhumación en tierra. Este experto codirigirá la exhumación con el responsable del equipo médico forense y emitirá el informe correspondiente sobre su actividad que se adjuntará al informe del equipo Médico Forense.* [Our emphasis]

[6]Data obtained from UN Office on Drugs and Crime, available at: http://www.unodc.org/ (last accessed October 2013).

Figure 21.1 Logo of the Spanish National Police Corps (*Cuerpo Nacional de Policía*) (© CNP).

and Scientific Support (*Comisaría General de Policía Científica*). Although the CNP mainly undertakes its work in provincial capitals and any urban centre, the Civil Guard, which is military in nature but with police functions too, undertakes its work in the rest of the national territory and its seas, as well as specific tasks like the control of the communication routes or the protection of dignitaries. Reciprocal cooperation often occurs between the national, state, regional and local forces.

The CNP comprises an 'identification' section (*Técnicas Identificativas*), which will deals with cases relevant to forensic archaeology and which can be deployed 24/7 to any point of the country dealing with cases which include illegal burials and any structure (*zulo*) used to hide kidnapped people or material such as drugs or weapons. This section will also deal with mass fatalities nationally and internationally such as those relating to the incidents in Madrid, the tsunami in Thailand or to the earthquake in Algeria. It is in the section of the Scientific Police (*Policía Científica*) that the forensic anthropologists are based, all of whom are also trained police officers. Due to the continued changing pattern and behaviour of crimes and criminals, it is essential to always have up-to-date professional development and competency and for this reason the professional development area of the CNP (*División de Formación y Perfeccionamiento del Cuerpo Nacional de Policía*) plays an important role. Within their teaching, there is training regarding how to deal with clandestine graves in a methodical and scientific manner.

The Civil Guard[7] in its Criminalistics Section (*Servicio de Criminalística*) has its own department for victim identification, and its identification team also manages a mobile laboratory (*laboratorio móvil de criminalística*), which has been used primarily for mass fatalities.

Professionals outside the armed forces have also been consulted for a number of cases and this includes technical support for the search and location of clandestine graves. For example, the company Condor Georadar,[8] directed by Luis Alvial, has provided technical support (e.g. GPR) for a number of cases run by the CNP, some of which have yielded positive results. Collaborations between professionals outside the armed forces, whether in private companies or universities, have also been possible with the Civil Guard in the search for missing (and presumably dead) persons. Research has also been conducted in Spain with forensic applications (Novo et al. 2011; Serrulla 2013; Solla et al. 2012), promoting the use of these techniques and the necessary collaboration of armed forces with non-police personnel.

The armed forces provide support to the forensic pathologist (*médico forense*) who will order the recovery of a body in an advanced state of decomposition, according to the Criminal Procedure Law (*Ley de Enjuiciamiento Criminal*; M. Polo, personal communication). The recovery and identification of the victim has always been part of forensic medicine but with the essential participation of the armed forces; and as stated earlier other experts outside the forces may also be required (see overview in Etxeberria 2004; Prieto Carrero 2008). In addition, two institutions must also be mentioned as they form part of the Ministry of Justice: the National Toxicological Institute (*Instituto Nacional de Toxicología y Ciencias Forenses*) and the Forensic Anatomical Institute (*Instituto Anatómico Forense de Madrid*). There are also forensic anthropology laboratories in a number of institutes of legal medicine (e.g. Catalonia, Galicia, Palmas de Gran Canaria), as well as universities. Those practising forensic anthropology, and thus recommending the presence of a forensic archaeologist or employing archaeological techniques, tend to be qualified forensic pathologists. These professionals tend to meet at the Spanish Association of Forensic Anthropology and Odontology association meetings (*Asociación Española de Antropología y Odontología Forense* – AEAOF)[9] and a number of presentations are on exhumations and

[7]For more information, see: www.guardiacivil.es (last accessed October 2014).
[8]For more information, see: www.condorgeoradar.es (last accessed October 2014).
[9]For more information, see: www.aeaof.com (last accessed October 2014).

clandestine graves, again providing an insight into the potential use of archaeology in forensic cases.[10]

With regard to buried human remains in clandestine graves and the use of forensic archaeology, a number of media releases have shown the different types of scenarios in which buried bodies have been presented (e.g. a body buried inside a barrel or a body buried within concrete). Examples of the types of cases are presented in the following sections. Although the focus of this volume is forensic archaeology with regard to buried remains, and, specifically, human remains, it is worth noting that both the CNP and Civil Guard each have a team which deals with cultural heritage and which investigates any violations of the cultural heritage (art work, sculpture, paintings, archaeological sites, etc.). For a more detailed overview of the judicial context in Spain refer to other publications (e.g. Lucena-Molina et al. 2012).

The first steps of archaeological contribution to criminal investigation in Spain

Although the number of clandestine burials as a result of homicide has not decreased in number, there is a rise in the participation of police officers, medico-legal experts and judges in exhumations for both criminal and human rights violations. This results in an increased number of buried corpses that fall under the umbrella of legal medicine. Often the exhumations or excavations of a buried body or skeletonised remains have fallen into the able hands of a forensic pathologist with expertise in forensic anthropology, and these individuals have been able to appreciate the value of archaeology in forensic contexts.

Hence, in Valencia (M. Polo, personal communication), the collaboration between forensic medicine and archaeology goes back to 1996 for clandestine burials in two contexts: the forensic or judicial one (although there are very few cases annually) and those related to the Francoist regime and particularly dating between 1946 and 1952 in this region. In both situations, the forensic pathologist (in this case, Dr Manuel Polo) has always worked with archaeological methodology, whose knowledge he has gained from working in 'traditional' archaeology for many years alongside other archaeologists. In fact, when police forces have been requested to undertake an exhumation of skeletal remains, the police have gone for assistance to the forensic pathologists who are based in the institutes of legal medicine (*Institutos de Medicina Legal* – IML). Although not all IMLs will have specialists in forensic anthropology, their staff can request the collaboration of colleagues in other institutions. In the case of this forensic pathologist working in Valencia,[11] in the forensic or criminal (or judicial) context, the 'presence of an archaeologist' has been requested formally through legal channels (through the courts). This was especially the case recently in the exhumation of infant human remains in the context of possible irregular adoptions. In these cases, most often requests for assistance have gone to archaeologists working for the local government, although, since these lack forensic experience and forensic knowledge regarding the chain of custody for example, this involvement may risk the value of archaeology if not done correctly within a forensic framework. Dr Manuel Polo has indicated that in his 14 years in the IML in Valencia, a judge (*Juez de Guardia*) has unfortunately never requested the presence of a (forensic) archaeologist in the excavation of human remains of a recent date.[12]

In correspondence with another forensic pathologist, Dr Ignasi Galtés of the IML in Catalonia (personal communication), this expert has always used archaeologists based at the Autonomous University of Barcelona (UAB) for forensic cases relating to clandestine burials whether in fields, inside houses or within wells. One such case in which an archaeologist was used was to recover a victim who had been buried and partially covered in concrete for c. 11 months. Dr Galtés indicates that archaeologists have also assisted and aided him in cases of surface remains so that the most complete recording and recovery can be undertaken (alongside other police methods). Thus, this forensic pathologist works together in forensic cases with an archaeologist, Dr Núria Armentano, who is also trained in physical anthropology and who has also undertaken a number of courses in forensic science. Dr Armentano is also part of a group which undertakes taphonomic research (e.g. Armentano et al. 2012). The work by archaeologists is voluntary at present, but this collaboration between forensic pathologists and archaeologists has been positive and well received by other colleagues at the IML as well as judges, attorneys and the police (*Mossos d'Esquadra*).

[10]In fact, in the last association meeting -at the time of this publication- in October 2014 in Madrid, it was agreed that a written statement should be sent to the Forensic Medical Council (*Consejo Médico Forense*) to ask that Institutes of Legal Medicine (*Institutos de Medicina Legal*) consider collaborations with archaeologists in the recovery of human remains from judicial contexts (Serrulla, personal communication).

[11]An email was sent out by the first author of this chapter (NMG) to a few forensic pathologists/anthropologists in a number of regions in Spain asking them whether they had ever worked with remains buried in a clandestine grave, whether they had used archaeological techniques or archaeologists, and so on. The correspondence was sent in September 2013. Acknowledgements have been provided in the Acknowledgement section of this chapter.

[12]The legal time frame in which a crime such as a homicide is of 'forensic interest or relevance' in Spain is 20 years according to the Penal Code (*Código Penal*) although there are exceptions to this (e.g. genocides).

Dr Santiago Crespo, a forensic pathologist with specialisation in forensic anthropology, has also worked with archaeologists previously. In a recent case involving the exhumation of infants relating to cases of 'irregular adoptions' (or stolen babies), this forensic anthropologist recommended that the judge contact the department of culture of the Catalonian government (*Generalitat*) to request the presence of an archaeologist; hence an archaeologist (Dr Maria Adserias) was involved in the exhumation (S. Crespo, personal communication). Other forensic pathologists and anthropologists have also dealt with clandestine graves and have required the expertise of an archaeologist. Dr Fernando Serrulla (personal communication) has worked in the region of Galicia in two forensic cases where archaeologists were part of the investigative team.

Finally, archaeological research and experimental studies in the fields of search and taphonomy have also been carried out in Spain, and this reflects an increasing awareness of the potential value of forensic archaeology. Examples of these studies are Fernando Serrulla's thesis (2013) on the use of GPR in the search for buried human remains as well as other buried items (e.g. Solla et al. 2012), and experimental studies on taphonomy (e.g. Armentano et al. 2012).

Figure 21.2 Anonymous victim, which helps to illustrate some of the cases where archaeology can be of benefit. In this case burnt human remains were found on the surface (© CNP).

Case studies from the Spanish National Police (CNP)

The CNP, throughout recent years, has investigated a number of cases which involve archaeological methods and theory. These cases include partially buried or buried bodies (or body parts in cases of dismemberment) in urban centres and these may be located in a number of contexts including under patios, in a basement or under a shed in private land. Some of the bodies are wrapped, whilst others are naked. In many cases these are shallow graves, most commonly between 30 and 80 cm and usually not deeper than 1.30 m in the cases reviewed by the authors. Other cases involving the use of archaeology have also related to skeletal remains on the surface.

Three anonymous case studies are presented here to preserve the integrity of the victim and the case. The first case relates to human remains found on the ground surface and is used to illustrate the scene protocol. The other two relate to buried human remains.

Case study 1: human remains found in an urban wasteland

On discovery of a skeleton (Figure 21.2) by a third party walking in the area, a call was received on the 091 number (the call centre of the CNP), after which the protocols for securing the perimeter and search for witnesses were put in place by officers from Scientific Support (*Policía Científica*) and the Homicide Unit (*Grupo de Homicidios*). The presence of human remains was confirmed by the police, and notified to the Judicial Commission, which is comprised of an on-call judge (*Juez de Guardia*), a secretary (*Secretario Judicial*) and a forensic pathologist (*médico forense*). This was followed by an examination of the scene (*inspección ocular*) prior to lifting or recovering the remains and transporting them to the IML.

The Scientific Support team described the context in which the remains were located, the position of the remains and the state of decomposition, in the relevant police body recovery forms. During a first examination of the area around the body, a number of items such as a watch found 40 cm from the body (Figure 21.3) or a hand bone (metacarpal) found 3 m away were noted and detailed in a plan. After the body was recovered, a detailed examination of the entire area (*inspección ocular técnico-policial*) was undertaken for any further evidence, such as blood.

Case study 2: burial in a back garden

This was a case of multiple kidnapping and the investigation was multidisciplinary, comprising the Scientific

Support team and a number of other police brigades or units (*Grupo de Secuestros y Extorsiones, Grupo de Estupefacientes* and *Grupo de Homicidios*). The suspect was arrested and questioning revealed information about his activities. It was, once again, the Judicial Commission mentioned previously which provided the approval to enter and register the house and its land.

A particular area of the property was investigated partly from intelligence information but also from observations of the ground: disturbed earth, different soil colour and texture from its surroundings, and absence of vegetation compared to its surroundings. This potentially disturbed area had the dimensions of a grave. From then onwards, the procedure was to investigate the area in detail and undertake the necessary examinations to search and find any evidence on the surface, any evidence regarding the sequence of events leading to the potential deposition and to undertake all the necessary recording. Once the upper fill of the grave was excavated, the presence of two corpses was observed at a depth of 1.30 m. These were recorded *in situ* by the Scientific Police and employing CNP's scene and body recording forms. The information registered included the position of the corpses, the clothing present, a description of blindfolds and tied limbs, the depth at which the corpses were buried, and so on. After this documentation had been undertaken and the bodies recovered, further excavation and recording of the grave was conducted whilst examining the area for any other evidence that might be relevant to the investigation. Other areas of the house were examined such as the bins and rooms inside the house, in the presence of the arrestee and his barrister.

Figure 21.3 Item (watch) found near the body and potentially associated with it (© CNP).

Case study 3: dismembered body in a dumping site

A dog walker alerted the police when she discovered human bones in the town suburbs. The police confirmed the presence of a human mandible (Figure 21.4), originally within a plastic bag, in a dumping site with much building material. This mandible had almost all the teeth present and a further search found the remaining teeth.

During the first assessment of the surroundings by the police, two separate rubbish tips c. 8 m apart were observed, both having similar building material or debris, which was mainly concrete, bathroom and kitchen tiles. On some of these tiles, the Scientific Police observed the presence of hair and textiles. No further remains were found but concrete blocks or sections were present which led the police to believe, after reconstruction (Figure 21.5), that the body had been buried in a concrete 'sarcophagus' c. 1.8 m in length.

Figure 21.4 First discovery of human remains (© CNP).

Figure 21.5 Concrete 'sarcophagus' in which the body would have originally been buried (© CNP).

Figure 21.6 The body was found under the garage of another property at approximately 1 m depth (© CNP).

In the area of the dumps the police had found degraded paper, but a section under a stone was preserved and included the letterhead. This letterhead revealed an invoice with a phone number and the name of a local ironmonger. This item was exhibited and later during the investigation these materials were linked to a suspect. After further investigation, the suspect was detained and the suspect's house searched. At the back of the living room, a kitchen was under construction with some of the material and concrete which matched that found where the mandible had been discovered. After a confession, the perpetrator had indicated where the body had been transported and buried. The body was found at c. 1 m deep under the garage of another house (Figure 21.6) where the perpetrator had previously worked as a builder. The remains were excavated by police and taken to the INTCF for the post-mortem examination.

Although the above cases do not outline in detail the archaeological techniques, recording and interpretation made for each case, they do illustrate a number of scenarios where the value of archaeology has been applied and recognised by CNP. This value continues to grow today.

Concluding remarks

A brief account of the medico-legal framework in Spain has been provided, describing in particular how forensic archaeology may fit into this framework. We have shown that there has certainly been an increase in the last two decades regarding the value that archaeology can bring to criminal investigation. Unfortunately, homicides and clandestine graves are not just a thing of the past, but will sadly continue in the future too. Hopefully, however, the value of archaeology will show its full potential in years to come in order to recover the victims and bring the perpetrators to justice. Continued research in forensic archaeology will without doubt contribute to the development of the discipline. In addition, students and professionals from Spain participate in training programmes abroad as well as conferences and this attitude is excellent regarding exchange of knowledge and experience.

In criminal investigation, forensic pathologists and forensic anthropologists, as well as police officers, have been calling upon archaeologists. Archaeologists themselves must also promote the discipline and young generations of students are currently adding to this contribution. Certainly, within the context of mass graves from the Spanish Civil War (Etxeberria et al., Chapter 55, this volume), although at present mainly humanitarian in nature rather than for the courts, the concept of *forensic archaeology* is now established both in theory and in practice, and has been consolidated in the published literature.

We recognise that it is not about how to use a tool to dig or about digging the ground to find something, but about how to dig well, how to record and interpret. It must not be forgotten either, that on discovery of human remains, although the police are notified, when these appear more likely to be archaeological in date, archaeologists in museums or local governments are called to confirm that remains are indeed archaeological. This has occurred on a number of occasions and highlights already a professional collaboration between police and traditional archaeologists based in museums and local governments. Some of the first cases using archaeologists have derived from forensic pathologists with expertise in forensic anthropology; thus the overlap and connection between archaeology and anthropology has strengthened. The top professionals in the forensic field and outside archaeology have recognised their limitations and have worked within their remit of expertise, and therefore when exhumations in cemeteries and excavations of clandestine graves have had to take place, they have recommended the involvement of experienced personnel in archaeological techniques or archaeologists themselves. However, archaeologists requested to take part in police work must also recognise their limitations and ensure that their work helps to promote the discipline rather than lead to any negative effects which can result. Thus, it is encouraged that archaeologists working alongside other professionals in forensic practice in Spain are made aware of the work they are requested to do, their responsibilities, the State and any regional legal framework and police and forensic protocols, especially with regard to scene attendance, confidentiality and chain of custody.

Perhaps forensic archaeology is not yet fully established in Spain, and its real value not fully explored; however, there is an impression that archaeologists are slowly assisting the armed forces, and at the moment their (voluntary) work has been well received. This involvement is increasing at the time of this publication. We must not forget either the research or publications devoted to the discipline and the work done by those investing their efforts in recovering and identifying victims of the Spanish Civil War and the dictatorship that followed. Therefore, we are happy to say that the concept of forensic archaeology in Spain *does* exist, not only regarding its presence in literature (whether archaeological, anthropological, medical or police), but also step by step in practice too.

Acknowledgements

We would like to express enormous gratitude to the Spanish National Police (*Cuerpo Nacional de Policía*) for their assistance, and within this force, in particular, the *División de Formación y Perfeccionamiento, Comisaría General de Policía Científica, Brigada Provincial de Policía Científica de la Jefatura Superior de Policía de Madrid*. Special thanks are also due to the *Brigada de Policía Científica de la Comisaría Local de la Laguna – JSP de Canarias*, without whom this chapter would not have been possible. In addition, Nicholas Márquez-Grant would like to thank the following members of the *Asociación Española de Antropología y Odontología Forense*, in no particular order: José Antonio Sánchez Sánchez, Francisco Etxeberria, Fernando Serrulla, José Luis Prieto, Manuel Polo, Santiago Crespo, Ignasi Galtés and Almudena García for their help, answering a number of questions throughout the years; Teresa Cabello Panades for sending some literature; and also Luís Alvial of Condor Georadar for some information regarding ground-penetrating radar as well as other geophysical techniques.

References

Armentano, N., Nociarova, D. and Malgosa, A. 2012. TAPHOS-m. Taphonomical and anthropological project. Human osteobiography using Sus scrofa domestica model. *Revista Funeraria* 109, 58–59.

Crespo, S. and Polo, M. 2013. Levantamiento-exhumación restos óseos. In F. Serrulla (ed.), *Recomendaciones en Antropología Forense*, 15–22. Asociación Española de Antropología y Odontología Forense.

Cubero Santos, C. (ed.) 2012. *Guía de Recomendaciones Para la Práctica de la Exhumación en los Casos de Posible Sustracción de Recién Nacidos*. Ministerio de Justicia.

Etxeberria, F. 2004. Panorama organizativo sobre antropología y patología forense en España. Algunas propuestas para el estudio de fosas con restos humanos de la Guerra Civil Española de 1936. In A. Álvarez (ed.), *La Memoria de los*

Olvidados. Un Debate Sobre el Silencio de la Represión Franquista, 183–219. Valladolid, Ámbito Ediciones.

Herrasti Erlogorri, L. and Jiménez Sánchez, J. M. 2012. Excavación arqueológica de los enterramientos colectivos de la Guerra Civil. In F. Serrulla (ed.), Antropología forense de la Guerra Civil Española. *Boletín Galego de Medicina Legal e Forense* 18, 29–45.

Lucena-Molina, J.-J., Pardo-Iranzo, V. and Gonzalez-Rodriguez, J. 2012. Weakening forensic science in Spain: from expert evidence to documentary evidence. *Journal of Forensic Science* 57, 952–963.

Márquez-Grant, N., Robledo Acinas, M. M. and Sánchez Sánchez, J. A. 2011. El papel de la arqueología en la investigación criminal. *Revista de la Escuela de Medicina Legal* 16, 14–22.

Márquez-Grant, N., Litherland, S. and Roberts, J. 2012. Forensic archaeology in Europe. In D. Dirkmaat (ed.), *A Companion to Forensic Anthropology*, 598–625. Chichester, Wiley-Blackwell.

Novo, A., Lorenzo, H., Rial, F. I. and Solla, M. 2011. 3D GPR in forensics: finding a clandestine grave in a mountainous environment. *Forensic Science International* 204, 134–138.

Ortega Ruiz, R. 2011. *Sobre la Aplicación del Método Arqueológico en Contextos Forenses: Actuaciones Arqueológico-Forenses en el Yacimiento de Sariegos Durante las Campañas 2009– 2010.* Madrid, Servicio de Publicaciones Universidad Autónoma de Madrid.

Otero Soriano, J. M. (ed.) 2011. *Policía Científica. 100 Años al Servicio de la Justicia.* Ministerio de Interior.

Polo Cerdá, M. 2002. Arqueología y medicina forense. *7DM* [*Siete Dias Médicos*] 533, 85.

Polo Cerdá, M. (ed.) 2008. *Arqueología Forense en el Territorio A .G. L. A.* Valencia, Asociación la Gavilla Verde y Grupo Paleolab.

Prieto, J. L. 2008. La antropología forense en España desde la perspectiva de la medicina forense. *Cuadernos de Medicina Forense* 53–54, 189–200.

Puchalt Fortea, F. J. 2000. Hallazgos y excavaciones. In J. D. Villalaín Blanco and F. J. Pucalt Foretea (eds.), *Identificación Antropológica Policial y Forense*, 31–39. Valencia, Tirant lo Blanch.

Reverte Coma, J. M. 1999. *Antropología Forense*. 2nd edition. Madrid, Ministerio de Justicia.

Robledo Acinas, M. M. and Sánchez Sánchez, J. A. 2010. Antropología forense. Investigación criminal en restos óseos. In M. J. Anadón Baselga and M. M. Robledo Acinas (eds.), *Manual de Criminalística y Ciencias Forenses. Técnicas Forenses Aplicadas a la Investigación Criminal*, 17–52. Madrid, Tébar.

Sánchez Marcos, I. 2009. Arqueología Forense. Aportación Metodológica de Campo. Unpublished Msc thesis, University of Granada.

Serrulla, F. 2013a. Utilidad del Georradar en la Búsqueda de Restos Humanos y Otros Objetos de Interés Criminalístico. Unpublished Master's thesis, Universidad de Granada.

Serrulla, F. (ed.) 2013b. *Recomendaciones en Antropología Forense.* Asociación Española de Antropología y Odontología Forense.

Solla, M., Riveiro, B., Álvarez, M. X. and Arias, P. 2012. Experimental forensic scenes for the characterisation of ground-penetrating radar wave response. *Forensic Science International* 220, 50–58.

Vázquez Díaz, M. A. 2011. La arqueología como instrumento forense. *Ciencia Policial* 105, 5–21.

CHAPTER 22

Forensic archaeology and anthropology in Switzerland

Sandra Lösch[1], Christian Jackowski[2] and Christian Zingg[3]

[1] *Department of Physical Anthropology, Institute of Forensic Medicine, University of Bern, Bern, Switzerland*

[2] *Department of Forensic Medicine and Imaging, Institute of Forensic Medicine, University of Bern, Bern, Switzerland*

[3] *Forensic Crime Scene Unit, Cantonal Police, Bern, Switzerland*

Introduction

Archaeological disciplines are closely linked to geographical and climatic conditions within the area of research. Local historical aspects also have a big influence on the discipline, this being especially true for forensic archaeology and anthropology, as do aspects of the legal system. This chapter provides an overview of Switzerland's geographical and legal characteristics referring to forensic anthropological work, education and related institutions and societies. Future trends are mentioned and recommendations are given by the authors.

Overview of Switzerland

Switzerland is situated in western and central Europe with borders to Germany, Austria, Italy, France and Liechtenstein. It is landlocked and geographically divided between the Alps, the Swiss Plateau and the Jura. Mountains occupy a great part of the territory; the population of *c.* 8 million[1] is mostly concentrated on the Plateau, where large cities like Zurich and Geneva are located. Four official languages are spoken in Switzerland: most people speak German while French, Italian and Romansh are minority languages.[2]

Switzerland is a federal parliamentary confederation. It comprises 26 independent states (*Cantons*) in an area of 41,285 km^2. Although the city of Bern hosts the federal authorities; it is not possible to write an article about the forensic archaeology strategies which apply to Switzerland as a whole. The authors of this chapter therefore focus on the canton of Bern, including its capital city Bern. The majority of people in the Bern canton speak Bernese German, a Swiss German dialect.

Medico-legal framework in Switzerland

Due to the federal system which divides Switzerland into sovereign cantons, each of Switzerland's 26 cantons has its own courts and police corps. Some municipalities also possess their own Police Units (*Stadt- und Gemeindepolizei*). The coordination between the Cantonal Police (*Kantonspolizei*) within Switzerland and with other countries is provided by the Cantonal Police Commanders Board and the Federal Office of Police (*Bundesamt für Polizei*).

When a case involving a dead individual arises, the responsible uniformed (Canton or Municipal) police unit is the first on site. They call other required external units such as the fire brigade or ambulance service. It is their responsibility as well to call other specialised internal units like crime investigation, homicide units or the forensic crime scene unit. These units are present in different sizes at all cantonal police organisations. In the Canton of Bern it is the crime investigation unit (*Regionalfahndung*) which is responsible for all investigative matters such as the questioning of people. The forensic crime scene unit (*Kriminaltechnischer Dienst*) is responsible for technical aspects such as collection and analysis of traces. When the case is more serious, it is also their responsibility to request specialised police officers. In Bern this is called the 'escalation' of the case to the homicide unit (*Dezernat Leib und Leben*), which takes over all responsibility for the case.

When a body is found in an extraordinary situation (e.g. in the field, long post-mortem interval and in advanced state of decomposition, young individual, assumed suicide) a forensic crime scene officer (*Kriminaltechniker*) is always on site, together with a district medical examiner

[1]Swiss Federal Statistical Office, Neuchâtel 2012.

[2]For more information, see: https://www.cia.gov/library/publications/the-world-factbook/geos/sz.html (last accessed October 2013).

Forensic Archaeology: A Global Perspective, First Edition. Edited by W.J. Mike Groen, Nicholas Márquez-Grant and Robert C. Janaway.

(*Rechtsmediziner*), for documentation and securing of medical evidence for subsequent analysis. In this case the responsibility becomes that of the prosecutor on duty. He is called immediately; in the canton of Bern this occurs *c.* 550 times per year, for a population of nearly 1 million. A legal inspection of the body is performed at the scene. This is done by either the district medical examiner, who is a general physician with forensic training, or the physician in charge from the Institute of Forensic Medicine, together with the forensic crime scene officer. District medical examiners cover cases that are further away from the urban area of Bern. If bones are found at a scene they are recovered by them as well. Archaeological principles are rarely used in forensic practice in Switzerland. For further investigations the bones are brought to the Department of Physical Anthropology (*Abteilung Anthropologie*) at the Institute of Forensic Medicine (*Institut für Rechtsmedizin*) of Bern University.

Within the Institute of Forensic Medicine in Bern procedures are defined for cases of casual findings of bones. Normally, the prosecutors give the order to start the process. The forensic physician in charge or the crime scene officer brings the findings to the Institute or directly to the Department of Physical Anthropology for investigation. Basically, the following questions are addressed by the Department:

- Are we dealing with human or animal bones?
- If the bones are human, what skeletal elements are present, how are they preserved and how many individuals are represented in the findings?
- Are the bones of forensic or historical context? In Switzerland, usually no criminal prosecutions are initiated if the findings are determined to have been lying in or on the ground for more than 30 years.
- If the bones are of forensic interest, are we able to narrow down the circle of missing persons or even identify the person through our investigation?
- Is it possible to identify the cause of death? This may certainly be possible if there are any lesions or agents which have been manifested on or in the bones.

Forensic archaeology and anthropology: background and practice

Forensic archaeology is defined as the application of archaeological principles and methods to the search, recovery and excavation of human remains and other buried evidence within a forensic, medico-legal and/or humanitarian setting (Litherland et al. 2012). According to this definition *forensic archaeology* is rarely applied in Switzerland. In most cases from mountain regions, human remains are found on the surface, due to melting of the glaciers. If an individual is already (partly) skeletonised, the bones are often scattered because of the slopes and wild animal scavenging activities. Mostly it is impossible to recover the entire skeleton. If human remains are found buried and criminal investigations show evidence of a historical/archaeological date, the 'case' is transferred to the cantonal Archaeological Services.

Forensic anthropology is defined as the 'application of methods and principles of physical anthropology (the study of human remains from the point of view of biology and physical characteristics), to cases of medico-legal or forensic interest' (Ramsthaler et al. 2009; Roberts and Márquez-Grant 2012). In practice, not many cases are assigned to Swiss forensic/physical anthropologists for the following reasons:

- First, the (physician) colleagues of the medical departments deal with the cases themselves. This can be due to the internal structures of an institute or a lack of forensic anthropology specialists. Forensic anthropologists are also often called in late when the examination has already begun. Many such cases happen to fall outside the legal time frame and/or are of archaeological interest. To save costs, molecular genetic analyses for identification purposes in archaeological cases should be avoided and experienced anthropologists should be consulted as early as possible.
- Second, at *c.* 0.003% the percentage rate for confirmed homicides is relatively low when taken in relation to the total population (taken from a study for the years 2000–2004).[3] The total estimated number of firearms in private Swiss households is, however, *c.* 2.2 million.[4]
- Third, forensic anthropologist expertise is only necessary if homicides remain undetected for a certain amount of time. In Switzerland, this is especially rare as habitable areas are either densely packed or massively cultivated. Due to the local geography and topography, the majority of Swiss cases for forensic anthropologists are surface findings from mountain or forest regions.

Very few physical anthropologists are employed in Switzerland, some of them at universities. Some archaeologists, with a physical anthropological background, work for the archaeological services of different cantons. There are also some freelancers who work on archaeological burial sites or on skeletal material from archaeological excavations. There is currently no system to accredit these physical anthropologists. A book written by Swiss colleagues describes

[3]Schweizerische Eidgenossenschaft. Verzeigungen – Analysen. Tötungsdelikte: Ausmass und Struktur. Fälle, Opfer und Tatverdächtige. Bundesamt für Statistik, Neuchâtel 2013.

[4]Eidgenössisches Departement für Verteidigung, Bevölkerungsschutz und Sport VBS, Factsheet vom 21.06.2007.

excavation techniques, recovery and basic physical anthropological information for archaeological exhumations (Ulrich-Bochsler et al. 2008). This book is widely used by Swiss archaeologists.

Currently, there are some initial efforts to establish national guidelines for working with skeletal material (Cooper and Lösch 2013). However, these guidelines are designed for historical skeletal material rather than for forensic cases.

Higher education

Forensic archaeology and anthropology are structurally not taught at any of the 12 universities in Switzerland. The University of Zurich offers courses in physical anthropology, integrated in the study of biology, with a main focus on primatology and palaeoanthropology. At the universities of Basel and Bern, archaeological students can take introductory courses in physical anthropology. The University of Geneva also offers physical anthropology courses. The Institute of Forensic Medicine at Bern University has, as mentioned earlier, a special department of physical anthropology with a scientific working group. This group works on forensic cases as well as on archaeological skeletal material; the staff is very often in the field at archaeological burial sites. Finally, the Centre Universitaire Romand de Médecine Légale offers a forensic anthropology training course.

Overview of Swiss societies

Several Swiss physical anthropological, archaeological and medical societies are involved in (forensic) archaeological and physical anthropological research. These are described in the following sections.

Swiss Society of Anthropology

The Swiss Society of Anthropology (*Schweizerische Gesellschaft für Anthropologie* – SGA or *Société Suisse d'Anthropologie* – SSA) was founded in the year 1920 as the Society for Anthropology and Ethnology (Sauter 1981) and acknowledged by the Swiss Academy of Sciences (SCNAT) in the same year. Since 1924/1925, the *Bulletin of the Swiss Society for Anthropology and Ethnology* (*Bulletin der Schweizerischen Gesellschaft für Anthropologie und Ethnologie*) has been the official journal of the society. In 1971 the ethnologists founded their own society. Hence the remaining members redefined the society as Swiss Society for Anthropology (*Schweizerische Gesellschaft für Anthropologie* or *Société Suisse d'Anthropologie*). From 1974 to 1983 the Society's journal was published under the title *Swiss Archives of General Anthropology* (*Archives Suisses d'Anthropologie Générale*) and from 1995 to the present day as *Bulletin of the Swiss Society for Anthropology* (*Bulletin der Schweizerischen Gesellschaft für Anthropologie* or *Bulletin de la Société Suisse d'Anthropologie*). Articles about archaeological skeletal series from Switzerland and Germany comprise the majority of its content. The texts have open access and are mostly written in German and French. It is conceivable that there will be more contributions in English.

In 1982 the Working Group for Historical Anthropology in Switzerland (*Arbeitsgemeinschaft Historische Anthropologie der Schweiz* – AGHAS) was established within the SGA/SSA (Cooper and Lörcher 2012). All of the founding members are still active today. There is no separate working group for forensic anthropologists, probably because there are not enough forensic anthropologists working in the forensic field in Switzerland to form a dedicated section.

Swiss archaeological societies

There are several archaeological societies in Switzerland, for example the Society of Swiss Archaeology (*Archaeologie Schweiz* – AS), the Swiss Prehistoric Society (*Arbeitsgemeinschaft für die Urgeschichtsforschung in der Schweiz* – AGUS or *Groupe de Travail pour les Recherches Préhistoriques en Suisse* – GPS), the Swiss Society of Archaeology of the Roman Provinces (*Arbeitsgemeinschaft für die Provinzial-Römische Forschung in der Schweiz* or *Association pour l'Archéologie Romaine en Suisse* – ARS) and the Swiss Society of Archaeology of the Middle Ages and Modern Times (*Schweizerische Arbeitsgemeinschaft für Archäologie des Mittelalters und der Neuzeit* or *Groupe de Travail Suisse pour l'Archéologie du Moyen Age et de l'Époque Moderne* – SAM). Here, physical anthropological topics are not the main focus. The groups mostly deal with conventional archaeological investigations.

Swiss Society of Forensic Medicine

The Swiss Society of Forensic Medicine (*Schweizerische Gesellschaft für Rechtsmedizin* – SGRM or *Société Suisse de Médecine Légale* – SSML) was founded in 1980 in the course of the seven institute directors' annual meetings. There are SGRM/SSML institutes in Basel, Bern, Chur, Lausanne and Geneva (which amalgamated with the *Centre Universitaire Romand de Médecine Légale*), St. Gallen and Zurich. The Institute of Forensic Medicine at Bern University is the only one to have a Department of Physical Anthropology with a scientific working group.

Disaster victim identification team Switzerland

During the 1990s, the Swiss cantons' police commanders founded a working group with the aim of establishing a national Disaster Victim Identification (DVI) team as recommended by the Interpol. After experiences such as the terrorist attack in Luxor (Egypt) and two missions dealing with mass graves in Kosovo (former Yugoslavia) the project was approved in the year 2000. On 1 January 2001 the DVI Team

Figure 22.1 The alpine site with a gradient of 40%. The flags indicate the locations where human bones were found.

Switzerland was founded, cooperating between all cantonal police organisations, the SGRM/SSML institutes and the Federal Office of Police. Liechtenstein became an official associate member of the team in 2002.[5] On the DVI team there are two physical anthropologists. Until now, there are no (forensic) archaeologists on the Swiss DVI team.

Case study: human remains found in an alpine region

In August 2011, forest workers found bones in an alpine wood close to Lauterbrunnen at a height of 1350 m. Next to the bones was an open jackknife. There were also heavily weathered fabric remnants which had probably once been clothes and a backpack. The area of the discovery is a good example of the difficulty of the working environment in mountain regions. A gradient of 40% complicated the recovery of the bones and other findings (Figure 22.1). The recovery was performed by the forensic crime scene unit of the police and the district forensic physician. The forensic anthropological examination in the laboratory revealed that the bones belonged to one human individual. Many bones were missing, probably due to steep rock slopes and wild animal activity. The remaining bones showed signs of small rodent teeth.

The bones were assigned to a male individual between 20 and 30 years of age-at-death, with an estimated body height of 175 cm. Due to the bone preservation and the associated fabrics, a post-mortem interval (PMI) of more than 2 but less than 10 years was assumed. There were no bone lesions that indicated peri-mortem blunt or sharp force trauma. Some bones showed fissures but none of them clearly indicated evidence of a peri-mortal origin. The results of the forensic anthropological examination helped the police to narrow down candidates within the circle of missing persons in the canton. They soon identified a potential young male who had been missing. A comparison was made of the dentition with ante-mortem radiographs of the missing person's dentist. It indicated a probable or likely match. This was finally confirmed with DNA analysis after obtaining a sample from the deceased and from the deceased's mother.

Conclusion and future trends

In Switzerland, the general situation of forensic archaeology and anthropology has to be improved in the future. This is true for higher education at universities as well as for integration into forensic medicine institutes, police organisations and the DVI team. Concepts must be developed to make these specialists routine members during excavation or in special cases in the field.

In particular, climate change leads to melting of the glaciers and we expect a number of human remains to emerge there. The identification of these bodies is a major concern, especially when the individuals have already been missing for a long time, but the appropriate assessment and recording of the scene can maximise the potential to identify these victims.

[5]For more information, see: http://www.dvi.ch/ (last accessed October 2013).

Acknowledgements

Thanks to Mr Korbinian Seitz for preparatory editing.

References

Cooper, C. and Lörcher, M. 2012. 30 Jahre historische Anthropologie im Fürstentum Liechtenstein. *Denkmalpflege und Archäologie im Fürstentum Liechtenstein – Fund- und Forschungsberichte 2010*. Vaduz 01/2012.126–143.

Cooper, C. and Lösch, S. 2013. Preservation and representation of human bones and its importance for anthropological analysis – an introduction. *Bulletin der Schweizerischen Gesellschaft für Anthropologie* 19(2), 5–7.

Litherland, S., Márquez-Grant, N. and Roberts, J. 2012. Forensic archaeology. In N. Márquez-Grant and J. Roberts (eds.), *Forensic Ecology Handbook: From Crime Scene to Court*, 23–48. Chichester, John Wiley & Sons, Ltd.

Ramsthaler, F., Jopp, E., Krumm, P., Bratzke, H. and Verhoff, M. A. 2009. Forensische Anthropologie. Aufgaben im Rahmen der Identifizierungskommission des Bundeskriminalamtes. *Rechtsmedizin* 19, 83–84.

Roberts, J. and Márquez-Grant, N. 2012. Forensic anthropology. In N. Márquez-Grant and J. Roberts (eds.), *Forensic Ecology Handbook: From Crime Scene to Court*, 49–67. Chichester, John Wiley & Sons, Ltd.

Sauter, M. R. 1981. Les 60 ans de la Société suisse d'anthropologie (et d'ethnologie). *Archives Suisses d'Anthropologie Générale* 45(1), 1–7.

Ulrich-Bochsler, S., Cueni, A., Cooper C. et al. 2008. *Grabungstechnik. Einführung in die Archäoanthropologie für das Archäologisch-Technische Grabungspersonal*. Basel, Vereinigung des Archäologisch-Technischen Grabungspersonals der Schweiz (VATG).

Websites

http://www.aim.uzh.ch/index.html

http://www.irm.unibe.ch/content/services/anthropology/index_eng.html

http://ipna.unibas.ch/studium/studium.htm

http://www.unige.ch/forel/lap/Labo.html

http://ua.unige.ch/fr/

http://www.curml.ch/en/curml_home/curml-qui-sommes-nous/curml-umf-3.htm

http://www.anthropologie.ch/

http://www.scnat.ch/

http://www.anthropologie.ch/d/Publikationen/

http://www.archaeologie-schweiz.ch/

http://www.sgrm.ch/de/allgemein/home.html

http://www.bfs.admin.ch/bfs/portal/de/index/themen/19/03/02/dos/02/01.html

CHAPTER 23

Introduction to forensic archaeology in the United Kingdom

John Hunter[1] and Cecily Cropper[2]

[1] *School of History and Culture, Arts Building, University of Birmingham, Birmingham, UK*

[2] *Private Consultant, Melksham, Wiltshire, UK*

Background

In 1988 John Hunter and Charlotte Roberts, on behalf of West Yorkshire Police, excavated the remains of a young boy murdered by his stepfather some 25 years earlier. This was the result of a proactive campaign to bring the forensic value of archaeological techniques to the attention of local law enforcement professionals. By careful excavation and use of stratigraphy they were able to demonstrate that a particular sequence of events had occurred: the boy had been wrapped in sacking, laid on the ground next to a stone wall in woodland and covered with stones from the wall. Natural processes of decomposition and soil formation had effectively caused the body to become buried beneath the stones. The same process of deposition was subsequently admitted by the stepfather. This was the first time in the United Kingdom that archaeological evidence had been used in a Crown Court. The stepfather was subsequently imprisoned (Hunter et al. 1996, 55–56). This marks the first stage in a lengthy process to gain professional operational acceptance for archaeology in the search for clandestine graves and the recovery of victims.

Medico-legal context in the United Kingdom

The United Kingdom is composed of over 40 different police forces, each effectively autonomous, led by a Chief Constable or equivalent who is responsible to a Local Police Authority, most of which are now headed by a Police Commissioner. These police forces come under the auspices of a government department known as the Home Office, which acts as a coordinating authority and which operates a series of centralised facilities, one of which is the National Crime Agency (NCA), a renaming and restructuring of the former National Policing Improvement Agency (NPIA). The NCA maintains a list of named experts in various fields, anything from fire investigation to knot-tying or from archaeology to black magic. Issues of validation and competency that allow individuals to appear on this list are dealt with elsewhere in this volume (Janaway, Chapter 24, this volume).

Any police force can contact the NCA, day or night, and receive names and contact details. That said, many police forces have their own preferred experts and make personal contact with them as the occasion requires. Each police force has a Scientific Support Manager (SSM) or coordinator, familiar with scientific developments, technical equipment and individual areas of expertise, who may act in this capacity. They also have Police Search Advisors (PoLSAs), originally set up for counter-terrorism purposes, who are now familiar with most of the prospection techniques that archaeologists tend to use. There is also a National Police Search Adviser who can be called upon at any time.

Most forensic archaeologists are employed outside the forensic community – in universities, museums or archaeological field units – and are called out as and when required. At scenes they work closely with Crime Scene Investigators (CSIs) and usually under the jurisdiction of the Crime Scene Manager (CSM) who controls the scene. There is often a close working relationship with the pathologist and/or the anthropologist.

Statistics

Last year in the United Kingdom some 240,000 individuals were reported missing (ACPO 2011); these included runaways, teenagers, children who wandered off, suicides, elopements, dementia sufferers and walkers who became disorientated on mountains. One way or another most were found again. Fewer than 600 of them ended up as homicide victims, most resulting from domestic violence. About 5% of the 600, *c.* 30, seem to have involved burial. Of course there will be others that will not have been found and that may or may not have been buried. This provides opportunities for searches, but overall the number of buried victims presents little scope for forensic archaeological work full time. In fact there is, at the time of writing, just one full-time practitioner in the entire United

Forensic Archaeology: A Global Perspective, First Edition. Edited by W.J. Mike Groen, Nicholas Márquez-Grant and Robert C. Janaway.

Kingdom. There are about a dozen who, on the basis of a validation process (Janaway, Chapter 24, this volume), are deemed competent to operate at crime scenes.

Historical developments

There are some classic historic cases which help to showcase the development of the approach to the search and recovery of buried remains in the United Kingdom. In 1953 police searched Number 10 Rillington Place, London, the home of serial killer John Christie who murdered at least eight women including his wife. Searches at the time were neither systematic nor thorough; for example a human thigh bone was later found propping up the garden fence. Although the garden was dug over using spades, the searches missed many of the buried bones. Christie later admitted that his dog had unearthed a skull in the garden shortly after the police searches; he removed it and disposed of it in a nearby bombed-out house. In fact, the skull was handed in to Notting Hill police station, London, during the investigation, but ignored (Oates 2012).

In 1964 on the Lancashire/Yorkshire moors police searched for the remains of murdered children, victims of the 'moors murderers' Ian Brady and Myra Hindley (Hunter and Cox 2005, 55–57; Staff 2013). One victim, Keith Bennett, has yet to be found. The investigation was renewed in 1988, and again some 20 years later, using a series of formal searches applying more up-to-date technology. The case is almost 50 years old but still attracts tabloid newspaper headlines on a regular basis.

The year 1983 saw the investigation into the serial killer Dennis Nilsen who preyed on teenage and young adult boys. After killing them he dismembered them and buried their remains in the back gardens of various places he had lived in London. There was much press coverage and images showing recovery techniques that finally prompted archaeologists to make their concerns known publicly (Hunter et al. 1996, 11–13). The investigation of Nilsen's back gardens prompted a letter to *The Times* newspaper (14 February 1983) by a professional archaeologist who criticised the garden excavation as lacking in basic archaeological method. Whilst this did not elicit a great deal of comment it did help to promote the role of the archaeologist in the investigation of buried human remains.

In 1994 the investigation into serial killers Fred and Rosemary West at 25 Cromwell Street, Gloucester, involved the excavation of their garden and various areas of countryside in the locality. The couple had killed at least 12 young vulnerable women including their own daughter. The remains of eight individuals were found in the garden and others in the house. Ground-penetrating radar (GPR) was used and the case made national headlines for weeks as body after body was unearthed (Hunter and Cox, 2005, 119). GPR was a relatively untried forensic technique at that time; it remains unclear if, or how, the radar responses distinguished between graves, structural foundations, service trenches and earlier cultural archaeological remains.

All these scenarios dealt with buried victims. The first three used neither archaeologists nor archaeological techniques to any great extent, but the Cromwell Street investigation brought in an archaeologist to help search, not in the house itself, but in a suspected rural location. The archaeologist had little awareness of operational crime scenes or understanding of what was expected and, as a result, the police suffered ridicule in what was a high-profile case which was followed by millions in the media.

About 13 years later, in 2007, another serial killer, Peter Tobin, had deposited two of his victims in graves in a garden in Margate, Kent. Their recovery was also the subject of massive media coverage but this time it was very different.[1] Live coverage on national radio gave us phrases such as 'Work in the garden won't commence until the forensic archaeologists arrive'. Suddenly forensic archaeologists were acceptable and the discipline became not only respectable but also essential. Moreover as the case went to court a forensic archaeologist was brought in by the defence team to review their findings. So what had happened in the intervening 13 years to make forensic archaeology professionally valid?

It has been largely a process of mission, for example gaining a place on the syllabus of training courses for senior detectives, setting up workshops for scene of crime officers, making forensic scientists aware of the nature of archaeological evidence and, most of all, demonstrating the value of the work operationally. The few archaeologists involved in this area have written papers, published books and delivered lectures at forensic, missing persons and police conferences. They have tried to ensure that no scene that needed an archaeologist was undertaken without one wherever possible. Papers have been published concerning the use of specific archaeological techniques at scenes of crime and about methodology, illustrated by case studies (e.g. Blau and Ubelaker 2009). Archaeology also has a widely accepted role in the recovery of victims from mass graves where the scale of the application has necessitated adaptations in techniques and protocols.

Current remits

Forensic archaeology in the United Kingdom now involves, fairly routinely, the investigation of clandestine graves. By adapting standard archaeological techniques such as aerial photography, geophysics and field

[1]See for example: http://www.dailymail.co.uk/news/article-1294006/Peter-Tobin-police-search-victims-garden-serial-killers-homes.html (last accessed 30 March 2014).

walking, they help to locate burial sites and then employ excavation strategies to recover the human remains they contain. On occasions other types of buried objects may be searched for and excavated, typically drugs, firearms and even ransom money packed into a holdall. Archaeologists have also been asked to resolve issues of date when human remains are discovered during building operations or when disarticulated human bones are encountered as 'stray' finds by members of the public walking their dogs. They may also be asked to take part in formal exhumations undertaken by the police as a requirement for a post-mortem examination, or for DNA or toxicological sampling. There have also been instances where archaeologists have been deployed in mass disaster recovery or in the search of fire debris, for example in the restoration of Windsor Castle (Kerr 2008), where stratigraphic investigation is required to ascertain the sequences of events. This can include the recovery of victims. In short, they have found themselves involved in any matter involving buried or sealed remains, or remains which may have been buried, and which then becomes part of a criminal investigation and requires expert operational input or opinion. It has been quite a remarkable development.

Case studies demonstrate a wide range of archaeological input, and examples include searching a quarry for a missing person that involved the archaeological removal of 37,000 tons of quarry waste (Figure 23.1); finding and recovering a murder victim from a container that had been buried in woodland (Figure 23.2);

Figure 23.1 Archaeologists excavating a quarry in the search for a missing person. The quarry had been infilled and needed to be returned to its original configuration of terraces and scree (loose stone) at the time the person went missing over 25 years earlier.

Figure 23.2 The careful excavation of a burial container hidden in woodland.

Figure 23.3 A mechanical excavator being used to strip the edge of a field in order to locate the disturbance caused by a burial.

Figure 23.4 Information that a person had been buried beneath a drainage pipe, which required a section of the pipe to be removed before archaeologists could begin excavating the subsoils.

locating a neonate buried in a plastic bag; recovering a murder victim from a cellar; dating a fence post in a boundary dispute; searching for a buried victim at the edge of a field (Figure 23.3); excavating a potential burial site under a pipe trench (Figure 23.4); recovering a murder victim from a building site; recovering dismembered remains buried in a pit; searching a back garden for a murder weapon; and recovering the victim of a shooting.

The breadth of involvement and the interdisciplinary nature of archaeology itself have also generated novel research areas, notably in geophysics and remote prospection (e.g. Ruffell and McKinley 2008; Pringle et al. 2011) and in taphonomy (Janaway 2002, 2008). That said, the discipline is still essentially 'hands on'. It adapts conventional archaeological techniques involving fieldwork and excavation in an integrated approach (Figure 23.5). But UK forensic archaeologists have also been quick to recognise a much wider picture of evidence capture: the subject requires integration with other, often unrelated, disciplines from which other types of evidence are drawn. These can include a wide range of forensic interests, some of which will be familiar territory for cultural archaeology, for example pedology, palynology and diatoms (e.g. Pye and Croft 2004). Other areas are less familiar and less frequently encountered, such as entomology and DNA (e.g. Gennard 2007; Gunn 2009). Some will be new to an archaeologist, such as fibres, paint, blood and pathology. The work has also involved an introduction to behavioural sciences such as offender and geographical profiling (e.g. Godwin 2001; Canter 2003), which archaeologists need to understand and integrate into a larger evidential equation. The overall picture is a wide one drawing on many disparate skills and areas of expertise, of which archaeology is often merely one small element.

Archaeology is an annoyingly connective discipline. Whilst it is a science in its own right, it feeds upon and integrates with a host of other disciplines. As one eminent academic is reputed to have said, 'Being an archaeologist is like working in the hedgerows, it lies in neither one field nor the other'. It is an impure discipline that has few firm boundaries. Forensic archaeologists have been quick to learn that the discipline is also a two-way process. They need to know the evidential requirements of other

Figure 23.5 Archaeologists, geophysicists and police search officers integrating their skills in searching the concrete base of a barn in a search for a buried victim. The floor was surveyed using ground-penetrating radar (GPR) and selected areas opened up and excavated.

Figure 23.6 An unusual case where a victim was found part buried and part on the surface requiring a combination of archaeological and anthropological skills.

professions as much as other scene professionals need to know about those of archaeology. They also need to be aware of the limitations of their own expertise in this interdisciplinary approach.

It is worth mentioning the relationship with the anthropologist briefly here. This tends to occur in contexts where the victims are substantially or completely skeletal and where matters of identification and specific trauma require expert interpretation (Figure 23.6). In some instances, notably in post-conflict environments and the excavation of victims from mass graves, practitioners tend to be experienced in both archaeology and anthropology. There is often confusion between the terms archaeology and anthropology particularly in discussions between US and UK practitioners. In the United States, archaeology emerged as a secondary discipline under the umbrella of physical anthropology (e.g. Cabo and Dirkmaat, Chapter 31, this volume), whereas in the United Kingdom, archaeology and anthropology both emerged as primary disciplines but with anthropology being more dominantly 'social' as opposed to 'physical' – hence the scope for confusion. A working definition might be that forensic archaeologists are expert in field skills but with an awareness of physical anthropology whereas forensic anthropologists are expert in the examination of skeletal tissue but with only a basic understanding of excavation field methods. However, some might argue with that. As all forensic work is open to cross-examination in court, individual competence therefore tends to be very skill-specific, with practitioners taking care not to drift outside their fields of expertise. Staying within the limits of one's discipline competency, but being aware of the evidential requirements of the case as a whole, is one of the prerequisites of successful forensic investigation.

Awareness

In the United Kingdom forensic archaeology has grown up together with a public enthusiasm for all things 'forensic' fuelled by television programmes such as *CSI* and *Silent Witness*. The effect of this has resulted in a rise in student numbers for certain courses, such as chemistry, particularly if the word *forensic* is in the course title. Anything 'forensic' is sexy and attractive. It is a pity that the hundreds of students who graduate every year with a degree in something 'forensic' have no jobs to go to in a shrinking forensic science and crime scene personnel job market. But forensic archaeology is a little different. It has managed to find its way into university undergraduate programmes as a component of existing courses. It is seen as a valid aspect of current archaeological studies in the same way as, for example, Roman archaeology. It has become academically respectable. It exists and needs to be recognised as part of the wider discipline of archaeology itself. What is important, however, is to remember that the study of forensic archaeology requires the study and particularly the practice of conventional archaeology as a prerequisite.

It is at postgraduate level, or as master's degrees, where forensic archaeology is now studied more seriously, and there are four main university institutions which provide teaching in the United Kingdom. Most universities offer related courses but these four are the key ones from an archaeological point of view. They each have their own different academic flavour, some being more practically biased than others. Some are more anthropologically enthusiastic but most importantly they all employ staff members who are mostly operationally active. None of these courses, however, would profess to turn out forensic archaeologists who on graduation could walk straight into a crime scene. However, courses do need a minimum number of students to be viable; it is better to teach forensic archaeology to a wider student audience, and thus to increase awareness, than to not teach it at all. In the same way we have to remember that when forensic archaeologists deliver courses for other crime scene professionals, such as crime scene investigators, it is not to enable them to become archaeologists, but to give them awareness of how archaeology works so that they have some understanding of the theory and the processes.

Evidence

It is always interesting to hear archaeologists giving evidence in court. Traditionally, cultural archaeologists measure their comments with terms such as *could*, *might*, *may* or other expressions of relative probability. Courts generally prefer a more precise opinion and police forces typically require clear factual statements which will allow them to take the next step in an enquiry. Unlike conventional archaeology which produces a final report setting out method, listing data and posing hypotheses for future consideration, the forensic requirement is part of a larger spectrum of data. Its importance can be increased or diminished according to the scenario and its contributing weight in achieving what police may refer to as a 'result'.

In court, archaeological evidence is preferred in the form of one single narrative with a chronological list of events, a requirement that sits uncomfortably with most current accepted archaeological theory which prefers evidence to be open to complex and multiple interpretations. However, this is not usually an issue in determining the relationships between the few layers that tend to characterise most forensic excavations. Theory may conceivably be more relevant in complex circumstances involving, for example, mass graves or human remains discovered during building operations; but even then, these rarely approach the multiple-layered, multi-period types of site exhibiting vast databanks covering artefacts, ecofacts and stratigraphies. More awkwardly, the archaeologist can be drawn into unchartered waters, in being required to comment as to whether a grave might have been dug hurriedly by a perpetrator or whether it was more likely or less likely that a particular scenario occurred in an attempt to fix opinion or likelihood into a particular spectrum of Bayesian probability. In short, the archaeologist can be placed under some pressure to be specific and that is not always a comfortable position in which to be.

It is well to point out also that in the United Kingdom criminal investigation is subject to tight legal constraints; barristers are quick to identify even the slightest breach of protocol. There are numerous *Rules* and *Codes*, but there are two central relevant pieces of legislation of which any archaeologist at a crime scene or potential crime scene will need to be aware. First is the *Police and Criminal Evidence Act 1984* (HMSO 1984), usually known as PACE, which can impose time constraints on archaeological work. The second is the *Criminal Procedure and Investigations Act 1996* (HMSO 1996), usually referred to as the CPIA, which covers the complex issue of disclosure and admissibility of evidence.

Commercialisation

In the last few years there has been a major change in the way police forces utilise forensic experts. From the early 1980s there was a national service known as the *Forensic Science Service*, centrally funded, to which police forces could go to seek specialist support in such routine areas as fingerprints, firearms, biology, marks, blood spatter and so on. This effectively became privatised and allowed the establishment of commercial companies and consultants to operate in the forensic environment. The difference was that police forces now had to buy these services in an open and highly competitive market (Janaway, Chapter 24, this volume).

Today there is what is known as a National Framework for forensic science whereby police forces are contractually obliged to work with forensic science partners for a fixed period of years. This is a process undertaken by competitive tendering by individual forensic companies for bundles of forensic services. Police forces are therefore committed to use only certain companies for their forensic services for which they have to pay. These forensic services comprise the routine areas of expertise such as firearms or marks but not the more minority areas such as archaeology, anthropology and ecology.

Police forces are therefore still free to choose their own archaeology practitioners irrespective of the provider that they are tied to for mainstream services. It is reassuring to be able to say that the small number of archaeologists who work in this sector have resolutely maintained high standards of discipline, camaraderie, competence and quality of work above matters of commercial consideration. Getting the work done effectively and professionally is still seen as fundamental.

In summary, forensic archaeology in the United Kingdom has found an important and respected niche in criminal investigation. But it has taken time and it is still incomplete. Some police forces think twice before calling in a service they often believe they can undertake themselves. Forensic archaeology has academic acceptance in universities and a validation process of competence under the auspices of the Institute for Archaeologists (IfA; Janaway, Chapter 24, this volume). The discipline has progressed since the recovery in 1988 of the small boy mentioned at the beginning of this chapter. Techniques have been developed, lessons learned, criticism levied and the forensic world has moved on (Hunter et al. 2014). There are still very few practitioners but they maintain a strong belief that the importance of the discipline itself, and of the scientific contribution it can make, is paramount in a forensic environment constantly plagued by cuts in public spending and commercial pressures.

References

ACPO (Association of Chief Police Officers). 2011. *Police Search Management – Missing Persons*. Bramshill, Hook, NPIA (National Centre for Policing Excellence). Restricted.

Blau, S. and Ubelaker D. H. 2009. *Handbook of Forensic Anthropology and Archaeology*. Walnut Creek, Left Coast Press.

Canter, D. 2003. *Mapping Murder*. London, Virgin Books.

Gennard, D. E. 2007. *Forensic Entomology: An Introduction*. Chichester, John Wiley & Sons, Ltd.

Godwin, G. M. (ed.) 2001. *Criminal Psychology and Forensic Technology*. Boca Raton, CRC Press.

Gunn, A. 2009. *Essential Forensic Biology*. 2nd edition. Chichester, John Wiley & Sons, Ltd.

HMSO (Her Majesty's Stationery Office). 1984. *Police and Criminal Evidence Act 1984*. London, HMSO.

HMSO (Her Majesty's Stationery Office). 1996. *Criminal Procedure and Investigations Act 1996*. London, HMSO.

Hunter, J. and Cox, M. 2005. *Forensic Archaeology: Advances in Theory and Practice*. London, Routledge.

Hunter, J., Roberts C. A. and Martin, A. 1996. *Studies in Crime: An Introduction to Forensic Archaeology*. London, Routledge.

Hunter, J., Simpson, B. and Sturdy Colls, C. 2014. *Forensic Approaches to Buried Remains*. Chichester, John Wiley & Sons, Ltd.

Janaway, R. C. 2002. Degradation of clothing and other dress materials associated with buried bodies of archaeological and forensic interest. In W. D. Haglund and M. H. Sorg (eds.), *Advances in Forensic Taphonomy*, 379–402. Boca Raton, CRC Press.

Janaway, R. C. 2008. The decomposition of materials associated with buried cadavers. In M. Tibbett and D. O. Carter (eds.), *Soil Analysis in Forensic Taphonomy: Chemical and Biological Effects of Buried Human Remains*, 153–202. Boca Raton, CRC Press.

Kerr, B. 2008. Windsor Castle: destruction and salvage. In L. Rakoczy (ed.), *The Archaeology of Destruction*, 152–175. Cambridge, Cambridge Scholars Publishing.

Oates, J. 2012. *John Christie of Rillington Place: Biography of a Serial Killer*. London, Wharncliffe Books.

Pringle, J. K., Jervis, J. R., Hansen, J. D., Jones, G. M., Cassidy, N. J. and Cassella, J. P. 2011. Geophysical monitoring of simulated clandestine graves using electrical and ground penetrating radar methods: 0-3 years after burial. *16th European Meeting of Environmental & Engineering Geophysics of the Near Surface Geoscience Division of the EAGE. Leicester, 12–14 September 2011.*

Pye, K. and Croft, D. J. (eds.) 2004. *Forensic Geoscience: Principles, Techniques and Applications*. Geological Society Publication 232. London, Geological Society.

Ruffell, A. and McKinley, J. 2008. *Geoforensics*. Chichester, John Wiley & Sons, Ltd.

Staff, D. (2013). *The Lost Boy*. 2nd edition. London, Bantam Press.

CHAPTER 24

Forensic archaeology in the United Kingdom and quality assurance

Robert C. Janaway
School of Archaeological Sciences, University of Bradford, Bradford, UK

Introduction

This chapter discusses the establishment of regulatory standards for forensic practice in the United Kingdom and will examine how forensic archaeology fits into this wider framework. In recent years the United Kingdom has seen a period of rapid change in policing, provision of forensic science services and, consequent to this, regulation of forensic practice. The important and significant difference in forensic practice between the United Kingdom and other jurisdictions worldwide is the development of a privatised forensic market (Lawless 2010). This is in marked contrast to the model where routine forensic services are delivered through a single state organisation which is either part of the police (e.g. France; Schuliar et al., Chapter 8, this volume) or independent of the police but part of the criminal justice system (e.g. the Netherlands[1]; de Leeuwe and Groen, Chapter 14, this volume). The role of this chapter is to explain how this has developed in the United Kingdom, and where specific forensic services such as forensic archaeology and forensic anthropology work within these structures.

Before discussing the role of forensic archaeology, Forensic Service Providers and the British system it is important to put this into context in terms of administration, political authority and law, land mass, population density and crime rates.

United Kingdom: government and law

The United Kingdom (England, Wales, Northern Ireland and Scotland) is currently nationally governed by the Parliament of the United Kingdom and Northern Ireland from Westminster (London). Following popular support in referendums of 1997 and 1998 the parliament passed three devolution acts: the *Scotland Act* (1998); the *Northern Ireland Act* (1998); and the *Government of Wales Act* (1998), which was superseded by the *Government of Wales Act* (2006).[2] These acts established the three devolved legislatures: the Scottish Parliament (Holyrood, Edinburgh), The National Assembly for Wales (Cardiff) and the Northern Ireland Assembly (Stormont, outside Belfast). This process transferred limited powers over, for instance, policies on education and health away from the Westminster Parliament, which nonetheless currently retains overall sovereignty. With respect to Scotland this was subject to a referendum on 18 September 2014, which did not result in a mandate for full independence rather than devolution from Westminster.[3] Due to how the United Kingdom developed in terms of government and law there are three distinct legal systems that operate: England and Wales, Scotland and Northern Ireland. This has an effect both in terms of police structure and governance but also the law that underpins the criminal justice systems. For instance, since the *Union with England Act* (1701) there has been a shared legislature between Scotland/England and Wales, although Scotland has retained a fundamentally different legal system. It is important, especially for external readers, to be mindful that what pertains to the jurisdiction of England and Wales does not necessarily follow for Scotland or Northern Ireland (see the role of the Home Office Forensic Science Regulator later in this chapter).

[1]The Netherlands Forensic Institute (NFI) does not have a monopoly, although it does conduct the bulk of the work for Dutch police; other forensic institutes are allowed to perform forensic work too, although they have to be paid for directly from the police budget.

Forensic Archaeology: A Global Perspective, First Edition. Edited by W.J. Mike Groen, Nicholas Márquez-Grant and Robert C. Janaway.

United Kingdom: homicide statistics

As has been discussed elsewhere in this volume (e.g. Introduction and Concluding Remarks, this volume) a country's response to the problem of the excavation and recovery of bodies as part of a medico-legal process is driven by a number of factors, including offender behaviour, terrain and time period, as well as established police and legal structures. This is true of the United Kingdom, which is a relatively small island of *c.* 243,500 km² and a population of 63.2 million.[4] It is thus relatively densely occupied and with the exception of areas such as the Scottish Highlands lacks large tracts of unfrequented land (wilderness). It also has relatively modest homicide rates (see Table 24.1).

Importantly it has been estimated that less than 5% of homicides involve burial (Hunter and Cropper, Chapter 23, this volume). Thus in the United Kingdom the police are likely to deal with less than 40 buried bodies per year. Based on the author's case experience, a significant proportion of these will not be skeletonised due to relatively short time intervals between deposition and recovery. Thus in the United Kingdom we have a relatively modest number of occurrences where the police will require an excavation specialist (forensic archaeologist) or a skeletal specialist (forensic anthropologist). Of course these data do not include other cases involving search and recovery for targets that are not clandestine human burials and which may require a forensic archaeologist. These include, for instance, suspicious burials on public land that turn out to be buried animals. Most practicing UK forensic archaeologists have excavated a number of dog/pet burials in differing locations including public parks, wasteland, farmland and even cemeteries. As practiced in the United Kingdom not all forensic archaeology involves buried bodies: specialist archaeological assistance may be required for the search and recovery of buried/concealed weapons, stolen goods, contraband items, etc. (e.g. Hunter and Cox 2005). In addition to burial, bodies are also subject to surface deposition; in a crowded island with a temperate climate and some 8.5 million dogs being walked[5] surface depositions are often found prior to full skeletonisation. That is not to say that United Kingdom–based forensic specialists do not deal with burials or surface depositions that have been reduced to skeletal elements, but that the absolute numbers and proportion of these cases is less compared to parts of the world with less densely used open spaces. This has two principal results, first, in terms of decisions made by perpetrators that some form of concealment (burial, under rubble piles, etc.) may be preferential to surface dumping in relatively unfrequented woods etc., and second, shallow burials (that might be dug back up by scavengers) or surface depositions may well be discovered by dog walkers etc. prior to extensive skeletonisation and scattering.[6]

Table 24.1 UK homicide statistics.

	England and Wales	Scotland	Northern Ireland
2011/2012	551	121	23
2010/2011	638	122	28
2009/2010	619	106	22
2008/2009	662	134	26

Sources: Office for National Statistics Crime in England and Wales, year ending September 2012 (released January 2013), The Scottish Government Recording Crime in Scotland, 2011/2012 (released June 2012), Police Service of Northern Ireland Trends in Police Recorded Crime in Northern Ireland 1998/1999 to 2011/2012 (released July 2012).

UK policing

The United Kingdom does not have a national police force, and has since the early 20th century been based around a number of constabularies.[7] *The Police Act*

---

[2]For more information, see: https://www.gov.uk/devolution-of-powers-to-scotland-wales-and-northern-ireland (last accessed December 2014).

[3]For more information, see: http://www.scotreferendum.com/ (last accessed December 2014).

[4]Last UK census 2011.

[5]According to the Pet Food Manufacturer's Association 2013 annual Pet Population Report 25% of households in the United Kingdom own a dog (http://www.pfma.org.uk/pet-population/, last accessed December 2014).

[6]One of the key points to come out of the European forensic archaeology meetings (EMFA) held in The Hague, the Netherlands, in 2012 and 2013 (e.g. Groen, Chapter 14, this volume) was how local circumstances will affect both offender behaviour, patterns of deposition and thus variable response from law enforcement agencies. For instance in Finland, with extensive woodland and frozen soils which cannot be dug for much of the year there is a very low incidence of clandestine buried bodies but much more surface deposition and extensive dispersal of skeletal elements due to scavenger behaviour.

[7]In addition to the regional/county-based constabularies there are, and have been, some policing agencies that have a national coverage but with a specific remit: for instance British Transport Police (who cover the rail network) and the Royal Military Police. For more information, see: http://www.army.mod.uk/agc/provost/23207.aspx (last accessed December 2014).

(1919) established over 100 police forces in England and Wales and following a series of police strikes formalised national pay and conditions and forbade the police to strike. *The Police Act* (1946) began the process of merging smaller town forces with county constabularies, leaving 117 forces. The Police Act (1964) set the basis for current police structures, with the Home Secretary (Westminster) responsible for UK policing and a Police Authority, comprised of councillors and magistrates, responsible for each force. Each force is headed by a Chief Constable, and there was an extension of police powers of a Constable from their own force area to the rest of England and Wales. This reform gave impetus for the eventual amalgamation of over 100 forces down to 42.

During the 1980s large-scale civilianisation of a number of policing duties, in a 1988 Home Office Circular to all Chief Constables, identified 25 different duties that could be conducted by civilian staff including clerical, administrative and, importantly, Scene of Crime Officers. This civilianisation of Scene of Crime roles led to a greater degree of specialisation and professionalism of the role compared to the old regime where the scene of crime role was often one taken up at the end of an active police career and a prelude to retirement. Until recently there were 52 constabularies: 39 in England, 4 in Wales, 8 in Scotland and 1 in Northern Ireland. The latter was originally the Royal Ulster Constabulary (RUC) but as part of the Northern Ireland Police Process and subsequent to the Independent Commission on Policing for Northern Ireland[8] it has become the Police Service of Northern Ireland (PSNI) from 4 November 2001. Until 1 April 2013 there were eight constabularies in Scotland but these have now merged into a single force following the *Police and Fire Reform (Scotland) Bill* (2012).[9] Policing in England and Wales has also been subject to recent change; in 2006 the government contemplated further mergers of police constabularies in the interests of greater operational efficiency. This met with considerable opposition from within the police service and although force cooperation regarding specialist functions was encouraged (Scene of Crime, Air Support and Underwater search) forced mergers were dropped.[10] The *Police Reform and Social Responsibility Bill* (December 2010) had three main themes:

1 Reconnecting the police with the public through the election of local Police and Crime Commissioners (PCCs); linked to this was the abolition of national (Home Office) targets and the PCCs to create local Crime and Disorder Plans.
2 The establishment of the National Crime Agency (NCA)[11] to provide a stronger national approach to serious and organised crime and phasing out of the National Policing Improvement Agency (some functions to be transferred to NCA).
3 Managing severe fiscal constraint as part of ongoing austerity measures.

Since the UK Government's Comprehensive Spending Review of 2010 there has been a £1.9 billion cut (equivalent to a 20% year-on-year cut) to the UK police central budget. This has resulted in both loss of staff (both police officers and civilian staff) and local reviews of bought-in specialist services, including forensic archaeology.[12] Despite the relative autonomy of individual police constabularies there have been for many years centralised structures to provide guidance, share ideas and best practice. Most important is the Association of Chief Police Officers (ACPO). This is an independent, professionally led strategic body which brings together the expertise and experience of chief police officers from the United Kingdom and provides a national policing overview.[13] The National Policing Improvement Agency (NPIA)[14] was created by the *Police and Justice Act* (2006) and formed in April 2007 with the remit to improve public safety through critical services for police forces, such as the national fingerprint and DNA databases, and providing professional expertise. Included with its remit of Operational Policing Services was a National Search Adviser, who was there to advise Senior Investigating Officers on search technology,

[8]The *Independent Commission on Policing for Northern Ireland* was established in 1988 as part of the Belfast Agreement. Its terms of reference were to consult widely and address issues of bias in Northern Ireland policing. It produced its report, entitled *A New Beginning: Policing in Northern Ireland (Patten Report)* in September 1999.

[9]Now known as the Police Service of Scotland.

[10]For more information, see: http://news.bbc.co.uk/1/hi/uk/4645472.stm (last accessed December 2014).

[11]Became operational in October 2013. For more information, see: http://www.nationalcrimeagency.gov.uk/about-us (last accessed December 2014).

[12]For more information, see: http://www.publicfinance.co.uk/news/2011/07/thousands-of-officers-to-go-as-police-budget-cuts-hit/ (last accessed December 2014).

[13]ACPO provides an overview through chief officers across the police service in England, Wales and Northern Ireland to a number of national policing units, agencies and projects. The *ACPO Criminal Records Office* provides operational support to forces in relation to criminal records and associated biometric data, including DNA and fingerprint information. The National Ballistics Intelligence Service provides an intelligence resource that is available to police forces and other law enforcement agencies that focuses entirely on the criminal use of firearms. For more information, see: http://www.acpo.police.uk/Home.aspx (last accessed December 2014).

[14]Took over work of precursor agencies including CENTREX (police-training agency).

offender profiling and patterns of disposal. This advice was based on restricted data sets that, for instance, related offender and victim to patterns of transport and disposal including burial. Following the last UK general election (2010) part of government-spending cuts saw the closure of just under 200 Quasi Autonomous Non-Governmental Organisations (QUANGOs),[15] including the NPIA, some of whose functions will be taken over by the newly formed NCA.[16] This is currently divided into six commands/units: Border Crime, Economic Crime, Organised Crime, Cyber Crime, sexual abuse, and exploitation of children and young people.[17]

Development and privatisation of forensic science in the United Kingdom

Established forensic science laboratories in England and Wales can trace their history back to the 1930s with the establishment of the Metropolitan Police Laboratory in 1935. This was built upon the pioneering work of Arthur Dixon, the Assistant Secretary at the Home Office, who promoted the use of scientific approaches to crime investigation. In 1929 Dixon submitted a proposal to the Home Secretary that argued for the establishment of police college laboratories that would have twin functions of both scientific research and investigation. This national forensic science service would utilise a wide range of scientific methods for both the collection and analysis of evidence. Police would receive advice and support from regional laboratories, with further research and training provided by a central establishment.[18] This was to a large extent based on the pioneering French model of '*Police Scientifique*'. Since the 1930s there was an expansion of regional Forensic Science Service Laboratories to conduct casework to which police could submit material for examination. By 1996 these included Birmingham, Chepstow, Chorley, Huntington, Wetherby and London (as the old independent Metropolitan Police laboratory was taken into the Forensic Science Service). In addition to the operational laboratories there was a research laboratory in Birmingham to maintain Dixon's original vision of Casework and Research. Scotland and Northern Ireland have their own publicly funded forensic service providers: the Scottish Police Services Authority (SPSA), Forensic Services and Forensic Science Northern Ireland (FSNI). FSNI is an agency within the Ministry of Justice. It is independent of the police and, importantly, due to the politics of Northern Ireland, independent of other forensic science services in the rest of the United Kingdom.

Thus from the 1930s to the 1990s in England and Wales there was essentially one provider of Forensic Services: the Forensic Science Service (FSS). This had a virtual monopoly on prosecution work (for the police),[19] with the exception of experts engaged on an *ad hoc* case-by-case basis. These experts were usually, but not exclusively, academics with a niche specialism – such as forensic archaeology. By around 2010 there were several private Forensic Science Providers (FSPs) and an emerging market in forensic science provision that reflected successive governments' policies of creating competition.[20] These included the FSS, which by 1991 had Executive Agency Status,[21] Forensic Alliance[22] (founded in 1987, taken over by LGC in 2005) and Manlove Forensics (MLF), a small private company which started with a highly focused remit but has expanded rapidly in recent years.[23] By the time of the closure of the FSS in 2010 the organisation had gone through a number of financial and managerial models (see Table 24.2) and was finally a government-owned company delivering around 60% of forensic services to

[15]Known in the press as 'Bonfire of the Quangos'. See for example: http://www.bbc.co.uk/news/uk-politics-11538534 (last accessed December 2014).

[16]For more information, see: http://www.nationalcrimeagency.gov.uk/ (last accessed December 2014).

[17]Having only recently become operational (October 2013) and with the next general election set for May 2015 it is entirely possible that this remit may change or even grow in the near future.

[18]In 1931 Dixon organised an informal chief constables' conference to consider the value of scientific aids in police work. In 1934 a Committee of Enquiry was set up to investigate the conditions and practices of detectives in the United Kingdom. A sub-committee was formed to consider the use made of scientific aids to police work. As a result, the first Police Laboratories were established.

[19]House of Commons Science and Technology Committee, 2011 *The Forensic Science Service*. For more information, see: http://www.publications.parliament.uk/pa/cm201012/cmselect/cmsctech/855/85502.htm (last accessed December 2014).

[20]The marketisation of forensic science in the United Kingdom needs to be seen against the general debate over the efficient delivery of a range of local and national government services. This of course has been reflected in the ideology of different political administrations. Starting with Compulsive Competitive Tendering (CCT) in the 1980s these policies have developed into a range of full and partial privatisation of former government agencies.

[21]Executive Agency Status – a branch of government which has independent managerial and budgetary control – in simplistic terms can be viewed as a halfway house to privatisation.

[22]For more information, see: http://www.lgcgroup.com/lgc-forensics/ (last accessed December 2014).

[23]For more information, see: http://www.manloveforensics.co.uk/ (last accessed December 2014).

Table 24.2 Recent history of Forensic Science Service (FSS).

1991	Became an Executive Agency of the Home Office
1999	Gained Trading Fund status
2002	Stopped being the 'preferred supplier' of forensic services for the Association of Chief Police Officers (ACPO)
2003	Home Office's review of the FSS recommended the FSS become a public–private partnership (PPP), via the government-owned, contractor-operated (GovCo) model
2005	FSS changed from a Trading Fund to a GovCo company
2008	£50 million government grant, the FSS launched a transformation programme to reduce costs, aimed to deliver by mid 2011
2010	Government announced closure
2012	Closure complete

For more information, see: http://www.publications.parliament.uk/pa/cm201012/cmselect/cmsctech/855/85505.htm (last accessed December 2014).

police forces in England and Wales.[24] The principal justification for closure was a loss of £2 million per month, although this figure has subsequently been challenged.[25]

It should be noted that although a number of United Kingdom–based forensic archaeologists worked closely over the years with scene-going FSS scientists, the FSS did not formally offer forensic archaeology or anthropology amongst its services.

The forensic market was made possible by the development of National Forensic Framework Agreements (NFFA). There is no space to go through the different iterations of funding arrangement that pertained to the 'virtual monopoly' of the old relationship between police and the FSS (Lawless 2010). That being said it was normal for a particular force to use their local FSS laboratory; for instance, West Yorkshire police would use the Wetherby laboratory for the bulk of their submissions, and, where appropriate, Wetherby-based scientists would attend crime scenes.[26] Of course if the appropriate scientific speciality was not available from Wetherby, assistance could be called upon from other laboratories. The arrangements for NFFAs were finalised in August 2008. These were a formalised mechanism by which police forces in England and Wales enter into service agreements with commercial FSPs, and are therefore committed to use only certain companies for their forensic services, for which they have to pay. The contracts are for a fixed period and are undertaken by competitive tendering by individual forensic companies for 'bundles' of forensic services (Lawless 2010). The NFFA covers routine expertise such as toxicology, DNA, firearms or marks, but *not* usually the more minority expertise such as forensic archaeology, anthropology and ecology (e.g. entomology, palynology, geology). Of course a company can include these in their 'bundle' if they have capacity and feel that it would make their tender more competitive. In the last round of tenders at least one service provider included forensic archaeology, ecology and anthropology within its 'bundle' but has subsequently outsourced in these areas.

Regulation of forensic practitioners

In November 1997 the Forensic Science Working Group, chaired by Lord Jack Lewis, produced a report that recommended an independent registration for forensic practitioners (this was to include police-based crime scene investigators (CSIs), fingerprint examiners and external experts such as forensic scientists, forensic anthropologists and forensic archaeologists).[27] It recommended that an independent registration council for forensic practitioners was necessary to secure the confidence of the courts and the public in the competence of forensic practitioners, coming after much public and legal debate concerning expert witnesses. This resulted in the formation of the Council for the Registration of Forensic Practitioners (CRFP). 'Alongside each name on the register you will find the name of at least one specialty. This describes the broad area of forensic work we believe that person is competent to do'. 'The Register is designed to cover all the regular forensic specialties' (CRFP 2003, 1). The CRFP register was therefore focused on the individual

[24]The provision of forensic science has been recently considered by the House of Commons Science and Technology Select Committee, which published its second and most recent report on 26 July 2013. Available at: http://www.publications.parliament.uk/pa/cm201314/cmselect/cmsctech/610/610.pdf (last accessed December 2014).

This considered in some detail the current Forensics Market and the implications of the closure of Forensic Science Service.

[25]For more information, see: http://www.publications.parliament.uk/pa/cm201012/cmselect/cmsctech/855/85505.htm (last accessed December 2014). Example of challenge to government costs, see: http://www.bbc.co.uk/news/science-environment-21251162 (last accessed December 2014).

[26]A good example of this would be a scene that required blood pattern analysis. Although the police would have scene of crime officers, the BPA expert would usually be a biologist from the FSS.

[27]For more information, see: https://www.gov.uk/government/uploads/system/uploads/attachment_data/file/117634/Forensic_Practitiioner_Stan1.pdf (last accessed December 2014).

Table 24.3 List of CRFP specialties (CRFP, 2003).

Incident investigation
Archaeologists
Fingerprint development specialists
Fingerprint examiners
Scene examiners (including those working in volume crime)[a]
Medicine
Anthropology
Forensic odontology
Science and engineering
Drugs
Firearms
Human contact traces
Questioned documents
Toxicology

[a]In UK police management, crime is divided between major crime, which includes homicide, rape, assault, etc., and volume crime, which includes theft, taking a vehicle without consent, burglary, etc.

practitioner, their knowledge base and experience, rather than the organisational systems within which they were working, including workplace quality management protocols. It was stated that '[a]ll forensic practitioners are expected to demonstrate adequate understanding of the law as it applies to their field of practice, and procedures which will be followed if a case with which they are involved comes to court' (CRFP 2003, 2).

Forensic specialties covered by CRFP (unpublished CRFP documentation 2003)

The CRFP divided up forensic practice under three broad areas (Table 24.3):

1 Incident investigation
2 Medicine
3 Science and engineering

As we can see from the outset this was designed to cover both investigative and evaluative areas of forensic endeavour.

It should be noted that, in keeping with developments in the United Kingdom, forensic archaeology and anthropology were separate disciplines, although it was open to individuals, depending on their skill sets, to register as a forensic archaeologist, a forensic anthropologist or both. The CRFP skills descriptions clearly demonstrate the distinctions in role in UK practice and how these mesh with other specialists such as pathologists and crime scene examiners:

- *Forensic archaeologists are concerned with finding and recovering buried human remains. In looking for these archaeologists are able to work with a search team, advising on appropriate methods or sequences of methods for searching. They use specific archaeological search skills such as field craft, geophysical survey, etc. as appropriate. In attending a scene where buried human remains have been discovered (for example at a building site), or where there is considered to be a clandestine grave, forensic archaeologists can devise, implement and lead a strategy for investigation that will maximise the available buried evidence. Forensic archaeologists support the pathologist in the excavation of a body and apply archaeological skills and recording techniques to assist the enquiry* (CRFP 2003, 3).
- *Forensic anthropology is the identification of human remains in a medico-legal context. Anthropologists can establish that remains are indeed human and assist in confirming the time–death interval. Primarily, they retrieve information pertinent to the identity of a dead person, to assist investigators to assign a name to them. Anthropologists assess the person's sex, age at death, stature and ethnicity and establish any features particular to their personal identity, including previous injury, pathology, abnormities, etc. Anthropologists usually work within a team including a forensic pathologist, odontologist and radiographer* (CRFP 2003, 4).
- *All registered forensic anthropologists are competent to proffer a professional opinion on identity from skeletal remains whether they are intact, fragmented or burned. Not all anthropologists have experience in extracting this information from remains which contain flesh. For this reason there is a sub-category of osteology, which identifies the specialists who work with dry skeletal remains but not with fresh or badly decomposed remains. Those practitioners who are competent to work with both categories of remains appear in the register under the heading of general forensic anthropology* (CRFP 2003, 4).

For each CRFP specialty there was a lead assessor and a number of assessors (drawn from established practitioners in the field). The scale for each specialty varied greatly from the potentially large number of fingerprint examiners down to the smaller number of forensic archaeologists, anthropologists or odontologists. An applicant submitted documentation for scrutiny by the assessors which consisted of evidence of training and qualifications, a case log and case summaries and references (usually from senior investigating officers, prosecuting council, etc.). The references and case files were used to evidence a detailed set of criteria for each specialty. The weakness of the system was that in addition to being a paper-based system, bias could be weighted towards court appearance (which would vary depending on case and evidence type). More significantly, not all police constabularies were keen to adopt a system that would require the registration (which costs) for a significant number of crime scene examiners with little perceived benefit to the force. In addition it was not uncommon, although this varied from specialty to specialty, that practitioners giving evidence in court were not asked if they were CRFP-registered. The CRFP was wound up in March 2009.[28]

Home Office Forensic Science Regulator

The Home Office Forensic Science Regulator was set up in 2008 against the background of the competitive forensic market to ensure an appropriate regime of scientific quality standards across the criminal justice system.[29] The Regulator is sponsored by the Home Office, but is an independent public appointee. The remit for the Regulator is England and Wales, and as already noted Scotland and Northern Ireland have their own autonomy concerning forensic services and criminal justice; currently Scotland and Northern Ireland follow the Regulator's standards on a voluntary basis. The Regulator's role and objectives were outlined in detail in the consultation document *Manual of Regulation* (FSR 2008), and from the beginning it was clear that with the remit of ensuring confidence and integrity in the criminal justice system it was necessary to ensure a level playing field for all forensic suppliers including police in-house services. The principle mechanism adopted by the Regulator was via the implementation of international standards[30] at an organisational level, whether that is a commercial Forensic Service Provider, a police Scene of Crime (crime scene examination) unit or an in-house police laboratory.[31,32] For traditional laboratory-based forensic work accreditation to ISO/IEC 17025 and certified to ISO 9001 has been adopted, while ISO/IEC 17020 has been used (in line with European standards) (e.g. Groen, Chapter 25, this volume) for crime scene examination. By 2011 the Regulator had published *Codes of Practice and Conduct for Forensic Service Providers and Practitioners in the Criminal Justice System* (FSR 2011), which reflects that greater impetus had been achieved with the external providers working in a laboratory setting (ISO/IEC 17025). To date, in addition to uptake of ISO/IEC 17025 by the main providers for laboratory based work, some scene-deployed private FSPs have also been accredited to ISO/IEC 17020,[33] as have some police scene of crime/scientific support departments. From 2008 to 2014 the Regulator has operated without statutory powers or the ability to enforce compliance with his standards. In January 2014 there was a consultation regarding whether the Regulator should have these statutory powers.[34] It is perhaps pertinent to note that contained within the strongly worded report on the House of Commons Scientific Select Committee published in July 2013 is a reiteration of the need for police in-house activity, whether laboratory- or crime scene–based, to comply with the same quality standards as work commissioned from outside providers.[35]

Forensic archaeology and the Chartered Institute for Archaeologists

Since 1988 and the Stephen Jennings Case (Hunter and Cropper, Chapter 23, this volume) a number of forensic archaeologists have been recognised and used by British Police Forces. In the early days they were brought in on an *ad hoc* basis rather than embedded in the FSS or the emerging independent Service Providers.

With the demise of the CRFP a working group of former CRFP-registered forensic archaeologists and assessors was set up to assess how forensic archaeology should consider the future formal organisation of forensic archaeology and the setting of standards in line

[28]This was precipitated by the decision of withdrawal of participation and hence finance from a number of police forces and organisations (NPIA, ACPO and Metropolitan Police), which finally led to the withdrawal of Home Office finance. The whole process took from 4 February 2009 until March (source letter CRFP Board 11 March 2009) and left a hiatus in regulation until the initiative of the Home Office Forensic Science Regulator came into force. For more information, see Early Day Motion 1849, House of Commons 7 September 2009.

[29]For more information, see: https://www.gov.uk/government/organisations/forensic-science-regulator (last accessed December 2014).

[30]For more information, see: http://www.iso.org/iso/home/about.htm (last accessed December 2014).

[31]This work was carried out working with the UK standards agency – UKAS.

[32]The implication of this organisational as opposed to individual accreditation is that an individual practitioner, whether freelance or attached to a university department, needs to operate through an organisation that has met the relevant standards. Since accreditation to ISO/IEC 17025 or ISO/IEC 17020 is not an inconsiderable investment; it is only really an appropriate route for organisations whose core business is delivery as opposed to teaching and research.

[33]In 2012, Cellmark Forensic Services became the first organisation to achieve this accreditation, House of Commons Science and Technology Committee, 2nd report on Forensic Science, 17 July 2013.

[34]For more information, see: https://www.gov.uk/government/uploads/system/uploads/attachment_data/file/256614/New_statutory_powers_for_the_forensic_science_regulator.pdf (last accessed December 2014).

[35]Some police forensic laboratories have failed to make sufficient progress towards achieving accreditation to the same quality standard (ISO/IEC 17025) as private providers, House of Commons Science and Technology Committee, 2nd report on Forensic Science, 17 July 2013.

with the proposals coming from the Forensic Regulator.[36] At this meeting the role of the Forensic Regulator and his recent review was clarified, which identified the need for the following:

- Quality standards that work
- Competent practitioners
- Reliable and valid methods
- Technical competence – people and equipment

These requirements could be achieved by the majority of organisations through accreditation under ISOs/IECs (ISO/IEC 17025 2005 – Laboratory, ISO/IEC17020 – Crime Scene). It was agreed, however, that niche disciplines, which may not be directly covered by the mainstream Forensic Service Providers, might struggle to operate under ISO/IEC 17020, which is essentially an organisational standard, unlike the old CRFP scheme which did not easily or economically cover small consultancies. It was also agreed that it was appropriate that niche disciplines while conforming to the requirements of the Regulator should be under the auspices of their professional bodies. The Chartered Institute for Archaeologists (CIfA) formerly known as the Institute for Archaeologists (IfA)[37] is the professional organisation for archaeologists in the United Kingdom.[38] In 2011 it was established that the CIfA should be the professional body for forensic archaeology and this was recognised by the Forensic Science Regulator.[39] As an organisation it already had a number of advantages, it was a professional body and not a learned society, it had an overarching Code of Conduct, a code of approved practice for the regulation of contractual arrangements in archaeology and a set of disciplinary procedures. It already had a set of published Standards and Guidance documents.[40] The working party developed *Standards and Guidance for Forensic Archaeologists* (written by Natasha Powers and Lucy Sibun).[41] This was produced in consultation with the Forensic Regulator with the draft Standards document based on former CRFP and CIfA guidelines, and on the existing template used by the forensic pathologists. These were approved on an interim basis at CIfA's 2011 annual general meeting (AGM) and subsequently confirmed in 2012 and endorsed by the Forensic Science Regulator.

The CIfA has three levels of professional membership, with membership applications being judged against a set of criteria by a centrally constituted membership (validation) committee. A matrix of forensic archaeology competency standards has been drawn up to assist the CIfA Membership Committee; there are three levels of membership:

1. Practitioner (Forensic Archaeology) PCIfA
2. Associate (Forensic Archaeology) ACIfA
3. Member (Forensic Archaeology) MCIfA

The latter is the highest grade, equivalent to 'Reporting Officer', and the matrix has also been linked to National Occupational Standards.[42] The benefits of the multiple membership grading are that it provides a progression route for younger practitioners (one of the failures of the old CRFP model) and allows for recognition of mentored working and succession planning within the discipline.

The CIfA has a number of special interest groups (e.g. Geophysics, Standing Buildings, Underwater and Nautical Archaeology) that hold lectures and meetings and are open to all CIfA members. There is a Forensic

[36]The first meeting was on 4 September 2009, and in attendance were forensic archaeologists, police personnel, representatives from the Home Office, Institute for Archaeologists and the Forensic Regulator.

[37]For more information, see: http://www.archaeologists.net/ (last accessed December 2014).

[38]The Chartered Institute for Archaeologists (CIfA) is a professional body for the study and care of the historic environment. It promotes best practice in archaeology and provides a self-regulatory quality assurance framework for the sector and those it serves. CIfA has over 3000 members and more than 70 registered practices across the United Kingdom. Its members work in all branches of the discipline: heritage management, planning advice, excavation, finds and environmental study, buildings recording, underwater and aerial archaeology, museums, conservation, survey, research and development, teaching and liaison with the community, industry and the commercial and financial sectors.

[39]There has been general agreement in the United Kingdom that the division between forensic archaeology and forensic anthropology should be maintained. It was felt that the discipline distinctions that had been established under the old CRFP system were still valid. With this in mind, for forensic archaeology this working party and the professional body for archaeologists (CIfA) established standards and guidance. The British Association for Forensic Anthropology (BAFA), established in 2011, and the Royal Anthropological Institute (RAI) are working to establish Code of Practice, Practitioner Levels and CPD guidelines for forensic anthropology. For more information, see: http://www.bahid.org/bafa/ (last accessed December 2014).

[40]Current Standards and Guidance Documents include archaeological advice; desk-based assessment; field evaluation; excavation; archaeological watching brief; archaeological investigation and recording of standing buildings or structures; collection, documentation, conservation and research of archaeological materials; stewardship of the historic environment; nautical archaeological recording and reconstruction; creation, compilation, transfer and deposition of archaeological archives; geophysical survey; and forensic archaeology.

[41]Available at: http://www.archaeologists.net/sites/default/files/node-files/Forensic2010-v1.pdf (last accessed December 2014).

[42]National Occupational Standards (NOS) are UK standards of performance for personal work–based performance including the knowledge and skills they need to perform effectively.

Archaeology Special Interest Group (FASIG) to promote the discipline generally; however, within this is a closed operative working group of forensic archaeologists practising as expert witnesses: the CIfA Forensic Archaeology Expert Panel ('the Expert Panel'). The Expert Panel provides the mechanism for accrediting and regulating the work of those forensic archaeologists acting or seeking to act as expert witnesses, as well as considering issues arising in the course of such work. Membership of the Expert Panel is open to all practising forensic archaeologists who are members of the CIfA at Member level (MCIfA) and who demonstrate competence against CIfA's forensic archaeology competency matrix.[43] All members of the CIfA are bound by the codes of conduct,[44] the most important of which are 1.3 'A member shall not offer advice, make a public statement, or give legal testimony involving archaeological matters, without being as thoroughly informed on the matters concerned as might reasonably be expected' and 1.4 'A member shall not undertake archaeological work for which he or she is not adequately qualified'. Failure to heed these aspects of the code or to deviate without well-considered and documented justification from the Standards and Guidance for Forensic Archaeologists makes the individual liable to sanction via the CIfA's disciplinary procedures.[45]

University education and quality standards in the United Kingdom

The broad curricular coverage of UK university courses is within the remit of the Quality Assurance Agency (QAA), which produces subject benchmarks for both undergraduate and master's degrees.[46] All UK university courses through approval and review procedures must address their synergy with subject benchmarks.[47] For master's degrees there is a benchmark for forensic science but not currently for forensic archaeology or forensic anthropology. For undergraduate (honours degrees) there are benchmark standards for forensic archaeology,[48] anthropology[49] (encompasses both social and biological), criminology and forensic science.[50]

In addition to the QAA benchmarks (which are mandatory) there is also a voluntary course validation that is available through the Chartered Society of Forensic Sciences (CSFS), which runs an accreditation scheme for forensic-related courses. These are more detailed than the QAA benchmarks. Usually a course, content and delivery will be judged against two or three component standards and are verified by a site inspection team. Component standards include interpretation, evaluation and presentation of evidence (which is the core standard to which all courses must comply), crime scene investigation, laboratory analysis, digital forensics, forensic archaeology (new 2013) and forensic anthropology (new 2013).[51]

For instance a typical undergraduate forensic science course will be examined against the core standard, crime scene investigation and laboratory analysis. Within this structure it is possible to accredit a master's level forensic archaeology course against the core standard plus the archaeology component standard.

Conclusions

The United Kingdom has seen a rapid development of forensic archaeology over the last 25 years, with archaeological techniques and practice becoming firmly embedded in UK police procedure (Hunter and Cropper, Chapter 23, this volume). In the United Kingdom forensic archaeology is taught and practised as a standalone discipline, in contrast to other jurisdictions (e.g. Cabo and Dirkmaat, Chapter 31, this volume). There are a number of distinct reasons why the UK approach has been different. First, in British universities there is no tradition of teaching archaeology as a subset of anthropology, as witnessed by the division of QAA benchmarks.[52] While the QAA benchmarks are

[43]There are currently (January 2014) 15 members within the Expert Panel.

[44]For more information, see: http://www.archaeologists.net/sites/default/files/node-files/Code-of-conduct-revOct2013.pdf (last accessed December 2014).

[45]For more information, see: http://www.archaeologists.net/sites/default/files/node-files/Disciplinary_by-law_revised_Oct_2012.pdf (last accessed December 2014).

[46]For more information, see: http://www.qaa.ac.uk/AssuringStandardsAndQuality/subject-guidance/Pages/Subject-benchmark-statements.aspx (last accessed December 2014).

[47]Although universities through their charters have a level of autonomy, they are required to conform to QAA audit processes.

[48]For more information, see Last benchmark reviewed and published 2007 (due for review 2014).

[49]For more information, see Last benchmark reviewed and published 2007.

[50]First published in 2012 for implementation by all courses with Forensic Science in title by academic year 2013/2014.

[51]For more information, see: http://www.forensic-science-society.org.uk/Accreditation/Component%20Standard (last accessed December 2014).

[52]In fact, physical anthropology, whether taught as individual undergraduate modules or as a standalone master's, is most likely to be embedded either with an archaeology- or a medical-related department (e.g. anatomy) within the United Kingdom.

mandatory on university courses they are generated by consensus working groups of established UK academics taken from across the sector. So in the first instance there has been no desire generally within UK archaeological practice or education to embrace the US four-field approach. Second, professional archaeology in the United Kingdom is an established profession in its own right,[53] already embedded in the planning/development process of heritage management. The approach taken in the United Kingdom, which mirrors the way forensic services are commissioned, is to use a combination of individuals with the right skill sets and experience for the specific job. This has been the case right from the very beginning. As has already been documented, the first case where archaeological expertise was used evidentially in a UK court was that of Stephen Jennings in 1988 (Hunter and Cropper, Chapter 23, this volume). While this excavation and post-excavation processing predated much of the current quality standard documentation it is instructive to examine how well this early piece of work meshes with current practice. In the first instance the team despatched to the scene comprised two individuals with complementary skill sets: Professor John Hunter, an experienced excavator, with a good working knowledge of police procedures, and Professor Charlotte Roberts, an experienced osteologist, also with extensive excavation experience but not at the same level as John Hunter. This fulfils the underlying principle that everyone should be working within their individual capabilities/remit. Taking this old case as an example, John Hunter had a working knowledge of human skeletal anatomy but was not a specialist, while Charlotte Roberts was an osteologist but not an excavation specialist with the same level of expertise as John Hunter. In addition to the work carried out on site the post-excavation sieving operation was carried out by Andrew Addison, an experienced field archaeologist, with professional experience of carrying out sieving operations and who as it happens later left archaeology to retrain as a crime scene examiner.

Finally it is important to remember that not all the endeavours of forensic archaeologists lead to the uncovering of skeletal human remains. Thus, generally in the United Kingdom, forensic practitioners are happy with dual standards for forensic archaeology and forensic anthropology. There will of course be individuals whose skills and expertise rest in both disciplines, although rarely will these directly balance. With both forensic archaeology via the CIfA and forensic anthropology via the British Association for Forensic Anthropology (BAFA)/Royal Anthropological Institute (RAI), both with three practitioner levels, it is possible to reflect an individual's personal skill sets.

This chapter has tried to capture the immense period of change in policy and structure that has affected the criminal justice system and in particular the police and forensic science; forensic archaeology has not been immune to these changes as they have profound effects on procurement of service and how service providers are regulated. It is our belief that mechanisms have been put into place whereby we can work with the policy makers, and in particular the Forensic Regulator, to provide a service to the Criminal Justice System that is accountable and fit for purpose.

References

CRFP. 2003. *Forensic Specialties Document*. London, Council for the Registration of Forensic Practitioners. Unpublished.

FSR (2008). *Manual of Regulation*. https://www.gov.uk/government/uploads/system/uploads/attachment_data/file/118892/Manual_of_Regulation_22.9.08.pdf (last accessed 17 December 2014).

FSR (2011). *Codes of Practice and Conduct for Forensic Service Providers and Practitioners in the Criminal Justice System*. https://www.gov.uk/government/publications/forensic-science-providers-codes-of-practice-and-conduct (last accessed 17 December 2014).

Hunter, J. and Cox, M. 2005. *Forensic Archaeology: Advances in Theory and Practice*. London, Routledge.

Lawless, C. 2010. *A Curious Reconstruction? The Shaping of 'Marketised' Forensic Science*. Centre for Analysis of Risk and Regulation, London School of Economics and Political Science, London, UK. Discussion Paper no 63.

[53]This separation of archaeology and anthropology is the norm for a number of other European countries; for instance, in Spain, anthropologists come from biology or medical departments, while archaeologists are embedded within geography and history.

CHAPTER 25

Forensic archaeology: the European collaboration

W.J. Mike Groen

Netherlands Forensic Institute (NFI), The Hague, The Netherlands

Introduction

This chapter discusses the establishment and development of the annual European Meeting on Forensic Archaeology (EMFA) since 2012, and the subsequent wish of the participants in these meetings to collaborate within a European network regarding the use of forensic archaeological theories and methodologies in a legal context. This desire resulted in a request made to the European Network of Forensic Science Institutes (ENFSI) to explore the feasibility of establishing a European Expert Working Group (EWG) on Forensic Archaeology within the ENFSI community. Although the final approval from the ENFSI Board and Membership to this request will not be given before May 2015, the EMFA meetings have already offered a platform that will be used for further structuring of the European forensic archaeological collaboration.

European meetings on forensic archaeology

In order to understand how forensic archaeology – defined here as a forensic discipline that uses archaeological theory and methodology in a legal context – is organised and practised within the different European countries, to meet and learn from foreign colleagues and to discuss the possibility of establishing a European forum for forensic archaeology in order to develop this discipline even further, the author and the Netherlands Forensic Institute (NFI) initiated the first EMFA in 2012. The desire for such a meeting was based upon several European developments, such as the fact that the application of archaeological theory and methodology at crime scenes was variable across Europe, and the European desire for accreditation and standardisation of Crime Scene Investigation (CSI) processes.

- Firstly, the publication by Nicholas Márquez-Grant et al. (2012) showed that the practice of forensic archaeology was scarcely applied at most European incidents or crime scenes, and the excavation and recovery of human remains from forensic contexts in Europe was mostly done by police officers with no archaeological training, forensic anthropologists or forensic pathologists.
- Secondly, a memorandum of understanding existed between the ENFSI[1] and the European Co-operation for Accreditation (EA),[2] selecting the international quality standard for inspecting bodies, ISO/IEC 17020, as the most appropriate standard for crime scene investigation in the forensic process at the time of writing.[3] This memorandum, which was ratified by both institutes in 2008, correspondingly intended to harmonise the assessment of European CSI services for the purpose of accreditation.
- Thirdly, in 2011 the Council of the European Union (EU) stated its ambition to create a European Forensic Science Area by 2020, and the development of forensic science infrastructure in Europe, all based on minimum European forensic science standards.[4]
- Fourthly, the British forensic archaeologists were starting to unite themselves under the umbrella of the Institute for Archaeologists (IfA) to fulfil the wish of the British Forensic Science Regulator (FSR) for quality and competence (QCC) assurances, and to promote the use of forensic archaeology in Britain (Janaway, Chapter 24, this volume).

[1]For more information, see http://www.enfsi.org/ (last accessed 28 December 2013).

[2]For more information, see http://www.european-accreditation.org/ (last accessed 28 December 2013).

[3]For more information, see http://www.european-accreditation.org/publication/ea-5-03-ta (last accessed 28 December 2013). This document will be revised in 2014.

[4]For more information, see http://www.consilium.europa.eu/uedocs/cms_data/docs/pressdata/en/jha/126875.pdf (last accessed 28 December 2013).

Forensic Archaeology: A Global Perspective, First Edition. Edited by W.J. Mike Groen, Nicholas Márquez-Grant and Robert C. Janaway.

- Finally, the NFI was also preparing its forensic archaeological service for accreditation according to the international ISO/IEC 17020 standard, a process that, in all probability, will be finalised in 2015 (De Leeuwe and Groen, Chapter 14, this volume).

All these developments made it necessary to promote the visibility, quality and use of forensic archaeology across Europe.

The first EMFA was held on 22 August 2012, as an additional event to the 6th European Academy of Forensic Science (EAFS2012) conference. This meeting was hosted by the NFI and organised as a joint venture between the NFI and the Forensic Archaeology Expert Panel of the British IfA (Janaway, Chapter 24, this volume).[5] The meeting had 14 oral papers on (quality assurances in) forensic archaeology and was attended by about 50 delegates, covering 12 countries and representing ENFSI member institutes, police forces, humanitarian organisations, forensic science providers, universities and freelance professionals. Representatives of six additional (south European) countries were not able to attend the meeting, but they supported its outcomes. One important outcome was the wish to establish a scientific forensic archaeological platform for European practitioners. It was also felt that it would be most convenient for the forensic community, and for forensic archaeologists, if this platform were not a stand-alone entity. The most logical options for such a platform were, according to the participants, the ENFSI or the European Association of Archaeologists (EAA).[6] It was agreed to contact ENFSI first. This is because the ENFSI Membership would not only underline the forensic nature of the forensic archaeological platform to be established, but also provide a direct access to the European forensic community.

The second EMFA was also held at the NFI, on 30–31 August 2013.[7] This meeting had 15 oral papers on forensic archaeology and four oral papers on forensic taphonomy, and was attended by about 45 delegates from 14 countries. The second EMFA also saw the inauguration of the ENFSI Project Group (PG) Forensic Archaeology (see later). The third EMFA (August 2014), being planned at the time of writing, will be held at Cranfield University, UK. The fourth EMFA (August 2015) will be hosted at the Forensic Science Institute of the French National Gendarmerie. It was a deliberate choice to move the venue from the Netherlands to a different European country, in order to stress the European format of the EMFA. The future venue will be changed on a voluntary basis within Europe, with different forensic institutes or universities acting as hosts.

European network of forensic science institutes

In 1992 an agreement was established between several directors of Western European governmental forensic laboratories to hold regular meetings. The first meeting was represented by 11 forensic laboratories and was held at the Dutch Forensic Laboratory (*Gerechtelijk Laboratorium*)[8] in Rijswijk, the Netherlands, in 1993. It was agreed that the Membership of the (future) ENFSI should be open to all European forensic science institutes. The formal founding of ENFSI took place on 20 October 1995, also at the Dutch Forensic Laboratory, Rijswijk, the Netherlands.[9]

The ENFSI has been considered as the sole voice of the forensic science community in Europe by the EU since 2009. ENFSI's main goals are to share knowledge and exchange experiences, to ensure the quality of development and delivery of forensic science throughout Europe, to encourage all ENFSI laboratories to comply with best practice and international standards for QCC assurance, to establish and maintain working relationships with other relevant forensic science institutes or organisations all over the world and to expand its Membership throughout Europe while maintaining the development and credibility of ENFSI.[10] ENFSI also holds the patronage over the EAFS Conference that is organised triennially by an ENFSI member institute.

ENFSI structure and Membership

ENFSI is governed by a five-member Board, elected by the ENFSI Membership from the directors of its member institutes,[11] and accountable to the ENFSI Membership. At the time of writing ENFSI had three Standing

[5]For more information, see http://www.forensicinstitute.nl/about_nfi/news/conferences_and_symposia/first-european-meeting-on-forensic-archaeology.aspx (last accessed 20 December 2013).

[6]For more information, see http://www.e-a-a.org/ (last accessed 20 December 2013).

[7]For more information, see http://www.forensicinstitute.nl/about_nfi/news/conferences_and_symposia/second-european-meeting-on-forensic-archaeology.aspx (last accessed 28 December 2013).

[8]This laboratory merged with the Dutch Laboratory for Forensic Pathology (*Laboratorium voor Gerechtelijke Pathologie*) to form the NFI in 1999.

[9]Source: http://www.enfsi.eu/about-enfsi/history (last accessed 28 December 2013).

[10]Source: http://www.enfsi.eu/about-enfsi (last accessed 28 December 2013).

[11]The Board members are elected by the ENFSI Membership at the Annual Meetings for a 3-year term, except the Chair and the Chair-designate who are elected for a 4- year term.

Committees, 17 EWGs and several PGs.[12] The three Standing Committees cover QCC, Education and Training (E&T) and Research and Development (R&D). The 17 EWGs are the scientific backbone of ENFSI, covering a broad range of forensic disciplines, and offering a scientific platform to exchange experience and expertise in these disciplines (ENFSI 2012).[13] An ENFSI Secretariat, currently hosted at the Polish Central Forensic Laboratory of the Police (*Centralne Laboratorium Kryminalistyczne Policji* – CFLP) in Warsaw, Poland, supports the ENFSI community in general and the ENFSI Board in particular in its duties. The Secretariat is accountable to and operates under the supervision of the ENFSI Board.[14]

At present, the ENFSI Membership includes 62 governmental and non-governmental forensic laboratories from 35 European countries.[15] ENFSI recognises only an institutional Membership. A forensic laboratory can become an ENFSI Member if it fulfils a number of criteria: it has to be European; it has to cover a broad spectrum of forensic expertise; it has to be ISO/IEC 17025 accredited, or planning to become so in the near future; it has to have a creditable status in its own country; and it has to employ at least 25 forensic experts who are allowed to give expert testimony in court (ENFSI 2010).

ENFSI Forensic Archaeology Project Group

In December 2012 the author sent an application letter to the 17th ENFSI Board with a request to launch a new ENFSI Forensic Archaeology PG, to explore the feasibility of the establishment of an ENFSI Forensic Archaeology EWG in the near future. The primary goal of forensic archaeology was defined in the letter as:

> *a scientific-based reconstruction of the human and natural activities that occurred on and around the crime scene or place incident, especially during the surface recovery of fragmented human remains and related finds and features, the survey for clandestine buried persons or objects, the excavation of clandestine buried persons or objects and related finds and features, the exhumation of persons at regular cemeteries for additional examination and* the dating of (buried) objects of skeletonised human remains (Groen 2012).

The 17th ENFSI Board agreed with the author's proposal during its annual meeting in Berlin, December 2012. This approval was communicated to the entire ENFSI Membership at the ENFSI annual meeting held in Belgrade in May 2013, and, as no objection was raised by the ENFSI Membership, the Forensic Archaeology PG was officially recognised by ENFSI.

Aims and objectives of the Forensic Archaeology PG

The first meeting of the Forensic Archaeology PG took place at the NFI, on 29 August 2013. This meeting was attended by three PG Founding Members and one Associate Founding Member: the Dutch NFI (De Leeuwe and Groen, Chapter 14, this volume), the Crime Scene Unit of the German Federal Criminal Police Office (*Bundeskriminalamt* – BKA; Neumann et al., Chapter 9, this volume), the Forensic Sciences Institute of the French National Gendarmerie (*Institut de Recherche Criminelle de la Gendarmerie Nationale* – IRCGN; Schuliar et al., Chapter 8, this volume) and the Forensic Archaeology British Expert Panel of the IfA (IfA 'Expert Panel'; Janaway, Chapter 24, this volume). It was agreed that the author would act as the Chair of the PG and that forensic archaeology should be defined within the PG as a 'scientific discipline that uses archaeological theory and methodology in a legal context. It combines archaeological, taphonomical and criminalistic knowledge to localise, document and interpret pedological, ecological and osteological finds and patterns at a (possible) place of incident or a crime scene'.

The key aims of the Forensic Archaeology PG are to raise awareness of forensic archaeological possibilities at places of incident or scenes of crime within the ENFSI Membership and to explore the achievability of the establishment of Forensic Archaeology EWG within the ENFSI network. At the time of writing there are only a few ENFSI member institutes that have incorporated forensic archaeological support in their casework, or that cooperate with forensic archaeologists in their countries. The decision to establish – or not – the Forensic Archaeology EWG will not be taken by the ENFSI Board before May 2015. This decision will depend on the extent of support within the ENFSI Membership for this potential EWG and on the delivery of a Forensic Archaeology Best Practice Manual and Proficiency Tests that can be carried out among European forensic archaeologists, or, at least, concrete assumptions for the designing of such tests. If formed, the key aims of the Forensic Archaeology EWG would be to promote cooperation between the ENFSI Membership and other European (non-)governmental

[12]Source: http://www.enfsi.eu/about-enfsi/structure (last accessed 28 December 2013).

[13]At the time of writing these disciplines are Animal, Plant and Soil Traces, Digital Imaging, DNA, Documents, Drugs, Explosives, Fingerprints, Firearms and Gunshot Residue, Fire and Explosion Investigation, Forensic Information Technology, Forensic Speech and Audio Analysis, Handwriting, Marks, Paint and Glass, Road Accident Analysis, Scene of Crime and Textile and Hair. For more information, see http://www.enfsi.eu/about-enfsi/structure/working-groups (last accessed 28 December 2013).

[14]Source: http://www.enfsi.eu/about-enfsi/structure/secretariat (last accessed 28 December 2013).

[15]Source: http://www.enfsi.eu/about-enfsi/members (last accessed 26 November 2014).

organisations or institutes (e.g. the National Archaeological Societies and Academia) and to increase the use and effectiveness of forensic archaeology during the investigation of the place of incident or scene of crime and/or the administration of justice.

The secondary aims and objectives of the PG (and the potential EWG) are:

- promoting the use of forensic archaeology in medico-legal and humanitarian investigations,
- continuing the annual EMFA meetings,
- exchanging case information, knowledge, expertise and working experience through a web-based forum,
- establishing and maintaining contacts between ENFSI member institutes and the national operating archaeological organisations,
- establishing and maintaining contacts between the PG/EWG and other European or non-European forensic archaeological organisations or institutes,
- combining forensic archaeological and taphonomic research activities,
- providing E&T in (forensic) archaeological theory and methodology,
- harmonising forensic archaeological principles and methods,
- promoting quality assurance in forensic archaeology,
- developing (new) professional standards in the field of forensic archaeology,
- producing a best practice manual on forensic archaeology and
- considering collaborative forensic archaeological exercises.

To summarise, the PG (and the potential EWG) aims to become a Centre of Excellence for forensic archaeology in Europe. It aims to be a platform for the development of forensic archaeological awareness and for sharing knowledge and experience of forensic archaeology. It plans to do this, among other things, by creating links between the (non-)governmental ENFSI member institutes, the local police forces and the national archaeological organisations and academia.

Structure of the Forensic Archaeology PG

Although the consensus in the Forensic Archaeology PG is that forensic archaeological casework should, in an ideal situation, be practised by qualified forensic archaeologists, the Membership of the PG (and the potential EWG) is not limited to (forensic) archaeologists only, but is open to all professional forensic scientists who apply forensic archaeological theories, methods and principles during their casework and who represent a European forensic laboratory, a (non-)governmental organisation or a university. The PG therefore contains, besides forensic archaeologists, also forensic anthropologists, forensic pathologists and police officers who regularly use archaeological theories, methods and principles in their casework. The PG believes that such a mix of professionals is necessary to succeed in introducing and maintaining forensic archaeological theories, methods and principles at places of incident and scenes of crime across Europe.

The Membership of the Forensic Archaeology PG (and the potential EWG) reflects the ENFSI Membership structure, consisting of Members, Associate Members and Guests. The Members are representatives of the ENFSI member institutes and function as representatives between the PG and these institutes. The Associate Members are representatives from other (non-ENFSI) organisations or institutes that are involved in forensic archaeological casework[16] within the context of medico-legal, humanitarian or civil law context in Europe, for example, police forces, (non-)governmental organisations and universities. Guests are representatives from non-European institutes, (non-)governmental organisations or universities that are involved in forensic archaeological casework instructed by prosecution and/or law enforcement, or representatives from a European non-ENFSI Member or Associate Member Institute that are involved in forensic archaeological casework instructed by prosecution and/or law enforcement. Guests are only admitted to the PG (and the potential EWG) meetings at the discretion of the Chair and Steering Committee of the PG.

The Steering Committee, elected from the PG Membership, is responsible for the strategic planning, monitoring of the PG's progress and the exploring of the feasibility of launching the Forensic Archaeology EWG in 2015. All Members and Associate Members are eligible for the Steering Committee and have voting rights. Guests are not able to be elected to the Steering Committee and have no voting rights.

[16]Forensic archaeological casework, as defined by the PG Steering Committee, includes (i) support in domestic police service cases (CSI), (ii) support in mass fatality events recovery work, (iii) support in medico-legal investigation related to human rights violations, (iv) support in humanitarian investigation related to human rights violations, (v) support in humanitarian investigation related to the recovery of missing military service personnel for the determination of the legal personal identity, (vi) support in civil law investigations, (vii) controlled exhumations of conventional burials at cemeteries for DNA sampling purposes outside the criminal, medico-legal or humanitarian setting and (viii) support in on-site police investigation related to the destruction of archaeological sites, monuments and artefact looting (e.g. Introduction, this volume).

Conclusion

This chapter has focused on the founding history of the annual EMFA and the wish to set up a European platform for forensic archaeology. It is the author's opinion that the ENFSI would be the best institute to provide such a platform. Therefore, a request has been sent to the ENFSI Board and Membership to form a Forensic Archaeology PG, this to examine the feasibility of setting up an official Forensic Archaeology EWG within the ENFSI community. This request has been granted and the Forensic Archaeology PG was officially launched in May 2013. Although the decision to launch the Forensic Archaeology EWG (or not to do so) is unknown at the time of writing, the future of forensic archaeology in Europe seems bright. The EMFA meetings, the establishment of the Forensic Archaeology PG and the contacts acquired during the editing of the current forensic archaeological volume have already established sufficient support for European forensic archaeological cooperation, independently of the outcome of the ENFSI mission. Nevertheless, it is self-evident that the launch of the Forensic Archaeology EWG would greatly benefit European cooperation.

References

ENFSI. 2010. *Brochure 2010*. The Hague, ENFSI Secretariat.

ENFSI. 2012. *Annual Report 2012*. Warsaw, ENFSI Secretariat.

Groen, W. J. 2012. *Letter of application for the establishment of an ENFSI Project Group 'Forensic Archaeology'*. Sent to the 17th ENFSI Board on December 3rd 2012.

Márquez-Grant, N., Litherland, S. and Roberts, J. 2012. European perspectives and the role of the forensic archaeologist in the UK. In D. C. Dirkmaat (ed.), *A Companion to Forensic Anthropology*, 598–625. Chichester, Wiley-Blackwell.

Websites

European Network of Forensic Science Institutes. Available at: http://www.enfsi.eu/. Accessed 15 August 2014.

CHAPTER 26

Forensic archaeology and anthropology in Brazil

Marco Aurelio Guimarães[1], Raffaela Arrabaça Francisco[1], Rafael de Abreu e Souza[2] and Martin Paul Evison[3]

[1] *Department of Pathology and Legal Medicine, Ribeirão Preto Medical School, Centro de Medicina Legal (CEMEL), University of São Paulo, São Paulo, Brazil*

[2] *LAP, Centre of Environmental Studies and Research, University of Campinas, Campinas, Brazil*

[3] *Northumbria University Centre for Forensic Science, Newcastle Upon Tyne, UK*

Introduction

It is usual when reviewing a particular subject in a particular locality to begin with a definition and summary of practice. Consideration of forensic archaeology in Brazil, however, requires some understanding of Brazilian history in relation to this important – but neglected – area of knowledge, and how it is located in the context of contemporary Brazilian society. Importantly, forensic archaeology in Brazil has been closely intertwined with the development of forensic anthropology, although contributions from more traditional archaeological thought and practice have become a more recent feature.

This chapter therefore begins with a brief overview of Brazil's somewhat hectic past and some key developments in legislation that have led to the rather incongruous state of forensic archaeology in a country whose economy is ranked the world's sixth largest and which has been chosen to host major sporting events such as the FIFA World Cup in 2014 and the Olympic Games in 2016. Discussion of the contemporary situation in forensic archaeology in Brazil then follows with reference to illustrative examples.

Brief historical background

The significance of recent history to forensic science and medicine in Brazil has been considered by Guimarães (2003) and Soares and Guimarães (2008). Brazil began as a Portuguese colony in AD 1500. Europeans initially subjugated indigenous peoples and subsequently imported slaves from Africa. Coexistence led to intense admixture between these populations. After independence in 1822, Brazil became an imperial monarchy that had only two emperors – Dom Pedro I and II. In 1888, Brazil was the last country in the world to abolish slavery, and in 1889 it became a republic. In the 20th century, from 1930 to 1945, the country had its first period of dictatorship under the control of Getúlio Vargas. A new wave of migration followed, comprising mainly World War II refugees from Japan, Italy, Germany and Eastern Europe, but with others from the Middle East, leading to a further period of considerable admixture and intermarriage. In 1964, another dictatorship was established. Leftist political parties were banned and civil rights limited. This dictatorship lasted until 1985 – making advanced democracy a recent acquisition for Brazil.

The criminal law is defined robustly in the Brazilian Penal Code (Brasil 1940) and Brazilian Penal Process Code (Brasil 1941), both of which were established during the Vargas dictatorship and which have received only minor modification since. These codes specify that all forensic investigations are the responsibility of the Civil Police (*Polícia Civil*). Although this arrangement is not entirely without merit, the resulting degree of governmental control made investigations vulnerable to political manipulation, both during the Vargas years and again during the military dictatorship of 1964–1985. As a consequence of this legislation, research and teaching in all branches of the forensic sciences were badly affected. Forensic cases were kept away from the universities, which were considered centres of political subversion. Very poor conditions of work in forensic medicine became the rule, as did the lack of up-to-date technology for criminal investigation. In many important respects, human identification was one of the worst-affected areas. Keeping victims unidentified meant that government institutions could avoid being the target of criticism or investigation. Political crimes could be hidden and members of the political opposition – mainly

Forensic Archaeology: A Global Perspective, First Edition. Edited by W.J. Mike Groen, Nicholas Márquez-Grant and Robert C. Janaway.

from left-wing political parties – could be 'disappeared' (Guimarães 2003, 215).

Within the vast 8,515,767 km^2 of the Brazilian interior (IBGE 2010), however, it was not an easy task for the military government to keep all opposition groups under control. Armed resistance spread to the countryside, and both urban and rural guerrilla networks developed. While confrontations resulted in deaths sustained by both sides, it was the military government that was accused of continuous human rights violations – through exile, torture, execution and the 'disappearance' of political prisoners.

Eventually, gradual liberalisation led to the Amnesty Law (Brasil 1979), enabling the exoneration of some Brazilian citizens who had been convicted of political crimes between 1961 and 1979. While the military dictatorship finally ended in 1985 with the indirect election of a civilian president, it was the establishment of the *New Constitution* (Brasil 1988) that was ultimately the most significant step in the process of re-democratisation and restoration of civil and human rights. The Amnesty Law (Brasil 2002) was also amended, enabling exoneration of those convicted of political crimes committed between 1946 and 1988.

Restorative actions on behalf of victims also formed part of the re-democratisation process. The Special Commission for the Political Dead and Disappeared (*Comissão Especial de Mortos e Desaparecidos Políticos* – CEMDP) was the first formal government initiative in the investigation of the political crimes of the dictatorship (Brasil 1995). This was followed by the establishment of the office of the National Secretary for Human Rights (*Secretaria Nacional dos Direitos Humanos* – SNDH) (Brasil 1997) – both within the Ministry of Justice. The SNDH was later elevated to ministry status (Brasil 2003) and the CEMDP was incorporated within its structure (Brasil 2004). In 2010, the SNDH was further elevated to become part of the President's Office and its name amended to the Secretary of Human Rights of the President of the Republic (*Secretaria de Direitos Humanos da Presidência da República* – SDH/PR) (Brasil 2010). The main contemporary national initiatives in the use of forensic archaeology and anthropology in the investigation of alleged human rights violations in Brazil are linked to SDH/PR-CEMDP.

In 2011 the President, Dilma Rousseff, herself a former political prisoner of the military government, signed into law the establishment of the National Commission of Truth (*Commisão Nacional da Verdade*) (Brasil 2011a), mandated to investigate human rights violations occurring between 1946 and 1988. Under the auspices of this Commission, independent investigations are to be undertaken which are intended to bring to light the widest possible range of findings relating to human rights violations in the country. The Commission's work is to be completed by 2014.

Academic, professional and legal aspects

According to Zarankin and Funari (2008, 310), archaeology in the Americas has traditionally focused on the study of prehistoric societies and their lifestyles, dietary habits and economic activities. In the public imagination, however, there is a gap between the exotic and distant past that archaeologists analyse and the present world. Frequently, it was the Indiana Jones representation of the archaeologist that was used to fill this gap.

This situation began to change when, some years ago, archaeologists began to question the nature of the knowledge they produced, and its wider social consequences. Archaeology became a political tool for opening new lines of inquiry regarding marginal groups in history – slaves, women, children, gays, lesbians, workers, aboriginals, prisoners, the elderly and Afro-descendants – whose importance is now more widely accepted. It was believed that this critical discussion of past domination, exploitation and resistance would lead archaeologists to political action in the present. It was thought that the democratic potential of archaeology could be co-opted in order to create alternative histories for invisible, minority and oppressed groups (Zarankin and Funari 2008, 310). In this context, it is not surprising that academic archaeology only began to expand in the last years of the military government, when steps towards democracy had already occurred.

Perhaps the most significant development in academic archaeology in Brazil occurred in 1980 with the creation of the Society for Brazilian Archaeology (*Sociedade de Arqueologia Brasileira* – SAB), which had its first scientific meeting in 1981 at the Estácio de Sá university (*Universidade Estácio de Sá*) in Rio de Janeiro. This university offered a unique undergraduate degree in archaeology at that time – although archaeology courses were sometimes delivered elsewhere from various Departments of Anthropology, Geography and History. Although this particular archaeology degree did not survive past the beginning of the last decade (SAB 2013) there are today 11 undergraduate courses at public institutions in Brazil – the first of which was established in 2004. Six of these are at specialisation level and, additionally, there are 14 master's and 6 PhD programmes (Costa 2013).

Given the historic absence of dedicated undergraduate degree courses in archaeology, many professionals who work in the field have a degree in a related area such as social science, history, geography, biology or geology. The SAB accepts affiliation of members who do not have a degree in archaeology, but in an alternative specialisation, master's or PhD degree and, occasionally, those with formal experience working in the area for at least 5 years. Most work in Brazil, however, is still focused on academic research in prehistoric and historical archaeology, preservation of the national historical and cultural heritage and, recently, in assessments for construction engineering where potential archaeological sites need to be investigated before building work commences.

Forensic archaeology

Although it is clear that archaeological techniques are sometimes essential in criminal investigation, the role of the archaeologist in the forensic arena is still very limited in Brazil. There are two main reasons for this.

The first reason is related to the earlier-mentioned legislation that controls forensic investigation in Brazil. The *Brazilian Penal Code* (Brasil 1940) and the *Brazilian Penal Process Code* (Brasil 1941) – both from the Getúlio Vargas dictatorship – limit forensic investigation of crimes to 'official experts' who are police staff. However, occasionally a non-official expert can be appointed by the police or judicial authorities to participate in a forensic investigation as an ad hoc expert — a geophysicist or some other academically qualified professional, for example. The legislation predates the arrival of professionals with a degree in archaeology, however, and there is no legal requirement for police forces to recruit or appoint archaeologists to apply their skills in criminal cases. Archaeologists can apply along with other graduates to join the police service with the aim of becoming an 'official expert', but even if selected there is no guarantee they will be deployed to work in their specific area of interest. There are, simply, no official posts for archaeologists on police staff to work in forensic archaeology.

The second reason is related to specialisations in qualifications. Among the 11 undergraduate courses in archaeology mentioned earlier, only 2 offer formal content in forensic archaeology. One is compulsory – a 30-h module with the Universidade do Estado do Amazonas. The other is optional – a 60-h module with the Universidade Federal de Sergipe. It is possible that other courses are offered in private institutions, but these do not typically serve potential professionals. There are as yet no standards for the qualification and experience of university teachers in forensic science, curriculum content or the methods of theoretical and practical instruction used.

A final point to be considered is that death certificates relating to violent deaths can only be signed by medical doctors who are also 'official experts' – the equivalent of the forensic pathologist in some jurisdictions, limiting the role of the professional forensic archaeologist and anthropologist in the forensic investigation of human remains.

The overall consequence is that archaeologists are not typically seen as the most suitable professionals to work in forensic cases. This very limiting vision is the result of the late origin and lack of a tradition of archaeology as an academic or professional occupation in the country. Changes in this perception have been marked by the publication of *Arqueologia: Direito e Democracia* (Archaeology: Law and Democracy, Carvalho et al. 2009) and *Memories from Darkness: Archaeology of Repression and Resistance in Latin America* (Funari et al. 2010). Both books highlight the importance of forensic archaeology in the investigation of human rights violations that occurred during the dictatorship years in Brazil and Latin America. These are probably the most relevant texts to the application of archaeology in the interests of the courts in Brazil, a field still considered to be at an 'embryonic stage' by one of the authors.

Technical contributions on bioarchaeology, biological anthropology and forensic anthropology have been produced by the archaeology team from the National School of Public Health of the Oswaldo Cruz Foundation – as described by Mendonça de Souza (2009). Bioarchaeologists have contributed sporadically to forensic science and medicine, having delivered courses to the Police Academy of São Paulo in 2006 (Silva and Oliveira 2009, 171) and participated in the recent foundation of the Brazilian Association of Forensic Anthropology (*Associação Brasileira de Antropologia Forense* – ABRAF) in September 2012 (ABRAF 2012).

Forensic anthropology

Forensic anthropology is a relatively new area of science, having originated during the 20th century (Burns 1999). It applies methods from physical anthropology and archaeology in the collection and analysis of evidence related to apparent crimes, with the aim of establishing the identity of the victim and the circumstances relating to the individual's death (Soares and Guimarães 2008, 7; Francisco et al. 2011, 231).

Despite – or, perhaps, because of – its relevance to criminal justice, the development of forensic anthropology was also badly affected in the years of dictatorship in Brazil. It was not convenient for government institutions involved in political repression and the violation of human rights – like torture and homicide – to have a well-established infrastructure for forensic anthropology, which could make such abuses public knowledge. During the military dictatorship, the bodies of political prisoners who died in the large urban centres were autopsied, as required by law, but the death certificate was liable to be modified to disguise the real cause of death. This practice was sometimes condoned or supported by the official medical expert, some of whom supported the dictatorship. If not, the medical examiners concerned could find themselves harassed into changing the final diagnosis, or substituted by other experts willing to cooperate with the deception. Probably the most widely known case of this type concerned the journalist Mr Vladimir Herzog, who died after his arrest in 1975. His body was found in a prison cell in a military institution in São Paulo City. The official cause of death was given as 'mechanical asphyxia by hanging'. Suicide was inferred even though signs of torture were evident on his body. It was not until 13 March 2013 when, as a consequence of a judicial application on behalf of the National Commission of Truth and the Herzog family, the cause of death recorded on the death certificate was corrected to include 'lesions and maltreatment' while in the custody of the II Army DOI-CODI (Borges 2013).

Again, it is not surprising that forensic anthropology, like forensic archaeology, could only emerge after the end of the dictatorship in 1985 and the establishment of the New Constitution, when the first groups in Brazil – such as those located in Campinas (São Paulo State) and Brasília (the Brazilian capital) – began to establish expertise. The forensic anthropology group in the Department of Legal Medicine at the University of Campinas (*Universidade de Campinas* – UNICAMP) was founded in 1986, and worked on cases of national importance, such as the identification of the remains of the Nazi doctor Josef Mengele. The Department was dissolved in 1999 for academic reasons mainly related to limited scientific productivity, but specialist expertise is retained by the School of Odontology located at the Piracicaba campus of the university. The second group, linked to the Medico-Legal Institute of the Secretariat of Public Security in Brasilia, is part of the civil police structure. It was established in 1992 on the initiative of three official experts – Drs Malthus Galvão, Eduardo Reis and Aluísio Trindade Filho – who recognised the necessity for expertise the area. It is significant that it was individual, rather than government, initiatives that led to the establishment of this expertise. The group now has six members and deals with routine cases from Brasília and surrounding areas. This group has also worked on cases of national importance, such as the investigation of GOL flight 1907 (CENIPA 2008), and participates in the search for remains of victims of the military dictatorship as part of the Araguaía Working Group (*Grupo de Trabalho Araguaia* – GTA) (see later).

Other groups have since arisen around the country, including – among others – in Salvador (Bahia State), Goiânia (Goiás State), Rio de Janeiro (Rio de Janeiro State), Porto Alegre (Rio Grande do Sul State) and Recife (Pernambuco State). Most of these are linked to police institutions, except for the one in Recife, which offers a postgraduate course (a master's in Forensic Expertise) including a module in forensic anthropology.

In Ribeirão Preto, a city in the interior of the state of São Paulo, a significant change arose in 1996, when post-dictatorial changes in legislation in the state allowed the establishment of partnerships between public institutions. Originally conceived by Dr Carmen Martin, the Medical Medicine Centre (*Centro de Medicina Legal* – CEMEL) was established in the city in 1999 as the result of a partnership between the Ribeirão Preto Medical School (previously known as the Faculty of Medicine of Ribeirão Preto), University of São Paulo (FMRP-USP), and the Medico-Legal Institute, Secretary of Public Security of São Paulo (IML/SSP-SP). CEMEL became the first centre in Brazil to bring officially recognised forensic expertise into the university sector. This partnership offers better facilities and a higher-quality scientific environment for forensic experts, and access to forensic data for teaching and research in the university – something unimaginable during dictatorship years (Guimarães 2003, 215). Expertise was extended to include forensic DNA profiling of skeletal remains via collaboration with the Sheffield Medico-Legal Centre in the United Kingdom. A unique institution in Brazil, CEMEL gained both national and international acknowledgement when its work was the subject of an article by Adam (2003, 13) in the scientific journal *Nature*.

In 2005, a new Laboratory for Forensic Anthropology was established at CEMEL as a result of the UK collaboration and financial support from the UK Foreign and Commonwealth Office Global Opportunities Fund (FCO-GOF). This capacity-building partnership resulted in not only laboratory infrastructure, but also bilateral exchanges and training in forensic autopsy, forensic anthropology, forensic facial reconstruction and forensic DNA profiling. Practical and pragmatic procedures for anthropological analysis of human remains (Soares and Guimarães 2008, 7; Crocco et al. 2008; Guimarães et al. 2009; Francisco et al. 2011, 231) were developed by CEMEL, specifically focused on forensic human identification in the challenging tropical environments of Brazil. These proved useful in local conditions and were adopted by the regional state Medico-Legal Institute (*Instituto Médico-Legal* – IML), leading to a substantial increase in the rate of identification of skeletonised and partially skeletonised human remains (Soares and Guimarães 2008, 7; Francisco et al. 2011, 231). In 2008, the forensic anthropology protocol was enhanced via a partnership with Dr Ricardo Alves da Silva from the Faculty of Odontology of Ribeirão Preto, University of São Paulo (FORP-USP), to permit extended odontological analysis.

In 2010, the Laboratory for Forensic Anthropology was approached by the Federal Police (*Policia Federal*) – a national civilian police agency whose role is equivalent to the US Federal Bureau of Investigation – with a request to provide training in forensic anthropology for its official experts. This resulted in a new partnership offering the prospect of academic qualifications for federal police scientists, and giving the university access to new forensic anthropology cases. The partnership between these institutions was essential in enabling them to participate in the work of the GTA in its search for the remains of victims of the military dictatorship.

Finally, CEMEL has recently been tasked with establishing national reference standards for forensic anthropology (FAPESP 2013), a particularly significant issue given the diverse ancestry and extent of admixture and intermarriage in the Brazilian population. These guidelines, however, address methods for analysis of remains. Standards for recovery of remains are anticipated to be included in a separate protocol.

Examples of forensic archaeology and anthropology in Brazil

Archaeological and forensic investigations of buried human remains typically rely on the application of a near-identical suite of methods. They represent the interface between archaeology and forensic sciences (Santos 2012, 1) and the suite of methods employed and potential for investigative use vary from country to country (Evison 2009). It is difficult to establish the extent of professional practice in forensic archaeology in Brazil. While forensic investigation of clandestine graves is a regular feature in the Brazilian media, these investigations tend to be conducted by police agencies. CEMEL is a notable exception, in that its experts are frequently asked by the police to assist in recovery and analysis of buried remains. Funding for development of the field is limited, with some academic research funding being potentially available as well as central government support for the investigation of recent human rights abuse allegations. It is the latter agenda which presently drives the development of forensic archaeology and anthropology in the country, with historical investigations also being prominent in the popular consciousness. Some examples from Brazil are presented here.

Araguaía Working Group

Location of the remains of political prisoners who disappeared in rural areas represents a particular problem in Brazil. It is widely believed that many were buried clandestinely in mass graves in legal cemeteries and their bodies mingled with those of vagrants, in an attempt to pre-empt future recovery and identification. It is believed that others were buried in clandestine cemeteries or other hidden locations. This practice is described in the book *Brasil: Nunca Mais* [*Brazil: Never More*] (Arns 1996), written following the secret investigation of 707 cases from the archives of the Superior Military Tribunal dating from 1961 to 1979. This book exposes the extent of political repression in Brazil during the dictatorship years.

The Araguaía Working Group (GTA) was established in 2011 with the aim of locating and identifying the remains of the dead from one such rural locality as a consequence of the Araguaia Guerrilla War (1966–1974). This war was the result of an insurrection movement formed by the Communist Party of Brazil (*Partido Comunista do Brasil* – PCdoB) in opposition to the military dictatorship, with the aim of instigating a socialist revolution in Brazil similar to those of Cuba and China. The movement started during the late 1960s and early 1970s in a region of the Araguaía River known as *Bico do Papagaio* (Parrot's Beak), where the Brazilian states of Pará, Tocantins and Maranhão meet. The guerrilla group numbered about 70 members – the exact number is still uncertain – and had the support of part of the local population, which was also involved in the conflict. The guerrillas were gradually eliminated by troops from the military dictatorship between 1972 and 1974. Their remains are anticipated to be spread within an area of about 7000 km^2, but most are probably concentrated between the cities of Xambioá (Tocantins State), São Geraldo do Araguaia and Marabá (Pará State).

The GTA was mandated as the consequence of an agreement between the First Federal Court of Brasília and the Inter-American Court of Human Rights of the Organisation of American States (OAS) and established following the enactment of Inter-Ministry Ordinance no 1 (Brasil 2011b) by signatories from the Ministry of Justice and Ministry of Defence and the National Human Rights Secretary (SDH/PR). The GTA replaced a pre-existing group founded in 2009 (Brasil 2009) and it comprises forensic medical experts, forensic anthropologists, archaeologists, geologists and geophysicists, sociologists, historians, journalists and other university representatives and independent observers (including relatives of the victims), and has the logistical support of the Brazilian Army. Professionals from the humanities and social sciences work on information collection from witnesses who lived – or still live – in the area, as well as from technical reports from previous investigations, and specialised literature from libraries, public institutions and private companies. Their main objective is to locate burials in official or clandestine cemeteries or in open areas like fields and forests (the location is inside the Amazon region). Professionals from geology and geophysics work on surveying areas of interest for possible human remains using Ground Penetrating Radar (GPR). Forensic anthropologists from the Medico-Legal Institutes of Brasília and Goiânia, the Brazilian Federal Police and CEMEL are responsible for the excavation and exhumation of remains using the established techniques of forensic archaeology and anthropology.

In an innovative approach to forensic investigation, the archaeology team led by Drs Valéria Cristina Ferreira e Silva and Rafael de Abreu e Souza has established a systematic survey of surface and subsurface finds as a precursor to excavation at the military bases of Xambioá and Urutu, which were used as prison camps during the guerrilla war. The objective has been to establish the pattern dispersal of artefacts in order to characterise different areas of activity, which can then be used to construct a contra-discursive memory and history of events. This novel perspective is part of a movement intended to enhance understanding of wider contexts of recent internal conflict in Latin America – via an 'Archaeology of Repression'.

The GTA is probably the most substantial public initiative in Brazil undertaking forensic archaeological investigation. There are two archaeologists contributing to the project, whose backgrounds are in historical archaeology – especially that relevant to recent political conflict – and who have some training in forensic procedures. Up to this date, 25 individual human remains have been located and recovered for further investigation – such as textile analysis and DNA profiling – in order to establish whether or not they are victims of the guerrilla war.

Historical investigations

Despite much sociopolitical interest in the forensic archaeological investigation of the crimes of the military dictatorship, the most well-known work among the general public in Brazil probably relates to the investigations of the Luz Monastery and of the first emperors of Brazil.

Funerary archaeology of the Luz Monastery

The excavation of well-preserved human remains from the Luz Monastery in São Paulo City is described by Fuzinato et al. (2009, 17). One of the most interesting finds – and one which caused a national sensation in Brazil – was that of two female bodies discovered buried in an embrace. Difficulties arising from ambiguous legislation that affects forensic archaeological investigation are also described, and the authors recount the list of laws and regulations involving various different institutions that can be encountered. They also emphasise the important contribution forensic pathologists and other forensic experts can make to the preservation of the archaeological heritage.

Studies in forensic archaeology applied to the human remains of the first emperors of Brazil

Deterioration of the funerary monuments of the first Emperor of Brazil, Dom Pedro I (Pedro IV of Portugal), and his two wives, Empress Dona Maria Leopoldina von Habsburg-Lorraine and Empress Dona Amélia de Beauharnais-Leuchtenberg, led to the excavation and analysis of their remains. Although initially intended to establish the state of preservation of the remains, the study revealed details of forensic significance. Dona Maria Leopoldina's bones showed no signs of fractures, contrary to a popular belief that she may have died as a consequence of falling from the stairs of the palace during an argument with her husband, the Emperor. The skeleton of the Emperor, however, presented with two fractured ribs compatible with a riding accident, which may have resulted in a pneumothorax (Ambiel 2013).

This forensic archaeological and anthropological study was probably the first to receive considerable attention not only from the academic world, but also from the general public, leading to wider popular interest in the field. Contributions of forensic archaeology and anthropology to prehistoric and historical studies can be found in Lessa (2004, 279), Silva (2005, 2008), Fuzinato et al. (2009, 17), Bendazzoli et al. (2009, 381), Palinkas et al. (2010, 75), Bastos et al. (2010, 68), Fischer (2012) and Mendonça de Souza (2013, 127). While other examples may exist, they are not readily revealed in searches of national databases.

Other studies

While the work of the GTA offers an outstanding example of the contribution of forensic archaeology and anthropology to criminal justice and the safeguarding of human rights, its wider role in public health and safety is frequently forgotten. Preliminary models for the study of utility and efficacy in forensic anthropology and archaeology have been offered by Evison et al. (2012a,b), which compared patterns of practice in Brazil in relation to other international centres. These studies suggest effectiveness can be significantly enhanced via improvements in feedback from investigative agencies, and better communication and integration in the investigative and prosecutorial use of forensic archaeology and anthropology. The authors suggest that changes in the law in Brazil may assist in the investigation and prosecution of homicides relating to organised crime and 'extra-judicial executions'. The authors also note, for example, the hugely disproportionate number of male fatalities encountered in forensic anthropology casework, whether due to homicide, suicide or natural causes – raising the question of whether gender discrimination is resulting in the neglect of the human rights of men and boys in many countries.

Conclusions

Practice in Brazil conforms to broad definitions, including both 'the application of archaeological theory and methodology for the search and excavation of remains in a crime scene' (Hunter and Cox 2005; Santos 2012, 1) and 'the use of archaeological practices to search, identify and analyse human remains from crimes as well as to recover evidences of how, when and who promoted that fact' (Santos 2012, 1). The close interface between forensic archaeology and anthropology in Brazil makes both areas almost indistinguishable. Practitioners can come from either subdiscipline or may originate from specialisations such as history, anthropology, sociology, biology, biomedicine, odontology or medicine. The few training opportunities available are spread around the country, and there are no national standards or system of accreditation. It is necessary to keep in mind that while forensic archaeology and anthropology expanded in other countries – like the United States and the United Kingdom – from the early 1970s (Santos 2012, 1), Brazil was under a military dictatorship. The development of scientific tools and techniques useful to solving crimes that could include those of the government was undesirable. It was not until the sociopolitical environment became favourable to the development of sciences formerly threatening to the dictatorship status quo that progress could begin.

Contemporary practice does recognise, however, that forensic archaeology and anthropology represent more than excavation and osteology. Forensic facial reconstruction from the skull, forensic facial comparison and low-template DNA analysis of skeletal remains are also undertaken in Brazil, and practitioners conduct relevant research in these areas, reflecting the cross-disciplinary nature of the field (Evison et al. 2012a, 85). Furthermore, there is considerable opportunity to develop dialogue between more traditional archaeologists and forensic practitioners, who have legal authorisation to deal with crime scenes but not necessarily with archaeological sites – and vice versa – with the aim of defining common objectives, responsibilities and proposals for changes in legislation that will lead to their formal acceptance.

The wider significance of forensic archaeology and anthropology to the rule of law and the safeguarding of human rights is of contemporary as well as historical importance, in Brazil as it is elsewhere. There is now no excuse for forensic archaeology and anthropology to remain forgotten sciences, as there was during the time of political repression.

References

ABRAF. 2012. *Associação Brasileira de Antropologia Forense [Brasilian Association of Forensic Anthropology]*. Available at: http://antropologiaforense.com.br/index.asp (last accessed 7 February 2013).

Adam, D. 2003. Back from the dead. *Nature* 423, 13–14.

Ambiel, V. C. 2013. Estudos de Arqueologia Forense Aplicados aos Remanescentes Humanos dos Primeiros Imperadores do Brasil Depositados no Monumento à Independência. MSc thesis, University of São Paulo. Available at: http://www.teses.usp.br/teses/disponiveis/71/71131/tde-27032013-173516/pt-bra (last accessed 2 February 2013).

Arns, P. E. 1996. *Brasil: Nunca Mais – Um Relato Para a História*. 3rd edition. Petrópolis (RJ), Vozes.

Bastos, M. Q. R., Mendonça de Souza, S. M. F., Santos, R. V., Cook, D. C., Rodrigues-Carvalho, C. and Santos, R. V. 2010. Da África ao Cemitério dos Pretos Novos, Rio de Janeiro: um estudo sobre as origens dos escravos a partir de análise de isótopos de estrôncio no esmalte dentário. *Revista de Arqueologia* 24(1), 68–97.

Bendazzoli, C., Francisco, R. A. and Guimarães, M. A. 2009. Arqueologia de um sambaqui em abrigo, Ilhabela-SP. *Revista do Museu de Arqueologia e Etnologia São Paulo* 19, 381–391.

Borges, B. 2013. Família de Herzog recebe novo atestado de óbito; veja certidão. *Jornal Folha de São Paulo online edition*, 15 March 2013. Available at: http://www1.folha.uol.com.br/poder/1246463-familia-recebe-novo-atestado-de-obito-de-herzog.shtml (last accessed 17 April 2013).

Brasil. 1940. *Decreto-Lei no 2.848, de 7 de Dezembro de 1940 – Código Penal*. Brasil, República Federativa do. Available at: http://www.planalto.gov.br/ccivil_03/decreto-lei/del2848compilado.htm (last accessed 10 April 2013).

Brasil. 1941. *Decreto-Lei no 3.689, de 3 de Outubro de 1941 – Código de Processo Penal*. Brasil, República Federativa do. Available at: http://www.planalto.gov.br/ccivil_03/decreto-lei/del3689.htm (last accessed 10 April 2013).

Brasil. 1979. *Lei no 6.683, de 28 de Agosto de 1979 – Anistia*. Brasil, República Federativa do. Available at: http://www.planalto.gov.br/ccivil_03/leis/L6683.htm (last accessed 10 April 2013).

Brasil. 1988. *Constituição da República Federativa do Brasil de 1988*. Brasil, República Federativa do. Available at: http://www.planalto.gov.br/ccivil_03/constituicao/constituicao.htm (last accessed 10 April 2013).

Brasil. 1995. *Lei no 9.140, de 04 de Dezembro de 1995 – Reconhece Como Mortas Pessoas Desaparecidas em Razão de Participação, ou Acusação de Participação, em Atividades Políticas, no Período de 2 de Setembro de 1961 a 15 de Agosto de 1979*. Available at: http://www.planalto.gov.br/ccivil_03/leis/L9140.htm (last accessed 7 April 2013).

Brasil. 1997. *Decreto no 2.193, de 7 de abril de 1997 – Aprova a Estrutura Regimental do Ministério da Justiça*. Available at: http://www.planalto.gov.br/ccivil_03/decreto/D2193.htm (last accessed 7 April 2013).

Brasil. 2002. *Lei no 10.559, de 13 de Novembro de 2002. Regulamenta o art. 8o do Ato das Disposições Constitucionais Transitórias e dá Outras Providências*. Brasil, República Federativa do. Available at: http://www.planalto.gov.br/ccivil_03/leis/2002/L10559.htm#art22 (last accessed 10 April 2013).

Brasil. 2003. *Lei no 10.683, de 28 de maio de 2003. Dispõe Sobre a Organização da Presidência da República e dos Ministérios, e dá Outras Providências*. Available at: http://www.planalto.gov.br/ccivil_03/leis/2003/l10.683.htm (last accessed 7 April 2013).

Brasil. 2004. *Lei no 10.875, de 1° de junho de 2004. Reconhece Como Mortas Pessoas Desaparecidas em Razão de Participação, ou Acusação de Participação, em Atividades Políticas*. Available at: http://www.planalto.gov.br/ccivil_03/_ato2004-2006/2004/lei/l10.875.htm (last accessed 7 April 2013).

Brasil. 2009. *Portaria No 567/MD, de 29 de Abril de 2009. Criação do Grupo de Trabalho Para localização, Recolhimento e Identificação de Mortos da Guerrilha do Araguaia*. Brasil, República Federativa do Brasil. Available at: http://pfdc.pgr.mpf.mp.br/atuacao-e-conteudos-de-apoio/legislacao/direito-a-memoria-e-a-verdade/portarias/portaria%20567.pdf (last accessed 10 December 2014).

Brasil. 2010. *Lei no 12.314, de 19 de Agosto de 2010. Dispõe Sobre a Organização da Presidência da República e dos Ministérios*. Available at: http://www.planalto.gov.br/ccivil_03/_ato2007-2010/2010/lei/l12314.htm (last accessed 7 April 2013).

Brasil. 2011a. *Lei no 12.528, de 18 de Novembro de 2011. Cria a Comissão Nacional da Verdade*. Brasil, República Federativa do. Available at: http://www.planalto.gov.br/ccivil_03/_Ato2011-2014/2011/Lei/L12528.htm (last accessed 10 April 2013).

Brasil. 2011b. *Portaria Interministerial no 1. Reformula o Grupo de Trabalho Criado pela Portaria no 567-MD, de 29 de Abril de 2009*. Brasil, República Federativa do. Available at: http://www.agu.gov.br/sistemas/site/PaginasInternas/NormasInternas/AtoDetalhado.aspx?idAto=267180&ID_SITE (last accessed 25 April 2013).

Burns, K. R. 1999. *Forensic Anthropology Training Manual*. Upper Saddle River, Prentice Hall.

Carvalho, A. V., Soares, I. V. P. and Silva, S. F. S. M. (eds.) 2009. *Arqueologia, Direito e Democracia*. Erechim, Habilis.

CENIPA. 2008. *Final Report A-00X/CENIPA/2008*. Available at: http://www.skybrary.aero/bookshelf/books/546.pdf (last accessed 7 March 2013).

Costa, D. M. 2013. *Arqueologia Digital – Cursos e Instituições de Arqueologia*. Available at: http://arqueologiadigital.com/page/cursos-e-instituicoes-de (last accessed 15 April 2013).

Crocco, L. G., Brondi, G. O., Soares, A. T. C., Felipe, J. C., Evison, M. P. and Guimarães, M. A. 2008. LAF 1.0: implantação de um sistema imformatizado para laboratórios de antropologia forense. *Medicina (Ribeirão Preto)* 41, 17–23.

Evison, M. P. 2009. Forensic anthropology and human identification. In J. Fraser and R. Williams (eds.), *Handbook of Forensic Science*, 84–112. London, Willan.

Evison, M. P., Francisco, R. A. and Guimarães, M. A. 2012a. Approaching utility in forensic anthropology. *Forensic Science Policy and Management: An International Journal* 3, 85–104.

Evison, M. P., Francisco, R. A. and Guimarães, M. A. 2012b. Utility in forensic anthropology: findings contributing to case conversion. *Forensic Science Policy and Management: An International Journal* 3, 113–125.

FAPESP. 2013. *Agência de Notícias da Fundação de Amparo à Pesquisa do Estado de São Paulo. Antropólogo Forense Busca Parâmetros Nacionais para Análise de Ossadas*. Agência FAPESP. Available at: http://agencia.fapesp.br/17328 (last accessed 7 March 2013).

Fischer, P. F. 2012. Os Moleques do Morro e os Moleques da Praia: Estresse e Mortalidade em um Sambaqui Fluvial (Moraes, vale do Ribeira de Iguape, SP) e em um Sambaqui Litorâneo (Piaçaguera, Baixada Santista, SP). MSc thesis, University of São Paulo. Available at: http://www.teses.usp.br/teses/disponiveis/71/71131/tde-28082012-143626/pt-br (last accessed 15 April 2013).

Francisco, R. A., Velloso A. P. S., Silveira, T. C. P., Secchieri, J. M. and Guimarães, M. A. 2011. Forensic anthropology at Medico Legal Centre of the Faculty of Medicine of Ribeirão Preto/USP – comparative study of cases from 1999 to 2009. *Medicina (Ribeirão Preto)* 44(3), 231–238.

Funari, P., Zarankin, A. and Salerno, M. 2010. *Memories from Darkness: Archaeology of Repression and Resistance in Latin America*. New York, Springer.

Fuzinato, D. V., Fontes, L. R. and Silva, S. F. M. 2009. O papel do médico legista e de outros profissionais forenses para a preservação do patrimônio arqueológico brasileiro. *Saúde, Ética and Justiça* 14(1), 17–25.

Guimarães, M. A. 2003. The challenge of identifying deceased individuals in Brazil: from dictatorship to DNA analysis. *Science and Justice* 43(4), 215–217.

Guimarães, M. A., Soares-Vieir, J. A., Alves Da Silva, R. H. and Evison, M. P. 2009. A standard procedure for accommodating forensic anthropological and genetic analysis of decomposing human remains from tropical climates. *Forensic Science International: Genetics* 2, 165–166.

Hunter, J. and Cox, M. 2005. *Forensic Archaeology: Advances in Theory and Practice*. London, Rutledge.

IBGE. 2010. *Instituto Brasileiro de Geografia e Estatística. Área Territorial Brasileira*. Available at: http://www.ibge.gov.br/home/geociencias/cartografia/default_territ_area.shtm (last accessed 15 April 2013).

Lessa, A. 2004. Arqueologia da agressividade humana: a violência sob uma perspectiva paleoepidemiológica. *História, Ciências, Saúde – Manguinhos* 11(2), 279–296.

Mendonça de Souza, S. 2009. Bioarqueologia e antropologia forense. *Anais I Encontro de Arqueologia de Mato Grosso do Sul*, 89–113. Campo Grande, Museu de Arqueologia da UFMS.

Mendonça de Souza, S. 2013. Escavar e interpretar lugares de deposição de mortos. In M. Gaspar and S. Mendonça de Souza (eds.), *Abordagens Estratégicas em Sambaquis*, 127–254. Erechim, Habilis.

Palinkas, M., Semprini, M., Francisco, R. A., Simões, C. B., Guimarães, M. A. and Silva, R. H. A. 2010. Análise morfológica de remanescentes dentais de uma ossada humana encontrados em sambaqui no arquipélago de Ilhabela, litoral norte do Estado de São Paulo, Brasil. *Saúde, Ética and Justiça* 15(2), 75–79.

SAB. 2013. *Sociedade de Arqueologia Brasileira* (*Brazilian Archaeology Society*). Available at: http://www.sabnet.com.br/conteudo/view?ID_CONTEUDO=604 (last accessed 15 April 2013).

Santos, A. B. 2012. Estudos arqueológicos a serviço de contextos criminais: arqueologia forense. *Revista de Criminologia e Ciências Penitenciárias* 2(2), 1–13.

Silva, A. L. 2008. Osteoartrose Temporomandibular em Crânios de Brasileiros e Portugueses de Coleções Históricas. PhD thesis, Escola Nacional de Saúde Pública – Fundação Oswaldo Cruz, ENSP/FIOCRUZ.

Silva, S. F. S. M. 2005. Arqueologia das Práticas Mortuárias em Sítios Pré-Históricos do Litoral do Estado de São Paulo. PhD thesis, University of São Paulo. Available at: http://www.teses.usp.br/teses/disponiveis/71/71131/tde-11072007-151325/pt-br (last accessed 15 April 2013).

Silva, S. F. S. M. and Oliveira, M. A. S. 2009. Arqueologia em meio forense: estudos sobre o estado da arte da disciplina e sua implantação no Brasil. In A. V. Carvalho, I. V. P. Soares, P. P. A. Funari and S. F. S. M. Silva (eds.), *Arqueologia, Direito e Democracia*, 171–203. Erechim, Habilis.

Soares, A. T. C. and Guimarães, M. A. 2008. Two years of forensic anthropology at the Medico Legal Centre (CEMEL) of the Faculty of Medicine of Ribeirão Preto-USP. *Medicina (Ribeirão Preto)* 41(1), 7–11.

Zarankin, A. and Funari, P. P. A. 2008. Eternal sunshine of the spotless mind: archaeology and construction of memory of military repression in South America (1960–1980). *Archaeologies: Journal of the World Archaeological Congress* 4(2), 310–327.

PART 2
The Americas

CHAPTER 27

Canadian forensic archaeology: a Mari Usque ad Mare, ad hoc

Derek Congram

Trudeau Centre for Peace, Conflict and Justice, Munk School of Global Affairs, Trinity College Site, University of Toronto, Toronto, Ontario, Canada

Introduction

This chapter draws upon publications, personal experience and a survey of others who have conducted forensic archaeological/anthropological fieldwork in Canada. This work typically involves the search for and recovery of human remains and associated objects and the contextual interpretation of their relative positions and condition. I will use the term forensic archaeology/forensic archaeologist throughout the text to refer to forensic search and recovery scene work. However, forensic archaeology as a distinct discipline and practice is not well established in Canada; many view it as a part of forensic anthropology and, in general, forensic archaeological work is performed by those who consider themselves to be biological anthropologists or biological anthropologists as well as archaeologists.

Canada's vastness, provincial administration of death investigation and lack of professional standardisation in the subject area mean that what is said here will inevitably be a generalisation and ultimately fail to capture all experience. Nevertheless, the relatively small number of cases that require archaeological expertise and the excellent response rate to the survey suggest that one can know with reasonable certainty how forensic archaeology is perceived and practised in Canada.

Skinner and Bowie provide a thorough discussion of forensic anthropology in Canada, in which they consider archaeology as a part of forensic anthropology (Blau and Ubelaker 2009), and readers are directed to their chapter as a complement to this one. Here, I will take a narrower view by focusing on those activities that could be considered to be the sole responsibility of the forensic archaeologist in Canada.

Medico-legal framework

Canada is an expansive, sparsely populated and relatively peaceful place of about 35 million people. The murder rate is low (1.6 per 100,000 people in 2010, which is one-third of the rate in the United States, UNODC 2011). Although a large majority of the population clings to the southern border, a relatively short drive due north will usually get you to a large, remote lake and/or wooded area. It is not surprising, then, that a large number of human remains recovered in the course of medico-legal investigation are simply scattered across the surface (and are often scavenged by animals), rather than buried in clandestine graves as appears to be the primary focus of forensic archaeologists in more densely populated countries (e.g. the United Kingdom; Hunter and Cropper, Chapter 23, this volume, and the Netherlands; de Leeuwe and Groen, Chapter 14, this volume). Of course, we cannot know with certainty that there are not many clandestine graves because, as the adage goes, absence of evidence is not necessarily evidence of absence (Morse et al. 1976). Indeed, the disturbingly large number of missing First Nations (Native American) women from northern British Columbia along the so-called *Highway of Tears* (CBC 2009; Wilson 2004) and, first officially recognised in 2002, missing sex trade workers and drug users from the Vancouver area that were the centre of the William Pickton serial murder trial suggest that there may remain many undiscovered burials of murder victims (Skelton 2010).

Death investigation in Canada is a provincial or territorial responsibility and its administration shows the dual influence of British and American systems. Of the 10 provinces and 3 territories, Alberta, Manitoba, Nova Scotia and Newfound and Labrador use a medical examiner system. All other provinces have a coroner system. In Ontario, coroners are medical doctors (as are medical examiners). There is not enough work to sustain full-time forensic archaeological expertise except, perhaps, in and around Canada's largest city of Toronto (the fourth largest city in North America). An average of only 15% of deaths in the country are investigated by a coroner or medical examiner (Statistics Canada 2012), and only a very small proportion of these would ever benefit from archaeological expertise. In Ontario,

Forensic Archaeology: A Global Perspective, First Edition. Edited by W.J. Mike Groen, Nicholas Márquez-Grant and Robert C. Janaway.

Canada's most populous province, only 1.1% of deaths investigated are homicides and of these, almost 50% occur in residences (Statistics Canada 2012, 26, 27).

Founding fathers

Although there were early applications of what could be deemed 'archaeological' techniques in crime scene examination in Canada (e.g. Skinner and Bowie 2009, 89), Jim Anderson at the University of Toronto laid the foundation for forensic archaeological work, despite not having practised it himself. Anderson taught anatomy and biological anthropology but also conducted extensive bioarchaeological work. Evidence of his contribution to both biological anthropology and archaeology is his publication: *The Human Skeleton: A manual for Archaeologists* (1962). In the late 1960s and early 1970s, Anderson supervised the first PhDs in biological anthropology in Canada (Meiklejohn 2012) and his combination of knowledge and experience helped produce cross-trained biological anthropologists/archaeologists that would later serve as consultants for medico-legal purposes (e.g. Jerry Melbye, Mike Pietresewsky, Michael Spence, Jerome Cybulski).

By virtue of geography, politics and history, Canada is heavily influenced by its southern neighbour. In the United States, the first publications on forensic archaeology were Morse et al. (1976) and (1983). Reflective of the times, whereby biological (forensic) anthropologists generally received cases in their labs, which had been collected by local law enforcement agents or death investigators, the 1976 article suggests that simply training police in archaeological techniques – rather than employing a trained, experienced archaeologist – may be sufficient for medico-legal investigation.

In Canada, Mark Skinner and Richard Lazenby published: *Found! Human Remains: A Field Manual for the Recovery of the Recent Human Skeleton* (1984). Three years later, spurred by the discovery in Argentina of mass graves of victims of systematic political killings, Skinner (1987) published a prescient and oft-cited article titled *Planning the archaeological recovery from recent mass graves.* This article followed the initial work by the Argentine Forensic Anthropology Team (EAAF; Fondebrider and Scheinsohn, Chapter 43, this volume), but preceded by almost a decade the massive effort by the United Nations to excavate primary and secondary mass graves in the former Yugoslavia (on which members of EAAF, Skinner and two generations [teachers and students] of other Canadians worked for over a decade). Based on his experience in the former Yugoslavia, Afghanistan and East Timor, Skinner continued to publish on forensic grave excavations, emphasising the critical role of archaeology with a focus on making contextual observations – mainly associations and provenance – as an essential part of certain medico-legal investigations involving human remains (Blau and Skinner 2005; Skinner and Jessee 2005; Skinner 2007; Skinner and Sterenberg 2005; Skinner et al. 2002, 2003). Skinner's earlier publications seemed to echo that of Morse et al. in the United States, stating that those using archaeological techniques need not be archaeologists (e.g. Skinner 1987, 272). Later, however, he would advocate a specialised role and standards for the archaeologist in directing mass grave excavations (e.g. Skinner et al. 2003).

Another key figure in the development of forensic archaeology in Canada is Jerry Melbye. Both Skinner and Melbye were biological anthropologists but they had education, training and experience in archaeology and were active advocates of its use for forensic work. Unlike Skinner, however, Melbye made his mission to preach to the 'home crowd'. Melbye began working with the Chief Coroner in Ontario in 1990, and he helped developed the forensic science programme at the University of Toronto at Mississauga, which continues today with a specialisation in anthropology (Katzmarzyk 2001). Melbye has several publications that advocate archaeological recovery of remains in a medico-legal setting (e.g. Melbye and Jimenez 1993, 1997; Melbye et al. 1999). Importantly, he has also given dozens of talks to coroner services and at professional meetings in Canada and the United States. That both Skinner and Melbye became Diplomates of the American Board of Forensic Anthropology – the highest level of professional achievement in the field – reinforced their expertise and authority. This along with their advocacy of forensic archaeology worked to ensure that archaeological practice was integrated with forensic anthropological work within their spheres of influence in Canada and abroad.

Important cases and precedents

Stratton and Beattie (1999) discuss the archaeological approach used to recover the remains of 10 people who died during a 1986 train collision, which caused a very destructive chemical fire. Having occurred before the regular use of DNA analysis for identification purposes, the recorded provenance of cremated remains became a critical element in reconstructing events and identifying some of the victims (Mayne Correia and Beattie 2002; Stratton and Beattie 1999). The use of archaeological techniques in Alberta could have served as a model for a recent investigation of a similar train derailment and devastating oil-fuelled fire in Lac Mégantic, Québec, which resulted in almost 50 deaths. Unfortunately, this seems not to have been the case, highlighting the regional administration and poor national coordination of these types of efforts, despite the terrible implications for successful identification of victims.

Melbye and Jimenez (1997) discuss a case where anthropologists were asked to return to a body disposal site years after the coroner and police had examined and removed remains from it. At the behest of the police, subsequent investigation using archaeological techniques recovered further human remains and material evidence that resulted, finally, in a determination of cause and manner (homicide) of death.

Around the same time that Melbye was demonstrating the utility of archaeology at crime scenes, a group of officers from the York Regional Police, part of the Forensic Identification Unit, was organised and trained to conduct search and recovery using archaeological techniques. This team continues to exist but is the only one of its kind in Canada (Olsen, personal communication, 2013).

In 2002, with the discovery of material evidence from a missing woman at a pig farm in British Columbia, a massive investigation was staged that would uncover evidence of serial killings by Robert Pickton. Although an incredible amount of soil was excavated during the investigation, and many students of archaeology and anthropology were employed throughout the fieldwork that was directed by two accomplished forensic anthropologists, it is unclear how 'archaeological' were the techniques employed. A publication ban was instituted throughout the investigation and subsequent trial and to date no detailed account of the procedures used has been published. As such, it is difficult to assess the contribution of the case to the development of forensic archaeology in Canada, but the scale and involvement of a relatively large number of professional and developing anthropologists make it an important precedent of sorts.

A final mention should be made of the innovative work of Margaret Kalacska at McGill University in Montréal who, with Lynne Bell and others, has undertaken research on burial prospection using multispectral analysis (Kalacska and Bell 2006; Kalacska et al. 2009). It remains to be seen if this line of inquiry will prove its worth but forensic archaeological research in Canada is virtually nil and this work warrants recognition.

In 1999, Michael Spence, an anthropologist and archaeologist at the University of Western Ontario, reflecting on a forensic case involving the recovery of a young girl's remains said:

> it is important to have both archaeological and physical anthropological expertise represented in the field and as early as possible in the course of the investigation... These skills may be embodied in one individual; many forensic anthropologists are basically physical anthropologists who have accumulated a good deal of archaeological field experience in the course of their research on prehistoric or early historic societies (Spence 1999, 180).

Despite such calls as well as great and early efforts by Skinner and Melbye, the use of archaeology and archaeologists for medico-legal investigation has not been formally and routinely accepted. In 2006 I met a Canadian pathologist from one of Canada's largest cities and she asked me why one might need an archaeologist to assist with a medico-legal investigation. This pathologist had been working with a very well-known forensic anthropologist, but failed to appreciate how archaeological techniques and knowledge were useful (presumably either because the anthropologist with whom she worked did not use any or, if they had, because the pathologist presumed that such skills were part of the regular skill set of the forensic anthropologist).

Current state of forensic archaeology in Canada

Given the mixed administration of death investigation across the country alongside little demand for routine forensic archaeological expertise, a lack of development and use of archaeologists for medico-legal investigation should not be surprising. Of course, archaeologists may be involved in search, recovery, scene documentation and interpretation for other manners of death: suicides, accidents or deaths from undetermined causes, but the number of these that warrant investigation are also relatively low and presumably the pressure to employ specialised expertise in these investigations (when there is good evidence prior to remains discovery/recovery of manner of death such as a suicide note left by a missing person) is less than for homicides.

Nevertheless, local and regional coroners or medical examiners in some jurisdictions routinely rely on archaeologists or anthropologists to help determine if remains are of medico-legal interest (i.e. they are *not* archaeological) and to conduct search and recovery at death scenes, which include sites of fire, suicides, surface-scattered remains, those washed ashore or discovered underwater and cemetery exhumations of cold cases that have been nominated for re-examination. Although the situation varies by provincial/territorial jurisdiction, generally the coroner or medical examiner takes jurisdiction of found remains. Assessment of whether or not remains are historic or archaeological can be a vague process and may include proximity to known archaeological sites, physical traits that indicate aboriginal identity such as cranial deformation or material culture associated with the remains. This process is sometimes done in consultation between members of heritage preservation agencies and medico-legal investigators (Al Mackie, personal communication, 2013).

In 2008, an ad hoc committee of the Canadian Association for Physical Anthropology (CAPA, or ACAP in French) produced a document advising police and death investigators on the minimum qualifications of those used for forensic anthropological analysis in Canada (Hoppa et al. 2008, 1). The authors stated that:

> forensic anthropologists today should be able to oversee searches for evidence, human remains, and graves and be

> able to determine whether the found remains are forensically significant and utilize proper crime scene protocols to document relevant information and evidence... evidence relevant to forensic anthropological investigations consist not only of physical human remains but also contextual evidence such as grave features, natural processes and site formation and site transformation processes, for which other specialists may contribute their expertise (e.g., archaeologists, entomologists, geologists, botanists, etc.).

In response to the continuing but sporadic use of archaeological and anthropological expertise in Canada, alongside other concerns about professional forensic practice in the United States (e.g. the National Academy of Sciences 2009 report on forensic sciences), Congram and Mundorff (2009) called for the professional organisation of forensic archaeology and anthropology at an annual meeting of CAPA. This call was met with stoic silence and soon thereafter both authors were hired to work in the United States: the latter at the University of Tennessee (famous for its forensic anthropological research) and the former as a postdoctoral research fellow with the US Department of Defense's Joint POW/MIA Accounting Command's Central Identification Laboratory (JPAC-CIL; Pietruszka, Chapter 51, this volume).[1] In 2013 a report was released on forensic sciences in Canada. The report chapter on forensic anthropology accentuated the lack of professional organisation, standardisation and accreditation in the discipline (Gruspier and Rogers 2013).

Nevertheless, local and regional expertise is generally available. Those called upon, as will be seen from the survey data later, are almost always archaeologists or anthropologists who are based at universities (e.g. Simon Fraser University, the University of Northern British Columbia, the University of Western Ontario, the University of Toronto Mississauga, or St. Mary's). It is not uncommon for qualified graduate students to assist. The federal police agency, the Royal Canadian Mounted Police (*Gendarmerie Royale du Canada* in French), also has a crime scene examiner, Dr Diane Cockle, who recently completed her PhD in archaeology at Simon Fraser University with a thesis on post-mortem intervals based on decomposition in Canada.

Training opportunities

In stark contrast to the United Kingdom where forensic graduate degree programmes abound, there is only one graduate-level programme in forensic anthropology (an MSc) in Canada, and it incorporates archaeological recovery. This is at St Mary's University in Halifax, Nova Scotia, under the direction of Tanya Peckmann. A few universities offer undergraduate degrees with a forensic anthropology focus (e.g. University of Toronto Mississauga, St Mary's, Memorial and Lakehead Universities) and many offer at least one course on forensic anthropology, some of which include teaching on archaeological recovery scene work. On two occasions, in 2008 and 2009, Simon Fraser University offered an undergraduate course specifically on forensic archaeology. There are many excellent graduate programmes in archaeology and anthropology, some of which provide students with an opportunity to get involved in mentored forensic casework and specialised course work on the application of archaeological and anthropological methods to medico-legal investigation as well as forensic-oriented research. Given the light caseload in Canada, the educational opportunities and course offerings seem appropriate. It is irresponsible for many students to be trained up in a discipline for which there is little work.

This said, Dirkmaat and colleagues in the United States have exemplified the utility of experimentation and training for mass fatality response (e.g. Cabo and Dirkmaat, Chapter 31, this volume; Chapman et al. 2012; Dirkmaat 2012). Canadian practitioners and researchers have done nothing comparable. Recently foiled terrorist plots in Canada, the Lac Mégantic train disaster and the past deployment of Canadian experts abroad for UN missions or disaster response should remind us of the value of this type of preparedness.

Also of educational note is the website *Investigating Forensics*, which was created with a grant from Virtual Museums Canada to Barbara Winter, the curator of the Simon Fraser University Museum of Archaeology and Ethnology. The site guides the visitor through a forensic case, starting with a scene search and grave excavation. The website includes text, video and still photographs that outline different forensic roles, including that of the forensic archaeologist (Investigating Forensics, online).

Survey of Canadian 'forensic archaeologists'

A multiple-choice, online survey was sent to 32 people who have experience with forensic archaeological fieldwork in Canada. The list of potential recipients was discussed with two colleagues who have relevant experience and who have been teaching forensic anthropology at the post-secondary level for many years. Some potential recipients of the survey were excluded: (i) those who worked only on the Pickton

[1] Congram moved back to Canada in 2013 and divides his time between teaching and consulting on international forensic investigations.

case, because the investigation appeared to employ little that could be considered archaeological and because many of those who worked there have not worked on other, more typical cases in Canada; and (ii) professionals from the United States who have consulted in Canada on only one or two cases, as they may skew results by having practised their own (though probably very similar) form of forensic archaeology. One Canadian recipient who has remarkably extensive experience in other countries did not complete the survey because they reported having no forensic fieldwork experience in Canada. There are some potentially relevant recipients that may have been overlooked, but in consulting with others and due to the small community of practitioners, the results should represent the discipline very well.

The response rate was 90%, with 28 of 31 eligible recipients completing most or all of the survey. In general, respondents have a lot of forensic experience: almost 80% have worked on forensic cases for at least 11 years; close to half (43%) have worked on over 20 cases in the field; 50% have worked on at least 6–10 burials and only 2 of the respondents have never excavated a burial as part of forensic fieldwork. When burials are successfully found, it is usually because there are some remains on the ground surface (71.4%) and/or a witness has identified the location (75%). This leads one to wonder how many unmarked graves exist undiscovered for lack of witnesses and because they remain undisturbed/completely buried. At the same time, the abundance of open and unpopulated areas in Canada allows for easy disposal of remains (in a homicide case, for example) without a high probability of recent discovery, thus removing the killer from the victim (in time–space, association). It may be that victims are seldom buried.

Although over a quarter (28.5%) of respondents reported having used (or worked with others who used) geophysics to search for burials, only two (7%) report it having been successful. Unfortunately the survey was not specific enough to establish how many times geophysics was used and failed to locate a burial, which was found by other methods (akin to a Type I error) so the reliability of geophysical prospection for forensic work in Canada is not known.

Despite almost half of the practitioners (43%) self-identifying primarily as biological anthropologists (even with the option of identifying as both a biological anthropologist and an archaeologist), nearly all respondents routinely report recording basic soil characteristics such as type, colour and stratigraphic relationships, and most report that either they or another on the scene regularly create a scale map. Three-quarters of those who completed the survey are based at universities. Half of the respondents have given testimony about the methods they used for fieldwork or the subsequent interpretations, and 60% of them indicated that the methods or interpretations were challenged during a trial or preliminary hearing. Nevertheless, almost half of the respondents (44%) indicated that they believed forensic fieldwork was not being conducted to a sufficient standard in Canada, which is worrying. This suggests that challenges at preliminary hearings or during trial might not be effectively identifying shortcomings in the standard of work. When these responses were tested against the years of experience of practitioners using a chi-squared test, there was no statistically significant correlation, indicating that it is not only those of a certain cohort who feel one way or another about the quality of work being performed.

Melbye and Jimenez (1997, 67) emphasised that investigations often result in the recovery of artefacts such as bullets, clothing and personal effects, the examination of which they deemed to be within the experience of the forensic anthropologist. The experience of this author and the survey results show that the examination of such artefacts by anthropologists/archaeologists who do recovery work in Canada does occur often. Nevertheless, such analysis is seldom a topic of discussion in the forensic literature (for recent exceptions, see Anderson 2008; Birkby et al. 2008; Skinner et al. 2009).

Conclusions

Despite low murder and disappearance rates in Canada and little demand for forensic archaeology, there are many historic cases of those who can be considered 'missing' for whom forensic archaeological expertise could be useful. One group of missing are those who died in past aircraft crashes and whose remains were never recovered from the crash site. During and following the Second World War there were a number of military and commercial aircraft crashes in the mountain ranges of British Columbia and Alberta, which resulted in dozens of deaths (e.g. Eldridge et al. 1994). Following the discovery of a commercial aircraft crash site, a newspaper reported that 'bodies … lie deep in a snow pocket … safe from desecration and buried so completely that man [sic] cannot hope to improve on nature's job … permanently buried in ice and snow which will last as long as the mountains remain' (Vancouver Sun, 1943). Both historically and recently, avocational hikers have discovered these sites, including that to which the earlier quote relates, and observed skeletonised remains lying across the landscape (Figure 27.1). It is remarkable to consider that this is acceptable, particularly when one thinks that many of those who died – despite some being war time losses – went 'missing' in a place where there were few significant impediments (beyond prohibitive seasonal weather) to the recovery of the remains.

Figure 27.1 Semi-articulated skeletonised remains from victims of a commercial aircraft crash in western Canada. This photo was recently taken by an avocational hiker (Photo: R. Marshall).

The second group of those whose remains are 'missing' are First Nations (aboriginal) children who were removed from their native homes and communities to be raised at residential schools, where recent research shows that at least 4100 of them died (Alex Maass, personal communication, 2013; Milloy 1999; The Canadian Press 2013). These schools were instituted by the Canadian government and administered by churches from the 1840s to 1996. The dead often lie in unmarked burials at the site of the school, and not in the communities from which the children were removed (Alex Maass, personal communication 2013). Forensic archaeologists could certainly assist with the location and exhumation of these remains although this must be done in association with and at the behest of the victim families and communities if they deem it appropriate. The existence of these burials and the remains of aircraft crash victims might be symptomatic of a general apathy about treatment of the dead in Canada, but they are more likely a result of disingenuous or lack of factual reporting by the authorities in charge at the time of the deaths. With the passage of time, families of the dead may become resigned to the seeming impossibility of recovery and repatriation of remains for culturally appropriate rites.

Overall forensic archaeology in Canada exists, albeit in various forms and with no particular standard operating procedures. There is certainly room for research and development as well as unexplored opportunity for those who are properly trained. Current practitioners demonstrate and advocate archaeological approaches, although many express dissatisfaction with the standard to which the work is being done. In terms of who practices forensic archaeology, a segment from a poem that was written about Jerry Melbye by his first anthropology PhD student gives us a pretty good idea:

...But perhaps what I got from my turn at the wheel
Was a burr that has pushed me along.
A phrase that he said, more than once, that I thought
Was simply and utterly wrong.

The osteologist, Melbye opined, has the job
of Handmaiden to the archaeologist.
Surely not! Thought my brain. Our work must stand
fast, without leaning on any apologist.

Like my colleagues, I've worked to define our perspective
To say, "this is OUR kind of question."
But now, as I survey the work that I do
And I ponder what brings satisfaction,

I go back to those words, and I have to admit
That alone none of us holds a candle
For finding and shaping the tale of our past
Is more than any one group can handle.

So handmaiden? Maybe. Colleague, for sure.
I'm pleased that I followed the call.
My thanks go to Jerry for urging me on
And I think that I speak for us all.

Susan Pfeiffer 2001

References

Anderson, B. E. 2008. Identifying the dead: methods utilized by the Pima County (Arizona) Office of the Medical Examiner for undocumented border crossers: 2001–2006. *Journal of Forensic Sciences* 53(1), 8–15.

Anderson, J. E. 1962. *The Human Skeleton: A Manual for Archaeologists*. Ottawa, National Museum of Canada.

Birkby, W. H., Fenton, T. W. and Anderson, B. E. 2008. Identifying southwest Hispanics using nonmetric traits and the cultural profile. *Journal of Forensic Sciences* 53(1), 29–33.

Blau, S. and Skinner, M. 2005. The use of forensic archaeology in the investigation of human rights abuse: Unearthing the past in East Timor. *The International Journal of Human Rights* 9(4), 449–463.

CBC. 2009. *BC's Infamous 'Highway of Tears'*. Available at: http://www.cbc.ca/archives/categories/society/crime-justice/cold-cases-unsolved-crimes-in-canada/bcs-infamous-highway-of-tears.html (last accessed 14 April 2013).

Chapman, E. N., Kenyhercz, M. and Cabo, L. L. 2012. *Enhancing Scene Protocols to Improve Victim Identification and Field Detection of Human Remains in Mass Fatality Scenes*. National Institute of Justice, Award number #2008-DN-BX-K133. Available at: https://www.ncjrs.gov/pdffiles1/nij/grants/238744.pdf (last accessed 13 May 2013).

Congram, D. and Mundorff, A. 2009. A call for accreditation in forensic archaeology and anthropology in Canada. *Canadian Association for Physical Anthropology Annual Meeting, Simon Fraser University, Vancouver.*

Dirkmaat, D. C. 2012. Forensic anthropology at the mass fatality incident (commercial airliner) crash scene. In

D. C. Dirkmaat (ed.), *A Companion to Forensic Anthropology*, 136–156. Madlen, Wiley-Blackwell.

Eldridge, M., Owens-Baird, D. and Mackie, A. 1994. *Mt. Slesse Air Crash Site Archaeological Investigation*. Report prepared for Chilliwack Forest District. Sidney, Millennia Research.

Gruspier, K. and Rogers, T. 2013. Forensic anthropology. In M. S. Pollanen, M. J. Bowes, S. L. Van Laerhoven and J. Wallace (eds.), *Forensic Science in Canada; A Report of Multidisciplinary Discussion*, 21–30. Centre for Forensic Science & Medicine, University of Toronto.

Hoppa, R. D., Rogers, T., Lazenby, R. et al. 2008. *The Canadian Association of Physical Anthropology/L'Association Canadienne D'Anthropologie Physique*. President's Ad-Hoc Committee Report on Minimum Levels of Qualifications for Forensic Anthropology in Canada (18 June 2008).

Kalacska, M. E. and Bell, L. S. 2006. Remote sensing as a tool for the detection of clandestine mass graves. *Canadian Society of Forensic Science Journal* 39, 1–13.

Kalacska, M. E., Bell, L. S., Sanchez-Azofeifa, G. A. and Caelli, T. 2009. The application of remote sensing for detecting mass graves: an experimental animal case study from Costa Rica. *Journal of Forensic Sciences* 54(1), 159–166.

Katzmarzyk, C. 2001. The academic career of Dr. Jerry Melbye. In L. Sawchuk and S. Pfeiffer (eds.), *Out of the Past: The History of Human Osteology at the University of Toronto*. University of Toronto Scarborough, CITD Press. Available at: https://tspace.library.utoronto.ca/citd/Osteology/Katzmarzyk.html (last accessed 30 March 2014).

Mayne Correia, P. and Beattie, O. 2002. A critical look at methods for recovering, evaluating, and interpreting cremated human remains. In W. D. Haglund and M. H. Sorg (eds.), *Advances in Forensic Taphonomy*, 435–450. Boca Raton, CRC Press.

Meiklejohn, C. 2012. From Lawrence, Kansas, to Victoria in 40 years. Some thoughts on the history of physical anthropology in Canada, CAPA, and a aareer in bioarchaeology. *Oral Presentation Given at the Annual Meeting of the Canadian Association for Physical Anthropology, Victoria, Canada.*

Melbye, J. and Jimenez, S. 1993. The integration of the metal detector with standard archaeological recovery. *Proceedings of the American Academy of Forensic Sciences*, Boston, MA.

Melbye J, and Jimenez, S. 1997. Chain of custody from the field to the courtroom. In W. D. Haglund and M. H. Sorg (eds.), *ForensicTaphonomy: The Post-Mortem Fate of Human Remains*, 65–75. Boca Raton, CRC Press.

Melbye, J., Chiasson, D., Wood, R. and Blenkinsop, B. 1999. Death on the Danforth. In S. I. Fairgrieve (ed.), *Forensic Osteological Analysis: a Book of Case Studies*, 89–106. Springfield, Charles C. Thomas.

Milloy, J. S. 1999. *A National Crime; The Canadian Government and the Residential School System, 1879 to 1986*. Winnipeg, The University of Manitoba Press.

Morse, D., Crusoe, D. and Smith, H. G. 1976. Forensic archaeology. *Journal of Forensic Science* 21(2), 323–332.

Morse, D., Duncan, J. and Stoudamire, J. 1983. *Handbook of Forensic Archaeology and Anthropology*. Tallahassee, Rose Printing Company.

National Academy of Sciences. 2009. *Strengthening Forensic Sciences in the United States: A Path Forward*. National Research Councils. Washington DC, National Academies Press.

Pfeiffer, S. 2001. Dr. Melbye's revenge. In L. Sawchuk and S. Pfeiffer (eds.), *Out of the Past: The History of Human Osteology at the University of Toronto*. University of Toronto Scarborough, CITD Press.

Skelton, C. 2010 Pickton won't face remaining 20 murder charges, *The Vancouver Sun* [online]. Available at: http://www.vancouversun.com/news/Crown+drops+remaining+murder+charges+against+Pickton/3360046/story.html (last accessed 8 September 2014).

Skinner, M. 1987. Planning the archaeological recovery of evidence from recent mass graves. *Forensic Science International* 34, 267–287.

Skinner, M. 2007. Hapless in Afghanistan: forensic archaeology in a political maelstrom. In R. Ferllini (ed.), *Forensic Archaeology and Human Rights Violations*, 233–265. Springfield, Charles C. Thomas.

Skinner, M. F. and Bowie, K. 2009. Forensic anthropology: Canadian content and contributions. In: S. Blau and D. Ubelaker (eds.), *Handbook of Forensic Anthropology and Archaeology*, 87–103. Walnut Creek, Left Coast Press.

Skinner, M. and Jessee, E. 2005. A typology of mass grave and mass grave-related sites. *Forensic Science International* 152, 55–59.

Skinner, M. F. and Lazenby, R. 1984. *Found! Human Remains: A Field Manual for the Recovery of the Recent Human Skeleton*. Burnaby, SFU Archaeology Press.

Skinner, M. F. and Sterenberg, J. 2005. Turf wars: authority and responsibility for the investigation of mass graves. *Forensic Science International* 151, 221–232.

Skinner, M. F., Alempijevic, D. and Djuric-Srejic, M. 2003. Guidelines for international forensic bioarchaeology monitors of mass grave exhumations. *Forensic Science International* 134, 81–92.

Skinner, M., Fernández, A. and Congram, D. 2009. Material culture analysis in forensic cases: a call for formal recognition by forensic anthropologists. *Proceedings American Academy of Forensic Sciences* 15, 336–337.

Skinner, M. F., York, H. P. and Connor, M. A. 2002. Postburial disturbance of graves in Bosnia-Herzegovina. In W. D. Haglund and M. H. Sorg (eds.), *Advances in Forensic Taphonomy*, 293–308. Boca Raton, CRC Press.

Spence, M. 1999. An anthropological investigation of a rural homicide scene. In S. I. Fairgrieve (ed.), *Forensic Osteological Analysis*, 173–182. Springfield, Charles C. Thomas.

Statistics Canada. 2012. *Canadian Coroner and Medical Examiner Database: Annual Report 2006–2008*. Available at: http://www.statcan.gc.ca/pub/82-214-x/2012001/int-eng.htm (last accessed 19 May 2013).

Stratton, S. U. and Beattie, O. B. 1999. Mass disasters: comments and discussion regarding the Hinton train collision of 1986. In S. I. Fairgrieve (ed.), *Forensic Osteological Analysis*, 267–286. Springfield, Charles C. Thomas.

The Canadian Press. 2013. *At Least 3,000 Died in Residential Schools, Research Shows*. Available at: http://www.cbc.ca/news/canada/story/2013/02/18/residential-schools-student-deaths.html (last accessed 9 June 2013).

Vancouver Sun. 1943. 21 August 1943, page 1.

Wilson, D. 2004. The lonely road of Matty Wilson, *United Church Observer Magazine*. Available at: http://www.ucobserver.org/justice/2004/11/the_lonely_road_of_matty_wilson/ (last accessed 30 May 2013).

Website

Investigating Forensics. Virtual Museum of Canada and Simon Fraser University Museum of Archaeology and Ethnology. Available at: http://www.sfu.museum/forensics. Accessed 15 August 2013.

CHAPTER 28

A brief account of the past and present circumstances of forensic archaeology in Costa Rica

Roxana Ferllini
Forensic Anthropologist, Independent Researcher and Author, Tettenhall, West Midlands, UK

Introduction

In this chapter, the necessity for the application of forensic archaeology in the Costa Rican context is discussed as a matter of priority, due to a variety of reasons including the broad range of taphonomic factors present in the country's highly varied ecosystems, certain manners of disposal practices connected with homicide victims and adjustments with respect to crime patterns and trends, which collectively present a wide array of challenges to the authorities on a recurring basis. However, it may be safely accepted that forensic archaeology in Costa Rica has not attained a solid foundation within the judicial framework; instead, the discipline has been applied sporadically via the intervention of forensic anthropologists possessing archaeological backgrounds and associated in part with the country's historical context during the 20th century, albeit through efforts made within the judicial system.

The introduction of forensic archaeology in the area of forensic investigations may yet materialise in the foreseeable future in Costa Rica and become a routinely applied discipline in the context of the search and retrieval of human remains.

Historical antecedents

In recent times, many Latin American countries have suffered the effects of massive violations of human rights; a common denominator here is the notable toll with respect to civilian casualties, as with the cases of Argentina, Chile, Peru (Baraybar and Mora, Chapter 52, this volume; Collins et al. 2013; Fondebrider and Scheinsohn, Chapter 43, this volume; Garrido Varas and Intriago Leiva 2012; Itriago Leiva et al., Chapter 45, this volume), Colombia (Gómez Lopez and Patiño Umaña 2007; Guatame et al., Chapter 46, this volume) and, more specifically in Central America, the cases of Guatemala (Congram and Fernández 2006; Isaacs 2010) and El Salvador (Scott 2001); however, with respect to Costa Rica, its citizens have not been placed in the position of confronting violent episodes of such large magnitude, such as the arbitrary patterns of abductions and systematic killings typical of the cases stated earlier. During the 20th century, the decade of the 1940s witnessed violence and repression directed towards the civilian population of Costa Rica, culminating in a civil war during March 1948 lasting 40 days; as a consequence of the said conflict, the military was entirely abolished from the structure of the state. Thousands of civilian casualties resulted from this conflict, estimated at between 2000 and 4000, mostly men, but with exact numbers unavailable. The majority of these casualties remained unconfirmed and were never accounted for publicly. Consequently, a notable lack of initiative was evident with respect to specifying the accurate whereabouts of the deceased (Huhn 2009; Solís 2008; Villalobos 2013). Solís (2008) reported the existence of a mass grave in which bodies had been discarded and burnt; however, in the Costa Rican consciousness, the connotation of mass graves related to an earlier historical context for the country or even the concept itself is virtually absent from public awareness. As a result, such conditions have not led to the necessity or desire to train qualified investigators or organise formal forensic teams within the country (Congram and Fernández 2006; Delgado 2013a; Huhn 2009), of the type present in countries such as Argentina, Peru and Guatemala (Juhl and Olsen 2006), consisting of, among other professionals, forensic archaeologists and anthropologists. These two disciplines are interrelated with the former in charge of applying modern techniques towards the search, location and retrieval of the victims and the latter dealing with the victims in the mortuary during the post-mortem examination as an aid to the identification process. As a consequence, when the archaeological intervention is not done

Forensic Archaeology: A Global Perspective, First Edition. Edited by W.J. Mike Groen, Nicholas Márquez-Grant and Robert C. Janaway.

appropriately, the post-mortem work can suffer negative outcomes.

Although the discipline of forensic archaeology (later as an integrated part of forensic anthropology) evolved steadily in the United States during the late 1970s and early 1980s (Morse et al. 1976, 1983), its application was late in arriving in many countries throughout the globe, including those within Latin America, with the exception of Argentina, where the practice was introduced in 1984 in response to the necessity of formally investigating the whereabouts of victims of the Dirty War (*Guerra Sucia*) between 1976 and 1983 (Joyce and Stover 1992).

In the Costa Rican context, attempts to formally implement the discipline as part of the judicial apparatus were made by creating a forensic anthropology section aimed at victim identification and research purposes, initiated and supported in 1989 through the efforts of Dr E. Vargas Alvarado, then the country's Chief Medical Examiner, and the current author working as a forensic anthropologist based at the University of Costa Rica. Lobbying was set in motion by the author among various magistrates of the Costa Rican Supreme Court, and although she was involved with scene investigations in addition to post-mortem examinations, the work was typically requested on a consultative basis, with a permanent post not receiving support at the time by those retaining the direct influence to approve it (Delgado, 2013a). Consequentially, active involvement in such activities remained on a consultative level throughout the intervening period, and focused primarily upon work within the mortuary.

Additionally, during the early 1990s, interest was expressed on the part of the Distance State University (Universidad Estatal a Distancia – UNED) with respect to forensic archaeology and anthropology; this culminated in UNED starting a bachelor's degree in Criminological Sciences with the objective of enrolling judicial employees who would be instructed in part by experienced members of the judicial system, in addition to qualified forensic consultants. The said programme required the production of accompanying texts which were specific to each module, and focused upon challenges which could be expected when operating in conjunction with the existing state system in the Costa Rican context. The textbook on forensic archaeology associated with the programme was presented in general terms (Ferllini 1993), and focused primarily upon informing judicial employees about the discipline, in order that they were better able to effectively assist professionals when in the field, whilst not involving themselves directly with the work at hand. This educational background instilled a desire in judicial investigators to apply the discipline; however, interest and goodwill from higher authorities was not always displayed with shared enthusiasm.

Costa Rican legal framework

Legislation in Costa Rica covers, among several aspects, the subject of judicial investigations, in addition to the involvement of forensic consultants when required, with the objective of promulgating the support and intervention of science for the benefit of justice. Such interventions can be commissioned by judges, in the context of requesting the involvement of required experts to intervene in a given case; the resulting investigations are then coordinated via a centralised organisation, the Judicial Investigative Bureau (*Organismo de Investigación Judicial* – OIJ), which is charged with overseeing the implementation of correct procedures in relation to any type of criminal investigation.

The creation of the OIJ came about in 1974 through the passing of the Organic Law of the Judicial Investigative Bureau 5524, created by the Republic of Costa Rica Legislative Assembly; it contains 15 Chapters, of which Chapter I, Article 1, Chapter II, Articles 3, 4 and 9, and Chapter III, Article 11, are of most relevance to the topic of this chapter (Red Hemisférica 2013). A summary of these Chapters and Articles is presented here:

- *Chapter I* – Article 1 refers to the creation of the OIJ, its jurisdiction and functions, with the aim of aiding the courts and the Public Ministry by applying scientific methods in the investigation of crime *[Será, asimismo, cuerpo de consulta de los demás tribunales del país]* (Red Hemisférica 2013).
- *Chapter II* – Article 3 addresses the OIJ's powers to guarantee the application of scientific methods when gathering evidence pertaining to crime investigation. *[Si el delito fuere de acción o instancia privada, solo actuará en acatamiento a orden de autoridad competente, que indique haber recibido la denuncia o acusación de persona legalmente facultada.]* Article 4, subparagraph 2, refers to the OIJ's responsibility at a scene, ensuring that only the competent authority investigates the scene, for the secure and successful outcome of any investigation; subparagraph 10 indicates the responsibility for a smooth process at the scene; and subparagraph 11 highlights the need for forensic consultants when appropriate (Red Hemisférica 2013). Article 9 addresses the various avenues by which the investigative actions can be recorded, through scientific methods (Red Hemisférica 2013).
- *Chapter III* – Article 11 establishes the component sections of the Judicial Investigative Bureau, including three different departments; Department of Criminal Investigations, Department of Legal Medicine and the Department of Laboratory of Forensic Sciences. Each of these departments has the ability to create the sections and offices deemed necessary (Red Hemisférica 2013).

The earlier-cited Chapters and Articles acknowledge OIJ's responsibilities with respect to properly processing and recording the steps taken during any

Figure 28.1 Members of the Red Cross and the Judicial Police rescue the body of a missing man in the Zurquí sector, outside the capital city San José (image courtesy: Grupo Nación, photo: G. Anrango).

criminal investigation and utilising, when necessary, the intervention of specialised forensic consultants from outside of the Bureau. Additionally, each department within OIJ is permitted to develop appropriate sections as deemed necessary. In this context, forensic archaeology should not be seen as an exception to these provisions; however, in the past there have been instances where the services of a forensic archaeologist were directly required, but declined, or no forensic archaeologist was available at the time within the country. In the latter case, this was no doubt influenced by the lack of opportunities in this field within Costa Rica.

Yet, the intervention of a forensic archaeologist in the capacity of an external consultant within the context of a scene dealing with surface remains would often be highly advantageous; however, in the current circumstances, such work is normally conducted via the Judicial Police (part of the OIJ), the Public Force of Costa Rica and the Red Cross. The Public Force (*Fuerza Pública*) is a police force created in 1996 in response to various national and regional police identities being reorganised or eliminated. As such, the Public Force is subdivided into a variety of specialised units and as part of its various duties it coordinates directly with the Judicial Police when attending to operational activities (Fuerza Pública de Costa Rica 2013), including those associated with situations akin to forensic archaeology, such as searches, aiding with the retrieval of the body and guarding crime scenes when required (Delgado 2014; Parrales 2012; Segura 2012). The Costa Rican Red Cross Search and Rescue Unit participates in the search and location of missing individuals (Chávez and Delgado 2012) under various circumstances, including aircraft accidents in remote mountainous areas (author's personal observation); the means by which such searches are carried out is varied, and includes the utilisation of cadaver dogs (Cabezas, 2013), with the said organisations working in cooperation (Delgado 2014; Segura 2012) (Figure 28.1). In cases dealing with clandestine burials, the said authorities may participate directly; however, certain members of the OIJ who possess basic knowledge of the archaeological discipline may also intervene (Delgado 2013b).

While the involvement of these organisations is of the utmost importance in forensic interventions, in cases concerning human remains in which the integrity of the cadavers has been compromised, skeletonised, and/or when they represent juveniles, the presence of a forensic archaeologist would considerably enhance the location and rescue process, particularly if the professional in question possesses proper osteological knowledge, as is the current trend in many countries. It is necessary to emphasise here that the judicial system retains a Forensic Biological Section as part of the Department of Laboratory of Forensic Sciences, in which entomological, botanical, hair and fibre specialists operate in the appropriate infrastructure. These specialists would benefit greatly from supporting forensic archaeological interventions when and where appropriate.

Certifications and academic degrees

At present, no system of accreditation exists in the country for forensic archaeologists and forensic anthropologists to be placed within a centralised registry (Congram and Fernández 2006), whether to practise within the judicial system, as an independent consultant, and/or to present testimony in a court of law. Due to the said lack of a centralised system, no national standards presently exist, with those wishing to practise not being expected, encouraged or supported by the system to move forward within the arenas of research and publication. The latter circumstances place practising professionals within a stagnating situation that is not entirely ideal, especially considering that these are disciplines in which new technologies, techniques and local knowledge of taphonomic factors may be of assistance in the context of the search and recovery of human remains.

To the author's knowledge, within the academic literature, publications related to forensic archaeology related to the Costa Rican context are few. Despite utilising various robust search engines, only three articles were identified, one case report by Congram (2008), two articles pertaining to remote sensing techniques by Kalacska and Bell (2006) and Kalacska et al. (2009). To this literature, only two books can be added (Ferllini 1993, in press) used within a specific module at UNED's programme.

Furthermore, no academic programmes are currently being offered at any level pertaining specifically to the subjects of forensic archaeology and anthropology for those interested in learning and working within these disciplines; however, many current students have expressed strong interest in following such lines of study, but with the choice of studying abroad not an option for the majority (Congram and Fernández 2006), as scholarships are typically rather limited in availability.

Figure 28.2 Premontane wet forest in the south area of the country, along the Pacific coast. Note the darkness due to the tree canopies, uneven terrain and massive tree roots – taphonomic factors to consider during a search operation.

Need for forensic archaeology

Archaeologists at the National Museum have been involved with the police and relevant authorities as part of investigations pertaining to archaeological sites which have been looted, but their intervention within criminal investigation has not been the norm (Congram 2008). However, archaeology is a discipline that should be applied to crime scene processing as a matter of necessity, and not exercised as a potential option. Such needs arise in response to a number of taphonomic factors, crime profiles and patterns of body disposal witnessed in the country.

Costa Rica is located in the tropical region of Latin America, and under the Holdridge Life Zone system, the 51,042.8 km^2 of territory has been divided into 12 Life Zones and 11 Transition Zones based upon environmental aspects such as relative humidity, precipitation, temperature and geographical and topographic factors influenced by both latitude and altitude (Holdridge 1967; Kohlmann et al. 2010). Consequentially, direct environmental conditions vary (Ross and Cunningham 2011) from tropical dry forest, to premontane wet forests (Figure 28.2), rainforests, cloud forests (Figure 28.3) and páramo, in addition to a variety of transitional zones, all of which present a wide range of taphonomic factors which affect the contexts of crime scenes and the human remains in question.

It is the experience of the author that in the Costa Rican context, bodies that have been left exposed to the elements, or within very shallow burials, normally present rapid rates of decomposition, skeletonisation, disarticulation and dispersal, primarily due to factors related to tropical climatic conditions, scavengers, rapid insect colonisation and rugged topography (author's personal observation; Vargas Fonseca 1999; INBIO 2014a; Jirón and Catín 1981; Kohlmann et al. 2010; Pape no date).

Various scavengers acknowledged to occur in Costa Rica may directly affect forensic scenes (Bravo 2014), including the coyote (*Canis latrans*) (INBIO 2014b; Rodríguez and Chinchilla 1996), the habitat of which has increased due to forest clearing, resulting in its occurrence within most areas of suitable habitat, with exception of regions of tropical moist forest located mainly in the southern and Caribbean zones of the country. Additionally, a further increase in the coyote population is most likely as more habitat becomes available (Hidalgo Mihart et al. 2004; Monge Nájera and Morera Brenes 1986). This species operates both as lone animals or in groups (Bekoff and Wells 1986), and may constitute a major factor by its direct effect upon human

Figure 28.3 Thick tree coverage in a cloud forest, accompanied by fog and rough topography, creates difficulties for search parties.

Figure 28.4 *Coragyps atratus* (commonly known as black vulture) on the Pacific coast line.

remains with reference to both soft and hard tissues, but also in connection to dispersal (Haglund 1997; Turhon 1997), thereby complicating efforts of search and recovery. Furthermore, a variety of carrion birds inhabit a wide range of the country's habitats, including turkey vulture (*Cathartes aura*) and black vulture (*Coragyps atratus*) (INBIO 2014c) (Figure 28.4). These scavengers are known to feed in unison, in some instances in large numbers upon a given carcass, depending upon its size, whether fresh or decomposing; these birds are capable of inflicting alterations and rapid consumption in relation to their food sources, and are recognised as being associated with areas of human habitation (author's personal observation; Coutiño and Enríquez 2009). Some taxa of carrion birds possess excellent senses of sight and smell, permitting them to locate potential carcasses concealed under the cover of tree canopies (Barron 2013), a common scenario within tropical settings, and with further local variations (Laska 1997).

In one particular area, the Zurquí sector – outside of the capital, an evergreen forest with thick vegetation (Figure 28.5) – is used upon occasion as a 'dumping

Figure 28.5 Zurquí sector during the dry season. The river can easily swell when the wet season returns.

ground', where human remains are discovered in various states of preservation, including highly incomplete bodies (author's personal observation; Chávez and Delgado 2012; Delgado 2012).

Additional scenarios which may require the intervention of forensic archaeological techniques are accidents involving small aircraft; it is the experience of the author that in circumstances in which bodies are located in remote regions, the remains are frequently scavenged before recovery can be attempted, and/or widely dispersed within the area of impact. Due to the topographic and geological setting of the country, the region is exposed to mudslides, earthquakes and swelling of rivers, all of which present further variations which may adversely affect recovery scenarios.

Finally, the national level of violent crime remains relatively low in comparison to other countries within the region; however, violent crime is presently on the rise (Dudley 2011; Vargas Sanabria et al. 2009), and in some instances, the context of such events is changing, such as the use of hired killers (La Jornada 2011), or the recent discovery of a grave which contained the bodies of two foreign nationals (BBC 2012). Such dynamics have never been published in association with crime scene contexts where forensic archaeology would be needed. Nonetheless, if such approaches were contextualised in conjunction with the increase in organised criminal groups, incursion of drug cartels and drug trafficking through land and sea, the presence of *maras* (street gangs, although in lower numbers than in other Central American countries, except for Panamá), in addition to an increase of undocumented foreign nationals (Dudley 2011), then situations will inevitably arise whereby forensic archaeology will constitute an essential element within crime scene investigations, in order to more comprehensively preserve the context of the finds and bodies, and aid in the accurate interpretation of events.

Perceptions of forensic archaeology

The OIJ and forensic personnel often associate the work of a forensic archaeologist and anthropologist solely with skeletal remains, whilst leaving those remains with soft tissue to other forensic personnel (author's personal observation; Delgado 2013b), thereby markedly limiting the contribution of both disciplines within the implementation of justice.

Based solely on skeletonised remains, statistics obtained from the OIJ spanning from the year 2008 to 19 October 2012 (D. Delgado, personal communication 2013) indicated that a total of 47 skeletal remains were discovered throughout the country, with 27 (57.5%) remaining unidentified; of these, in 25 cases (92.57%), the cause and manner of death was not accurately ascertained. Only in the cases of two individuals was it possible to determine the cause of death due to head trauma; one associated with homicide, whilst the other case is still pending due to further investigation being required. Whilst this information does not indicate the circumstance in which each case was discovered and how complete each individual was, it is feasible to postulate that perhaps with the regular intervention of both disciplines, statistics pertaining to the number of successfully identified remains may have been improved.

Discussion

The taphonomic factors present throughout the various ecosystems within Costa Rica, in association with changes in trends related to crime characteristics, suggest an urgent requirement to implement forensic archaeology as a discipline in order to preserve the context in the field, thereby permitting more accurate interpretation of events. Furthermore, the legal framework within the judiciary currently permits forensic archaeologists to be utilised as an investigative element of any crime scene when required by the authorities, paid on a consultative basis. At present, the central mortuary is contemplating opening a part-time post for a forensic anthropologist (Delgado 2013b); it is hoped that this placement will also require participation in the context of crime scene investigations, and concurrent cooperation with the authorities, serving as an integral part of investigative efforts when required. It has been the direct experience of the author on many occasions that the performance of work within the mortuary in Costa Rica frequently becomes problematic, due to the lack of both direct participation and deficient contextual knowledge being conveyed from the field.

Acknowledgements

The author wishes to thank Mr S. Laidlaw of the Institute of Archaeology, University College London, for his support in producing the images for publication; Grupo Nación for allowing Figure 28.1 to be used in this publication and Mr D. Delgado for his help in obtaining the permit. Finally, my thanks to Dr D. Congram for his comments on academic literature relating to Costa Rica and to Mr J. Monge-Nájera for guidance on coyote studies within Costa Rica.

References

Barron, K. 2013. *Costa Rica's Vultures....so Prevalent They Could be the National Bird!* Available at: http://eyeoncostarica.blogspot.co.uk/2013/01/costa-ricas-vultures-so-prevalent-they.html (last accessed 29 April 2013).

BBC. 2012. *Costa Rican Police Find Remains Allegedly Belonging to Missing Mexican Reporter*. Available at: http://www.accessmylibrary.com/article-1G1-307246544/costa-rican-police-find.html (last accessed 8 May 2013).

Bekoff, M. and Wells, M. 1986. Social ecology and behaviour of coyotes. *Advances in the Study of Behavior* 16, 251–325.

Bravo, J. 2014. Cocodrilos despedazan a peón nicaragüense en Costa Rica. *Hoy Diario*. Available at: http://www.hoy.com.ni/2014/05/01/cocodrilos-despedazan-a-peon-nicaraguense-en-costa-rica/ (last accessed 11 December 2014).

Cabezas, Y. 2013. Perro adiestrado ayudó a encontrar víctimas de deslizamiento. Available at: http://www.crhoy.com/perro-adiestrado-ayudo-a-encontrar-victimas-de-deslizamiento/ (last accessed 3 September 2014).

Chávez, K. and Delgado, D. 2012. Hallado cuerpo con ropa igual a la de enfermero desaparecido. *La Nación*. Available at: http://www.nacion.com/2012-10-22/Sucesos/hallado-cuerpo-con-ropa-igual-a-la-de-enfermero-desaparecido.aspx (last accessed 29 April 2013).

Collins, C., Balardini, L. and Burt, J. 2013. Mapping perpetrator prosecutions in Latin America. *The International Journal of Transitional Justice* 7, 8–28.

Congram, D. 2008. A clandestine burial in Costa Rica: prospection and excavation. *Journal of Forensic Sciences* 53, 793–796.

Congram, D. and Fernández, A. 2006. A. Introducción a la antropología y arqueología forense. *Cuadernos de Antropología* 16, 47–57.

Coutiño Molina, J. and Enríquez Rocha, P. 2009. Zopilotes y cóndores de América. *Ecofronteras* 37, 22–25. Available at: http://www.ecosur.mx/ecofronteras/ecofrontera/ecofront37/apuertasabiertas.pdf (last accessed 25 April 2013).

Delgado, D. 2012. Cuerpo hallado en el Zurquí es de enfermero. *La Nación*, 22 October 2012. Available at: http://www.nacion.com/2012-10-22/Sucesos/cuerpo-hallado-en-el-zurqui-es-de-enfermero.aspx (last accessed 1 May 2013).

Delgado, D. 2013a. Roxana Ferllini: 'No ha habido voluntad para promover antropología forense'. *La Nación*, 21 January 2013. Available at: http://www.nacion.com/2013-01-21/Sucesos/Roxana-Ferllini---No-ha-habido-voluntad-para-promover-Antropologia-Forense-.aspx (last accessed 16 April 2013).

Delgado, D. 2013b. Seis de cada 10 osamentas se vuelven un enigma para el OIJ. *La Nación*, 20 January 2013. Available at: http://www.nacion.com/2013-01-20/Sucesos/seis-de-cada-10-osamentas-se-vuelven--un-enigma-para-el-oij.aspx (last accessed 16 April 2013).

Delgado, D. 2014. Hallan restos óseos y ropa en finca de desaparecido. *La Nación*. Available at: http://www.nacion.com/sucesos/crimenes-asaltos/Hallan-restos-oseos-finca-desaparecido_0_1439256102.html (last accessed 10 December 2014).

Dudley, S. 2011. Central America besieged: cartels and Maras country threat analysis. *Small Wars and Insurgencies* 22, 890–913.

Ferllini, R. in press. *Técnicas de Arqueología Forense*. San José, Editorial Universidad Estatal a Distancia.

Ferllini, R. 1993. *Principios de Arqueología Forense*. San José, Editorial Universidad Estatal a Distancia.

Fuerza Pública de Costa Rica. 2013. Available at: http://www.fuerzapublica.go.cr/funciones/ (last accessed 29 April 2013).

Garrido Varas, C. and Intriago Leiva, M. 2012. Managing commingled remains from mass graves: considerations, implications and recommendations from a human rights case in Chile. *Forensic Science International* 219, e19–e24.

Gómez Lopez, A. and Patiño Umaña, A. 2007. Who is missing? Problems in the application of forensic archaeology and anthropology in Colombia's conflict. In R. Ferllini, (ed.), *Forensic Archaeology and Human Rights Violations*, 170–204. Springfield, Charles C. Thomas.

Haglund, W. 1997. Dogs and coyotes: postmortem involvement with human remains. In W. D. Haglund and N. H. Sorg (eds.), *Forensic Taphonomy: The Postmortem Fate of Human Remains*, 367–381. Boca Raton, CRC Press.

Hidalgo Mihart, M., Cantú Salazar, L., González Romero, A. and López González, C. 2004. Historical and present distribution of coyote (*Canis latrans*) in Mexico and Central America. *Journal of Biogeography* 31, 2025–2038.

Holdridge, L. 1967. *Life Zone Ecology*. Revised Edition. San José: Tropical Science Center. Available at: http://cct.or.cr/publicaciones/Life-Zone-Ecology.pdf (last accessed 24 April 2013).

Huhn, S. 2009. *Contested Cornerstones of Nonviolent National Self-Perception in Costa Rica: A Historical Approach*. German Institute of global and area studies working papers 101. Available at: http://www.giga-hamburg.de/workingpapers (last accessed 11 April 2013).

INBIO (Instituto Nacional de Biodiversidad). 2014a. *Biodiversity of costa Rica*. Available at: http://atta2.inbio.ac.cr/neoportal-web (last accessed 11 December 2014).

INBIO (Instituto Nacional de Biodiversidad). 2014b. *Canis latrans*. Available at: http://atta2.inbio.ac.cr/neoportal-web/species/Canis%20latrans (last accessed 11 December 2014).

INBIO (Instituto Nacional de Biodiversidad). 2014c. *American vultures*. Available at: http://atta2.inbio.ac.cr/neoportal-web/groupNav?gni=770 (last accessed 11 December 2014).

Isaacs, A. 2010. At war with the past? The politics of truth seeking in Guatemala. *The International Journal of Transitional Justice* 4, 251–274.

Jirón, L. and Catín, V. 1981. Insect succession in the decomposition of a mammal in Costa Rica. *New York Entomological Society* 89, 158–65.

Joyce, C. and Stover, E. 1992. *The Stories Bones Tell: Witnesses from the Grave*. New York, Ballentine Books.

Juhl, K. and Olsen, O. 2006. Societal safety, archaeology and the investigation of contemporary mass graves. *Journal of Genocide Research* 8, 411–435.

Kalacska, M. and Bell, L. 2006. Remote sensing as a tool for the detection of clandestine mass graves. *Canadian Society of Forensic Science Journal* 39, 1–13.

Kalacska, M., Bell, L., Sanchez-Azofeifa, A. and Caelli, T. 2009. The application of remote sensing for detecting mass graves: an experimental animal case study from Costa Rica. *Journal of Forensic Sciences* 54, 159–166.

Kohlmann, B., Roderus, D., Elle, O., Solís, A., Soto, X. and Russo, R. 2010. Biodiversity conservation in Costa Rica: a correspondence analysis between identified biodiversity hotspots (Araceae, Arecaceae, Bromeliaceae, and Scarabaeinae) and conservation priority life zones. *Revista Mexicana de Biodiversidad* 81, 511–559. Available at: http://scielo.unam.mx/pdf/rmbiodiv/v81n2/v81n2a23.pdf (last accessed 17 April 2013).

La Jornada. 2011. *Se Triplicaron Asesinatos a Manos de Sicarios en Costa Rica*. Available at: http://www.lajornadanet.com/diario/archivo/2011/septiembre/2/9.php (last accessed 18 March 2013).

Laska, M. 1997. Structure of understory shrub assemblages in secondary and old growth tropical wet forests. Costa Rica. *Biotropica* 29, 29–37.

Monge Nájera, J. and Morera Brenes, B. 1986. La dispersión del coyote (*Canis latrans*) y la evidencia de los antiguos cronistas. *Brenesia* 25–26, 251–260 Available at: http://www.tropinature.com/cvitjmn/publications/artcient/coyotes/dispersion.pdf (last accessed 25 April 2013).

Morse, D., Crusoe, D. and Smith, H. 1976. Forensic archaeology. *Journal of Forensic Sciences* 21, 323–323.

Morse, D., Duncan , J. and Stoutamire, J. (eds.) 1983. *Handbook of Forensic Archaeology and Anthropology*. Tallahassee, Florida State University Foundation.

Pape, T. no date. *Familia Calliphotidae*. Available at: http://www.inbio.ac.cr/papers/insectoscr/Texto374.html (last accessed 17 April 2013).

Parrales, F. 2012. Policía halla saco con huesos humanos. *La Nación*. Available at: http://www.nacion.com/sucesos/Policia-halla-saco-huesos-humanos_0_1276472382.html (last accessed 11 December 2014).

Red Hemisférica de Intercambio de Información para la Asistencia Mutua en Materia Penal y Extradición. 2013. Available at: http://www.oas.org/juridico/mla/sp/cri/sp_cri-int-text-loij.html (last accessed 18 March 2013).

Rodríguez, J. and Chinchilla, F. 1996. Lista de mamíferos de Costa Rica. *Revista de Biología Tropical* 44, 877–890.

Ross, A. and Cunningham, S. 2011. Time-since-death and bone weathering in a tropical environment. *Forensic Science International* 204, 126–133.

Scott, D. 2001. Firearms identification in support of identifying a mass execution at El Mozote, El Salvador. *Historical Archaeology* 35, 79–86.

Segura, J. 2012. *Autoridades Hayan cuerpo de dombre desaparecido en Bagaces. La Nación*. Available at: http://www.nacion.com/2012-04-05/Sucesos/Autoridades-hallan-cuerpo-de-hombre-desaparecido-en-Bagaces.aspx (last accessed 10 April 2013).

Solís, M. 2007–2008. El 48 como desborde trágico. *Anuario de Estudios Centroamericanos* 33–34, 261–295.

Turhon, M. 1997. The utilization of faunal evidence in the recovery of human remains. In W. D. Haglund and M. H. Sorg (eds.), *Forensic Taphonomy: The Postmortem Fate of Human Remains*, 395–404. Boca Raton, CRC Press.

Vargas Fonseca, J. 1999. Distribución y Morfología de Adultos e Inmaduros de Moscas Califóridas (Diptera: Calliphoridae) de Importancia Forense en Costa Rica. Unpublished Licenciatura thesis, University of Costa Rica. Available at: http://www.libreroonline.com/costa-rica/libros/17971/vargas-fonsecajohn-f/distribucion-y-morfologia-de-adultos-e-inmaduros-demoscas-califoridas-diptera-calliphoridae-de-.html (last accessed 13 May 2013).

Vargas Sanabria, M., Solano Calderón, L. and Bonilla Montero, R. 2009. Análisis médico legal de los homicidios en Costa Rica en el 2008. *Medicina Legal de Costa Rica* 26, 7–27.

Villalobos, G. 2013. *En Detalle la Guerra Civil de 1948: Una Síntesis*. Museo Nacional de Costa Rica Boletín Electrónico 6. Available at: http://www.museocostarica.go.cr/es_cr/en-detalle/la-guerra-civil-de-1948-una-s-ntesis.html?Itemid=115 (last accessed 16 April 2013).

CHAPTER 29

Forensic archaeology in Mexico: the intermittent and unfinished application of the forensic archaeological techniques and methods

Carlos Jácome Hernández[1] and Lilia Escorcia Hernández[2]

[1] *Department of Sociology and Anthropology, University of Concepcion, Concepcion, Chile*

[2] *Instituto de Investigaciones Antropológicas, Circuito exterior s/n, Ciudad Universitaria, Coyoacan, Mexico*

Introduction

To talk about forensic archaeology and its application in Mexico really means to talk about a concept which is not well understood and which requires clarification. Although much has been published worldwide on forensic anthropology, the publications arising from Mexico are limited. The media has certainly raised an interest in this latter subject and forensic science in general. This is not quite the case for forensic archaeology, although there is a misconception which assumes that when forensic anthropology is spoken about, this also includes archaeology. This should not be the case. On the website of the *American Board of Forensic Anthropology* it can be read that 'forensic anthropology is the application of the science of physical or biological anthropology to the legal process', and the quote ends saying that 'physical or biological anthropologists who specialise in forensics primarily focus their studies on the human skeleton'.[1] This simply reflects that when we talk about forensic anthropology it is not in any way the same as talking about forensic archaeology. This distinction is necessary since in this chapter we address forensic archaeology and in particular its use in Mexico.

In Mexico, archaeology is a discipline that falls under the umbrella of general anthropology. Archaeology seeks to understand and explain humanity through its material culture. Everything that leaves a trace of its past, organic or inorganic, is an object of study through archaeology. In the international context today, forensic archaeology is defined, according to Hunter (1996, in Dupras et al. 2006, 3), as 'the application of archaeological theory and methods to crime scene investigation and recovery'. Dupras et al. (2006, 3) define this further by citing Dirkmaat and Adovasio (1997), who define the field as 'data collection activities carried out during the field recovery aspect of the entire discipline of forensic anthropology'. As can be read, forensic archaeology in the eyes of these specialists is well defined or constrained only to the site of excavation or exhumation at the crime scene, ignoring the potential it has in the laboratory or post-excavation phase with regard to the reconstruction of the events leading to that deposition by examining contexts (stratigraphy), artefacts and their interaction with the environment.

In the case of Mexican archaeology, the earlier-mentioned concept is very limited and leaves aside the important aspect of forensic or legal archaeology with regard to protecting the heritage on which Mexican archaeologists have been working and developing in recent years. Therefore, prior to dwelling on the current status of forensic archaeology in Mexico, it is necessary to have a better understanding to take into account the concept of forensic science in its widest sense; according to *Forensic Science: An Illustrated Dictionary* (Brenner 2004, 120), forensic science is 'the application of scientific facts to legal problems. The field of science that is used in the judicial process. Some are derived from the physical, medical, and dental sciences, and the best-qualified workers specialise in the court-oriented aspects of each discipline'. Thus, following this definition of forensic science, we conclude that forensic archaeology is the application of the knowledge, theory and methods of archaeology used to solve problems which are of judicial interest. With this definition of archaeology used to address judicial problems, we can now proceed to present forensic archaeology in Mexico in a more complete way.

---

[1] Available at http://www.theabfa.org/ (last accessed 30 March 2014).

Forensic Archaeology: A Global Perspective, First Edition. Edited by W.J. Mike Groen, Nicholas Márquez-Grant and Robert C. Janaway.

Two types of criminal investigation in which archaeology is used

In Mexico, the involvement of archaeologists in legal cases is not limited to the recent involvement in searching and excavating clandestine graves. There is another area which has a history of more than four decades in Mexico; since this is not well recognised, or is poorly recognised, this will be outlined here prior to dwelling on the more recent work on clandestine graves.

Mexican archaeology and the protection of the national cultural heritage

The use of archaeology in criminal investigation can first of all include the protection of the cultural heritage, taking as a basis a series of national and international decrees or laws on the protection of archaeological and historical sites, artistic monuments, and so on.[2] Mexico has a great cultural heritage and Mexican archaeologists as professionals dedicate themselves to the study and scientific conservation of their heritage, but are also involved in its legal protection. The archaeologist is called upon at times to provide an opinion in cases of robbery, destruction, fraud and illegal trafficking of movable and immovable cultural heritage objects. Such a task falls under the current Federal Laws. Within the *Law of Monuments* of 1972[3] is stated not only the way in which ancient monuments and artefacts have to be studied, recorded and reported, but also rules regarding any damage or illegal activities to which national monuments may be subject and the penalties or punishment for perpetrators. Within this legal framework, the National Institute for Anthropology and History (*Instituto Nacional de Antropología e Historia* – INAH) has positively intervened at the federal or state level on cases of infraction of the laws. Therefore, archaeologists on many occasions have appeared in the 'forensic context' as experts to assist the judicial system with any of these issues of protection of the cultural heritage. With this in mind, Mexican archaeology has assisted the courts since the beginning of these legal bases of protection of the cultural heritage (Cottom 2001; Gertz 1976, 1980; González Oropeza 1980; López Wario 1996, 2005; López Zamarripa 2000, 2003; Lorenzo 1998; Paredes 2007). The archaeologist is thus requested to assist the judicial system when it is necessary to assess damage, whether intentional or unintentional, to an archaeological site, or when it is necessary to determine whether an artefact is authentic or whether it is a modern imitation. The archaeologist is also called upon to establish the origin of archaeological artefacts which exist outside the nation (García 1996; Gertz 1996; Nalda 1996). In fewer cases, archaeologists have been called upon to confirm whether an archaeological site really exists in a particular location and the extent of its boundaries.

Mexican archaeology in the resolution of criminal cases, in particular regarding clandestine graves

To place forensic archaeology into context in Mexico it is necessary to talk about the beginnings of forensic anthropology, since although these are different areas of specialism, as is also highlighted later, their origins fall under the umbrella in general terms of anthropology. In Mexico, the formation of these specialisms has mainly followed the North American tradition where anthropology is generally taught including social, cultural and biological aspects[4]. Within these general anthropology degrees in Mexico, physical anthropology as well as archaeology are delivered over a minimum of eight semesters at the undergraduate level. This significant input of both these disciplines in the undergraduate degree is to allow students to eventually specialise in one of the disciplines of anthropology. Unlike in other countries, this means that students will graduate not with a degree in general anthropology but with a specific degree based on the subject they have specialised in. The way the system works also means that those who specialise as archaeologists will have obtained a basic knowledge of physical anthropology (and vice versa, physical anthropologists will have been taught some archaeology). The options of forensic archaeology or forensic anthropology cannot be taken in any university. However, a number of optional papers or modules are available on forensic science and these are mentioned here. In order to understand the historical absence and current lack of archaeologists at crime scenes where anthropologists have been and are involved it is necessary to provide a historical overview.

To start talking about forensic anthropology in Mexico it is necessary to refer back to the 19th century, when there were a number of scientific publications in Europe

[2]For example, Constitución Política de los Estados Unidos Mexicanos, La Ley Orgánica de la Administración Pública Federal de 1976, la Ley Federal sobre Monumentos y Zonas Arqueológicas, Artísticos e Históricos de 1972, el Registro Público de Monumentos y Zonas Arqueológicas, el Código Penal Federal vigente, el Código Federal de Procedimientos Penales and in particular Chapter IV (Aguirre 1980; González 1980; Litvak 1980; Matos 1980; Olivé 1980; Sánchez-Cordero 1980; Valdés 1982; Valencia 1980; Williams 1980).

[3]*Ley Federal sobre Monumentos y Zonas Arqueológicos, Artísticos e Históricos de México de 1972*, which belongs to the *Instituto Nacional de Antropología e Historia* (INAH).

[4]In Mexico there is only one university that teaches physical anthropology at an undergraduate level, whilst archaeology is taught at a number of universities: *Escuela Nacional de Antropología e Historia, Universidad Autónoma de Yucatán, Universidad Veracruzana, Universidad Autónoma de Zacatecas, Universidad Autónoma de San Luis Potosí, Universidad Autónoma del Estado de México* and *Universidad de las Américas.*

and a positive approach to research; particularly relevant were studies on criminology by Italian criminologist Dr Cesare Lombroso. Amongst the Mexican scientists at the time were Dr Francisco Martínez Baca (Lagunas 2006; Lagunas and Reyes 2009), especially with the work he undertook with Dr Manuel Vergara. Dr Martínez Baca was a military physician who was assigned to the penitentiary of the state of Puebla, *c.*1891. There he founded the first laboratory of criminal (forensic) anthropology and the first cranial reference collection in the country. The skeletal specimens, mainly skulls, were of the prisoners who had died there and it meant therefore that apart from the anatomical study of the skulls, there was information regarding the social, cultural and criminal background of each individual. The data was published in 1892 in *Estudios de Antropología Criminal* (Studies in Criminal Anthropology), which was positively acknowledged by Dr Cesare Lombroso and, through his influence, translated into Italian. In 1900 Dr Martínez Baca was made director of the penitentiary of Mexico City, which also had a department of physical anthropology and a cranial collection which today is curated at the INAH. He also undertook research on tattoos and on any link between the physical and biological characteristics of individuals and their social behaviour, therefore attempting to understand the criminal phenomenon from a biosocial perspective. Lagunas and Reyes (2009) remind us of other scientists of the time, one of whom was Dr Fernández Ortigosa, who published his work *Identificación Científica de los Reos* (Scientific Identification of Criminals) in 1892 on the scientific identification of prisoners.

Since the 1940s a number of physical anthropologists have worked on the identification of human remains and the study of skeletal collections. Such scientists include Professor Javier Romero Molina, Dr Eusebio Dávalos, Professor Felipe Montemayor García, anthropologist Anselmo Marino and Dr Carlos Serrano (Lagunas and Reyes 2009). However, it was not until the 1970s that forensic anthropology was recognised more formally thanks to Dr Arturo Romano Pacheco and his work on the identification of individuals from their skulls. Partly influenced by his work, physical anthropology was admitted into criminalistics in 1975 (Jáen et al. 1998; Lagunas and Reyes 2009). Dr Romano Pacheco actually makes reference, however, to an earlier work which was influential in physical anthropology in Mexico prior to 1975; this was the work undertaken by Drs Luis Alberto Vargas and Mario Alva Rodríguez (Talavera and Lara 2007). These experts worked on the radiographical superimposition of the skull in a criminal context and their results were published in the Mexican journal *Criminalia* in 1973 (Lagunas and Reyes 2009). Other physical anthropologists involved in the identification and research of human remains in Mexico include Dr Luis Alberto Vargas, anthropologist José María Luján, Dr Zaid Lagunas, anthropologist María Elena Salas, Dr Carlos Serrano, Dr María Villanueva and a large number of other anthropologists working in forensic but also in historical contexts such as the identification of Moctezuma II (*c.*1466–1520) and Cuauhtémoc (*c.*1495–1525), Aztec rulers of Tenochtitlan, as well as Sor Juna Inés de la Cruz (1651–1695), a Hieronymite nun and poet (Lagunas and Reyes 2009). The latter, although historical cases, have aided the promotion of the use of physical anthropology and raised the reputation of our national anthropologists.

In recent years the participation of forensic anthropologists has increased. On the one hand there are the physical anthropologists who have dedicated their efforts to developing methods of identification for the Mexican population today. On the other hand, there are those educating and training as forensic anthropologists and those who work in medico-legal or forensic institutions throughout the country. Although the number of forensic anthropologists is relatively low, there are a number working in the Attorney's Office (*Procuradurías Generales de Justicia*) in the states of Guerrero, Morelos, Chihuahua, Oaxaca, Michoacán, Campeche, Estado de México and Distrito Federal. Of these, it is the *Procuraduría General de Justicia* of the state of Chihuahua which has the most specialists, with a total of six forensic anthropologists to date. At the federal level, the *Procuraduría General de la República* (PGR) has only one specialist with a background in physical anthropology, Ms Yadira Reyna, although within the forensic anthropology team there are specialists in other areas of identification of human remains. All these forensic anthropologists undertake the task of identifying victims as well as the search, recording, excavation and recovery at the scene, that is, forensic archaeology. In the best of cases, the archaeological experience of these teams has been obtained through courses specifically on archaeology, which is important as it results in them being qualified to act as archaeologists and to be present in all forensic cases involving an element of search, excavation, recovery and recording not only of the human remains but also of any associated material or artefacts, amongst the other tasks undertaken by the professional archaeologist (e.g. Haglund 2001). The participation of archaeologists is especially significant bearing in mind that in Mexico as a result of organised drug crime there have been more than 2000 clandestine mass graves in the last 7 years.[5] Families of the

[5]Estimated number based on the field study by journalist Roberto Meléndez and published on 23 August 2013. For more information, see http://www.unomasuno.com.mx/2013/08/23/en-los-ultimos-siete-anos-mas-de-dos-mil-fosas-clandestinas/ (last accessed August 2013).

disappeared and human rights organisations suggest that this number could be underestimated and that there are many more clandestine graves throughout the country's 32 federal entities. One example of this situation is the municipality of San Fernando, in the state of Tamaulipas, northeast Mexico, where a number of massacres relating to the Mexican drug war have taken place. In 2011 there was the mass murder of 193 people, who were then buried in over 40 clandestine graves.[6] In this case, unfortunately, as in many others, no professional or qualified archaeologist participated in the search, excavation or recovery of the bodies.

In the academic sphere in the speciality of forensic anthropology there are different institutions where physical anthropologists train new generations of scientists and undertake research on methods to identify individuals in the diverse Mexican populations. Amongst these institutions we include the Institute for Anthropological Research (*Instituto de Investigaciones Antropológicas* – IIA), the Faculty of Medicine of the National Autonomous University of Mexico (*Universidad Autónoma Nacional de México* – UNAM), the National School of Anthropology and History (*Escuela Nacional de Antropología e Historia* – ENAH), the Department of Physical Anthropology (*Dirección de Antropología Física* – DAF) and several other institutions such as the INAH and the Autonomous University of Yucatán (*Universidad Autónoma de Yucatán* – UADY). Apart from the physical anthropologists at these institutions, two physical anthropologists who work within forensic science are based outside Mexico: one of them at the University of California, US, and the other at the University of Concepción (*Universidad de Concepción*), Chile. In these universities there is no specialism in the subject of forensic archaeology as such, but, nevertheless, there are a number of short courses on the use of archaeology in forensic contexts and the techniques employed in criminal investigation.

With regard to reviewing the published literature on forensic archaeology, this is unfortunately very scarce and the published works have been mainly written by anthropologists Mr Arturo Talavera and Mr Israel Lara and archaeologist Mr Juan Martín Rojas (Talavera and Martín Rojas 2006). In the 1990s, amongst the efforts of academia to promote forensic anthropology as well as forensic archaeology, a Bioarchaeology Team (*Equipo de Bioarqueología*) was created at the Department of Physical Anthropology (INAH). This was founded in 1996 by Mr Arturo Talavera and Mr Martín Rojas; a number of dissertations were produced in this area of forensic archaeology (Jácome 2000, 2007).

In the judicial context, the current cases require the need to not only identify the victims from a forensic anthropological point of view, but also apply archaeology to the increasing discoveries of human remains in clandestine graves, as well as in other locations where there are surface depositions, since the contextual information is, as always, so important. One of the most significant examples from the 1990s is the hundreds of assassinated women in Ciudad Juárez (Álvarez 2003). In addition, at the end of the 1990s a number of investigations were opened when secret files became declassified with regard to past political crimes by the authorities and the state itself, known as the Dirty Waror *Guerra Sucía* (1965–1982). This latter resulted in the need to locate and excavate clandestine graves of victims who died as a result of the internal war between the governing party and other groups commencing in the 1960s, with a peak in the 1970s and continuing into the 1980s. In fact, one of the first cases in which an archaeologist was involved in the tasks of search and recovery took place in 2003, with the exhumation of Professor Lucio Cabañas Barrientos, commander of the *guerrilla* and leader of the Party for the Poor (*Partido de los Pobres*). In this case, the authors of this chapter (CJE, LEH), who have participated as expert witnesses (*peritos*) since 2000, were involved in the search on behalf of the relatives of the deceased Professor Cabañas Barrientos. In this case as in others, therefore, archaeological expertise has significantly contributed to solving some judicial issues where there is an element of search, location, recording, excavation and recovery as well as other analyses.

Today, forensic archaeology is applied by those expert witnesses (*peritos*) with a background in physical anthropology in each of the state and federal Attorney's Office.[7] We understand that today there are two archaeologists who work directly in this context; one works for

[6]Statements made on 7 June 2011, in a press conference by the then Attorney General of the Republic (*Procuradora de la República*), Marisela Morales. For more information, see http://www.milenio.com/cdb/doc/noticias2011/a83771a907f9b3b0aaf6153c163b67ca (last accessed August 2013).

[7]Scientific analysis of evidence is meant to be part of the responsibilities of the forensic scientist or expert witness, depending on their field of expertise, all of it under the command of the Public Prosecution Office (*Ministerio Público*) (e.g. the Constitution of the United Mexican States, Articles 20, 21 and 102; Federal Code of Criminal Procedures Art. 1 123, 128, 136, 141, 168 bis, 208, 219, 220 to 239, 324 Quintus). Such studies are carried out by the official, partly depending on the judicial circuit in which each case is managed. In local cases it will be the Expert Witness Services of the General Attorney of each state of Mexico; in the larger judicial circuit it will be the General Attorney's Office in the Federative field (*Procuraduría General de la República*). Non-official defenders, victims or accusers are allowed to present evidence and expert witness testimony from non-official expert witnesses belonging to various scientific institutions charged with the legal task at the time.

the Attorney General of Chihuahua (*Procuraduría General de Justicia de Chihuahua*) and the other for the Attorney General of the state of Guanajuato (*Procuraduría General de Justicia del Estado de Guanajuato*), although another three had worked previously in the state of Chihuahua. All of these archaeologists, in their role as expert witnesses, have to provide their expert inputs into the case, go into the field, write reports and provide statements when required. With regard to external experts for these judicial governmental institutions, we know of only two professional archaeologists, Mr Arturo Talavera and the first author, Dr Carlos Jácome. These two experts have worked in forensic cases on behalf of the attorneys (*procuradurías*) or as experts on behalf of Human Rights organisations.

Discussion

The current situation is that the institutions which are in charge of criminal investigation with regard to the search, recording, exhumation and recovery of human remains which have been found either buried or on the surface, and the gathering of other evidence related to a deposition site, are largely staffed by people who are not qualified or, in the best case, have a very basic knowledge of forensic anthropology and archaeology. As we have seen earlier, there are only a few general Attorney Offices that have (forensic) physical anthropologists and an even lesser number who have personnel formally qualified in archaeology and who participate in forensic casework.

In this chapter we prefer not to address the criticisms that can be raised with regard to the lack or misuse of archaeological methods and techniques by people who are not qualified or have received very little professional training. We prefer to talk about the benefits that can be brought by professional archaeologists to criminal investigation; by professionals we mean those trained and experienced in the fields of physical anthropology and archaeology and not crime scene investigators or police officers who apply archaeological methods without the necessary experience or qualifications. As a reminder, professional archaeologists can bring a more reliable analysis and interpretation to the issues surrounding the burial context and are better prepared to address specific questions asked during the investigation, in particular with reference to the different layers or contexts. However, the archaeologist must work together with a wider investigation team including forensic anthropologists, other forensic scientists and crime scene investigators in order to construct the sequence of events leading to burial or deposition. Since the archaeologist has the theoretical and practical knowledge to interpret stratigraphy and the material found within the different layers or contexts, he/she can come up with some hypotheses as to the formation of a scenario or scene (context). One problem, however, is that the level of organised crime and other forms of crime in Mexico is overwhelming compared to the level of response or resources of the federal institutions. In the archaeological context, assassinations and the volume of discovered clandestine graves and of human remains in other types of deposition are higher in number than the resources available for search, location, excavation and recovery.

The effort required and challenges faced when promoting the use of archaeology in criminal investigation teams does not only lie with the authorities, but also lies with physical anthropologists, the upcoming archaeologists from the academic field and the professional archaeologists themselves, who in many cases are not interested in working in forensic contexts. The forensic archaeologist also has a responsibility to be up-to-date within the field and to provide and propose the best advice regarding the most effective methods and techniques for a particular case. The professional archaeologist also faces the challenge of getting the right balance between the correct recording procedures (both archaeological and forensic) within the time constraints of a criminal investigation.

Certainly, thanks to the use of archaeology in forensic contexts, we have obtained information about the different types of clandestine graves made by the different drug cartels; these range from a variety of graves to the manner of depositing human remains, including dismemberment, feeding human remains to animals and chemically destroying human remains. With the different types of contexts or scenarios, the archaeologist also needs to work in an office and laboratory so he/she can independently enable a reconstruction of the events leading to the deposition site by archaeological analysis of any artefacts or associated materials within the

On 9 March 2012, the Scientific Investigation Division of the Federal Police, a suboffice of the Ministry for the Public Security, was inaugurated, which also supports scientific investigation for the General Attorney's Office in the Federative field (e.g. Regulations of the Law of the Federal Police). This division has several scientific areas and laboratories with the latest technology, including a department of forensic anthropology and forensic reconstruction, with a team of two physical anthropologists and which is chaired by the social anthropologist Dr Hugo Soto Escutia. However, sustained political conflicts in the legal intricacies of the institution, including the absence of certified laboratories, have stopped its operation and performance (e.g. Castillo García 2011).

context (stratigraphy) in which they were found. Because of the nature of drug crime in Mexico in particular, it seems that archaeology should have a duty to help in the forensic field. Communication with other scientists can only help promote the use of archaeology and although archaeologists are not being used at present this also should be viewed as positive for future archaeologists, who can work on promoting the discipline in criminal investigation.

With this demand in mind, there have been advances in the training of archaeologists. Although this subject of education was touched upon earlier, it is worth mentioning a few promising advances. The expert witness diploma in Anthropological Science (*Diplomado Peritaje en Ciencias Antropológicas*) delivered by INAH, covering topics in forensic anthropology, criminological anthropology, forensic linguistics and forensic archaeology (with regard to heritage) has existed since 2004. Training in the search and recovery of either buried or unburied human remains has been taught since 1998 in the diploma on Forensic Anthropology (*Diplomado en Antropología Forense*), also at INAH. More recently, 2013 saw the degree of Forensic Sciences at the Faculty of Medicine at the National Autonomous University of Mexico (UNAM). For many years this institution has delivered workshops and organised seminars and conferences on the use of forensic anthropology and archaeology. Similar programmes and workshops have also been delivered at the National School of Anthropology and History (ENAH) where a post degree Diploma in the speciality of forensic anthropology has been opened in this early August 2014. All these developments partly stem from the gap or niche in higher education, which until now has largely been covered by schools or academies which are not accredited or have teaching staff with no forensic experience. However, the positive outcome of this is that the large institutions have now realised that there is a demand and popularity for learning these forensic disciplines. These different courses and teaching institutions, however, have provided training which appears to be more at an individual level and not within an established forensic teaching and research academy. This means though that in Mexico there are no standard protocols at present for forensic archaeology. Neither do we have a national body for accreditation to guarantee the highest standards of professionalism in forensic anthropology and archaeology.

Conclusion

Through this chapter we have contextualised the use of forensic archaeology in the judicial scene in Mexico, with regard to heritage cases and also regarding homicides or suspicious deaths. We as authors have wanted to be honest in the information provided and also to respect the discipline as much as possible when mentioning the current status both with the advances and with the delays in forensic archaeology. We have tried to be unbiased and neither emphasise its importance nor criticise it too much. We are in fact at a stage where forensic archaeology has not had the opportunity to flourish, develop and show its true potential. Yet it is also necessary to recognise the work of those who are in the 'front line', using archaeology and promoting it within the difficult and challenging world of forensic science. There are only a few forensic archaeologists and anthropologists in Mexico who have been brave enough to work in an environment which is demanding at both a professional and a personal level. Working in Mexico in these forensic situations is dangerous not only for the specialist but also carries a risk to his/her family and circle of friends.

There is a need today to narrow the gap between practitioners and academics in the same field. As stated earlier, the practice of forensic anthropology in Mexico is quite unique and there are at least three streams of work in different fields embraced by anthropology. On the one hand, there are those who are either physical or social anthropologists or archaeologists who work for attorneys; on the other hand, there are those who work as external experts for NGOs or as freelance experts. There are also those based primarily at universities who undertake research regarding new methods and techniques which address some of the problems faced by practitioners. There needs to be more communication and exchange between these three fields as well as an increase in resources to aid communication between those in the front line (practitioners) with the academics. Practitioners could then transmit their needs and issues that the research scientists with their laboratories and resources can perhaps address and develop. If we isolate ourselves from each other, neither physical anthropology nor archaeology will have the impulse needed in the forensic sphere. Society needs the intervention of professional anthropologists and archaeologists committed to solving some of these social issues of crime in Mexico and we have the tradition and capacity to undertake such a task. To conclude, therefore, the necessary means need to be generated to undertake and achieve these aims through a better communication between archaeologists and anthropologists and between practitioners and academics.

References

Álvarez Díaz, J. A. 2003. Lasmuertas de Juárez: bioética, género,poder e injusticia. *Acta Bioethica* 9, 219–228.

Brenner, J. C. 2004. *Forensic Sciences: An Illustrated Dictionary*. Boca Raton, CRC Press.

Cottom, B. 2001. Patrimonio cultural nacional: el marco jurídico y conceptual. *Derecho y Cultura* 79–107.

Dirkmaat, D. C. and J. M. Adovasio. 1997. The role of archaeology in the recovery and interpretation of human remains from an outdoor forensic setting. In W. D. Haglund and M. H. Sorg (eds.), *Forensic Taphonomy: The Postmortem Fate of Human Remains*, 39–64. New York, CRC Press.

Dupras, T. L., Schultz, J. J., Wheeler, S. M. and Williams, L. J. 2006. *Forensic Recovery of Human Remains: Archaeological Approaches*. Boca Raton, CRC Press.

García Bárcena, J. 1996. La autentificación de piezas arqueológicas. *Arqueología Mexicana* 21(IV), 62–67.

Gertz Manero, A. 1976. *La Defensa Jurídica del Patrimonio Cultural*. México, Fondo de Cultura Económica.

Gertz Manero, A. 1980. La defensa jurídica y social del patrimonio cultural. In J. Litvak King, L. González Rodríguez and M. del Refugio González (eds.), *Arqueología y Derecho en México*, 9–18. México, Universidad Nacional Autónoma de México.

Gertz Manero, A. 1996. El saqueo arqueológico. Lento Suicidio. *Arqueología Mexicana* 21(IV), 22–27.

González Oropeza, M. 1980. Aplicabilidad de la legislación federal sobre el patrimonio cultural en la Universidad Nacional Autónoma de México. In J. Litvak King, L. González Rodríguez and M. del Refugio González (eds.), *Arqueología y Derecho en México*, 151–180. México, Universidad Nacional Autónoma de México.

Haglund, W. D. 2001. Archaeology and forensic death investigations. *Historical Archaeology* 35(1), 26–34.

Jáen Esquivel, M. T., López Alonso, S., Márquez Morfín, L. and Hernández Espinosa, P. O. 1998. *Tiempo, Población y Sociedad. Homenaje al Maestro Arturo Romano Pacheco*. México, Instituto Nacional de Antropología e Historia.

Jácome Hernández, C. A. 2000. Arqueologíaforense. Unpublished BSc thesis, Escuela Nacional de Antropología e Historia.

Jácome Hernández, C. A. 2007. Un Equipo de Especialistas en Antropología Forense Como Proyecto de Investigación. Memorias, Reflexiones y Propuestas. Unpublished MSc thesis, Instituto de Investigaciones Antropológicas, UNAM.

Lagunas, Z. 2006. La antropología física forense, una especialidad necesaria. *Ciencia Ergo Sum* 13(2), 211–217.

Lagunas, Z. and Reyes, A. M. 2009. Apuntes para la historia de la antropología física forense en México. *Criminalidad* 51(2), 61–79.

López Wario, L. A. 1996. El patrimonio arqueológico de México. *Arqueología Mexicana* 21(IV), 14–21.

López Zamarripa, N. 2000. *Los Monumentos Históricos Arqueológicos, Patrimonio de la Humanidad en el Derecho Internacional*. México, Editorial Porrúa.

López Zamarripa, N. 2003. *El futuro del Sistema Jurídico Nacional e Internacional del Patrimonio Cultural*. México, Editorial Porrúa.

López Wario, L. A. 2005. *¿Qué es eso de la arqueología de salvamento en México? Resultados de una encuesta y algunas propuestas*. México, Instituto Nacional de Antropología e Historia.

Lorenzo, J. L. 1998. El material arqueológico como propiedad cultural de la nación. Su defensa jurídica y social en el caso de Estados Unidos Mexicanos. In L. Mirambell and J. Litvak (eds.), *La Arqueología y México*. México, Instituto Nacional de Antropología e Historia.

Nalda, E. 1996. Coleccionismo, saqueo y legislación. *Arqueología Mexicana* 21(IV), 48–53.

Paredes Gudiño, B. 2007. La riqueza del patrimonio arqueológico de México en riesgo. In P. Cabello Carro (ed.), *Patrimonio Cultural e Identidad*, 49–57. Madrid, Ministerio de Cultura.

Talavera, A. and Lara, I. 2007. El papel de la antropología forense en la investigación de asesinos seriales. *Diario de Campo* 95, 64–87.

Talavera, A. and Martín Rojas, J. 2006. Actualidades de la arqueología y la antropología física forense, una estrategia interdisciplinaria contra el crimen. *Diario de Campo* 83, 64–87.

Further Reading

Aguirre Valdés, Ó. 1980. Registro público de monumentos y zonas arqueológicas. In J. Litvak King, L. González Rodríguez and M. del Refugio González (eds.), *Arqueología y Derecho en México*, 133–150. México, Universidad Nacional Autónoma de México.

Castillo García, G. 2011. Laboratorios de criminología de la PF carecen de certificación. *La Jornada*, 11 de Mayo de 2013, No. 31. Available at: http://www.jornada.unam.mx/2013/05/11/politica/015n1pol (last accessed December 2013).

Código Federal de Procedimientos Penales. 1934. *Diario Oficial de la Federación*. Published 30 August 1934, México. Last reform published 3 May 2013.

Código Federal Penal. 1931. *Diario Oficial de la Federación*. Published 14 August 1931, México. Last reform published 22 July 2013.

Constitución Política de los Estados Unidos Mexicanos. 1917. *Diario Oficial de la Federación*. Published 5 February 1917, México. Last reform published 27 December 2013.

Del Refugio González, M. 1980. La protección de los bienes arqueológicos en México y su relación con la jurisprudencia. In J. Litvak King, L. González Rodríguez and M. del Refugio González (eds.), *Arqueología y Derecho en México*, 71–82. México, Universidad Nacional Autónoma de México.

Ley Federal Sobre Monumentos y Zonas Arqueológicas, Artísticas e Históricos. 1972. *Diario Oficial de la Federación*. Published 6 May 1972. Last reform published 9 April 2012.

Ley Orgánica de la Administración Pública Federal. 1976. *Diario Oficial de la Federación*. Published 29 December 1976. Last reform published 2 April 2013.

Ley Sobre Protección y Conservación de Monumentos y Bellezas Naturales 1930. Published 31 January 1930.

Ley Sobre Protección y Conservación de Monumentos Arqueológicos e Históricos, Poblaciones Típicas y Lugares de Belleza Natural 1934. Published 19 January 1934.

Litvak King, J. 1980. Algunos conceptos sobre el problema de la acción legal en la arqueología mexicana. In J. Litvak King, L. González Rodríguez and M. del Refugio González (eds.), *Arqueología y Derecho en México*, 47–54. México, Universidad Nacional Autónoma de México.

Matos Moctezuma, E. 1980. Las normas jurídicas y la investigación arqueológica en México. In J. Litvak King, L. González Rodríguez and M. del Refugio González (eds.), *Arqueología y Derecho en México*, 125–132. México, Universidad Nacional Autónoma de México.

Olivé Negrete, J. C. 1980. Reseña histórica del pensamiento legal sobre arqueología. In J. Litvak King, L. González Rodríguez and M. del Refugio González (eds.), *Arqueología y Derecho en México*, 19–46. México, Universidad Nacional Autónoma de México.

Registro Público de Monumentos y Zonas Arqueológicas. 1972. *Instituto Nacional de Antropología e Historia.*

Reglamento de la Ley de la Policía Federal. 2010. *Diario Oficial de la Federación.* Published 17 May 2010. México.

Sánchez-Cordero Dávila, J. A. 1980. La ilicitud de la transmisión de la propiedad de monumentos arqueológicos. In J. Litvak King, L. González Rodríguez and M. del Refugio González (eds.), *Arqueología y Derecho en México,* 55–70. México, Universidad Nacional Autónoma de México.

Valdés Rodríguez, J. J. 1982. *La Protección Jurídica de los Monumentos Arqueológicos e Históricos en México.* México, Instituto Nacional de Antropología e Historia.

Valencia, A. 1980. La coordinación federal en materia de bienes culturales. La nueva legislación. In J. Litvak King, L. González Rodríguez and M. del Refugio González (eds.), *Arqueología y Derecho en México,* 83–92. México, Universidad Nacional Autónoma de México.

Williams García, J. 1980. Los delitos en la ley federal sobre monumentos. In J. Litvak King, L. González Rodríguez and M. del Refugio González (eds.), *Arqueología y Derecho en México,* 93–112. México, Universidad Nacional Autónoma de México.

CHAPTER 30

Forensic scientific practice in Panama

Ann H. Ross[1] and José Vicente Pachar Lucio[2]

[1] *Department of Sociology and Anthropology, NC State University, Raleigh, USA*

[2] *Instituto de Medicina Legal y Ciencias Forenses, Departamento de Patologia Forense, Panama City, Panama*

Introduction

Unlike in the United States and other countries, the police in Panama do not work crime scenes. This is under the mandate of the Public Ministry and the tasks are performed by the Institute of Legal Medicine and Forensic Sciences (*Instituto de Medicina Legal y Ciencias Forenses* – IMLCF) Criminalistics officials. Although needed as a priority, there are no qualified personnel such as archaeologists and forensic anthropologists; there are no training programmes in Panama and there is little interest in studying these fields. In addition, there is no institutional policy to develop areas of forensic science. There have been a few instances where the public prosecutor has recommended employing the services of anthropologists/archaeologists to conduct excavations in cases of clandestine burials, but these recommendations have not been followed through as a result of the lack of funds. The Institute is completely dependent upon government budget allocations and each year there are more funding cuts, as politicians do not consider the development of forensic science to be a priority.

Medico-legal system in Panama

In Panama the fundamental legal entities are the judiciary and the public prosecutor's office or Attorney General's Office (*Órgano Judicial/Ministerio Público*). Prosecutors address the prosecution of legal offences and to accomplish this mission police entities (judicial investigative branches) and scientific experts of the IMLCF are enlisted.

The public prosecutor's office is organised into the district attorney's office and attorneys at the national level. When there is information on the commission of a crime, specifically in cases defined in the penal code as crimes against life and personal integrity, the public prosecutor directs the investigation at the scene as established by the judicial code. The National Police guarantee security at the location and detectives begin the investigation under the direction of the judicial investigative branch. Medico-legal death investigators of the IMLCF are present at the scene, have jurisdiction over the body and are responsible for transporting the body, associated evidence and maintaining the chain of custody as well as the delivery of evidence to the representative of the public prosecutor's office.

Forensic archaeologists and forensic anthropologists are not part of the IMLCF personnel. Panama does not have forensic archaeologists and there are no university programmes or any possibility of training in the country. The first author is the only active forensic anthropologist in the country. Forensic pathologists and rarely more generalised physical anthropologists conduct the tasks of a forensic anthropologist. When skeletal remains, surface or buried, are discovered, it is the forensic physician from the IMLCF (the only certified forensic pathologist in the country is the second author) who, when judicial authorities consider it necessary, attends the scene to coordinate the recovery, proper collection, transport and subsequent analysis in the judicial morgue. Remains less than 20 years old are considered to be of forensic significance; however, no legal provision exists to make this determination. Recovery methods are empirically based and do not follow a standard or systematic approach; they are usually made in hostile environmental conditions such as mangroves, areas of dense tropical vegetation and distant beaches. To further impede recoveries in a harsh environment, the personnel conducting the recoveries are under extreme pressure from officials leading the investigation who do not know or understand the importance of a scientific approach. There are still instances in which the remains are excavated in a haphazard manner, placed in plastic garbage bags and sent to the judicial morgue for study by the coroner or medical examiner without recovery, provenance or scene information and documentation such as photographs (Figure 30.1). Unfortunately, no archaeological techniques or methods are utilised in the recovery of human remains.

Forensic Archaeology: A Global Perspective, First Edition. Edited by W.J. Mike Groen, Nicholas Márquez-Grant and Robert C. Janaway.

Figure 30.1 Photograph adapted from La Prensa depicting the 'excavation' of the remains at Punta Barco.

Once cases are entered into the judicial morgue system, a basic forensic anthropological analysis is conducted by forensic pathologists who have received some training during their academic preparation through the IMLCF and the School of Medicine at the University of Panama, which includes anthropometric analysis. However, radiographic analysis – a standard protocol in most laboratories – is not conducted due to the lack of adequate facilities and equipment.

The number of skeletal cases per year reported in the archives of the judicial morgue is low; many of them remain unidentified as ante-mortem information does not exist in order to make the identification. These (usually traumatic) deaths are thought to be related to human trafficking of individuals illegally making their way to the United States or foreign victims of organised crime.

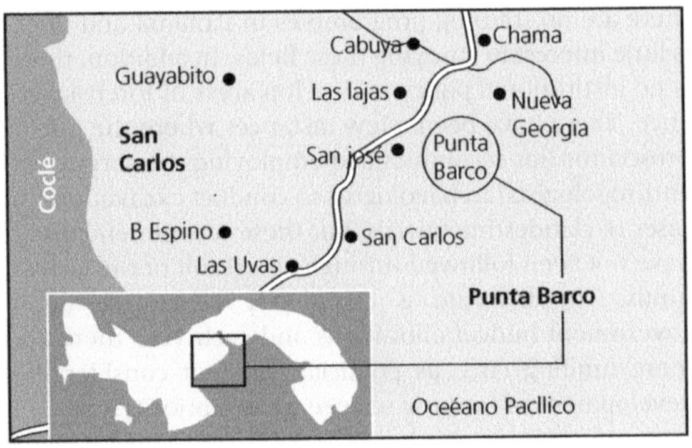

Figure 30.2 Photograph adapted from La Prensa showing the location of the clandestine burial at Punta Barco.

Case example: Punta Barco

In October of 2003, a clandestine burial was accidentally discovered in Punta Barco close to one of Dictator Manuel Noriega's (former military junta leader from the 1980s) enclaves when a containment wall was being constructed in a private residence (Figure 30.2). Although the Panamanian Truth Commission (*La Comisión de la Verdad de Panamá*) had jurisdiction over crimes committed by the military juntas, they were not allowed access to the site. The Judicial Technical Police (*Policía Técnica Judicial* – PTJ) cordoned off the area and proceeded to excavate the site with shovels without following a standard crime scene or forensic archaeological protocol (Marcel Chery 2003, La Prensa, see Figure 1). As a result of this chaotic approach much of the evidence was lost and many of the remains exhibited post-mortem damage. There was no associated evidence such as clothing or personal effects and thus it was impossible to determine the antiquity of the remains or provenance without adequate scene information. Because of the absence of associated evidence and artefacts and poor excavation, a bone sample was sent for radiocarbon testing. The results showed that the sample was dated between 1682 and 1933, with 95.4% confidence interval, and thus the remains were unlikely to be associated with crimes committed by the military regimes of the 1970s or 1980s (Figure 30.3). Furthermore, local indigenous populations were known to have buried their dead on beaches.

Interaction institute of legal medicine – truth commission

Panama's democratic history came to an abrupt halt in 1968 after a coup d'état toppled President Arnulfo Arias 10 days and 11 hours after his administration began. This coup set in motion Panama's 21 years of military

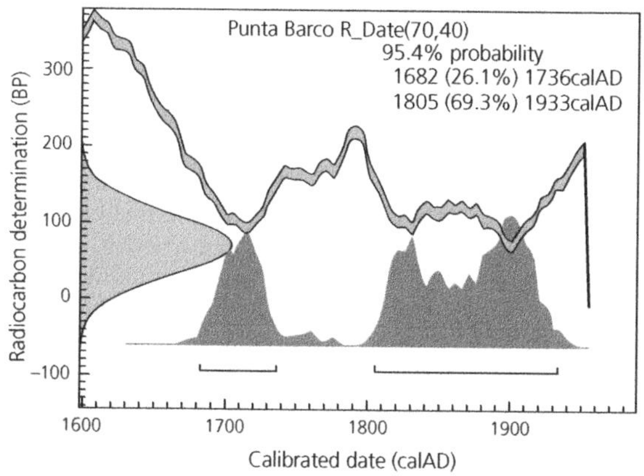

Figure 30.3 Radiocarbon calibrated dates for Punta Barco remains (OxCal, Ramsey 2013).

dictatorship that began with General Omar Torrijos (1968–1981) and continued with General Manuel Noriega (1981–1989). Forced disappearances, torture and arbitrary execution of its victims characterised the military regimes of the 1970s and 1980s (Cotes et al. 2004; Jemmott et al. 2004; Ross et al. 2004; Suarez Silva et al. 2004).

Chronology

At the end of the 1990s interest increased in establishing the actual number of victims of the military dictatorship during the period 1968–1989, which ended with the US military invasion of Panama on 20 December 1989.

In 1999, several clandestine graves were discovered, one of which was later identified as the remains of Heliodoro Portugal. His remains were positively identified via DNA on 21 August 2000. Heliodoro Portugal had been identified as a *leftist* by the military junta and was last seen being forcibly pushed into a car on 14 May 1970 (Cotes et al. 2004; Jemmott et al. 2004; Ross et al. 2004; Suarez Silva et al. 2004). As a result of these findings, the Panamanian Truth Commission was formed on 18 January 2001 by Executive Order issued by the lady President Mireya Moscoso (Suarez Silva et al. 2004). The objective of the Truth Commission as written in the Executive Decree 'is to contribute to the clarification of the truth regarding human rights violations fundamental to life, including the disappearances committed during the Military Regimes that governed Panama beginning in 1968'.[1]

On 22 September 1999 excavations were undertaken in the former military barracks in the capital city of Panama, with assistance from a medical examiner. On 24 September 1999 another three sets of remains were found in the same area. These four cases were analysed at the Institute of Legal Medicine. The excavations were suspended. On 10 December 2000 excavations were restarted on the initiative of the Catholic Church; excavations were carried out by *huaqueros* (looters who plunder archaeological sites for huacas or pre-Columbian artefacts) hired by the Church, and the medical examiner made the anthropometric assessment. Work continued for several months with a few scattered finds. On 18 January 2001 the Truth Commission was formed, as a result of the shortcomings of the Institute of Legal Medicine with regard to scientific experts, equipment and insufficient materials to conduct the investigations. On the same day (18 January 2001) an Executive Decree, N° 2, was issued, establishing the Truth Commission for a period of 6 months, which was later extended until 2002. The mission of the Commission was to establish a complete picture of the disappearances and murders committed by the military dictatorship.

As part of its mandate, it would gather background information that would allow the identification of the victims and establish their whereabouts. It also specified that the Commission could not assume judicial functions typical of the courts, nor infer proceedings pending before them. Thus, the investigations were purely humanitarian in nature and would not result in prosecutorial actions as in other Truth Commissions such as in Chile. Therefore, it could not rule on criminal acts of the perpetrators while investigating the facts. If the Commission came into the possession of information about known criminal acts, they would make the facts available to the Attorney General.

The commissioners were empowered to accept and conduct any investigation they deemed appropriate, including requesting reports, documents or records from authorities and public institutions, and to ensure the confidentiality of sources and the safety of witnesses and informants.

The Commission had the support of several North American and Panamanian anthropologists, who conducted the excavations of over 30 sites, recoveries and analysis of the remains found in several provinces. The Truth Commission created a Department of Anthropology within its organisation. Cultural anthropologists were tasked with the preliminary investigation, which included examining documents, interviewing informants and developing a socio-cultural profile of the victim within the historical context (Almanza et al. 2002, 198). After the initial investigative phase was conducted, an archaeological phase led by Loreto Suarez (a Chilean trained archaeologist working for the Truth

[1]Decreto Ejecutivo, #2, 2001 Por la cual se crea la comisión de la verdad, Ministerio de Gobierno y Justicia. Available at http://www.usip.org/files/resources/Panama-Charter.pdf (last accessed 30 March 2014).

Commission) followed where remains were discovered, recovered and preserved; this was the excavation phase. The identification phase included developing a biological profile of the victim and identification when possible by forensic anthropological and mtDNA analysis (Almanza et al. 2002, 198).

By 18 April 2002, the Truth Commission had amassed enough information to identify 110 persons who had been assassinated and disappeared (Suarez Silva et al. 2004). However, these numbers changed as new information was gathered, including the positive identification of Jerónimo Díaz Lopez, who disappeared in 1985, in June 2003. About 50% of the victims were murdered or disappeared between 1968 and 1972, 20% between 1973 and 1983, 28% between 1984 and 1989 and 2% with no known information (Suarez Silva et al. 2004).

The recovery and identification efforts that yielded the most positive results have been from the island of Coiba. In efforts to locate the remains of Floyd Britton (a student leader), arrested in 1968 and sentenced to the prison in Coiba, others have been inadvertently identified who were not known to have perished there. The remains of Sergeant Sánchez Tenas, who was killed in 1975 at the hands of another member of the military police and whose murder was covered up by the military, were identified via mtDNA analysis while testing the skeletal samples in the hope of finding Floyd. The identification of Jerónimo Díaz Lopez was made via dental comparison and traditional forensic anthropological techniques (e.g. biological profile, dentition). Floyd Britton has yet to be identified (Ross and Broce 2003).

On 18 April 2002 the term of operation of the Truth Commission expired and an Office of *Seguimiento* or continuation was created, which operated until 31 December 2004. Subsequently, all the material gathered was placed in the custody of the Institute of Legal Medicine.

Years later, after the enactment of Law 50 of 13 December 2006, the Institute of Legal Medicine was reorganised into the Institute of Legal Medicine and Forensic Sciences, which includes forensic anthropology as one of its operating units. Later, with the disappearance of the Judicial Technical Police, Forensic Services and Forensic Laboratories became part of the Institute, an operational and organisational model unique in the region that brings together all the technical expert services and scientists at a single institution assigned to the Attorney General.

In search of Floyd Britton – bringing forensic anthropology and archaeology to forensic investigations

Floyd Britton was a *leftist* university student leader who was arrested on 12 October 1968 and was sentenced by the military government of Omar Torrijos (1968–1981) to the penal colony on the island of Coiba on 3 November of the same year. He died in November 1969, allegedly beaten to death by prison guards under the direct order of General Omar Torrijos. His body was flown to Panama City for an autopsy and his death was determined to be from natural causes. Purportedly, his body was then sent back to Coiba and interred at the Marañon Cemetery.

Previous attempts to locate Floyd Britton occurred in May of 1991 and then again in 2001. The first excavation was concentrated in the northeast sector of the cemetery and was conducted by Dr Clyde Snow. New eyewitness testimonies led to another exhumation on 2–3 August 2001 by the Truth Commission and another team of US forensic anthropologists (Drs Frank and Julie Saul and Dr Murray Marks). Skeletal remains were recovered from four burials in the northwest sector of the cemetery. During this phase, however, two of the burials were only partially excavated.

Continued efforts to locate Floyd Britton during a third excavation and exhumation phase took place between 26 February and 6 March 2002 by the first author as Project Director and the Truth Commission. Three burials were identified for excavation from information derived by the Truth Commission from several eyewitness accounts and the remains of the three burials (Ross and Broce 2003).

Excavation protocols

Burials (*tumba*), one and two in the northwest section of the cemetery, were partially excavated in 2001 by another team (Sauls and Marks) and burial three, due south of burials one and two, was undisturbed. Standard excavation protocols were followed. A tree located just south of the cemetery boundary (at GPS coordinates N 07°30.182′, W 081°41.789′) was chosen as the primary datum point. The subdatum (one) point is on the southwest corner of burial one and two is 49.15 m northwest from the primary datum point. Burials one and two consist of an area of 5×6 m, which was subdivided by 1 m^2 (Figure 30.4). Five rows running from west to east were designated 1E–5E. The rows running from north to south were designated 1N–6N. Thus, the 1 m^2 in the southeastern corner was designated 6E1N. Burial three is concentrated in an area measuring 3×2 m and the subdatum (two) is on the southwest corner 35.70 m northwest from the datum point (Figure 30.5). Burial three was also further subdivided into 1-m^2. Burial contents for each 1 m^2 were sifted and the contents were packaged separately in brown paper bags for future analysis. The skeletal remains encountered were left in situ until they were almost fully exposed. When identifiable, human bone was individually packaged by skeletal elements to facilitate reconstruction (Ross Site Report 2002; Ross and Broce 2003).

Tumba uno (burial one)

Decomposed and oxidised zinc sheet fragments were found immediately above the skeletal remains along with nine plastic sheet fragments measuring about

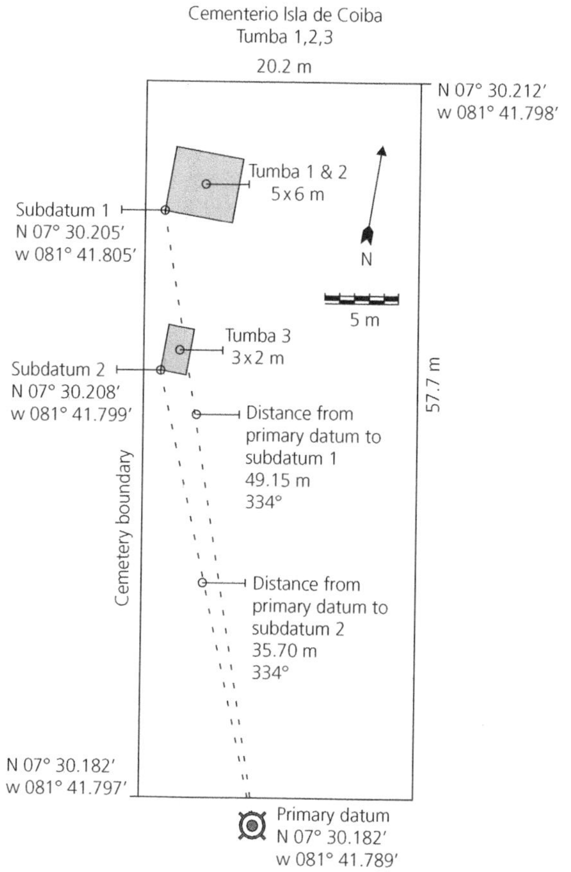

Figure 30.4 Cementerio Marañonat La Central map with burial locations (drawing: J. Hefner).

70–74 mm in length. These artefacts were placed on top of the remaining skeleton as a 'covering' by the Sauls during the previous excavation. The skeletal remains were encountered at a depth of 77 cm (3E2N–3E3N). The skeletal remains were in a poor state of preservation with a fine root system growing around and within the bones. The bones were very moist and chalk-like, disintegrating to the touch. The taphonomic variables (e.g. red clay soil, high humidity, soil pH and acidity, insect and bacteria) on Coiba are ill suited to the preservation of human skeletal remains.

This burial primarily consisted of the lower portion of an adult male skeleton lying in an extended position. The upper portion of the skeleton was exposed and removed by Frank and Julie Saul in 2001. The adult male was lying on his back with arms and legs extended, the legs pointing northwards. The femoral heads were oriented laterally, probably from shifting during decomposition. In addition, decomposed wood and oxidised nails (#41) were recovered from within the grave. The nails were bilaterally positioned in rows (*c.* 7 cm distance between nails) along the body indicating that this was a coffin burial. Before removal, the bones were first left to dry and then a thin coat of varnish was applied in order to extract the bones as completely as possible. This procedure was performed as bones and teeth had previously been obtained for DNA analysis in an earlier excavation (Ross Site Report 2002).

Tumba dos (burial two)

Burial two was contaminated with refuse (plastic bottle, aluminium foil and a cardboard core of a roll of aluminium foil). Five zinc sheets (4 × 8 cm), large decomposed cardboard sheets and aluminium foil were covering the bones, which were found at a depth of 117 cm. The remains were in a worse condition of preservation than Tumba uno because the above-mentioned tomb refuse trapped moisture and accelerated decomposition as observed by the recent insect activity (Ross Site Report 2002).

Tumba tres (burial three)

The third burial, or Tumba tres, was undisturbed and the remains of a wooden coffin were located at a depth of 92 cm. However, there was no obvious evidence for a lid although all other walls of the coffin were present; it is likely that the lid decayed at a faster rate due to taphonomic processes (e.g. soil acidity, soil weight and pressure). This grave consisted of an adult male skeleton lying in an extended position and resting on top of a folded blanket with head facing north (Figure 30.5). A cross necklace fashioned out of woven burlap was found around the neck area with the cross in the left hand resting over the chest region. All dentition was present in varying degrees of preservation with the exception of the left first maxillary molar and right second mandibular molar. The dentition showed minimal if absent occlusal wear. In addition, the left mandibular canine has an unusual apical wear pattern on the lingual surface. The molars of this individual are heavily crenulated, which is consistent with someone of African ancestry. Table 30.1 presents the results of the biological profile (Ross Site Report 2002).

Role of the convicted dog handler in planting evidence, the loss of the nation's trust and the collapse of the Truth Commission

The infamous Mrs Sandy Anderson (Michigan, US) and her cadaver dog Eagle were retained by the Truth Commission to help locate the remains of the victims of the military junta. She was brought to Panama several times in 2001, and was treated as a celebrity, with even the presidential helicopter at her disposal. She was found guilty of planting evidence in the United States in 2004 and was under Federal Bureau of Investigation (FBI) investigation. She was sentenced to 21 months in

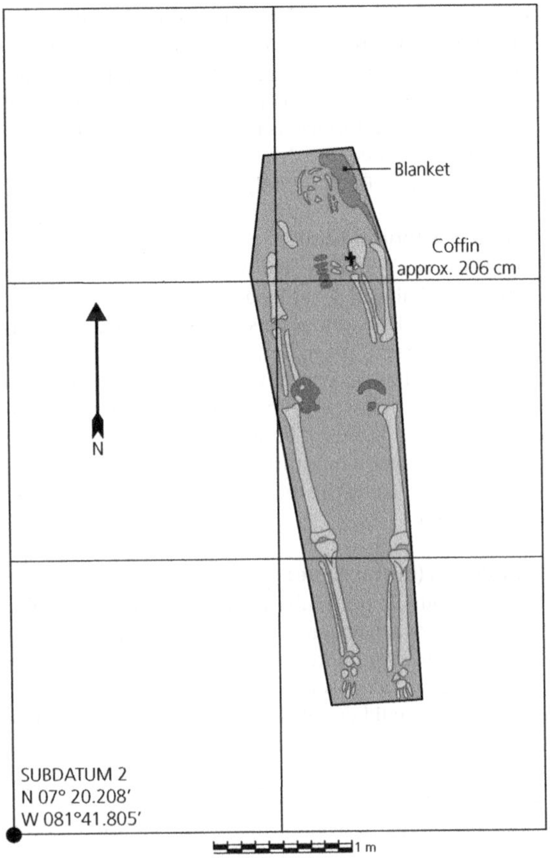

Figure 30.5 Detail of burial three (Drawing: J. Hefner).

prison and had to repay $14,500 in damages to law enforcement agencies. Her conviction provided the stimulus for the PRD (*Partido Revolucionario Democratico*), with strong ties to the military dictatorship, to negate and dismiss the Truth Commission's findings. They asserted that as the dog Eagle was a fraud everything that was investigated by the Truth Commission was also invalid and, thus, nobody had ever died, disappeared or been tortured at the hands of the dictatorship (Linares Franco, La Prensa, 28 March 2004). It has been claimed that the Truth Commission spent $97,485 on the various Operation Eagles. However, the work conducted by the Department of Anthropology of the Commission was independent of Anderson and her dog. Many of the sites and the 60 so-called boxes of remains currently housed in the Institute of Legal Medicine are not of the disappeared or dead and were 'discovered' by Anderson and her dog Eagle.

Thirty-four excavation sites were identified in the provinces of Panamá, Chiriquí, Veraguas, Coclé, Bocas del Toro and Colón. However, much of the resistance against the military regimes was in the province of Chiriquí (Almanza et al. 2002, 214). Many of these sites were identified by Anderson.

Table 30.1 Biological profile burial three.

Sex and age: The remains are consistent with an adult male. Sex was assessed via gross visual morphology. The remains of this individual are rugose (e.g. heavily marked *lineaaspera*) and the intercondylar notch of the distal femur is U-shaped.
Ancestry: Molar crenulations are characteristic of individuals of African ancestry and were quantitatively substantiated using FORDISC 2.0 using the maximum humerus length and femoral subtrochanteric measures.
Stature: The length of humerus (365 mm) was used to estimate stature. The predictive stature equation for African males derived by Trotter (1970) was utilised. The mean predictive stature is 181.09 cm ± 4.43 cm with a prediction interval of 176.66–185.52 cm.
Post-mortem modification: There is extensive post-mortem weathering. The bone surface is coarse, rough, brittle and fragile. The internal matrix of the long bones has completely decayed leaving the bones hollow.
Summary: The biological profile determined from the skeletal remains is consistent with the biological information made available for Floyd Britton.
DNA results: Unfortunately, the samples submitted did not yield any DNA. At present, additional samples are being submitted for re-testing. Recently, other victims have been identified through DNA methods from remains recovered on Coiba and other areas of Panama.

In the light of Anderson's conviction, every case that was associated with Operation Eagle was re-examined by the first author and graduate assistant and is summarised in Table 30.2. Interestingly, many of the skeletal elements recovered from the mainland were hand and foot bones that generally do not have a high frequency of survivability (Galloway et al. 1997; Waldron 1987; Willey 1990; Willey et al. 1997). Many of the well-preserved foot and hand bones did not exhibit signs of weathering or decay consistent with tropical environments. Skeletal identifications are extremely difficult because of various taphonomic processes (e.g. soil acidity, insect activity and bacterial activity, roots, humidity) and conditions that are not conducive to good skeletal preservation, and therefore the remains sustain considerable post-mortem damage (Ross and Cunningham 2011).

Conclusion

In 2010, the Institute of Legal Medicine had 60 boxes containing what were presumed to be unidentified remains. Because of the distrust that Anderson's planting of evidence caused, a cloud of doubt has surrounded all of the Truth Commission's investigations. The family members of the victims are convinced that the 60 boxes housed at the Institute of Legal Medicine contain the remains of their loved ones, as no one has presented them with actual evidence. The first author re-examined all of the remains discovered/recovered as the result of the various Operation Eagles and concluded that many of the sites were fake, the majority of the remains were non-human and those that are human are mostly of dubious origin (Table 30.2). Eight individuals were identified during the era of Truth Commission: Heliodoro Portugal, Reinado Sanchez, Lindbergh Gante, Ever Quintanar, Alfredo Serracín, Jerónimo Díaz, Cecilio Hazelwood and Gerardo Olivares (Ross et al. 2004). The family members are still requesting that the investigations continue, but investigations have ceased due to changes in government, changes in the Institute of Legal Medicine leadership and corruption.

Twenty-three years after the fall of the military dictatorship, not a single conviction has occurred for the crimes committed by the military regime. Of the 110 cases of deaths and forced disappearances documented

Table 30.2 Skeletal element recovery/survivorship by site.

Site	Human	Non-human	Skeletal elements	Preservation	Operation eagle
Tocumen*	×	×	l. patella, r. calcaneus, l. talus, r. proximal femur fragment, long boneshaft fragment, three cranial fragments	Poor earlier finds, good subsequent finds during Operation Eagle	Later finds
David†	×	×	One first metatarsal	Good and still greasy	×
Miraflores	×	×	r. second metatarsal, proximal hand phalanx; l. femur fragment, proximal hand phalanx; r. maxillary fragment, *second premolar with unique restoration, which is consistent with restoration on tooth found at another site, Piso Fundarte*	Good	×
San	×		Three human maxillary incisor fragments, calcined mandibular premolar enamel, calcined cranial fragments	Fragmentary	
Enrique Maleq	×		r. calcaneus	Good. Rodent gnawing and adhered brown soil	×
Las Ajuntas Barranco	×		Proximal foot phalanx and foot phalanx fragment	Weathered	
Piso Fundarte‡	×		r. and l. tali, r. second rib, l. maxillary canine with unique silver amalgam restoration, *restoration is consistent with the restoration on tooth found at Altos de Miraflores*, several maxillary incisor fragments, proximal foot and hand phalanx	Good	×
Mata del Chayote	×		Mandibular premolar with carious lesion	Good	×
Cuesta de Piedra§	×		l. and r. patellae, l. talus, two r. third metatarsals, three long bone fragments	Weathered, good	×
Is. Coiba	×		Partial skeletons from burials	Variable	

*Skeletal remains were first discovered in Tocumen in 1999 and 2000 prior to the formation of the Truth Commission. These remains were very weathered, consistent with remains having been buried in a tropical environment. Subsequent findings yielded non-human remains and the human material found was inconsistent with remains having been exposed to a tropical environment.

†The condition and preservation of the remains are inconsistent with what you would expect with remains exposed to a tropical environment.

‡The condition and preservation of the human bones recovered are inconsistent with what you would expect with buried remains or remains exposed to a tropical environment.

§Human remains found at Cuesta de Piedra are very weathered, light in colour and display thin, flaky cortical bone. These remains are consistent with having been exposed to a tropical environment. However, later remains recovered from the same site are inconsistent with what one would expect to find with remains exposed to tropical environments (e.g. extensive weathering and cortical flaking). Some even had evidence of patina.

by the Truth Commission, 84 were presented to the Justice Department. Of these 84 cases, 18 were declared prescribed or unenforceable (despite constituting crimes against humanity), 4 were dismissed and 18 were closed temporarily. In three cases there were pardons (despite the fact that pardon does not apply to criminal offenses) and in two cases the accused were acquitted. In eight cases there were first-degree convictions, which have been appealed, so the accused remain free. The remaining 31 cases, according to the Committee, 'are pending' in the Attorney General's Office and the Judicial Branch (translated from Guevara Mann, La Prensa, 22 May 2013).

References

Almanza, A., Tejadas Mora, J. A., Velasquez, O., Thompson, J. E. M. and Berguido, G. F. 2012. *Informe Final Comision de la Verdad.* 18 April 2002, Panama.

Cotes, L. M., Suarez Silva, L., Jemmott, K. and Ross A. H. 2004. The archaeology of tyranny. *Presentation at the American Academy of Forensic Sciences*, AAFS 2004, Dallas.

Galloway, A., Willey, P. and Snyder, L. 1997. Human bone mineral densities and survival of bone elements: a contemporary sample. In W. D. Hanglund and M. H. Sorg (eds.), *Forensic Taphonomy: Postmortem Fate of Human Remains*, 295–318. Boca Raton, CRC Press.

Guevara Mann, C. 2013. Los crímenes de la dictadura: Carlos Guevara Mann. *La Prensa*, 22 May 2013. Available at: http://www.prensa.com/impreso/opinion/los-crimenes-de-la-dictadura-carlos-guevara-mann/179245 (last accessed 10 June 2013).

Jemmott, K., Ross, A. H., Suarez Silva, L. and Cotes, L. M. 2004. Preservation in paradise II. A Pre-Columbian burial in a contemporary cemetery. *Presentation at the American Academy of Forensic Sciences*, AAFS 2004, Dallas.

Linares Franco, A. E. 2004. El PRD, el Perro 'Eagle' y la Comisión de la Verdad. *La Prensa*, 28 March 2004. Available at: http://mensual.prensa.com/mensual/contenido/2004/03/28/hoy/opinion/1594990.html (last accessed 10 June 2013).

Marcel Chery, J. 2003. Ministerio Público Desafía Orden de Mireya Moscoso. *La Prensa*, 22 October 2003. Available at: http://mensual.prensa.com/mensual/contenido/2003/10/22/hoy/portada/1314868.html (last accessed 10 June 2013).

Ramsey, B. 2013. *OxCal v. 4.2.2, r.2* [computer software program]. Atmospheric data from Reimer et al. 2009. Available at: https://c14.arch.ox.ac.uk/oxcal/OxCal.html (last accessed 10 June 2013).

Ross, A. H. 2002. *Human Remains from El Marañon, Isla de Coiba, Panama.* Site Report, Comision de la Verdad.

Ross, A. H. 2004. Use of digital imaging in the identification of fragmentary human skeletal remains: a case from the Republic of Panama. *Forensic Science Communications* 6(4). Available at: http://www.fbi.gov/about-us/lab/forensic-science-communications/fsc/oct2004/index.htm/case/2004_10_case01.htm (last accessed 10 June 2013).

Ross, A. H. and Broce, B. 2003. In search of Floyd Britton: investigations of human rights issues on the Island of Coiba, Republic of Panama. *Presentation at the American Academy of Forensic Sciences 2003*, Chicago.

Ross, A. H. and Cunningham, S. 2011. Time since death and bone weathering in a tropical environment. *Forensic Science International* 204, 126–133.

Ross, A. H., Jemmott, K, Suarez, L. and Cotes, M. 2004. Preservation in paradise I: El Marañon cemetery, Isla de Coiba, Republic of Panama. *Presentation at American Academy of Forensic Sciences*, AAFS 2004, Dallas.

Suarez Silva, L., Ross, A. H. and Jemmett, K. 2004. In the name of the dead: the Panamanian Truth Commission's search for the "disappeared". *Presentation at the American Academy of Forensic Sciences*, AAFS 2004, Dallas.

Trotter, M. 1970. Estimation of stature from intact limb bones. In T.D. Steward (Ed), *Personal Identification in Mass Disasters*, 71–84. Washington, DC, National Museum of Natural History.

Waldron, T. 1987. The relative survival of the human skeleton: implications for palaeopathology. In A. Boddington, A. Garland and R. Janaway (eds.), *Death, Decay and Reconstruction: Approaches to Archaeology and Forensic Science*, 55–64. Manchester, Manchester University Press.

Willey, P. 1990. *Prehistoric Warfare on the Great Plains: Skeletal Analysis of the Crow Creek Massacre Victims.* New York, Garland Publishing Co.

Willey, P., Galloway, A. and Snyder, L. 1997. Bone mineral density and survival of elements and element portions in the bones of the Crow Creek massacre victims. *American Journal of Physical Anthropology* 104, 513–528.

CHAPTER 31

Forensic archaeology in the United States

Luis L. Cabo and Dennis C. Dirkmaat

Department of Applied Forensic Sciences, Mercyhurst University, Erie, USA

Introduction

If we were to point out a defining characteristic that could set apart North American forensic archaeology from its conception in other countries, it would be that forensic archaeology is more often considered as an integral part of forensic anthropology in the United States, rather than as a standalone discipline (e.g. Crossland 2013; Dirkmaat et al. 2008). In a recent vote carried out on February 2013 at Washington, DC, US, during the 65th Scientific Meeting of the American Academy of Forensic Sciences (AAFS), the members of the Physical Anthropology section of AAFS decided to change the name of the section to simply *Anthropology* (thus understood as *Forensic Anthropology*, as the section is enclosed within the Forensic Academy). The main reason invoked to justify this change was that the new section name provides a better description of the current duties and practices of North American forensic anthropologists, which involve fields beyond physical anthropology, particularly forensic archaeology.[1] In a poll carried out by the authors to aid in this decision, 78% of the 165 members of the anthropology section of AAFS participating in the survey declared their preference for processing burials and outdoor scenes themselves; the same percentage expressed the opinion that archaeological methods are the most appropriate for that task. The respondents actually considered a good knowledge of archaeological and mapping techniques as the third most valued skill within the forensic anthropology toolkit, just behind human anatomy (including osteology) and forensic taphonomy – the latter, as we will discuss later, intimately related to forensic archaeology. Therefore, a large majority of North American forensic anthropologists appear to regard forensic archaeology as not only a key discipline, but also an integral part of their work. In contrast, teams that are exclusively devoted to forensic archaeological tasks and routinely called to the scene to excavate buried bodies or scattered remains just to turn them over to pathologists or forensic anthropologists are extremely rare in the United States.

From this viewpoint, we have defined forensic archaeology as the implementation of archaeological methods and theory in the processing of crime scenes that may not lend themselves well to established indoor crime scene protocols, such as burials, surface scatters, fire scenes, mass disasters and other outdoor crime scenes. The addition of forensic archaeology within a forensic anthropologist's purview allows for not only an osteological analysis of a forensic case, but an analysis of crime scene context and reconstruction of past events (Dirkmaat 2012c).

Throughout this chapter we will describe some of the key factors behind this trend – namely, the inclusion of forensic archaeology within the larger discipline of forensic anthropology – and discuss what we perceive as some of its main practical and conceptual outcomes. This being said, the disposition of the field as a component of forensic anthropology, while clearly predominant in current North American practice, does not go completely unchallenged. Its appropriateness has been recently discussed in academic forums, including two recent special symposia devoted to forensic archaeology in the 2007 (Chicago, Illinois) and 2013 (Honolulu, Hawaii) meetings of the Society for American Archaeology (SAA). Any description of the current practice and state of affairs of forensic archaeology in the United States would be incomplete without referring to this debate.

Moreover, apart from providing a useful contrast to highlight some of the peculiarities of the North American model, the comparison with the nature of the field in the United Kingdom (*the British model*), where forensic archaeology is viewed as a more independent field (e.g. Crossland 2013, Hunter and Cropper, Chapter 23, this volume; Janaway, Chapter 24, this volume; Márquez-Grant et al. 2012) is also relevant and interesting in its

[1]The main arguments and the opinions of many sections members in the discussion preceding this change are presented at http://panthsectionnamechange.wordpress.com (last accessed November 2013).

Forensic Archaeology: A Global Perspective, First Edition. Edited by W.J. Mike Groen, Nicholas Márquez-Grant and Robert C. Janaway.

own right for several reasons. For example, from a practical point of view, the United States and the United Kingdom still seem to constitute the two main foci of forensic archaeological practice, although fortunately this trend seems to be changing at a rapid pace, as illustrated by this volume. Márquez-Grant et al. (2012) have recently contributed an outstanding multinational survey of current forensic anthropological and forensic archaeological practice, revealing that while the systematic application of forensic archaeology is gaining converts around the globe, it still remains a relatively rara avis in most other countries. Additionally, North America and the United Kingdom concentrate a large portion of the classic bibliography on the subject. Thus, the direction taken by forensic archaeology in these two countries will likely have a heavy impact on the immediate future of the field at a global scale, especially if the two views come to be interpreted in a dogmatic way as irreconcilable options.

However, in our opinion, the main motivation behind the comparison of the two seemingly opposed conceptions lies in the fact that both represent sensible and valid intellectual alternatives that, importantly, have provided excellent results in terms of both successful casework and the advancement of forensic archaeology as a scientific discipline. This is somehow surprising and certainly worth examination, as we might have expected some severe consequences to result from the notable differences in their conceptual points of view. The divide actually dictates the very first line of the definition of the field as well as the parent discipline from which forensic archaeology must build its conceptual framework; either 'it is a branch of archaeology' or 'it is a branch of forensic anthropology'. The source of the two diverging perspectives is even more puzzling in view of the similarities between the two countries in terms of the conception of anthropology as a social science, more or less related to archaeology, in comparison with some other European countries where physical anthropology is instead a branch of biology, or in which anthropologists are not even considered in the discussion, as it is mainly pathologists carrying out forensic anthropological analysis. Furthermore, we cannot blame the disparate philosophies on language barriers or a lack of connection between the academic literatures produced in both countries, as most key publications are widely distributed across both sides of the Atlantic.

It is for these reasons and more that we believe that the roots of the split are not so much conceptual, but based primarily on the historical paths followed by the field in each country, marked by the peculiarities of the respective legal systems, the different organisation and structure of law enforcement bodies and, as with any historic narrative, by chance events and the influence of individual personalities. Possibly, the key elements to understanding why forensic anthropologists are nowadays the standard bearers of forensic archaeology in the United States are the number of practitioners and their degree of involvement in everyday forensic investigation, as well as the level of respect realised by forensic anthropology in this country in the past 40 years. In the United States there are a relatively large number of practicing forensic anthropologists, and they have been the professionals of choice for many decades in cases involving severely altered or completely skeletonised human remains, predating the development of forensic archaeology as a common practice and fully mature field. Not only do these cases often include the most common scenarios in which forensic archaeology is particularly useful, but most forensic anthropologists were also North American physical anthropologists trained under the traditional four-field approach to anthropology, which combines cultural, linguistic, and biological anthropology with archaeology, and therefore familiar with archaeology theory and practice. Thus, it appears almost inevitable that forensic anthropologists would be among the first to realise the utility and importance of introducing archaeological methods into scene recovery and incorporate them into their everyday practice in this country.

One of the key points that we will try to develop along this chapter is that the forensic archaeology component, if largely stemming solely from historical accident, still resulted in very important practical and theoretical contributions that might have been missed if the field had followed the same historical path as in the United Kingdom. We will focus primarily on discussing the contributions spanning from the North American model, but that is not to say the British model is without its own unique contributions. In our view, the British and American schools represent, in reality, just two ends of a single conceptual spectrum, rather than antagonistic, largely incompatible models of forensic archaeology. This would explain the aforementioned convergence of methods, practice and results coming from two conceptual frameworks so apparently divergent. For this reason, we are convinced that a potential dismissal of one model by adopting a dogmatic view of the other would result in a dramatic impoverishment of the field, both as a scientific discipline and as a profession.

To be completely clear, we do not propose that the correct view lies on some theoretical midpoint, but rather that forensic archaeology must exploit and encompass the entirety of the spectrum revealed by the American and the British schools. If we had to argue for a potential advantage of the North American model, it would be that it represents a broader and more inclusive framework for forensic archaeology, bringing to the table more elements and scientific disciplines, and involving the forensic archaeologist to a much larger degree in the analytical process, both at the crime scene and in the laboratory. Conversely, the British model provides a more rigorous treatment and consideration of the strictly archaeological component, stressing and taking full advantage of the classic archaeological theory, methodology, training and tradition. Therefore, it is not a case of choosing between two incompatible positions, but rather of utilising the whole array of techniques, findings and observations realised within the discipline.

In the remaining sections we will first briefly describe how the North American model came into being as well as the main outputs of this historical development and how they affected and came to enrich the field, particularly in relation to its general scope, conceptual framework and target subjects. We will also discuss our view of how a reductionist adoption of either the American or the British model, either by identifying forensic archaeology as just a subset of applied field techniques for the osteologist or by considering it a discipline completely detached from the goals of anthropological investigation, would, in our opinion, adversely affect the usefulness and effectiveness of forensic archaeology, handicapping its future development. We close the chapter with a reflection on the immediate challenges faced by the field at present, during its transition from a period in which most of our efforts were directed towards explaining the need for forensic archaeology to one in which the task ahead consists instead of defining and refining clear methodological and academic standards for an already widely accepted field. We believe that the integration of the analytical goals of the American school with the rigorous archaeological standards of the British model must and will play a central role in our success in confronting these challenges, which consist of no less than developing forensic archaeology into a fully fleshed scientific field.

Development of forensic archaeology in the United States

As discussed earlier, the histories of forensic archaeology and forensic anthropology are practically one and the same in the United States, although forensic anthropology had already attained a large degree of recognition and popularisation in forensic circles long before forensic archaeology was to take its first steps. Although the practice of forensic anthropology in the United States can be traced back to the early 1900s (for brief overviews of the early history of the field see Dirkmaat and Cabo 2012; Snow 1982; Tersigni-Tarrant and Shirley 2012a), forensic anthropologists did not come to be organised as a professional body until the early 1970s. In 1972, a small group of forensic anthropologists met at the annual meeting of the AAFS and succeeded in creating a new section within the Academy (Dirkmaat and Cabo 2012; Snow 1982). Although they would have preferred the name *Forensic Anthropology* for the new section, the inclusion of the word *Forensic* in a section's name went against the tradition of the Academy (which already includes the adjective in its name), and thus they settled on the less musical name, *Physical Anthropology Section* (Snow, personal communication, 2012). Admittedly, all the founding fathers were indeed physical anthropologists, most with day jobs in museum settings. Typically, their role in forensic investigations at that time was limited to osteological analysis in the laboratory and was not considered an appropriate business for other branches of anthropology (i.e. for cultural anthropologists and archaeologists), further justifying the more restrictive name for the section.

The embrace by AAFS represented the official acceptance of forensic anthropology as a legitimate member of the forensic sciences; the backing of forensic anthropologists by AAFS credentials in American courts and in their relationship with law enforcement was an extremely important development, particularly in the credentials-ruled pre-Daubert era. More importantly, the new AAFS section also provided a scientific forum for the discussion and exchange of information and experience among forensic anthropologists, as well as between forensic anthropologists and other forensic specialists. Shortly after the creation of the new section a flurry of articles and even books started to provide working definitions and practical instructions for those who wished to be called forensic anthropologists. Perhaps the most influential of these publications was Dr T. Dale Stewart's *Essentials of Forensic Anthropology*, published in 1979. It provided the guiding light for many years, indeed well into the 1990s. The common nexus of virtually all of these publications was a scope of the field based on the description of what forensic anthropologists were already doing, with little conceptual flourishes or discussion of potential new tasks or future developments. In nearly all cases, forensic anthropology was presented as a subdiscipline of physical anthropology, focused exclusively on aiding in the identification of unknown individuals through osteological analysis. Within this framework, the field was seen as a purely applied and strictly laboratory-based activity, which, in retrospect, severely constrained its evolution as a true scientific discipline for many decades (for a deeper discussion of the problem, see Dirkmaat et al. 2008). As discussed later, we believe that the development of forensic archaeology as a discipline independent from forensic anthropology would produce similar results, essentially reproducing the mistakes and lack of foresight that afflicted modern forensic anthropology in its origins.

However, forensic anthropology in the United States would soon outgrow this narrow original definition, benefitting from what we consider the two main driving forces in its transition from a technical application to a more scientific field: (1) its already strong entrenchment in the rapidly evolving forensic practice, and (2) the development of vertebrate taphonomy and its incorporation into the discipline. The latter would also play a decisive role in the incorporation of forensic archaeology into forensic anthropological practice.

Apart from the immediate benefits discussed earlier, the wide acceptance and complete integration of forensic anthropology within the forensic sciences came to provide a baseline for comparison regarding what could and should be expected from a forensic anthropological investigation. In particular, during the same decades in which forensic anthropology was cutting its baby teeth, the criminalistics technique for indoor crime scene investigation underwent a dramatic metamorphosis, resulting in increasingly refined and comprehensive protocols for their analysis and documentation. For example, the initial editions of the classic criminalistics textbook by Dr Richard Saferstein (2010), first published in 1977, focused exclusively on laboratory analysis of different types of evidence. However, by 1990 its fourth edition already included a chapter entirely devoted to crime scene investigation and documentation. In its current incarnation, it places special stress on the necessity of producing an accurate map ('sketch') of the scene, discussing advanced mapping methods and instrumentation such as the Total Station or 3D scanners (Saferstein 2010).

While these advances were being incorporated into the investigation of conventional indoor scenes, forensic anthropologists faced a very different reality when investigating the type of cases in which they were often involved. As specialists in bone tissue, they were most often called when the victim was already skeletonised or severely decomposed, and thus the forensic pathologist, fingerprint specialist or even the sketch artist were unable to assess trauma or identity from soft tissue. This implied that the body had remained undiscovered for a long period of time and could not be readily associated with an address or identifying personal effects. The scenarios in which all these circumstances concur most often are burials and outdoor scenes; thus, these were the scenes more often confronted by forensic anthropologists.

The problem was that the sophisticated indoor protocols simply did not translate well to outdoor scenes. In an environment devoid of permanent, definite reference points, such as the walls or heavy furniture of a room, scene investigators found little use for the simple but powerful techniques that they used to create precise maps indoors. The problem lay not only in mapping the scene but also in choosing which objects or features to map. When confronting buried bodies, standard indoor techniques did not address issues such as stratigraphic relationships or even the most basic excavation techniques. In addition to, and partially derived from, these technical problems there was a perception that little could be gained from a more meticulous treatment of the scene. The complex interactions resulting from the exposure of the remains and other evidentiary materials to environmental factors and biological agents complicated the analysis and documentation of outdoor scenes and were therefore interpreted as disturbances that would have already erased any information relevant to the reconstruction of past events. For this reason, careful documentation of the outdoor scene was simply considered not worth the time and energy.

Thus, potential improvements in outdoor protocols were scarcely considered even after the advent of rigorous indoor protocols, and outdoor scenes were still processed by law enforcement largely as they were in the 1930s, when forensic anthropologists first started operating on a regular basis in the United States (Dirkmaat and Cabo 2012; Snow 1982). The modus operandi for law enforcement was to remove the bones from the scene and bring them to the forensic anthropologist in a box. The forensic anthropologist was then given the task of generating a biological profile of the victim (Sigler-Eisenberg 1985; Snow 1982). Morse et al. (1976, 323) describes how 'nearly all anthropologists and many physicians in various communities in the US have had a law official bring them a pile of human bones, badly broken or with many parts missing, usually in a bushel basket or a plastic bag after having been removed from the ground with a long-handled shovel or a pickaxe, or both'. Regarding the techniques utilised by law enforcement to collect the remains, some early authors politely referred to them as excavations 'under less than optimum conditions' (Sigler-Eisenberg 1985, 650). Dr Clyde Snow jokingly described the practice in less charitable terms: 'Having a policeman excavate a skeleton, I felt, was a bit like having a chimpanzee perform a heart transplant' (Snow 1995, 17–18).

The high standards set for indoor scenes, however, did provide a baseline and the right mindset for law enforcement to appreciate what archaeological techniques could bring to the table. Both law enforcement and magistrates were familiar with the strong inferences that other forensic experts, dealing more often with indoor scenes, were able to produce. Aided by precise scene data and scene reconstructions, forensic pathologists (who, in the view of the legal community, based their diagnoses on similar materials as forensic anthropologists) were able to integrate elements such as the position and location of the body in their interpretations. Their hypotheses and inferences could also be confirmed through their further integration with the work of other professionals, such as blood spatter analysts, serologists, and, later, geneticists examining blood evidence, or criminalists tracing projectile trajectories. As a consequence, forensic anthropologists were asked some of the same tough questions that could be increasingly answered at the less hastily processed and more properly documented indoor scenes: How long was the body there? Why are some parts missing? Why are the bones scattered? Why are some bones broken? Did this happen during the death event or after it? What is the sequence of events that occurred at this scene?

As mentioned in our introduction, the North American forensic anthropologists confronting those questions had usually been educated under the 'four-field approach' championed by Dr Franz Boas, which in its current configuration includes physical anthropology, archaeology, cultural anthropology and linguistics as sister fields under the umbrella of general anthropology (see Hicks 2013 for a discussion on the origin of this view from a historical perspective). Even though there are reasons to be sceptical of the real motivation behind the integration of the four fields in either practice or education (e.g. Borofsky 2002), this means that most physical anthropologists, and, consequently forensic anthropologists, were familiar with archaeological theory; in some cases, they even had solid archaeological backgrounds and experience themselves or worked in close collaboration with regular archaeologists in their academic practice. Thus, it does not come as a surprise that a few of these professionals soon realised that 'techniques for the location and removal of burials have been developed over a long period of time by those in the field of archaeology' (Bass and Birkby 1978, 6) and, therefore, outdoor scenes could be processed best 'by suitably modifying methods long employed by archaeologists to solve similar problems' (Snow 1982, 118).

Morse et al. (1976) appear to provide the first literary contribution explaining this view, constituting the foundational reference for forensic archaeology in the United States and likely forensic archaeology at large. After exposing the central arguments in favour of implementation of archaeological techniques and illustrating the inadequacy of the methods employed at the time using two case examples, the authors provide a basic forensic archaeological protocol that, in its main elements, we could still endorse today. Dr Donald Crusoe and Dr Hale Smith were archaeologists, the former with the US National Park Service, and the latter at the Department of Anthropology at Florida State University, actually serving as the founding member of the department. Dr Dan Morse, the main force behind the article, was a medical doctor and amateur archaeologist (Kwas 1999) working as a forensic anthropologist at the same institution. Interestingly, Morse's son, Dr Dan F. Morse, is a renowned archaeologist who was working at that time for the Arkansas Archaeological Survey. He is acknowledged in the article for his technical assistance (Morse et al. 1976, 331), and it is likely that he provided not only the first case example discussed in the paper (an excavation by prison inmates at Arkansas), but also part of the impetus for the article, which expresses the complaint that 'even though the state of Arkansas employed at least twelve expert field archaeologists, none were asked to help' (Morse et al. 1976, 324).

Another unsung hero of forensic archaeology revealed in the article is Dr Dick Ping Hsu, a US National Park Service archaeologist who in 1972 processed a shallow grave at a murder scene in Rome, New York, at the request of the State Police (Morse et al. 1976, 325). Even though it is more than likely that other archaeologists performed similar work at earlier dates, Dr Hsu is probably the first American archaeologist whom we know by name to process a real outdoor crime scene.

Morse et al. (1976) was quickly followed by a second paper written by two leading forensic anthropologists, Bass and Birkby (1978). Apart from the stature of both authors within the forensic anthropology community, the paper is especially significant because of the journal chosen for its publication, the *FBI Bulletin*. The clear goal of the paper was therefore revealing the arguments laid by Morse et al. (1976) to the law enforcement community. The strategy appeared to work like a charm, as only one year later Mr Robert M. Boyd, an instructor at the FBI Academy in Quantico, VA, presented the methods proposed by Morse et al. (1976) and Bass and Birkby (1978), referring directly to them as the best-practice crime scene protocols for law enforcement (Boyd 1979). Even though at this point forensic anthropologists could theoretically begin processing burials and outdoor scenes using archaeological methods, which would allow them to work towards the next objective of developing and perfecting the field, that is unfortunately not how things worked – forensic archaeology still had a long and winding road ahead before it could become accepted as a common practice.

Boyd (1979) provides some clues about the reasons behind the slow initial acceptance of forensic archaeology by both law enforcement and a substantial portion of the forensic anthropology community, which are relevant to our current debate on the British and American approaches. While Boyd (1979) presents basically the same arguments and methods as the preceding articles, recommending the inclusion of archaeologists in the scene processing team, he extends the argument to a wide array of other professionals. He mentions specific scene tasks for archaeologists, pathologists, botanists and entomologists, in addition to photographers and the usual crime scene technicians. He also provides a long list of other professionals to have on call, including forensic anthropologists, psychiatrists or toxicologists, not always clarifying whether they should attend scene recoveries too. In other words, although the article focuses on archaeological techniques, it is easy to imagine some law enforcement officials misinterpreting its central argument to be that they should bring to the scene as many specialists as possible. In a country where a large portion of cases are processed by small agencies with limited resources, such as county coroner's or medical examiner's (ME's) offices, that is often seen as a very unrealistic goal.

Thus, all the foundational articles of the 1970s presented the argument that archaeologists should be brought to the scene, making the very initial conception of forensic archaeology in the United States very similar to the current British one. However, the authors failed to foresee that, with closely related professionals already involved in everyday forensic casework, the law enforcement community would be quicker and more inclined to buy the old dog a new collar than to add new puppies to the crime scene kennel. Nevertheless, the fact remained that several forensic anthropologists with archaeological training who sought to answer questions which required solid contextual data had already started utilising archaeological methods to process their scenes as early as 1970 (Snow 1995, 18). Probably the best among the early expressions of this view is a masterful article by Dr Clyde Snow (1982) in which, after reviewing the origins and evolution of the field up to that moment, he lays the conceptual foundations of modern North American forensic anthropology as we understand it today. Although in his final remarks he still offers a definition of the field focused on victim identification ('the application of the physical anthropologist's specialised knowledge of human sexual, racial, age, and individual variation to problems of medical jurisprudence', Snow 1982, 128), he also stresses the legitimacy and necessity of expanding the array of problems targeted by the forensic anthropologist and, more relevant to our discussion, broadens decisively the role of forensic anthropology to include forensic archaeology work. More specifically, in an article largely aimed at aspiring forensic anthropologists, rather than calling for the presence of an archaeologist, Snow advises the reader to 'brush up on any archaeological skills … acquired in [their] academic training' as well as to keep a field kit, as 'systematic recovery of the materials from burials and surface sites is best accomplished by suitably modifying methods long employed by archaeologists to solve similar problems' (Snow 1982, 118). This introduces two key concepts: (1) that the archaeological methods to be employed at forensic contexts go beyond the classic ones, and (2) that the recovery of the remains through those methods is now one of the duties of forensic anthropologists. He reveals that, since he travelled often, he had two Death Investigators of the Oklahoma Medical Examiner's Office trained in basic archaeological techniques process the scenes when he was out of town and could not do so himself (Snow 1982, 118). Likely as a consequence of this field experience, Snow also places searches and surface remains, which were not considered in the preceding articles, within the forensic archaeological scope and, as we will discuss later, makes the first explicit mention of the link between archaeologically retrieved data and taphonomic studies.

Continuing with this pattern, the main foundations of North American forensic archaeology were put in place by the early 1980s through several publications, including the first two manuals on the subject by Morse et al. (1983) and Skinner and Lazenby (1983) (even though the latter was published in Canada and authored by Canadian authors, we feel that it must be included in our narrative due to the tremendous influence that both the volume and its authors would have on North American forensic anthropology and archaeology). The title of Morse et al. (1983), *Handbook of Forensic Archaeology and Anthropology*, confirms the early integration of the two disciplines earlier hinted by Snow (1982). In similar fashion, Krogman and Işcan (1986) included a section on crime scene techniques, detailing archaeology-based methods, in their osteology manual. This trend has survived to this day, with most modern forensic anthropology manuals and edited volumes including sections on forensic archaeology and field methods (e.g. Blau and Ubelaker 2009; Burns 2012; Byers 2010; Dirkmaat 2012a; Komar and Buikstra 2008; Steadman 2003; Tersigni-Tarrant and Shirley 2012b), while the number of volumes focusing specifically on scene recovery from this perspective is increasing at a slower pace (but see Connor 2007; Dupras et al. 2006; Killam 2004).

Work environment: academy and agency settings

We can conclude from the earlier discussion that one of the key elements facilitating these developments, as well as the interrelation of forensic archaeology and forensic anthropology in the United States, is that from a historical point of view, forensic anthropologists were better positioned than archaeologists to demonstrate and introduce forensic archaeology to law enforcement and prosecutors due to their already established working relationship. This was tremendously important, as some misconceptions, such as the idea that archaeological techniques would increase processing times to impractical levels, or that minimal evidence could be recovered from highly altered human remains or outdoor scenes, were more easily corrected through practical demonstrations than through academic articles. When law enforcement and legal professionals were shown that archaeological techniques permitted the processing of outdoor scenes and burials in a timely and efficient manner, providing information as relevant and detailed as that obtained at indoor scenes, they could hardly keep settling for the old standards. Their work at indoor scenes placed them in a position to understand the importance of the contextual and associational relationships revealed by archaeological inquiry. Ultimately, they felt much more comfortable presenting archaeological maps in court, which were much closer to their detailed indoor crime scene documentation than the traditional coarse sketches, drawings and murky field photographs.

For forensic anthropologists, this was a long war that was fought door to door. The strategy of spreading the gospel by demonstrating the virtues of forensic archaeology one agency at a time was favoured by the peculiar and fragmentary organisation of the American system, comprising 2342 death investigation jurisdictions in 2004 (National Research Council 2009, 243). Two different types of agencies are in charge of investigating and responding to all deaths, including those derived from terrorism and mass disasters – coroners and ME's offices. Coroners (C) are generally elected officials, while ME are medical professionals, most often forensic pathologists.[2] Most of these professionals operate at the local level; as of 2004, only 16 of the 50 states had a centralised statewide ME system, with half of those 16 states utilising a hybrid ME/C system which included coroners (National Research Council 2009, 245). All ME/C agencies are subject to budgetary constraints, which are particularly limiting for the large proportion of the ME/C offices that serve small communities; roughly 53% of coroners in 2004 hailed from jurisdictions with less than 25,000 inhabitants (National Research Council 2009, 245). This means that they are generally happy to accept all the help they can get, including that coming from archaeologists and anthropologists.

This environment favoured a working relationship between forensic anthropologists and an increasing number of ME/C agencies, developing through cooperation agreements which included a pledge to be contacted in the very early stages of the investigation, whenever possible, before the scene was processed. Large and mid-sized ME offices started including forensic anthropologists among their personnel as well (Berryman and Lanfear 2012). Small agencies, such as coroners who often ran barebones operations, asked other law enforcement agencies for help with their investigations, especially state police officials who, in turn, after becoming familiar with the advantages of forensic archaeological recoveries, would start calling forensic anthropologists to their scenes.

This dynamic has survived to the present day in the form of a system in which academy-based laboratories coexist with facilities run by state or federal agencies to provide forensic anthropological and archaeological services to law enforcement in a consulting capacity. Warren et al. (2008) provides a fantastic overview of the wide array of forensic anthropology laboratories operating nowadays in the United States. Notably, even when the volume is devoted to lab operations, forensic archaeological services, including training, are mentioned for six of the eight facilities presented as examples in the volume. Apart from the university-based laboratories, these range from small and large ME offices to the gargantuan Joint Prisoner of War/Missing in Action Accounting Command's Central Identification Laboratory (JPAC-CIL) of the US Department of Defense, which carried out its first field recovery in 1976 and currently keeps 18 standing recovery teams that can be deployed anywhere in the world for extended periods of time (Holland et al. 2008, 54). Emanowsky and Belcher (2012) provide a closer look at the nature and protocols of JPAC-CIL recoveries (e.g. Pietruszka, Chapter 51 this volume). Apart from the government agencies described in the volume, the practice and contributions to forensic archaeology of FBI personnel, particularly Special Agent Michael Hochrein, are well known (Hochrein 2011, 2012). Since 2010, the FBI Forensic Anthropology Program (FAP) also offers full forensic archaeology services (Christensen 2010).

Modern university-based laboratories are experiencing a quick evolution, stirring away from the dismal panorama of small, underfunded operations found in many US institutions as well as the Canadian institutions described by Skinner et al. (2010). However, the protocols of the University of Indianapolis, presented by one of the main stalwarts of North American forensic archaeology in the last decades (Nawrocki 2008), serve to illustrate the growing capabilities and extreme level of professionalism with which many academic laboratories are currently managed in the United States. Following the lead of JPAC-CIL and motivated by a scolding report on the state of the forensic sciences in the United States by the National Research Council (2009), there is now a push for institutions to pursue accreditation by the American Society of Crime Laboratory Directors/Laboratory Accreditation Board (ASCLD/LAB). Presently, several forensic anthropology laboratories at academic settings are already pursuing this goal, displaying enough capabilities, quality facilities and funding to fulfil the same requirements expected of government laboratories.

Taphonomic approach

If opportunity and historic inertia played a role in the adoption of forensic archaeology by North American forensic anthropologists, it also had much deeper and serious motivations. All the early articles discussed in the previous section already placed forensic archaeology squarely in a forensic anthropological context and justified the need for archaeological techniques based on their impact on osteological analysis. Morse et al. (1976) open their foundational article with a description of

[2]For an updated critical review of the tasks and characteristics of each type of office as well as their interworkings with the police and other law agencies, see Strengthening Forensic Science in the United States: A Path Forward (National Research Council 2009, 241–252).

how forensic anthropologists often handled decontextualised and altered samples due to the lack of appropriate recovery techniques. In that same manner, each subsequent contribution discussed with increasing detail the different ways in which poor recoveries negatively affected forensic anthropological interpretation, slowly revealing a common theme: contextual data recovered and documented through archaeological techniques were crucial to interpreting samples and bone alteration, and that context may be the key motivation for forensic archaeology. Bass and Birkby (1978, 9) utilise an example involving the integration of scene and laboratory analysis to interpret cut marks on bone and Sigler-Eisenberg (1985, 650) mentions the problem of distinguishing between peri-mortem trauma and post-mortem damage without sufficient scene context. Snow (1982, 118) frames the question of context in relation to the interpretation of the degree of skeletonisation and bone weathering in estimating post-mortem intervals and is probably the first author not only to mention the magic word *taphonomy*, but also to point out the promise of a thorough study and documentation of forensic contexts to advance taphonomic research.

Taphonomic analysis was, therefore, one of the leading motivations behind the development of North American forensic archaeology from its origins. Taphonomy was born as a branch of palaeontology, originally presented by Dr Ivan Efremov (1940) as 'the study of the transition of animal remains from the biosphere to the lithosphere'. For decades following this definition, the bulk of the taphonomic literature dealt mostly with invertebrate fossils and focused on the interface between diagenesis, fossilisation and bed formation. At the end of the 1960s, just as that gang of physical anthropologists was plotting and scheming to create the anthropology section of the AAFS, vertebrate species started providing a new focus for taphonomic research. Notably, many of the taphonomic publications reflecting this trend in the late 1970s and early 1980s were related to fossil hominid sites, where humans were key taphonomic agents affecting vertebrate remains (Binford 1981; Boaz and Behrensmeyer 1976; Brain 1981). By the early 1980s, volumes on taphonomy directly addressed some of the purely anthropological and archaeological applications with which we are familiar today, such as analysis of bone modification and determination of whether an assemblage could be attributed to a human or a non-human origin. During that decade, taphonomy manuals began to present vertebrate taphonomy as a constituting part of archaeological practice (e.g. Grayson 1984; Klein and Cruz-Uribe 1984). Research goals and techniques were redefined in the ecotone between the palaeontological and archaeological analytical dominions (Gifford 1981), and taphonomic studies of archaeological sites and assemblages began to be labelled under the emerging subdiscipline of zooarchaeology (Grayson 1984). By the mid-1990s, vertebrate taphonomy was a mature field, covering all of the subjects with which we are familiar in forensic anthropology today. The publication of Lyman's (1994) *Vertebrate Taphonomy* probably represents the best illustration of this maturity.

As physical anthropologists, many forensic anthropologists were aware of these developments and soon realised the striking parallels between the goals of the new field of vertebrate taphonomy and many of their own questions concerning bone modification, trauma analysis, preservation and transport potentials, diagenesis, site formation, animal alteration, and so on. As a matter of fact, aside from the estimation of the biological profile (age, sex, ancestry, stature) in the attempt to aid in the identification of the unknown victim, many of the questions currently addressed by forensic anthropologists can be formulated in strictly taphonomic terms.

Legal developments provided further incentive for embracing vertebrate taphonomy. In the early days, forensic anthropologists could rely on silverback wisdom and support their guesses in appeals to authority or experience. Once the authority of a forensic anthropologist had been established, experience could often justify his/her opinions on a particular case simply with statements like 'I have seen this a hundred times'. However, the 1993 US Supreme Court decision in the case *Daubert* vs. *Merrell Dow Pharmaceuticals* (113 S.Ct. 2786) would decisively alter this landscape. Dirkmaat et al. (2008) discusses the Daubert ruling and its impact on US forensic anthropology more in depth, but its main consequence was that it called for scientific testimony to be based on reliable, tested and well-established scientific foundations rather than merely on the credentials of the expert witness. This placed a burden on forensic anthropologists to justify their methods with arguments beyond prior experience. Just as the palaeopathology literature provided the initial scientific backing to trauma analysts in the absence of studies developed specifically for forensic contexts, forensic anthropologists realised that vertebrate taphonomy studies could serve the same purpose in answering questions about body position, bone alteration and whether these alterations had occurred peri- or post-mortem. These parallels and advantages led forensic anthropologists to embrace taphonomy rapidly and rather enthusiastically. Research specifically addressing taphonomic applications in forensic contexts was already being carried out by the mid-1980s (Sorg et al. 2012), and the first key publication on forensic taphonomy, Haglund and Sorg's (1997a) edited volume *Forensic Taphonomy*, appeared only 3 years after Lyman's (1994) tome on vertebrate taphonomy.

The adoption of the taphonomic approach had major consequences. One of the key elements of the new field of vertebrate taphonomy was that it seamlessly joined assemblage and site analysis, which could no longer be approached as separate activities to be performed by different professionals operating independently in different observational venues. Taphonomic analyses performed at the laboratory required very specific field data collected with those analyses in mind. In this manner, the new forensic taphonomy volumes included several chapters on forensic archaeology and scene recovery techniques (Dirkmaat 2002; Dirkmaat and Adovasio 1997; Hochrein 2002; Mayne Correia and Beattie 2002; Saul and Saul 2002; Scott and Connor 1997).

Thus, forensic anthropologists were dragged out of their comfy labs and into the field, and forensic archaeology was to become one of their basic tools, primarily as the best means to record and collect taphonomic information. In exchange for this sacrifice, they would broaden their professional horizon and would transition from little more than laboratory technicians aiding in the process of victim identification to scientists analysing pre- and post-depositional processes and products. We have referred elsewhere (Dirkmaat et al. 2008) to this change as a true Kuhnian paradigm shift, as it does not represent just a methodological improvement, but a 'shift in the problems available for scientific scrutiny' (Kuhn 1970, 6) within the field. In their first volume, Haglund and Sorg (1997b, 13) define forensic taphonomy as:

> that part of forensic anthropology which focuses on reconstructing events during and following death by collecting and analysing data about the depositional context, discriminating peri- and post-mortem modification of the remains, and estimating the post-mortem interval. It includes the application of archaeological search and recovery techniques, the laboratory analysis of the remains, and an understanding of unique and overlapping agencies of soft tissue and bone modification and distribution.

Far from focusing exclusively on victim identification and laboratory procedures and methods (forensic osteology), within the new paradigm the analysis of human remains from forensic contexts also requires optimal recovery and field-derived contextual information (forensic archaeology), in order to provide scientifically valid reconstructions of past events and processes (forensic taphonomy). It is also worth noting that Haglund and Sorg's (1997b) definition does not mention a limitation to buried bodies and also places search techniques as part of the forensic anthropologist repertoire, an aspect that had been largely absent from the foundational articles of the 1970s. Boyd (1979, 2–3) advocated for calling the archaeologist once the body had been located, limiting his/her role to excavation while recommending the presence of other specialists (e.g. botanists) during the search. Apart from the references quoted earlier, Sorg et al. (2012) and Beary and Lyman (2012) discuss the taphonomic approach in detail, providing updated bibliographies. The references in Hochrein (2011) provide a comprehensive view of the wide array of taphonomic subjects and issues that North American forensic anthropologists nowadays consider relevant to their field.

Archaeology, but a bit different

If the focus on taphonomic issues resulted in dramatic changes for forensic anthropology, it would also decisively affect the conception of forensic archaeology in the United States. Snow (1982) and Sigler-Eisenberg (1985) had already pointed out that forensic archaeology required the modification of classic archaeological techniques. The nature of these modifications goes beyond the adaptation of mapping or excavation techniques to adjusting for time or personnel constraints. Haglund (2001) provides a brief but particularly meaningful discussion on the differences between forensic and classical archaeological contexts taking into account issues such as time frames or the presence of soft tissues. The task of recovering and contextualising materials that are strange to the classically trained archaeologist, such as soft tissue and bodily fluids, certainly plays a major role for forensic anthropologists. Still, it is only when we factor the nature of the contextual information necessary to analyse the recovered materials, and consider that in many cases they must be studied and evaluated at the scene, that we realise the true dimensions of the divide.

In our opinion, there are at least three major factors that extend the background of the forensic archaeologist well beyond classic archaeology: (1) the nature of the physical and contextual evidence under consideration; (2) the medium in which that evidence is stored; and (3) the paramount importance of properly evaluating the forensic significance of that evidence at the field in order to choose and implement the appropriate protocols. In general, rather than discreet elements, the three factors are intimately related and share many of the same underlying principles. Factors (1) and (2) are both related to the much more limited time frame of the archaeological record in a forensic case (biological time at the hours, days, and weeks scale, rather than geological time at the century or millennium scale), which in turn dictates the type of evidence present at the scene and the medium in which the relevant information is preserved. Factor (3) refers to the continuity of field and laboratory analyses, in particular regarding taphonomic inference.

Concerning the nature of the evidence, the most frequently invoked difference is that forensic archaeology often involves the recovery of human remains in various stages of active decay and decomposition. This makes critical the documentation of the condition of the body and the stages of decomposition in order to get a better idea of how long the body was in the ground (i.e. the post-mortem interval). Thus, the forensic archaeologist must be familiar with decompositional processes and the contextual data necessary to interpret the stage and pattern of the decomposition. Some of the data necessary for these interpretations may appear in stratigraphic relationships, spatial patterns or physical evidence such as plant or insect specimens. At first glance, forensic archaeologists would not appear to be in a worse position in this respect than archaeologists working in other contexts. Even if they usually are only in charge of analysing the stratigraphic relationships and a fraction of the other materials that they are excavating, archaeologists daily identify, document and handle a myriad of other organic and chemical samples at archaeological sites. The primary way in which they recognise these unfamiliar materials at palaeoanthropological sites is through their imprint on the sedimentological context. They appear as discreet phenomena intersecting the stratigraphic continuity or as anthropogenic alterations of the sedimentological continuum.

From this perspective, the direct introduction of classic field archaeology into the forensic arena seems like a match made in heaven; archaeologists are at an advantage over other professionals due to their training and ability to recognise subtle changes in sediment composition and texture rapidly. The traditional archaeologist is able to separate and interpret the pages of the stratigraphic volume by carefully exposing (excavating) the sedimentological matrix layer by the microlayer, using specific methods developed in archaeology to focus the stratigraphic lens properly. These efforts provide significant high-resolution evidence about the relative relationships between sets of events based on their position within the sedimentological space and timescales. However, the medium in which this information is recorded, namely, the stratigraphic record, is created by sedimentological processes affecting the feature over the course of prolonged time spans; these long-term sedimentological processes are largely absent or are much less relevant in forensic contexts.

From the archaeological point of view, forensic features most often represent single temporally circumscribed events. Usually depositional episodes have not spanned decades or centuries, but rather consist of a lone, fleeting moment that may have taken place over the course of just a few minutes. As a consequence, the sedimentological context is often extremely simple and stratigraphic resolution of microstrata is not of the utmost importance. This partially shifts the main focus to other components of the archaeological gamut, such as excavating, mapping and documenting a variety of evidence within the excavated matrix which can be reliably and confidently attributed to the specific burial episode. Elements like the back-dirt pile and its contents now become important as a reflection of the past event.

For example, it can be argued that stratigraphic depositional contexts do exist in forensic sites in the form of leaf litter or organic soil horizons. Yet these elements are not consistently addressed in archaeology, falling instead within the realm of other fields, such as edaphology, the branch of ecological soil science dealing with soil–organism interactions. On the other hand, the forensic archaeological scene is not defined solely by subsurface sedimentary deposits as in classic archaeology, but must also include a consideration of aboveground evidence. The types and distribution of living vegetation may be integral to establishing the post-mortem interval or interpreting the degree of decomposition of the remains. For example, dead twigs or branches over the grave may indicate attempts to hide the evidence. Surface elements – such as trampled vegetation, upturned sediment, shoe impressions in soft sediment, discarded cigarette butts, bottles, cans and shovels – are all potentially relevant and must be integrated with the classic archaeological, sedimentological and depositional information.

In other words, a large fraction of the relevant contextual relationships are not spatial or stratigraphic, but biological; the environmental information necessary for their interpretation goes far beyond the biological specimens or environmental signals trapped in the sedimentological milieu with which traditional archaeologists are familiar. Soil granulometry and chemical characteristics, diatoms or pollen trapped in the soil all provide us with information regarding the palaeoenvironmental conditions at the time of deposition. However, although some of these elements can be important at forensic scenes, the forensic context expands the limits of the archaeological feature to all current environmental factors and conditions surrounding it. Whereas in an archaeological setting the current environmental context may be dramatically different from the one present at the time of original deposition, in forensic contexts both environments are likely similar, calling for sampling and documentation techniques more related to field ecology than archaeological methods. The recordation of relevant environmental data requires instrumentation, techniques and sampling strategies radically different from those utilised in archaeological settings, such as multiple temperature readings, estimates of vegetation coverage or alteration, measurements of light exposure or traces of animal activity. While it is possible to develop step-by-step standard protocols to recover this kind of evidence, in order to be efficient recoveries must also involve a large dose of on-site decision-making as well as a deep understanding of the processes under consideration and the analyses to be performed with that evidence. In these cases, North American forensic anthropologists are better positioned than classically trained archaeologists, as most of the environmental data and processes related to the interpretation of, for example, entomological or botanical evidence, are intimately related to those relevant for taphonomic analysis and, in particular, to tissue decay and decomposition.

Understanding processes and analyses is also particularly important if we view forensic archaeologists as scientists capable of researching and developing their own methods, rather than as mere technicians. The first step in developing and improving new protocols to document a particular type of evidence is recognising that it exists and understanding why and how it will be analysed. The necessity for the forensic archaeologist to be more than a topographer and excavator, being instead familiar with the analysis of at least some of the evidence he/she is recovering, is essential due to more practical and immediate reasons, such as the extreme importance of establishing forensic significance at the scene.

A particularly important role performed by North American forensic anthropologists at the outdoor crime scene is recognising and understanding the relevance of different types of evidence, in order to avoid missing or damaging it. This goes beyond being aware of the fact that some types of materials can be sent for analysis, but includes understanding how and why the particular item can provide evidentiary information so that all appropriate scene and environmental data can then be documented in a manner allowing for comprehensive analysis. These steps constitute what is known as 'establishing the forensic significance' of the materials. In the case of human skeletal remains, their forensic significance is largely related to taphonomic issues, such as the antiquity of the remains, the presence of peri-mortem trauma, atypical patterns of heat alteration (for a recent review on the issue, see Schultz 2012a). However, distinguishing human from animal remains is often the only requirement in the extremely common case in which surface scatters of bones are discovered. In this case, the assessment of forensic significance serves to determine whether a forensic effort should be initiated at all, rather than the next step to take in an ongoing one. Errors of omission (mistakenly identifying a human bone for an animal one) or of commission (mistaking animal elements for human remains) can be devastating. The former results in a failure to recognise the victim, while the latter leads to a waste of time and resources since the find will be unnecessarily processed as a crime scene. The ability of North American forensic anthropologists to recognise the lack of forensic significance early in the process, saving important time and resources, is one of the main arguments promoting law enforcement to call forensic anthropologists to the scene rather than recover and send them the remains.

As will be discussed later, the detection and identification of severely altered, small, or fragmentary human remains, which would likely be missed by the untrained eye, is also extremely important at some of the most common scenes, such as surface scatters or fatal fires. In these situations, it becomes particularly crucial to be able to understand the extensive range of environmental factors that may have played a role in the spatial distribution of the remains, the specific type of alteration they exhibit (e.g. thermal modification, staining, animal alteration) or the determination of the events surrounding death. These inferences will be related mostly to interpretation of taphonomic processes which can help explain why some remains are missing, damaged or scattered from their original anatomical position. This means that the spatial distribution of the human remains relative to topographical factors such as slope or depth must be recorded and analysed. Importantly, these notations are also made in comparison with current biotic factors such as vegetation cover, shade area and intensity, edaphological conditions, temperature regimes and even insect activity. The relative significance of each of these factors and the exact data collection protocols to be employed in each case will depend on elements such as the degree of decomposition of the soft and hard tissues at the time of recovery, which will need to be assessed at the scene.

Not just burials

We described earlier how the development of the field in the United States was largely driven by the analytical needs of forensic anthropologists rather than by law enforcement's recommendation. We think that this is actually the most fruitful approach to discuss the future state of the field, basing it on the analytical needs required at the scene and the materials recovered from it, rather than on the academic degree of the professionals processing it. In this sense, we find it useful to describe briefly some of the scenes most commonly processed by North American forensic anthropologists, discussing some of the characteristics that we consider to have key analytical and methodological implications. We are leaving out the discussion of burials, as we believe that there is a general agreement on the way in which they are processed across the globe, and focusing instead on common scenes in which forensic archaeologists are likely to play different roles, depending on the country. These scenes include searches, surface scatters, mass disasters and fire scenes.

Searches

After initial focus on graves in the 1970s literature by nouveau forensic archaeologists, anthropologists in the United States turned to extending these archaeological principles and practices to other common types of police work. Among these, one of the most frequent requests received by forensic anthropologists/archaeologists in the United States was assistance with outdoor searches for missing individuals or associated evidence (e.g. guns, shell cases). Law enforcement is not particularly well trained to deal with these types of extensive searches, while archaeologists have developed very efficient and effective surveying techniques that are well-tested and routinely utilised in a variety of terrains and situations.

Still, archaeological and forensic searches present some differences, namely, in terms of the range of materials sought. If the feature being located is a burial, archaeological surveying techniques can be applied almost seamlessly (although, as mentioned earlier, forensic anthropologists must pay close attention to signals of recent alteration of soil surfaces and vegetation that may be irrelevant in archaeological contexts). Improved electronic surveying techniques also play an increasingly important role in burial searches (Schultz 2012b).

However, in the forensic setting the victim is not necessarily buried and in a complete and/or unaltered state. As a consequence, an additional skill making forensic searches both efficient and effective is the ability to determine forensic significance accurately and in real time. The evaluation of forensic significance in these cases is based primarily on osteological skills, specifically the ability to identify precisely and accurately not only complete human and animal skeletons or complete bones, but also chewed, weathered, or burned bone fragments. In addition, other associated evidence including clothing, environmental and ecological evidence, and shoe impressions are critical to providing relevant and accurate determinations of significance. Forensic anthropologists involved in searches at specialised scenarios, such as mass disasters or fatal fires, often receive additional training to recognise relevant materials such as parts of explosive devices, vehicles or electric components, all of which may be important in determining fire sources.

Surface scatters

Another type of forensic scene commonly encountered in forensic work in the United States are situations in which the body was disposed of on the ground surface and was subsequently scattered by a variety of taphonomic agents, including animals, gravity, slope wash. Archaeological methods in mapping the spatial distribution of evidence provide a very valuable resource at these scenes. However, the waters are muddied by the deposition of evidence in one episode over a landscape full of non-related evidence or material. In these situations, the key skill again becomes the evaluation of forensic significance and the association of evidence tied to the deposition event.

In these types of situations, an understanding of the extensive range of environmental factors that play a part in the reconstruction of the events is crucial. This means that forensic anthropologists need to analyse the spatial distribution of the human remains relative to scene factors such as slope, vegetation cover, amount and density of shade, soil conditions, temperature regimes, or entomological and botanical evidence. In addition, they need to note carefully and thoroughly the degree of decomposition and alteration of soft and hard tissues at the time of recovery. All the relevant data must be recorded in a manner allowing for their direct introduction in the analyses.

Even though the body may originally be deposited on the surface of the scene, there are still stratigraphic relationships related to vegetal deposits (leaf litter) over and under the remains. This information relates to the timing of the depositional event, at least relative to seasonal indicators. There is also a possibility of partial burial through slope wash, particularly if the body is located in a depression. In this sense, this first phase of the forensic archaeological recovery of the outdoor scene becomes more of a field ecology exercise than an archaeological excavation. All of these new assessments relate to biological and ecological issues that are typically outside the training regime of classical archaeologists, and are, in our opinion, better addressed from a background in the biological sciences. Additionally, the working knowledge of anatomy often possessed by forensic anthropologists is extremely useful in cases involving soft tissue.

Mass disasters and fatal fire scenes

Other types of outdoor forensic scenes in which forensic anthropologists are usually involved absolutely require an archaeological perspective and training, but do not necessarily require an archaeologist. These scenes include fatal fire scenes and mass fatality scenes, the recovery protocols of which are receiving increased attention (Dirkmaat 2012b; Dirkmaat et al. 2012a,b; Symes et al. 2012).

Mass fatality scenes are characterised by the presence of severely altered, and often co-mingled, human remains interspersed with large amounts of burned debris, large vehicle parts, man-made structures, natural environment structures and other objects. The high density of materials and the severe time and personnel constraints associated with these types of scenes exponentially increases the importance of establishing forensic significance rapidly and in situ. While processing normal crime scenes, when in doubt, we can adopt the conservative approach of collecting everything that could be deemed relevant by one of the experts that will later examine the evidence; that luxury is not possible in mass fatality scenes. Utilising that approach with the sheer volume of materials present at these scenes would simply collapse most laboratory capabilities. For this reason, mass fatality scenes require the presence of the main types of analysts in the field, rather than trusting the scenes to criminalists, as is often the case in conventional crime scenes.

Thus, knowledge of archaeological principles, methods and practices is absolutely required at these scenes, both to map and to avoid damaging the evidence, while forensic significance of the evidence must still be established rapidly and in situ, just as it is being excavated. In our view, the best way of attaining this goal is by making the excavator and the specialist who is establishing forensic significance and determining how the evidence should be subsequently treated to be one and the same. Once again, the profile emerging from this situation is that of a professional who combines proper training in archaeological techniques with a comprehensive background in osteology and anatomy.

Very similarly, fatal fire scenes require the two key elements of accurate and timely assessment of forensic significance, as well as the ability to recognise and make decisions regarding extremely altered and co-mingled biological tissues. As in mass disasters, implementation of some archaeological techniques is absolutely critical. However, the relative weight of advanced archaeological and anthropological skills demanded by these scenes is overwhelmingly tilted towards the latter.

Discussion

In the previous sections, we have tried to provide an outline of the history of forensic archaeology in the United States, along with some basic information on the venues in which its North American practitioners operate, the conceptual framework leading their efforts and the types of scenes in which they are involved. The model outlined presents forensic archaeology as an essential component of forensic anthropology, inextricably entrenched with taphonomic interpretation and practised by professionals who are not only tasked with recovering and documenting the evidence, but also with establishing forensic significance, and who are actively involved in its posterior interpretation. Our defence of this model is based on some major characteristics of forensic scenes that, in our opinion, make them not a special form of an archaeological site, but a type of forensic feature subject to contextual regimes fundamentally different from those inspiring the development of classical archaeological theory and practice. Key among them is the diminished importance of the sedimentological context and the inclusion of the current environmental regime as an essential contextual component.

Probably the best way of explaining our view is by briefly describing the curriculum of our Masters programme in Forensic and Biological Anthropology at Mercyhurst University. The students in our programme are selected primarily on the basis of their science background, whether it be in chemistry, biology or archaeology, and not exclusively on their anthropology background. The curriculum is a sequence of different classes in forensic archaeology, GIS, forensic osteology, zooarchaeology, biostatistics, forensic taphonomy and human skeletal trauma analysis. In addition to class work, the graduate students are involved in all aspects of the forensic cases processed by the department, after the appropriate controls, evaluations and clearance, and under appropriate supervision. These include field recoveries in which they participate as team members in the multidisciplinary effort to document context and association at the scenes. They are also involved in all aspects of the laboratory analyses of these remains, including serving in the role of case manager, overseeing and ensuring that the standard operating protocols are followed and all analyses are done properly, prior to thorough review by the forensic anthropology faculty. By the end of 2 years, they are well-trained and experienced forensic anthropologists who can work equally well in the field and in the laboratory.

From our perspective, the North American model would be, at least in principle, more inclusive than the British one and, in this sense, superior. Based on our earlier description, North American forensic anthropologists would be able to do everything at a crime scene that a British forensic archaeologist can do, in addition to anthropological analyses. However, that is far from a widespread reality. In our introduction we mentioned a survey in which an overwhelming majority of members of the Anthropology Section of AAFS stated that they preferred to process their own scenes and that forensic archaeology was the best tool to do so. In the very same survey, when asked about the skills more relevant for forensic anthropology, the members gave very high scores to taphonomy and archaeological techniques, but very low ones to subjects like stratigraphy or archaeological theory. That is to say, there still seems to be a widespread perception of forensic archaeology as an auxiliary, strictly technical field, requiring little training other than in very basic techniques.

This is probably due to a trend taking hold in a large proportion of North American forensic archaeology literature along the last three decades; starting with Bass and Birkby (1978) and Boyd (1979), a very high proportion of the publications were aimed primarily at persuading law enforcement and other forensic anthropologists of the need to utilise forensic archaeological techniques. Thus, they focused more on presenting case examples than detailed protocols or research on specific technical issues. The same is largely true for forensic taphonomy. We have argued that taphonomy provides the conceptual framework and scientific tradition to articulate forensic anthropology as a full-blown scientific field. However, as noted by Bristow et al. (2011), we have yet to take full advantage of that framework and, although to a lesser extent than for forensic archaeology, a large proportion of the contributions on forensic taphonomy are theoretical or based on case examples.

Spreading the gospel among target audiences that the application of forensic archaeology techniques is a necessary requirement in a wide variety of outdoor forensic scenes and contexts has therefore been a very necessary enterprise. But, as noted by Schultz (2008), in spite of the four-field approach, the training of physical anthropologists is very variable in the United States, and many of them have little or no training in archaeology. Thus, convincing a forensic anthropologist to use archaeological techniques is not enough if he/she does not fully understand what that entails. Sigler-Eisenberg (1985, 650–651) warns against instructing law enforcement in archaeological mapping and excavation techniques, pointing out that 'archaeology is more than just digging a neat square hole' and technical training devoid of the appropriate background only creates the illusion of precision. We think that the same can be said of anthropologists who lack the appropriate archaeological background; the next challenge is defining the best practices and what can and cannot be considered as a proper forensic archaeology intervention. From that perspective, the rigorous training in archaeological background demanded by the British model is the best reference and must act as a baseline.

We have also stressed the idea that forensic taphonomy should serve as the backbone for the development of forensic anthropology, to the point at which we could maybe define forensic anthropology as being constituted by osteology and forensic taphonomy. In this regard, the improvement and standardisation of forensic archaeological techniques is also crucial for the further development of forensic taphonomy and even of taphonomy at large. As already noted by Snow (1982), forensic cases provide a unique opportunity for actualistic studies in taphonomy. The forensic anthropologist is able to observe natural taphonomic processes in all their stages, as they are taking place, and place them into a detailed environmental background. We mentioned earlier how much of the literature on forensic taphonomy is largely based on case examples. However, as noted by Bristow et al. (2011), the only thing separating those isolated examples from becoming true study samples is the consistent recording of contextual data. This makes the development of appropriate archaeological protocols for data retrieving, recordation and sharing one of the key goals for forensic anthropology, archaeology and taphonomy in the next decades.

Finally, we have tiptoed insofar over one of the main questions posed in the introduction: if both models are so conceptually different, why are their results are so similar? Those similarities go beyond the appearance of the site maps or the instruments used to produce them. Through discourse with British forensic anthropologists, we frequently discover that we seem to have developed almost identical modifications of the standard archaeological techniques. Part of the explanation can be found by examining the foundational papers of North American forensic archaeology.

As discussed earlier, Morse et al. (1976), Bass and Birkby (1978) and Sigler-Eisenberg (1985) all recommended bringing archaeologists to the scene, much in the fashion of the British model. Still, those same authors, and especially Morse et al. (1976), also stress an important element that is less often remembered: multidisciplinary team work.

Even when the debate surrounding the North American and British models sometimes focuses on the degree that a forensic archaeologist should hold, the reality is that the times of the individual professionals processing scenes or analysing human remains by themselves is gone for good. In general terms, here and in Booty Lane[3] proper forensic archaeological recoveries are being carried out by multidisciplinary teams rather by a single actor. In forensic anthropology the increasing specialisation is not just a trend, but an increasing need. The methods and body of knowledge applied to the analysis of human remains have already achieved a level of sophistication in which it is virtually impossible for a single individual to be completely proficient in all of them (trauma analysis, archaeology, biometry, etc.). Still, the development of all those subfields is far from independent, and requires that all actors share a basic common background, which in the case of forensic anthropology is mostly related to human osteology. We believe that the key requirement for our fields to attain scientific maturity is the definition and development of a similar common background for all the actors involved in forensic archaeological recoveries.

A recurring theme in the previous sections is that the professionals in charge of scene recoveries must have a solid archaeological background, plus a number of other skills. In our view, those professionals can be archaeologists who have also received extra training in physical anthropology, or physical anthropologists who have a solid archaeological background. From our experience, both from our very different backgrounds and from having worked in the field with students with degrees ranging from geography to chemistry or biophysics, those do not represent two distinct profiles, but rather two extremes within a single continuum. We have found that all the colours within that spectrum are necessary and bring important elements to the field, and it is experience and scene requirements that best define the specific tasks that each individual will adopt as their main vocation. In addition, we must also be aware that the combination of traditional physical anthropology and archaeology does not suffice in covering the needs of forensic archaeological recoveries, and we are still in dire need of both developing and borrowing new methods from other disciplines (e.g. field ecology) to address many of the materials and contextual relationships that, as discussed earlier, fall beyond the realms of both fields.

[3]Street roadat Womersley, North Yorkshire, UK.

Still, we strongly believe that the combination of those two facets (physical anthropology and archaeology) provides the optimal common background and language to start defining the field in a more rigorous and concerted effort. We are convinced that this would be an almost impossible task if forensic archaeologists and anthropologists confronted the challenge independently and if the divide between both conceptions of the field was interpreted in a dogmatic manner based on appeals to credentials or imagined ownership rights, rather than on the analytical needs of the forensic scene.

Acknowledgements

The authors would like to thank Kaitlyn E. Sanders for her assistance in editing and preparing this chapter. We also thank Dr Emma Brown for her thoughtful comments on a previous version of the manuscript, which largely improved its quality.

References

Bass, W.M. and Birkby, W.H. 1978. Exhumation: the method could make the difference. *FBI Law Enforcement Bulletin* 47(7), 6–11.

Beary, M.O. and Lyman, R.L. 2012. The use of taphonomy in forensic anthropology: past trends and future prospects. In D.C. Dirkmaat (ed.), *A Companion to Forensic Anthropology*, 499–527. Chichester, John Wiley & Sons, Inc.

Berryman, H.E. and Lanfear, A.K. 2012. Forensic anthropologists in medical examiner's and coroner's offices: a history. In D.C. Dirkmaat (ed.), *A Companion to Forensic Anthropology*, 534–548. Chichester, John Wiley & Sons, Inc.

Binford, L. 1981. *Bones: Ancient Men and Modern Myths*. New York, Academic Press.

Blau, S. and Ubelaker, D.H. 2009. *Handbook of Forensic Anthropology and Archaeology*. Walnut Creek, Left Coast Press.

Boaz, N.T. and Behrensmeyer, A.K. 1976. Hominid taphonomy: transport of human skeletal parts in an artificial fluviatile environment. *American Journal of Physical Anthropology* 45(1), 53–60.

Borofsky, R. 2002. The four subfields: anthropologists as mythmakers. *American Anthropologist* 104, 463–480.

Boyd, R.M. 1979. Buried body cases. *FBI Law Enforcement Bulletin* 48(2), 1–7.

Brain, C.K. 1981. *The Hunters or the Hunted? An Introduction to African Cave Taphonomy*. Chicago, Chicago University Press.

Bristow, J., Simms, Z. and Randolph-Quinney, P. 2011. Taphonomy. In S. Black and E. Ferguson (eds.), *Forensic anthropology 2000 to 2010*, 279–318. Boca Raton, CRC Press.

Burns, K.M. 2012. *The Forensic Anthropology Training Manual*. 3rd edition. New York, Pearson Education.

Byers, S.N. 2010. *Introduction to Forensic Anthropology*. 4th edition. New York, Pearson Custom Anthropology.

Christensen, A. 2010. The FBI laboratory division's new forensic anthropology program. *FBI Law Enforcement Bulletin* 79(8), 14–15.

Connor, M.A. 2007. *Forensic Methods: Excavation for the Archaeologist and Investigator*. Lanham, Rowman Altamira.

Crossland, Z. 2013. Evidential regimes of forensic archaeology. *Annual Review of Anthropology* 42, 121–37.

Dirkmaat, D.C. 2002. Recovery and interpretation of the fatal fire victim: the role of forensic anthropology. In W. D. Haglund and M. H. Sorg (eds.), *Advances in Forensic Taphonomy: Method, Theory, and Archaeological Perspectives*, 451–472. Boca Raton, CRC Press.

Dirkmaat, D.C. (ed.) 2012a. *A Companion to Forensic Anthropology*. Chichester, John Wiley & Sons, Inc.

Dirkmaat, D.C. 2012b. Forensic anthropology at the mass fatality incident (commercial airliner) crash scene. In D.C. Dirkmaat (ed.), *A Companion to Forensic Anthropology*, 136–156. Chichester, Wiley-Blackwell.

Dirkmaat, D.C. 2012c. Documenting context at the outdoor crime scene: why bother? In D.C. Dirkmaat (ed.), *A Companion to Forensic Anthropology*, 49–65. Chichester, John Wiley & Sons, Inc.

Dirkmaat, D.C. and Adovasio, J.M. 1997. The role of archaeology in the recovery and interpretation of human remains from an outdoor forensic setting. In W.D. Haglund and M.H. Sorg (eds.), *Forensic Taphonomy: The Postmortem Fate of Human Remains*, 39–64. New York, CRC Press.

Dirkmaat, D.C. and Cabo, L.L. 2012. Embracing the new paradigm. In D.C. Dirkmaat (ed.), *A Companion to Forensic Anthropology*, 3–40. Chichester, John Wiley & Sons, Inc.

Dirkmaat, D.C., Cabo, L.L., Ousley, S.D. and Symes, S.A. 2008. New perspectives in forensic anthropology. *American Journal of Physical Anthropology* 137(S47), 33–52.

Dirkmaat, D.C., Chapman, E., Kenyhercz, M. and Cabo, L.L. 2012a. *Enhancing Scene Processing Protocols to Improve Victim Identification and Field Detection of Human Remains in Mass Fatality Scenes*. Washington, DC, National Institute of Justice (NIJ).

Dirkmaat, D.C., Olson, G.O., Klales, A.R. and Getz, S. 2012b.The role of forensic anthropology in the recovery and interpretation of the fatal-fire victim. In D.C. Dirkmaat (ed.), *A Companion to Forensic Anthropology*, 113–135. Chichester, John Wiley & Sons, Inc.

Dupras, T., Schultz, J., Wheeler, S. and Williams, L. 2006. *Forensic Recovery of Human Remains*. Boca Raton, CRC Press.

Efremov, I.A. 1940. Taphonomy: new branch of paleontology. *Pan-American Geologist* 74, 81–93.

Emanowsky, P.D. and Belcher, W.R. 2012. The many hats of a recovery leader: perspectives on planning and executing worldwide forensic investigations and recoveries at the JPAC Central Identification Laboratory. In D.C. Dirkmaat (ed.), *A Companion to Forensic Anthropology*, 567–592. Chichester, John Wiley & Sons, Inc.,.

Gifford, D.P. 1981. Taphonomy and paleoecology: a critical review of archaeology's sister disciplines. In M.B. Schiffer (ed.), *Advances in Archaeological Method and Theory*, Volume 4, 365–438. New York, Academic Press.

Grayson, D.K. 1984. *Quantitative Zooarchaeology: Topics in the Analysis of Archaeological Faunas*. Orlando, Academic Press.

Haglund, W.D. 2001. Archaeology and forensic death investigations. *Journal of Historical Archaeology* 35(1), 26–34.

Haglund, W.D. and Sorg, M.H. (eds.) 1997a. *Forensic Taphonomy: The Postmortem Fate of Human Remains*. New York, CRC Press.

Haglund, W.D. and Sorg, M.H. (eds.) 1997b. Method and theory of forensic taphonomy research. In *Forensic Taphonomy: The Postmortem Fate of Human Remains*, 13–25. Boca Raton, CRC Press.

Hicks, D. 2013. Four-field anthropology. *Current Anthropology* 54(6). Available at: http://www.jstor.org/stable/10.1086/673385 (last accessed 30 March 2014).

Hochrein, M.J. 2002. An autopsy of the grave: recognizing, collecting, and preserving forensic geotaphonomic evidence. In W.D. Haglund and M.H. Sorg (eds.), *Advances in Forensic Taphonomy: Method, Theory, and Archaeological Perspectives*, 45–70. Boca Raton, CRC Press.

Hochrein, M.J. 2011. *A Bibliography Related to Crime Scene Interpretation with Emphases in Geotaphonomic and Forensic Archaeological Field Techniques*. Johnstown, PA.

Hochrein, M.J. 2012. Crime scene perspective: collecting evidence in the context of the criminal incident. In D.C. Dirkmaat (ed.), *A Companion to Forensic Anthropology*, 101–112. Chichester, John Wiley & Sons, Inc.

Holland, T., Byrd, J. and Sava, V. 2008. Joint POW/MIA accounting command's central identification laboratory. In M.W. Warren, H.A. Walsh-Haney and L. Freas (eds.), *The Forensic Anthropology Laboratory*, 47–63. Boca Raton, CRC Press.

Killam, E.W. 2004. *The Detection of Human Remains*. Springfield, Charles C Thomas.

Kuhn, T. 1970. *The Structure of Scientific Revolutions*. Chicago, University of Chicago Press.

Klein, R.G. and Cruz-Uribe, K. 1984. *The Analysis of Animal Bones from Archeological Sites*. Chicago, University of Chicago Press.

Komar, D.A. and Buikstra, J.E. 2008. *Forensic Anthropology: Contemporary Theory and Practice*. Oxford, Oxford University Press.

Krogman, W.M. and Işcan, M.Y. 1986. *The Human Skeleton in Forensic Medicine*. Springfield, Charles C. Thomas.

Kwas, M.L. 1999. A retrospective on the careers of archaeologists Dan Franklin Morse and Phyllis Anderson Morse. In R.C. Mainfort and M.D. Jeter (eds.), *Essays in Honor of Dan and Phyllis Morse*, 1–14. Fayetteville, University of Arkansas Press.

Lyman, R. L. 1994. *Vertebrate Taphonomy*. Cambridge, Cambridge University Press.

Márquez-Grant, N., Litherland, S. and Roberts, J. 2012.European perspectives and the role of the forensic archaeologist in the UK. In D.C. Dirkmaat (ed.), *A Companion to Forensic Anthropology*, 598–625. Chichester, John Wiley & Sons, Inc.

Mayne Correia, P. and Beattie, O. 2002.A critical look at methods for recovering, evaluating, and interpreting cremated human remains. In W.D. Haglund and M.H. Sorg (eds.), *Advances in Forensic Taphonomy: Method, Theory, and Archaeological Perspectives*, 435–450. Boca Raton, CRC Press.

Morse, D., Crusoe, D. and Smith, H.G. 1976. Forensic archaeology. *Journal of Forensic Sciences* 21(2), 323–332.

Morse, D., Duncan, J. and Stoutamire, J. 1983. *Handbook of Forensic Archaeology and Anthropology*. Tallahassee, Rose Printing.

National Research Council 2009. *Strengthening Forensic Science in the United States: A Path Forward*. Washington, DC, National Academies Press.

Nawrocki, S.P. 2008. The university of Indianapolis archeology and forensics laboratory. In M.W. Warren, H.A. Walsh-Haney and L. Freas (eds.), *The Forensic Anthropology Laboratory*, 65–93. Boca Raton, CRC Press.

Saferstein, R. 2010. *Criminalistics: An Introduction to Forensic Science*. Englewood Cliffs, Prentice-Hall.

Saul, J.M. and Saul, F.P. 2002. Forensics, archaeology, and taphonomy: the symbiotic relationship. In W.D. Haglund and M.H. Sorg (eds.), *Advances in Forensic Taphonomy: Method, Theory, and Archaeological Perspectives*, 71–97. Boca Raton, CRC Press.

Schultz, J.J. 2008. The contribution of forensic archaeology to homicide investigations. *Homicide Studies* 12(4), 399–413.

Schultz, J.J. 2012a. Determining the forensic significance of skeletal remains. In D.C. Dirkmaat (ed.), *A Companion to Forensic Anthropology*, 66–84. Chichester, John Wiley & Sons, Inc.

Schultz, J.J. 2012b.The application of ground-penetrating radar for forensic grave detection. In D.C. Dirkmaat (ed.), *A Companion to Forensic Anthropology*, 85–100. Chichester, John Wiley & Sons, Inc.

Scott, D.D. and Connor, M. 1997. Context delicti: archaeological context in forensic work. In W.D. Haglund and M.H. Sorg (eds.), *Forensic Taphonomy: The Postmortem Fate of Human Remains*, 27–38. Boca Raton, CRC Press.

Sigler-Eisenberg, B. 1985. Forensic research: expanding the concept of applied archaeology. *American Antiquity* 50(3), 650–655.

Skinner, M. and Lazenby, R. 1983.*Found! Human Remains: A Field Manual for the Recovery of the Recent Human Skeleton*. Burnaby, Archaeology Press – Simon Fraser University.

Skinner, M.F., Clegg, L., Congram, D. et al. 2010. Taking the pulse of forensic anthropology in Canada. *Canadian Society of Forensic Science Journal* 43(4), 191–203.

Snow, C.C. 1982. Forensic anthropology. *Annual Review of Anthropology* 11, 97–131.

Snow, C.C. 1995. Murder most foul. *The Sciences* 35(3), 16–20.

Sorg, M.H., Haglund, W.D. and Wren, J.A. 2012. Current research in forensic taphonomy. In D.C. Dirkmaat (ed.), *A Companion to Forensic Anthropology*, 477–498. Chichester, John Wiley & Sons, Inc.

Steadman, D.W. (ed.) 2003. *Hard Evidence: Case Studies in Forensic Anthropology*. New Jersey, Prentice Hall.

Symes, S.A., Dirkmaat, D.C., Ousley, S. and Chapman, E. 2012. *Recovery and Interpretation of Burned Human Remains*. Washington, D.C., National Institute of Justice (NIJ).

Tersigni-Tarrant, M.T. and Shirley, N.R. 2012a. Brief history of forensic anthropology. In M.T. Tersigni-Tarrant and N.R. Shirley (eds.), *Forensic Anthropology: An Introduction*, 1–16. Boca Raton, CRC Press.

Tersigni-Tarrant, M.T. and Shirley, N.R. (eds.) 2012b. *Forensic Anthropology: An Introduction*. Boca Raton, CRC Press.

Warren, M.W., Walsh-Haney, H.A. and Freas, L. (eds.) 2008. *The Forensic Anthropology Laboratory*. Boca Raton, CRC Press.

CHAPTER 32

Forensic archaeology and the recovery of human remains in Venezuela

Livia Margarita Muñoz Andrade

Dirección de Asesoría Técnico Científica e Investigaciones del Ministerio Público, Caracas, Venezuela

Introduction

Forensic archaeology is rarely recognised or used in the Bolivian Republic of Venezuela for several reasons, including a shortage of clandestine burials. However, if resources are available regarding archaeologists or forensic anthropologists with knowledge of archaeological techniques, these are used. In any case that may require the use of forensic archaeology, both disciplines of archaeology and forensic anthropology are employed. Yet, the concept of forensic archaeology in Venezuela is very limited and therefore although some use of archaeological techniques in forensic investigations will be mentioned, this chapter largely focuses on presenting a brief history of legal medicine and the role of forensic anthropology in Venezuela.

Medico-legal context and a brief history of forensic anthropology in Venezuela

The history of legal medicine in Venezuela has a chronology that dates from the days of the Liberator Simón Bolívar (1783–1830) and the beginnings of the Republic (1810–1812) to the present day, coupled with the creation of public and private institutions and laws that mould the present state of medico-legal framework in our country. The main authors of the medical jurisprudence of Venezuela have boosted the legal aspects governing medical practice in Venezuela today. Nevertheless, legal medicine in Venezuela is a product of history and culture of the times in which it developed, and reflects the values prevailing in medical and legal practice in the country.

The Chair of Legal Medicine in Venezuela was first included in the very first university founded in the country (1721, University of Caracas), a World Heritage site, the Central University of Venezuela (*Universidad Central de Venezuela* – UCV). Yet Legal Medicine was already established in the Republican Statutes of the Liberator (*El Libertador*) in which Article 83 provides:

> Medicine classes are divided in the following order: first, one of general and descriptive anatomy; second, one of physiology and hygiene...third, one of denosography and internal pathology or medical practice; fourth, one of nosography and external pathology or surgery; fifth, one of therapeutics, *materia medica* and pharmacy; sixth, one of obstetrics or births; seventh, one of legal medicine. There will also be courses in clinical medicine and surgery which will take place in hospitals with the respective teachers ... [RFM v.26 n.2 Caracas, July2003]. [author's translation]

In Article 91, it is stated that Legal Medicine will be the responsibility of the teachers of Clinical Medicine and Surgery:

> Clinical Medicine, Surgery and Legal Medicine. In these departments will be taught clinical medicine and the application of theoretical principles to practice. Equally, clinical surgery or external in all its branches; the same Chairs [Professors] will also teach Legal Medicine, at such times as required in the timetable of the courses. [RFM v.26 n.2 Caracas, July 2003]. [author's translation]

The Chair of Legal Medicine was opened for the first time 15 years after the establishment of the Constitution of the UCV, in the year 1841, appearing together with *Materia Medica* and Therapeutics, among others. However, by the late 1950s the Judicial Technical Police (*Policía Técnica Judicial* – PTJ) was created in Venezuela, and it is there where the part of Legal Medicine and its specialities or branches are related to the forensic arena. Throughout time, Legal Medicine has developed and the Venezuelan Society of Forensic Medicine (*Sociedad Venezolana de Medicina Forense*) was founded on 6 January 1964; in 1966 the forensic anthropologist Dr Maritza Garaicoechea, who had graduated from the UCV, joined the PTJ and become the founder of forensic anthropology in the country. In the beginning

Forensic Archaeology: A Global Perspective, First Edition. Edited by W.J. Mike Groen, Nicholas Márquez-Grant and Robert C. Janaway.

Dr Garaicoechea dedicated her work on the skeletal remains recovered by the PTJ throughout the national territory.

These cases are often associated with people reported missing by their families and which were sometimes associated with homicides. For the forensic anthropology cases, obviously the techniques of physical anthropology were employed regarding the calculation of Minimum Number of Individuals (MAI), identifying the bones present and providing a biological profile where possible including sex, age at death, height and ancestry or population affinity. This profile alongside unique identifying features in some cases allowed a positive identification. Cases like that in the suburb of Mamera in Caracas where three young men were murdered in 1980[1] and buried allowed through anthropological study the identification of the three victims.

In 1974 the Judicial Police Act (*Ley de Policía Judicial*) was published. This law relates to Forensic Medicine and disciplines such as dentistry, forensic anthropology, and forensic radiology amongst others. Partly as a result of this, in June 2012 a decree which also relates to Forensic Science and Medicine (*Decreto con rango, valor y fuerza de Ley Orgánica del servicio de Policía de Investigación, el Cuerpo e Investigaciones Científicas, Penales y Criminalísticas y El Servicio Nacional de Medicina y Ciencias Forenses* – SENAMECF), assigned to the Vice Ministry of Interior (*Vice Ministerio Integral de Investigación Penal y Jurídica del Ministerio; Poder Popular paralas Relaciones del Interior, Justicia y Paz*) was promulgated. This Act states in its Article 72:

> The National Service of Medicine and Forensic Sciences (*Servicio Nacional de Medicina y Ciencias Forenses* – SENAMECF) is the main body in forensic science and forensic medicine at the service of criminal investigation and public security, administratively and functionally dependent on the Ministry of Popular Power [*Ministerio del Poder Popular*] with responsibility for public safety. [author's translation]
>
> The National Institute of Forensic Medicine and Sciences is civil in nature, not police, public, permanent, professional and organised. It will be deployed throughout the country to ensure the practice of criminal investigation. The National Service of Medicine and Forensic Sciences is the main body for expertise in the field of criminal investigation. [author's translation]

In addition, Article 73 indicates that this body has competence in all national territories where scientific and technical support is necessary for criminal investigation. The duties of such service are outlined in Article 74, stating that the SENAMECF will [summarised, modified and translated by the author]:

- collect, organise and scientifically ensure the evidence and information which is gathered,
- ensure and maintain, in coordination with other relevant agencies and entities, the chain of custody of all the items gathered and which falls under the area of expertise of the SENAMECF,
- employ the areas of expertise that are present to assess the requirements on a case by case basis of the specialties necessary, requesting the cooperation of national and international experts in certain areas of expertise if required,
- determine the cause, manner and date of death, as well as establish the identification of the deceased,
- undertake assessments on living persons, by way of physical examinations and/or mental health evaluations,
- undertake DNA analysis in living persons, deceased, human skeletal remains, dental remains or any other human tissue if required,
- perform autopsies and exhumations in those cases of forensic or criminal interest,
- undertake research and development into methods of forensic identification,
- provide medical and forensic science support in cases where this is required by the Public Ministry and institutions and authorities relating to criminal or unexplained death investigation,
- become established as the scientific centre of reference in all matters relating to medicine and forensic science,
- serve as a monitoring and quality assurance or control body of expert evidence and medico-legal examinations performed by other officials and agencies at the request of the competent authority,
- provide scientific and forensic advice to the judiciary, the Public Ministry, competent bodies and authorities,
- provide advice and consultancy on a scientific or medico-legal cases,
- serve as the accreditation and certification body for forensic testing laboratories of public and private entities, as well as the competence of people engaged in these activities.

Currently, there is an Integrated Police, in operation since 2010, with the aim of creating a single police force which also includes other agencies such as the Fire and Rescue Department, Civil Protection, Traffic Police and the local and regional police forces throughout the country. This Integrated Police was termed National Police (*Policía Nacional*) and it

[1]For more information, see: http://cronicasdeltanato.wordpress.com/el-triple-crimen-de-mamera/ (last accessed October 2013).

undertakes a number of functions although some of the other departments such as Fire and Rescue which are at present adopting themselves to this plan still retain their original functions. One of the main functions of this National Police is to prevent crime; however, at present therefore it does not have any forensic anthropologists amongst its staff.

The equivalent to Scientific Support or Scientific Police is called *Policía Científica* or *Cuerpo de Investigaciones Científicas, Penales y Criminalísticas* (CICPC), and legally it follows under the decree unique to the Police Service (*Ley Orgánica del Servicio de Policía de Investigación*). When there is notification of a loss of life, the CICPC as well as the Public Ministry (*Ministerio Público*) is notified immediately. Thus, the CICPC is in charge of investigating all homicides nationally as well as originally investigating the crime scene, gathering the evidence and producing police exhibits. These police exhibits are then sent following appropriate chain of custody to the relevant specialist laboratories which might include criminalistics as well as the SENAMECF.

When forensic anthropological expertise is requested the CICPC as well as the Public Ministry contact their own experts in the area of forensic anthropology (*División de Antropología Forense*). In Caracas alone, the forensic anthropology section has 14 forensic anthropologists. These experts write a report on the examination they have undertaken, and may be required to attend court as an expert witness, especially when there is a comparison between a specific's person ante-mortem data with the post-mortem data, rather than simply for general biological profiling. It is worth noting that in Venezuela, the forensic anthropologists do not attend the (crime) scene (it's the Scientific Police or CICPC), except for mass fatality incidents as a result, for example, of air disasters, traffic fatalities or natural catastrophes (e.g. earthquakes, landslides, floods).

Anthropological and archaeological training

As for the training of anthropologists in Venezuela, this tends to take place at the School of Anthropology (*Escuela de Antropología*), which belongs to the Faculty of Economics of the UCV, as it is considered a Humanities or Social Sciences rather than a Medical or Clinical career. This degree covers ten semesters spread over five years. Subjects which are taught include general osteology, physical anthropology and biodiversity, and it also includes archaeology amongst others fields of study. However, the qualification provided at the end of the degree is that of anthropologist (*Título de Antropólogo*) and graduates end up in public bodies including the Division of Forensic Anthropology of CICPC in the city of Caracas. This team of forensic anthropologists examines unidentified bodies, human skeletal remains or bodies in an advanced state of decomposition, dismembered bodies and fire victims. As stated earlier, there are 14 forensic anthropologists working in Caracas as part of CICPC. There are also another four in the state of Miranda, three in the state of Aragua and one in Vargas and Anzoátegui. Although all of those practising forensic anthropology in Venezuela have an anthropological qualification, some have other backgrounds such as in Law, Nursing, Psychology, Radiology and other areas related to forensic science such as Criminalistics, Criminology, Police Administration and Logistics, Statistics and Genetics, amongst others; but none have a degree in Medicine.

The Venezuelan Public Ministry has several forensic anthropologists in the area of Human Rights (*Unidades Criminalísticas contra la Vulneración de Derechos Fundamentales*) in Caracas and Barquisimeto and two in the Department of Scientific–Technical Advice and Investigations (*Dirección de Asesoría Técnico Científica e Investigaciones*). In the Bolivarian National Guard (*Guardia Nacional Bolivariana*), which belongs to the Armed Forces, there are also forensic anthropologists; as well as at the Ministry of Popular Power for Interior Justice and Peace of the Bolivarian Republic of Venezuela in the area of Crime Prevention.

Forensic anthropologists are taught archaeological theory, methods and excavation techniques during their degree and this includes a practical element. Most people who are interested in archaeological fieldwork end up focusing mainly on the historical context rather than the forensic side of archaeology.

With regard to the criminal investigator (*Investigador Criminalista*), his/her main function is to advise the different national territory Fiscal Representation in a variety of areas. These include criminology, ballistics, document analysis, medical malpractice, fraud, toxicology, dentistry and forensic anthropology. By channelling this through one individual (*Investigador Criminalista*), there is a coordinated and comprehensive response and advice for Prosecutors.

The author has attended several International Conferences of the Latin American Association of Forensic Anthropology (*Asociación Latinoamericana de Antropología Forense* – ALAF) and delivered a number of papers on the subject, such as identifications through forensic anthropology (ALAF Conference, Argentina 2009) and the anthropological approach to be followed in air disasters (ALAF Conference, Colombia 2010). The author has also participated as a speaker at the International Courses run by the Criminology and Forensic Science Department of the Public Ministry with lectures on the subject of forensic anthropology, including recovery, followed by hands-on practical workshops. The subject of forensic anthropology has also been included in the Diploma of Criminalistics and Forensic Sciences, Criminal Investigation and Criminal Process, which have been promoted by the National School of the Public Ministry of Venezuela, and delivered to the National Guard amongst other forces. The author has also collaborated in a number of publications in the magazine of the ministry (*Ministerio Público*) to promote the discipline (Rivero 2009, Rivero Nuñez 2012). In addition, anthropology has played an important part and appeared in the media, for example, with the author's participation alongside Dr Lourdes Pérez and Dr Maritza Garaicoechea from the CICPC, in the exhumation and bioanthropological study of the remains of the Liberator Simón Bolívar in 2010 as a request from the Ministry of Justice.

Homicides and clandestine burials

The homicides that occur in Venezuela are mostly violent deaths caused by gunshot wounds or knives amongst others, and the rate is 50 for every 100,000 inhabitants.

There have not been many cases of clandestine burials including mass graves in Venezuela. One known case is that known as *El Caracazo*, an incident which started in the city of Guarenas in the state of Miranda and then extended to Caracas. The year was 1989 and about 300 people died, most of whom were buried in mass graves in the southern cemetery (*Cementerio General del Surs*). By 1992 this particular case was ruled as a violation of human rights by the Venezuelan Armed Forces, which led to a criminal investigation being launched by a criminal court (*Tribunal décimo de Primera Instancia en lo Penal*) and which led to the recovery of the human remains from the mass graves by forensic anthropologists from Venezuela alongside members from the Argentine Forensic Anthropology Team (EAAF; Fondebrider and Scheinsohn, Chapter 43, this volume) who had been invited to assist. Later these remains were reburied in defined niches in the same cemetery. In 2009, the Public Ministry led by the Attorney General of the Bolivarian Republic of Venezuela, Dr Luisa Ortega Diaz, took over this investigation and the remains were exhumed once more from the niches in which they had been reburied. This exhumation had taken place in an organised and orderly manner following scientific protocols by a team of forensic anthropologists, dentists, medical doctors, pathologists and two archaeologists from the UCV. During the exhumation process, the bones were exhibited separately and the chain of custody was followed from the site to the laboratory where all the forensic anthropological, dental and genetic analyses were undertaken in order to obtain a biological profile for the deceased.

During the course of analysing the remains of those who had been buried in the mass graves at this southern cemetery of Caracas, forensic anthropological and dental analyses yielded a total of 72 individuals. They were reburied once again in the same cemetery but in a dignified and respectful manner. Formal identification via DNA is currently being carried out with the samples extracted from the victims and this identification is undertaken by the Public Ministry and a number of other scientific institutions (*Cuerpo de Investigaciones Científicas Penales y Criminalísticas, Instituto Venezolano de Investigaciones Científicas* and the *Instituto de Estudios Avanzados*).

Another case which will be remembered was the massacre at Cantaura (*La Masacre de Cantaura*) in 1982. A total of 25 individuals were killed by the armed police and military forces and buried in a cemetery. Forensic anthropologists were requested to identify the remains by a number of techniques including image superimposition. Although in these cases no forensic archaeology excavation techniques were employed, the investigators did follow a number of international protocols such as that of the United Nations and Minnesota. However, the exhumation was undertaken by the cemetery workers or undertakers under the supervision of experts for preservation of the remains and for ensuring the recovery of all evidence. These experts formed a team comprising forensic pathologists, a dentist, a forensic anthropologist, sometimes a radiologist and the police.

Excavation at Jacumuparo

To the author's knowledge only one case appears to have used archaeology in a forensic setting in Venezuela. The case relates to the presumed killing in the village of Jacumuparo, in the state of Falcón. In the 1970s two amongst a group of young revolutionaries were allegedly killed. A group of archaeologists and physical and forensic anthropologists, all graduates from the UCV, worked together to survey and evaluate the area that some witness accounts had pointed out as the place where the depositions took place (Figure 32.1). After a number of trenches (Figure 32.2), the human remains were located (Figure 32.3) and since excavating them one by one would have significantly damaged the remains, the retrieval was a 'block' excavation where the earth and bones were placed in a wooden frame in which they could then be sent to a forensic anthropology laboratory for analysis. This included careful recovery of the bone, radiographic examination and forensic anthropological analysis to obtain as much information

Figure 32.1 Presumed location where the remains would have been buried.

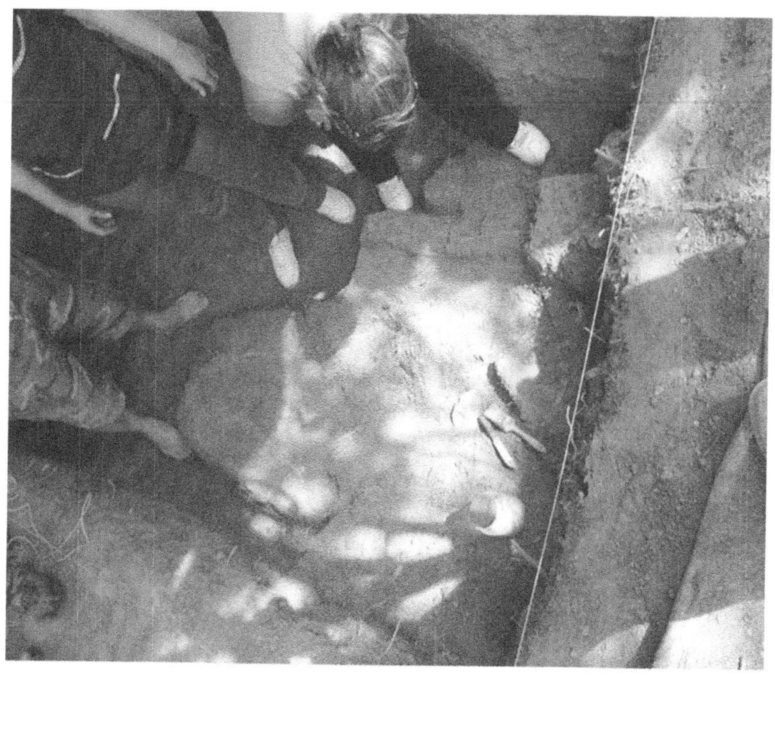

Figure 32.2 Excavation of the area in which the remains were presumably buried.

Figure 32.3 Human remains in a poor state of preservation.

as possible on age, sex and stature as well as other parameters. Samples were also obtained for DNA analysis and once the remains had been identified, they were submitted to the relatives for reburial.

Conclusion

As to whether there is a future for forensic archaeology in Venezuela, this is unclear at present as this field of expertise is not used in the country. The Central University of Venezuela (UCV) does not currently teach archaeology applied to the forensic context; however, delivering workshops or courses in forensic archaeology would certainly benefit those working in the area of forensic anthropology in Venezuela. With this in mind, the author feels that it should be compulsory that forensic anthropologists in Venezuela be more aware of the value of forensic archaeology and this can nicely overlap with forensic anthropology.

References

Rivero, G. 2009. Tras la identidad desconocida. *Ministerio Público* 2, 15–18.

Rivero Nuñez, G. 2012. Gracias a la antropología forense. *Ministerio Público* 13, 50–52.

CHAPTER 33

The use of (forensic) archaeology in Australia in the search and recovery of buried evidence: a review

Soren Blau[1] and Jon Sterenberg[2]

[1] *Victorian Institute of Forensic Medicine/Department of Forensic Medicine, Monash University, Southbank, Victoria, Australia*

[2] *Archaeological Contractor, Bendigo, Victoria, Australia/Institute for Archaeologists (IFA), UK*

Introduction

While clandestine burials involving human remains are occasionally reported in the Australian media (e.g. The Australian 2012; The Irish Echo 2012), the use of archaeologists at a crime scene has not been routinely recognised by any Australian police force as a professional resource for forensic investigators. This is unlike the situation in the United Kingdom and other countries across the globe and may be because 'the detection of clandestine graves is not perceived in Australia as a frequent, substantial or resolvable problem' (Powell 2006, 426). A national survey of techniques used over a period of 7 years by Australian police to locate bodies showed that the three main methods of locating human remains were accidental discovery, further information being given to police and police ground search (Powell 2006, 30–31).

Legal framework concerning the investigation of a crime scene in Australia

The British settlers who colonised Australia in 1788 were subject to decisions made by the British government, which meant that Australia followed the 'body of English law, including the criminal law in force in England at the time' (Plueckhahn and Cordner 1991, 39). As a result, modern-day Australia's six states and two territories have coronial systems of medico-legal death investigations, each with their own *Coroner's Act*. There is, however, 'a great deal of variation in the manner in which each system operates' (Australian Royal Commission into Aboriginal Deaths in Custody 1991, 4.5.17). The states of Queensland, Victoria, New South Wales (NSW), South Australia (SA) and Western Australia (WA) have a centrally administered coronial service under the control of a state coroner. In contrast, Tasmania, the Australian Capital Territory (ACT) and the Northern Territory (NT) have decentralised systems where 'coronial functions are performed by the chief magistrate and all stipendiary magistrates who are coroners by virtue of their office as magistrates' (Australian Royal Commission into Aboriginal Deaths in Custody 1991, 4.5.28). Most magistrates in all Australian states can act as coroners, as can some judges.

Each state and territory has its own government forensic science and medicine service providers (Table 33.1). While some organisations operate under the auspices of Departments of Justice (e.g. the Victorian Institute of Forensic Medicine [VIFM]), others (such as Path West in WA and the Queensland Health Forensic and Scientific Operations) function under the Department of Health. In addition, there is a national Forensic and Data Centre run out of the Australian Federal Police (AFP).

There are also differences in the legislation between the states and territories as to when human skeletal remains can be legally considered of 'forensic significance' (Blau 2009a, 10). For example, in the states of Victoria and NSW the legislation clearly defines a time depth in which human remains are of medico-legal significance. A coroner in Victoria may investigate a death that is or may be a reportable death if the death appears to have occurred within 100 years before the death was reported to a coroner. However, a coroner must investigate a death if the death occurred within 50 years before the death was reported (Victorian Coroners Act 2008). Similarly, in NSW, a coroner does not have jurisdiction to investigate the death unless the death occurred within the last 100 years; if they are found to be non-human

Forensic Archaeology: A Global Perspective, First Edition. Edited by W.J. Mike Groen, Nicholas Márquez-Grant and Robert C. Janaway.

Table 33.1 Summary of the forensic science and medicine service providers in Australia.

State/Territory	Forensic medicine	Forensic science
Australian Capital Territory (ACT)		Toxicology and Forensic Chemistry
New South Wales (NSW)	Institute of Forensic Medicine; Department of Forensic Medicine, Institute of Clinical Pathology and Medical Research, Westmead Hospital	Division of Analytical Laboratories; Forensic Services Group (NSW Police)
Northern Territory (NT)	Forensic Pathology, Royal Darwin Hospital	Forensic Services, NT Police
Queensland	Queensland Health Forensic and Scientific Operations	Forensic Services, Queensland Police Service
South Australia (SA)	Forensic Science SA	Forensic Services Branch, South Australia Police
Tasmania	State Forensic Pathologist, Royal Hobart Hospital	Forensic Science Service Tasmania; Forensic Services, Tasmania Police
Victoria	Victorian Institute of Forensic Medicine	Victoria Police Forensic Services Centre
Western Australia (WA)	PathWest	Forensic Division, WA Police
	Forensic Services – Pathology, PathCentre	Forensic Science Laboratory, ChemCentre WA

remains or if the remains found have no connection with NSW (NSW Coroners Act 1980). The majority of other states' and territories' legislation make no specific mention of a defined time period. Most practitioners make assumptions that remains older than between 50 and 70 years are of no medico-legal significance.

The legislation in both Queensland and Tasmania specifically outlines, however, that remains believed to be ancient indigenous remains are of no medico-legal significance. For example, in Queensland, a coroner must stop investigating a death if the coroner's investigation shows that the remains are believed to be indigenous burial remains (Queensland Coroners Act 2003). In this context, indigenous burial remains are defined as burial remains to which the Cultural Record, Landscapes Queensland and Queensland Estate Act 1987, section 3453 applies. In addition, each of the Australian states and territories has its own police force. There is also the AFP which acts as a national (within the ACT) and international law enforcement agency and is the direct territory police service in the ACT.

Australian forensic archaeologists and investigation of international mass graves

Australian archaeologists have played a significant role in the development of archaeological techniques being incorporated into the forensic investigation of crime scenes internationally. Between 1990 and 1991, the highly experienced field archaeologist Richard Wright (Emeritus Professor of Anthropology, University of Sydney) employed archaeological techniques to investigate three mass graves in the Ukraine. The three graves were dated to 1942 and excavated almost 50 years later. The work was undertaken at the request of the Special Investigations Unit (SIU) of the Attorney General of the Commonwealth Government of Australia as part of prosecution cases of alleged war criminals residing in Australia (Bevan 1994, 21–25; Dayton 2000; Tatz 1997, 329–331; Wright 1995).

A witness from the Ukraine provided information to Australian investigators about the size and ramped nature of a clandestine grave, manner and sequence of deaths and the numbers of individuals in the grave. Although no convictions were achieved (e.g. Fraser 2010 for further explanation), the evidence recovered using forensic archaeology was unchallenged and provided vivid physical support for the testimony of the eyewitness of the event (Wright 2010a, 100–101). Wright's work highlighted the detail of evidence that could be recovered by employing meticulous excavation techniques at a crime scene. Such evidence not only tested and confirmed information obtained from eyewitness accounts but also added detail to the understanding of what happened.

Wright was subsequently employed as the Chief Archaeologist for the United Nations International Criminal Tribunal for the Former Yugoslavia (ICTY) (1997–2000) investigating mass graves in the former Yugoslavia and providing forensic archaeological evidence in The Hague (Anon 2000; ICTY Transcripts Database: 2003, 2007, 2011, 2013). In both contexts Wright worked closely with forensically trained archaeologists, anthropologists, pathologists and crime scene personnel participating from many countries to collect and recover evidence that was significant for ongoing investigations and prosecutions. The protocols that Wright and his team developed during the work for the ICTY laid the foundations for one of the seminal texts for forensic archaeologists, 'The Scientific Investigation of Mass Graves' (Cox et al. 2008).

Australian archaeologists and anthropologists have also been pivotal to investigations related to missing persons from both World Wars (1914–1918 and 1939–1445). Emeritus Professor Richard Wright was appointed as the Senior Forensic Advisor to Oxford Archaeology during their recovery of Australian and British war dead from mass graves dating back to 1916 at Fromelles in northern France (Anon 2011; Oxford Archaeology 2013). Consultant archaeologists[1] and anthropologists from the Army Recovery Team have been actively involved with the location and recovery of remains from the World War II and recent conflicts, for example Papua New Guinea (Donlon et al., Chapter 44, this volume). In more recent times Australian archaeologists and anthropologists have worked on international cases where the excavation, recovery and identification of human remains have been undertaken to recover missing persons who died as a result of political and/or ethnic conflict, for example Timor-Leste (Blau and Fondebrider 2010) and the Solomon Islands.

Forensic archaeology in Australia

Despite the obviously significant contributions Wright and his forensic archaeology colleagues have made to the collection and recording of evidence of single, multiple and mass graves, the impact of this work has had relatively little influence on the incorporation of archaeology in the investigation of Australian crime scenes involving buried evidence. As a result, there are currently no professionally recognised forensic archaeologists (as opposed to forensic anthropologists) permanently employed in this capacity in Australia. Practitioners with relevant forensic archaeological skills are employed as either forensic anthropologists or consultants on an ad hoc basis (see below).

While North and Latin America do not differentiate between the disciplines of forensic archaeology and anthropology, Australia, like Scandinavia, the United Kingdom and Europe in general, treats archaeology and anthropology as two separate disciplines (Kuhl and Olsen 2006, 417). Currently only three of the six states and two territories, (Victoria, SA and WA) have medico-legal service providers that employ full-time forensic anthropologists. NSW and Tasmania have access to consultants that are based in universities. In 2006 the executive of the Senior Managers of Australian and New Zealand Forensic Laboratories (SMANZFL) supported the formation of a Scientific Advisory Group (SAG) made up of forensic anthropologists, mortuary managers, forensic odontologists and forensic entomologists. This group developed a Guideline for Forensic Anthropology Practitioners in which it was agreed that in order to practise effectively as a professional forensic anthropologist interested parties should have:

a an undergraduate degree in science majoring in anatomy and a PhD in physical/biological anthropology or anatomy;

b formal association with a recognised SMANZFL-approved institute;

c current casework experience, and

d publications in relevant peer-reviewed journals on the subject of physical/biological/forensic anthropology are also desirable (SAG 2009).

However, no such guidelines aimed at forensic archaeologists have so far been put in place.

As an employee of a forensic medical service provider, forensic anthropologists may be requested to provide expert evidence in court. In most instances opinion is requested about interpretations of skeletal trauma rather than questions about biological profile as related to identification. The majority of forensic anthropologists have some skills in archaeology (e.g. Donlon 2009, for a review of forensic anthropology in Australia; also Donlon 2008). There are examples of cases where forensic anthropologists have been called to assist in the recovery of buried human remains. However, in most cases, the anthropologist, having confirmed the located remains are human (often an image is sent via mobile phone from investigating officers for comment), is requested to attend the scene to find that the recovery is being undertaken by police, search teams or scene of crimes officers, perhaps with the assistance of State Emergency Service (SES) teams.

The attendance of a state forensic anthropologist/archaeologist at a potential crime scene within the same state is considered part of the practitioner's professional responsibility to assist police investigations. Therefore, forensic anthropologists and archaeologists generally undertake these services on a gratis basis. However, should a practitioner be required to travel interstate (e.g. to provide a second opinion or additional assistance in the case of large-scale mass disasters), travel costs and salaries are generally requested to be covered by the host state.

Depending on the nature of the case, site investigations for human remains may involve a combination of search by teams of volunteers from SES followed by police search using shovels or probes to undertake subsurface tests. If available a police cadaver dog may also be brought into the investigation. The use of geophysical techniques in attempts to locate clandestine graves (e.g. ABC Sydney 2012; Pringle et al. 2012; Thomas 1999) has also been employed to assist and aid search teams. This has led in some part to an emerging trend

[1]Archaeological and Heritage Management Services (AHMS), Sydney, Melbourne and Perth.

for Australian police agencies (as well as consultant archaeologists – Wright 2010b; NSW National Parks and Wildlife Services 2003) responsible for the investigation of human remains (but not trained in archaeology) to rely on the results of geophysical investigation prior to excavation. While geophysical techniques may play a role in the investigation of landscape anomalies (e.g. Cheetham 2005), the equipment is expensive and requires specific expertise (often many years of experience on one piece of equipment) to locate anomalies that may be of forensic interest from a background of false signals and anomalies. In the majority of cases a far more time-effective and practical approach to the search of a suspect area is to implement a carefully controlled removal of the upper surface of an area to identify potential grave cuts. The effectiveness of physically testing the anomaly using archaeological techniques to guarantee no false negatives and no false positives is commonly underestimated by police (Wright 2010b).

Given the multitude of variables that influence the detection of buried human remains, it is incorrect to assume there is only one reliable method of detection (cf. Powell 2006, 31). Further, the decision to rely on geophysical techniques ignores one of the major contributions made by the archaeologist to a timely investigation of a scene where a clandestine burial is suspected: the application of a suite of skills to evaluate and then systematically plan and implement the most appropriate search and detection methods for that specific site (Hanson 2008; see Ashby 2013 for a similar discussion in the New Zealand context).

The number of buried remains within Australia as a proportion of homicides is relatively small (exact figures unknown). However, in cases involving burial, police jurisdictions across Australia typically do not incorporate archaeologists with experience and expertise dealing with buried human remains into their investigations, this in spite of repeated offers of assistance by archaeologists. It is therefore very rare that police forces will ask for the assistance of an archaeologist at a scene and even rarer to invite an archaeologist to assist in an investigation. There is a common belief amongst police agencies that scene of crime officers who are responsible for the recovery of buried evidence have all the necessary required expertise. In reality, however (at least in the authors' experience), that expertise has been undertaken on an ad hoc basis. For example, human remains have been recovered by police using household spoons (as no suitable tools were available) and unnecessary digging has continued in cases where understanding of stratigraphy was non-existent (e.g. Wright et al. 2005, 151, for discussions about recognising the true bottom of a grave). In the case of 9-year-old Samantha Knight, who went missing in the city of Sydney in 1986, Michael Guider a confessed paedophile admitted killing her but initially refused to provide information about the location of her body (Newscom 2004). In 2001, after 17 years of searching, Guider told the police that he had buried Samantha's body in the gardens of the Royal Sydney Yacht Squadron. A newspaper article at the time reported that they believed the human remains 'were gouged from the harbor-side grave by a giant excavator during construction of a car park about 18 months after Guider buried her at the squadron, where he worked as a gardener' (Cornford 2003). While police worked with a cadaver dog and dug and sieved the remains, had an archaeologist been involved in the investigation process it may have been possible to provide more detailed information about the sequence of activities at the site, including possible evidence of grave cuts and the subsequent construction work.

While investigations must remain 'body focused', it is important for scene of crime officers and investigators as well as forensic pathologists to appreciate the potential value of the surrounding scene and the types of information an archaeological approach can potentially add to an investigation. This could potentially include information about when the grave was dug (recently or some time ago), how the grave was dug (planned, haphazardly, by hand with a specific type of tool or by machine) and whether the grave was disturbed since the body was initially interred.

In cases where the skills of an archaeologist have been requested by police, the understanding of how an archaeologist may assist has come about either informally through word of mouth, typically as a result of the individual police officer having previously studied archaeology (Powell 2006, 19), or through the more enlightened younger generation of detectives involved in a case where an extra set of eyes can often lead to a better understanding of a site. To date only the NSW police force has a register of experts that includes at least one archaeologist who can be contacted if required. The number of domestic cases where archaeologists have assisted police with their investigations, although sporadic, has begun to increase and includes archaeological assistance with the recovery of human remains discovered at a rock shelter that were confused as a coronial case (e.g. McDonald and Ross 1990),[2] the large-scale search of an area for a suspected burial of a long-term missing person (Anon 2012) and support and advise on a possible burial (Silvester 2012). Archaeological advice has also been provided to police regarding building structural changes possibly concealing a burial. However,

[2]While very few unsuccessful cases of forensic searches for graves are published (Powell 2006, 22) it should be remembered that the ability to exclude a site using archaeological techniques is powerful.

there are many more examples of cases in Australia where police have not included an archaeologist that unfortunately has resulted in time wasted on fruitless digging (e.g. Wright 2003).

Education and training opportunities in forensic archaeology in Australia

Over the past 10 years there has been a shift in universities to offer courses in forensic archaeology at undergraduate level. These courses are now run within departments of archaeology at the Australian National University (ACT), the University of New England (NSW), Flinders University (SA) and the University of Western Australia (WA). However, in the majority of cases introductory courses are taught by archaeologists with little or no forensic experience. It may be argued that the inclusion of forensic archaeology is a result of the so-called *CSI effect* where the 'forensic tag' attracts students to courses (Blau 2004, 13). While technical methodology is essential for good practice, it is also vital that the legal and moral implications of the work are fully understood by students (Blau 2009b, 459).

Forensic anthropologists with archaeological expertise employed by Australian forensic medical service providers have been active in developing training for both Australian police and forensic pathologists in order to raise awareness of the advantages of including an archaeologist at a scene involving human remains or other buried evidence. Training for police in the recovery of human remains occurs regularly in WA (A. Buck, personal communication 2012) and has also been offered to Tasmanian Police. The VIFM has delivered exhumation workshops for forensic pathologists and police in the Asian Pacific region. In 2012 the AFP requested staff from the VIFM to develop and deliver a training programme for AFP crime scene examiners in the recovery of buried evidence. A site was prepared which included a series of clandestine burials of various sizes. The burials included drugs caches, weapons and three graves containing plastic human remains complete with associated clothing and personal effects. A 4-day recovery course based around a suggested scenario was repeated 5 times over 4 months to groups of 12–14 AFP crime scene examiners from across Australia. The first day consisted of lectures outlining the theory associated with archaeological recovery of buried remains together with a field exercise demonstrating the appropriate tools to use and an example of a small-scale excavation. The remaining three days focused on field exercises designed to demonstrate to participants how to assess field anomalies and highlight the advantages and limitations of using metal detectors and geophysical techniques such as Ground Penetrating Radar (GPR) prior to physically investigating the anomalies. The course offered by the VIFM to the AFP crime scene examiners provided an introduction to broadening appreciation of how archaeologists can contribute to the recovery of buried evidence. Since the delivery of this training, archaeologists have increasingly been incorporated into investigations (Anon 2013). However, the differences between state and federal legislation mean that similar education of state crime scene officers is still required.

In 2012 the VIFM was also contracted to provide training in the investigation of mass graves to staff from the Iraqi Human Rights Ministry of Human Rights (MoHR). Undertaken through World Wide Project Management, the training and discussions provided perspectives into how future investigations of mass graves known to be located across the governorates of Iraq could be undertaken. The training was spread over several weeks with a small component focused on how archaeological and anthropological methods and techniques could be employed within future fieldwork. The training was undertaken with the assistance of Victoria Police, specialists at the VIFM and visiting lecturers that included a simulated excavation of human remains from three small mass graves.

Conclusion

The fact that archaeology has much to offer crime scene investigations of landscape anomalies believed to be clandestine burials is now well recognised outside the Australian context (Bernardi and Fondebrider 2007; Blau and Skinner 2005; Congram and Sterenberg 2009; Cox 2001; Flavel and Barker 2009; Haglund 2001; Hunter and Cox 2005; Renshaw 2011; Wright et al. 2005). The disposal and burial of all types of evidence including human remains will, no doubt, continue to be a modus operandi for criminals. However, the relatively low homicide rate in Australia (figures for 2010 are 1 death per 100,000 persons [count=229] compared to, for example, 4.8 deaths per 100,000 [count=14,748] in the United States) (UNODC 1995–2011; e.g. Chan and Payne 2013), the small number of discoveries of clandestine burials and the low numbers of long term missing[3] (>1600; AFP 2013) will mean that the demand for involving an archaeologist with specialised skills in locating and recovering human remains in Australia will continue to be relatively low.

'Forensic' archaeology within Australia is slowly becoming recognised as a developing discipline. However, the time of writing, 2014, forensic archaeology was neither

[3]In Australia, the term 'long term missing' refers to those individuals who have not been seen by friends of family for 6 months or longer.

systematically employed by state and federal police nor disregarded as a discipline that may assist in investigations. The overall response to the 2012 AFP training course was positive and a comment on some of the techniques taught being used in ongoing cases was seen as favourable. At this stage a central contact person has been identified for cases that require archaeological input.

How many 'forensic' archaeologists are in Australia today? Unlike in the United Kingdom, the Netherlands, the United States and Latin America where there now seems to be a glut of practising professionals, there are very few practising archaeologists who have been asked by police to assist in forensic casework within Australia. As stated, Australian forensic archaeologists and forensic anthropologists have been employed by various international teams in countries such as Iraq, Bosnia and Herzegovina, Timor-Leste and the Ukraine. However, it is unclear whether many of these highly experienced professionals have had the opportunity to undertake domestic police casework. Certainly, professional forensic anthropologists are few with those practising being placed at forensic institutes, universities or acting as experts in their own right.

In conclusion, while there may not be the numbers of domestic cases of buried remains in Australia to justify a formal post-graduate degree in forensic archaeology in Australia (cf. Blau 2004), it may still be beneficial for stakeholders (police, judiciary and families) to facilitate a register in each of the jurisdictions of professionally trained archaeologists whose everyday work involves excavating and recording different types of evidence. Such a registry, similar to the register of experts existing in NSW, could greatly assist Australian Federal and State police agencies who are largely responsible for the recovery of buried evidence including human remains. A register could provide an additional tool to investigations where site evaluation and excavation are required. With the assistance of experienced professional archaeologists a coordinated multidisciplinary approach would augment the location, recovery and identification process.

Acknowledgements

The authors are grateful to Emeritus Professor Richard Wright for the comments and references he provided. We also appreciate the comments provided by Professor Stephen Cordner and Professor David Ranson.

References

ABC Sydney. 2012. *'Part of a Hand' Found in Backyard Search.* 13 April 2012. Available at: http://www.abc.net.au/news/2012-04-13/27part-of-a-hand27-found-in-backyard-search/3947688/?site=sydney (last accessed 3 March 2013).

AFP. 2013. *National Missing Persons Coordination Centre.* Available at: http://www.missingpersons.gov.au/about-us/faqs.aspx (last accessed 19 March 2013).

Anon. 2000. *Krstic (II-98-33) Srebrenica-Drina Corps.* Transcripts 26 May 2000, 3632–3672; 29 May 2000, 3673–3721. Available at: http://www.un.org/icty/ind-e.htm (last accessed 8 June 2013).

Anon. 2011. *Identifying the WW1 dead in Fromelle.* Available at: http://www.bournemouth.ac.uk/applied-sciences/news-and-events/news/2011/mar/ne003-identifying-dead-in-fromelles.html (last accessed 20 July 2012).

Anon. 2012. *Search for Body of Prue Bird at Bega Schoolgirl Murder Site.* 14 February 2012. Available at: http://www.theage.com.au/victoria/search-for-body-of-prue-bird-at-bega-schoolgirl-murder-site-20120213-1t28k.html (last accessed 3 February 2012).

Anon. 2013. *NSW Police Search for Donald Mackay's Body.* Available at: http://www.smh.com.au/nsw/after-35-years-has-donald-mackay-been-found-20130612-2o46w.html (last accessed 11 December 2014).

Ashby, E. 2013. Forensic archaeology in New Zealand: review and future directions. *Australian Journal of Forensic Sciences* 45(1), 25–35.

Australia Royal Commission into Aboriginal Deaths in Custody. 1991. Structure and administration of coronial systems. *National Report* Volume 1 paragraphs 5.18–5.19. Available at: http://www.austlii.edu.au/au/other/IndigLRes/rciadic/national/vol1/103.html (last accessed 3 July 2013).

Bernardi, P. and Fondebrider, L. 2007. Forensic archaeology and the scientific documentation of human rights violations: an Argentine example from the early 1980s. In R. Ferllini (ed.), *Forensic Archaeology and Human Rights Violations*, 205–232. Springfield, Charles C. Thomas.

Bevan, D. 1994. *A Case to Answer For: The Story of Australia's First European War Crimes Prosecution.* Adelaide, Wakefield Press.

Blau, S. 2004. Forensic archaeology in Australia: current situations, future possibilities. *Australian Archaeology* 58, 11–14.

Blau, S. 2009a. Forensic anthropology and police investigations. *Australian Police Journal* 63(1), 8–14.

Blau, S. 2009b. More than just bare bones: ethical considerations for forensic anthropologists. In S. Blau and D. H. Ubelaker (eds.), *Handbook of Forensic Anthropology and Archaeology*, 457–467. Walnut Creek, Left Coast Press.

Blau, S. and Fondebrider, L. 2010. Dying for independence: proactive investigations into the 12 November 1991 Santa Cruz massacre, Timor Leste. *The International Journal of Human Rights* 15(8), 1249–1274.

Blau, S. and Skinner, M. 2005. The use of forensic archaeology in the investigation of human rights abuse: unearthing the past in East Timor. *The International Journal of Human Rights* 9(4), 449–463.

Chan, A. and Payne, J. 2013. *Homicide in Australia: 2008-09 to 2009-10. National Homicide Monitoring Program Annual Report.* Monitoring Report 21. Available at: http://www.aic.gov.au/publications/current%20series/mr/21-40/mr21.html (last accessed 18 March 2013).

Cheetham, P. 2005. Forensic geophysical survey. In J. Hunter and M. Cox (eds.), *Forensic Archaeology: Advances in Theory and Practice*, 62–95. London, Routledge.

Congram, D. and Sterenberg, J. 2009. Grave challenges in Iraq. In S. Blau and D. H. Ubelaker (eds.), *Handbook of Forensic Anthropology and Archaeology*, 441–453. Walnut Creek, Left Coast Press.

Cornford, P. 2003. Gone forever: Sam's grave yields only more mystery. *Sydney Morning Herald*, 12 July 2003. Available at: http://www.smh.com.au/articles/2003/07/11/1057783360705.html (last accessed 20 June 2012).

Cox, M. 2001. Forensic archaeology in the UK: questions of socio-intellectual context and socio-political responsibility. In V. Buchli and G. Lucas (eds.), *Archaeologies of the Contemporary Past*, 145–167. London, Routledge.

Cox, M., Flavel, A., Hanson, I., Laver, J. and Wessling, R. 2008. *The Scientific Investigation of Mass Graves: Towards Protocols and Standard Operating Procedures*. Cambridge, Cambridge University Press.

Dayton, L. 2000. Unearthing evil. *Quantum Special*, 1 June 2000. Available at: http://www.abc.net.au/quantum/stories/s124137.htm (last accessed 15 February 2002).

Donlon, D. 2008. Forensic anthropology in Australia: a brief history and review of casework. In M. Oxenham (ed.), *Forensic Approaches to Death and Disaster and Abuse*, 97–110. NSW, Australian Academic Press.

Donlon, D. 2009. The development and current state of forensic anthropology: an Australian perspective. In S. Blau and D. H. Ubelaker (eds.), *Handbook of Forensic Anthropology and Archaeology*, 104–114. Walnut Creek, Left Coast.

Flavel, A. and Barker, C. 2009. Forensic anthropology and archaeology in Guatemala. In S. Blau and D. H. Ubelaker (eds.), *Handbook of Forensic Anthropology and Archaeology*, 426–440. Walnut Creek, Left Coast Press.

Fraser, D. 2010. *Daviborshch's Cart: Narrating the Holocaust in Australian War Crimes Trials*. Lincoln, Nebraska Press.

Haglund, W. D. 2001. Archaeology and forensic death investigations. *Historical Archaeology* 35(1), 26–34.

Hanson, I. 2008. Forensic archaeology: approaches to international investigations. In M. Oxenham (ed.), *Forensic Approaches to Death and Disaster and Abuse*, 17–28. NSW, Australian Academic Press.

Hunter, J. and Cox, M. 2005. *Forensic Archaeology: Advances in Theory and Practice*. London, Routledge.

ICTY Transcripts Database. Available at: http://www.ictytranscripts.org/ (last accessed 20 March 2014). See transcripts for 2003, 2007, 2011, and 2013.

Kuhl, J. and Olsen, O. E. 2006. Societal safety, archaeology and the investigation of contemporary mass graves. *Journal of Genocide Research* 8(4), 411–435.

McDonald, J. J. and Ross, A. C. 1990. Helping the police with their inquiries: archaeology and politics at Angophora reserve rock shelter, N.S.W. *Archaeology in Oceania* 25(2), 114–121.

Newscom. 2004. *We Want to Bury our Daughter.* 22 January 2004. Available at: http://www.theage.com.au/articles/2002/06/07/1022982768795.html (last accessed 11 December 2014).

NSW Coroners Act. 1980, Section 13B & 13C.

NSW National Parks and Wildlife Services. 2003. *Lost but not Forgotten: A Guide to Methods of Identifying Aboriginal Unmarked Graves*. New South Wales.

Oxford Archaeology. 2013. *Remembering Fromelles*. Available at: http://thehumanjourney.net/index.php?option=com_content&task=view&id=501&Itemid=40 (last accessed 30 March 2013).

Plueckhahn, V. D. and Cordner, C. M. 1991. *Ethics, Legal Medicine and Forensic Pathology*. 2nd edition. Melbourne, Melbourne University Press.

Powell, K. J. 2006. *The Detection of Buried Human Skeletal Remains in the Australian Environment*. Unpublished PhD thesis, University of Adelaide.

Pringle, J. K., Ruffell, A., Jervis, J. R. et al. 2012. The use of geoscience methods for terrestrial forensic searches. *Earth Science Reviews* 114(1–2), 108–123.

Queensland Coroners Act. 2003: Section 12(2) and Section 23(1).

Renshaw, L. 2011. *Exhuming Loss: Memory, Materiality, and Mass Graves of the Spanish Civil War*. Walnut Creek, Left Coast Press.

SAG. 2009. *Guideline for Forensic Anthropology Practitioners*. Medical Science Scientific Advisory Group. Unpublished document in possession of the authors.

Silvester, J. 2012. Teenager's murder linked to Russell Street bombing. The Age. Available at: http://www.theage.com.au/victoria/teenagers-murder-linked-to-russell-street-bombing-20120214-1t4a5.html (last accessed 20 February 2013).

Tatz, C. 1997. Genocide and the politics of memory. In C. Tatz (ed.), *Genocide Perspective 1: Essays in Comparative Genocide*, 308–361. Sydney, Macquarie University.

The Australian. 2012. *Rayney Wept When Told of Wife's Bush Grave*. 12 September 2012. Available at: http://www.theaustralian.com.au/news/rayney-wept-when-told-of-wifes-bush-grave/story-e6frg6n6-1226472179235 (last accessed 2 March 2013).

The Irish Echo. 2012. *Jill's Body Found in Shallow Grave, Man Charged*. 28 September 2012. Available at: http://www.irishecho.com.au/2012/09/28/jills-body-found-in-shallow-grave-man-charged/20778 (last accessed 3 February 2013).

Thomas, D. G. 1999. Investigating sub-surface search: the pros and cons of some instrumented search technologies available to police in Australia. *Australian Police Journal* 53(1), 62–72.

UNODC. 1995–2011. Intentional homicide, count and rate per 100,000 population.

Victorian Coroners Act. 2008. Part 4 Division 1. Section 14.1 and Section 15c.

Wright, R. 1995. Investigating war crimes: the archaeological evidence. *The Sydney Papers* 7(3), 39–44.

Wright, R. 2003. Shallow and grave. *Letter to The Australian*, 2 September 2003.

Wright, R. 2010a. Where are the bodies? In the ground. *The Public Historian* 32(1), 96–107.

Wright, R. 2010b. *Guidance for the Archaeologist Considering Using Geophysics for the Discovery of Single Scattered Graves*. Unpublished document in possession of the authors.

Wright, R., Hanson, I. and Sterenberg, J. 2005. The archaeology of mass graves. In J. Hunter, and M. Cox (eds.), *Forensic Archaeology: Advances in Theory and Practice*, 137–158. London, Routledge.

PART 3
Africa, Asia and Oceania

CHAPTER 34

Forensic archaeology: an Indian perspective

Anil Aggrawal

Department of Forensic Medicine and Toxicology, Maulana Azad Medical College, New Delhi, India

Introduction

Archaeology is the systematic study of human societies from the past using the items they left behind. In India, as in the United States, archaeology is a subfield of anthropology, which is the study of humans in general, whether modern or ancient. In general, forensic archaeology is the application of archaeological principles, techniques and methodologies for the purposes of law and administration of justice. Forensic archaeology in India as practised by the present author, a forensic pathologist, combines the knowledge of osteology and human remains with archaeological techniques to help recover finds and provide vital evidence for the investigative team. With a background in osteology, the Indian forensic archaeologist, in the opinion of the author, provides a field assessment on the age at death, sex and other physical characteristics of the remains, while as an experienced excavator he/she will not only examine the scene, but lay out a grid, excavate, screen or sieve, and plot the human remains and the artefacts so that they will be accurately located, recovered, identified and catalogued. He/she has the training, the tools and the equipment to undertake the task.

Legal framework in India

In India, investigation of most criminal cases starts with a police inquest, which refers to an inquest held by a police officer. It is held under Section 174 of the Criminal Procedure Code (CrPC) of India. The CrPC was enacted in 1973 and came into force on 25 January 1974. Earlier CrPC was passed by the British in 1861, which continued till 1969, when it was amended. It was finally replaced by the current Code. Under Section 174 of the CrPC, generally the officer-in-charge of a Police Station (Station House Officer – SHO) or Police Post conducts the inquest. He/she is usually of the rank of sub-inspector (SI), but no such rank has been specified in the CrPC. In a minority of cases, the inquest is not conducted by the officer-in-charge, but by a magistrate (Section 176[1] of the CrPC). Examples of such cases are:

- suicide of a woman within 7 years of marriage;
- death of a woman within 7 years of marriage in any circumstances raising a reasonable suspicion that some other person has committed an offence in relation to said woman, (homicide, etc.);
- exhumation, or unearthing the remains of a legally buried body, where the grave is properly identified by the relatives, priest, and so on.

If a criminal has buried the body of his/her victim, and the investigation is starting ab initio, it is not an exhumation in a legal sense. The inquest in such cases would be done by the police officer-in-charge. The police officer-in-charge or magistrate conducting the inquest is known as the Investigating Officer (IO). In most cases involving forensic archaeological techniques, a police officer is the IO, but in some cases when a legally buried body needs to be unearthed, the IO is a magistrate.

Forensic archaeology in India

In India, forensic archaeology is being perceived as a part of forensic medicine. Indian medical education is imparted at three levels. Level 1, the base level, takes five-and-a-half years to complete. It has to be passed by any individual wishing to undertake medicine as a career. After passing this level, this individual obtains the Bachelor of Medicine/Bachelor of Surgery (MBBS) degree. It is not essential to go to level 2, if one does not wish to specialise in any single subject. However, if someone wants to specialise in a particular subject, say, surgery, gynaecology, obstetrics or forensic medicine, he/she has to study for three additional years and pass an additional examination to obtain a Doctorate of Medicine (MD) degree. If one wants to super-specialise, he/she can go for a Doctor in Medicine (DM) or Magister Chirurgiae (MCh) degree, say, in paediatric surgery, in vitro fertilisation (IVF) obstetrics and so on.

Unfortunately, in India there are no super specialty subjects under forensic medicine, although there are several attractive candidates, for example forensic odontology, forensic radiology, forensic archaeology. Before such courses can start, they have to be approved by the

Forensic Archaeology: A Global Perspective, First Edition. Edited by W.J. Mike Groen, Nicholas Márquez-Grant and Robert C. Janaway.

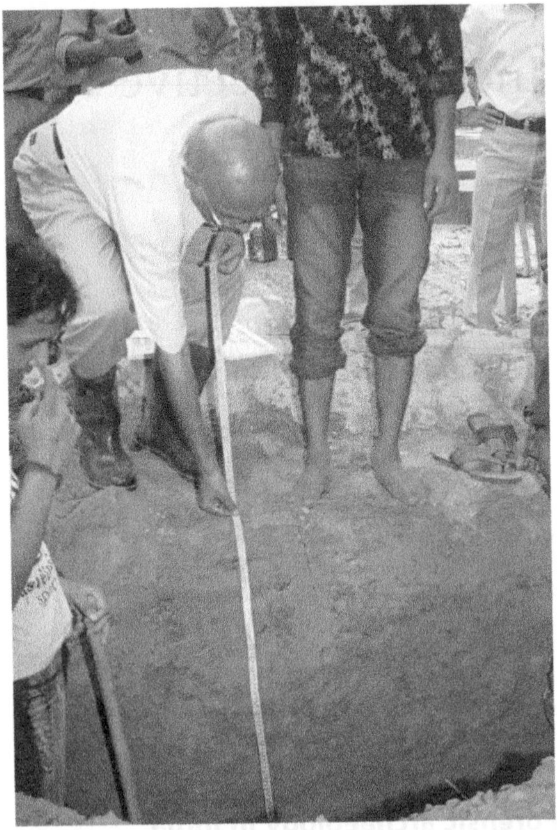

Figure 34.1 Author applying forensic archaeology techniques in one of his cases.

Medical Council of India (MCI), which is the regulator of undergraduate and postgraduate education in India. The author is in the process of framing detailed guidelines on the course structure and other formalities for starting a DM course in forensic archaeology, which will then be submitted to MCI. But it could take some time before such a course receives final approval and implementation.

Thus currently forensic archaeology does not exist in India as a separate discipline. Work related to forensic archaeology is undertaken mainly by forensic pathologists themselves (Figure 34.1), who have learned the archaeological techniques in a more or less informal way from their mentors, who in turn learnt it either by experience or from their own seniors.

Training opportunities

Training opportunities are minimal, and, as stated earlier, mainly depend on the initiatives taken by senior pathologists. All this might change once the MCI approves a DM course in forensic archaeology. It is proposed that a minimum qualification of MD in forensic medicine may be required for admission to a DM course.

Accreditation

Accreditation of forensic science laboratories in India is done by the National Accreditation Board for Testing and Calibration Laboratories (NABL).[1] There are currently no NABL guidelines for forensic archaeology, which is understandable, because the discipline is not fully established as such in India.

Forensic archaeological casework

Currently, archaeological techniques employed in India relate mainly to the unearthing of mass graves. These could be historical graves or in some cases graves created by perpetrators of mass murder (discussed further on in this chapter). In most cases, services of a trained archaeologist are not sought. As stated, the forensic pathologist himself/herself undertakes the task in association with the IO.

Archaeological techniques employed by the author

Proper excavation methods have already been detailed in various texts (e.g. Hester et al. 2009), and the protocols employed by the author in forensic casework in India are given here:

1 *Search team completes investigation*: The first step involves the police and forensic search team completing the investigation of the surface area.
2 *Location*: The approximate location of the grave or graves is then established by intelligence information, disturbed ground and other indicators.
3 *Photographs*: A photograph is taken at every stage with an identifying number, a scale and an arrow pointing to the magnetic north.
4 *Vegetation*: The vegetation over the grave is observed as to its height, distribution and depth of root system and compared with that of the immediate surroundings to get some idea of the time elapsed between the digging of the pit and the present. A botanist is helpful in interpretations. Usually an informal request to the IO is made, who is normally able to arrange a botanist from a university.
5 *Clearing of extraneous material*: Extraneous material is now cleared from the surface. If necessary, some surface material and topsoil is scraped off using a trowel or shovel with a flat blade, thus allowing a clearer observation of the grave boundaries or profile.
6 *Map*: After the extent of the area is established, a map or plan is made. A reasonably satisfactory plan of the area can be made with the following basic equipment: 100 ft (*c.*30 m) tape, Brunton or lensatic compass, graph paper, drawing board, hard lead #4 pencils, plumb bob, protractor, scaled ruler, spirit level and string (Figure 34.2). More complicated and precise equipment, such as a Total Station, is used if a trained surveyor or engineer is available.
7 *Datum point and a grid around it*: A datum point is established, which is outside the area selected for

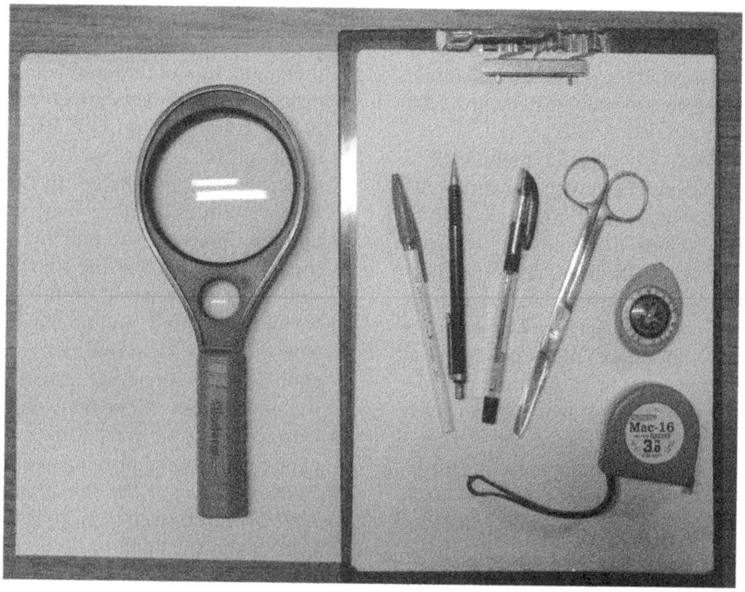

Figure 34.2 Basic equipment used by the author for laying out a forensic archaeological grid.

excavation but close to it, to which all measurements are referred. It is marked by an item such as a wooden stake with a nail in the top and should be protected so that it is not disturbed. Vertical distance or depth is measured from the datum point with the use of a level, a string, and a measuring tape. To get the horizontal distance a grid system is established by dividing the whole area into 5 ft (*c.* 1.5 m) squares (Figure 34.3).

8 *Numbering of grid*: Each square is assigned a number which is placed on the lower left corner. The square just to the right of and above the datum point is given the number 00. Other points are self-intuitive. There is no unanimity in these points, and the reader is free to use his/her own system as long as it is internally consistent in his/her own work.

9 *Marking of each square*: The corner of each square is now marked by a stake. If possible grid lines must be oriented north–south and east–west, but it is by no means necessary. The importance of this elaborate exercise is that all subsequent finds and features are accurately noted in reference to the grid coordinates as well as depth below datum. For example, bullets and pellets in the body will drop downward with the decomposition of the cadaver. Their location should be recorded in relationship to the skeleton, or, if the criminal has lost something, say, a lighter or perhaps a button, it is more meaningful to know if that object was in the grave or on the surface. If it was in the grave, quite possibly the perpetrator was the one who buried the body (unless someone else stole that item and put it in the grave to send investigators off-track).

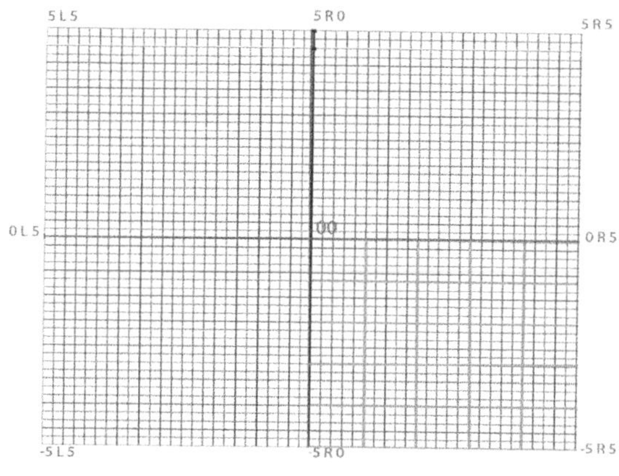

Figure 34.3 A typical 5 × 5 ft grip employed by the author in his forensic archaeological excavations.

10 *Examination of peripheries*: The potential for tool marks around the grave should always be noted, which could indicate the type of tool used by the perpetrator. The same assessment should be undertaken during excavation of the grave, as tools marks may be present on the grave walls and at the base of the grave.

11 *Excavation*: An excavation of the burial pit and its contents begins now. Small hand tools are used to avoid any inadvertent damage to the remains. The author has seen some workers using large mattocks for digging. This should be strictly avoided, because once this damage occurs to, say, a bone, it becomes very difficult or even impossible to tell if it was peri-mortem or post-mortem trauma. As digging goes on, constant visual inspection is done to identify any artefact of value. Extreme care should be exercised to maintain the exact limits of the grave so that only the grave fill is excavated.

12 *During the digging process*: As digging progresses, a botanist is in constant consultation with the author, IO and locals, who are conversant with the vegetation of the area. The size of any roots of identifiable trees and shrubs growing in the pit usually gives additional information. A root growing over the body and covering it obviously formed *after the body had been laid down.* Its age estimation can give important clues regarding time of burial. It should necessarily be of *lesser age than the time of burial.* Conversely, a root growing underneath the body had formed before the body was buried there, and *its age should be greater than the time of burial.* A botanist is of great help in such interpretations.

13 *Artefacts left by backfilling*: It is common knowledge that whenever pits are dug and backfilled, the earth originally from within the pit becomes mixed or mottled. Some material originally on the surface will always be found in the bottom of the pit. A soil sample from the base of the grave should be sent to experts for examination for the presence of pollen, seeds and insects. In this way it might be possible to tell the season of the year the deposition took place. More soil from the area of the stomach and intestines should be collected and sent to the toxicology laboratory for analysis.

14 *Removal and sifting of earth*: The earth from the grave is removed using arbitrary levels or layers (spits), about every 2 in (5.1 cm). The levels are marked in sequence beginning from 0. Thus 0 represents surface; 1, material recovered up to 2 in; 2, material recovered from 2 to 4 in and so on. Each level is profiled and the dirt removed is sifted through a quarter inch (6.35 mm) screen. It helps recover such items as small calibre bullets and shotgun pellets. The soil is then resifted with standard window screens. Anything found by this method should be recorded by its level number.

15 *Mapping and photographing of recovered items*: If anything significant is found, it is mapped and photographed in situ. When the excavation reaches the body, smaller and softer tools should be used, with only a hard bristle brush (depending on the soil) used around the body. After exposure of the body has been accomplished, the remains are catalogued and photographed and plans and sketches are made.

16 *Segregation of samples*: All samples (soil, vegetation, bullets, pellets, knife tips, prostheses, artefacts, etc.) are collected in separate containers and tagged as evidence.

17 *Cataloguing or inventory*: Sufficient records of all finds should be made throughout the entire excavation, preferably in a bound notebook so that no pages can be lost. Some workers prefer loose pages, and there is no absolute objection to it, except that one has to be more careful not to lose the pages and in ensuring that pages are numbered. In the process, the papers can sometimes become dirty, which in the author's opinion only serves to enhance the value of the document, in as much as the court is convinced the documents were prepared on the spot when everything was fresh in mind, and no manipulations were done. Notes must be clear and not erased. Any corrections should have a single line drawn through them so that the original can still be read, and initialled.

18 *Original base of the grave*: One should be careful when exposing the burial so as not to disturb the original floor.

19 *Further digging of the base of pit*: After the remains have been removed, it is advisable to excavate a portion of the pit floor to be certain that nothing has been overlooked.

20 *Examination of remains*: After an assessment in the field, examination of the remains in the mortuary or laboratory follows. Injuries to the bone at the time of death may be ascertained by careful examination of the skeleton in situ. This may be impossible after the skeleton has been removed to the laboratory. More often than not, merely the process of removing the skeleton damages, fractures and fragments bone, if the skeleton is too fragile. The person examining should be knowledgeable and competent in forensic anthropology.

21 *Further examination by a forensic pathologist*: If a body is not completely skeletonised, it is desirable for the forensic pathologist to have the remains removed in their entirety. This is accomplished by various methods, depending on the degree of decomposition. It may be necessary to place plastic, sheet metal or plywood under the body for removal. In one case dealt with by the author, a young 17-year-old boy was unearthed from a proper legal burial. Initially it was thought that he had died of some natural disease, and because of some social and legal constraints an autopsy could not be done. Nor was it considered absolutely necessary at that time. Later evidence gathered that the boy had been electrocuted. The body was putrefied but in a fairly good shape to allow a reasonably good post-mortem examination. The body was first X-rayed to look for 'osseous pearls' which are sometimes seen in electrocution victims. No such pearls were found. A thorough examination of the skin failed to reveal any electrocution marks. Thus the original opinion of death by natural disease was adhered to, although its nature could not be determined.

---

[1]For more information, see http://www.nabl-india.org/. For the NABL guidelines, please see http://www.nabl-india.org/nabl/file_download.php?filename=201206281231-NABL-113-doc.pdf (last accessed October 2013).

It must be stressed that the techniques outlined here are by no means standard. These can be varied to suit the case and the experience of the excavator. The only thing to keep in mind is the philosophy behind each step. The degree of accuracy and the extent of recording should be determined by the criminal investigator who has the duty of steering the evidence through the courts. Since forensic archaeology has not been tested adequately, extensive practical experience in the field may disclose other information. The author has always maintained that forensic archaeology is a judicious mix of art, science and experience.

Case examples: the 1984 riots

The 1984 anti-Sikh riots were a series of pogroms directed against Sikhs in India, by anti-Sikh mobs, in response to the assassination of Prime Minister Indira Gandhi (1917–1984) by her Sikh bodyguards. There were more than 8000 deaths, including 3000 in Delhi. Many dead bodies were burnt, many were buried and others were left to rot. One case related to a skull brought in to a forensic pathologist by the police, days after a riot. The police said it had been recovered from under some bushes. It bore a signature fracture on the occipital bone, possibly indicating that the deceased had been killed by a blunt instrument, potentially an iron rod. From the peculiarities or unique identifying features of the dentition (gold filling in the second lower left molar), he could be identified as one of the missing Sikh casualties. The pathologist then went to the scene of discovery and applying the archaeological techniques outlined earlier helped to search and recover further human remains. It led to the identification of several more bodies and the remains were finally handed over to the relatives. DNA profiling had just been discovered at the time and its use was not popular anywhere in the world; thus identification depended more upon crude techniques to estimate age at death, sex and any other identifying features from the skeleton or associated artefacts. In some cases, bodies could be positively identified based on peculiar tooth fillings, prostheses and personal items such as diaries, watches, leather bags.

More and more mass graves relating to that massacre are continually being discovered. In January 2011, the burned and abandoned village of Hondh-Chillar, where 32 Sikhs were killed on 2 November 1984, was discovered in northern Haryana state.[2] In March 1984 the site of another killing of 17 people in nearby Pataudi was discovered. How those bodies were dealt with by the authorities has not been ascertained by the present author.

Future of forensic archaeology in India

The future of Indian forensic archaeology appears bright, as the government is becoming more aware of the needs of application of scientific methods in crime detection. Although currently forensic science departments are suffering from staff crunches and poor budgetary allocations,[3] there has been positive pressure on the government from several quarters, including the judiciary. Recently a Lucknow bench of the Allahabad High Court asked the state government to find out whether the working and functioning of a forensic science laboratory was satisfactory and to check the details of the budget utilised by the director of the forensic science laboratory in the past three fiscal years.[4] It is hoped that in the next few years, the discipline of forensic archaeology will be far better developed, valued and established.

References

Hester, T. R., Shafer, H. J. and Feder, K. L. 2009. *Field Methods in Archaeology*. 7th edition. Walnut Creek, Left Coast Press.

[2]Human Rights Watch. India: Bring Charges for Newly Discovered Massacre of Sikhs. 25 April 2011. For more information, see http://www.hrw.org/en/news/2011/04/25/india-bring-charges-newly-discovered-massacre-sikhs (last accessed October 2013).

[3]For more information, see http://articles.timesofindia.indiatimes.com/2012-12-17/hyderabad/35868412_1_forensic-dept-apfsl-staff-crunch (last accessed October 2013).

[4]For more information, see http://articles.timesofindia.indiatimes.com/2013-06-01/lucknow/39674408_1_dna-test-supplementary-budget-sessions-court (last accessed October 2013).

CHAPTER 35

Forensic archaeology in Lebanon

Lynn Maalouf[1] and Rita Clovis Maalouf[2]

[1] *Institute for the Study of Human Rights, Columbia University, New York, USA*

[2] *Forensic Advisor*

Introduction

On 27 September 2013, in a small theatre on the outskirts of Beirut, located a few hundred metres away from the Ministry of Justice, the Palace of Justice and the Beirut's Public Prosecutor's office, a dozen people heeded the call of the Committee of the Families of the Kidnapped and Missing in Lebanon, which was to make its latest statement to the press.

A small-framed woman sat down, and after smiling at the people around her, carefully put on her reading glasses and held up her handwritten notes: 'I am Najat Hashisho, the wife of the kidnapped Muhieddine Hashisho, who was abducted from his home in broad daylight and in front of all his family members, by force, on September 15th 1982'.[1] Mrs Hashisho had filed a lawsuit against three persons she had identified as the abductors of her husband. That was in January 1991, after 9 years of individual efforts to search for her husband had led her nowhere. It took close to 23 years for the Criminal Court of South Lebanon to issue its decision, concluding that there was insufficient evidence against the suspects. Evidence gathered by Mrs Hashisho, that is. To say that for 23 years Mrs Hashisho had been waiting would be inaccurate. In a meticulous and detailed inventory, Mrs Hashisho listed all the steps, files, documents and declarations she undertook over the years in her efforts to find out what happened to her husband. Several pages and no mention of the judiciary undertaking any investigation.

The sheer length of the list, each document numbered, each file registered, the full names and positions of people solicited, and on what dates, exemplifies what the term 'waiting' means in Lebanon for the family of a missing person. Her case is one of only two known cases that were brought before the judiciary by individual family members to clarify the fate of their missing relatives. In a context framed by a near-blanket amnesty law, failure to redress civic trust in the state's institutions, including in its judiciary, and very scant initiatives to address the legacy of the successive armed conflicts in Lebanon, this latest judicial decision came as a strong symbolic blow to the struggle of the families of the missing in Lebanon. And yet, in the past 5 years or so, a number of initiatives by various non-state entities are managing to build incremental steps, carving their way towards what will no doubt be a long process of clarifying the fate of the missing people in Lebanon.

The present chapter will seek to provide a short introduction to the current medico-legal framework existing in Lebanon, with its legal structure, the role of forensic experts during trials, existing capacity and resources. Additionally, it will present an overview of the latest efforts in Lebanon to push forward the issue of the missing, including enforced disappearances. It will, moreover, outline current efforts to build a forensic framework that could feed into a potential future process of recovering and identifying remains of missing persons in Lebanon, and refer to the few cases in which excavations of human remains were conducted. The chapter will conclude with an assessment of future prospects related to the field of forensic science in Lebanon.

Lebanon's medico-legal framework

In Lebanon, the medico-legal investigation of unnatural death follows the Medical Examiner (ME) system, which was developed from the European Continental Law.

The crime investigation is led by a Prosecutor General (PG), who is an appointed Judge within the Ministry of Justice. In some cases, the PG delegates the lead to an Investigative Judge under his/her supervision. The PG

[1] Press statement made by Mrs Najat Hashisho, on 27 September 2013, in Beirut, at Tournesol Theatre. For more information (in Arabic), see http://legal-agenda.com/article.php?id=529&folder=articles&lang=ar#.UlpRYFCmhD0 (last accessed October 2013).

Forensic Archaeology: A Global Perspective, First Edition. Edited by W.J. Mike Groen, Nicholas Márquez-Grant and Robert C. Janaway.

or the Investigative Judge then appoints a ME, who is an independent practitioner and not an appointed official. The ME is a physician who is not required to have a specialty or training in pathology.

It is noteworthy that despite Lebanon's high number of mass graves (primarily as a result of the 1975–1991 war), the country has no forensic archaeologists.

Crime investigation in Lebanon

According to statistics dating from the early 1990s, based on an unofficial review of the criminal files in the archives of the criminal courts, over 50% of violent criminal activities in the Lebanese territories are of a homicidal nature.

All suspicious deaths are first reported to the local police station in the district where the body is located and the first responder is a patrol unit that will identify and secure the crime scene. The police conduct interviews with eyewitnesses and others on the scene and record all the information in their report. The police are not authorised to collect or touch any evidence from the scene. The police then notify the PG and he/she goes to the crime scene to lead the investigation; in some cases, the PG appoints an Investigative Judge to do so. In this chapter the PG, the Investigative Judge and the Lead Investigator all refer to the same person.

Once at the crime scene, the Lead Investigator will request the presence of the Crime Scene Investigation (CSI) team. The CSI team includes the detectives who will document and analyse the crime scene through the various means of documentation (photography, sketching, blood spatter analysis, etc.) and will collect and preserve the pertinent physical evidence. The CSI team and the police are affiliated with the Internal Security Forces (ISF) under the jurisdiction of the prosecutorial body (Ministry of Justice) and of the Ministry of the Interior.

The PG will also request an ME at the crime scene. The ME will try to fulfil all his/her duties on site in terms of evaluating the time and cause of death and will recommend to the PG if an autopsy is required. Usually, most unnatural, unexplained and suspicious deaths will require an autopsy, which will be done by the ME. However, even though the decision for an autopsy is a matter of law determined by the PG, Lebanon's strong religious beliefs and family pressure are sometimes capable of stopping that decision even at the unfortunate cost of burying the truth with the body.

Once the evidence is collected by the CSI team, who must follow an established protocol to protect the chain of custody, it is sent to the Government forensic laboratory in Beirut whose different areas of expertise are ballistics, explosives, trace analysis, DNA typing, toxicology and photography. Fingerprint analysis is sent for identification to a different specialised government facility which has developed an impressive database of suspects and criminals. Once completed, the police report along with the forensic laboratory results, the ME's report and the CSI team's findings are then presented to the PG for his/her review and decision. This of course will include any suspects in the crime. If the PG deems that there is evidence that a crime was perpetrated, he/she will transfer the file to an Investigative Judge and also issue an arrest warrant for the suspect(s). The Investigative Judge will follow the judicial process, which is based on French civil law and is mainly an inquisitorial system.

If the Investigative Judge is convinced that the suspect(s) have committed the crime, he/she will indict the defendant(s), order their incarceration and turn the file over to a Criminal Court Judge (CCJ) for the trial to begin.

In Lebanon, the CCJ is the absolute authority and runs the entire trial – he/she acts as the jury and the Judge. The defence lawyers submit their pleadings in writing prior to the trial and may also present oral arguments to the CCJ at the beginning of the court hearing. Once the witnesses or the accused take the stand, the CCJ asks all the questions and instructs the court clerk to write down the questions and the answers. Defence lawyers are not allowed to object, nor are they authorised to question their clients or witnesses, or to cross-examine the prosecution's witnesses.

In the investigation, the main body of evidence is naturally the victim's body. Pursuant to the PG's instructions, the final recovery of the body is at the morgue of either a public or a private hospital depending on the next of kin's will. In the event that the victim is not identified by anyone, a public hospital is obligated to admit the corpse.

It is important to note that the judicial system in Lebanon is archaic, procedurally slow and heavily influenced by politics and personal connections. It is also overburdened by frivolous lawsuits primarily due to the fact that the fees and expenses ordered to be paid by the plaintiff in case he/she loses are insignificant. As a result of these factors, some cases have dragged on for decades, including some criminal defendants whom the present authors have knowledge of that have been incarcerated for more than 18 years without a final ruling in their case for conviction or acquittal. We are all shocked when we hear of individuals who have been convicted and incarcerated for that long, and then released because they were wrongly accused. How shocked are we when we hear of individuals incarcerated for that long during their trial?

Forensic scientist and ME licensing

Forensic scientists need to be competent in the science of the CSI process – the collection, testing and evaluation of the evidence – and should have a good understanding of the legal criminal process to assist in the proper and factual presentation of the evidence so the judicial system can reach a fair and just opinion.

Until recently, there were no private forensic science advisers as all the forensic science experts in Lebanon were government employees (members of the ISF) and were not required to hold degrees in forensic science; in 2010, the Lebanese Ministry of Justice created a new public category of expertise under the name of 'forensic science Expert', which currently has only one such certified member.

The licensing requirement for an ME has remained unchanged since it was first established under the Ottoman Empire rule; essentially any qualified medical doctor can apply for a licence without the need for further specialisation such as in pathology, as is the case, for example, in the United States. Currently there are around 90 licensed MEs in Lebanon.

Growing public discussion but lack of official action

'The decision issued today raises a greater question', said Mrs Wadad Halwani, sitting next to Mrs Hashisho, and who has taken the lead in voicing the demands of the families of the missing since 1982. Her husband was abducted in similar circumstances from his home a few days after Mr Hashisho's abduction. 'What has the state done, in all of its legislative, executive and judiciary branches, to provide justice to the victims?'[2]

This overpowering sense of isolation, helplessness and fatigue is emblematic of the situation that has plagued the families of the missing in Lebanon for over three decades now. A recently published report on the needs of the families of the missing in Lebanon, based on interviews conducted with 324 families of diverse geographical, social and personal status background, found that 'the main problem facing the individual family members was the emotional distress created by the absence of their loved one and the psychological difficulty of coping with uncertainty about his fate. This is particularly remarkable given the average time elapsed since the disappearance'. The assessment report, carried out by the International Committee of the Red Cross (ICRC), the first of its kind to be conducted on this issue, concludes that 'hearing the truth' and 'doing something to find him and get him back' were the families' most important need expressed, over and above other administrative, legal, financial or material considerations (ICRC 2013, 11).

The armed conflict that broke out in 1975 saw a number of local, regional and international non-state and state parties fighting each other on Lebanese territory, dragging the country into 15 years of continuous politically motivated violence, which were followed by 10 more years of Israeli occupation and 15 years of Syrian occupation. A report issued by the Lebanese government in March 1992 gave an estimate of the conflicts' casualties, as follows: 144,240 killed; 197,506 wounded, including 13,455 with permanent disability; 17,415 missing, including 13,968 as a result of kidnappings (Human Rights Watch 1993, 1).

These figures in no way result from a thorough investigation, including the figure of the missing, and subsequent academic research has yielded differing results. One of the chief demands voiced by the families of the victims today remains the need for a comprehensive and centralised list of missing persons. The missing persons in Lebanon generally include Lebanese and other nationals, including Palestinians, who were abducted and thereafter disappeared at the hands of local Lebanese militias, or by the Israeli or Syrian armies or their local proxies, before being transferred to either Syria or Israel. This figure further includes those who went missing during wide-scale killings or in combat.

When the conflict ended in 1991, the country remained subject to the occupation of its two powerful neighbours, Syria and Israel, the latter controlling the country's south, in effect isolating that region from the rest of the country, which itself came under Syria's military, economic and political hegemony. During this time, political violence continued, and was marked by several Israeli large-scale attacks, including a fully fledged war in July 2006, and numerous serious violations of international human rights and humanitarian rights, including enforced disappearances, forced displacement, car bombs and targeted assassinations, torture and arbitrary detention (e.g. ICTJ 2013). Israel eventually withdrew in May 2000 and Syria in April 2005.

This departure of foreign troops from the country heralded a new phase with a potential to start addressing the legacy of the conflicts, accompanied by a sustainable and legitimate institution-building process. This included the issue of missing persons in Lebanon: in June 2008, a joint memo addressed by 17 non-governmental organisations (NGOs) demanded that the incoming President, Mr Suleiman, prioritise the issue of the missing and establish a national commission for the missing. The President heeded the call and pledged in his oath to address the issue; his call was echoed in the ministerial declarations of the three governments that succeeded his pledge.

Prior to this, two official commissions had been formed but failed to deliver any form of meaningful response to the families, let alone conduct any serious investigations, despite the testimonies of former detainees who were released from Syrian prisons and of families (Maalouf 2010, 276; Mermier and Varin 2010). The first commission, in 2000, did, however, mention that there were mass

[2]Press statement by Mrs Wadad Halwani, on 27 September 2013, in Beirut, at Tournesol Theatre. For more information (in Arabic), see http://legal-agenda.com/article.php?id=530&folder=articles&lang=ar#.UlpRhlCmhD0 (last accessed October 2013).

graves all across the Lebanese territory, explicitly mentioning three in the capital city, Beirut.

Excepting these two commissions and a third joint Syrian–Lebanese one formed in 2005, which also failed to deliver any answers, no official initiative was taken until October 2012, when the Minister of Justice submitted a draft decree[3] for the creation of a commission. The government appointed a ministerial committee to examine the draft, which was also shared with various stakeholders and NGOs working on the issue, including the ICRC and the International Centre for Transitional Justice (ICTJ). In February 2013, the ministerial committee submitted the final copy to the government, but the government resigned before being able to examine it. In the process, however, the decree drew criticism from the Committee of the Families of the Kidnapped and Missing and the Legal Agenda, a legal watchdog association, on the basis that a commission formed by ministerial decree would not have the necessary prerogatives to undertake any meaningful progress on the issue, among other issues. Moreover, the State Constitutional Court also issued its decision, making clear that such a commission would need a parliamentary ratification in order to fulfil its stated mission, which would include subpoena and investigative powers. The ICTJ further published general principles to take into consideration in the discussion.[4]

This decree came at the heels of a civil society initiative, led by the ICTJ, and in conjunction with the two main family associations, which had undertaken to develop a draft law through a 2-year consultative process with over 15 international and local organisations, that would set the institutional, legal and technical framework for addressing the issue of the missing, including the forcibly disappeared.[5] The draft law was modelled to a large extent on the ICRC Model Law, and drew on certain aspects of the Law on Missing Persons in Bosnia and Herzegovina (Hanson, Chapter 48 this volume), and the Iraqi Law on Protection of Mass Graves. It seeks to set the legal framework to enable a process of creating a comprehensive list of victims, acknowledges the families' right to know the truth, protect suspected and confirmed sites of individual and communal graves and allow for the excavation of remains and their identification. The text, however, has failed to garner any interest from Lebanon's parliamentary members to date. In the foreseeing months, it would be highly surprising if this situation were to change, considering the near paralysis of state institutions, including a resigned government, a parliament that self-extended its own mandate and has been failing to meet and a growing social and economic crisis resulting in part from the conflict in neighbouring Syria.

It remains, however, the chief demand and main advocacy tool of the Committee of the Families, which, in light of the latest judicial decision in Mr Hashisho's case, announced that the draft law would be henceforth baptised the law of Muhieddine Hashisho.[6]

ICRC's missing persons project in Lebanon

One recent initiative worth noting, and that has managed to make headway regardless of political considerations, is the project being led by the ICRC (Tidball-Binz and Hofmeister, Chapter 49 this volume). Since April 2012, after consultation with Lebanese authorities, the ICRC has been collecting pre-disappearance data on the missing through one-to-one interviews with the family members. The ICRC reached out to the families through a public call, by setting up a dedicated phone line and by coordinating with local authorities (municipalities and other parties) in the regions. To date, over 1000 families have been interviewed.[7] The information collected will remain confidential, only to be shared once a national mechanism, mandated to carry out the identification process, has been formally agreed upon by the Lebanese government and the ICRC.[8]

As this process continues, the ICRC has in parallel entered into discussions with the government towards reaching an agreement for the collection of Biological Reference Samples (BRS) from suitable familial donors for subsequent DNA testing, which will be conducted at a later date determined by a national mechanism. While cooperation between the ICRC and ISF is facilitating the necessary planning for the commencement of this endeavour, a formal agreement has not been approved due to the government's resignation, but it is likely to be addressed once a new government is set in place. The ICRC has provided the ISF, which will be responsible for collecting the BRS, with training on the

[3]Draft decree found here: http://ictj.org/sites/default/files/Decree-National%20Commission-Forcibly%20Disappeared-10oct2012-EN.pdf (last accessed 14 October 2013).

[4]For more information, see http://ictj.org/news/lebanon-principles-dealing-missing-including-forcibly-disappeared (last accessed 14 October 2013).

[5]The key provisions of the draft law can be found here: http://www.actforthedisappeared.com/assets/documents/Key-Provisions-Law.pdf (last accessed 14 October 2013).

[6]Halwani, press statement, 17 September 2013.

[7]Author's interview with ICRC, Beirut, 1 October 2013.

[8]Author's interview with ICRC, Beirut, 10 October 2013.

ICRC's software to manage the ante- and post-mortem information on the missing persons or human remains found (ICRC 2012, 440). The ICRC is working with the ISF to identify the necessary capacity, technical expertise in the forensic science field and logistical requirements to undertake this endeavour, and they are jointly developing standard operating procedures to provide a framework for collecting and preserving DNA samples, with a rigorous chain of custody approach necessary for demonstrating reliable sample control measures in a joint-organisational project.[9]

In its concluding recommendations, the ICRC echoes the call of the Committee of Families in demanding the ratification of the draft law, namely, by calling on the Lebanese authorities to set up a mechanism mandated to search for the missing, clarify their fate and whereabouts and inform the families, with the necessary resources and powers to carry out the process of tracing and identifying missing persons, including the excavation of individual and mass graves and recovery of human remains (ICRC 2013, 21).

Forensic archaeology

From an archaeological standpoint, Lebanon is renowned as a haven for archaeological findings. But despite having internationally renowned archaeologists, the country has no forensic archaeologists. In the event a mass grave is found during an archaeological expedition or during an excavation, the site is immediately turned over to the police, who then call the CSI team and the ME to exhume the bodies; the crime scene is then dealt with in the same manner as is done for a regular crime scene.[10]

Unfortunately, the lack of forensic archaeologists (and also forensic anthropologists) in Lebanon has often led to the improper handling of human remains, resulting in the difficulty and sometimes the impossibility of proper identification.

Accordingly, it may be appropriate at this point to introduce the field of forensic entomology in Lebanon, where we can use our scientific knowledge of insects and the collection and analysis of scientific evidence of necrophagous insects for use in crime investigation, to assist the prosecution or the defence to identify, convict or exonerate suspects.

In Lebanon, forensic entomology is relatively new and the only forensic entomologist is Dr Danny Azar, who is internationally renowned in this field. Taxonomy studies of the local necrophagous insects in different zoogeographical areas in Lebanon are now under way to establish a scientific database to use in crime investigation. Eventually, these insects will provide a range of valuable scientific information which can be used to locate a missing body, specify the exact time of death, identify drugs in the body and determine whether a body has been moved.

An experiment was conducted this past summer as the first of a series of experiments, using a domestic pig on which the five stages of decomposition were followed and observed to identify the main species of necrophagous insects. The findings were presented on 21 November 2013 at the fifth Annual Zoological Congress in Bucharest, Romania (Maalouf et al. 2013).

Selective cases of exhumations

When, in 2000, the first official commission published its two-and-a-half page report, it concluded that all persons missing were considered to be deceased, and where remains were exhumed, it would be impossible to identify them on account of the nature of the remains and the time that has elapsed.[11] No mention was made about what was done with the remains exhumed, nor on what basis the scientific conclusion was reached. At the time, Lebanon did not have a forensic laboratory or the human resources to carry out any identification process. A lawsuit carried out by the families of missing persons in 2008, on the basis of their right to have information, granted them access to the reports of the two medical forensic doctors who had contributed to the commission's conclusion. One said that it was impossible to identify on account of the passage of time, and the other said that it would be, pending the completion of the forensic laboratory that was in the making at the time.

The families contested the findings of the report, more pointedly the forensic doctors' conclusions, and have since demanded that the sites explicitly mentioned in the report be protected until the time they can be excavated. The litigation process is ongoing, and the state authorities have not taken any steps to protect and guard these sites, nor shown any willingness to do so. Moreover, it has already happened that remains have been found on construction or archaeological sites; however, the judicial authorities responsible for the exhumation and identification process have never disclosed what they have done with the remains or if they undertook any related measures.

[9]Author's interview with ICRC, Beirut, 10 October 2013.

[10]In such case, it may be also beneficial to call on a Forensic Entomologist (FE) where the knowledge of the indigenous necrophagous insects could reveal valuable forensic evidence on buried and decomposed corpses that a Medical Examiner (ME) may not be qualified to provide.

[11]The commission's report (in Arabic) can be found here: http://www.actforthedisappeared.com/assets/documents/Report/Report-Commission-Part-Ar.pdf (last accessed 14 October 2013).

And yet there have been successful cases of recovery of remains, their identification and return to their families. In November 2005, following the withdrawal of the Syrian army from Lebanon, the Army command ordered the opening of a suspected mass grave located on the site of the Ministry of Defence, in Yarzeh. The opening and exhumation was carried out under the aegis of the military court, in the presence of the military tribunal Judge, a forensic medical doctor and a delegation of military police and Red Cross personnel. The remains of 18 bodies, later identified as Lebanese soldiers, were exhumed, identified by DNA analysis and handed over to their families. It is believed that the soldiers were killed during a land and air attack by the Syrian army in October 1990, during which summary executions of prisoners and arbitrary detentions followed by disappearances took place (ICTJ 2013, 67). An official funeral ceremony was held in their honour.[12]

One year later, the remains of Mr Michel Seurat, a French researcher who had been abducted in 1985 and subsequently disappeared, were recovered in the southern suburbs of Beirut, and were handed over to his family. In 2009, the remains of Alec Collett, a British journalist, who had been abducted in Beirut in 1985 while on a mission for the United Nations Relief and Works Agency for Palestine Refugees in the Near East (UNRWA), were located in the Bekaa Valley, in the town of 'Ayt al-Foukhar, exhumed, identified and returned to his family. A UK-dispatched mobile unit was able to identify the remains of Mr Collett, later confirmed by DNA. This was done with the support and cooperation of the Lebanese authorities. In both cases, the respective families of the victims, with the help of the French and UK diplomatic missions, exerted pressure so that the Lebanese authorities would undertake the necessary steps to locate, recover and return the remains of their missing family members.

In the case of Mr Collett, however, the remains of another body, in military clothes, were found some 20 m away, but there has been no communication by the Lebanese authorities as to what was done with these remains. Reports suggest that these remains were reburied. This tragically attests to the selective will to carry out the process of tracing, identifying and return of specific cases of missing persons.[13] 'The apparent inability of the Lebanese authorities to identify the second body highlights their failure to establish a database of DNA samples from family members of those who went missing. Associations of families of civil war victims have been campaigning for such a database for more than a decade', said Amnesty International in a statement.[14]

Moreover, the ICRC coordinated several rounds of exchanges between Israel and the Lebanese armed and political party, Hezbollah, which allowed the recovery of the remains of 185 Hezbollah fighters. Though both parties subsequently announced that they deemed the file to be complete, some families still claim that their relatives, believed to have been disappeared at the hands of Israelis or their Lebanese proxy, have not been accounted for.

In August 2011, three associations – the Committee of the Families, Support of Lebanese in Detention and Exile (SOLIDE 2012) and CLDH (Lebanese Centre for Human Rights) – issued a press release to the effect that their delegation was denied access to the site of a suspected mass grave, and were calling on the authorities to take the necessary measures to protect the site. There had been media reports that human remains were found in the town of Shbaniyyeh, in the Chouf region in Lebanon, and the authorities had quickly stated that these were bones of animals. The delegation that went, accompanied by a forensic medical doctor, was denied access to the site by the municipality and the military intelligence service, and notified by the ISF, according to the group's press release.[15] Family members of disappeared persons in the area who were interviewed said they were worried about the authorities' conclusion, especially since the human cranium and bones were found wrapped in nylon bags, according to witnesses.

Conclusion

Lebanon is a country which is still recovering from almost two decades of civil war and ensuing years of continuing politically motivated violence, including a devastating war with Israel. The issue of the missing in Lebanon, and the process to clarify their fate and meet some measure of the families' needs and rights, is contingent primarily upon a still non-existent political will to address the issue of the war in its entirety.

However, Lebanon has come a long way with the establishment of the aforementioned forensic laboratory, and it is worth noting that currently two universities – the American University of Science and Technology (AUST) and the Lebanese University (LU) – have started offering degrees in forensic sciences.

[12]An Nahar, 14 November 2005, 7.

[13]Media report can be found on the homepage of Memory at Work: http://www.memoryatwork.org/ (last accessed October 2013).

[14]Amnesty International, *Lebanon must investigate all civil war mass grave sites*, 25 November 2009. For more information, see http://www.amnesty.org/en/news-and-updates/news/lebanon-must-investigate-civil-war-mass-grave-sites-20091125 (last accessed 15 October 2013).

[15]For more information, see http://www.actforthedisappeared.com/assets/documents/Press-release-Speech/Press-release-Potential-MassGrave.pdf (last accessed 15 October 2013).

However, in its continued quest to improve its forensic competencies, Lebanon is in dire need of a new morgue and a properly structured Forensic Institute, with state-of-the-art equipment and laboratories specialising in the various scientific processing and identification techniques. More importantly, it needs to have at least one forensic archaeologist and to keep improving its educational standards. Furthermore, Lebanon needs to raise the licensing requirements for the forensic science and the Forensic Pathology fields to improve the qualification and efficiency of its criminal investigation experts and of its ME.

References

Committee of the Families of the Kidnapped and Disappeared in Lebanon and Support of Lebanese in Detention and Exile (SOLIDE). 2012. *Law for Missing and Disappeared Persons.* Beirut, Arab Printing Press. Available at: http://www.actforthedisappeared.com/assets/documents/Draft-Law-Eng.pdf (last accessed October 2013).

Human Rights Watch. 1993. *World Report.* Lebanon, Human Rights Watch.

International Committee of the Red Cross (ICRC). 2012. *ICRC Annual Report 2012 – Lebanon,* May 2013, available at: http://www.refworld.org/cgi-bin/texis/vtx/rwmain?page=search&docid=51d52c1d0&skip=0&query=ICRC Annual Report 2012, Lebanon (last accessed 2 December 2014).

ICRC. 2013. *The Families of People Missing in Connection with the Armed Conflicts that have Occurred in Lebanon since 1975, an Assessment of their Needs,* May 2013, available at: http://www.icrc.org/eng/assets/files/2013/lebanon-missing-06-2013-icrc.pdf (last accessed 8 September 2014).

ICTJ. 2013. *Lebanon's Legacy of Political Violence.* Available at: http://ictj.org/publication/lebanon-legacy-political-violence (last accessed October 2013).

Maalouf, L. 2010. Les disparitions forcées au Liban: l'héritage immuable d'une nation. In F. Mermier and C. Varin (eds.), *Mémoires de Guerres au Liban (1975-1990),* 265–284. Arles, Actes Sud.

Maalouf, R., Shayya, S. and Bassil, C. 2013. The importance of Calliphora, Sarcophaga and Coleoptera in forensic investigations in Lebanon. CZGA 2013 Programme, 20 November 2013.

Mermier, F. and Varin, C. (eds.) 2010. *Mémoires de Guerres au Liban (1975-1990).* Actes Sud, Arles. English translation available at: http://www.actforthedisappeared.com/assets/documents/Report/Article_LynnMaalouf_ENG.pdf (last accessed October 2013).

CHAPTER 36

Forensic sciences in Libya and mass grave investigation

Amin Attia Alemam

Libyan Society of Forensic Odontology, University of Benghazi, Benghazi, Libya

Introduction

Forensic archaeology is not a recognised discipline in Libya, although much archaeological, anthropological and forensic expertise is present in the country. Recently, with the work of a number of scientists and the fall of the previous regime, the investigation of mass graves and the training and formation of the judicial and security forces has been undertaken. The excavation of clandestine graves has slowly been carried out and with the increase presence of forensic scientists, albeit the lack of forensic archaeologists. This chapter summarises the judicial system and the attempts to use forensic disciplines in mass grave investigation in Libya. Recently, the presence of international organisations has also highlighted and introduced the role and work of forensic archaeology, and training is under way to promote the value of the discipline, at least at the moment in mass grave investigation.

Background on the Libyan political and criminal justice system

Libya was a country based on the views, instructions and beliefs of one person after the Libyan Constitution was no longer in effect from 1977. Colonel Qadhafi (*c.* 1942–2011) replaced the Constitution after taking power with his Green Book and with what he called the People's Declaration of 1977 (DPADM 2004). During Qadhafi's regime, which lasted for 42 years (1969–2011), the Ministry of Justice and National Police experienced widespread corruption. The majority of security institutions were deliberately destroyed throughout that period. However, there were a number of security organisations that had authority and provided a high standard of facilities. This was because they were strongly supported, as they were originally founded mainly for protection purposes and for internal and external investigations for the benefit of that regime.

In the field of criminal investigations, there were Libyan institutions that had already been created during the period of the monarchy (1951–1969) of King Idris I, for example, the National Centre of Legislative and Criminal Research (المركز القومي للبحوث التشريعية والجنائية) (Alshawari 2012). The Centre was founded in 1964. It included six branches distributed over six different areas: Tripoli, Benghazi, Sabha, the Green Mountain, Sebratah and the West Mountain Branch. It was concerned with all the legal issues that needed specialist investigation in different fields, forensic sciences among them.

In 2002 its name was changed from the Centre of Expert Witnesses to the Court of Laws and Research and (مركز الخبره القضائية و البحوث) it became more organised, with a separate forensic medicine department. The last available statistics for the number of cases in this department were for 2005, when 15,616 cases required examination (clinical cases); 12,979 cases were processed in that year, which represented about 83% as a percentage of completion. Statistics show that the highest numbers of cases were recorded by the Benghazi branch with 7897 cases, which represents half of the total number (50%), while the Tripoli branch took second place in terms of caseload, with 5503 cases.

The first officially recognised Libyan specialist in forensic sciences was Dr Fawzi Benomran. As noted by Benomran (*Forensic Pathology in Libya*, Personal Interview/Personal Comment, 7 May 2013, Derna, Libya), he was the first forensic pathologist in Libya. He held the post of Director of the Centre of Expert Witnesses to the Court of Laws and Research, and the Head of Department of Forensic Medicine and Toxicology at the Faculty of Medicine of Benghazi University until July 1997, when he left Libya for a job in Dubai, United Arab Emirates. Prior to Dr Benomran's involvement, all forensic specialists at the Centre were expatriates from different nationalities (e.g. Egypt, India, Poland and Bulgaria). However, Libya still has a shortage of experts in the field of forensic investigation, where the domestically available specialties are restricted

Forensic Archaeology: A Global Perspective, First Edition. Edited by W.J. Mike Groen, Nicholas Márquez-Grant and Robert C. Janaway.

to one main forensic science – forensic pathology. Only four forensic pathologists currently hold a PhD, while some other sciences are completely absent, such as forensic anthropology, forensic archaeology, forensic odontology and forensic entomology. There are a few forensic toxicologists, and, lastly, since the revolution, there are now two specialists in forensic genetics, in DNA profiling and DNA fingerprinting respectively.

There are currently two forensic medicine departments at Libyan Universities. The first one is in the School of Medicine at the University of Benghazi, which opened in 1974, and the second is in the School of Medicine at the University of Tripoli, which opened in 1978. Both have an academic teaching function (Benomran 2013).

The facilities and equipment inside the forensic departments in the justice and education sectors are still conventional and very simple. This shortage was very apparent during the liberation war in 2011.

Status of forensic archaeology in Libya

There are no forensic archaeological specialists in Libya at the moment. However, there are regular archaeologists present in Libya with experience in the excavation of (mass) graves. Since some of the excavated archaeological human remains are mummified, archaeological excavation experience could also be of use during forensic investigation of (mass) graves.

There have been a number of discoveries made by Libyan archaeologists of faunal and human skeletal remains. For instance, five mummies were discovered in 1995 at El-Jaghbub by Dr Fadel A. Mohamed, Advisor to the State for Antiquities and lecturer at the University of Omar al-Mukhtar. First he found well-preserved human remains in the area and when he sent samples to France for radiocarbon tests, the results were dated between 196 BC and AD 126 (Mohamed 2007). There have been a number of other discoveries made by international individuals and organisations, such as a child's mummified body which was discovered in 1959 inside the Uan Muhuggiag cave in the Libyan desert by Professor Fabrizio Mori. A two and a half year old child was found bound in animal skin, and this skin has been radiocarbon dated to be between 3275 and 3635 years BC (Aufderheide 2003). Another example is the skeletal remains of two individuals who were earthquake victims during Emperor Gallinus's fifth consulship in AD 262, exhumed from the Sanctuary of Demeter and Persephone at Cyrene, by the University of Pennsylvania Museum of Archaeology and Anthropology between 1973 and 1981 (White 1990). Moreover, human osteological material was excavated by C. M. Daniels and housed at the Jarma museum. This consists of 56 human skeletons retrieved from 68 archaeological features (Mattingly 2010). Recently, archaeologists have uncovered 20 Stone Age skeletons in and around a rock shelter in Libya's Sahara desert. A new programme of territorial study was launched in the area of Wadi Takarkori, which is located in southwestern Libya on the border with Algeria in a strategic position between the Tassili and the Acacus Mountains. As part of the activities of the archaeological mission in the Sahara, a team from Sapienza University in Rome was supported by Libya and led by Dr Salah Agab who is the chairman of the Department of Antiquities in Tripoli (Lernia and Tafuri 2013).

Due to its strategic location and large surface area, about 1.8 million km^2, Libya has been strongly characterised by its history and archaeology. For millennia Libya has been a land of very different civilisations, including Greek, Roman, Islamic, Ottoman and Italian colonialism, as well as its original history as an African country. Therefore Libyan scientists believe that in Libya many archaeological discoveries are possible.

Although this example is archaeological in nature and not forensic, it illustrates and emphasises that there are many experienced and qualified archaeologists and anthropologists in Libya whose skills should not be undervalued for forensic and/or criminal investigation in the future.

Identification process during the Libyan revolution

The early days of the Libyan revolution (February 2011) clearly showed a deficit in the area of identification for the rebels' unidentified bodies, but a great effort was made and is still being made locally, in an attempt to compensate for this lack of identification of the victims, despite the absence of subspecialties and unavailable facilities. The Centre of Expert Witnesses to the Court of Laws and Research in Benghazi, under the auspices of the Libyan Ministry of Justice at the beginning of the revolution, was one of the official institutions that belonged to the National Transitional Council (المجلس الوطني الانتقالي), when the east of Libya was liberated on the revolution's sixth day. While the other parts of the country were not yet liberated, the forensic medicine department of this centre was responsible for dealing with all the different cases of the victims on the Eastern Front, with a restricted forensic team and a lack of facilities. The team consisted of four forensic pathologists and one dentist. All members were official staff of this centre except for the dentist, as he was a volunteer during that period.

Unidentified bodies presented with different injuries and even if they had clear body and facial features they sometimes could not be identified because of an absence of ID. Furthermore, if there were no relatives who asked about them at the mortuary, they were usually buried in numbered individual graves, without a death certificate. Only photographs and a DNA sample were taken from this first group. The second type of unidentified victims was those whose facial and physical features were partially or completely lost due to the severity of their trauma. For example, on 2 April 2011, NATO mistakenly attacked the rebels; 13 people were killed and their bodies were severely burned and charred. For forensic anthropologists obtaining a biological profile in those cases is possible since forensic anthropologists can deal with such cases even if the remains are modified by the heat (Blau and Ubelaker 2009, 23). With the absence of dental records, as well as the lack of a DNA database and facilities for analysis, the identification process in this 2011 incident was difficult to apply.

This incident emphasised the challenge that the team faced regarding the increasing problem of identification. The situation made the team consider finding a substitute for DNA analysis, rather than collecting samples; to solve this problem the team proposed to start dental diagnostic work at the conflict line by building up a dental record system for all the soldiers at the Eastern Front. This proposal was promoted by a group of dentists from the University of Benghazi Dental School. Another idea was to introduce a proposal to the military council and rebel leaders to make metallic military identification plates for all soldiers at the front line. Neither of these solutions was implemented and the number of unidentified bodies increased dramatically. The number of missing rebels also increased, starting with the first incident at Binjawad on 8 March 2011, when about 200 rebels were captured by Qadhafi's forces, the outcome unknown. In other conflict zones, mortality rates were not documented, but predictions based on previous experience were frightening. During that time new discoveries of multiple mass graves were also made, of people previously killed by Qadhafi's forces. The first mass grave to be investigated was at Zueitina village.

Zueitina mass grave

Zueitina is a coastal village 150 km west of Benghazi. News of a mass grave in that area reached one of the rebel battalions from an eyewitness in April 2011. Some battalion members then went to the site at Zueitina and after searching they uncovered their first evidence. They kept searching until three skeletonised human bodies were exhumed non-scientifically. They then decided to complete this mission under legal jurisdiction and the case was therefore handed over to the Centre of Expert Witnesses to the Court of Laws and Research in Benghazi, where the forensic department recruited a forensic team (Figure 36.1) led by a forensic pathologist, Dr Khaled Almgasbi. He was the Centre President and the Head of its forensic department. After that all the victims' remains were exhumed from the grave (Figure 36.2), and then transferred to an autopsy laboratory in the Benghazi Medical Centre (Figure 36.3).

Seven skeletons were arranged in order from one to seven, post-mortem dental records were made, photographs were taken and dental samples were collected for DNA analysis. Dental identification was attempted, but found impossible as ante-mortem dental records were absent. During the first days of the revolution the internal security headquarters, which most represented the repression of Qadhafi's security system, was invaded

Figure 36.1 The Zueitina mass grave investigation team which includes the forensic team (e.g. forensic pathologists, odontologists), rebels, prosecutors, and members of human rights organisations, April 2011.

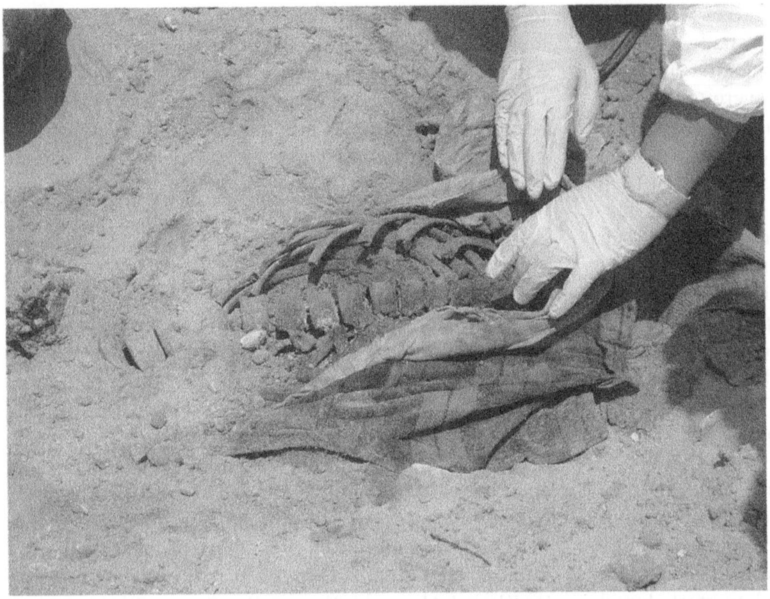

Figure 36.2 Exhumation of the Zueitina mass grave (2011).

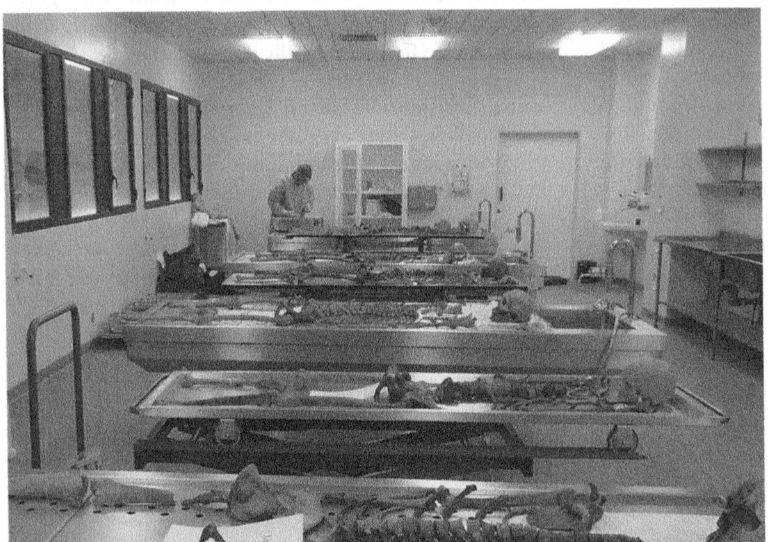

Figure 36.3 Autopsy laboratory of the Benghazi Medical Centre where the examination process of the Zueitina mass grave was held (2011).

and destroyed by rebels. Some of the files detailing the regime's crimes were preserved by the rebels. These files held many secrets and one of these files related to the Zueitina mass grave. It had contained all the necessary information about the crime, one peri-mortem photograph of one of the seven victims (Figure 36.4) and also their names.

This file reached the crime investigator directly from the rebels and after that the seven families were informed as to what had happened to their sons. They accepted the news of their sons' fate as they had suspected the cause of the disappearance for about 15 years. In 1996 a group of seven friends, two of them brothers aged 17–25 years old, were secretly executed because they disagreed with Qadhafi's regime. The murder happened away from the burial place as recent stories from eyewitnesses mention the crime taking place near a small city east of Benghazi called Alabyar, about 220 km from Zueitina. These seven skeletal remains belonged to this group of friends, but the

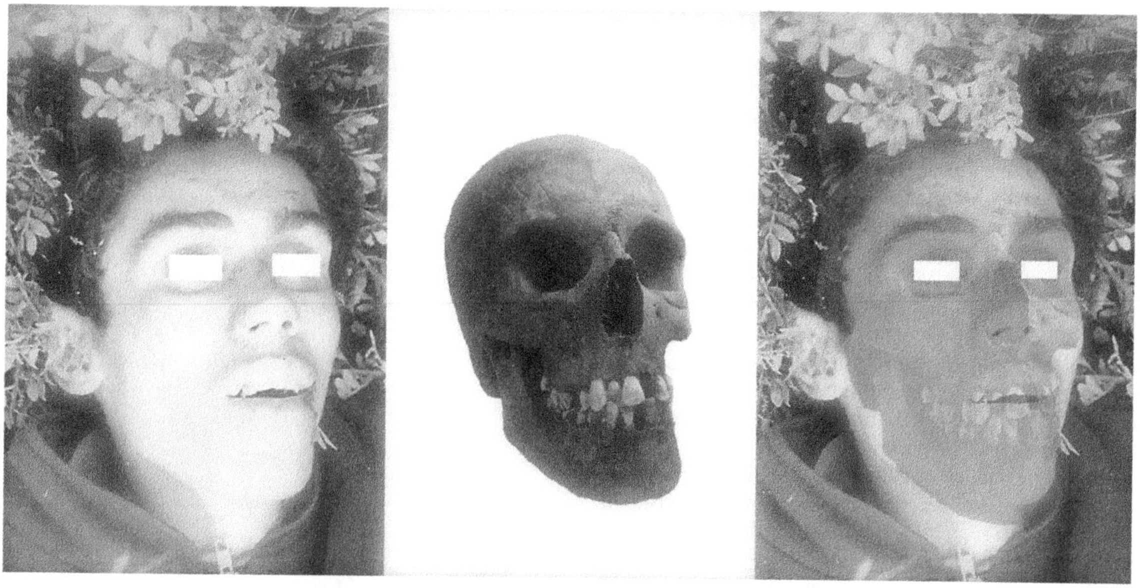

Figure 36.4 Superimposition of two photographs. The first one is a peri-mortem picture which was found within the internal security headquarters' files. The second one is a post-mortem picture of one of the seven victims' skulls of the victims of the Zueitina mass grave. This process was applied before the DNA testing had been conducted.

Figure 36.5 The funeral ceremony for the Zueitina Martyrs was held in Benghazi's Liberation Plaza and they were buried in Alhawari Cemetery in May 2011. This picture was taken inside the Martyrs Battalion (Benghazi Protection).

forensic team found it difficult to differentiate between them and thus issue a death certificate for each of them. Libyan forensic specialists testified as to their findings to the Centre of Expert Witnesses to the Court of Laws and Research. The sample collection instructions for mitochondrial DNA analysis were given by the American Society of Forensic Odontology. After samples had been taken a funeral ceremony for the Zueitina Martyrs was held in Benghazi's Liberation Plaza and they were buried in Alhawari Cemetery in May 2011 (Figure 36.5). DNA analysis for the seven cases and their families was conducted in the Genoma laboratory in Rome, Italy, and the results were finally disclosed on 8 July 2012.

Identification process after the Libyan revolution

Multiple mass graves were discovered in different places in Libya during and after the liberation. The largest one is the Ben Jawad grave, which includes 157 bodies of rebels killed by Qadhafi's forces in March 2011. Ben Jawad village is located 150 km east of Sirte. Forensic investigation of this grave started on 2 March 2012 by the Centre of Expert Witnesses to the Court of Laws and Research, Benghazi branch.

The Libyan Ministry of the Affairs of the Families of Martyrs and Missing Persons وزارة شؤون أسر الشهداء و المفقودين estimates that there are around 10,000 people missing in Libya. This number includes people lost during the revolution as well as from previous events, such as the 1270 prisoners killed in 1996 in Abu Salim prison. There has been a great effort made by the Libyan provisional government to search for and identify the missing people. This has been done with the cooperation of international organisations. For example, the International Committee of the Red Cross (ICRC; Tidball-Binz and Hofmeister, Chapter 49 this volume) and the Physicians for Human Rights (PHR; Schmitt et al., Chapter 53 this volume) supported the Ministry of Affairs of the families of Martyrs and Missing Persons (MAFMM) by reuniting families, dealing with human remains, collecting and storing personal details and/or advising on the handling of missing person cases (ICRC 2013; PHR 2013).

The International Commission on Missing Persons (ICMP; Hanson, Chapter 48 this volume) director, General Kathryn Bomberger, and the Libyan Minister for MAFMM, Naser Jibril Hamed, agreed to cooperate in Tripoli in November 2012 to try to solve missing person cases from the Qadhafi's regime and the latest conflicts (ICMB 2012).

This agreement includes the ICMP providing help in creating a Libyan Identification Centre (LIC). This is essential in developing a sustainable means of dealing with missing person cases in Libya in the future. The LIC plans to have a DNA laboratory system which will house a facility to manage biological samples for DNA identity testing and which will have the capacity to develop further in other areas. This centre should allow for better coordination of internal testing in Libya and the ability to provide assistance internationally.

Full training in successful recovery and identification has been provided by the ICMP for Libyan scientists involved in the identification process of mass grave victims, including archaeology and anthropology. Demonstrating the value of archaeology has certainly been focal in the last 2 years. In addition, a Libya-specific version of the Forensic Data Management System (FDMS), a specialised software solution internally designed by the ICMP to record identification, will be donated by the commission. In terms of legal support, the ICMP will assist Libya in writing specific missing person legislation.

Figure 36.6 Members of the Libyan Society of Forensic Odontology of the National Health Systems Conference held on 29 August 2012.

Future of forensic sciences in Libya

Currently there are many Libyan students studying forensic sciences outside the country. Many of these sciences are completely absent in Libya. Meanwhile, there are others currently training in Libya to be a domestic forensic team able to deal with war victims and graves and who are receiving training including forensic archaeology. In addition, related civilian organisations have been founded during and after the liberation war, such as the Libyan Society of Forensic Odontology (Figure 36.6). Moreover, archaeologists from universities may receive training in forensics; this will be of value in the search, location and excavation of human remains buried in clandestine graves. Therefore it is anticipated that the field of forensics in Libya will grow significantly during the few next years.

Acknowledgements

I wish to express my sincere gratitude to Professor Fadel Ali Mohamed, Tariq Eljahmi, Wanysa Massoud, Rachel Embury, Dr Fawzi Benomran, Dr Khaled Almgasbi and Dr Mahmud Kaddura for their contribution during the time of research and writing of this chapter.

References

Alshawari, A. 2012. *The Libyan Ministry of Justice.* Available at: http://www.aladel.gov.ly/main/modules/sections/item.php?itemid=313 (last accessed 25 April 2013).

Aufderheide, A. C. 2003. *The Scientific Study of Mummies.* Cambridge, University of Cambridge.

Blau, S. and Ubelaker, D. H. (eds.) 2009. *Handbook of Forensic Anthropology and Archaeology.* Walnut Creek, Left Coast Press.

DPADM (Division for Public Administration and Development Management) 2004. Department of Economic and Social Affairs, UN. 2004. *Country Report.* Available at: http://www.unpan.org/DPADM/ProductsServices/ThematicPortals/PublicAdministrationCountryProfiles/tabid/677/Default.aspx (last accessed 20 April 2013).

ICMB. 2012. *ICMP and Libyan Government Sign an Agreement on Cooperation Concerning Missing Persons.* November 2012. Available at: http://www.ic-mp.org/press-releases/icmp-libya-sign-agreement/ (last accessed 1 May 2013).

ICRC. 2013. *Libya: What the ICRC Did in 2012.* Available at: http://www.icrc.org/eng/where-we-work/africa/libya/facts-figures-libya-long.htm (last accessed 1 May 2013).

Lernia, S. and Tafuri, M. A. 2013. Persistent death places and mobile landmarks: the Holocene mortuary and isotopic record from Wadi Takarkori (SW Libya). *Journal of Anthropological Archaeology* 32, 1–15.

Mattingly, D. J. (ed.) 2010. *The Archaeology of Fazzan.* Volume 3. London, The Society for Libyan Studies.

Mohamed, F. A. 2007. Trail Excavations at El-Jaghbub. In L. Gasperini and S. M. Marengo (eds.) *Cirene e la Cirenaica nell'antichità. Atti del convegno internazionale di studi.* Roma – Frascati.

Physicians for Human Rights (PHR). 2013. *Libyan Human Identification Needs Assessment and Gap Analysis.* Contributors: Schmitt, S., Sozer, A., Haglund, W., Peerwani, N., Varney, H., and Lamburne, R. Cambridge, MA. Available at: https://s3.amazonaws.com/PHR_other/annual-report-2013.pdf (last accessed 10 November 2014).

White, D. (ed.) 1990. *The Extramural Sanctuary of Demeter and Persephone at Cyrene, Libya.* Final Reports IV. Philadelphia, University of Pennsylvania.

CHAPTER 37

Forensic archaeology in Nepal

Susan Appleyard

Independent Human Rights Researcher, UK

Introduction

Nepal is a small landlocked country, about 800 km in length, between 150 and 250 km in width with a total area of 147,000 km^2. The country's geography is highly variable with the low-lying plains of the Tarai stretching 50 km from the Indian border, leading into the hill areas, before rising dramatically into the world's tallest mountain ranges towards the Chinese border. As a result, transport, by road and air, is a complex and dangerous endeavour, leaving many villages extremely isolated and only accessible on foot. Nepal's extreme seasons, the 4-month wet season from June to September and the winter from December to February, and lack of infrastructure, further impede access and communications. Nepal is highly vulnerable to natural disasters as the country's rivers are prone to flooding and Nepal is positioned in a major fault zone, making earthquakes a regular occurrence.

Nepal, which has a population of 26.5 million (Ekantipur 2012), is extremely poor. The country's annual per capita gross domestic product is just $535 (USD) (UN Data 2013) of which 23% derives from remittances, placing Nepal in the top five countries in the world in terms of remittances (Kathmandu Post 2010). Governance in Nepal lacks stability, as political power struggles among the country's leading politicians continue to block progress towards completion of the peace process and a return to normalised governance. Local elections have not taken place since 1997. Infrastructure and governance at the local level suffer from the political stalemates at the national level. Historically, Nepal's governance has been largely through absolute rule by the monarchy with two brief periods of democracy in the 1950s and again between 1990 and 2002. Democracy was once again restored in April 2006 and Nepal became a republic soon after.

Nepal experienced a 10-year armed conflict beginning in 1996 when the Communist Party of Nepal (नेपालकम्युनिष्टपार्टी) (hereafter 'the Maoists') began the Peoples' War after the government ignored their 40 demands which included an end to discrimination against women, an end to racial exploitation, elimination of 'untouchability', language rights, freedom of expression, land rights, housing rights and access to healthcare. The conflict escalated significantly in late 2001 when the Royal Nepal Army (RNA) was deployed to fight the Maoists. The United States, the United Kingdom and India labelled the Maoists 'terrorists', shortly after the commencement of the US-led global *War on Terror*, and significantly stepped up their military aid to Nepal. In this context human rights violations perpetrated by both parties to the conflict significantly escalated. Both the Maoists and the government's security forces were responsible for more than 1400 enforced disappearances (International Committee of the Red Cross [ICRC] 2012), in addition to extrajudicial killings, torture, rape and arbitrary detentions. The conflict officially came to an end in November 2006 with the signing of the Comprehensive Peace Agreement, 6 months after the political parties and Maoists had successfully led the Peoples' Movement against King Gyanendra's absolute rule.

The Comprehensive Peace Agreement committed the government and the Maoists to making public the status of every individual who had disappeared during the conflict and to establishing a Truth and Reconciliation Commission. There was no progress in either regard until March 2013 when the *Ordinance on the Investigation of Disappeared Persons, Truth and Reconciliation Commission* was issued by the country's president. The Ordinance has been strongly criticised for its focus on providing amnesties for perpetrators (Human Rights Watch [HRW] 2013) and has been challenged in the Supreme Court by relatives of the disappeared (National Network for Families of the Disappeared [NEFAD] 2013). Likewise, relatives of the disappeared are facing obstacles within Nepal's criminal justice system as they attempt to seek justice. To date, Nepal's Police have only conducted five excavations of those who disappeared during Nepal's conflict and even those exhumations were under significant pressure from civil society and the National Human Rights Commission (NHRC), which is an independent human rights body mandated by the

Forensic Archaeology: A Global Perspective, First Edition. Edited by W.J. Mike Groen, Nicholas Márquez-Grant and Robert C. Janaway.

Parliament to promote and protect human rights in Nepal established in 2000.[1]

Non-conflict-related homicides also occur in Nepal. Homicides as a result of domestic violence and organised crime are commonly reported in Nepal's newspapers. Due to Nepal's extreme geography and weather, humanitarian disasters resulting in multiple deaths are frequent. Although forensic archaeology skills are much needed in the context of both crime and humanitarian disasters, this chapter is focused on the application of forensic archaeology principles in the context of investigations into conflict-related enforced disappearances and extrajudicial killings. The medico-legal system applied in criminal cases is explained in detail and can be applied to either conflict-related or criminal cases.

Medico-legal context in Nepal

Nepal's legal system is principally a common law system with many aspects of the Hindu religion and culture reflected in the law. The *Muluki Ain* (1963) is the primary legal code for the country. The *State Cases Act* (1993) allocates the responsibilities of investigation and prosecution to the Nepal Police[2] and the attorney general, respectively.[3] Nepal's criminal justice system is broadly criticised for its weak investigations and corruption on multiple levels. These obstacles to justice are exacerbated for conflict-related crimes, due to political interference and a lack of cooperation from the political parties (the Nepal Army and the Maoists), often resulting in a complete failure of the Police to investigate (Advocacy Forum and HRW 2010). Police sometimes refuse to file complaints regarding conflict-related crimes on the grounds that a future truth mechanism will address such cases, completely denying victims any access to justice (Advocacy Forum 2011, 27).

Nepal's court structure has three levels, district, appellate and the Supreme Court, with criminal and civil cases heard in the same courts. The administrative district chief (Chief District Officer – CDO) is empowered to hear cases of minor offences; however, some security-related legislation also empowers the CDO to order administrative detention without judicial review, which several organisations have found amounts to arbitrary detention (Terai Human Rights Defenders Alliance 2013). In Nepal there is no jury trial system.

There are two legal avenues through which human remains can, and have been, exhumed in Nepal – as part of a criminal investigation undertaken by the Nepal Police or as part of an investigation into a human rights violation by the NHRC as part of that institution's mandate. The legal framework for both types of exhumations lacks clarity. A third avenue was introduced through the introduction of the *Truth, Reconciliation and Disappearance Ordinance* in March 2013; however, this remains to be tested.

Police investigations into crimes are governed by the *State Cases Act* (1993).[4] District Police Offices (DPO) have the responsibility to investigate scenes of crime in their local area and a Police officer from the DPO is usually appointed as the investigating officer for a specific case. Police officers at the Assistant Sub Inspector level (junior officers) are given 3 months' training as Scenes of Crime Officers (SOCOs) at the National Police Academy with the intention of deploying trained SOCOs to the DPOs throughout Nepal. SOCOs are usually now deployed at crime scenes in Kathmandu and other major cities in Nepal. Crime scene sketches are not required as part of the crime scene investigation report.

While not providing explicit guidance on exhumations, the *State Cases Act* has some relevant clauses. Firstly, when a Police officer receives information about a suspicious death, an Assistant Police Inspector, or above, should 'go to the place where the body is located and shall examine the body and prepare a body examination report' (State Cases Act, Section 11(1)). This should include: identification, location, wounds, possible cause of death and 'any remarkable things' (State Cases Act, Section 11(1) (a–f)), and a dead body inventory form is referred to in Appendix 7 of the *State Cases Regulation 2055*. The *State Cases Act* requires that if the death appears to be the result of criminal activities then a government medical doctor should conduct a post-mortem. However, the *Country Code* only requires that the Police have the nearest, most senior medically qualified person complete the dead body examination report (Country Code (*Muluki Ain*), Chapter on Homicide). The Country Code also requires that the Police protect the body. The *State Cases Act* further requires that 'if the body is not in a condition to be examined or is found in a state of decomposition, the relevant Police personnel shall prepare an examination report mentioning the same' (State Cases Act,

[1]It was established in 2000 under an Act passed by the Parliament in 1997.

[2]In addition to the Nepal Police, Nepal also has an Armed Police Force, which was established in January 2001 in response to the conflict. Its responsibilities are primarily in the areas of terrorism, armed conflict, riot control and responding to natural disasters.

[3]For a more in-depth description of the development of Nepal's legal system see International Commission of Jurists, *Human Rights and Administration of Justice: Obligations Unfulfilled*, June 2003.

[4]For a detailed analysis and text of relevant legislation, see: Advocacy Forum, *Exhumations of Bodies of the Disappeared: In Need of a Policy Framework*, 2011.

Section 11(4)). However, this clause allows the Police to not refer the body for a post-mortem.

The *State Cases Act* provides further direction relating to the general collection of evidence such as the taking of photographs, fingerprints and footprints and taking possession of any physical evidence relevant to the crime. The *State Cases Act* (Section 8) further requires that any evidence collected be inventoried at the crime scene in the presence of two witnesses and a representative of the appropriate village development committee. In relevant cases doctors are required to collect physical and/or biological evidence during an autopsy, and hospitals have protocols in place for the collection and storage of such evidence. The courts tend to call the doctor who has conducted the autopsy to provide expert testimony in relevant cases.

Within its criminal justice framework, Nepal does have a National Forensic Science Laboratory (NAFOL), a forensic laboratory within the Nepal Police and a Forensic Medicine Department within the Tribhuvan University's Teaching Hospital. The Central Police Forensic Science Laboratory only had the capacity for fingerprint analysis and photography, prior to its upgrade to a fully fledged laboratory in 1995 (Karki 2010).

Investigations into human rights violations are conducted by the NHRC under the *NHRC Act* (2012). The NHRC has, as part of an investigation into a human rights violation, conducted exhumations. The NHRC, for example, conducted its first exhumation in August 2003 in Doramba and has since been involved in 11 exhumations, 4 of which involved the remains of multiple individuals. However, it is unclear if any evidence collected during an exhumation can be referred to the Attorney General's Office for further investigation and prosecution. Currently, the NHRC submits its reports and recommendations on investigations to the Office of the Prime Minister, but such recommendations are rarely implemented. Given that excavations are inherently destructive, there is concern that evidence collected during an NHRC investigation cannot be recollected during a Police investigation and thus could potentially weaken future criminal prosecutions. The NHRC has, as far as possible, attempted to ensure that the exhumations it is involved in officially form part of a Police investigation (Gauri Pradhan, personal communication 2012). However, only 5 of the 11 exhumations conducted by the NHRC have been in the capacity of technical assistance to the Police. When the exhumation does not occur under the auspices of a Police investigation its purpose could be viewed as humanitarian and truth seeking. In light of its ongoing involvement in exhumations, the NHRC developed and published *Exhumation Guidelines* in 2012 (see later) and in March 2010 the NHRC proposed the establishment of a Forensic and Body Exhumation Unit (United Nations Department of Political Affairs [UNDP] 2010).

The *Ordinance on the Investigation of Disappeared Persons, Truth and Reconciliation Commission*, issued in March 2013, establishes a five-member commission to conduct investigations into disappearances which took place during the armed conflict, serious human rights violations and crimes against humanity; to be involved in reconciliation between the perpetrator and victim and to make recommendations on reparations for victims. The Commission is empowered by Article 14(5) to carry out an excavation if they are convinced that the disappeared person has already been killed and the dead body is buried in a particular place, to ascertain the reality of the allegations. The Ordinance (Article 15(6)) requires that the excavation be carried out in a systematic manner and if a body or remains are found then the Commission should carry out a DNA test of the body or autopsy. The dead body or remains should then be handed over to the closest family member of the deceased person. As discussed earlier, the Ordinance has been strongly criticised by human rights groups for its focus on providing amnesties for perpetrators. It therefore remains to be seen if these powers to excavate will be effectively used for the purpose of establishing the truth and securing justice and reparations for the relatives of the disappeared.

Forensic archaeology in Nepal

Expertise in forensic science, including forensic archaeology, is needed in Nepal not only to respond to the 1400 cases of conflict-related disappearances, but also to improve Nepal's criminal investigation methods and to prepare Nepal to respond to human identification needs in the event of a humanitarian or natural disaster. Nepal has some of the building blocks for effective forensic investigations in place: in the capital there is a team of competent forensic pathologists at the Teaching Hospital, a NAFOL and a Central Police Forensic Science Laboratory. In addition, Nepal has experienced archaeologists working for the Ministry of Culture's Department of Archaeology and also for the Archaeology Department at Tribhuvan University in Kathmandu. In recent years, Nepal's archaeologists have begun to be involved in forensic excavations and related training courses. While the knowledge of forensic archaeology and use of its principles was very limited during the first exhumation conducted in Doramba in August 2003, the 2010/2011 excavation at Dhanusha reflects a significant increase in awareness and application of forensic expertise including archaeology techniques. However, major obstacles prevent the delivery of professional forensic services, including forensic archaeology, in Nepal. Both the NAFOL and the Central Police Forensic Science Laboratory identify major human and resource capacity constraints. The Senior Superintendent for the Police

Forensic Science Laboratory raised concerns that equipment was not being updated and stated that:

> for some 3600 crime investigation cases per year, the Police forensic lab has strength of 70 to 75. Some of our forensic units like toxicology, bio and serology are operating on outdated equipment, which limit our efficiency. For instance, our toxicology unit can only test 30 to 40 kinds of poisons, while the varieties have proliferated in the market (Karki 2010).

Until recently the NAFOL had no capacity to analyse DNA from bone samples and had relied on blood samples. While Mr Jiwan Prasad Rijal, a scientist at NAFOL, stated that the laboratory would now attempt to do DNA profiling from bone, he was cautious and has requested that samples from the exhumation in Dhanusha to also be sent to an international laboratory to allow a crosscheck for the results obtained in Nepal (Karki 2010). Mr Jiwan Prasad Rijal has also raised concerns about a lack of guidelines for forensic procedures hampering forensic work in Nepal (Karki 2010).

Forensic work, especially forensic archaeology, is seriously affected by Nepal's difficult terrain and weather conditions. In the future, human remains will need to be excavated from clandestine burial sites in areas of the country that have no road access and require up to several days of hiking or the use of helicopters. Equipment required for the exhumation will need to be carried into such sites and infrastructure necessary for exhumations such as water and electricity will need to be procured. Remains will also need to be exhumed from complex locations such as on steep hills or mountain sides or from riverbeds. This will require logistic capabilities and involvement of individuals with relevant experience. The extremes of climate in Nepal ranging from the oppressive heat in the Terai, the extreme cold in the mountains and the onslaught of the wet season will significantly limit the periods of the year in which exhumations can be conducted. The climate will have caused significant decomposition of remains, often leaving only the skeleton. Further compounding these natural obstacles will be Nepal's general lack of reliable infrastructure, such as electricity, water and roads, all of which will be needed to enable professional excavations.

Overriding all other concerns is the lack of qualified forensic anthropologists or archaeologists in Nepal.

Efforts to address some of these obstacles have been made. Firstly, the NHRC has developed *Exhumation Guidelines* (2012) which include direction on:

- field inspection forms;
- sequenced use of excavation tools;
- mapping methods, including mapping on a slope and mapping a gridded excavation area;
- essential excavation scene equipment, including digging, packing and general scene equipment;
- packing skeletal remains in a container;
- ante-mortem data collection form;
- body recording forms and dental recording forms;
- field inventory form; and
- chain of custody form.

The NHRC proposed that security personnel, the then proposed Commission of Inquiry on Disappearances (CoID) and others could make use of the guidelines. The NHRC reported that the Office of the Prime Minister has instructed the Home Ministry, the Defence Ministry and the Nepal Police to implement the guidelines (NHRC 2012).

In addition, training has been provided both within Nepal and internationally to a variety of participants. In 2010, the American Bar Association provided training on forensic science to around 50 people, including lawyers from the Nepal Bar Association and the Nepal Bar Council, state prosecutors, representatives from local human rights organisations and investigators from the Nepal Police Force and the NHRC. It included classroom-based teaching on collection of ante-mortem data, burial site preservation, recovery of evidence, crime scene assessment and post-mortem analysis techniques to determine the most probable cause and manner of death and a practical excavation experience to apply the training (ABA 2010).

The ICRC (Tidball-Binz and Hofmeister, Chapter 49, this volume) is helping to strengthen the capability of national forensic specialists in the excavation of human remains, the identification of the deceased and determination of the circumstances of death. Since 2008, ICRC reports that it has conducted annual forensic training for specialists from the Departments of Forensic Medicine and Archaeology, as well as for representatives of the Nepal Police and the NHRC (ICRC 2011). The ICRC also facilitated a practical 2-week work experience for one medical doctor from the Teaching Hospital and one staff member from the Department of Archaeology (ICRC, personal communication 2012). This exposure of practitioners and government officials to forensics, especially forensic anthropology and archaeology, has resulted in an increased interest in forensics within the medical profession and more awareness of the range of expertise required during a forensic excavation.

In addition to providing expertise during the excavations in Dhanusha and Shivapuri, the Department of Forensic Medicine in Ruskeasuo, Helsinki, provided training for a Nepalese forensic pathologist and a medical doctor working in the area of DNA in November 2010 (Ministry of Foreign Affairs of Finland 2010).

A German forensic pathologist provided expertise over a period of 18 months in Nepal through an agreement between the German Development Service and the NHRC (Karki 2010).

Despite Nepal's forensic institutions and other relevant participants increasing their skills, improving their resources and adopting some basic protocols, it is still the case that capacity, infrastructure and geography remain significant obstacles to professional forensic work, including forensic archaeology, in Nepal. While a lack of political commitment to identifying remains and returning them to the relatives, establishing the truth behind the victim's disappearance and death and ensuring justice remain entrenched in Nepal, work to build capacity and address resource constraints can only have a limited impact on addressing Nepal's enforced disappearances.

Case studies

A full list of exhumations in Nepal and details on those exhumations can be found in Advocacy Forum's 2011 publication *Exhumations of Bodies of the Disappeared: In Need of a Policy Framework.*

Doramba: Nepal's first excavation

On 17 August 2003, 19 people were extrajudicially executed by the RNA in Doramba, Ramechhap District in the Central Region of Nepal. The 17 unarmed Maoist cadres and 2 civilians, not associated with the Maoist Movement, were arrested at a house in the village area. With their hands bound they were forced to march to the top of a nearby hill where they were lined up and shot dead at close range. Their dead bodies were pushed down the side of the hill and left exposed on the surface. One man survived the shootings and the tumble down the hillside. He could be heard crying out for several hours before succumbing to his injuries. The Maoists arrived 3 days later to conduct a burial ceremony for their dead comrades (Dixit 2012). Other reports suggest at least some of the bodies were buried by locals, as people from the village were among the dead.

These killings took place in the 7th month of a ceasefire and during the third round of negotiations, at a time when both the Maoist Peoples' Liberation Army and the RNA were restricted to within 5 km of their barracks. The killings were identified by analysts as a significant factor in the Maoists' decision to end the ceasefire and return to war (M. Shrestha, personal communication 2008). Questions were also raised in regard to who authorised the killings during the ceasefire and for what purpose (International Crisis Group [ICG] 2005).

A preliminary report on the incident issued by the Army Human Rights Cell (AHRC) stated that the Maoists had led two armed confrontations against a security patrol with 5 and 12 Maoist deaths in the two attacks (Thapa 2003). Leading up to the killings, there had been an increasing number of reports of 'encounter killings', which locals and the Maoists claimed to be extrajudicial killings (M. Sharma, personal communication 2008). Having received information indicating that this incident was in fact an extrajudicial killing, Nepal's NHRC established a subcommittee, which included forensic and legal experts, to investigate. A review of the NHRC Act concluded that the NHRC had the same powers as other investigating authorities and was therefore empowered to conduct an excavation. This investigation was the first to include forensic expertise, in the person of a forensic pathologist, Dr Harihar Wasti. The team did not include an (forensic) archaeologist; however, the team had received some basic training from the ICRC, prior to departure, on exhumation principles.

The team travelled to Doramba by helicopter, having to land about an hour's hike from the village due to low cloud. The following day the team hiked about 2 hours to the alleged location of the killings, following the same path the victims had been forced to take. Along the way, witnesses came forward and shared their recollections of the incident which were taken as formal depositions by the lawyer and judge in the investigation team. Locals were also able to identify the specific burial location as they had been involved in burying some of the bodies after the security forces left the location. A roll of film was handed to one team member, which, once developed in Kathmandu, provided pictures of the bodies 1 day after the killings.

Despite the absence of a crime scene expert or a forensic archaeologist, and this being the first exhumation ever conducted by the NHRC, several forensic techniques were employed. The area was secured using tape brought from Kathmandu and only those involved in the investigation or assisting with digging were allowed to enter the cordoned area. Relatives and locals watched the exhumation from outside the secured area. Written permission was given by the relatives to exhume the bodies and as burial rituals had been carried out at the time of burial, there was no request for rituals to take place prior or during the exhumations or during the reburial.

Locals willingly assisted with the digging of the first 3 graves, which held people from the village. Some encouragement was required to gain their assistance with digging the remainder of the graves and they were collectively financially compensated for their work at the end of the day. Tools for digging were provided by the villagers. In total, 19 graves were exhumed with human remains located at a depth of about 5 ft (1.5 m). The soil was removed from above the bodies as well as digging out the soil on the sides of the bodies, to allow the back of the body to be seen better. The bodies were each covered by a white cloth and the flag of the Maoists. Buddhist cloths were found with some bodies, suggesting they were of Tamang ethnicity. The bodies were not removed from the graves. Due to the altitude (2130 m) the bodies remained quite fresh despite having been buried for about 1 week, though decomposition rapidly took place once the bodies were exposed to the air.

Dr Wasti entered the graves one by one to examine each body. He measured the depth and length of the graves. He also examined wounds, measuring their length and width, and any other marks or scars on the bodies. As a forensic pathologist he was also able to determine the cause of death. All bodies, with the exception of one, were assessed to have been shot dead, with their hands tied behind their backs, at close range in the head as there was evidence of an entry wound to the front of the skull and most with parts of the back of the skull missing due to the exit of the bullet. Some bullets were also found inside the bodies. Detailed notes of Dr Wasti's findings were taken by Mr Hari Phuyal, an officer of the NHRC, standing outside the grave and photographs and video were taken by Mr Kanak Mani Dixit, a leading journalist who was a member of the subcommittee. The bodies were then reburied in the position they had been found. The investigation was focused on gathering evidence related to the killings, rather than on identification as the identity of many of the individuals was already known.

A search was also conducted of the area where the shootings had taken place, about 100 m from the burial site. Some bullet shells and bullets were collected from this area. These were submitted to a ballistics expert upon return to Kathmandu and a report provided. Some clothes, diaries, letters and other personal belongings, such as combs, were found near the location where the people had been killed. Some of these were partly burned and the investigation team was told that some documents and personal belongings had been completely burned. All evidence was collected by the investigation team and transported to the NHRC office in Kathmandu for analysis.

The exhumation was conducted over 1 day and interviews with witnesses were conducted over 2 days. The investigation team's departure from Doramba was delayed by a day as the conflict had recommenced, in part as a result of the killings at Doramba, and the helicopter companies were not initially willing to fly into a conflict area.

The report on the killings at Doramba written by the investigation team dramatically altered the international community's perception of the conflict and the role of the RNA in the conflict. Pressure on the RNA began to increase as their human rights violations continued to escalate. The impact of the report is in part attributed to the forensic nature of the investigation as it was able to produce technical, scientific information on the killings, supported by professionally documented witness statements.

The details of this case study are based on interviews with two members of the investigation team and a Commissioner from the NHRC.

Maina Sunuwar

Maina Sunuwar, a 15-year-old girl, was arrested and tortured to death by the RNA in February 2004 in Kavrepalanchowk District.[5] The soldiers who arrested Maina said they were looking for her mother and would release Maina if her mother reported to the Lamindanda Army Barracks. The authorities denied any involvement with her arrest and death and she became one of the hundreds of people enforcedly disappeared in Nepal. In April 2004, her mother visited the Nepal Army Headquarters in Kathmandu and was told that Maina had been killed. As a result of concerted national and international pressure, Maina's body was exhumed in March 2007 from its clandestine grave inside the Birendra Peace Operations Training Centre, an army camp in Panchkal. The Centre is used for training members of the Nepal Army before they are deployed on United Nations (UN) peacekeeping missions. The excavation team did not include an archaeologist.

Following her arrest, Maina was tortured for about an hour and a half in the presence of seven Nepal Army officers and soldiers. Her head was submerged for 1 min six or seven times. She was electrically shocked on her wet hands and feet four or five times. Maina was then detained, blindfolded and handcuffed, in a building at the Training Centre. Later she began vomiting and foaming at the mouth, but died before medical help could arrive. In an attempt to cover up the murder, her body was shot in the back and buried inside the Centre. A report saying she was shot whilst trying to escape was then fabricated.[6]

As a result of sustained pressure, the RNA conducted its own investigation through a Court of Inquiry Board and in September 2005 brought three soldiers before a court martial. They were found guilty of minor offences such as not using proper interrogation techniques and not following procedures for the proper disposal of her body. They were sentenced with 6 months in detention. Not satisfied with this outcome, Maina's mother filed a case with the Police in November 2005. Despite the extreme non-cooperation of the Nepal Army with the

[5]Maina Sunuwar's name has been used widely in international papers and has appeared extensively in local and international newspapers.

[6]These details of Maina's torture, death and burial are based on the United Nations Office of the High Commissioner for Human Rights (OHCHR) public report which summarises the Court of Inquiry Board's report, which the Office gained access to. For more information, see *The Torture and Death in Custody of Maina Sunuwar: Summary of Concerns*, December 2006.

Police investigation, the Police, with an observer from the Office of the High Commissioner for Human Rights (OHCHR), were eventually able in June 2006 to enter the Training Centre and mark out the grave site with the objective of future exhumation.

In March 2007, Maina's body was exhumed from a shallow grave at the Training Centre, by the Nepal Police, reportedly only after receiving permission from the Home Ministry (Tamang 2007), as part of the criminal investigation into her death. The Police sought the assistance of the Tribhuvan University Teaching Hospital, where forensic pathologist Dr Wasti is employed (Tamang 2007). An international expert, brought in by the NHRC, also assisted as an advisor, and OHCHR provided technical assistance. The exhumation was observed by OHCHR, the NHRC and Maina's parents. Maina's mother had provided ante-mortem data to OHCHR prior to the exhumation. There was no archaeologist present during the excavation.

Advocacy Forum, a legal organisation that represents Maina's mother, reported that Maina's remains were taken to the Teaching Hospital Forensic Department and a sample from the remains was sent to India, along with DNA provided by Maina's mother, for analysis in November 2007. The analysis of the samples confirmed the remains were those of Maina in July 2008 (Advocacy Forum 2011).

The Kavre Public Prosecutor, under orders from the Supreme Court of Nepal, filed murder charges against four army officers suspected of being responsible for her death and the Court issued a summons for their arrest. Only one of the four accused appears to remain in the Nepal Army. He was serving in a UN Peacekeeping Mission in Chad, when in September 2009, the District Court ordered him to be suspended from the Nepal Army. He has since been dismissed from the Mission and repatriated to Nepal, but was taken into Army Police control upon landing at Nepal's international airport (Advocacy Forum 2013a).

Shivapuri National Park and the search for the disappeared from Maharajgunj barracks

In 2003, hundreds of individuals suspected of association with the Maoists were detained by the RNA in their Maharajgunj barracks in Kathmandu. OHCHR has documented (OHCHR 2006b, 45) in detail the 'severe and prolonged ill-treatment and torture' experienced by most of those detained at Maharajgunj barracks by the Bhairabnath and Yuddha Bhairab battalions. OHCHR was able to confirm the identity of nearly 50 individuals who had been in the custody of the Bhairabnath battalion between September and December 2003 and remained disappeared at the time of the UN's investigation in 2006.

It was reported that the NHRC received information indicating a location in Shivapuri National Park where remains of those who disappeared from Maharajgunj barracks might be located. In December 2008, what appeared to be human remains were discovered in Shivapuri National Park. The NHRC called on the government to secure the site to ensure the preservation of potential evidence for future investigation. However, it took over a week for the government to secure the site with a 24-hour Police guard (UN Mission to Nepal [UNMIN] 2008). The NHRC subsequently conducted a search of the area, recovering clothing, sacks, charred items and plastic bags. The NHRC requested support from Finnish forensic scientists as advisors, who then visited Nepal. Despite their assistance, the tests done in Nepal on some of the items recovered reportedly did not return any useful information and the items were sent for further testing in Finland. DNA could only be extracted from one of the six samples. The tests revealed that the samples included remains of at least one male (Aryal 2008).

Five students excavated in Dhanusha

On 8 October 2003 in Janakpur, Dhanusha District (Eastern Nepal), at a picnic organised by fellow students, 11 people were arrested by the RNA, the Armed Police and the Nepal Police. They were blindfolded and beaten during their transport to the then Regional Police Office. Six of the 11 were reportedly released the next day (Advocacy Forum 2011, 4) and the remaining five (JitendraJha [23], Sanjeev K Karna [25], SailendraYadav [18], DurgeshLav [23] and Pramod N. Mandal [19]) were enforcedly disappeared until their exhumation in September 2010.[7]

The families reported the case to the NHRC, and numerous other organisations, on the day of the disappearance. In January 2003, the NHRC received a letter from the Nepal Army's Human Rights Cell which stated that the five men had been killed in a Police operation in Janakpur on 8 October 2003. The Police claimed the young men were handed over to the Bhiman Barracks, while the Nepal Army claimed the Police were responsible for the disappearances and killings (Advocacy Forum 2013b). The NHRC's exhumation report concluded that the men had been arrested, blindfolded, shot dead and buried beside the Kamala River in Dhanusha in October 2003. The report names those responsible, including Police, military and civilian authorities in Dhanusha (Ekantipur 2011).

[7]The names of the victims have already has been widely used in international and national reports and in local and international newspapers.

Despite complaints being filed with the Police in July 2006, the Police did little to investigate and the Nepal Army obstructed investigations. However, the Police were taken to the alleged burial site in July 2006 and demarcated it with barbed wire, but failed to secure the site, and the wire was removed. Advocacy Forum, a legal organisation, then hired a villager to watch over the site (Advocacy Forum 2011, 9).

Due to the lack of Police commitment in the investigation, the NHRC decided to go ahead with the exhumation. The NHRC wrote to the Home Ministry requesting directives be given to the Police and seeking government support for the NHRC to secure assistance from national and international experts. The NHRC and experts then conducted a feasibility study of the suspected burial site in June 2010 (NHRC 2010a, 1).

The 18-member exhumation team formed by the NHRC included two Finish and one German expert, experts from Tribhuvan University's Teaching Hospital Forensic Medicine Department (including Dr Wasti), the National Forensic Laboratory, a former NHRC member, OHCHR, representatives from civil society and, significantly, experts from the Ministry of Culture's Archaeology Department (NHRC 2010a, 2). This was the first time archaeologists had been involved in an exhumation in Nepal. Training in Nepal on excavation of human remains has emphasised the importance of archaeological techniques and archaeologists have been included in trainings. It is therefore likely that increased awareness of the role of an archaeologist at an excavation led to the request that the archaeologists join this excavation.

In preparation for the exhumation, the NHRC, with the assistance of non-governmental organisations, informed the relatives of the victims and the local landowner about the exhumation. The NHRC asked the relatives of the victims to complete an ante-mortem form on 2 September 2010. The NHRC also reported that it provided psychosocial counselling to the relatives; however, non-governmental organisations have raised serious concerns about respect for the relative's rights throughout the exhumation process such as keeping them informed and providing counselling (Advocacy Forum 2011, 10–15).

The NHRC reported that the burial site was cordoned off by the Nepal Police, and work by the exhumation team began on 6 September 2010. Fifty-eight trenches, nine extensions and three blocks were excavated, with four of the five skeletons located at the burial site on 8, 9, 10 and 16 September, respectively (NHRC 2010a, 2). Archaeological methods were employed by the team, including detailed measurements of the location of the remains, and documented by the Dhanusha Police. The skeletons were recovered from the burial site and stored as evidence by the Police along with 21 other pieces of evidence including cartridge cases, bullets, worn clothes and footwear and jewellery (Advocacy Forum 2011, 10). The evidence was collected and stored in line with the advice of the experts (Advocacy Forum 2011, 10).

The Advocacy Forum reported:

> Observing the skeletal remains, it reportedly appeared that the victims had been murdered: the head of one of the bodies appeared to have been severed and there were what appeared to be bullet holes observed in another body. All the bodies were reportedly lying face down and two of them were said to have been blindfolded (Advocacy Forum 2011, 10).

The remains did not show evidence of having been burned prior to burial, despite Nepal being dominantly a Hindu country in which the dead are usually burned. Dr Wasti postulated that the security forces had not burned the bodies because burying the bodies would require less time and drawn less attention than igniting a fire (NHRC 2010b, 4).

It was reported that the process to determine the identities of the bodies took place at the NAFOL (a government institution under the Ministry of Science and Technology), but that Laboratory staff had requested the samples also be sent to international laboratories as a countercheck of the results of the Nepal Laboratory (Karki 2010). The identification took place at the University of Helsinki in Finland (*Nepalnews* 2011), where one of the experts involved in the exhumation works was based.

The fifth body, which could not be located during the initial exhumation in September 2010, was recovered during a follow-up exhumation in February 2011. This excavation took place over 3 days, with the remains located on day 2. Six trenches and two blocks were cleared in the process of locating the fifth body.

Relatives of the victims have not been asked to identify any of the items recovered during the 2010 and the 2011 excavations or to identify the remains recovered.

Conclusion

While the 2010/2011 excavation of the five bodies in Dhanusha is, to date, the most technical excavation in Nepal, numerous political obstacles and technical weaknesses in the medico-legal system still impede further excavations and identification of the hundreds of people who disappeared during the decade-long armed conflict in Nepal. Technical weaknesses will also hamper the application of forensic archaeology, and other forensic disciplines, in the criminal justice context in Nepal.

Awareness of the role of archaeology in excavations has greatly increased in Nepal for three reasons. Firstly, forensics training has included archaeology skills and excavation exercises applying those skills. Secondly, international forensic experts, who understand the role of archaeologists in forensic contexts, have taken part in exhumations since the conflict ended in 2006 and shared knowledge about the role of archaeologists. Thirdly, we have the NHRC's 'Exhumation Guidelines' which provides guidance on archaeological techniques to be applied during excavations.

Therefore, if the political obstacles that currently impede conflict-related excavations and if the resource issues that hamper criminal investigations are overcome, and excavations do begin to take place more frequently, it is likely that archaeologists will be requested to take part and their unique skills will begin to professionalise the excavation of human remains in Nepal.

References

ABA (American Bar Association). 2010. *Forensics Trainings Conducted in Nepal.* Available at: http://www.americanbar.org/advocacy/rule_of_law/where_we_work/asia/nepal/news/news_nepal_forensics_training_0510.html (last accessed 5 September 2014).

Advocacy Forum. 2011. *Exhumations of Bodies of the Disappeared: In Need of a Policy Framework.* Kathmandu, Advocacy Forum.

Advocacy Forum. 2013a. *Case Update on Maina Sunuwar.* Available at: http://advocacyforum.org/emblematic-cases/2011/01/maina-sunuwar.php (last accessed 16 December 2014).

Advocacy Forum. 2013b. *Case Update on Sanjeev Kumar Karna.* Available at: http://advocacyforum.org/emblematic-cases/2010/12/sanjeev-kumar-karna.php (last accessed 16 December 2014).

Advocacy Forum and Human Rights Watch. 2010. *Indifference to Duty: Impunity for Crimes Committed in Nepal.* New York, Human Rights Watch.

Aryal, M. 2008. Unearthing the truth. *Nepali Times*, 430.

Country Code (*MulukiAin*) 1854.

Dixit, K. 2012. *Remember Doramba.* Report, Ekantipur.

Ekantipur. 2011. *Five Youths Murdered by Government Forces.* Report, Ekantipur.

Ekantipur. 2012. *Census Puts Nepal's Population at 26.49 million.* Report, Ekantipur.

Human Rights Watch (HRW). 2013. *Nepal: Truth and Reconciliation Law Betrays Victims.* New York, Human Rights Watch.

International Committee of the Red Cross. 2011. *ICRC Action in Nepal for Missing Persons and their Families.* Geneva, ICRC.

International Committee of the Red Cross. 2012. *Nepal: Over 1400 People Still Unaccounted for.* Geneva, ICRC.

International Crisis Group. 2005. *Nepal: Dealing with a Human Rights Crisis.* Brussels, International Crisis Group.

Karki, S. 2010. *Of Disappearances, and Forensic Science.* Republica. Available at: http://archives.myrepublica.com/portal/index.php?action=news_details&news_id=26449 (last accessed 5 September 2014).

Kathmandu Post. 2010. Nepal among top five countries. *Kathmandu Post.*

National Human Rights Commission (NHRC). 2010a. *Preliminary Summary Report on Exhumation: Godar VDC, Janakpur, Dhanusha District*, 19 September 2010, Janakpur.

National Human Rights Commission (NHRC). 2010b. *International Community in Nepal Updated on Janakpur Exhumation.* NHRC Bulletin.

National Human Rights Commission. 2012. *e-Newsletter* 7, 12.

National Network for Families of the Disappeared and Missing in Nepal. 2013. Available at: http://nefad.wordpress.com (last accessed 20 May 2013).

Nepalnews.com. 2011. NHRC deploys exhumation team at Dhanusha. Available at: http://www.nepalnews.com/archive/2011/feb/feb13/news17.php (last accessed 5 September 2014).

Ministry of Foreign Affairs of Finland. 2010. *Finnish DNA Expertise Appreciated in Nepal.*

Office of the High Commission for Human Rights (OHCHR). 2006. *The Torture and Death in Custody of Maina Sunuwar: Summary of Concerns.* Available at: http://nepal.ohchr.org/en/resources/Documents/English/reports/IR/Year2006/2006_12_01_HCR%20_Maina%20Sunuwar_E.pdf (last accessed 19 August 2014).

OHCHR. 2006. *Report of Investigation into Arbitrary Detention, Torture and Disappearances at Maharajgunj RNA Barracks, Kathmandu, in 2003–2004.* Geneva, Office of the High Commission for Human Rights.

State Cases Act. 1992 and Regulations.

Thapa, M. 2003. Storm over Doramba. *Nepali Times.* Available at: http://nepalitimes.com/news.php?id=4639 (last accessed 5 September 2014).

Tamang, K. S. 2007. Police to exhume Maina's remains. *Kathmandu Post.* Available at: http://www.ekantipur.com/the-kathmandu-post/2007/03/14/related_articles/police-to-exhume-mainas-remains/103542.html (last accessed 5 September 2014).

Terai Human Rights Defenders Alliance (THRD Alliance). 2013. *Arbitrary Detention and Torture in the Terai.* Kathmandu, Terai Human Rights Defenders Alliance.

UN Data. 2013. *Nepal.* Available at: http://data.un.org/CountryProfile.aspx?crName=Nepal (last accessed 18 May 2013).

United Nations Mission to Nepal (UNMIN). 2008. Disappearances – Shivapuri find. *Newsletter* 4.

CHAPTER 38

The current status of forensic archaeology in New Zealand

Edward Ashby[1] and Beatrice Hudson[2]

[1] *Independent Consultant Archaeologist, Auckland, New Zealand*

[2] *Independent Consultant Archaeologist and Osteologist, Auckland, New Zealand*

Introduction

Forensic archaeology is a new concept in New Zealand, and its presence as a distinct professional discipline has not yet been established. However, archaeological techniques have been applied to scenes of crime, and recent calls have been made for its use in routine scenes involving buried or dispersed human remains. The aim of this chapter is therefore to give an outline of the context in which forensic archaeology must operate, its current status and applications, the obstacles it faces and its future potential in New Zealand. Forensic archaeology can be broadly defined as the application of archaeological theories, principles, and methods to the process of justice (Cox 2011). Although the term *forensic* relates to courts of law, this wider definition encompasses humanitarian contexts. While forensic archaeology also relates to the archaeological examination of artefacts as part of an investigation into looting or forgery, this chapter deals specifically with archaeology as applied to scenes involving human remains. In this context, archaeological skills are applied to the search, excavation and recovery of buried or dispersed human remains and other related evidence within a medico-legal or humanitarian setting.

Archaeological and medico-legal framework

Archaeological framework: legislation and operation

Often described as the last major landmass to be colonised by humans, New Zealand has a comparatively short history of human occupation. The archaeological record begins with the arrival of the Maori within the last 1000 years and the 'historic' era commences from the arrival of Europeans in 1769 (Smith 1990, 86; Walter and Jacomb 2008). The relative youth of New Zealand's archaeological sites is reflected by the primary legislation governing archaeology in New Zealand. The *Heritage New Zealand Pouhere Taonga Act* (2014)[1] defines an archaeological site as a place that is associated with pre-1900 human activity, where investigation by archaeological methods may provide evidence relating to the history of New Zealand. Modification of an archaeological site is illegal, unless pursuant to an archaeological authority granted by the Heritage New Zealand Pouhere Taonga (HNZPT).[2]

Nationwide, consultant archaeologists tend to work as sole traders or in small companies providing heritage management services (currently 60 archaeologists are listed on the New Zealand Archaeological Association Consultants Directory, NZAA 2013). Two larger consultancy firms (Opus International Consultants Ltd; VCS Environmental Ltd.) employ archaeologists, and archaeologists also hold positions at the HNZPT, the Department of Conservation, museums and the Auckland Council. Two New Zealand universities (Auckland and Otago) have anthropology departments with academic archaeologist positions. There is no national professional registration or accreditation system, though archaeological authorities from the HNZPT will name the archaeologist legally responsible for conducting the required work. To be named in this way, the archaeologist must have a recognised level of qualification and experience (c.f. AGS5 Guidelines for Section 17 Approval, HNZPT).[3] The sole association of archaeologists is the New Zealand Archaeological Association (NZAA), which has open membership that does not relate to

[1] Formerly the *Historic Places Act* (1993).

[2] Formerly the *New Zealand Historic Places Trust* (NZHPT).

[3] Note that Section 17 refers to the Historic Places Act (1993) and the guideline will soon be updated to refer to Section 45, as per the new Act (2014).

Forensic Archaeology: A Global Perspective, First Edition. Edited by W.J. Mike Groen, Nicholas Márquez-Grant and Robert C. Janaway.

professional registration. The NZAA has a hortatory code of ethics published on its website (NZAA 1999) but does not oversee or enforce standards.

Neither the NZAA nor the HNZPT issues manuals or detailed directives to standardise how sites are excavated or recorded. Heritage New Zealand Pouhere Taonga authorities list general components of excavation and recording required, which are to be conducted in accordance with 'current archaeological practice'. There are no common pro forma recording sheets or standardised terminologies, such as given by the MoLAS manual that is widely recognised in Britain (Museum of London Archaeology Service 1994) and such as are recommended for use in forensic archaeology (IfA 2011, 15). Archaeologists therefore adopt a variety of context recording methods, often tailored to the excavation at hand.

Police and archaeologists frequently come into contact over the discovery of human remains. When human remains are encountered during an archaeological excavation, the standard requirement of any HNZPT authority is that all work must cease within 20 m of the discovery and the New Zealand police must be informed, in addition to the HNZPT and local *Iwi* (Maori tribal group) representatives. *Iwi* representatives will usually conduct a blessing of the site and oversee cultural protocol in relation to the human remains. Therefore, the identification of bone as human, and the estimation of its broad ancestry (Polynesian, European or Asian being the key ancestries to identify for historic skeletal remains in New Zealand), has important legal and procedural implications. In such circumstances, the scene is rarely, if ever, cordoned off with restricted access in the way a standard crime scene would be managed, despite police first needing to rule out that a crime has taken place.

In New Zealand, many physical anthropologists, particularly osteologists, come from an archaeological background, having come to the discipline through study in the anthropology departments at Otago or Auckland universities. Many adopt the term 'bioarchaeologist' for this reason and have experience in participating in (though generally not directing) archaeological excavations for the purpose of excavating and studying the human skeletal remains.

The youth of archaeology and small size of the archaeological community in New Zealand contribute to a generally low public profile and lack of awareness; many laypeople express surprise to find that there are archaeologists in this country, or even that New Zealand has any archaeology at all. This, to some degree, feeds into the lack of awareness of the potential of forensic archaeology as a field in this country.

Medico-legal framework

The medico-legal framework in which a crime, fatality or disaster scene is investigated in New Zealand is largely based upon the British model. This includes the roles of coroners, pathologists, police, judges, Crown Prosecutors, defence lawyers and forensic scientists. The level of engagement and type of involvement of these various roles depends upon whether the death or deaths were the result of criminal behaviour, or are sudden deaths resulting from accident, misadventure or some other non-criminal activity. The main legislation which guides these processes includes the *Coroners Act* (2006), the *Crimes Act* (1961), the *Evidence Act* (2006) and the *Burial and Cremation Act* (1964).

When a homicide is discovered in New Zealand, law enforcement and forensic response follows a series of set protocols which incorporates a chain of command and investigative hierarchy. The New Zealand police are responsible for responding to and processing crime scenes. This organisation is the national police force and is divided into 12 districts, each containing a central station and a number of suburban or localised stations. Typically, in an incident involving human remains all police and forensic personnel ultimately report to the Officer in Charge (OIC). In the case of homicide, this will be an officer responding from the regional Serious Crime unit. Other police personnel include the OIC of Exhibits, specially trained police photographers and Fingerprints Officers. The police also have Scene of Crime Officers (SOCOs), but unlike in the United Kingdom, these officers do not attend serious crime and are not currently permitted to give opinion evidence in court. In addition to police personnel, civilian staff responding to a homicide scene will include forensic scientists, who will process and collect evidence such as shoe prints, biological samples, physical evidence or blood spatter evidence. These personnel tend to have molecular biology or chemistry backgrounds and are supplied by regional centres (Auckland, Wellington, Christchurch) from Environmental Science and Research (ESR), a government-owned Crown Research Institute. The Crown Prosecutor may also attend the scene, and a forensic pathologist may be called to view the body or remains in context, though in practice forensic pathologists are rarely invited to the scene in cases involving buried or dispersed skeletal remains.

For all cases, police will manage and lead the investigation, with ESR forensic scientists providing support. On rare occasions other specialists may be involved to help interpret the scene or gather evidence, though the exhumation and/or collection of the remains themselves and processing of the scene will be carried out by police and ESR personnel. Once the scene is processed, and assuming a suspect has been charged by police, the Crown Prosecutor will bring the prosecution to a criminal hearing which is overseen by a District or High Court Judge under an adversarial system with a jury. Defence lawyers and independent forensic scientists may become involved at this stage to cross-examine and give expert testimony on the evidence. The *Evidence Act* (2006) governs the rules of evidence including expert witness evidence. The excavation of human remains can be considered to be a type of expert witness evidence, yet currently this excavation evidence has the potential to fail in court should it ever be challenged, as the excavator may not be considered an 'expert'.

In contrast, in cases where death was the result of non-criminal (or at least not the result of homicide) activity, such as a mass fatality, disaster scene or the finding of remains which may pertain to a missing person, the medico-legal process is governed by coroners and guided by legal and humanitarian aims. Coroners are responsible for legally determining the causes and circumstances of death. The New Zealand police are first responders and are responsible for coordinating the recovery and identification of the deceased. This includes securing the scene if necessary, recovering evidence, uplifting and transporting the body to the mortuary, and arranging, in discussion with the coroner and pathologist, for the identification method needed. The pathologist may attend the scene and take part in the recovery process, especially in Disaster Victim Identification (DVI) scenarios, though it is far more common for the remains to be uplifted by police and transported to the mortuary where the pathologist will conduct a post-mortem examination to establish the medical cause of death. The coroner's role is to authorise the post-mortem examination and manage the investigation following positive identification.

Identification of the deceased usually involves visual identification by the next of kin or other visual comparison, fingerprints or dental identification. In cases where the remains are skeletonised, burnt, have been subject to massive physical trauma or have undergone severe decomposition, other methods of identification including biological anthropology or DNA analysis may be carried out by relevant specialists (though anthropological identification is rare). In terms of recovery, as mentioned earlier, the police coordinate and manage this phase, including the decision process of what, if any, experts are required. In some cases a DVI response team may be deployed (this includes specialist police officers, a pathologist and odontologist, but can also include ESR forensic scientists and other specialists) though in general attending police officers will undertake the recovery themselves.

Application of archaeology to the forensic arena

Forensic archaeology in New Zealand is in the earliest stages of its development. It is not yet recognised as a distinct area of forensic or archaeological specialisation, and it is therefore not defined at all within the archaeological or forensic communities. Forensic archaeologists as recognised professionals do not yet exist, though there are several archaeologists in the country who could be considered to have various levels of expertise in this field: Ms Andrea Scott is based with the Auckland police as a Forensic Supervisor and is an accredited forensic archaeologist in the United Kingdom where she worked previously; Mr Chris Mallows is based at Auckland Council and has experience working within an international forensic archaeological setting; while the authors have groundings in archaeology, human osteology and forensic science.

A review of published and unpublished (university theses) material relevant to the topic of forensic archaeology in New Zealand reveals only five entries. Two of these pertain to forensic anthropology (Cox et al. 2006; Master 2006), one concerns archaeological human remains and legislation (Tayles and Halcrow 2011) and one details the use of geophysics in clandestine grave investigation (Nobes 2000). The first paper published specifically on forensic archaeology in New Zealand was written by Ashby (2013) and called for greater use of archaeology in forensic casework. Subsequently there is no system of accreditation for forensic archaeologists, and very little in the way of training opportunities. This shouldn't be surprising given that forensic anthropology (which more often than not precedes the development of forensic archaeology) is still in the early stages of development as a profession in New Zealand. Certainly the situation is compounded by the fact that even traditional archaeology is not well known as a profession here.

Yet despite this seemingly gloomy picture of the state of the discipline, ostensibly archaeological techniques or approaches have been applied to serious scenes of crime involving human remains. The application of archaeological techniques to scenes of crime, notably clandestine graves, by police and ESR first appeared in the early 2000s and has been used sporadically since. This is a positive move and demonstrates that interest in such approaches exists and can be useful here. These techniques and approaches have been employed by police and ESR on a number of occasions involving dispersed skeletal remains and clandestine graves with some success, and range from the simple use of grid systems and exhumation using trowels to the employment of 3D mapping and Ground Penetrating Radar (GPR) equipment.

The problem here, however, is a lack of appreciation for the role archaeology plays in *excavation* as opposed to merely more careful *exhumation*. The archaeologist's expertise in identifying a sequence of modifications to soil and in helping to establish the relationship between items of evidence and the events represented by those modifications is not widely recognised. For example, the ESR's Methods Manual section on gravesite examination (Forensic Service Centre Methods Manual, S.19 2011) outlines a number of archaeological methods, such as gridding areas and excavating in level spits, which allow for good control of spatial and depth information. But it does not mention the importance of distinguishing different layers of soil within and around the grave, which may allow for the identification of any successive cut and fill events that can be vital to the reconstruction of events.

This trend mimics the earlier US experience in the 1970s and 1980s, where the role of archaeology was limited to the use of field techniques, and these techniques were taught in ways that did not acknowledge the need for thoroughly trained and experienced professionals (Connor 2007). Experience has shown that this kind of problematic divorcing of archaeological theory from the field methods employed in forensic work means that 'such training only generates the illusion of precision in the excavation of buried bodies – if one starts with the premise that archaeology is more than just digging a neat square hole' (Sigler-Eisenberg 1985, 650–651).

Another way in which archaeology is applied to the forensic arena in New Zealand is through clarifying the legislative responsibilities and respective jurisdiction of the police and heritage agencies, in the context of differentiating historic remains from those of recent or forensic interest by helping to determine the post-mortem interval (PMI). The main legislation which covers the management of human remains is divided between heritage organisations, empowered by the *Heritage New Zealand Pouhere Taonga Act* (2014), and the coroners, empowered by the *Coroners Act* (2006). All remains which predate 1900 fall under the jurisdiction of the *Heritage New Zealand Pouhere Taonga Act* (2014), and all other more recent remains under the *Coroners Act*. In practice, archaeologists have been called by police and coroners when skeletal remains are unearthed and thought to be historic, and their nature has needed to be established in order to rule out a crime scene or missing person. Unfortunately, in many cases (e.g. about 20–30 known instances in the wider Auckland region alone in the last decade, based upon personal experience and coronial cases) the reality is that the remains are removed from the site by attending police or laypeople and transported to the mortuary for assessment by the pathologist.

Part of the reason for the variable way in which archaeology is applied to both known forensic cases and those involving skeletal remains where their nature is not immediately known, is that these situations are relatively uncommon, so the body of casework is slow to build and is disorganised. In New Zealand, the number of homicides is relatively low compared to other countries, although the frequency is similar to that of Australia and Canada (1.64 homicides per 100,000 people). Police statistics indicate a total of 72 homicide victims in 2010 (New Zealand Police 2011). Of the total number of homicides, it is estimated that only one to two of these (<3%) per year will involve an attempt to conceal the body, such as a scene involving a clandestine grave, based upon a review of ESR case files and personal communications with ESR staff. This figure is in accordance with the figure of 1 in 50 homicides involving a burial cited in international literature (e.g. Blau 2004; Hunter 1994). Other cases involving human remains which are not related to modern homicide, but which need to be ruled out from an investigation, are much more common, with estimates ranging between two and six per month nationally (Meeting with HNZPT, Coroners, and police 2013, personal communication February 2013).

One of the difficulties faced in taking stock of the development of forensic archaeology in New Zealand is tracking the rates and types of interactions archaeologists have had or are having with forensic professionals and the state of knowledge among the forensic community about the potential use of archaeological methods. Since there is currently little standardised interaction between these professionals in New Zealand, a brief questionnaire was circulated in order to gather information about informal interactions related to forensic archaeology.

Comments from archaeologist respondents showed that many had been consulted by police in relation to identifying skeletal remains as human or non-human and of archaeological or forensic interest. Therefore, it appears quite common to involve archaeologists in the definition of whether or not the remains are part of a potential crime scene, but very few archaeologists had been involved beyond that stage. Few respondents (5/35, 14%) had formal experience or training in forensics or forensic archaeology, though a number (21/35, 60%) expressed an interest in assisting with police operations, if an appropriate situation should arise. General lack of forensic experience and training indicates that many archaeologists would require careful collaboration and instruction from crime scene managers regarding crime scene protocol and the admissibility of evidence or testimony to court. The only current avenue for formal forensic training in New Zealand (outside of police work) is via specific degree, diploma or certificate programmes in Forensic Science offered by the Universities of Auckland or Otago, though forensic topics are taught as elements of general science degrees at a number of other universities. The most accessible basic forensic training for professionals from other disciplines looking to apply their skills to the forensic sphere is the Certificate of Proficiency offered by the University of Auckland. To the authors' knowledge, no formal archaeological training is available to police or forensic scientists.

Physical anthropologists and forensic odontologists are more often consulted in relation to police investigations than archaeologists in New Zealand. A small number of respondents ($n=4$) from these disciplines showed that they were rarely called to the crime scene but each reported awareness of at least one case involving buried evidence, at which archaeologists or archaeological methods could have, in their opinions, been beneficial. These respondents were supportive of greater use of forensic archaeology in this country.

Comments from respondents among police, forensic practitioners and coroners generally noted that archaeological expertise could potentially be beneficial – though there did appear to be some confusion between the roles of archaeologists and anthropologists. Comments also indicate some difficulties had been encountered with the availability of such experts and knowing who to contact.

One cautionary comment from this group raised the issue of the importance of clear professional boundaries and guidelines to the roles of such experts if they were to be involved in forensic work, so as not to jeopardise credibility in court. This is a particularly important point in relation to the conflation of archaeologists and anthropologists – an understandable confusion, since there will often be overlap between these areas in traditional archaeology/anthropology. For involvement in forensic work, it would be necessary for experts from each sphere to be very clear about the boundaries of what their expertise allows them to comment on, in order for their work and opinions to stand up to courtroom scrutiny.

In general, from all parties there appeared to be support of the concept of forensic archaeology and willingness, in principle, to develop the use of archaeological methods or expertise in this way, but comments also indicated that at present such collaboration is hampered by a lack of appreciation of each other's roles, skills and legal positions. This is something that will only likely be bridged by education of all parties and relationship-building between the fields.

Case studies

In spite of the lack of formal forensic archaeology or forensic archaeologists in New Zealand, ostensibly archaeological techniques or approaches have been applied to a number of different settings or case types. These include serious scenes of crime involving surface skeletal remains or clandestine graves, and scenes involving buried or dispersed skeletal remains which are of unknown age (i.e. it is not known whether the remains are historic or forensic). Archaeologists and archaeological techniques are not currently used in scenes involving mass fatalities or disasters.

The use of archaeologists is reported in cases throughout the country where police and coroners are faced with skeletal remains of unknown age (though always in cases where the remains are suspected to be historic) and archaeologists have been consulted in determining their archaeological context. This experience is, however, highly variable, with no clear protocols or national list of archaeologists on which police and coroners can call. The reality is that use of archaeologists varies depending on the region, the police staff or coroner involved, the availability and knowledge of local archaeologists and the specific scenario. This type of situation, while not strictly forensic, is important as it is often the demarcation point for whether a coronial inquiry commences or not. The archaeologist's involvement at this juncture is also critical as it is equally important that the scene is left undisturbed irrespective of whether it is archaeological or criminal.

In purely forensic settings, archaeological techniques and approaches have been employed by police and ESR on a number of occasions. Review of ESR case files going back to 2002 reveals a wide range of archaeological techniques applied to clandestine burials (case details cannot at this time be specified).

In one case involving a clandestine burial in a rural–industrial area, police received information of a victim buried in an area of the bush line at the rear of an industrial site.

An initial assessment was carried out by police, noting vegetation markers and using aerial photographs to establish scene parameters. A suspect burial location was identified close to a spoil heap, and separate excavation and sieving areas were established. The surrounding bush was cleared to ground level in a 5-m radius, and the ground was searched before the topsoil was removed. A grid system was established and soil from each square was placed in a bucket with a tag referencing the respective grid number before being sieved. The suspect area was probed and found to be soft, and an area 3×4 m was staked out as the potential grave. The surface was cleared and a GPR survey conducted which identified an anomaly 1–1.2 m below the surface. The cleaned subsoil was noted as a clay mixed with topsoil/humus, and the grave was subsequently excavated by hand, using trowels and working within the grids. Unfortunately, the method of excavation was not recorded. Artefacts/evidence were retrieved in the fill above the body, and the bones were exposed, having been subject to fire damage. As the grave was excavated, planks were placed over the grave so that personnel could reach the body without damaging it. The body was then removed, moving from the cranium to the feet (the body was noted as having some articulated long bones), though it is unclear what the exact method of body excavation and removal was. Beneath the body a newspaper was found which was dated, and two bullets were located at the base of the grave. The scene and exhumation was mapped by police personnel using a Sokkia 3030R3 Electronic Distance Measuring (EDM) unit.

The approaches used in this case example were well-recorded relative to other files and clearly had incorporated a number of archaeological techniques. However, the case also suffers from a number of issues. One issue is that, despite the use of excavation grids, trowels and 3D mapping equipment, the grave does not appear to have necessarily been excavated using the stratigraphic method. This is a key issue to optimal interpretation and reconstruction of the scene events. Another issue is that many details were not reported, and despite the use of a reasonably sophisticated electronic mapping system, the maps produced were uninformative, and did not record or make use of the matrix or contexts within the deposit. This case demonstrates the use of many archaeological techniques, but without a solid understanding of the theory which underpin them.

Other cases varied in the type and quality of archaeological techniques used. In some cases (such as a case involving surface remains) consideration was made to recording the entire remains in situ, excavating in arbitrary layers or spits, and considering the possibility of an earlier primary grave and site formation processes. In other cases GPR was used, grid systems were established and core samples were systematically taken before excavation, but the stratigraphy of the scene was largely ignored (the nature of the soil layers and the depth of the remains and other items were not recorded) and no archaeological/layer context numbers were assigned to exhibits. The use of pedestrian or walk-over survey and visual assessment for depressions, mounds or vegetation markers also featured, and in one case excavators noted 'vertical layering' (presumably natural horizontal strata) of the soil, which they interpreted as being undisturbed. However, there also appear to be instances of over-cutting (the excessive removal of material into the natural substrate, or cutting into underlying deposits) and 'chasing' natural features such as tree roots, in one instance fully excavating an area through 50 cm of undisturbed clay subsoil. These processes could have been made more efficient, saving the investigators time and effort, had archaeological excavation techniques and theory been employed to complement forensic protocols.

Regarding the presence of archaeology in court for criminal trials, at the time of submission of this chapter the second author (BH) is involved in preparing evidence for the defence in a criminal case that involves the burial and scattering of human remains. For this particular case however, the evidence from the clandestine grave itself is not an issue for the defence, and therefore the methods and expertise used to excavate it are not under scrutiny. Rather, the archaeologist's evidence surrounds the existence of archaeological sites, and the potential for skeletal remains related to them, in the vicinity of the crime scene. It is perhaps only a matter of time before evidence from the grave itself becomes the focus for critical attention in such a case. No other examples of New Zealand criminal trials requiring evidence from archaeologists in relation to buried remains is known to the authors.

Future of forensic archaeology in New Zealand

The potential for forensic archaeology in New Zealand has to date remained unrealised, yet it presents a worthwhile area of research and practice that can contribute meaningfully to the forensic arena. Recent discussions between the authors, police, coroners, forensic pathologists, biological anthropologists, ESR and the HNZPT have highlighted the issues and potential, and provided a forum of cross-organisational dialogue from which to build a national policy for the investigation and management of scenes involving skeletal remains.

Some of the challenges which are inhibiting the development of forensic archaeology in New Zealand include low caseload numbers, the low profile of traditional archaeology, confusion over what archaeological skills are, a lack of standardisation in archaeology, the unfamiliarity of archaeologists with forensic and criminal courtroom processes, a lack of accreditation and a lack of training or experience opportunities. Additionally, although the Evidence Act requires experts to carry out or oversee an expert activity (such as excavating a grave and interpreting the archaeological evidence), this point of the rules of evidence has so far gone unchallenged in a criminal proceeding involving the recovery of buried remains.

Future trends in the development of forensic archaeology in New Zealand may involve the establishment of a national benchmark for assessment of such remains to require expert advice, even if by remote means (e.g. via scene photographs and GPS coordinates emailed to an expert), and before the scene is disturbed in all cases where practical. Other opportunities lie in the development and establishment of forensic archaeology consultants, who could be contracted by police or ESR in either a practical or advisory capacity at short notice.

Alternatively, or in addition, professionally drafted forensic archaeological guidelines for police and forensic scientists could be established; this could be coupled with a short annual education programme as part of existing quality management. Education also needs to be targeted at coroners as well as the wider archaeological community in order to raise the profile of forensic archaeology in New Zealand. At its core, there needs to be understanding about the role archaeology plays in *excavation* – the retrieval of human remains and the reconstruction of human activity at the site and beyond (Connor 2007; Hunter and Cox 2005), as opposed to merely more careful *exhumation*. To date, archaeology as evidence and archaeologists as experts, either for the prosecution or for the defence, have been absent from the criminal courts (with the exception of the author's upcoming involvement as noted earlier). This situation is unsustainable given the admissibility and importance of such evidence in other jurisdictions and the reality of inexpert use of archaeological methods as applied to domestic homicide cases.

References

Ashby, E. 2013. Forensic archaeology in New Zealand: review and future directions. *Australian Journal of Forensic Sciences* 45(1), 25–35.

Blau, S. 2004. Forensic archaeology in Australia: current situations, future possibilities. *Australian Archaeology* 58, 11–14.

Connor, M. A. 2007. *Forensic Methods: Excavation for the Archaeologist and Investigator*. Lanham, AltaMira Press.

Cox, M. 2011. Forensic anthropology and archaeology: past and present – a United Kingdom perspective. In S. Blau and D. H. Ubelaker (eds.), *Handbook of Forensic Anthropology and Archaeology*. Walnut Creek, Left Coast Press.

Cox, K., Tayles, N. and Buckley, H. 2006. Identification of "race" the issues in New Zealand. *Current Anthropology* 47(5), 869–874.

Environmental Science and Research Quality Documents. 2011. *Forensic Service Centre Methods Manual Section 19. Grave Site Examination*. Version 5.0, September 2011. ESR Service Centre Reference Material – Uncontrolled copy for reference only.

Hunter, J. 1994. Forensic archaeology in Britain. *Antiquity* 68, 758–769.

Hunter, J. and Cox, M. 2005. *Forensic Archaeology: Advances in Theory and Practice*. London, Routledge.

Institute of Forensic Archaeology. 2011. *Standards and Guidance for Forensic Archaeologists*. Reading, Institute for Archaeologists and Forensic Science Regulator. Unpublished Institute Standards Document.

Master, P. 2006. *Time since Death: The Gap between Forensic Anthropology and Legislation*. Unpublished MA thesis, University of Auckland.

Museum of London Archaeology Service. 1994. *Archaeological Site Manual*. 3rd edition. London, Museum of London.

New Zealand Archaeological Association. 1999. *NZAA Code of Ethics*. Unpublished Association Document. Available at: http://www.nzarchaeology.org/ethics.htm (last accessed 26 May 2013).

New Zealand Archaeological Association. 2013. *Consultants Directory*. Available at: http://nzarchaeology.org/cms/index.php?option=com_content&view=article&id=52&Itemid=98 (last accessed 17 May 2013).

New Zealand Historic Places Trust. 2009. *Archaeological Guidelines Series No. 5: Guidelines for Section 17*. Approval, NZHPT ISBN 978-0-908577-95-8. Available at: http://www.heritage.org.nz/protecting-heritage/archaeology/-/media/ac8b13188a5748e48da3a0f4cf00b779.ashx (last accessed 21 November 2014).

New Zealand Police. 2011. *Crime Statistics*. Available at: http://www.police.govt.nz/service/statistics/index.html (last accessed 26 May 2013).

Nobes, D. C. 2000. The search for "Yvonne": a case example of the delineation of grave using near-surface geophysical methods. *Journal of Forensic Sciences* 45(3), 715–721.

Sigler-Eisenberg, B. 1985. Forensic research: expanding the concept of applied archaeology. *American Antiquity* 50(3), 650–655.

Smith, I. W. G. 1990. Historical archaeology in New Zealand a review and bibliography. *New Zealand Journal of Archaeology* 12, 85–119.

Tayles, N. and Halcrow, S. 2011. New Zealand. In N. Márquez-Grant and L. Fibiger (eds.), *The Routledge Handbook of Archaeological Human Remains and Legislation*, 647–656. Abingdon, Routledge.

Walter, R. and Jacomb, C. 2008. New Zealand. In D. M. Pearsell (ed.), *Encyclopedia of Archaeology* 3, 1738–1747. New York, Academic Press.

CHAPTER 39

The archaeological investigation of crime scenes and humanitarian cases that involve graves and human remains in South Africa

W. Coen Nienaber

Forensic Anthropology Research Centre, Department of Anatomy, School of Medicine, Faculty of Health Sciences, University of Pretoria, Pretoria, Republic of South Africa

Introduction

South Africa has a unique socio-political make-up largely due to its recent liberation, ongoing transformation and empowerment of previously disadvantaged communities. The impact of this particular history on forensic anthropology was noted as long ago as 1997 by Steyn et al. (1997). High rates of violent crime, political violence and human rights abuses by the former Apartheid government, rapid, uncontrolled urbanisation and large numbers of illegal immigrants complicate the social landscape of the country. In this context, the role of forensic anthropology in identifying the victims of crime, and that of forensic archaeology in the recovery of remains and crime scene information, is crucial.

The medico-legal framework in South Africa fails to recognise forensic archaeology beyond the principal function of body recovery by technicians. These technicians are morgue staff and play no role in the investigation of the scene. Their primary function is to collect and transport the body to the medico-legal facility. There is no stipulated requirement for the use of any specialist techniques when buried bodies or decomposed human remains scatters are recovered. There is also no set standard for recovery reports and no criteria for when cases should be investigated with the use of archaeological methods in addition to the normal protocols in place. Furthermore, there is a dearth of awareness among law enforcement officers regarding the need for in situ observation and documentation of decomposed or decomposing remains. Although this is slowly changing, the predominant attitude among investigating officers appear to be that if there is no blood on the scene and if the body cannot be autopsied, then there is very little evidence of any value.

Conversely, the exhumation of victims' bodies is often ordered by courts to reinvestigate cases in dispute. This is usually limited to post-mortem sampling for DNA for identification purposes, but some have also been exhumed in order to reassess trauma or cause of death. Unfortunately, these exhumations are often conducted by cemetery staff using earth moving machinery.

As a general observation, very little, if any, heed is paid to the principles of archaeology when bodies are exhumed and bones recovered in South Africa.

Legislation and structures that govern the recovery of forensic human remains in South Africa

As part of the transformation of the country after the first democratic elections in 1994, the existing legislation was reviewed and subsequently transformed and modernised. However, this process is ongoing and several pre-democracy regulations (albeit mostly minor) and by-laws are still in place. Because these were enacted under different circumstances to the current dispensation, in many cases they do not integrate well with new legislation, or with the aims of a progressive society. Legislation is also not always interpreted and applied uniformly in the different provinces. This leads to problems, particularly when a forensic activity involves more than one province (Nienaber and Steyn 2011).

Exhumation and body recovery as a medico-legal function of the South African Judicial System

The responsibility for the investigation of deaths due to unnatural causes lies with the Forensic Pathology Service in the province where the incident occurred.

Forensic Archaeology: A Global Perspective, First Edition. Edited by W.J. Mike Groen, Nicholas Márquez-Grant and Robert C. Janaway.

Under the *Inquest Act* (Act 58 of 1959), this Service makes provision for rendering medico-legal investigation of the cause of death and serves the judicial process. Up until 2006 this function was performed by, and fell under, the South African Police Services. As stipulated by the *National Health Act* (Act 61 of 2003), the operational management of the medico-legal laboratory facilities was subsequently transferred to the different provincial Departments of Health.

Within this structure the investigation of deaths due to unnatural causes, including body recovery, is controlled by the *Regulations Regarding the Rendering of Forensic Pathology Service* (R363 of 2007) and the *Criminal Procedures Act* (Act 51 of 1977). The latter comprises a comprehensive legislative framework that regulates the procedures at a scene of death, or at a crime scene (Burger 2010).

Jurisdiction over inadvertently discovered human remains is governed by the *National Heritage Resources Act* (Act 25 of 1999) which stipulates that all discoveries of human remains should be reported to the local South African Police Services and the relevant Heritage Resources Agency (be it the Provincial Heritage Resources Agency or the South African Heritage Resources Agency for national and priority graded sites). Human remains identified by the Act, or proclaimed by the minister of Arts and Culture, should be reported to the South African Heritage Resources Agency Burial Grounds and Graves Unit. Jurisdiction, that is, whether the remains are forensic in nature or of heritage value, and whether the cause of death was non-natural and judicially relevant, is then assigned after consultation between officials. As a general rule, although specified exceptions to this are indicated in the *National Heritage Resources Act* (Act 25 of 1999), human remains older than 60 years are not forensic, and remains older than 100 years are considered to be archaeological.

Human rights abuses and restitution investigations in South Africa

The *National Heritage Resources Act* (Act 25 of 1999) also identifies categories of human remains, such as Victims of Conflict (referring to victims of the pre-1994 political violence in South Africa), which are classified as human rights abuses and deserving of special investigation and commemoration. Authorisation for archaeological investigation of these remains should, however, still comply with other legislation, such as the *National Health Act* (Act 61 of 2003). The relevant jurisdictions hold sway where crimes were perpetrated.

The human remains identified as Victims of Conflict in the *National Heritage Resources Act* (Act 25 of 1999) include, among others, those who died in the present territory of the Republic of South Africa as a result of any war or conflict, certain persons who died in the 'liberation struggle' in the present territory of the Republic of South Africa and outside South Africa and individuals indicated by the Minister of Arts and Culture in notices in the *Government Gazette*. This excludes those covered by the *Commonwealth War Graves Act* (Act 8 of 1992), who died in the present territory of the Republic of South Africa as a result of any war or conflict after 4 August 1914 and were citizens of Commonwealth countries other than South Africa (Nienaber and Steyn 2011). This framework provides for the protection and special identification of victims of war, war crimes and human rights abuses. The exhumation of remains from such graves, as well as the housing, transport and handling of the remains, may only be done once a permit from the South African Heritage Resources Agency has been issued in compliance with the *National Heritage Resources Act* 25 of 1999.

In order to apply for a permit to exhume the remains identified by the *National Heritage Resources Act* (Act 25 of 1999), a public participation and social consultation process is required. This involves a concerted effort to identify and trace any person or community with an interest in the remains by means of documentary and archival research and the placing of specified notices. The stipulations set by bona fide interested and affected parties must be agreed and complied with during the recovery of the remains in question (Nienaber and Steyn 2011).

National Prosecuting Authority Missing Persons Task Team

The Truth and Reconciliation Commission (TRC) recommended the investigation of nearly 500 unsolved cases of missing persons reported to it during its tenure mandated by the *Promotion of National Unity and Reconciliation Act* (Act 34 of 1995). The TRC was established in 1995 with the purpose of promoting national unity and reconciliation in a spirit of understanding, which goes beyond the conflicts and divisions of South Africa's political past, specifically Apartheid. To this end, a Missing Persons Task Team (MPTT) was established in the Priority Crimes Litigation Unit of the National Prosecuting Authority in order to conduct the investigation of persons who disappeared in political circumstances between 1 March 1960 and 10 May 1994 (Notice 1539 of 2008). The Priority Crimes Litigation Unit is tasked with the implementation of the Rome Statute of the *International Criminal Court Act* (Act 27 of 2002) and with the management and direction, amongst others, of investigating and prosecuting crimes against humanity and war crimes.

Legislation in general

Over and above the requirements of the *National Heritage Resources Act* 25 of 1999 and the *National Health Act* 61 of 2003, remains from graves that are located in South African National Parks may only be recovered with specific permission from the landowner in line with applicable policy. This is relevant as 3926 ha are proclaimed South African National Parks.[1] Municipal bylaws also apply in cases that are conducted in municipal jurisdictions (Nienaber and Steyn 2011). The handling, storage and transport of any and all human remains, whether they are of historic, forensic or humanitarian case origin, is further regulated by the *Graves and Dead Bodies Ordinance* (Ord. 7 of 1925; reinstituted by Proclamation 109 of 17 June 1994) and the *Exhumations Ordinance* (Ord. 12 of 1980) (Nienaber and Steyn 2011). These provisions remain subject to a direct court order and jurisdiction established by the *Inquest Act* (Act 58 of 1959) and the *National Health Act* (Act 61 of 2003).

Forensic archaeology in the South African context

From the legal context, it is evident that the forensic archaeologist in South Africa works in a supporting role as a specialist in any investigation that involves clandestine graves and decomposed or decomposing remains of the victims of crime and human rights abuses. The inclusion of archaeological techniques for crime victim recovery from buried contexts and decomposed surface scatters and even mass disaster management improves the success of the investigation and may also serve to ensure that all evidence is recovered and documented while preserving the context. Steyn et al. (1997) reported several cases where improper recovery of remains referred for physical anthropological analysis led to false reporting of the number of victims. In one case the remains of a 7–8-month-old foetus was found comingled with the remains of an adult male who was sent for analysis. In another case the skeletal remains of two individuals were submitted by the police as one. Such discrepancies may easily be avoided by using suitable (forensic) archaeological methods during body recovery. A further case involved an inadvertently discovered skeleton of an individual at Mathibestat, showing clear signs of trauma to the skull, and assumed to be a victim of violent crime. After investigation by an archaeologist it was found to be of archaeological origin and that it represented a case of ancient interpersonal violence (Nienaber et al. 2009) (Figure 39.1).

The most valuable contribution of archaeology to forensics in South Africa is, ironically, not forensic in nature. The confluence of history, Southern Africa's long human habitation, the abundance of cultural relics and material remains spanning human prehistory, a recent past of dispossessed and undocumented communities and high numbers of unidentified illegal immigrants contributes to the regular inadvertent discovery of unidentified human remains. These cases are taken up in the judicial process and clog the system with irrelevant bureaucracy and high volumes of non-forensic remains. Archaeological methods and techniques are able to distinguish quickly and accurately between victims of crime and human rights abuses and between remains from historical or prehistorical origin. Thus irrelevant cases are effectively solved and resources may be used to investigate and prosecute crime. At present archaeologists are consulted by the police on an ad hoc basis, and depending on the nature of the finds in question assessments are made either in the field or later on in the laboratory.

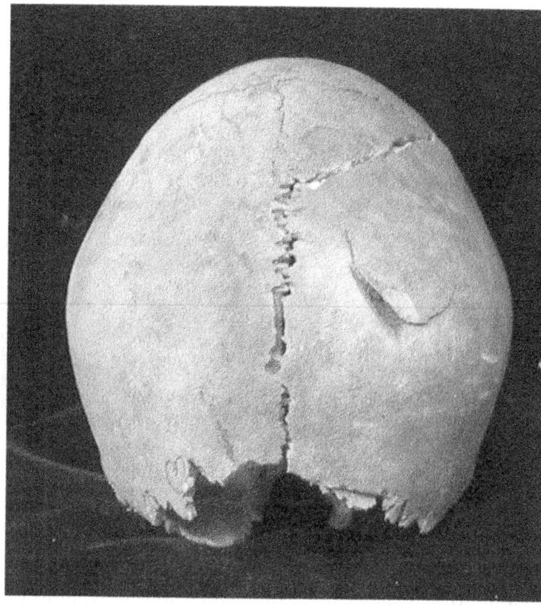

Figure 39.1 The Mathibestat archaeological skull from the back. Note the sharp force trauma on the right parietal bone (with bone wastage) and lambdoid suture.

The recovery and handling of prehistorical and culturally significant remains by law enforcement personnel is also detrimental to heritage conservation and best left to archaeologists in the relevant scientific field of study. Of the 317 individuals included in a forensic anthropology profile from 1993 to 2006 at the Department of Anatomy, University of Pretoria (Van Rooyen et al. 2007), 12 were of archaeological origin but had been taken up into the judicial process and were investigated as crimes instead.

In addition, cultural anthropology and culture historical archaeology often contribute in interpreting evidence in so-called *muti* (or medicine) cases where

[1]For more information, see: http://www.sanparks.co.za/about/ (last accessed 30 March 2014).

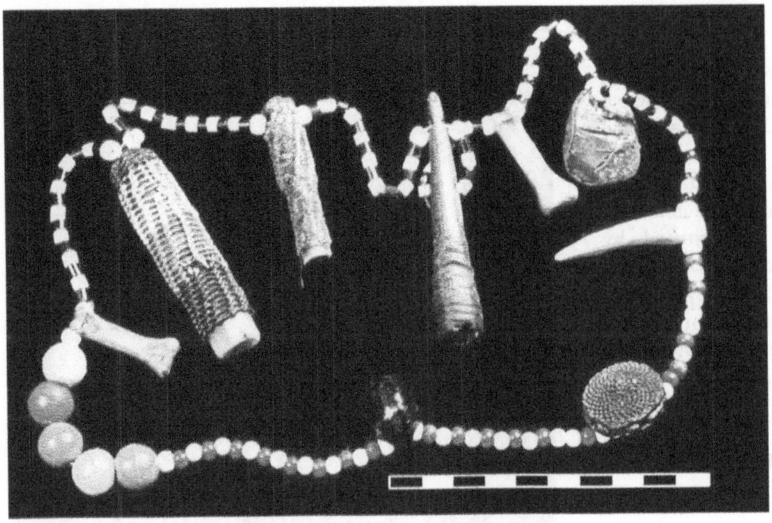

Figure 39.2 A necklace of strung together objects, including human bone and a lion tooth, with series of beads in traditional Tsonga magic colours and sequence from a 'muti' murder case (Photo: M. Loots).

human body parts are used in black magic based on ancient African practices. These often follow traditionally known practices that may be identified and contextualised by archaeologists (Steyn 2005) (Figure 39.2).

Forensic archaeology in South Africa

Steyn et al. (1997) recognised that various authors (e.g. Bass and Brikby 1978; Boyd 1979; Brooks and Brooks 1984; Levine et al. 1984; Morse et al. 1976, 1984; Stoutamire 1983; Warren 1979) point to the use of archaeological techniques when retrieving human remains of forensic nature, but noted that there were insufficient suitably qualified archaeologists in the country to handle all buried body and decomposed surface scatter cases. A suitable legal and institutional framework did not exist for them, even if the necessary capacity could be developed. Therefore Steyn et al. (1997) proposed that crime scene investigators already in place at the various law enforcement and judicial institutions be trained and equipped with the required skills to fulfil this function. This also addresses the immediate question of legal mandate to undertake cases such as these.

The established centres for forensic anthropology in South Africa, mainly at the Universities of Pretoria and Cape Town, have a degree of forensic archaeological specialisation. These institutions have a long established relationship with the South African Police Services and the South African Heritage Resources Agency. It is on this basis that specialist assistance for the recovery of forensic human remains is offered. Mostly this assistance is arranged by memoranda of understanding and in some cases by long-term consultation appointments between the institutions and law enforcement and legal compliance agencies (Nienaber and Steyn 2011). The assistance, however, remains collaborative between the case officers and the archaeologist involved in the case. The work of the National Prosecuting Authority MPTT is mainly conducted in conjunction with the Argentine Forensic Anthropology Team (EAAF; Fondebrider and Scheinsohn, Chapter 43, this volume) but also includes South African professionals and students, some of whom now work in the field (Figure 39.3).

Besides the Association of Southern African Professional Archaeologists' minimum standards of practice and code of conduct which ethically binds members of the association, there are no legally mandated standards for excavation in South Africa. The professional ethic is based, among others, on respect for the remains themselves and applies to forensic and humanitarian contexts.

Case studies

Investigation into the presence of an alleged mass grave at Laingsburg municipal refuse dump

Laingsburg in the Western Cape Province of South Africa was devastated by a severe flood on 25 January 1981. At least 100 people lost their lives and 72 bodies were never recovered.[2] Allegations were made that the Coloured (in South Africa this general term indicates

[2]For more information, see: http://www.sahistory.org.za/dated-event/least-100-people-drown-flood-laingsburg (last accessed 30 March 2014).

Figure 39.3 National Prosecuting Authority Missing Persons Task Team exhumation of the 'Langa 6' at Rebecca Street Cemetery, Pretoria in 2010 (Photo: W. C. Nienaber).

individuals of mixed population descent) victims of the flood were buried disrespectfully in a mass grave in the town rubbish dump, in black plastic body bags, while the white victims were buried properly and commemorated. To investigate these allegations, the Western Cape Provincial Government followed a process that included Ground Penetrating Radar (GPR) scanning of the old town rubbish dump by the South African Council for Geoscience and thereafter, in 2003, an archaeological investigation of the location by the University of Pretoria[3] to probe the allegations and the possible existence of a mass grave at this location.[4]

The archaeological investigation of the site commenced after a foot survey of the area was conducted. A mechanical digger-loader and manual labour were used to excavate 10 test trenches in the indicated area (Figure 39.4). These trenches were placed to ensure that the calculated minimum size of a possible mass grave would be encountered, should it exist as alleged. The products of these excavations were sorted and indicative materials were recovered and documented by means of proven permanent methods. All objects from the trenches were collected and sorted and relevant finds that served to give an indication of date, such as preserved newspaper, products with a sell-by date indicated, special edition products that were only manufactured for a short period, were marked with an accession number and location in permanent ink and were photographed and described.

Figure 39.4 Excavations at the old Laingsburg refuse dump (Photo: H. Steyn).

[3]For more information, see http://www.polity.org.za/article/dowry-press-conference-to-announce-outcome-of-laingsburg-mass-grave-investigation-03092003-2003-09-03 (last accessed 30 March 2014).

[4]For more information, see http://www.polity.org.za/article/dowry-alleged-mass-grave-in-laingsburg-western-cape-to-be-investigated-19122002-2002-12-19 and http://www.info.gov.za/speeches/2003/03021715461003.htm (last accessed 30 March 2014).

This investigation established the true extent of the post-1980 refuse dump, which was considerably smaller than the area indicated as a possible location of the mass grave, and located at the western side of the indicated area (Figure 39.5). No disturbances of the bedrock of the valley were observed. East–west trenches in the bedrock into which the bodies were reportedly placed to form the alleged mass grave could therefore not have existed. Rather, abundant evidence indicated the dumping of whole and butchered animal carcasses from butchery cold rooms and drowned animals. These were recovered from the matrix of the refuse dump and not from trenches allegedly dug in the bedrock.

No black body bags nor any part or remnant thereof was encountered. Refuse-type black bags occurred in abundance and these may have been mistaken for black body bags thought to have contained the remains of human flood victims. No human remains were encountered during the investigation and no anomalies of the stratigraphy of the investigated area indicating the presence of the alleged mass grave were observed.

This investigation concluded that the post-1980 refuse dump that was created shortly after the flood contained nothing but household refuse dating from the time to 2000/2001. Subsequently, it was publicly accepted that the archaeological investigation proved conclusively that there was no evidence to back the allegations.[5]

The Argentine Forensic Anthropology Team (EAAF) 2005 second mission to South Africa in conjunction with the National Prosecuting Authority Missing Persons Task Team

During 2005 the Argentine Forensic Anthropology Team (Equipo Argentino de Antropologia Forense – EAAF) (EAAF 2006) conducted missions in the KwaZulu-Natal, Mpumalanga and Gauteng provinces of South Africa together with the MPTT of the National Prosecuting Authority. During these missions, they also trained South African professionals and students.[6]

Piet Retief Thandokukhanya cemetery (Mpumalanga province)

From the TRC hearings[7] and subsequent additional investigations by the MPTT of the National Prosecuting Authority, the following incident was recounted. In 1983 Richard Mzwamadoda Bonga (member of *Umkhonto we Sizwe* – MK), the former armed wing of the

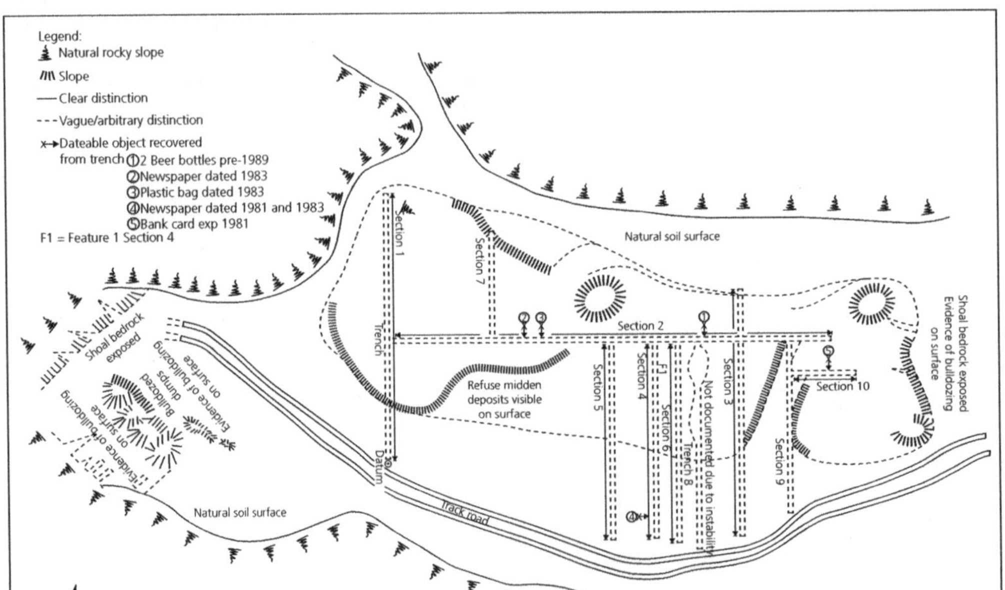

Figure 39.5 Mapped results of the investigation into the existence of a mass grave at Laingsburg.

[5]For more information, see http://www.info.gov.za/speeches/2003/03090314461002.htm (last accessed 30 March 2014).
[6]For more information, see http://eaaf.typepad.com/cr_south_africa/ (last accessed 30 March 2014).
[7]For more information, see http://www.justice.gov.za/trc/report/finalreport/victims_list_vol7.pdf (last accessed 30 March 2014).

African National Congress (ANC) disappeared near the South African border with Swaziland. This was reported by a former member of the ANC. MPTT investigators found police photographs and documents describing the shooting of two ANC members on Madola Farm on the outskirts of the town of Piet Retief by security police. The ANC members reportedly killed in this incident were given paupers' burials in the Thandokukhanya Cemetery in Piet Retief. The MPTT deduced that the buried individuals might be Richard Mzwamadoda Bonga and Vusumzi Justice Ngwema (also an MK member).[8]

During 2005 these graves were excavated by members of the EAAF (EAAF 2006) and the MPTT, with the Bonga and Ngwema families present. Staff and students of the Forensic Anthropology Research Centre of the University of Pretoria (FARC)[9] also participated in the excavations. Human remains were exhumed and analysed the following day. The physical anthropological characteristics observed were consistent with antemortem information for Richard Mzwamadoda Bonga and Vusumzi Justice Ngwema. Peri-mortem lesions and peri-mortem gunshot wounds were also observed on the remains. Bone samples were taken and DNA analysis of the remains was recommended to confirm the identities of the recovered remains.[10]

On 10 July 2005 the remains of five MK members, including those of Richard Mzwamadoda Bonga and Vusumzi Justice Ngwema, were handed to their families by the Minister of Justice for reburial in their hometowns during a ceremony at the Freedom Park in Pretoria. The identities of these remains were confirmed by DNA analysis (Beeld, 11 July 2005).

Exhumation for repatriation of the remains of the Ebo 4, Ebo, Kwanza Sul Province, Angola

As part of Operation Savannah during the South African 'Border War' (1966–1989) and in the aftermath of the Portuguese withdrawal from Angola on 11 November 1975, the South African Defence Force Battle Group Foxbat focused its attention on the area around the village of Ebo, southeast of Luanda (Du Preez 1989; Spies 1989). In the period 23–25 November 1975 four South African soldiers died in combat in the area. Trooper Niel Lombard (South African Army) died in an ambush of an armoured car convoy on 23 November 1975 at the Massaba River north of Ebo. Captain Daniël Jacob Taljaard, (South African Army), second Lt Keith Arthur Williamson and second Lt Eric Bryan Thompson (both of the South African Air Force) were together in a Cessna 182 reconnaissance aircraft that was shot down by Cuban forces on 25 November 1975. All these soldiers were reportedly buried in the area by members of the local community, because it was impossible for the South African forces to recover and evacuate their bodies from the battlefield (unpublished documents and reports collected in his private capacity by WO 1 (Rtd) Rowley Medlin).

Towards the end of January 1976 it was reported in the *London Times* that the wreckage of an aircraft was seen north of Ebo. These reports were later corroborated by members of the Ebo community. A first round of excavations to exhume and repatriate the remains of these soldiers was conducted by the Heritage Foundation with the FARC of the University of Pretoria accompanying as specialists during May 2012. Efforts were abandoned after the South Africans were expelled from the grave sites by the Angolan army and police. Following negotiations between the Angolan and South African governments, the team returned in June 2012 and the excavations were completed.

The location indicated as the grave of the South African soldiers who died in the aircraft was at the foot of a cut tree and was marked by several pieces of aircraft wreckage visible on the surface and on several photographs of the site, some of them taken not long after the incident. The infill of the grave contained various objects that could be associated with an aircraft. These included several metal, plastic and rubber objects. The first human remains were encountered at a shallow depth of about 0.5 m (Figure 39.6). Even with careful excavation, no complete bones could be found. All bones were fragmentary and poorly preserved. This poor preservation was probably the result of the soil conditions (clay), rodent and termite activity and the state of the remains when they were buried, as the bodies had most likely fragmented and burned during and after the crash.

The remains of three individuals were identified from the grave pit. From medical records it was known that Captain Daniël Jacob Taljaard wore a dental prosthesis. The remains associated with the denture found in the grave could therefore be positively identified. The findings also attested to the violent nature of the crash and impact of the aircraft after it was shot down. The haphazard way in which the remains were buried, the fact that parts of the aircraft were found between the remains and the severed limb present in the grave indicated that this was

[8]For more information, see http://eaaf.typepad.com/cr_south_africa/ (last accessed 30 March 2014).

[9]FARC is a Research Centre of the University of Pretoria that consolidates the staff at the Department of Anatomy who have a research interested in forensics and are active in the field. It functions parallel to the department and shares its infrastructure and capacity.

[10]For more information, see http://eaaf.typepad.com/cr_south_africa/ (last accessed 30 March 2014).

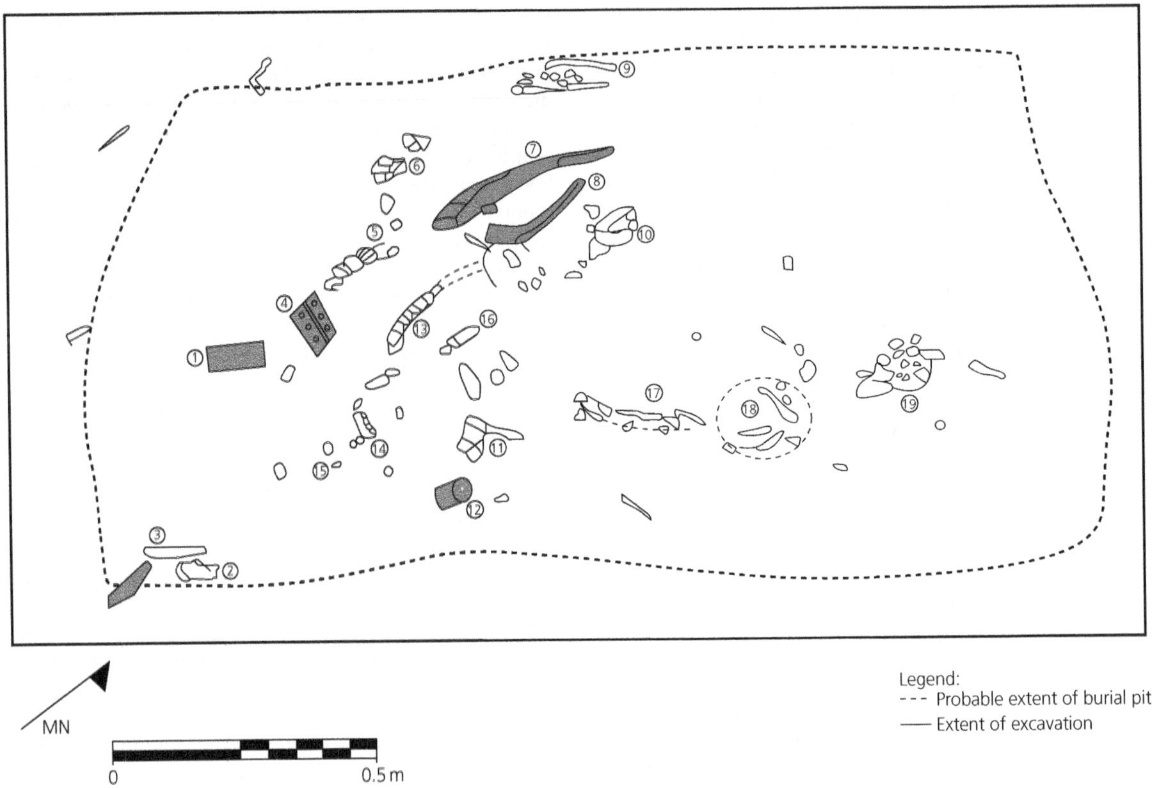

Figure 39.6 Measured drawing: reconstruction of human remains found at Ebo4/1–3. Key to Figure 39.6: 1, metal box; 2, calcaneus; 3, distal tibia; 4, metal box; 5, emerging vertebral column; 6, bone fragments; 7, leather belt; 8, plastic from aircraft (possibly a door handle); 9, unassociated upper limb; 10, fragment of oscoxa and femur head (possibly right side); 11, emerging oscoxa and femur head; 12, cylindrical metal object (possibly a spent flare); 13, vertebral column; 14, dentures, 15, small cranial fragments; 16, shaft of long bone; 17, emerging vertebral column; 18, shoulder girdle; 19, cranial fragments.

not a formal burial. A reconstruction of events suggested that the three individuals probably died inside the aircraft, and that their remains as well as parts of the aircraft were dragged into a communal grave pit with spades, shovels or similar implements. DNA samples were taken from bones associated with specific individuals identified through burial position. Although DNA for comparative purposes was obtained from the families of the deceased, the quality of the DNA isolated from the bone samples from the grave was so poor that no conclusive identifications could be made of the remains of second Lt Keith Arthur Williamson and second Lt Eric Bryan Thompson. Nonetheless, the families of these individuals indicated that they accept that the remains were those of their sons and that specific identification of the bones was not required, even if it was preferred.

Several possible localities in a specific general area were indicated for the grave of Trooper Niel Lombard who died in the armoured car (unpublished documents and reports collected in his private capacity by WO 1 [Rtd] Rowley Medlin). These localities were documented and archaeologically investigated by the FARC to establish any indications for the presence of human remains at each. No evidence for the presence of a grave or any human remains could be established.

Since the remains of Trooper Niel Lombard could not be recovered, his brother, who was present in Angola during the mission, took soil and flowers from the area thought to be the grave site and this was placed in a coffin for reburial (Beeld, 26 July 2012).The 'remains' were ceremonially reburied in the Wall of Remembrance at the Voortrekker Monument in Pretoria on 8 July 2012 (Boshoff 2012a,b).

Taking forensic archaeology forward in South Africa

Conducting cases that involve human remains in clandestine graves, buried body cases and the recovery of decomposed or decomposing surface scattered remains entail the retrieval, excavation, analysis and personal identification of the remains and the associated evidence. To accomplish this a multidisciplinary approach, involving law enforcement specialists, crime scene technicians and also archaeologists, anthropologists, pathologists, entomologists and botanists, is required (Steyn et al. 2000).

Essentially, the legal framework for collaboration between archaeologists and law enforcement personnel and judicial institutions is in place. Archaeological involvement, although limited, is already taking place and some positive contributions have been achieved. However, it is essential that law enforcement agencies responsible for the recovery of bodies appoint suitably qualified investigators and train and equip these individuals to apply archaeological methods where appropriate in the recovery of buried bodies, clandestine graves and decomposed or decomposing surface scattered remains. These arrangements and case investigation protocols should be formally developed and implemented through legislative regulations and standard operating procedures.

Acknowledgements

The author wishes to acknowledge the members and staff of the South African Police Services Victim Identification Centre, the Forensic Anthropology Research Centre, Department of Anatomy, University of Pretoria, the Missing Persons Task Team of the National Prosecuting Authority, EAAF and the Heritage Foundation.

Marinda Pretorius produced the graphic art. Kim Outhoff and Maryna Steyn assisted with editing.

References

Bass, W. M. and Birkby, W. H. 1978. Exhumation: the method could make the difference. *FBI Law Enforcement Bulletin* 47, 6–11.

Beeld, 11 July 2005. *5 MK-'Helde' kan Uiteindelik Tuis Gaan Rus.* Available at: http://152.111.1.88/argief/berigte/beeld/2005/07/11/B2/04/03.html (last accessed July 2013).

Beeld, 26 July 2012. *Drie se Oorskot en 'n Hopie Grond. Gestorwe Soldate ná 37j. Terug in SA.* Available at: http://152.111.1.88/argief/berigte/beeld/2012/06/12/B1/2/tegebokry.html (last accessed July 2013).

Boshoff, W. 2012a. Die repatriasie van die Ebo-4: die lokalisering en opgrawing van die grafte van vier Suid-Afrikaanse soldate in die Ebo-distrik, Kwanza Sul, Angola, 1975–2012. *Journal of Contemporary History* [*Joernaal vir Eietydse Geskiedenis*] 37(2), 191–223.

Boshoff, W. 2012b. *Stof is jy… Die Opgrawing en Repatriasie van die Ebo-4.* Available at: http://teo.co.za/artikel/articles/488/1/*Stof-is-jy---Die-opgrawing-en-repatriasie-van-die-Ebo-4*/Bladsy1.html (last accessed July 2013).

Boyd, R. M. 1979. Buried body cases. *FBI Law Enforcement Bulletin* 48, 1–7.

Brooks, S. T. and Brooks, R. H. 1984. Problems of burial exhumation, historical and forensic aspects. In T. A. Rathburn and J. E. Buikstra (eds.), *Human Identification: Case Studies in Forensic Anthropology*, 64–86. Springfield, Charles C. Thomas.

Burger, L. 2010. The death notification form. In K. Joyner (ed.), *Aspects of Forensic Medicine: Introduction for Health Care Practitioners*, 138–152. Claremont, Juta.

Criminal Procedures Act (Act 51 of 1977).

Commonwealth War Graves Act (Act 8) of 1992.

Du Preez, S. 1989. *Avontuur in Angola. Die Verhaal van Suid-Afrika se Soldate in Angola 1975–1976*, 134–145. Pretoria, Van Schaik.

EAAF. 2006. *Annual Report.* Available at: http://eaaf.typepad.com/ar_2006/88-97_southafrica-4.pdf (last accessed July 2013).

Exhumations Ordinance (Ord. 12 of 1980).

Graves and Dead Bodies Ordinance (Ord. 7 of 1925; re-instituted by Proclamation 109 of 17 June 1994).

Health Act (Act 61 of 2003).

Inquest Act (Act 58 of 1959).

International Criminal Court Act (Act 27 of 2002).

Levine, L. J., Campbell, Jr., H. R. and Rhine, J. S. 1984. Perpendicular forensic archaeology. In T. A. Rathburn and J. E. Buikstra (eds.), *Human Identification: Case Studies in Forensic Anthropology*, 87–95. Springfield, Charles C. Thomas.

Morse, D., Crusoe, D. and Smith, H. G. 1976. Forensic archaeology. *Journal of Forensic Sciences* 21, 323–332.

Morse, D., Daily, R. C., Stoutamire, J. and Duncan, J. 1984. Forensic archaeology. In T. A. Rathburn and J. E. Buikstra (eds.), *Human Identification: Case Studies in Forensic Anthropology*, 53–63. Springfield, Charles C. Thomas.

National Heritage Resources Act (Act 25 of 1999).

Nienaber, W. C. and Steyn, M. 2011. Republic of South Africa. In N. Márquez-Grant and L. Fibiger (eds.), *Physical Anthropology and Legislation: European Perspectives and Beyond*, 501–502. New York, Routledge.

Nienaber, W. C., Malopyane, K., Steyn, M. and Myburgh, J. 2009. *SAPS Matibestat MAS 93/03/2009 Rescue Excavation. The Rescue Excavation of Inadvertently Discovered Archaeological Human Remains from Matibetstat (North-West Province).* Report to South African Heritage Resources Agency and the South African Police Services.

Notice 1539 of 2008. Department of Justice and constitutional development. Exhumation policy: cases of missing persons reported to the Truth and Reconciliation Commission (TRC). *Government Gazette*, 12 December 2008, No. 31723.

Promotion of National Unity and Reconciliation Act (Act 34 of 1995).

Regulations Regarding the Rendering of Forensic Pathology Service. *Government Gazette*, 20 July 2007, No. 30075 31, R. 636.

Spies, F. J. Du T. 1989. *Angola. Operasie Savannah. 1975–1976.* Chapters 14–15, 177–202. Pretoria, SA Weermag (Direktoraat Openbare Betrekkinge).

Steyn, M. 2005. Muti murders from South Africa: a case study. *Forensic Science International* 151, 279–287.

Steyn, M., Meiring, J. H. and Nienaber, W. C. 1997. Forensic anthropology in South Africa: a profile of cases from 1993 to 1995 at the Department of Anatomy, University of Pretoria. *South African Journal of Ethnology* 20(1), 23–26.

Steyn, M., Nienaber, W. C. and Iscan. M. Y. 2000. Excavation/retrieval of forensic remains. In J. A. Siegel, P. J. Saukko and G. C. Knupfer (eds.), *Encyclopaedia of Forensic Sciences*, 235–242. London, Academic Press.

Stoutamire, J. 1983. Excavation and recovery. In D. Morse, J. Duncan, J. and J. Stoutamire (eds.), *Handbook of Forensic Archaeology and Anthropology*, 20–47. Tallahassee, Bills Book Store.

Van Rooyen, C., L'Abbé, E. N. and Steyn, M. 2007. Forensic anthropology in South Africa: a profile of cases from 1993 to 2006 at the Department of Anatomy, University of Pretoria. *Proceedings of the 37th Annual Meeting of the Anatomical Society of Southern Africa*, Mount Grace Hotel, North West Province, South Africa, 22–25 April 2007.

Warren, C. P. 1979. Verifying identification of military remains: a case report. *Journal of Forensic Sciences* 24, 182–188.

Websites

http://www.justice.gov.za/trc/report/finalreport/victims_list_vol7.pdf0000a

http://www.sahistory.org.za/dated-event/least-100-people-drown-flood-laingsburg

http://www.polity.org.za/article/dowry-press-conference-to-announce-outcome-of-laingsburg-mass-grave-investigation-03092003-2003-09-03

http://www.polity.org.za/article/dowry-alleged-mass-grave-in-laingsburg-western-cape-to-be-investigated-19122002-2002-12-19

http://www.gov.za/speeches/2003/03090314461001.htm

http://www.gov.za/speeches/2003/03090314461002.htm

http://www.sanparks.co.za/about/

CHAPTER 40

Anthropology module of Mass ID Manager (MIM) in the Republic of Korea: potential for forensic archaeology

Nak-Eun Chung[1], Yi-Suk Kim[2] and U-Young Lee[3]

[1] *Division of Forensic Medicine, National Forensic Service, Seoul, Republic of Korea*

[2] *Ewha Womans University, School of Medicine, Seoul, Republic of Korea*

[3] *Department of Anatomy, College of Medicine, The Catholic University of Korea, Seoul, Republic of Korea*

Introduction

This chapter focuses on the use of an anthropological Mass Identification Manager (MIM) module and its potential for forensic archaeology within mass fatality incidents. Although forensic archaeology has not yet been established in the Republic of Korea, our experience shows the potential for such a discipline primarily in the framework forensic anthropology cases. In the Republic of Korea, the NFS (National Forensic Service, 국립과학수사연구원)[1] oversees the victim identification project by setting up a task force team, the Korea Disaster Victim Identification (DVI) team,[2] in the event of mass disasters. We also recruit the attending staff from various institutes (the police, the prosecutor's office, relevant universities and NGOs, etc.), and organise the joint investigation team.

The NFS has been involved in several mass fatality incidents, including the Sampoong Department Store Collapse in June 1995 (Chung et al. 1996), the Gimhae Air China Flight 129 Crash in April 2002, the Daegu Subway Fire in February 2003 (Chung 2004; Park 2009), the Southeast Asia Tsunami Disaster in December 2004 (Chung and Yoon 2009), the mass exhumation associated with the Jeju 4.3 massacre (1948–1954) in 2007 and the mass burial in Daehakro in 2009 (Chung et al. 2009). This mass grave was found in an underground space of a building demolition site, near the site where the Medical Department of the Kyeongseong Imperial University stood during the Japanese colonial rule (1910–1945). Our experiences have shown that the amounts of data related to mass disaster victims or mass graves are usually too large to collect or compare; it is essential to do the identification with software that makes the process faster and more efficient, both in the field during the process of recovery (forensic archaeology) and later in the laboratory or morgue (forensic/physical anthropology, pathology). Therefore, in early 2013, the Korea DVI developed a new software named *Mass Identification Manager* (MIM), especially focused on small- and medium-sized disasters. This has shown itself to be invaluable during the (forensic archaeological) recovery of victims from mass disasters and mass graves. During the development of MIM, we developed several modules which are quite distinct from other compatible systems, such as dental, DNA, fingerprint, forensic anthropology (and archaeology), familial assistance and information management. Using data restricted to each disaster or mass grave, we can make a very reasonable identification process by combining various modules. The MIM system is a portable compact system which consists of three notebooks, one copy of Oracle DB and three copies of MIM. We believe that it could be a powerful total solution for identification purposes and become the standard programme used by many other countries, for both forensic archaeologists and anthropologists.

In MIM, we also designed a unique forensic/physical anthropology module with new coding systems to manage skeletons effectively during exhumation, and to

[1]The NFS is an independent and the largest forensic institute in Korea which is under the ministry of Security and Public Administration.

[2]The Korea DVI (Disaster Victims Identification Team) is a temporary task force team which is organised when there are many victims, usually more than 20 persons in a single disaster.

Forensic Archaeology: A Global Perspective, First Edition. Edited by W.J. Mike Groen, Nicholas Márquez-Grant and Robert C. Janaway.

facilitate skeletal inventory and anthropologic examination in the laboratory.

Medico-legal system and the DVI

Prior to exploring the MIM programme further, we provide an overview of the medico-legal system in which we work in the Republic of Korea. When quantities of unidentified skeletal or buried remains are found in suspicious circumstances, the scene investigators from the National Police Agency (NPA) investigate and recover the remains. After getting an order from the prosecutor and a warrant from the court, the remains are transferred to the NFS to identify individuals and determine the manner and cause of death. For skeletonised remains, the medical examiners cooperate with the forensic/physical anthropologists (hereafter anthropologists) based at universities.

In the late 1990s, organisations for identification of human remains from historical events were established, such as the Ministry of National Defence Agency for Killed in Action Recovery and Identification (MAKRI) during the Korean War (1950–1953) (Korea Joint POW/MIA Accounting Command – KJPAC) (국방부 유해발굴단), the Presidential Truth Commission on Suspicious Deaths (의문사진상규명위원회) and the Jeju 4.3 Research Institute (제주 4.3 연구소) for the massacre which occurred during the 1948–1954 uprising on Jeju Island.[3] These organisations have served to identify the deceased killed during these historical events and have engendered cooperation between (forensic) archaeologists, forensic anthropologists and other investigators. Apart from these mass graves, the first use of anthropologists (who also assist with the recovery) in mass fatalities took place in 2002 during the airline crash at Gimhae.

Since then, the NFS has formed the temporary task force team, the Korea DVI, which includes medical examiners, odontologists, DNA experts and other specialists in various fields in the event of mass disasters, and has cooperated with forensic anthropologists, archaeologists and fingerprint experts based at universities or other agencies. The Korea DVI has taken charge of the affairs requested by the government for human identification of the victims of mass disaster or remains in mass graves.

The exact structure of the medico-legal system associated with DVI operations is determined by the location of each disaster. When the mass disaster happens within the territory of the Republic of Korea, the NFS will cooperate with other national institutes, set up the structure for the DVI recoveries and organise the joint investigation DVI team. On the other hand, when the mass disaster happens in a foreign country and there is a suspicion that citizens of the Republic of Korea are among the victims, the rapid deployment team of the Ministry of Foreign Affairs will ask the NFS to form the DVI team.

Mass Identification Manager and the anthropology module

Although forensic archaeology isn't established, recoveries undertaken by anthropologists have used archaeological techniques (Haglund and Sorg 1996). Therefore, we explore here the anthropology module of MIM. This programme consists of three stages; the Rough, Detail and Analysis stages. The Rough stage is made up of lower-graded inventory to classify skeletons roughly, so that you can input basic data set directly into the MIM using mobile devices in the field. The Detail stage contains higher-graded inventory for performing more precise analysis of collected skeletal remains at the laboratories. The Analysis stage facilitates the process of coming to a decision and visualising biological profiles for skeletal remains, based on analysing the results of the Detail stage.

To sort and standardise the osteological constituents of skeletons, the concept of *Class Category* is introduced here, which standardises the overall categorising process for entering data of skeletal constituents. Furthermore, the *NFS code* is built for base formatting of inventory construction, considering various exhumation situations and different groups of participants.

NFS code

A new coding system called the *NFS code* has been invented to sort skeletal constituents briefly and efficiently, and has been applied to the anthropology module in MIM. The NFS code makes the digital storage or recording of human skeletons possible. It is a very simple and powerful method, with which we can communicate easily with software programmers and graphic engineers. The Basis Structure of New Code consists of three parts: front for two digits, middle for short osteological term and last for anatomical position if necessary. In the middle part, the abbreviation of osteological term has three types: one large letter, three large letters and four small letters. For the front two digits, we classified the central axis as 0, the upper limb as 1, the lower limb as 2, the left side as 1 and the right side as 2, so that we can make further combination of codes (Figure 40.1). The central skeletons

[3]The Jeju Uprising was a revolt led by the residents on Jeju Island, off the south coast of the Korean Peninsula, against the government of the Republic of Korea during the period of political instability and Korean War. It is estimated that about 34,000 individuals were killed during this uprising.

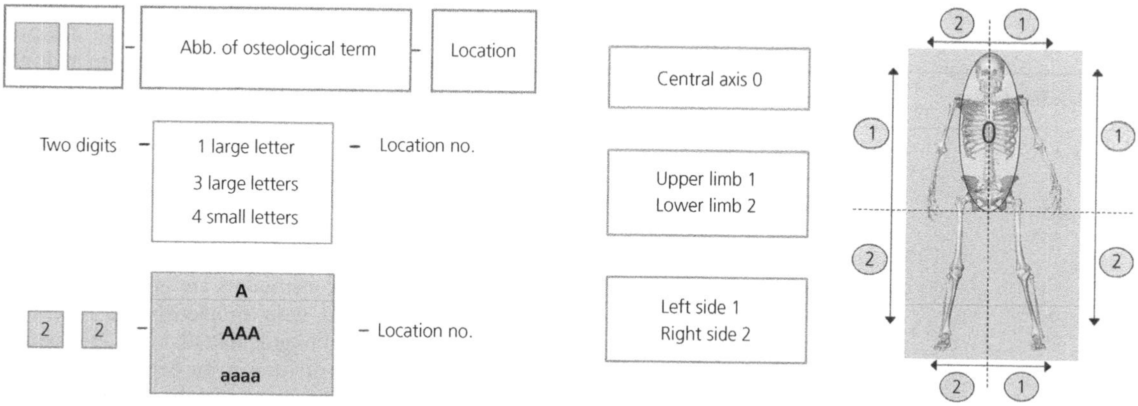

Figure 40.1 Basic structure of coding system (left) and concept of making frontal two digits (right) in the NFS code.

can be further classified as 00, 01, 02, with 00 for the central axial skeleton, 01 for the left-side intermediate bone attached to the central skeleton and 02 for the right-side intermediate bone attached to the central skeleton. The appendicular skeletons can be further classified as 11, 12, 21, 22, with 11 for the left upper limb, 12 for the right upper limb, 21 for the left lower limb and 22 for the right lower limb. As a result, each bone is assigned with two digits for the anatomical position and all human bones can be assigned with the NFS code. To clarify, Table 40.1 presents the examples of NFS codes for the bones of central and appendicular skeletons. Meanwhile, four small letters, such as 'luna' for lunate or 'hdpp' for hand phalanges proximal, are used to identify small bones.

To classify whole skeletons more effectively, we adopt the concept of the 'Class' system in the anthropology module. To distinguish between whole skeletons and individual bones, six classes were introduced to the module, following the sequence of classes which are designated from whole skeleton as Class 1 to individual bone parts as Class 6. At the level of Class 5, the NFS code identifies individual bones (Table 40.2). Moreover, in the case of fragmented bones which cannot be designated by the NFS code, seven groups of unclassified code (UC; Table 40.3) are used. Using this classification system, we can express skeletal remains variously according to the level of works and analysis.

Table 40.1 Examples of NFS codes and descriptions.

NFS codes	Descriptions
00CRA	Cranium
00T12	12th thoracic vertebra
01R07	7th rib (left)
02CLA	Clavicle (right)
12HUM	Humerus (right)
12luna	Lunate (right)
12mtca02	2nd metacarpal bone (right)
12hdpp02	2nd hand phalanges proximal (right)
12hdpm02	2nd hand phalanges middle (right)
12hdpd02	2nd hand phalanges distal (right)

Table 40.2 Inventory category of anthropology module.

Category	Subject	Stage
Class 1	Whole skeleton	Rough
Class 2	Axial and appendicular skeletons	
Class 3	Regional bones of skeleton	
Class 4	Subregional bones	
Class 5	Individual bones (NFS code)	Detail
Class 6	Parts of individual bone	

Rough stage

The Rough stage is the process dealing with the Class 1–4 inventorial data set, and each directory has a check box to hide and open the list. At this stage, brief comments and photos related to exhumed bones can be uploaded and managed. Since this stage is performed in the field, the interface is intuitively organised for prompt action, to save time in response (Figure 40.2). This stage will often be performed by (forensic) archaeologists in many countries.

For input data at the Rough stage, a skeleton exposed during the (forensic) archaeological exhumation needs to be classified as one individual and should be given a unique post-mortem (PM) number, allocated in the MIM anthropology module. It is important that this module be used when exhumed remains are deemed likely to be one person. If the exhumed skeletons seem to be made up of several individuals and are intermingled, groups of bones that appear to be one person should be kept separate and allocated separate PM numbers. Several PM numbers can then

Table 40.3 Explanation of unclassified (UC) category for Rough stage.

Unclassified bones	Descriptions
UC skull	Count the fragments when difficult to discriminate the parts of skull
UC vertebrae	Count the number when difficult to discriminate the type of vertebrae
UC ribs	Count the number when difficult to discriminate the side and order of ribs
UC hands	Count the number when difficult to discriminate the side and order of hand bones
UC feet	Count the number when difficult to discriminate the side and order of foot bones
UC hands and feet	Count the number when difficult to discriminate the parts of hand or foot bones
UC unknown	Count the number of packets when difficult to discriminate which parts of bones

be reassociated later into one number, according to the results of various tests. If the side (left, right) of bones such as ribs, hands and feet are recognised, but their correct anatomical order cannot be designated (e.g. for vertebrae T1, T2, T3), they can simply be numbered at Class 4 in the Rough stage. These records are then transferred to the Detail stage and can be further classified.

In the tree structure of skeletons on the left side of the screen of MIM, the presence of bones can be checked. Photos of exhumed bones can be uploaded and annotated in a pop-up window. In the pop-up window, particular photos can be selected for use in the Analysis stage later. A memo icon allows the addition of brief and important comments about bone condition, for example, its taphonomic stage.

If the bones are severely fragmented and cannot be identified correctly, the number of fragments or packets can simply be recorded using UC. After attaching photos and comments, these records are transferred to the Detail stage and can be further classified there. The UC can be revised through identifying osteological characteristics at the Detail stage, through further examination by osteologists or anthropologists.

The 'save' button at the bottom of the screen will store all the data for each unique PM number, and will activate the 'next' button leading to the Detail stage.

Detail stage

The Detail stage is the process dealing with the Class 5–6 inventorial data set. At this stage, exhumed bones are transported from the field to the laboratory for more detailed osteological examination. The Class 5 content corresponds to the NFS code, and the more delicate parts of bone such as the cranium, the sternum and the hip bone that the NFS code cannot reflect are managed in Class 6. When you check the bones in Class 4 of the Rough stage, the subordinate bone codes of Class 5 and 6 are selected by default. After reviewing and examining the skeleton in more detail, the presence and status of each bone are revised and expressed on the scheme (Figure 40.3).

When osteological constituents are entered, selected bones are colour-coded, with complete bones as yellow, burnt bones as red and fragmented and damaged bones as blue on the tree structure in the Detail stage. This scheme and visualisation process of the NFS code helps the worker to recognise overall anthropological examination results at a glance. Comparing bone specimens with the colour coding allows skeletal inventory, which was insufficient at the Rough stage to be improved. After saving all of this information, the next step, the Analysis stage, is reached.

Analysis stage

The Analysis stage is the process where we can input basic information regarding personal identification (e.g. age, sex). Considering the characteristics of victim identification in mass disasters, rapidity is one of the most important factors. Therefore, simple methods which are generally recognised by anthropologists are used, so that information on individuals can be effectively supplied.

Sex, height and age are estimated using methods which are generally accepted in the fields of anthropology. Sex and age are estimated using non-metric methods which make it possible to analyse intuitively, referring to the methods suggested in *Standards for Data Collection from Human Skeletal Remains* (Buikstra and Ubelaker 1994). The anthropologist responsible for analysis of sex and age can input the estimated results with the observed features on the programme. The height range is automatically calculated using maximal length of long bones, referring to the methods suggested by Trotter (1970). It is also possible for others to see all the estimated information with photos on the screen, which makes peer review effective.

Sex estimation

The non-metric method based on skull and hip bones is used for sex estimation, which is more convenient in the field (Figure 40.4). Five parts of the skull and six items of the hip bone are observed (Buikstra and Ubelaker 1994; Walker 2005, 2008). Sex is estimated from the characteristics determined in the observations discussed earlier. Viewing photos from the Rough stage, the result can be confirmed more accurately. The process of estimation of sex is not automatic; therefore the anthropologist who is responsible determines the sex based on data, and inputs the result in person.

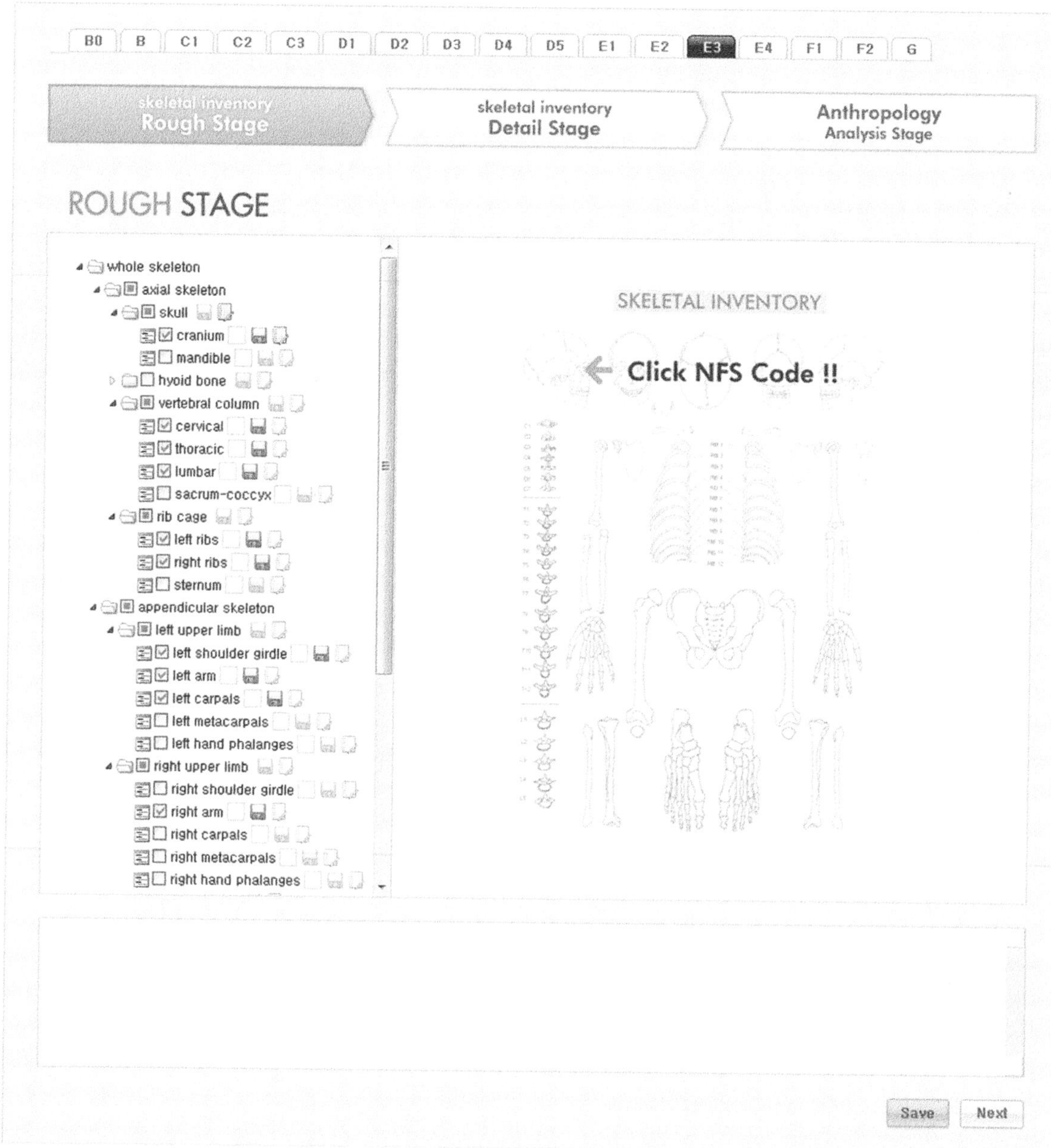

Figure 40.2 Display of Rough stage of the MIM anthropology module.

Height estimation

For height estimation, the maximum lengths of femur, humerus and tibia are measured. The mean and range of height are calculated automatically and displayed when this data is fed as input (Figure 40.5). To estimate the height, it is a principle that we should use separate equations for corresponding populations. However, in this programme we have used the equations by Trotter (1970) for stature estimation applied to several populations. In the future, the MIM anthropology module will be revised to reflect the equations of different populations and height can then be estimated more accurately.

Age estimation

For age estimation, the pubic symphysis and auricular surface of the hip bone, in which the age-related changes are relatively clear, are used (Todd 1920; Lovejoy et al. 1985; Katz and Suchey 1986). As the purpose of MIM is to manage the compilation of data quickly and efficiently in a variety of situations, age is

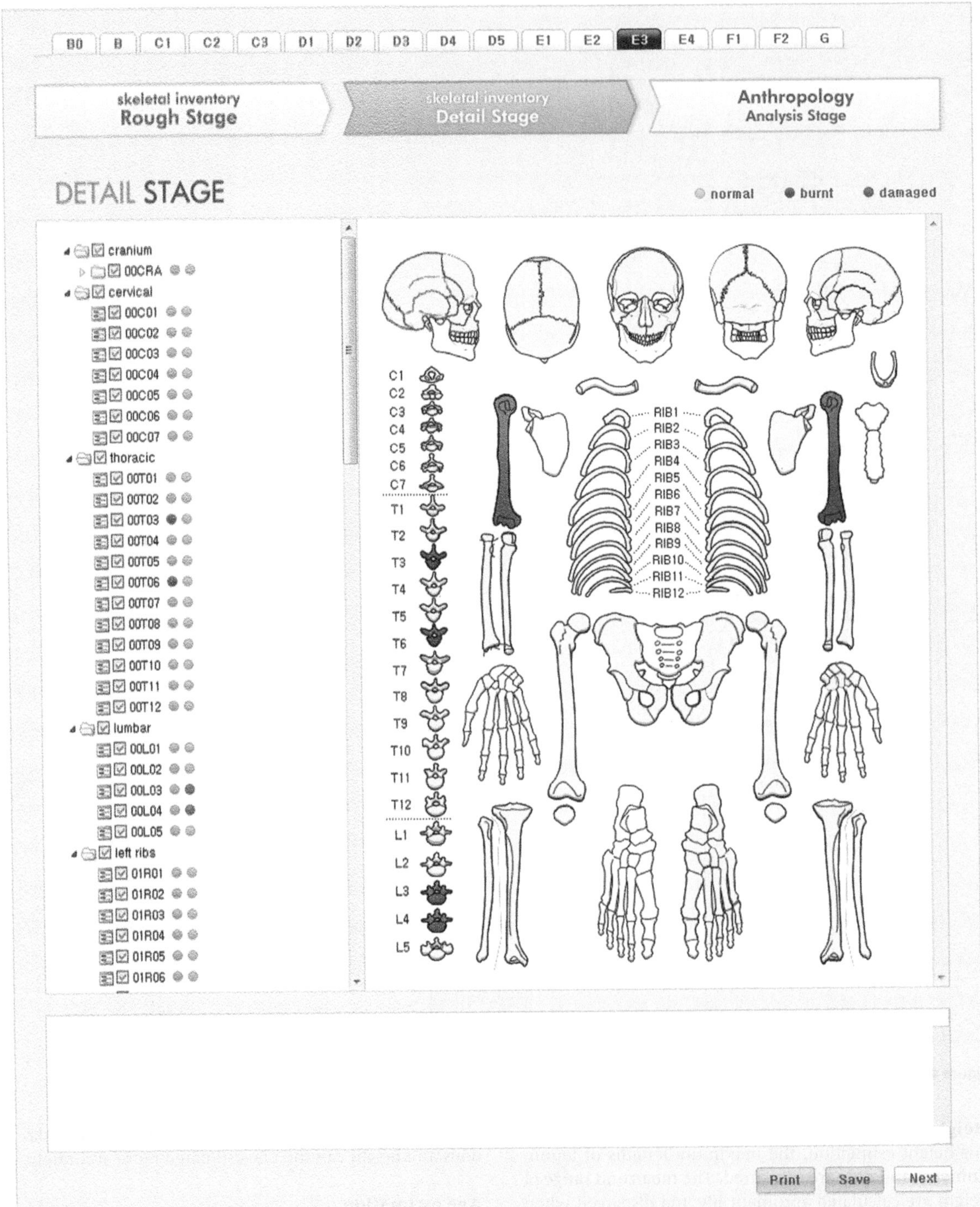

Figure 40.3 Display of Detail stage of the MIM anthropology module. If you check on the left side, the colour of that code can be changed on the scheme.

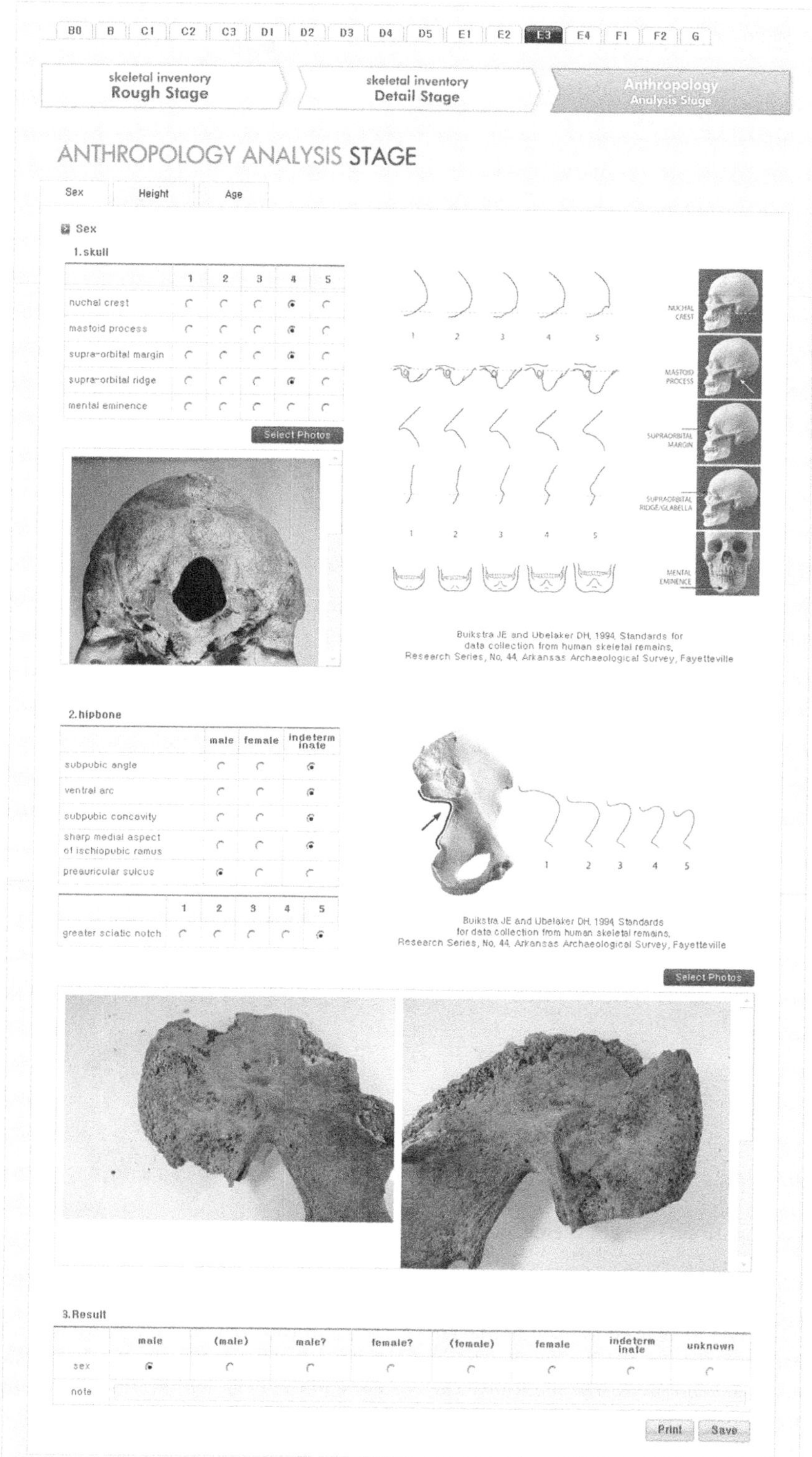

Figure 40.4 Display of Analysis stage for sex determination in the MIM anthropology module.

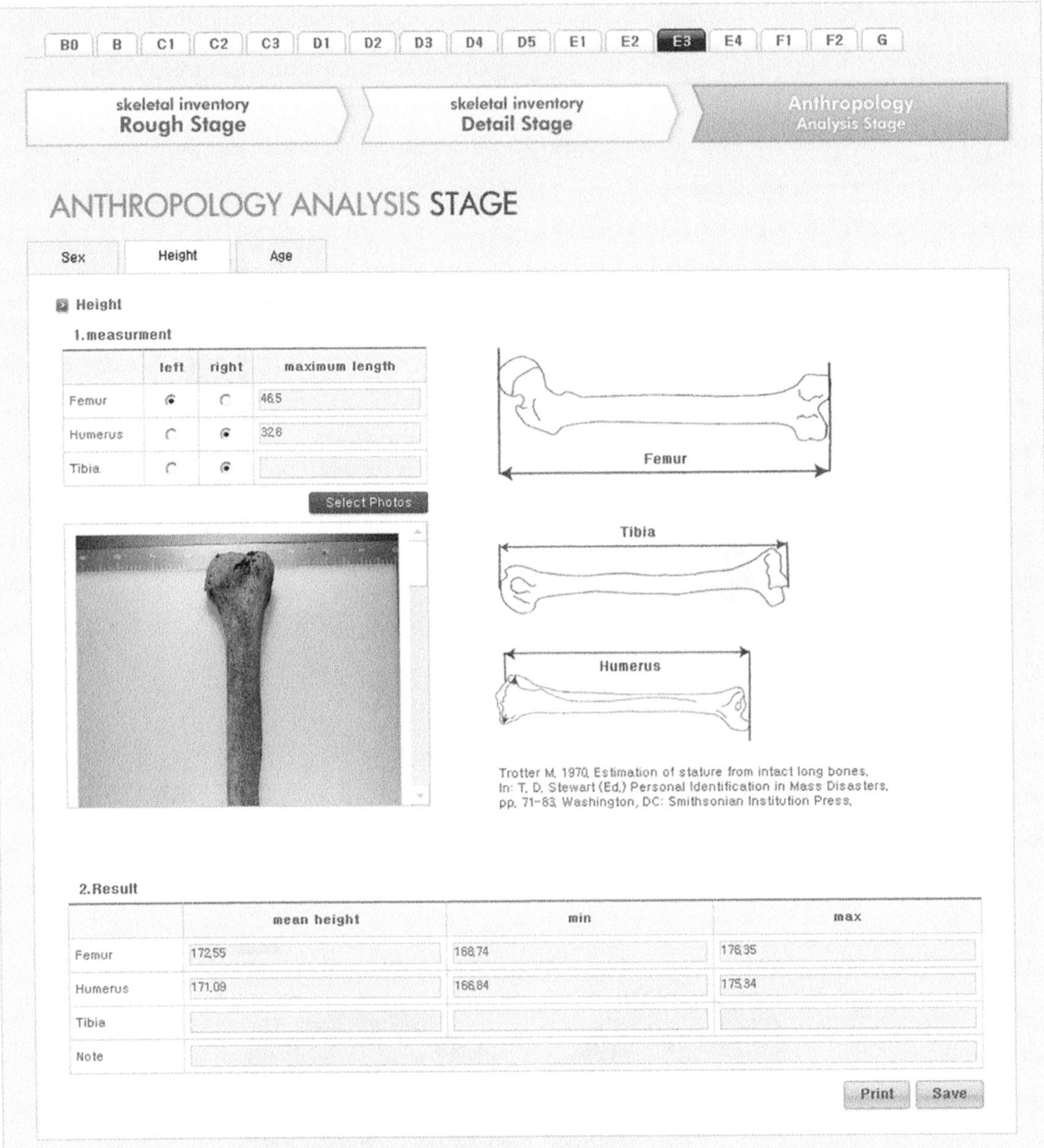

Figure 40.5 Display of Analysis stage for height estimation in the anthropology module.

currently only estimated for adults. In the near future, however, the module will be revised to include the age estimation of subadults.

The estimation of age is not done automatically. The anthropologist who is responsible inputs the estimated figure using the pop-up windows of 'auricular surface' and 'pubic symphyseal surface' based on observed features (Figure 40.6).

Report of additional analysis

The anthropology module in MIM has been developed focusing on the work on mass disasters which should be done in the field, within time constraints, and has been designed for these circumstances with simple metric or non-metric methods. Moreover, additional test results can be entered by anthropologists if necessary. Peer review can also be used to reduce errors in analysis.

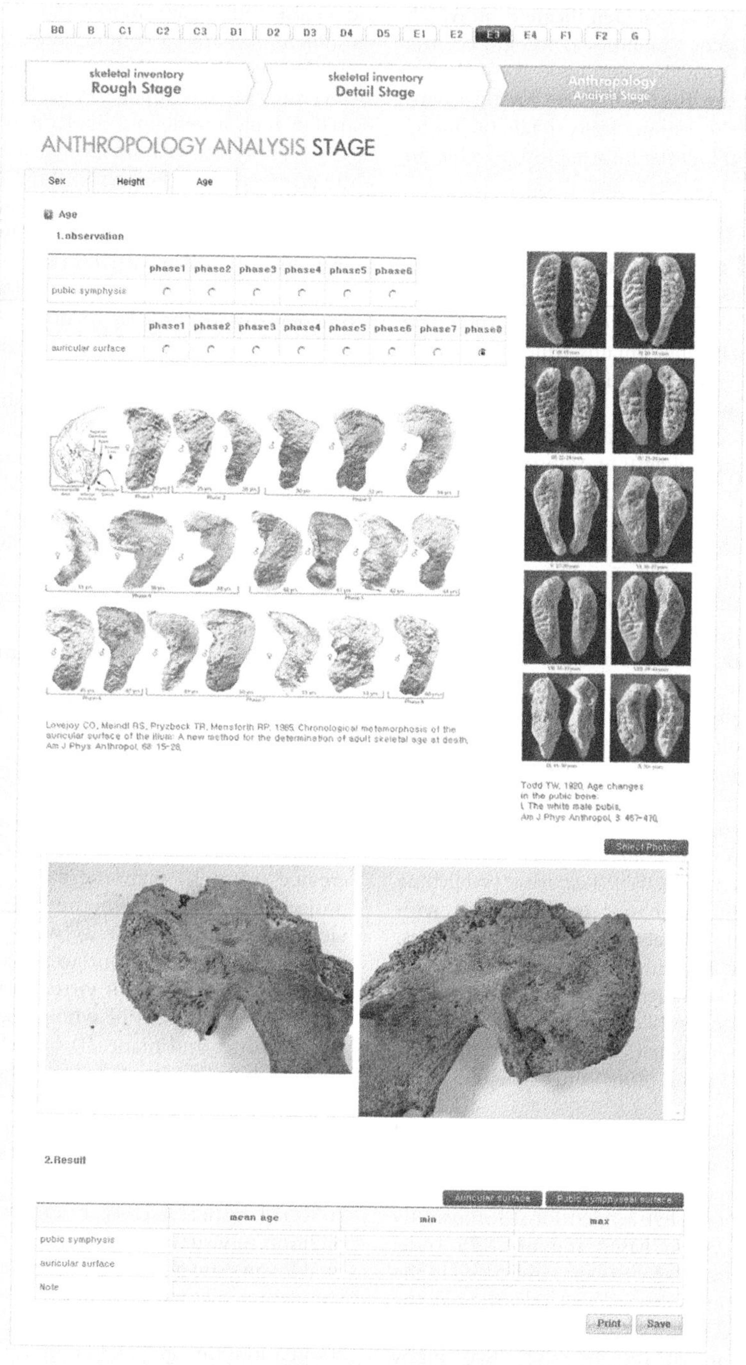

Figure 40.6 Display of Analysis stage for age estimation in the anthropology module.

In the final stage of individual identification, in which all information from other modules is integrated, the anthropology module provides only basic skeletal constituents of estimated sex, height and age. An anthropological report can then be automatically made, including a skeletal inventory and all the information possible on the biological profile.

Discussion and conclusion

Forensic and/or physical anthropologists record a 'biological profile' of skeletal remains which consists of inventory of bones present, Minimum Number of Individuals (MNI), ancestry, age, sex, stature, metric and non-metric characteristics, trauma and pathology. Forensic/physical anthropologists and (forensic) archaeologists generally prefer manual recording using recording forms which show an outline image of all the bones. They can be coloured in or annotated, and check boxes or tables allow inputting of appropriate data. For inventory, some of these anthropologists also list the bones by element. Recording forms and protocols of *Standards* by Buikstra and Ubelaker (1994) are frequently used among anthropologists. Institutions, museums and universities often develop their own recording form or computer programme which better suits their needs, and many of these are based on the *Standards*. Computer software and databases for electronic recording of skeletons are being developed around the world in order to manage large numbers of skeletal remains better. The *WORD database* (Wellcome Osteological Research Database)[4] is a database with records of over 11,000 archaeological skeletal remains, created by the Centre for Human Bioarchaeology at the Museum of London, UK. Researchers can download and utilise it to seek samples of archaeological skeletal remains. *Osteoware*,[5] created by the Smithsonian Institute, US, is a data input programme which is freely distributed.

The NFS, while processing over a 100 cases of skeletal remains per year ranging from clandestine burials to mass disasters, at the request of the police or relevant government department, felt a need for a forensically oriented recording system based the on NFS code. Although (forensic) archaeologists are rarely used in the Republic of Korea, this software will ensure that the police will record the bones in situ and will therefore improve identification of the remains. Not many recording systems employ a code for each bone element. Even if some systems do have a code such as the WORD database and use a numeric system, using a sequence of numbers is hard to comprehend. Furthermore, many existing recording systems are not forensically oriented since they are developed to suit the recording of regular archaeological remains. Skeletal remains sent to the NFS for forensic examination will be first subjected to the primary process using NRP (NFS Report Processor), which is developed for autopsy reports. During the process using NRP, the focus of examination will be providing the police with information regarding positive identification and cause of death as soon as possible. The time-consuming process of documenting which completes the biological profile, including information which is unnecessary for the police investigation, is performed in the secondary process using the anthropology module in MIM and the related data is stored in NSD (NFS Skeletal Database). The anthropology module, NRP and NSD should be linked and can also be used to create various statistical data, to link cases and/or individuals automatically and to match the information with the missing persons database automatically.

Clandestine remains are often found in a completely skeletonised state in old burial grounds or fields. Identification of such remains starts with categorising relevant evidence and various non-invasive examinations such as collection of metric data. Damage to the remains is often inevitable at the end because of invasive identification methods. Skeletal information contained in the remains can be lost during such a process. To address this issue, the NFS launched a project whereby a virtual model of the skeletal remains was created using 3D scanning data. The objective of this project is to find out whether it is possible to create a virtual model of intact as well as already damaged human skeletal bodies and to build a stepping stone for a relatively new field of virtual forensic anthropology. We scanned two sets of whole body skeletons using a microscanner and made 3D models of them, and then aligned them in virtual space using software. By comparing the metric data collected from actual skeletons and virtual models, we made RPs (Rapid Prototypes) using 3D modelling data. In the near future, it is recommended that 3D scanning data of skeletal remains be collected using microscanners and CT scanners, in addition to visual evidence from crime scenes. This will enable investigators to re-create 3D remodelling and simulation in more detail, improving reliability of scientific examination methods. It can also provide the foundation for application in the fields of medicine, forensic/physical anthropology, forensic archaeology and engineering.

[4]For more information, see: http://archive.museumoflondon.org.uk/Centre-for-Human-Bioarchaeology/Database/ (last accessed November 2013).

[5]For more information, see: http://osteoware.si.edu/ (last accessed November 2013).

References

Buikstra, J. E. and Ubelaker, D. H. 1994. *Standards for Data Collection from Human Skeletal Remains*. Fayetteville, Arkansas Archaeological Survey. Research Series No. 44.

Chung, N. E. 2004. *Daegu Subway Disaster – Mass Disaster and Management for Victims*. Seoul, National Institutes of Scientific Investigation.

Chung, N. E. and Yoon, C. Y. 2009. *Southeast Asia Tsunami Disaster – Korea DVI*. Seoul, National Institute of Scientific Investigation.

Chung, N. E., Lee, H. Y., Seo, J. K. et al. 1996. Individual identification of dead bodies in Sampoong department store collapse. *Annual Report of NISI* 28, 3–32.

Chung, N. E., Park, D. K., Kim, Y. S. and Lee, W. Y. 2009. *Burial Skeletal Remains in Daehakro*. Seoul, Korea, Official Report of NISI.

Haglund, W. D. and Sorg, M. H. (eds.). 1996. *Forensic Taphonomy: The Postmortem Fate of Human Remains*. Boca Raton, FL, CRC Press, pp. 39–64.

Hunter, J., Roberts, C. and Martin, A. 1996. *Studies in Crime: An Introduction to Forensic Archaeology*. London, Routledge.

Katz, D. and Suchey, J. M. 1986. Age determination of the male Os pubis. *American Journal of Physical Anthropology* 69, 427–435.

Lovejoy, O., Meindl, R. S., Pryzbeck, T. R. and Mensforth, R. P. 1985. Chronological metamorphosis of the auricular surface of the ileum: a new method for the determination of adult skeletal age at death. *American Journal of Physical Anthropology* 68, 15–28.

Park, D. K., Park, K. H., Ko, J. S. et al. 2009. The role of forensic anthropology in the examination of the Daegu subway disaster (2003, Korea). *Journal of Forensic Sciences* 54(3), 513–518.

Scott, D. D. and Connor, M. 2001. The role and future of archaeology in forensic science. *Historical Archaeology* 35(1), 101–104.

Todd, T. W. 1920. Age changes in the pubic bone. *American Journal of Physical Anthropology* 4, 1–70.

Trotter, M. 1970. Estimation of stature from intact long bones. In T. D. Stewart (ed.), *Personal Identification in Mass Disasters*, 71–83. Wahington, DC, Smithsonian Institution Press.

Walker, P. L. 2005. Greater sciatic notch morphology: sex, age and population differences. *American Journal of Physical Anthropology* 127, 385–391.

Walker, P. L. 2008. Sexing skulls using discriminant function analysis of visually assessed traits. *American Journal of Physical Anthropology* 127, 39–50.

CHAPTER 41

Forensic archaeology: an introduction from the United Arab Emirates

Khudooma Saeed Al Naimi

Forensic Biology Section, Forensic Evidence Department, Abu Dhabi Police General Directorate, Ministry of interior, Abu Dhabi, United Arab Emirates

The principles of forensic archaeology are regarded, generally speaking, as the location, documentation, recovery and examination of evidence. Whilst traditional archaeology deals with the more ancient past, forensic archaeology focuses on recent events and specifically in medico-legal contexts. In Arthur Conan Doyle's book *The Musgrave Ritual*, Sherlock Holmes may have used forensic archaeology when entering a crime scene: 'From this starting point I proceeded to step, having first taken the cardinal points by my pocket compass' [surveying and identifying the north at a crime scene]; and 'Ten steps with each foot took me along parallel with the wall of the house, and again I marked my spot with a peg [locating the area of interest]and "an under" he cried[examining any *buried* or hidden evidence]' (Doyle 2001, 168).

The United Arab Emirates (UAE) is a federation state comprising seven Emirates (equivalent to Principalities) named Abu Dhabi, Dubai, Sharjah, Umm al-Quwain, Ajman, Ras al-Khaimah and Fujairah. The country gained its independence on 2 December 1971. Today, the UAE has achieved tremendous progress in a number of fields, including forensic sciences, and this continues to progress favourably in accordance with the needs of society.

Archaeologically, some of the earliest evidence in the UAE dates to the late Middle Stone Age or Middle Palaeolithic 130–150,000 years ago (Armitage et al. 2011; Mark Beech, personal communication 2013). Today archaeological surveys and excavations are undertaken by UAE specialists as well as foreign scientists.

This archaeological tradition and previous archaeological fieldwork will have a strong influence on the development of forensic archaeology in this country. In short, the current status of forensic archaeology in the UAE will be briefly discussed.

Medico-legal framework

In the UAE the medico-legal framework consists of Federal and Local Forensic Services which can be summarised as follows.

At the *federal level* Abu Dhabi is the centre of administration of the federal authorities for forensic medicine. At the federal level, there is the Forensic Medical Administration إدارة الطب الشرعي. The forensic medical service covers the emirates of Sharjah, Ajman, Fujairah and Umm al-Quwain. In the Emirates of Ajman there is also a 'crime scene village' which is a central training facility to prepare crime scene investigators in the Northern Emirates (Sharjah, Ajman, Fujairah, Ras al-Khaimah and Umm al-Quwain). This training centre is linked to the Federal Ministry of the Interior in Abu Dhabi In addition to the current facilities and resources, there is a plan to establish a federal centralised Forensic Laboratory (Emaratalyoum 2013).

At the *local level* the following Emirates have their own forensic capabilities:

- *Abu Dhabi* has a Forensic Medicine Department (إدارة الطب الشرعي) and a Forensic Toxicology Laboratory (مختبر الطب الشرعي). These two departments are part of the Judicial Department of Abu Dhabi, General Attorney's Office. The Forensic Toxicology Laboratory processes samples and evidence received from Abu Dhabi and the other Emirates. There is also a Crime Scene Department and Forensic Evidence Department (laboratory) (إدارة الأدلة الجنائية) and the Criminal Medical Office (مكتب الطب الجنائي), based at the Abu Dhabi Police General Directorate. The laboratory has branches in the western area of Abu Dhabi and the city of Al Ain. The responsibilities of the Criminal Medical Office include attending crime scenes to assess whether a case is of

Forensic Archaeology: A Global Perspective, First Edition. Edited by W.J. Mike Groen, Nicholas Márquez-Grant and Robert C. Janaway.

forensic or non-forensic interest, and especially to provide advice and support to the police (Police General Directorate) if there are human remains at a crime scene. There is also a crime scene training centre run by Abu Dhabi Police connected to Crime Scene Department.

- *Dubai* has a Forensic Medicine Department (الطب الشرعي) and a Forensic Laboratory المختبر الجنائي related to the Dubai Police General Directorate and specifically its Public Administration of Criminal Evidence and Criminology.
- *Sharjah* has a Forensic Laboratory (المختبر الجنائي) that is connected to the Police General Headquarters; forensic medicine is attached to it but is actually part of the Federal Ministry of Justice.
- *Ras Al Khaimah* and *Fujairah* Emirates also have their own Forensic Laboratories, linked to their own Police Forces. *Ras Al Khaimah* also has its own section of forensic medicine.

Legal and expert witness systems

The UAE legal system consists of federal and local courts in each Emirate. Its court system is divided into three levels which are the First Instance Court, the Court of Appeal and the Cessation Court. The *Sharia Court* (Islamic Court) deals with civil cases regarding personal status such as divorce, inheritance and marriage.

There is a Federal Law which regulates scientific expertise in the country. This Law is issued by the H. H. president of UAE and describes the qualifications or accreditation needed to become an expert. It also describes the regulations regarding penalties, fees and the formation of a committee of Expert Affairs (Bou Malhab and Abdel-Nabi 2013).

In the Federal Ministry of Justice there is a separate administration for experts, which holds a database of their contacts in case a particular expertise is required for a certain case. On the website of the Ministry there is a link providing information on how to register as an expert. An expert is allowed to apply to be considered by the Ministry of Justice (2013).

The Emirate of Abu Dhabi has its own expert administration. One of the systems in place is to send a text message to the expert to inform them about a case assigned to that person and the requirement to attend the administration office to receive the case file. That results in a more rapid response (Judicial Department 2013).

Archaeology as a field of forensic science

Forensic archaeology can be defined in general terms as stated earlier and is primarily used to search for and recover buried forensic evidence, in assisting in the investigation of a case, in providing dating information where possible and in providing assessment of archaeological artefacts which have been looted and have been traded illegally.

In the UAE forensic archaeology is not an established stand-alone forensic science discipline. Currently, there are no forensic archaeologists in the UAE, but there is knowledge concerning its theories and methods. This knowledge has been gained by specific scientists and experts (including forensic anthropologists) working in police laboratories and cultural/archaeological institutions, such as museums. There is indeed an increased potential for forensic archaeologists to be present in the UAE in the near future, due to continual training and the recognisable need to use forensic archaeology in the field of crime scene investigation.

Forensic archaeological theories and principals could be employed in the UAE in several types of forensic cases, such as:

- searching for buried human remains or objects using geophysical techniques;
- documenting buried human remains or any other types of evidence;
- recovery of buried human remains or other types of evidences;
- recovery of human remains and other types of evidence from burned cars and other fire scenes;
- recovery of humans remains and other types of evidence from water environments;
- estimation of post-mortem interval (PMI), for example, by assessing the contextual deposition of human remains and any associated personal effects such as clothing;
- participation in the excavation of mass graves in neighbouring countries; and
- discovery of looted archaeological artefacts.

In 1983 an air crash accident happened in Abu Dhabi sadly resulting in the deaths of 112 individuals (Clark 1986). During the examination, Clark (1986) indicated that the accident site had not been mapped with a grid, that the remains had not been recorded in situ before removal and that the body bags were unnumbered. This accident shows how forensic archaeological techniques could have helped in the recovery and documentation of human remains at the scene of the accident. Today, there have been positive developments in the forensic field in the UAE which will eradicate any past problems regarding the documentation and recovery of human remains.

Case studies from the UAE

This section discusses several case studies from the UAE where forensic archaeology was or could have been employed to help process the scene. Therefore, archaeology is promoted here for the different scenarios which have been appearing in recent years in the UAE.

Washed-up body on Red Island

Jazirat al-Hamra, or Red Island, is located in the Emirates of Ras Al Khaimah. On 14 August 2009, the dead body of a female was found on the shore of the island. The female was wearing a coloured T-shirt (Emaratalyoum 2009). In this case, the body was found well preserved on the shore. Washed-up bodies have been found on several occasions in the UAE. Sometimes these bodies are naturally buried afterwards in the sand or scattered between rocks. Although forensic archaeology has not been applied in these cases until now, these are scenarios where surface documentation and interpretation by a forensic archaeologist would have been useful.

Dead infant found in the desert

On 24 March 2013, a dead infant was found near the Al-Daid-Sharjah highway. The body of the infant was wrapped in newspaper. The infant's age was estimated as being 2–3 weeks old and the PMI was estimated approximately as 2 weeks. The body was sent to the Forensic Laboratory in Sharjah for autopsy and DNA sampling (Al Kitbi 2013). Although no forensic archaeology was required, this case provides some future planning. If the remains had been in a more advanced state of decomposition and scattered due to animal scavenging, then forensic archaeology (and anthropology) would have been useful.

Decapitated body in Al Samha area

On 20 March 2013, a decapitated body was found in Al Samha in Abu Dhabi. The head was found under a tree and the rest of the body was found buried in a nearby location. The body had been deposited in a shallow grave. The body was exposed after workers discovered it whilst removing rubbish from that area (Gulf News 2013). Forensic archaeological techniques were used here by the police (author and crime scene staff), documenting the remains as found in situ and recovering them. Identification was aided by an ID card in a T-shirt found near the body. Clothes recovered from the scene were examined in the laboratory for name, cuts, damages, laundry number, plant evidence and so on (Figure 41.1). After further investigation, a person who had been reported missing was deemed likely to be the deceased. A DNA test was carried out with a body sample and with DNA from a toothbrush and the results provided a positive identification.

Body of an infant at Al Mamzar Beach (Dubai)

On 18 December 2013, a male found the wrapped body of an infant partially exposed at Al Mamzar Beach (Dubai). The body had been buried, but had been exposed by the tide. The police attended the scene and after a post-mortem examination manner and cause of death were established as well as an age of 30–40 days for the infant (Fuda 2013). In this case, although archaeology was not clearly employed, it was recognised that methodological excavation around the body would have revealed the original position of the body when buried, the depth of the grave and an understanding of the deposition environment influencing the possible formation of the adipocerous tissue in the infant's body.

Woman killed and buried in Oman

The body of a UAE national female was found buried in a village on the UAE and Oman border. The body had been buried at a farm and the burial was located after a visual search of the grounds and with the use of police dogs (Emaratalyoum 2010). The documentation by the police in this forensic archaeology clandestine grave case was important in indicating how the grave was dug and how the remains were deposited (Feder 2009). Three individuals were detained and charged with this murder.

Buried body in Ras Al Khaimah

A man was killed in Ras Al Khaimah by two individuals who worked in construction. After killing the person they transported the body to an area of Shimal in Ras Al Khaimah. The murder had occurred at Al Dhait, a sandy area south of the Emirates, while the burial was in the Shimal area in the north, which is a mountainous area. The distance between both sites is about 10 km. During interrogation the suspect confessed that one of them held the victim and the other strangled him with a rope. In this case, the burial site was reached using information provided by the suspects and the body was found in an area of vegetation, rocks, gravel, dry and green grasses, trees and waste around the burial site. The forensic staff of the police dug around the body and revealed a shallow grave up to 30 cm deep (Ameen 2011). Good forensic archaeological techniques helpful in reveal the condition of the burial which useful in build the case with more materialistic evidence.

Burned human remains in a car

One of the special situations where forensic archaeology has also been useful in the UAE is its application to fire scenes where human remains were contained in a vehicle and where much fragmentation of the skeleton occurred, including the mixing with debris from the burned vehicle. Careful recovery and documenting of the burned human remains will have an impact on the solution of the case (Symes et al. 2012). One case involved a forensic anthropologist (the author) when a burned car was moved to a secure police area (Figure 41.2). Whilst the initial recovery of the burned human remains was undertaken by medical and police staff the forensic anthropologist using archaeological techniques was able to recover further human skeletal

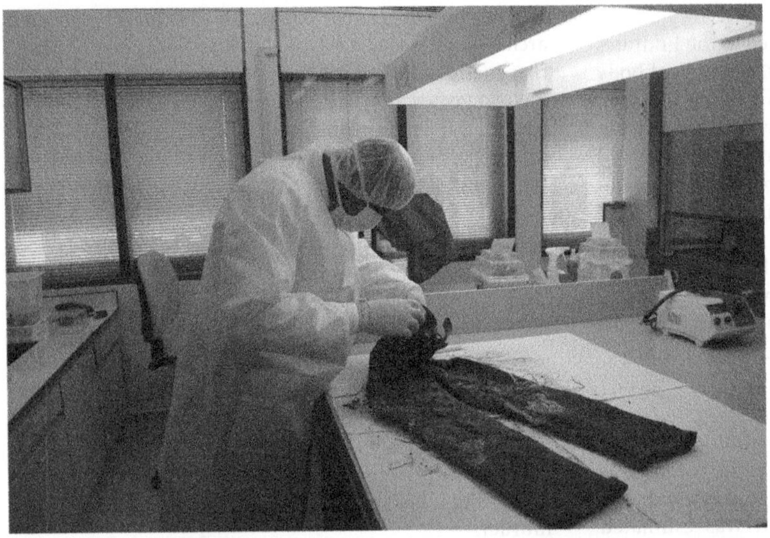

Figure 41.1 The author examine a trouser of body in the laboratory to extract for identification and possibly to reach the condition of burial and death.

Figure 41.2 The author examining a burned car during the recovery of human remains. It is recommended that examination begins in the driver's location where the body was found. Other parts of the car should also be examined for osteological or other evidence (Image courtesy: Abu Dhabi Police).

material and other possibly associated evidence. Arson experts also examined the car at a later stage to recover any possible evidence related to the cause of the fire. There should be a strong cooperation between forensic archaeologist and arson expert as some evidence can be examined by both, for instance a piece of cloth can be examine for identification and for hydrocarbon present.

Skeletonised body on the beach

In this case, partially buried skeletal remains were discovered on a beach. The police technicians, directed by a forensic anthropologist with knowledge of archaeological techniques (the author), worked around the body to locate the edges of the grave. Due to the fast-moving tides, part of the skeleton was recovered in bulk with sand so it could be examined in the morgue at a later stage. In the morgue it was decided that the wet sand, which also included botanical remains, should be wet sieved (Figure 41.3). This process enabled the recovery of small human bones such as phalanges prior to forensic anthropological examination.

Burnt human body in a house

Cooperation between the forensic archaeologist and the fire investigator during examination of a fire scene is critical. In one case related to the burned remains of a young man in a house the forensic evidence required good location and documentation, as the recovery had to be fast due to family pressure. After locating the human remains, a forensic anthropologist (the author) started

Figure 41.3 The author recovering human remains, after washing the soil that was removed from the body (Image courtesy: Abu Dhabi Police).

cleaning around the lower limbs, carefully removing any other burnt material first (e.g. wood, plastic, fabric). During this process, burnt electrical cables were found and prior to excavating further the arson expert was called to document these cables and recover them. This process was repeated until the whole body was freed from debris which would eventually be examined for analysis of accelerants. The subsequent work in the morgue by the forensic anthropologist, forensic pathologist and the arson investigation expert is also crucial; while the post-mortem examination is taking place material of interest to the fire investigator may be found. Likewise, the archaeological record can also be examined in conjunction with the forensic anthropology/pathology examination for example, when examining the burnt remains in a morgue and understanding the position of the body in relation to the fire.

Interaction between classical and forensic archaeology

Archaeologists can learn from forensic science and forensic scientists can learn from archaeological theories and methodologies. Here are a couple of examples regarding the cooperation within the UAE between forensic scientists and regular archaeologists in an archaeological context. Although these examples are archaeological in nature and not forensic, they illustrate and emphasise that there are many experienced and qualified archaeologists in the UAE whose skills should not be undervalued for forensic investigation in the future. What it also emphasises is the close collaboration between forensic science and archaeology in the UAE and that this collaboration can be the basis for establishing a strong ground for cooperation in the type of forensic archaeological scenarios outlined in the previous section.

There is a good level of interaction between forensic scientists/anthropologists and classical archaeologists in the UAE and the nearby countries which has produced publications. Some of these interactions are as follows:

aDNA studies

In 2004 the author was successful in building up a relationship between the Abu Dhabi Island archaeological survey represented by Dr Mark Beech and the head of the Abu Dhabi Police Forensic Laboratory in order to use forensic DNA techniques to examine Neolithic human remains from Marawah Island in the Western area of Abu Dhabi Emirates. This also provided a good opportunity for a forensic scientist to test and develop forensic kits and other methods when dealing with challenging samples (Beech et al. 2005).

To show the public interest in applying forensic science in archaeology, a press conference (Figure 41.4) was held in the Forensic Laboratory to present the findings from the skeletal and a DNA analysis from the remains found in Marawah Island to the public.

Hand print and stature estimation

Anthropological techniques were used to search and document hand prints found at an archaeological site in the Khutwa area in Oman. The hand prints were on dried *sarooj* material discs, which were used in building water channel systems (*falaj*) in the neighbouring country of Oman. After taking the measurements of the hand prints, forensic/physical anthropological equations were used to estimate the stature of the *falaj* builders, taking into consideration that this method can potentially also be used in forensic hand and foot print examination.

Figure 41.4 A press conference held at the Forensic Evidence Department in Abu Dhabi. The photograph shows police officers, archaeologists and forensic personnel presenting the findings from the DNA examination (Image courtesy: WAM, UAE).

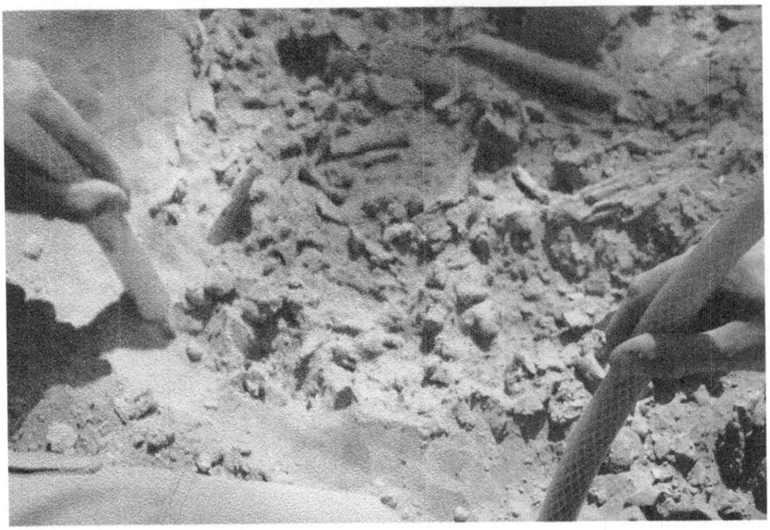

Figure 41.5 This process suction excavation process of a Broze-age tomb in Al Ain city, United Arab Emirates. The process can be use also in the forensic condition with precaution which can be use to remove sand with evidence around the body or the skeleton and collect it in a container which can be further examined in the laboratory.

Insect remains from a Bronze Age tomb

Insect remains from an archaeological site were documented and collected by a forensic anthropologist (the author) during volunteer work with the French archaeological mission in 2006 in Al Ain city at the site of a Bronze Age tomb (Al Naimi 2009). This is another example where forensic entomologists and other forensic scientists collaborated with archaeologists.

Archaeological techniques:

Classical archaeologists have vast experience in the environment which they search and recover archaeologists items. Forensic archaeological can learn and experience exchange at this stage such as the use of suction excavation. In this stage sand which can contain evidences, can be remove by suction from around the body. These are collected in a container which is examined by sieve or microscope (Figure 41.5). On the other hand, excavation techniques in desert condition can be exchanged between forensic and classical archaeologist. Desert condition can include dealing with soft, dry, and gravity moving sand that can close the unprotected excavated hole. One solution is to increase the size of the excavated hole around the body to reduce sand movement into the hole (Mark Beech, personal communication 2008), and possibly to use physical buriers around the working area.

Smuggled artifacts:

In addition, the archaeologist can assist with detecting smuggling of archaeological and historical artefacts. In 2008, archaeologists pressed for a Federal Law to be drafted to prosecute the illegal trade of antiquities in the UAE (Al Serkal 2008). Most of the smuggled goods entering the UAE come from Iran, Iraq, Turkey, Pakistan and Afghanistan (Al Serkal 2008). In addition, there is also other expertise that can be of assistance in a forensic archaeological context.

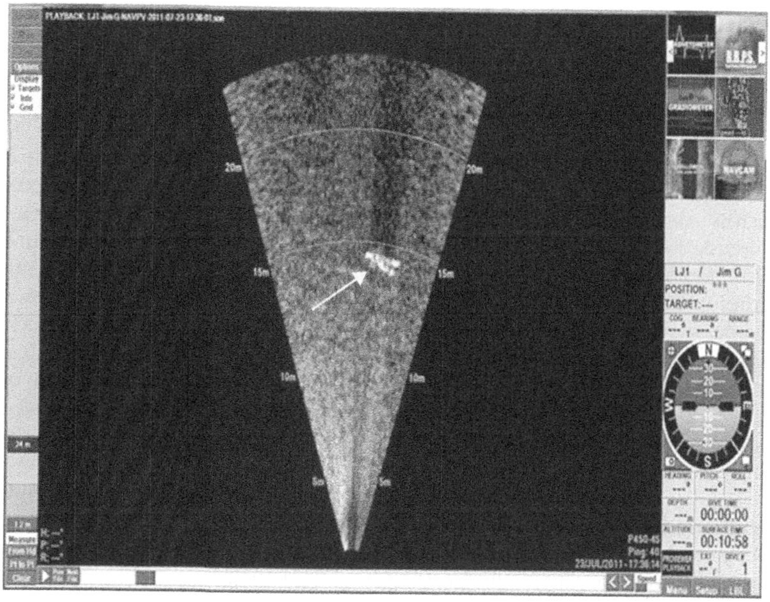

Figure 41.6 The image Show a body in deep water as indicated by the arrow. Image from an underwater radar (Image courtesy: M. Ferguson, Centre for Applied Science and Technology, Home Office, UK).

Supporting capabilities

This section outlines some of the police resources present in the UAE that could be of use in a forensic archaeological setting. Apart from health and safety protocols in place for working at a crime scene and the use of personal protective equipment we follow a number of protocols in archaeological excavation (e.g. Litherland et al. 2012).

Abu Dhabi Police Geosciences Project

There is a strong relationship between forensic archaeology and forensic geology and it may be said that forensic geologists are good at searching and locating, whereas forensic archaeologists are better at the recovery of buried bodies. The connection between the two fields in the UAE has a practical positive effect in the area of crime scene management, search and collaboration between scientists. The Abu Dhabi Police General Directorate has initiated a project focusing on geosciences in order to test its application for forensic investigation in the UAE, such as the viability of Ground Penetrating Radar (GPR) (Alkathiri et al. 2010). The Abu Dhabi Police has also joined the International Union of Geological Sciences (IUGS) Initiative on Forensic Geology (IFG)[1] to gain more support and cooperation in the field of forensic geology. IFG was started on 22 February 2011 by the IUGS (Donnelly 2011).

Within the IFG project, training in using new ground and water search equipment was presented to the forensic department under Abu Dhabi Police. Mr Mike Ferguson (Centre for Applied Science and Technology, Home Office, UK) has used new equipment to train a UAE search team in underwater search, including the use of the Shark Navigator dual frequency sonar system (Shark Marine, Canada) (Figure 41.6).

Geological survey of the UAE

An important step in searching for buried bodies includes the understanding of the different geological structures within the UAE, including the mapping of soil and geological distribution in the UAE. This helps the geologist and archaeologist with the search and in deciding what equipment to use. There is a resource which can be accessed on the Internet, which provides a map outline of the different geological structures within the UAE.[2]

Abu Dhabi police GIS

In addition, the Abu Dhabi Police has opened a Geographical Information System Centre for Security (GISCS). This centre can be of use in conjunction with soil maps to help intelligence regarding the location of a clandestine grave. It also provides support for archaeological excavation and documentation.

[1]For more information, see http://facstaff.buffalostate.edu/bergslet/ForensicGeology/index.html (last accessed 25 October 2013).
[2]For more information, see http://www.uaesis.ae/ (last accessed 25 October 2013).

Education and professional development

Training opportunities

In 2005 a crime scene village was created in Abu Dhabi. This village runs an academic programme to train crime scene technicians from a number of different police stations across Abu Dhabi. The academic programme includes forensic documentation of a crime scene, fingerprint analysis, forensic photography and blood spatter analysis. After initial training, the trained police staff return to the crime scene village for additional development courses each year (Youssef 2009). The Abu Dhabi Police opened an additional crime scene village in the Ajman Emirate in 2010.[3] It is hoped that in the future this village will also include courses on forensic archaeology, in order to increase the proficiency of crime scene staff.

Higher education opportunities

As part of the educational targets which have been set, many police departments in the UAE have sent their upcoming forensic scientists and recent graduates to universities in the United Kingdom, Australia and the United States to undertake both undergraduate and postgraduate training in several fields of forensic science. In some of these universities, the UAE students will receive training in forensic archaeological theories and methodology. The latter is an excellent opportunity for the development of forensic archaeology in the UAE.

The United Arab Emirates University (UAEU) in Al Ain (Abu Dhabi) has a History and Archaeology Department within the College of Humanities and Social Sciences (CHSS).[4] This department focuses on three main areas: archaeology, public history and cultural tourism. There is no mention of forensic archaeology in the curriculum, but the CHSS does offer a course in Fundamentals of Archaeology and Archaeological Field Methods, this within the context of Cultural Resource Management (CRM). The latter course includes methods of recording field data including mapping, drawing and photography; practice in the use of field equipment; conservation of artefacts; surveying and if feasible excavation at an archaeological site too.

The Amity University Dubai, a private Indian-based university, is offering a BSc in Forensic Science.[5] Their syllabus does not include courses in forensic archaeology, but it is expected that this university will teach some forensic archaeological theories and methodologies in their forensic anthropology course.

Summary and conclusion

Forensic archaeology as a field in forensic science is not as yet established as a separate discipline in the UAE. It is, however, recommended that each Forensic Laboratory join forces with archaeologists in order to improve the procedure of crime scene investigation from the scene to the morgue. In addition, a number of bullet points can be highlighted:

- Forensic scientists working in the recovery of human remains have a general knowledge of archaeological excavation techniques.
- Forensic archaeological excavation will also require consideration of other evidence types, and therefore a team may need to include a forensic anthropologist and a fire investigator where relevant to document and recover evidence related to the case.
- There is potential cooperation between the universities and police departments, for example, the History and Archaeology Department of the UAEU and the police to design specialised programmes in forensic archaeology.
- There have been an increasing number of opportunities to hold workshops, training and conferences to develop the education and training of police in the field of forensic archaeology. In addition, inviting international forensic archaeologists for training is certainly a serious consideration. A short course on forensic archaeology with invited guests from abroad could certainly be added to the annual training scheme of the training departments in the police.
- There are many opportunities for cooperation between (regular) archaeologists and forensic laboratories in the UAE. Although this cooperation mainly focuses on the study of archaeological artefacts (e.g. illegal trade), it also enables the archaeologist and forensic scientist to exchange ideas and experiences. This is certainly something that in due course could further promote the use of forensic archaeology in the UAE crime scene work and analysis.
- There is pressure to ensure that any forensic archaeology practice follows a system of quality control as with other forensic science discipline.

Acknowledgements

I would like to thank HH Sheikh Saif bin Zayed for his continued support to the forensic sciences in the UAE. I thank Colonel Abdul Rahman Al Hammadi, Head of the Forensic Evidence Department in Abu Dhabi Police, for

[3]For more information, see http://www.khaleejtimes.com/DisplayArticle08.asp?xfile=data/theuae/2010/July/theuae_July399.xml&section=theuae (last accessed 25 October 2013).

[4]For more information, see http://webapps.uaeu.ac.ae/catalog/auto/department_HS_HS_HIST.asp#HIS120 (last accessed 25 October 2013).

[5]For more information, see http://www.amityuniversity.ae/courses.aspx (last accessed 25 October 2013).

his useful advice. I would like to thank my colleagues at work for their cooperation in this field. I would like to thank Dr Ahmed Rushdi, Forensic Section of the Judicial Department in Abu Dhabi, for his enriching discussions. I would also like to thank Mr Mike Ferguson (Centre for Applied Science and Technology, Home Office, UK) for allowing me the use of the image of water search training in the UAE. I thank Mr Peter Hellyer for his useful discussion. I would finally like to thank Dr Mark Beech, Head of Coastal Heritage and Palaeontology Section, Historic Environment Department, Abu Dhabi Tourism & Culture Authority, for his cooperation.

References

Gulf News. 2013. *Bulldozer Unearths Grisly Crime in Abu Dhabi.* Available at: http://gulfnews.com/news/gulf/uae/crime/bulldozer-unearths-grisly-crime-in-abu-dhabi-1.1160182 (last accessed 8 September 2014).

Alkathiri S. A., Al Naimi K.S., Al Kaabi A. S. and Baker H. A. 2010. Abu Dhabi Police Forensic Geosciences Project. *ASA CSSA SSSA International Annual Meeting.* Available at: https://a-c-s.confex.com/crops/2010am/webprogram/Paper63315.html (last accessed 27 October 2013).

Al Kitbi, S. 2013. *Dead infant body was found in Al-Daid.* Available (in Arabic) at: http://www.emaratalyoum.com/local-section/accidents/2013-03-24-1.559991 (last accessed 20 December 2013).

Al Naimi, K. 2009. The discovery of insect remains associated with a Bronze Age tomb in the United Arab Emirates: a preliminary study (poster). *Proceedings of the Seminar for Arabian Studies* 39, 303–306.

Al Serkal, M. M. 2008. *Federal Law Needed to Fight Smuggling of Antiquities in UAE.* Available at: http://gulfnews.com/news/gulf/uae/heritage-culture/federal-law-needed-to-fight-smuggling-of-antiquities-in-uae-1.105604 (last accessed 19 January 2014).

Ameen, M. 2011. *Ras Al Khaimah Police found to the Perpetrators by Credit Card; the Prosecution is waiting the Forensic Medicine Report on the Killed Person in Ras Al Khaimah.* Available (in Arabic) at: http://www.emaratalyoum.com/local-section/accidents/2011-12-13-1.444784 (last accessed 23 December 2013).

Armitage, S. J., Jasim, S. A., Marks, A. E. and Parker, A. G. 2011. The southern route 'Out of Africa' evidence for an early expansion of modern humans into Arabia. *Science* 331(453), 453–456.

Beech, M., Cuttler, R., Moscrop, D., Kallweit, H. and Martin, J. 2005. New evidence for Neolithic settlement of Marawah Island, Abu Dhabi, United Arab Emirates. *Proceedings of the Seminar for Arabian Studies* 35, 37–56.

Bou Malhab, N. and Abdel-Nabi, S. 2013. *New UAE Federal Expert.* Available at: http://www.clydeco.com/insight/updates/new-uae-federal-expert-law (last accessed 7 February 2014).

Clark, D. H. 1986. Dental identification problems in the Abu Dhabi air accident. *American Journal of Forensic Medicine and Pathology* 7(4), 317–321.

Donnelly, L. 2011. *History of the Development of the IUGS Task Group on Forensic Geology.* 2nd draft. Available at: http://www.forensicgeologyinternational.com/ (last accessed 21 December 2013).

Doyle, A. C. 2001. *The Complete Sherlock Holmes. The Musgrave Ritual.* New Lanark, Geddes & Grosset.

Emaratalyoum 2009. *Unknown Woman's Dead Body Found on the Jazirat al-Hamra.* Available (in Arabic) at: http://www.emaratalyoum.com/local-section/2009-08-14-1.154390 (last accessed 20 December 2013).

Emaratalyoum, 24 July 2010. *A 70 Year old Citizen was found dead on a Farm in an Ambiguous Condition.* Available (in Arabic) at: http://www.emaratalyoum.com/local-section/accidents/2010-07-24-1.269953 (last accessed 21 December 2013).

Emaratalyoum, 18 March 2013. *Search the Establishment of Federal Forensic Laboratory.* Available (in Arabic) at: http://www.emaratalyoum.com/local-section/other/2011-10-01-1.426949. (last accessed 23 December 2013).

Feder, K. L. 2009. Data preservation: recording and collecting. In T. R. Hester, H. J. Shafer and K. L. Feder (eds.), *Field Methods in Archaeology,* 114. Boca Raton, Left Coast Press.

Fuda, M. 2013. *Infant Body was Found Buried in Al Mamzar Beach.* Available at: http://www.emaratalyoum.com/local-section/accidents/2013-12-18-1.632884 (last accessed 20 December 2013).

Judicial Department. 2013. *Judicial Department in Abu Dhabi Organises a Meeting Between Judges and Experts.* Available (in Arabic) at: http://www.adjd.gov.ae/portal/site/adjd/news.detail/?document-friendly-id=Arabic.news111&language=ar (last accessed 23 December 2013).

Litherland, S., Márquez-Grant, N. and Roberts, J. 2012. Forensic archaeology. In N. Márquez-Grant and J. Roberts (eds.), *Forensic Ecology Hand Book,* 23–48. Oxford, John Wiley & Sons, Ltd.

Ministry of Justice. 2013. *Our Services.* Available at: http://ejustice.gov.ae/portal/page/portal/eJustice%20MOJ%20Portal/HomePages/Home%20Page%20HQ (last accessed 23 December 2013).

Symes, S. A., Dirkmaat, D. C., Ousley, S., Chapman, E. and Cabo, L. 2012. *Recovery and Interpretation of Burned Human Remains.* National Institute of Justice, Document No. 237966.

Youssef, M. 2009. *CSI Abu Dhabi – and no Expense Spared.* Available at: http://www.thenational.ae/news/uae-news/csi-abu-dhabi-and-no-expense-spared (last accessed 13 August 2013).

CHAPTER 42

The heroic and the hidden dead: Zimbabwe and exhumations

Shari Eppel

Solidarity Peace Trust, Port Shepstone, South Africa

Introduction

In Zimbabwe, while archaeology is currently a well-established field with a long history, forensic archaeology as a subdiscipline is barely known and not officially practised. However, this has not precluded a limited number of forensic exhumations from taking place in Matabeleland, in the western part of Zimbabwe, under the guidance of the Argentine Forensic Anthropology team (Equipo Argentino de Anthropologia Forense (EAAF); Fondebrider and Scheinsohn, Chapter 43, this volume). These occurred between 1998 and 2001. In addition, there have also been exhumations conducted under the guidance of community leaders and spirit mediums at different times since 1980. The focus of these exhumations was not forensic in nature but was aimed at appeasing the spirits of those who died in combat. In Zimbabwe, the dead – in particular the murdered dead – carry political, cultural and social significance beyond the grave (Eppel 2006). Where the ancestral spirits are intricately linked to the living, the ramifications of not honouring the dead are complex and long-lasting. The need for expert exhumations is urgent and communities desire this, but the path towards achieving this has been complicated by recurring patterns of violence and the continued presence of an oppressive state. Lack of awareness of the benefits of professional exhumations, as opposed to culturally conducted reburials, is a further inhibiting factor. Prosecutions are not possible in Zimbabwe, owing to general amnesties in 1979, 1980 and 1988, so that forensic report findings have been archived. The political constraints and unequal rights of some dead compared to others further complicate the issue, as does the continued senior presence in the army of past perpetrators.

This chapter will begin with a brief overview of political violence in the last 40 years. The state structures and legislation designated to curate the past will be indicated. The cultural significance of exhumations for spiritual purposes will be outlined, and the chapter ends by summarising the forensic archaeological exhumation of human remains in Zimbabwe. Conducted in the 1990s, these exhumations took cognisance of the principles of forensic archaeology and also of the community need to heal the dead. The chapter concludes with some recommendations for the future.

Historical context: counting the dead

The War of Liberation in the former Rhodesia lasted from the 1960s to 1980.Through a brutal war against the colonial regime, Zimbabwe achieved independence at the cost of an estimated 35,000 dead, many of them in neighbouring states (Catholic Commission for Justice and Peace 1997). Zimbabwe African National Union–Patriotic Front (ZANU-PF) convincingly won the first election. Almost immediately post-independence, a second period of killings ensued, this time restricted to the western half of the country, where the opposition Zimbabwe African People's Union (ZAPU) continued to have a stronghold. Prime Minister Robert Mugabe, in pursuit of a one-party state, deployed what became known as the *Gukurahundi* Brigade to force the region into submission.[1] An estimated 10,000–20,000 civilians were massacred between 1982 and 1985 (Raftopoulos 2012). This was the most intense period of violence ever experienced in the three affected provinces, and the era remains a dark stain on the nation's history. The crisis

[1]*Gukurahundi* is a Shona word meaning 'the first rain of spring that washes away the chaff from the last season'. See Catholic Commission for Justice and Peace and Legal Resources Foundation (1997) for full details of this era. The Ndebele perceive themselves as the 'chaff' that got 'washed away' by the Shona-speaking 5 Brigade. This Brigade, made up of former ZANLA soldiers, was trained by the North Koreans and deployed in Matabeleland from 1983 to 1985, where they beat, tortured and murdered civilians.

Forensic Archaeology: A Global Perspective, First Edition. Edited by W.J. Mike Groen, Nicholas Márquez-Grant and Robert C. Janaway.

ended in 1987 with the signing of a Unity Accord between the two parties, and for a decade there was apparent calm. However, the rise of a new popular opposition party in 1999, the Movement for Democratic Change (MDC), saw a new era of repression. Between 2000 and 2013, around 1000 activists died, thousands were tortured or lost property and the nation suffered extreme turmoil in the form of state collapse, massive inflation and widespread poverty, all of which has fuelled unprecedented diasporisation of the population.

There is not a province in the country that cannot lay claim to citizens that have died in one or another era of political violence in the last 40 years and many of these remain in shallow or mass graves. However, in Zimbabwe, all the dead are not equal, and the dead of different eras do not have equal access to being mourned and remembered.

Graves: legal and practical issues

National Museums and Monuments: archaeology

There is no specific legislation regarding forensic archaeology in Zimbabwe. However, the Department of National Museums and Monuments of Zimbabwe is the dominant structure officially tasked with overseeing archaeological activities in the country, and in terms of the enacting legislation, its mandate is primarily to oversee all historical sites and artefacts that predate 1890.[2] This date approximately coincides with the arrival of the first white colonisers in the country. The mandate of the Museums and Monuments is therefore primarily to maintain and preserve pre-colonial artefacts and sites, including (among others) the major historical complexes of Great Zimbabwe and Khami; early San cave painting sites around the country; palaeontological sites and fossils and relics of scientific interest. The department also has the power to designate as a national monument any building or site of any era that is of historical interest.

Memorialisation of mass graves from the 1970s

Museums and Monuments have been involved in the commemoration of mass graves linked to the War of Liberation that lasted from the 1960s until 1980. This is in keeping with the department's general powers to declare anything of historical significance to be a national monument. The graves of the war dead have always carried political weight, and ZANU-PF, in power since 1980, often evokes their existence to justify their continued political dominance, on the grounds that those whose cadres died for freedom must always run the country. The mass graves that have been designated as monuments include those in external guerrilla training camps and refugee camps. Such memorialisations have occurred at Nyadzonya and Chimoio in Mozambique, where supporters and cadres of the Zimbabwe National Liberation Army (ZANLA, the armed wing of ZANU-PF) perished in their hundreds during Rhodesian army raids of the 1970s, and at Victory Camp in Zambia, where cadres and supporters of the Zimbabwe People's Revolutionary Army (ZIPRA, the armed wing of ZAPU) perished similarly. The establishing of these graves as monuments has not involved forensic exhumations, but rather the entombing of the original mass graves in concrete to commemorate them. The interest in commemorating graves from the 1970s has recently been revived by Museums and Monuments. Memorialising procedures include 'identification of the liberation war sites, traditional acknowledgement of the souls of fallen freedom fighters, physical rehabilitation of the burials, erecting memorial shrines and site museums or interpreting centres as well as conservation and promotion of Zimbabwe's liberation heritage' (Shoko 2011, 3). Notably, there is no mention of intention to conduct forensic exhumations of the graves.

Zimbabwe Republican Police: forensic cases

The police force is responsible for forensic investigations of cases involving human remains or associated evidence. The police lack archaeological training and do not call on archaeologists in the event of finding human remains, or when needing to examine a potential clandestine burial. Confidential informants in the police force (June 2013) have confirmed that forensic archaeological methods are not applied in cases where human remains are discovered with an unknown cause of death, including suspected homicides. There is a general lack of awareness among the police of the advantageous role such skills could play in solving forensic cases.

Community-driven exhumations

Role of the ancestors

While forensic exhumations have generally not occurred in Zimbabwe, exhumations have at times taken place at the initiation of ex-combatants, as well as spirit mediums and local traditional leadership. These exhumations have been carried out in order to honour ancestral spirits by reburying their bones in the right place, traditionally speaking. In terms of both Shona and Ndebele

[2]National Museums and Monuments Act of Zimbabwe [Chapter 25:11], (revised 2001). Part I, 2, (b) defines 'ancient monument' as dated prior to 1 January 1890. Part IV further defines monuments and relics.

belief systems in Zimbabwe, the ancestral spirits guard the lives of the living. Daneel (1996, 358) illustrates how centrally the *Mwali* cult, practised in most of the country, places the ancestral spirits: 'Now that we come to address our ancestors we do so in the knowledge that the ancestors are the land, the ancestors are the water, the ancestors are the *sadza* [porridge] we eat, and the ancestors are the clothes we wear. Without the ancestors we will be without water, without food, without clothes. Our entire well-being will be lost without them'.

Werbner (1991, 95) defines the Ndebele *Sangoma* cult concept of the Tears of the Dead as being inseparable from the experiences of the living: 'Tears of the dead are shed by the living, when they cry in mourning. Yet the tears are *of* the dead, physically embodied in all the goods and livestock that come from them to the living'. Most notably, if an 'unarmed, innocent victim of war' does not have his spirit appeased, then his surviving family will suffer 'from a vengeful, aggrieved presence [known as] *ngozi*'. Werbner recounts in detail a case of *ngozi*, caused by failure to honour an uncle: 'The atrocity of his death, unmourned in any wake, haunted his family' (1991, 188/9). The haunting took the form of headaches, pains and swellings inflicted on the family spirit medium, who had to undertake rituals and make sacrifices in the name of her uncle in order to recover.

Mupinda (1995) has recounted the deep distress caused by the non-return of family members after the Zimbabwe War of Liberation. Whether a family member is dead in action, missing in action, or a disappeared person, the consequences for surviving relatives are severe, and families will go to great lengths to establish the whereabouts of their dead. In Matabeleland, communities blame droughts, infertility, failed marriages, badly behaved children and illnesses on the aggrieved spirits of those massacred in the post-independence brutality of *Gukurahundi* (Eppel 2002). These incorrectly buried dead continue to disturb the lives of their descendants in order to remind them that they need to be mourned. In particular, the rituals of *Umbuyiso* (Ndebele regions) and *Kugadzira* (Shona regions) need to be performed so that ancestral spirits can move from being malignant, trouble-causing outcasts and into the ancestral spirit hierarchy, where they can positively help the living.

Spirit mediums and uprisings

The struggle for freedom from colonial domination was always inextricably linked in Zimbabwe to the power of the ancestral spirits, with spirit mediums playing a key role in invoking the struggle. Spirit mediums are perceived to be part-person, part-ancestor, through whom the dead can speak (Lan 1985, 211). Ambuya Nehanda (*c.*1840–1898), a spirit medium who drove the First Chimurenga (uprising of the 1890s) with her prophecies, paid for her political activism with her life. After she was sentenced to death by the British colonial regime in 1898, Nehanda famously pronounced that her 'bones will rise again'. Her image was displayed prominently and songs were written in her honour when Zimbabwe achieved independence in 1980. Winning the war was seen as her 'bones resurrected' (Lan 1985, 217). Nehanda's spirit has once more been invoked since 2000, during the land seizures of the last decade, which are referred to as the Third Chimurenga.

Honouring the dead

In Zimbabwe, with its 'holistic African world-view in which the living and the living dead, the creator-divinity and all of creation are inseparably linked in a seamless totality on one continuum' (Daneel 1996, 348), it is fundamental for the dead to be buried in the correct way and place. In the case of men, this means burial by their cattle holding pen; for women, this means burial alongside their fields. The quest to recover and return the dead has therefore continued to drive the needs of many families, as every misfortune in their home is laid at the door of aggrieved spirits.

Every rainy season, bones become exposed and nearby villagers are faced with the dilemma of what to do. This dilemma plays out differently depending on the region concerned. In most of the country, exposed bones may receive massive media coverage as evidence of colonial cruelties,[3] whereas in Matabeleland, where the dead were mostly killed under the rule of the current government, bones are hastily covered up by the state and access to them sealed off (Bulawayo24.com 2012; Smith 2011). In Zimbabwe, some dead are heroic, others are hidden.

Gutu reburials, 1989

Bearing in mind the intricate interrelationship between the War of Liberation, the ancestral spirits of those who have died, and the living, it is unsurprising that there have been community-driven attempts to bring home the dead since Independence. Every district and province in Zimbabwe established Heroes' Acres and in some of these, informally exhumed combatants were reburied. In others, ex-combatants who have died since 1980 have been buried. Daneel (1995) recounts his attendance at the 1989 Gutu District reburial of 40 combatants who died during the war. There is no indication of how or where the combatants were exhumed, and none of them are identified by their actual name, but rather by their *Chimurenga* (struggle) names. The ancestral spirits drove the process: 'Once Tazivei, senior spirit medium of

[3]See the Mount Darwin exhumations for a good example.

the land, had revealed the wishes of the ancestors, fencing, grave digging, terracing and building of the heroes' acre could commence' (Daneel 1995, 30). The chief headed the reburial ceremonies, which were also attended by President Robert Mugabe to underline the significance of honouring the war dead. Chief Gutu praised the ancestors for facilitating the processes of reburial: 'I want all of you chiefs to know that in fetching these boys' bodies we did not encounter any problems. The vehicles we used got through without a single puncture. I am extremely proud of our ancestors in this district. They did not put us to shame in any way' (Daneel 1995, 36).

Beer was shared with the ancestors by being poured on the grave mounds. However, it was noted that 'even our reburial ceremony is imperfect. The real identities of the heroes, for instance, are not known ... what on the face of it is a successful ceremony is but a faint echo of a true commemoration' (Daneel 1995, 44).

Mount Darwin exhumations, 2011

In March 2011, the government-controlled media in Zimbabwe gave extensive daily coverage to the attempts of a group of ZANLA war veterans called the Fallen Heroes Trust to exhume possibly thousands of skeletons from a long-abandoned mine shaft in the northern part of the country.[4] The war veterans were local residents of Mount Darwin with no forensic training or expertise, and the exercise showed the state propaganda machine in full swing; the main role of the exhumations seemed to be to proclaim the dead to be victims of colonial repression, and to denounce the current opposition MDC as being colonial-sponsored (Louden 2011; Sithole 2011).[5] Television footage showed crowds including school children being forced into the mine shaft to see for themselves the piles of skeletons – and these same crowds walked over these very bones, crushing them underfoot. Images of veterans irrevocably commingling remains by throwing them from all parts of the mineshaft into common sacks filled the screens night after night (Figure 42.1). Veterans brandished detached, mummified limbs for the cameras.[6]

Hundreds of damaged and disarticulated remains were laid out for crowds to witness, and spirit mediums went into intense trances and played a central role in conducting messages from the murdered dead to the living. One spirit spoke through his brother: 'All Zimbabweans must help in according us decent burials. I want to be buried where my ancestors are. We died trying to free this country from colonial rule and all patriotic Zimbabweans owe us a decent burial'. Another [dead] freedom fighter pleads, 'I want to be buried in my home area here in Mt Darwin so that my soul will find peace and rest at last' (Shoko 2011, 8).

Figure 42.1 Commingled remains in Mount Darwin, Zimbabwe, after amateur exhumations. March 2011.

However, the state failed to maintain control of this exercise, both in practical and in propaganda terms. The war veterans of ZIPRA, which operated predominantly but not exclusively in the west of the country during the war, went to the High Court and were successful in stopping the exhumations on the grounds that some of their cadres could be among the ZANLA dead and they had not been consulted. Furthermore, the recovery of some bodies that still oozed fluids led the political opposition party, the MDC, to state publicly that they believed some of these bodies could be of their disappeared activists, murdered since 2000. The Mount Darwin exhumations literally had skeletons tumbling out of

[4]Exact numbers were never established because of the chaotic nature of the exhumation. Nor was/were the era/s of the dead irrevocably established, although most if not all were most likely killed during the 1970s war; army personnel confirmed to the author that it was well known that the Rhodesian army used this shaft to dispose of the war dead. This would not have precluded the same shaft having been used later for the same purpose.

[5]These are two of many media articles covering the event both nationally and internationally in 2011, which include the following: The Standard, Comment 2011, 'Unearth Truth on Human Remains', Harare, *The Standard*, 26 March 2011; T. Madzongwe 2011, 'Hundreds of Bodies Removed from Zimbabwe Mass Grave', *ipsnews.net*, 25 March 2011; J. Makumbe 2011, 'Skeletons to the Rescue', *Zimbabwe Mail*, 23 March 2011.

[6]Zimbabwe Broadcasting Services showed footage nightly on their 8p.m. news bulletins in March 2011.

cupboards, as people linked the dead to various eras and contexts of political violence – many of them post-independence (Guma 2011). The High Court ruled that the digging had to stop as ZIPRA requested, and the area was suddenly closed down (Sithole 2011). From having been a very public process, it became difficult to access the site, and the situation was uneasily resolved a few months later when the bones were reburied in a new mass grave, adjacent to the mine-shaft, taking any forensic secrets with them back under the ground.

The very public destruction caused by these ZANLA exhumations resulted in the ZIPRA veterans, whose legal case had halted the Mount Darwin dig, issuing this additional warning: 'We call upon the so-called Fallen Heroes Trust to limit their activities to the graves of their own fallen heroes and not to tamper with those of ex-Zipra and MK[7] cadres'. ZIPRA went on to say that ordinary citizens of Matabeleland 'had appealed to ZAPU to protect the graves of their relatives who were killed during *Gukurahundi*' (Mlotshwa 2011).

Matabeleland exhumations, 1998–2001

It is thus apparent that those who died in the War of Liberation at the hands of the Rhodesian colonial forces are seen as heroes, whose spirits and remains must be acknowledged and honoured, even though many of these dead remain in mass graves and very few have been accurately identified through reburials. The president regularly presides over burials of recently dead 'Heroes' at the National Heroes Acre, and has on occasion attended Heroes' ceremonies in the rural districts, such as the one at Gutu.[8]

However, thousands of murdered dead are still largely denied, and their spirits remain unmourned. These are the *Gukurahundi* dead in the west of Zimbabwe. There are no Heroes' Acres for them, and their relatives cannot even refer to these graves without fear. In some instances, human remains literally lie scattered on rock shelves, and local villagers know whom and where they are, but are too afraid to gather them up for burial even now, 30 years later (Figure 42.2). As recently as June 2013, President Mugabe once more denied the need to face the facts of this era, even while acknowledging at some level that 'bad' things happened: 'Yes, it was very bad. We don't want to talk about [the *Gukurahundi* killings], but it turns up a story which has not been told in full, how it started and so on, you know, what was happening. It's involving, it's not a story we should continue' (Phiri 2013).[9]

Figure 42.2 Remains of an abducted headmaster dating to 1985 lie still unrecovered in 2013: one of Zimbabwe's many 'hidden' and denied dead.

[7]MK – Umkhonto we Sizwe, armed wing of the South African ANC, which lost cadres in Zimbabwe in the 1970s.
[8]The Politburo has to decide who deserves to be called a 'Hero' and at what level (National, Provincial or District), and the process has been increasingly criticised as a form of party patronage, with only ZANU-PF stalwarts getting the title, regardless of their role in the actual war. Norma Kriger (2003) has written on the contested notion of national heroes (see references).
[9]South African TV personality Dali Tambo conducted a long interview with Mugabe in late May 2013. The quote cited by *Daily News* is from this interview.

Amani Trust, Matabeleland

It is against this background of national denial of the need to deal with *Gukurahundi*, that in 1998, Amani Trust, Matabeleland, a small non-governmental organisation with an office in Bulawayo, began to confront the problem of the angry dead. Focused on repairing the social fabric after political violence in the region, and with good knowledge of the events of *Gukurahundi*, Amani Trust consulted local communities about what needed to be done. They expected to find Western-defined syndromes of psychosocial distress, such as posttraumatic stress disorder (PTSD). However, the overwhelming request was for help with aggrieved spirits. The EAAF was contacted, and agreed to help both with exhuming and with beginning to train a Matabeleland-based, Zimbabwean forensic team. For the following 4 years, Amani Trust documented the sites of graves, recorded the incidents of murder and burial from eyewitnesses and gathered pre- and peri-mortem information about the dead. Each year, the EAAF sent over a small team to exhume a few sites, while training Amani Trust staff in basic forensic archaeological and anthropological skills. This was not without incident, and the first exercise faced government interference. The dig was stopped with a mass grave open in the field, as the ZANU-PF Politburo argued over what to do, before finally allowing the exercise to be completed. Ways of continuing with exhumations legally but without much visibility were found for ensuing exercises, and the fact these forensic exhumations took place remains not widely known. Graves exhumed included both mass (more than one) and single graves.

Sitezi grave

The most complicated grave exhumed involved a grave situated within what had been a *Gukurahundi* detention and murder camp in Matabeleland South. Amani Trust had been told of eight civilians, who had been forced to dig their own shallow grave and then lie down in it, while the local commander listened to the radio and casually beat and shot people in the grave. Seeing they had nothing to lose, two men out of the eight jumped up and ran away, one sustaining gunshot injuries as he fled. It was these survivors who were primary informants as to the whereabouts and occupants of this grave. However, what they did not know was that soldiers had returned at some later point and had torched the grave. On exhumation, all that was found were bone fragments and not the complete skeletons that had been anticipated. In addition, a wedding ring, a distinctive silver cigarette lighter, a Zimbabwe national identity card and several bullets and cartridge cases were exhumed. The personal effects confirmed that this was indeed the assumed grave, and the presence of Zimbabwe coins and the identity card confirmed the era, while the bullets confirmed the violent nature of the deaths. The evidence supported the eyewitness accounts. The EAAF was able to confirm that the manner of bone fragmentation was consistent with the bodies having been burnt when the bones still contained collagen, thus confirming an attempt by the state to make this grave clandestine, after murdering its occupants. The bone fragments were grouped into piles depending on what type of bone they were from (specific long bones, vertebrae, ribs), and the finding of six right proximal ulna fragments confirmed Minimum Number of Individuals (MNI) as six.

The families and the chief were consulted, and a decision was made to reinter all the bones in one coffin, with skull fragments grouped at the top, down to toes at the bottom, in the original grave site. A very moving ceremony was held, with the presence of multiple community leaders including several Christian priests. This funeral was a true reclaiming of the past, and an honouring of the dead, witnessed by hundreds from far and wide. A year later, in a solemn but celebratory ceremony, a headstone was erected (Figure 42.3). This remains the only formal commemoration of any grave from the *Gukurahundi* killings.

Forensic archaeology and cultural healing: complementary processes

Amani Trust Matabeleland and the EAAF oversaw exercises that simultaneously paid respect to the cultural needs of families to heal their dead, and followed forensically meticulous exhumation principles at the same time. Families were encouraged to conduct family rituals before, during and after any exhumation, and to observe the process if they wished. They also participated in sifting soil and other simple tasks linked to the exhumations. Relatives were allowed to sit with the bones at particular times during the analysis phase, in order to conduct the equivalent of a wake, decades after the actual deaths of their beloved. This also allowed family members who had not been able to attend the exhumations to share in the process in some way. Families would accompany the bones, now in a coffin, back to their homesteads for traditional reburial – finally, in the right place. In the years following, Amani Trust noted significant changes in family functioning after these reburials, as the spirits, no longer anguished, allowed families and communities to move on in various ways.[10]

[10] These have been described in other publications, see Eppel (2002, 2006, 2013).

Figure 42.3 Sitezi gravestone is the only official memorial to 6 out of the more than 10,000 massacred in western Zimbabwe in the 1980s.

2002 to 2014

By 2002, a new phase of political violence linked to the rise of the MDC meant that exhumations were no longer pragmatic, in particular for rural communities who were and continue to be extremely vulnerable in the hands of an oppressive state. Amani Trust moved its focus to current torture and abuses. However, the presence of graves and exposed remains has continued to be documented. Over the last decade the old team has continued to make efforts to achieve training in forensic archaeology and anthropology, both formally through academic institutions and informally through the support of the EAAF. It is the team's intention to resume exhumations for both forensic and healing purposes once the political space allows.

Recommendations

Our Zimbabwe team could not have undertaken their exhumation exercises without the support of the EAAF. The EAAF policy of always seeking to establish local expertise and of always operating through a locally based organisation or structure is one that should be adhered to by all who intend to exhume in the context of nations that are foreign to them. Sub-Saharan Africa has possibly 10 million dead in mass graves, placed there over the last 50 years by various civil and cross-border wars.[11] As many cultures in Africa believe in the continuity of the spirits of the dead with the well-being of the living, there is a huge task to be done to heal the dead, as well as to reclaim histories and bring genocidal leaders to justice. However, precisely because the dead are embodied with such intense and regionally varying cultural beliefs, and such complicated and often very localised political realities down to the village level, any exhumations need to be primarily community-driven and should give families the ultimate say in whether and when graves should be exhumed, as well as allowing space for local rituals. Acknowledging and facilitating local cultural rituals where exhumations are wanted does not have to conflict with forensically accurate exhumations needed for purposes of accountability.

In some cultures, on the other hand, exhumations are not considered necessary or helpful in healing the dead, as it is possible to remove and rebury the spirit without disturbing the bones. As a general rule, in such contexts,

[11]Nobody knows the actual numbers of African war dead, but this estimate is based on these very approximate figures for deaths in recent wars: Mozambique, 400,000; Angola, 500,000; Rwanda, 800,000; Burundi, 300,000; Democratic Republic of Congo, 5.4 million+; Sudan, 600,000–2.5 million; Algeria, 1 million; Sierra Leone, 100,000; Liberia, 350,000plus hundreds of thousands of casualties in multiple wars/uprisings in Somalia, Ethiopia, Namibia, Uganda and many other countries.

exhumations should not happen, as the cultural needs of communities should be paramount.[12]

Furthermore, as the digging to be done exceeds what can be accomplished by overseas summer schools or International Criminal Court processes, it is imperative that those from outside Africa and Asia with skills and the desire to exhume in the developing world do not neglect their responsibility to contribute their concerted efforts towards the establishment of self-sustainable expertise in the countries where they dig. There is a need to link any digs by Western/Latin American teams to the training of individuals who are citizens of our developing nations, and who understand the local histories, contexts and beliefs. In this way in a decade from now, following in the footsteps of Latin America, Africa will hopefully have several highly competent indigenous and self-sustaining teams capable of exhuming using the principles of forensic archaeology. Zimbabwe aims to have one of these teams.

References

Bulawayo24.com, 27 January 2012. *Mass Grave at Zimbabwe Police Post*. Bulawayo.

Catholic Commission for Justice and Peace in Zimbabwe and the Legal Resources Foundation. 1997. *Breaking the Silence, Building True Peace: A Report on the Disturbances in Matabeleland and the Midlands 1982–1988*. Harare, CCJPZ and LRF.

Daneel, I. 1995. *Guerrilla Snuff*. Harare, Baobab Books.

Daneel, I. 1996. Environmental reform: a new venture of Zimbabwe's traditional custodians of the land. *Journal of Legal Pluralism and Unofficial Law* 37–38, 347–376.

Eppel, S. 2002. Reburial ceremonies for health and healing after state terror. *The Lancet* 360, 9336.

Eppel, S. 2006. Healing the dead: exhumation and reburial as a route to truth telling and reclaiming the past in rural Zimbabwe. In T. A. Borer (ed.), *Telling the Truths: Truth Telling and Peace-building in Post Conflict Societies*, 259–288. Notre Dame, University of Notre Dame Press.

Eppel, S. 2013. Repairing a fractured nation: challenges and opportunities in post-GPA Zimbabwe. In B. Raftopoulos (ed.), *The Hard Road to Reform: The Politics of Zimbabwe's Global Political Agreement*, 211–250. Harare, Weaver Press.

Guma, L. 2011. *Mass Graves Raise More Questions than Answers*. 23 March 2011. London, SW Radio Africa.

Kriger, N. 2003. *Guerrilla Veterans in Post-War Zimbabwe: Symbolic and Violent Politics 1980–1987*. Cambridge, Cambridge University Press.

Lan, D. 1985. *Guns and Rain: Guerrillas and Spirit Mediums in Zimbabwe*. Harare, Zimbabwe Publishing House.

Louden, B. 2011. Dead become a tool for Mugabe. *The Australian*, 31 March 2011.

Mlotshwa, K. 2011. Zapu plans parallel exhumations. *News Day Southern Edition*, 4 June. Bulawayo.

Mupinda, M. 1995. Loss and grief among the Shona: the meaning of disappearances. *Paper Presented to the 7th International Symposium on Torture as a Challenge to the Medical Profession, Cape Town*.

Phiri, G. 2013. 5th brigade did not follow instructions. *Daily News*, 5 June 2013. Harare.

Raftopoulos, B. (ed) 2013. *The Hard Road to Reform: the Politics of Zimbabwe's Global Political Agreement*. Harare, Weaver Press.

Shoko, T. 2011. *'My Bones Shall Rise Again': War Veterans, Spirits and Land Reform in Zimbabwe*. Leiden, African Studies Centre.

Sithole, Z. 2011. *Audit Human Remains – Colonel*. London, The Zimbabwean.

Smith, D. 2011. Grave containing up to 60 people found at Zimbabwe school. *The Guardian*, 5 October 2011. London.

Werbner, R. 1991. *Tears of the Dead: the Social Biography of an African Family*. Harare, Baobab Books.

[12]On a field visit to Liberia in March 2012, the author witnessed 'reburial' ceremonies in Liberia involving the Mandingo, Lorma, Kissi and Gbandi ethnic groups in the small village of Kambolahun deep in the jungles of the northeastern border. They all strongly believe in a ritual in which the spirit of the deceased is removed from a mass grave using an 'iron' – small metal rod – to be transferred to a place appropriate for him/her to then 'cross to the other side', with the help of further rituals. The bones of mass graves were considered irrelevant organic matter that could be ploughed under or built over. 'Reburying' to these ethnic groups simply means moving of the spirit alone. Furthermore, these communities professed no interest in prosecuting the commander responsible for the deaths of over 100 civilians in their village, who still lived nearby. They stated that if the perpetrator would simply come and prostrate himself on the ground and ask for forgiveness, they would accept this as enough of an apology. Therefore the bones held neither forensic nor cultural value for these particular villagers.

PART 4

(Non-) Governmental Organisations

CHAPTER 43

Forensic archaeology: the Argentinian way

Luis Fondebrider[1,2] and Vivian Scheinsohn[3,4]

[1] *The Argentine Forensic Anthropology Team (EAAF), Buenos Aires, Argentina*

[2] *Forensic Anthropology, Faculty of Medicine, University of Buenos Aires, Buenos Aires, Argentina*

[3] *Department of Anthropology, Facultad de Filosofía y Letras, University of Buenos Aires, Buenos Aires, Argentina*

[4] *Instituto Nacional de Antropología y Pensamiento Latinoamericano (INAPL) – National Scientific and Technical Research Council (CONICET), Buenos Aires, Argentina*

Introduction

The death of a human being has material and immaterial consequences. Among the former, one of the most important involves making special arrangements to dispose of the corpse, since decomposition starts upon death and, from a sanitary point of view, decomposing bodies should not be kept inside the dwelling. This need to take corpses away from dwelling places gave rise to mortuary practices that still live on today, the earliest ones recorded being those of the hominines from the archaeological sites of Skhul and Qafzeh, more than 100,000 years old (Tillier 2009). In addition to their origin associated with the materiality of a decomposing corpse, mortuary practices also have an emotional and ritual component. But besides these conscious and deliberate consequences, the death of a human being bears unconscious and involuntary consequences.

When faced with mass deaths, materiality becomes overpowering. In 1982, under the military dictatorship, the Argentine writer Alberto Laiseca published a volume of short stories entitled *Matando Enanos a Garrotazos* (*Beating Dwarfs to Death*). This book includes the short story *La Solución Final* (*The Final Solution*), in which Laiseca (1982) presents what could be regarded as an economic analysis of the consequences of a massacre. Devoid of any emotion, the narrator sets out to calculate and envision how to dispose of 1400 million corpses from a slaughter organised by the Monitor in the fictional but clearly Nazi-echoing country of *Tecnocracia* (*Technocracy*). This is similar to the context in which Laiseca wrote the story, that is, Argentina at the time of the last military dictatorship. Laiseca's calculations may well have taken place in the minds of those who perpetrated the massacre of thousands of their fellow citizens.

The development of forensic archaeology (understood as the application of archaeological principles, methods and techniques in a legal context) in Argentina is associated with such tragedy. During the last military dictatorship (1976–1983), between 10,000 and 30,000 people, depending on the source, were victims of enforced disappearance. The concept of the desaparecido (*the disappeared*) could not disguise the material and immaterial consequences of the military regime. It was precisely these consequences that led to the creation of the Argentine Forensic Anthropology Team (*Equipo Argentino de Antropología Forense* – EAAF), the starting point of forensic archaeology in Argentina.

Argentine Forensic Anthropology Team (*Equipo Argentino de Antropología Forense*)

From 1984, after democracy was restored, it was felt necessary to investigate what had happened to the victims of enforced disappearance. At first, this need was part of the political programme that took Raúl Alfonsin to the presidency. Hence, one of his first acts of government was the creation of the National Commission on the Disappearance of Persons (*Comisión Nacional Sobre la Desaparición de Personas* – CONADEP), which produced a report known as *Nunca Más* (Never Again). Upon its publication, investigation into these crimes was passed on to forensics. These circumstances brought about the need to find the victims' bodies. One of the first clues was that many bodies were buried without identification as NN (No Name, equivalent to 'unknown' or the American John/Jane Doe) either in individual or in mass graves in cemeteries all over the country. Faced with this, the judges decided as they usually did in criminal cases: whenever a body had to be exhumed in a cemetery, the task was commissioned to gravediggers under the guidance of forensic physicians; should the body be in a clandestine grave, the task was assigned to the fire brigade, as was normally the case where there was a need to recover a body after an accident. Given the lack of

Forensic Archaeology: A Global Perspective, First Edition. Edited by W.J. Mike Groen, Nicholas Márquez-Grant and Robert C. Janaway.

personnel trained in recovering skeletal remains the result was a major catastrophe. Remains were recovered only partially (particularly in the case of skeletonised bodies), the bones suffered post-mortem damage, associated relevant objects such as bullets were not retrieved, or even discarded and overall there was a lack of understanding of burial contexts and spatial associations. In addition, from a humanitarian point of view, such practices prevented the victims' relatives from learning what had happened to their loved ones. Thus, hundreds of bodies and their respective contexts were either jeopardised or completely missed. The problem was that, for recovery purposes, archaeological techniques needed to be applied.

In Argentina, as in many other parts of the world, the disciplines within a forensic or medico-legal investigation field have traditionally focused around medicine, odontology, radiology and toxicology. With few exceptions, officials in the justice system (i.e. judges, prosecutors, police officers, forensic experts) did not see the need to incorporate non-traditional disciplines into the forensic field, either out of ignorance of their usefulness or simply because they did not know where to seek appropriate assistance. Argentinian universities had long-standing degree courses in subject areas such as archaeology, entomology or biology, but they had almost never been summoned to work on forensic cases. This dissociation of the scientific disciplines from their possible applications, particularly from the forensic field, was also a consequence of the last dictatorship. In a society clearly devoid of justice, the judiciary acted only through inertia, uninterested in introducing any improvement or sophistication. All this led to the complete absence of archaeology in the forensic context of the time. As stated previously, both forensic archaeology and forensic anthropology came to light in Argentina with the foundation of the EAAF in 1984.

The EAAF was born out of a practical need. The Grandmothers of the Plaza de Mayo (*Abuelas de Plaza de Mayo*) is an organisation made up of relatives of victims who forcibly disappeared during the dictatorship. Its main goal is to promote the search for around 500 children who had been kidnapped together with their mothers. They started asking for help to solve the issue of how to identify those children. They came in contact with the American Association for the Advancement of Science (AAAS), since they have a Science and Human Rights Department, and its director at that time was especially concerned with the Argentinian case. In mid-1984, the AAAS sent a delegation of forensic scientists to Argentina to attempt a practical recovery of these grandchildren, on the one hand, and to implement an exhumation method which prevented the destruction of evidence, on the other (Doretti and Fondebrider 2001; Fondebrider 2002, 2009; Salado and Fondebrider 2008; Snow 1984; Snow and Bihurriet 1992).

Among the members of the delegation was Dr Clyde C. Snow, an American forensic anthropologist and one of the most prominent figures of the discipline in his country. Dr Snow was one of the first to use archaeological techniques in the forensic field. His mission was to devise a scientific methodology that would prove useful to recover the buried bodies properly and analyse them for identification purposes.

While in Buenos Aires, the capital city of Argentina, Dr Snow asked members of the Association of Professional Anthropologists (*Colegio de Graduados en Antropología*) for help with a first exhumation to be carried out in a cemetery in the province of Buenos Aires. The association members, possibly afraid of the uncertain political context that still prevailed, were rather reluctant to participate. Therefore, Dr Snow decided to resort to undergraduate students of anthropological sciences. Morris Tidball-Binz, a student of medicine acting as a translator during a lecture given by Dr Snow at the School of Medicine of the University of La Plata (*Universidad de La Plata* – UNLP), helped him get in touch with a group of archaeology and social anthropology undergraduate students from the University of Buenos Aires (*Universidad de Buenos Aires* – UBA)[1] and the UNLP. Many of them were receiving training at the Association for Anthropological Research (*Asociación de Investigaciones Antropológicas* – AIA), a non-governmental organisation (NGO) devoted to archaeological research, under the direction of archaeologists Luis Orquera and Ernesto Piana. These researchers, like many others in different fields, had found themselves in a delicate situation after they had been forced to quit their academic positions in the 1970s. So they created the AIA in order to continue their ongoing research projects. After the dictatorship, both began to gain institutional recognition. Piana moved to the city of Ushuaia, where he had been admitted as a researcher by the National Scientific and Technical Research Council (*Consejo Nacional de Investigaciones Científicas y Técnicas* – CONICET).[2] Orquera, who during dictatorship had been teaching at the University of

[1]Among them were the already mentioned Morris Tidball-Binz (student of medicine, UNLP); Douglas Cairns (a UBA student of anthropology and friend of the former) and Mercedes Doretti (student of anthropology, UBA); Teresa Acedo, Patricia Bernardi, Luis Fondebrider, Vivian Scheinsohn, and Hernán Vidal (students of anthropology at UBA and members of AIA); and Osvaldo Herrera, and Darío Olmo (students of anthropology at UNLP and members of AIA).

[2]CONICET is one of the institutions that make up the scientific and technical system in Argentina. Founded in 1958, it was designed after the French CNRS model.

Comahue (*Universidad del Comahue*) – in the south of the country and far away from academic centres – was offered a chair at the UNLP and was admitted by the CONICET as a researcher. Since 1975, the AIA had been allowing them to conduct archaeological research work in Tierra del Fuego and, by the same token, to train dozens of anthropology students from the UBA and the UNLP, who were looking for alternatives to what universities had to offer at the time of the dictatorship. Simultaneously, these students had embarked on an archaeological project of their own, led by Hernán Vidal, who had been trained by Orquera and Piana and was soon to graduate from the UBA. Vidal's thesis consisted of an archaeological study of Valentín Bay (Mitre Peninsula, Tierra del Fuego). His project, funded by the Tierra del Fuego Territorial Museum (*Museo Territorial de Tierra del Fuego*), involved the participation of young researchers from various disciplines, as it was conceived as a multidisciplinary project (Scheinsohn and Muñoz 2011).

At the time that Dr Snow was ready to conduct his first exhumation, Vidal was making arrangements for his trip to Tierra del Fuego, where he was to settle as the official of the Tierra del Fuego Territorial Museum responsible for the Archaeology Department. As Dr Snow needed an Argentine professional to carry out such an exhumation, this group of students, convinced Vidal to participate on the very date of his departure since he was the only one of the group to have a degree. Vidal went to the Boulogne cemetery in the morning, from where he was taken directly to the airport in the afternoon in a car provided by the court ordering the exhumation. Thus, the first exhumation using archaeological techniques was carried out in an individual grave located at the Boulogne cemetery, province of Buenos Aires, in June 1984. Orquera and Piana did not take part directly in the hands-on work but they gave support by making their excavation tools available to the participating students. The group of students who participated in this first exhumation was the original core of the EAAF, with some further additions and dropouts.

The chaotic start of forensic archaeology in Argentina, with no official or institutional backing, without any official involvement of university anthropology departments (only by their students), and with no interest from the forensic system, is consistent with the history of most academic disciplines in Argentina. A considerable contribution to Argentina science was made from outside main institutions and archaeology was not an exception. This explains the EAAF conformation, and makes sense in the context of the conformation of archaeology as an academic field in Argentina. So, in order to explain the development of forensic archaeology in Argentina we have first to briefly review the history of archaeology here.

In so doing we will review three main episodes: the role of archaeology in the creation of the nation-state (1812–1880), Ameghino's project (1880–1930) and the establishment of processualism (1970–1980).

Role of archaeology in the creation of the nation-state

The origins of archaeology in Argentina can be traced back to 200 years ago, contemporaneous to the advent of scientific archaeology in Europe (Daniel 1967).

The first archaeologists in the country were, in fact, naturalists collecting all kinds of objects from the natural world, including animals, which were either embalmed or sold live to flourishing European or American zoos, fossils and 'antiquities'. All these objects belonged to the past; therefore, from these researchers' viewpoint, a fossil was no different from any other 'antiquity'. The history of indigenous peoples also played a part in the creation of the nation-state in the 19th century. While the nation-state was being established after the European model, the history of the indigenous peoples would provide the fledgling nation with some ancient past or an invented tradition (Hobsbawm and Ranger 1983). This focused on the archaeology of the northwestern region of the country, given the existence of pre-Inca and Inca settlements in that area, or in the remote past as natural history and fossils.

Museums also did their part in creating a tradition for the future Argentina. Proof of this is that the first museum in what was then called the United Provinces of the Río de la Plata (*Provincias Unidas del Río de la Plata*), known as the Museum of the Country (*Museo del País*), was founded in 1812, only 2 years after the first autonomous government took office and in the middle of the war of independence. Run under successively different names, this museum is known today as the Bernardino Rivadavia Argentinean Natural Sciences Museum (*Museo Argentino de Ciencias Naturales* [MACN] *'Bernardino Rivadavia'*).[3] The underlying idea, as pointed out by Podgorny and Lopes (2008), was to create institutions comparable to their counterparts in Europe and America.

> Possessing 'a museum' symbolised civilisation and a place in the world in line with the spirit of the time ... . As felt by both politicians and science enthusiasts, the need for a museum was also associated with the exploration of the territory and with a seemingly unattainable goal: getting to know all the riches of these peoples (Podgorny and Lopes 2008, 12). [Our translation]

[3]The Museo del País was successively designated as Museo Público de Buenos Aires (1823–1882), Museo Nacional (1883–1911) and Museo Nacional de Historia Natural (1911–1931) until its current name.

History prior to the arrival of Europeans in Argentina and outside the Argentinian north west was basically understood as natural history. In other words, indigenous history was only equated with those classified as 'high cultures', such as the Diaguita or the Inca,[4] located at the northwest of the country. This indigenous history, deemed of interest, had no relationship with the nomadic native peoples occupying large areas of the northeastern and Patagonian regions at the time. These peoples were perceived as typifying the barbarism that had to be overcome in order to raise Argentina to a European level of civilisation. Moreover, if it was worth considering the remote past outside north western Argentina, it was only because of its extraordinary fauna, the fossil remains of which were the main interest to international museums (Podgorny 2009; Podgorny and Lopes 2008). This fauna was thus a source of wealth and notoriety for the country. Florentino Ameghino (see later) was the naturalist who connected such extinct mega fauna with the early presence of the human species since he proposed that the origin of the human species had taken place in the Pampas. Thus, Argentina invented a past for itself, and with it, the country could boast of being the birthplace of mankind, as in an Argentine joke.[5]

Ameghino's project

While fossils found in Argentina were taken to museums around the world, the Public Museum of Buenos Aires (*Museo Público de Buenos Aires*) waned gradually. It achieved some stability only with the arrival in 1862 of the German naturalist Hermann Burmeister (1807–1892), who was its director for 30 years. Burmeister became the guardian of national antiquities: he prohibited the export of fossils and exerted firm control over the museum collections and library (Podgorny and Lopes 2008). This zeal for control led a new generation of naturalists to work under his aegis, at first accepting this situation, but later rising up against it. Among the rebels was Florentino Ameghino (1854–1911).

Ameghino had built his career from scratch, supported by the efforts of his family and the influence of his country folk. He was the eldest son of an Italian family that had settled in Luján, a locality near the city of Buenos Aires. As a child, he was fond of walking by the ravines along the Luján River, where he used to find fossils (Mercante and Ambrosetti 1913). Eventually, these fossils grew into what would become a family business (Podgorny 2009) devoted to the sale of fossils and archaeological objects. In 1876, Ameghino, with an extraordinary boldness, submitted a report to the Argentine Scientific Society (*Sociedad Científica Argentina*) in which he stated that he could provide evidence that:

> the human species has inhabited the Argentine pampas in a previous geological period, when the flat marshes of this part of the Americas still swarmed with such animated colossuses as the ones that many thousands of years later would be designated as Megatheriums, Glyptodonts ... etc. (Ameghino 1914, 21 cited in Podgorny and Lopes 2008). [Our translation]

Ameghino did not succeed in arousing the interest of this society to publish his work. Nevertheless, he went to Paris in 1878 to participate in the International Exhibition of Anthropology and Palaeontology. He stayed there for three years working with Paul Gervais at the French Museum of Natural History (*Muséum National de Histoire Naturelle* – MNHN), and financed his stay in Paris with the proceeds of the sale of fossils he had taken to the exhibition (Podgorny and Lopes 2008). This is where he finally published the book he had been unable to release in Argentina: *La Antigüedad del Hombre en el Plata* (*The Antiquity of Man in the River Plate*).

Ameghino resorted to material evidence of two types to account for the existence of a 'tertiary man' in the Pampas: human skeletons and lithic assemblages were considered by him to be in Tertiary sediments (Politis and Bonomo 2011). In his opinion, the *Homo* genus and the *Homo sapiens* from the Old World were descendants of a small biped or *Homunculus* from the Patagonian Tertiary period (Podgorny 2009). Although his proposal had been criticised in Argentina, it was Aleš Hrdlička who finally overturned his thesis. The international reputation of Hrdlička (as curator of the Smithsonian Institution National Museum) and his examination of Ameghino's evidence during the International Congress of Americanists in 1910, held in Buenos Aires, discredited Ameghino's reputation and led to the consideration of human settlement in the Americas at a later time. However, after Ameghino's death in 1911, his disciples, basically his brother Carlos and a series of researchers, kept this debate alive until the 1930s.

As can be concluded from the previous paragraphs, Ameghino as a researcher was not affiliated to an institution but, on the contrary, he build his career outside the main institutions until he was admitted first to University of Córdoba, then to the La Plata Museum

[4]This readiness to connect the fledgling nation to the 'high cultures' was already clearly evident in the complete National Anthem lyrics adopted in 1813, which read: 'The dead Inca are shaken/and in their bones the ardour revives/which renews their children/of the Fatherland the ancient splendour.' [Our translation]

[5]Argentine jokes, seen as narcissistic and arrogant, are popular in Mexico and Spain, countries which received waves of Argentines in exile as a result of the military dictatorship during the 1970s.

and finally when he became director of the National Museum (see note 3). From 1902 to his death, while he was in that chair, he merged himself with this institution. As Podgorny and Lopes posited:

> Even though the organisers' personalities and identities strongly influenced the development of these institutions, upon their deaths they remained as structures and objects inherited by generations who created new settings. However, in the years that followed, the fabric of identity between institutions and founders woven by their protagonists stood safe and sound. Such founders became icons of different scientific positions and opposing political affiliation – very often at odds with the conflicts of the time (Podgorny and Lopes 2008, 251). [Our translation]

Establishment of processualism

In the years following Ameghino's death, and especially in Patagonia and Pampas, archaeological studies focus on the issue of the antiquity of the human presence. The recent past was left in the hands of history (which may explain the minimal development of historical archaeology in Argentina until 1980). In this division of intellectual labour, archaeology was reduced to a mere technique, and prehistory was the scientific discipline that would explain and interpret what archaeologists did (Sanguinetti de Bórmida and Orquera 1975). In fact, in 1976, the UBA branch within the anthropological sciences curriculum which would deal with archaeological issues was named 'Prehistory'.

Since 1948, when Austrian archaeologist Oswald Menghin arrived in Argentina and introduced the cultural–historical school of thought, professional practice was imbued with this theoretical framework (Kohl and Perez 2002). Two disciples of Menghin, José Imbelloni and Marcelo Bórmida, would extend the prevalence of this school until the 1980s.

The first voices challenging this official theoretical framework started to be heard at the beginning of the 1980s, reaching out to the students that would later form the EAAF. They were being trained in the cultural–historical school at the UBA, and were dissatisfied with it.

According to Luco (2010), it was archaeologist Carlos Aschero who set this process in motion at the UBA. Even though he had been trained in the cultural history approach, and did not altogether reject it, Aschero's research and teaching practices gradually started to take interest in a new perspective closer to the innovations introduced by French archaeologist Leroi-Gourhan. From his chair, shared with Ana María Aguerre, at the UBA, they began to introduce New Archaeology or processualist texts into the course syllabus. This initiative – which, according to Luco (2010) was merely a methodological rebellion – was followed by theoretical texts, concepts and topics for discussion slowly introduced by Luis Borrero in his classes and by a group of young researchers, amongst whom were Hugo Yacobaccio, Hugo Nami and Guillermo Mengoni.

While this was taking place, several private centres were created in order to offer to anthropology students what was lacking in the university curriculum, due to political and ideological exclusion. In this chapter we are focusing our concerns on the archaeological field, but the situation in the field of social anthropology was even worse, UBA students having to supplement the very basic UBA syllabus either through private centres or on their own. Amongst those centres the earlier-mentioned AIA offered a more practical training: archaeology students worked on the lab the material recovered from excavations carried out in Tierra del Fuego and were offered the opportunity to do fieldwork. But also, at a time when institutional libraries were very understocked and new books were slow to arrive, the role of professors' private libraries, such as that of Orquera and Piana, was key in their students' academic training (Farro et al. 1999; Fiore 2006; Scheinsohn 2009). In addition, Orquera devoted himself to translating into Spanish the texts that aroused his interest. These translations were given as photocopies to students attending AIA training, and from there to the students at the UBA and the UNLP. Farro et al. (1999) also noted Orquera's role in spreading the New Archaeology at the UNLP when he was appointed as a professor there.

The introduction of processual archaeology to Argentina meant that it came to terms with the recent past and the present. Investigations, although employed to interpret a more remote past, encouraged the idea that archaeology was neither exclusively prehistorical nor committed necessarily to the remote past, but was also concerned with any historical moments, including the present.[6] This would be very significant for the EAAF future members, as they had to first overcome the Argentinean archaeological prejudice against working with the contemporary time (see earlier).

Peculiarities of forensic anthropology in Argentina

After this journey through the history of archaeology in Argentina, we reach December 1983, when a new president was democratically elected in the country. The political climate became favourable to investigate the fate of those who had disappeared during the military dictatorship.

[6]Evidence of this was that in 1984, with the dictatorship over, the curriculum at the UBA was modified, and the curriculum branch called 'Prehistory' (see earlier) was renamed as 'Archaeology and Prehistory'.

At this stage, it is relevant to make a brief reference to the forensic system in Argentina. Forensic experts, mostly physicians, report to the judiciary or the police. In other words, they have no relationship at all with the medico-legal departments of the Schools of Medicine or with any other university. Argentina features a republican presidential system with a strict division of powers – the executive (the government), the legislative (the Parliament), and the judiciary (the system of justice) – but under a dictatorship this division is less clear, and the system of justice, under which forensic physicians work, may find its independence at risk. The same holds true for the police, which served as one of the executing arms of military dictatorship.

Therefore, added to the lack of expertise and experience of official forensic physicians in exhuming bodies and analysing skeletons, is the lack of social credibility, particularly for the victims' relatives, as forensic experts were seen, many times justifiably, as part of the system that caused the disappearance of their sons and daughters.

This context, which differs altogether from the one in which forensic archaeology developed in the United States (to mention one of the countries that took the lead in this application of archaeology), at first puzzled Dr Snow, who did not understand why the students he had recruited were so distrustful (especially of the police, forensic physicians and judges).

Another striking difference, which may largely account for the path followed by forensic archaeology in Latin America, was that in 1984 in Argentina it was not a question of investigating an individual murder whose body could have been buried in the woods, nor a plane crash killing hundreds of passengers, but what came to be known as 'cases of human rights violation' (or crimes against humanity, war crimes or genocides), that is, contexts in which the state decides to kill and disappear citizens for political reasons.

Another feature derived from this context was the close relationship established with the victims' relatives. In a traditional forensic context, experts – archaeologist, anthropologist or physician – have little or no contact with the relatives seeking their loved ones; the decision to get in touch rests with the homicide detective or prosecutor. However, in Argentina, and then in all Latin American countries, this was different. Contacting the victims' relatives was vital, not only to create a climate of trust and transparency, but also to gather valuable data for the investigation. In other words, forensic archaeology in Argentina is not connected to the police, since all efforts have been made to humanise the context of the tasks performed (see examples later).

Finally, the greatest difference, and probably the one that made the investigations most successful, has been the integration of forensic archaeology with both forensic and social anthropology. This means that the archaeological recovery of a skeleton and its associated elements is combined with the analysis of remains at the lab and with the ante-mortem data collected by social anthropologists during their interviews with victims' relatives. Hence, unlike the usual practice in the United Kingdom, archaeologists and anthropologists in Argentina are integrated, this being upheld by the very university curricula, since, as mentioned earlier, students attend a single course of studies combining various branches (social anthropology, archaeology, biological anthropology, etc.).

In the light of all this, the development of forensic archaeology in Argentina, closely linked with the creation of the EAAF, is the result of some random events, together with the quest for truth and justice by hundreds of victims' relatives.

Subsequent development of forensic archaeology and its regional impact

The EAAF has stood as an independent scientific institution since 1986, as a result of proceedings brought to the Argentine courts and, of course, the support of the victims' relatives, who saw in this independent forensic body a concrete opportunity to find out what had happened to their loved ones.

In Argentina the medico-legal framework is under the judiciary and responds to a prosecutor system, where the attorney has the responsibility to investigate and present the evidence to the judge. The judge has the right to nominate whoever they want as an expert witness. There is an official list of expert witnesses which does not include a forensic archaeologist. Most of the experts are forensic pathologists, odontologists, toxicologists and so on, although there is one physician working as a forensic anthropologist. If the prosecutor is not satisfied with the official forensic physician or the police, he or she can call on another expert. That is the way in which the EAAF is normally involved.

From those initial students of medicine, archaeology and anthropology, the team currently comprises 60 persons, including biologists, information techniques and external consultants (such as odontologists and forensic physicians). Forensic archaeologists comprise approximately half of the team, but there is no strict separation among the different specialists at the EAAF. Interested undergraduate and graduate students start as volunteers and after a while some of them can be hired. Currently there is a long waiting list, local and international, to be taken on as a volunteer.

In Argentina the EAAF was mostly committed to the recovery of human remains. 1200 bodies were recovered, some of them very commingled, of which 589 have been identified. Most of those bodies were buried in cemeteries, 65% of them in individual graves, or graves with up to five bodies, one on top of the other. Around 30% were recovered from two mass graves and 5% from military/police compound mass graves. The EAAF worked in most of the 24 provinces of Argentina but most of the bodies were recovered in Buenos Aires, Córdoba, Rosario and Tucumán cities and their surrounding areas.

The EAAF has also taken the Argentine experience to Chile (1989) (Intriago Leiva et al., Chapter 45, this volume), Guatemala (1992) and Peru (2001) (Baraybar and Mora, Chapter 52, this volume), where major human rights violations with thousands of victims had been committed and where groups of young archaeologists and anthropologists had decided to create independent organisations. Colombia (Guatame García et al., Chapter 46, this volume), Venezuela (Muñoz Andrade, Chapter 32, this volume) and México (Hernández and Escorcia-Hernández, Chapter 29, this volume), to mention only a few, already had anthropologists working for the state. Later on, a team of Uruguayan archaeologists would join these efforts to find the victims of the dictatorship in their country (López Mazz and Lusiardo, Chapter 56, this volume). In 2003, all these regional developments converged with the creation of the Latin American Forensic Anthropology Association (*Asociación de Antropología Forense de América Latina* – ALAF), an organisation gathering together forensic anthropologists and archaeologists concerned with regional issues from the entire subcontinent.[7] Every year since 2004 ALAF has organised an international congress in a Latin American country. A certification programme for its members, similar to the one run by the American Board of Forensic Anthropologists (ABFA), is scheduled to be launched at the end of 2013.

Over time, the EAAF has extended its work to some 45 countries in Latin America, Africa, Asia, Eastern Europe and Oceania, summoned by national and international courts, Truth Commissions, local prosecutors, UN Special Commissions of Inquiry, the International Committee of the Red Cross (Tidball-Binz and Hofmeister, Chapter 49, this volume), organisations of victims' families and so on.[8]

Furthermore, at the beginning of 2000, the EAAF's work in Argentina,[9] carried out in isolation for many years, witnessed the creation of others locals groups dealing with forensic archaeology as the Interdisciplinary Group of Archaeology and Anthropology of Tucumán (*Grupo Interdisciplinario de Arqueología y Antropología de Tucumán* – GIAAT) (Arenas et al. 2003–2005, 2005; Ataliva 2004). This is an organisation similar to the EAAF, but since they are linked to the University of Tucumán, they decided to work separately from the EAAF. They aim to work on cases of victims of enforced disappearance in that northern province.

At the same time, other archaeologists, summoned by local authorities, NGOs or by judicial order (see later), started to engage in excavations and reconstructions of facilities serving as clandestine detention centres during the military dictatorship. These facilities, which had usually been under police or military control, were later abandoned; in some cases they began to serve as sites for memory and reflection and archaeological work was conducted, allowing the location of relevant material. A survey conducted by Salerno et al. (2012) identified more than 20 archaeological interventions in former clandestine prisons in Argentina (in preparation, cited in Salerno et al. 2012). They have different origins, geographical locations and trajectories. But most of them followed the EAAF model and constituted themselves as an NGO not depending on academic or other institutions, since, Argentina being a federal republic, there is no overall state organisation or institute that supervises forensic archaeological work. Among them, the Club Atlético research team was led by a Work and Consensus Commission (*Comisión de Trabajo y Consenso*). This gathered together human rights organisations, survivors, victims' families and departments of the City of the Buenos Aires government working at the Club Atlético (a former clandestine detention centre in Buenos Aires city) location. More recently, teams of archaeologists who commenced works in 2002 (Duguine et al. 2013; Pafundi and Tessone 2005; Zarankin and Niro 2009) where incorporated and continue today.

We also have to mention the Anthropological and Archaeological Group Memory and Identity (*Grupo Antropológico-Arqueológico Memoria e Identidad* – GAAMI), which started to work at the clandestine centre known as Mansión Seré in 2000, in Morón, near Buenos Aires city;[10] and the Investigation Team for the Political–Cultural Memory (*Equipo de Investigación por la Memoria Político-Cultural* – EIMePoC), concerned with the reconstruction of the former detention centre known as El Pozo, in Rosario city (Compañy et al. 2011), 400 km from Buenos Aires. Also, certain publications, though addressing forensic issues concerned with the military dictatorship, aim to go beyond the forensic field by using the concept of 'archaeology of the dictatorship and political repression' (Funari and Zarankin 2009; Salerno 2007; Zarankin and Salerno 2008; Zarankin et al. 2012).

[7] For more information, see http://eaaf.typepad.com/alaf/ (last accessed October 2013).

[8] For more information, see EAAF (1991–2009).

[9] For more information, see EAAF (1991–2009).

[10] Bozzutto et al. 2004; Di Vruno 2012; Di Vruno et al. 2006; Dirección de Derechos Humanos, Municipio de Morón 2002–2003/2006–2008, 2007; Doval and Giorno 2010; Doval et al. 2008, 2010; Proyecto Antropológico Mansión Seré 2005.

Conclusion

Forensic archaeology in Argentina was born with the investigations into the human rights violations that had been committed during the last military dictatorship. But archaeology already had a considerable history here. The constitution of the nation-state used some of the 'antiquities' found in Argentinean territory to build up a tradition for its sake. Thus, concern for the remote past and prehistory took root in the country. For forensic archaeology to emerge it was necessary to do away with that concern for the remote past and focus instead on the contemporary. This was made possible largely due to the introduction of processualism at the UBA and the UNLP, which influenced the group of undergraduate students that were to shape the EAAF. We also believe that the long-standing tradition in Argentine archaeology of working outside main official institutions – from Ameghino to AIA – allowed the EAAF to stay independent from the state and to work independently of political and academic circumstances. Inside the state, chances were scarce for forensic archaeology given the initial resistance and political ups and downs. Much progress has been made in Argentina as to the inclusion of forensic archaeology in the academic and forensic fields, but it is still far from the ideal situation. No medico-legal institute has incorporated forensic archaeology; nor has this action been taken by the police force. Some judges and prosecutors regard this as a problem and resort to the EAAF, or try to work more carefully, but ultimately this relies on voluntarism. We can say that most judges understand why archaeological methods are needed in order to recover *desaparecidos* remains but this is not yet automatically translated to the rest of crime research. As we wrote this chapter, and as an example of the inability of police and judges to understand the need for archaeological methods, and the inability of archaeologists to communicate their proficiency, the recovery of a body, supposedly buried clandestinely in a cemetery near Buenos Aires city after a murder case, is being recovered by police officers employing a mechanical shovel.

In Argentina, the academic field includes neither a major in forensic anthropology or archaeology nor a regular course, except the one given by the EAAF at the UBA School of Medicine, which began 17 years ago. From time to time, lectures are delivered at the university level, but this is always thanks to the efforts of individual archaeologists rather than an institutional decision. To conclude, the development of forensic archaeology has primarily focused on the search for those who disappeared 35 years ago. Present cases of disappearances, which would fall within the category of ordinary criminal homicides, would justify a more institutional development and greater interest from academia.

Finally, it is our belief that the context of archaeology in Buenos Aires at the beginning of the 1980s was crucial for the creation of the EAAF and, hence, for the development of forensic archaeology in Argentina. Salerno et al. (2012) explained the time gap between the foundation of the EAAF and the creation of subsequent teams concerned with clandestine detention centres. According to these authors the latter started this work after the academic changes that took place around 2000, associated with the introduction of post-processual archaeological paradigms in Argentina. According to them, this is the paradigm that advocates the removal of time barriers in archaeology and the advent of political commitment. Our interpretation is different. As already stated, we think that processualism was instead the theoretical framework that enabled jumping over the fence that had confined archaeology to prehistory and connecting archaeology with the contemporary.

As for political commitment, our belief is that this is not related to a post-processualist approach, but to individual positions that go beyond any theoretical framework. Working on Patagonian hunter-gatherers is not less political than working on clandestine detention centres. The problem does not lie in the subject matter, but in the manner in which any subject matter is approached. In this sense, processualism, as already stated, should not necessarily be associated with conservative policies. During the military dictatorship, the resistance expressed by UBA archaeologists drew on New Archaeology (Luco 2010). Indeed, the fieldwork and training given by the AIA, basically processualist as stated earlier, enabled these students to take a leap forward and create the EAAF.

Looking ahead, the true challenge of forensic archaeology in Argentina today is to achieve an official place on the judiciary in order not to be exclusively confined to investigations into human rights violations, as it is an invaluable instrument for criminal law in general. This will be up to future generations of archaeologists and judges.

References

Arenas, P., Ataliva,V., López Campeny, S. et al. 2003–2005. Arquitectura del terror: los lugares de la no-memoria en San Miguel de Tucumán (Argentina). *Cuadernos del Instituto Nacional de Antropología y Pensamiento Latinoamericano* 20, 27–45.

Arenas, P., Ataliva, V., López Campeny, S. and Noli, E. 2005. La arqueología y la antropología en la búsqueda de identidades: el caso de los desaparecidos durante la última dictadura militar. *Estudios Sociales del NOA* 8(8), 136–158.

Ataliva, V. 2004. Disputas territoriales de las memorias: apuntes para una arqueología del terrorismo de Estado en Tucumán (Argentina). *Resúmenes. XV Congreso Nacional de Arqueología*

Argentina, 86. Río Cuarto, Universidad Nacional de Río Cuarto.

Bozzutto, D., Diana, A., Di Vruno, A., Dolce, N. and Vazquez, V. 2004. Mansión Seré: debates y reflexiones. Resúmenes. *XV Congreso Nacional de Arqueología Argentina*, 207. Río Cuarto, Universidad Nacional de Río Cuarto.

Compañy, G., González, G., Ovando, L. and Rosetto, D. 2011. A political archaeology of Latin America's recent past: a bridge towards our history. In A. Myers and G. Moshenska (eds.), *Archaeologies of Internment*, 229–244. New York, Springer.

Daniel, G. 1967. *The Origins and Growth of Archaeology*. Harmondsworth, Penguin Books.

Dirección de Derechos Humanos, Municipio de Morón. 2002. *Proyecto Mansión Seré. Encuestas en el Barrio Seré*. Morón, Municipio de Morón.

Dirección de Derechos Humanos, Municipio de Morón. 2002–2003/2006–2008. *Proyecto Mansión Seré. Informes de Gestión*. Morón, Municipio de Morón.

Dirección de Derechos Humanos, Municipio de Morón. 2007. *Proyecto Mansión Seré. Reconstrucción Arqueológica del Ex CCD Mansión Seré o Atila*. Morón, Municipio de Morón.

Di Vruno, A. 2012. La Praxis Arqueológica. El Caso Mansión Seré. In A. Zarankin, M. Salerno and M. C. Perosino (eds.), *Historias Desaparecidas: Arqueología, Memoria y Violencia Política*, 101–115. Córdoba, Brujas.

Di Vruno, A., Diana, A., Seldes, V. et al. 2006. Arqueología en un centro clandestino de detención. El caso Mansión Seré-Atila. In *Actas de Resúmenes del 3° Congreso Nacional de Arqueología Histórica*. Rosario, Universidad Nacional de Rosario.

Doretti, M. and Fondebrider, L. 2001. Science and human rights: truth, justice, reparation and reconciliation: a long way in Third World countries. In V. Buchli and L. Gavin (eds.), *Archaeologies of the Contemporary Past*, 138–144. London/New York, Routledge.

Doval, J. and Giorno, P. 2010. Análisis de los procesos de formación cultural en el sitio Mansión Seré. Un abordaje a partir del proceso destructivo de la casona (1978–1985). *La Zaranda de Ideas* 6, 37–55.

Doval, J., Giorno, P., de Haro, M. and Diana, A. 2008. Una reconstrucción arquitectónica desde la imagen fotográfica. In *Actas de Resúmenes del 5° Congreso de Arqueología de la Región Pampeana*, 111. Santa Rosa, Facultad de Ciencias Humanas.

Doval, J., Giorno, P., de Haro, M. and Diana, A. 2010. Mansión Seré: una reconstrucción arquitectónica desde la imagen fotográfica. In M. Berón, L. Luna, M. Bonomo, C. Montalvo, C. Aranda and M. Carrera Aizpitarte (eds.), *Mamül Mapu: Pasado y Presente desde la Arqueología Pampeana*, 215–226. Buenos Aires, Editorial Libros del Espinillo.

Duguine, L., Durán S., Contissa V. and Carreras, M. 2013. Experiencias desde la arqueología y la conservación para la recuperación material de los ex centros clandestinos de detención, tortura y exterminio (Ciudad Autónoma de Buenos Aires, Argentina). In L. Adad, A. Villafañe and C. Ferrer (eds.), *La Antropología social hoy: a 10 años del nuevo siglo*, 723–734. Olavarría, Universidad Nacional del Centro de La Provincia de Buenos Aires.

EAAF. 1991–2009. *Informes Anuales*. Available at: http://eaaf.typepad.com/eaaf_reports/ (last accessed October 2013).

Farro, M., Podgorny, I. and Tobías, D. 1999. Notas para un ensayo sobre la recepción de la 'Nueva Arqueología' en la Argentina. *Revista do Museu de Arqueologia e Etnologia*, Suplemento 3, 221–234.

Fiore, D. 2006. Comment to Gustavo Politis'. The theoretical landscape and the methodological development of archaeology in Latin America. *Arqueología Suramericana* 2(2), 188–190.

Fondebrider, L. 2002. Reflections on the scientific documentation of Human Rights violations. *International Review of the Red Cross* 84(848), 885–891.

Fondebrider, L. 2009. The application of forensic anthropology to the investigation of political violence in South America. In S. Blau and D. H. Ubelaker (eds.), *Handbook of Forensic Anthropology and Archaeology*, 49–55. Walnut Creek, Left Coast Press.

Funari, P. and Zarankin, A. 2009. *Arqueología de la Represión y Resistencia en América Latina (1960–1980)*. Córdoba, Brujas.

Hobsbawm, E. and Ranger, T. (eds.) 1983. *The Invention of Tradition*. Cambridge, Cambridge University Press.

Kohl, P. and Pérez Gollán, J. 2002. Mixing religion, politics, and prehistory: the life and writings of O. Menghin. *Current Anthropology* 43(4), 561–586.

Laiseca, A. 1982. *Matando Enanos Garrotazos*. Buenos Aires, Editorial de Belgrano.

Luco, S. 2010. Tensión político-académica en la Universidad de Buenos Aires (1975–1983): el cambio de paradigma en la arqueología patagónica. *Revista del Museo de Antropología* 3, 211–224.

Mercante, V. and Ambrosetti, J. 1913. *Vida y Obra del Doctor Florentino Ameghino: Contribución a su Conocimiento*. Buenos Aires, Imprenta Metodista.

Pafundi, L. and Tessone, A. 2005. Trabajo arqueológico in Proyecto de Recuperación de la Memoria Centro Clandestino de Detención y Tortura 'Club Atlético'. In A. Madariaga (ed.), *El Porvenir de la Memoria. Segundo Coloquio Interdisciplinario de Abuelas de Plaza de Mayo*, 103–122. Buenos Aires, Abuelas de Plaza de Mayo.

Podgorny, I. 2009. *El Sendero del Tiempo y de las Causas Accidentales. Los Espacios de la Prehistoria en la Argentina, 1850–1910*. Rosario, Prohistoria ediciones.

Podgorny, I. and Lopes, M. 2008. *El Desierto en una Vitrina. Museos e Historia Natural en la Argentina, 1810–1890*. México, DF, Editorial LIMUSA.

Politis, G. and Bonomo, M. 2011. Nuevos datos sobre el 'Hombre Fósil' de Ameghino. *Publicación Especial Asociación Paleontológica Argentina* 12, 101–135.

Proyecto Antropológico Mansión Seré. 2005. Proyecto antropológico Mansión Seré. In A. Madariaga (ed.), *El Porvenir de la Memoria. Segundo Coloquio Interdisciplinario de Abuelas de Plaza de Mayo*, 137–152. Buenos Aires, Abuelas de Plaza de Mayo.

Salado, M. and Fondebrider, L. 2008. El desarrollo de la antropología forense en Argentina. *Cuadernos de Medicina Forense* 14(53–54), 213–221.

Salerno, M. 2007. "Algo habrán hecho…" La construcción de la categoría "subversivo" y los procesos de remodelación de identidades a través del cuerpo y el vestido (Argentina, 1976–1983). *Revista de Arqueología Americana* 24, 29–65.

Salerno, M., Zarankin, A. and Perosino, M. 2012. Arqueologías de la clandestinidad. Una revisión de los trabajos efectuados en los Centros de Detención Clandestinos de la última dictadura militar en Argentina. *Revista Universitaria de Historia Militar on-line* 2. Cádiz, Centro de Estudios de Historia Militar.

Sanguinetti de Bórmida, A. and Orquera, L. 1975. *Las Fuentes para el Estudio de la Prehistoria*. Buenos Aires, Ed. Glauco.

Scheinsohn, V. 2009. Evolución en la periferia. El caso de la arqueología evolutiva en la Argentina. In M. Cardillo and G. López (eds.), *Teoría, Métodos y Casos de Análisis en Arqueología Evolutiva*, 73–86. Buenos Aires, Editorial SB.

Scheinsohn, V. and Muñoz, A. 2011. La gran aventura de la arqueología. Las investigaciones arqueológicas en el marco del programa extremo oriental del Archipiélago Fueguino. In A. Zangrando, M. Vazquez and A. Tessone (eds.), *Los Cazadores-Recolectores del Extremo Oriental Fueguino*, 115–142. Buenos Aires, Sociedad Argentina de Antropología.

Snow, C. 1984. The investigation of the human remains of the 'disappeared' in Argentina. *American Journal of Forensic Medicine and Pathology* 5, 297–300.

Snow, C. and Bihurriet, M. 1992. An epidemiology of homicide: Ningún Nombre burials in the province of Buenos Aires from 1970 to 1984. In T. Jabine and R. Claude (eds.), *Human Rights and Statistics. Getting the Record Straight*, 328–363. Pennsylvania, University of Pennsylvania Press.

Tillier, A. 2009. *L'Homme et la Mort : l'Émergence du Geste Funéraire durant la Préhistoire*. París, CNRS.

Zarankin, A. and Niro, C. 2009. La materialización del sadismo: arqueología de la arquitectura de los centros clandestinos de detención de la dictadura militar argentina (1976–1983). In P. Funari and A. Zarankin (eds.), *Arqueología de la Represión y Resistencia en América Latina (1960–1980)*, 159–182. Córdoba, Brujas.

Zarankin, A. and Salerno, M. 2008. Después de la tormenta. Arqueología de la represión en América. Complutum 19(2), 21–32.

Zarankin, A. Salerno, M. and. Perosino, M. 2012. *Historias Desaparecidas: Arqueología, Memoria y Violencia Política*. Córdoba, Editorial Brujas.

CHAPTER 44

Forensic archaeology and the Australian war dead

Denise Donlon[1], Anthony Lowe[2] and Brian Manns[3]
[1]*Shellshear Museum, Discipline of Anatomy and Histology, University of Sydney, Sydney, New South Wales, Australia*
[2]*Casey & Lowe Pty Ltd, Marrickville, New South Wales, Australia*
[3]*Army Headquarters, Australian Capital Territory, Canberra, Australia*

Introduction

This chapter provides an overview of the history, current practice and legal requirements that apply when forensic archaeology is used in the recovery of Australian war casualties outside of Australia.

Since the creation of the federated nation of Australia in 1901, Australia has committed significant forces, naval, land and air, to two World Wars (1914–1918 and 1939–1945), the Korean War (1950–1953) and ;the Vietnam War (1962–1975). In addition, Australian military forces have served in Malaysia during and after the Malayan Emergency (1950–1960) and during the period of Confrontation with Indonesia (1963–1966). Since the end of World War II (WWII), Australia has also made significant contributions to peacekeeping and peace-enforcing missions throughout the world. Thus far in the 21st century, Australia has been a member of military coalitions in Iraq (2003–2009) and Afghanistan (since 2001).

Australia and its war dead

Since 1966 Australia's policy in respect to combat deaths has been to repatriate the bodies of slain servicemen and women to Australia and afford them a burial in accordance with their families' wishes. Prior to that, servicemen and women who died overseas under any circumstances were buried in foreign soil. Prior to World War I (WWI), soldiers killed in action were buried in the closest and most convenient cemetery and, in the main, forgotten. However, the carnage of the Western Front during WWI caused some to stop and recognise that the sacrifices being made deserved better treatment. The result was the creation, by Royal Charter in 1917, of the Imperial War Graves Commission (IWGC), renamed the Commonwealth War Graves Commission (CWGC) in 1960.[1] From the beginning, it was intended that the Commission would collect and provide a dignified and egalitarian environment in which the thousands of war dead of the Commonwealth could lie at rest in perpetuity. Australia is among the member nations represented on the Commission and contributes funding (and other) support to the Commission in proportion to the number of Australians who rest in the Commission's cemeteries. Australia also manages all CWGC burials in Australia and Papua New Guinea.

There are 20,802 Australians buried in CWGC cemeteries around the world, and another 9,181 Australians with no known graves are commemorated on CWGC memorials. There are a total of 1,148,963 Commonwealth burials in the care of the CWGC around the world.

There were 281 Australians killed in action during the Korean War, and they are buried in the United Nations Memorial Cemetery at Tanggok near the southern Republic of Korea city of Busan. Also commemorated there are the names of another 44 Australian servicemen from that war who remain unrecovered on the Korean Peninsula.

Australia committed forces to the Malayan Emergency from 1950 until after the emergency was officially declared over in 1960. During that time, 39 Australians were killed although only 15 of the deaths occurred as a result of offensive operations. They are buried in CWGC cemeteries in Malaysia.

Between 1962 and 1966, Indonesia and Malaysia fought a small, undeclared war that is commonly referred to as the Indonesian Confrontation. Australian forces stationed in Malaysia as part of Australia's contribution to the Far East Strategic Command were involved, firstly on the Malaysian peninsula in September and October 1964 and later (March 1965–August 1966) in

[1]For more information, see: http://www.cwgc.org (last accessed March 30 2014).

Forensic Archaeology: A Global Perspective, First Edition. Edited by W.J. Mike Groen, Nicholas Márquez-Grant and Robert C. Janaway.

the Malaysian state of Sarawak on the island of Borneo. During Confrontation, 23 Australians died but only seven of them were on operations. Two Australians from a Special Air Service (SAS) Regiment patrol into the Indonesian state of Kalimantan were lost in 1966 when they were swept away whilst attempting to cross a swollen river. They remained officially dead but with no known grave, until they were found by a combined Australian Army and Indonesian Defence Force team that included an anthropologist and archaeologist, in October 2009. They were repatriated to Australia in April 2010, reunited with their families and were buried with full military honours in Perth, Western Australia and Brisbane, Queensland.

During the early years of Australia's involvement in the Vietnam War, those killed were also buried in CWGC cemeteries in Malaysia and Singapore. One Australian was buried in Kranji War Cemetery in Singapore, and all of the remainder (24) were buried in the Terendak Military Cemetery. With pressure mounting on the Australian government, in March 1966, the government policy was amended to allow for burial in the closest CWGC cemetery or repatriation to Australia in response to a family's request. A total of six Australians were listed as missing from the Vietnam War: four lost in the southern part of the country were serving in the Australian Army and two lost in central Vietnam were the crew of a Royal Australian Air Force (RAAF) aircraft. Between 2007 and 2009, several Australian Army teams searched for, found and recovered the remains of all four Army personnel. Forensic archaeologists and anthropologists were present in the teams for all recoveries. An Army team also discovered the crash site of the RAAF aircraft with its two-man crew, and their remains were recovered by a RAAF team that employed appropriate archaeological techniques and under the direction of an archaeologist with considerable experience in the recovery of wartime human remains. All six were repatriated to Australia, reunited with their families and buried with full military honours.

Today, all Australian servicemen and women who die overseas whilst on military service are returned to Australia and are buried in the place chosen by their families.

Individual Australian services' responsibility

Current Australian Defence Force (ADF) policy (Commonwealth Government of Australia 1996) requires that each individual Service (Navy, Army and Air Force) is to provide an appropriate response to the discovery of human remains that are believed to be those of a previously unaccounted for serviceman or woman.

The ADF policy directs also that each of these services is responsible for the recovery, repatriation and burial of those servicemen and women who served in it and who remain unaccounted for.

Australian Army

The Australian Army, which has the majority of unaccounted for personnel, is the only Australian service that has a permanent unit tasked with the accounting for all of the Army's unaccounted for soldiers. Prior to 2010, most Australian Army responses were tasked to the Australian Army History Unit (AAHU). The AAHU, officially established in 1996, comprises full-time civilian and Army staff, part-time Army reserve staff and utilises the expertise of forensic specialists when required. Over the past 15 years, the AAHU has investigated and accounted for a number of Australian soldiers whose remains were discovered, mostly in France and Belgium.

In the late 1990s, compelling evidence was produced by an Australian amateur historian, Mr Lambis Englezos, that there were many Australian and British soldiers buried in mass graves at Pheasant Wood near Fromelles in Northern France. In 2008, a joint Australian Army and UK Ministry of Defence project team engaged Glasgow University Archaeological Research Division (GUARD) to confirm the location and number of burial pits and to confirm the presence of human remains. This included the use of ground-penetrating radar (GPR) followed by exploratory excavation of the site by forensic archaeologists and forensic anthropologists from GUARD. In May 2009, phase two was commenced by a British archaeology company – Oxford Archaeology, supervised by the CWGC on behalf of the Australian and British governments. Using a specialist team of forensic and investigative professionals including British and Australian archaeologists, forensic anthropologists, British crime scene recorders and X-ray specialists, all of the pits were opened and the remains of 250 Australian and British soldiers were successfully exhumed. During January and February of 2010, 249 of the 250 soldiers were reinterred at the Fromelles (Pheasant Wood) Military Cemetery, the first new cemetery built by the CWGC in over 50 years. To date, 119 have been identified by name – all Australians – and the joint identification work will continue until 2014 in the hope that more might be identified.[2] The size and complexity and geographic separation along with the joint Australian and British nature of the project meant that using European-based specialists with sufficient resources was the most practical course of action.

[2]For more information, see: http://www.army.gov.au/Our-work/Unrecovered-War-Casualties-Army/Fromelles/Remains-discovered-recovered-and-reinterred-at-Fromelles (last accessed March 30 2014).

In September 2006, and in response to mounting pressure from Australian interest groups, staff from AAHU were given the task of investigating information that it was alleged would lead to discoveries and recoveries of Australian servicemen who remained unaccounted for from the Vietnam War. Between early 2007 and late 2009, AAHU-led teams, which included archaeologists, anthropologists and Army investigators, went on to locate all six Australians who remained unrecovered from Vietnam.

In early 2010, the need for a permanent capability to respond to the increasing notifications of the discoveries of human remains was identified by the Australian Army. In July 2010, the establishment of Unrecovered War Casualties – Army (UWC-A) was approved.[3] This decision removed from the AAHU the responsibility to respond to any notifications of human remains. The role of UWC-A is to investigate all discoveries of human remains that are believed to be those of Australian soldiers and to investigate all other information that might result in the discovery of human remains of Australian soldiers from earlier conflicts (WWI, WWII, Korean War). UWC-A comprises a small permanent civilian (a middle-level manager and specialist investigative case managers) and a part-time uniformed Army Reserve staff. This small team is supplemented by additional Reserve (part-time) staff from across all three Australian services and other specialists from outside the Australian Defence Force (ADF) when fieldwork to search for, recover and identify human remains is undertaken. UWC-A utilises the skills of a broad pool of investigators, archaeologists, anthropologists, odontologists, pathologists, scenes of crime specialists and others from within the ADF. Without exception, these specialists are highly credentialed and possess extensive experience in their field of expertise. Outside of their Reserve Force employment, they hold senior positions in universities and private consultancies (Manns 2012).

UWC-A carries out detailed historical research, interviews witnesses and carries out excavations and recovers human remains. The collection of ante-mortem records is an important part of this process. However, it was only after WWI that dental records and metal dog tags were used. This expertise ensures the accuracy and veracity of any identifications that result from the work of UWC-A. This, in turn, allows the Army to provide each Australian soldier with a burial in an appropriate place with dignity and respect.

Royal Australian Air Force

The Royal Australian Air Force (RAAF), previously the Australian Flying Corps (AFC), has taken part in many of the 20th century's major conflicts including WWII, the Korean War and the Vietnam War. The AFC saw action in New Guinea, Egypt, Palestine and on the Western Front throughout WWI. During WWII, Australian aircrew served with the Royal Air Force (RAF) over Europe and the RAAF operated throughout the South Pacific, often without the support of immediate search-and-recovery aircraft. Many aircraft were lost over Papua New Guinea, and it is estimated that there are around 50 Australian aircraft still missing there. Since 1994, the RAAF has recovered the remains of 23 WWII Australian servicemen, from Buru in Indonesia, Irian Jaya, and from Kimbe, Bugaiu, Kewieng and New Britain in Papua New Guinea, successfully identifying 21 (Griffiths and Duflou 2000).

Royal Australian Navy

During WWI, the Royal Australian Navy (RAN) was involved with Germany's South Pacific colonies and later as part of Royal Navy forces in the Mediterranean and North Seas. In WWII, RAN ships operated as part of Royal Navy flotillas, serving in the Mediterranean, the Red Sea, the West African Coast, the Persian Gulf and the Indian Ocean. In the Pacific War, the RAN operated more independently and saw action in many Cold War era conflicts in the Asia-Pacific region off Korea, Malaysia and Vietnam. The bulk of the RAN war dead for WWI, WWII and Korea are either still listed as missing (lost with ship or buried at sea) or were buried ashore in war graves at time of death. There have been a few cases where bodies were exhumed from original burial sites and moved to centralised war cemeteries in Bagdad after WWI and in Singapore, Jakarta and Ambon after WWII. Since the end of the Cold War, the RAN has been part of Coalition forces in the Persian Gulf and Indian Ocean and in East Timor and the Solomon Islands. The recovery of Australian Naval personnel from offshore has been a rare occurrence. Sunken ships, when discovered, may become Protected Wrecks. A Japanese midget submarine from WWII just north of Sydney is a Protected Wreck, making it illegal to disturb the crew of two still onboard. Described below is the recovery on Christmas Island of a crewmember of HMAS Sydney II that sank with all hands in 1941 in the Indian Ocean.

Legislation, permits and negotiations

Before any ADF recovery team can be deployed to a foreign country to recover remains approval from the host country must be negotiated. These negotiations are generally carried out by the staff of the appropriate Australian diplomatic post and where possible by ADF representatives.

[3]For more information, see: http://www.army.gov.au/Our-work/Unrecovered-War-Casualties-Army (last accessed March 30 2014).

In most circumstances, recovery work must be done in conjunction with host country agencies. In Vietnam, Australian search and recovery teams operated under the scrutiny of several national agencies. These included that country's Ministry of Defence, Ministry of Foreign Affairs and others. In Malaysia, where a large area was excavated in search of a suspected WWII mass burial, work required the approval of the Director of National Heritage and the search team was a combined Malaysian Heritage Commission and Australian Army one.

Without exception, approval is negotiated before any teams are sent to a foreign country. These negotiations are normally carried out by the Australian High Commission or Embassy located in the country, or with diplomatic credentials for the country where remains are reported. Often, the lead in such negotiations is managed by the Australian Defence staff posted to the diplomatic post (High Commission or Embassy). At all times, there is close coordination and cooperation between the appropriate ADF agency and the diplomatic post.

The ADF, and in particular UWC-A, works in close cooperation with similar agencies from other nations, in particular the United States and the United Kingdom. This cooperation includes the exchange of information and expertise, as well as complementary support and assistance in conjunction with field work to recover and identify human remains.

The Joint POW/MIA Accounting Command (JPAC) is the US agency, with its headquarters near Honolulu in Hawaii, with a mandate to search for and recover all of those Americans who have no known grave (Pietruszka, this volume). Once JPAC has recovered and identified an unaccounted for American, the remains are transferred to the appropriate service's casualty accounting unit in order that the family can lay the body to rest in the place of its choice.

The British Ministry of Defence Joint Casualty and Compassion Cell (JCCC) does similar work, as does the Republic of Korea Ministry of National Defence Agency for KIA Recovery and Identification (MAKRI).

The active Australian agency, UWC-A, maintains regular lines of communications with each of these agencies and that includes close cooperation when required. UWC-A staff may be embedded in JPAC field teams, spend time working in the JPAC Central Identification Laboratory (JPAC-CIL) in Hawaii or exchange research assistance with counterparts in JPAC. Similarly, Australian recovery and identification work will be carried out with the British JCCC. Often, this will include cooperation to identify, and later bury, Australian servicemen who were members of the crew of a recovered WWII RAF aircraft. In the case of MAKRI, UWC-A has provided information that allowed Australian servicemen to be excluded during the identification of human remains recovered in the Republic of Korea.

Private searches

Occasionally, interested parties and possible relatives have made their own investigations and searches for those missing. These activities probably began in Papua New Guinea in the 1980s with the discovery of WWII Australian aircraft. Such activities have increased, especially in Papua New Guinea and in Europe, possibly as a result of the finding of the previously unknown mass graves at Fromelles. Despite often good intentions, there is a danger that private (amateur) excavations, because of a lack of suitable forensic expertise, will compromise the positive identification of any recovered remains.

Current practice – archaeological techniques used

Traditional archaeological techniques used in the recovery of the war dead may be modified to deal with the casework that typifies such recoveries. The following are two case studies that illustrate the methods and challenges involved in such recoveries.

Case study 1 – The Vietnam War

The Vietnam War was Australia's longest war of the 20th century, running from 1962 until 1973. While 521 Australians died during the war, at its end there were six men who had been killed in action but whose bodies had not been recovered from the battlefields on which they fell. They were to remain unaccounted for until the early years of the 21st century.

On the 17 April 1971, an RAAF helicopter A2-767, UH-1H Iroquois was hit by enemy ground fire and crashed and burned in the Minh Dam Mountains of then Phuoc Tuy province. Lance Corporal (LCPL) John Gillespie of 8 Field Ambulance was the Medic on board that dust-off helicopter (medical air evacuation). A crewmember attempted to free him from the aircraft wreckage but could not due to his legs being trapped under the side of the aircraft. He died in the fire and the aircraft burned for several hours. Three other soldiers also died as a result of the crash and were recovered at the time. The next day, the aircraft still radiated intense heat and rescuers could not get closer than 4 ft to it. It was reported that there was no trace of human remains visible in the wreckage.

After 1971, the crash site was not revisited by non-Vietnamese until it was re-identified by Mr Peter Aylett of Operation Aussies Home (OAH) with the assistance of locals in 2004. OAH is a non-government interest group dedicated to the discovery and recovery of Australia's missing in action from the Vietnam War and other wars. The Department of Defence subsequently organised a team of archaeologist and anthropologist, two odontologists and Army investigators to investigate the site, in order to determine whether human remains might be present. The team initially visited the site on 20 March, with work taking place from 21 March to 23 March 2007.

The archaeology

The use of archaeological techniques to investigate the site meant that the crash site and therefore the area potentially retaining human remains could be defined and the process and results documented. As the crash site location was initially based on the evidence of eyewitnesses, the archaeological testing was also a test of their claims, arriving at results that could be independently measured.

In March 2007, preliminary testing was conducted at the crash site as identified by OAH. This indicated the presence of metal debris, leading to a more comprehensive testing programme in November 2007. As the location of the crash site was the subject of differing opinion, the focus of the archaeological input was to determine, if possible, where the helicopter came to rest after it crashed and to determine whether any human skeletal remains were present in or around the crash site. While the actual helicopter site was to be the focus of the investigation, it was also important to determine the extent of debris, in order to ensure that deeper deposits that might have retained human remains could be identified.

The identification of the actual crash site was complicated by eyewitness accounts. A former Vietnamese soldier, Mr Hung, who inspected the wreckage approximately 1 year after the crash and who apparently participated in its dismantling, attended the site on 15 November 2007, and identified an area some way above the location tested in March 2007. The soldier had also previously discussed and inspected the location with Mr Roy Zegers, crewman on the crashed helicopter, and Mr Zegers concurred with the site identification.

The newly identified location was a large relatively flat area immediately adjacent to the top of the hill. The overall area was cleared of vegetation and was about 750 m^2 (Figure 44.1). Five 1 m^2 test trenches were set out in the Upper Area with the intent of recovering helicopter debris and identifying whether this was either the crash location or where the helicopter came to rest. More trenches were set out on the slope below to pick up the anticipated 'wash' of debris down slope and to determine the extent of the debris field.

Each trench was excavated stratigraphically, the thin layer of leaf litter first being removed as a unit, and in turn the humic topsoil and the upper subsoil. All soil was sieved in two nested 450 mm sieves, with mesh sizes of 5 and 2 mm. Once the area's characteristic strata were determined, the relatively thin soil profile in each square could be quickly excavated, without going deeper than necessary. This meant that areas could be efficiently 'crossed off', therefore keeping valuable time to focus on the crash debris area once that had been identified.

The Upper Area, being the location identified by Mr Hung and Mr Zegers, produced no helicopter debris. In archaeological terms, the area was sterile and no evidence of the crash was found in the five squares (A–E) in this location. Most of the squares, however, did produce shrapnel which, in most cases, was located immediately below the leaf litter. In Square E, a large piece of shrapnel was found embedded vertically in the soil just below the leaf litter. The implication of the depth of the suspected wartime shrapnel was that the development of the humic topsoil layer was somewhat slower than expected. Consequently, any skeletal remains would be found quite close to the present surface.

The squares set out immediately below the Upper Area to intercept any wash of debris down the slope revealed nearly no helicopter debris. Square F had only one shell fragment, with G having three. Square H had small fragments of helicopter skin. Square I had a length of wire and two cartridge cases.

Squares were set out to the north (K) and south (N, O, P) in order to determine the limits of helicopter debris. All these squares had little or no helicopter debris although K had some fragments of ceramic heat shield. This allowed the work to concentrate on the main area of helicopter debris in the vicinity of Trenches 1 and 2 dug in the March 2007 testing. In the current programme, this area was Squares J and L, which were expanded as the spread of debris continued, making up an area of about 32 m^2. Square L had been recently disturbed, presumably by persons looking for helicopter debris. In this area, a concentration of helicopter debris was found including engine parts, fabric and metal flooring from the cabin, and 'cooked off' rounds. Some items can be linked directly to Gillespie – medicine vials, one half of a pair of scissors or clamp, and harness brackets. In J West were found other items likely to be connected to LCPL Gillespie (Figure 44.2; Lowe 2007a).

The human remains

Bones, showing evidence of exposure to an extremely high temperature, were found amongst this debris, mostly scattered through L but also in J West. The bones' context is directly associated with the helicopter and its debris and therefore with LCPL Gillespie. Square L also had a high level of magnesium thought to represent ash from the combustion of magnesium alloys commonly used in aircraft, indicating that the helicopter came to rest in the immediate vicinity of Squares J and L. Debris was consequently scattered to the south and west of this location, through dismantling of the wreck and by the action of wind and rain. It was thought extremely improbable that any further human remains, washed from the wreck site, had survived in locations further downhill of the crash location.

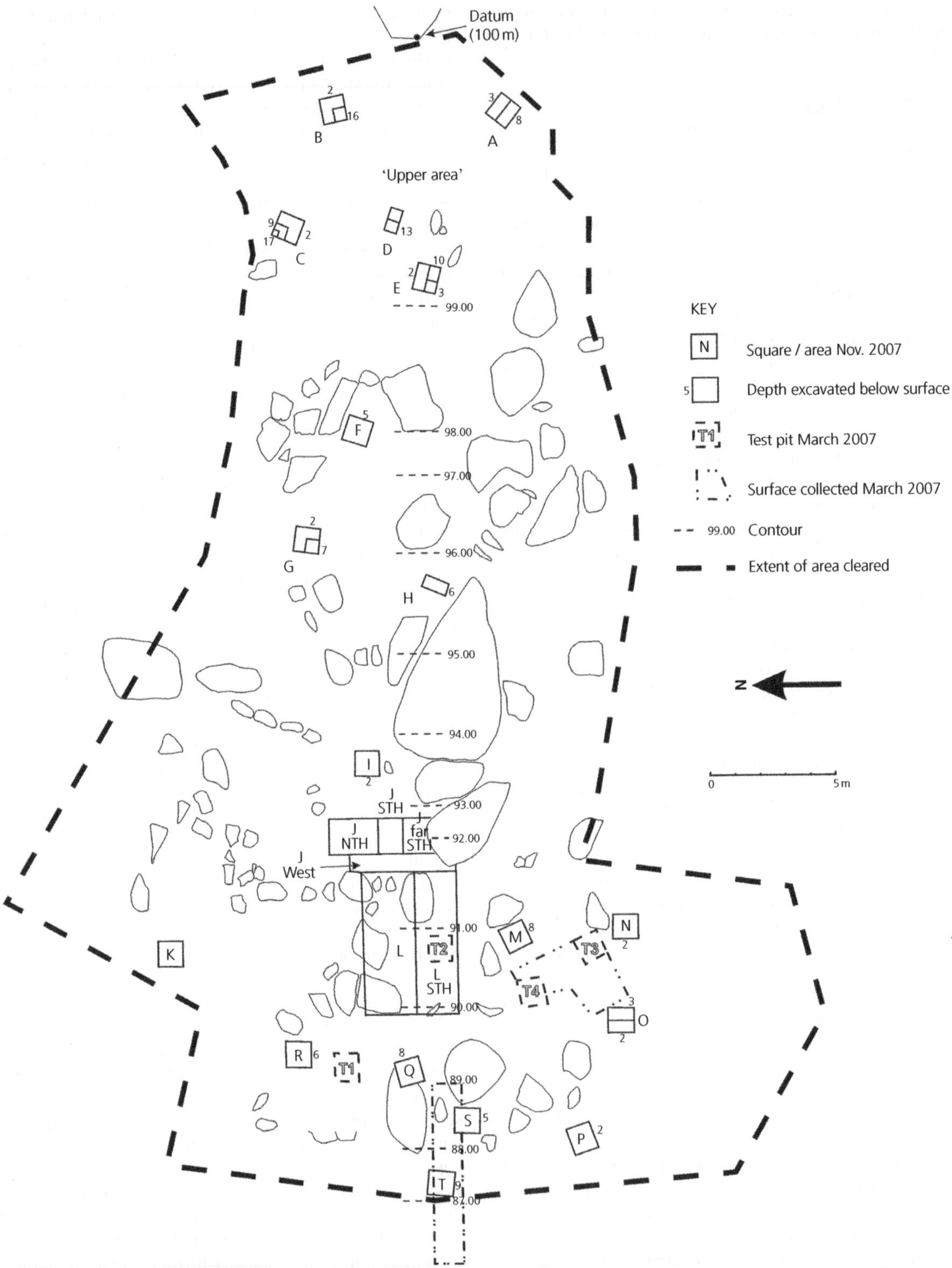

Figure 44.1 Plan of area investigated and squares excavated. A temporary height datum (top) of 100 m was used. The crash debris was concentrated in Squares J and L.

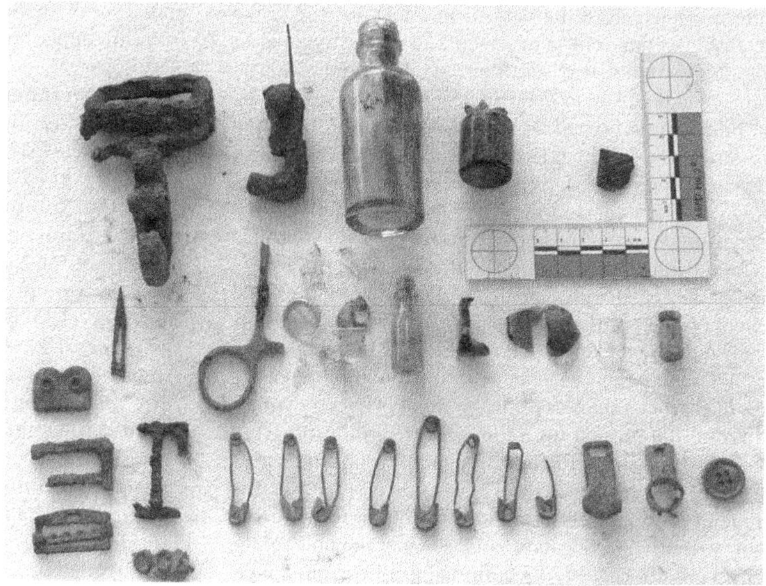

Figure 44.2 Items likely to be connected to Gillespie – a zip fastener, scissors, scalpel blade, medicine bottles and safety pins.

The bones found within the area of wreckage were fragmented and some showed signs of heat-induced distortion of the cortical bone. The condition of the bones is also consistent with bones dating to the period of the Vietnam War, in that the unburned bones were leached and somewhat fragile. However, the pH of the soil at the Vietnam site was 8, which is slightly alkaline and therefore quite good for the preservation of bone.

Some of the bones also showed evidence of possible high impact fracturing, consistent with those likely to occur in a helicopter crash. The bones were later examined by Professor Nguyen Trong Toan, Director of the Military Forensic Institute in Hanoi. Professor Toan reviewed the Australian team's findings and agreed with the assessment that, in all probability, the bones were those of LCPL Gillespie. There was a ramp ceremony for LCPL Gillespie in Hanoi in December 2007 after which he was repatriated to Australia and buried in Melbourne.

From 2007 until 2009, Australian teams recovered another five Australian servicemen in Vietnam, and no Australian servicemen remain missing in action from the Vietnam War.

Case study 2 – WWII: the unknown sailor from HMAS Sydney II

Background

On 19 November 1941, HMAS *Sydney*, a light cruiser of the Royal Australian Navy with an impressive record of war service, was lost following a battle with the German raider HSK *Kormoran* in the Indian Ocean off the Western Australian coast. The loss of the *Sydney* with 645 on board was Australia's worst naval disaster (National Archives of Australia Fact sheet 111). Almost 3 months later, a corpse of an unidentified sailor was recovered from a Carley float as it drifted by Christmas Island. The corpse was buried in the Old European cemetery, overlooking Flying Fish Cove, on Christmas Island. As a result of public pressure, in 1997 there was a Parliamentary Enquiry into the loss of HMAS Sydney. They recommended attempts be made to search for both the *Sydney* and the grave, which should then be exhumed and identified (Parliamentary Enquiry 1999).

The archaeology

2001 expedition

In June 2001, as a result of the Parliamentary Enquiry and the recollections of a former engineer on Christmas Island, a reconnaissance was made of the site on Christmas Island of the possible grave of the unknown sailor. Later that year, a team of forensic specialists, including an anthropologist/archaeologist, an odontologist, two pathologists and a Navy investigator, was taken to excavate the potential site and to recover the remains for reburial. An area of about 35 m^2 was excavated by hand to a depth of between 0.5 and 1.5 m. Depth varied depending on the presence of limestone pinnacles. The area of the possible grave was also surveyed using GPR. No grave or remains were found (Donlon 2001).

2006 expedition

A second expedition in 2006, led by Captain James Parsons RAN, travelled to Christmas Island in another attempt to locate the burial. This team comprised an archaeologist, an anthropologist, two odontologists and a Navy investigator. The archaeological challenge was to determine which of the various locations for the grave given by several informants who had seen the grave in the early 1950s was accurate, while doing as little damage to the place as possible. The location provided by an informant who had taken a photograph of the grave in 1950 was tested first. This location in the Old European cemetery was tested by excavating narrow trenches down through the 400 mm thick layer of relatively friable humic topsoil to compacted clayey brown subsoil.

All the initial trenches showed that the slope in this section of the cemetery was made up of horizontally stratified layers of deposit, with no sign of vertical cuts or disturbance which would indicate the presence of a grave. The trenches were then widened with the intent of making it less likely that a short grave was present between them.

When the precipitous nature of the terrain in part of the cemetery made further investigation unsafe, it was decided to test in an adjacent vacant plot within the cemetery. Initial digging showed the strata to be mixed and without stratification and several possible grave cuts were noticed. Work continued until corroded nails and fragments of what appeared to be decayed timber were found, before human bone was exposed. The grave was found placed at right angles to the previous graves in the row and excavation of the grave revealed a rectangular timber coffin (1.5 × 0.8 m) at a depth of about 2 m (Figure 44.3).

Subsequent excavation of the grave exposed a human skeleton, flexed at the knees, and buried face down. The skeleton's arms were separated at the elbow joint, with the forearms and hands underneath the body, while the upper arms were splayed out. Five metal eyelets lying adjacent to the western end of the coffin gave the impression that the body might have been wrapped in a hessian or canvas sheet. Four large press-stud buttons and several smaller press-stud buttons were recovered from the upper body area (Lowe 2007b).

The human remains

The entire skeleton was found although parts were fragmented. The skeleton was flown to the Shellshear Museum at the University of Sydney where it was analysed by an anthropologist, odontologists and a pathologist. There was shrapnel embedded in the frontal bone of the cranium. Numerous restorations in both amalgam and gold were present. Cranial and pelvic features suggest the skeletal remains were Caucasoid and male. An age range of 22–31 years is indicated and stature was estimated at 168.2–187.8 cm (5′6″–6′2″). Additional DNA and stable isotope analysis provided successful results. His dentition was compared with about 300 surviving dental records (Donlon 2008). However, this sailor remains unidentified. In 2008, a Commission of Enquiry into the loss of the *Sydney* concluded that this skeleton was probably that of a sailor from the *Sydney* (Cole 2008).

Also in 2008, the wreck of HMAS *Sydney* (II) was found by the Finding Sydney Foundation of about 207 km (c. 128 miles) from the west coast (Steep Point) of Western Australia at a depth of about 2468 m, and the wreck of the HSK *Kormoran* (which was scuttled) was found nearby. Later in 2008, the unknown sailor was interred with full military honours at the Geraldton War Cemetery, Western Australia (Figure 44.4).

Future trends

The future of UWC-A is clear, and it can be expected that its roles and tasks and its methods of operation will mature and evolve over time. It is unlikely that the

Figure 44.3 Testing in area in the Old European cemetery as indicated by eyewitness. The actual grave location was in the vacant space to the right of the tent in the midground.

Figure 44.4 Headstone of the unknown sailor in the Geraldton War Cemetery in Western Australia.

principle role of reacting to notifications of the discovery of remains and the submission of information will change. There is no apparent dwindling of work well into the foreseeable future; in fact, the number of reports of human remains and the frequency of those reports has been increasing in recent years. Such is the increase in discoveries in Papua New Guinea that UWC-A has installed a temporary morgue/storage facility at the CWGC Bomana War Cemetery near Port Moresby to enable it to properly process the volume of remains being recovered. All of the remains recovered in Papua New Guinea are buried in CWGC cemeteries in that country. It is likely that UWC-A might eventually be given an ADF wide responsibility for the recovery of human remains and a more direct management of the ADF's forensic specialists.

Conclusions

The history of the use of forensic archaeology in Australia is very recent – probably only a matter of a decade or two (Blau and Sterenberg, Chapter 33 this volume). Its use in the excavation of the Australian war dead has proved to be extremely important in their successful recovery and identification. As well as being able to document the methods used at each site and the results obtained, the use of archaeological techniques to investigate sites has been a useful tool to test eyewitness claims about the sites, particularly as even in the case of the Vietnam War many years have now passed and the locations have often been subject to changes that may have led to confusion among those returning to the scene. The growing public interest in, and awareness of, such recoveries, will ensure the ongoing use and development of forensic archaeology in the recovery of Australia's war dead into the future.

Acknowledgements

We thank Commander Greg Swinden, Royal Australian Navy (RAN), for information about the RAN war dead.

References

Cole, T. R. H. 2008. *HMAS Sydney II Commission of Enquiry 2009.* Available at: http://www.defence.gov.au/sydneyii/finalreport/index.html (last accessed 30 March 2014).

Commonwealth Government of Australia, National Archives of Australia. *The Sinking of HMAS Sydney, November 1941* – Fact Sheet 111. Commonwealth Government of Australia, National Archives of Australia. Canberra.

Commonwealth Government of Australia, The Commonwealth War Graves Commission – Charter of Incorporation dated 21 May 1917 and Supplemental Charter dated 8 June 1964.

Commonwealth Government of Australia. *The Defence Instructions (General) Missing in Action Presumed Killed: Recovery of Human Remains of Australian Defence Force Members* PERS 20-4, issued on 12 December 1996.

Donlon, D. 2001. *Excavation of the Old European Cemetery Christmas Island: A Possible Site for the Grave of the Unknown*

Sailor of HMAS Sydney. Canberra, Report to the Royal Australian Navy.

Donlon, D. 2008. *Report on the Examination of Skeletal Remains from the Minh Dam Mountains*, Vietnam 2007. Canberra, Report to the Army History Unit, Department of Defence.

Griffiths, C. J. and Duflou, J. 2000. Recovery of Australian service personnel missing in action from World War II. The work of the ADF forensic recovery team. *ADF Health* Volume 1 Number 2.

Lowe, T. 2007a. *Results of Archaeological Program. Gillespie Crash Site, Minh Dam Mountains, Vietnam*. Canberra, Draft Report to Army History Unit, Department of Defence.

Lowe, T. 2007b. *Locating the Grave of the Unknown Sailor, Christmas Island 2006*. Canberra, Report to the Royal Australian Navy.

Manns, B. 2012. Creating and managing multi-disciplinary, multi-function forensic teams to recover and identify Australia's wartime missing in action. *ANZFSS Symposium*, Hobart, Tasmania, Australia, September 2012.

Parliament of the Commonwealth of Australia, Joint Standing Committee on Foreign Affairs, Defence and Trade 1999. *Report on the Loss of HMAS Sydney*. Canberra, AGPS.

Websites

Australian Army. *Unrecovered War Casualties-Army*. Available at: http://www.army.gov.au/Our-work/ (accessed 11 September 2014).

Commonwealth Government of Australia, Office of Australian War Graves. Available at: http://www.dva.gov.au/commems_oawg/OAWG/Pages/index.aspx (accessed 11 September 2014).

Commonwealth of Australia. *Australian War Memorial*. Available at: http://www.awm.gov.au/ (accessed 11 September 2014).

Commonwealth War Graves Commission. Available at: http://www.cwgc.org/ (accessed 11 September 2014).

Commonwealth War Graves Commission. Available at: http://www.cwgc.org/ (accessed 9 August 2014).

Ministry of Defence, UK. *Joint Casualty and Compassionate Centre (JCCC)*. Available at: https://www.gov.uk/joint-casualty-and-compassionate-centre-jccc (accessed 11 September 2014).

United States Department of Defense. *Joint POW/MIA Accounting Command*. Available at: http://www.jpac.pacom.mil/ (accessed 11 September 2014).

CHAPTER 45

Forensic archaeology in Chile: the contribution of the Chilean state to our memory, truth and justice

Marisol Intriago Leiva[1], Joyce Stockins Ramírez[2] and Claudia Garrido Varas[3,*]

[1] *Anthropologist, Head of the Special Unit of Forensic Identification, SML, Santiago, Chile*

[2] *Forensic Archaeologist in the Special Unit of Forensic Identification, SML, Santiago, Chile*

[3] *Odontologist, Ms in Human Identification in Special Unit of Forensic Identification, SML, Santiago, Chile*

Introduction

The Medico-Legal Service (*Servicio Médico Legal* – SML) of Chile is a centralised public service under the Ministry of Justice, which follows the provisions of Law No. 20.065, which establishes in its Article 2 that 'The purpose of the SML is to provide technical and scientific advice to the courts and research institutions throughout the national territory, in the fields of legal medicine, forensic science and other related matters' (Lagos Escobar et al. 2005, http://www.leychile.cl/Navegar?idNorma=243150). By judicial and governmental order (Exempt Resolution No 3153 2007, 1), the SML has emphasised the identification of victims of human rights violations in the period from 11 September 1973 to 11 March 1990, thus executing public policies regarding truth, justice and reparation of the aforementioned cases.

The Special Forensic Identification Unit (*Unidad Especial de Identificación Forense* – UEIF) of the SML was created in 2011; its main function is the following:

> to assist the jurisdictional and investigative authorities in human identification and determination of cause of death in complex cases, in order to perform expert analyses, actions and procedures in line with quality standards, coordinating and collaborating with organisations and institutions, both public and private, national and international, related to the field of Forensic Identification (Exempt Resolution No 004742 2011, 1).

Among its tasks, the UEIF must 'perform expert analysis pertaining to partially skeletonised remains including complete, incomplete, single and commingled individuals of forensic interest. The areas of expertise include evidence-gathering processes, anthropological, dental, associated evidence and forensic analysis, besides other relevant aspects' (Exempt Resolution No 004742 2011, 1). The UEIF must also'[c]ontinue with forensic activities in cases of human rights violations for the period September 1973 to March 1990, in line with the guidelines of the Human Rights Program of the SML' (Exempt Resolution No 004742 2011, 2).

Two things may be deduced from the preceding paragraphs. First, the UEIF continues with the work of the Human Rights Program of the SML, in operation between 2008 and 2010. Second, the approach to complex cases is comprehensive and multidisciplinary, including a forensic approach from the time of evidence gathering to the various analyses from different disciplines, all of which must work together to provide information in a comprehensive and coordinated manner to the judicial body, the victim's families and society as a whole. In this model, the contribution and participation of forensic archaeology is present from the time of discovery to laboratory analysis by qualified and trained professionals, along with the implementation of its methods and approaches in the development of protocols and procedures. This incorporates, from the time of its initial intervention, the concept of chain of custody, a protocol which, in Chile, establishes norms for evidence collection and its treatment or management, under the direction of prosecutors and judges, who are responsible for guiding the investigation and protecting the site where the finding took place, according to the provisions contained in Articles 80 and 83 of the Criminal Procedure Code (*Código Procesal Penal*) of Chile.

In our country, the development and contribution of archaeology to the forensic field is closely linked to the

*Currently Forensic Advisor in the International Committee of the Red Cross.

Forensic Archaeology: A Global Perspective, First Edition. Edited by W.J. Mike Groen, Nicholas Márquez-Grant and Robert C. Janaway.

violent and abrupt break of democracy in September of 1973, which involved the murder and disappearance of supporters of the socialist regime of President Salvador Allende (1970–1973) and many civilians by the Armed Forces, with the support of key members of powerful economic groups in the country. The military coup that put an end to nearly a century of democratic tradition in Chile initiated a terror dynamic that divided, and still divides, this nation where illegal detentions, torture, exile and forced disappearance became everyday issues in people's lives. The return to democracy after a plebiscite was called in 1988 allowed a cautious, still under military disclosure, of the horror experienced by thousands of families, who despite fear and threat, organised themselves to search for their missing relatives and demand truth and justice. Since the beginning of the 1990s, archaeologists and anthropologists have joined their efforts voluntarily and, following a few judicial instructions, collaborated in the search and recovery of the remains of the victims illegally buried in cemeteries, ravines, mine shafts, furnaces, military land and desert plains (Cáceres Roque 2011).

However, in addition to the weak democratic structure and the non-existence of institutional coordination, the systematised judicial secrecy and lack of state guidelines, there was no organisation that could take scientific and methodological responsibility for the analyses of these complex cases, unlike what happened in Argentina, with the formation of the Forensic Anthropology Team (Fondebrider and Scheinsohn, Chapter 43, this volume). In view of these circumstances, the SML assumed responsibility for the recovery and analysis of cases demanding technical and methodological capabilities that were far from the reality of the institution. Without real political will and financial support that would facilitate the required technical standards to address these cases, an impoverished SML that had been mutilated by the same dictatorship took on the daunting task of identifying hundreds of bodies, with more limitations than capabilities.

Despite these conditions, an archaeological perspective was applied to the expert tasks, but not in the optimal way. In 2000, with the incorporation of archaeologist Pamela Brito,[1] there was for the first time the urgent need to comply strictly with the methodological standards of the discipline, both in terms of recovery of evidence and the recording of the excavations, elements that so far had been met irregularly, with foreseeable consequences for laboratory analysis. In 2003, with the arrival of the archaeologist Mrs Ximena Novoa, together with a technical team made up of two anthropologists, two odontologists and one physician, archaeological methodology began to be applied systematically in terms of the approach to the sites, as well as the proper written and photographic record of each stage of the excavation and evidence-gathering process.

Patio 29 – the turning point for the incorporation of archaeology in forensic investigation

One of the most emblematic cases in investigations associated with human rights in our country is the Patio 29 case. During the first weeks following the military coup, an attack on the civil population took place in the capital city, Santiago. At that time, anyone who did not respond to orders from the military or the uniformed police risked being killed and his or her body left on the street, thrown into the Mapocho River or left at the entrance of cemeteries or the Medico-Legal Institute (*Instituto Médico Legal*).[2]

The bodies piled up at the premises of the SML, which could not cope with carrying out the autopsies as well as identifying the bodies. In most cases, the bodies could not be returned to their families, and had to be referred for burial in the General Cemetery, one of the oldest and largest cemeteries in the country, in the vicinity of the SML. Thus, with just a number assigned to the unidentified corpse, the bodies were frequently buried in so-called Patios, large lots where individuals who had died unexpectedly or did not have the resources to be buried in family tombs were temporarily buried. About 400 of these victims were buried in Patio 29;[3] and because these were temporary graves, in 1979 the Cemetery began to remove the bodies to reuse the graves (Human Rights Program Report 2007–2010, 37). In view of this situation, the Vicariate of Solidarity (*Vicaría de la Solidaridad*) denounced the fact and managed the restriction of this operation, which was partially achieved: only 108 graves for unidentified people were preserved.

From 2 to 14 September 1991, a team of volunteer archaeologists and anthropologists who formed the Forensic Anthropology Group (*Grupo Anthropologia Forense* – GAF) exhumed 107 graves, where 125 bodies[4] were found. The bodies were sent to the SML; however, it was not until 1992, due to the dissolution of the GAF, that this institution began the analysis aimed at identifying victims and determining their cause and manner of death. By 2002, 96 individuals had been identified by 'traditional' anthropological methods, including the controversial use of craniofacial superimposition. However, since 1994, there have been doubts about the quality of the processes and methodologies used to

[1]Deceased in April 2003.

[2]Name of the SML at the time.

[3]According to the Complete List of Patio 29, issued by the General Cemetery of Santiago, 24 June 1991.

[4]Grave 108 was exhumed in 1997, totaling 126 bodies.

reach those identifications, doubts that were accepted by Minister Sergio Muñoz, who ordered the SML to perform genetic analyses (mitochondrial DNA) to verify identifications already made. By April 2006, the results delivered were categorical (Bustamante and Ruderer 2009): of 94 cases analysed, 48 were exclusionary, 37 cases uncertain and the rest did not give useful results for comparison.

The response was immediate. The associations of families of victims of political violence demanded a radical response from the State of Chile, which lead to an audit of the SML that revealed the scarcity of its resources, as well as limited support for technical and methodological development necessary to approach the complex human rights cases. A panel of internationally renowned experts from different areas related to human identification was convened, and presented a proposal for comprehensive intervention. Then, the Human Rights Program was formed which, by virtue of the power vested in it, raised the need to develop a multi-disciplinary expert technical area that should be trained to work with a holistic approach.

Since 2007, with the incorporation of Alejandra Didier Perez, archaeology has become a comprehensive and permanent part of the majority of the cases studied by the UEIF. The application of archaeological methodology has enriched the analysis of bone evidence and associated cultural elements, contextualising the findings; and due to the precision of the records generated, it has become an essential element of the chain of custody. In 2008, and in close connection with the Los Arrayanes Ravine case, a new methodology to deal with associated evidence, implemented by archaeologist Mrs Isabel Martínez Armijo, was incorporated. Specifically, a methodology of textile analysis was designed, which was extrapolated to other associated evidence of forensic interest. This methodology has become a hallmark for the Unit, which proves the importance of this discipline in analyses aimed at identifying the victims, as well as determining the cause and manner of death.

The UEIF understands forensic archaeology as the application of traditional archaeological theory and methods to the investigation of forensic cases, where there is a possibility of finding the perpetrators of a crime, and moreover, bringing them to justice. Currently, the UEIF, in accomplishing this objective, has forensic archaeologists that lead excavations, search areas and recovered evidences from the crime scene incorporating otherwise traditional fieldwork techniques, legal and criminalistic procedures such as the use of chain of custody and the expertise of professionals from a variety of disciplines: geology, botany, marine biology and cartography . The exercise of this area of study within the UEIF incorporates work both on site and in the laboratory.

While forensic archaeology can be applied to different types of cases, the UEIF currently incorporates within its range of activities criminal, mass disaster, posthumous paternity establishment and human rights cases. Additionally, and given that the population that has inhabited this land has always enjoyed access to many natural resources, there are numerous archaeological sites often found, especially within the Central Valley and northern part of the country, which the UEIF team needs to evaluate in order to discard its medico-legal interest.

Given the variety of sites this unit faces, and taking into account that each one of them is unique, these are dealt with on the basis of their particular characteristics, such as geography, climatic conditions and the nature of the evidence, whose recovery is intended, the possible methods to be used and the resources available to maintain custody and secure conservation of the evidence.

In all phases of the fieldwork at hand (search, detection and recovery of human remains and associated evidence), steps are taken to ensure that the process adheres to strict quality work parameters, which comply both with internationally approved procedures[5] and with the methodology proposed in the 1989 United Nation's Minnesota Protocol: Manual for the Prevention and Investigation of Extra-Legal, Arbitrary and Summary Executions. Among these steps are complete written, photographic and occasionally audio-visual records of all fieldwork, site plans and relevant measurements, storage of the evidence using custody seals, and constant safekeeping of it until its final transport to the UEIF.

Regarding laboratory work, the archaeology field within this Unit specialises in the analysis of cultural evidence found in association with human remains, in an attempt to contribute to the objectives of the investigation: determining the cause and manner of death, and the circumstances in which this took place. As previously stated, this procedure was standardised by Isabel Martinez Armijo from 2007, after the finding of numerous remains of human rights victims and their associated evidence in a site called Los Arrayanes Ravine. From this location, around 500 pieces of cultural evidence were recovered, including small fragments of clothing, shoes and personal effects.

Today, the process entails a quantitative and qualitative analysis and recovery of trace evidence, as well as written and photographic records of any pertinent finding. Additionally, the examination comprises a description of the type of materials and fibres that compose the cultural evidence, specification of their models, patterns and colours, and determining their state of conservation and/or degree of degradation. Last, the evaluation of damage suffered by the evidence is of primary importance, especially if they transcend destruction caused naturally by the passing of time or

[5]The procedures are explained in the Section Fieldwork.

the environmental conditions to which they have been exposed, such as fire arm trauma. In all these processes, care is taken to maintain quality control, by appointing a responsible and a control party.

In fact, this type of laboratory analysis has come a long way, demonstrating its relevance in aiding the investigation, but also given the value that the recovery and reconstruction of the material culture holds for the family of the victim. Through the associated evidence, the families can even re-establish a link with their beloved ones, seeing them in a favourite piece of clothing that they helped to choose, or a pair of glasses that the person always wore. Many times, the cultural evidence will become more representative to them than the remains themselves, especially if what are being handed back to them are only fragments.

The Los Arrayanes Ravine case

On 5 September 2007, an incomplete long bone, a shoe and a shoe heel were sent to the SML in Santiago by the Court of Appeals in San Miguel, in order to perform an urgent study of the date of the evidence submitted. In relation to the bone, it was also requested 'to establish whether it corresponds to male or female sex, height and other anthropomorphic characteristics of the subject it would belong to'.[6]

In the report submitted to the court, it is pointed out that the bone piece corresponds to the human remains of an adult; however, it was impossible to estimate sex, height, the presence of individualising traits or perimortem lesions, or the time of death.

In relation to the footwear remains, the visual and physical inspection report states that:

'it is a nationally manufactured shoe, for the left foot, made of leather, male moccasin model, apparently black colour, size 40 (...), it corresponds to a model that was very popular from 1965 to 1980, made by a craftsman (hand-made)'.[7]

The findings of Judge Héctor Solís Montiel, whose investigation partly related to the abduction of 22 peasants from the town of Paine – Case No. 04–02 'F' Paine – located south of Santiago, give rise to one of the most complex field campaigns in the history of the SML, where, under its coordination and organisation, professionals and technicians of the SML together with the Investigations Police (Civil Police), Uniform Police (*Carabineros de Chile*), as well as national and foreign professionals, collaborated in this endeavour.

In relation to the victims associated with the case, the National Commission on Truth and Reconciliation (*Comisión Nacional de Verdad y Reconciliación*) states that

> In the town of Paine, between September and November of 1973, there were serious violations of human rights by state agents, specifically officers from the Carabineros and the Army, accompanied by local civilians who collaborated in the repression that was mainly directed towards the peasant sector (...) on October 16th 1973, 23 people were arrested in Campo Lindo, 24 de Abril and Nuevo Sendero settlements, 22 of which are missing (...) The morning of that day an operation was carried out (...) searching the homes and sometimes acting with unnecessary violence (...) the detainees were taken to the police station of Paine, where some of them were seen by their families. From there, the detainees were taken to the Infantry Regiment of San Bernardo, being ignorant since then of their whereabouts, despite the many administrative and judicial efforts made by the families (National Corporation of Reparation and Justice 1996, 225).

The place is Los Arrayanes Ravine, located in the interior of Fundo Los Quillayes, northern sector of Rapel Lake, VI Region of Chile.

On 7 September, Mrs Alejandra Didier Perez, archaeologist, and Mr Christian Cornejo Flores, technician assistant, both from the Special Unit for Human Rights (Unidad Especial de Derechos Humanos (UEDDHH))[8] of the SML of Santiago, established the area of interest where the evidences sent to the SML had been found, conducted a reconnaissance of the ravine and gathered the necessary information in order to design the intervention to the site, aimed at detecting and recovering the evidence deposited there.

The UEDDHH team began the second phase of the field campaign on 10–13 September, resuming its work on 21 September and concluding it on 19 October 2007.

Fieldwork

The aim of the fieldwork[9] was to detect, document and recover, with the proper archaeological methodology, all bone and cultural evidence present at the origin and in the upper course of Los Arrayanes Ravine (Figure 45.1).

The archaeological methodology that was followed (Gallardo 1987; Gallardo and Cornejo 1986, 409–420) focused on the delimitation, superficial and subsuperficial evidence recovery and excavation of a site, complemented by a forensic archaeological procedure established by Dupras et al. (2006), Hunter and Cox

[6]Translation of Writ No 41–2007, issued by the Judge Mr Héctor Solís Montiel, dated 5 September 2007.

[7]Visual and physical inspection, dated 26 September 2007, signed by the shoemaker Mr Enrique Ricardo Samur Muñoz.

[8]Name of the UEIF between 2007 and 2010.

[9]Field Work Report, Protocol No 81–07 UE, Case No 04–02 'F' Paine, Court of Appeals of San Miguel, signed by Alejandra Didier Pérez and Angel Medina Bejarano.

Figure 45.1 General view of Los Arrayanes Ravine.

(2005) and Ubelaker (1999), all adapted according to the particularity of the case, which is broken down as follows.

Site investigation

It included a preliminary inspection visit, field reconnaissance with a photographic record, the intervention strategy design, site evaluation by a geologist, a botanist and the canine division of the Investigations Police; surveying[10] with ground-penetrating radar (GPR), metal detector, superficial and sub-superficial recovery, in addition to the photographic and planimetric record using the Global Positioning System (GPS) and Total Station of all evidence recovered (Figure 45.2).

The excavation included in-depth evaluation of pits of 1 × 1 m in areas identified by GPR with evidence of stratigraphic changes; the recovery of evidence through systematic excavation in trenches along the bottom of the ravine (Figure 45.3); the excavation of natural strata with minor tools (trowel, spatula and brush); sieving of 100% of sediments with 3 × 3 mm mesh; and sterility control of the units by ground coring.

The records included photography and mapping, using GPS, of all the evidence recovered during the survey with a metal detector, top view photography of the evidence and planimetric view with three coordinates, top view and profile drawings with relevant information, survey with a Total Station of the ravine, evidence recovered during the survey with a metal detector of the points marked by GPR of the four vertexes of the excavation units and of the most relevant evidence details.

Figure 45.2 View of the NE slope with flags indicating the probable presence of metal items.

[10]Surveying is the method through which it is possible to discover the archaeological record of a locality (translated from Gallardo et al. 1986).

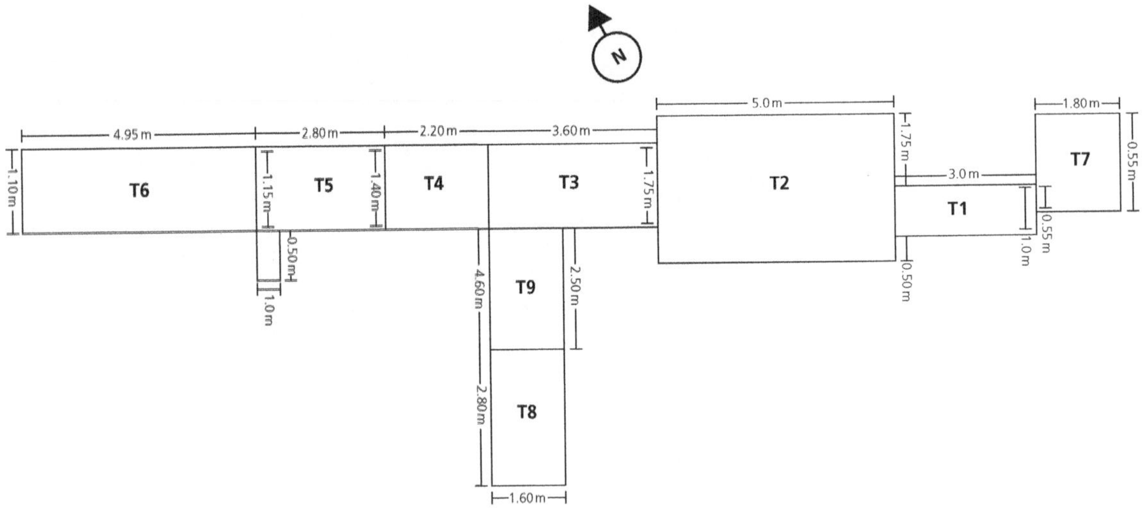

Figure 45.3 Scheme that shows the nine excavated trenches.

Field laboratory and evidence handling

This includes the individualisation of the evidence with an acronym formed by the identification of the unit of origin and an individual consecutive number. If association was found between pieces of evidence, a unique number was assigned, coupled with letters in alphabetical order. The evidence was packed in a Ziploc-type bag, wrapped in tin foil if necessary to ensure conservation, and placed in corrugated boxes according to the nature of the evidence and protected by sheets or small balls of expanded polystyrene when appropriate. An inventory was made of the bags, duly closed with an evidence seal and placed in each box, and the boxes were sealed with the relevant chain of custody and dispatched with a delivery certificate to the custodian responsible for the transportation of the boxes.

The work to recover bone and cultural remains in Los Arrayanes Ravine followed a methodological design with the application of archaeological techniques, which ensured the full recovery of the skeletal remains and cultural evidence associated with them. Post-mortem damage of the remains was minimised as far as possible, and the necessary information to account for the burial context was gathered.

A total of 546 ballistic elements, 1016 pieces of bone evidence, 79 pieces of dental evidence and 567 associated cultural elements were recovered from the terraces and slopes of the ravine.

The incorporation of evaluations by natural science professionals, such as geologists and botanists, allowed the characterisation of the site's natural environment as well as factors that influenced the deposition of the remains, and those taphonomic processes that could have generated natural disturbances to the site and therefore to the evidence.

The geology report established that the upper zone of Los Arrayanes Ravine had not been significantly modified by natural processes over the past 30 years or by the use of earth-moving machinery. The botany report indicated that tracks of local animals were observed in the ravine, as well as the effects of current geological erosion due to runoff. Finally, the GPR report established that in the bottom of the ravine, there were at least two areas that indicated artificial removal of the ground and subsequent filling.

The careful handling of evidence in terms of labelling, packaging and transportation safeguarded the conservation, security and chain of custody of the materials, meeting the expert work and judicial system requirements.

From the information gathered in the field, it was possible to determine that the area of Los Arrayanes Ravine corresponds to a place of execution by a firing squad and the primary burial site of more than one individual. Regarding the time period of the events that took place at the site, the associated cultural material allows us to circumscribe the facts as post-1973 and an intervention in 1975 or thereafter.

Human intervention was detected, that is alterations made intentionally by humans, resulting in at least one event of removal of bones and associated personal items. This removal process would have been done manually, ruling out any use of heavy machinery.

Additionally, the site is affected by taphonomic processes related to the action of climatic and orographic agents and wild and introduced fauna, which takes account of site disturbance such as the interment of materials.

Associated evidence

The expert analyses[11] carried out by the Expert Technical Area of the Unit also included the personal items and cultural materials associated with the victims found, and separate reports were prepared for metal fragments, footwear, personal items, lenses and frames, as well as recovered textile fragments, shirt collar structures, buttons, zipper sliders and metal rivets, which it would be appropriate to discuss further.

This expert analysis, by archaeologist Mrs Isabel Martínez, began on 15 April 2008 and ended on 13 June of the same year. The overall objective was to determine the number and type of the garments found in the Los Arrayanes Ravine, when they were worn, and sought to identify the origin and fabric type of textile fragments; identify the material of buttons, rivets and collar structures; and determine the type and model of garments they belonged to.

Within the universe of evidence, 318 textile fragments, 120 buttons, metal rivets, zipper sliders and 6 collar structures were analysed.

A methodological procedure relevant for the analysis and classification of archaeological cultural material was used. The textile fragments were grouped based on similar attributes such as raw material, shape, colour and texture, that is by similarities and differences among these evidences. The purpose was to make a qualitative and quantitative description of the universe of evidence, determine the state of conservation of these and the raw material, associate the fragments corresponding to a particular piece, determine the minimum number of the same garment and reconstruct the latter from the universe of fragments, estimating the model and time when they were fashionable.

To achieve the aforementioned objectives, technical datasheets were developed for each type of evidence. The elaboration of the Textile Technical Datasheet was based on forms made and used for pre-Hispanic textiles, adapting them to the requirements of contemporary textile analysis, while taking into account variables that differ from the antique evidence.

Thus, the form includes the following points:

1. Name of the specific case.
2. Number of the sheet, to control the number of items analysed.
3. Number of prototype only related to this specific case.
4. Evidence: number the fragment found during the excavation.
5. Code: assigned by the Identification Unit team to the different evidences found.
6. Unit: that is, the number of the Excavation Unit where the item was found.
7. Date of the analysis.
8. Box for the picture of the individual fragment with the respective protocol numbers, excavation unit, code and scale in centimetres.
9. Description: presentation of the main qualitative characteristics of the item.
10. Measurements: quantitative description of the item.
11. State of conservation: determination of the state of the fragment and the possibility of determining the causes of the deterioration.
12. Type of fibre: natural, synthetic or artificial and whenever possible, specification of the same (e.g. cotton, wool, polyester and acrylic).
13. Colour: determined by a colour pallet such as a textile pantone.
14. Type of garment: if possible to determine.
15. Model: if possible to determine.
16. Comments: if necessary, enter data or information related to the item that is not included in the other sections. The manufacturing of the garments is also specified.
17. Responsible person: name of the person(s) who prepared the datasheet.

In order to analyse successfully the different fragments recovered and proceed in a second phase to the possible reconstruction of the garments, it was necessary to form different groups including parts of similar characteristics, where the criteria for the formation of each group were the following:

1. Weaving technique
2. Characteristics of the yarn[12] (number of cords,[13] twist[14] and doubling[15] that determine the texture of the yarn)
3. Type of fabric
4. Colour of the yarn
5. Design, if any

The initial classification was performed using a macroscopic visual analysis of the items, with the help of a thread counter, an instrument that comprises a support, a ruler in centimetres and a magnifying glass. In this way, it was possible to observe in detail the weaving technique and the formal characteristics of the yarn.

On the other hand, the qualitative description of the fragments was mainly focused on their shape, the colour

[11]Pericia de Objetos Personales y Materiales Culturales Asociados, Protocolo 81–07 UE Causa Rol UE N° 04–02 'F' Paine, Corte de Apelaciones de San Miguel, signed by Isabel Martínez Armijo.

[12]Group of twisted and many times doubled threads that form a thin cord or yarn that once woven will form the textile piece. The yarn can be twisted in an 's' or 'z' shape depending on the direction of the same (Cornejo Lacroix 1996).

[13]Twisted threads that form a thicker thread, that is a thread can be formed by one or more cords (Cornejo Lacroix 1996).

[14]Direction of the twist to join textile threads and form one yarn that can be in an 's' or 'z', that is to the right or to the left.

[15]Direction of the twist of the set of cords that form a yarn that could be in an 's' or 'z' and generally opposed to the cord twist.

of the fabric, design, presence of typical garment folds and evidence of stitches. When it was possible to identify the item, for example shirt collar or cuff, trouser clip, this is mentioned in the description. Otherwise, or when identification was not certain, just the aforementioned description was reported (Figure 45.4).

As for the quantitative description, a metal measuring tape was used to obtain maximum and minimum height, length and width.

Finally, to determine the state of conservation, analysis was focussed on the current condition of the fragments, using the qualitative criteria as very good, good, fair to good, fair, fair to poor, bad and very bad. Then the alterations of the items were specified: cuts, earth impregnation and that of other organic and non-organic elements, structural deformations caused by missing parts, folds and/or wrinkles, unwoven and frayed fabric, untwisting of the yarn, alteration of the original colours (discolouration, stain, etc.) and others. Burns or stains from being in contact with other objects are mentioned among the causes of the alterations.

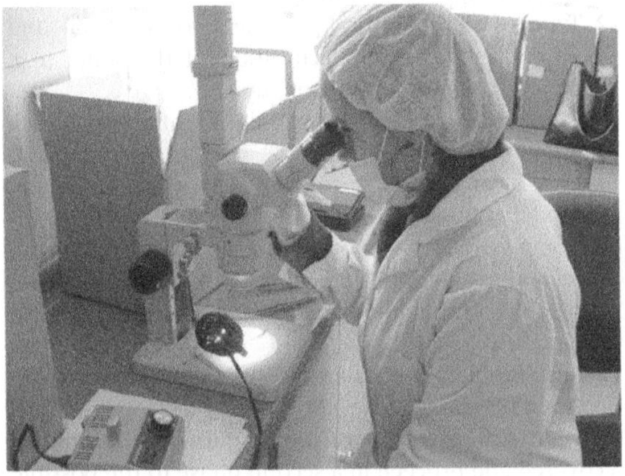

Figure 45.4 Visual analysis of textile fibres under the stereoscopic magnifier.

Among the group of evidence analysed, 23 elements and fragments of personal items, 10 pieces of evidence associated with glasses and lenses, 66 non-ballistic metal fragments and 82 footwear pieces and fragments were included.

Among the sample of garments, it was possible to identify a high percentage of shirt remains, followed by remnants of trousers, undetermined clothes, upper garments, sweaters, jackets, boots, a sock and a hoodie; 13 textile garments were partially and/or completely restored (Figure 45.5).

The universe of fragments analysed corresponded to some adult male elements worn in a period ranging from 1960 to 1975, or in subsequent years. The state of conservation is fair/poor due to the environmental conditions to which the fragments were exposed. Many of the elements analysed show individualising characteristics, allowing comparison with ante-mortem information provided by the families of the victims and recognised later by them.

Likewise, it should be pointed out that evidence T5E28 and T2E63 correspond to a pair of glasses, which have a fracture as a result of a gunshot whose probable trajectory goes from the inside to the outside of the item (Figure 45.6).

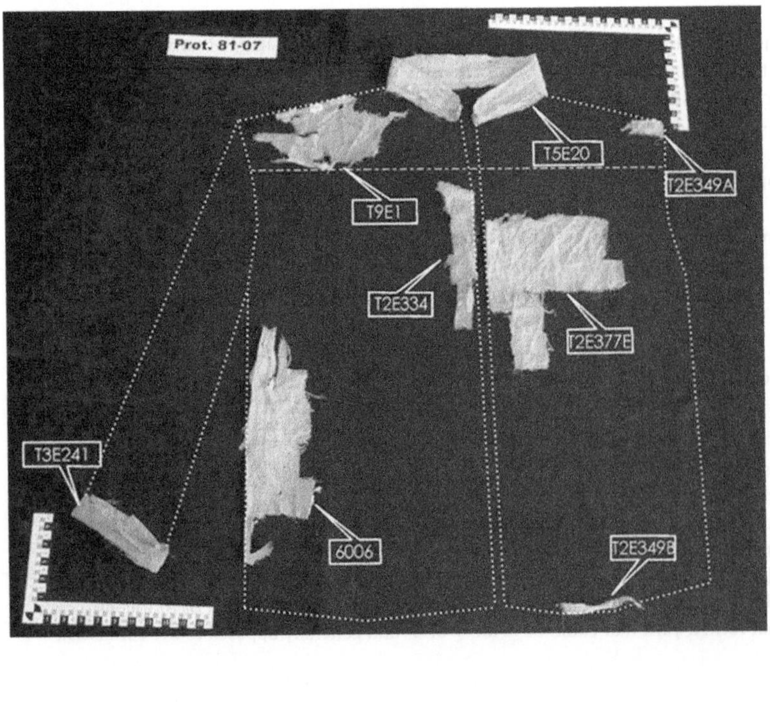

Figure 45.5 Reconstruction of the shirt whose fragments are part of Group 1.

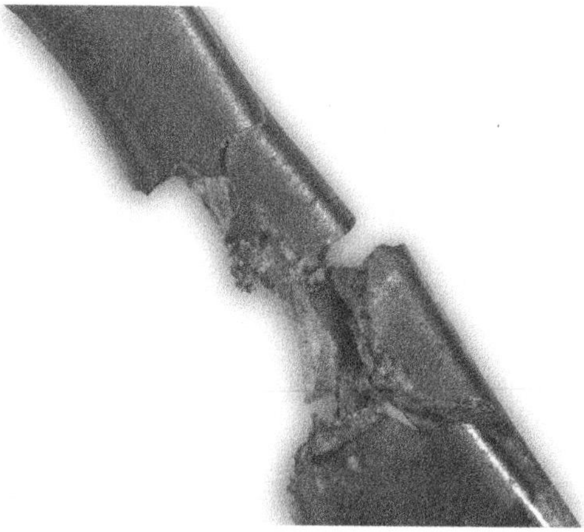

Figure 45.6 T5E28. Detail of the outer face of the left earpiece.

The Los Arrayanes Ravine case is still in process, pending the results of genetic analysis. As of September 2013, 13 genetic profiles have been obtained from which 12 victims associated to the Paine case have been identified. The application of forensic archaeology from the time of search for the remains to the analysis of the associated cultural evidence led to success, considering the adverse geographical conditions of the site, the poor state of conservation of the bones and teeth remains and the intervention of the military, who removed the physical evidence in order to eliminate the traces of these victims.

References

Bustamante, J. and Ruderer, S. 2009. *Patio 29. Tras la Cruz de Fierro*. Santiago, Ocho Libros Publishing Company.

Cáceres Roque, I. 2011. Missing Detainees in Chile-Archaeology of the Denied Death. Academic thesis. Available at www.cybertesis.uchile.cl/tesis/uchile/2011/cs-caceres_i/pdfAmont/cs-caceres_i.pdf (accessed on 20 September 2014).

Cornejo Lacroix, M. 1996. *Procesos de Producción Textil I Course*. Course of Design, Universidad de Valparaíso.

Dupras, T.L., Schultz, J.J., Wheeler, S.M. and Williams, L.J. 2006. *Forensic Recovery of Human Remains: Archaeological Approaches*. Boca Raton, CRC Press.

Exempt Resolution No 3153, 30 April 2007.

Exempt Resolution No 004742, 15 April 2011.

Gallardo, F. 1987. *Dónde, Cuánto y Cómo Excavar?: Acerca del Diseño de Excavación*. Arqueologíay Ciencias: Segundas Jornadas. Santiago de Chile, Museo Nacional de Historia Natural.

Gallardo, F. and Cornejo, L. 1986. El diseño de la prospección arqueológica: un caso de estudio. *Chumgará* 16–17, 409–420.

Hunter, J. and Cox, M. 2005. *Forensic Archaeology. Advances in Theory and Practice*. London, Routledge.

Human Rights Program Report, 2007–2010.

Lagos Escobar, R., Bates Hidalgo, L. and Eyzaguirre Guzmán, N. 2005. *Title I, Article Nr°2*, Promulgated in Santiago, 4 October 2005.

National Corporation of Reparation and Justice, 1996. *Report of the National Commission on Truth and Reconciliation*, 11th edition. Andros Impresores, Chile.

Ubelaker, D.H. 1999. *Human Skeletal Remains. Excavation, Analysis, Interpretation*. 3rd edition. Manuals on Archaeology 2. Washington, DC, Taraxacum.

CHAPTER 46

The role of forensic archaeology in revealing the truth of Colombia's armed conflict: a critical perspective

Ana Carolina Guatame García, Carolina Puerto Valdivieso and Eileen Buitrago Pérez
Colombian Interdisciplinary Team on Forensic Work and Psychosocial Assistance, EQUITAS, Bogotá, Colombia

Introduction

Forensic archaeology is the application of archaeological methods and techniques to the recovery of human remains in judicial investigations for legal and humanitarian purposes. Forensic archaeology needs to be defined as distinct from forensic anthropology, as its critical contribution is made prior and during the actual finding of human remains, without which the work of forensic anthropologists could not even begin, especially in contexts such as the investigation of clandestine graves where the location of burials is paramount. However, due to the academic tradition of the Americas where archaeology is taught as part of anthropology programmes, forensic anthropologists are also normally considered to be forensic archaeologists (Congram 2010).

The practice of forensic archaeology in Colombia responds to the historical particularities of the country. Throughout recent history, there have been countless human rights violations in the entire territory; many of these violations are the result of the internal armed conflict, characterised by the combination of acts of common criminals, insurgent groups operating outside the law (left-wing guerrilla groups and right-wing paramilitary organisations), and the Military themselves, who are also responsible for crimes either by direct action or omission. In this particular scenario, forensic sciences have the challenge of contributing to the attainment of justice by providing reliable evidence for reconstructing the truth as a *sine qua non* condition for the construction of peace.

One of the most complex crimes in the context of the Colombian armed conflict is the enforced disappearance. Disappearances in Colombia were first manifested as a systematic tool for terror employed by the Public Force (*Fuerzas Militares de Colombia*) with the occasional participation of paramilitary forces, as a strategy to persecute political opposition. Enforced disappearance became a mechanism to frighten and subjugate civilians under paramilitary control, which consolidated its position in most of the country. These armed groups have been protected again and again by omission by, or tolerance of, the Public Force, and have committed collective disappearances since the 1990s in the context of other human rights violations such as massacres, extrajudicial executions and enforced displacements (Albaladejo 2009, 11–14).

From the legal viewpoint, the complexity of investigating enforced disappearance is due to the difficulty of identifying the perpetrators and motives of crimes accurately; from a technical viewpoint, there is a big challenge in establishing the whereabouts of the victims, most of them killed and disposed in clandestine graves. Figure 46.1 illustrates relatives of the victims demanding their search.

Action patterns of criminal groups identified during criminal investigation reveal that disappearances/murders have been associated with practices such as torture, dismemberment, scattering and disposal of bodies in remote areas, among other concealment techniques. Some of the perpetrators have confessed that the bodies of missing persons had been thrown into rivers, incinerated or buried in a second burial to prevent their discovery by the authorities. This marks the starting point for forensic archaeological research.

This chapter will present the professional, technical and political challenges faced by forensic archaeology in Colombia in its mission to contribute to unravelling the history of violence in the country.

The chapter also focuses on the work of EQUITAS.[1] EQUITAS is the Colombian Interdisciplinary Team on

[1]For more information, see: http://www.equitas.org.co (last accessed August 2013). Also visit: http://equitascolombiablog.wordpress.com (last accessed August 2013).

Forensic Archaeology: A Global Perspective, First Edition. Edited by W.J. Mike Groen, Nicholas Márquez-Grant and Robert C. Janaway.

Figure 46.1 Relatives of victims of enforced disappearance in a pacific mobilisation of black veils and colourful flowers in front of the Attorney General's Office, Bogota, Colombia. In the picture, a woman showing the face of her son, a 13-year-old child forcibly recruited and then disappeared by paramilitary groups in 2004 (© EQUITAS).

Forensic Work and Psychosocial Assistance (*Equipo Colombiano Interdisciplinario de Trabajo Forense y Asistencia Psicosocial*), a scientific and humanitarian organisation focused on victims and based on evidence. It performs independent forensic contributions and provides psychosocial support to families of victims of crimes committed in the context of human rights violations in Colombia. Since its inception in 2004, EQUITAS has primarily worked on technical assistance in the processes of search, identification and analysis of the bodies of enforced disappeared persons. In the course of our work, we have identified structural, methodological and scientific issues that demonstrate the challenges of working in the context of an ongoing armed conflict, parallel to transitional justice processes and a complex State bureaucracy.

Who are the professionals that perform forensic archaeology in Colombia?

To understand how forensic archaeology is involved in the investigation of crimes related to Colombia's armed conflict, it is necessary to understand who practices the profession. Currently, all the practitioners of forensic archaeology have local undergraduate degrees in anthropology, and work mainly at two state institutions: the Attorney General's Office (*Fiscalía General de la Nación*) and the National Police (*Policía Nacional de Colombia*). Very often, these undergraduate programmes in anthropology also offer instruction in archaeology; students select courses and internships in order to specialise their degrees in cultural or biological anthropology or archaeology. However, the availability of courses offered relating to forensic archaeology is quite limited. There are no undergraduate or postgraduate forensic archaeology degrees; there have not been any academic meetings in this field; and there are no specialists' guilds in this area to date.

Five years ago, the only graduate program in forensic anthropology that had existed in Colombia was closed at the National University. A few years ago, the first archaeology program with emphasis on classic archaeology was founded at the private Externado University of Colombia (*Universidad Externado de Colombia*) in Bogotá, although the first cohort has not graduated yet. Given these conditions, it is not yet possible to glimpse a space for training new forensic archaeologists.

Forensic anthropologists who have been carrying out the work of forensic archaeologists have had limited training in specific matters such as criminal and forensic investigation or human rights (EQUITAS 2011, 9–16).[2] Thus, the forensic anthropologists working at state institutions have gained their expertise in forensic archaeology by performing forensic archaeological interventions on a regular basis, since the number and diversity of relevant cases is quite significant. Further, they have complemented their training by participating in academic meetings and courses offered through international cooperation.

The very few professionals in the country with academic training in forensic archaeology have had their training in foreign universities, and are mostly based at universities and non-governmental organisations. However, due to the structure of forensic investigation in the country (see the following text), they are not fully allowed to carry out independent field searches and recoveries, meaning that these personnel apply their

[2]EQUITAS authoring documents are available at: http://www.equitas.org.co/index.html?modulo=documentos&articulo_id=28 (last accessed 13 August 2013).

expertise from the theoretical viewpoint, or are restricted to sending technical recommendations to anthropologists employed by the aforementioned state institutions.

Forensic archaeology and the investigation of crimes related to the armed conflict

General background

Given the Colombian legal structure, the Attorney General's Office is the sole authority responsible for investigating crimes and bringing charges against alleged offenders. This implies that it is primarily responsible for obtaining evidence in the criminal investigation. Before 2005, when a new Criminal Procedural Code of accusatory tendency was implemented, only the State's experts were allowed to collect evidence, so they were the only ones authorised to carry out exhumations both related to the armed conflict and to other regular death investigations. To date, a reduced number of exhumations mostly related to 'cold cases' have been conducted for humanitarian purposes.

With the new code, non-state experts are also allowed to carry out exhumations (e.g. independent forensic organisations such as EQUITAS). Both state and non-state experts should fulfil the same requirements set by the new code for expert witnesses regarding either having an academic title specific to the matter of expertise or prominent knowledge and experience of it. However, the bureaucratic process to obtain permissions, as well as the lack of knowledge of the rule by many prosecutors, makes non-state exhumations occur only very rarely.

Forensic anthropologists doing forensic archaeology for the State are assigned to any of the institutions of national jurisdiction with judicial police functions. Whenever a prosecutor requests technical support to locate and/or recover a corpse that represents a forensic case, they are randomly assigned a 'field criminalistics team' that usually consists of an anthropologist in charge of the archaeological work, a photographer, a topographer and a field assistant, at the very least. These teams cater to the specific request given by the authority and are rarely involved in the entire process of investigation, making it hard to provide structural and scientific contributions to the search process. Unofficial information suggests that about 80 people are working country-wide as part of these teams at the Attorney General's Office, but the specific number of forensic anthropologists among them is unknown.

The search for the missing

The internal armed conflict in Colombia began in the 1960s with the formation of peasant guerrillas seeking agrarian reform, ever since the government started an armed war in order to get the country back to political stability. In the late 1980s, the establishment of paramilitary groups formed by landowners, anti-communist factions and retired and active military intensified the war; since then, they have been responsible for the majority of human rights violations in the country. It is hard to establish an approximate number of fatal victims and survivors because under-documentation of crimes is extensive, and registration as public policy started late (Grupo de Memoria Histórica 2013, 31). However, the last report of the Historical Memory Group (*Grupo de Memoria Histórica*) released in July 2013, gives some figures on several crimes. It reports around 220,000 confirmed violent deaths, of which 80% correspond to civilians; 5,700,000 people displaced, which represents about 15% of the total population of the country; 27,023 kidnappings; 10,189 people affected by unexploded ordnances and anti-personnel mines; 6,421 children forcibly recruited and 1,754 victims of sexual violence, among others.

Numbers regarding enforced disappearance are problematic; the Unified Registry of Victims (*Registro Único de Víctimas*)[3] accounts for 25,007 forcibly disappeared victims (Grupo de Memoria Histórica 2013, 33), but the National Registry for Missing People (Registro Nacional de Desaparecidos 2013)[4] reports only 19,924 people.

In the context of a transitional justice process that seeks the end of the conflict, several legislative measures have been developed, some transient and others permanent, such as the *Law 975* of 2005, also named the Justice and Peace Law (*Ley de Justicia y Paz*). This transitional law was created to facilitate the demobilisation of right-wing paramilitary groups by offering them reduced prison sentences in exchange for their full confession of the crimes committed. Because a critical part of this process is the confession of the whereabouts of the missing by paramilitaries who expected the benefits of the law, there was an enormous and unmethodical increase in exhumations after their confessions, hence, a significant impact on the development of forensic archaeology in the country.

[3]This centralised registry is intended to contain the records of the non-lethal victims and relatives of lethal victims recognised by several laws that have been enacted since 1997. However, it only recognises victims from 1 January 1985, leaving behind an significant number of people affected by the conflict. It is expected that the registry crosschecks registers of other state data management systems such as the one created for victims related to the Justice and Peace process (*Justicia y Paz*) and the National Registry for Missing People.

[4]This is a technical data management and repository centralised system created in 2007 to contain the reports on missing persons and unidentified decedent records. It is administered by the National Coroner's Office and can be accessed by any public institution related to the search for the missing.

The dizzying increase of 'body recoveries' in a context in which preliminary documentation on the missing has been precarious,[5] has meant that despite the successful discovery of the bodies, only about 50% of the bodies recovered have been identified and returned to their loved ones.[6] In addition, a serious situation occurs with the contextual information that might be accessed from the graves in order to reconstruct the circumstances of death: the exhumations have been carried out for the practical purpose of verifying a death as proof of the confessed crimes, but not with the aim of reconstructing the fatal events or identifying the victim. With different intervention logic, forensic archaeology could be providing valuable information on burial patterns and systematic use of specific geographical areas for the concealment of corpses. It could also be analysing circumstantial evidence that could help the subsequent establishment of crimes such as sexual violence and torture, since the bodies are not the only evidence recovered from a burial.

In many cases, locating the clandestine grave is difficult because the forensic anthropologist/archaeologist has little information to guide a field survey. Most of the time, the only information available is the testimony of a perpetrator who claims not to remember accurately or to have difficulty in recognising the area, given the changes in the landscape with the passage of time. There are also cases in which the perpetrators were not demobilised under the Justice and Peace Law; and therefore, they testify with the possibility of obtaining sentence reductions in mind, as demobilised people do.

It is not often that the forensic anthropologist/archaeologist has the opportunity to analyse the case prior to the field survey, so that the possibility of identifying alternative ways of searching, proposing different survey strategies than the one guided by witnesses, and carrying out a planned intervention is minimal.

Despite the significant progress in standardising procedures and the adoption of international protocols to raise quality standards, an interdisciplinary criminal and comprehensive investigation has yet to win back lost ground in the country, so that the potential of forensic archaeology can be recognised as part of the legal investigation of the crimes and not only as a digging tool. EQUITAS believes that the current results of exhumations do not allow the reconstruction of the truth, in a process where it is essential when talking about reparation and reconciliation.

Another important legislative progress in the search for the missing was the typification of the crime by the *Law 589* of 2000. This law was the result of over a decade of work by human rights and victims' organisations, which led to the later creation of a number of technical instruments for the search of the missing including the National Missing Persons Search Plan (*Plan Nacional de Búsqueda de Personas Desaparecidas*).

Presented to the public in February 2007, the plan aims to locate the disappeared, identify them and establish the circumstances of their deaths. It consists of four phases, including data collection (ante-mortem and location of burial), data analysis, field recovery and identification activities, and the final return of bodies to their relatives. However, 6 years after its creation, its implementation is still a challenge.

Until very recently, specific search plans are being developed aside of the rule of the justice and peace process, thanks to the encouragement of victims' organisations and independent forensic teams. These plans include the systematisation of information obtained by state institutions (testimonies, geographical data on field surveys and exhumations, tracking of DNA samples, etc.), the design of technical proposals for regional field searches (especially in complex cases where the victims were disappeared individually, but such disappearances describe systematic patterns that may be reflected in the arrangement of the clandestine burials)[7] and the insistence on the formation of criminalistics groups that could get involved in the process in a non-circumstantial way. The adoption of these recommendations challenges the witness-finding intervention logic that has been extended to other search processes, thus broadening the technical possibilities in cases where no testimonial information is available or where there are complex settings of disposal such as rivers. Regarding the last, EQUITAS has made proposals that explore technical methodologies for the search in fluvial environments based on successful search experiences in river settings worldwide and following methods accepted by the international forensic community (EQUITAS 2007).

[5]For example, back in 2007 the *Human Rights Data Analysis Group* in partnership with EQUITAS published a study that provides a scientific estimation of the number of unreported missing people in the Department of Casanare, a rural state in Colombia located in the foothills of the Andes and on the eastern plains, that has a long history of violence. The study estimates that the total number of missing persons in Casanare from 1986–2007 is 2553 compared to the 1500 persons reported missing during this period. This analysis suggests that between 30 and 40% of missing persons in Casanare were unreported during this period.

[6]According to data from the Attorney General's Office, as of 30 April 2013, 5258 bodies have been recovered, of which 725 are being identified; 2038 have been fully identified and returned to their relatives. For more information, see: http://www.fiscalia.gov.co:8080/EXH/EXHUMACIONES.htm (last accessed 5 August 2013). The identity ofabout 2400 recovered bodies (about 45%) is still unknown. Those bodies are stored in official laboratories or public cemeteries.

[7]Such is the case of the disappearances of Chámeza and Recetor, municipalities of the department of Casanare, where about 60 people were disappeared between November 2002 and March 2003, in a criminal action committed by the Self-Defense Forces of Casanare. Of this group of people, only 11 bodies have been found, identified and returned to their loved ones.

Besides the technical recommendations, these studies have permitted increased awareness of the duty of the State to exhaust all means of searching for the missing persons, even knowing the constraints that these search processes involve for successful findings.

Searching for the missing in public cemeteries

Another under-explored scenario in the search for the missing in Colombia is that of the public cemeteries; these include cemeteries under the administration of the State and those that arise informally under the charge of local communities. The work in these settings is quite important since a number of bodies of missing persons have been buried in public cemeteries as 'John Doe' or NN, after having passed the required post-mortem examinations, or as a result of official exhumations of bodies that are not being identified and have then had a 'State burial' when the storage capacity of the laboratories is surpassed. The precarious documentation, preservation and custody of the corpses in public cemeteries have led to an extensive loss of bodies, resulting in a second disappearance, now institutional (EQUITAS 2008). Many bodies are transferred to common ossuaries without appropriate packaging and individualised marking after an initial burial period that does not exceed 4 years, so that the commingling of human remains creates great difficulties for later recovery (see Figure 46.2). In cases in which the body is held in the first burial, there are no standards for labelling grave walls to facilitate the posterior localisation of the body and to maintain the information available for indefinite periods of time.

As stated earlier, it has been an important issue for EQUITAS to promote public policies for the documentation, preservation and furtherance towards the identification of unidentified bodies buried in the cemeteries through the project Seal Narces (*Sello Narcés*).[8] This is a quality seal that aims to promote best management practices for cemeteries and other state institutions that are legally responsible for the management and conservation of unidentified bodies. Methods for the systematisation of information, geospatial analysis and funerary archaeology have been the basis for designing action plans that ensure a proper technical intervention for the recovery of bodies, rescue of valuable information to the judicial investigation and obtaining their full identification.

Additional perspectives of forensic archaeology in Colombia

The role of independent forensic experts

As mentioned earlier, there are few occasions where forensic experts from non-governmental organisations are the direct agents of archaeological field actions. Most of the time, the role of these teams is to accompany and independently observe how fieldwork is carried out so that the procedures are performed according to national and international protocols.

Further, EQUITAS has been involved as technical forensic advisor for human rights and victims' organisations in the legal investigation of human rights abuses. The forensic archaeological contribution from a non-State perspective in these cases has been to formulate

Figure 46.2 Burials of unidentified people in a public cemetery on the west plains of the country. As can be seen, technical standards for labelling and conservation are not followed (© EQUITAS).

[8]For more information, see: www.narces.org (last accessed 5 August 2013).

strategies for the collection and analysis of data for the search and to provide recommendations for the technical planning of field surveys and exhumations that improve the practices of State teams. Given the need for development of new techniques for the search in complex settings, EQUITAS has developed different research initiatives regarding remote sensing, archaeology and statistics, search in rivers and location of unidentified bodies in cemeteries and waste dumps, among others (EQUITAS 2009a; Guberek et al. 2009). Another important contribution has been the training of relatives of victims and their legal representatives so that they can make informed decisions about their participation in technical activities (exhumations mainly) and so that the information derived from the field of forensic science can have an effective impact on the litigation strategy and the judicial process itself. The goal is that the information derived from a serious archaeological work would become evidence of the serious crimes committed in Colombia, as has happened in international tribunals.

Finally, it is key to mention the role of non-State forensic teams as promoters of the self-thinking of the forensic task. In this regard, EQUITAS has developed a preliminary study that analyses the exercise of different forensic specialities from the academic, professional and ethical perspectives (EQUITAS 2011). From the academic standpoint, the study identified the need for specialised forensic graduate programmes that could be supported both financially and technically by international organisations, leading to the development of local capacity to ensure the sustainability of the processes. These academic projects will allow professionals not only to have knowledge derived from experience in the field but also an academic background that will strengthen their work. From the professional perspective, the study identified the need to optimise the supply of forensic science services so as to avoid duplication of functions between institutions, and to build indicators not only on results but also on its impact on the criminal investigation. From the ethical viewpoint, the reflection pointed out the need to evaluate how forensic science responds to the investigation of human rights violations, and hence, the need to create specific mechanisms to monitor, evaluate and report malpractices and to resolve disputes or consequences related to the action or inaction of the experts in particular cases.

Psychosocial dimension of the work of forensic archaeologists

The Report of the Office of the United Nations High Commissioner for Human Rights (UNHCHR) *Study on the Right to the Truth* (Organización de Estados Americanos 2006), states that in the case of enforced disappearances, the right to justice and truth includes knowing the fate and whereabouts of disappeared persons. In consequence, a thorough and serious effort that leads to the return of the victims to their families must be carried out.[9]

Since relatives' participation is key in the search process, several psychosocial and forensic organisations working with victims of human rights violations worldwide wrote in 2010 the *International Consensus on Principles and Minimum Standards for Psychosocial Work in Search Processes and Forensic Investigations in Cases of Enforced Disappearances, Arbitrary or Extrajudicial Executions*.[10] This is an instrument that brings together a series of parameters for psychosocial work in forensic investigations that contribute to the location, identification and return of the missing for reburial. In 2012, the Organisation of American States recognised it as a binding international instrument.[11]

The document begins by recognising the strong psychosocial impact of forensic investigations on victims, and how they can be repaired or re-traumatised depending on how technical procedures, including planning and the subsequent delivery of results, are performed. Making the psychosocial impact 'positive' or 'reparatory' implies the appropriate involvement of the families to the process before any field activity is developed (standard 2), the informed decision of the relatives on their participation in technical activities and their knowledge of any activity carried thereon (standards 3 and 8) and the development of actions to ensure the rigour, transparency and objectivity of forensic work through independent expert participation and coordination between public and private organisations of legal, technical and psychosocial functions (standards 14, 15 and 16).

The forensic work of EQUITAS and victims' organisations such as the Association of Colombian relatives (*Asociación Familiares Colombia*)[12] and the *Nidya Erika Bautista Foundation*[13] have been developed with this perspective in mind, revealing the reparatory nature of the direct relation between victim and expert (in this case,

[9]Inter-American Court of Human Rights, Case of the 19 Merchants vs Colombia, Judgment of 5 July 2004.

[10]For more information, see http://www.equitas.org.co/docs/55.pdf (last accessed 5 August 2013).

[11]For more information, see: http://scm.oas.org/IDMS/Redirectpage.aspx?class=CP/CAJP&classNum=3052&lang=s (last accessed 5 August 2013).

[12]The Association of Colombian Relatives: Relatives of Victims of Enforced Disappearance for Their Mutual Support (*Familiares de Desaparecidos Forzadamente por el Apoyo Mutuo* – Familiares Colombia) is a civil organisation with nearly 10 years of experience in the development of activities of solidarity, support and assistance to the relatives of enforced disappeared people.

[13]The Nidya Erika Bautista Foundation (*Fundación Nydia Erika Bautista para los Derechos Humanos*) is a non-profit organisation that since 2007 has worked with an integrated and participatory approach to the protection and empowerment of women and families of the missing.

the forensic archaeologist). There is a change in the perspective because victims are recognised as part of the search process, their information and participation requirements are validated, and the expert gives a different meaning to his/her work to the extent that the product of such work has a known recipient expecting accountability. These considerations change a process that was purely technical into a reparatory process, even in those cases in which, despite enormous technical and human efforts, the experts do not succeed in locating the whereabouts of the missing (EQUITAS 2009b, 2–9).

Perspectives and challenges

In a context of truth, justice, reparation, guarantees of non-recurrence and respect for the rights of the surviving victims, the search for thousands of missing persons in Colombia and the identification of the unidentified recovered bodies depend on improving the quality of the technical processes (understood as a set of well-planned actions), and on the operational effectiveness of the State to optimise its resources and counter the current fragmentation of the investigative process. The search strategy on a case-by-case basis in which forensic archaeology is limited to the excavation of a grave that follows a results-based evaluation model is an obstacle to planning large-scale forensic archaeological interventions in the context of a comprehensive process of search, identification and return of the missing to their families.

The involvement of forensic archaeology in criminal investigations, not only as a technical discipline but as a science, includes recognising its potential for developing strategies to intervene in complex settings such as regional contexts, cemeteries and rivers, to identify activity patterns of criminal groups, and to recover an d interpret physical evidence beyond the bodies themselves. To do so, a dialogue and mutual understanding between prosecutors and forensic scientists is needed to identify the technical tools that can lead to successful searches and make them available to the criminal investigation, both for clandestine graves of armed conflict and for homicides related to other kinds of violence.

Finally, forensic archaeology in Colombia has the opportunity and the challenge to become psychosocially oriented work that meets the needs of victims in order to establish the truth of the conflict as a way to access justice.

References

Albaladejo, I. A. 2009. *La Desaparición forzada de personas en Colombia. Guía de normas, mecanismos y procedimientos.* Bogotá, Oficina en Colombia del Alto Comisionado de las Naciones Unidas para los Derechos Humanos.

Congram, D. 2010. Spatial analysis and predictive modelling of clandestine graves from rearguard repression of the Spanish Civil War. PhD thesis, Simon Fraser University.

EQUITAS. 2007. *Primer documento sobre búsqueda forense de cadáveres y restos humanos en ríos colombianos.* Bogotá, EQUITAS.

EQUITAS. 2008. *Reflections on Preserving the Skeletonized Remains of Unidentified Persons as a Historical Record of the Violence in Colombia.* Bogotá, EQUITAS.

EQUITAS. 2009a. *Methodological Proposals for Documenting and Searching for Missing Persons in Colombia.* Bogotá, EQUITAS.

EQUITAS. 2009b. *Desafíos psicosociales en la búsqueda de personas desaparecidas en Colombia.* Bogotá, EQUITAS.

EQUITAS. 2011. *Fortalecer el gremio científico forense en Colombia. Balance y Retos.* Bogotá, EQUITAS.

EQUITAS. 2012. *Estándares para el impulso de la identificación de personas no identificadas en cementerios* [online]. http://narces.org/ (last accessed 5 August 2013).

Grupo de Memoria Histórica. 2013. *¡BASTA YA! Colombia: Memorias de guerra y dignidad.* Bogotá, Centro Nacional de Memoria Histórica.

Guberek, T., Guzmán, D. and Vejarano, B. 2009. El uso de información de cementerios en la búsqueda de desaparecidos: Lecciones de un estudio piloto en Rionegro, Antioquia. In: Guberek, T., Guzmán, D., Price, M., Lum, K. and Ball, P. 2010. *Los que faltan por contar: Una estimación de la violencia letal en Casanare, Colombia.* Colombia, Benetech Human Rights Program.

Organización de Estados Americanos. 2006. *Informe de la Oficina del Alto Comisionado de las Naciones Unidas para los Derechos Humanos. Estudio sobre el Derecho a la Verdad, U.N. Doc. E/CN.4/2006/91.*

Registro Nacional de Desaparecidos. 2013. http://sirdec.medicinalegal.gov.co:58080/rnd/ (last accessed 12 August 2013).

Bibliography

Comisión Nacional de Búsqueda 2007. *Plan Nacional de Búsqueda.* Available at: http://www.comisiondebusqueda.com/joomlacbpd/images/PDF/CARTILLAS2012/b_plan_nacional.pdf (last accessed 1 August 2013).

Coordinación Colombia-Europa-Estados Unidos, Observatorio de Derechos Humanos y Derecho Humanitario 2012. *Desapariciones Forzadas en Colombia: En Búsqueda de la Justicia.* Bogotá, Mesa de trabajo sobre Desaparición Forzada de la coordinación Colombia-Europa-Estados Unidos. Available at: http://www.corporacionavre.org/files/documentos%206%20FINAL%20mayo%2031.pdf (last accessed 5 August 2013).

Corte Interamericana de Derechos Humanos. 2004. *Sentencia Caso 19 Comerciantes vs. Colombia.* Fondo, reparaciones y Costas.

EQUITAS. 2006. *Innovative Contributions to the Documentation of Missing Persons and Clandestine Cemeteries in Colombia's Conflict.* Bogotá, EQUITAS.

International Commission on Missing Persons. 2008. *Informe de ICMP: Respuesta de Colombia a las Desapariciones Forzadas. Panorama General y Recomendaciones.* Available at: http://www.ic-mp.org/wp-content/uploads/2008/10/colrep-distrspa.pdf (last accessed 5 August 2013).

Ley 589 de 2000. *Por medio de la cual se tipifica el genocidio, la desaparición forzada, el desplazamiento forzado y la tortura; y se dictan otras disposiciones.* Santa Fe de Bogotá.

Ley 975 de 2005. *Por la cual se dictan disposiciones para la reincorporación de miembros de grupos armados organizados al margen de la ley, que contribuyan de manera efectiva a la consecución de la paz nacional y se dictan otras disposiciones para acuerdos humanitarios.* Bogotá, D.C.

Organización de las Naciones Unidas (ONU). A/Res/60/147. *Resolución de la Asamblea General de la Organización de las Naciones Unidas del 21 de marzo de 2006. Principios y directrices básicos sobre el derecho de las víctimas de violaciones manifiestas de las normas internacionales de Derechos Humanos y de violaciones graves del Derecho Internacional Humanitario a interponer recursos y obtener reparaciones.* Available at: http://www.un.org/es/comun/docs/?symbol=A/RES/60/147 (last accessed 10 December 2014).

CHAPTER 47

Forensic archaeology and the independent commission for the location of victims' remains

Niamh A. McCullagh and Geoffrey C. Knupfer
ICLVR, Ireland

Introduction and context

In the course of their long and inter-related histories, Ireland and Great Britain have encountered periods of political and civil strife, focused largely on Ireland's desire for independence from Britain. This gradual process, occasionally violent, came to a head in the late 19th and early 20th centuries and culminated in the formation of the Irish Free State in 1921 (later to become the Republic of Ireland in 1937). However, not all the then citizens of Ireland supported this development and, as part of a political accommodation, the country was partitioned along broadly religious lines, with the largely pro-British Protestant North (the ancient province of Ulster) electing to remain a province of Great Britain, rather than becoming part of an independent (Catholic) Ireland.

Many citizens of the newly formed independent Irish State, supported by numbers of the significant Catholic minority in the province of Northern Ireland, totally rejected this artificial division of their country and continued to seek independence for a fully 'united Ireland'. Over the years, this movement prompted periods of civil unrest in Northern Ireland and phases of paramilitary activity, the latter initiated by the Irish Republican Army (IRA). In 1969, the Northern Ireland Civil Rights Movement, in its desire for true equality for all members of the population, took on the Northern Ireland State in a campaign of civil disobedience. The IRA seized this opportunity to launch a military offensive against the British State. The civil police (the Royal Ulster Constabulary), totally overwhelmed by the substantial civil rights campaign and associated paramilitary activity by the IRA, sought the support of the UK's military forces. Thus, the seeds of Ireland's 'troubles' were sown. They were to last from 1969 to 1998. In this time, in excess of 3720 individuals lost their lives (McKittrick et al. 2007).

A complex political solution involving many strands was negotiated in 1998 between the two governments and the various political factions, resulting ultimately in paramilitary disarmament and the release of 'political' prisoners. This landmark settlement is known as the Belfast (or Good Friday) Agreement (English 2012). It marked the beginning of the peace process, and the formulation of numerous measures to address a range of important aspects, including constitutional and political issues and also the then existing security and political difficulties. Nevertheless, human rights and humanitarian issues lie at the very heart of this peace process. One of the initiatives taken by the governments of Ireland and the United Kingdom was the establishment of the Independent Commission for the Location of Victims' Remains (ICLVR). This is a body tasked with the search for, recovery and repatriation of a small number of individuals who had been abducted and murdered during the course of the conflict, the whereabouts of their remains being unknown (Woods 2013).

Legislation

The structure and functions of the ICLVR are set out in largely parallel legislation enacted by the two governments (Ireland: *The Criminal Justice (Location of Victims' Remains) Act, 1999* and UK/Northern Ireland: *The Northern Ireland (Location of Victims' Remains) Act, 1999*). Whilst the Commission was established and is funded by the Ireland and UK governments, it is, as its title suggests, a truly independent body, its work being overseen by two appointed commissioners. To summarise, the Commission's role and responsibilities are enshrined in the Agreement and legislation as follows:

- To facilitate the location of the remains of victims of violence;
- To receive information in relation to the location of the remains of victims;
- To disclose this information for the purpose of locating the remains of victims;
- To provide reports annually to the two governments on progress made.

Forensic Archaeology: A Global Perspective, First Edition. Edited by W.J. Mike Groen, Nicholas Márquez-Grant and Robert C. Janaway.

Victims of violence are defined as 'those killed before the 10 April 1998 (the date of the Belfast Agreement) by or on behalf of an unlawful (i.e. paramilitary) organisation'. Whilst there is no start date insofar as the adoption of cases by the Commission is concerned, this strict cut-off date does create some administrative ambiguities, since at least one incident involving the abduction and murder of a young man occurred after the signing of the Belfast Agreement.

To protect the work of the Commission and to encourage the flow of information, the legislation imposes strict limitations on how information received by the Commission can be used:

- Evidence obtained directly or indirectly by the Commission is not admissible in any criminal proceedings (however, this does not apply to admissions adduced in criminal proceedings).
- Any remains recovered shall not be subjected to forensic examination other than to establish the identification of same, or for safety reasons (e.g. improvised explosive devices, IEDs).
- Information received by the Commission cannot be disclosed to any person except for the purpose of facilitating the location of remains to which the information relates.

The legal provisions under which the Commission undertakes its business are wide-ranging and effective. They were framed with a view to encouraging former paramilitaries, and indeed anyone with relevant information, to provide it to the Commission in the knowledge that it would be used solely for the purpose of recovery and repatriation and, more importantly, that it would not be passed on to other agencies or the governments or result in prosecution.

The disappeared

Between 1969 and 1998, and as a result of the conflict, a number of individuals were abducted and murdered by the paramilitary groups – the majority of cases occurring in the island of Ireland, but one case, attributed to the Irish National Liberation Army (INLA), occurring in France. There is no definitive figure because new cases do come to light from time to time; however, at the time of writing, there are 17 known cases, and the remains of 11 victims have been recovered and repatriated. A total of 16 of these cases appear on the Commission's list of victims, with 10 victims recovered and repatriated (ICLVR 2012).

Responsibility for a number of these cases has been accepted by two of the former paramilitary groups, the IRA and INLA. Other cases, however, remain unattributed, albeit they too are strongly suspected to be the work of paramilitaries, possibly individuals or groups acting without the authority of their central command.

The current list of those recognised by the ICLVR as *the Disappeared* (Figure 47.1) is presented in Table 47.1.

Figure 47.1 'The Disappeared of Northern Ireland' families pin (© WAVE).

In terms of victimology and statistical profiling, 15 of the 16 victims are male and the total age range is from 17 to 54. The average age at the time of disappearance is the early twenties, with six of the victims being in their twenties when they disappeared.

Victims disappeared between 1972 and 1985, with 1972 and 1981 representing the highest concentration of disappearances. Within the group are two double graves and the remaining cases are of single disappearances. To date, the remains of 10 of these victims have been returned to their families and searches continue for those still missing; however in some cases, a complete absence of information has remained.

History of the search approach

On 28 May 1999, the legislation that established the ICLVR was signed and enacted by government ministers. On 29 May 1999, information was passed to the Commission via intermediaries in relation to the location of nine bodies in six locations around Ireland (Wilson and Bloomfield 1999). On this same day, one of these victims was presented to the ICLVR in a coffin at a cemetery in Faughart, County Louth (ICLVR197501).

On 30 May 1999, searches began simultaneously at all the locations disclosed via intermediaries to the Commission. Since the Commission did not, at that stage, possess its own physical search capability, this process was undertaken by officers of the Irish Police Force (*An Garda Síochána*) acting on behalf of the ICLVR. In the beginning, search teams began with shovels and wheelbarrows (Cusack 1999); and in a short space of time, these were exchanged for smaller mechanical diggers and finally for larger mechanical excavators (Figure 47.2). It was believed that search would be straightforward. Such was the level of confidence that in the early days of search undertakers and families

Table 47.1 ICLVR case data (Hill 2013; ICLVR 2012).

Case reference	Age	Gender	Missing since	Located	Searches prior to 2006
ICLVR197201		M	Mid 1972		Not applicable
ICLVR197202	25	M	October 1972		Yes
ICLVR197203		M	October 1972		Yes
ICLVR197204	37	F	December 1972	August 2003	Yes
ICLVR197301	21	M	August 1973	November 2010	No
ICLVR197501		M	July 1975	May 1999	No
ICLVR197502	17	M	October 1975		Yes
ICLVR197701	29	M	May 1977		Not applicable
ICLVR197801	23	M	April 1978	October 2014	Yes
ICLVR197802	18	M	May 1978	May 1999	Not applicable
ICLVR197803	22	M	May 1978	May 1999	Not applicable
ICLVR197901	24	M	March 1979	October 2010	No
ICLVR198102		M	July 1981	November 2008	Yes
ICLVR198103	54	M	August 1981	July 2010	Yes
ICLVR198101		M	January 1981	May 1984	Not applicable
ICLVR198501	33	M	May 1985		Yes

Figure 47.2 An Garda Síochána searches in 1999 (Image courtesy: Irish Times).

waited at the edge of numerous sites (Cusack 1999) anticipating an early recovery. The searches continued at these locations for 30 days after which activity was suspended (Newman and Keogh 1999). In this time, one double grave was located (ICLVR197801 and ICLVR197802), but all other searches proved unsuccessful (Keogh 1999).

Over the intervening years, search was intermittent and dependent on local police. A number of cases were returned to, some more than once, for example ICLVR197204 and ICLVR197502 (Humphreys 2003; *Irish Times* 1999; Moriarty 2003; Moriarty 2008); and in one case, the victim's family privately funded a search (family member, personal communication, 2008).

In 2005, a juncture was reached when calls for independent advice in the search for the disappeared came through government channels as a result of pressure from families and politicians (*Irish Times* 2006). The issue was debated a number of times both in the UK's Houses of Parliament and in the Oireachtas, the Irish Parliament (Keenan 2003), as being necessary to bring closure to the families of the victims.

In 2005, a conscious decision was taken by the leadership of the Commission to progress from a reactive organisation to a proactive one. Up to that point, the Commission had relied entirely on the receipt of information from intermediaries and former paramilitary organisations, and the search capability of local police forces. In 2006, an independent advisor was invited to review the Commission's operations up to that date and make recommendations on how the organisation might more effectively undertake its role in the future. The resultant key recommendations related to the establishment of a relative's DNA database; improving existing family liaison arrangements; adopting a proactive media strategy and, most significantly insofar as this paper is concerned, the establishment of a team of specialists and experts working directly for the Commission. On this list was the employment of advice from the field of forensic archaeology. This was the first time that independent forensic archaeologists had been consulted in the search for these victims. Following a case-by-case assessment fieldwork recommenced in late 2007 and search continued at full pace until 2011. At the time of writing, a programme of search for one victim is taking place and fresh appeals are being made for information in respect of a number of outstanding Commission cases.

Renewed search strategy

The search strategy is developed for each site, based on the specific information available, the value placed on the information by the investigation team and the terrain concerned. From this process, a costed project plan is then prepared and submitted to the two sponsoring governments in order to obtain the necessary funding in support of the proposed operation. This entire procedure is covered by the ICLVR confidentiality legislation; thus, the documentation concerned and details of associated discussions between the ICLVR and governments are not publicly available.

The ICLVR operates on the principal of least intrusive to most intrusive search techniques with search only taking place if there is sufficient evidence to do so (*Irish Times* 2006). A search will begin with the analysis of information available and attempts to validate or corroborate that information. Relevant contemporary records, mapping and imagery will always be sought and, where it is available, examined. Information in relation to the location of a victim can come to the Commission in a number of ways, either as a result of public contact and media appeals (Breen 2009) or via intermediaries and interlocutors acting on behalf of other organisations.

The use of forensic archaeology

The ICLVR is a transitional rather than a permanent body, and it does not employ a fixed workforce. It obtains the services of all its staff only on a contractual basis. The numbers of staff, including forensic archaeologists, working at any given time depends entirely on the nature and number of sites being processed at that stage. The primary roles and responsibilities of forensic archaeology as an investigative tool for the ICLVR have been in four key areas: preliminary investigations, taphonomic assessment, excavation and forensic recovery. Once a case has been established and information has been passed to the ICLVR search team, a preliminary desktop survey is undertaken, during which historic and current photographic and cartographic resources are assembled to assess and analyse landscape and environmental changes at time of burial (TOB) and time since burial (TSB). This includes the assembly of historical environmental data and geological information. The time frame of cases ranges from 30 to 40 years since victims were buried and the landscapes in which they were buried have long since been abandoned and their physical nature has changed, for example estuarine erosion and prolonged landscape saturation through extension of flood plains. In eight of the current cases, landscape assessments have been influenced heavily by previous searches prior to 2006 (Figure 47.3 and Table 47.1).

Figure 47.3 Landscape disturbance due to previous searches (© N.A. McCullagh, ICLVR).

It is also the role of the forensic archaeologist to conduct a taphonomic assessment of each location. The specific burial environment of each location has to be considered and pre-emptive studies have been undertaken at all remaining sites to evaluate the potential for human remains to survive in location.

Once a desktop assessment is complete, the next phase of assessment of the potential of the search location is to conduct field walking and a topographical survey. This survey is undertaken by members of the forensic archaeology team, acting under the overall direction and control of the head of the ICLVR investigation team. If it is deemed relevant, an auger survey will be undertaken to corroborate stratigraphic information and assist in limiting the potential search area. In the next phases, a cadaver dog search is conducted alongside a remote sensing survey, depending on the site potential for these methods. Resistivity, magnetometry, ground-penetrating radar (GPR), infrared and LIDAR are all considered at each search location. The results are collated in mapping prepared by the survey suppliers. These remote sensing methods have been deployed by the ICLVR with hugely varying degrees of success.

Excavation

Once a primary search area has been established by the team, the site will be taken to the invasive stage of excavation. Since 2007, 19 searches have been taken to the excavation phase of search. Excavations have taken place in three different jurisdictions – Ireland, Northern Ireland and France – and have ranged in size from 20 to 94,600 m^2 (Figure 47.4). During this phase, the ICLVR practises complete excavation and conclusive search (Figure 47.5).

The types of sites that the ICLVR has excavated have varied from coastal to woodland to peat bog, each with its own challenges. Relatively speaking, 90% of all time spent on site conducting excavation has been in saturated peat land. This requires significant site preparation in some cases. For example, case ICLVR197901 required the renewal of 4.2 km of drainage to allow access to a 100 × 100 m initial search area.

During the course of excavation, the forensic archaeologist must identify and establish the importance of any physical evidence encountered. For example, evidence of previous search activity (Figure 47.6, left) and the identification of human and non-human osteological remains (Figure 47.6, right). The forensic archaeologist must also establish the historic nature of illegal dumping, for example, domestic and industrial waste, and in one case a buried car.

Once human remains have been located, it is the responsibility of the forensic archaeologist to maintain the forensic integrity of the site and, working in conjunction with the pathology service concerned, it is the responsibility of the forensic archaeologist to recover human remains to the highest possible standards. Given the joint legislation under which the ICLVR operates, it does have primacy in both jurisdictions in respect of these particular cases. Notwithstanding, the coronial process (the State's investigation into the circumstances of any sudden or unexpected death, both in Ireland and the United Kingdom) runs largely in parallel to this recovery process. For that reason, post-mortem examinations of the remains are carried out by the State Pathology Service for the jurisdiction in which the remains are discovered. Whilst the ICLVR and the Pathology Service will jointly pursue the question of identification, the cause of death is a matter solely for the pathologist. Once identified, the remains are returned to their families for formal burial.

Figure 47.4 Size range of sites excavated (© N.A. McCullagh, ICLVR).

Figure 47.5 Complete excavation (© N.A. McCullagh, ICLVR).

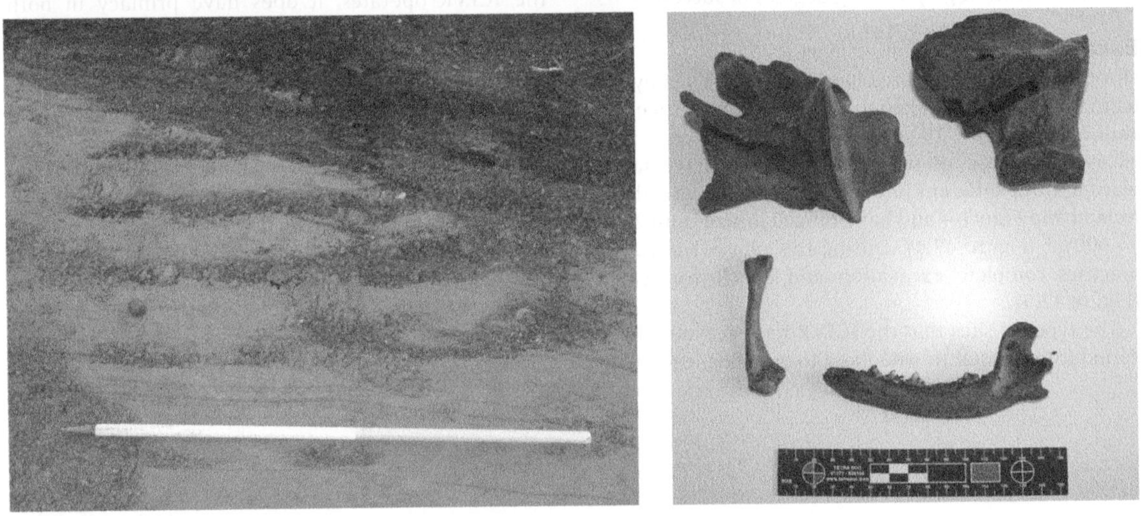

Figure 47.6 Examples of evidence of previous search activity and non-human osteological remains (© N.A. McCullagh, ICLVR).

Conclusion

The use of forensic archaeology in the search for *the Disappeared* in Ireland was first called for in 2003 (Keenan 2003). It was formally introduced as a skill to the team in 2006 by the second author (GK); and since 2007, forensic archaeology has been an integral tool used in support of the ICLVR search processes. As many as 10 (forensic) archaeologists have been deployed at some stages of the search process, qualified staff being provided by specialist university departments and also private consultancies.

Since the appointment of a forensic expert to steer this renewed search approach, five victims have been found through active search. Prior to this just one grave, containing two victims, was located through active search. Search continues at the time of writing. ICLVR searches are always information led, and further assistance is always sought from members of the public and, preferably, those individuals who were directly involved in the events.

Given the complex political context and the lengthy timescales involved, it has been suggested that the ICLVR has achieved significant success in locating and recovering several victims of conflict. So much so that both the International Committee of the Red Cross (ICRC) and the United Nations High Commission for Refugees (UNHCR) have expressed a degree of interest in exploring further and possibly exporting this unique 'Ireland' model. The ICLVR maintains a regular and well-established dialogue with officials of the ICRC; and in 2012, senior representatives of the ICLVR team held meetings with members of the UNHCR in Brussels and Geneva.

Acknowledgements

This chapter would not have been possible without the consistent support and patience of our Commissioners Sir Ken Bloomfield and Mr Frank Murray and members of the ICLVR team, including Jon Hill, John McIlwaine and the University of Bradford, Robert Friel, Aidan Harte and Aidan Boyle and his dedicated staff. Thank you also to Sandra Peake, CEO of the WAVE Victims Organisation, for her unending support and enthusiasm and to the *Irish Times* for permission to use images.

References

Breen, S. 2009. IRA killer of 'disappeared' man reveals burial place. *The Sunday Tribune*, Sunday, 18 January 2009.

Cusack, J. 1999. Gardaí to start digging for bodies of nine IRA victims. *The Irish Times*, Friday, 28 May 1999.

English, R. 2012. *Armed Struggle: The History of the IRA*. Oxford, Pan Books.

Hill, J. 2013. *The Victims* [conversation], 30 January 2013.

Humphreys, J. 2003. Search for remains in bog. *The Irish Times*, Tuesday, 9 September 2003.

Independent Commission for the Location of Victims' Remains 2012. *The Disappeared*. Available at: http://www.iclvr.ie/en/ICLVR/Pages/TheDisappeared (last accessed 10 December 2012).

Keenan, D. 2003. Hopes grow of finding bodies of 'disappeared'. *The Irish Times*, Wednesday, 3 September 2003.

Keogh, E. 1999. Gardaí find bodies of two missing men in double grave. *The Irish Times*, Wednesday, 30 June 1999.

McKittrick, D., Kelters, S., Feeney, B. and Thornton, C. 2007. *Lost Lives: The Stories of the Men and Women who died as a Result of the Northern Ireland Troubles*. Edinburgh, Mainstream Publishing.

Moriarty, G. 2003. Search resumes for body of 1975 abductee. *The Irish Times*, Monday, 8 September 2003.

Moriarty, G. 2008. Search for remains of man killed in INLA dispute fails. *The Irish Times*, Wednesday, 23 July 2008.

Newman, C. and Keogh, E. 1999. Search for six IRA victims suspended by commission. *The Irish Times*, Monday, 19 July 1999.

The Irish Times 1999. Harrowing week of digging finds little to comfort families of 'disappeared'. *The Irish Times*, Saturday, 5 June 1999.

The Irish Times 2006. New policy announced in hunt for 'disappeared'. *The Irish Times*, Friday, 4 August 2006.

Wilson, J.P. and Bloomfield, K. 1999. Statement on victims. *The Irish Times*, Monday, 31 May 1999.

Woods, D. 2013. Independent Commission for the Location of Victims' Remains. *Administration* 61(1), 99–109.

CHAPTER 48

Forensic archaeology and the International Commission on Missing Persons: setting standards in an integrated process

Ian Hanson

Internet Control Message Protocol (ICMP), Sarajevo, Bosnia and Herzegovina

Historical background

The International Commission on Missing Persons (ICMP) was established at the initiative of US President Clinton in 1996 at the G-7 Summit in Lyon, France. Its primary role is to ensure the cooperation of governments in locating and identifying those who have disappeared during armed conflict or as a result of human rights violations. The organisation was established to support the Dayton Peace Agreement, which ended the conflicts in Bosnia and Herzegovina scientific and investigation support operations started in 2001 (Hanson et al., Chapter 3 this volume). Headquartered in Sarajevo, the mainstay of ICMP's work has been in Bosnia and the Western Balkans. However, ICMP is now actively involved in helping governments and other institutions across the world. This includes supporting identification of missing persons, for example in Chile (Intriago Leiva et al., Chapter 45 this volume), Cyprus, Kuwait and South Africa (Nienaber, Chapter 39 this volume), assisting with DVI operations after natural disasters, such as the 2004 Asian Tsunami and Hurricane Katrina, and transport disasters, for example in the Philippines, Cuba, Cameroon and the Republic of Congo.

The ICMP undertakes capacity building in post-conflict countries to assist governments in addressing the issue of decades of large-scale disappearances, and unidentified casualties from war. Programmes in Iraq and Libya (Alemam, Chapter 36 this volume) are currently providing training and support to ministries to undertake investigations and missing persons' identifications. The ICMP also supports governments in the provision of evidence for prosecutions, in developing legislation relevant to missing persons' issues, and supporting family associations in the pursuit of their rights.

The ICMP has developed the biggest programme of its kind in the world, utilising a DNA-led identification system that successfully locates and examines and accurately identifies large numbers of persons missing from armed conflict and disaster. The effective use of archaeological approaches for search and investigation of crime scenes and recovery of the missing has been a driving force in the success of programmes.[1]

Organisation

Main responsibilities and functions

Archaeological methods and techniques utilised by the ICMP straddle the investigation process from planning site work to evidence identification and excavation, and overlap with forensic anthropological analysis and examination processes. This process is discussed in the following text. By supporting the implementation of this process, the ICMP is able to help international and national authorities undertake effective investigations. These activities include training and capacity building that provide understanding, advice and standards for investigating authorities, medical-legal entities and judiciaries to improve reliability of procedures, evidence management and documentation of sites, remains and associated evidence.

The ICMP undertakes data analysis and modelling to assist in determining site locations. Data gathered over 17 years is providing information and patterns to assist in predicting, guiding and prioritising site location efforts. Effective management, organisation and search of data are achieved through the use of dedicated database modules that are part of the ICMP's Forensic Database Management System (fDMS) (discussed in the following text and in Hanson's et al. Chapter 3, this volume).

---

[1]For more information, see: http://www.ic-mp.org (last accessed 30 March 2014).

Forensic Archaeology: A Global Perspective, First Edition. Edited by W.J. Mike Groen, Nicholas Márquez-Grant and Robert C. Janaway.

The ICMP provides support in the planning, organisation and management of the investigation process, assisting in determining and estimating resources, costs and timeframes of work, and advising on the integration of the archaeological and related processes in a wider investigative and identification system. ICMP staff report on activities and outcomes of capacity building and provide reports for relevant authorities, and may be called upon to provide evidence of findings for courts and tribunals.

The archaeology and anthropology division

These responsibilities are undertaken by the Archaeology and Anthropology Division (AAD) of the ICMP. The division is part of the Forensic Science Department.[2] Led by a Deputy Director (the author), the division aims to form common teams across programmes. These include forensic archaeology, forensic anthropology and crime scene investigation trainers, analysts and researchers. These teams are augmented with specific support staff depending on operational need. For example in Bosnia since 2013, a team is dedicated to supporting the systematic review of some 9000 unidentified cases held in 12 mortuary facilities across the country, and another team is supporting excavation of large complex grave sites such as Tomasica, near Prijedor.

The organisation of the division allows capacity building and mentoring to be undertaken, while also providing technical support, data analysis and advice to authorities in process, discipline and management matters. Currently contributing to the division are seven forensic archaeologists, twelve forensic anthropologists, a forensic pathologist, a crime scene manager, six case managers and an analyst. Additionally, interns and researchers are undertaking experimental and research work with the ICMP on a regular basis. The division is equipped for large-scale mass grave excavations and field support, and to undertake high-throughput skeletal examinations and sampling.

The ICMP follows best practice in archaeological excavation and recording by following definitions and descriptions including those used by the Museum of London Archaeology Service (MoLAS), widely used in the United Kingdom, Scandinavia and elsewhere (Museum of London Archaeology Service 1994). For example, units of record, usually defined stratigraphically, are called 'contexts'. These may be described by their properties, for example as 'deposits' and 'cuts'. Planning and drawing conventions for archaeology are also followed (e.g. Barker 1987).

Data recording, organisation and management

The forensic archaeologists and others in the division employ a simple-to-complex data documentation and organisation system that is straightforward to teach, and allows collection of data in difficult and demanding circumstances. Paper forms guide application of standard operating procedures (SOPs), and prompt thorough identification of evidence and data sources as well as data collection. The forms feed into simple intermediary databases based on Excel. Finally, data feeds into the linked, searchable and analytical ICMP's fDMS database.

The standardised forms are based on best practice and exemplar discipline examples. They have been developed over time through a legacy of UK archaeological field work recording systems, International Criminal Tribunal for the former Yugoslavia (ICTY) forensic field team work and ICMP experience. For example, to record data on archaeological deposits, surfaces and features, adapted versions of Museum of London Archaeology Service (MoLAS) context recording sheets are used, which were developed from the 1970s to record single archaeological contexts and stratigraphic information. To record the properties and location of human remains in the field a 'body form' is used based on those developed by the ICTY field team from 1998 and subsequently developed in convergent versions by the ICMP and the author while at Bournemouth University, UK (e.g. Cox et al. 2008; Wright et al. 2005).

Similarly, scaled archaeological sections and plan recording is undertaken using formatted and standardised gridded weatherproof drafting film (widely used in rescue and research archaeology). Technical progression of three-dimensional data recording is achieved through use of dumpy levels, and Total Stations, using software such as Arcview (GIS) and CorelDraw to produce scale plans.

This system allows best practice recording of data in a range of appropriate formats, and can also be taught in a stepped sequence from simple paper forms, planning with pencil and ruler through to digital recording and computerised data entry, to complete fDMS database entry and management. This has allowed data recording to be achieved and successfully taught and mentored in operational and difficult circumstances, and from basic to advanced technical levels.

The data collected in standard forms and formats allows consistent checking and quality assurance to be undertaken in the field and also when training new users. It also allows archiving of data from the raw records that can then be made available for review as disclosed evidence to courts, for quality checks, and so it is available to be re-interpreted in the future.

The ICMP produces standard excavation reports that summarise investigation findings in the field as public records and have been provided at the request of prosecutors and courts. These record the site location, site formation data and history, methods of excavation and recording, the

[2]For more information, see: http://www.ic-mp.org/administration/icmp-organization-chart/ (last accessed 30 March 2014).

excavation process, archaeological record, evidence identified and recorded, as well as interpretations. Formal statements and press releases are produced to inform authorities, family groups, the media and public of general findings.

Another output from the excavation process is interaction with the searchable ICMP on-line enquiry database.[3] This has an Excavation Site Inquiry Tool that allows authorised users to see summary information on the sites from which DNA sampled remains were recovered. The sites are designated by country, site name and the grid coordinates corresponding to the site if available. Not all DNA samples come from sites excavated or managed by the ICMP. Outcomes of DNA testing are also provided with the excavation information such as status and numbers of DNA profiles obtained from sites and whether a DNA match has been made.

Principles

The ICMP's forensic efforts: a collaborative scientific process of investigation

Best practice in the use of scientific techniques to assist in identification of the missing has developed in tandem with domestic forensic science capability and the work of international criminal investigations over the past 30 years. Progressive homicide investigation and achieving identifications of individuals with limited circumstantial information has been achieved through multidisciplinary approaches. The ICMP follows this principle and has expanded it to embrace a coordinated multi-agency cooperative approach to delivering multidisciplinary investigative support. Operational synchronicity between investigative authorities is vital to undertake complex scene investigations. It is however too often lacking, with the result that standards of work vary, and experience and intelligence are not shared.

The AAD employs forensic pathologists, forensic archaeologists, forensic anthropologists and crime scene managers as necessary to deliver coordinated support and advice for mass grave and crime scene investigations. Consultants from a range of disciplines support and advise on specific scientific analysis. The contributions of each discipline within the scientific process are vital to ensure evidence is identified and effectively documented, analysed and managed. Consistent definition of responsibility and communication ensures efforts overlap and do not conflict. Recognition of the limitations to the expertise and competence of individual disciplines and practitioners is important in ensuring efficient and effective investigation. Coordinated planning, procedures and team input are crucial to solving the problems that always arise because each scene investigation is unique.

Investigative problems

Key to the capacity for the ICMP to successfully investigate mass graves and other scenes has been identifying technical approaches to several consistent problems:

- Most of the crime scenes and the missing are either buried or in outdoor environments.
- The missing have been dead for some time or are affected by post-mortem (PM) changes (e.g. Haglund 2001).
- Tissues normally used to determine cause of death and identity are degraded or absent.
- Deposits and remains are often obscured, commingled, disturbed or damaged.
- There is limited witness information or other documentary evidence as to the location of graves, circumstances of death and identity of the dead.
- There is a massive scale of crime scenes, graves, evidence and numbers of missing.
- There is often a lack of dedicated resources on the part of domestic authorities to undertake appropriate specific technical work to acceptable standards.
- There is multi-agency jurisdiction and responsibility over investigations.

Inter-disciplinary approaches

Innovative use of existing disciplines and the management of several key coordinated inter-disciplinary approaches provided the methods to tackle these problems:

- Combining crime scene and archaeological search methods with remote sensing techniques to locate graves;
- The use of archaeological methods and experienced field archaeologists to identify, interpret and manage large, complex scenes in tandem with crime scene managers, identifying, controlling, recording and securing high volumes of evidence and cases;
- Application of archaeological excavation and osteological assessment techniques to identify individual cases at the grave from the complex associations encountered;
- Determining cause and manner of death through combined pathology-led autopsy and forensic anthropologically based observation and documentation, both at the scene and during examinations;
- Evidential exhibiting, recording and storage, combining principles of criminal evidence custodianship, mortuary practice, museum archiving and cultural anthropological description and documentation to accepted standards;
- Application of bone sampling and DNA profiling techniques to generate data from the hard skeletal tissues of cases to allow identifications, case associations,

[3]For more information, see: http://www.ic-mp.org/fdmsweb/index.php?w=intro&l=en (last accessed 30 March 2014).

physical links between scenes and provide evidence to help date events;

- Combining of witness information and interviewing techniques to gather ante-mortem (AM) data on the missing as well as where and when they disappeared, to feed analysis to determine site locations;
- Implementing database systems that document and analyse AM, crime scene analysis and PM data to allow matching of information to provide positive identifications and provide additional data for continuing investigation and prosecutions.

Process

The problem solving undertaken by key disciplinary approaches has developed into the structured and sequenced scientific process that AAD undertakes. The typical journey of investigating a case should follow the sequence listed:

- Planning for investigation of suspected scenes using available intelligence and undertaking estimates of work requirements;
- Potential grave locations pinpointed through analysis of available multi-source intelligence. For example, witness information and analysis of aerial images;
- Grave site located and confirmed by prioritising most effective search techniques after permissions and court orders for search and excavation are issued;
- Scene examination and assessment of excavation and investigation requirements;
- Excavation, search for and identification of evidence. Definition and recovery of cases and evidence. Documentation and recording. Excavation and ancillary reports produced;
- Examination in the mortuary, with multi-disciplinary autopsies including forensic anthropological assessment, inventory and determination of cause and manner of death. Assessment, documentation and analysis of any evidence for identification and investigation purposes. Examination and ancillary reports produced;
- Sampling of bone and tissues most likely to yield DNA;
- Data checking, entry and management of the entire process;
- Identification assessment undertaken using all available investigative, AM and PM data by forensic pathologist, including that generated by the DNA sample processing in the lab: DNA profile generation, profiles matched to reference samples and match reports generated;
- Positive identification made, family informed, identification accepted, remains signed for and repatriated;
- Case review to determine if identification data lead to need for re-assessment of other cases to determine associations, re-association requirements, potential case mis-identifications, mis-associations and requirements for re-exhumations;
- Case intelligence review to determine if results can contribute to further investigative progress, analysis or statistical assessments;
- Long-term conservation, preservation, storage, organisation and management for non-identified cases, personal effects and clothing, as well as relevant evidence for investigations, documentation and other records.

Standards and legal requirements

ICMP recognises that the evidence and data produced by this process are intrinsically linked to both criminal investigations and the identification of the missing. Therefore, any standard used to undertake this process effectively to identify, collect and analyse evidence must meet the requirements of prosecutors, judicial enquiries and scientific analytical techniques. Failure to meet standards in one part of the process has serious knock-on effects to the rest, impacting on integrity and accuracy of data, evidence and interpretations, costs, time, resources and the ability to complete investigations, prosecutions and identifications.

As the archaeological component forms the start of the process in searching for, identifying and excavating mass graves and other scenes, and assists in the management of the recovery of remains and evidence, there is a gravitas to this work. Failure of investigations to ensure appropriate archaeological techniques are utilised is a common cause in investigations of evidential loss and increased complexity of case examinations.

Assessment of the appropriate techniques to use in investigations is an increasingly frequent occurrence in forensic science, as highlighted in the NAS Report (Committee on Identifying the Needs of the Forensic Sciences Community 2009). The ICMP therefore expects examination and scrutiny of the archaeological methods they use, their application to forensic and investigative matters, as well as results and interpretations reached. With the aim of archaeological applications being the maximising of evidence identification, collection and analysis, the reconstruction of events and provision of intelligence to progress investigations, work needs to be of a high enough standard to allow scientifically verifiable and independent analysis, reinterpretation and auditing of any records and conclusions (Cheetham and Hanson 2009).

A useful standard approach is to conduct all work in accordance with the established principles of the professions, using methods of proven validity and appropriate equipment and materials (Forensic Science Regulator 2011). The ICMP's DNA Laboratory and Identification Coordination Division have been ISO/IEC 17025 accredited since 2007, and the AAD is developing standards and competency to map onto accreditation requirements (e.g. ENFSI 2007; ISO/IEC 17025 and 17020). While methods and procedures need to be demonstrably suitable and follow evidential guidelines, in many jurisdictions there have been no or limited applications of archaeological approaches within investigations to use as a benchmark. The ICMP provides assistance in developing understanding of how archaeology can assist investigations and what standards and methods are appropriate. These may exceed current legal needs under what may be limited criminal code descriptions. However, it is paramount that the principle adhered to is that all possible relevant information is documented and collected, and that it can be demonstrated that maximum evidential recovery has been attempted, and if possible achieved.

Archaeological principles

To assist in achieving the standards described earlier, the ICMP follows principles for archaeological and excavation work, which guide practice and ensure that staff undertake work in a thoughtful, logical and organised way that allows clear identification and understanding of the archaeological record for any site. These 'golden rules' are summarised here:

- Clearly identify the investigative and research questions being asked;
- Define the terminology and use of nomenclature for archaeological and scientific purposes in any investigation;
- Utilise and apply the Laws of Archaeological Stratigraphy (e.g. Harris 1979) as a standard approach;
- Identify, delineate and treat each identified archaeological context as a unique and separate entity;
- Identify and record all site formation processes, and the processes leading to formation of all contexts;
- Identify and describe all pertinent contexts and stratigraphic relationships using single context recording systems and a Harris Matrix;
- Record and document the nature and properties of all contexts in three dimensions using appropriate methods;
- Justify and record all archaeological destruction;
- Use excavation methods that can identify, determine and test all contexts and their relationships;
- Use excavation methods that maximise evidence identification, survival and integrity;
- Define, describe and justify all methods and techniques used, considered and or rejected. Justify interpretations and review alternatives;
- Apply mechanisms to allow checking of methods and interpretation, and that assist in identifying and limiting bias;
- Demonstrate staff have appropriate levels of qualification, skill and experience;
- Ensure that the methods, recording, interpretations and documentation undertaken are acceptable to the legal authority in charge of work.

These rules assist (forensic) archaeologists in developing a mindset to master understanding of the archaeological record present in any excavation. For example, using a context recording sheet that prompts stratigraphic description of neighbouring contexts leads the archaeologist to fully identify the stratigraphic record.

Archaeological technical support

The archaeological principles implemented by the ICMP allow for the thorough search, identification and recording of the surviving archaeological record. Providing capacity in this task is a main aim of the technical support of AAD to authorities.

Archaeological approaches

Search, location excavation and recovery is a continuous process from macro to micro, focusing on ever smaller areas of interest, defined by the perimeters of surviving anthropogenic and environmental stratigraphy (Cheetham and Hanson 2009). The ICMP prioritises search techniques based on those most likely to locate and identify sites and evidence, and which are cost and time effective. In terms of site location, these have focused on gaining multiple sources of intelligence to provide increased certainty of location and properties of sites. Knowing what is likely to be found evidentially and how remains will be affected by given environments assists estimates of planning. Witness information, aerial imagery and predictive modelling from data analysis have been most successful in pinpointing mass grave sites.

Practical excavation begins with probing and testing sites to assess and locate areas of interest. A key technique is to determine the 'natural' stratigraphy of the site and the site history by excavating test trenches that do not impact the structure and evidence of graves and sites. This 'forewarns' archaeologists of the expected stratigraphic record, and it helps identify what is anomalous when excavating.

Excavations by the ICMP focus on revealing the stratigraphic sequence of deposits, and where possible excavating them in their depositional sequence. Excavating in plan across the complete area of interest to expose as much as of each context as is possible and practical is the ideal. Excavation of each context by reversing as exactly as possible the deposition and formation sequence as it was laid down is the aim. Location and exposure of the surfaces upon which perpetrators and victims operated and were moved is vital. It is here that trace evidence, tool marks and artefacts accumulate. These surfaces both within and without graves are often sealed by backfilling, spreading of excess spoil and landscaping, and can be found easily if stratigraphic excavation principles are followed.

They are far harder to find if arbitrary excavations methods are used. The ICMP only advocates using techniques such as removal of soils in spits when excavation of undifferentiated deposits is needed to remove layers to pinpoint visible stratigraphy, when an identified context is excavated in spits to control evidence location and soil removal within the context boundaries, or for safety or access reasons once deposits have been identified. Use at other times makes identification and understanding of the stratigraphic sequence far harder to determine, and more difficult to interpret.

Trenching is the most common way for those excavating to locate graves and remains, and often where work begins to unravel. Many excavators focus on using trenches to pinpoint remains, and then expand trenches to expose limits of bodies. This often leads to loss of stratigraphic understanding and under-excavation of graves, resulting in limited or inaccurate interpretation as well as loss of evidence. The ICMP excavates trenches to analyse the stratigraphy revealed. This provides insight into structure of graves and dating sequences of later deposits. It is more difficult to see deposits and cuts and gain clear stratigraphic understanding in a narrow trench than in more open excavation, but it does allow more rapid testing and search of a given area.

A key objective of trenching is to determine the length, breadth and depth of deposits and graves so that estimates of time and cost of excavation can be determined. Accurately determining how long site work will take depends on accurately assessing the volume of soil to be moved, and the number (and condition) of cases and other evidence to be collected. The ICMP assists in estimating and planning the excavations that it supports. There has often been limited assessment, which leads to underestimates of time needed to complete work. Speed of excavation is often rushed to compensate (among other reasons). There is a misconception that rapid removal of bodies saves money. The contrary is true, rushed excavation costs; it leads to loss of evidence and commingling of remains. Complex commingled cases need extensive additional examination time and sampling costs, exceeding the days and costs saved by hurrying excavation.

Guidance in use and requirements of heavy machinery and site engineering (e.g. stepping battering, drainage and safe work practice) is something for which the ICMP provides support on larger excavations. The use of machinery can speed site preparation, leaving adequate time for cleaning and recording of remains. Often mass graves have been dug and landscaped with heavy machinery by perpetrators, and similar equipment has to be used for excavation if work is to be undertaken in a reasonable timeframe.

Anthropological approaches in the field

ICMP forensic archaeologists are trained in human osteology; but during mass grave excavations, both forensic archaeologists and forensic anthropologists are normally deployed to work together. Forensic anthropologists have the critical skills in dealing with skeletal remains. Forensic archaeologists remove soil and identify grave structure and stratigraphy of interest. The skills of both disciplines overlap in removing deposits to expose remains and assessing taphonomic effects. The osteological skills of forensic anthropologists determine how best to recover cases, record them and identify trauma and other evidence before lifting of cases.

The ICMP considers the autopsy to begin in the grave, with forensic pathologist, CSIs, forensic anthropologist and forensic archaeologist working to interpret the context of events. Recording case evidence and any information on cause and manner of death at the scene where body disposal (and often killings) took place builds the basis for developing interpretation of the cases during subsequent examination. Lack of understanding of context can lead to misinterpretation. Evidence and the nature of cases is changed once moved. Ballistic material in soil where soft tissue once was, blindfolds, ligatures, fractured and fragmented bones are all examples of evidence affected by case recovery. This needs to be balanced against the biasing effects of knowing the context of events before interpretation and examination take place (e.g. Nakhaeizadeh et al. 2014).

Recovery and packaging of cases in organised anatomical sections is standard ICMP practice, for example placing the left and right arms in separate bags. This is vital in allowing checks and an inventory to be made as the body is recovered, to assessing and inventory what is present, which saves time and prevents confusion in the mortuary. Examination is also efficient if cases are well organised from point of recovery. Recording the position and properties of the body before recovery is necessary to prevent the case becoming more complex through mixing and commingling. The systematic planning of each body is undertaken using a 15-point anatomical survey, using Total Station, body form and photography, and provides understanding of the body location to aid recovery, and relationships between all cases, evidence and grave structures. Three-dimensional plans show the position and properties of bodies' masses in graves that cannot be captured using two-dimensional photography.

A typical speed of excavation in mass grave investigations is for each forensic archaeologist and forensic anthropologist to recover two bodies a day, or five body parts a day for commingled assemblages. This takes into account full surveying and documentation of remains and the grave, and proper identification and handling of related evidence by the multidisciplinary team, working together to maximise effective recovery.

Evidence

The focus of ICMP forensic archaeologists is not just to recover the remains of the missing but also to recover associated evidence that will assist with dating and reconstruction of events that aid in identifications. All evidence collected has potential to be used for identifications and prosecutions, and should always be evaluated to see if it is relevant to assist identifying the missing. This includes evidence of perpetrators as well as individual victims among the many found in mass graves. For example, stratigraphic relationships and datable artefacts may differentiate graves from separate events at the same burial location. Artefacts disposed of in graves and personal effects may corroborate witness statements that link events concerning specific victims to specific graves. Evidence of machinery tool marks may link series of graves together, thus connecting the victims within those graves to the same events. To prove genocide or a crime against humanity, prosecutors need to demonstrate not only of what happened to each individual but also how a related group of individuals, evidence, crime scenes and perpetrators are connected. Patterns need to be identified and assessed, and data collected concerning:

- Related execution and burials distributions;
- Grave construction and properties;
- Time of death for all victims;
- Cause and manner of death;
- Demographic make-up of the dead;
- Relationships between individuals as provided by identification evidence;
- Evidence for the status of the dead (being military or civilians, for example).

The aim of such analysis is to determine whether there had been organised, planned and controlled crimes that involve groups, organisations and governments, and to provide evidence that indicates where the missing originated, who they are and how they are connected. The breadth of evidence sought for must be considered at the start of work through investigative questions. This should lead to the appropriate evidence being searched for, identified and collected, so that relevant analysis can be undertaken to provide answers to these questions. For example, evidence of perpetrators at a mass grave site may consist of shell case distributions recovered using metal detectors, showing firing positions and number and type of weapons used. Shell cases give dates of manufacture for ammunition. Bullets may be recovered from inside and outside graves, which can be matched. Rubber gloves, drinks containers, cigarettes and other evidence dropped in and around graves during body disposal may contain perpetrator DNA or provide other indications of perpetrator identification or origin. This physical evidence can link victims to perpetrators to scenes. The practical location and recovery of such evidence begins with excavation by archaeologists.

Capacity building

The ICMP's AAD has developed a comprehensive training system for the process of investigation of mass graves from field to mortuary. The courses provide investigation skills ranging from searching for graves to sampling remains for DNA analysis. This system has been used in a successful programme of capacity building in Iraq and Libya, where courses and manuals are provided in Arabic and English, and are pre-prepared. Delivery is undertaken by AAD training staff and national staff instructors, who can deploy to a country and undertake new course delivery in under a month. A system of interlinked modules develops skills from basic knowledge to advanced technical competency. The courses link into the wider ICMP identification system.

Training

The key principles that the ICMP promotes in its training are understanding, competency and sustainability. Too often, short courses provided by agencies and organisations in the spirit of goodwill and support leave authorities and attendees with limited understanding of issues, resources and skills needed to achieve results, and a belief that they have gained competency. This has implications for legal investigations and ability to positively identify the missing.

The ICMP's training courses are designed to develop minimum competency in undertaking the investigation process with the application of necessary technical skills, in as short a time as possible. Mentoring of trainees is vital to achieve consistent competency. The basic training course provides 80 h of teaching, with an additional 120 h of study and practice expected. This gives an underpinning of understanding. The ICMP expects mentoring and further training to be undertaken over a minimum period of 18 months to 3 years, as skills are developed. The training modules are designed to map onto Institute of Higher Education (IHE) credit units/ modules. This provides potential for trainees to further develop and gain qualifications at national institutes and overseas universities. Courses are designed for specific country and authority needs, with the modular delivery providing flexibility and focus on the specific skill sets needed in any programme. An assessment of the current scientific and practical capacity and facilities is made so that subsequent training can be tailored to investigative needs.

The training programme has a three-fold approach: to provide scientific processes to multidisciplinary staff so that they can undertake investigations, to provide management training and understanding to authorities so that investigations can be competently legislated for, led and organised, and last to provide training in resource and logistics support needs for investigations and departments. It is vital that awareness and understanding of the scientific process among government and legal entities is developed, so that adequate central and departmental support for field and mortuary investigations is put in place.

This rapidly builds a functional capacity that can be supported and mentored. Mentoring is necessary; problem solving and the experience to undertake interpretation, analysis and consistent standards of work come only with time and advice. The training programme typically leads to practical work being undertaken within 3 months of basic course completion. The dynamic in post-conflict countries is often that pressure to begin investigations is overwhelming and cannot be delayed while full-fledged institutions are developed. The key is to supervise, support and mentor development while investigations begin, and experience develops from a minimum practical competency.

Another dynamic in post-conflict countries is security and stability. To ensure momentum in training and development, the ICMP employs a combination of classroom training and practical exercises using simulations. This is undertaken in a controlled and safe environment. It also ensures trainees are not learning basic skills on actual crime scenes. Simulations have been developed by the author for training since 2001, and provide realistic training and mentoring exercises for mass grave, death scene, disaster scene and mortuary scenarios (Figure 48.1).

Figure 48.1 Mass grave simulation in Iraq, 2009; learning basic skills in a safe, controlled and measured environment. Coordinating mass grave investigation procedures between MHR and Ministry of Defence de-mining team staff who will conduct site searches.

Mentoring and advising

ICMP staff physically mentor and provide technical assistance at excavation sites and in mortuaries, aiming to do so until consistent standards are achieved, and national self-sustaining systems are in place. This additional training and mentoring covers processes and methods, management and logistics, legal standards, reporting, analysis and post-excavation requirements and is needed to ensure independent consistent standards are developed and maintained. The mentoring develops the following:

- Scientific requirements for identifications;
- Standards of evidence collection for criminal cases;
- Legal requirements under national and international law.

Assistance also includes advising on facility development and investigation support. The ICMP also advises on planning strategies, coordination and management of mass grave investigations and analysis. This includes advising on how field and mortuary operations interlink with identification and prosecutorial systems, how to determine and conclude identifications, what specialist requirements are needed and how to work with and provide understanding to family and community groups.

Monitoring

Trainees finish the courses being able to undertake the basic skills required for mass grave excavation and examination in teams. They are able to undertake process, evidence gathering and reporting under supervision. However implementation, as well as requiring mentoring, also requires monitoring. The ICMP undertakes systematic and thorough review of teams and staff to check that standards are implemented, to determine what shortfalls there are and what additional development or reinforcing of training is required. Training impact is assessed and feeds back to continual development of courses suitable for the authorities being supported. Monitoring, as with training courses, is standardised, which allows comparison of the training results and operational implementation across investigations, time, organisations and departments.

Monitoring also determines the attrition rate within departments for staff trained, and identifies resource and staffing gaps that further basic training courses can fill. Hence, there is a need for consistent and committed support for ministries and their departments. This requires funding to ensure capacity is developed and maintained.

Training in ICMP Operations

The ICMP has run eight basic training courses and numerous advanced courses in Iraq since 2009. Over 300 trainees have undertaken courses, both men and women and from all parts of Iraq. The Ministry of Human Rights (MHR) and in the Kurdistan region Ministry of Martyrs and Anfal Affairs (MoMAA) now have fully functioning and equipped field teams that undertake mass grave investigations, cooperating with the Medical-Legal Institute (MLI) who undertake examinations and assist in case recoveries from their offices across Iraq. Many investigations concern on-going prosecution cases, and are coordinated under the Law on Protection of Mass Graves (Ministry of Human Rights 2006). MHR has investigated 60 mass graves and recovered 4000 bodies since 2008 concerning the missing from the Saddam Hussein regime era (1979–2003). The ICMP has not provided support for investigations into the missing from the Iran—Iraq war (1980–1988). The data collected during investigations is being used to identify the missing and to provide evidence for the courts. Training and standards are geared towards the Iraq criminal code and relevant laws governing investigations, as well as responsibilities towards the missing and families. Teams have been mentored and monitored, developing both technical skills and experience, despite the trying security conditions and environment in which they operate. Some 2000 bone samples and several thousand blood reference samples are being provided to the ICMP under agreement, for DNA analysis to be undertaken in their labs in Bosnia as part of the effort to identify the remains recovered through mass grave excavations.

The ICMP began their Libya programme in 2012, with an initial assessment of requirements, and briefings to staff of the newly formed Ministry for the Affairs of Families of Martyrs and Missing (MAFMM). In March 2012, the Ministry's newly formed forensic team was guided through basic procedures, and provided with practical training. The team were mentored though the taking of samples – from skeletal and mummified fleshed remains – so that the ability to undertake further anthropological assessment would not be impacted (e.g. Hines et al. 2014; ICMP 2013). Formal training began in March 2013 with two basic courses at facilities provided by the Ministry. The courses have been completed by 40 trainees, with advanced courses on-going. Two teams are operating nationally based in Tripoli and Benghazi, with plans for more staff and teams to be trained. Advice on national facilities development is being provided, together with planning and coordination assistance between various ministries with responsibility for missing persons and investigations. Mentoring at excavations has begun, in collaboration with the Republic of Korea's Ministry of National Defence Agency for KIA Recovery and Identification (MAKRI) staff, with sites investigated in Tripoli, as the security situation permits. Political and family pressures led to some excavations in 2012, for which the ICMP provided more than 100 DNA identifications through analysis of samples at their labs in Bosnia.

Case studies

Iraq

In 2011, MHR and MLI undertook excavations near Ramadi and Abu Ghraib prison. An area several kilometres in area was assessed and found to contain 25 mass graves, shown to be dug by heavy machinery as extended lines. They contained bodies, clothing and personal effects. The remains recovered were reputed to be of the missing held in prison and then executed during the Saddam Hussein regime era. The graves were systematically excavated and recorded with 954 cases recovered. The site investigation was monitored by the ICMP (Figure 48.2), with weekly visits and monitoring

Figure 48.2 ICMP monitoring and mentoring MHR staff at a mass grave excavation near Ramadi, Iraq, in 2011.

reports. The basic principles of process and documentation taught in the training courses were implemented. Remains and evidence were planned to scale and were secured in a documented chain of custody. Bodies were collected as individual cases through assessment by osteologists and medical doctors from MHR and MLI. Details of grave construction and tool marks from grave creation were recorded. ICMP provided recommendations concerning implementation of training, for technical and process issues, for management, for SOPs and guidelines and documentation standards. The site was secured by both Iraqi police and army, as the area is volatile and there are frequent bombing and small arms attacks on the authorities.

Libya

ICMP forensic technical support was requested in 2013 to assess human remains discovered at a construction site in Tripoli. Prosecutors wanted to know if the site was of forensic interest. The ICMP undertook an assessment with MAFMM field team staff, mentoring them in archaeological techniques. Four sections in already excavated foundation trenches were cleaned and examined. They consistently showed that beneath 2 m of recent concrete and building deposits were layers of sand and mud brick with no modern inclusions. Several truncated single burials were visible in these layers aligned West to East, and lying in a supine position. Remnants of coffin wood and nails were identified with the burials, and no modern artefacts or materials were present. The conclusion was that the site was a disused legitimate cemetery, which is of archaeological and not forensic interest, and that the remains did not fall under the mandate of prosecutors or MAFMM.

Bosnia

A grave site was excavated in 2012 near Rogatica. The victims were reported to be Bosniak civilians killed in 1992 in the area of Višegrad. The mass grave was reportedly hidden under a farm pond, on property next to a road. A test trench found human remains. The pond was then drained and an excavation began. The remains however were found to be dis-articulated. A cleaned section and stratigraphic assessment demonstrated the deposit in which the remains were found lay underneath the pond, and extended from the road. The section was drawn and photographed. It was determined from the landowner that the pond existed before the conflict started in 1992; therefore, the remains could not be from that war. Numerous artefacts found in the same deposit with the remains – military webbing, a *Luftwaffe* dog tag, German 1943 pfennig coin, knife made in Germany, army boots, tinned beef – all indicated the dating of the deposit to World War II. Vintage telegraph pole porcelain insulators were also found in the deposit. It was determined the road was re-made in the 1980s. It is likely the remains were disturbed from a grave when the road was widened at that time. The cases were therefore excluded from investigation, and the archaeological analysis precluded the need for examination or DNA sampling. The offices of the Missing Persons Institute in Bosnia and Herzegovina coordinate with national war graves commissions to repatriate war dead from previous conflicts. See Chapter 3 for additional case studies.

Serbia

During 2001–2002, a series of five mass graves and three related features were excavated at Batajnica, Belgrade. ICMP provided archaeological assistance to the investigating judge, together with a team from the Forensic Institute of Belgrade, the Institute of Anatomy and archaeologists from the University of Belgrade (Djurić and Starović, Chapter 18 this volume). Eight graves were excavated by defining and recording stratigraphic relationships, including deposits of remains that indicated sequences of deposition. Remains were examined and recovered together with all related evidence, and fully recorded in three dimensions, including deposits that had undergone burning. Surfaces were exposed and recorded that provided evidence of events concerning grave construction, movement of remains and back filling of graves. Landscaping and post-deposition events were revealed and recorded across the whole area (ICMP 2004). The sequence of a complex series of events at the site was determined using archaeological, physical anthropological and forensic methods, and greatly assisted the court's understanding of the crime scene, and assisted examinations of the missing by discretely identifying separate cases of remains, and plotting the bodies in three dimensions. This produced accurate maps showing the location of the bodies themselves and any associated evidence that might relate to identification. Altogether, 705 bodies were recovered from eight mass graves, with identifications greatly aided by DNA matching at ICMP labs and Identification Coordination Department (ICD). They were identified as individuals killed in Kosovo in 1999 (Kron 2006).

Conclusions

The ICMP undertakes forensic archaeological investigations and provides technical support to authorities and government ministries globally. It provides capacity building expertise, and successfully assists governments in setting up investigative teams using archaeological, multi-disciplinary and inter-disciplinary cooperation, expertise and processes to collect evidence and identify the missing. The ICMP undertakes technical support and training to standards that meet the requirements of national and international courts and presumes that all mass grave, crime scene and case investigations will be subject to prosecutorial, political, media and community scrutiny at some point in the future. Work that does not meet accepted evidential needs, court needs and scientific standards potentially compromises prosecutions, the chance for justice and the ability to positively identify the missing. If defined national standards are lacking, then the ICMP uses its own standards by default that are suitable for international courts.

Perpetrator agendas can aim to obscure the truth and try to destroy and obliterate the past, the present and the future of the missing. Many families want to know what happened to those who went missing and want opportunities for justice. Not being able to achieve this continues the violation of the rights of the missing and their families. The work of the archaeologist helps to reveal events and a person's identity, not only to give it back to them, their family and their community, but also to help provide a narrative for courts and for the future, as a historical record. Archaeologists help to reveal the story through their observation, recording and interpretation.

Best practice in stratigraphic excavation, recording and analysis is utilised by the ICMP as the preferred way to fully identify, define and understand the archaeological history of any site. In doing so, the ICMP's forensic archaeologists frustrate efforts to hide and eradicate the past and the missing that are concealed.

Acknowledgements

This chapter includes description of cases studies illustrating the cumulative experience, operating standards, working policies and integrated forensic sciences that have been established by large numbers of individuals working both within and outside the ICMP. The number of past and current employees whose immense work and remarkable dedication have contributed to forensic archaeology and the integrated scientific process at ICMP is unfortunately too large to list in entirety, but particular acknowledgement is due to Jon Sterenberg, Adnan Rizvic, Edin Jasaragic, Zlatan Bajunovic and Cheryl Katzmarzyk, and to ICMP Directors Thomas Parsons, Andreas Kleiser, Adam Boys and Kathryne Bomberger. James Fenn, David Hines, James Murphy, Caroline Barker, Dale Roberts and Javier Naranjo Santana have contributed substantially to development of the ICMP AAD training programmes in Iraq and Libya, which have been generously funded by the United States, the United Kingdom, the German and Danish Governments, and the United Nations.

References

Barker, P. 1987. *Techniques of Archaeological Excavation*. London, Batsford.

BS EN ISO/IEC 17025. 2005. *General Requirements for the Competence of Testing and Calibration Laboratories*. Geneva, ISO/IEC.

Cheetham, P. and Hanson, I. 2009. Excavation and recovery. In S. Blau and D. H. Ubelaker (eds.), *Handbook of Forensic Anthropology and Archaeology*, 141–151. Walnut Creek, Left Coast Press.

Committee on Identifying the Needs of the Forensic Sciences Community, National Research Council. 2009. *Strengthening Forensic Science in the United States: A Path Forward*. Washington, DC, National Academy of Sciences.

Cox, M., Flavel, A., Hanson, I., Laver, J. and Wessling, R. 2008. *The Scientific Investigation of Mass Graves*. Cambridge, Cambridge University Press.

ENFSI. 2007. *Guidance for Best Practice Sampling in Forensic Science*. Available at: http://www.enfsi.eu/sites/default/files/documents/bylaws/guidance_document_for_best_practice_manuals.pdf (last accessed 10 May 2013).

Forensic Science Regulator. 2011. *Codes of Practice and Conduct for Forensic Science Providers and Practitioners in the Criminal Justice System*. Version 1.0. Birmingham, The Forensic Science Regulator.

Haglund, W. D. 2001. Recent mass graves, an introduction. In W. D. Haglund and M. H. Sorg (eds.), *Advances in Forensic Taphonomy*, 243–261. Boca Raton, CRC Press.

Harris, E. 1979. *Principles of Archaeological Stratigraphy*. London, Academic Press.

Hines, D., Venemeyer, M., Amory, S. et al. 2014 (in press). Prioritized sampling of bone and teeth for DNA analysis. In B. J. Adams and J. E. Byrd (eds.), *Recovery, Analysis, and Identification of Commingled Human Remains*. 2nd edition. Totowa, Humana Press.

ICMP. 2004. *Exhumation and Examination Summary Report on the Forensic Monitoring Activities Relating to the Excavation and Recovery of Human Remains from Several Related Features Located at Batajnica Serbia and Montenegro August to December 2002*. ICMP Unpublished Report. Document number ICMP. FSD.16.04.2.doc. Available at: http://www.ic-mp.org/wp-content/uploads/2008/02/icmp-fsd-16-04-2-doc.pdf (last accessed 10 May 2013).

ICMP. 2013. *Standard Operating Procedure for Sampling Bone and Tooth Specimens from Human Remains for DNA Testing at the ICMP*. ICMP.SOP.AA.136.1.doc. ICMP Unpublished Standard Operating Procedure.

Kron, A. 2006. Determining the fate of missing persons in post-conflict society: role of judiciary, ad hoc bodies, and international actors. Case study. *Justice in Transition* 7. Available at: http://www.tuzilastvorz.org.rs/html_trz/(CASOPIS)/ENG/ENG07/1614.htm (last accessed 10 May 2013).

Ministry of Human Rights. 2006. *Law on the Protection of Mass Graves*. Law number 5, Official Gazette 2006. Baghdad, Ministry of Human Rights, Iraq.

Museum of London Archaeology Service. 1994. *Archaeological Site Manual*. 3rd edition. London, Museum of London.

Nakhaeizadeh, S., Hanson, I. and Dozzi, N. 2014. The Power of contextual effects in forensic anthropology: a study of biasability in the visual interpretations of trauma analysis on skeletal remains. *Journal of Forensic Sciences*, 59(5), 1177–1183.

Wright, R., Hanson, I. and Sterenberg, J. 2005. The archaeology of mass graves. In J. Hunter and M. Cox (eds.), *Forensic Archaeology: Advances in Theory and Practice*, 137–158. London, Routledge.

CHAPTER 49

Forensic archaeology in humanitarian contexts; ICRC action and recommendations

Morris V. Tidball-Binz and Ute Hofmeister

The International Committee of the Red Cross (ICRC), Geneva, Switzerland

The tragedy of persons missing as a result of armed conflicts and catastrophes

> *'For a long time I had realised that this uncertainty was the greatest agony of all.'*

The above quotation from Dr Marcel Junod, referring to the suffering of the relatives of missing persons[1] whom he met during his work as a delegate of the International Committee of the Red Cross (ICRC) in the Spanish Civil War (Junod 1951, 114–115; Anasagasti 2007), anticipated today's universal recognition of the kind of suffering affecting those who have lost a loved one due to armed violence or other catastrophic events and do not know their whereabouts. Such recognition is nowadays enshrined by substantive national and international jurisprudence (e.g. Nicholas Chapman Blake vs. Guatemala).[2]

From such recognition springs the obligation, under international humanitarian law, for participants of armed conflict to ensure the proper and dignified management of the remains of the deceased and the protection of the families' right to know the fate and whereabouts of their loved ones. Humanitarian forensic action[3] plays an increasingly important role in helping to fulfil these obligations.

This chapter summarises some of the practical considerations in this novel field of application of forensic archaeology, the search of missing persons in international and non-international armed conflicts. The principles and practice behind the need to resolve and prevent the tragedy of the missing, and ensuring the proper and dignified recovery and identification of the dead are also applicable to mass fatalities unrelated to armed conflicts, such as natural catastrophes.

The International Committee of the Red Cross

The ICRC is an impartial, neutral and independent organisation whose exclusively humanitarian mission is to protect the lives and dignity of all victims of armed conflict the world over.[4]

The ICRC was created in 1863 following an international campaign launched by Jean Henry Dunant (1828–1910), a Swiss citizen from Geneva, after witnessing the battle of Solferino (1859) in present-day Northern Italy, where thousands of wounded soldiers died for lack of medical care. Dunant's calls for the creation of an organisation able to offer protection and assistance to the war wounded, without any distinction and strictly for humanitarian purposes, led to the founding of the ICRC and to the creation of national relief societies in each country (e.g. the French Red Cross and the Tunisian Red Crescent).

---

[1] In ICRC definition, *missing person* is a person whose whereabouts are unknown to his/her relatives and/or who, on the basis of reliable information, has been reported missing in connection with an international or non-international armed conflict, a situation of internal violence or disturbances, natural catastrophes or any other situation that may require the intervention of a competent State authority. This broad category of victims includes the victims of enforced disappearances.

[2] For more information, see: http://www.worldcourts.com/iacthr/eng/decisions/1998.01.24_Blake_v_Guatemala.pdf. (last accessed 30 March 2014).

[3] The ICRC defines humanitarian forensic action as the field of application of forensic science to humanitarian action (i.e. fulfilling international humanitarian law), notably for the search, recovery, management and identification of the dead from armed conflicts. Other applications include investigations of allegations of torture and ill-treatment, deaths in custody related to armed conflict and the identification of the living.

[4] For more information, see: http://www.icrc.org/eng/ (last accessed 30 March 2014).

Forensic Archaeology: A Global Perspective, First Edition. Edited by W.J. Mike Groen, Nicholas Márquez-Grant and Robert C. Janaway.

The ICRC is also a source and custodian of international humanitarian law, a special body of international public law applicable at times of armed conflict, aimed at reducing the suffering caused by war.

The ICRC's mandate for carrying out its global humanitarian activities derives from the Geneva Conventions by which every state in the world has agreed to be bound, their Additional Protocols and from the Statutes of the Movement. The ICRC is active in nearly 100 countries around the world, and its work is coordinated from its Geneva headquarters in Switzerland. The ICRC is a non-profit organisation, funded principally by governments, regional organisations, national Red Cross and Red Crescent societies and members of the public.

International humanitarian law on the dead and missing from armed conflict

In consideration of the importance of the dead and missing from armed conflicts, the four *Geneva Conventions of 1949* (GC I to IV) (ICRC 2002), their Additional Protocols I and II (AP I and AP II) (ICRC 1977) and customary international humanitarian law (Henckaerts and Doswald-Beck 2006) include specific provisions dealing with the deceased, gravesites and the missing from armed conflict.

The handling of the remains of those killed in armed conflict is often a highly sensitive issue, and their desecration is considered shameful and deeply offensive. In effect, international humanitarian law protects the dignity of the dead, and it requires their identification whenever possible. It includes detailed obligations concerning the treatment of the dead and their burial sites, the collection of information on the deceased, their identification, the registration and protection of grave sites and the repatriation of remains (Petrig 2009).

On a more fundamental level and in terms of humanity, the right of human beings not to lose their identity after death is nowadays universally recognised (Interpol 1996), which implies that the dead are identified, that something is known about how they died and that funerary rituals are carried out whenever possible.

In addition to the loss of human life and the destruction caused by war, one of the tragedies resulting from armed conflict is that large numbers of people go missing and cannot be accounted for.

For the families of the missing,[5] the combination of lack of news and uncertainty about the fate of their loved ones often amounts to serious and long-lasting suffering, which remains active as long as 'closure' is not possible.

The impact of the missing also often transcends the intimacy of the bereaved and permeates their wider communities, who also aspire to know. For example, in August 2011, members of a remote community in the mountainous north-western region of Libya approached the ICRC for forensic assistance in recovering and identifying their dead (Alemam, Chapter 36 this volume). They had been killed 2 months earlier by members of the opposing warring party, who had buried them in an unmarked mass grave, which was then mined. The community explained that the recovery and proper burial of their loved ones were for them more important than any other humanitarian assistance they were receiving, including medical aid and food. They insisted on the urgent need for forensic expertise, which was unavailable in the region as a result of ongoing conflict, in order to know the fate of their dead and to mourn and bury them according to their traditions and religion.

The core element of international humanitarian law that addresses this consequence of armed conflict is the bereaved families' right to know the fate of a relative who is missing (Article 32 of AP I). This means that families have a right to know whether the missing relative is dead or alive; and if the relative is dead, they have a right to know something about how the death came about and the whereabouts of the deceased.

A global agreement on best practices: the 2003 international conference on the missing and their families

The right of families to know the fate of their missing relatives and the need for the dignified and proper management of the dead from armed conflict and other forms of violence were highlighted in a process launched by the ICRC between 2002 and 2003.

This aimed to consolidate the lessons learnt worldwide for preventing and resolving the tragedy of missing and to raise awareness of the issues among the community of States and other key actors – including forensic scientists – and to provide political and practical solutions to the tragedy of the missing. The recommendations were adopted by the international community during an International Conference of Governmental and Non-Governmental Experts on the Missing and Their Families (the Conference), held in Geneva,

[5]The terms 'family' and 'relatives' must be understood in their broadest sense, including family members and close friends, and taking into account the cultural environment.

Switzerland, in February 2003. The ultimate objective was to ensure that families of missing people are assisted in finding their loved ones, that all the dead from armed conflict are managed in a proper and dignified way and to prevent people becoming unaccounted for in the future.

The Conference recognised that forensic science plays an essential role in the recovery and identification of the dead and the documentation of facts, which may lead to accountability of perpetrators and reparations for the victims and – some argue – may also help prevent their repetition. It also recognised that forensic science can help uphold the families' right to know the fate of their missing relatives. In other words, the Conference helped recognise forensic science as a necessary tool for humanitarian action (ICRC 2003a).

However, while in contexts of armed conflict or other situations of widespread armed violence, the responsibility to investigate deaths, identify the victims and inform the families, in theory lies fully with the authorities, all too often, either through lack of capacity or lack of will, this responsibility is not fulfilled. As a result, international forensic action is increasingly called upon by the concerned communities, the authorities and also by international agencies to help monitor and safeguard provisions of international humanitarian law.

In carrying out such operations, however, forensic practitioners, including archaeologists, often face unique challenges, including ethical and legal dilemmas and technical constraints seldom experienced in their domestic settings. The recommendations on forensic best practices from the Conference and the experience gained since by the ICRC's forensic services can provide useful and practical guidance for those involved or willing to participate in humanitarian forensic work (Tidball-Binz 2007).

The recommendations include advice and guidelines on multidisciplinary team efforts for the recovery, management and identification of the dead in war-torn and challenging contexts. These include defining the roles, duties, responsibilities and applicable ethical standards for forensic practitioners and teams; guidelines for documentation and storage of human remains and associated evidence; the use and integration of the various forensic disciplines, including forensic archaeology; methods and criteria for forensic human identification; principles for ethical, effective and efficient information management, including the collection and comparison of ante-mortem and post-mortem data; and advice on the relationship between forensic practitioners and bereaved families and communities.

In the years that followed the Conference, it became growingly apparent that many of the recommendations related to forensic sciences are also valuable for the investigation of the missing in catastrophes.

Forensic archaeology in humanitarian forensic action

Forensic archaeology only relatively recently became a regularly applied method for the search and identification of missing persons in humanitarian and human rights contexts. The first recorded systematic use of forensic science for the recovery and identification of large numbers of victims of armed violence took place in the 1980s in Argentina, where thousands of people were abducted, killed and buried in unmarked graves during a military regime which ruled the country between 1976 and 1983 (Snow et al. 1984).

The outcome of those early pioneering investigations, carried out by the Argentine Forensic Anthropology Team (EAAF; Fondebrider and Scheinsohn, Chapter 43 this volume), helped catapult forensic science – in particular forensic archaeology and anthropology – in its application to humanitarian and human rights investigations and went beyond resolving cases in specific contexts. In subsequent years, archaeologists were the main specialists to be found working in mass grave exhumations in other Latin American countries, such as Guatemala (Figure 49.1) and Colombia (Guatame et al., Chapter 46 this volume). The large-scale exhumations in the Balkans in the second half of the 1990s had a heavy archaeological component, dealing with the complex scenarios of combined secondary and primary mass graves, heavy commingling and multiple deposits. This work, carried out mainly by ICTY and later ICMP (Hanson, Chapter 48 this volume), also contributed to the development of new forensic archaeological methodologies applied to complex contexts (e.g. Tuller and Duric 2006, Tuller et al. 2008).

Forensic archaeology in the ICRC

For the implementation of the Missing Conference's recommendations, in 2003 the ICRC acquired for the first time its own forensic capacity, to promote and help implement forensic best practices applied to humanitarian operations, principally for the search, recovery, identification and adequate management of the remains of those killed or reported missing as a result of armed conflict. Like all other ICRC activities, these services are provided free of charge. At the time of writing, the ICRC is still the only organisation in the world providing global forensic services exclusively for humanitarian purposes.

The ICRC's forensic services focus primarily on building local and regional forensic capacity and fostering regional and international cooperation among forensic practitioners and institutions, especially among countries affected by armed conflict and catas-

Figure 49.1 Families at an exhumation site in Guatemala (Photo: U. Hofmeister).

trophes, to help prevent and resolve the humanitarian consequences of these events. In addition, the ICRC also carries out a range of forensic training activities, often in collaboration with forensic institutes and universities; it helps develop and promote standards of best practice, and it develops specialised tools, including Disaster Victim Identification (DVI) equipment and software.

ICRC forensic experts, as are all ICRC staff, are bound to the ICRC confidentiality agreements and exemption from providing evidence, and thus cannot give expert testimony in court.[6] For this reason, actual forensic work is only carried out in exceptional circumstances or via other service providers.

The ICRC's forensic services include forensic professionals from the fields of medicine, anthropology, archaeology, odontology and criminalistics. Experts with a background in forensic archaeology/anthropology presently make up the majority of the ICRCs forensic team,[7] at least two of them having originally been trained and worked in traditional archaeology before specialising in forensics. The often very extensive background of archaeologists, particularly those trained in the Americas, (including aspects of social and physical anthropology) and thorough knowledge of documentation methods and information management, provide a good basis for understanding issues of forensic search and identification.

Although the ICRC's forensic experts are usually not directly involved in forensic investigations, they may do so in specific situations, including as neutral intermediaries in situations of armed conflicts or at the request of state authorities, communities and families, albeit for purely humanitarian purposes, always with the consent of the authorities in charge. These services have mainly been in the field of forensic archaeology/recovery of human remains, including supervising exhumations at a complex burial site (in a cave setting) in Cyprus, related to the Greek–Turkish Cypriot conflict, supporting the recovery of remains from the Iran–Iraq war (1980–1988), joint exhumations associated with the Georgian–Abkhazian conflict with local forensic experts in Abkhazia, and the emergency recovery of human remains associated with the ongoing internal conflict in Colombia, Libya and other contexts.

In Colombia in particular, the ICRC has a team of three forensic archaeologists/anthropologists ready to carry out, when required, exhumations of human remains in areas that, due to the internal armed conflict, are not accessible to the authorities. Usually in these cases, it is armed groups who – on a confidential basis – hand over bodies or information on burials to the ICRC for humanitarian reasons; sometimes, the request comes directly from the family of the supposed victim. These exhumations are carried out under the ICRC's headquarter agreement (Ley 42 de 1981) and mandate and in coordination with the Colombian authorities.

[6] For more information, see: www.icrc.org/eng/resources/documents/misc/5wsd9q.htm (last accessed 30 March 2014).

[7] At the time of writing, this team comprised 16 forensic specialists, from the fields of medicine, odontology, archaeology, anthropology and criminalistics.

Such operations are only carried out with the express consent of the parties of the conflict. ICRC experts recover the remains, assuring the necessary quality of recovery and then, always maintaining ICRC's principles of confidentiality, hand them over to the authorities together with the hypothesis of identity for subsequent scientific and official identification.

An emblematic case was the recovery of the remains of 11 parliamentarians from Cali killed during captivity, recovered by the ICRC and then identified by a joint team of Colombian and international experts. But there are many other such cases, albeit not receiving such media attention. In the past 16 years, the ICRC has recovered 105 human remains in Colombia in such a way. The ICRC in Colombia has also trained non-forensic ICRC colleagues in the basics of dead body recovery (archaeological principles and techniques, principles of chain of custody, legal framework, health and safety), in case they should be in a situation where recovery of a body is an emergency, and no forensic colleagues are at hand. It sometimes happens that armed groups hand over human remains for humanitarian reasons during an ICRC field trip, but refuse to wait for the arrival of the forensic experts. Clearly, these are exceptional situations. If in any way possible, the ICRC strives to enable the state's forensic experts to recover the remains in question. Nevertheless, the ICRC's humanitarian recovery activities have made it possible to bring answers to dozens of families that have been waiting for news about the fate of their missing loved one.

Humanitarian forensic action: roles and responsibilities of forensic practitioners

As recognised by the 2003 International Conference on the Missing and confirmed by the ICRC's own experience thereafter, the role that forensic specialists play in their domestic context cannot be automatically extrapolated to humanitarian forensic action in international contexts involving investigations into the dead and missing from armed conflicts. These situations require special consideration.

Legal and ethical framework

Before embarking on investigations into the dead and missing from armed conflicts and catastrophes, forensic practitioners need to understand what the mandate and legal standing of the their employer is, and need assurance that the work to be done might not in fact be considered unlawful in domestic law.

No matter what the purpose of the investigations, practitioners have an ethical duty to observe and record all information potentially relevant to the identification of human remains under their responsibility, just as much as all information is useful to establish cause and circumstances of death. They should also familiarise themselves with and be respectful of the provisions of local culture and religion regarding the treatment of the dead and funeral rituals and consider the families' rights and needs before, during and after the investigation. Special consideration should be given to the management and disposal of unidentified remains in a way appropriate to the context.

Forensic experts called to take part in exhumations should advocate and recommend that an identification system be put in place, and that identified remains should be swiftly returned to their families, either by the authorities or by some other relevant stakeholder who is competent to do so. Thought must be given to the whole process before the forensic practitioner becomes involved; it cannot be assumed that the entire chain of responsibility that usually exists in a domestic context is in place and will be effectively operational in war-torn contexts. Practitioners also have to ensure that their activities are actually considered lawful in the specific settings.

The ICRC's own recommendations and operational best practices (ICRC 2003b) complement and expand existing standards and guidelines for investigations into the missing, including the 1991 *UN Manual on the Effective Prevention and Investigation of Extra-Legal, Arbitrary and Summary Executions* (Minnesota Protocol) (UN Doc 1991), the 1995 *Guidelines for the Conduct of United Nation Inquiries into Allegations of Massacres* (UN 1995) and Interpol *Disaster Victim Identification (DVI) Guide* (Interpol).

Existing standards and best practice guidelines, including those described in this chapter, have universal application. They were designed to help forensic practitioners involved in humanitarian operations to act within the ethical and professional boundaries applicable to investigations into the dead and missing, especially where the legal and institutional frameworks for forensic investigations are collapsed or eroded as a result of armed conflict.

Such guidelines should, wherever possible, accommodate local skills and expertise, and they should also consider the need for local forensic capacity-building, including the training of non-specialists, which should be planned in the early stages of any mission or project.

Adapting to constraints

Forensic practitioners involved in humanitarian operations in contexts of active armed conflict may sometimes be forced to work with much less time and resources available than they would in their domestic practice or in post conflict situations, due to extreme constraints faced, including threats to their security. When the remains in question are buried, and there is no immediate threat to their integrity, it may be preferable not to carry out substandard exhumations and possibly risk loss of evidence. It is important that such recovery operations are well planned and respect minimal standards. On the other hand, there are situations where examinations even under difficult conditions and time restraints may be indicated and are necessary. This could be for humanitarian reasons, for a window of opportunity that may not arise again anytime soon, and if the remains are endangered by human or natural forces.

In such extreme circumstances, the forensic specialist may find that 'the best may be an enemy of the possible'. However, performing an abbreviated procedure may be fully compatible with professional conduct and existing guidelines (such as those developed by the ICRC), given the constraints, as long as the supporting reasons are duly noted and recorded and some minimum standards are observed in order to keep remains and evidence intact and provide the minimum necessary documentation, even in the most adverse conditions.

Health and safety concerns

Apart from the usual health and safety concerns encountered in domestic forensic archaeology, forensic archaeologists working in conflict-related contexts will often be confronted with issues of weapons contamination, such as unexploded ordnances (UXOs), mines, booby traps or even remnants of chemical, biological or nuclear warfare. These serious threats require appropriate and professional management to ensure satisfactory health and safety conditions and acceptable levels of risk for the investigators. Clearance activities should be combined with training investigators with recognition of such risk and safe conduct.

Experts in chemical, biological, radiological and nuclear (CBRN) threats and weapon contamination, such as those of the ICRC, should be consulted for advice in the preparation of missions in the field and, if required, for assistance during operations (ICRC 2007).

Other risks for the forensic practitioners may arise from the findings of the investigations and lead to threats and attacks against the investigators by those under investigation. Adhering to strict principles of independence, neutrality and impartiality will substantially reduce such risks.

Working in contexts of armed conflict is often stressful. Special guidelines have been developed to help minimise both the danger and stress faced by humanitarian staff, including forensic investigators, in armed conflict (Roberts 1999; Bierens de Haan 2001).

Forensic specialists and their support staff, as well as staff working with the families of missing people, might find their health affected by the work they are doing. Because of the emotionally charged nature of such work, especially the interaction with the bereaved, it is essential that staff are duly trained and briefed for this highly sensitive job (e.g. US Army Centre for Health Promotion and Preventive Medicine).

Forensic archaeology in humanitarian contexts: principles

Search and recovery of the remains is often one of the first steps in the identification of the dead and missing. However, for a successful recovery operation, preliminary investigation is indispensable to help locate the sites, creating hypotheses of identity, but also to plan aspects such as priorisation, scheduling, logistics and security.

Contrary to other phases of the investigation, forensic archaeology is (as all archaeological excavation/recovery) a destructive process and cannot be repeated. Mistakes made during this crucial stage may imperil or impede even the most thorough and technologically advanced identification at the laboratory stage. It is therefore paramount that the recovery is carried out to standards and provides all documentation that is necessary to reconstruct the excavation/recovery process later. Good standards of recovery and documentation are required not only for the collection of evidence for judicial criminal investigations but also for issues of identification.

Therefore, the search and recovery of the remains of victims of armed conflict should be handled with the same care and detail as used in crime scene management in domestic settings. This requires the availability of experts at the scene and the coordination between the principal investigator and the participating specialists, particularly scene of crime officers (SOCOs), forensic archaeologists and anthropologists, in order to avoid the remains and associated evidence being handled by law enforcement officers unskilled in the required techniques.

The following general procedures should be followed during search and recovery investigations, bearing in mind that every scene is unique and poses specific problems that require adapting the procedures accordingly.

In complex cases, such as those related to armed conflict or internal violence, it is important that the search start with thorough preliminary investigations. These preliminary investigations, which should be using as wide a variety of sources as possible and necessary,[8] will help to establish better the exact location of the remains, the possible number, origin and identity of the

[8]The most common ones include government and other archives, press, witness interviews, visual documentation (photos, videos), geophysics, analysis of surface evidence and geological and taphonomic features.

human remains, and with which event they might be connected. Particularly with buried remains, it is important to establish an identification mechanism before proceeding with exhumations. Otherwise, unless the remains are on the surface or are in danger of being damaged or destroyed by human or natural influences, there is a considerable risk that the redundant remains, once recovered, will merely get damaged or lost in storage, without real possibility of identification.

With the necessary background information on the site, a preliminary site assessment should be conducted, in order to establish the exact location and to understand logistical and security needs.

The recovery of remains itself is an important step in the identification process and – if performed correctly – will produce important evidence. If the recovery is not carried out to standards, this information may be lost forever, the remains compromised and damaged, and possibilities for their identification greatly reduced. For this reason, it is important that the recovery of human remains be performed by trained experts with experience in the application of (forensic) archaeological techniques and crime scene analysis.

Forensic archaeologists have the necessary skills for finding buried remains, recovering them without damage together with the associated evidence, and for documenting and interpreting all the evidence. This applies particularly for the recovery of buried remains, but also for other complex settings and recovery scenarios (i.e. caves, wells and commingled remains) in which archaeologists are of added value. Complex cases, such as mass graves with numerous depositional events, primary and secondary, and commingling, such as many of the mass graves exhumed in Bosnia, can only be solved by applying advanced archaeological methods and analyses (Tuller et al. 2005, 2008). In case no forensic archaeologists are available in a certain context, (local) traditional archaeologists should be employed to work together with forensic anthropologists.

The recovery of remains should consist of the basic steps of initial documentation of the site, careful exposure of the remains, detailed documentation of all remains and related evidence. Evidence includes all objects, but also burial features such as the shape of the grave and tool marks. Since the recovery/exhumation of remains cannot be repeated, thorough documentation is paramount, as only documentation will later allow the reconstruction and interpretation of the findings at the scene. Before being removed, all evidence should be sufficiently cleaned and photographed *in situ*. Documentation should consist of sketching, mapping (including 3D measurements), photography and verbal description in standard forms and if necessary, sampling.

Time restraints (due to security situation, lack of resources or political pressure) should not be a reason to digress from the basic principles of recovery and documentation of the remains. Unless dealing with complex sites, the minimal standards of recovery and documentation can be applied in very little time. Sites that require a more complex methodology should only be exhumed when the necessary minimal conditions for not losing evidence for further identification can be assured.

Recovery operations in a humanitarian context tend to deal with complex sites that present many issues such as tampering with burial sites, diachronic sites with multiple burial events and thus multiple deposits and commingled and highly fragmented remains. Such sites need special attention, and recovery methodologies adapted to the specific situation and detailed documentation are particularly important in such cases.

Sufficient attention should also be given to coding of sites, remains and all other recovered evidence. Codes must be unique and should be maintained throughout the operation in order to avoid confusion and loss of information on the origin of remains and associated evidence.

The ICRC has produced several guidelines outlining the basic steps of recovery and/or documentation for a variety of situations, a set of minimum standards (ICRC 2003b), a recommendation on dealing with remains found during mine clearance operations (TNMA 10.10), recovery of remains by non-experts such as humanitarian workers or military (ICRC 2004), or the recovery of remains in large scale after disasters (Morgan et al. 2006).

Documentation and information management

As mentioned earlier, documentation is an indispensable part of forensic archaeology. Documentation relies on a variety of formats (e.g. maps, descriptions and photos) and may create a large amount of data. In order for this data to be complete, useful and easily available later on in the process, there is a need for standardised forms and an appropriate data management system. Internationally, there are many examples of forensic operations where good archaeology is applied during recovery, but the information never reaches those in charge of the analysis of all elements.

Responding to the recommendations from the International Conference on the Missing in 2003, the ICRC developed standard forms and the AMPM software, an electronic tool for the management of data collected for the identification of human remains of missing persons, including ante-mortem (AM) and post-mortem (PM) data. The AMPM software supports the archiving, standardisation, reporting, searching and analysis of forensic data, as well as the automated basic matching of AM and PM data in order to facilitate the identification process. It also implicitly provides and promotes guidelines for good standards of data collection and the use of appropriate methods. The AMPM manages information about missing persons and the events related to their disappearances, as well as recovered bodies (or body parts) and the sites where they were found. It was designed for use by investigators and institutions involved in the search for persons reported missing as a result of armed conflict, disasters or other situations of violence and in the forensic identification of human remains.

Contrary to many of the other available electronic tools, the AMPM has an extensive module on forensic archaeology. The module contains information from preliminary site assessments, descriptions of the exhumation process, a form for the description of the site, point of recovery (grave or other), specific features and all items and human remains recovered, with functions to manage different associations, manage multi-deposit mass graves, a detailed field inventory of human remains and artefacts including basic descriptions, and a module for commingled elements. It is possible to link photos, videos and maps. Further, for use in large mass grave operations, there is a function for import of Total Station data into the database, which automatically creates items such as site, recovery points and the single set of human remains in the database, based on the codification used in the database (for the recommended codification, see Tuller et al. 2008, 7–29). Associations that were wrongly observed in the field can later on be modified without losing the original information.

The standard reporting forms include witness information on gravesites, site assessment form, grave form, human remains form and PM analysis. All the ICRC forms and the AMPM were developed by analysing and consolidating a large variety of existing forms used in contexts across the world, and have gone through a process of validation by international experts of different backgrounds and specialities.

Training

A basic understanding of forensic archaeological recovery methods is important not only for the personnel involved in the recovery, but is also helpful for other specialists involved in the investigations, such as forensic doctors. By understanding the basics of recovery processes, they will better appreciate the history and complexity of the remains they have to analyse. A basic explanation of forensic archaeology will also highlight the importance of applying the appropriate recovery methods to those in charge of planning forensic operations (Figure 49.2). A forensic archaeology/recovery module, with theoretical and practical modules, is usually incorporated into ICRC training for a variety of forensic specialists.[9] It is also an integral part of ICRC's training on Management of Dead in Mass Disasters and Armed Conflict.

The identification of human remains

The identification of the dead person is an integral part of any investigation into a suspicious death, and it goes hand-in-hand with ascertaining the cause, manner and circumstances of death. However, in the case of investigations into the dead and missing from armed conflict,

Figure 49.2 Exhumation training in Kathmandu, Nepal (Photo: U. Hofmeister).

[9]ICRC training is usually tailored to the specific needs in a given context and to varying audiences, such as pathologists, judicial experts, first responders and military in local, regional or international courses.

especially when these involve victims of war crimes, it is usually easier to determine their cause and manner of death than ascertaining their identity. In many contexts, the identification of the deceased is the most challenging and resource-intensive forensic task. As a result, simple recovery and analysis procedures may readily satisfy the need for evidence of the cause and manner of death of the deceased, even if these are not identified. This can lead to the unfortunate situation whereby remains are recovered and their cause and manner of death established; but because the process of identification is much more time- and resource-consuming, the bodies remain forever unidentified.

From a humanitarian viewpoint, this situation is unacceptable, as it prevents the bereaved from knowing the fate of missing relatives and to recover their remains (Stover and Shigekane 2002, 845–847).

Community and family participation

Unlike most domestic criminal investigations, forensic investigations into the dead and missing from armed conflict should be carried out in constant interaction with the concerned communities and with the families or their representatives, who have the right to be kept informed throughout. This right is duly protected under international humanitarian law (OAS AG/RES 2729, Consenso Mundial 2011).

In addition, ensuring the participation of and information for the bereaved families is usually essential for the success of the investigation and for fulfilling its humanitarian objective, including ensuring the understanding and acceptance of results, regardless of whether these satisfy expectations or not.

Good interaction and dialogue with affected families is also essential for obtaining information for the identification of the remains of their loved ones. Therefore, building trust and liaising positively and constructively with concerned families should be a central consideration of forensic practitioners involved in these investigations.

Forensic practitioners should also be aware that communities and families are usually deeply affected when their members are killed or go missing in the context of armed conflict, and that the process of identifying remains may simply add to the trauma if not managed properly. For example, any handling of remains and information perceived as undignified or unskilful (according to local customs and sensitivities) may further traumatise the families of the missing and imperil the investigation. The cultural (including religious), social and psychological background of investigations and their effect on communities and families should therefore be assessed as part of their planning (ICRC 2012).

The extent to which the communities or families are involved in the investigation and their different stages should be decided on a case-by-case basis following consultation with the bereaved, community and religious leaders and other concerned stakeholders. The decision should always consider the possible benefit for the families, the avoidance of any interference with the investigation and security issues.

The notion of 'family', including its composition and the roles of those included in it, may vary considerably in different cultural contexts. Awareness of this factor will help ensure best possible interaction with the families of the missing persons.

In addition, the concerned communities or families may:

- Be a source of valuable information on the location of human remains or burial;
- Aid in the identification of some remains after their recovery, including through the recognition of unique traits and belongings;
- Offer valuable advice on particular health and safety issues.

Informing the communities and families about the forensic investigation always requires a communication strategy. If possible, families and communities should already be duly informed before the beginning of an exhumation. Realistic briefings must be given of the possible outcome of the investigation and information should be updated regularly.

Participating investigators should be aware that:

- Family participation, often in the form of observation of some stages of the forensic investigation (e.g. exhumation), may lead to easier acceptance of the results.
- Religious or community leaders should be contacted and consulted in some contexts, including for the approval and authorisation of forensic procedures (e.g. handling of human remains).
- Building trust and establishing a good relationship with the families of those missing is essential for the adequate collection of AM data and reference samples.

Unlike in most domestic criminal investigations, in humanitarian forensic contexts it is quite common throughout the world that families of victims are or wish to be present at an exhumation. This wish is sometimes little understood or supported by forensic investigators, who are not used to working with families on site, and who fear for the integrity of evidence and the psychological effect that seeing the remains may have on the families. Nevertheless, in most settings, experience has shown that these fears are unfounded. On the contrary, the presence of the families will often have a positive impact both on the investigation, and in the longer term, on the families' psychological well being as well.

Families or communities will want to see with their own eyes, in order to gain trust in the work. Presence at the site may also be a sign of respect for the dead. In many contexts, families and communities need to conduct certain ceremonies to ensure that the dead will not be angered by their disturbance or will be able to pass over to the other world in peace. Furthermore, by being present and maybe supporting the forensic team with food, shade, and so on at the exhumation site, families often feel that they can contribute to the search effort, a psychologically important factor. Forensic experts can contribute to the families' acceptance of the investigation and to their process of coming to terms, by explaining to them the steps of the exhumation process and the different findings (without of course providing baseless or premature conclusions).

In some cases, security or logistical constraints may prevent families' access to the recovery site. In this case, it is important to communicate these constraints to the families, and to give them as much information as possible by other means (e.g. explanations, photos or video, if requested).

Staff working in forensic exhumations of the dead and missing from armed conflict should be prepared for this interaction with families. The better forensic investigators understand the importance for families of being at the exhumation site, and the more familiar they are with possible reactions, the better and more fruitful the interaction between experts and families will be.

Conclusions

In the ICRC's forensic humanitarian action forensic archaeology is an important component. Based on International Humanitarian Law and consolidated international experience; and up to date, scientific standards, the ICRC guidelines and recommendations on forensic investigations including forensic archaeology aim at ensuring appropriate standards in forensic investigations in armed conflict related contexts in order to achieve the humanitarian objective of preserving the dignity of the dead and bringing answers to the Missing Persons' families and communities.

References

Anasagasti, I. 2007. *Marcel Junod: Delegate of the International Committee of the Red Cross, his Mediation with the Basque Government and the Rebels During the Civil War in Euskadi*. Victoria-Gasteiz, Central Service of the Basque Government Publications.

Bierens de Haan, B. 2001. *Humanitarian Action and Armed Conflict: Coping with Stress*. Geneva, ICRC.

CIDH. *Nicholas Chapman Blake v. Guatemala*. Available at: http://www.worldcourts.com/iacthr/eng/decisions/1998.01.24_Blake_v_Guatemala.pdf (last accessed December 2012).

Consenso Mundial de Principios y Normas Mínimas sobre Trabajo Psicosocial en Procesos de Búsqueda e Investigación Forenses para Casos de Desapariciones Forzadas, Ejecuciones Arbitrarias o Extrajudiciales. 2011. Available at: http://www.equitas.org.co/docs/53 (last accessed June 2013).

Henckaerts, J.-M. and Doswald-Beck, L. 2006. *Customary International Law Vol. 1: Rules*. Geneva, Cambridge University Press.

ICRC. 1977. *Protocols Additional to the Geneva Conventions of 12 August 1949*. Geneva, ICRC Publications.

ICRC. 2002. *The Geneva Conventions of August 12 1949*. Geneva, ICRC Publications.

ICRC. 2003a. *The Missing and their Families. Summary Conclusions Arising from Events Held Prior to the International Conference of Governmental and Non-Governmental Experts (February 19–21 2003)*. Available at: http://www.icrc.org/eng/assets/files/other/icrc_themissing_012003_en_10.pdf (last accessed October 2012).

ICRC. 2003b. *The Missing and their Families*. ICRC Report. Geneva, ICRC Publications. Available at: http://www.icrc.org/eng/resources/documents/misc/5jahr8.htm (last accessed 6 October 2011).

ICRC. 2004. *Operational Best Practices Regarding the Management of Human Remains and Information on the Dead by Non-Specialists, for all Armed Forces, for all Humanitarian Organisations*. Geneva, ICRC Publications.

ICRC 2007. Weapon contamination manual: reducing the impact of explosive remnants of war and landmines through field activities. Geneva, ICRC Publications. Available at: https://shop.icrc.org/reference-publications-humanitarian/weapon-contamination-manual-reducing-the-impact-of-explosive-remnants-of-war-and-landmines-through-field-activities.html (last accessed October 2014).

ICRC. 2012. *Accompanying Families of Missing Persons, a Field Guide*. Geneva, ICRC Publications.

Interpol. 1996. ICPO-Interpol General Assembly, 65th Session. Resolution AGN/65/RES/13. Available at: https://www.interpol.int/Public/ICPO/GeneralAssembly/Agn65/Resolutions/AGN65RES13.asp (last accessed June 2013).

Interpol. *The DVI Guide*. Available in electronic version only, Interpol, Available at: http://www.interpol.int/INTERPOL-expertise/Forensics/DVI-Pages/DVI-guide (accessed June 2013).

Junod, M. 1951. *Warrior without Weapons* 114–115. London, Jonathan Cape Ltd. 1st edition. Reprinted by the ICRC, Geneva, 1982.

Ley 42 de 1981, Diario Oficial. Año CXVIII. N. 35776. 8. Junio 1981, Colombia.

Morgan, O., Tidball-Binz, M. and Van Alphen, D. 2006. *Management of Dead Bodies after Disasters: A Field Manual for First Responders*. Washington, DC, PAHO/WHO, ICRC, IFRC.

OAS. 2012. *Las Personas Desaparecidas y la Asistencia a sus Familiares*. AG/RES 2729 (XLII-O/12) par. 2. Available at: http://scm.oas.oeg/42AG/Documentos/VOL_SPA.doc (last accessed June 2013).

Petrig, A. 2009. The war dead and their gravesites. *International Review of the Red Cross* 874, 341–369.

Roberts, D. L. 1999. *Staying Alive: Safety and Security Guidelines for Humanitarian Volunteers in Conflict*. Geneva, ICRC.

Snow, C., Levine, L., Lukash, L., Tedeschi, L., Orrego, C. and Stover, E. 1984. The investigation of the human remains of the 'disappeared' in Argentina. *American Journal of Forensic Medicine and Pathology* 4, 297–303.

Stover, E. and Shigekane, R. 2002. The missing in the aftermath of war: when do the needs of victims' families and international war crimes tribunals clash? *International Review of the Red Cross* 848, 845–847.

Tidball-Binz, M. 2007. Managing the dead in catastrophes: guiding principles and practical recommendations for first responders. *International Review of the Red Cross* 866, 421–442.

TNMA 10.10. Technical Notes for Mine Action. *Guidelines on the Management of Human Remains Located During Mine Action Operations*. Available at: http://www.mineactionstandards.org/ (last accessed June 2013).

Tuller, H. and Duric, M. 2006. Keeping the pieces together, comparison of mass grave excavation methodology. *Forensic Science International* 156, 192–200.

Tuller, H., Hofmeister, U. and Daley, S. 2005. The importance of body deposition recording in event reconstruction and the re-association and identification of commingled remains'. *Proceedings of the American Academy of Forensic* Sciences 2005, 313.

Tuller, H., Hofmeister, U. and Daley, S. 2008. Spatial analysis of mass grave mapping data to assist in the reassociation of disarticulated and commingled human remains. In B. J. Adams and J. E. Byrd (eds.), *Recovery, Analysis, and Identification of Commingled Human Remains*, 7–29. Totowa, Humana Press.

United Nations. 1991. *Manual on the Effective Prevention and Investigation of Extra-Legal, Arbitrary and Summary Executions*. U.N. Doc. E/ST/CSDHA/.12. Available at: http://www1.umn.edu/humanrts/instree/executioninvestigation-91.html (last accessed October 2012).

United Nations Office of Legal Affairs. 1995. *Guidelines for the Conduct of United Nations Inquiries into Allegations of Massacres*. New York, United Nations Publications.

US Army Centre for Health Promotion and Preventive Medicine. *Dealing with the Stress of Recovering Human Dead Bodies*. Available at: http://nvmassfatality.com/images/Dealing-with-the-stress-of-recovering-human-dead-bodies.pdf (last accessed 3 October 2011).

CHAPTER 50

The Inforce Foundation

Roland Wessling

Inforce Foundation, Cranfield Forensic Institute, Cranfield University, Shrivenham, Swindon, UK

Introduction

The Inforce Foundation, a charity founded in 2001, was based at Bournemouth University, UK, until 2007 and has since moved to Cranfield University, UK.[1] This chapter looks at Inforce's past activities relating to forensic archaeology, as well as its code of conduct and ethical guidance.

Background

The Inforce Foundation is a non-profit-making organisation and is registered as a charity (1097435) and as a company (4371179). The organisation was founded in 2001 by a group of forensic scientists and legal academics. The idea of funding Inforce came from the forensic archaeologist and anthropologist Professor Margaret Cox. At that time, Professor Cox was the academic leader of the world's first Masters-level programme in Forensic Archaeology based in Bournemouth University, UK. This MSc programme began in 1996 and coincided with the first systematic forensic investigation by the International Criminal Tribunal for the Former Yugoslavia (ICTY). In 1997, the ICTY decided to create its own forensic investigation team; and over the years, more and more graduates from the Bournemouth University Forensic Archaeology MSc became its team members.

Reasons for founding Inforce

The forensic investigations by the ICTY in Bosnia and Herzegovina, first carried out by Physicians for Human Rights (PHR) (Schmitt et al., Chapter 53, this volume) in 1996 and followed by its own forensic team in 1997, were the first of their kind by an international criminal tribunal to use hard forensic evidence. Previous international tribunals had always relied on documental evidence and witness statements. Although similar forensic investigations had been carried out for some time in a number of South American countries (e.g. Fondebrider and Scheinsohn, Chapter 43, this volume), the use of forensic archaeology and anthropology in international war crime investigations was still very much a blank canvas. The learning curve for both the forensic exhumation team and the mortuary team was therefore a steep one, but significant progress had been made over the years in Bosnia and Herzegovina; and by the time the ICTY decided to extend its investigations to Kosovo, a set of methods and procedures had been well established.

The main reason why Inforce was founded revolved around the nature of the forensic investigations in Kosovo in 1999, especially in the light of the forensic investigations since 1996 in Bosnia and Herzegovina (Hanson et al., Chapters 3 and 48, this volume). Despite the considerable progress made towards developing methodologies of mass grave investigations in Bosnia and Herzegovina, political time pressures led the international forensic community to reinvent the wheel, rather than build on the success of earlier investigation. The result was a series of uncoordinated investigations carried out using differing forensic teams with non-compatible methodologies and non-compatible aims and objectives. Although individual team efforts may have been very successful and professional, the overall forensic investigation, both from a legal and scientific perspective, was dogged by problems due to its inconsistency.

This triggered Professor Cox to contact fellow forensic scientists and members of the legal profession with an interest in human rights investigations to try to change this situation so that the same mistakes would not be repeated in future forensic investigations.

[1]For more information, see: http://www.inforce.org.uk/ (last accessed December 2013).

Forensic Archaeology: A Global Perspective, First Edition. Edited by W.J. Mike Groen, Nicholas Márquez-Grant and Robert C. Janaway.

Charitable aims

Inforce's main charitable aims are as follows:

- Fast response to mass fatalities (including natural disasters, man-made disasters and mass atrocities) by a world-wide network of experienced forensic practitioners.
- Empowering nations and regions to investigate their own mass fatalities through capacity building in such countries that have experienced mass fatalities, especially mass atrocities, and have little or no current expertise.
- Development and promotion of international standards in mass fatality investigations.

Mission statement

Inforce's mission statement is: 'To provide a centre of expertise for the location, recovery and identification of victims of atrocity crimes and mass fatality incidents on a world-wide basis. To enable legitimate legal authorities to proceed with the prosecution of alleged perpetrators. To satisfy the humanitarian need of families and communities to bury their dead. To provide education for practitioners and as a means of empowering survivor groups'.

Code of conduct and ethical guidance

Inforce considers the adoption of this code of conduct and ethical guidance by the organisation, and any who work for us,[2] to be imperative. Inforce believes that ethical guidance can be broken down into several broad areas, including overriding concerns that govern component parts.[3]

Overriding code of conduct

- To uphold respect for human life and dignity at all times;
- To act with integrity and honesty in all circumstances;
- To be apolitical;
- To provide confidential, informed and impartial advice;
- To practice within relevant current legal and regulatory frameworks;
- To respect the cultural and religious values of the host country, community or society;
- To uphold rules of confidentiality and, where appropriate, of subjudice;
- To promote the improvement of standards and services through the development and adoption of protocols and standard operating procedures (SOPs), as well as professional bodies, education, research and best practice;
- To keep up to date with developments in field and/or laboratory techniques as appropriate;
- To refrain from issuing statements that appear to represent the position of the organisation as a whole without the specific authority to do so;
- To refrain from issuing statements that appear to represent the position of the relevant profession as a whole without the specific authority to do so;
- To prevent and outlaw malpractice;
- Not to accept core or programme funding from any organisation considered to be inappropriate in any given context.

Contractual and operational involvement

- To provide services to the highest standards of excellence within the organisation's and the individual practitioner's field of competence;
- To uphold the terms of service agreed at the outset of any contract;
- To work within defined resource constraints (time, personnel, financial);
- To set 'reasonable' fees consistent with those charged by other forensic scientists, or other relevant professionals; these will reflect any given security situation or other specific considerations in overseas missions;
- To refrain from undertaking work on a contingency-fee basis;
- To refrain from taking instructions from any party or organisation that is legally unacceptable, or that conflicts with Inforce's organisational values and ethics, or that precludes good scientific practice;
- To recognise and advise on techniques only from an informed basis;
- To maintain the highest level of objectivity in all cases and to accurately present the facts involved based on the limitations of the evidence itself;
- While adhering to the Inforce protocols and SOPs where possible, to accept the need to adapt methodology when warranted by particular circumstances;[4]
- To ensure appropriate reporting and archiving/storage of findings and data;
- To refrain from working with non-police or other informal investigative agencies or to jeopardise on-going police or other formal enquiries.

---

[2]Inforce predominantly recruits from a database of experts who contacted Inforce or were contacted by Inforce after being recommended by a colleague. Inforce considers a wide variety of knowledge, skills and experience to be significant when it comes to team selection.

[3]These ethical guidelines are developed from those set out in *Forensic Archaeology: New Approaches* (Hunter and Cox 2004). Inforce is grateful to Professor John Hunter for his contribution to its development.

[4]But when it is agreed as necessary to vary, then the rationale and process must be logged.

Treatment of human remains in investigations, analysis and research

- To accord human remains decency, dignity and respect under all circumstances;
- To accord survivors and relatives respect and have due regard to their emotional, religious and cultural needs;
- To make all possible efforts to obtain the consent of communities and families for tissue sampling, where to obtain such is possible;
- To refrain from removing samples from human remains for forensic or research purposes unless commensurate with legal, religious and cultural dictates where such a judgement is possible;
- To ensure, wherever possible, that all human material taken for sampling, or removed in the process of sampling, is ultimately interred with the remains;
- To avoid undertaking research using material or data derived from unethical contexts;
- To undertake research based only on sound scientific principles; such research should be based on research designs approved by the Inforce executive;
- To disseminate, where possible, the results of research and fieldwork that may increase knowledge or provide beneficial information for future work;
- To respect the fieldwork, research and intellectual property of others;
- To refrain from undertaking research using animal remains outside current legislation and regulation and without due regard to the environment and public health;
- To adopt and adhere to international and relevant national and local regulations and legislation governing the use of human remains in research.

Acting as an expert witness

- To offer opinions only on matters within one's own area of specialism and competence;
- To state explicitly the limitations of the evidence itself;
- To state explicitly the limitations of the methodologies employed;
- To make every effort to use language and terminology that can be understood by the court;
- To differentiate clearly between scientific results and expert opinion;
- To disclose all findings, irrespective of their implications;
- To comment on the work of another expert in good faith, objectively and not maliciously;
- To recognise the over-riding duty to the proper administration of justice.

Education and public liaison

- Only to use human remains in teaching if their provenance is acceptable both legally and ethically;
- To avoid using human remains in education in any way that might detract from the value of human life and dignity;
- Only to use illustrative material of human remains when necessary in publication or lecture, irrespective of the level of the intended readership or audience;
- To make efforts to ensure that illustrative material will not be offensive from any legal, political, cultural or religious viewpoint;
- Only to use shocking, horrific or explicit illustrations where such is beneficial, and only to professional audiences;
- To include tuition on ethics in forensic practice in programmes at all levels of education.

Key Inforce activities

The key activities are grouped into three sections according to Inforce's primary aims:

1 Operations – Actual investigations of areas covered by the charitable aims, such as crimes against humanity, mass atrocities or genocide. Exhumations of cemeteries or domestic homicide investigations are not part of the core activities; however, they are not entirely excluded and have been performed on rare occasions.

2 Standards – Collating, editing and publishing of standards in the areas covered by the charitable aims.

3 Education and Training
   - **(a)** Capacity Building – This 'reactive' type of education and training tries to assist scientists, investigators and others from regions where atrocity crimes or mass fatalities have taken place in building up the capacity to investigate and deal with those incidents themselves.
   - **(b)** Workshops – This 'proactive' and UK-based part of education and training invites anyone interested in mass fatality investigations to participate in workshops and exercises that range from simulated mass grave excavation to mass fatality mortuary workshops.

However, before these three distinct areas are discussed, a brief and largely anecdotal aspect needs to be addressed; which shaped and defined Inforce's entire existence and with it its principles. These principles have, over the years, influenced many students and professionals who have subsequently provided feedback by email and other personal correspondence.

One of the basic principles specifically referred to was The Inforce Code of Conduct (e.g. see Section 'Code of conduct and ethical guidance'). As far as Inforce is aware it was, for a long time, the only such text freely available on the Internet. Inforce has always had a policy of transparency, which shows in the code of conduct as well as later in the publication of the Inforce protocols and SOPs (for details, see Section 'Standards').

A further sign of the willingness to share its intellectual property is the set of forms developed over the years. The forms were inspired originally by those of various organisations ranging from the ICTY to the Museum of London Archaeology Service (MoLAS), but have been very heavily developed and modified to fit the specific needs on forensic archaeological sites (field forms) and in temporary mass fatality incident mortuaries (mortuary forms), as well as operational forms coordinating processes and audit trails. It would take too much space to list them all in this publication; however, they are available on request. Inforce's forms have been adopted by other organisations and adapted by them into other formats by adding their logo and by transforming them, for example, into letter format (from A4) or by translating them into a bilingual Spanish/English form for use in South American forensic investigations. The International Association of Forensic Radiographers (IAFR) based in the United Kingdom worked with Inforce to develop a radiology recording form. This form has subsequently been adopted by the UK Disaster Victim Identification (DVI) Forensic Radiography Response Team and has been used in mass fatality response in the United Kingdom. There may be many others who use them or have based their own versions on them.

Operations

This section contains all major operations that were started and finished while Inforce was based at Bournemouth University, UK.

Iraq assessment operation 2003

Between 24 May and 26 June 2003, the Inforce Foundation, on behalf of the UK Foreign and Commonwealth Office and the US State Department, carried out a series of site visits, assessing the nature and history of suspected mass graves related to the regime of Saddam Hussein (1979–2003), in the Baghdad–Hillah–Kerbalah–Najaf area in Iraq. The graves investigated allegedly spanned a period of 20 years, with the youngest having been only 3 months old, which placed them towards the very end of the second Gulf War.

The aims of the operation were the following:

- To locate and assess the nature of suspected mass grave sites;
- To assess how local Iraqi communities can be assisted in exhumation processes;
- To determine what practical steps may be required to build a forensic investigation and humanitarian capacity given the recent developments across the forensic landscape of mass graves and execution sites in Iraq;
- To assess the forensic potential left within sites already exhumed by local communities.

The core team consisted of four forensic archaeologists and anthropologists, one forensic photographer, and one scene of crime officer. The skills covered by the group, apart from the obvious, included geophysical and optical surveying, DNA sampling, navigating, surface scatter surveys and *ad hoc* anatomy teaching. The team was led by a forensic archaeologist and worked closely with US military liaison officers as well as other NGOs throughout the deployment. All core team members had built up most of their experience in the Balkan investigations (ICTY forensic teams in Bosnia and Herzegovina, Croatia and Kosovo).

The first aim was achieved by visiting 14 different sites and assessing a variety of suspected mass graves. On some sites, the presence of mass graves could be confirmed; on others, it could be confirmed that no mass graves were present or that graves were most unlikely to have originated from any mass atrocity; and on some sites, the presence of mass graves could not be positively confirmed but neither could their absence. The Inforce team found human remains and associated artefacts were very well preserved on all sites where assessment was possible.

The Inforce team visited several on-going as well as completed exhumations carried out by teams of local volunteers. None of those teams had any forensic capacity, and the only relevant skill sets present on some sites were of a medical and engineering nature. The Inforce team was frequently asked to take over the excavation or to return later to do so, but since that was not in Inforce's mandate or capability, the local volunteers had to be informed that this would not be possible. In order to improve the exhumation standards to a small degree, Inforce offered to demonstrate some basic anthropological skills, such as skeletal inventory and rudimentary trauma analysis (Figure 50.1). This offer was always accepted and warmly received.

The following recommendations were made to the Coalition Provisional Authority or CPA:

- **a** For the highest profile prosecutions, a rigorous scientific programme should be implemented to investigate a small number of selected sites. That for such sites the CPA should adopt SOPs that are internationally acceptable, and should ensure that all evidence collected will satisfy evidential requirements of the court. Inforce is supplying these standards.
- **b** That a multifaceted capacity enhancement programme be implemented to enable the Iraqis to develop and own an indigenous forensic science capacity and to be able to investigate and analyse evidence for their own judicial process.
- **c** That an identification programme be implemented to seek to identify as many of the human remains recovered as possible, to ensure that the bereaved are reunited with their dead and help them move forward with their lives.

Figure 50.1 Two Inforce staff give an *ad hoc* basic skeletal anatomy lesson for members of a local exhumation team.

d That a set of protocols and SOPs be established, which had to be adopted by any Iraqi or foreign forensic team carrying out mass grave investigations and post-mortem examinations.

Cyprus commission for missing persons operations 2004–2005

Between October 2004 and September 2005, various Inforce teams or individual staff members were sent to Cyprus. It all started with a deployment of a brief reconnaissance mission in late 2004 to visit, view and report on three potential grave sites, associated with the Cyprus dispute (1974–2014), making recommendations for how they could be approached, and preparing risk assessments. It continued in the deployment of a further mission in January 2005 to assess one large reported grave site, determining that in fact it was not a grave site. The most substantial operation was the bi-communal Emergency Exhumation Programme (EEP) that included the provision of a senior forensic archaeologist to oversee this emergency work throughout June and July 2005. This operation was directed by an Inforce scientist, who worked with a core team of between five and six archaeologists and anthropologists from both communities and a team of criminal investigators and technical support workers. The excavations saw the recovery of 24 individuals from four separate sites. Due to the purely humanitarian, rather than forensic, nature of the recoveries, the events that caused the graves, their dates and other circumstances were not addressed. The human remains were exhumed, cleaned and prepared for storage. In addition, one further site was assessed, one site received a reconnaissance visit and another one site (previously visited in 2004) was re-visited, once again with both Cypriot teams working with the Inforce scientist. During the mission, the Inforce scientist continued to provide advice, presentations and briefings to the Committee on Missing Persons (CMP)[5] in Cyprus on how to progress the work, and helped develop documentation that could be used for the purposes of discussing needs with potential donors.

In summary, the aims of this operation were the following:

- To assess a number of sites potentially containing mass graves;
- To carry out emergency excavations of sites most endangered by erosion, agricultural use or building developments;
- To lead a bi-communal team and establish a mid- to long-term working relationship between experts from both Cypriot communities.

The results of the project included working through a list of suspected sites put together by investigators in an order suggested by the CMP. A total of 24 individuals were exhumed with their associated artefacts. All remains and artefacts were prepared for medium-term storage for later detailed anthropological and DNA analyses.

The exhumations referred to earlier were also used to establish the first attempt in Cyprus for archaeologists

[5]For more information on CMP, see: http://www.cmp-cyprus.org/nqcontent.cfm?a_id=1 (last accessed December 2013).

and anthropologists from both Cypriot communities to work together on exhumations. Despite considerable logistical, environmental, legal and diplomatic challenges, the team and its internal dynamics developed extremely well. Since then, the CMP has established a professional and well-respected team of forensic archaeologists and anthropologists from both communities without any need for an international individual to coordinate the work.

Standards

One of Inforce's main charitable aims is to help establish industry standards. Inforce does not 'set' standards, but it tries to collate best practices from practitioners across the world and to edit them into one coherent set of protocols and SOPs.

The development of the standards finally published in 2007 can be segmented into three distinct phases, which will be looked at in detail in the following.

Development of standards in the forensic investigation of war crime investigation

In 2002, Inforce invited forensic scientists, law enforcement experts and legal professionals from all over the world to attend a workshop in December held at Bournemouth University, UK. The aim of the group of participants, from as far afield as Australia or the United States, was to kick-start a process to collate best practices in a variety of scientific practices and to draw on deployment experiences of delegates to develop protocols. The detailed aims were as follows:

- To start the development of mass grave investigation and victim identification protocols based on delegates' operational experiences;
- To start collating best practices for all techniques and methodologies needed in mass grave investigations and victim identification.

During the workshop, several issues about the protocols were discussed and previously prepared drafts discussed. This led to a second draft being circulated, with comments collated and incorporated.

Working groups for various areas, such as forensic archaeology, anthropology or pathology, collated and presented published materials on their state-of-the-art techniques and methods. The work of every group was collected by Inforce for later editing.

Development of the field manuals of protocols and SOPs

On 11 December 2003, Inforce proposed to the UK Foreign and Commonwealth Office (FCO) to complete the Inforce protocols (version four), which would be the first working version. During December 2003 and January 2004, detailed negotiations took place around the intellectual property clauses of the protocols contract and its extension to cover development of SOPs.

The intellectual property rights for the protocols and SOPs remained firmly with Inforce. However, the FCO, having funded the editing of the considerable amount of material collated prior to and since the workshop in 2002, was granted a licence to use the protocols and SOPs specifically in Iraq but also in similar scenarios in the future. Such matters are often overlooked by scientists working on scientific projects but are of great importance when a non-profit-making organisation, such as Inforce, enters into a contractual agreement with a governmental body.

The aims of the consolidation of the material into protocols and SOPs were as follows:

- To deliver a set of protocols for locating, assessing, excavating and investigating mass graves and to analyse and attempt to identify the victims. This protocol is designed to be used by any forensic team, Iraqi or international, operating in Iraq to ensure legal and scientific consistency;
- To deliver a set of SOPs covering all methods and techniques necessary to conduct the work set out in the protocols. These SOPs are designed to be used by any forensic team, Iraqi or international, operating in Iraq to ensure legal and scientific consistency.

In March 2004, this resulted in the final draft of the protocols and SOPs being produced, printed and sent to the FCO in London. One copy was kept there and others sent on to Baghdad.

In March 2004, the final drafts of the SOPs were produced, printed and sent to the FCO in London. One copy was kept there and others sent on to Baghdad.

Conversion of the field manuals into a textbook

In June 2004, discussions with CRC publishing began regarding a textbook version of the protocols and SOPs. Due to various reasons, Inforce changed publishers to Cambridge University Press (CUP) and finally produced a first draft in October of 2006. After appearing first on the US market in 2007 and then later in 2008 in the rest of the world as Cox et al. (2008), *The Scientific Investigation of Mass Graves – Towards Protocols and Standard Operating Procedures*. A total of 421 copies had been sold by the end of 2012 (latest available figures). The aim was to disseminate the Inforce protocols and SOPs to the largest possible audience, especially students at universities with relevant forensic programmes.

Whether 421 copies sold in 6 years is a lot or very little is difficult to judge. On the one hand, the number seems very small considering a world-wide availability. On the other hand, it is only available in English, costs almost $200 and the scientific and professional communities interested in mass grave excavations and victim identification is not a particularly large one. In any case, Inforce is glad that it had the opportunity to publish the book, and it has since been used successfully on many occasions in mass grave investigations.

Capacity building

There is no doubt that the deployment of international teams of forensic experts to investigate scenes of atrocities in post-conflict regions can be an appropriate response on some occasions, and in some contexts. However, Inforce considers it to be more appropriate for countries to lead their own investigations. Countries and regions should be empowered to be in charge of their own investigation; and if they are, they can still choose to invite foreign experts to take part. International involvement should be a choice rather than an imposed necessity.

Inforce assists in this by delivering multidisciplinary training programmes that are aimed at building local capacity. Courses can be short- and intensive skill-enhancement programmes or can be longer and more detailed programmes involving practical experience and professional placements. Inforce has delivered most of its capacity building in the United Kingdom because it was either unsafe to do it in the relevant region or because it was economically more efficient.

Inforce works with a range of professional partners in the United Kingdom and abroad. Inforce's primary partner organisations within the United Kingdom have been Cranfield and Bournemouth University, the International Association of Forensic Radiographers (IAFR) and the Association of Anatomical Pathology Technologists (AAPT). Overseas, Inforce has worked with the *Asistencia Forense para la Protección de los Derechos Fundamentales y el Avance de la Investigación Científica* (AFFIC) in Colombia, the International Commission on Missing Persons (ICMP; Hanson, Chapters 3 and 48, this volume), and the South African Universities of Witwatersrand, Pretoria (Nienaber, Chapter 39, this volume) and KwaZulu-Natal. It is part of Inforce's philosophy that working with a competent, specialist partner organisation is always preferable, rather than trying to cover a field of expertise outside its own area of competence. Inforce will always consider working with further organisations as appropriate.

The knowledge and skills that are at the heart of Inforce's capacity building try to span the entire spectrum needed in mass fatality investigation, including finding scenes, investigating them, recovering human remains and associated evidence, analysing them, identifying the victims and finally repatriating them to their loved ones. Scientific, operational and logistic issues are all addressed to leave teams of professionals who can operate independently and sustainably. If a forensic framework already exists, isolated areas, such as forensic archaeology, may be taught separately but as a general rule, Inforce tries to teach a holistic and complete process.

Another important aspect is that Inforce tries to teach profession-specific knowledge not only to those who are going to practise it, that is forensic archaeology to the archaeologist, but Inforce always attempts to explain the role of each professional to all of the other professions who work with them. That way, the scene of crime officer will work better with the forensic archaeologist and the surveyor better with the photographer, because they all understand the issues involved with their colleague's role in the team.

Inforce has a number of fundamental philosophies that characterises its approach to training and exercising:

- Essential but minimal theoretical content is delivered by experienced practitioners;
- Processes and exercise set-ups are not imposed on trainees but developed by them with minimal assistance by Inforce supervisors;
- Trainees are allowed and, in some cases, invited to make mistakes. If mistakes are made, it is crucial that the trainees (i) identify the mistake themselves, (ii) analyse the mistake and (iii) find a solution to it;
- A training session or exercise must be specifically tailored for the group receiving it, depending on their previous experience and future needs;
- Training and exercises must be delivered cost effectively, to be affordable and sustainable.

Iraq capacity building project

Inforce delivered three capacity-building programmes designed specifically to enable Iraq to develop its own forensic science and crime scene management teams. Altogether, 72 individuals have been trained in the skills needed to locate, record, excavate and analyse human remains and other evidence from mass graves, and to investigate the sites of atrocity crimes, as well as to enable them to train others in all these aspects. Each programme was designed for a specific trainee group.

All three programmes were delivered in the United Kingdom, although the third project involved trainees undergoing professional placements in South Africa and Bosnia and Herzegovina as well as in the United Kingdom. The different phases were taught by differently structured teams; but at the core of it was a team of four to five archaeologists and anthropologists, who participated in varying roles in all phases of the Iraq Capacity Building Project. Some individuals who were trained have stayed in regular contact with Inforce and each other.

Iraq training programme 2004–2005

The training programme started in October 2004 and ended late February 2005. Term 1 (the theoretical phase) and Term 2 (the practical phase) were separated by a break from mid-December to mid-January. Six groups of professionals were invited consisting of 7 archaeologists, 13 anthropologists, 4 radiographers, 1 anatomical pathology technologist (APT), 7 Crime Scene Investigators (CSIs) and 2 project managers. All were, of course, Iraqi nationals and represented all major ethnic groups, age ranges and both sexes. All were professionals (not students) and worked at the time in jobs closely related to what they were about to learn during the training. The selection process was carried out in a fair and unbiased manner. Each group had a different combination of lecture units in Term 1 and different practical elements in Term 2.

Term 1 (theoretical phase) was mainly hosted by Bournemouth University, except for some modules that were taught either in the Inforce temporary mortuary facility or in London. Some of the units were existing modules from the Bournemouth University MSc Forensic Archaeology and the MSc Forensic and Biological Anthropology programmes, while other units had to be specially created. Every unit was delivered in English[6] and fully assessed to Master level.

For Term 2 (practical phase), the groups of CSIs and anthropologists were split into two. One half was working in the field on the first grave (Figure 50.2), while the other half worked in the mortuary. For the second grave, the groups changed places. Equally, the project managers were split up most of the time between field and mortuary.

Figure 50.2 Iraqi archaeologists and Science of Crime Examiners during a simulated mass grave excavation.

Every group had supervisors in a ratio 1:2–1:4 to the students. The emphasis was on applying the theoretical knowledge gained in Term 1. Elements that could not easily be taught in Term 1 were demonstrated and trained on site. All supervisors were experienced practitioners in their own fields.

The two mass graves were put in place on different sites representing very different soil conditions. The graves contained in total 50 adult, 10 juvenile and 6 infant plastic skeletons. Most skeletons were dressed, blindfolded, had their hands tied, and had associated evidence such as ID papers, glasses or keys, as well as bullets and shell cases. The skeletons were laid out in small groups representing different killing scenarios (killed in the grave, killed on the edge of the grave and fallen in, killed somewhere else and being thrown into the grave, etc.).

Any evidence produced in the field was handed over from the field CSIs to the mortuary CSIs with full handover documentation. The 'bodies' then underwent standard post-mortem examination procedures, during which the plastic skeletons were exchanged with archaeological remains at the appropriate point. For the mortuary technician and the radiographers, visits to the field were arranged, so they could experience first-hand how the operation there related to their own operation in the mortuary. Both the field and mortuary team had to produce reports for both graves.

During the intense theoretical and practical training and exercising of the various skill sets, with considerable emphasis on core skills, such as archaeology, the overarching aim was to produce a long-term, sustainable capacity for Iraq. Although this could only be truly achieved after the follow-on project described later (training of trainers project), the fact that some of those Iraqi participants who have stayed in touch are still working in the field using the skills they learned during the project is very encouraging. This does not mean that the work of the group after their return to Iraq was ideal; much more could have been achieved if the team had been given a structure/framework to work in. Nevertheless, this should not negate the positive work that has taken place since 2005 by those individuals who have managed to establish themselves back in Iraq.

Criminal investigation training programme 2005

The second course was an intensive 3-week programme (March to April 2005) designed to train 39 lawyers working as investigators for the Iraq Special Tribunal. This was delivered in association with the Halo Partnership, Connecticut, US, and the Defence

[6]Not all participants spoke or understood English well. Lecture material, where possible and available, was translated into English before the lecture. All lectures were recorded, transcripted and translated. Regular peer learning groups with Iraqi and non-Iraqi students were organised to ensure that all participants were capable of following the lecture material.

Institute of International Legal Studies (DIILS), Rhode Island, US.

Inforce delivered a series of lectures introducing the group to the forensic side of international mass atrocity investigations as well as the issues around how to deal with the enormous wealth of information that would arise from their investigations and how to link criminal with forensic investigations.

During a later meeting in Iraq between an Inforce representative and those investigators, it appeared that they had indeed changed their attitude towards 'hard' evidence resulting from forensic investigations, and they fully admitted that this was because of the integrated and pragmatic approach in which they were introduced to the topics. This is, of course, only anecdotal information but still demonstrates that the education of law enforcement professionals and other legal professions is of vital importance if forensic archaeology wants to be involved in future atrocity crime investigations.

Iraq training of trainers programme 2005

The third course was a 3-month programme (April to June 2005) designed to train the most appropriate of the first group of trainees to be trainers. These 12 Iraqis were partly working in education, archaeological services and the police, and represented all professions mentioned in the earlier section. They received 1 month of pedagogy (the science of teaching) training and then 2 months of additional training in their various sciences and/or placements with organisations such as the ICMP, Dorset Police, the UK and the South African Universities of Witwatersrand, Pretoria and KwaZulu-Natal. The aim was to set the foundation for sustainable, long-term capacity of forensic atrocity crime investigation in Iraq. By training 12 of the original 34 Iraqis in (i) how to teach, (ii) enhanced skill sets in their discipline and (iii) by giving placements in the most ideal environments possible, no doubt a great foundation was created. As mentioned earlier, some of those trained are still practicing their skills and passing it on to the next generations of atrocity crime investigation scientists.

Rwanda capacity building project

Inforce's involvement in Rwanda, related to the Rwandan genocide of 1994, began in 2003 with a capacity building feasibility study and has been ongoing ever since.

Rwanda capacity building feasibility study 2003

In late 2003, the Inforce Foundation conducted a feasibility study to establish the potential contribution a forensic capacity building programme in Rwanda could have. The Inforce team interviewed and discussed with genocide survivors, ministers, police, prosecutors, other NGOs concerned with various aspects of the genocide, international donors, educationalists and others. The project aimed at the following:

- To investigate how necessary, welcomed and feasible a capacity building programme for Rwanda would be;
- To develop a capacity building proposal to create an atrocity crime investigation team for Rwanda and possibly the wider region;
- To assess the practical issues around potential team member selection.

All Rwandans and NGOs with whom the Inforce team met were unanimous in their view that they welcomed the prospect for a capacity building initiative, felt that it would make a major contribution and wanted it to proceed. The representatives of the donors were also extremely positive, and an opportunity clearly exists for Inforce to make a significant contribution to the (long-term) development of the emergent justice sector strategy.

Inforce prepared a proposal to run a pilot programme in association with a Rwandan higher education institution. The pilot was designed to equip up to 40 Rwandese (similar spread of professions as in the Iraq capacity building projects) with the technical skills necessary to locate and excavate mass graves, and to perform some analysis of the remains and other evidence recovered. In collaboration with the Prosecutor General's Office, the pilot programme would have also excavated one grave and provided evidence to be used in court.

Teaching and mentoring on the training and excavation would have been provided by an Inforce managed team of international experts. The training was to use international protocols and SOPs, and would have been subject to rigorous quality assurance. Successful completion of the course was designed to be certified by Rwanda's partner higher education (HE) institution[7] in cooperation with Inforce.

Candidates for the training were to be drawn from a variety of sources – some were to be students, whilst others would have already been qualified in relevant disciplines (i.e., medicine, surveying or civil engineering). After training they were meant to be coordinated by the HE institution. Inforce had pledged to continue to provide technical advice and support whilst the capacity grew. In particular, Inforce was determined to raise funding to bring Rwandans to the United Kingdom for master's degree-level training so that they could have returned to Rwanda and formed a core of experts to nurture Rwanda's forensic capacity. In the longer term, Rwanda could have exported forensic training throughout their region.

[7]Details are yet to be decided, but are likely to be the National University of Rwanda.

The use of locally trained forensic scientists and technicians would have made the location, excavation and analysis of forensic evidence a cost-effective option for courts in the poor countries of the region. At the time of the study, justice was being denied to Africans in part because forensic evidence was simply too costly to acquire.

Rwanda mobile laboratory project

Over an extended period, discussion of the issues arising from the study led to a proposal for a mobile laboratory for Rwanda. Plans for this were developed in 2009 when two students from Cranfield University, UK, were given the opportunity to accompany Inforce staff to go to Rwanda to collect data for their dissertation research projects. Initially, there were two key thoughts: (1) the unique memorial site at Murambi, where hundreds of genocide victims were preserved with lime, had to be studied in order to preserve it, and (2) there are half a dozen key memorial sites throughout Rwanda that would benefit greatly from the presence of a laboratory to help with the preservation of both victims' remains and associated artefacts. In conclusion, there had to be (i) a multi-purpose laboratory and (ii) it should be mobile. While fully equipped to enable a small team to work on limited numbers of anthropological identification cases, the primary function of the mobile laboratory was to assist Rwanda with the 'preservation of the memory of the genocide' using photography, scanning and X-rays. Alongside the 'hardware', Inforce had planned to supply teams of at least three specialists in the various disciplines relevant to the functionality of the laboratory and for those experts to train and mentor Rwandan scientists and students.

Apart from this, Inforce developed and built 20 acrylic display containers, which are capable of either being flooded with nitrogen or maintaining a vacuum. These display containers are for a selected number of victims' remains from the Murambi memorial site. The nitrogen or vacuum is designed to minimise any chemical and insect activity that is currently destroying the remains.

Apart from sending the first Inforce team out to start operations, all the above aims have been completed. At the end of 2011, the containerised laboratory was initially delivered to Cranfield University, UK, where it was stocked with all the equipment it was to carry. Meanwhile, the acrylic containers were developed, tested and then produced by a specialist company in the south of England. They were transported to Rwanda first, followed by the laboratory, which safely reached Rwanda, where it was then commissioned by an Inforce team in 2012 and handed over officially to Rwanda (Figures 50.3 and 50.4). Since then, detailed negotiations have been taking place to ensure that the medium- and long-term future of the project will be a success.

Inforce conferences and workshops

As well as reacting to conflicts aboard and trying to build capacity in affected countries or regions, Inforce has always tried to find means to educate and train forensic practitioners in the United Kingdom or other countries through conferences and workshops.

Inforce conferences 2005 and 2006

By 2005, topics such as forensic archaeology, anthropology and entomology had become academically well established; Inforce felt it was time to establish an international annual forensic conference and started

Figure 50.3 The 'Rwanda Mobile Laboratory', designed and built in the United Kingdom, arrives at its first destination Murambi, Rwanda.

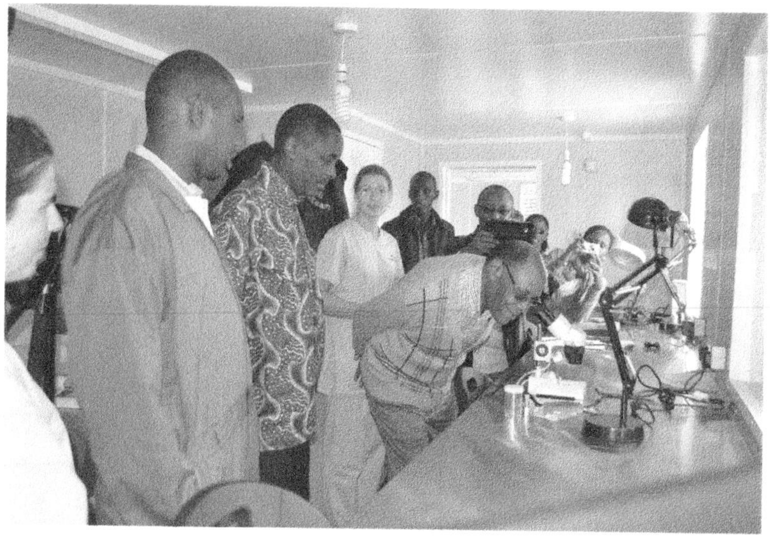

Figure 50.4 Inforce hands over the Mobile Laboratory to the CNLG during an official commissioning ceremony.

with the first of that kind in December 2005. The aims for these conferences were as follows:

- To establish an annual or biennial (every 2 years) forensic conference in the United Kingdom;
- To create an affordable forum for students to attend;
- To create a professional environment for the exchange of experiences for forensic practitioners;
- To establish an international forum for forensic disciplines relevant to mass fatality investigations.

In 2005, a total of 133 delegates from over 15 countries came to Bournemouth and saw 28 presentations in 5 different scientific fields. The 2006 conference tried to develop the foundation laid in 2005 further, including more forensic disciplines. Although that was not quite achieved and forensic archaeology and anthropology still represented the core of the presentations, the conference was still considered a success by the organisers and delegates.

The foundation for an annual international forensic conference in the United Kingdom was undoubtedly laid with these two conferences. However, Inforce moved in the summer of 2007 away from Bournemouth and needed time to establish itself at its new base. This disrupted the momentum of running the Inforce conference. Until the present day, significant logistical challenges have prevented Inforce from re-igniting the idea of a regular forensic conference. However, this could change as soon as solutions for the challenges are found.

The high proportion of 37% students at the 2006 conference indicates that there is definitely a need for such events. The proportion should probably not be much higher, since otherwise the students have less opportunity to learn from and network with professionals, but it should also not be much lower.

The fact that so many professionals from so many countries are willing to travel to the United Kingdom to participate in such an event shows that there is a need for it. Two conferences do not provide a sufficient sample size to draw too many conclusions, but it would still be encouraging enough to re-launch the conferences.

Inforce mass atrocity workshops

Based on the experience of training the 34 Iraqis in 2004–2005, Inforce established modified versions of practical workshop experiences for anyone. Inforce has so far developed seven different workshops, which are as follows:

- Mass Grave Excavation
- Mass Fatality Incident Mortuary
- Advanced Mass Grave Excavation
- Advanced Mass Fatality Incident Mortuary
- Forensic Photography
- Forensic Anthropology for Radiography
- Forensic Radiography for Anthropologists

The aims of these workshops were the following:

- Train professionals from various backgrounds in the processes and methods of forensic mass fatality mortuary investigations;
- Provide an opportunity and a venue for fundraising activities;
- Test practitioners who are interested in working on Inforce operations in the future;
- Conduct research during the exercise;
- Further test the practicality of the protocols, SOPs and recording forms.

Two main benefits resulted from the workshops. First, many students and professionals were given a chance to have very realistic experiences, but still in an

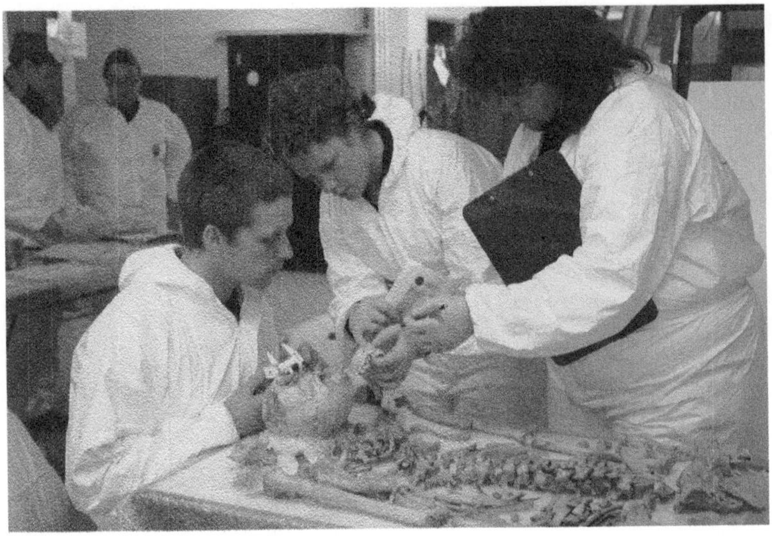

Figure 50.5 Mortuary workshop participants trying to establish a biological profile of skeletonised human remains.

environment in which they could make mistakes without real and considerable consequences (Figure 50.5). Second, each workshop was used to test the protocols and SOPs, and the development can easily be traced by the new version of the Inforce forms, which of course are directly linked to the methods and techniques.

Inforce police DVI workshops

In 2008, the DVI coordinator for Nottinghamshire Police visited an Inforce Mortuary Workshop and was determined that a modified version would benefit his DVI officers greatly. At the time, each police force in England and Wales was required to have a certain number of officers trained in DVI operations to form part of the UK DVI Team. In total, around 500 officers had been trained across the 43 police forces in England and Wales, with each force, depending on its own size, having between 5 and 15 officers. However, it was recognised that as the UK DVI Team would only be activated in major mass fatalities, it was desirable for each force to have at the very least 50 officers to deal with any minor mass fatality. Therefore, individual forces had to train further officers from various departments who volunteered for the force's DVI Team. Most of those had only little or no in-house training, and hardly any would have any real operational experience and some limited exercising.

For such forces, Inforce developed a workshop model, in which Inforce provided all the scientific personnel, such as pathologists, anatomical pathology technologists (APTs), anthropologists, radiographers and odontologists, while a large number of officers could be trained and exercised, being supervised both by the force's trained DVI officers and Inforce personnel. Various different versions of these exercises were developed depending on the force's needs.

The exercises provided officers who were already DVI trained and/or experienced with a chance to put their theoretical skills into practice, to refresh their previous operational experiences, to test operational procedures and SOPs and to lead less experienced officers. Officers who volunteered to assist in a DVI incident but had little formal training and operational experience were able to experience many aspects of DVI procedures in a 'safe' exercise environment, to get accustomed to DVI-related paperwork and to draw on the experience and expertise of their more experienced colleagues and Inforce supervisors.

Between 2008 and 2013, Inforce worked with five forces of the East Midlands Police Collaboration (Derbyshire, Leicestershire, Lincolnshire, Northamptonshire and Nottinghamshire) and the six forces of the East of England Region (Bedfordshire, Cambridgeshire, Essex, Hertfordshire, Norfolk and Suffolk). The total number of officers included in these workshops will be somewhere over 300 (Figure 50.6).

Future developments

An organisation's purpose and activities must regularly be assessed and developed. Whilst some purposes remain significant, others may become obsolete. New activities may be needed to address emerging needs, and Inforce therefore monitors the relevance of its activities constantly and reviews possible developments for the future.

The most straightforward issue is that of standards. The publication of Inforce's Protocols and SOPs addressed this element of its charitable activities very well. Naturally, methods and techniques constantly evolve, new ones appear and need to be considered and

Figure 50.6 DVI officers of Dorset Police recovering a light aircraft crash simulated by Inforce.

some may become outdated for various reasons. Inforce therefore proposes to publish a second edition at an appropriate point in the future. This may be both in the form of a hardcover and an electronic edition to be more accessible especially for students.

It is impossible to predict in what operational activities Inforce will become involved. Inforce will always offer its assistance when it believes it has the appropriate experience and expertise. In a perfect world, Inforce, as a charity, should be able to offer its services free of charge; but for that, it would require core funding to pay for equipment, consumables and salaries. Although everyone who works for Inforce does so for significantly reduced rates compared to their commercial work, Inforce still needs to be able to pay its staff something. Currently, this is done by budgeting all this into operations, but Inforce is continually seeking opportunities to secure independent core funding.

The need to build capacity abroad and to run conferences and workshops in the United Kingdom or other countries is still as high as ever. This side of Inforce's work has never stopped, and they will always try to supply according to demand and circumstances. At the time of writing this chapter, Inforce is just about to launch its next workshop programme.

All those involved in working for or with Inforce have always believed that there is a significant need for a non-profit-making, reliable, independent, impartial and international organisation, and that is what Inforce has always tried to be and will continue to aim for.

Although Inforce is clearly a multidisciplinary organisation and aims at promoting better inter-disciplinary understanding and cooperation, it started out with forensic archaeology and anthropology at its core, and many students and professionals of those scientific fields from various countries have benefited from Inforce's work on standards and capacity building. Currently, Inforce does not concentrate on an active database of practicing professionals, science that would only be legal and ethical if there was a significant amount of international operations to utilise the registered individuals. And while there is an enormous need for forensic mass fatality investigations in most parts of the world, forensic sciences, such as archaeology and anthropology, have not yet managed to be routinely part of investigations and most cases are not investigated at all. However, this should not deter anyone from preparing for future investigations and from constantly promoting forensic archaeology and other relevant sciences by setting good, professional examples.

References

Cox, M., Flavel, A., Hanson, I., Laver, J. and Wessling, R. 2008. *The Scientific Investigation of Mass Graves – Towards Protocols and Standard Operating Procedures*. Cambridge, Cambridge University Press.

Hunter, J. R. and Cox, M. (eds.) 2005. *Forensic Archaeology: Advances in Theory and Practice*. London, Routledge.

CHAPTER 51

Forensic archaeology underwater: JPAC's inventory, investigation and recovery of US casualties of war from submerged sites

Andrew T. Pietruszka

Joint POW/MIA Accounting Command-Central Identification Laboratory, Joint Base Pearl Harbor-Hickam, Hawaii, USA

Introduction

This chapter focuses specifically on the US Department of Defence Joint Prisoners of War, Missing in Action Accounting Command-Central Identification Laboratory's (JPAC-CIL)[1] investigation and recovery of underwater losses. Given the critical role underwater sites play in JPAC's forensic mission, there is a surprising dearth of information on underwater applications in the major relevant forensic archaeology and anthropology literature (e.g. Blau and Ubelaker 2009; Dirkmaat 2012; Komar and Buikstra 2008). This suggests that JPAC-CIL is somewhat unique in its pursuit of forensic underwater archaeology. In this chapter, such operations are briefly contextualised within the organisation's history and overarching mission (e.g. Emanovsky and Belcher 2012, 569–572; Holland and Tersigni-Tarrant 2013). A case study provides a detailed example of how standard forensic and archaeological techniques are integrated and applied to underwater sites, as well as some of the challenges unique to working in this environment.

JPAC's mission is to conduct global search, recovery, and laboratory operations to identify unaccounted for Americans from past conflicts in order to support the US Department of Defence's personnel accounting efforts. Commanded by a flag officer (currently Major General Kelly McKeague of the US Air Force), JPAC is staffed by about 500 handpicked soldiers, sailors, airmen, marines and Department of the Navy civilians. JPAC's organisational structure is typical of most US military commands including directorates responsible for personnel, intelligence, operations, logistics, policy and information technology. Three detachments – based in Laos, Vietnam and Thailand – facilitate travel and operations in South East Asia (e.g. Emanovsky and Belcher 2012, 569). JPAC is headquartered on Joint Base Pearl Harbor-Hickam, Honolulu, Hawaii, US. From here, members of JPAC Investigation and Recovery Teams travel throughout the world to search for and recover Americans missing from World War II (WWII; 1939–1945), the Korean War (1950–1953), the Vietnam War (1966–1975) and the Cold War. Currently, over 83,000 US service members remain missing from these conflicts.

The laboratory portion of JPAC, referred to as the CIL, is the largest forensic anthropology laboratory in the world with a staff of over 40 forensic anthropologists and archaeologists[2] as well as three forensic odontologists. The primary functions of the laboratory include: directing scientific and forensic recoveries in the field; analysis of osseous remains and non-biological material evidence; the scientific identification of individual remains; researching forensic scientific methods and techniques; providing humanitarian support during national and international mass disasters; consultation to foreign governments and international organisations; forensic support to law enforcement and investigative agencies; and to advance the field of forensic anthropology in collaboration with national and

[1]For more information, see: http://www.jpac.pacom.mil/index.php?page=cil (last accessed October 2013).

[2]In the United States, the discipline of anthropology is generally subdivided into four subfields – archaeology, physical anthropology, cultural anthropology, and linguistics – with practitioners of each receiving cross-training among each of the sub-disciplines (e.g. Cabo and Dirkmaat, Chapter 31 this volume). At JPAC, forensic anthropology is the sub-discipline that applies the principles and methods of physical anthropology to legal issues, while forensic archaeology is defined as the application of archaeological principles, methods and techniques to the legal process. While JPAC forensic anthropologists do have a primary laboratory function, both archaeologists and physical anthropologists are qualified to conduct recovery scene work in the field.

Forensic Archaeology: A Global Perspective, First Edition. Edited by W.J. Mike Groen, Nicholas Márquez-Grant and Robert C. Janaway.

international forensic organisations (Holland et al. 2008, 48). Since JPAC's inception in 2003, scientists at the CIL have identified over 730 US service members and reunited their remains with their families.

Historical overview of the Central Identification Laboratory

During WWII, the task of recovering, identifying, and interring US war casualties was carried out by the US Army Quartermaster's American Graves Registration Service (AGRS) (Wood and Stanley 1989, 1365). After the war, the AGRS carried out a large-scale effort to search for and recover the thousands of US service members still missing as a result of the conflict. These efforts centralised in each of the war's major theatres – Europe and the Pacific – mark the beginning of the military's use of professionally trained physical anthropologists for the scientific identification of remains.

In 1947, the first central identification point was established in Strasbourg, France. Dr Harry L. Shapiro, then the curator of Physical Anthropology at the American Museum of Natural History in New York, was hired on as a consultant (Wood and Stanley 1989). A Pacific theatre Central Identification Laboratory was established at Schofield Barracks, territory of Hawaii, that same year, with Dr Charles Snow, professor of Physical Anthropology at the University of Kentucky, serving as the Laboratory Anthropologist from 1947 to 1948. Although brief, Dr Snow's tenure is significant as it marks the first permanent physical anthropologist position in the US military's identification process (Holland and Tersigni-Tarrant 2013, 18). In 1948, Dr Snow's obligations to the University of Kentucky forced him to return to his faculty position. Dr Mildred Trotter of Washington University (St Louis, MO) was hired to replace Dr Snow as the CIL Scientific Director and continue the task of identifying the thousands of US service members recovered throughout the Pacific theatre. By 1949, Dr Trotter and her staff had identified almost 7000 individuals; however, limitations in forensic and anthropological techniques at the time prevented any further identifications (Holland and Tersigni-Tarrant 2013, 19). The remaining unidentified individuals were interred in the National Memorial Cemetery of the Pacific (NMCP) in Honolulu, Hawaii, as 'unknowns', and the first CIL was officially closed.

The peace that followed the end of WWII was short-lived and with the outbreak of war on the Korean peninsula in 1950, the US military once again found itself in need of a large-scale recovery and identification effort for war casualties recovered from the battlefield. To meet this need, the Army Quartermaster Corps established a Central Identification Unit (CIU) in Kokura, Japan, in 1951. While physical anthropological data and methods developed from the post-WWII identification effort were utilised, the rapid recovery of battlefield dead precluded the need of physical anthropologists in the identification process. This changed, however, with the 1953 Armistice and the subsequent exchange of US Ally, North Korean and Chinese dead. As part of the bilateral exchange over 4000 sets of remains were repatriated to the United States. Once again the US Army Quartermaster Corps found itself in need of a physical anthropologist to assist in the identification of America's war dead. In 1953, the Corps hired a team of physical anthropologists including Dr T. Dale Stewart, Dr Ellis R. Kerley, Dr Charse P. Warren, Dr Thomas McKern, and Dr Tadao Furue to study and identify the remains. By 1955, the team had identified all but 840 of the repatriated individuals and the remainder were interred in the National Memorial Cemetery of the Pacific (NMCP) as unknowns (Holland and Tersigni-Tarrant 2013, 20).

As in previous conflicts, the task of recovering and identifying US war dead during the Vietnam War fell to the US Army Quartermaster Corps. Initially, the remains of soldiers were processed at a small mortuary located on Clark Air Force Base in the Philippines by civilian morticians. However, as the war escalated and the death toll rose, so too did the need of in-country mortuary facilities. The first was established in 1965 outside of Saigon at the US Air Force Base at Tan Son. Two years later, a second facility was established at the air base in Da Nang. As was the case during the Korean War, the identification of battlefield casualties remained straightforward and did not require the expertise of a trained physical anthropologist. As America's role in the war began to wane in the early 1970s, the need for and ability to support the area of operation facilities declined and by 1973 both in-country mortuary facilities were closed. In 1973, a new CIL was opened at Camp Samae San, Bangkok, Thailand. The facility, referred to as CIL-THAI, remained in operation until 1976 when it was again moved, this time to Honolulu, Hawaii, and renamed CIL-HI. The post-Vietnam era marks a significant transition in the US military's recovery and identification mission. Whereas in the past, CILs were temporarily established and specifically tasked with the identification of remains from a particular conflict, the mission of the CIL-HI was expanded to include the recovery and identification of missing and unaccounted-for Americans lost in all past military conflicts, with an indefinite mandate.

Amidst the domestic political turmoil following America's involvement in Vietnam, the mid-1980s saw increased scrutiny into the scientific practices and identification performed by CIL-HI, and as a result subsequent restructuring of the overall operation. In 1987, Dr Ellis R. Kerley was hired as the Scientific Director to address many of the issues confronting CIL-HI. In an effort to bolster scientific credibility, an internal peer-review process was implemented for all identifications and outside consultants were brought in to further validate final case reports. This important change began the process of surety and reliability critical to the CIL's forensic mission (e.g. identification for legal purpose). Another significant change came in the forensic anthropologist's/archaeologist's role in recovering remains. Initially restricted to the laboratory and the identification of remains, it had become apparent that more systematic and scientific field recoveries were needed to ensure successful identifications. In response, for the first time in the US military's recovery effort, physical anthropologists and archaeologists were included as members of recovery teams deployed in the field. In 1994, Dr Thomas D. Holland became the Scientific Director and implemented further changes to the role of the team forensic expert. First and foremost was a dramatic shift in the duties of deploying physical anthropologists and archaeologists from what was formerly an advisory role to that of a Recovery Leader. Henceforth, the CIL physical anthropologist/archaeologist was recognised as the subject matter expert charged with maintaining forensic integrity and scientific methods while overseeing site excavation.

In 2003, CIL-HI merged with the Joint Task Force-Full Accounting to form the newly commissioned Joint POW/MIA Accounting Command (JPAC). In homage to its historic ancestry, the JPAC forensic laboratory retained the title of CIL. JPAC's mission was expanded to include the recovery and identification of missing unaccounted-for Americans lost in past military conflicts to include WWII, the Korean War, Vietnam, and the Cold War. In 2003 JPAC-CIL became the first skeletal identification laboratory to be certified by the American Society of Crime Laboratory Directors – Laboratory Accreditation Board (ASCLAD-LAB). In 2008, the CIL was reaccredited by ASCLAD-LAB under the International Program in Crime Scene and Trace Evidence; at the time, it was only the second laboratory in the United States to obtain a perfect assessment. The CIL's international accreditation was expanded in 2013 to include crime scene, trace evidence and forensic biology (DNA sampling).

Forensic underwater investigations and recovery at JPAC

A growing concern at JPAC over the past 15 years has been the recovery and identification of remains from submerged sites. Currently, worldwide, some 3400 unique loss incidents, accounting for over 9000 individuals, are believed to be underwater. In addition to the sheer volume of individuals contained within, underwater sites in general often provide a greater degree of preservation in comparison to terrestrial losses. For example, cold waters and anaerobic environmental conditions, such as those provided by the rapid burial of objects in silt or mud, retard the biological and chemical decomposition of materials including biological remains (Ferrari and Adams 1990; Haglund and Sorg 2002, 203; Mays 2008, 125; Stewart 1999, 578–581; Ward et al. 1999). Contrary to early assumptions (i.e. Arnaud et al. 1980, 53), the recovery of human remains from historic shipwreck sites is well documented (e.g. Bruseth and Turner 2005, 115–122; During 1997; Nuorala 1999; Stirland 2000), and human remains over 10,000 years old have been discovered in fresh water springs (Clausen et al. 1975). The level of preservation of the bone recovered at many of these sites not only allows standard biometric research (i.e. sex, age and stature) of individuals, but has also produced viable results on the biomolecular level. Mitochondrial DNA (mtDNA) has been successfully extracted from preserved human remains recovered from shipwrecks dating from the 16th and 17th centuries (Ariffin et al. 2007; Hagelberg and Frame 2005). The successful research carried out on remains recovered from such sites bodes well for the success of JPAC's underwater mission, whose sites are significantly more recent. Remains recovered by the JPAC-CIL from submerged sites have a very high success rate in DNA extraction and ultimately identification. Many of JPAC's underwater sites are also often located in remote areas with little to no human disturbance. And the historical practice of 'ditching' – or emergency landing a crippled plane on the water – suggests a greater propensity for discovering more intact aircraft sites with a higher expectation for recovering remains contained within.

Modern-day underwater operations at JPAC-CIL began in earnest in the mid-1990s with the earliest activities focused on Vietnam War-era aircraft wreck sites in Southeast Asia (specifically Vietnam and Cambodia). Missions have subsequently expanded into other regions, encompassing earlier conflicts, including: the United Kingdom, France, Tunisia, Italy, the Netherlands, Philippines, Canada, Papua New Guinea, Palau, the Republic of Korea, and the United States. Underwater operations typically focus on overwater military aircraft losses in marine, lacustrine, riverine, estuarine and aquaculture environments. Logistical, technical, environmental, safety and fiscal factors combine to make it difficult to conduct underwater operations. Thus, an emphasis is placed on shallow water sites (<30 m); however, utilising US Navy capabilities, diver-assisted recoveries are feasible up to 90 m, while submersible vehicles may provide access at even greater depths. JPAC-CIL forensic underwater archaeologists also undertake missions in littoral zones and on land at locations related to underwater losses as the situation warrants. And on a few occasions, JPAC-CIL forensic underwater archaeologists have advised or consulted with external cultural resource management entities and law enforcement agencies.

The underwater programme at JPAC-CIL includes historical research, site investigation and archaeological recovery. Although many general concepts are identical to standard terrestrial archaeology procedures, an underwater-specific standard operating procedure (SOP) guides all JPAC-CIL work at submerged sites. This SOP requires the use of appropriate scientific staff with specific training in underwater archaeology and marries technical underwater archaeological practices (e.g. Dean et al. 2000; Green 2004) with forensic methods. Since 1997, JPAC-CIL has maintained at least one, and as many as four, professionally trained forensic underwater archaeologists on staff. In addition to these civilian professionals, JPAC employs a designated Underwater Search and Recovery Team comprising an active duty US Army Dive Officer, Master Diver, NCO Diver, Explosive Ordnance Disposal (EOD) technicians and dive medical technicians. Field operations are further supplemented with active duty dive-qualified US military personnel augmented on a mission-by-mission basis (i.e. dive qualified combat cameramen for photography). Such personnel – who are not typically available to civilian forensic underwater archaeology teams – are highly professional and competent in their given fields; however, their lack of previous archaeological or forensic experience presents a unique challenge for JPAC-CIL's civilian forensic underwater archaeologist overseeing operations. To mitigate complications JPAC-CIL employs systematic search, survey, and excavation strategies developed to incorporate best archaeological practices with standard military procedures.

JPAC-CIL underwater operations utilise an interconnected two-phase approach in the field consisting of investigation and recovery, both of which are led by forensic archaeologists with advanced degrees in underwater archaeology. Investigations are primarily information gathering expeditions focused on finding sites, correlating them to known loss incidents associated with unaccounted-for individuals, and collecting detailed site data. For loss locations reported to JPAC by outside sources, witness interviews and diver reconnaissance are often enough to provide a precise site location and correlation with a known loss incident. JPAC-CIL forensic underwater archaeologists also conduct focused hydrographic surveys utilising multiple remote-sensing capabilities – including side-scan sonar, magnetometer, multibeam echosounder and autonomous underwater vehicle (AUV)/unmanned undersea vehicles (UUV) – to locate previously undiscovered sites (Figure 51.1). Information gathered during the investigation phase, such as site integrity, extent, potential threats to the site, environmental conditions, weather patterns, currents and navigation hazards is used to determine if a potential site warrants excavation and provides details critical to planning the recovery phase.

Recoveries are carried out by active duty US military divers under the supervision of one of JPAC-CIL's forensic underwater archaeologists. Like terrestrial sites, horizontal provenience is controlled and recorded in reference to a standard archaeological grid and site datum, while vertical provenience is defined by either arbitrary or defined stratigraphic levels. During excavation, an innovative system designed by JPAC-CIL's forensic underwater archaeologists, comprising venturi suction dredges and catchment lifting baskets, is used to remove, contain and segregate the matrix. The variable water-powered suction produced by the venturi dredge allows the diver to excavate in a controlled and uniform manner while ensuring minimal impact on fragile remains and material evidence, since they pass through no moving mechanical parts (Figure 51.2).

Figure 51.1 Side-scan sonar image and JPAC diver investigation of a WWII B-17 off the coast of Corsica, France.

Case study: a WWII era B-24J Liberator crashed off the coast of Palau

On 1 September 1944, a US Army Air Forces B-24J Liberator bomber (Tail No. 42-73453) carrying a crew of 11 individuals was shot down during a bombing reconnaissance mission of enemy targets near the town of Koror, Republic of Palau. Crew members in accompanying aircraft reported that the aircraft broke up in the air before crashing into the water. At least two parachutes were observed prior to impact. Japanese war documents later confirmed three individuals had successfully exited the aircraft, but all three later died during captivity.

The aircraft was originally discovered by Dr Patrick Scannon and members of the Bent Prop Project[3] team just off the south-western coastline of Babelthaup Island, Republic of Palau, in 2004. The site consists of a broken-up and dispersed debris field separated by a large coral head (80 m in diameter) ranging in depth between 7 and 23 m below the water's surface. Several key features, including three propellers, the starboard wing, and an oval vertical stabiliser were easily identified as belonging to a B-24 Liberator (Figure 51.3).

Figure 51.2 Diver excavating with venturi suction dredge around aircraft wreckage, B-24J Liberator, off the coast of Palau.

Figure 51.3 Rear vertical tail stabiliser, B-24J Liberator, off the coast of Palau.

[3]The Bent Prop Project is a non-profit organisation dedicated to locating and assisting with identifying American prisoners of war and missing in action from WWII within the Palau Islands. For more information, see: www.bentprop.org/docs/vision-mission-values.htm (last accessed October 2013).

The geographic location and the type of aircraft observed on the seafloor tentatively correlated to the loss incident described in Missing Air Crew Report (MACR) 8641, which involved the loss of 11 individuals who remained unaccounted for. JPAC conducted preliminary investigations at the site in January and February of that same year. The debris field was inventoried and mapped, and limited testing was carried out to evaluate key areas most likely to contain human remains and probative material evidence. The team recovered possible human remains and recommended two areas – designated Locus A and Locus B – for excavation. A third area – Locus C – situated about 200 m southeast along the adjacent reef was also chosen for excavation during subsequent missions.

The site was excavated by JPAC Underwater Recovery Teams over the course of three missions that took place in 2005, 2007 and 2008. Overall, the horizontal distribution of wreckage exceeded 500 by 500 m; however, the full extent of the site was indeterminate. Although several large portions of aircraft wreckage were readily discernible, other portions were obscured by significant coral growth and several components including the port-side wing and tail turret were never located. All work on site was overseen by a JPAC-CIL forensic archaeologist with specialised training in underwater archaeology. US Navy divers from Mobile Diving Salvage Unit 1 (MDSU-1) and members of the Pearl Harbor Naval Shipyard (PHNSY) assisted in the recovery effort. A locally contracted barge functioned as the team's base of operations and dive platform throughout the entire project.

Field operations commenced with pre-disturbance documentation across the site utilising diver reconnaissance, photo-documentation and video. This was followed by a risk assessment by the team's EOD technician who conducted a seafloor and sub-seafloor metal detector sweep to ascertain the presence of unexploded ordnance (UXO). Large aircraft oxygen tanks, mounted weapons (0.50 calibre machine guns) and unfired ammunition were deemed unsafe and had to be removed from the site. Test pits and subsurface probing delineated the site's vertical extent and revealed a matrix comprised of three distinct stratigraphic levels. An uppermost zone comprising light-suspended silt marked the oxic interface between the water column and seafloor, an anoxic silty clay loam defined the second level, and the third was characterised by a well-defined base of dead corals extending to an undetermined depth. Metal, glass, composites and other items in level one were heavily concreted and exhibited high levels of corrosion, while the anaerobic properties of the second level offered the greatest potential for preservation. The coral base in level three marked the beginning of incident sterile soil and marked the site's lower limits.

As is standard in most archaeological excavations, divers established a site datum and reference grid to maintain horizontal control and to document proper provenience for all features, excavated units and diagnostic evidence. The grid was extended throughout the site using fixed baselines extending from the site datum. Units typically ranged in size from 2 by 2 m to 5 by 5 m depending on the complexity of the deposit. For the most part, finds were plotted using triangulation and offset distance measurements; however, a 1 × 1 m planning frame subdivided into 50 × 50 cm or 20 × 20 cm quadrants was utilised to further refine provenience of and precisely document highly complex and probative areas (i.e. those containing possible human remains and material evidence) (Figure 51.4).

Vertical control was established utilising a temporary benchmark installed into the coral head separating Locus A and B referenced to the site datum and the water's surface. The contour of each unit was recorded, each unit related to datum, datum to temporary benchmark and benchmark to water's surface, thus providing bathometry for the entire site. With the contour of the seafloor known, all materials encountered were then simply measured as depth below seafloor. At the conclusion of the project, the temporary coral benchmark was tied into a nearby officially recognised land elevation point using the same principle.

Figure 51.4 Diver recording provenience during excavation, B-24J Liberator, off the coast of Palau.

Excavation was carried out using trowels, venturi-powered suction dredges and hand fanning. When possible, exposed human remains were left *in situ* in order to preserve associated context prior to removal. Evidence removal was largely conducted by the JPAC-CIL Recovery Leader/Anthropologist (RL/A) unless precluded by safe diving protocols (such as during required surface intervals for off-gassing between dives). When prevented from diving, the RL/A directed the excavation and recovery via underwater communications and live video feeds provided by the diver's helmet mounted cameras. Excavated sediment was collected in large metal lift baskets placed on the seafloor adjacent to each excavation area. Each basket was lined with 0.25 in. (about 0.63 cm) wire mesh inserts and was equipped with a lid to ensure no material was lost. Once each basket was filled or an excavation level was completed, these baskets were lifted by crane from the seafloor and placed on the deck of the salvage barge. On the surface the matrix was then sifted through 0.25 in. wet screens. All materials of evidentiary value were examined by the RL/A, placed in plastic bags marked with provenience information and sealed with evidence tape, stored within a locked case or a secured area, and a chain of custody of these materials was initiated and maintained. Excavations expanded until a 1 m buffer of incident sterile soil could be established along the perimeter of the outermost units.

The site was divided into three loci each containing a single feature. Two features – Locus A, Feature 1 and Locus B, Feature 2 – were further subdivided based on crew members' stations identifiable in the wreckage, the placement of which could provide a line of evidence as to the identification of human remains found within.

Locus A, Feature 1 consisted of a large section of aft fuselage extending from just forward of the ball turret to the rear window frame inferior to the horizontal stabiliser of the tail. The wreckage rests on the seafloor and coral head with a steep (60–80°) transitional slope. Coupled with a compromised structural integrity, this area was initially determined unsafe for extensive excavation as the removal of matrix from beneath presented a high level of threat for collapse. To mitigate the risk a stabilisation cradle had to be prefabricated in Hawaii and installed on site. The cradle was anchored into the seafloor using concrete footpads and an opposing force counterweight system. Belly straps and chain falls interconnected between the cradle and fuselage supported the weight of the wreck and allowed for safe excavation underneath.

The forward portion is associated with the waist and belly gunner positions of the aircraft. Human remains were recovered in close association with identification media (two identical identification tags), life-support and survival equipment, and other diagnostic material evidence including: a pair of sunglass frames, lens fragments, flak vest material, radio receiver earpiece, the heel lift of a boot, a few coins, match case, pistol grip, survival knife and boot sole. Also discovered was a 0.50 calibre machine gun, the serial number of which indicated it to be the aircraft's starboard waist gun. The MACR lists the individual to whom the identification tags belonged to as a 'Gunner'. The rear portion of Feature 1 was associated with the tail gunner position. It did not include the actual tail turret, which was never located. Human remains and material evidence were recovered; they are believed to represent the lower extent of the forward portion rather than being associated with the tail gunner's position.

Locus B, Feature 2 consisted of large fragments of a forward section of fuselage from the forward most bomb bay (just aft of the top turret) to the nose turret. This area includes crew positions for the top turret gunner, radio operator, pilot and co-pilot. Upslope lay wreckage associated with the aircraft's nose compartment, including the navigator's workspace and nose turret. A high concentration of navigational equipment, flak vest material, armour plating, ammunition cans, and two 0.50 calibre machine guns were clearly visible. The uppermost portion of this feature contained an identification tag matching that of the assistant engineer, a gold ring, buttons, coins, boot fragments, sunglass frames, jewellery chain, flak gear and zipper in association with skeletal remains. A second group of human remains was concentrated down slope in proximity to an illegible identification tag, relatively intact boot, boot fragments and flak vest material. The serial numbers from two 0.50 calibre guns recovered mid-slope correlate to the left and right nose turret guns. Further down-slope human remains, the pilot's identification tag, a boot sole and button were recovered in association with the pilot's seat. Additional human remains, as well as two hack watches, a pair of sunglass frames, lens fragments and portions of a 'Mae West' life preserver were recovered in association with the co-pilot's seat. The top turret seat and guns were identified nearby; however, no human remains were recovered in the immediate vicinity. Additional concentrations of wreckage including a portion of the starboard wing, two engines and their propellers were discovered to the northwest but no human remains or evidentiary material were associated.

Locus C, Feature 3 was a relatively isolated intact portion of the horizontal stabiliser and the superior stabiliser of the portside tail. The inferior portion of the vertical stabiliser rests down-slope just a short distance away. The area was of particular interest due to its structural proximity to the still missing tail turret and its operator. Unfortunately, the tail turret was not located and excavations yielded no human remains or evidentiary material evidence.

In total, the recovery operations spanned 34 weeks over the course of three field seasons. During 1401 archaeological dives, the teams excavated 488 m^2 to an average depth of 67 cm below surface. In addition, divers surveyed 2880 m^2 of seafloor documenting the open spaces interspersed between the three loci. Forensic and historical evidence establish that 8 of the 11 men aboard a B-24J Liberator (Tail No. 42-73453) died on, or about, 1 September 1944 when their aircraft broke apart and crashed into the sea off the coast of Babelthaup Island, Republic of Palau. The wreckage dispersed throughout the site is consistent in size, form, and assembly with a US Army Air Forces B-24J Liberator and the geographic location matches that of the loss incident described in MACR 8641, which details the loss of the specific aircraft. Furthermore, serial numbers from five 0.50 calibre machine guns recovered at the site correspond to those on record as having been mounted on the aircraft, and three identification tags recovered bear the names of missing crew members. Coins recovered from the site provide a *terminus post-quem* of 1944.

The identification of human remains was based on multiple lines of evidence. mtDNA sequence data obtained from 53 bone and tooth samples represented five unique sequences; each matched to an individual crew member to the exclusion of all others on board. Dental remains associated with four of these individuals were consistent with their historic dental records. Three identification tags bearing the names of unaccounted for crew members were found in association with human remains. Careful control in the recording of provenience during the excavation process allowed analysts to correlate discrete sets of human remains with assumed crew positions. Finally, several of the human remains recovered could not be attributed to a specific individual with any significant degree of certainty and were thus identified as Group Remains. These remains may represent any, or all, of the eight men on board the aircraft when it crashed into the ocean.

Conclusion

Since the mid-1990s, JPAC-CIL has demonstrated an increasing awareness of the importance of underwater operations in our mission to provide the fullest possible accounting of individuals missing as a result of this nation's previous conflicts. In this vein, the JPAC-CIL is taking several steps to continue growing our capabilities and effectiveness in this sector. One way we are doing this is the development of our Underwater Geographical Information System (UGIS). The primary goal of UGIS is to develop a comprehensive global inventory and data repository for all underwater US military losses from previous conflicts. This single database will allow us to assess, analyse, identify and manage underwater military losses and archaeological site information; determine the environmental feasibility of conducting underwater investigation and recovery activities; prioritise investigation and recovery efforts in order to achieve the best possible accounting results; deliver mission planning and post-mission reports and map products; and preserve historical information and knowledge, including storage and warehousing of underwater investigation survey and recovery data.

Over the years, JPAC has been fortunate to receive mission essential support from a multitude of US Government sources and our future success hinges upon the expansion of inter-agency cooperation. Operationally, JPAC recently began receiving support from the US Naval Oceanographic Office (NAVO) both in terms of hydrographic survey platforms as well as data acquisition and post-processing. Future plans with NAVO include additional missions scheduled through 2016, with plans to extend our cooperation beyond. In terms of intelligence and planning, the Naval History and Heritage Command (NHHC) continues to assist JPAC through data sharing, including site location information, as well as providing archaeological permits for US naval sites under their jurisdiction. A Memorandum of Understanding (MOU) is in the works between JPAC and the National Oceanic and Atmospheric Administration allowing for a freer flow of information (particularly survey data) between our two organisations, as well as the potential for provision of additional platforms and field assets for JPAC investigations and recoveries.

Last, it is critical that we continue to expand our efforts to publicise JPAC, particularly in this case its underwater mission, and engage third-party organisations, foreign national archaeological agencies, and individuals working around the world who may come in contact with submerged sites. This is being accomplished by engaging in the wider archaeological discourse through presentations and publication as well as continuing our outreach and cooperation with local archaeologist and advocacy groups within the areas in which we conduct missions. The efficacy of this was poignantly demonstrated on a recent recovery in Corsica, France, when a group of local WWII enthusiasts and archaeologists handed over a comprehensive investigation of a P-47, including correlating historical documentation for the aircraft and unaccounted-for individuals and a complete photomosaic plan of the site. With the help of our partners, JPAC will continue to have a high rate of success in forensically recovering and identifying unaccounted US service members from underwater sites. This past year, we successfully recovered six individuals from two sites while carrying out investigations at eight others, and another eight missions are currently being planned through 2016.

References

Ariffin, S. I. Z., Wahab, R. M. A., Zamrod, Z. et al. 2007. Molecular archaeology of ancient bone from 400 year old shipwreck. *Asian Pacific Journal of Molecular Biology and Biotechnology* 15(1), 27–31.

Arnaud, G., Arnaud, S., Ascenzi, A., Bonucci, E. and Graziani, G. 1980. On the problem of the preservation of human bone in sea-water. *The International Journal of Nautical Archaeology and Underwater Exploration* 9(1), 53–65.

Blau, S. and Ubelaker, D. H. (eds.) 2009. *Handbook of Forensic Anthropology and Archaeology*. Walnut Creek, Left Coast Press Inc.

Bruseth, J. E. and Turner, T. S. 2005. *From a Watery Grave: The Discovery and Excavation of La Salle's Shipwreck, La Belle*. College Station, A&M University Press.

Clausen, C. J., Brooks, H. K. and Wesolowsky, A. B. 1975. The early man site at Warm Mineral Springs, Florida. *Journal of Field Archaeology* 2(3), 191–213.

Dean, M., Ferrari, B., Oxley, I., Redknap, M. and Watson, K. (eds.) 2000. *Archaeology Underwater: The NAS Guide to Principles and Practice*. Portsmouth, Nautical Archaeology Society.

Dirkmaat, D. C. (ed.) 2012. *A Companion to Forensic Anthropology*. Chichester, Wiley-Blackwell.

During, E. M. 1997. The skeletal remains from the Swedish man-of-war *Vasa*: a survey. *Journal of Comparative Human Biology* 48, 135–160.

Emanovsky, P. D. and Belcher, W. R. 2012. The many hats of a recovery leader: perspectives on planning and executing worldwide forensic investigations and recoveries at the JPAC Central Identification Laboratory. In D. C. Dirkmaat (ed.), *A Companion to Forensic Anthropology*. 567–592. Chichester, Wiley-Blackwell.

Ferrari, B. and Adams, J. 1990. Biogenic modifications of marine sediments and their influence on archaeological material. *The International Journal of Nautical Archaeology and Underwater Exploration* 19(2), 139–151.

Green, J. N. 2004. *Maritime Archaeology: A Technical Handbook*. New York, Academic Press.

Hagelberg, E. and Frame, I. 2005. The genetic affinities of the Mary Rose crew: DNA analysis of the skeletal remains. In J. Gardiner and M. J. Allen (eds.), *Before the Mast: Life and Death Aboard the Mary Rose*, 557–563. The Archaeology of the Mary Rose, Volume 4. Portsmouth, Mary Rose Trust.

Haglund, W. D. and Sorg, M. H. 2002. Human remains in water environments. In W. D. Haglund and M. H. Sorg (eds.), *Advances in Forensic Taphonomy: Method, Theory, and Archaeological Perspectives*, 201–218. Boca Raton, CRC Press.

Holland, T. D., Byrd, J. and Sava, V. 2008. Joint POW/MIA Accounting Command's Central Identification Laboratory. In M. W. Warren, H. A. Walsh-Haney and L. E. Freas (eds.). *The Forensic Anthropology Laboratory*, 47–63. Boca Raton, CRC Press.

Holland, T. D. and Tersigni-Tarrant, M.-T. A. 2013. Joint POW/MIA Accounting Command/Central Identification Laboratory (JPAC/CIL) history. In M.-T. A. Tersigni-Tarrant and N. R. Shirley (eds.), *Forensic Anthropology: An introduction*, 17–23. Boca Raton, CRC Press.

Komar, D. A. and Buikstra, J. E. 2008. *Forensic Anthropology: Contemporary Theory and Practice*. New York, Oxford University Press.

Mays, S. 2008. Human remains in marine archaeology. *Environmental Archaeology* 13(2), 123–133.

Nuorala, E. 1999. Tuberculosis on the 17th century man-of-war Kronan. *International Journal of Osteoarchaeology* 4, 149–163.

Stewart, D. J. 1999. Formation processes affecting submerged archaeological sites: an overview. *Geoarchaeology* 14(6), 565–587.

Stirland, A. 2000. *Raising the Dead: The Skeleton Crew of King Henry VIII's Great Ship the Mary Rose*. Chichester, John Wiley & Sons, Ltd.

Ward, I. A. K., Larcombe, P. and Veth, P. 1999. A new process-based model for wreck site formation. *Journal of Archaeological Science* 26, 561–570.

Wood, R. W. and Stanley, L. A. 1989. Recovery and identification of World War II dead: American graves registration activities in Europe. *Journal of Forensic Sciences* 34(6), 1365–1373.

CHAPTER 52

Forensic archaeology in Peru: between science and human rights activism

José Pablo Baraybar and Franco Mora
Equipo Peruano de Antropologia Forense (EPAF), Lima, Peru

Introduction

Forensic archaeology, understood as a branch of forensic science applying the concepts of archaeology in processing crime scenes of buried or scattered remains, is relatively new, and began to be part of forensic investigations in the United Kingdom in the late 1980s (Hunter and Cox 2005, 2). The application of forensic archaeology to the investigation of human rights violations cases in Latin America began in Argentina in 1984 with the creation of the Argentine Forensic Anthropology Team (EAAF; Doretti and Snow 2003; Fondebrider and Scheinsohn, Chapter 43, this volume); spreading to Chile in the early 1990s with the creation of the Chilean Forensic Anthropology Group (GAF)[1] in 1989 (Cáceres Roque 2011) and Guatemala with the Guatemalan Forensic Anthropology Foundation (FAFG) in 1992 (Ferllini 2007, 15). In Peru, forensic archaeological work began in 1997 with the creation of the so-called Technical Group within the National Coordinator of Human Rights Organisations (*Grupo Técnico de la Coordinadora Nacional de Derechos Humanos*), which later became the Peruvian Forensic Anthropology Team (*Equipo Peruano de Antropología Forense* – EPAF). Most of the members of EPAF came from the ranks of human rights activism and professional training in archaeology and physical anthropology. In 2001, at the request of the Public Ministry (*Ministerio Público*), the newly created Peruvian team conducted the exhumation and examination of the bodies of 14 guerrilla fighters of the Túpac Amaru Revolutionary Movement (*Movimiento Revolucionario Túpac Amaru* – MRTA); a few years earlier, in 1996, the terrorists started a hostage crisis that ended 3 months later when the Armed Forces stormed the Japanese embassy, where they kept 72 people hostage. All 14 terrorists were killed, but allegations were made shortly after that some would have been killed after surrendering.

In 2001, the creation of the Truth and Reconciliation Commission (TRC) (*Comisión de la Verdad y Reconciliación* – CVR), established to investigate the internal armed conflict in Peru between 1980 and 2000 between the so-called Communist Party of Peru's Shining Path (*Partido Comunista del Peru-Sendero Luminoso*), The Túpac Amaru Revolutionary Movement (MRTA) and the State, necessitated the implementation of a methodology allowing the location and eventually the exhumation of hundreds of clandestine burial sites where thousands of missing persons were presumed to be buried.[2]

In January 2002, under a cooperation agreement with the TRC, EPAF exhumed the remains of five peasants abducted and executed by the military at the site of Sillaccasa, province of Ayacucho, in 1983. This was the first scientific exhumation of remains dating to the internal armed conflict in Peru. The methodology used in this intervention was derived from that developed by the International Criminal Tribunal for the Former Yugoslavia (ICTY) during the previous decade.

The concept of *forensic archaeology* as an academic specialty does not exist in Peru and, as elsewhere in Latin America, the recovery of human remains from mass graves is performed primarily by archaeologists with a bioarchaeology or physical anthropology background, based on their investigations of skeletonised human remains from pre-Columbian or historical contexts.

---

[1]The Chilean Forensic Anthropology Group was dissolved in 1994 (Cáceres Roque 2011, 62).
[2]The CVR or TRC (in English) reported in its Final Report (2003) 8555 missing persons and 3500 burial sites. In 2007, EPAF recalculated the number of missing persons with available lists and got a much higher figure: 13,721 (EPAF 2007). In 2011, the Peruvian government acknowledged to the Organization of American States (OAS) the existence of 15,731 missing persons (Ministry of Foreign Affairs 2011). In addition, the existence of 6400 clandestine burial sites has been reported (COMISEDH 2012).

Forensic Archaeology: A Global Perspective, First Edition. Edited by W.J. Mike Groen, Nicholas Márquez-Grant and Robert C. Janaway.

In 2002, EPAF ceased working with the TRC. As a consequence, the TRC formed a temporary ad hoc team with the support and participation of the Argentine Forensic Anthropology Team (EAAF), the Guatemala Forensic Anthropology (FAFG) and a member of what was once the Chilean Forensic Anthropology Group (GAF). This situation allowed in turn the formation of the Andean Centre for Forensic Anthropological Research (*Centro Andino de Investigaciones Antropológico Forenses* – CENIA) by former EPAF members and the Specialised Forensic Team of the Institute of Legal Medicine (*Instituto de Medicina Legal*), a division of the Public Ministry.

Since its creation in 2001, EPAF has participated in 55 cases, 15 of them as expert for the prosecution and the judiciary, and in the remaining 40 cases on behalf of the families of the victims of the internal armed conflict. Over the years, EPAF has recovered 157 bodies, carried out the analysis of 468 bodies, and identified 206, using both DNA and traditional methods.[3] All those cases date back to the Peruvian internal armed conflict (1980–2000) and involve forced disappearances or extra judicial killings.

Forensic archaeology in Peru and the work of EPAF

In our country, forensic archaeology can be practiced in two ways: working for the Public Ministry (Institute of Forensic Medicine) or as an expert for non-governmental organisations representing family members or victims' associations. EPAF is a non-governmental organisation based in Lima, Peru, and focuses in three main areas: forensic expertise, historical memory, and training and human development. EPAF's main work is carried out in Peru but has also expanded to other countries with a stress on forensic and human rights in Africa, South East Asia and elsewhere in the Americas. EPAF comprises 12 staff including four archaeologists/anthropologists, one forensic doctor, one geneticist, one historian, one outreach worker, two project designers and one administrator. State as well as non-state actors regularly contact EPAF in the first instance in delicate or highly controversial cases in which conflicts of interest may be present.

While EPAF primarily works in judicial cases, it understands the need for humanitarian exhumations to enforce the Right to Know of families who wish to bury their relatives with dignity and without prejudice to the right to access justice. However, regardless of the context in which a forensic intervention takes place, EPAF identifies three basic phases.

The first phase of any forensic investigation is what we call the preliminary investigation or assessment. This could be compared to the background search carried out in traditional archaeology prior to intervening in a site. At this stage, information is sought on the facts, either from media reports, victims' testimonies or in de-classified reports from the military. At this stage, we also compile all information pertaining to the victims in order to ascertain whether we are dealing with an open or closed case; ante-mortem information on all potential victims is also collected at this stage. The archaeological survey is usually performed immediately prior to the exhumation, due to the need for a prosecutor (*fiscal*) to be present throughout the process, and to avoid potential tampering with the evidence once the site is identified.

The second phase is the recovery, which consists of the exhumation of the remains and associated objects (clothing, personal items, shell casings, etc.), applying traditional archaeological methods. The procedures and recommendations of best practice were included in the manual on the effective investigation of graves in Peru, *Defensoría del Pueblo y Equipo Peruano de Antropología Forense* (2002), and complement other publications and protocols (i.e. *Manual on the Effective Prevention and Investigation of Extra-Legal, Arbitrary and Summary Executions* (United Nations 1989), e.g. Mendonça and Fondebrider 2001).

The third stage is the analysis of the evidence, in which bioarchaeologists or physical anthropologists will process the recovered remains and associated artefacts in order to define the biological profile of the victims, as well as determine the pathological conditions and injuries that occurred during lifetime; this typically takes place in a State morgue. Traumata that occurred around the time of death are used to establish the most probable cause of death of the victims. A comprehensive report is then submitted to the authority that requested the expertise in the first place. If samples are taken during the process, proper chain of custody forms are also completed and attached to the specimens. When acting as defence experts, EPAF will maintain direct communication with family members, keeping them informed of the findings as appropriate.

In the following text, we present the results of a forensic intervention in the Andean community of Putis, in the Province of Ayacucho, where after 25 years the remains of almost 100 people were recovered from a mass grave.

[3]Out of the total of the identified ($n = 206$), 87 people were identified by comparison ante-mortem/post-mortem, and 119 were identified by DNA.

Putis

Putis is a community located in the district of San José de Santillana, Ayacucho Province, at 3500 m above sea level and 6 hours from Huamanga, the capital of the province.

With the start of the armed struggle by the Shining Path (*Sendero Luminoso*) in 1980 against the Peruvian State, violence quickly spread through the Province of Ayacucho. With the advancement of the Shining Path and the ineffectiveness of the National Police (*Policia Nacional del Perú*) in re-establishing order in the Province, the area was taken over by the Army in December 1982. In November 1983, a military base was installed in the community of Putis.

Upon reaching Putis, the military summoned the inhabitants of the areas around the community who had been displaced by the Shining Path to the upper parts of the valley to return to Putis. The villagers, tired of living in subhuman conditions, decided to heed the call of the military, thinking they would be safe.

Having arrived at Putis with all their belongings, the villagers were received by the military, who assured them they would be provided with a safe environment to resettle and carry on with their lives. After separating the men from the women, the military ordered the men to dig a pond, allegedly to build a fish farm. When the hole was finished, men, women and children in groups of six were shot, killed and thrown inside (CVR 2003, Volume VII, 143–154).

In May 2008, EPAF was commissioned by the Public Ministry to start the intervention in Putis, and 15 archaeologists (EPAF and EPAF associates) were involved in the recovery efforts.

During the survey, a slight depression behind the ruins of the old community church, human remains and clothing were observed on the surface. The evidence was confirmatory of the alleged burial site.

Work began on 17 May 2008, identifying the area to be exhumed and recording all surface evidence (clothing, projectiles, etc.'; see Figure 52.1). Every artefact or human remain was given a unique number and photographed (Figure 52.2).

In the absence of a Total Station to manage the spatial location of the findings, a grid system was used throughout the site.

According to preliminary information, the bodies of 123 victims were buried near to the surface. Since the information could not be corroborated through other sources, the removal of the surface layer was carried out with picks and shovels, and all sediment was sieved in order to retrieve small artefacts such as shell casings.

Unlike traditional archaeology, excavation was carried out removing (disturbed) natural stratigraphic levels rather than arbitrary ones. The stratigraphy was somewhat uniform and predictable, the surface layer then the fill of the grave containing the bodies. The latter are usually found over the natural or sterile layer. Additionally, if dealing with a closed context, that is a finite number of victims killed and buried at one time, it is presumed that all the victims were buried in a single episode and a single level of bodies, though superimposed, would be found. A key step in this process is to define the boundaries of the grave.

Once the first signs of bodies were identified, they were marked with flags to indicate the existence of evidence of forensic interest there. An evidence number was assigned after having partly exposed the remains or associated objects and determined their nature. While the absence of survey equipment required us to use a grid system, the strings often hindered the work during

Figure 52.1 General view of the grave before the exhumation.

Figure 52.2 General view of evidence found on the surface.

Figure 52.3 General view of the bodies found in the grave.

exhumation; to facilitate the work, we removed most of the internal strings of the grid, keeping an X and Y axis for general measurements. Then the exposure of bodies continued, assigning numbers to each and replacing the grid when necessary to locate the bodies in our drawing (Figure 52.3).

Once bodies, body parts or artefacts are given a code, the information is recorded in a case sequence log. Case logs contain information pertaining to the nature of the evidence collected, location within the grave, day of collection, relationship with other pieces of evidence or bodies, photo number and the person responsible.

While every archaeologist in the grave has the responsibility of digging, each has a role in the excavation. The chief archaeologist is responsible for the devising of the exhumation strategy, the collection of the field notes and the submission of evidence for trial. Another person is responsible for all graphic records of the evidence, including photography and drawings. When the number of bodies is great, however, we tend to only photograph and reconstruct the excavation from those images.

Since in a mass grave bodies are not disposed in an orderly manner, their recovery depends rather on a principle of opportunity, that is the ease with which they can be removed while maintaining their integrity. The numbering of the bodies is not therefore correlative.

When the body is ready to be recovered, an exhumation form which includes the code of the body or body part (as applicable) briefly describes the type of burial and its dimensions, the shape of the matrix, the position of the body, as well as their depth, and associated objects is completed. As far as possible, a preliminary estimation of sex and age is also included using general categories such as male, female or indeterminate, adult or subadult. General categories prevent contradictions between field and laboratory reports.

A photograph of the body delimited by rulers is taken in order for it to be distinguished from surrounding bodies (Figure 52.4). The remains are recovered in full and keeping their associations intact, that is clothing and other associated artefacts, such as shells, caps or other items. If bodies are dressed, they are lifted as a single entity, trying to keep the anatomical structure of the chest and arms inside the shirt or upper garments and pelvis and legs as units within the trousers.

When the remains are not clothed, they are lifted carefully, bone by bone, and sided (determining the side, if is left or right) whenever possible. Bones are placed in carefully labelled bags with the case code, case number, bag contents and date (Figure 52.5). Finally, all bags containing remains and associated elements are stored in properly labelled cardboard boxes.

After the last piece of evidence has been lifted, we scrape the bottom of the grave for any elements that may have been overlooked; a metal detector is useful when looking for metal particles such as casings or bullets. The area around the grave should also be carefully examined as victims may have been executed nearby and disposed of in the pit. That is what happened in Putis, where large concentrations of shell casings of the

Figure 52.4 Detailed view: flexed body found inside the grave.

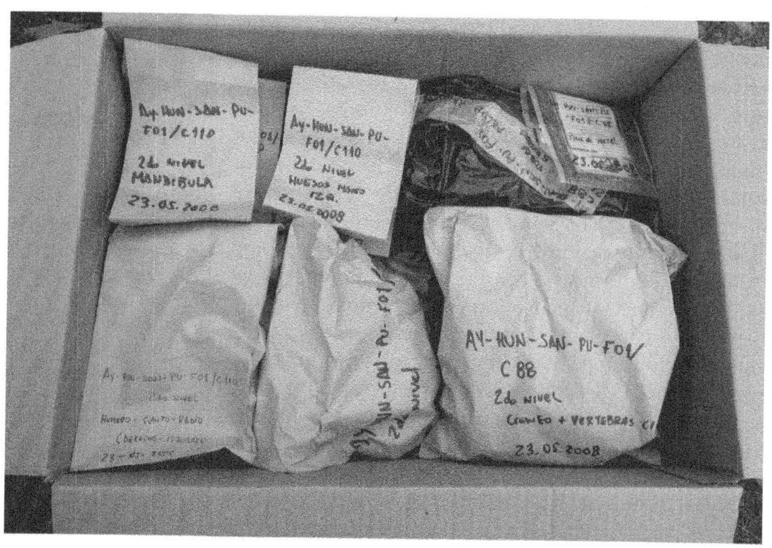

Figure 52.5 Labeled bags in box.

Figure 52.6 General view of the grave. The lines crossing the trench indicate the possible places where the shooters stood.

same calibre (7.62 × 51 mm) were found in an area close to the grave. According to the ejection pattern of the rifle used to fire those rounds (FN FAL), we were able to reconstruct the probable positions of the shootings (Figure 52.6).

Challenges to forensic archaeology in Peru

The problem of the disappeared in Peru is not academic but rather humanitarian and certainly practical. Strangely enough, a country with a 150-year-old archaeological tradition seemed uninterested in applying that knowledge to uncover the recent past, but rather continued investigating our remote past. In fact, the majority of university graduates in archaeology from public or private universities seek employment in archaeological projects or research activities. This in turn generates many complex situations: forensic archaeology considers a series of assumptions that traditional archaeology does not, namely validating or substantiating hypotheses to exclude evidence of specific crimes and victim identity hypothesis, among others. The interaction with the relatives of victims and the need to perform tasks considered outside archaeology are also important in the formation of this discipline. Forensic archaeologists/anthropologists are multifaceted and multifunctional; they investigate documentary and oral sources, interview people, survey and excavate, analyse and identify people. It should be emphasised that this discipline is immersed in the field of human rights activism, and shares the lack of financial and technical resources with traditional archaeology. Our practice could benefit greatly from improved technical resources, such as the use of Total Station, the use of the 3D-scanner, the use of balloons and drones for aerial shots, the use of satellite photographs and the use of geo radar, among many other advancements.

Finally, it is important to note that as a response to the disproportion between the courses in Andean archaeology compared to those in forensics and bearing in mind the need to regulate a practice that grows in the region through activism in human rights and the need to provide answers to the families, the Latin American Forensic Anthropology Association (*Asociación Latinoamericana de Antropología Forense* – ALAF) has created the Latin American Board of Forensic Anthropology (*Directorio Latinoamericano de Antropología Forense* – DLAF) to start the certification of its partners in the region with the intention of promoting best practices and standardising the methodologies and the systems that make up the discipline.

References

Cáceres Roque, I. 2011. Detenidos Desaparecidos en Chile: Arqueología de la Muerte Negada. Unpublished B.A. thesis, Department of Anthropology, University of Chile.

Comisión de Derechos Humanos – COMISEDH. 2012. *Los Muertos de Ayacucho: Violencia y Sitios de Entierro Clandestinos*. Lima, Perú.

Comisión de la Verdad y Reconciliación – CVR. 2003. *Informe Final*. Lima, Peru.

Doretti, M. and Snow, C. C. 2003. Forensic anthropology and human rights: the Argentine experience. In D. W. Steadman (ed.), *Hard Evidence, Case Studies in Forensic Anthropology*, 290–310. Upper Saddle River, Prentice Hall.

Defensoría del Pueblo y Equipo Peruano de Antropología Forense – EPAF. 2002. *Manual Para la Investigación Eficaz ante el Hallazgo de Fosas con Restos Humanos en el Perú*. Lima, Peru.

Equipo Peruano de Antropología Forense – EPAF. 2007. *Proyecto Memoria de los Desaparecidos*. Report submitted to the International Committee of the Red Cross (ICRC). Peru.

Ferllini, R. 2007. Human rights violations, past and present: consequences and interventions. In R. Ferllini (ed.), *Forensic Archaeology and Human Rights Violations*, 3–23. Springfield, Charles C. Thomas.

Hunter, J. and Cox M. (eds.) 2005. *Forensic Archaeology: Advances in Theory and Practice*. London, Routledge.

Mendonça, M. and Fondebrider, L. 2001. *Protocolo Modelo para la Investigación Forense de Muertes Sospechosas de Haberse Producido por Violación de los Derechos Humanos*. Mexico City, Office of the High Commissioner for Human Rights (OHCHR).

Ministry of Foreign Affairs. 2011. *Las Personas Desaparecidas y la Asistencia a sus Familiares*. Lima, Ministry of Foreign Affairs.

United Nations. 1989. *Manual on the Effective Prevention and Investigation of Extra-Legal, Arbitrary and Summary Executions*. New York, United Nations.

CHAPTER 53

Physicians for human rights: the role of forensic archaeology in transitional justice contexts

Stefan Schmitt[1], Amanda Sozer[1,2], Gillian Fowler[1] and Dallas Mazoori[1]

[1] *Physicians for Human Rights International Forensics Program (PHR IFP), Cambridge, USA*

[2] *SNA International, Alexandria, USA*

Introduction

Physicians for Human Rights (PHR) was founded in 1986 as an independent non-governmental organisation, fostering the idea that health professionals, with their specialised skills, ethical duties and credible voices, are uniquely positioned to prevent human rights violations.[1] Since its founding, PHR has mobilised forensic scientists and other experts worldwide to respond to enquiries by governments, organisations, families, and individuals. These experts represent an array of scientific disciplines, including forensic pathology, archaeology, anthropology and genetics, and include scientists in forensic laboratories, such as firearms examiners. These individuals volunteer their time and come from universities, public forensic laboratories and private organisations.

PHR's International Forensic Program (IFP) directed the forensic exhumations and analysis of human remains for the International Criminal Tribunal for the former Yugoslavia (ICTY) and for the International Criminal Tribunal for Rwanda (ICTR) in the late 1990s. Since then, PHR forensic experts have been appointed by the United Nations (UN), international tribunals, human rights courts and national jurisdictions. Our experts have also been active in forensic human identification projects in Cyprus, Guatemala, Colombia and, most recently, in Afghanistan and Libya.

Mass fatalities resulting from conflict and past repressive regimes leave many unanswered questions for families searching for their missing loved ones. Human remains in these contexts are often buried either as a result of the inability to identify and repatriate the remains at the time the bodies were collected, or in an attempt to conceal evidence of atrocities. Forensic archaeological excavations and the identification of human remains therefore has become a critical part of transitional justice processes.

Countries transitioning from conflict and/or state repression have implemented different methods, both judicial and non-judicial, to redress human rights abuses that occurred in their past. These transitional justice measures attempt to address the rights of victims through different means, ranging from prosecutions through special tribunals/courts, to truth-seeking mechanisms such as truth commissions, to reparations and institutional reforms by national governments. The desired goal for any country experiencing such a transition is to reach a stage in the future where no new human rights violations occur and where both the rights of victims and the obligations of the state are addressed. This poses judicial and technical, as well as educational, challenges in establishing the necessary forensic infrastructure in transitional justice contexts.

This chapter identifies the challenges of implementing forensics in a transitional justice setting and provides examples of PHR's International Forensic Program at work. The ideas presented later are based on the authors' personal experiences working on projects in international transitional justice contexts.

Identifying, securing, documenting and recovering evidence of past human rights violations is a critical element in addressing transitional justice needs. In order to accomplish this, forensic archaeology (the application of archaeology in a legal context) serves as a necessary part of any immediate response to addressing mass fatalities resulting from conflict. At the same time, those forensic experts working in such settings must recognise transitional justice as the defining legal context in order to maximise the impact of their work.

[1]For more information see: www.physiciansforhumanrights.org (last accessed March 30th 2014).

Forensic Archaeology: A Global Perspective, First Edition. Edited by W.J. Mike Groen, Nicholas Márquez-Grant and Robert C. Janaway.

The right to the truth

The scientific identification of human remains following periods of conflict and gross human rights violations has increasingly become an expected standard to be implemented in such mass fatality situations. At the individual level, surviving family members want to know what happened and lay their loved ones to rest according to their cultural and/or religious norms. At a societal level, there is also now wide recognition of the importance of understanding the circumstances of past human rights violations in order to prevent their recurrence. The *right to the truth* developed in response to these needs, initially in international humanitarian law. The right of families to know the fate of their missing or dead relatives as a result of international armed conflict is codified in Article 32 of Additional Protocol I of the Geneva Conventions. At customary international law, it also applies to non-international armed conflicts (Henckaerts and Doswald-Beck 2005, 421). International human rights law now recognises the right to the truth about gross human rights violations as 'an inalienable and autonomous right, linked to the duty and obligation of the state to protect and guarantee human rights, to conduct effective investigations and to guarantee effective remedy and reparations' (OHCHR 2006, 2). It is expressly provided for in the preamble and Articles 18 and 24(2) of the International Convention for the Protection of All Persons from Enforced Disappearance. The UN General Assembly Resolution on Basic Principles and Guidelines on the Right to a Remedy and Reparation for Victims of Gross Violations of International Human Rights Law and Serious Violations of International Humanitarian Law also provides for victims' right to the truth about these violations (Article 24, see also Article 22(b)) and includes the search for the disappeared and identification of those killed as means of satisfaction (Article 22(c)).

The right to the truth is central to the development of a society that upholds the sanctity of human rights. For societies in transition from a period of conflict or gross human rights violations, forensic archaeology can make an important contribution to upholding the right to the truth. However, from a technical and scientific perspective, mass fatalities require responses that by their catastrophic nature generally fall outside the existing capacity of a country's forensic infrastructure. This is especially true in countries that are coming out of conflict and are willing to reconcile with their past.

The technical and scientific requirements in human identification operations though are quite uniform in their approach and various guidelines have been published to assist in human identification responses to mass fatality incidents (AABB 2010; Interpol 2009; Morgan et al. 2009; NIJ 2005).

The role of forensic science in transitional justice

Forensic science assists in the determination of truth in legal contexts. In mass fatality incidents, it plays critical roles in determining human identity and in the determination of the cause and manner of death of a person. Forensic science consequently falls into the purview of a larger investigation, defined by a specific legal framework. The methods used in identifying, securing, documenting and collecting evidence have to demonstrate transparency and objectivity.

Scientific enquiry is based on the principle that an adequate theory must be falsifiable, refutable or testable (Popper 1963, 37). Therefore, scientists collect and secure data to allow for the independent verification of results. In a forensic setting, the level of expected scrutiny of data and results is defined by a binding legal framework. This legal framework often provides for adversarial debates as to the legitimacy of the scientific data being presented. This approach to the evaluation of data obliges forensic scientists to demonstrate their competence in a particular field of enquiry and also demonstrate that data collection and analysis (i.e. chain of custody) was conducted in accordance with rules/standards of evidence as defined by applicable courts of law (AAAS 2012). In democratic states, this means that forensic scientists have to submit to clearly defined procedures subject to legal and public scrutiny. This legal framework defines the rights of victims and perpetrators, the obligations of the State, and the consequences that follow the determination of truth. The latter can be criminal prosecutions, repatriation of remains to families, reparation measures and the like.

As a democratic approach to law enforcement is often a new concept to countries transitioning to democracy, it is especially critical that forensic services provide accurate results and that they be both reliable and transparent. Capable academic institutions are critical in providing the pool of scientists necessary for sustainable forensic operations. Countries that are emerging from conflict often lack the necessary academic and forensic expertise, nor is there a legal framework in place which defines the scope of the necessary forensic work to address the crimes of the past.

In the effort to reduce the psychological burden on families, the retrieval of human remains for the purposes of identifications and repatriations is considered a priority (Tidball-Binz 2007, 7). The pressure of families demanding the repatriation of the remains of their loved ones is often coupled with the misconception that DNA analysis is the main factor in achieving expedient human identifications. In transitional justice settings, it is not uncommon that exhumations of remains and DNA sample collections are carried out under this misconception. However, this often tends to marginalise the legal aspects of the identification of human remains, such as chain of custody of evidence, samples and remains, as well as the judicial determination of cause and manner of death. This can result in identification attempts that do not follow standard forensic practices, and the element of truth seeking and accountability in regards to the circumstances leading to the deaths is not addressed (PHR 2013a, 11).

From a forensic archaeological perspective, conditional evidence (Lee et al. 2001, 28), such as ligatures around necks or the extremities, are often the only means to establish cause and/or manner of death. Without forensic evidence collection and documentation, this conditional evidence can be lost in these types of *DNA-centric* exhumations. This leads to less than satisfactory results for all those families who do not receive the remains of their loved ones, or who do not receive answers as to how their loved ones died. The search for truth and justice is hampered, as evidence is either lost or compromised, and above all the expectations of families are not met.

Forensic archaeology is the foundation of a multidisciplinary approach to mass fatality human identification

Archaeologists are typically part of a multidisciplinary forensic team focussing on the collection of buried and/or surface evidence. Their work is governed by rules of evidence that dictate the method in which data and samples are shared for analysis and reporting purposes within an existing legal system. For instance, human remains can sometimes involve soft tissue, and it is important that forensic archaeologists are familiar with these types of conditions and have been exposed to working with forensic pathologists and forensic anthropologists (Dirkmaat et al. 2008, 41). PHR and Human Rights Watch (HRW) conducted an investigation into the use of chemical weapons in Iraq in 1992 where PHR forensic archaeologists contributed crucial evidence by documenting patterns of destruction of households, collecting cartridge cases and recording their distribution on the ground to provide evidence of a firing squad, and collecting physical evidence of the use of chemical weapons described by witness testimony (HRW and PHR 1993, 42).

As forensic laboratory services are necessarily an extension of forensic field investigations, it is necessary for forensic archaeologists to have a clear understanding of procedures and protocols as they relate to forensic laboratory analysis. Archaeology as a discipline in developed countries is found in a wide variety of institutions from local government to commercial enterprises, as nations make every effort to preserve their heritage. This increased professionalisation of the field has eased the transition for traditional archaeology to be used in a forensic context (Hunter and Cox 2005, 1). Standard operating procedures for forensic archaeology are now written into documents such as the UN Minnesota Protocols (United Nations 1991); the Scientific Working Group for Forensic Anthropology, Scene Detecting and Processing, US (SWGANTH 2013); and the British Institute for Archaeologists (IfA) Forensic Archaeology Special Interest Group, UK (IfA 2011; Janaway, Chapter 24, this volume). Skinner and Sterenberg (2005, 231) point out that forensic experts need to be integrated within a criminal investigation, in order to ensure the proper collection and examination of evidence, as well as identifying the remains of victims.

In countries that lack both the necessary expertise and legal framework to process the forensic evidence, securing evidence until the country develops the forensic capability is a prerogative. To do so, the evidence has to be identified, documented and secured in such a way that can be addressed within a controlled process, which allows for the concurrent development of laws and technical and scientific capacity. Forensic archaeology needs to be part of a *first response* to mass fatalities in transitional justice contexts in supporting the development of a legal framework, as well as developing a country's technical capacity to identify, document, secure and collect evidence of a mass fatality. Such *first responders* need to recognise danger in the tendency to sacrifice forensic standards for the sake of expediency. Forensic archaeologists will need to become involved with managing family expectations about the expediency of human identification processes from the point of securing evidence as a first step in being able to maximise the success of any human identification effort.

Forensic archaeology: defining the scope of the mass fatality human identification effort

Both from legal, technical and scientific perspectives, it is necessary to devise means by which the scope of the mass fatality may be defined and determined. A relatively accurate assessment of the scope of the identification effort is needed on various levels: from planning and resource allocation purposes, to the numbers of missing persons used in the statistical analysis of the DNA kinship analysis reports.

In most transitional justice settings, the number of disappeared and/or dead is not only unknown, but might also be of political relevance, and is a difficult number to obtain in most mass fatality settings of this type. In Libya, the first estimates on the number of disappeared and/or dead during the armed revolution in 2011 were most likely inflated, ranging from 20,000 to 50,000 missing persons. In December of 2011, the Libyan National Transitional Council created the Ministry for the Affairs of Families of Martyrs and

Missing (MAFMM) to lead the identification of the missing (Alemam, Chapter 36, this volume). The Ministry created a Technical Department that was tasked with exhuming human remains, collecting DNA reference and family samples and establishing a DNA laboratory. Estimates of the number of missing conducted by this Technical Department in 2013 were based on the number of DNA samples that had been collected by families reporting missing loved ones. This DNA-centric approach to estimating the number of missing in 2013 reported about 2100 persons for whom family members had come forward to donate DNA reference samples. This number, though, most likely underestimated the total number of missing.

The political affiliation of the MAFMM with the concept of *Martyrs* (those who died fighting Colonel Qadhafi's regime (1969–2011)) led to some families, who lost loved ones fighting on the side of the Qadhafi regime, not donating samples because they were afraid of the repercussions (PHR 2013a, 37). Furthermore, no provisions had been made for the collection of DNA reference samples of family members of foreign nationals who had died during the conflict, some of whom were alleged to have been mercenaries in the service of Qadhafi. There were reasonable grounds to believe that sampling bias was taking place and affecting the efficiency with which human identifications could be generated. Consequently, PHR recommended in its Libyan Human Identification Needs Assessment and Gap Analysis Report that an independent body such as a Commission be formed to lead the human identification effort (PHR 2013a, 27).

In Afghanistan, on the other hand, there are no estimates on the number of dead, disappeared and missing. Politically, many of those in power in the country are alleged to have perpetrated crimes in the past, and some have been implicated in ongoing abuses. The 2008 *National Reconciliation, General Amnesty and National Stability Law* purportedly granted blanket immunity to those involved in the perpetration of crimes during the country's conflict. This is not consistent with Afghanistan's obligations under international law to prosecute (or extradite) alleged perpetrators of serious international crimes. The resolution was amended based on the Sharia principle that only victims can forgive, and that this right cannot be exercised by the state. The law places the unrealistic burden of pursuing justice upon the victims in an environment in which there are no provisions for victims to approach the judiciary safely and demand that there be investigations for these past crimes (PHR 2013b, 13).

Another characteristic highlighting the need for surveying of physical evidence, that is mass graves, is that in countries such as Afghanistan, 'bearing witness' is linked closely to oral tradition and customary practices of conflict resolution. Culturally, individuals 'bear witness' as a social responsibility towards the community they identify with. Accounts are often related via representatives, such as community elders. Relating defining events, such as massacres, then take on the function of representing communal consensus. The influence of external factors, such as whether it is politically and/or socially 'safe' to relate such accounts, becomes a factor in how a community's history is defined.

It is therefore not surprising that in Afghanistan individuals often relate witness testimony from a first person perspective, although they are in actuality hearsay accounts. Questioning such accounts for the purposes of objective verification can be considered culturally offensive, as it is perceived that doing so places in doubt the 'truth' as related in testimonies by representatives of a particular social group. This culture of 'truth telling by proxy' also has the potential to marginalise the victims in the process.

This type of hearsay testimony is of little judicial value and cannot be compared to societies where verifiability is at the core of how individual rights and responsibilities are defined within the law. This is not surprising, given that in Afghanistan most people have not had access to a reliable and stable judicial system and tend to rely on ethical codes that are transmitted via oral tradition within communities.

Mass graves though are recognised as a physical reality. In Afghanistan, these are often identified by symbolic means, such as posts with coloured flags conveying religious and cultural values. These sites are distinguished in a community primarily as a result of the oral accounts of the events leading to the mass grave. These sites are where physical reality meets oral tradition. Forensic archaeological survey methods are the first means by which both judicial and scientific concepts of verifiability can be introduced into a community's discourse on truth seeking, repatriation of remains, restitution and accountability. It is also a first step in beginning a transitional justice process by confronting current judicial authorities with demands to secure, protect and investigate mass graves and thus begin addressing victims' demands for justice. In a context where there is little or no trust in a judicial system, this may also assist in establishing a dialogue and building trust over time. From a technical perspective, forensic archaeological surveys and assessments are necessary prior to any excavations and exhumations of human remains (Schmitt 2002, 280).

Building capacity in Afghanistan

In Afghanistan, the rule of law faces serious challenges. Certain areas are inaccessible due to ongoing conflict. Further, the country lacks the legal, technical and scientific infrastructure for a full forensic response, such as exhumations, evidence storage, post-mortem examinations, DNA analysis and other forensic methods.

As an initial step towards addressing these challenges, PHR's International Forensic Program developed and implemented a three-and-one-half-year project Securing Afghanistan's Past: A Forensic Program to Enhance Transitional Justice and Promote Dialogue, between 2009 and 2013. The project was funded by the US Department of State, Bureau of Democracy, Human Rights and Labour and included training in crime scene documentation, forensic anthropology and archaeology, two conferences on truth seeking and the role of forensic science in Kabul, and a human identification needs assessment and gap analysis report – *Securing Afghanistan's Past – Human Identification Needs Assessment and Gap Analysis* (PHR 2013b).

In 2010, 18 Afghans from the Afghan National Police, the Afghanistan Independent Human Rights Commission (AIHRC), Forensic Medicine Department, archaeologists from the Ministry of Culture and Information and other civil society groups participated in a 5-week training course in basic crime scene documentation and human osteology. The students also participated in the exhumation of a set of human remains in a single grave that had been located in the Ministry of the Interior compound. At the conclusion of the course, all students were able to photograph and sketch crime scenes, use professional camera equipment, operate a Global Positioning Device (GPS), distinguish human skeletal remains from animal bones and to identify and name individual human bones.

In 2011, the students who had participated in PHR's course founded the Afghanistan Forensic Science Organisation (AFSO) with the stated objective to document and secure the country's mass grave sites. In 2012, members of AFSO documented 13 mass grave sites through photography, sketching, GPS surveying and forensic reports. These reports were issued to local and judicial authorities, civil society and victim organisations. They included information on the background of the incident that led to the mass grave and forensic/physical anthropological and archaeological findings, along with recommendations on how the grave site should be protected and secured. This is particularly important when there are no evidence storage and management solutions (i.e. chain of custody and storage facilities for human remains) for surface depositions. In some instances, documentation through photography and sketching, and the subsequent reburial of scattered human remains and associated evidence, such as clothing at the site, are the only means of securing this type of evidence for future analysis.

Concurrent with these surveys, AFSO conducted awareness raising workshops in the communities where mass graves were surveyed and documented. Participants were members of law enforcement, judicial, religious and community representatives (e.g. elders), and representatives of victim and civil society organisations. Workshops covered the importance of forensic documentation of mass graves and the responsibilities of police and local authorities in securing them. Discussions included legal and religious aspects of mass graves. AFSO also developed and distributed a number of brochures and presentations on the role of forensic science in truth seeking.

As argued earlier, forensic archaeological surveys of physical locations and evidence necessarily need to form part of any effort aimed at estimating the scope of a human identification effort. A first step in a country's decade-long process of reconciling with its violent past needs to include a controlled survey of mass grave sites to assess the scope of the mass fatality problem scientifically. This also needs to be done to prepare for subsequent technological, scientific and legal measures. Relying mainly on DNA sample collection efforts, or reporting of missing persons by those who are willing to come forward, does not suffice.

From a developmental perspective, the introduction of forensic survey, documentation, and evidence and sample collection methods also prepares the ground for more complex technologies, such as DNA sample collection and analysis, and forensic laboratory services. Forensic archaeology, both from a scientific and legal perspective, is well positioned to do this.

The importance of forensic human identification: human identity

Another important aspect in developing a country's capacity to identify and repatriate human remains resulting from past conflicts and/or repressive regimes is the legal framework and administrative implementation through which a country defines a citizen's identity. This is defined as *civil identity* in PHR's Human Identification Needs Assessment Reports for Libya and Afghanistan (PHR 2013a, 9):

> *Civil identity is generally the responsibility of a state (i.e., the state issues a birth certificate, which in turn grants the individual a name linked to rights and responsibilities within society and the state). In much the same way, the certification of death is a state's responsibility, as the death of an individual has a legal impact on living family members, such as a woman's marital status, custody of children, inheritance, etc. A 'death certificate' also generally includes the determination of cause and manner of death (natural, accidental, homicide, suicide), which can have further legal implications, such as the launching of a criminal investigation. Both birth and death certifications therefore are part of a state's manner to exert the norms and regulations of the society it represents on the individual. This is the context in which a human identification effort has to be understood.*

The process of generating one's civil identity is performed through forensic human identification. For forensic purposes, an identity in such a case can be based on various factors, ranging from documentary evidence (adoption papers), to fingerprints, to DNA (affiliation with biological parents). In some cases, a subjective identification based on recognition of the remains in a controlled environment by witnesses and circumstantial evidence (i.e., someone died in his bed surrounded by family members) is confirmed judicially by a forensic expert, usually the medical examiner. The exact method of forensic human identification depends on the circumstances surrounding the death and the available evidence.

Shortly after the fall of the Colonel Qadhafi's regime in 2011, exhumations were conducted without the necessary expertise in an effort to repatriate human remains as an immediate response to family requests. The inexpert and often extra judicial handling of remains and collection of DNA samples at the time, both from the remains and from family members, led to misidentifications in some cases, where remains were repatriated simply on the basis of family pressure. DNA reference samples had also been collected from remains that were not repatriated and subsequently reburied in marked plots without implementing proper chain of custody measures. This absence of implementing a failsafe chain of custody on the remains led to later questions about the reliability of the information on the provenance of the samples collected from these reburied human remains.

With the formation of the MAFMM in December of 2011, who then took on the task of a human identification effort, exhumations continued despite the fact that there was no capacity in the country to properly identify, collect, document and store evidence – whether for truth-seeking or for human identification purposes. PHR International Forensic Program (IFP) Director (the first author) in February 2012 made a series of recommendations to the Libyan government, one of which was to suspend exhumations and secure mass graves until forensic resources and capacities were available in Libya (PHR 2013a, 8). The Libyan Forensic Medicine Department also stated its concerns about inexpert exhumations and sample collections and at the time withdrew from the MAFMM's human identification operations (PHR 2013a, 8).

Due to a lack of resources, the MAFMM then contracted out post-mortem examinations of the remains that they exhumed to Forensic Medical Specialists from Sudan. These examinations though did not follow international standards for medico-legal examinations and took place outside the routine practice of standard forensic examinations conducted by Libya's Forensic Medicine Department (PHR 2013a, 34). International support for a human identification operation poured into Libya, each offering to provide DNA laboratory services and help establish a DNA laboratory at the MAFMM (PHR 2013a, 10).

This particular situation, where external DNA laboratories or human identification operations offered their support, created internal political pressures that were based on the expectation that outsourcing DNA analysis would expedite human identifications. The Ministry in effect was becoming the source of all Libyan and international attention, with the result that existing national forensic and scientific infrastructure was being neglected as Libyan forensic scientists and academics were either unable or unwilling to participate in the Ministry's human identification effort.

From a human identification perspective, short-term goals of expediting some human identifications were prioritised, without allowing for a more deliberate, independent, all-inclusive and credible process. Exhumations continued in 2013 under the auspices of the Ministry, even though the problems regarding chain of custody and evidence collection for accountability purposes had yet to be addressed. The input of forensic experts is critical in highlighting the consequences of such misguided expediency. Under these circumstances, forensic archaeologists might find themselves in situations where it is more prudent to concentrate their efforts on preventing excavations from taking place.

Forensics and international law

Inherent to any transitional justice context is the realisation that the country has reached a point where it has identified 'its past' and endeavours to embark on a process leading to a better future. Because human identification efforts in this context could take decades, plans should be made for the critical question as to when, and under which circumstances, the work may be concluded. Typically, the discussions on an 'exit strategy' should incorporate mechanisms under which any unresolved cases are transitioned to routine law enforcement and judicial operations (PHR 2013a, 11).

In Libya, the political landscape soon after the fall of Qadhafi was defined in some ways by the victims who had suffered under the previous regime and were politically motivated to construct a new future. Unlike Libya, in Afghanistan the political landscape is dominated by many alleged perpetrators of human rights violations, past and present. In both countries, PHR recommended acceding to and implementing within national law, the International Convention for the Protection of All Persons from Enforced Disappearance. The Convention provides the framework upon which the scope of a missing persons problem and its integration into national forensic infrastructure can be defined.

Forensic experts responding to mass fatalities in transitional justice settings need to recognise the importance of their contribution in the implementation of such international legal instruments. Implementing the Convention on a national level requires the domestic criminalisation of enforced disappearance and the enactment of legal provisions covering their investigation, the obligations of the state and the rights of victims to repatriation of remains, reparations, truth seeking and accountability. Forensic science, and especially forensic archaeology, can initially provide the scientific means to establish the scope of a mass fatality in conflict situations on a physical scale, contributing to discussions regarding the allocation of resources and the design of these laws themselves.

Aside from establishing reported missing persons registry efforts – which aren't covered in this chapter – there is an immediate need to archaeologically survey and assess sites at which human remains have been buried. This allows for the adequate planning and management of a comprehensive forensic human identification effort, while simultaneously initiating a process through which evidence regarding such sites is placed on the record and where these initial surveys can be submitted as official reports into a nation's judicial system. This becomes particularly important in countries such as Afghanistan, where there is neither political will nor adequate infrastructure to implement a truth-seeking or human identification effort. Establishing a scientific record through factual investigation is a first step towards acknowledging the truth.

Conclusions

Forensic archaeologists responding to mass fatality human identification operations in transitional justice settings are often faced with the lack of appropriate legal frameworks within which they can work. Meaningful responses to mass fatalities resulting from past conflicts require specialised laws, and it is critical that forensic experts be part of the development of such legal frameworks. Rather than simply providing support in excavating evidence and exhuming remains, a forensic archaeologist might be faced with the task of raising awareness on the limitation of science in order to ensure that appropriate steps are taken in securing evidence.

Within transitional justice contexts, ownership of human identifications – and truth seeking – needs to be integrated from the beginning within a country's legal and forensic system. Forensic archaeologists need to engage in raising awareness regarding the limitations and strengths of forensic evidence management with a focus on building national forensic capacity.

Forensic archaeology has a critical role to play in responding to mass fatality operations in transitional justice settings. It provides the means with which to begin assessing the scope of a human identification and truth seeking efforts, as well as the necessary tools for addressing the identification, documentation and collection of evidence within a legal framework.

References

American Association for the Advancement of Science (AAAS). 2012. *Human Rights Projects: Guidelines for Scientists and Human Rights Organizations.* Contributors: Sozer, A., Schmitt, S., Wyndham, J. et al. Science and Human Rights Coalition, AAAS. Available at: http://www.aaas.org/sites/default/files/reports/Scientists_Human_Rights_Orgs.pdf (last accessed July 2013).

American Association of Blood Banks (AABB). 2010. *Guidelines for Mass Fatality DNA Identification Operations.* Contributors: Sozer, A., Baird, M., Beckwith, M. et al. Maryland, Bethesda. Available at: http://www.aabb.org/programs/disasterresponse/Documents/aabbdnamassfatalityguidelines.pdf (last accessed July 2013).

Basic Principles and Guidelines on the Right to a Remedy and Reparation for Victims of Gross Violations of International Human Rights Law and Serious Violations of International Humanitarian Law, UN Doc A/RES/60/147 (adopted 16 December 2005).

Dirkmaat, D. C., Cabo, L. L., Ousley, S. D. and Symes, S. A. 2008. New perspectives in forensic anthropology. *American Journal of Physical Anthropology* 137, 33–52.

Henckaerts, J. M. and Doswald-Beck, L. 2005. *Customary International Humanitarian Law. Volume 1: Rules.* Cambridge, Cambridge University Press. Available at: http://www.icrc.org/eng/assets/files/other/customary-international-humanitarian-law-i-icrc-eng.pdf (last accessed July 2013).

Hunter, J. and Cox, M. (eds.) 2005. *Forensic Archaeology: Advances in Theory and Practice.* London, Routledge.

Institute for Archaeologists (IfA). 2011. *Standards and Guidance for Forensic Archaeologists.* Available at: www.archaeologists.net (last accessed July 2013).

International Convention for the Protection of All Persons from Enforced Disappearance, opened for signature February 6th 2007, UN Doc A/61/177 (entered into force 23rd December 2010).

Interpol. 2009. *Interpol Handbook on DNA Data Exchange and Practice.* Recommendations from the Interpol DNA Monitoring Expert Group. 2nd edition. Lyon, ICPO-Interpol.

Lee, H. C., Palmbach, T. and Miller, M. T. 2001. *Henry Lee's Crime Scene Handbook.* San Diego/London, Elsevier/Academic Press.

Middle East Watch and Physicians for Human Rights. 1993. *Iraqi Kurdistan: The Destruction of Koreme During the Anfal Campaign.* HRW/PHR.

Morgan, O., Tidball-Binz, M., and Van Alpen, D. 2009. *Management of Dead Bodies after Disasters: A Field Manual for First Responders.* 2nd edition. Washington, DC, Pan American Health Organization.

National Institute of Justice. 2005. *Mass Fatality Incidents: A Guide for Human Forensic Identification.* Washington, DC, US Department of Justice, Office of Justice Programs.

OHCHR. *Promotion and Protection of Human Rights: Study on the Right to the Truth.* UN Doc E/CN.4/2006/91 (8 February 2006).

Physicians for Human Rights (PHR). 2013a. *Libyan Human Identification Needs Assessment and Gap Analysis.* Contributors: Schmitt, S., Sozer, A., Haglund, W., Peerwani, N., Varney, H., and Lamburne, R. Cambridge, MA. Available at: https://s3.amazonaws.com/PHR_Reports/Libya-human-remains-id-assessmt-report-Mar-2013a.pdf (last accessed July 2013).

Physicians for Human Rights (PHR). 2013b. *Securing Afghanistan's Past- Human Identification Needs Assessment and Gap Analysis.* Contributors: Schmitt, S., Sozer, A., and Mazoori, D. Cambridge, MA. Available at: https://s3.amazonaws.com/PHR_Reports/afghan-human-id-needs-assessment-April2013.pdf (last accessed July 2013).

Popper, K. R. 1963. *Conjectures and Refutations: The Growth of Scientific Knowledge.* London, Routledge and Kegan Paul.

Protocol Additional to the Geneva Conventions of 12 August 1949, and relating to the Protection of Victims of International Armed Conflicts, opened for signature June 8th 1977, 1125 UNTS 3 (entered into force 7 December 1978).

Schmitt, S. 2002. Mass graves and the collection of forensic evidence: genocide, war crimes, and crimes against humanity. In W. D. Haglund and M. H. Sorg (eds.), *Advances in Forensic Taphonomy: Method, Theory, and Archaeological Perspectives,* 277–292. Boca Raton, CRC Press.

Scientific Working Group for Forensic Anthropology (SWGANTH). 2013. *Scene Detection and Processing*. Available at: www.swganth.org (last accessed July 2013).

Skinner, M. and Sterenberg, J. 2005. Turf wars: authority and responsibility for the investigation of mass graves. *Forensic Science International* 151, 221–232.

Tidball-Binz, M. 2007. Managing the dead in catastrophes: guiding principles and practical recommendations for first responders. *International Review of the Red Cross.* 89(866), 421–442.

United Nations Manual on the Effective Prevention and Investigation of Extra-Legal, Arbitrary and Summary Executions, UN Doc E/ST/CSDHA/.12 (1991).

CHAPTER 54

Recovering memories of the Portuguese Colonial War through forensic anthropology

Eugénia Cunha[1], Maria Teresa Ferreira[2], Sónia Codinha[2], Gonçalo Carnim[3], Carina Marques[4] and Cláudia Umbelino[4]

[1] *Departamento de Ciências da Vida (Antropologia), Universidade de Coimbra, Coimbra, Portugal*

[2] *Forensic Sciences Centre (CENCIFOR), Department of Life Sciences, University of Coimbra, Coimbra, Portugal*

[3] *Delegação do Centro, Instituto Nacional de Medicina Legal e Ciências Forenses IP, Coimbra, Portugal*

[4] *Centro de Investigação em Antropologia e Saúde, Department of Life Sciences, University of Coimbra, Coimbra, Portugal*

Introduction

One of the projects promoted by the Portuguese League of Combatants (*Liga dos Combatentes*), a subsection of the Portuguese Ministry of Defence, is called *Conservação das Memórias* (Memories Preservation) which aims to retrieve the greatest possible number of Portuguese soldiers who died during the Portuguese Colonial War in the 1960s and 1970s in Africa, namely in Guinea-Bissau, Angola and Mozambique. The purpose is to dignify the memory of the Portuguese soldiers deceased in battle whose remains have been buried not only in cemeteries but also in clandestine graves at the former battle fields.

For that reason, a protocol between the League of Combatants (Ministry of Defence, Lisbon), the Department of Life Sciences of the University of Coimbra (*Universidade de Coimbra*) and the National Institute of Legal Medicine and Forensic Sciences (*Instituto Nacional de Medicina Legal e Ciências Forenses I.P.* – INMLCF, I.P.), based in Coimbra, was established. Between March 2008 and February 2010, five forensic anthropological missions were accomplished, all of them to Guinea-Bissau, with a total of 50 bodies recovered. In two missions, it was necessary to perform a geophysical prospection to locate the clandestine graves at a former battle field. The remaining three missions were carried out at regular cemeteries.

The available ante-mortem data on the Portuguese soldiers was quite scarce for some individuals, while for other individuals data on stature, age at death, cause of death and photographs were available. None of the soldiers had odontograms available. Overall, the state of preservation of the human remains was highly variable. While some individuals were quite complete and well preserved, others were represented by a scarce amount of bones. The cause of death and the extrinsic taphonomic factors such as the effects of temperature, soil type, water and plant roots played a major role in the deterioration of the human remains. However, some individuals still preserved their clothing and other personal belongings, which contributed to their circumstantial identification. These items helped, for example, to distinguish between the Portuguese of European and African ancestry. The positive identifications that were obtained until now were mainly based on anthropological features. With regard to genetic identification, some genetic profiles have been obtained from the remains and are awaiting comparison with the DNA profile from the relatives of the victims.

Forty-four skeletons recovered are now deposited in a chapel at the Bissau main cemetery. The remaining six bodies were brought to Portugal and returned to their families, who have waited almost 40 years for them, at the Portuguese Union of Paratroopers' expense (*União Portuguesa de Paraquedistas*), since the deceased were paratroopers.

The different procedures applied in the course of the field work, namely for the location, recovery and excavation of the burial sites, as well as the methodologies used during the anthropological expertise on the five missions, are described and discussed later.

Forensic anthropology in Portugal

Since the missions that will be described here involved expertise in forensic anthropology, it is paramount to contextualise it within forensic sciences in Portugal. In this country forensic medical services are provided by a single National Institute of Legal Medicine and Forensic

Forensic Archaeology: A Global Perspective, First Edition. Edited by W.J. Mike Groen, Nicholas Márquez-Grant and Robert C. Janaway.

Sciences, an autonomous administrative entity dependent on the Ministry of Justice. It is based in Coimbra and has three branches (Oporto, Coimbra and Lisbon) and a network of 31 forensic medical offices scattered throughout the country (Vieira 2008). It is mandatory that all human remains found in a suspected forensic context are sent to the INMLCF, I.P. This is done mainly by the police or by the courts who ask for post-mortem forensic examination to answer several questions such as who, how and when. This implies that the forensic experts, including forensic anthropologists, will work in collaboration with the police (*Polícia Judiciaria* in particular). From excavation to the comparative phase of identification (confrontation of ante- and post-mortem data), the complicity is important. The expert gives key clues to be followed by the police.

The INMLCF, I.P. structure includes four technical departments in each of the above-mentioned branches, one of them being the Forensic Pathology service where forensic anthropology is located. Currently, the INMLCF, I.P. has two forensic anthropologists: one in Lisbon (the first author), who, although employed in the academic realm, has also been national consultant for this institution since 1997 and, much more recently, the fourth author (GC) who is a technician in the Central Branch (Coimbra). Other forensic anthropologists exist (e.g. the second and third authors) mainly as a consequence of the masters, postgraduate and PhD courses on forensic anthropology existing nowadays in the country. Although they do not work on forensic cases on a regular basis, they participate sporadically in cases at the INMLCF, I.P., and they perform important research in the domain (within post-doc grants). Basically, the background of the Portuguese forensic anthropologists is physical anthropology (Cunha and Pinheiro 2007; Kranioti and Paine 2011). In a way, it is like the American practitioners who mainly derived from physical anthropology as well, but they do work on a regular basis with forensic pathologists (Cunha and Pinheiro 2007). Therefore, in the country, there are physical anthropologists who deal with skeletal remains from past populations and forensic anthropologists who deal with forensic skeletons, bodies in several states of preservations, cremains, performing identification and assessing traumatic injuries to assist the forensic pathologists in cause and manner of death. Furthermore, they do prospection, excavation, time since death evaluation, taphonomic criticism as to the manner of death and also identification of the living. The *modus pensandi*, the expertise and even some specific background differs between physical and forensic anthropology (Cunha and Cattaneo 2006). Goals and tasks are not the same. Recent developments of this latter discipline lead to some authors (Dirkmaat 2012; Dirkmaat et al. 2008) stating that forensic anthropology is not a sub-discipline of physical anthropology but a sister discipline. Unlike physical anthropology, forensic anthropology cases can end in a courtroom. Therefore, concepts such as chain of custody are paramount, and every step we take cannot be undertaken only with osteological analysis, or even be undertaken by someone with years of experience with bones from archaeological contexts.

In addition, it should be borne in mind that in Portugal an archaeologist has no experience with human bones during graduation. Even after graduation, those skills can only be acquired by some archaeologists on masters and postgraduate courses in skeletal biology and/or forensic anthropology. Furthermore, since 1999, there is a law in Portugal, which requires the presence of a physical anthropologist whenever skeletal remains are retrieved in archaeological contexts (Umbelino and Santos 2011). Therefore, in our country there are no forensic archaeologists. We have some archaeologists with competences with human remains acquired after graduation, but without any type of experience or academic education on the forensic domain. Ultimately, it is the forensic anthropologist who is called to assist with mass disasters and crimes against humanity. That was what happened with the forensic expertise described in this chapter. The military got in touch directly with the first author, at the INMLCF, I.P. to form a team. By then, she had been working there for 10 years and her forensic anthropology work was recognised. The selection of the team relied on the scientific and academic background of the discipline and their experience with human remains excavation, a common element to all the team (with the exception of the geophysicist).

The project of the League of Combatants

By 2006, the League of Combatants (*Liga dos Combatentes*) engaged in the creation of a project for the recovery of the bodies of the Portuguese soldiers deceased during the so-called Overseas, or Colonial, War (*Guerra do Ultramar* or *Guerra Colonial Portuguesa*), that took place in Africa between 1961 and 1974. The Portuguese Colonial War was fought between the Portuguese army and the emerging nationalist movements in the Portuguese colonies, namely Angola, Guinea-Bissau and Mozambique. It is estimated that a total of 8831 Portuguese soldiers died (Brandão 2008), with about 2500 of them still unaccounted for; that is, their bodies are buried in unknown parts of the above-mentioned countries, at the site of the battlefield or in ancient or abandoned cemeteries.

The Portuguese military forces have a motto that nobody is left behind; it is also the duty of any country to bring back the bodies of its combatants. Thus, the missing bodies of the Colonial War soldiers need to be both retrieved and identified. Taking into account the

Figure 54.1 Cemetery of Farim before the excavation: the state of disrepair can be observed.

large amount of unaccounted deaths, the League of Combatants has decided to initiate the Memories Preservation project (*Conservação das Memórias*), aiming to recover the soldiers' bodies and to centralise their remains in appropriate and known cemeteries (Figure 54.1), such as the Bissau main cemetery. If the families reclaim the bodies of their relatives, then these bodies could be repatriated to Portugal.

This project started in Guinea-Bissau, a country in West Africa bordered by Senegal to the north, Guinea-Conakry to the south and east, and by the Atlantic Ocean to the west. It covers 36,125 km^2 and has an estimated population of 1,600,000 inhabitants. Nowadays, it is one of the poorest countries in the world. The period of the Colonial War in Guinea-Bissau extended from the beginning of the 1960s until their independence, recognised by Portugal in 1974.

The missions

The organisation of the missions developed in Guinea-Bissau followed a strict strategy. There were two distinct teams that interacted in order to fulfil the missions' aims. One team was called the Mission Team (*Equipa de Missão*), directed by a General (on reserve) from the Portuguese army and members of the League of Combatants. The Mission Team was responsible for all the planning, which was quite detailed and strict, as well as for the legal and logistics aspects of the missions. The Mission Team did exhaustive reconnaissance work in order to evaluate which sites should be chosen for the anthropological intervention. First they did careful documentary research concerning the Guinea-Bissau war. They then went to Guinea-Bissau to evaluate the potential sites, namely to see the type of site (an open field or an ancient cemetery) and to obtain the local permissions needed to create the appropriate conditions that allowed the second team (Technical Team),which was responsible for the detection and retrieval of the human remains, to work.

This second team, or the Technical Team (*Equipa Técnica*), was coordinated by the first author (EC). The previous work undertaken by the Mission Team, which proved to be essential for the success of the missions, took some time, and the necessary conditions to start the technical work were only established in 2008. In total, five missions were sent to Guinea-Bissau between 2008 and 2010. These missions covered different parts of Guinea-Bissau, namely Guidage (mission 1), Farim (mission 2), Gabu (mission 3), the South of Guinea (mission 4) and Cheche (mission 5).

The purpose of this chapter is to describe the work performed by the Technical Team, and how the team members were able to retrieve a total of 50 bodies by means of field anthropology methods.

Operation procedures

The five missions were quite different from each other since the sites and contexts were different. The Technical Team comprised several experienced physical and forensic anthropologists with academic background in both the excavation and identification of human remains. The number of team members varied in each mission as dictated by the type of intervention and financial constraints. For example, the mission to the

South of Guinea employed only three experts (all anthropologists), while the mission to Guidaje employed six experts (four anthropologists, one archaeologist and one geophysicist who was included whenever prospection and survey was needed).

During the first mission an archaeologist was included in the team (Dr Conceição Vitoriano) not only because of her skills but also as she was a relative of one of the dead soldiers. One geological engineer, who was responsible for the geophysical survey, participated in two of the missions (Eng Hélder Hermosilha) where a survey was needed, as well as Dr Maria Luís Carvalho, another physical anthropologist who was asked to join the team in one mission involving many skeletons.

We will discuss each mission separately later. Yet, besides the field work, the Technical Team was also involved in the recovery of ante-mortem data (Figure 54.2). We will discuss each of these phases, highlighting the methodologies used for each.

Phase 1: obtaining/retrieving ante-mortem data

This phase was accomplished by two teams, mainly in Portugal. After being informed by the Mission Team who the probable victims buried in a specific place were, a registration or case file was created for each the soldiers. This basically followed Interpol Guidelines, in an attempt to assemble the maximum amount of ante-mortem data possible. Besides the generic factors of identity, namely sex, date of birth, ancestry, stature and health, we also tried to gather data on dentition, medical files, ante-mortem fractures and earlier diseases. We also asked for photographs of the victims, preferably smiling, in order to access anterior dentition features. Gathering this data was not an easy task, mainly because of the time that had elapsed. While during the 1960s and 1970s, the military were undertaking medical examinations before going to war, the archives were not complete: whereas for some individuals we had data on body measurements and weight, for other individuals it was impossible to find these records. Odontograms were not included in the military medical record because they were not performed during the medical examinations undertaken by the soldiers. Besides searching the military archives, contact with the relatives was also attempted in order to ask for details that could help identify their deceased relatives, such as photographs.

A field data sheet was created based on Interpol Guidelines and reflecting these specific contexts.

Phase 2: field work

Field work could be divided in sub-phases depending on the type of sites and contexts, namely in open fields (missions 1 and 5) or ancient cemeteries (missions 2, 3 and 4).

When the remains were reported to be in an open field, a geophysical survey was needed. This was the case for missions 1 and 5, the geological engineer going to Guinea-Bissau before the rest of the Technical Team in order to have the site ready for excavation. Ground-penetrating radar (GPR) was used during the geophysical prospection. A local grid was used, taking into account the available area, and was created *in situ* using lines separated from one another by 0.5 m. Profiles were made with GPR antennas with different frequency signals (500 and 800 MHz).

For mission 1, the profiles obtained were subjected to pre-processing in the field, in order to provide information to the rest of the Technical Team (who arrived on site 1 day later). The radargrams obtained revealed several diffractions resulting from the presence of empty fields (ancient decomposed roots), tree roots and several cracks caused by the characteristics of the clay soil. The edges of the graves, although difficult to interpret, were also exhibited by the radargrams. These

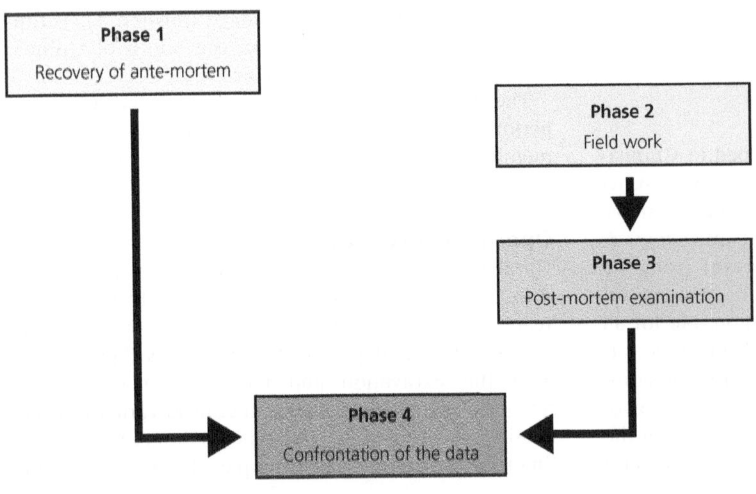

Figure 54.2 Phases of the anthropological work.

limits were confirmed by the archaeological prospection and the later excavation.

For mission 5, the processing was undertaken in Portugal, several months before the Technical Team (four anthropologists) arrived at the site. The resulting radargrams were not very specific, showing cracks caused by the characteristics of clay soil and several anomalies caused by tree roots. Although a lower limit (perhaps the bottom of a grave) was apparent, the lateral boundaries indicative of grave edges were not clearly visible in the radargrams. In fact, after excavation, we concluded that no grave existed at this site. The anomalies observed in the radargrams derived from roots of jungle trees, and the bottom limit was caused by the limit of these roots penetrating into the clay soil. We could see the same process in a river bank near the site.

During missions 1 and 5, after the GPR survey, the grave limits were located by observation of the surface soil, namely the differences in colour and texture of the sediment. During mission 1, after observation, excavation started following the stratigraphic method, that is the grave sediment was excavated but the graves' boundaries were preserved. The archaeologist helped in the excavation of the initial layer of sediment; but since skeletal remains started to appear, the excavation had to be made only by anthropologists. The skeletal elements and associated items (e.g. boots and remnants of uniforms, amongst others) were kept *in situ* until the end of the excavation (Figure 54.3). After that, a photographic record was made. All associated items and skeletal remains from one grave were recovered and placed into the same body bag. A preliminary anthropological analysis was performed in the field and recorded on the field data sheets (Figure 54.4).

A careful taphonomic analysis was performed in the field in order to make the correct distinction between the severe taphonomic skeletal changes and the peri-mortem injuries caused by the potential violent death of several of the individuals.

During missions 2, 3 and 4, since the graves were dug in existing cemeteries, the upper layer of sediment was removed by local workers under the supervision of anthropologists. The sediment surrounding the skeletons was always removed by anthropologists in order to recover as many bones as possible and to record their position *in situ*. The exhumation and recording procedures used during missions 2, 3 and 4 were the same as those used in missions 1 and 5.

Phase 3: post-mortem examination

After the field work, still in Guinea-Bissau, a post-mortem examination of skeletal remains was carried out by the anthropologists in a temporary mortuary located at the team's accommodation. The bones were cleaned and photographed before skeletal analysis.

Regarding the biological profile, the methods employed followed international standards. Estimation of sex was achieved by the analysis of the pelvic region followed by the skull (Buikstra and Ubelaker 1994). To estimate age, the subsequent elements were analysed: sternal end of the clavicle; epiphyseal fusion; calcification and eruption of the third molars; and differential dental wear on first, second and third molars (Cunha et al. 2009; Cunha and Wasterlain in press). For the evaluation of ancestry, mainly morphological traits of the face (spachnocranium) were taken into account (Byers 2011; Hefner 2009). Among the traits analysed, the most useful were prognathism; nasal width; nasal sill; anterior nasal spine; inter-orbital breadth; nasal root;

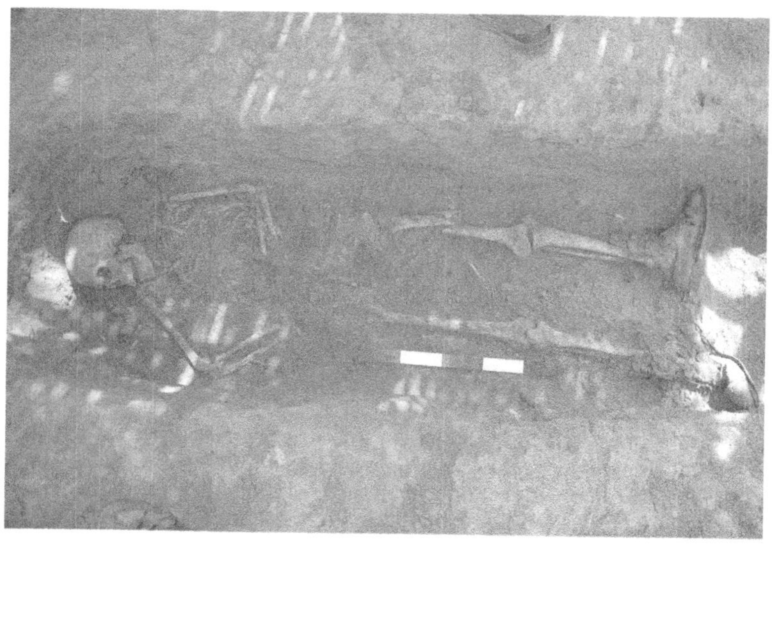

Figure 54.3 The skeletal elements and the associated items were kept *in situ* until the end of the excavation. The military boots were present. A peri-mortem trauma can be seen in the left femur.

Figure 54.4 The preliminary anthropological analysis was made in the field: metric analysis for ancestry estimation.

and nasal bridge. The ancestry evaluation was successful in recognising individuals in the group with a sub-Saharan African origin (in missions 1 and 2). Stature was estimated, on the basis of long-bone measurements taken during field work, applying the formulae by Mendonça (2000) for the Portuguese population. Skeletal lesions were described and photographed.

Phase 4: comparison of the ante- and post-mortem data

Comparison of the ante-mortem and post-mortem data was also made in Guinea-Bissau. Individual field records were checked one by one. Both biological and pathological profiles of skeletal remains were compared with ante-mortem data in order to achieve a positive identification. This process worked mainly by exclusion until we could reach the best possible match between the location of burial, the biological profile, the ante-mortem fractures and the compatibility between the general facial profile or morphology displayed by the facial bones and the one showed in the available photographs. We could not perform a craniofacial superimposition, but details such as wrongly positioned teeth were particularly helpful in querying identity. On the other hand, parameters such as age at death could lead to exclusion. The majority of the missing soldiers aged between 18 and 23 years, and these ages were easily obtained by post-mortem. Whenever there was an indication of an older individual, around 30 years of age, skeletal indicators of age were used to exclude individuals. Ancestry was also effective in discriminating between the European and African individuals. Sex was not helpful for obvious reasons (all were males). Stature estimations did not work because of the unavailability of ante-mortem data. Moreover, this parameter was too subjective whenever the soldiers' relatives tried to provide a stature estimate. For this reason, stature was not taken into account. Moreover, when the families were able to provide data on old ante-mortem trauma, these fractures were paramount for the identification process. As mentioned earlier, personal belongings and clothing were powerful circumstantial indicators. Finally, still regarding identification, the knowledge of the cause of death of some of the individuals and the possibility of confirming it through the skeletal remains corroborated the process. It has to be stated that bone and dental samples were taken from some skeletons in order to perform genetic analysis (both nuclear and mtDNA) in Portugal, at the INMLCF, IP. These analyses were difficult to perform, due to the bad state of collagen preservation; but after several attempts, the DNA profiles were obtained. Currently, two complete STR individual genetic profiles of two soldiers, and partial STR genetic profiles in three corpses have been achieved (Amorim et al. 2012, 2013).

Once the above-mentioned process was accomplished, the skeletal remains and corresponding personal belongings were placed in small coffins. The coffins were labelled and transported to the Guinea-Bissau capital, Bissau, where they were reburied in a purpose-built grave or tomb stone at a Catholic cemetery adjacent to the League of Combatants' chapel.

The five missions

First mission: Guidage (March 2008)

This was the most difficult and challenging mission, not only because it was the first mission, but also because of the expectancy of the present soldiers about the forensic science and the retrieval of skeletal remains. Guidage can be found in the north of the country near Senegal. A hand-sketched map with the location of the burials in relation to each other and in relation to a tree and a house – which luckily were still in place – was used to locate the burials. This sketch was drawn in May 1973 by a couple of soldiers who participated in this mission and buried the remains after the battle (Calheiros 2010). Moreover, one of the members of the mission team had been in charge of the combat mission in 1973, which led to the death of the soldiers whose bodies were buried (Calheiros 2010). This combination of factors offered a good chance for a successful mission. But the task was not an easy one.

Once provided with the information on the probable location of the burials, local workers removed the most recent layers of earth. Essentially, we followed the stratigraphic method. Then the archaeologist delimited the location of the burials using their specific expertise, based on the observation of surface soil, as explained earlier. Thereafter, the physical and forensic anthropologists performed the excavation since these are the experts with the required skills. As previously referred to, in Portugal archaeologists are not supposed to perform excavations of human remains.

Roots were indeed the main obstacle, and it was possible to confirm that the field where the soldiers were buried had been used for agriculture in the past 20 years (Figure 54.5). Burials were found in the same location registered on the 1973 sketch, providing clues to identification. In addition, pieces of military tent fabric were recovered, and this fabric had been reported by witnesses as being used at the time to wrap the bodies. The soldiers who survived the May 1973 battle and who performed the original inhumations could still remember some important details. These details turned out to be helpful in the identification process and are described later.

As a rule, when a soldier was killed his body should be returned to Portugal. Unfortunately, when the above-mentioned individuals died, their companions were under attack and could not transport their fallen colleagues to the city of Bissau, from where the bodies would be sent home. Facing an increasing danger of health problems because of the decomposing bodies, the surviving soldiers felt obliged to bury the bodies at the battle field. While they were burying the bodies, they suffered another attack. Some soldiers had to even jump over some of the cadavers who were already inside the graves to protect themselves from the gun shots, while others had to quickly throw the bodies inside the graves in order to run (Calheiros 2010). In a way, the excavation team was able to confirm this episode since some bodies were prone, while other bodies were not. It was also perceptible, through the analysis of the relative positions of the bones, that something had fallen over some bodies at the time of death, leading to an opening of both upper and lower limbs and even to some bone depressions. Therefore, the meticulousness with which the excavation was performed was paramount to detect this key evidence.

All the bodies were completely skeletonised although the bone preservation was diverse due to the taphonomic alterations related mainly to root growth, and also because of the cause of death. The worst preserved skeleton was the one that was buried near a tree, followed by the skeletons of individuals who had died due to severe traumatic injuries from landmine or howitzer explosions.

Additional artefacts regarding circumstantial identification were retrieved, in particular clothes and

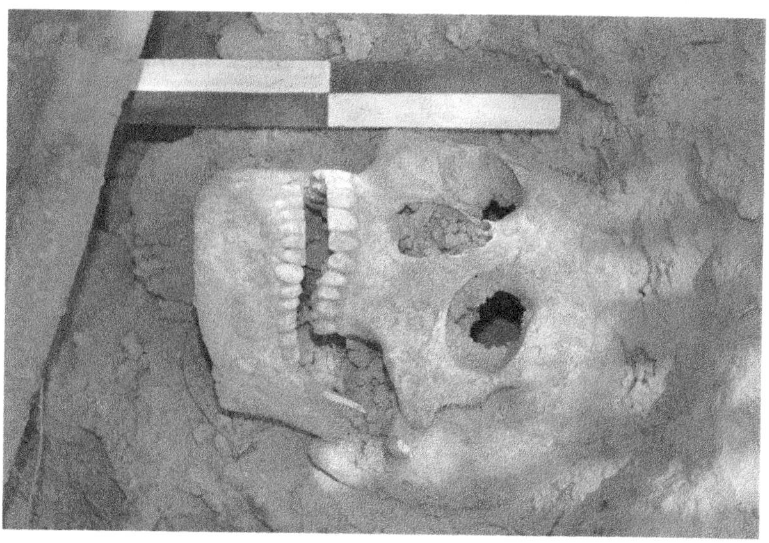

Figure 54.5 This skeleton was disturbed by roots, whereas the skull was well preserved, and dental characteristics helped in the identification.

personal belongings. Military boots were present in three cases, preserving the foot bones (Figure 54.3); a bracelet located on a forearm presented the possibility that this was a native person (the Portuguese army had soldiers from the metropolis (Portugal) and also from other colonies, and two soldiers were identified as belonging to this region of Guinea-Bissau) since this kind of bracelet is still being used today in the very small village of Guidaje (Figure 54.6). Instead of the 10 expected bodies, one more was recovered, namely the partial remains of a skeleton that had been covered with lime. One of the witnesses said he remembered that the remains of a soldier (whose name or military rank was unknown) who was killed by a landmine was also inhumed there. The body was lying face down, in prone position, with the lower limbs located near the skull and displaying peri-mortem fractures, namely in the femur. These features were consistent with the information as provided by the witnesses.

For this assemblage of soldiers (originally 10, later turning out to be 11), there was some ante-mortem data which proved to be paramount. Photographs were available for five individuals and some displayed the anterior dentition. Two individuals had known ante-mortem fractures. Cause of death and peri-mortem injuries were known for all five.

In all, it took 5 days to excavate the human remains which were then taken to the base camp (a local house in a village 30 km away from the excavation) where they were subject to a general cleaning process as well as to a re-evaluation of the biological profile, identity factors and traumatic injuries. The comparison of ante- and post-mortem data successfully identified 10 individuals. Unfortunately, the lack of ante-mortem data related to the eleventh skeleton precluded its identification. At the end of this first mission, all the skeletal remains of the 11 individuals were buried in the League of Combatants grave in the Bissau Catholic cemetery. Some months later, the skeletal remains of six soldiers were returned to their relatives in Portugal with military honours.

Missions in cemeteries (Farim, Gabu and South of Guinea-Bissau)

As mentioned earlier, three missions were concentrated on the remains of soldiers that were buried in former Portuguese cemeteries, some of them abandoned since the independence of Guinea-Bissau in 1974. Missions 2 and 3 took place in the cities of Farim (December 2008) and Gabu (March 2009), and Mission 4 (November 2009) covered cemeteries in four small villages in the south of Guinea-Bissau. Not all the soldiers who were buried in the abovementioned cemeteries died during combat; some died in accidents, for example car crashes or drowning, during the 13 years of the war.

In Farim, the team recovered the remains of 15 individuals, 14 of them skeletonised and 1 in a mixed state of decay. In fact, two individuals had been buried in lead coffins. One of these coffins had deteriorated over the years, allowing roots and sediment to penetrate; the human remains were skeletonised. The corpse in the intact lead coffin was saponified. The remaining 13 individuals were buried in wooden coffins. Several objects were found associated with the skeletal remains, such as Catholic religious items, bottles of beer, combs, bracelets and rings. The field work, the data collection and comparison process were made as described earlier. After that process, the corpse of the saponified individual (born in Guinea-Bissau) was reburied in the same grave. The other 14 individuals were transported to the Bissau League of Combatants Ossuary Chapel.

From the cemetery at Gabu, the team exhumed 14 skeletons and in the 4 villages south of Guinea-Bissau a total of 10 skeletons. The state of preservation of these

Figure 54.6 Bracelet found on a forearm, which suggests that the skeleton belongs to the one of the Guinea soldiers inhumed in Guidage.

latter remains was poor, and the worst of all the sites. Bone fragmentation was considerable; and in some cases, the bodies were reduced to small bony pieces, which precluded the necessary anthropological analysis. Yet, the field work, data collection and comparison process (whenever possible) followed the same procedures as with the other sites. The discovery of metallic military insignias (the cavalry weapons in a beret) associated with the some of the excavated skeletons in Bolama (south of Guinea-Bissau) was also very helpful in the identification process.

Search for a mass grave (mission 5: Cheche, February 2010)

This was the mission with the least probability of success and, in fact, no human skeletal elements were found. In February 1969, 49 soldiers drowned crossing the Corubal River during a military operation (Brandão 2008; Catarino 2010). Their bodies were recovered by marines in the following weeks and buried in a mass grave in the jungle near the river bank. The exact location of the mass grave was not properly recorded in the army archives. Consequently, the Mission Team tried to find witnesses of this episode. Some witnesses pointed to a large area of jungle, without great certainty. Nevertheless, the Mission Team cleared an area in the jungle and a GPR survey was performed, as previously described. Some months later, the Technical Team performed prospection and excavation in the cleared area without any results. The exact location of the mass grave is therefore still unknown. This is as example of how the absence of results, in this case, the absence of human skeletons, could be seen as a positive result, although, we would of course have preferred to find the soldiers' bodies. But now, it is at least known that the place where the witnesses believed the bodies were buried was not the right one. Most probably, the mass grave was originally located very near the river margins that have altered during the past 30 years. Consequently, it is very probable that the mass grave (and the bodies within it) has been eroded by the river water.

Concluding remarks

It is well known that identification of the deceased is dictated by the post-mortem condition of the body and by the availability of ante-mortem information, both in terms of quantity and quality. We have tried to correlate several sources of evidence, namely body location, biological profile, personal belongings and cause of death. *A priori*, we were ready to perform identification by exclusion since we knew that all the deceased were young males in their early twenties, originating both from Portugal and Guinea-Bissau.

Ante- and post-mortem comparison was most often hampered by the inadequate ante-mortem photograph quality and by the absence of good ante-mortem data regarding features that could be used as unique identifiers. The time elapsed since the deaths, 30–40 years, also played an important role in this failure. Relatives were not abundant, and the photographs present were particularly old and of bad quality. In addition, memory betrayed the relatives when they tried to remember particular details. Nevertheless, attending to the bad state of preservation of some of the excavated remains, the time since death was not the only important factor. Roots, soil acidity and the very high temperatures contributed to disintegration of bones in some cases (e.g. mission 4). Even in bones that showed apparently good preservation (e.g. mission 1), the preservation of the collagen was not as good as expected. Again, environmental conditions dictated the preservation.

The recovery of the remains of soldiers fallen on duty is much more than just opening their graves and retrieving their bones. Ante-mortem data collection and a correct anthropological post-mortem analysis are of paramount importance in order to identify these individuals. Besides, forensic anthropologists with knowledge of both anthropological and archaeological field methods and the help of a geophysicist were key elements for grave location.

Guinea-Bissau missions showed that the Portuguese Technical Team had the necessary experience to be involved in the search, recovery and identification of military personnel missing from past conflicts. They could also operate in different contexts like crimes against humanity or war crimes such as the case of East Timor, in 2003, where a mass grave was excavated to exhume a Portuguese soldier and where the first author of this publication was involved (Cunha et al. 2005). The research and analysis of such a situation is very complex; it being necessary not only to have great experience in laboratory anthropological analysis but also in anthropological excavation in difficult environments. Both experiences were revealed to be of major significance. The awareness of the importance of teamwork in hard conditions is also crucial for a positive outcome. The League of Combatants plans to proceed with this type of work in Mozambique and Angola, also in ancient Portuguese colonies affected by war, and to call us whenever unidentified graves or bodies' prospection will be needed. Currently, the League is working in Mozambique with identified burials.

It has to be borne in mind that the forensic work performed here cannot be directly compared with the work performed in the context of crimes against humanity. In effect, in our situation there are no committed crimes and, implicitly, no military police involved, and there is no possibility of going to prosecution. The soldiers died during the war and were buried according to available resources at the time. The main aim was to dignify the soldiers' death, giving them a more noteworthy, known and deserved place of burial; in the case of Guinea Bissau, a special place in Bissau cemetery was built for that purpose. The remains are only returned to the families when they request them; and in these cases, their relief at finally retrieving peace and being able to end their grief are the most compensatory results of this work. In the meantime, both genetic and anthropological data are kept at the INMLCF, I.P., waiting for families who wish to retrieve the remains of their relatives who died around 40 years ago in Guinea-Bissau.

References

Amorim, A., Costa Santos, J. and Cunha, E. 2012. Portuguese Colonial War (1616–1975): the role of forensic genetics on recently exhumed soldiers' identification – preliminary results. *International Journal of Legal Medicine* 126 Suppl. 1, S121–S384.

Amorim, A., Costa, H., Silva, C. et al. 2013. PowerPlex ESI17 performance on Portuguese skeletal soldiers remains of the Portuguese Colonial War. *Proceedings of the 14th European Forensic DNA Working Group Meeting*, Lisbon, March 19–21.

Brandão, J. 2008. *Cronologia da Guerra Colonial: Angola-Guiné-Moçambique*, 1961–1974. Lisboa, Prefácio.

Buikstra, J. and Ubelaker, D. 1994. *Standards for Data Collection from Human Skeletal Remains. Proceedings of a Seminar at the Field Museum of Natural History.* Archaeological Survey Research Series 44, Fayetteville, Arkansas.

Byers, S. 2011. *Introduction to Forensic Anthropology*. 4th edition. Boston, Prentice Hall.

Calheiros, J. 2010. *A Última Missão*. Lisboa, Caminhos Romanos.

Catarino, M. 2010. *As Grandes Operações da Guerra Colonial, 5: A Retirada de Madina do Boé*. Lisboa, Presselivre.

Cunha, E. and Cattaneo, C. 2006. Forensic anthropology and forensic pathology: the state of the art. In A. Schmitt, E. Cunha and J. Pinheiro (eds.), *Forensic Anthropology and Medicine: Complementary Sciences from the Recovery to the Cause of Death*, 39–53. Totowa, Humana Press.

Cunha, E., Martrille, L., Ramsthaler, R. et al. 2009. The problem of aging human remains and living individuals: a review. *Forensic Science International* 193, 1–13.

Cunha, E., Mendonça, M. C. and Vieira, D. N. 2005. Exhumation and identification of a particular individual in a mass grave. *Proceedings of the American Academy of Forensic Sciences, New Orleans*, 314.

Cunha, E. and Pinheiro, J. 2007. Forensic anthropology in Portugal: from current practice to future challenges. In M. B. Brickley and R. Ferllini (eds.), *Forensic Anthropology. Case Studies from Europe*, 38–57. Springfield, Charles C. Thomas.

Cunha, E. and Wasterlain, S. (in press). Estimativa da idade em ciências forenses: os métodos dentários. In A. T. Corte-Real and D. N. Vieira (eds.), *Medicina Dentária Forense*. Coimbra, Imprensa da Universidade.

Dirkmaat, D. C. (ed.) 2012. *A Companion to Forensic Anthropology*. Chichester, Wiley Blackwell.

Dirkmaat, D. C., Cabo, L. L., Ousley, S. D. and Symes, S. A. 2008. New perspectives in forensic anthropology. *Yearbook of Physical Anthropology* 51, 33–52.

Hefner, J. 2009. Cranial nonmetric variation and estimating ancestry. *Journal of Forensic Sciences* 54, 985–995.

Kranioti, E. F. and Paine, R. R. 2011. Forensic anthropology in European assessment of current status and application. *Journal of Anthropological Sciences* 89, 71–92.

Mendonça, C. 2000. Estimation of height from the length of long bones in a Portuguese adult population. *American Journal of Physical Anthropology* 112, 39–48.

Umbelino, C. and Santos, A. L. 2011. Portugal. In N. Márquez-Grant and L. Fibiger (eds.), *The Routledge Handbook of Archaeological Human Remains and Legislation*, 341–352. Oxon, Routledge.

Vieira, D. N. 2008. Forensic medicine in Portugal. In B. Madea and P. Saukko (eds.), *Forensic Medicine in Europe*, 317–341. Lubeck, Schmidt Romhild.

CHAPTER 55

Contemporary exhumations in Spain: recovering the missing from the Spanish Civil War

Francisco Etxeberria[1,2], Lourdes Herrasti[2], Fernando Serrulla[3] and Nicholas Márquez-Grant[4,5]
[1]*Medicina Legal y Forense, Facultad de Medicina, Universidad del País Vasco UPV/EHU, San Sebastián, Spain*
[2]*Sociedad de Ciencias Aranzadi, Donostia/San Sebastían, Gipuzkoa, Spain*
[3]*Unidad de Antropología Forense, Instituto de Medicina Legal de Galicia, Hospital de Verín, Ourense, Spain*
[4]*Cranfield Forensic Institute, Cranfield University, Defence Academy of the United Kingdom, Shrivenham, UK*
[5]*Institute of Human Sciences, School of Anthropology and Museum Ethnography, University of Oxford, Oxford, UK*

Introduction

In the past decade, interest has grown in Spain with regard to recovering the remains of the victims of the Civil War (1936–1939) and the Francoist regime that followed (1939–1975). With the arrival of democracy in Spain in 1978, numerous exhumations were undertaken although unfortunately without technical or institutional support, and hence little information is available about them. At the same time, on a few occasions the remains were studied by forensic scientists; perhaps one of the clearest examples followed the accidental discovery of human remains in Casa de Campos in Madrid, published by Reverte (1984–1985), who had an expertise in forensic anthropology.

After the end of the transition to democracy in Spain, several civil associations were formed and set up projects to recover the Historical Memory (*Memoria Histórica*) of those who had suffered the most and who had been obliterated from memory in contemporary history. These were mainly deceased who had been killed in extrajudicial executions.

The policy of the exhumation of victims of the Civil War is not new, however, if we recall the legislation of the Francoist Government in 1939 and 1940. After that time, and until the *Valle de los Caídos* (Valley of the Fallen) was opened in 1959, around 30,000 skeletons were exhumed and buried in this place, which was built to honour the victims on the side that won the war.

Contemporary exhumations

In 2000, a group of specialists in the fields of archaeology, physical anthropology and forensic medicine carried out the excavation of a Civil War mass grave in Priaranza del Bierzo[1] (León) where the remains of 13 civilians, murdered on 16 October 1936, were exhumed. This was the first Civil War grave to be excavated with scientific methodology and qualified experts, enabling the DNA identification of one of the individuals.

To date (2000–2011), a total of 302 mass graves have been exhumed (Figure 55.1), and over 5471 skeletons have been recovered. From the excavation of one grave in 2000 (at Priaranza del Bierzo, León; Prada et al. 2003), followed by two graves in 2001, there has been an increase with 27 graves excavated in 2011 and a maximum reached per year of 43 graves in 2008 and 2009. Over 95% of the graves are associated with extrajudicial executions, 4% contain remains of those who died in combat and 1% of graves include those who died while imprisoned. Technical reports have concentrated on different aspects of the matter: historical,

[1]The work was supervised by Julio Vidal, an archaeologist, and Encina Prada, a physical anthropologist, who wrote a report and produced a first widely distributed paper with the suggestive title of *Archaeology of Reconciliation*. For more information, see: http://www.derechos.org/nizkor/espana/doc/arqueo.html (last accessed October 2013).

Forensic Archaeology: A Global Perspective, First Edition. Edited by W.J. Mike Groen, Nicholas Márquez-Grant and Robert C. Janaway.

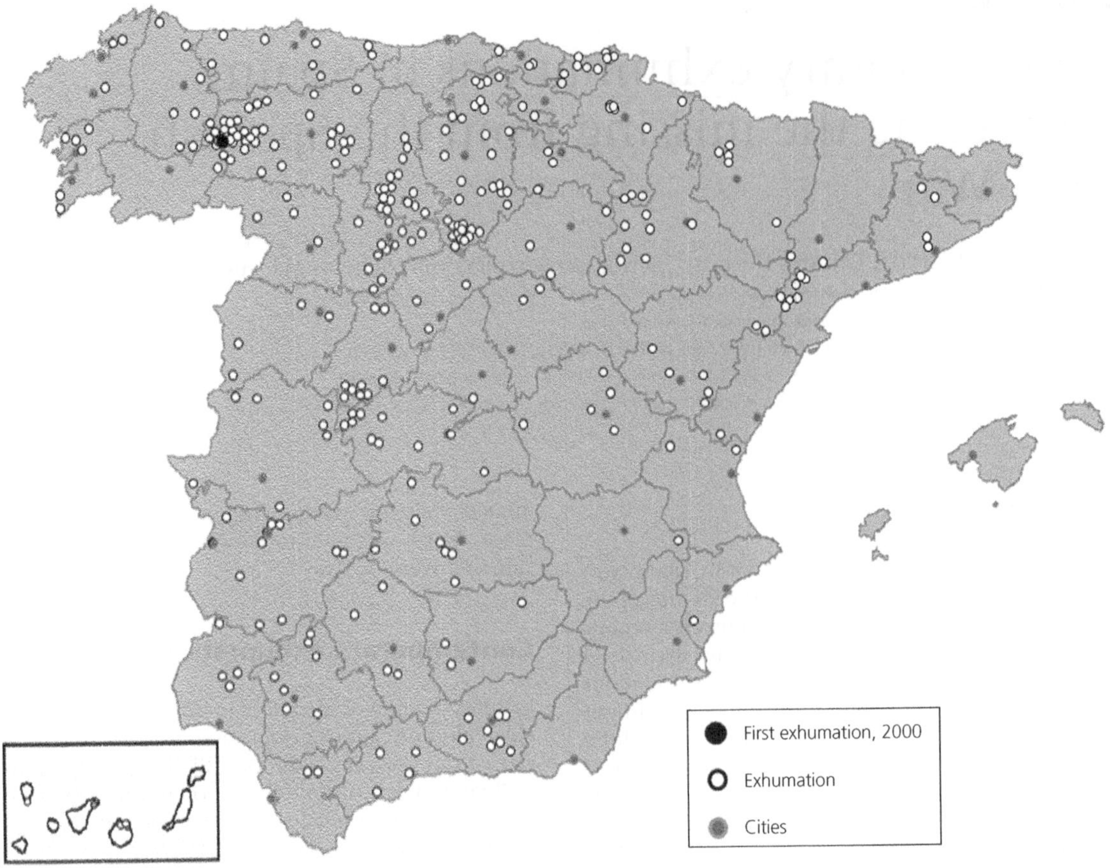

Figure 55.1 Civil War (1936–1939) exhumations carried out in Spain since 2000.

biographical, archaeological, physical anthropological, pathological, genetic and ballistic.[2]

Regarding the biological profile of the deceased, both males and females from a range of age groups, from adolescents to the elderly, were buried in these mass graves (Herrasti and Jiménez 2012). In the largest mass grave identified to date, that of San Rafael in Malaga, over 300 children have been recovered, many of whom had died in custody. Although the large majority of the victims were males, women were also amongst the deceased, as is the case in the mass grave in Valdediós (Asturias) where 11 of the 17 victims were female nurses from a nearby psychiatric hospital.[3]

Amongst the deceased, most (>80%) had died as a result of extrajudicial executions; less than 5% had died in combat and less than 10% in custody. Peri-mortem fractures (gunshot wounds) to the skull (including the mandible), vertebrae and other bones have been recorded on most victims; this provides evidence of manner and cause of death.

Exhumation protocols

According to a number of specialists and in the recommendations compiled by Etxeberria (2004) (e.g. Etxeberria 2012; Herrasti and Jiménez 2012), the main stages in the process of the exhumation of these burials are:

a Proof of the legitimate interest of the person or group of people proposing the exhumation. In order to undertake an exhumation, it is necessary to have the expressed wish of the family or relatives of the victims

---

[2]Since 2009, we have been compiling all the reports published, and these have been included in a database. This project is funded by the Ministry of the Presidency in their policy of supporting Historical Memory. At the same time, monitoring is being carried out from the perspective of social anthropology within the project 'Politics of memory in contemporary Spain: analysis of the impact of exhumations of the Civil War in the first years of the 21st century', reference CSO2009-09681 (MICINN) supervised by Dr Francisco Ferrándiz at the Higher Council of Scientific Research (CSIC).

[3]For more information, see: http://www.sc.ehu.es/scrwwwsr/Medicina-Legal/valdedios/ (last accessed October 2013).

who may be buried in a particular common grave. If this cannot be proved, all the information about the case that is known through historical documentation or other evidence will be considered. Permission to exhume is also required.

b Preliminary technical report or desk-based assessment. This will explain the background to the case, the historical information and the evidence of those witnesses who know about the case, as well as information about the location of the grave and the feasibility of the exhumation. It also includes the human and technical resources needed for the exhumation.

c Exhumation and study of the remains. A field evaluation may already have taken place to locate the remains prior to full excavation and recovery. The exhumation is performed following internationally acknowledged scientific methods[4] by qualified archaeologists and forensic anthropologists. It is, however, often led by forensic pathologists with an expertise in forensic anthropology. This guarantees (i) the appropriate completion of the tasks; (ii) correct sequence of safekeeping, continuity and chain of custody of all the evidence seized; (iii) application of ethical principles (including dignity and respect) regarding the victims and their relatives; (iv) transfer of the remains to a laboratory where they can be stored and studied appropriately; and (v) a technical exhumation report with photographic and video documentation.

It is particularly important to take into account the following points:

a Basic excavation methods (e.g. drawing, photography and written descriptions) should be followed regarding recording the grave, skeletons and any associated materials, careful excavation of the remains, sampling and sieving of sediments and recording contexts (e.g. fills and cuts of the grave).

b It is vitally important to establish a suitably marked and protected security perimeter, where only authorised personnel have access, to avoid damage and plundering of the remains. Special care and a meticulous approach must be taken to protect and avoid the deterioration of the materials found. Appropriate conservation and storage of materials is also undertaken by the archaeologists who within this context may take the role of forensic archaeologists.

The final report also includes all the historical documentation known about the case as well as the evidence provided by relatives and others. These reports tend to include a historical background on the site and the context in which the individuals were executed; a list of the individuals presumed buried in a particular location and their biographical and biological details; an archaeological report on the location and excavation of the site; and the results from the physical anthropological and palaeopathological analysis in order to aid victim identification and a pathological report regarding the manner and cause of death. Most reports are available to the public either through a number of websites,[5] or archived in local governmental institutions or through other publications (e.g. López García and Ferrándiz 2010). Although the results have been uneven, these reports are continually improving, complementary appendices with graphics and documents in the form of specialist technical reports and guidelines having been provided (e.g. Etxeberria 2012). The results have been presented at specialised meetings, such as the conferences of the Spanish Association of Forensic Anthropology and Odontology (*Asociación Española de Antropología y Odontología Forense* – AEAOF) and a specific literature exists that is listed at the end of this chapter. Some of these results have also been presented at talks to the community and the relatives of the deceased, and some popular publications to honour those victims have also been published.

From then onwards, protocols and guidelines based on Etxeberria's 2004 protocol have been developed (e.g. Order PRE/2568/2011 of 26 September 2011 – see Annex in *Boletín Oficial del Estado*, 232: 101916–101923; Herrasti and Jiménez 2012; Polo Cerdá 2009). These provide further detail with more specifics regarding requests to exhume, permission to exhume, desk-based assessments, archaeological excavation and how they are to be notified (e.g. local judge, town hall, police and Department of Health), the analysis of human remains, report writing and reburial.

The guidelines recommend that qualified personnel undertake the work. It is recommended, moreover, that the team should comprise professionals from a variety of relevant fields including history, archaeology, anthropology (social and physical), forensic medicine, odontology, geophysics and psychology. Geneticists may also be involved as some DNA analysis may be required (e.g. Alonso 2006; Alonso et al. 2012; Cardoso et al. 2008; Crespillo et al. 2004; Ríos et al. 2010). Other logistical staff and a number of other volunteers are also involved. Within archaeology itself, the role of the archaeologist is to search and locate the grave usually by excavation, whether by hand or by undertaking a watching brief of machine excavation. Archaeologists will supervise the excavation of the grave, undertake the recording of the grave, the human remains and any associated artefacts.

Legal aspects

The Law of Historical Memory (Law 52/2007 of December 26), which recognises and enlarges rights and establishes measures in favour of those who suffered

[4] UN Manual on the Effective Prevention and Investigation of Extra-Legal, Arbitrary and Summary Executions (New York, 1991).

[5] For example, see: http://www.sc.ehu.es/scrwwwsr/Medicina-Legal/ (last accessed October 2013).

persecution and violence during the Civil War and Dictatorship, states in its Article 13 thus:

> The competent public Administrations will authorise the work of exploration to locate the remains of the victims described in Section 1 of Article 11, in accordance with regulations on historical heritage and the action protocol approved by the Government. The discoveries will be immediately reported to the competent administrative and legal authorities. [authors' translation]

More precisely, Article 12 of the same law, about the measures for the identification and location of victims, states thus:

1. The Government, in collaboration with all the Public Administrations, will develop a protocol of scientific and multidisciplinary action, ensuring institutional collaboration and the appropriate procedure in the exhumations. [authors' translation]

Equally, in its Article 14, the law adds:

1. The competent public Administrations will produce and make available to the interested parties described in Article 13, within their respective territories, maps showing the places where the remains of the people described in the previous Article are located, including complementary information about the same.
2. The Government will determine the procedure for the production of an integrated map covering the whole of Spain, which will be equally accessible to the interested parties and which will include the data which, in the terms to be determined, must be submitted by the various competent public administrations.
3. The areas included in the maps will be the object of special preservation by their owners, on terms to be determined by the regulations. [authors' translation]

This map of the mass graves was presented by the Government on 4 April 2011.

The guidelines alluded to in this law were approved by the Government on 26 September 2011 and published as Order 2568/2011 by the Ministry of the Presidency. The law establishes the guidelines governing exhumations and forensic anthropological analyses. This protocol transfers much of the authority in the research to the field of Forensic Anthropology and Pathology, within the general framework of Forensic Sciences.

In addition to the above, specific regulations exist in the Autonomous (Regional) Communities, which have authority in these matters from the administrative viewpoint, but not in the legal aspect. These included legal regulations in 1999 in Aragon; 2002 in Extremadura; 2003 in Asturias, Basque Country and Andalusia; 2008 in Galicia; 2009 in Catalonia (as well as Andalusia again) and 2011 in Navarre.

A number of clandestine graves case studies are presented in the following, with a focus on wells, potholes and caves as these are not widely reported in the literature.

Case studies

A number of case studies related to the victims of the Civil War and the Francoist regime which followed are discussed.

Mass Grave of Loma de Montija (Burgos)

The first case study to be discussed is the mass grave of Loma de Montija (Burgos), a clandestine grave located within a cemetery. This common grave was excavated over 7 days in April 2011 by a multidisciplinary team from Aranzadi Science Society (*Sociedad de Ciencias Aranzadi*) consisting of 10 archaeologists, 4 forensic anthropologists and another 4 social anthropologists, all of whom are widely experienced. The grave was dug in a field with a subsoil of clayey soil, with a neutral or slightly alkaline pH, with high calcium levels, a low amount of organic matter and high sodium and iron levels.

A total of 24 bodies were buried at a depth of 1 m in a grave 6.5 m long and 2.5 m wide. They all possessed personal objects. It was also found that some of the victims' hands were together, suggesting that their hands had been tied. The remains were in a variety of positions, but many of them were prone (facing down), a few in a supine position or on their side (Figure 55.2).

The remains were studied at the University of the Basque Country (*Universidad del Pais Vasco/Euskal Herriko Unibertsitateko*), where some of the victims could be identified through DNA analysis. They all exhibited gunshot wounds to the head, typical of the repression exercised on the civil population in 1936.

Pits, caves and shafts with human remains from the Civil War

As well as burials in the earth, human remains have been found in natural caves, artificial shafts and abandoned mines (Table 55.1, Figure 55.3).

These are less well known and seldom published and, therefore, comprise the case studies presented in the following text.

Sima El Grajero (Lario, León)

This is a natural pothole about 20 m deep into which an indeterminate number of people were thrown in 1936. In 1998, the media reported the discovery of remains in the shaft belonging to individuals executed in the Civil War and Francoist repression. The law court at Cistierna was informed, ordered the recovery of the bones and initiated legal proceedings.[6]

[6] Following this discovery, the term *historical memory* was coined and applied to the study and vindication of the victims of the Civil War and Francoism.

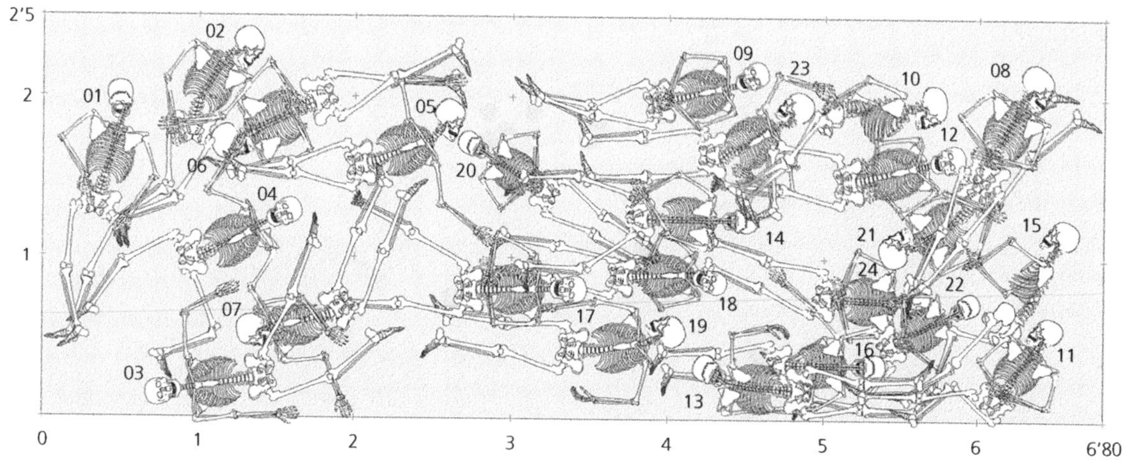

Figure 55.2 Distribution of the remains in the common grave at Loma de Montija.

Table 55.1 Deposition sites of individuals killed during the Civil War.

Natural feature	Town	Province	Number of individuals
Sima El Grajero*	Lario	León	13
Sima de Otsoportillo	Sierra de Urbasa	Navarre	?
Sima de Kurtzetxiki-Bedoña*	Arrasate	Gipuzkoa	2
Jinamar Volcanic Shaft	Telde	Gran Canaria	?
Sima de Kristoleze*	Lizarraga-Andía	Navarre	?
Sima del Raso de Urbasa*	Sierra de Urbasa	Navarre	10
Sima de Ardaitz	Valle de Erro	Navarre	2
Simas de Dolencias	Sotoscueva	Burgos	?
Sima de Gaztelu	Gaztelu	Navarre	?
Sima Torca Palomera	Mozuelos de Sedano	Burgos	?
Cova Arcoia*	Sierra del Caurel	Lugo	2
Cueva de Humarraña*	Loma de Montija	Burgos	2
Human-made feature			
Well of Aguadillas de la Fuente de la Rosa	Aldeaseca	Ávila	7
Pozos de Caude	Llanos de Caudé	Teruel	?
Pozo Ventafarinas	Tamarite de Litera	Huesca	?
Llano de las Brujas well*	Arucas	Gran Canaria	24
Valdihuelo mine shaft*	Alburquerque-San Vicente	Badajoz	15–17
Las Cabezuelas mine shaft*	Camuñas	Toledo	+50
El Salamanco Chico mine shaft	La Parra	Badajoz	+2
Covarrubias limekiln	Covarrubias	Burgos	8
Bodega Peña Tejada	Medina del Campo	Valladolid	?

The asterisk indicates the sites where human remains have been recovered following scientific methodology. This information has been obtained from a number of unpublished and published sources for each individual site (sources can be made available on request).

The study was carried out at the National Institute of Toxicology (*Instituto Nacional de Toxicología*) in Madrid, which determined a minimum number of 13 individuals present. Following the wishes of relatives, the remains were finally buried in Lario cemetery in 2000.

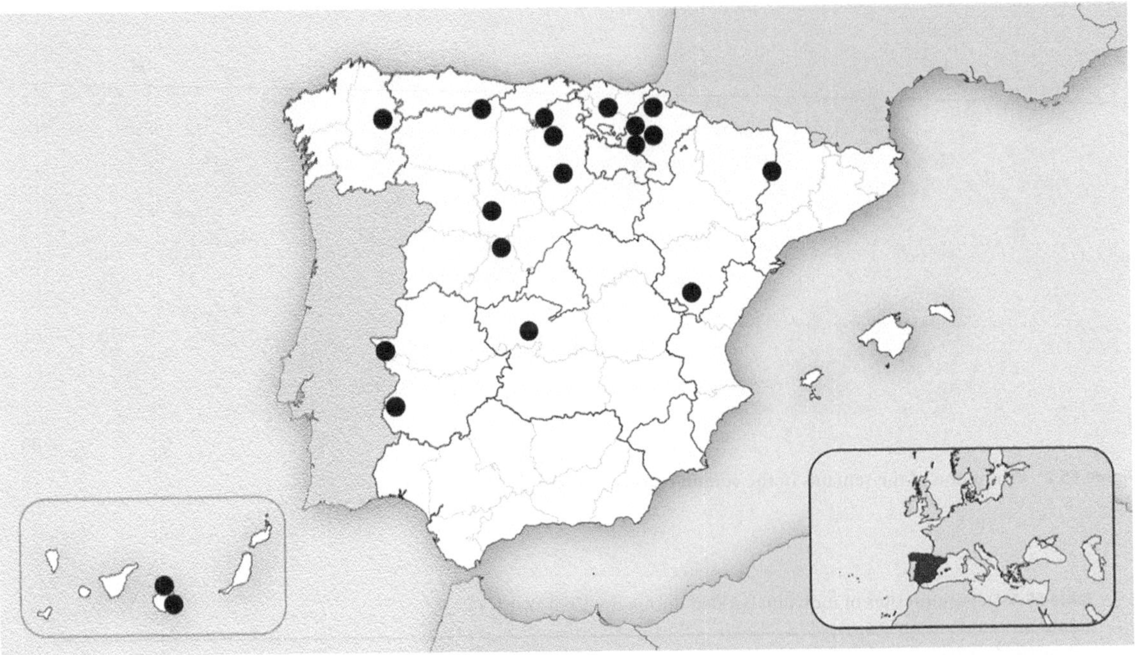

Figure 55.3 Location of the sites included in Table 55.1.

Sima de Kurtzetxiki-Bedoña (Arrasate, Gipuzkoa)

In 1970, Besaide Caving Club found a human skull inside this shaft. From information available from witnesses at the time, it was known that the remains dated from 1935. In 1988, another human skull was found as were the remains of a leather shoe. As a result, the shaft was explored and all the osseous remains recovered in 2002. The pothole consisted of a vertical shaft 6 m deep, which then continued down a steep slope 20 m long (Figure 55.4). The human skeletal remains recovered in this pothole belonged to two male individuals, with gunshot wounds to the skull and spinal column.

Sima de Kristoleze (Lizarraga-Sierra de Andia, Navarre)

This pothole is narrow for the first 15–18 m, and it then opens up into a chamber at a depth of 40 m and finishes with a slope. The human remains were found on the slope among waste thrown down the shaft throughout the years. In 2010, specialists from the Armed Forces (*Guardia Civil, Policía Nacional*) recovered the remains of about 10 individuals that had been found by cavers. Although their age has not been fixed precisely, they are supposed to date to the time of the Civil War. The remains were inspected *in situ* and later taken to the Central Identification Unit of the Scientific Police HQ in Madrid.

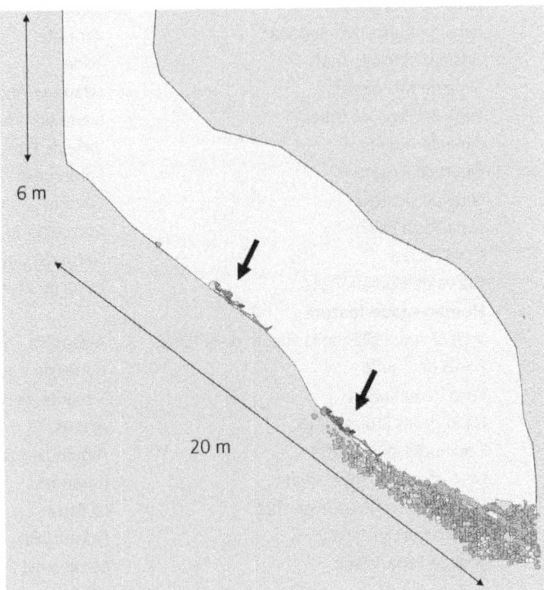

Figure 55.4 Plan of Sima de Kurtzetxiki, indicating (arrow) the location of the remains.

Sima de Raso de Urbasa (Sierra de Urbasa, Navarre)

This is a natural pothole with a vertical entrance 10-m deep dropping into a large chamber, which was first explored in 1950. Two or three human skeletons in very badly deteriorated clothes were discovered on the floor of the chamber. Local farmers knew that several inhabitants of the town of Eulate had been shot and their bodies hidden in the Autumn of 1936. Around 1956, their relatives covered the pothole with stones and placed a tombstone with the names of some of the victims. In 2013, the pothole was reopened and the remains of 10 individuals were found in a good state of preservation. They were recovered from this pothole and at least three individuals have been identified to date. All are males and have gunshot wounds to the skulls. A 9 mm bullet was also found. All the remains display evidence of scavenging.

Cova Arcoia (Sierra del Caurel, Lugo)

In 1992, a multidisciplinary team from Laxe Geological Institute (A Coruña) discovered two human skulls, some loose teeth and several long bones in this cave. The physical anthropological study determined that they belonged to a minimum number of three individuals: a female, a male and the remains of a juvenile individual of unknown sex. The skulls displayed signs of violence (Serrulla and Etxeberria 1995). AMS radiocarbon dating was carried out in the Svedberg Laboratory (Sweden), determining time of death consistent with the timeframe of the period of the Civil War.

More human remains were found in 2009, together with other objects and a used rifle bullet case. The competent Court of Law, the Civil Guard and the Forensic Anthropology Unit at the Institute of Legal Medicine of Galicia (*Instituto de Medicina Legal de Galicia* – IMELGA) intervened on this occasion. The remains were found in a funnel-shaped area of collapsed rock, which could be reached in two ways: either by crawling along a free hanging drop of 5 m to finally reach the chamber with the bones, or down a winding descent between large rock faces. The temperature inside the cave was between 7 and 9°C (July, estimated altitude 1800 m), with a relative humidity of about 90%. The bones were disarticulated, except for the left leg of a sub-adult individual that was connected to a leather boot. Many domestic animal bones were mixed with the human remains. All the bones were found in the surface layer. The chemical analysis of the sediment found it was alkaline, with a mean pH of 7.8, with high calcium levels. A fired case was found near the bones and sent to the Civil Guard's Ballistic Laboratory, which determined it was from a Remington Berdan (41 × 15 mm) 0.58 calibre round. These were first manufactured in Spain in 1867, mainly at the Asturias Weapons Factory, and were principally in use from the third Carlist War (1872–1876) until the Civil War.

The inventory of the remains found in 1992 and 2009 reveals two almost complete skeletons. One of these was a young adult male (25–30 years) with signs of severe cranial trauma (not compatible with a firearm wound), fracture of the femur shaft and signs of minimal survival (days). The other skeleton belonged to a sub-adult individual with an estimated age of 10–14 years corresponding genetically to a male. This individual exhibited severe cranial trauma with an orifice in the right occipital compatible with a bullet exit wound (the area of the entry wound was not present). This individual also exhibited fractures in two vertebrae, as well as a rib fracture. The boot found in connection with this sub-adult individual's leg was made wholly of leather (including laces and sole), without any marks or logotypes.

Well of Aguadillas de la Fuente de la Rosa (Aldeaseca, Ávila)

The archaeological excavation performed in 2003 was able to determine that only a few bone fragments remained in this well, into which seven individuals from Pajares de Adaja (Ávila) had been thrown in August 1936. In fact, this well, which was not in use, had been emptied in 1959 in order to transfer the remains to the pantheon in the *Valle de los Caídos*, where over 30,000 skeletons from all over the country were deposited.

Well of Llano de las Brujas (Arucas, Gran Canaria)

Several wells on the island of Gran Canaria were used to hide murdered bodies during the first months of the Civil War, with some evidence of use in March 1937. These are the wells of Llano de las Brujas (Montaña Blanca), Barranco de Tenoya, Puente del Barranco de Arucas, Vuelta del Ayuntamiento (del Francés) and Martorell. Of these, Llano de las Brujas, in the town of Arucas, has been investigated and the remains of 24 complete individuals were recovered in 2009. The remains were deposited in a circular well, 3 m in diameter and 55 m deep, into which the bodies were thrown on two different occasions, as demonstrated by the separation of a group of 14 skeletons from a second group of 10 skeletons above it. Nine individuals have been identified after analysis at the Genetics Laboratory at the University of Las Palmas in Gran Canaria. Numerous personal objects and lime were found together with the human remains, as well as 36 bullets and 30 cartridge cases. A further three cases and two bullets were found on the surface, around the top of the well. The physical anthropological study was able to determine that the direct causes of death were the gunshot wounds, mainly to the skull.

Las Cabezuelas mine shaft (Camuñas, Toledo)

This mine shaft 30 m deep (Figure 55.5) was visited on three occasions from 2008 to 2010 in order to determine the characteristics of a place where an indeterminate number of individuals were murdered by the Republicans during the Civil War.

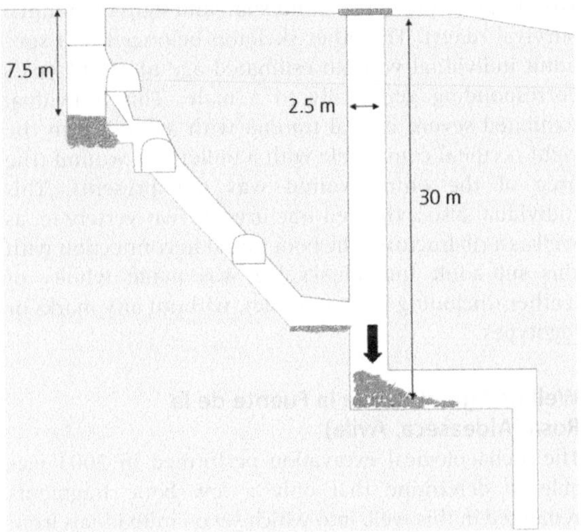

Figure 55.5 Section of Las Cabezuelas Mine, indicating (arrow) the location of the human remains.

The archaeological work was designed to expose the largest possible number of human remains, so that they could be interpreted without removing them from the shaft. After removing several tons of earth, it was found that the last bodies to be thrown into the shaft were carbonised by the fire deliberately lit inside the mine, probably with petrol, as some testimonies affirm. Over 50 human skeletons were located at the bottom of the vertical shaft, into which they must have been thrown in at least two episodes, separated by a thick layer of lime. The cause of death was violent murder, with clear evidence of firearm wounds.

Covarrubias limekiln (Covarrubias, Burgos)

In 2005, eight skeletons were exhumed from the bottom of a 4 m deep limekiln (Figure 55.6). After mapping the area and establishing a grid with Cartesian coordinates within the circular walls of the limekiln, the sediment around the skeletons was excavated. The bottom of the limekiln was filled with large stones that had been thrown inside to cover the bodies. Ashes and lime also

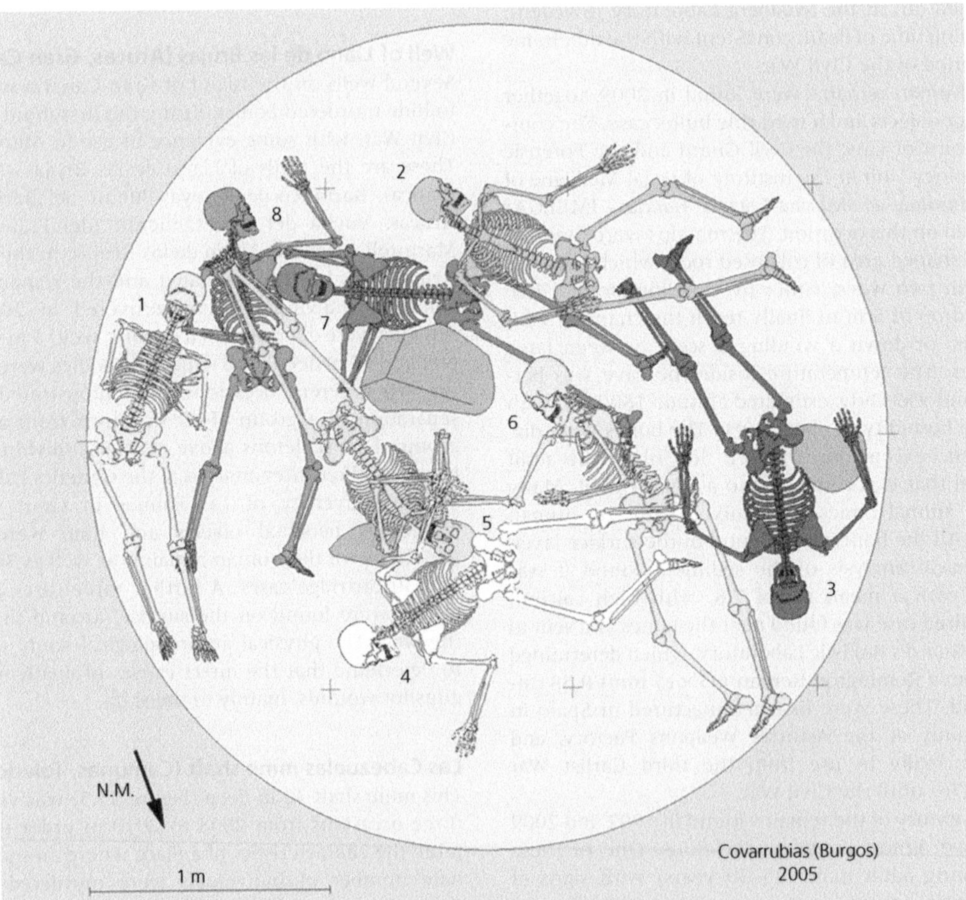

Figure 55.6 Distribution of the cadavers in the bottom of the limekiln at Covarrubias.

formed a very hard level in the first layers of the sediment. The remains were found articulated (i.e. in anatomical connection) at depths of less than 50 cm on an incline corresponding to the original sedimentation in the bottom of the kiln.

All the bodies had fractured skulls as a consequence of shots which, judging by their respective trajectories, were fired from the back of the skull. Two bullets were found corresponding to different calibre pistols (7 and 11 mm).

Conclusions

Thousands of victims of the Spanish Civil War (1936–1939) remain buried in mass graves all over the country. The recovery of the human remains of victims in the Civil War is always a complex task that requires specialised techniques developed by archaeologists and using internationally proven methodology. The excavation of more than 300 mass graves since 2000 has certainly triggered the concept and awareness of the value of forensic archaeology.

However, in addition to such clandestine graves dug in peripheral areas or cemeteries, wells and natural caves were also used to hide the evidence of these crimes. Such places have been used throughout history in conflict situations and with the common aim of hiding the bodies as well as possible. With regards to recovery, these same scientific protocols, when applied to mine shafts and natural caves, become even more necessary, and often require the specific design of resources adapted to each particular case, due to the intrinsic difficulty of these kinds of sites, where little experience has been acquired. Appropriate conditions of safety and illumination and small well-trained teams enable the correct exhumation of these remains, which are characterised by their great fragility and deterioration as a consequence of the special environmental conditions.

Advancements in archaeological techniques in the field of Forensic Science as well as advances in other disciplines have made it possible to search, locate and recover these remains and identify the victims. Today, the use of archaeology in these contexts is extremely important not only for the 'mere' excavation but also for the correct recovery and interpretation that may later facilitate the identification of the human remains in the laboratory. Ultimately, it brings respect, dignity, memory, closure and the healing of wounds.

References

Alonso, A. 2006. La identificación genética de las víctimas de la Guerra Civil Española. In ARMH Valladolid, *La Represión Franquista: Mito, Olvido y Memoria*, 183–193. Valladolid, Universidad de Valladolid.

Alonso, A., Martín, P., Albarrán, C., García, P., Aguirre, A. and Fernández, C. 2012. La identificación genética de víctimas de la Guerra Civil Española: la experiencia del Instituto Nacional de Toxicología y Ciencias Forenses. *Boletin Galego de Medicina Legal e Forense* 18, 117–123.

Cardoso, S., Etxeberria, F., Alfonso-Sánchez, M. A. et al. 2008. Contribution of forensic genetics to the recovery of historic memory of the Spanish Civil War. *Forensic Science International Genetics Supplement Series* 1, 454–456.

Crespillo, M., Paredes, M., Arimany, J., Guerrero, L. and Valverde. J. L. 2004. Guerra Civil Española (1936–1939): identificación de restos humanos procedentes de fosas comunes en Cataluña mediante análisis de ADN Mitocondrial. A propósito de un caso. *Cuadernos de Medicina Forense* 38, 37–46.

Etxeberria, F. 2004. Panorama organizativo sobre Antropología y Patología Forense en España. Algunas propuestas para el estudio de fosas con restos humanos de la Guerra Civil española de 1936. In Ambito (ed.), *La Memoria de los Olvidados. Un Debate Sobre el Silencio de la Represión Franquista*, 183–219. Valladolid, Ambito.

Etxeberria, F. (ed.) 2012. Antropología forense de la Guerra Civil Española. *Boletín Galego de Medicina Legal e Forense* 18. Asociación Galega de Médicos Forenses.

Herrasti Erlogorri, L. and Jiménez Sánchez, J. M. 2012. Excavación arqueológica de los enterramientos colectivos de la Guerra Civil. In F. Etxeberria (ed.), Antropología forense de la Guerra Civil Española. Boletín Galego de Medicina Legal e Forense 18, 29–45.

López García, J. and Ferrándiz, F. 2010. *Fontanosas, 1941-2006. Memoria de Carne y Hueso*. Ciudad Real, Imprenta Provincial.

Polo, M. 2009. *Métodos Internacionales Empleados para la Identificación de Restos Óseos Humano*. Revista d'Estudis de la Violència no 8.

Prada, E., Etxeberria, F., Herrasti, L., Vidal, J., Macías, S. and Pastor, F. 2003. Antropología del pasado reciente: una fosa común de la Guerra Civil española en Priaranza del Bierzo (León). In Mª P. Aluja, A. Malgosa and R. Mª Nogués (eds.), *Antropologíay Biodiversidad*, Volumen I, 431–446. Barcelona, Edicions Bellaterra.

Reverte, J. M. 1984–1985. Informe emitido por la escuela de medicina legal en su sección de antropología forense al Ilmo. Sr. Juez del Juzgado de instrucción no 10, Madrid. Los esqueletos de la Casa de Campos de Madrid. *Anales de la Escuela de Medicina Legal de la Universidad Complutense de Madrid* 1, 33–48.

Ríos, L., Casado Ovejero, J. I. and Puente Prieto, J. 2010. Identification process in mass graves from the Spanish Civil War I. *Forensic Science International* 199(1/3), e27–e36.

Serrulla, F. and Etxeberria, F. 1995. Estudio antropológico forense de los restos óseos aparecidos en cova Arcoia (O Caurel, Lugo). *Boletín Galego de Medicina Legal e Forense* 1, 9–13.

CHAPTER 56

The development of forensic archaeology and anthropology by the Uruguayan Forensic Anthropology Team

José M. López Mazz and Alicia Lusiardo

Universidad de la República, Facultad de Humanidades y Ciencias de la Educación, Montevideo, Uruguay

Introduction

In the past 20 years, legal scenarios linked to violations of human rights have given renewed impetus to the systematisation of forensic field and laboratory work in Uruguay. At the level of field work, fragmentary information about the location of the Disappeared Detainees (*Detenidos Desaparecidos*) of the last military dictatorship (1973–1985), together with archaeological survey strategies, led to the finding of several clandestine cemeteries (López et al. 2007, 9).

The total number of missing persons is difficult to quantify precisely for different reasons. There are about 40 political Disappeared Detainees in the Uruguayan territory, while there are about 245 disappeared Uruguayans in Argentina. To that number must be added the detainees of other nationalities in Uruguayan territory, and an important but difficult-to-estimate number of disappeared of other nationalities, who were the subject of 'removals' by Condor Operation. The Condor Operation was the coordinated repression among the anti-communist militaries in the region (McSherry 1999).

In relation to laboratory techniques, the systematic comparative study of bone remains from these burials helped us identify the suffering and torture endured by these political prisoners, simultaneously facilitating the identification of their causes of death. This information allowed us to recognise patterns of torture applied to Disappeared Detainees as part of a systematic activity by the oppressors.

Concurrently, the established scientific systematic facts facilitated the recognition of execution of prisoners. Up until this point, military speech alleged that those deaths were the result of the occasional excesses of torture (Rico et al. 2007).

Prior to the creation of the Forensic Anthropology Investigation Team (*Grupo de Investigación en Arqueología Forense* – GIAF), the judicial system in Uruguay dealt with the investigation of skeletonised remains with plenty of flaws. There was a single anthropologist, working at the capital city Medical Examiner's office, analysing all the remains found throughout the country. No archaeologists worked for the judicial system, and the exhumations and field work related to those cases were performed by untrained police officers and/or firefighters. No chain of custody was implemented. No international standardised forensic protocols were used. The anthropological reports were faulty and incomplete, revealing the lack of appropriate methodologies and techniques both in the field and in the laboratory. Moreover, identifications were performed using skull identification through video superimpositions, with the obvious result of misidentification.[1] All these deficiencies resulted in mistrust and pain for the relatives of the victims.

The administration of updated forensic protocols forced the Uruguayan State to review some of the identification procedures used hitherto, since they produced contradictory results, and did not give judicial guarantees. In this context, the need to develop protocols where positive identification must be achieved through DNA analysis (performed either by international or national, private or governmental labs) arose. Forensic protocols did not exist until the issue of human rights was assumed as a matter of State. In 2010, the Inter-American Court of Human Rights condemned Uruguay for its actions relating to the forced disappearance of

[1]For more information, see: http://www.lr21.com.uy/politica/337692-justicia-solicita-examen-de-adn-por-restos-hallados-en-vichadero, http://www.ultimasnoticias.com.uy/hemeroteca/270809/prints/act02.html. (last accessed 30 March 2014).

Forensic Archaeology: A Global Perspective, First Edition. Edited by W.J. Mike Groen, Nicholas Márquez-Grant and Robert C. Janaway.

a woman in the 1970s, in a case that human rights experts see as a watershed for ending impunity for crimes against humanity committed under Uruguay's military dictatorship. The Court asked the country to guarantee the quality of the search through the use of protocols. The Secretariat for Human Rights wrote a protocol that was endorsed by the Public Prosecutor of the nation in 2013.

The present work shows different aspects of the investigation by the GIAF in Uruguay from 2005 to 2013 and will discuss the scope of the results.

History and development of the GIAF

The GIAF was created in the bosom of the Institute of Anthropology of the University of the Republic in 2005, to accommodate the request for collaboration of the President of the Republic, Tabaré Vásquez, and to address social demands in relation to human rights. The Uruguayan police and judicial system lacked and unfortunately still lacks trained forensic anthropologists and archaeologists.

The GIAF scientific mission has been to produce original methodologies and direct information regarding disappeared detainees. The team is integrated by forensic archaeologists and anthropologists. Its mission is to support justice with more rigorous procedures, to collaborate on respect for human rights and to update a historical narrative for that period. The objectives of the team are to search, locate, retrieve, analyse and identify remains belonging to the missing detainees. Since 2005, the GIAF have excavated different military fields, finding and identifying the remains of four missing detainees. The resulting information allowed us to reconstruct some crime patterns of the political repression.

The archaeological survey

The search for the Disappeared Detainees comes to a critical point when choosing a geographical space in which to perform the search. The places where field archaeology techniques were applied generally arise from a database set up in 2005 by the GIAF, containing documentary and testimonial information of a diverse nature and from different sources (governmental, NGOs, and other files). In the case of Uruguay, the critical address of this type of information led to a categorisation between official and unofficial testimonies as well as between direct and indirect testimonies. A direct testimony is a testimony from a direct participant in the crime or from a crime witness, while an indirect testimony is an account of someone who did not participate in the crime or did not witness the crime. Despite this methodological concern, the evaluation of the quality of the information will always be part of a long process, where the results on the ground have the last word (López et al. 2012).

Much *a priori* encouraging information, due to its official origin, was eventually found to be deliberately false with the intention to mislead the archaeological search for remains. In 2005, at the training fields of the 14th Parachute Battalion, Uruguayan Army sources voluntarily pinpointed the burial location of María Claudia Garcia de Gelman, an Argentinean political detainee, kidnapped in Argentina and transferred to Uruguay. After several days of extensive searching, we were able to confirm that there had never been any kind of burial at the indicated area.

The area selection should be based on direct testimonies if possible. Then, a careful aerial photograph study (from the military geographical, years 1966, 1975, 1980, 1981, and 1985) should be made, trying to recognise changes in the landscape under investigation (López et al. 2007, 27–32). This methodology has been successful if different images are available, if they are temporally successive and if they directly cover the time period linked to cases of disappearances of political detainees.

The information obtained by the aerial photograph study proves to be essential as it enables the spatial accuracy and identification of features and site changes within a previously larger and vaguely defined zone. These landscape modifications could be clandestine burials. We were able to observe changes in vegetation of the training fields at the 13th and 14th Battalions in Uruguay, which were later matched to large ground sub-stratigraphic disturbances.

Depending on the spatial scale where the search was conducted, classic archaeological field techniques were applied, seeking a detailed subsurface exploration of the area (Harris 1991). Forensic archaeology tries to optimise the location of clandestine cemeteries and burials. It also combines techniques to record the crime scene, facilitating detailed spatial and positional analysis of mass graves, human remains and objects. This facilitates, by inference, the interpretation of the events. The forensic archaeological field work in Uruguay entailed large areas, in some cases comprising 12 ha (13th Battalion) and in other cases more than 100 ha (14th Battalion).

In order to cover large areas, trenches (excavation units) of 3 × 1 m were dug every 0.5 m to ensure complete and uniform coverage. In some areas, trenches were manually excavated; whereas in large areas, backhoes were used. A 250 m^2 per day of coverage was accomplished in some areas, depending on topography, weather conditions and vegetation (Figure 56.1). The testimonies of clandestine cemeteries and graves are often vague or refer to military premises from 4 to 400 ha.

Figure 56.1 Excavation units at a farm in Pando, Canelones.

Aerial photos allow us to recognise changes in the designated spaces and to complete field observation. They also help us to recognise changes in different spatial scales and to propose casual relationships with the clandestine activities of execution, burial and digging.

The operations of body concealment

As fieldwork developed, the results highlighted a series of operations related to the concealment of clandestine graves of the Disappeared Detainees. These procedures with deliberate intent to conceal were found at different stages of our investigation. The concealment by the military was active and can be considered permanent, since it still has an effect on most of the burials that have not been located.

First, the preferred locations for concealment were remote locations with restricted access (wetlands, forests), which were generally located at the back of military bases. Second, concealment is demonstrated by the preparation of sub-surface pits of different depths often carved into the rock. The third episode of concealment refers to the desire to destroy the body by covering it with quicklime, with the (wrong) assumption that this ensures the destruction of the skeleton. Fourth, and according to an established criminal pattern in Uruguay, a cement slab was placed over the remains.

So far, four individual graves have been located in military bases, as well as different partial remains, corresponding to testimonies of 'cleaning' activities of the clandestine cemeteries, on the eve of the return to democracy, between 1983 and 1985.

In some cases, the concealment operations continued with a careful forestation of the field, in an attempt to hide any evidence that could guide a future search. In a few cases, buildings and other structures were built over clandestine graves, in particular at the headquarters of the 13th Battalion (the Battalions are still active). Some graves were primary, while others were secondary, depending on specific dates. Around 1984, when democracy returned to our country, bodies were exhumed and reburied under military buildings (sheds, ammunition depots, firing ranges, etc.) by the military with the intent to further conceal the bodies. Some military accounts indicate that some bodies were cremated and the ashes were thrown in the Bay of Montevideo (Rico et al. 2007).

Another form of concealment has to do with the placement of bodies in rural cemeteries, mixing the remains with those from legal burials. Many bodies of the Disappeared Detainees reached the Uruguayan coast, presumably from death flights (flights in which victims were drugged before being thrown from planes, still alive, into the sea or the Río de la Plata River). The bodies were buried as NN (*Nomen Nescio* or No Name) in public cemeteries. In an effort to confirm the location and identification, the majority of these bodies were dumped into ossuaries, as part of a policy involving different cemeteries (López et al. 2012).

The systematic concealment policy, closely linked to the denial of the committed crimes, sets up a separate chapter in the absolute silence of the perpetrators and their police and military colleagues. This silent agreement combines with threats and calls to respect the military hierarchy, even after retirement.

Clandestine grave excavation

Clandestine graves are, in a way, *memory reservoirs* analogous to the archaeological sites. The excavation of a clandestine grave is done by forensic archaeologists following technical procedures and forensic protocols to secure as much information as possible with little destruction. However, the excavation activity is a destructive activity by nature, and a clandestine cemetery can only be excavated once.

A good excavation procedure allows the recovery of human bone without damaging the material in order to secure further analysis and identification. The burial context analysis, through a careful and controlled observation, generates valuable information about the circumstances of the death and burial. The objects associated with clandestine burials are critical, as they contribute information that is necessary in order to interpret the crime and strengthen the value of the evidence.

This contributes to a better recording of the history of these crimes and supports the justice actions, offering signs and empirical evidence. Moreover, the handling of independent lines of evidence gives more accuracy to the analysis of crimes under study and improves the design of strategies for the validation of scientific hypotheses.

Recognising torture

The most widely accepted definition of torture can be found in Article 1 of the United Nations Convention against Torture and other Cruel, Inhuman or Degrading Treatment or Punishment (UNCAT):

> *For the purposes of this Convention, torture means any act by which severe pain or suffering, whether physical or mental, is intentionally inflicted on a person for such purposes as obtaining from him or a third person information or a confession, punishing him for an act he or a third person has committed or is suspected of having committed, or intimidating or coercing him or a third person, or for any reason based on discrimination of any kind, when such pain or suffering is inflicted by or at the instigation of or with the consent or acquiescence of a public official or other person acting in an official capacity. It does not include pain or suffering arising only from, inherent in or incidental to lawful sanctions (Nowak* 2006, 817*).*

Due to the wide range of methods of inflicting pain and to the deliberate attempt to reduce any physical evidence in order to evade its detection, positive confirmation of an act of torture is a complex task for the forensic anthropologists (Vogel et al. 2007, 188). Moreover, forensic anthropologists analyse hard tissues, a material that will not necessarily exhibit all signs of inflicted pain. Other reasons that limit the analysis are poor recovery and/or bad preservation of the remains.

Physical evidence can corroborate an eye witness testimony or, on the contrary, can undermine someone's statement. Ligatures to the hands and feet, as well as blindfolds of different material, have proven to be valuable tools in establishing relationships between execution sites and primary and secondary mass graves. They are also proof of civilian deaths not related to combat in any way, as intended and planned by the perpetrators (Tyers 2009, 74).

Careful documentation and recovery of all the evidence relevant to abuse, such as cloths used for blindfolding or ropes, wires and scarves used for handheld ligatures, is essential to prove and corroborate eyewitness accounts of torture. The mere finding of human remains within a grave is not enough to demonstrate the occurrence of human rights abuses (Blau and Skinner 2005, 456).

In the case of Uruguay, the archaeological evidence was able to corroborate the victim's accounts in relation to places, dates, physical harassment and ill-treatment. In the burial sites uncovered in a farm in Pando (Canelones), and in the training fields at the 14th Parachute Battalion in Toledo (Canelones), the GIAF recovered several items showing a direct relationship to physical harassment, such as ligatures, blindfolds and cords used as necklaces holding ID numbers given to prisoners by the military. These items were analysed in relation to burial context and other findings such as lack of clothing, peri-mortem lesions and hand position, allowing us to reconstruct the detention condition of prisoners as well as their deaths (Figures 56.2 and 56.3).

Sometimes, burial conditions do not allow for the recovery of evidence related to ill-treatment since preservation condition varies according to the type of material. However, body position has been interpreted by others as evidence that the victims were buried handcuffed (Komar 2008, 124). Objects found in the pit and associated with the remains, such as papers, documents, coins and bills aid the task of determining a relative chronology of the events (Figure 56.4).

Examination of executions

The identification of bone trauma requires very careful recovery of both bones and associated physical evidence (shells and bullets). It is necessary to differentiate between taphonomic alterations and/or post-mortem

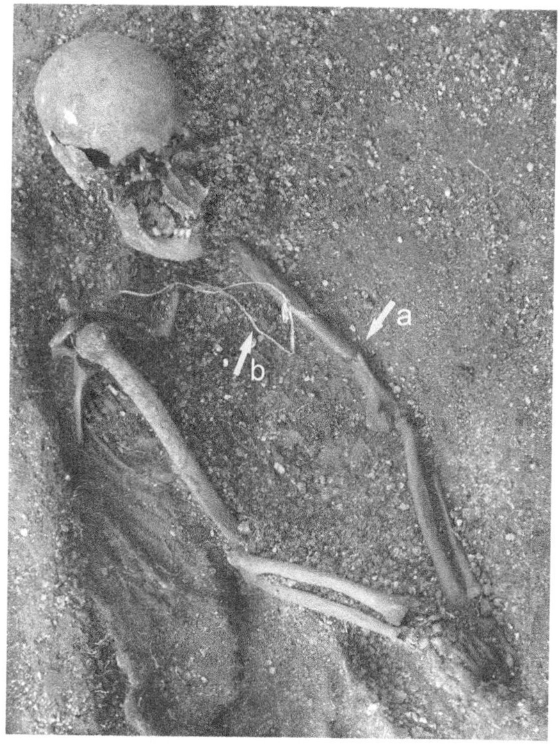

Figure 56.2 Skeleton exhibiting peri-mortem trauma (a) and a cord used as necklace for an ID tag (b).

Figure 56.3 Skeleton with hands restrained by a ligature.

Figure 56.4 Recovered evidence associated with the remains.

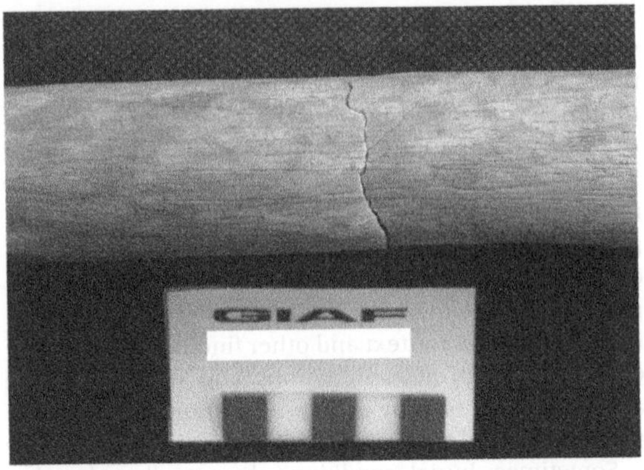

Figure 56.5 Butterfly peri-mortem fracture of a right femur.

Figure 56.6 Rib with peri-mortem fracture.

fractures that might resemble lesions in order to diagnose correctly the mechanism that may have contributed to the death of an individual.

Fractures that do not exhibit evidence of healing and have a series of typical features are classified as peri-mortem, and they are the result of an episode of violence whose occurrence took place around the time of death. The distinctive characteristics of a peri-mortem injury are the staining and the morphology of the fracture (Kimmerle and Baraybar 2008, 58). The bone colour change (staining) is attributable to decomposition fluids, blood and sediment. The difference in colour between the bone surface and the inner and outer bone fracture surface is one of the diagnostic features. If all are homogeneous in colour, the fracture corresponds to a peri-mortem fracture that may present some pigmentation due to body fluids and sediment from burial. The morphology of the fracture is related to the response of bone material, whether this is fresh or dry. Fresh bone, unlike dry bone, is still surrounded by muscles, skin and periosteum, and has considerable tensile strength. When it breaks, there are typically greenstick, concentric, circular, spiral, butterfly or oblique fractures, all with irregular chipped edges (Figures 56.5 and 56.6).

The cases analysed in Uruguay, at our university laboratory, are clear examples of the degree of cruelty to which victims were subjected during their detention, not only by the aforementioned finding of ligatures and blindfolds but also due to skeletal evidence of peri-mortem trauma (both blunt force and gunshot wound trauma).

Identification problems

Although positive identification of a set of human remains must be carried out by comparing genetic profiles or dental records, the reconstruction of the biological profile and other relevant data provides a hypothesis of identity that helps narrow down the number of comparisons to be made. This step comprises age-at-death, sex, height and ancestry estimation, as well as the analysis of the pathological conditions, individualising characteristics and occupational stress markers.

The number of possible identities is greatly reduced if we produce relevant information concerning the biological profile of the remains under analysis. If we add up all those normal but individualising traits, a skeleton might have (accessory bones, epigenetic traits, degree of development of muscle insertion sites, diseases that leave marks on bones) the hypothesis of identity is built with greater precision.

The analysis of occupational stress markers can provide information on daily life activities. Any repetitive activity sustained over time leaves a mark on the skeleton and can be quantified and interpreted. While this type of analysis does not infer the exact activity performed by the individual, we can describe the type of repetitive motion involved as occupational, recreational or sport related. The skeletons recovered in Uruguay allowed genetically guided studies, providing concrete data on sex, age, stature, pathology and occupational activities of the victims.

Conclusion

Since its inception, the activity of the GIAF has been followed closely by the media. Information is disseminated regularly, and has been the subject of books, articles and two film documentaries. The archaeologists and forensic anthropologists that comprise the GIAF are graduates from the School of Humanities and Education Science (*Facultad de Humanidades y Ciencias de la Educación* – FHCE), University of the Republic (*Universidad de la Republica*) and have received specialised training (in some cases, postgraduate degrees) in the United States, Europe and Argentina. One of the GIAF members is Board Certified by the Latin American Forensic Anthropology Association (*Asociación Latinoamericana de Antropología Forense* – ALAF). Some regularly teach courses within the framework of the activities of the Postgraduate Unit of the FHCE, distance learning programmes, and also travel abroad to teach workshops.

The GIAF has consolidated an area of forensic expertise, which answers the University's demands, the need for legal expertise and the reformulation of historical memory through new data.

The identification of four Disappeared Detainees to date has had a great impact on society. The team also accompanied the relatives of missing persons in the processes of appropriation of the burial sites as *places of memory*. The GIAF regularly produces reports and technical expertise, as well as books, book chapters and scientific articles.

In relation to their future expectations, the GIAF, within the University, concerns the training and specialisation in forensic topics and their scenarios. Our University basis allows us to try different routes once the agreement with the Presidency of the Republic of Uruguay ends. There is regular collaboration with the Argentine Forensic Anthropology Team and the Secretariat of Human Rights of Brazil.

Piecing together a criminal investigation, especially dealing with compromised human remains, is a complex task; it entails multidisciplinary teams, validated forensic protocols, skills, training and experience. Despite the evident deficiencies and problems mentioned in the introduction of this chapter, up to the present, nothing has changed in the Uruguayan judicial system. The GIAF remains working independently, strengthening the human rights investigations in the country.

References

Blau, S. and Skinner, M. 2005. The use of forensic archaeology in the investigation of human rights abuse: unearthing the past in East Timor. *The International Journal of Human Rights* 9, 449–463.

Harris, E. 1991. *Principios de Estratigrafía Arqueológica*. Barcelona, Editorial Crítica.

Kimmerle, E. H. and Baraybar, J. P. 2008. *Skeletal Trauma: Identification of Injuries Resulting from Human Rights Abuse and Armed Conflict*. Boca Raton, CRC Press.

Komar, D. 2008. Patterns of mortuary practice associated with genocide: implications for archaeological research. *Current Anthropology* 49, 123–133.

López, J. M., del Puerto, L., Erchini, C. et al. 2007. *Investigación Arqueológica sobre Detenidos Desaparecidos. En cumplimiento del Artículo 4° de la Ley 15.848*, Tomo V. Montevideo, Presidencia de la República-IMPO.

López, J. M., Lusiardo, A., Nadal, O. et al. 2012. *Investigaciones Antropológicas sobre Detenidos Desaparecidos en la Última Dictadura Cívico-Militar*. Informe de Actividades Año 2011 – 2012. Available at http://sdh.gub.uy/wps/wcm/connect/0aa20e004f86a212a716ef747e17f7b4/Investigaciones+antropologicas+sobre+detenidos+desaparecidos+en+la+%C3%BAltima+dictadura+c%C3%ADvico-militar.pdf?MOD=AJPERES&CACHEID=0aa20e004f86a212a716ef747e17f7b4. (last accessed 30 March 2014).

McSherry, J. P. 1999. Operation Condor: clandestine Inter-American system. *Social Justice* 26, 144–174.

Nowak, M. 2006. What practices constitute torture? US and UN standards. *Human Rights Quarterly* 28, 809–841.

Rico, A., Alonso, J., Figueredo, M. et al. 2007. *Investigación Histórica sobre Detenidos Desaparecidos. En Cumplimiento del Artículo 4° de la Ley 15.848*, Tomo I. Montevideo, Presidencia de la República, IMPO.

Tyers, C. A. 2009. Hidden atrocities: the forensic investigation and prosecution of genocide. PhD thesis, University of Tennessee.

Vogel, H., Schmitz-Engels, F. and Grille, C. 2007. Radiology of torture. *European Journal of Radiology* 63, 187–204.

Further Reading

Jessee, E. 2003. Exhuming conflict: some recommendations for the creation of a series of experimental mass grave and mass grave-related test sites. PhD thesis, Simon Fraser University.

Jordana, G., García, C. and Malgosa, A. 2007. Marcadores de actividad en restos óseos. *Cuadernos de Medicina Forense* 13, 179–189.

Krenzer, U. 2006. Compendio de métodos antropológico forenses para la reconstrucción del perfil osteo-biológico. *Serie de Antropología Forense*. Centro de Análisis Forense y Ciencias Aplicadas, Guatemala, CAFCA.

Madres y Familiares de Detenidos Desaparecidos. 2004. *A Todos Ellos*. Montevideo, Caligráficos S.A.

Ubelaker, D. H. 2006. Introduction to forensic anthropology. In A. Schmitt, E. Cunha and J. Pinheiro (eds.), *Forensic Anthropology and Medicine: Complementary Sciences from Recovery to Cause of Death*, 3–12. Tottowa. Humana Press.

Wieberg, D. A. M. and Wescott, D. J. 2008. Estimating the timing of long bone fractures: correlation between the post-mortem interval, bone moisture content, and blunt force trauma fracture characteristics. *Journal of Forensic Sciences* 53, 1028–1034.

CHAPTER 57

The Returning Casualty: the excavation of a communist re-education camp cemetery at Lang Da, Yen Bai Province, Vietnam

Julie Martin

Archaeological Consultant, The Returning Casualty, Houston, Texas

Introduction

> *The prison cemetery, called Cay Khe, held the remains of many bad-luck prisoners. Their mates wrapped the bodies in rotten cloth and buried them hurriedly with a crystal bottle containing a small piece of paper recording personnel details of the victim such as his name and date of death. This was done to help family members identify the body as a later date (Truong* 2010*, 214).*

While the convoluted struggle known as the Vietnam War in the West has received wide attention historically and culturally, the fallout of the war after 30 April 1975 and the fate of the defeated populace of South Vietnam garnered little interest from those not directly involved in the conflict. This chapter covers one small charity created by a survivor of the post-war communist re-education camps, and the development of the charity as it progressed with the help of archaeological and anthropological guidance both in the field and the laboratory, leading to the successful resolution of uniting families with the remains of their lost relatives.

Vietnam after the fall of Saigon: a brief history of the South Vietnamese people from 1975 to 1979

On 30 April 1975, Saigon, the capital of South Vietnam, fell to the communist forces of the north after the unconditional surrender of General Duong Van Minh, the last president of the South Vietnamese Republic. Soon after the fall, radio and loudspeaker announcements throughout the south declared that all military personnel from the defeated Army for the Republic of Vietnam (ARVN) (*Lục quân Việt Nam Cộng hòa*) should present themselves to the Communist authorities in their home district for re-education. On average, announcements stated that all military officers should present themselves for a re-education programme that would last between 1 and 4 weeks and the officers should bring enough clothing, money, food and medicines for that time period. Survivor accounts vary, but Hoa Minh Truong, in his book *The Dark Journey – Inside the Re-education Camps of Vietcong* recounts 'that the "tolerant" policy would require me to undergo learning for seven days, after which I would return home as normal' (Truong 2010, 17). Mr Truong's imprisonment in a number of camps lasted 6 years. In his book, *A Gift of Barbed Wire – America's Allies Abandoned in South Vietnam,* Robert S. McKelvey interviewed a number of re-education camp survivors and their families, and reported that although the Communist government announcements stated that the re-education programme would last 1 month, the average stay in the camps was 7–8 years, with a range of 1–2 years to over 20 years (McKelvey 2002, 5).

Although exact numbers of prisoners and re-education camps are unknown, Truong (2010, 72) writes, 'According to Amnesty International and the Human Rights Watch organisation, 193 prison camps were established in 36 provinces from North to South.' In McKelvey's book, a former South Vietnamese intelligence officer in the Central Intelligence Organisation (CIO) in South Vietnam who spent 21 years in the camps recounts that, 'There were over 600 district re-education camps, one or two per district. Then there were more than 100 provincial camps and more than 20 national camps. Each camp had between 500 and 800 prisoners' (McKelvey 2002, 86). This disparity in the exact number of camps (and its victims) as recorded in the aforementioned books illustrates the lack of accountable evidence from this episode in the history of Vietnam.

Along with former military personnel from the defeated South Vietnamese regime, other individuals considered enemies of the Socialist Republic of Vietnam (*Cộng hòa Xã hội chủ nghĩa Việt Nam*) government, and therefore liable for re-education, included anyone with

Forensic Archaeology: A Global Perspective, First Edition. Edited by W.J. Mike Groen, Nicholas Márquez-Grant and Robert C. Janaway.

past affiliations with the Americans, public servants of the former South Vietnamese government, Buddhist and Catholic monks and nuns and members of two other Buddhist sects, the Cao Dai and the Hoa Hao. Repercussions of the defeat of the South extended to wives and children of the military. Children were barred from attending school, and wives often had to resort to selling anything they could to survive while their husbands were imprisoned (McKelvey 2002, 5 and 95). Military personnel who survived the camps found they were barred from work after their release and stripped of Vietnamese citizenship, and these families were treated with suspicion and scorn by their neighbours and communities (McKelvey 2002, 4 and 211). Many survivors of the war sought escape in the diasporas from 1978 and 1979 in a desperate attempt to flee the national food shortages that occurred after the fall of Saigon after the Socialist Republic of Vietnam shut its borders to outsiders. Those who escaped on boats often found themselves victims of armed Thai pirates who boarded the boats to steal money and possessions from the refugees. Women and girls were raped and some taken by the Thais, never to be seen again (Truong 2010, 100).

The Orderly Departure Program

In 1979, in an effort to quell the attacks on the refugee boat people, a Memorandum of Understanding was negotiated between the Socialist Republic of Vietnam and the United Nations High Commission for Refugees (UNHCR) (USGAO 1990, 2). The Orderly Departure Program (ODP) was instigated and adopted by over 40 receiving countries and lasted until 1994. The United States accepted applications for the program from a number of individuals including children, spouses and parents of US citizens or permanent residents, former US Government employees and political prisoners and others held in re-education camps. In 1995, with the continuing release of more detainees from the camps despite the ending of the ODP, the Humanitarian Resettlement Program (HR) was implemented in the United States to allow former soldiers or officials of the former South Vietnamese Government before 30 April 1975, who had spent 3 years or more in a re-education centre after 30 April 1975, to apply for the Humanitarian Offensive (HO) Program (US Department of State 2005). This process was limited to those who were unable to apply, such as through imprisonment in a re-education camp, or were unable to complete the application process before the ODP closed on 30 September 1994. A further US program, The McCain Amendment, was launched in 1996 allowing unmarried children over the age of 21 and widows of former re-education camp detainees to apply for resettlement to the United States as refugees of special humanitarian concern due to their family's association with the former South Vietnamese Government and the United States. This program was extended to the 17 December 2007 (US Department of State 2005).

> *We know now from a 1985 statement by Nguyen Co Tach that 2 500 000, rather than 1 000 000, people went through re-education....in fact, possibly more than 100 000 Vietnamese people were victims of extrajudicial executions in the last ten years ... it is likely that, overall, at least one million Vietnamese were the victims of forced population transfers (Desbarats* 1990).

The communist re-education camps and its prisoners

Many of the re-education camps used by the victorious communist regime were sited at previous prisoner of war camps from the First Indochina War (1946–1950) between the French colonialists and the nationalist Viet Minh, including the camp at Lang Da, Yen Bai Province (Thanh Dac Nguyen, personal communication 2010) where The Returning Casualty charity (further details later) conducted its excavation in July 2010. With hundreds of re-education camps in existence throughout Vietnam, prisoners were often moved between a number of camps during their imprisonment, with the northern jungle camps used especially to house South Vietnamese officers with a rank of captain and above (McKelvey 2002, 62 and 82; Truong 2010, 131 and 158). Camp life consisted of forced heavy labour including jungle clearance, road building, land mine clearance and crop cultivation during the day and hours of communist manifesto education and exercises in self-criticism late into the evening (McKelvey 2002, xii and 83; Thanh Dac Nguyen, personal communication 2010). The regimen was offset with, on average, three small handfuls of rice per day, which was on rare occasions supplemented by parcels of food provided by family members if they could afford to make the long and treacherous journey to the camps. The combination of starvation rations, poor sanitation and hygiene and lack of medical care resulted in diseases such as beri beri, tuberculosis and malaria that were further exacerbated by bouts of influenza, amoebic dysentery and pneumonia (McKelvey 2002, 89; Truong 2010, 114 and 182).

There is no accurate record of the death toll of prisoners in these camps which ran from 1975 to 1998, but it is estimated that at least 50,000 deaths could be attributed to starvation, disease, execution, torture and, as discovered in the Lang Da cemetery, work-related accidents (Truong 2010, 122).

The Vietnam: American Foundation and The Returning Casualty

In 1984, Mr Thanh Dac Nguyen, a major in the former Army for the Republic of Vietnam (ARVN), was released from the Lang Da camp after spending 9.5 years in a number of re-education camps. In December 1993, after moving to the United States under the ODP, Mr Nguyen established the Vietnamese American Foundation (VAF) (originally known as the Mutual Assistance Association of HO, or *Tổng Hội HO* in Vietnamese). He wanted to assist other refugees who came to live in the United States under the humanitarian resettlement program, and help with the transition into their new lives as American citizens. Today, Association chapters are located throughout the United States, Germany, France and Australia where large Vietnamese expatriate communities have become established. The charity is specifically a non-political, humanitarian organisation that does not seek to apportion blame or press for prosecution of human rights violations against the Vietnamese government.

December 2006 welcomed a new chapter in the life of the Foundation as The Returning Casualty (*T. R. CTử Sĩ Trở Về*)[1] initiative began to take shape. Through this US-based project, the charity sought to bring closure and peace of mind to the many Vietnamese who lost their relatives in the post-war re-education camps, while honouring those who perished in the jungle camps. Since December 2007, The Returning Casualty has successfully located nearly 300 re-education camp graves and helped over 68 families recover the remains of their loved ones.

Excavations by The Returning Casualty

Excavations of re-education camp graves before archaeological consultation

An archaeological approach to the retrieval of human remains had, at first, not been achieved by the charity. Since commencement of exhumation work began in 2007, the organisation had relied on local labourers to excavate specific graves of individuals that were marked by headstones. The grave sites were located through death certificates issued by the government, which included the location site, and the labourer would dig into the grave and retrieve the bones, pulling the skeletal elements from the grave fill and handing them to the family members to wrap in red or gold paper as part of the Buddhist practice for honouring the dead. Any personal effects were often left unrecovered or considered of little consequence.[2]

Archaeological excavation of the Lang Da cemetery for mtDNA retrieval

From the 21 to the 23 of July 2010, The Returning Casualty undertook its first archaeological excavation of a burial site at a former camp at Lang Da, Yen Bai Province, northwest of Hanoi. Under the author's supervision as the archaeological advisor to the charity, the organisation successfully exhumed the remains of 12 former prisoners whose death certificates identified them as being buried at the Lang Da camp. Samples of each individual were taken for mtDNA analysis and brought to The University of North Texas, Centre for Human Identification, Forensic Division. In addition, the remaining skeletal elements were placed in individual ceramic ossuaries and taken to a temporary burial site near the original cemetery until the results of the DNA analysis and familial matches were completed and the remains returned to their families.

For the Lang Da excavation, each grave was fully excavated as per the British Institute for Archaeologists' (IfA) codes, standards and guidelines. This British organisation is considered the benchmark for maintaining professional standards and ethics throughout all aspects of archaeological work in the United Kingdom (Janaway, Chapter 24, this volume), and their standards and guidelines cover subjects such as *Standard and Guidance for Excavation* and *Standard and Guidance for the Collection, Documentation, Conservation and Research of Archaeological Materials*. In 2011, the IfA produced its standard and guidance for forensic archaeologists, allowing for continuity throughout the discipline which is often utilised by British archaeologists who work outside the country in both forensic and humanitarian excavations.

In keeping with the IfA's guidelines, each grave and skeleton at the Lang Da cemetery was given a discrete context number; and after the grave fill was removed, the skeleton and personal effects were photographed *in situ*. Skeleton recording forms were kept for each grave, which listed not only the artefacts retrieved from the graves, but any visible pathology or trauma evident from the initial site analysis of the skeleton as identified by the author. The personal effects included makeshift burial shrouds, clothing, rice bowls, medicine vials and mosquito nets that were recovered and taken back to the charity's headquarters in Texas for further analysis.

The cemetery site was located on a steep hillside overgrown with vegetation overlooking Thac Ba Lake in Yen Bai province, about 170 km northwest of Hanoi. The dirt road to the site was originally cut into the hillside by the prisoners of the Lang Da camp, sometimes without the use of tools (Thanh Da Nguyen, personal communication 2010). The actual location of the site was rediscovered by one of The Returning Casualty's Vietnamese members with the help of a hand-written map written by a former prison guard.

[1]For more information, see: www.vietremains.org (last accessed 30 March 2014).

[2]For a video footage of some of these excavations, see: The Returning Casualty project videos on You Tube, available at: https://www.youtube.com/user/thereturningcasualty (last accessed 30 March 2014).

Local labourers were brought in to clear the site of undergrowth and to remove the upper deposits of the grave fill. The cemetery site had seen previous exhumations of marked graves by family members; but by the time the Lang Da excavation commenced, many of the grave stones had been moved to the periphery of the site, leaving the remaining graves unmarked. Of the 31 grave plots at this particular site, at least eight had been previously excavated. The graves excavated in the Lang Da project were graves 2, 3, 5, 6, 8, 13, 15, 16, 21, 22, 23 and 30.

In agreement with Ms Dixie Peters, the forensic anthropologist responsible for performing the DNA analysis at the University of North Texas Centre for Human Identification, it was decided that at least one femur would be retained for mtDNA analysis, with tibia also included if taphonomic alterations were severe. Southeast Asia is well noted for its acidic soils and high humidity making bone preservation very poor, as attested by the Joint Pacific Accounting Command's (JPAC) work in the region recovering the remains of US military personnel (Pokines 2009). Of the 12 skeletons exhumed, 10 provided viable mtDNA; and as this publication goes to print, three familial matches have been made from families who provided samples through DNA kits provided by The Returning Casualty free of charge.

Due to time limitations, the fieldwork was undertaken in 2.5 days, resulting in the excavation of up to five graves per day with a small team of labourers, while the author completed the final cleaning back of the grave fills to expose the skeletons and the lifting of artefacts and skeletal elements, as well as any recording. Time constraints like this are not ideal, but one must be adaptable to the changing conditions on site, including inhospitable weather. July in Vietnam is extremely hot, humid and wet. Despite the inclement weather, the language barrier between the local workforce and the author, the underlying tensions between the South and North Vietnamese and the constant monitoring of our actions throughout the trip by local government officials, the excavation proved successful.

In keeping with Buddhist religious practice, an altar was placed at the site with food offerings and incense. As no Buddhist monks would take part in the proceedings due to fear of repercussions by the local government, Mr Nguyen donned saffron robes to recite prayers before and after the day's excavation work. All graves being dug that day had incense burning at the head of the grave, and paper money was burned and placed in the empty graves after the exhumation process. Dr Mai Lan Gustafsson, assistant professor of anthropology at Christopher Newport University in Virginia, US, writes 'Many Vietnamese believe that if someone dies violently or far from home without a proper burial, that person becomes trapped in hell' (Gustafsson 2009, Houston Chronicle). Family members of the prisoners, some of whom came from California for the excavation, were present throughout the project and even took part in non-forensic fieldwork. Allowing family members this opportunity to take part in the project appeared to offer many of them a sense of empowerment, as they could finally play a part in reclaiming their loved ones after over 30 years of separation.

Field results of the excavation

All 12 skeletons were buried in individual graves originally marked with carved gravestones that included their name, date of birth and death, and home town or village. The cemetery was laid out in a north – south alignment in three rows with the first row at the east end of the site containing graves 1–14, starting with grave 1 at the southern end. The second row contained graves 15–29, with grave 15 at the northern end and the third row contained graves 30 and 31, with grave 30 at the northern end. It appears that there was room for more graves in the third row, but inhumations ceased after grave 31 for reasons unknown to the author or the charity. Each grave was cut to a depth of about 1.3 m with vertical sides and a flat base suggesting that great care was taken by the fellow prisoners who were ordered to dig the graves of the deceased.

The skeletons were buried in a supine position with their heads facing east except for skeleton 6 which was buried facing west. One possible explanation for this anomaly is included in the summary below. Along with the bodies, a number of grave goods were also deposited within the graves of individuals.

Below is a brief summary of the initial observations and actions undertaken during the 2.5 days of fieldwork.

Grave 2 – The condition of the remains were fully skeletonised and in a poor state of preservation. Both femurs and the right tibia were retained for DNA analysis. Clothing and personal effects included a burial shroud consisting of a cloth and plastic tarpaulin, one pair of cloth shorts, one small enamelled bowl, a toothbrush and tube of toothpaste and one cloth bag with draw string filled with a number of other items (Figure 57.1).

Grave 3 – The condition of the remains were fully skeletonised and in a moderate state of preservation. Both femurs were retained for DNA. Grave goods included a fabric bag with drawstring and a blue and white floral pattern plastic raincoat.

Grave 5 – The condition of the remains were fully skeletonised and in a poor state of preservation. Both femurs were retained for DNA analysis. Grave goods included a blue-and-white patterned ceramic rice bowl, two coffin nails and two strips of cloth from a hat.

Grave 6 – The body was fully skeletonised and in a poor state of preservation. This was the only burial facing west, suggesting a Catholic priest or someone who had taken on the role of priest for the Catholic prisoners within the camp. Vietnam has maintained a strong Catholic population since the 16th century, when the

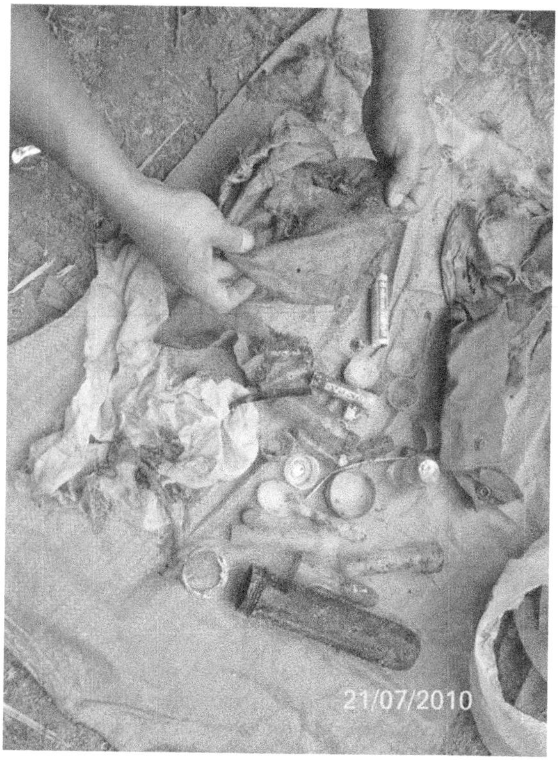

Figure 57.1 Grave 2, personal effects.

religion was first brought to the country by Portuguese missionaries and later through French colonialism. Today, about 6.8% of the total population of the country are practicing Catholics. In countries with a Christian tradition, ordained clergy are usually buried facing west so they can minister to their congregation after the Great Resurrection. Both femurs and the left tibia of this individual were retained for DNA analysis. Personal effects included one black shirt, one mosquito net and a piece of cloth placed under the head.

Grave 8 – This was a fully skeletonised body in a moderate state of preservation. During excavation, it was noted that the distal ends of the left tibia and fibula were missing along with the left foot, and there was little evidence of osteoblast formation at the fracture sites. In addition, a scatter of small pits marked the right femur, suggesting that the individual suffered a traumatic amputation, possibly from stepping on a land mine. Many survivor accounts mention re-education camp prisoners being forced to clear land mines as part of their work duties. The personal effects buried with this body included a blue plastic valise, a bright blue knitted scarf with yellow detail, a number of coffin nails and buttons and one mosquito net.

Grave 13 – This was a fully skeletonised body in a poor state of preservation. The body was buried with one ceramic celadon-style rice bowl, coffin nails and buttons and a foam cushion placed under the head.

Grave 15 – The condition of the remains were fully skeletonised and in a poor state of preservation. Grave goods included a mosquito net placed over the body from the waist to the feet.

Grave 16 – The remains of this individual were fully skeletonised, in a poor state of preservation and buried with no possessions except for a piece of cloth placed under his head.

Grave 21 – These remains were fully skeletonised and in a poor state of preservation. There was a large assemblage of artefacts buried with this individual including one mosquito net, a plastic sheet, a dark blue valise, two plastic bowls – one red and one green – one ceramic bowl placed in a larger white bowl, one toothbrush, one net-type undershirt and one t-shirt. This skeleton was successfully identified through mtDNA as the remains of Artillery Captain Luong Van Hoa. His son Dien (Daniel) Luong has granted permission for his father's name and the image in the photo below to be included in this chapter (Figure 57.2).

Grave 22 – This body was fully skeletonised and in such a poor state of preservation that both femurs and tibia were retained for DNA analysis. Personal effects included eighteen coffin nails, six buttons, one zipper, one small copper alloy object, four metal (nonferrous) reinforcement rings/grommets, one small plastic bag and one thin plastic sheet used as a burial shroud.

Grave 23 – These remains were fully skeletonised and in a poor state of preservation. The burial contained one of the largest assemblages of personal effects recovered from the excavation, including a pair of black rubber sandals with buckles, one mosquito net, one rope belt, one blue plastic folded tarp, four brown glass medicine bottles including two still containing pills, a plastic pipe fragment with an iron attachment, one clear glass medicine bottle, one small mirror, two buttons, one toothbrush, six coffin nails, three buckles and eleven grommets for a mosquito net.

Grave 30 – This grave differed from the others due to a thin layer of lime that covered the entire grave and was found roughly half-way down, between two deposits of grave fill. A cloth had been placed over the mouth and then plastic placed over the entire face. This individual had been buried in a plastic raincoat, and other personal effects included one pair of black rubber sandals in a plastic bag, one large orange plastic bowl, one beige plastic rice bowl, one brown glass bottle, a number of coffin nails, a blue and white woven plastic mat and a large piece of material, possibly a mosquito net. The use of lime in the grave fill and the covering of the mouth with a cloth and plastic suggested this individual may have suffered and died from one of the many communicative diseases found in the camps (Figure 57.3).

Figure 57.2 Grave 21, Artillery Captain Luong Van Hoa.

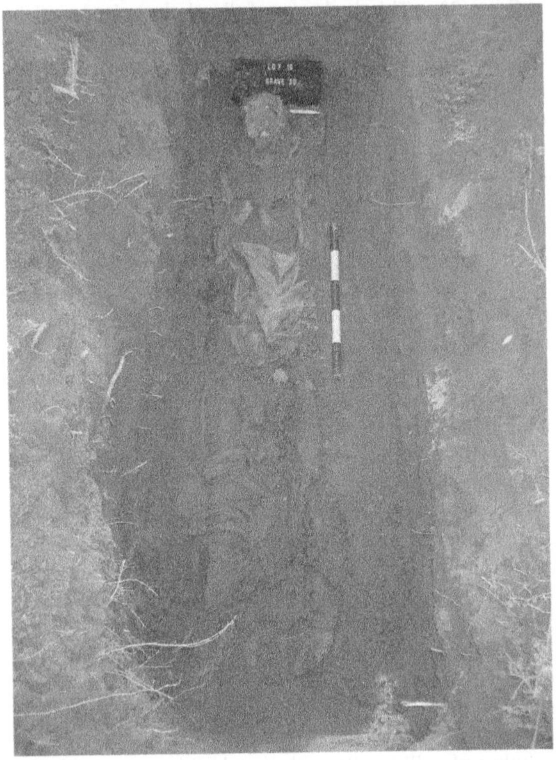

Figure 57.3 Grave 30 (0.5 m scale).

Summary of the excavation

The Returning Casualty's first excavation utilising archaeological techniques proved successful on a number of counts. With the full excavation of each skeleton, as opposed to digging into the grave to remove individual bones, which was the technique used before archaeological consultation, a complete view of the skeleton *in situ* offered additional information about the individual and allowed for the retrieval of all the skeletal elements including bone fragments and smaller bones. In addition, the recovery of grave goods allowed for secondary information about the individual, especially unique items such as the knitted scarf found in grave 8. With the use of archaeological techniques such as photo records and individual skeleton recording sheets, a primary archive was produced which sets the standard for further work by The Returning Casualty.

Further work

The Returning Casualty has two main objectives, the recovery of those buried in the post-war re-education camps and the restoration of the cemetery called Bien Hoa (now referred to as Binh An) as a final resting place for former South Vietnamese soldiers of the Republic of Vietnam. The cemetery was over run after the fall of Saigon and badly vandalised, with around 300 bodies of South Vietnamese soldiers who fell in that final battle removed from a climate-controlled morgue and unceremoniously buried outside the cemetery to allow the communists to store their dead in the facility. The charity would like to restore this military cemetery and use it to inter the remains of the unidentified re-education camp victims exhumed during past and future excavations as a lasting memorial to those who gave their lives in a conflict that divided a nation and its people.

Conclusion

The Returning Casualty is an example of how one individual can create a humanitarian charity for a specific episode in history. Mr Nguyen's promise to his comrades in the camps over three decades ago to one day return to Vietnam to find their bodies and return them to their families has compelled him develop his small ad hoc charity. The writing of this chapter is the author's first opportunity to introduce The Returning Casualty to the forensic and archaeological community in an attempt to further the charity's goals and achieve its missions to reconcile the haunted past of a vanquished people and let them find closure.

References

Desbarats, J. 1990. Repression in the Socialist Republic of Vietnam: executions and population relocation. In J. Norton Moore (ed.), *The Vietnam Debate: A Fresh Look at the Arguments*. Lanham, University Press of America. Available at: http://jim.com/repression.htm. (last accessed 30 March 2014).

Gustafsson, M. L. 2009. *War and Shadows: The Haunting of Vietnam*. Ithaca, Cornell University Press.

McKelvey, R. 2002. *A Gift of Barbed Wire: America's Allies Abandoned in South Vietnam*. Seattle, University of Washington Press.

Pokines, J. T. 2009. Forensic recoveries of U.S. war dead and the effects of taphonomy and other site-altering processes. In D. W. Steadman (ed.), *Hard Evidence: Case Studies in Forensic Anthropology*, 141–154. 2nd edition. Upper Sadle River, Prentice Hall.

Truong, H. M. 2010. *The Dark Journey: Inside the Re-education Camps of Vietcong*. Durham, Eloquent Books.

United States General Accounting Office – National Security and International Affairs Division 1990. *Refugee Program: The Orderly Departure Program from Vietnam*, Washington DC, The Office.

Further Reading

Do, A. and Phan, H. T. 2001. *Camp Z30-D: The Survivors*. Orange County Register, 29th April 2001.

Mason, M. 2011. Vietnamese re-education camp prisoner keeps promise. *Associated Press*, 9th September 2011.

Sagen, G. and Denney, S. 1982. *The Indochina Newsletter 'Re-education in Unliberated Vietnam: Loneliness, Suffering and Death'*. Draft Report for the Aurora Foundation.

Toai, D. V. and Chanoff, D. 1986. *The Vietnamese Gulag*. New York, Simon and Schuster.

Websites

G. Neville, *Thought reform: the curriculum of Vietnamese re-education*. Available at: http://www.scribd.com/doc/16601184/Thought-Reform-The-Curriculum-of-Vietnamese-Reeducation. Accessed 08 August 2014.

The forgotten victims in VietNam. Available at: http://www.vietquoc.com/0003vq.htm. Accessed 08 August 2014.

The Returning Casualty. Available at: http://www.vietremains.org./. Accessed 08 August 2014.

US Department of State 2005. *Joint U. – Vietnamese Announcement of Humanitarian Resettlement Program*. Available at: http://www.usvtc.org/us-vietnam/issues/hr/HumanitarianResettlement15Nov05.pdf. Accessed 08 August 2014.

L. Wise, *Pearland man wants to ensure Vietnam victims rest in peace*, Houston Chronicle. Available at: http://www.chron.com/news/houston-texas/article/Pearland-man-wants-to-ensure-Vietnam-victims-rest-1735675.php. Accessed 08 August 2014.

PART 5
Concluding Remarks

Concluding remarks

W.J. Mike Groen[1], Nicholas Márquez-Grant[2,3] and Robert C. Janaway[4]

[1] Netherlands Forensic Institute (NFI), The Hague, The Netherlands

[2] Cranfield Forensic Institute, Cranfield University, Defence Academy of the United Kingdom, UK

[3] Institute of Human Sciences, School of Anthropology and Museum Ethnography, University of Oxford, Oxford, UK

[4] School of Archaeological Sciences, University of Bradford, Bradford, UK

The chapters of this volume have described the status and perception of forensic archaeology in several countries and organisations across the globe. The first section of this chapter – The global perspective of forensic archaeology: a summary – concentrates therefore on the worldwide perception of forensic archaeology by providing answers to a set of questions that were asked of the contributors to this volume.[1] Archaeology has once been described by Clarke (1973, 17) as 'the discipline with the theory and practice for the recovery of unobservable hominid behaviour patterns from indirect traces in bad samples.' Although this description mirrors modern crime scene investigation (CSI), the chapters in this volume show that – with the exception of a limited number of specific jurisdictions – archaeological theories and methodology are sparsely used across most of the globe, if related to criminal, disaster or civil law setting.

The second section of this chapter – Forensic archaeology: an interpretative framework – is intended to show how forensic archaeology could become more grounded in archaeological theories and methodology and more *forensic* by integrating theories and methodologies from affiliated behavioural and forensic sciences into its framework. This section also shows that forensic archaeological casework should not be an end in itself; it should also be used in the generation of models for understanding past human criminal behaviour. It is regrettable that the discourse of forensic archaeology, with some noteworthy exceptions, has remained largely outside the scientific debate regarding the theoretical framework of forensic archaeology. Consequently, there also seems to be little agreement concerning the fundamental nature of this discipline. Most of the non-archaeologically educated forensic specialists who apply archaeological techniques – be it forensic anthropologists, forensic pathologists, or police officers – interpret the retrieved forensic record (i.e. the sum of all archaeologically retrieved forensic evidence)[2] from a purely materialistic perspective (e.g. entirely focusing on the recovered human remains); they seem to ignore the theoretical concepts needed to reconstruct the behavioural patterns that have caused this record. Archaeological theories, as mentioned in the introductory chapter, are hereby perceived as too *academic* and therefore irrelevant to the *practical*-oriented police and prosecution needs. Additionally, archaeological methods and techniques are frequently applied by the non-archaeologically educated practitioners to scenes of crime or places of incident without acknowledging the taphonomic transformations (taphonomy[3] and material degradation) that affect the visibility and the evidential value of the retrieved record. Interpretation of the retrieved forensic record is not based on a solid pre-emptive research strategy, but on the *ad hoc* availability of methods and techniques learned in a short course or during past casework. The used 'methodology' is regularly uncritical concerning the availability of potential evidence and often without a solid criminalistic basis. A *practical* approach is used to excavate clandestine graves, to recover human remains or to predict locations of clandestine (mass) burials. Forensic archaeological

[1] See Part 3 of the Introduction to this volume.

[2] The forensic record consists of the physical remains of humans, animals, other organisms (e.g. plants, insects and diatoms), material evidence (finds and traces) and non-portable soil features (e.g. grave pit).

[3] Taphonomy can be defined as the 'context related study of organic decomposition'. In traditional archaeology taphonomic studies address all stages of research: 'from site formation process through diagenesis and sampling procedures to analytical techniques and interpretative perspectives' (Stallibrass 2000, vii).

Forensic Archaeology: A Global Perspective, First Edition. Edited by W.J. Mike Groen, Nicholas Márquez-Grant and Robert C. Janaway.

knowledge, which has been acquired in previous – similar – casework by other forensic archaeological specialists, is therefore frequently ignored. No wonder that most of the police officers, forensic experts and prosecutors across the world think that forensic archaeology is all about 'the application of archaeological field methods and techniques' – mostly related to (stratigraphic) digging with appropriate tools and (contextual) mapping – and that 'it' can be learned during a short training course.

The global perspective of forensic archaeology: a summary

This section focuses on summarising the answers to eight questions that were asked of the contributors to this volume. These summaries are, if not specified otherwise, based on information acquired from the individual chapters. It should be kept in mind that this overview is not intended to be all-embracing, but is only intended to describe general trends. For country-specific in-depth information, the editors refer to the relevant chapters. We also apologise for possible omission of information in the answers provided.

Description of the medico-legal framework

The legal traditions in which the contributors to this volume operate differ per country and organisation. For example, most of the countries in the Commonwealth of Nations (former British colonies) use Common Law, or law tradition based on the idea of precedent and developed by judges in courts and tribunals. This is in contrast to the Civil Law, or law tradition based on governmental legislation and codified in procedural law, used by (most of) the European, Asian and Latin American countries (e.g. Glenn 2010). Remaining contributors are associated with mixed traditions, blending Civil and Common Law (e.g. South Africa), or incorporating Islamic Law (*Sjarī'a*) with other law traditions (e.g. Libya and the UAE). The internationally operating NGOs and intergovernmental organisations are sometimes also affected by a number of international conventions, declaration and treaties (e.g. the United Nations (UN) Convention on Crime of Genocide, the UN Declaration of Human Rights, the Geneva Conventions and the Rome Statute that led to the established International Criminal Court (ICC) in The Hague, the Netherlands, in 2002). There are also country-specific differences regarding the presentation of evidence in court, the potential of introducing external experts in legal proceedings and court procedures (e.g. Broeders 2003; Crombag 2003; Diamond 2003; Van Koppen and Penrod 2003; Hodgson 2006). For example, most Common Law countries have an Adversarial legal system where two parties (prosecution and defence) present their case before an impartial judge or jury. This is in contrast to most Civil Law countries that have an Inquisitorial legal system where a judge is in charge of the (police) enquiry and the gathering and preparation of evidence before the actual trial by a different judge or jury. A number of countries have a blend of the Adversarial and the Inquisitorial legal systems. The legal differences mentioned earlier will influence the manner of reporting and the possibility of being called before a judge or jury to give evidence. For example, the chance that an expert witness will be called before a judge or jury to clarify his/her findings will be – generally speaking – higher in the Adversarial legal system; in the Investigatory legal system most of the evidence will be presented to the court in written reports.

Of importance is also that some countries have unitary (centralised) governments,[4] while others are more federally oriented.[5] This dissimilarity could, for example, affect the possibilities to obtaining enough casework, since different legal requirements could be required in different states/regions. Additionally, if the forensic archaeological specialists are not positioned in a national (or large state/region) operating organisation, they will be – generally speaking – too infrequently needed to assist in casework and, consequently, will not have much case experience. Finally, the lack of a centralised government could also introduce a variable forensic archaeological approach to crime scenes or places of incidents and a lack of a standardised national examination process.

It should be clear that the legal traditions and systems mentioned earlier are applicable if the investigation is being performed in a criminal, medico-legal or civil law setting. However, if the investigation is being performed in a humanitarian (NGO) or archaeological setting (e.g. artefact looting), different legal rules and proceedings will apply. In the last-mentioned setting, it could for example be compulsory (by law or organisational statutes) that an archaeologist leads the field recovery part of the investigation.

Finally, there are also differences in the country-specific forensic science system that will influence the availability of external forensic scientists at a crime

[4]E.g. Bulgaria, Chile, Colombia, Costa Rica, Croatia, Czech Republic, Denmark, France, Greece, Hungary, Italy, Lebanon, Libya, Lithuania, the Netherlands, New Zealand, Panama, Peru, Poland, Portugal, Romania, Serbia, Slovakia, Slovenia, South Africa, Spain, Republic of Korea, the United Kingdom, Uruguay, Zimbabwe.

[5]E.g. Argentina, Australia, Austria, Belgium, Bosnia and Herzegovina, Brazil, Canada, Germany, India, Mexico, Nepal, Russia, Switzerland, the UAE, the United States, Venezuela.

scene or place of incident. For example, in countries where the providing of forensic science is privatised (e.g. the United Kingdom) or strongly linked with academia (e.g. Austria, Canada, Denmark, Switzerland and the United States), the police officers will already be used to working with *external* forensic scientists at crime scenes or places of incident. This is in contradiction to countries with police laboratories (e.g. France, Germany, the UAE) or countries with centralised governmental medico-legal laboratories (e.g. the Netherlands).

The definition of forensic archaeology

In Africa and Asia, the concept of forensic archaeology is mostly unknown; and if known, it's mainly through the presence of international teams. A survey among the Member-Institutes of the European Network of Forensic Science Institutes (ENFSI) has shown that forensic archaeology in Europe is not *officially* being practised or recognised in Albania, Armenia, Azerbaijan, Belarus, Estonia, Georgia, Latvia, Sweden, Turkey and Ukraine – this according to the addressed contacts in these institutes.

If the concept of forensic archaeology exists, it is defined differently across the world (see also the introductory chapter):

- In North America, Australia, New Zealand, South Africa and North-Western Europe, forensic archaeology is primarily defined as the application of archaeological (and taphonomic) theories and methodology – mostly related to buried or otherwise concealed human remains – in criminal or medico-legal casework. In some countries (e.g. Austria, Finland[6] and the United States), the definition of forensic archaeology also includes the recovery of missing military service personnel from past military conflicts (e.g. World Wars I and II (WWI and WWII), the Korean War and the Vietnam War). However, the latter is not always the case in other countries; in Western Europe for example the recovery of missing military service personnel from WWI and/or WWII is mostly performed by Army personnel (e.g. Belgium, France, Germany and the Netherlands), occasionally with the assistance of academically educated and trained archaeologists (e.g. Belgium and the United Kingdom).
- In Central and Eastern Europe, forensic archaeology is primarily associated with the recovery of human remains associated with WWI and/or WWII and the Communist-era and is interpreted as the application of forensic methods and techniques to the study of atrocities which had occurred during the periods mentioned earlier. Additionally, in some of these countries, the identification of historical individuals and the study of archaeological record associated with historic execution sites may also be perceived as a part of forensic archaeology. As already mentioned in the introductory chapter, the distinction between forensic archaeology and traditional archaeology is somewhat unclear in the last-mentioned definition. However, the indistinctness between forensic archaeology and the use of forensic methods and techniques in traditional archaeology is understandable from the Central and Eastern European perspective, where both types of investigation are often performed by the same experts. These experts may be working in the forensic field and applying their forensic methods and techniques to the study of the past. It should also be acknowledged that this approach could lead to further exposure, increasing interest and development of forensic archaeological possibilities in Central and Eastern Europe, by exposing its potential to the forensic and judicial community.
- Some Central and Eastern European countries (e.g. Bulgaria, Croatia and the Slovak Republic) also include investigation associated with illegal excavation and the associated illicit trade of archaeological artefacts within the definition of forensic archaeology. Other countries (e.g. Costa Rica, Mexico, New Zealand, the UAE and the United States) seem to have a similar policy. Additionally, there are countries (e.g. the Netherlands, Spain) where the illegal trade of archaeological and historical artefacts is undertaken by specialists belonging to Heritage Sections of the regular police force.
- In Latin America, forensic archaeology is primarily associated with the recovery of victims from (mass) burials related to human right violations (crimes against humanity, war crimes and genocide) committed by former dictatorial regimes and/or paramilitary units. In this context, forensic archaeology is integrated with forensic anthropology and cultural/social anthropology into one operational approach. This type of casework is generally performed by the Latin American NGOs (e.g. EAAF, EQUITAS, EPAF, FAFG and GIAF)[7] and some other international operating NGOs (e.g. International Committee of the Red Cross (ICRC), Inforce, Physicians for Human Rights (PHR)).
- Finally, in some countries, the application of a selection of forensic archaeological methods and techniques at a crime scene or place of incident may be predominantly undertaken by a forensic pathologist (India may be an example).

[6] Source available at: http://fafaa.fi/index_en.html (last accessed 20 February 2014).

[7] These NGOs are: the Argentine EAAF (*Equipo Argentino de Antropología Forense*), the Colombian EQUITAS (*Equipo Colombiano Interdisciplinario de Trabajo Forense y Asistencia Psicosocial*), the Peruvian EPAF (*Equipo Peruano de Antropología Forense*), the Guatemalan FAFG (*Fundación de Antropología Forense de Guatemala*) and the Uruguayan GIAF (*Grupo de Investigación en Arqueología Forense*).

Summarising, the definition of forensic archaeology varies across the globe. Whilst some countries focus mainly on the search and recovery of human remains from clandestine graves in domestic police cases; other countries and organisations see forensic archaeology mainly in the context of search and recovery of human remains from (mass) graves or places of incident associated with historical (military) events. The definition of forensic archaeology is sometimes widened even further, for example to include the examination of cultural property in cases of looting and illegal trade. The used definitions seem to correlate with the legal setting (see earlier) and the educational background of the forensic specialists that use forensic archaeology in their casework and the history of the country/region where they practise (see later).

Brief background and development of forensic archaeology

As mentioned in the Introduction and in other chapters in this volume, most of the forensic archaeological casework done prior to the application of archaeology to the mass graves of Bosnia in the late 1990s was done by the US-based PHR, the Argentinian EAAF (*Equipo Argentino de Antropología Forense*), the Chilean GAF (*Grupo Antropología Forense*) and the Guatemalan EAFG/FAFG (*Equipo/Fundación de Antropología Forense de Guatemala*). The US-based Joint POW/MIA Accounting Command – Central Identification Laboratory (JPAC-CIL), a governmental organisation specially developed to locate, recover, repatriate and identify its missing military personnel from past conflicts, also regularly employed forensic archaeology in its casework. On the national police service level, almost all archaeological casework in the pre-2000 era was performed in the United States and the United Kingdom.

This country-specific development of forensic archaeology is strongly linked to the educational background of its practitioners and historical developments. For example, the relation between forensic archaeology and forensic anthropology (the first being related to search, location and retrieval, and the second to the examination of human skeletal remains) seems to correlate with the educational traditions regarding the archaeological and anthropological sciences in the Americas versus Europe and some of Europe's former colonies. In the American Boasian 'four-field' approach, archaeology is seen as an anthropological sub-discipline. Most of the American physical/forensic anthropologists will therefore have (some basic) training in archaeology. In most of Europe and its former colonies, archaeology and anthropology are perceived as separate disciplines and are taught at different departments. In this setting, physical anthropology is taught as a module within an archaeological degree (e.g. the Netherlands and the United Kingdom), or at a medical or biology department (e.g. Spain). Consequently, while forensic specialists in the Americas – generally speaking – do not perceive forensic archaeology and forensic anthropology as separate disciplines, many countries in North-Western Europe as well as South Africa, Australia and New Zealand do define – generally speaking – forensic archaeology and forensic anthropology as two separate disciplines. This does not mean that the forensic archaeological/anthropological practice is perceived uniformly across the Americas. In Latin America, forensic archaeology/anthropology is intertwined with cultural/social anthropology. Latin American forensic archaeologists/anthropologists have a background predominantly in cultural/social anthropology, traditional archaeology, or physical anthropology/bioarchaeology. The cultural/social anthropologists, for example, will make the initial contact with the relatives of the victims, explain the goals and procedures of the planned investigation, compile witness reports, and collect the DNA samples from the relatives and ante-mortem data needed for a positive identification (Snow 2011). It is also not uncommon to find Latin American forensic archaeologists/anthropologists that have a background in biology or medicine.

The forensic archaeological specialists in Central and Eastern Europe are mostly archaeologists, although sometimes forensic archaeology may be practised by medical doctors (e.g. forensic pathologists) or police officers. Forensic archaeology is associated here predominantly with the excavation of WWI and WWII (mass) graves and the graves related to the extra-judicial executions that were performed during the Communist-era after WWII. The Central and Eastern European perception of forensic archaeology is therefore (as in Latin America) strongly intertwined with investigation of crimes performed by former totalitarian governments.

There are also legal differences regarding the perception of forensic archaeology across the world. For example, the access to most crime scenes or places of incident in Europe and North America is strictly regulated; the survivors of criminal acts and families of the victims are generally not involved in criminal or medico-legal investigation. The primary goal of forensic archaeology in the geographical regions mentioned earlier is to help prosecute crimes. This is however not the case in the NGO-run investigations in Latin America. In the Latin American framework, the survivors and relatives are – where possible – integrated in the investigation and are often able to visit the excavation site. In this framework, the forensic archaeological specialists also engage in the social and cultural dimensions of the society they are working in (e.g. Crossland 2011). This framework, mainly promoted by the Argentinian EAAF, the Guatemalan FAFG (F. Peccerelli, personal communication 2013), the ICRC and the PHR, has been integrated into other parts of the world, for example during the NGO-run excavations in Bosnia and

Herzegovina, Iraq and South Africa (e.g. Stover and Shigekane 2002; Rainio et al. 2007).

The organisational positioning of forensic archaeologists

The organisational positioning of forensic archaeologists in a country or organisation depends on the country/organisation-specific definition of forensic archaeology. Forensic archaeologists – strictly defined as academically educated archaeologists working within (or providing consultancy to) the criminal or medico-legal context as forensic archaeological specialists – seem to exist only in North-Western European countries, NGOs (e.g. Inforce, The Returning Casualty) and intergovernmental organisations (e.g. European Union Rule of Law Mission (EULEX); C. Cropper, personal communication 2012, International Commission on Missing Persons (ICMP)). Forensic archaeologists in North-Western Europe are employed by national operating medico-legal laboratories (e.g. France, the Netherlands), private forensic providers or archaeological units (e.g. the United Kingdom), academic institutions, or simply as freelance. At times (e.g. Costa Rica, Finland (N. Söderholm, personal communication 2013), Italy and the United Kingdom), the distinction between a forensic archaeologist and a forensic anthropologists will be blurred, since some of the forensic anthropologist will also have a traditional archaeological education and work experience.

If the forensic context is defined to include regular recovery of missing military service personnel and/or humanitarian investigation of human rights violations (as it should), it could be said that academically educated forensic archaeologists exist in most European Countries (e.g. Austria, Ireland and Poland), Australia, New Zealand, South Africa and the United States (i.e. JPAC-CIL). Some European countries (e.g. Austria and Finland) possess Forensic Archaeological Working Groups with special focus on the recovery of missing WWI and/or WWII military personnel. The WWI and WWII contexts also encounter a lot of amateur-led digging, ranging from a people's movement to recover the remains of the WWII dead (e.g. Russia), through looting of bodies forsaleable items (e.g. Poland, Russia and Ukraine) to amateur enthusiasts/private collectors of military equipment (e.g. Belgium, Germany, France and the Netherlands).

Finally, the number of forensic archaeologists per country/organisation will not only be dependent on the definition of forensic archaeology, but also on the volume of casework that is (perceived as) forensic archaeology related. For example, there are several forensic archaeologists working throughout the United Kingdom, in other countries there may be only one or two.

If forensic archaeologists are lacking, who is engaging in forensic archaeology?

In countries that do not employ forensic archaeologists within their criminal or medico-legal settings, the forensic archaeological recoveries are performed by archaeologically skilled forensic anthropologists (e.g. Austria, Brazil, Colombia, Denmark, Peru, the UAE and the United States), forensic pathologists (e.g. India) or archaeologically trained police officers (e.g. Belgium and Germany). In some countries (e.g. Australia, Canada, Denmark, Mexico and Spain), most of the recovery work within the criminal or medico-legal setting is performed (besides the police) by a forensic anthropologist (some of whom are also forensic pathologists) working – generally speaking – within governmental medico-legal institutes, although at times archaeologists are also used. It is in fact often a push from forensic anthropologists and pathologists, which is enabling a wider use of forensic archaeology within criminal or medico-legal settings.

On occasions, there will be police staff with academic degrees in archaeology (e.g. Belgium, the Netherlands, Spain and the United Kingdom). Although these police officers may also work in cases where forensic archaeology is required, their day jobs are not as forensic archaeological specialist; they have another role within the police force.

Systems of accreditation and training in forensic archaeology

Forensic archaeological practice is hardly certified or accredited across the globe. In the United States, the *Daubert v. Merrell Dow Pharmaceuticals Inc.* (1993), the *General Electric Co. v. Joiner* (1997) and the *Kumho Tire Co. v. Carmichael* (1999) US Supreme Court rulings had a huge impact on the admission of (non)scientific expert testimonies in the US federal courts (e.g. Berger 2011). These rulings led to the formation of best-practice guidelines and minimum standards in forensic science across the United States. Regarding forensic anthropology, two scientific working groups were formed: the Scientific Working Group for Forensic Anthropology (SWGANTH) formed in 2008 and the Scientific Working Group on Disaster Victim Identification (SWGDVI) formed in 2010. Both these groups have developed – and are still developing – several forensic anthropological best practice manuals and guidelines. For example, the SWGANTH has published guidelines on scene detection and processing.[8]

In Europe, the United Kingdom has forensic archaeological standards and guidance documents that are recognised by the UK government, and there is a professional body, the Institute for Archaeologists (IfA),

[8] For more information, see: http://swganth.startlogic.com/Scene%20Detection%20and%20Processing%20Rev%200.pdf (last accessed 15 February 2014).

that regulates the quality of forensic archaeologists in the United Kingdom. In the Netherlands, forensic archaeological practice is in the process of becoming ISO/IEC 17020 accredited at the Netherlands Forensic Institute (NFI), this in accordance to the wish of the European Union (EU) to have its Scene of Crime Investigation (CSI) accredited by 2020.[9]

In Latin America, the Latin American Forensic Anthropology Association (*Asociación Latinoamericana de Antropología Forense* – ALAF), founded in 2005, has created the Latin American Board of Forensic Anthropology (*Directorio Latinoamericano de Antropología Forense* – DLAF) to start the certification of its partners in the region, with the intention of promoting best practices, and standardising the methodologies and the systems that make up the Latin American discipline. ALAF membership is open to (forensic) archaeologists and cultural/social anthropologists, as well as forensic/physical anthropologists/bioarchaeologists that conduct research or active investigation in the field of forensic archaeology/anthropology.

Regarding training opportunities, only few countries across the globe offer (short) training courses in forensic archaeology. Most of the nationally operating forensic scientists, prosecutors, lawyers, judges and police officers are therefore unaware of the possibilities that this discipline has to offer in the legal setting. Police training in forensic archaeological recovery is given in most countries with a forensic archaeologist or a forensic anthropologist with archaeological skills. Short academic courses or modules in forensic archaeology are offered in some American and European countries (e.g. Argentina, Brazil, Canada, France, the Netherlands, Poland, Spain, the United Kingdom and the United States). Higher academic degrees such as Master programmes in forensic archaeology can be obtained in the United Kingdom, although it is expected that higher forensic archaeological degrees will be offered in other European counties in the near future.

Case scenarios and context where forensic archaeology is being used

In the introductory chapter, it was argued that (modified) archaeological theories and methodology could be used within the context of law in nine areas of engagement: domestic police service cases; mass fatality events (Disaster Victim Identification (DVI) or Mass Fatality Incidents (MFI)); investigations of human rights violations in a medico-legal setting; investigations of human rights violations in a humanitarian setting; recovery and repatriation of missing military service personnel; controlled exhumations at regular cemeteries outside a criminal, medico-legal or humanitarian setting; archaeological investigations in the context of civil law; on-site investigation related to the destruction of archaeological sites or monuments; and investigations related to illegal selling of archaeological or historical artefacts. The chapters in the volume show that all these nine areas of engagement are being perceived as forensic archaeology, although not consistently across the globe.

Important is also that boundaries between the nine areas of engagement can be blurred at times. For example, forensic archaeological investigation of human rights violations in humanitarian setting can lead to an official recognition that crimes against humanity were committed and therefore to a criminal investigation. Evidence gathered during humanitarian investigation can therefore also be used in prosecution of wrongdoers and/or in lifting of legal restrictions imposed by former governments on survivors and victims' families. Another example is a DVI/MFI-run investigation that converts into a criminal investigation after encountering evidence that points towards a terrorist attack.

As mentioned previously, forensic archaeology is being used in domestic police service cases predominantly in the United States and North-Western Europe. Controlled exhumations at regular cemeteries outside a criminal, medico-legal or humanitarian setting seem to be mainly practised in the Netherlands, Spain, the United States and the United Kingdom. The investigations related to the destruction of archaeological sites or monuments, or the illegal selling of archaeological or historical artefacts, seem to be almost universal, although not all countries would define these investigations as being part of forensic archaeology. The archaeological possibilities regarding investigations in the context of civil law are not widely known and seem to be restricted to a couple of countries (e.g. the United Kingdom and the United States). DVI/MFI recovery by means of archaeological methods and techniques (sometimes called 'disaster archaeology', e.g. Gould 2007) seems to be restricted to the United States and the NGOs working internationally (e.g. air disasters). Forensic archaeology, as most widely known and practised, is related to the medico-legal or humanitarian investigations of (mass) graves that are associated with human rights violations, and the recovery and repatriation of missing military service personnel from the past military conflicts or places of incident (Table C.1).[10]

There is a parallel between the Latin American and European countries that had a violent dictatorial or

[9]For more information, see: http://www.european-accreditation.org/publication/ea-5-03-ta (last accessed 31 July 2013).

[10]Table C.1 only includes countries represented in this volume that have (mass) graves related to past human right violations within their territories and/or that (at times) use archaeologists to localise and retrieve their missing military service personnel.

Table C.1 The use of forensic archaeology in medico-legal and humanitarian setting associated with human rights violations, and in missing military service personnel settings, per country.

Country	Medico-legal investigation of (mass) graves	Humanitarian investigation of (mass) graves	Recovery of missing military service personnel
Argentina	Yes	Yes	—
Australia	—	—	Yes
Austria	—	Yes	Yes
Belgium	—	—	Yes
Bosnia and Herzegovina	Yes	Yes	—
Brazil	Yes	Yes	—
Chile	Yes	Yes	—
Colombia	—	Yes	—
Croatia	Yes	Yes	Yes
Czech Republic	—	Yes	Yes
Greece	Yes	Yes	—
Hungary	—	Yes	—
Italy	—	—	Yes
Ireland	—	Yes	—
Libya	Yes	Yes	—
Lithuania	Yes	Yes	—
Mexico	Yes	Yes	—
Nepal	—	Yes	—
Panama	—	Yes	—
Peru	Yes	Yes	—
Poland	—	Yes	Yes
Portugal	—	—	Yes
Romania	—	Yes	—
Serbia	Yes	Yes	—
Slovenia	Yes	Yes	—
South Africa	—	Yes	Yes
Spain	—	Yes	—
UK	—	—	Yes
Uruguay	Yes	Yes	—
US	—	—	Yes
Venezuela	Yes	Yes	—
Zimbabwe	—	Yes	—

Communist past and the availability of (NGO-based) archaeologists/anthropologists that engage in medico-legal or humanitarian forensic archaeological investigations in these countries. The relation between participation of a country in past military conflicts (e.g. WWI, WWII, the Korean War and the Vietnam War) and its active search for and retrieval of the remains of its missing military service personnel using archaeologically accepted methodology is less clear. While almost all countries that have participated in military conflicts have specialised departments for the recovery and repatriation (and identification) of its missing military service personnel, most of these departments are manned by non-archaeologically educated military personnel. Only a few countries seem to invest in archaeologists to perform the search for, and recovery of, its missing military service personnel. Prominent examples are the excavation of a WWI mass grave near Fromelles, France, in 2009,[11] and the deployment of the JPAC-CIL by the US government to locate and repatriate (and identify) its missing military service personnel all over the globe.[12]

Future trends in forensic archaeology

Almost all contributors to this volume state that there is a need for the implementation and/or improvement of forensic archaeology (and forensic anthropology) in their country or organisation. There is a belief that the application of forensic archaeology in their casework would contribute to additional forensic evidence; that it would make the responsibility of the forensic anthropological/medical examiners and prosecutors easier with regards to search, location and recovery aspects and, consequently, that it would solve more crimes as archaeology also helps to maximise the evidence that can be obtained from a deposition site. The main hindrances seem to be limited professional opportunities for a forensic archaeological specialist, for example too low a murder rate and the size of the country; the presence of financial, organisational or legal restrictions; the lack of relevant archaeological education and training or awareness of its potential; and consequently, the perception among police officers, prosecutors, lawyers and judges that archaeological theories and methodology are not relevant to modern crime scenes or places of incident. Moreover, the progress of forensic

[11]The excavated mass grave was related to British and Australian military casualties of the battle of Fromelles, Northern France, 19 July 1916 (e.g. Donlon et al., Chapter 44, this volume). For more information, see: http://www.rememberingfromelles.co.uk/ (last accessed 20 February 2014).

[12]An additional example is English Heritage (a non-departmental public body of the UK Government) that has developed several archaeological guidelines for processing and managing WWII sites. See, for example 'Monuments of War: The Evaluation, Recording and Management of Twentieth-Century Military Sites', available at: http://www.english-heritage.org.uk/publications/monuments-of-war/militarymonumentsofwarlores.pdf (last accessed 20 February 2014) and 'Military Aircraft Crash Sites: Archaeological Guidance on their Significance and Future Management', available at: http://www.english-heritage.org.uk/publications/military-aircraft-crash-sites/milaircsites.pdf (last accessed 20 February 2014).

archaeology in most countries seems to rest on the shoulders of a few individuals. Only few are embedded in forensic laboratories, private providers or academic forensic institutions and have, therefore, regular access to modern casework.

Despite the aforementioned restraints, most contributors also see possibilities for improvement in their countries or organisations. Several universities are planning to offer (under)graduate courses in forensic archaeology, and there are plans to set up specialised (academic) units that could assist other forensic specialists during casework. There is also the belief that the traditionally educated (forensic) archaeologists should work more closely with the non-archaeologically skilled forensic anthropologists and forensic pathologists. It is also believed that the last-mentioned forensic specialists are also in a good position to introduce forensic archaeology (and forensic archaeologists) to the forensic community.

Summarising

The application of forensic archaeological theories and methodology during medico-legal and humanitarian investigations associated with human rights violations seems to be well developed across the world. Several intergovernmental, governmental, and non-governmental organisations have forensic archaeologists or archaeologically educated forensic anthropologists on their payroll. Forensic archaeology is also being used by the organisations mentioned earlier to establish 'a historical record that can counteract historical revisionism' (Juhl and Olsen 2006, 422). Moreover, the organisations mentioned earlier employ teams that combine forensic archaeological and forensic anthropological knowledge.

Additionally, the editors fully acknowledge that forensic archaeology is also being practised in countries and organisations that are – due to different reasons – not represented in this volume. For example, the practice of forensic archaeology in medico-legal and humanitarian setting is being strongly promoted by the Guatemalan Forensic Anthropology Foundation (*Fundación de Antropología Forense de Guatemala* – FAFG),[13] as discussed earlier. Recent examples of exhumations/excavation of mass graves can be found in Cambodia and Malaysia,[14] the Ivory Coast,[15] Sri Lanka,[16] Pakistan,[17] and Western Sahara.[18] Additionally, the first-ever archaeological excavations at the Nazi death camp Treblinka (Poland) have not only located physical evidence that the camp held gas chambers, but also the presence of mass graves.[19] These mass graves were located using LiDAR survey and archival research and presence of three mass graves was confirmed by a minimally invasive excavation (C. Sturdy Colls, personal communication 2014).[20] It is hoped the earlier-mentioned and other applications of (forensic) archaeology in the criminal, medico-legal or humanitarian context will one day be integrated into the wider forensic archaeological network.

It is also hoped that the ENFSI initiative to set up a European platform for forensic archaeology, and the initiatives of the Latin American ALAF and the two US-based scientific working groups (SWGANTH and SWGDVI) to accredit/develop best practice field recovery standards, will improve the image of forensic archaeology worldwide by producing more awareness of the possibilities and limitations regarding the use of forensic archaeology in legal settings. It is also hoped that these and other initiatives will improve the level of communication between (forensic) archaeologists, forensic anthropologists, forensic pathologists, police officers, prosecutors and other legal officials concerning the potential of forensic archaeology at modern crime scenes and places of incident. Finally, it is expected that the earlier-mentioned initiatives will also lead towards a formalisation of the role of the forensic archaeological specialist.

The chapters in this volume also point out that forensic archaeological potential is hardly used at modern domestic crime scenes or places of incident; and

[13] For more information, see: http://www.fafg.org/Ingles/paginas/FAFG.html (last accessed 7 April 2014).

[14] E.g. F. Tay on Malaysia and C. Bennet on Cambodia. Available at: http://www.corpsesofmassviolence.eu/calendar/c2013/our-annual-workshop/ (last accessed 7 April 2014).

[15] For more information, see: http://www.aljazeera.com/news/africa/2013/04/201344184424107708.html (last accessed 7 April 2014).

[16] For more information, see: http://www.abc.net.au/news/2014-03-02/an-mass-grave-found-in-sri-lanka-ahead-of-united-nations-rights/5293140 (last accessed 7 April 2014).

[17] For more information, see: http://www.thenewstribe.com/2014/04/01/17-bodies-recovered-from-mass-grave-in-balochistan/ (last accessed 7 April 2014).

[18] For more information, see: http://press.resistenciasaharaui.com/2013/09/basque-forensic-and-research-team.html (last accessed 7 April 2014).

[19] For more information, see: http://www.huffingtonpost.com/2014/03/31/nazi-death-camp-treblinka-excavated-archaeologists_n_5062114.html (last accessed 7 April 2014).

[20] For more information on the Treblinka project, see: http://blogs.staffs.ac.uk/archaeology/projects/holocaust-landscapes/genius-and-genocide/finding-treblinka/ (last accessed 16 April 2014).

if used, it is almost always *body focused* and constrained to the search and excavation/exhumation, ignoring the potential this discipline has to offer in other types of criminal and civil law investigations. Another observation is that the educational background of the forensic archaeological specialists, who (could potentially) assist at a crime scene or place of incident, is not uniform across the globe. There are hardly any academic institutions that specialise in forensic archaeology and that offer relevant degrees at a Masters or PhD level. This among other things, due to the low number of cases that warrant specialised forensic archaeological investigation and – as importantly – to the absence of a grounding body of theory regarding forensic archaeology as an academic discipline.

Forensic archaeology: an interpretative framework

Looking at the forensic archaeological literature related to modern criminal or medico-legal settings, it could be said that forensic archaeology is predominantly seen as the application of archaeological methods and techniques, mainly related to the recovery of materials from buried (outdoor) contexts. Additionally, the common view is that the obtained forensic record is limited to site-specific reconstructions. To quote Connor and Scott (2001, 3), forensic evidence 'is not gathered to uncover the broad patterns of human behaviour, but rather to reconstruct the specifics of a single event'. The editors believe that archaeological knowledge can and should be more widely applied within the legal setting, especially knowledge of survey and excavation methodology, dating and the use of interpretative models developed to recognise, document, understand and reconstruct human behaviour from the forensic record. Additionally, the forensic record can also be used to contribute to criminological and criminalistic knowledge concerning the locations of clandestine graves and manners of interment. Forensic archaeology has therefore an important role to play not only in recovery of victims and associated evidence but also in providing a historical perspective for understanding the significance and potential of the recovered record within the context of law. Such studies will understandably be constrained due to legal restrictions regarding the disclosure of evidence (e.g. in an ongoing criminal investigation), the limited number of forensic archaeological case examples (small dataset) and the fact that most forensic archaeological case studies are not published. These restrictions are, however, common in all criminological and criminalistic analyses and should not be an excuse to refrain from research.

It is also important that forensic archaeology – in contrast to traditional archaeology – *has* a direct access to information about past human behaviour. We have access to testimonies, confessions and other documents. In addition, some forensic archaeological reconstructions are checkable after the conclusion of the investigation/trial. We can see if our interpretation of past human (criminal) behaviour was correct in the first place, something that is not possible within traditional archaeology of the more distant past. Forensic archaeology should therefore, as traditional archaeology does, use theories and methodologies from both the Sciences and Humanities. As a science, it should recognise the pedological, ecological, biological and physical processes that are needed to understand the site formation processes and taphonomic transformations (taphonomy and material degradation) that had helped to shape the scene of crime or place of incident. As a humanity-based discipline, it should try to reconstruct and interpret what actually happened at a crime scene or a place of incident. Since forensic archaeologists cannot observe the human behaviour they are trying to reconstruct directly – the retrieved evidence is not able to 'speak for itself' – they must, as all traditional archaeologists, infer human behaviour from the material record. To be able to do this, an underlying body of theory is needed to interpret how human beings behave and, above all, how this behaviour is reflected in the recovered forensic record.

The remaining part of this section focuses on the theoretical framework and methodology needed for a reliable reconstruction of past human criminal behaviour by means of the retrieved forensic record in criminal, medico-legal and humanitarian settings. Other areas of engagement in which archaeologists could be of use (i.e. destruction of archaeological sites or monuments, illegal selling of archaeological or historical artefacts and archaeological investigation in a civil law context) are not addressed. This is because these areas of engagement are archaeological in nature and therefore predominantly practised by archaeologists who are already familiar with archaeological theories and methodology. The archaeological potential concerning 20th century warfare is also not addressed, since this potential is already covered in battlefield / conflict archaeology (e.g. Scott et al. 2006; Vanin et al. 2009; Saunders 2012; Moshenska 2013; Gassend 2014).

The proposed theoretical framework is built around a middle range (MR) theory that combines archaeological and criminological theories and models. The proposed methodology is linked to the theoretical framework and integrates the archaeological field methods and techniques with the methods and techniques from criminalistics. For an introductory discussion of archaeological theory and methodology, see the introductory chapter.

Forensic archaeology: the theoretical framework

The editors propose an interpretative framework that is grounded in processualism[21] (e.g. Fondebrider and Scheinsohn, Chapter 43, this volume) and that acknowledges the taphonomic transformations that have taken place between the deposition of the forensic record during the actual crime or incident and the time of the actual retrieval of this record during investigation. However, the proposed theoretical framework should also incorporate certain post-processual views.[22] This is necessary since processual archaeology relied too much on logical positivism and a deductive methodology to be able to explain past human behaviour, leading to deterministic behavioural reconstructions. Mere correlations between the retrieved forensic record and the assumed human criminal behaviour cannot be viewed as an explanation. This is because cultural factors, thoughts and intentions structure human behaviour and are therefore a necessary part of understanding this behaviour, as proclaimed by the post-processual frameworks. Processualism therefore failed to acknowledge that interpretation of human behaviour should also be grounded in subjective, motivational, emic[23] concepts. Processualism also failed to acknowledge that archaeological knowledge is not entirely 'neutral' nor 'objective' since the detection of finds and features, and the subsequent interpretation and reconstruction, is also influenced by historical and sociocultural contexts. Differently educated and trained archaeologists can therefore produce somewhat dissimilar sets of archaeological data. This is also the case in forensic archaeology where the definition of forensic archaeology is context dependent and the object of its study, and the questions to be addressed are not academic but legal (and therefore also context dependent) in nature. To quote Gassiot Ballbé and Steadman (2008, 432) forensic 'scientists do not have the freedom which atrocities to investigate based on scientific or ethical principles. Instead, fluctuating political agendas significantly impact which projects are undertaken.'

MR-theory

To be able to explain human behaviour from the archaeological record, processual archaeologists generally use some kind of middle range theory (MR-theory).[24] These theories are defined as a set of models or propositions that link the empirical data to general, often abstract and empirically untestable, high-level conceptual schemes or theories. In other words, MR-theories seek regularities that occur within the archaeological record and link these regularities, while acknowledging the importance of site formation processes and taphonomic transformations, to human behaviour by creating hypotheses that are testable (and falsifiable) by means of the archaeological record.[25] MR-theories in traditional archaeology can be constructed from (actualistic) experimental studies, ethnoarchaeological observations of present-day societies, historical sources and taphonomic research (e.g. Binford 1977, 1981). MR-theories can be inductive, by linking the empirical reconstructions to higher conceptual schemes or theories, or deductive, by creating testable middle range hypotheses (MR-hypotheses) that can be derived from existing higher conceptual schemes or theories. However, successful theory-building seems to involve a combination of both approaches. It all depends on questions that need to be answered.

It is important to notice that not all (theoretical) archaeologists agree on how MR-theories should be used within archaeology, and that the use of MR-theories

[21] Processualism, also known as new archaeology, is strongly associated with a positivist view of the past, an ecosystemic approach, and a hypothetico-deductive research philosophy. It holds that archaeologists are able to develop accurate, objective information about past human behaviour by applying the scientific method and the ethno-historical approach to their investigations.

[22] Post-processualism, also known as interpretative archaeology, was developed in the early 1980s in response to the processual framework that, according to the post-processual archaeologists, treated cultural change independently of human social relations and the human beings as passive objects totally modified by external dynamics. Post-processualism refers to different theoretical frameworks (e.g. neo-Marxism, structuralism, contextual archaeology), all with their own theoretical thoughts. Generally speaking, post-processualism states that the interpretation of the archaeological record is infected by our own subjective interpretation and social factors (multiple interpretations of the past are therefore possible), sees the archaeological record as a communicative medium and considers the role of individuals (i.e. agents) as the driving force for all archaeological patterning.

[23] Emic concepts are developed within the mind of an individual or culture and therefore describe the 'native' categories of meanings, this as opposed to the Etic concepts that describe the meaning from the analytic view of the scientific observer (e.g. Darvill 2002, 132 and 137).

[24] The middle range (MR) theory was originally developed in sociology by Robert Merton as a means to guide empirical inquiry and to test parts of the empirically untestable high-level theories (Merton 1948, 1967, 2012). Merton (2012, 448) defines MR-theories as theories 'that lie between the minor but necessary working hypotheses that evolve in abundance during day-to-day research and the all-inclusive systematic efforts to develop a unified theory that will explain all the observed uniformities of social behaviour, social organization and social change.'

[25] See also Lovis (1992) and Boyd and Boyd (2011) on possible use of MR-theory in US forensic anthropology.

within archaeology is not without ontological and epistemological criticism.[26] A large part of this criticism is focused on the strong fixation of some MR-theories on the site-formation processes and the refutation of restrictions regarding the use of modern ethnoarchaeological regularities to explain past human behaviour. This criticism, although valid for traditional archaeology, does not seem that relevant for the use of MR-theories in forensic archaeology. A relevant criticism is the processual postulation that MR-theories should have a universal (cross-cultural) validity. This belief, as argued by post-processualists, seems to be invalid. It could even be said that context specific generalisations cannot be transformed to cross-cultural generalisations without a severe loss in context and significance (e.g. Trigger 1982). Therefore, forensic archaeological MR-theories do not need to have a universal validity *per se*; they could be limited to specific categories of casework or contexts. MR-theories are at times also used in criminology, to clarify the relation between the empirical observations of criminal behaviour and the higher theories concerning this behaviour (see below).

Archaeology and criminology

Human remains are some of the most significant archaeological finds, and archaeologists have a long history of studying past funerary practices 'not only to document ancient rituals by recovering the evidence of past funerary practices but also attempt to understand them within their historical contexts and to explain why they were enacted in the ways they were' (Parker Pearson 2003, 3). Consequently archaeology has developed a sub-discipline that focuses entirely on past funerary behaviour: mortuary archaeology.[27] Mortuary archaeology is all about excavating burials and interpreting mortuary architecture and associated grave goods. Although theories and concepts associated with mortuary archaeology are developed to explain historical phenomena, these theories and concepts can also be used to help explain modern human body deposition (e.g. Crossland 2000, 2013; Renshaw 2013a, 2013b). Archaeological theories show, for example, that mortuary contexts are the outcome of formal mortuary rituals, an accidental deposition or a formal or informal (clandestine) disposal related to malevolent circumstances, and that interplay exists between these contexts. Funerary rites and interment locations are being perceived as part of the active creation of social relations; the living manipulate the dead for their own interest, something that also continues to be the case today (e.g. Crossland 2000, 2013; Fondebrider 2002, 2009; Williams and Crews 2003; Juhl and Olsen 2006; Skinner 2007; Mark 2010; Eppel, Chapter 42, this volume; Etxeberria et al., Chapter 55, this volume; López Mazz and Lusiardo, Chapter 56, this volume). Mortuary archaeological studies further show that excavations of the dead could have an impact on modern society, and depending 'on the social conditions and present-day perception of the dead, their re-emergence into the living community may go relatively unnoticed, or may be highly controversial' (Crossland 2000, 147). Instigation of human (mass) graves is never socially detached or politically neutral. This is fully acknowledged by the Latin American NGOs. One of the objectives of the Argentinian EAAF is for example to 'assist the families of the victims in their right to recover disappeared loved-ones, so that they could carry out the customary funerary rites and mourn their dead' (EAAF 1992, 2).

Criminology is an interdisciplinary science that focuses on the study of crime, criminality, criminals, criminal behaviour and the criminal justice and penal systems (e.g. Newburn 2007). One of the main goals of criminology is to gain an understanding of causality of crime and criminal behaviour. As mentioned earlier, criminologists sometimes use MR-theories to develop a link between the empirical data and theories concerning human motivation and behaviour, this in order to produce a coherent description of criminal behaviour, crime and/or punitiveness (e.g. Steffensmeier and Allan 1996; Unnever and Cullen 2009; Sullivan 2011). One of the criminological research methodologies is offender profiling. 'At the heart of most profiling is the belief that characteristics of an *offender* can be deduced by a careful and considered examination of the characteristics of the *offence*' (Ainsworth 2001, 7). Offender profiling generally involves information acquired by psychological theories; the scene of crime; the location of the body deposition site; the age, sex and personal history of the victim; and the interaction between the victim and the (probable) offender, this to predict the characteristics of the offender with the aim of apprehending this

[26] For discussions concerning the use of MR-theories in archaeology, see for example Schiffer (1976, 1988); Binford (1977, 1981); Raab and Goodyear (1984); Pierce (1989); Wylie (1989); Salmon (1992); Maschner (1996); Tschauner (1996); Shott (1998) and Smith (2011).

[27] Mortuary archaeology (also known as funerary archaeology) studies uniformity and variability in the mortuary archaeological record to identify and explain cultural, social and economic aspects of the interred dead. Generally speaking, mortuary archaeology is all about the (non) existence of regularities in the archaeological record, the relationship between these (non) regularities and the individual's status and persona in life and his/her treatment after death. This archaeological sub-discipline is per definition interdisciplinary, as it integrates historical, ethnoarchaeological and bioarchaeological theories and methodologies. For more information on mortuary archaeology, see for example Chapman (2003); Effros (2003); Parker Pearson (2003); Rakita et al. (2005); Sayer and Williams (2009); Baadsgaard et al. (2011); Baker (2012); Tarlow and Nilsson Stutz (2013).

individual (e.g. Rossmo 2000; Ainsworth 2001). Some offender profiling studies also focus on the location of the body disposal sites, as related to the type of offender, the nature of the crime and the type of victim, and are therefore of importance to forensic archaeology (e.g. Lundrigan and Canter 2001a, 2001b; Morton and Lord 2002; Nethery 2004; Snook et al. 2005; Häkkänen et al. 2007; Hays 2008). In addition, criminological theories and models can also provide emic interpretation, as given by offenders themselves (although careful treatment is needed as offenders rarely give an entirely honest account of events), and can consequently improve our knowledge of human criminal behaviour at scenes of crime or places of incident, knowledge that is also needed for interpretation of the retrieved forensic record in the first place. Criminological generalities about the locations of body disposal and the manners of disposal, related to certain types of crimes and victims, can also serve as MR-hypotheses that could be integrated into future forensic archaeological investigation. Criminological knowledge, in the sense of understanding why, how and where people dispose of their victims (the pre-depositional and depositional processes), is for example as essential for the development of valid and reliable forensic archaeological search strategies as is the knowledge of site formation processes and taphonomic transformations (the depositional and post-depositional processes). This is far from new: comparable approaches – although more 'historically' orientated – are being practised by the Latin American NGOs, JPAC-CIL (D. Congram, personal communication 2013), and ICMP (I. Hanson, personal communication 2014).[28] Additionally, the criminological behavioural MR-hypotheses could also be fed and tested archaeologically, by combining (anonymised) evidence from past casework.

Summarising, forensic archaeological research should therefore not end with the delivery of an investigation report, it should also aim at reconstruction of sequential series of events that can be stored in a Geographic Information System (GIS) database and used in subsequent criminological analyses and forensic archaeological cases. This way we are able to use information from previous cases to guide our future inquiries. Such an approach is for example followed in the Netherlands where past forensic archaeological knowledge, as stored in a GIS database, is used by criminologists to develop a probabilistic geospatial model regarding the relationship between the victim and the offender, the category of murder committed and the location where the victim has been buried by the offender.

Forensic archaeology: the methodological framework

The forensic record as retrieved is a selection of the once deposited material evidence at a crime scene or place of incident. These sites are formed by human and/or natural actions (the pre-depositional processes, and the depositional and post-depositional or site formation processes), are subsequently distorted by human activities and/or natural processes (the post-depositional or site formation processes) and are finally recorded, sampled and processed (the retrieval processes) by forensic archaeological specialists.[29] The composition of the recovered forensic record therefore not only depends on all of the processes mentioned earlier, but also on the knowledge, interest and resources of the specialist responsible for the retrieval of this record. Knowing what happened during the pre-depositional, depositional, post-depositional and the recovery process is therefore essential for fully understanding the limitations, potential and significance of the retrieved record.[30] Knowledge of site formation processes and taphonomic transformations should be used to introduce the concept of (relative or absolute) time into the retrieved forensic record and to develop specific MR-theories for forensic archaeology that will be able to explain the presence or absence of material evidence at a crime scene or place of incident. However, it is also important to note that site formation processes and taphonomic transformations are highly context specific and that more research is needed to really understand the impact of these processes and transformations on modern crime scenes and places of incident.

[28] For additional discussion on the use of criminalistic theories and models in in predictive search for clandestine burial, see also Orengo (2007), Congram (2010) and Congram (2013).

[29] Pre-depositional activities comprise all past human behaviours that took place at an archaeological site. Depositional activities are associated with all cultural and natural activities that were expressed through the means of archaeological record, and that resulted in the insertion of this record in the archaeological context, for example by loss, abandonment or intentional burial. Post-depositional processes comprise all cultural and natural activities that have altered or destroyed the archaeological record after its inclusion in the archaeological context, and before the archaeological excavation. Retrieval processes deal with the relation between the survived archaeological record and the archaeological record that has been recognised and recovered by the archaeologist (e.g. Clarke 1973).

[30] For information about taphonomic transformations in forensic context, see for example Mann et al. (1990); Dirkmaat and Adovasio (1997); Haglund and Sorg (1997, 2002); Hochrein (1997, 2002); Scott and Connor (1997); Holland et al. (2002); Morton and Lord (2002); Dirkmaat et al. (2008); Nawrocki (2009); Boyd and Boyd (2011); Ross and Cunningham (2011); Vass (2011); Sorg et al. (2012).

In view of this, a forensic archaeological specialist operating in a legal context should at first be 'experienced and competent field archaeologist, in the same way that a forensic pathologist is a specialised pathologist' (Cheetham and Hanson 2009, 142). It is a truism that the evidentiary value of the forensic record that is analysed and interpreted in a laboratory is only as good as its recognition, documentation and recovery in the field. As mentioned earlier and in the introductory chapter, archaeological field methodology should not compromise the recovery of forensic evidence, be designed around legal research aims and goals and should be able to identify the site-specific site formation processes and taphonomic transformations that have altered the once deposited forensic record. 'There are no archaeological methods, no string grids or square holes, which can be a standard for archaeological work' (Connor and Scott 2001, 4). Forensic archaeological methodology cannot be entirely prescriptive. However, since forensic archaeology is firstly *forensic*, its field methodology should integrate criminalistic methods and techniques and 'provide a focus to maximise consideration for evidence distribution and identification' (Hanson 2008, 24). Additionally, the used methodology should also be linked to archaeological and criminological MR-theories that will be needed to interpret the retrieved forensic record.

Archaeology and criminalistics

Forensic archaeological field methodology entails field surveys (e.g. systematic surface 'walkover', geophysics and remote-sensing), subsurface tests to examine the localised soil features for presence of bodies and associated evidence (e.g. probing, auguring, hand excavated trenches or pits and machine-assisted removal of topsoil) and stratigraphic excavation techniques that – if performed correctly – are least destructive of grave shafts and other soil features and can provide (relative and/or absolute) a dating sequence. Some forensic archaeologists are moreover used to examine material culture from forensic settings (e.g. clothing and personal effects), in view of both physical and sociocultural evidence (e.g. Baraybar 2008; Komar and Lathrop 2008; Skinner et al. 2009; Intriago Leiva et al., Chapter 45, this volume). The forensic archaeological documentation methods and techniques are developed to record the contextual association of the (sub) surface stratigraphy, the site formation processes and taphonomic transformations, and the relationships between grave shafts, body position, (soil) features and finds (e.g. the use of total station aided photogrammetry and 3D laser scan technology). This documentation is needed since the forensic archaeological recovery destroys the spatial relations and associations between the individual evidence units within the forensic record.[31] The documented record should also be processed, analysed and visualised within a GIS. The use of GIS is fully integrated in modern archaeological field methodology and is essential to understand the (possible) patterns of evidence in the retrieved archaeological record.

However, as mentioned in the introductory chapter, forensic archaeology also differs from regular archaeology and should therefore be practised by individuals with complementary knowledge and understanding of law procedures and criminalistics. It is vital to realise that forensic archaeology, as opposed to traditional archaeology, is in the first place *forensic*; maintaining chain of evidence/custody regarding the retrieved forensic record is crucial and all retrieved evidence can be excluded from the legal proceedings after a mutual agreement between the prosecutor and defence lawyer, or by the decision of a judge. To quote Crossland (2013, 126) the 'decisions over evidence are based on the goal of reaching a final adjudication of guilt or innocence, rather than on what the evidence potentially contributes to more complete knowledge of the past.'

Criminalistics, or the 'discipline that embraces a holistic philosophy, the principles of science, the scientific method, and logic as it relates to the analysis and interpretation of evidence and its relationship to a set of alleged facts' (Shaler 2012, 17), is loosely based on Locard's exchange principle: *every contact leaves a trace*. As a result, the criminalistic methodology focuses on the possible transference (or lack thereof) and degradation of offence related (trace) evidence between the offender and victim at (or around) the scene of crime or place of

[31] For more information on the usability of archaeological methodology in a legal setting , see for example McLaughlin (1974); Bass and Birkby (1978); Boyd (1979); Morse et al. (1983); Skinner and Lazenby (1983); Killam (1990); UN (1991); France et al. (1992, 1997); Owsley (1995); Spennemann and Franke (1995); Hunter et al. (1996, 2001, 2013); Dirkmaat and Adovasio (1997); Haglund (1998); Webster (1998); Dirkmaat and Hefner (2001); Haglund et al. (2001); Scott (2001); Dirkmaat (2002, 2012); Mayne Correia and Beattie (2002); Schmitt (2002); Komar (2003); Skinner et al. (2003); Hunter and Cox (2005); Jessee and Skinner (2005); Menez (2005); Rogers (2005); Ruffer (2005); Wright et al. (2005); Dupras et al. (2006); Manheim et al. (2006); Tuller and Durić (2006); Connor (2007); Listi et al. (2007); Cox et al. (2008); Egaña et al. (2008); Fairgrieve (2008); Komar and Lathrop (2008); Reinecke and Hochrein (2008); Tuller et al. (2008); Blau and Ubelaker (2009); Holland and Connell (2009); Larson et al. (2011); Cabo et al. (2012); Dirkmaat et al. (2012); Hochrein (2012); Schultz (2012); Tuller (2012).

incident. This transference (or lack thereof) could be analysed at the source level or the activity level.[32] Criminalistic methodology is scenario driven and developed to recover the forensic record with the highest evidential value, as related to the kind of questions (hypotheses) that will have to be answered during the legal inquiry/trial. The incorporation of criminalistic methodology into the forensic archaeological framework can also reduce some of the ambiguity in the forensic record by evaluating the likelihood that a certain natural or human agent was responsible for a specific action in light of all the encountered evidence (i.e. the Bayesian interpretation framework of forensic evidence). Although an individual indication between one encountered type of evidence and a certain human action could be ambiguous, the picture could become much clearer if all independent types of evidence are analysed together. The stronger the relationship between the independent types of evidence, the stronger the possibility that this evidence could be used together in reconstructing past human (criminal) behaviour. Criminalistic methodology thus uses multiple, independent lines of reasoning to indicate the most likely causal agent.

Forensic archaeology, reconstruction and interpretation

The editors propose a forensic archaeological interpretative framework that links archaeological and criminological MR-theories with archaeological and criminalistic methodologies (Figure C.1). There are no rational reasons why forensic archaeological specialists should not integrate criminological models into their case studies, for example during a search for a missing and presumably buried person. Besides, most academically educated forensic archaeologists/anthropologists are also trained in the social sciences and should be able – after additional instruction – to understand the advantages and limitations of criminological theories and models. All archaeologists/anthropologists for example should already know that mortuary behaviour, although based on general sociocultural behavioural models, is highly variable. The variability in mortuary behaviour is also confirmed in modern criminological (GIS) studies

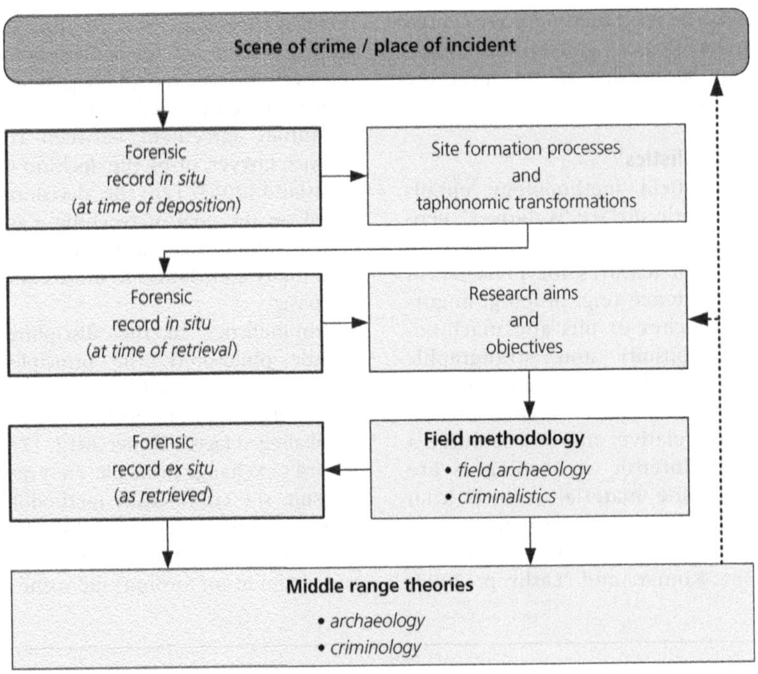

Figure C.1 Proposed structure of a forensic archaeological interpretation.

[32]Criminalists define three hierarchical levels of analysis of transference: the source level (the identification or classification of the transferred material in relation to its possible source), the activity level (the relation between the transferred material and human action that possibly causes this transfer) and the offence level (the relation between the transferred material and the crime committed). The offence level lies outside the domain of the forensic scientists and is addressed in the Court (e.g. Cook et al. 1998).

that show that there is a significant variation in victim disposal patterns among offenders. We should consequently be very sceptical about the possibility of being able to predict the exact location of a clandestine burial or mass grave. Nonetheless, an integration of archaeological and criminological theories and models will allow us to develop MR-hypotheses that will be able to explain a part of the encountered forensic record. New forensic archaeological casework will undoubtedly expose new (GIS) datasets, finding the current MR-hypotheses deficient. The use of MR-hypotheses will allow the development of new MR-hypotheses that will again be tested by the empirical datasets in the future. The continuing feedback corrections from new case studies (with understandable legal restriction) will surely result in a better understanding of human (criminal) behaviour at the activity level and, for example, the growth of predictive (region or country specific) models regarding the geographical location of a clandestine (mass) burial site and the manner of interment. Summarising, there exists a complementary relationship between forensic archaeology and criminology, although this relationship is hardly recognised by practitioners in both disciplines at the moment.

Additionally, there is the need for an integrated archaeological and criminalistic field methodology for the recognition, documentation, retrieval and analysis of the forensic archaeological datasets. It is also believed that forensic archaeology needs MR-theories on the relationship between the retrieved forensic record (i.e. the sum of all archaeologically retrieved forensic evidence) and the behavioural models that can be used to reconstruct and interpret human (criminal) behaviour from this record at the activity level. Additionally, MR-theories are needed to develop a context-specific field methodology that will offer the retrieved forensic record the highest evidentiary value at the activity level, as requested by the relevant legal setting. It should also be remembered that an explanation at the source level alone will not tell us how the retrieved forensic record came to be deposited as a result of human (criminal) behaviour. Archaeological theories have already shown that material record *an sich* is 'speechless', and that an 'atheoretical' reconstruction of human behaviour from this record will lead to simplistic interpretations of past human behaviour. Without proper MR-theories forensic archaeology will remain an 'applied discipline', performed by technicians rather than the scientists.

The ability to be able to recognise, document and reconstruct the natural and manmade site-formation processes and taphonomic transformations – which will affect our ability to reconstruct and interpret past criminal behaviour – is also essential. This is because these processes and transformations are not only a potential source of bias; they can also aid in reconstruction and interpretation, for example in providing evidence on the events surrounding the cause and manner of death. Forensic archaeological recoveries should therefore – ideally – be performed by individuals who understand why a certain archaeological or criminalistic method or technique is being applied at a crime scene or place of incident and what the context specific advantages and limitations of the applied technique or method are. It should be remembered that the use and knowledge of specific field methodology will not only affect what type of forensic record will be collected and the evidentiary value of this record, but also if the retrieved record will be adequate to answer legal questions and if it will stand the scrutiny of lawyers trying to discredit its legal value during court proceedings. Above all, it could also lead to not fulfilling the right of victims' families to thorough investigation; to justice; and to know the truth regarding what had happened to their loved ones. It should be acknowledged that not all forensic archaeological specialists possess comparable knowledge and experience. As mentioned earlier, there are important country-specific educational and legal differences. For example, traditionally educated archaeologists without a strong educational background and working experience in physical anthropology/bioarchaeology, although still very useful at some type of crime scenes or places of incident (e.g. Márquez-Grant et al. 2012), could be limited in their full forensic potential (e.g. Cabo and Dirkmaat, Chapter 31, this volume). Osteological knowledge will, for example, be needed for an accurate documentation of scattered, commingled or burned human skeletal material. The human remains to be recovered will be in various decomposition stages and almost every forensic search will result in finding bones that will have to be determined as soon as possible, preferably at the moment of their detection. Besides this, knowledge and experience will also be needed to recognise and interpret the taphonomic transformations (e.g. human taphonomy and material degradation) encountered at a scene of crime or place of incident. Additionally, all forensic archaeological specialists working within a criminal, medico-legal or humanitarian setting, be they archaeologists, forensic anthropologists, forensic pathologists or police officers, should have a good knowledge of, and working experience with, GIS, affiliated forensic sciences (e.g. forensic botany, forensic entomology, forensic geology and criminalistics including fibres, footwear marks and DNA), forensic practices (e.g. cadaver dog possibilities and tactics), as well a general knowledge of criminology.

Final remarks

This volume shows that forensic archaeology is defined differently across the globe and that it is, accordingly, practised by different professionals. Although forensic archaeological practice is reasonably grounded in medico-legal and humanitarian investigations, it is mostly performed by intergovernmental organisations or NGOs, and is hardly practised at modern domestic crime scenes or during recovery of human remains and associated evidence from mass fatality incidents. One of the reasons behind this omission is probably related to the second word in the name of this discipline: *archaeology*. Most people – and rightly so – associate archaeology with the study of the past and not with a scientific discipline that has developed a theoretical and methodological framework that can also be used at modern crime scenes or places of incident. To quote Houck and Siegel in *Fundamentals of Forensic Science* (2010, 31), the 'similarities between archaeology and crime scene processing are numerous and deep. Serious crime scene students would do well to study archaeological methods to enhance their forensic skills'. It is therefore regrettable that Dr Brenda Sigler-Eisenberg's observation that justice system 'warrants increased participation and support of forensic research by forensically trained professional archaeologists' (Sigler-Eisenberg 1985, 650), although nearly three decades old, is still valid in most countries.

In some countries and organisations, forensic archaeological recoveries are performed by forensic anthropologists, forensic pathologists or police (e.g. Scientific Police), some of them skilled in field archaeological methods and techniques. Traditionally trained archaeologists are hereby underrepresented, this due to country-specific differences in archaeological education and working experience; the legal restrictions in using external (non-police or civilian) experts; and the focus on the 'practical' part of forensic archaeology. Or it may be simply because there is no awareness that this discipline exists. It should be acknowledged that most of the non-archaeologists – although there are noteworthy exceptions – lack the theoretical background and broad archaeological field skills that come with a traditional archaeological education and working experience, and that is needed to be a good forensic archaeological specialist. The non-archaeologists generally do not keep up with (bio)archaeological publications, or the exchange of new theoretical and methodological ideas that takes place during traditional archaeological conferences, symposia and meetings. This is not intended to mean that all forensic archaeological practice should therefore be restricted to the traditionally educated forensic archaeologists only. As mentioned earlier, it all depends on the country-specific educational background and past working experience. However, this does mean that non-archaeologically educated specialists should become a part of the wider archaeological community and keep up with the theoretical and methodological progress within this community.

Acknowledging all these, the editors believe that forensic archaeology should be recognised as an archaeological specialisation (similar to historical archaeology, mortuary archaeology and bioarchaeology), and that it should also be grounded in academic departments. The question if these departments should be 'archaeological' as in most of Europe, or 'anthropological' as in the Americas, is not really relevant. What is relevant is that forensic archaeological investigation should be grounded in MR-theories, combining archaeological and criminological theories and models, and that it should include field methodology that combines archaeology (including taphonomy and material degradation) with criminalistics. It is fully acknowledged that the proposed framework will not eliminate all biases that can influence the interpretation of forensic record, but we are confident that the proposed framework will add to more rounded insights into what has really happened at a crime scene or place of incident. We also believe that the proposed framework will offer a vantage point from which the relations between archaeology, criminology, criminalistics and law can be further examined.

It is humbly hoped that this volume will help to change the outdated views of forensic archaeology as a 'practice' and that it will assist in further development of this discipline across the globe. Forensic archaeology – be it practised by forensic archaeologists, forensic anthropologists, forensic pathologists or police officers – has a collective experience of nearly 50 years of case studies. It's time, given the theoretical and methodological challenges forensic archaeology faces as a scientific discipline, to team up, acknowledge our professional strengths and weaknesses, learn from each other and move into a truly cooperative multidisciplinary mode of investigation and research.

Finally, in view of all these, the editors would like to specify the working definition of forensic archaeology, as used in the introductory chapter. We propose the following definition of forensic archaeology: *Forensic archaeology is the scientific discipline that uses archaeological theory and methodology in a legal context. It combines archaeological, criminalistic and criminological knowledge to search, localise, document, retrieve and interpret the forensic record (i.e. the sum of all archaeologically retrieved forensic evidence) at a crime scene or place of incident.*

References

Ainsworth, P. B. 2001. *Offender Profiling and Crime Analysis*. Uffculme, Willan Publishing.

Baadsgaard, A., Boutin, A. T. and Buikstra, J. E. (eds.) 2011. *Breathing New Life into the Evidence of Death: Contemporary Approaches to Bioarchaeology*. Santa Fe, School for Advanced Research Press.

Baker, J. L. 2012. *The Funeral Kit: Mortuary Practices in the Archaeological Record*. Walnut Creek, Left Coast Press.

Baraybar, J. P. 2008. When DNA is not Available, Can We Still Identify People? Recommendations for Best Practice. *Journal of Forensic Sciences* 53, 533–540.

Bass, W. M. and Birkby, W. H. 1978. Exhumation: the Method Could Make the Difference. *FBI Law Enforcement Bulletin* 47(7), 6–11.

Berger, M. A. 2011. The Admissibility of Expert Testimony. In National Research Council (ed), *Reference Manual on Scientific Evidence*. 3rd edition. 11–36. Washington, DC, The National Academies Press. Available at: http://www.au.af.mil/au/awc/awcgate/fjc/manual_sci_evidence.pdf (last accessed 15 February 2014).

Binford, L. R. (ed.) 1977. General Introduction. In *For Theory Building in Archaeology: Essays on Faunal Remains, Aquatic Resources, Spatial Analysis, and Systematic Modelling*. 1–10. London, Academic Press.

Binford, L. R. 1981. *Bones: Ancient Man and Modern Myths*. New York, Academic Press.

Blau, S. and Ubelaker, D. H. (eds.) 2009. *Handbook of Forensic Anthropology and Archaeology*. Walnut Creek, Left Coast Press.

Boyd, C. and Boyd, D. C. 2011. Theory and the Scientific Basic for Forensic Anthropology. *Journal of Forensic Sciences* 56, 1407–1415.

Boyd, R. M. 1979. Buried Body Cases. *FBI Law Enforcement Bulletin* 48(2), 1–7.

Broeders, T. 2003. The Role of the Forensic Expert in an Inquisitorial System. In P. J. van Koppwn and S. D. Penrod (eds.) *Adversarial versus Inquisitorial Justice: Psychological Perspectives on Criminal Justice*. 245–253. New York, Springer.

Cabo, L. L., Dirkmaat, D. C., Adovasio, J. M. and Rozas, V. C. 2012. Archaeology, Mass Graves, and Resolving Commingling Issues through Spatial Analysis. In D. C. Dirkmaat (ed.) *A Companion to Forensic Anthropology*. 175–196. Chichester, Wiley-Blackwell.

Chapman, R. 2003. Death Society and Archaeology: the Social Dimensions of Mortuary Practices. *Mortality* 8, 305–312.

Cheetham, P. N. and Hanson, I. 2009. Excavation and Recovery in Forensic Archaeological Investigation. In S. Blau and D. H. Ubelaker (eds.) *Handbook of Forensic Anthropology and Archaeology*. 141–149. Walnut Creek, Left Coast Press.

Clarke, D. 1973. Archaeology: the Loss of Innocence. *Antiquity* 47, 6–18.

Congram, D. 2010. Spatial analysis and predictive modelling of clandestine graves from rearguard repression of the Spanish Civil War. PhD thesis, Simon Fraser University.

Congram, D. 2013. Deposition and Dispersal of Human Remains as a Result of Criminal Acts: Homo Sapiens Sapiens as a Taphonomic Agent. In J. Pokines and S. A. Symes (eds.) *Manual of Forensic Taphonomy*. 249–286. Boca Raton, CRC Press.

Connor, M. and Scott, D. D. 2001. Paradigms and Perpetrators. *Journal of Historical Archaeology* 35, 1–6.

Connor, M. A. 2007. *Forensic Methods: Excavation for the Archaeologist and Investigator*. Lanham, Altamira Press.

Cook, R., Evett, I. W., Jackson, G., Jones, P. J. and Lambert, J. A. 1998. A Hierarchy of Propositions: Deciding which Level to Address in Casework. *Science & Justice* 38, 231–239.

Cox, M., Flavel, A., Hanson, I., Laver, J. and Wessling, R. (eds.) 2008. *The Scientific Investigation of Mass Graves. Towards Protocols and Standard Operating Procedures*. Cambridge, Cambridge University Press.

Crombag, H. F. M. 2003. Adversarial or Inquisitorial: do we have a Choice? In P. J. van Koppwn and S. D. Penrod (eds.) *Adversarial versus Inquisitorial Justice: Psychological Perspectives on Criminal Justice*. 21–25. New York, Springer.

Crossland, Z. 2000. Buried Lives: Forensic Archaeology and the Disappeared in Argentina. *Archaeological Dialogues* 7, 146–159.

Crossland, Z. 2011. The Archaeology of Contemporary Conflict. In T. Insoll (ed.) *The Oxford Handbook of the Archaeology of Ritual and Religion*. 285–306. Oxford, Oxford University Press.

Crossland, Z. 2013. Evidential Regimes in Forensic Archaeology. *Annual Review of Anthropology* 42, 121–137.

Darvill, T. 2002. *The Concise Oxford Dictionary of Archaeology*. Oxford, Oxford University Press.

Diamond, S. S. 2003. Convergence and Complementarity between Professional Judge and Lay Adjudicators. In P. J. van Koppwn and S. D. Penrod (eds.) *Adversarial versus Inquisitorial Justice: Psychological Perspectives on Criminal Justice*. 321–332. New York, Springer.

Dirkmaat, D. C. 2002. Recovery and Interpretation of the Fatal Fire Victim: the Role of Forensic Anthropology. In W. D. Haglund and M. H. Sorg (eds.) *Advances in Forensic Taphonomy: Methods, Theory, and Archaeological Perspectives*. 451–472. Boca Raton, CRC Press.

Dirkmaat, D. C. 2012. Forensic Anthropology at the Mass Fatality Incident (Commercial Airliner) Crash Scene. In D. C. Dirkmaat (ed.) *A Companion to Forensic Anthropology*. 136–156. Chichester, Wiley-Blackwell.

Dirkmaat, D. C. and Adovasio, J. M. 1997. The Role of Archaeology in the Recovery and Interpretation of Human Remains from an Outdoor Forensic Setting. In W. D. Haglund and M. H. Sorg (eds.) *Forensic Taphonomy. The Post-Mortem Fate of Human Remains*. 39–64. Boca Raton, CRC Press.

Dirkmaat, D. C. and Hefner, J. T. 2001. Forensic Processing of the Terrestrial Mass Fatality Scene: Testing New Search, Documentation and Recovery Methodologies. *Proceedings of the American Academy of Forensic Sciences* 7, 241–242.

Dirkmaat, D. C., Cabo, L. L., Ousley, S. D. and Symes, S. A. 2008. New Perspectives in Forensic Anthropology. *Yearbook of Physical Anthropology* 51, 33–52.

Dirkmaat, D. C., Olson, G. O., Klales, A. R. and Getz, S. 2012. The Role of Forensic Anthropology in the Recovery and Interpretation of the Fatal-Fire Victim. In D. C. Dirkmaat (ed.) *A Companion to Forensic Anthropology*. 113–135. Chichester, Wiley-Blackwell.

Dupras, T. L., Schultz, J. J., Wheeler, S. M. and Williams, L. J. 2006. *Forensic Recovery of Human Remains: Archaeological Approaches*. Boca Raton, CRC Press.

EAAF (EquipoArgentino de AntropologíaForense) 1992. *EAAF 1992 Annual Report*. BuenosAires. Available at: http://eaaf.typepad.com/ar_1992/AnnualReport1992.pdf (last accessed 15 February 2014).

Effros, B. 2003. *Merovingian Mortuary Archaeology and the Making of the Early Middle Ages*. Berkeley, University of California Press.

Egaña, S., Turner, S., Doretti, M., Bernardi, P. and Ginarte, A. 2008. Commingled Remains and Human Rights Investigations. In B. J. Adams and J. E. Byrd (eds.) *Recovery, Analysis and Identification of Commingled Human Remains*. 57–79. Totowa, Humana Press.

Fairgrieve, S. I. 2008. *Forensic Cremation: Recovery and Analysis*. Boca Raton, CRC Press.

Scott, D. D. 2001. Firearms Identification in Support of Identifying a Mass Execution at El Mozote, El Salvador. *Journal of Historical Archaeology* 35, 79–86.

Scott, D. D. and Connor, M. 1997. Context Delicti: Archaeological Context in Forensic Work. In W. D. Haglund and M. H. Sorg (eds.) *Forensic Taphonomy: the Postmortem Fate of Human Remains*. 27–38. Boca Raton, CRC Press.

Scott, D.D., Babits, L.E. and Haecker, C.M. (eds.) 2006. *Fields of conflict: battle archaeology from the Roman Empire to the Korean War*. Volume II. Santa Barbara, Praeger.

Shaler, R. C. 2012. *Crime Scene Forensics: a Scientific Method Approach*. Boca Raton, CRC Press.

Shott, M. J. 1998. Status and Role of Formation Theory in Contemporary Archaeological Practice. *Journal of Archaeological Research* 6, 299–330.

Sigler-Eisenberg, B. 1985. Forensic Research: Explaining the Concept of Applied Archaeology. *American Antiquity* 50, 650–655.

Skinner, M. 2007. Hapless in Afghanistan: Forensic Archaeology in Political Maelstrom. In R. Ferllini (ed.) *Forensic Archaeology and Human Rights Violations*. 233–265. Springfield, Charles C. Thomas.

Skinner, M. and Lazenby, R. A. 1983. *Found! Human Remains. A Field Manual for the Recovery of the Recent Human Skeleton*. Burnaby, Archaeology Press.

Skinner, M., Alempijevic, D. and Djuric-Serejic, M. 2003. Guidelines for International Forensic Bio-Archaeology Monitors of Mass Grave Exhumations. *Forensic Science International* 134, 81–92.

Skinner, M., Fernández, A. and Congram, D. 2009. Material Culture Analysis in Forensic Cases: a Call for Formal Recognition by Forensic Anthropologists. *Proceedings American Academy of Forensic Sciences* 15, 336–337.

Smith, M. E. 2011. Empirical Urban Theory for Archaeologists. *Journal for Archaeological Method and Theory* 18, 167–192.

Snook, B., Cullen, R. M., Mokros, A. and Harbort, S. 2005. Serial Murderers' Spatial Decisions: Factors that Influence Crime Location Choice. *Journal of Investigate Psychology and Offender Profiling* 2, 147–164.

Snow, C. C. 2011. Letter to Dr D. C. Dirkmaat regarding the proposal to change the name of the AAFS Forensic Anthropology Section, 29 July 2011. Available at: http://panthsectionnamechange.wordpress.com/a-letter-by-clyde-snow/ (last accessed 15 February 2014).

Sorg, M. H., Haglund, W. D. and Wren, J. A. 2012. Current Research in Forensic Taphonomy. In D. C. Dirkmaat (ed.) *A Companion to Forensic Anthropology*. 477–498. Chichester, Wiley-Blackwell.

Spennemann, D. H. R. and Franke, B. 1995. Archaeological Techniques for Exhumation: a Unique Data Source for Crime Scene Investigations. *Forensic Science International* 74, 5–15.

Stallibrass, S. 2000. AEA 1993 Conference at Durham: Editorial. In J. P. Huntley and S. Stallibrass (eds.) *Taphonomy and Interpretation: Symposia of the Association for Environmental Archaeology No. 14*. v–vii. Oxford, Oxbow Books.

Steffensmeier, D. and Allan, E. 1996. Gender and Crime: Toward a Gendered Theory of Female Offending. *Annual Review of Sociology* 22, 459–487.

Stover, E. and Shigekane, R. 2002. The Missing in the Aftermath: when do the Needs of Victims' Families and International War Crimes Tribunal Clash? *International Review of the Red Cross* 848, 845–866.

Sullivan, C. J. 2011. The Utility of the Deviant Case in the Development of Criminological Theory. *Criminology* 49, 905–920.

Tarlow, S. and Nilsson Stutz, L. (eds.) 2013. *The Oxford Handbook of the Archaeology of Death and Burial*. Oxford, Oxford University Press.

Trigger, B. G. 1982. Archaeological Analysis and Concepts of Causality. *Culture* 2, 31–42.

Tschauner, H. 1996. Middle-Range Theory, Behavioral Archaeology, and Postempiricist Philosophy of Science in Archaeology. *Journal of Archaeological Method and Theory* 3, 1–30.

Tuller, H. H. 2012. Mass Graves and Human Rights: Latest Developments, Methods, and Lessons Learned. In D. C. Dirkmaat (ed.) *A Companion to Forensic Anthropology*. 157–174. Chichester, Wiley-Blackwell.

Tuller, H. H. and Durić, M. 2006. Keeping the Pieces Together: Comparison of Mass Grave Excavation Methodology. *Forensic Science International* 156, 192–200.

Tuller, H. H., Hofmeister, U. and Daley, S. 2008. Spatial Analysis and Mass Grave Mapping Data to Assist in the Reassociation of Disarticulated and Commingled Remains. In B. J. Adams and J. E. Byrd (eds.) *Recovery, Analysis, and Identification of Commingled Remains*. 7–29. Totowa, Humana Press.

UN (United Nations) 1991. Model Protocol for Disinterment and Analysis of Skeletal Remains. In *Manual for the Effective Prevention and Investigation of Extra-Legal, Arbitrary and Summary Executions*. 30–41. New York, United Nations.

Unnever, J. D. and Cullen, F. T. 2009. Empathetic Identification and Punitiveness: a Middle-Range Theory of Individual Differences. *Theoretical Criminology* 13, 283–312.

Vanin, S., Turchetto, M., Galassi, A. and Cattaneo, C. 2009. Forensic Entomology and the Archaeology of War. *Journal of Conflict Archaeology* 5, 127–139.

Van Koppen, P. J. and Penrod, S. D. 2003. Adversarial or Inquisitorial: Comparing Systems. In P. J. van Koppen and S. D. Penrod (eds.) *Adversarial versus Inquisitorial Justice: Psychological Perspectives on Criminal Justice*. 1–19. New York, Springer.

Vass, A. A. 2011. The Elusive Universal Post-Mortem Interval Formula. *Forensic Science International* 201, 34–40.

Webster, A. D. 1998. Excavations of a Vietnam-era Aircraft Crash Site: Use of Cross-Cultural Understanding and Dual Forensic Recovery Methods. *Journal of Forensic Sciences* 43, 277–283.

Williams, E. D. and Crews, J. D. 2003. From Dust to Dust: Ethical and Practical Issues Involved in the Location, Exhumation and Identification of Bodies from Mass Graves. *Croatian Medical Journal* 44, 251–258.

Wright, R., Hanson, I. and Sterenberg, J. 2005. The Archaeology of Mass Graves. In J. R. Hunter and M. Cox (eds.) *Forensic Archaeology: Advances in Theory and Practice*. 137–158. London, Rutledge.

Wylie, M. A. 1989. The Interpretative Dilemma. In V. Pinsky and A. Wylie (eds.) *Critical Traditions in Contemporary Archaeology*. 18–27. Cambridge, Cambridge University Press.

Index

Forensic Archaeology: A Global Perspective, First Edition. Edited by W.J. Mike Groen, Nicholas Márquez-Grant and Robert C. Janaway.

Printed and bound by CPI Group (UK) Ltd, Croydon, CR0 4YY
21/09/2026
14965815-0001